WEST POINT *Leadership* PROFILES OF COURAGE

ABOUT THE BOOK

LETTER FROM THE PUBLISHER, CO-AUTHOR, AND EDITOR:

In 2004, I had the honor of returning to duty in the Army after nearly 13 years to deploy to Tikrit, Iraq, as an Infantry officer responsible for economic development/Civil Affairs work. In this role, I traveled throughout both Iraq and the entire region and experienced the war at the tactical, operational, and strategic levels. While I naturally assumed that West Point graduates would be involved at these particular levels within the Army from Second Lieutenant to General, I was surprised to find graduates engaged in nearly every other aspect of the war beyond the military: political, economic, and non-profit to name a few. West Point graduates were serving in the State Department, USAID, CIA, FBI, leading nearly every newly formed private security company (Triple Canopy and Sallyport for instance), and in nearly every one of the major contractors (Bechtel, KBR, etc.), all of whom were involved in the effort to re-build and develop the Iraqi economy. In fact, the informal West Point Society of Baghdad had thousands of members representing hundreds of organizations of all types. I later experienced that same unique network throughout Afghanistan.

It was then that I realized no other university has an alumnus so deeply involved at all levels of our national security apparatus – involvement reaching well beyond their official Army roles. I started to fully understand the value of the West Point education, not only for the individuals who are fortunate enough to be accepted and graduate, but the value to the nation of the network of graduates who help lead organizations throughout the United States and the world.

Several years later one of my best friends, Rick Minicozzi (USMA 1986), led the effort to turn around the Historic Thayer Hotel at West Point and to restore it to a standard worthy of West Point. Prior to Rick's incredible initiative, the hotel was in physical and financial distress having suffered from neglect and providing a very low standard of service.

Rick took over the day-to-day management of the hotel while also serving as the developer and general contractor of the restoration of the hotel. Rick led the recapitalization of the partnership that operates the hotel and immediately began developing peripheral feeder businesses for the business-starved hotel. The capital improvements were funded with a combination of his own capital and additional capital he raised from a select group of his partners. Rick's efforts are deserving of immense gratitude by all graduates and friends of West Point.

One of the ideas conceived is the room dedication program. This program is designed to make the hotel a unique hospitality experience, offering its guests a walk through American history and opportunity to celebrate the achievements of the graduates of West Point. This "museum in a hotel" concept is inspirational to the guests who are frequently found walking the guestroom halls and reading the plaques outside the guestroom doors while recognizing the generous corporations, families, and friends who sponsored those rooms.

The Thayer Hotel business plan was a challenge when Rick took charge of the hotel. At the time, the security at West Point was very tight for the public. For a while, the public was only allowed on post if traveling with a contracted touring company, attending specific athletic events such as Army football, visiting the Thayer Hotel, or as guests of those stationed at West Point. This created a perception by the public that West Point was completely inaccessible since it was a "closed post."

The Thayer Hotel also has a very seasonal business calendar due to the long winter at West Point. The hotel enjoys 20 or so "great days" during which it would be guaranteed to fill up. Days such as those during graduation week in May and for the five or so home football games in the fall. Beyond the great 20 days, the hotel was largely underutilized and had significant capacity during the weekdays and in particular during the winter.

The challenge existed to change the seasonal nature of the hotel and create a steady demand for its use. To achieve that, the decision was made to leverage West Point's greatest asset and its recognition as the world's premier leader development institute. Thus, in 2010, Thayer Leader Development Group (TLDG) was founded to help educate corporate executives on the leadership principles taught at West Point and in the Army, building full time leaders of character. TLDG focuses on many of the same leadership principles taught to the cadets who will one day be the future leaders of our nation.

TLDG was fortunate to find a great leader to serve as the Executive Director of Education. Dr. Karen Kuhla, former head of GE's global leader development program, joined the team. Karen methodically built a world-class faculty of instructors, nearly all of whom had military backgrounds and were predominantly West Point graduates with advanced degrees in the areas they were instructing. TLDG also created the Senior Advisors Program, a group of former General Officers, to serve as mentors and facilitators of dynamic classroom and field time learning.

TLDG offers executives customized training programs for existing teams within corporate America, government, NGO, and not-for-profit companies. TLDG also offers Open Enrollment programs for executives and emerging high potential leaders within these same organizations.

TLDG has been a tremendous success, both for itself and for the Thayer Hotel. Some of the greatest companies in the United States, and in fact the world, have sent their senior leadership teams to TLDG programs. TLDG currently enhances the lives of more than 5,000 leaders annually while tangentially exposing these same influential leaders to West Point, which has very positive second and third order effects.

It was during the creation of the TLDG that a plethora of literature and marking materials was inventoried – both public and private – highlighting West Point and her graduates. The material is voluminous and some of it incredible. Hundreds of outstanding books exist about individual West Point graduates while countless books exist on the various military campaigns that have been led by West Point graduates. Another category of books also exist that attempt to educate students about the principles of West Point leadership. In addition to the written works, numerous movies exist that highlight West Point graduates leading in the military.

What I could not find, however, was a single work that was both inspirational and comprehensive in highlighting the contributions of the individual members of the Long Gray Line across the entire breadth of our nation's history. Indeed both West Point and the West Point Association of Graduates need to be sensitive in not overly promoting the successes of graduates in the private sector at the expense of West Point's primary mission of creating military leaders of character. As a result, it was no surprise that few works exist primarily highlighting West Point graduates as leaders of America's greatest companies, yet we found numerous graduates who quietly and successfully lead large corporations today. It was these graduates who initially inspired us to highlight how West Point and its leadership education and principles transcend military application. Of course, the success of graduates leading global companies, like J&J, Procter and Gamble, the New York Stock Exchange Group, and other organizations, is only part of the Long Gray Line's story. West Point graduates have influenced every aspect of America's development, in addition to their obvious pre-eminent role in leading the nation's military.

Thus was formed the idea in 2010 to create this book, *West Point Leadership: Profiles of Courage*, in order to highlight an inspirational and comprehensive collection of graduates who, through their individual biographies, reveal how West Point graduates have shaped America's rich history. This was a private project that I personally funded. It is neither a Thayer Hotel nor TLDG project, yet we hope it will support both as well as USMA and the West Point AOG.

I asked a friend Greg Mathieson, Sr., to join the project as the photographer and another friend, Keegan Cotton, to help me manage the administration of the entire project.

Another one of my best friends, West Point classmate and company-mate, Lieutenant Colonel John Vigna (USA, Ret), was on his second tour at West Point as a professor (first in the History Department, then in the Social Sciences Department after his retirement), and I asked him to join me as a co-author. Without John's tireless and skillful work, this book would not have been possible. We then asked several friends if they would like to contribute one or more biographies of their favorite graduates and provided them a list of the grads we planned to highlight. Leading this group of incredible people was extremely rewarding to say the least.

We hope that this book will inspire future cadets, motivate tourists to visit one of America's greatest national treasures, and help educate the public on the incredible sacrifices and contributions that West Point graduates have made to our nation.

I hope you enjoy it, and I appreciate your confidence in us by purchasing this book.

Go Army!
Daniel E. Rice
USMA 1988
Publisher, Co-Author & Editor *West Point Leadership: Profiles of Courage*

"To call *West Point Leadership: Profiles of Courage* impressive would be a major understatement—it is awesome, almost to the point of being intimidating, in scope, certainly, and even in size. Seeking just the right word to describe your book, I decided on 'monumental.' It truly is that, both literally and metaphorically."

LIEUTENANT GENERAL DAVE PALMER (USA, RETIRED)
USMA 1956
Superintendent of West Point 1986-1991
Author "*The River and the Rock: The History of Fortress West Point 1775-1783*"

"*West Point Leadership: Profiles of Courage* is a moving, insightful look at the invaluable and timeless contributions West Point has made...and continues to make...to our country and the world. NO publication better captures the profiles of the Academy's graduates and the imprint they have made on our great country."

LIEUTENANT GENERAL DANIEL CHRISTMAN (USA, RETIRED)
USMA 1965
Superintendent of West Point 1996-2001

"*West Point Leadership: Profiles of Courage* is unique among works written about West Point, my alma mater: Like no other, it captures the story of West Point, the strategic Revolutionary War military garrison, and the United States Military Academy from the times of the founding patriots to contemporary times by featuring a selection of academy graduate-leaders, many of whom are still serving the nation today. A rich, diverse assembly of academy graduates from all corners of American society, including those breaking barriers of race and gender, are seen not only in the defense of the nation, but also across countless sectors from prominence in politics to Wall Street. I am honored to be among them. Primary author Dan Rice and his colleagues have done a superb job in providing a uniquely distinctive reflection of West Point and its graduates."

MAJOR GENERAL FRED A. GORDEN, (USA, RETIRED)
USMA 1962
First African American Commandant of Cadets

"*West Point Leadership: Profiles of Courage* is brilliant- it provides a depth and breadth of West Point's history as told through the lives of numerous graduates who have made incalculable contributions to our country."

LIEUTENANT GENERAL FRANKLIN "BUSTER" HAGENBECK (USA, RETIRED)
USMA 1971
Superintendent of West Point 2006-2010

"What a magnificent book! Clearly the most definitive collection of West Point graduate biographical summaries I have ever seen and I am sure there has never been anything like it ever published. Congratulations on a job well done!"

LIEUTENANT GENERAL ROBERT F. FOLEY (USA, RETIRED)
USMA 1963
Medal of Honor Recipient and former Commandant of Cadets at West Point

"Absolutely fantastic book! You've done an amazing job melding visuals and real intellectual content to produce a readable and thought-provoking work. It's also a value for the price."

LIEUTENANT GENERAL JOHN MOELLERING (USA, RETIRED)
USMA 1959
Retired Chairman of the Board, USAA 2007-2012 and former Commandant of Cadets at West Point

"I think this book is outstanding. I have bought several copies to give to young people considering applying for a nomination and appointment to West Point. The candidates I have given it to have all told me how inspired they were by the stories of the graduates in the book, and how much more motivated they were to get into West Point and to lead a lifetime of service to the nation. Thank you for preparing the book and providing a vehicle for us to tell the West Point story and to use it to attract outstanding young men and women to become part of the Long Gray Line."

ROBERT A. "BOB" MCDONALD
USMA 1975
Retired Chairman of the Board, President and Chief Executive Officer The Procter & Gamble Company (NYSE: PG)

"I expected a first class product, but this far exceeds my expectations. The printing, writing and photography are all superb; the presentation is spectacular. This is a book that every West Point graduate would be proud to own, and that every patriotic American would enjoy perusing."

DR. JOHN NAGL, LIEUTENANT COLONEL (USA, RETIRED)
USMA 1988
Rhodes Scholar and Counterinsurgency Expert

>> Contents

There were several authors who contributed to this book and each is acknowledged for their work at the site of the biography. Unless otherwise acknowledged, all writing was done by Daniel E. Rice, USMA 1988, and Lieutenant Colonel (USA, Retired) John A. Vigna, USMA 1988.

Published by the Leadership Development Foundation info@WPLPOC.com

This is a book about leadership. Its purpose, however, is not to catalog a set of rules or principles to follow that will guarantee a successful outcome; rather, it is to reveal how leadership manifests itself through the incredible and unique life stories of 180 West Point graduates and two of America's Founding Fathers. In doing so, the one constant among all of these stories is West Point. Founded by General Washington as a strategically important military post in 1778, and later established as the United States Military Academy by President Thomas Jefferson in 1802, West Point has evolved into the world's premier leadership-training institute. A rigorous and challenging four-year experience, West Point clearly articulates both an academic and military component in its mission statement:

"To educate, train, and inspire the Corps of Cadets so that each graduate is a commissioned leader of character committed to the values of Duty, Honor, Country and prepared for a career of professional excellence and service to the nation as an officer in the United States Army."[1]

As an academic institution of higher education, West Point provides a well-rounded and world-class education in a variety of academic disciplines. It has achieved the pinnacle of undergraduate status in being ranked as both America's top college by *Forbes Magazine* and America's top public liberal arts college by *U.S. News & World Report* while regularly maintaining a top-five status in those areas. Additionally, West Point ranks among the nation's top schools in terms of producing Rhodes Scholars, Marshall Scholars, Hertz Fellows, and White House Fellows. In light of these academic credentials and unlike most academic institutions, West Point's primary focus goes far beyond producing top-tier students. That focus is, most importantly, to produce commissioned officers and leaders of character to serve and guide the nation, with intellectual excellence as a critical component of those leaders. While there have been subtle changes to West Point's mission statement over the years, the end state of producing commissioned leaders of character remains

the same. For more than 210 years, West Point's success in accomplishing its mission is clearly visible through the lives of its graduates who have led the nation militarily, politically, economically, and academically. Clearly, many of America's most notable senior military leaders, strategic wartime commanders, and combat leaders at every level have been West Point graduates – this purpose is explicit in the mission statement and remains paramount. It is also evident in the numerous graduates who have given the ultimate sacrifice in the service of their country.

Yet, the leadership cadets learn and develop at West Point transcends the military and is applicable in a variety of other areas. Unsurprisingly, West Point has regularly produced successful leaders in these areas as well. West Point graduates have become politicians and public servants, to include two American presidents (both two-term), along with several governors, senators, representatives, cabinet members, and ambassadors. West Point graduates have become nation-builders and scientific pioneers who designed and built railroads, the Panama Canal, the Pentagon, and who became astronauts (18 in total to include two of the three *Apollo 11* crew members) and led the Manhattan Project. West Point graduates spearheaded the creation of many of our national institutions and infrastructure such as the Interstate Highway System, the commercial airport system, the National Rifle Association (NRA), and the National Collegiate Athletic Association (NCAA). Others have become All-American athletes and NCAA Hall of Fame coaches. West Point graduates have founded universities such as Howard University, City College of New York, Norwich University, and the U.S. Air Force Academy to name a few, and have been the university presidents of many universities.

Graduates have also become leaders of some of America's greatest corporations starting with the majority of the railroads in the 1800s and continuing through the current leaders of Johnson & Johnson, Foot Locker, Procter & Gamble, 7-Eleven, Mercedes-Benz USA, Medtronic, Bell Helicopter, SolarWorld

USA, the New York Stock Exchange, and many others. Thus, the collection of graduates highlighted in this book represents only a small sample of successful leaders in these various areas and across the span of West Point's existence. Through their individual stories, this book honors their personal experiences and provides inspirational examples of leadership through discipline, duty, intellect, ethics, service, courage, and sacrifice – the very same traits defining those leaders of character West Point seeks to develop. With their collective stories, this book provides a lens through which to view America's rich history and the leading role West Point's graduates have played in shaping every aspect of that history.

AUTHORS' NOTE ON GRADUATE PROFILES

It is important to note that this book is neither an attempt at, nor intended to be, a ranking in any way of the United States Military Academy's 180 most distinguished graduates. In fact, such an attempt would be impossible and would never gain consensus in any circle given the number and variety of contributions made by West Point's tens of thousands of graduates throughout the course of its existence. Arguably, some of those profiled in this book would likely have been considered by anyone selecting individual West Point graduates to profile – certainly Ulysses S. Grant, Dwight D. Eisenhower, Sylvanus Thayer, and Douglas MacArthur come to mind – but again, to "rank order" or provide a top listing of "distinguished graduates" is not our purpose. Rather, as stated in "Taking the Oath," our intent is to honor the individual stories and experiences of selected graduates across the breadth of West Point's existence and provide inspirational examples of leadership through discipline, duty, intellect, ethics, service, courage, and sacrifice. In doing so, we necessarily selected both historical and contemporary graduates so that their collective stories also provide a lens through which to view America's rich history and the leading role West Point's graduates have played in shaping every aspect of that history.

The selection process was not scientific. So exclusion from this book in no way is a statement about any West Point graduate's worthiness of being included here – either living or historical figure. In fact, there are likely hundreds, perhaps thousands, of graduates not appearing in this book who have led and inspired generations of Americans and are worthy of consideration amongst the cabinet members, generals, ambassadors, politicians, philanthropists, athletes, scholars, educators, CEOs, Medal of Honor recipients, and those making the ultimate sacrifice. This book provides only a small, representative sample of those graduates. While there are many historical figures profiled in this book, there are a disproportionate number of living and contemporary graduates. This is unsurprising given that nearly two-thirds of West Point's total alumni have graduated since 1960. This was also done intentionally to highlight that even today, at a time of enormous focus on national security, West Point graduates not only continue to lead the military, but they also lead in nearly every other aspect of American society after they complete their military service – just as they have throughout the Academy's existence.

Selection to West Point and earning the opportunity to join the Long Gray Line is a great honor, privilege, and opportunity for any young man or woman. It is a life changing event. We hope that this book will inspire young men and women to consider a future at West Point and in the Army. The opportunities available to West Point graduates are limitless as seen through the incredible life stories of those profiled in this book.

Likewise, many of these stories also reveal how many graduates have given back to West Point after their military service. Thus, we hope that their examples will inspire other graduates to continue to do so.

Finally, we hope that the leadership profiles in this book serve as an inspiration to all who read them.

TAKING THE OATH

Since the United States Army was founded June 14, 1775, millions of Americans have taken the oath to serve and protect the Constitution of the United States as soldiers and officers in the United States Army. Every cadet entering West Point takes the Cadet Oath on the Plain at the end of the first day, and for those who graduate four years later, take the Officer's Oath upon graduation and are commissioned in the United States Army. Both the Cadet and Officer Oath have plaques at West Point shown below.

CADET OATH AND OFFICER OATH:

"I, _____, do solemnly swear (or affirm) that I will support and defend the Constitution of the United States against all enemies, foreign and domestic; that I will bear true faith and allegiance to the same; and that I will obey the orders of the President of the United States and the orders of the officers appointed over me, according to regulations and the Uniform Code of Military Justice. So help me God."

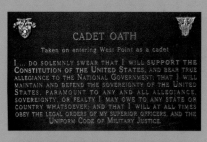

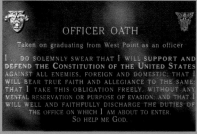

Above photos © 2013/Greg E. Mathieson Sr./MAI

Cadets take the Oath of Office as Officers in the United States Army at West Point graduation on May 21, 2011.

TO THE AMERICAN SOLDIER

MISSION OF THE
UNITED STATES MILITARY ACADEMY

The mission of the United States Military Academy is to educate, train, and inspire the Corps of Cadets so that each graduate is a commissioned leader of character committed to the values of "Duty, Honor, Country" and prepared for a career of professional excellence and service to the Nation as an officer in the United States Army.

Monument dedicated to the American soldier, located on the north side of Lusk Reservoir, West Point. Gift from USMA Classes of 1935 and 1936.

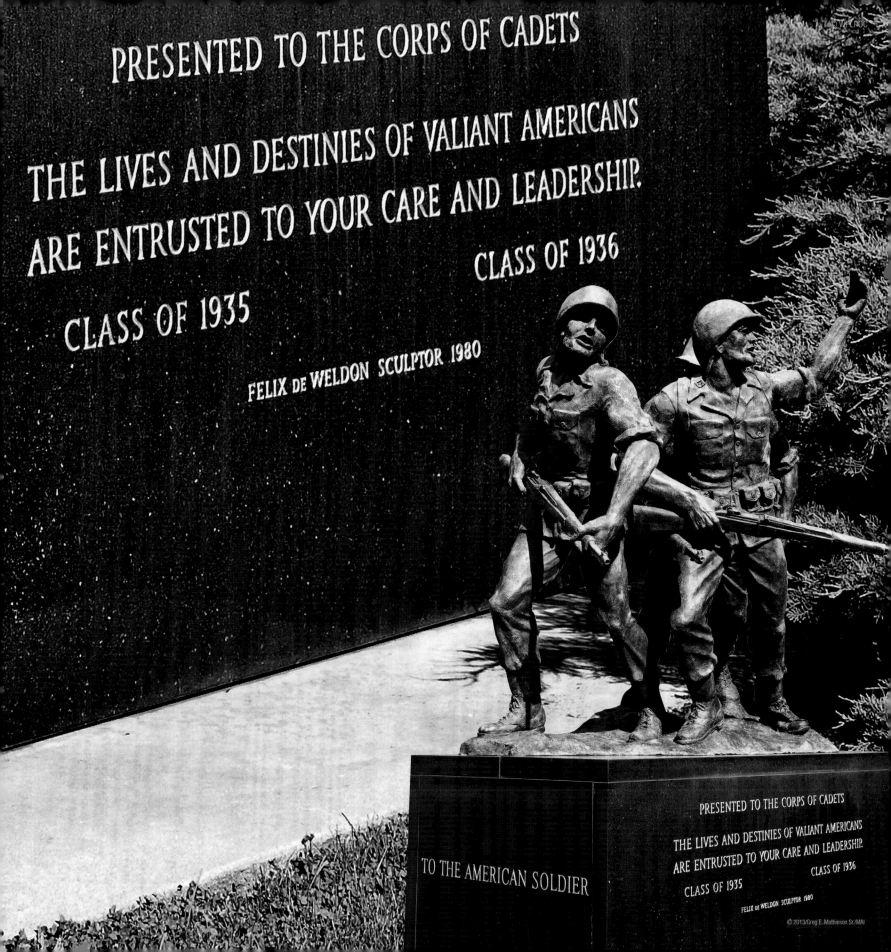

© WLPOC

PRESENTED TO THE CORPS OF CADETS

THE LIVES AND DESTINIES OF VALIANT AMERICANS
ARE ENTRUSTED TO YOUR CARE AND LEADERSHIP.

CLASS OF 1936

CLASS OF 1935

FELIX DE WELDON SCULPTOR 1980

TO THE AMERICAN SOLDIER

PRESENTED TO THE CORPS OF CADETS

THE LIVES AND DESTINIES OF VALIANT AMERICANS
ARE ENTRUSTED TO YOUR CARE AND LEADERSHIP.

CLASS OF 1935

CLASS OF 1936

FELIX DE WELDON SCULPTOR 1980

PRESENTIAL PERSPECTIVES ON
WEST POINT

During the American Revolution, General George Washington selected West Point as the most strategically important position in America, ordered Continental troops to occupy it on January 27, 1778, and eventually transferred his headquarters there in 1779. Since then, American soldiers have occupied West Point, making it the oldest continuously garrisoned post in the United States. President Thomas Jefferson next signed legislation in 1802 that officially established the United States Military Academy on West Point. Every President since has been involved with West Point and her graduates.

"No other educational institution in the land has contributed as many names as West Point has contributed to the honor roll of the nation's greatest citizens…. And of all the institutions in the country, none is more absolutely American."

–President Teddy Roosevelt, 1902

"You at West Point have established an example for the rest of the nation."

–President George H. W. Bush, 1991

"I feel in my heart a great confidence in the future of our country, for I know that you will defend that future. And it's true: The Long Gray Line has never failed us."

–President Ronald Reagan, 1987

"You are part of a long tradition stretching back to the earliest days of this country's history."

–President John F. Kennedy, 1962

"Graduates of this Academy have brought creativity and courage to every field of endeavor. West Point produced the chief engineer of the Panama Canal, the mind behind the Manhattan Project, the first American to walk in space."

–President George W. Bush, 2002

"The Long Gray Line has extended from here to the ends of the world."

–President Gerald Ford, 1975

"Generations of Americans have built upon the foundation of our forefathers – finding opportunity, fighting injustice, forging a more perfect union. Our achievement would not be possible without the Long Gray Line that has sacrificed for duty, for honor, for country."

–President Barack Obama, 2010

THE FOUNDING FATHERS OF WEST POINT

While most Americans typically know West Point as the home of the United States Military Academy, its rich history precedes the Academy's creation by nearly 25 years. It was during the American Revolution that West Point's strategic importance became apparent as the best location for denying the British access northward along the Hudson River and protecting lines of communication between New England and the rest of the colonies. General George Washington considered West Point "indispensably essential" to this end, and thus directed the construction of a fortifications system, which began on January 27, 1778, and continued through the end of the war when West Point then remained as one of only two garrisoned posts after the war.[1] By 1783, the experience during the American Revolution convinced America's Founders that the nation clearly lacked trained military leaders, engineers, and artillerymen and that some type of military school would be valuable and essential to the growing nation.[2] So was borne the idea to establish a national military school to train officers in the military arts and sciences, as well as in the technical disciplines, and West Point seemed a logical place to do so. Following years of debate, President Thomas Jefferson carried the torch of creating a Military Academy immediately after taking office in March 1801, and West Point still remained the logical choice. By April 1801, the Jefferson Administration quickly moved forward in conceptualizing and establishing the Military Academy, naming Major Jonathan Williams as its first Superintendent. As a final step on March 16, 1802, Congress officially sanctioned the Military Academy under the Military Peace Establishment Act, which also directed the formal establishment of the Corps of Engineers to be located at West Point. The United States Military Academy at West Point was officially created with Thomas Jefferson credited as its primary founder. Shortly thereafter, Joseph G. Swift graduated on October 12, 1802, to become West Point's first graduate.[3] Since those humble beginnings, West Point has evolved into its present state as the United States Military Academy, a top-rated undergraduate institute, and the world's premier leadership training institute developing commissioned leaders of character. Today, March 16th is celebrated annually by West Point Societies around the world as "Founders Day."

"In 1778, George Washington erected a fort high upon a granite point overlooking the Hudson to guard the region of New York in the event of a British attack. And now, for more than 180 years, the United States Military Academy, here at West Point, has in effect extended and carried on that first mission. For here we train the men and women whose duty it is to defend the Republic, the men and women whose profession is watchfulness, whose skill is vigilance, whose calling is to guard the peace, but if need be, to fight and win...More than 180 years, West Point in this time has established and added luster to a proud story, a story of courage and wisdom, a story of heroism, of sacrifice, and yes, very often the ultimate sacrifice. It is the story of men like Ulysses Grant, the son of a humble tanner in Ohio who went on from West Point to save the American Union. It's the story of Dwight David Eisenhower, a Kansas farm boy who learned the skills at West Point that enabled him to command the mightiest invasion force in history, and of Douglas MacArthur, an acknowledged genius in war who showed himself during the occupation of Japan to be a genius in peace, as well."

–President Ronald Reagan, October 28, 1987

Portrait of Washington Crossing the Delaware to attack the Hessians, painted by Emmanuel Leutze.

Photo: NARA

Washington Statue at West Point.

President George Washington

- FOUNDED MILITARY BASE AT WEST POINT, 1778
- COMMANDING GENERAL, CONTINENTAL ARMY
- LED THE CONTINENTAL ARMY TO VICTORY OVER THE BRITISH IN THE REVOLUTIONARY WAR, 1775–83
- PRESIDED OVER THE CONSTITUTIONAL CONVENTION, 1787
- ELECTED FIRST PRESIDENT OF THE UNITED STATES OF AMERICA, 1789
- WASHINGTON STATUE AND WASHINGTON HALL AT WEST POINT DEDICATED IN HIS HONOR

Photo: NARA

Washington Monument in Washington, D.C., both named in Washington's honor.

Courtesy: NPS

Washington Statue in front of Washington Hall, West Point.

>>> Spotlight

Washington's image has become representative of America, adorning the dollar bill, the quarter, several stamps, and the Purple Heart (the nation's first valor award for military heroism).

General George Washington established the Purple Heart Medal during the American Revolution at his Continental Army Headquarters in Newburgh, New York, August 7, 1782, as the first formal system of recognizing soldiers for individual gallantry. Following the American Revolution, the Purple Heart Medal fell into obscurity but was re-established by the Secretary of War in 1932 at the request of General Douglas MacArthur (USMA 1903), Chief of Staff of the United States Army as a combat decoration awarded to any American service member who is killed or wounded at the hands of the enemy. Since then, West Point graduates have been killed or wounded in every American conflict leading soldiers in combat. The National Purple Heart Hall of Heroes in New Windsor, New York, founded in 2010, honors those West Point graduates, as well as all other recipients of the Purple Heart Medal. The Purple Heart bears the profile of our founding father, General George Washington.

It is not often that a nation collectively holds one of its historical figures in such high regard throughout the entirety of its national history. For America, General George Washington is one such example. Although his life as the younger son within a family of Virginia's colonial gentry did not fore-shadow opportunities of historical greatness, Washington's life ultimately led him down a path of military and public service to the nation that would have monumental impacts on the direction of America and the world. Commander of the Continental Army and architect of victory during the American Revolution, delegate to the Constitutional Convention and the Constitution's first signer, and first President of the United States, Washington – the consummate soldier-statesman – rightfully earned his title as "Father" of the nation among America's "Founding Fathers." Where Washington's status could have easily led him to choose a life that was self-serving, he instead pursued a life of selfless-service, using a blend of positive temperament, experience, intellect, and tact, which made him the right leader at the right time in war and peace. Also under his leadership, Washington the General established the military base at West Point during the American Revolution, and Washington the President advocated for establishing a military school at West Point. While he never lived to see West Point's establishment, it is altogether appropriate that Washington's life was guided by the very tenets that are at West Point's foundation: "Duty, Honor, Country."[1]

Born on February 22, 1732, in Westmoreland County, Virginia, to tobacco farmers, Washington had five siblings – of which he was the oldest from his father Augustine's second marriage – and two older half-brothers. When Washington's father died in 1743, his eldest half-brother and childhood idol, Lawrence, became his surrogate father. Washington received various levels of informal education, to include home-schooling and the study of practical surveying. At age 17, he became a part of Lawrence's household at Mount Vernon and the heir to the estate. When his brother died in 1752, Washington thus inherited Mount Vernon.[2]

Washington's military experience prior to the American Revolution resulted from his service for the British in the French and Indian War from 1754 to 1758. Commanding Virginia militia forces on the colonial frontier, Washington first saw combat in 1754 at Fort Necessity in Pennsylvania – the opening action of the war – where he was captured by the French and then released. Next, in 1755, as General Edward Braddock's aide, he rallied British and Virginia militia forces for an organized retreat after a devastating ambush by the French

and their Indian allies during the Battle of Monongahela killed Braddock and threatened to annihilate the command. For his actions, Washington received a promotion to Lieutenant Colonel – the only native-born American to do so in the war – and command of the Virginia Regiment he then led during the capture of Fort Duquesne in Pennsylvania in 1758. Washington demonstrated excellent combat and leadership skills during the French and Indian War. He proved to possess a great command presence and to be adept at organizing, training, and disciplining soldiers, while at the same time fearlessly leading them under fire.[3] Following the French and Indian War, Washington married widow Martha Custis in 1759, bringing her and her children to his Mount Vernon estate. He spent the next 16 years as a well-respected and well-connected private citizen, amassing a large estate, becoming a successful planter, but also serving in Virginia's House of Burgesses from 1759 to 1774 as was expected from a man of his social and economic status. While his political and economic prudence aided in his success, Washington was among the first Virginians to publicly protest British colonial policy, underscoring his opposition

WASHINGTON CONSIDERED WEST POINT THE "KEY TO AMERICA," ESTABLISHING A MILITARY BASE AT ITS CURRENT LOCATION IN 1778 THAT IS THE LONGEST OCCUPIED BASE STILL IN EXISTENCE IN THE UNITED STATES.

with his acceptance as Virginia's delegate to the First Continental Congress in 1774 to 1775 on the eve of the American Revolution.[4]

By 1775, the Colonists began to organize to fight the British and the first shots were fired at Lexington and Concord. Washington seemed ideally positioned for selection as the Commander in Chief of the Continental Army, and he was unanimously chosen by the Second Continental Congress on June 15, 1775. Washington accepted the position and did so not for economic, social, or political status – he already had those – but out of a profound sense of duty as he commanded the Army for more than eight years and refused any salary. Every aspect of Washington's talent as a leader came to bear during the American Revolution. While he experienced more defeats than victories at the war's tactical and operational levels – Trenton, Princeton, and Yorktown were his three significant

victories – he won the war by focusing on the strategic level. Essentially, Washington knew that preserving the Continental Army so that it could continue to fight without undermining the ideological goals of the Revolution was key. He did just that through his constant interaction with the Continental Congress and by focusing his efforts on raising, equipping, training, and maintaining the Army, all the while leading by example in enduring the same hardships as his soldiers throughout the war. Washington also considered West Point to be strategically indispensable to the American effort and established a military base and fortifications system at its current location beginning in January 1778. In 1779, he even headquartered his Army at West Point before moving it to nearby Newburgh. The war ended in 1783 with the Treaty of Paris as Britain accepted the independence of the United States. On December 4, 1783, Washington gathered his officers in New York City's Fraunces Tavern, where he officially announced he would resign as Commander in Chief and bid farewell to his officers rather than seizing power. In doing so, he established the critical precedent of military subordination to civilian authority.[5] After the war, he returned to Mount Vernon and out of the public eye, but only for a short while.

In 1787, he re-entered public service as a delegate to the Constitutional Convention and was unanimously elected to preside over the convention. After the ratification of the Constitution, Washington was then unanimously elected as the first President of the United States in 1789 and again in 1793. His presidency was marked by the very same traits that had served him well throughout his life. Again realizing that everything he did as President was setting precedent and careful not to turn the office into a monarchy, Washington sought policies that would allow the United States to economically develop and gain international legitimacy as he balanced political factions, promoted national expansion, reduced the national debt and established a national bank, and pursued international neutrality. While careful not to usurp power at the federal level, he was quick to defend the federal government's authority. He also unsuccessfully urged Congress to establish a professional Military Academy at West Point, which would not come to fruition until 1802, three years after his death. Perhaps his most significant precedent as President was to willingly step down, just like he had resigned his military commission after the American Revolution, after two terms in office, even though the Constitution did not limit terms until the 22nd Amendment in 1951.[6] Washington finally returned home to a dilapidated Mount Vernon in 1797, the result of his previous 23 years of selfless service to the

new nation in both war and in peace. Over his final two years, he worked to restore his estate while also putting his personal affairs in order – most significant of which was to free his slaves upon Martha's death, which made him the only Virginia "Founding Father" to do so.[7] On December 14, 1799, George Washington died after a sudden bout with an extreme form of tonsillitis.[8]

Washington has been honored in countless ways, both nationally and at West Point, and his iconic image continues to be representative of America. The nation's capital is named after him, as is the state of Washington. One of the most prominent features in the Washington, D.C., skyline – The Washington Monument – also bears his name. A sculpture of his head is one of four different United States Presidents adorning Mount Rushmore National Monument in South Dakota. The George Washington Bridge in New York City bears his name. The Purple Heart, the nation's oldest military award still given to United States service members – its forerunner originally known as the Badge of Military Merit established by Washington in 1782 – bears his profile. His likeness appears on the quarter, the dollar bill, and several stamps. Prominent universities also bear his name to include Washington, D.C.'s George Washington University, St. Louis's Washington University, and Lexington, Virginia's Washington and Lee University. At West Point, the recognition of Washington's special place in the Academy's history is also clearly evident. His statue holds the most prominent, centrally located position on the Plain in front of the mess hall, where he overlooks the parade field upon which cadets regularly perform drill and ceremony, much like he would have observed Continental Army soldiers and militia training at this very same location more than 230 years ago. Fittingly, the cadet mess hall in front of which his statue stands bears the name Washington Hall – each day more than 4,000 cadets are served simultaneously during the three daily meals. Also, one of the Thayer Hotel's most exclusive conference rooms overlooking the picturesque Hudson River is dedicated to President Washington. Finally, in 1976 during America's bicentennial celebration, Congress approved a joint resolution posthumously promoting General Washington to "General of the Armies." It gave Washington a rank superior to General John. J. Pershing, who, at that point, had held the highest rank in the history of the Army. In doing so, the resolution's intent ensures that Washington forever remains the highest-ranking officer in the United States.[9]

Thomas Jefferson – scholar, lawyer, philosopher, statesman, President, and founder of the United States Military Academy – was born April 13, 1743, in Shadwell, Virginia, to a moderately wealthy family. Jefferson grew up with a passion for learning instilled in him by his father, who died when Jefferson was 14. At age 16, the bright young student attended the College of William and Mary and graduated with honors, going on to study law. In 1767, he was admitted to the bar in Virginia, and the next year he began construction of a neo-classical mansion on the estate, Monticello,

he had inherited from his father. In 1772, he married Martha Wayles Skelton. The happy couple eventually had six children.[1]

This Virginia gentleman was soon caught up in the swirling events of the American Revolution, however. In 1774, when the British Parliament first enacted the Coercive Acts in response to unrest in the Colonies, Jefferson published a response that suggested the Colonists had the natural right to govern themselves. The following year, Jefferson was appointed to the Second Continental Congress, eventually serving on the five-man team charged with creating a

statement declaring the American colonies as an independent nation. The team assigned Jefferson with the primary responsibility of drafting the document. Although Congress debated and made some edits, Jefferson's Declaration of Independence was officially approved and signed on July 4, 1776.[2]

After this monumental accomplishment, Jefferson served as Governor of Virginia from 1779 until 1781. During his time as Governor, the Revolutionary War finally came in force to Virginia. First, a British force led by the traitorous Benedict Arnold landed near the capital, forcing the Virginia govern-

ment to flee inland to Charlottesville.[3] In the waning days of the ill-fated British march toward Yorktown, British General Charles Cornwallis dispatched a raiding party led by the infamous Banastre Tarleton toward Charlottesville. Jefferson escaped only 10 minutes before the British arrived.[4]

After helping the United States secure its independence, Jefferson served as Ambassador to France from 1785 to 1789 and then as Secretary of State under President George Washington until 1793. He then somewhat reluctantly ran for President in 1796 but lost to his friend and rival John

President Thomas Jefferson

- **FOUNDER OF THE UNITED STATES MILITARY ACADEMY, 1802**
- **FOUNDER OF THE UNIVERSITY OF VIRGINIA, 1819**
- **THIRD PRESIDENT OF THE UNITED STATES, 1801–09**
- **VICE PRESIDENT OF THE U.S. UNDER PRESIDENT JOHN ADAMS, 1797–1801**
- **U.S. SECRETARY OF STATE UNDER PRESIDENT GEORGE WASHINGTON**
- **U.S. AMBASSADOR TO FRANCE, 1785–89**
- **GOVERNOR OF VIRGINIA DURING THE AMERICAN REVOLUTION, 1779–81**
- **AUTHOR OF THE DECLARATION OF INDEPENDENCE**

Photo: NARA

Jefferson Statue in Jefferson Library, West Point.

© 2013 Greg E. Mathieson Sr./MAI

Mount Rushmore. Presidents Washington, Jefferson, Teddy Roosevelt, and Lincoln.

Photo: AP

>>> Spotlight

Courtesy: U.S. Mint

Considered one of the founding fathers of the United States, Jefferson's image is reflected on the nickel, as well as the $2 bill and Mount. Rushmore beside George Washington, Teddy Roosevelt, and Abraham Lincoln.

© 2013 Greg E. Mathieson Sr./MAI

Adams. However, he had enough votes to become Vice President, a position he actually preferred.[5] During these years, Jefferson and other members of the growing "Republican" faction opposed many "Federalist" efforts to strengthen the Federal government. Among these Federalist initiatives was a drive to create a national Military Academy, which Jefferson opposed because he feared that such a school would create a permanent military caste that might threaten the fledgling nation's liberty.[6]

Jefferson ran for President again in 1800, defeating Adams, but tying Aaron Burr in the Electoral College. Congress broke the tie, choosing Jefferson to be the third President of the United States.[7] While Jefferson worked to keep the United States from becoming embroiled in the epic struggle between Napoleonic France and the rest of Europe, he did order the United States Navy to deploy military vessels to combat Algerian pirates in what became known as the Barbary Wars.[8] On March 16, 1802, Jefferson signed legislation establishing the United States Military Academy at West Point. Jefferson's reversal on the issue of a national Military Academy has puzzled many. Some theorize that Jefferson's longtime advocacy for higher education and his belief that the establishment of a national university would benefit society as a whole by providing scientific and practical knowledge had trumped his constitutional fears.[9] Others argued that Jefferson wanted to free the country from its need for foreign-born military experts, or that establishing the Academy himself, focusing on developing expert leaders for the nation's citizen-soldiers, would prevent the Federalists from establishing an isolated, self-perpetuating military elite.[10]

After his Presidency, he remained involved in public affairs and continued to be a strong proponent of higher education. He lobbied for years for a state university in Virginia, until the University of Virginia was founded in 1819. Jefferson designed the university's "academical village," centering the buildings on the library, not a church, in keeping with Jefferson's Enlightenment secularism.[11]

Jefferson died on July 4, 1826, exactly 50 years after the signing of the Declaration of Independence and passing within hours on the same day as his great rival and friend Adams.[12] Our grateful nation commemorates this centrally important founding father throughout the land in memorials, on mountainsides, and on currency. As one of the original American advocates of higher education, he will be forever memorialized as the founder of both West Point and the University of Virginia. The recently constructed library at West Point is named in his honor. When the library's statue of Jefferson, dedicated by the West Point Class of 1968, was being delivered to West Point in 2008, it was involved in a traffic accident, the transport vehicle caught fire, and the statue was slightly damaged. Tested by fire, just like Jefferson himself, the statue of the man who founded West Point and helped found the United States of America stands each day watching over our nation's future leaders.[13]

Written by: Major Joseph C. Scott and Daniel E. Rice, USMA 1988.

ON MARCH 16, 1802, JEFFERSON SIGNED LEGISLATION ESTABLISHING THE UNITED STATES MILITARY ACADEMY AT WEST POINT. JEFFERSON WAS A LONGTIME ADVOCATE OF HIGHER EDUCATION AND HAD BELIEVED THAT THE ESTABLISHMENT OF A NATIONAL UNIVERSITY WOULD BENEFIT SOCIETY AS A WHOLE.

Jefferson Library at West Point, built 2010.

The West Point Crest on the floor of the Jefferson Library in front of Jefferson Statue.

Jefferson Statue within the Jefferson Memorial, Washington, D.C.

Although President Thomas Jefferson holds the title as West Point's "founder" by formally establishing the United States Military Academy in 1802, Sylvanus Thayer is considered its "father." Thayer's impact on West Point cannot be overstated as he became renowned for resurrecting the Academy at a tenuous time in its early existence, thus setting it on a positive trajectory for future centuries. Holding the position of Superintendent for 16 years from 1817 to 1833, longer than any other Superintendent, Thayer rightfully earned the title "Father of the Military Academy" as he transformed the Academy from an institution uncertain of its purpose and inconsistent in its administration and execution, into the nation's premier leadership institution by codifying an enduring system that has intellectually, militarily, and ethically developed and shaped its graduates ever since.[1] The Academy Thayer built as Superintendent required him to create order from chaos through a blend of previous initiatives, his own vision, and his force of will, the end result of which successfully produced graduates who provided the core leadership for America throughout the nineteenth century and beyond.[2]

Thayer was born in Braintree, Massachusetts, on June 9, 1785 – only two years after America had gained independence, but still prior to the Constitutional Convention and the presidency of George Washington. At age 8, he moved to New Hampshire to live with his uncle, a Revolutionary War veteran. At age 18, he entered Dartmouth College and graduated as valedictorian in 1807. Rather than giving his valedictorian address at Dartmouth, Thayer instead headed to West Point after receiving a Presidential appointment from Thomas Jefferson. Because of the unstructured nature of the early Academy, Thayer graduated in only one year as part of the

Colonel Sylvanus Thayer, USMA 1808

- CONSIDERED "THE FATHER OF THE UNITED STATES MILITARY ACADEMY"
- SUPERINTENDENT OF WEST POINT, 1817–33
- ESTABLISHED CURRICULUM MAKING WEST POINT THE FIRST ENGINEERING COLLEGE IN THE U.S.
- ESTABLISHED CADET HONOR CODE, ACADEMIC BOARD AND BOARD OF VISITORS
- COMMANDER, NORFOLK, VIRGINIA, WAR OF 1812
- CHIEF OF ENGINEERS, NEW ENGLAND, U.S. ARMY, 1833–63
- SYLVANUS THAYER AWARD NAMED IN HIS HONOR
- THAYER HOTEL AT WEST POINT NAMED IN HIS HONOR
- FIRST PRESIDENT OF THE WEST POINT ASSOCIATION OF GRADUATES

Photo: NARA

SYLVANUS THAYER
BVT. BRIG. GEN'L U.S. ARMY.
BORN JUNE 9, 1785, AT BRAINTREE MASS.
DIED SEPT. 7, 1872, AT BRAINTREE MASS.
SUPERINTENDENT OF THE MILITARY ACADEMY
JULY 28, 1817, TO JULY 1, 1833.

Thayer grave at West Point Cemetery.

© 2013/Greg E. Mathieson Sr./MAI

>>> Spotlight

The Historic Thayer Hotel at West Point was opened May 27, 1926. The original West Point Hotel was a wooden structure, located on Trophy Point, built in 1929 by then-Superintendent Colonel Sylvanus Thayer. After World War I, as the Academy was expanding, the decision was made to tear down the wooden hotel and build a new granite-and-brick hotel near the gate at Highland Falls. Named after the "Father of the Military Academy," the Thayer Hotel was opened in 1926 and the old West Point Hotel was torn down in 1929. In 2009, the Thayer Hotel experienced a multi-million-dollar renovation and is now a 149-bed hotel ideally suited for conferences, weddings, reunions, and tourists coming to the Hudson River Valley.

THE THAYER

Class of 1808 – the Academy's 33rd graduate overall – and commissioned in the Corps of Engineers.[3] After graduation, he served as inspector of fortifications in New England, taught mathematics at the Academy, and then saw duty in War of 1812 on the Niagara Frontier, Lake Champlain, and in the defense of Norfolk, Virginia. While Thayer did not gain recognition during the war for combat valor, he did earn praise for his administrative performance and skills by senior leaders to include the Chief of Engineers and future West Point Superintendent, Joseph G. Swift, who also recommended him for a Brevet promotion to Major.[4]

After the war, President James Madison sent Thayer in 1815 to study at France's *École Polytechnique*, as well as tour Europe to observe a variety of military institutions and educational methods. Essentially, his charter was to learn firsthand about the European art of war, fortifications, military engineering, and history while gaining insights in military education and the operation of military schools. Additionally, he was also charged with acquiring as many books, maps, and materials as possible for West Point. Thayer welcomed this opportunity since his observations during the War of 1812 led him to conclude that American Army officers suffered from poor training, poor standards, poor discipline, and a lack of general military knowledge. After his return to the United States, he was directed by the new President, James Monroe, to become the fifth Superintendent of West Point. Thus, with Thayer's appointment came his vision to transform the Academy.[5]

During his 16 years as Superintendent, Thayer's transformation of the Academy centered on the key pillars of academics, military discipline, and ethical behavior. Careful not to turn West Point into a narrowly focused military school, his most durable legacy was his reform and standardization of the curriculum – a four-year program that heavily emphasized science, math, and engineering, which went against the conventional academic wisdom of the early-nineteenth century. In doing so, West Point became America's first and finest engineering school – so much so that some contemporary critics argued, for a time, that West Point produced better engineers than soldiers.[6] Along with this revised yet diversified curriculum – French, drawing, and traditional courses, such as history, grammar, and philosophy were required – Thayer further instituted other academic processes to include small classes, daily recitations, regular exams, and class rankings. In the realm of military discipline, Thayer established many policies that standardized and improved personal appearance, Academy conditions, and individual behavior, to include the earliest stages of the Honor Code, all of which were associated with various forms of reward and punishment. Military training also had its role in Academy life as cadets learned military tactics, drills, and participated in summer encampments. In essence, Thayer put his imprint on every aspect of the Academy in a role that now incorporates the current responsibilities of the Superintendent, Commandant, and Dean.[7] In order to emphasize Thayer's influence on West Point, historian Theodore Crackel notes, "Thayer's legacy went far beyond the system itself, for he embodied what was to become known as 'The Spirit of West Point.'"[8] By 1833 and despite his transformation of the Academy, however, Thayer resigned as Superintendent over philosophical differences with President Andrew Jackson – namely, over Jackson's concern that Thayer was turning the Academy into an undemocratic and elitist institution. Nevertheless, Thayer's system endured and many of the 711 cadets who attended the Academy during his tenure went on to found or staff many of America's colleges – 78 of his former cadets were on the faculty of American universities by 1860 – as well as provide the core pool of leaders who would continue to serve the Army and develop the nation.

THE HONORS BESTOWED UPON COLONEL THAYER ARE MANY – BOTH AT WEST POINT AND ELSEWHERE. AT WEST POINT, HE IS KNOWN AS "THE FATHER OF THE MILITARY ACADEMY," AND HIS STATUE STANDS ON THE PLAIN BY THE SUPERINTENDENT'S HOUSE, OVERLOOKING THE PARADE FIELD.

Thayer returned to the regular Army, where he served for 30 more years, primarily as the Chief Engineer in Boston, until his retirement in 1863 due to health reasons. In 1864, President Abraham Lincoln retroactively promoted him to Brevet Brigadier General. In a final, fitting role, Thayer helped establish and was elected as the first President of West Point's Association of Graduates in 1869. Thayer eventually died on September 7, 1872, at his home in Braintree, and even more fittingly, is buried at West Point, where he continues to keep watch over the institution he so greatly influenced.

In addition to the enduring systems he put into place at the Academy, Thayer's legacy remains in many other ways at West Point and elsewhere. At West Point, his statue stands on the Plain, directly across from the Superintendent's house, overlooking the parade field. Key structures, roads, and awards at the Academy also bear his name. Thayer Hall is the largest cadet academic building. The former West Point Hotel, located for nearly a century on Trophy Point, was relocated and opened in 1926 as the Thayer Hotel. It overlooks Thayer Gate, which links West Point with the village of Highland Falls. Thayer Road also links Thayer Gate with the main cadet academic area. Beyond West Point, the Thayer School of Engineering at Dartmouth College established in 1871 and the Thayer Academy in Braintree, Massachusetts, established in 1877 both honor their famous alumnus and native son respectively. In 1958, West Point named its most distinguished award the Sylvanus Thayer Award, which annually honors an outstanding citizen whose service to the nation best reflects the United States Military Academy's motto of "Duty, Honor, Country." Past recipients of this award include Henry Kissinger, General Douglas MacArthur, President Ronald Reagan, Walter Cronkite, Sandra Day O'Connor, and other influential American leaders. Ultimately, Thayer's legacy remains in every graduate by the time they receive their West Point diplomas. That legacy is established through the commonality of their West Point experience and their development into commissioned leaders of character who enter the Army to lead the nation's soldiers in peacetime and in war.

The historic hotel at West Point is named "The Thayer Hotel" in his honor.

Wedding photo at Thayer Hotel overlooking Hudson River.

Thayer Statue on the Plain at West Point.

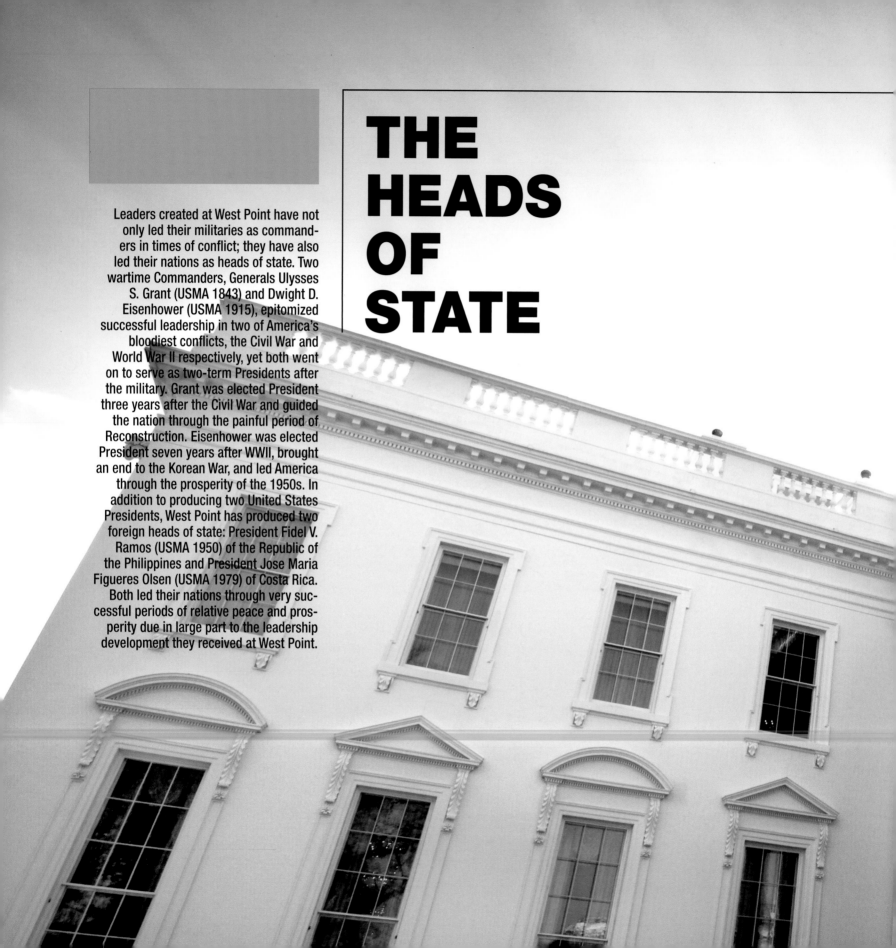

THE HEADS OF STATE

Leaders created at West Point have not only led their militaries as commanders in times of conflict; they have also led their nations as heads of state. Two wartime Commanders, Generals Ulysses S. Grant (USMA 1843) and Dwight D. Eisenhower (USMA 1915), epitomized successful leadership in two of America's bloodiest conflicts, the Civil War and World War II respectively, yet both went on to serve as two-term Presidents after the military. Grant was elected President three years after the Civil War and guided the nation through the painful period of Reconstruction. Eisenhower was elected President seven years after WWII, brought an end to the Korean War, and led America through the prosperity of the 1950s. In addition to producing two United States Presidents, West Point has produced two foreign heads of state: President Fidel V. Ramos (USMA 1950) of the Republic of the Philippines and President Jose Maria Figueres Olsen (USMA 1979) of Costa Rica. Both led their nations through very successful periods of relative peace and prosperity due in large part to the leadership development they received at West Point.

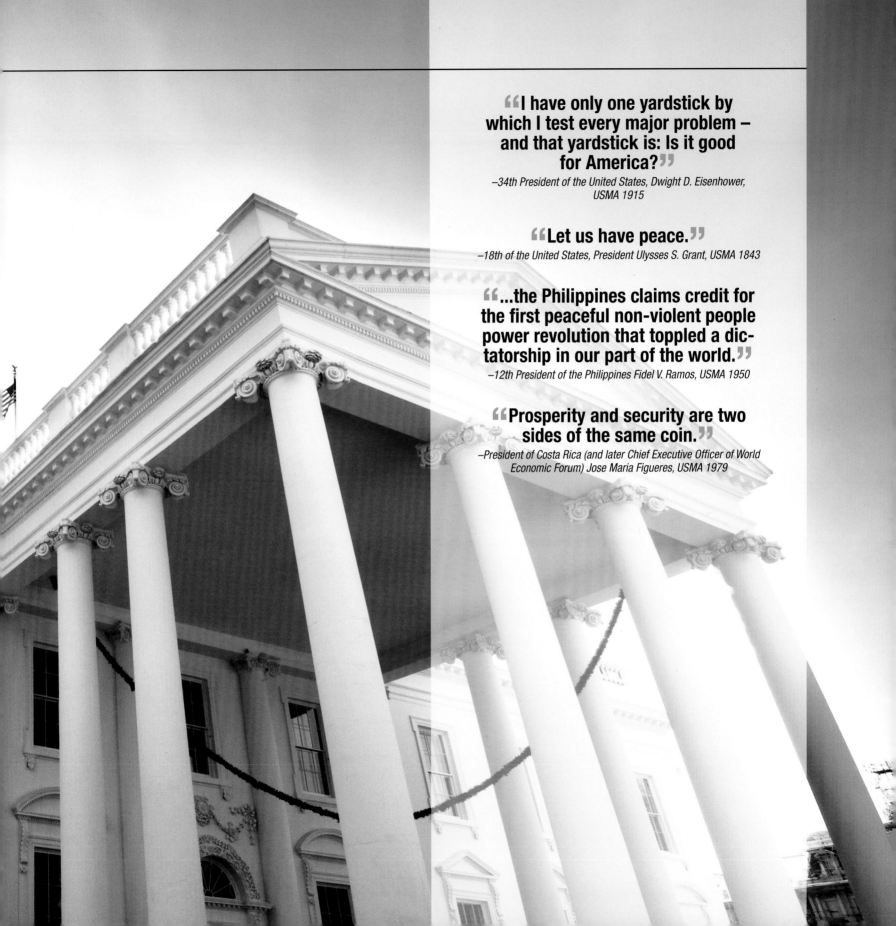

"I have only one yardstick by which I test every major problem – and that yardstick is: Is it good for America?"

–34th President of the United States, Dwight D. Eisenhower, USMA 1915

"Let us have peace."

–18th of the United States, President Ulysses S. Grant, USMA 1843

"...the Philippines claims credit for the first peaceful non-violent people power revolution that toppled a dictatorship in our part of the world."

–12th President of the Philippines Fidel V. Ramos, USMA 1950

"Prosperity and security are two sides of the same coin."

–President of Costa Rica (and later Chief Executive Officer of World Economic Forum) Jose Maria Figueres, USMA 1979

President Grant's official photo.
Photo: NARA

Grant Tomb in New York City.
Photo: NARA

President Ulysses S. Grant, USMA 1843

- **18TH PRESIDENT OF THE UNITED STATES**
- **COMMANDING GENERAL OF THE UNION ARMY, 1864–65**
- **LED MAJOR UNION VICTORIES IN THE WEST AT VICKSBURG, FORT DONELSON, FORT HENRY, AND SHILOH**
- **MEXICAN WAR VETERAN WITH DISTINGUISHED CONDUCT AT CHAPULTEPEC**
- **GRANT HALL AT WEST POINT NAMED IN HIS HONOR**
- **PRESIDENT, NATIONAL RIFLE ASSOCIATION (NRA)**

Ulysses S. Grant is one of the greatest American leaders to emerge from West Point. During his lifetime, the nation descended into civil war, underwent an imperfect reunion, and emerged a stronger democratic republic. Both as General and as President, Grant's leadership made the difference in guiding the United States through war, reconstruction, and recovery. When he died in 1885, Grant was easily the most popular figure in America. He had defeated General Robert E. Lee and the Confederacy in battle, and outlived President Abraham Lincoln in peace. Still, 125 years after his death, Grant's rise to power and renown in the United States remains enigmatic. Many have sought to understand Grant's complex legacy, one highlighted by his clarity of vision in battle, his political ascendancy after the war,

and his shortcomings in private business. Even William Tecumseh Sherman famously remarked, "Grant is a mystery, even to himself." Regardless, Grant's achievements distinguish him among his generation of Academy graduates.

Grant's modest roots in Galena, Illinois, and early military career only make his significance that much more compelling. Forced to attend the Military Academy after his father had secured Grant an appointment through a family friend, Grant proved to be a mediocre cadet. He dreamed of becoming a math professor, preferred to read novels, and hoped for Congress to close the Academy as a way to honorably avoid his service obligation. Graduating 21st out of 39 in the Class of 1843, Grant was commissioned as an Infantry Lieutenant and assigned to Jefferson Barracks, Missouri,

where he was relegated to the duties of the regimental quartermaster.

But Grant matured quickly as a young officer serving under Generals Zachary Taylor and Winfield Scott in the Mexican War. As a cadet, he had been impressed by the sharpness of Winfield Scott's uniform and appearance, but later, in Mexico, Grant appreciated how Taylor's soldiers admired the General for his actions and leadership. Grant also noticed that Taylor made the most with the means provided and did not gripe or leave problems to be solved by his higher command. In Mexico, Lieutenant Grant distinguished himself directing an artillery attack at Chapultepec but wrote that he preferred to avoid battle if it all possible, noting that the lure of combat was not in his nature.

After the war, Grant married Julia Dent,

then took assignments to Detroit, Michigan; Sackets Harbor, New York; and Fort Humboldt, Oregon. The drudgery of frontier duty, combined with the long separations from Julia and his young family, led Grant to resign his commission in 1856. For the next four years, Grant attempted farming and business pursuits in St. Louis, but despite his best intentions and hard labor, his efforts proved to be fruitless. In 1857, Sherman, while paying off debts of his own in St. Louis, visited Grant and commiserated, "West Point and the Regular Army aren't good schools for farmers, bankers, merchants, and mechanics." Grant's failure to produce a profitable harvest was certainly testimony to Sherman's observation. Humbled, Grant returned to Galena, Illinois, with his wife and four children, where, in the spring of 1861, Grant found himself

>>> Spotlight

President Ulysses S. Grant is pictured on the $50 bill, which was first issued in 1929. He joins $1 bill President Washington, $5 bill President Lincoln, $10 bill Alexander Hamilton, $20 bill President Andrew Jackson, and $100 bill Benjamin Franklin.

Grant Statue, Lincoln Park, Chicago.

employed in his father's tannery business.

At the outbreak of the Civil War, Grant secured an appointment as Colonel of the 21st Illinois Regiment of Volunteers. From the war's outset, Grant was resolute to serve in uniform again, pledging his loyalty and support to the Union above all else. Victories at Belmont, Fort Henry, and Fort Donelson in the winter of 1861 to 1862 earned Grant much celebrity as "Unconditional Surrender Grant," and gained the approval of Henry Halleck and Lincoln. By April of 1862, Grant was a Major General in command of the Army of Tennessee and repulsed the Confederate offensive at the Battle of Shiloh. At a cost of more than 13,000 Union casualties, Generals Sherman and Grant rallied 48,000 men to drive back Beauregard's forces. While some criticized Grant's tactics for getting so many Union

forces killed in battle and allowing the Confederate Army to escape, others noted that Grant's determination "to make war" set him apart from the other Union Generals.

President Lincoln, frustrated by George McClellan's ineffective campaigns in Virginia and Maryland, was naturally drawn to Grant and his victories. Over the course of the Vicksburg campaign in 1863, Grant demonstrated a keen steadiness in leading his troops and making operational decisions. Never flustered by setbacks nor overly exuberant from Union success, Grant persevered in capturing the Confederate fortress at Vicksburg and gave the Union control of the Mississippi River. At Chattanooga, Grant applied lessons learned in the previous battles, specifically the effectiveness of continuing the attack. Grant also realized that his Army could maintain the offense by

foraging off the land. Observers agreed that Grant had the gift of being able to see the war as "one big thing" and act accordingly.

Lincoln promoted Grant to Lieutenant General, made him Commanding General of the Union Army, and in 1864, brought Grant east to plan a comprehensive strategy to defeat Lee's Army of Virginia. Grant pursued Lee in the Overland Campaign by waging battles in the Wilderness and Spotsylvania, Cold Harbor, then laying siege at Petersburg. The bloody battles earned Grant the sobriquet of "the Butcher," losing nearly 53,000 men in May and June of 1864. By April of 1865, the Union forces had all but vanquished the expended Confederate Army. Grant dictated the generous terms of peace to Lee at Appomattox Court House. In less than five years, the Civil War had transformed Grant from a dismal business-

man to a national hero, not to mention, he was also the most victorious of all West Point graduates.

After the war, Grant remained in uniform as General of the Army of the United States. President Johnson tried to use Grant's popularity to placate the Radical critics of "Presidential Reconstruction." Racial violence and white resistance in the South undermined any genuine postwar stability. In 1868, Grant decided that he had to answer the call of the Republican Party and run for President, famously declaring, "Let us have peace." For Grant, the gains won for the Union by defeating the Confederacy were at risk. Grant wrote, "I could not back down without, as it seems to me, leaving the contest for power for the next four years between mere trading politicians, the elevation of whom, no matter which party won, would lose to us, largely, the results of the costly war which we have gone through."

Grant proved to be much better at negotiating the battlefields of Virginia than he was at navigating the treacheries of the Republican Party and national politics. Seeking to enforce the will of the people, President Grant more often than not pursued appointments and causes counter to those of Senators Charles Sumner, Carl Schurz, and other Republican members of Congress. Bids to annex the Dominican Republic, decrease the national debt, and stem racial violence in the South all met strong resistance from Democrats and conservative Republican rivals. While his foes accused him of lacking sound judgment, President Grant was also vulnerable to allegations of scandal and corruption, particularly in his second administration. Even so, when he left office in 1877, Grant had led the nation to a position of unprecedented stability after years of racial violence economic peril.

IN 1868, GRANT DECIDED THAT HE HAD TO ANSWER THE CALL OF THE REPUBLICAN PARTY AND RUN FOR PRESIDENT, FAMOUSLY DECLARING, "LET US HAVE PEACE."

In his final years, Grant enjoyed hero status around the world but would succumb to poor business acumen one more time. The scandalous failure of Grant and Ward, the ensuing bankruptcy, and Grant's race to write his memoirs before dying are well known. Ironically, though, it was Grant's *Memoirs* published after his death in 1885, that saved his family and his legacy. In spite of all of his achievements and shortcomings, Grant's strength of character, dogged determination, and loyalty made him a successful leader, family man. His example has endured for generations of American leaders and will likely continue to inspire those to come.

Written by: Lieutenant Colonel Jon Scott Logel, PhD (USA, Retired).

Grant Statue, Washington, D.C.

Grant Hall at West Point named in his honor.

Grant Statue, Washington, D.C.

© WPLPOC

Grant and staff.

Photo: Mathew Brady / NARA

Vicksburg Cannon, Battle Monument, West Point.

© 2013/Greg E. Mathieson Sr./NARA

Official portrait of President Dwight D. Eisenhower.

Photo: NARA

Cadet Dwight D. Eisenhower.

Photo: NARA

Photo: AP

Photo: AP

President Dwight David Eisenhower, USMA 1915

- 34TH PRESIDENT OF THE U.S.
- GENERAL OF THE ARMY
- CREATED NATIONAL AERONAUTICS AND SPACE ADMINISTRATION (NASA)
- CREATED THE U.S. HIGHWAY SYSTEM NOW CALLED THE EISENHOWER FEDERAL HIGHWAY SYSTEM
- PRESIDENT, COLUMBIA UNIVERSITY
- 16TH CHIEF OF STAFF OF THE ARMY
- 1ST SUPREME ALLIED COMMANDER OF THE NORTH ATLANTIC TREATY ORGANIZATION (NATO)
- SUPREME ALLIED COMMANDER, EUROPEAN THEATER OF OPERATIONS WORLD WAR II
- SUCCESSFULLY LED THE ALLIES TO VICTORY IN EUROPE IN WORLD WAR II
- EISENHOWER HALL, BARRACKS, AND STATUE AT WEST POINT NAMED IN HIS HONOR
- EISENHOWER CONFERENCE ROOM AT THE HISTORIC THAYER HOTEL NAMED IN HIS HONOR

Few West Point graduates are more synonymous with successful leadership, service to the nation, and the values of "Duty, Honor, Country" than Dwight David Eisenhower. In fact, Eisenhower's life and career may represent the greatest example of the type of graduate and leader West Point strives to produce – he served the nation in every capacity and achieved the highest level of both military service and public office. From his humble, middle-American roots in Abilene, Kansas, through his rise to the Army's highest rank in World War II, and to his two-terms as President of the United States, Eisenhower is certainly one of America's greatest leaders in every sense and arguably one of the twentieth century's most influential "soldier-statesmen."

Eisenhower was born in Dennison, Texas, on October 14, 1890, the third son of David and Ida Eisenhower's six boys. Faced with extreme economic hardships and with only 10 dollars to his name, David moved his family to Abilene, Kansas, in 1891 in order to take a job at a local creamery.[1] The Eisenhowers were a hardworking family and quickly became well-respected within their new community. Moreover, they were devout Mennonites who were, ironically, given young Dwight's future career, pacifists.[2] Eisenhower earned the nickname "Little Ike" as a child and was very popular proving to be an excellent student, athlete, and outdoorsman. In 1910, he gained acceptance to the United States Military Academy – he did not qualify for the Naval Academy – and he entered West Point the next year, crossing the Mississippi River for the first time in his life to join the Class of 1915.[3]

Where his family and the Abilene of his childhood and adolescence instilled within him the values, work ethic, and drive to succeed in

D-Day, Normandy Beach, June 6, 1945.

Eisenhower with 101st Airborne hours before D-Day invasion.

General Officer ranks — more than any other class — with Eisenhower and his good friend Omar N. Bradley each attaining Five-Star status as Generals of the Army.[5]

Shortly after graduation, Eisenhower went to Fort Sam Houston, Texas, where he met Mary "Mamie" Geneva Doud. They were married in 1916. Ike and Mamie would spend the next 54 years together and have two sons, Dwight and John. Dwight unfortunately died in 1921 of scarlet fever, while John would graduate West Point — coincidentally on D-Day, June 6, 1944 — and eventually become a Brigadier General in the Army. Although he was extremely frustrated to sit out World War I while training tank corps soldiers for deployment to France, Eisenhower's pre-World War II assignments and associations were unique, earned him a great reputation, and set the conditions for his World War II success.[6] Between the wars, Eisenhower served in Panama under General Fox Connor, who became his mentor and advocate. He attended Fort Leavenworth's Command and General Staff College in 1926 and graduated an impressive first in his class of 245 students. In 1933, he served as a military aid to Army Chief of Staff, General Douglas MacArthur (USMA 1903), with whom he then deployed to the Philippines in 1935 and remained there to train the Philippine Army until 1939. MacArthur recognized Eisenhower's talents and even labeled him the best staff officer in the Army, considering him particularly skilled at absorbing and conceptualizing information and viewing problems from the perspective of the highest command levels.[7] By now, Brigadier General Eisenhower had also long come to the attention of Army Chief of Staff General George C. Marshall, who summoned him to Washington, D.C. following the attack on Pearl Harbor and made him chief planner for the Pacific and Far East. Two months later, Marshall made him Chief of the War Plans Division and promoted him to Major General.[8] Eisenhower clearly thrived in this role, continuing to impress Marshall with his abilities as a planner, strategist, organizer, and diplomat because Eisenhower also interacted regularly with America's allies. As a result, Marshall named him Commanding General, European Theater on June 25, 1942, with a subsequent promotion to Lieutenant General — an act of intuition on Marshall's part since Eisenhower had never seen combat and had limited experience commanding troops.[9] That intuition proved to be a stroke of genius as Lieutenant General Eisenhower planned and led allied forces in the successful invasions of North

Africa (November 1942), Sicily (July 1943), and Italy (September 1943). In December 1943, Eisenhower, now a Four-Star General, was named Supreme Commander of Allied Expeditionary Forces and was directed to plan the invasion of Europe that would open the long-awaited second front. Eisenhower did so with brilliance as he led the successful invasion of Normandy, France, in Operation Overload on June 6, 1944, his signature operation and arguably the most important day of the war.[10] Continuing to drive across Europe with his "broad front" strategy, Eisenhower received his fifth star and promotion to General of the Army during the last German counter-offensive, the Ardennes Offensive, in December 1944, which the allies halted so they were able to continue their assault into Germany until the war in Europe ended on May 7, 1945.[11] Eisenhower's leadership at the strategic level was critical to the outcome of World War II as he more than validated Marshall's trust in him as the right leader, in the right place, at the right time.

SWORN IN DURING JANUARY OF 1953, EISENHOWER WAS THE 34TH PRESIDENT OF THE UNITED STATES, ENDING THE KOREAN WAR AND BEING RE-ELECTED FOR A SECOND TERM. HIS EIGHT YEARS AS PRESIDENT WERE PEACEFUL AND PROSPEROUS DURING THE TENSE TIMES OF THE COLD WAR WITH THE SOVIET UNION.

Immediately following the war, Eisenhower was appointed the Military Governor of the Occupied Zone in Germany. He then replaced his mentor, General Marshall, as Army Chief of Staff in November 1945 prior to his retirement in 1948, when he became President of Columbia University. While at Columbia, Eisenhower was recalled to active duty in 1950 by President Harry Truman and appointed as the first Supreme Allied Commander of the North Atlantic Treaty Organization (NATO) — the military alliance created to deter communist aggression in

life, West Point greatly built upon those same characteristics after entering his adult life at the Academy. At West Point, Eisenhower was a strong cadet who balanced academics and athletics while he was a member of the football team. After a disappointing knee injury ended his football career, however, he helped coach the football team, as well as became a cheerleader. Eisenhower honed his interpersonal traits as a cadet. His classmates saw him as a natural leader because he was

skilled at fostering cooperation, inspiring them, and earning their trust — all characteristics that would serve him well throughout his life.[4] Eisenhower eventually graduated 61st in his class of 164 cadets from the famed Class of 1915 and entered the Infantry branch. While his middle-third-class ranking might seem mediocre, Eisenhower's class was exceptional and became known as "the class the stars fell on" because 59 members (36 percent) would rise to the

a recovering, post-war Europe. This move also came at the request of America's European allies, who viewed Eisenhower as a man they could trust to lead the alliance in peace, just as he had successfully done in war. Eisenhower also viewed this command opportunity extremely unique since it was the first time, as he noted, that a multinational Army was created "to preserve the peace and not to wage war."[12]

Eisenhower was an international celebrity by 1952. He returned to the United States and successfully ran for President as the 1952 Republican Party candidate by overwhelmingly defeating the Democratic Party challenger Adlai Stevenson. Eisenhower then won re-election in 1956 in nearly identical fashion. The very same personal traits underlying his success as a wartime strategic leader also served him well as President where his eight years in office were economically prosperous and generally peaceful for America despite increased international tensions surrounding the Cold War, particularly with the Soviet Union. Internationally, Eisenhower ended the Korean War, supported anti-communist expansion in the Middle East with his Eisenhower Doctrine, led the creation of the International Atomic Energy Agency, endorsed an "Open Skies" policy with the Soviet Union, increased the United States strategic nuclear force, and preferred economic and military aid for allies over the use of United States ground forces. Domestically, he conceived and championed the Interstate Highway System – one of the most successful United States infrastructure programs in history with nearly 50,000 miles of highway – which sparked significant economic growth, established the National Aeronautics and Space Administration (NASA), balanced the budget, slowed inflation, and began integrating the public school system. As with any Presidential administration, however, there remains a wide range of critiques regarding Eisenhower's presidency. Some of those include a perceived detachment from actual policymaking while leaving too many decisions to his advisors, or point to negative long-term effects of certain domestic policy decisions on the economy and foreign policy decisions on increasing Cold War tensions. Whatever validity may or may not reside in such critiques, Eisenhower's presidency gave the nation a level of peace and prosperity unlike any other in the twentieth century.[13]

Eisenhower finally retired from public life and settled with Mamie at their small Gettysburg, Pennsylvania, farm in 1961 until his death on March 28, 1969. Although out of the public eye, he still remained active in the Republican Party and subsequent Presidents sought him out for policy advice. Eisenhower is also memorialized across America in many ways that honor one of the nation's greatest leaders. During his lifetime, he was a two-time selectee as *Time* magazine's "Person of the Year" in 1944 and 1959 and West Point's 1961 Thayer Award recipient. Since his death, hundreds of schools, parks, buildings, funds, and even geographic features bear his name. Among them are Washington, D.C.'s Eisenhower Executive Office Building, which houses the offices of the Vice President and staff; the St. Lawrence Seaway's Eisenhower Locks; Eisenhower State Park in Dennison, Texas; and the Eisenhower Institute. Most notably, America's federal highway system is denoted with markers throughout the country as the Eisenhower Interstate System.

President Eisenhower, President Kennedy, and Pakistan President Ayub Khan, July 13, 1961.

His profile also appears on the United States silver dollar and several United States stamps. An avid golfer, his visible love of the game is credited with helping to double the number of American golfers during his presidency, thus earning him induction in the World Golf Hall of Fame in 2009. At West Point, a statue of General Eisenhower stands overlooking the parade field on the Plain at the corner of Eisenhower Barracks. The largest cadet entertainment center bears the name Eisenhower Hall. The Thayer Hotel's main conference room also bears his name, the Eisenhower Conference Room.

In May 1966, Colonel Sylvanus Thayer (USMA 1808) was inducted into New York City's Hall of Great Americans with President Eisenhower providing the dedication. In his speech, Eisenhower concluded:

"'Duty, Honor, Country,' the code of the West Point of Sylvanus Thayer. Three simple words, but their application is universal. These enduring ideals can move Americans, whatever their age or walk of life, now, or in centuries hence, to strive for great goals, to endure tragic trial, to serve in devotion that others may gladly and grandly follow them. So doing, they will be faithful to the spirit of Sylvanus Thayer."[14]

In speaking about Thayer, Eisenhower just as easily, yet unintentionally, described his own life's example as one of the nation's greatest soldier-statesman who clearly lived by these same enduring ideals and the spirit of Thayer's West Point.

Photo: AP

General Eisenhower wearing Five-Star insignia

Eisenhower Statue at West Point.

General MacArthur and Colonel Eisenhower 1932 in the march on the Bonus Army, Washington, D.C.

Photo AP

Courtesy: MacArthur Memorial

Eisenhower putting at St. Andrews Golf Course, October 12, 1946.

>>> Spotlight

Eisenhower was *Time Magazine's* "Man of the Year" twice – first, in 1944, then again in 1959.

In 1971, the Eisenhower Dollar was minted to honor President Eisenhower, who died in 1969. Eisenhower silver dollars were minted from 1971 through 1978.

Magazine Cover Courtesy: Time, Inc., Coin Courtesy: U.S. Mint

Eisenhower Memorial, Frank Gehry Design for the Mall in Washington, D.C., May 2012.

Photo: AP

President Eisenhower and General MacArthur.

Photo: AP

President Fidel V. Ramos, USMA 1950

- **PRESIDENT OF THE REPUBLIC OF THE PHILIPPINES**
- **PHILIPPINE SECRETARY OF NATIONAL DEFENSE**
- **CHIEF OF STAFF OF THE PHILIPPINE ARMED FORCES**
- **SERVED IN KOREAN WAR, VIETNAM WAR, AND FOUGHT COMMUNISTS IN PHILIPPINES FOR FOUR DECADES**
- **WEST POINT DISTINGUISHED GRADUATE AWARD**

Fidel Ramos entered West Point as a foreign cadet from the Philippines in 1946 and graduated in 1950. He returned to his homeland after graduation to join the Philippine Army, where he served his country admirably for more than half a century with the same "Duty, Honor, Country" core beliefs he had learned at West Point while helping his country maintain an excellent partnership with the United States. He served in combat in the Korean War, Philippine counterinsurgencies, and the Vietnam War. He rose up the ranks to the top of Philippine Army as the Chief of Staff of the Philippine Armed Forces and then as the Secretary of National Defense. He was elected as the 12th President of the Republic of the Philippines and served as the Head of State from 1992 to 1998. He is considered one of the greatest Presidents in the Philippines's 100-plus-year history. He left public service after 51 years and is one the most successful graduates in West Point history.

He was born March 18, 1928 in Lingayen, Pangasinan, Philippines. His father, Narcisco, was a lawyer, five-term member of Philippine Congress, an Ambassador, and the Secretary of Foreign Affairs. His mother, Angela, was a public teacher and a university professor. When he was 12 years old, Japanese forces invaded the Philippines 10 hours after attacking Pearl Harbor. Philippine and American forces fought for six months before Lieutenant General Wainwright (USMA 1906) surrendered all United States and Philippine forces at the Bataan Peninsula on May 6, 1942, as they were out of ammunition, food, and medical supplies. The Japanese brutally occupied the Philippines for more than three years until General MacArthur (USMA 1903) returned to liberate it in 1945, fulfilling his famous "I shall return" promise. Only nine months after the end of World War II, 18-year-old Ramos traveled to New York to enter West Point in 1946.

While Ramos was at West Point, the Cold War was heating up as the United States, the West, and the Philippines were allied against the communist forces led and supplied by the Soviet Union and China. His class graduated June 6, 1950, with him ranking as 63rd in a class of 670. Three weeks after graduation, North Korean communist forces invaded South Korea and rapidly overwhelmed the United States and South Korean forces, pushing them south to the Pusan perimeter. He and his West Point class headed off to fight the communists: His American classmates deployed with the United States Army and United States Air Force to defend South Korea, while Ramos, in the uniform of the Philippine Army, returned home to fight the Philippine counterinsurgency campaign as a Platoon Leader from 1950 to 1951. For the next five decades, Ramos fought the communists at home and abroad starting as a Lieutenant and finishing as the Head of State.

He then deployed to Korea to fight the Chinese communists as an Infantry Platoon

Leader in the 2nd Battalion Combat Team in the Philippine Army from 1951 to 1952. In 1952, he was given the Reconnaissance Platoon in the Philippine 20th Battalion Combat Team in Korea. As the Recon Platoon Leader, he personally assaulted an enemy bunker and eliminated it. He was awarded the first of three Philippine Legion of Honor Awards for his actions.

After the Korean War ended, Ramos served in successive positions as a Battalion Staff Officer, Company Commander, Task Force Commander, Special Forces Group Commander, and Brigade Commander. As the Special Forces Group Commander, he led soldiers in Luzon (the largest island in the Philippines) in combat against communist insurgent forces from 1962 to 1965. In the Vietnam War, he headed the advance party and served as the Chief of Staff of the Philippine Civil Action Group. In 1972, during the Marawi Incident (Marawi is the only Muslim city in the Philippines and insurgents

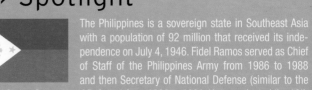

>>> Spotlight

The Philippines is a sovereign state in Southeast Asia with a population of 92 million that received its independence on July 4, 1946. Fidel Ramos served as Chief of Staff of the Philippines Army from 1986 to 1988 and then Secretary of National Defense (similar to the United States Secretary of Defense) from 1988 to 1991. He was elected the 12th President of the Philippines in 1992 and served until 1996.

President Ramos with President Bill Clinton.

rebels rose up to fight the Philippine government), he defended a camp besieged by 400 rebels.

He then served for 14 years in charge of the Philippine police. In 1986 to 1988, he was appointed as the Chief of Staff of the Philippine Armed Forces. From 1988 to 1991, he served as the Secretary of National Defense (similar to the United States Secretary of Defense), where he sought peace in a period of instability with communist and separatist movements. He was always an advocate of reconciliation and worked tirelessly to bring peace to his troubled country.

On June 30, 1992, Ramos was elected as the 12th President of the Philippines, which he served as until June 30, 1998. He assumed responsibility for a troubled country, working with Congress to implement a dramatic number of reforms. He was a soldier at heart, but an advocate of peace as his mentor and

RAMOS WAS A SOLDIER AT HEART, BUT AN ADVOCATE OF PEACE AS HIS MENTOR AND HERO OF THE PHILIPPINES GENERAL MACARTHUR ONCE SAID, "THE SOLDIER, ABOVE ALL OTHERS, PRAYS FOR PEACE."

hero of the Philippines General MacArthur once said "The soldier, above all others, prays for peace." He made peace with the military rebels and the secessionist Moro National Liberation Front (MNLF). In 1997, the Philippines won the UNESCO Peace Award. With renewed peace, investor confidence in the Philippine economy grew. The GDP of the Philippines grew an average of five percent during the first five years of his Presidency, and the reforms and policies he put in place

were credited with a drastic improvement in the life of the average Filipino. After 50 years of fighting communist forces, he left office with the communist insurgency at historic lows. He is one of the most beloved Presidents, and his time in office saw an economic rebound in the first five years, from 1992 to 1997, before the entire Asian economic crisis occurred in 1997.

In addition to a bachelor's in engineering from West Point, he received a master's of Science in Civil Engineering from the University of Illinois in 1961 and a master's of National Security from the National Defense College of the Philippines in 1969. Ramos also received an master's in Business Administration from the Philippine's Ateneo de Manila University in 1969. He received many military awards, including the Distinguished Conduct Star for Gallantry in Action for his actions in the Marawi Incident, three Philippine Legion of Honors, and the Master Parachute Badge with 116 jumps. In 2000, he returned to West

Point to join the most elite club amongst the Long Gray Line, when he was awarded the West Point Distinguished Graduate Award, along with Colonel Buzz Aldrin (USMA 1951) and General Fred Franks (USMA 1959).

He is currently the Founding Chairman of Ramos Peace and Development (RPDEV) Foundation. He and his wife, Amelita Jara Martinez, have five daughters: Angelita, Josephine, Carolina, Cristina, and Gloria. He holds 28 honorary degrees – 14 from Philippine Universities and 14 from international prestigious universities. He is an Honorary Director of the MacArthur Foundation.

U.S. President Clinton signs declaration of San Jose (Costa Rica), May 8, 1997, with President Figueres.

Photo: AP

President José María Figueres Olsen, USMA 1979

- **PRESIDENT OF COSTA RICA, 1994–98**
- **FIRST CHIEF EXECUTIVE OFFICER OF THE WORLD ECONOMIC FORUM**
- **HARVARD UNIVERSITY, MASTER'S IN PUBLIC ADMINISTRATION (MPA)**
- **COSTA RICAN COMMISSIONER OF THE NATIONAL RAILWAY SYSTEM, 1981–87**
- **COSTA RICAN MINISTER OF FOREIGN TRADE, 1987–88**
- **COSTA RICAN MINISTER OF AGRICULTURE, 1988–90**

Photo: NARA

Photo: AP

Photo: AP

>>> Spotlight

The Republic of Costa Rica is a Central American country bordered to the north by Nicaragua and to the south by Panama with a population of four million and a capital in San Jose. Jose Maria Figueres Olsen was elected President of Costa Rica and served the maximum four-year term from 1994 to 1998. His father, Jose Figueres Ferner, served three terms as President of Costa Rica, and his mother, Karen Olsen Beck, served as Ambassador from Costa Rica to Israel. His sister, Muni Figueres, is the current Costa Rica Ambassador to the United States.

Flag Courtesy: Costa Rica

Photo: AP

Photo: AP

José María Figueres Olsen is a West Point graduate who was elected President of Costa Rica and served with distinction in that role from 1994 to 1998. He is a progressive international leader who has served as the Chief Executive Officer of the World Economic Forum at Davos, Switzerland, and now serves on the boards of several for- and non-profits that are his passion.

Born December 24, 1954, in Costa Rica, Figueres Olsen grew up in a farming community before attending public high school in the capital of San José. His family had been public servants in Costa Rica for multiple generations, and he is the son of the three-time President of Costa Rica President José Figueres Ferner, who was called "Person of the 20th Century" in Costa Rica by the leading newspaper. His mother was First Lady Karen Olsen Beck, who served as Ambassador to Israel in 1982 and then later served in the Costa Rican Congress from 1990 to 1994. His sister, Muni Figueres, is the Costa Rican Ambassador to the United States.

After graduating from high school, Figueres Olsen worked for three years before being accepted to West Point as a foreign cadet. The international cadet program started

HE SERVED ONE TERM OF FOUR YEARS AS THE PRESIDENT AND FOCUSED HIS PRESIDENCY ON THE ENVIRON- MENT, SUSTAIN- ABILITY, AND INCREASING PRODUCTIVITY OF COSTA RICA.

at West Point in 1816 in order to promote better international relations with allied countries and help build partnership capacity in allied countries. Countries that have had the most graduates are the Philippines, Costa Rica, Thailand, and Panama. Two particularly distinguished foreign cadets are President José Figueres Olsen of Costa Rica and President Fidel V. Ramos President of the Philippines. Foreign cadets attend all the same courses and meet the same requirements as American cadets, but upon graduation, they return to their homeland. In some cases, they serve in their military. Currently, Congress authorizes each of the service academies to have up to 60 foreign cadets enrolled at any one time.

Figueres Olsen graduated from West Point in

1979 with an Industrial Engineering degree and returned to his homeland in Costa Rica. Costa Rica does not have a military, so upon his return, he went to work for the family business, Sociedad Agroindustrial San Cristobal (SAISC), where he worked for seven years. He also served in the Costa Rica government for six years in successive appointments, including the commissioner of the National Railway System (1986–87), minister of Foreign Trade (1987–88), and, finally, minister of Agriculture (1988–90).

In 1990, Figueres Olsen returned to the United States to attend Harvard University and received his master's in Public Administration (MPA) in 1991. While at Harvard, he announced his candidacy for President of Costa Rica in the 1994 election. He returned to Costa Rica and, in 1994, at age 39, won the primary against five other candidates. He then went on to win the general election, becoming the Head of State as President of Costa Rica. He was the youngest President of Costa Rica during the twentieth century and the youngest President of any Central American country in modern history.

He won the election based on five major principles of his leadership plan for Costa Rica:

1. Opportunity for all Costa Ricans.

2. Economic growth into the world economy.

3. Protect Costa Rica's natural resources and a focus on environmental issues.

4. Make government more efficient and eliminate waste.

5. Increase democratic institutions and public institutions.

Figueres Olsen served one term of four years as the President and focused his presidency on the environment, sustainability, and increasing productivity of Costa Rica. He was a very popular and successful leader and would likely have been re-elected. Unfortunately, at that time, the Costa Rican Constitution stipulated that a President could only serve one term (that law was later amended in 2003 to allow a second term).

After leaving office, he was named a Managing Director of the prestigious World Economic Forum. In 2003, President Figueres Olsen became the first Chief

Executive Officer of the World Economic Forum, responsible for the annual World Economic Forum in Davos, Switzerland, which brings together global business leaders, heads of state, and academia.

President Figueres Olsen's sister, Muni Figueres, was appointed the Costa Rican Ambassador to the United States in 2010. President Figueres Olsen is currently the Chief Executive Officer of CONCORDIA 21, based in Spain, dedicated to supporting organizations that promote development and democratic values around the world.

Currently, he also serves on the boards of World Resources Institute (USA), Earth Council Geneva (Switzerland), Discovery Channel Global Education Partnership (USA), Talal Abu-Ghazaleh Organization (Jordan), the Dubai Recycling Park, the ACIPP Qualification Advisory Board Committee of the Arab Society for Intellectual Property and Grupo San Cristobal SAISC (Costa Rica), among others. Together with former President Carter, he is also an international advisor at Global Environmental Action (Japan). In addition, Figueres Olsen is a member of the Dean's Alumni Leadership Council at the John F. Kennedy School of Government at Harvard University and a founding Member of the Club de Madrid. He serves as the Chairman of the Carbon War Room and previously served on the Boards of the World Wildlife Fund (WWF), The Stockholm Environment Institute (SEI), and FUNDES Internacional.

The Long Gray Line is proud to have President Figueres Olsen as another Head of State in its ranks, along with United States Presidents Grant and Eisenhower and President Ramos of the Philippines.

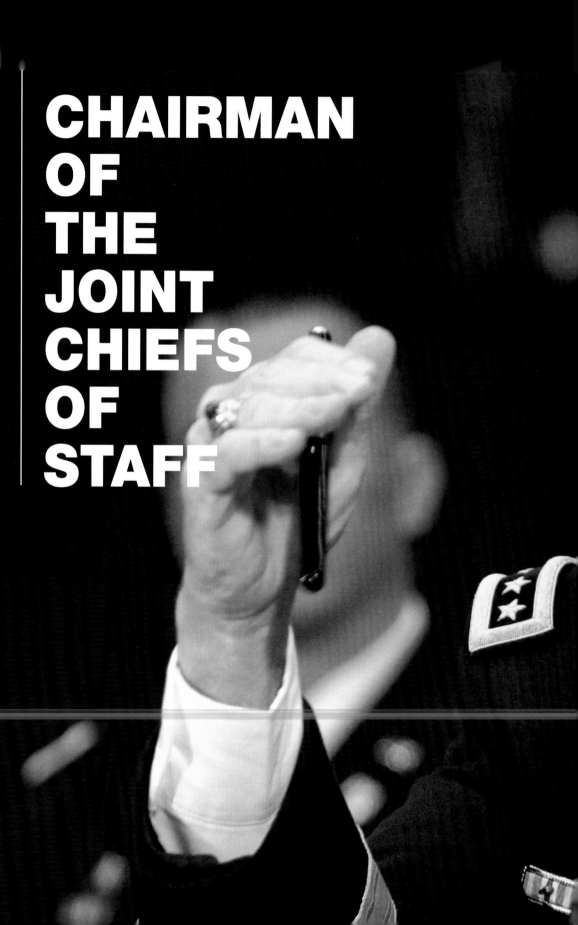

CHAIRMAN OF THE JOINT CHIEFS OF STAFF

The Chairman of the Joint Chiefs of Staff (CJCS) is the principal military adviser to the President, the Secretary of Defense, the National Security Council, and the Homeland Security Council. Created by 1949 amendments to the National Security Act of 1947, the Chairman is the highest-ranking officer in the United States Armed Forces by statute. The President appoints the Chairman, who must then be confirmed by the Senate, and serves a two-year term.

The Chairman continues to serve at the discretion of the President and may be appointed for continued two-year terms for up to six years. The table on the opposite page provides a list of Chairmen of the Joint Chiefs of Staff. Since the creation of the CJCS, 18 officers have held the position, of which seven have been West Point graduates – more than any other institution – to include current Chairman General Martin Dempsey (USMA 1974). The United States Naval Academy has produced five chairmen, while the remaining six commissioned through the Reserve Officer Training Corp (ROTC) and Officer Candidate School (OCS) as graduates of six different universities – Bradley, City College of New York, Kansas, Maryland, North Carolina State, and North Dakota.

Dempsey in Senate confirmation hearings
Chairman of the Joint Chiefs of Staff.

Chairmen of the Joint Chiefs of Staff since 1949

Name	Military Branch Undergraduate University	Dates of Service
General of the Army Omar N. Bradley	U.S. Army West Point, 1915	Aug. 16, 1949– Aug. 14, 1953
Admiral Arthur W. Radford	U.S. Navy Annapolis, 1916	Aug. 15, 1953– Aug. 14, 1957
General Nathan F. Twining	U.S. Air Force West Point, 1918	Aug. 15, 1957– Sept. 30, 1960
General Lyman L. Lemnitzer	U.S. Army West Point, 1920	Oct. 1, 1960– Sept. 30, 1962
General Maxwell D. Taylor	U.S. Army West Point, 1922	Oct. 1, 1962– July 1, 1964
General Earle G. Wheeler	U.S. Army West Point, 1932	July 3, 1964– July 1, 1970
Admiral Thomas H. Moorer	U.S. Navy Annapolis	July 2, 1970– June 30, 1974
General George S. Brown	U.S. Air Force West Point, 1941	July 1, 1974– June 20, 1978
General David C. Jones	U.S. Air Force University of North Dakota	June 21, 1978– June 17, 1982
General John W. Vessey, Jr.	U.S. Army University of Maryland	June 18, 1982– Sept. 30, 1985
Admiral William J. Crowe, Jr.	U.S. Navy Annapolis, 1947	Oct. 1, 1985– Sept. 30, 1989
General Colin L. Powell	U.S. Army City College of New York	Oct. 1, 1989– Sept. 30, 1993
General John M. Shalikashvili	U.S. Army Bradley University, Peoria, Illinois	Oct. 25, 1993– Sept. 30, 1997
General Harry Shelton	U.S. Army North Carolina State	Oct. 1, 1997– Sept. 30, 2001
General Richard B. Myers	U.S. Air Force Kansas State University	Oct. 1, 2001– Sept. 29, 2005
General Peter Pace	U.S. Marine Corps Annapolis, 1967	Sept. 30, 2005– Sept. 30, 2007
Admiral Mike Mullen	U.S. Navy Annapolis, 1968	Oct. 1, 2007– Sept. 30, 2011
General Martin Dempsey	U.S. Army West Point, 1974	Sept. 30, 2011– Present

President Truman promotes Bradley as the last Five-Star General, September 22, 1950.

Bradley, Eisenhower, and Patton.

Arlington National Cemetery.

OMAR NELSON BRADLEY
GENERAL OF THE ARMY
1893 — 1981
LOVING WIFE
ESTHER DORA BRADLEY
1922 — 2004

MARY QUAYLE BRADLEY
1892 — 1965

Official portrait in the Office of the Chairman.

General of the Army Omar Bradley, USMA 1915

- **GENERAL OF THE ARMY**
- **1ST CHAIRMAN OF THE JOINT CHIEFS OF STAFF**
- **CHIEF OF STAFF US ARMY**
- **1ST CHAIRMAN OF THE NATO MILITARY COMMITTEE**
- **COMMANDING GENERAL OF THE US 1ST ARMY AND 12TH ARMY GROUP IN WWII**
- **COMMANDING GENERAL OF THE 82ND AIRBORNE DIVISION AND 28TH INFANTRY DIVISION IN WWII**
- **M-2 BRADLEY FIGHTING VEHICLE NAMED IN HIS HONOR**
- **ARMY FOOTBALL PLAYER**
- **DIRECTOR OF THE VETERANS ADMINISTRATION**
- **CHAIRMAN OF THE BOARD OF DIRECTORS, BULOVA WATCH COMPANY**

Forever remembered as "the GI's General" or "the Soldier's General," thanks to war correspondent Ernie Pyle, Omar Nelson Bradley's life and career epitomize the highest ideals and aspirations of the West Point graduate and career Army Officer. Modest and unassuming, Bradley was one of the most successful General Officers of the Second World War and the fifth and last Army Officer to be promoted to the rank of General of the Army. His vast list of accomplishments includes being the Chief of Staff of the United States Army, the first Chairman of the United States Joint Chiefs of Staff, and the first Chairman of the NATO Military Committee. Bradley also holds the distinction of having commanded the largest number of combat troops ever assembled under a single command in the history of the United States.

Born into rural poverty – literally in a log cabin – near Clark, Missouri, on February 12, 1893, Omar's early life gave little indication of future greatness. Bradley's father, John S. Bradley, an itinerant rural school teacher, died when Omar was only 13. With his widowed mother, Mary Hubbard Bradley, he moved to Moberly, Missouri, where he established a record of academic and physical excellence (he was Captain of both the football and baseball teams) and graduated high school in 1910. Upon the advice of his Sunday-school teacher, Bradley took the entrance examination for West Point and joined the famed USMA Class of 1915, known ever since as "the class the stars fell on" because 59

of its 164 graduates attained the rank of General Officer, the highest percentage of any West Point class.

As a cadet, Bradley distinguished himself more on the fields of friendly strife than in the classroom, undoubtedly the result of his devotion to athletics, particularly baseball, at which he was one of the best college outfielders in the nation. Commissioned into Infantry, Bradley did not see combat during the First World War and instead served on the Mexican border and other assignments in the western United States. His wartime promotions came quickly, however, and he was promoted to Captain on August 27, 1917, and temporarily to Major on July 17, 1918, but reverted to his permanent rank of Captain on

November 4, 1922. He would return to the regular Army rank of Major on June 27, 1924, and remain at that rank for the next dozen years.

The United States Army of the interwar period possessed outdated and insufficient equipment, paltry budgets, and small troop strength that never approached 200,000 soldiers. Active service for Bradley reflected this reality and most of his service consisted of training and teaching. Although not glamorous, these experiences certainly contributed to his leadership style and ability to manage large organizations later in his career. Following a short tour as a military instructor at South Dakota State College in 1919, Bradley taught mathematics at West Point until 1924. At West Point when

>>> Spotlight

The M-2 Bradley Fighting Vehicle is named after General Bradley. The Bradley Fighting Vehicle was launched in 1981, and nearly 7,000 have been produced, costing more than $5 billion.

© 2013/Greg E. Mathieson Sr./MAI

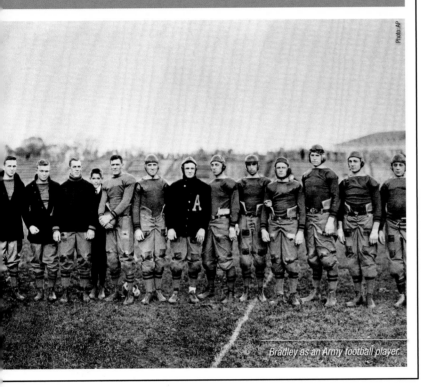

Photo: AP

Bradley as an Army football player.

time he left Fort Benning, Bradley's fundamental abilities as a tactician had been greatly improved, his understanding of his profession had grown considerably, and he had gained the support of the future Chief of Staff of the United States Army, George C. Marshall.

In 1934, Bradley again returned to West Point for a four-year tour, when he served in the tactical department. Many cadets whom he supervised and taught would themselves achieve high rank, among them William C. Westmoreland, Creighton W. Abrams, Jr., and Andrew J. Goodpaster, Jr. Interestingly, by the end of his assignment at USMA in the summer of 1938, Bradley had served 16 years in United States Army schools as a student and teacher. A Lieutenant Colonel since June 1936, Bradley next served on the General Staff as G-1 Chief of Operations Branch and Assistant Secretary of the General Staff from 1938 to 1941. During this time, the United States Army was growing rapidly and Bradley was instrumental in streamlining processes required to make expansion possible. In fact, General George C. Marshall, Chief of Staff, was so impressed that he promoted Bradley to Brigadier General (skipping the rank of Colonel) and placed him in command of the Infantry School at Fort Benning in February 1941. As Commandant of the Infantry School, Bradley set the foundation for many of the programs that would sustain the continued rapid expansion of the United States Army during World War II, the most significant of which was the Officer Candidate School (OCS) that allowed rapid commissioning and training of Infantry Officers.

Following the Japanese attack on Pearl Harbor and the declaration of war, Bradley briefly commanded the 82nd Infantry Division and then a second division, the 28th Infantry Division. After a short stint as General Dwight D. Eisenhower's deputy in North Africa, he replaced General George S. Patton as Commanding General of II Corps and led it during the final stages of the Tunisian Campaign and throughout the Sicilian Campaign from July 10 to August 17, 1943. Following Sicily, Bradley became Commanding General of the 1st Army, later the 12th Army Group. Following the allied landings at Normandy, Bradley's 1st Army grew to include three full Army corps. After weeks of being blocked on the Normandy beaches from June 6th until mid-July 1944, Bradley's bold plan, COBRA, used punishing air power in conjunction with a massive armored thrust to penetrate the German defenses. This operation was a huge victory that led a speedy liberation of France.

In August 1944, Bradley became Commander of the newly activated 12th Army Group, a mas-

sive formation consisting of 21 divisions and more than 900,000 soldiers. No other American Officer has commanded such a unit that at its peak exceeded one million soldiers.[3] Bradley led it superbly until the end of the war through the liberation of France, the Battle of the Bulge,

BRADLEY'S BOLD PLAN, COBRA, USED PUNISHING AIR POWER, IN CONJUNCTION WITH A MASSIVE ARMORED THRUST, TO PENETRATE THE GERMAN DEFENSES.

and the seizure of the Ruhr and destruction of the last major German Army remaining in western Germany, Field Marshall Model's Army Group B, in March 1945. It was Bradley's troops who linked up with Soviet soldiers on the Elbe River in April 1945. Bradley's 12th Army Group captured more than 315,000 German prisoners, making it the most successful of all American commands in the European theater during the Second World War.

After World War II, Bradley headed the Veterans Administration until December 1947, when he succeeded General Dwight D. Eisenhower as Chief of Staff of the United States Army in February 1948. He culminated his career as Chairman of the Joint Chiefs of Staff from 1949 until his retirement from active service in 1953 with the majority of his time being during the Korean War from June 1950. He was promoted to General of the Army on September 22, 1950.

Although considered neither a military genius nor a particularly original thinker, Omar Bradley was a superb tactician, excellent planner, and extremely capable organizer. Although success seemed to evade him early in his career, principally because of his lack of overseas service during World War I, Bradley never relented in his commitment to professional and personal development. His interpersonal skills and unassuming manner proved invaluable when working with more flamboyant peers and subordinates, as well as the other armed services and allied powers. Outwardly calm, courteous, and modest, Omar Nelson Bradley embodied fundamentally the principles of "Duty, Honor, Country," and exemplified selfless service to the nation to the final days of his life.

Written by: Colonel Kevin W. Farrell, PhD (USA, Retired), USMA 1986.

Douglas MacArthur was Superintendent, Bradley devoted himself to the study of military history and attended the Infantry School at Fort Benning, Georgia, after his tour at USMA. Bradley honed his abilities as an Infantry Officer and graduated second in his class. Convinced that the static war experience of World War I was irrelevant, he instead focused on maneuver warfare and studied the campaigns of Sherman during the United States Civil War. Bradley finished the course as a recognized expert in tactics, terrain, and fire and movement.

Following a tour of duty with the Hawaiian Department related to Reserve and National Guard Affairs, then-Major Bradley traveled

to Fort Leavenworth, Kansas, and graduated from the yearlong Command and General Staff School in 1929. Returning again to Fort Benning, Georgia, he was an instructor there until 1934. More than any other assignment, Bradley's time at Fort Benning set the conditions for future advancement. Later in life, Bradley asserted that Assistant Commandant George C. Marshall had a more profound influence on him personally or professionally than anyone else in his life. Marshall encouraged Bradley and his peers to think creatively about tactical problems and to simplify doctrine to be comprehensible to an Army of citizen-soldiers. During this tour, Bradley met many of the so-called "Marshall men" who would achieve high rank during the Second World War. By the

Ironically, Nathan Farragut Twining has been immortalized more by conspiracy theorists for his involvement in a 1940s-era UFO study he recommended than by his collective body of work in service to the nation – a body of work that is more deserving of that fame and culminated with Twining's rise to the highest levels of the U.S. military as Chairman of the Joint Chiefs of Staff. It is somewhat poetic justice, then, that because conspiracy theorists have kept his legacy and memory alive, Twining's interesting and impressive career has become much more visible.

Nathan Farragut Twining was born October 11, 1897. in Monroe, Wisconsin. He enlisted in the Oregon National Guard and served in the Infantry, rising to the rank of Sergeant and participating in the 1916 Punitive Expedition against Mexico. He received his appointment to West Point and entered in the summer of 1917 in a shortened "War Emergency" class that graduated on November 1, 1918, in anticipation of a continuing World War I. With the sudden end of the war, however, Twining's class was recalled to West Point to complete a "Student Officers' Course" that ended on June 11, 1919. While Twining and his class retained their 1918 diplomas and graduation credentials, this subsequent course did influence their branch assignments.[1] As a result, Twining was commissioned in the Infantry branch, served on occupation duty in Germany, and also served in Colorado and Texas before entering flight school in 1923.

After completing flight school, Twining remained as a flight instructor before transferring to the Army Air Corps and serving in a number of positions, including commander of the 26th Attack Squadron at Schofield Barracks, Hawaii. He also served in a number of command and staff roles prior to World War II. In August 1940, he was sent to the Pentagon's Inspection Division and then Air Operations Division before being sent to the South Pacific in August 1942. For the next three years, he would serve in key leadership positions in both the Pacific and European Theaters of Operation until the end of the war in September 1945.

Upon his arrival in the Pacific, he was named Chief of Staff for General M.F. Harmon (USMA 1912), the Commanding General of Air Forces in the South Pacific. He then followed that assignment in January 1943 as Commanding General of the 13th Air Force, then most notably, as Commander, Aircraft, Solomon Islands – one of the first joint commands in Air Force history – and provided critical air support to operations on Guadalcanal and Bougainville.[2]

In November 1943, he was transferred to the European Theater of Operations, first commanding the 15th Air Force in Italy and then of the Allied Strategic Air Forces in the Mediterranean in January 1944. While in this command, two of his most notable operations included the August 1944 bombing raid on the oil fields of Ploesti, Romania, and providing air support to ground forces during the Allied invasion of Southern France. Following the end of war in Europe in May 1945, Twining then took command of the 20th Air Force in the Pacific on August 2, 1945. Four days after assuming command, aircraft under Lieutenant General Twining embarked upon one of the most historic and destructive combat air missions in world history when two of his B-29 Superfortress bombers – the *Enola Gay* and *Bockscar* – dropped atomic bombs on Hiroshima and Nagasaki on August 6 and 9, 1945, respectively. These operations also served as a catalyst for Japan's surrender and the end of World War II. Immediately following the war, he served as both Commander, Air Materiel Command, then as head of the Unified Alaskan Command after transferring to the newly established, independent U.S. Air Force in September 1947.[3]

It was in 1947 as the Commander of the Air Technical Service Command, however, that Twining conducted an analysis and then recommended a study that would make him forever one of the conspiracy theorists most popular generals. With the onset of the Cold War, frequent occurrences in the night skies of strange phenomenon and unidentified flying objects (UFOs) began to increase in the United States. Lieutenant General Twining analyzed many of these initial sightings and recommended that a formal government program – eventu-

General Nathan Farragut Twining, USMA 1918

- THIRD CHAIRMAN OF THE JOINT CHIEFS OF STAFF
- THIRD CHIEF OF STAFF, UNITED STATES AIR FORCE
- VICE CHIEF OF STAFF, UNITED STATES AIR FORCE
- COMMANDER, 20TH AIR FORCE, DROPPED HIROSHIMA & NAGASAKI ATOMIC BOMBS
- COMMANDER, MEDITERRANEAN AIR FORCES, WORLD WAR II
- COMMANDER, AIRCRAFT, SOLOMON ISLANDS AS JOINT COMMAND
- COMMANDER, 13TH AIR FORCE, SOUTH PACIFIC
- SERVED AS AN INFANTRY NON-COMMISSIONED OFFICER PRIOR TO WEST POINT

>>> Spotlight

In 1947, General Twining ordered a study group to research several Unidentified Flying Objects (UFOs). This period of time was early in both aviation and jet aviation. The fact that the study was ordered by the Department of Defense fueled conspiracy theories regarding UFOs and extraterrestrial origins that still perpetuate today. The study was declassified in 1961 with no significant revelations.

NATHAN FARRAGUT TWINING
GENERAL
UNITED STATES AIR FORCE
1897 ---- 1982

BELOVED WIFE AND MOTHER
MAUDE McKEEVER TWINING
1907 ---- 1999

Arlington National Cemetery.

ally known as Project Sign – be established to collect, collate, evaluate, and distribute within the government all information relating to such sightings on the premise that UFOs might be real and of national concern.[4] Project Sign began on January 22, 1948, and found

TWINING AND 14 OTHERS SPENT SIX DAYS ON RAFTS AFTER DITCHING THEIR AIRCRAFT NEAR GUADALCANAL.

that UFOs were much more easily attributed to three major causes: mass hysteria and hallucination, hoax, or misinterpretation of known objects. The report did, however, recommend continued military intelligence control over the investigation and did not rule out the possibility of extraterrestrial phenomena because many of the sightings came from credible sources.[5] Although the Air Force discontinued Project Sign by late 1948, it did continue its study of these unusual occurrences via subsequent programs known as Project Grudge and Project Blue Book.[6]

Twining was eventually promoted to Four-Star General and appointed to Vice Chief of Staff of the U.S. Air Force before becoming the 3rd Chief of Staff of the U.S. Air Force on June 30, 1953, just prior to the end of the Korean War. As Air Force Chief of Staff during the heightened Cold War years of the 1950s, Twining presided over a period in which the U.S. Air Force's role – particularly with the Strategic Air Command (SAC) – in supporting America's strategic nuclear capabilities was paramount. Under Twining, the B-52A Stratofortress flew its first test mission in 1954 and then, at his direction, the Air Force initiated mass production of the B-52. This aircraft eventually took center stage of the U.S. strategic arsenal with its ability to deliver nuclear weapons, and has continued serving as the U.S. Air Force's main heavy bomber for over half a century.[7] To this day, Twining was and still remains the only commander to ever deploy nuclear weapons against an enemy.

On August 15, 1957, General Twining reached the pinnacle of his career when he was appointed by President Dwight Eisenhower as the third Chairman of the Joint Chiefs of Staff (CJCS). He was the first Air Force officer to assume the position and the first Chairman with prior enlisted experience. Of the 18 Chairmen of the Joint Chiefs of Staff to date, four have been Air Force Generals (Twining, Brown, Jones, and Myers) and only four have had prior service experience (Twining, Brown, Vessey, and Shalikashvili). As Chairman of the Joint Chiefs of Staff, Twining's three years experienced some of the Cold War's most notable events to include: the Soviet launching of *Sputnik* on October 4, 1957, which precipitated the "race to space;" the Cuban Revolution, which placed Fidel Castro in power on January 1, 1959, and still remains as one of the world's last Communist bastions; and the downing over the Soviet Union of U-2 pilot Frances Gary Powers on May 1, 1960.

Twining stepped down on September 30, 1960, after nearly 42 years of service and was succeeded as CJCS by General Lyman Lemnitzer (USMA 1920). Though he would not know it at the time, one of America's longest wars had begun on his watch. Two months prior to his retirement on July 8, 1960, two American advisors were killed in a country most Americans had never before heard of – Vietnam. Major Dale Buis and Master Sergeant Chester Ovnand were killed in Bien Hoa when their compound was overrun by communist guerillas. Of the 58,261 names on the Vietnam War Memorial in Washington, D.C., honoring those Americans killed in that conflict – which appear in chronological order – Buis is the first name and Ovnand the second name. The conflict in Vietnam had begun and would not see the final death of an American service member until nearly 16 years later on May 15, 1975.[8] After his retirement, Twining served as Vice Chairman of Holt, Rinehart, & Winston Publishing. He passed away on March 29, 1982, at the age of 84 and is buried in Arlington National Cemetery; and, while Twining has certainly appealed to generations of conspiracy theorists, his honorable and distinguished career should also be appealing to every American.

Official portrait in the Office of the Chairman of Joint Chiefs of Staff.

Lyman Lemnitzer graduated from West Point in 1920, just five years behind the famed Class of 1915, better known as "class the stars fell on," which had 36 percent of its class become General Officers, including legendary graduates Dwight Eisenhower, Omar Bradley, James Van Fleet, and several others. Lemnitzer would remain in the shadows of those legendary Generals for much of his career and serve under them in both World War II and the Korean War. After 35 years under their mentorship, however, he would take the baton and lead the United States Army and United States military for another 15 years rising to the highest offices in the United States military – Chief of Staff of United States Army and then Chairman of the Joint Chiefs of Staff. After reaching this pinnacle, Lemnitzer remained in uniform another six years as Commander of United States Forces in Europe and Supreme Allied Commander of NATO before retiring. While his time as Chairman of the Joint Chiefs of Staff was relatively short, it spanned two of the Cold War's most volatile years confronting international crises, such as the Bay of Pigs, the building of the Berlin Wall, and escalation in Vietnam.

Born at the end of the nineteenth century on August 29, 1899, in Honesdale, Pennsylvania, to German Lutheran parents, Lemnitzer's time in uniform spanned an amazing period of growth for American power and global influence. Lemnitzer graduated high school at the height of the Bolshevick Revolution that pulled Tsarist Russia out of World War I and marked the beginnings of the Soviet Union. He first donned cadet gray in 1918 as part of a two-year class during World War I and trained to enter an Army that still relied on literal horse power; however, he retired his Army uniform more than 50 years later in 1969, just weeks before Colonel Buzz Aldrin (USMA 1951) walked on the moon and when much of the United States military was fueled by nuclear power. In those 51 years after Lemnitzer took the oath on the Plain at West Point, the United States had become the world's major economic and military superpower, and he was personally at the forefront of many of the most significant international events of the twentieth century, signaling that ascendancy.

Lemnitzer was commissioned in the coastal artillery and served between the two world wars in a combination of operational units and in academia. He served in the Philippines, taught Philosophy at West Point, and attended the Army War College. Soon after World War II started, Eisenhower assigned Brigadier General Lemnitzer to his staff as Deputy Chief of Staff and later Chief of Staff for British General Harold Alexander (later Field Marshall). Lemnitzer proved to be a very talented soldier-statesman in this coalition-building role for the 15th Army Group.

Brigadier General Lemnitzer, along with General Mark Clark (USMA 1917), took part in a secret mission before the November 1942 allied invasion of North Africa. Lemnitzer and Clark went ashore in a small craft, after being dropped off by a British submarine, and successfully negotiated with the Vichy French to ensure that Vichy forces would not fire on the invading allied Army during Operation Torch. Later in the war, this time under the command of General Clark, Lemnitzer met secretly with the Italians behind enemy lines to help successfully negotiate the surrender of Italian forces in 1944. In one final effort, Lemnitzer met secretly in 1945 with the Germans in neutral Switzerland to successfully negotiate their final surrender. Lemnitzer proved multiple times during World War II that he was a skilled diplomat and negotiator who clearly earned the trust of America's senior leaders and that

he significantly influenced the outcome of the war in roles that did not involve directly leading soldiers in combat. After World War II, Lemnitzer would spend the remainder of his career confronting and fighting communist forces during the Cold War using both diplomacy and military force.

In 1951, he took command of the 11th Airborne Division as a Major General and impressively earned his jump wings at the age of 51. He then took command of the 7th Infantry Division in the Korean War and led the division through some of the toughest fighting of the war against communist Chinese and North Korean forces while earning the Silver Star for Valor. In Korea, he served under 8th Army General Van Fleet and United Nations Commanders General Matthew Ridgway (USMA 1922) and General Mark Clark.

Lemnitzer was promoted to Lieutenant General in 1952 and General in 1955. He commanded the United Nation Forces in Korea and Japan before being appointed Vice Chief of Staff of the United States Army in 1957, then Chief of Staff of the United States Army in 1959, and finally Chairman of the Joint Chiefs of Staff in September 1960 by President Eisenhower, his former Commander.

General Lyman Louis Lemnitzer, USMA 1920

- **FOURTH CHAIRMAN OF THE JOINT CHIEFS OF STAFF**
- **CHIEF OF STAFF U.S. ARMY/VICE CHIEF OF STAFF U.S. ARMY**
- **SUPREME ALLIED COMMANDER, NORTH ATLANTIC TREATY ORGANIZATION (NATO)**
- **COMMANDER, U.S. FORCES EUROPE**
- **UNITED NATIONS COMMANDER, KOREA AND JAPAN**
- **COMMANDING GENERAL, 7TH INFANTRY DIVISION, KOREAN WAR**
- **COMMANDING GENERAL, 11TH AIRBORNE DIVISION**
- **SILVER STAR, PRESIDENTIAL MEDAL OF FREEDOM**[1]
- **PARTICIPATED IN NEGOTIATING ITALIAN AND GERMAN SURRENDERS OF WORLD WAR II**
- **WEST POINT ASSOCIATE PROFESSOR**

As Chairman, Lemnitzer served only briefly under Eisenhower before John F. Kennedy was elected President and took office in January 1961. That year proved to be very trying for both the new President and the new Chairman as Cold War tensions escalated. The plans to invade Cuba and overthrow communist Fidel Castro had been well under way prior to Kennedy's administration; however, both Kennedy and Lemnitzer assumed responsibility for the failed April 1961 Bay of Pigs invasion. Later that year, on August 13, 1961, the Soviets isolated West Berlin and threatened access to it by building a wall, literally overnight, and sparking another significant international crisis. The Berlin Wall would isolate West Berlin for the next 28 years and become the iconic symbol of Cold War division and tension between East and West. As Chairman of the Joint Chiefs of Staff, Lemnitzer worked diligently throughout the crisis with United States Ambassador to Berlin, Lucius Clay (USMA 1918), United States Ambassador to France, James Gavin (USMA 1929), and Supreme Allied Commander Europe, General Lauris Norstad (USMA 1930) to arrive successfully at a diplomatic solution and defuse the tense situation with the Soviet Union.

In October 1961, Kennedy sent retired General Maxwell Taylor (USMA 1922) to Vietnam on a special mission as United States involvement in Southeast Asia continued to expand. Kennedy frequently used Taylor as an unofficial military advisor, creating an uncomfortable relationship between the President and Lemnitzer since, as Chairman, Lemnitzer was officially the President's primary military advisor. In the political fallout still surrounding the Bay of Pigs fiasco even a year later, Lemnitzer – an Eisenhower selection – was not reappointed by Kennedy. Instead, Kennedy, who had been using Taylor as his unofficial military advisor recalled the General to active duty and appointed him as Chairman of the Joint Chiefs of Staff, while General Lemnitzer stepped down on September 30, 1962, just two weeks prior to the Cuban Missile Crisis. More a political move on Kennedy's part than an indictment on Lemnitzer's performance, the President continued to maintain the highest regard for Lemnitzer and requested he remain in uniform on active duty and assume the role of Supreme Allied Commander of Europe and later of NATO – arguably the two most important command positions during the Cold War. Lemnitzer remained in these commands for the rest of the decade, finally stepping down in July 1969.

Of the 18 Chairman of the Joint Chiefs of Staff to date, Lemnitzer is the only one to remain in uniform after completion of his Chairman of the Joint Chiefs of Staff duties.[2]

West Point and its graduates clearly played a major role in both Lemnitzer's personal and professional lives. On the personal side, he was the first member of his family to attend West Point and established a legacy lasting three generations. His son, Brigadier General William L. Lemnitzer, graduated in 1951, and his grandson, Lieutenant Colonel William F. Lemnitzer, graduated in 1978. On the professional side, Lemnitzer's career throughout every stage was heavily influenced by numerous West Point graduates who were his commanders, mentors, peers, and subordinates. Lemnitzer, in turn, skillfully assumed each of those roles across the spectrum of his career from a newly commissioned Second Lieutenant in 1920, to the United States military's highest-ranking officer by 1960.

In one of his final speeches at the Army War College in the twilight of his career, General Lemnitzer spoke about the need for leaders to be themselves and be genuine in their leadership when he cautioned:

"It is a serious error for any officer to attempt to emulate one or more qualities of our great military leaders when such qualities are lacking in his own individual makeup. Any attempts in this regard are usually so transparent that anyone…can easily see through them. My advice is to turn in the very best performance you are capable of, but, above all, be yourself."[3]

Lemnitzer retired in July 1969 having clearly heeded his own advice for more than half a century in uniform. He was appointed as a member of the Rockefeller Commission, the commission established by President Gerald Ford and headed by Vice President Nelson Rockefeller, which examined Central Intelligence Agency (CIA) activities in the United States. General Lemnitzer died on November 12, 1988, at the age of 89 and is buried in Arlington National Cemetery. A year after his death, the Berlin Wall came down peacefully, followed by the peaceful dissolution of the Soviet Union. Unfortunately, Lemnitzer was not able to witness this relatively peaceful conclusion to the Cold War, a war against which he fought most of his career, as he had witnessed its violent beginnings.

Official portrait in the Office of the Chairman Joint Chiefs of Staff.

Secretary of Defense Robert S. McNamara and General Lemnitzer.

President John F. Kennedy with General Lemnitzer.

>>> Spotlight

From April 17 to 19, 1961, a Cuban paramilitary group of approximately 1,400 soldiers supported by the United States invaded Cuba in the Bay of Pigs. The invasion was unsuccessful, and the invaders were either killed or captured. The operation had been planned under the Eisenhower and conducted under the Kennedy administration. The failed invasion gave Fidel Castro increased power and was embarrassing to the United States. General Lemnitzer served one term as Chairman of the Joint Chiefs but did not receive a second term in 1962 — the Bay of Pigs fiasco was likely a contributing factor.

Arlington National Cemetery.

Major General Taylor, Commanding General 101st Airborne Division.

Major General Taylor boarding aircraft for D-Day invasion.

Ambassador Taylor with President Kennedy.

General Maxwell D. Taylor, USMA 1922

- **5TH CHAIRMAN OF THE JOINT CHIEFS OF STAFF, 1962–64**
- **COMMANDING GENERAL, 101ST AIRBORNE DIVISION DURING WORLD WAR II**
- **40TH SUPERINTENDENT OF THE UNITED STATES MILITARY ACADEMY**
- **ARMY CHIEF OF STAFF, 1954–59**
- **U.S. AMBASSADOR TO VIETNAM, 1964–65**

Major General Taylor as the Superintendent of West Point

Few West Point graduates have achieved such dramatic success as General Maxwell D. Taylor. An officer of the highest caliber, his career both reflected and informed key foreign policy issues during four crucial decades of the twentieth century. West Point graduates remember him as a reforming Superintendent, veterans, and students of the Second World War and the Korean War remember him as a Battlefield Commander and perhaps his role in the early stages of the Vietnam War overshadow everything else; however, every stage of his career was marked by outright excellence.

Like many officers who attained high military rank during the Second World War, Maxwell D. Taylor had strong Midwestern roots. Born an only child to a small-town lawyer with an ancestor who fought in the American Revolution and a mother whose father had fought for the Confederacy, money was always tight but he was not poor.[1] Maxwell demonstrated excellence in his elementary and high-school studies with a strong foundation in language — he had four years each of Spanish and Latin and two of Greek by the time he graduated — he demonstrated great interest in a military career, remarking in

sixth grade that his professional goal was to become a Major General.[2] Seeking admission either to Annapolis or West Point while World War I was ongoing, he passed the West Point entrance examination and ultimately graduated an impressive fourth in a graduating class of 102 with the Class of 1922.[3] The first class to resume a four-year program after the shortened classes of World War I, Douglas MacArthur served as Superintendent three of the four years Taylor was a cadet. While at West Point, he met his future wife, Lydia "Diddy" Happer, whom he would marry in 1925, and together they sustained each

other through 37 moves in 37 years of active service.[4]

The diversity and breadth of Maxwell Taylor's assignments in the interwar years allowed for continuous intellectual development and furthered his remarkable ability in language and history. Commissioned into the engineer branch, Taylor served in Maryland and Hawaii before transferring to field artillery in 1926. The following year he was sent to Paris to learn French with a follow-on assignment to West Point from 1928 to 1932 where he taught French and Spanish. More education followed with the Artillery School at Fort Sill, Oklahoma, from

>>> Spotlight

General Taylor commanded the 101st Airborne Division throughout most of World War II. The 101st has been an active-duty division since August 15, 1942, and is one of the most decorated divisions in American history.

Courtesy: US Army Historical Center

As the American military establishment expanded drastically in the months before World War II and during the war itself, Taylor experienced rapid promotion. His experience of working directly with the new United States Army Chief of Staff, General George C. Marshall, certainly helped his career. Artillery battalion command came in 1940 and promotion to Lieutenant Colonel in December 1941. Colonel soon followed when he became Chief of Staff for the Commanding General of the 82nd Airborne Division, Matthew Ridgeway, then Brigadier General in December 1942. Following combat service with the 82nd Airborne Division in North Africa and Sicily in 1943, Taylor took part in a daring secret mission to Rome, well behind enemy lines. Chosen because of his proficiency in foreign language, his task was to assess the feasibility of an allied airborne landing in Rome. His negative assessment, though controversial, prevented the operation.[8]

Taylor's mission attracted the highest favorable attention and he received command of the 101st Airborne Division, leading it heroically during the airborne assault into Normandy early in the morning of June 6, 1944. He remained in command of the division for the remainder of the war, once again demonstrating bravery and competence during the largest allied airborne operation of 1944, the failed attempt to end the war by a drive into Holland, Operation Market Garden. Unfortunately for Taylor, he missed the heroic defense of Bastogne during the Battle of the Bulge in December 1944 because he was in the United States attending a conference. Taylor's Assistant Division Commander, Brigadier General Anthony McAuliffe led the fight in Taylor's absence and is most remembered for the Battle of Bulge, even though Taylor returned to command shortly after Christmas 1944.

Following World War II, Maxwell Taylor became the 40th Superintendent of the United States Military Academy.[9] In addition to updating the curriculum, his most significant accomplishment was the adoption of a written honor code at West Point that remains in effect. Following his extremely successful tenure as Superintendent, he became the Commanding General of allied forces in Berlin from 1949 to 1951. Promoted to Lieutenant General, he next became the United States Army Deputy Chief of Staff for Operations, then assumed command of the 8th Army in Korea in 1953, was promoted to General, and led it through the conclusion of the armistice of July 28, 1953. In 1954, he assumed command of Allied Forces Far East and relinquished command to become Chief of Staff of the United States Army from 1954 until his retirement in 1959. Because of a strong disagreement with President Eisenhower's redirection of the United States Army and Taylor's perception of overreliance upon nuclear weapons, he retired from active service and wrote a book highly critical of the reshaped military entitled *The Uncertain Trumpet*. The essence of his criticism was that the Army had to rely on the cohesion, morale, and training of troops because nuclear war was quite unlikely. Labeled "flexible response," his approach still undergirds United States Army doctrine.

As a Presidential candidate John F. Kennedy took notice of Maxwell Taylor and recalled him to active duty to serve as Military Advisor to the President of the United States in the wake of the Bay of Pigs. He then named him Chairman of the Joint Chiefs of Staff, in which capacity he served from 1962 until 1964. His tenure marked the closest the United States ever came to nuclear war, the Cuban Missile Crisis of October and November 1962. Taylor also laid the foundation for the general strategy in Vietnam of employing counterinsurgency in South Vietnam and selective air and naval strikes against North Vietnam. Following Taylor's second military retirement, President Lyndon Johnson appointed him Ambassador to South Vietnam from 1964 to 1965, a period that witnessed a crucial escalation of United States involvement in the Vietnam War. He remained an advisor to the President on the war until the end of Johnson's term in 1968.[10] Afterward, Taylor continued work in think tanks and the corporate world, all the while writing extensively on defense issues. He died at Walter Reed Army Hospital in Washington, D.C., on April 19, 1987, from complications of Lou Gehrig's disease.

Without exaggeration, it can safely be said that General Maxwell D. Taylor was one of the great American military figures of the twentieth century. Although his career was not without controversy, he represented the last of the "heroic Generals" of the Second World War and a new breed of "managerial Generals" that have dominated the United States Army since the 1960s.[11] A man of extraordinary and diverse talents, General Maxwell D. Taylor dedicated his entire life to serving the United States of America and he never forgot that success for the United States Army meant quality conventional forces and good soldiers. He was truly one of the finest sons West Point has ever produced.

Written by: Colonel Kevin W. Farrell, PhD (USA, Retired), USMA 1986.

Photo: AP

Official portrait in the Office of the Chairman, Joint Chiefs of Staff.

Photo: 2013/Greg E. Mathieson Sr./MAI

Photo: AP

Photo: NARA

McNamara, Taylor, and President Johnson.

1932 to 1933, and the Command and General Staff School at Fort Leavenworth, Kansas, in 1935, out of which his class of 119 members produced 62 future General Officers.[5]

Interested in the Far East and wishing to learn additional foreign languages, Taylor requested and received a posting to the United States embassy in Tokyo in 1936. Within two years, he had mastered Japanese.[6] In 1937, he accompanied legendary "Vinegar Joe" Stilwell, then a Colonel, throughout northern China in an attempt to monitor the actions of the Japanese who had invaded China, after which he returned to Tokyo for the remainder of his four-year assignment in Japan. Upon the completion of his tour in Japan in 1939, still a Captain some 17 years after graduating from West Point, he wrote an important book on Japanese tactical doctrine that anticipated how the Japanese would fight and what their weaknesses would be in a future conflict.[7] Taylor then attended the National War College in Washington, D.C., but his time there was cut short when his former Spanish instructor from West Point, Matthew Ridgeway, selected him to serve with him in a sensitive diplomatic mission to Latin America.

Photo: AP

President Lyndon Johnson awarding General Wheeler the Distinguished Service Medal.

General Earle Gilmore Wheeler, USMA 1932

- SIXTH CHAIRMAN OF THE JOINT CHIEFS OF STAFF
- 23RD CHIEF OF STAFF, U.S. ARMY
- COMMANDER, III CORPS
- COMMANDER, 2ND ARMORED DIVISION
- PROFESSOR OF MATHEMATICS, WEST POINT
- BURIED AT ARLINGTON NATIONAL CEMETERY

★★★★

Photo: NARA

General Earle G. Wheeler reached the pinnacle of the United States Military as the sixth Chairman of the Joint Chiefs of Staff, serving in that position for six years, from 1964 to 1970 – longer than any other Chairman. While General Wheeler's tenure as Chairman spanned the height of United States involvement in the Vietnam War, it also culminated a career of military service spanning some of the most challenging years of the Cold War.

Wheeler was born January 13, 1908, in Washington, D.C. He entered the Academy just prior to The Great Depression, graduated from West Point in 1932, and commissioned as an Infantry Officer. He served at Fort Benning, Georgia; Fort Lewis, Washington; and in Tientsin, China. Prior to World War II, he also served as an instructor in the Mathematics Department at West Point. Although entering World War II as a Captain, Wheeler experienced rapid promotion to Colonel and arrived in Europe in November 1944 as Chief of Staff of the 63rd Infantry Division. After the war, he served in various key command and staff positions within the United States and abroad as the Cold War solidified between the United States and the Soviet Union. Some of his key staff assignments included Fort Sill, Oklahoma, United States occupation forces in Germany, the North Atlantic Treaty Organization (NATO)

Headquarters, and as the Director of the Joint Staff. His significant operational commands after the war included the 351st Infantry Regiment, the 2nd Armor Division, III Corps, and finally as Deputy Commander of United States forces in Europe.[1]

In October 1962, Wheeler became the United States Army's 23rd Chief of Staff during President John F. Kennedy's administration, only to be welcomed with the most dangerous Cold War confrontation – the Cuban Missile Crisis. Wheeler prepared ground troops for the possible invasion of Cuba after the Soviet Union placed offensive nuclear weapons on the island. Fortunately, U.S.– Soviet diplomacy prevailed and defused the

crisis as both nations came to the brink of war. Wheeler was also influential in persuading the other service chiefs to support an eventual limited nuclear testing ban as a result. Domestically, he deployed troops to Alabama and Mississippi to counter disturbances as the Civil Rights movement gained momentum. Wheeler next set the conditions for greater United States involvement in Vietnam in championing the development of the Army's air assault capability and advocating an increased United States presence in Vietnam. He would continue this advocacy in his final assignment.[2]

By 1964, President Lyndon Johnson appointed General Wheeler to succeed

General Wheeler advising President John F. Kennedy.

>>> Spotlight

General Wheeler served as Chairman of the Joint Chiefs of Staff for six years, from 1964 to 1970, during an incredibly challenging period of force modernization, Cold War struggles, Vietnam escalation, and public discord. He served longer as Chairman of the Joint Chiefs than any of the current 17 other Chairman of the Joint Chiefs of Staff and through some of the most difficult times.

Official portrait in the Office of the Chairman, Joint Chiefs of Staff

General Maxwell Taylor as the sixth Chairman of the Joint Chiefs of Staff. It was in his role as Chairman that Wheeler advised two Presidents — Johnson and later Richard Nixon — on United States involvement in Vietnam. General Wheeler worked closely with policymakers and successive Military Assistance Command Vietnam (MACV) Commanders, General William Westmoreland (USMA 1936), and General Creighton Abrams (USMA 1936) in conducting the war. Generally viewed as a "hawk," Wheeler was a strong proponent of escalating United States involvement through an increased and aggressive air campaign against North Vietnam augmented by an expanded ground presence in South Vietnam. Wheeler, however, opposed the gradual and limited nature in which Johnson heeded this advice believing that such an

IT WAS IN HIS ROLE AS CHAIRMAN THAT WHEELER ADVISED TWO PRESIDENTS — JOHNSON AND LATER RICHARD NIXON — ON U.S. INVOLVEMENT IN VIETNAM.

approach would not compel North Vietnam to end the war. Following the disastrous political fallout of the TET Offensive in January 1968, Johnson was even more unwilling to listen to his senior military leaders and Wheeler was marginalized, along with the rest of the Joint Chiefs for the remainder of Johnson's administration. Wheeler continued to serve under Nixon. The new President was determined to end the war on United States terms and withdraw United States forces. Nixon pursued this end through both a brief escalation of the war to bring North Vietnam to the negotiating table and his policy of "Vietnamization," which turned the war over to South Vietnam to manage and fight. As part of this plan, Wheeler later revealed in 1973 that he had been ordered by Nixon to conduct the secret and controversial bombing of Cambodia in 1969 through 1970, an act that further eroded public support for the war.[3]

General Wheeler retired on July 2, 1970, after 38 years in uniform. He died of a heart attack on December 18, 1975, at the age of 67 and is buried in Section 30 of Arlington National Cemetery. In his wake, he left a legacy of distinguished service at the nation's top leadership levels during the height of the Cold War. His wife, Betsy Howell ("Betty" Wheeler), died July 1, 2004. They had one son, Dr. Gilmore Stone "Bim" Wheeler.

West Point classes who graduate the year that a major war starts are destined for significant combat as Junior Officers. These classes, having been tested in combat as Junior Officers, have often produced our greatest Generals. The Classes of 1861 (Civil War), 1917 (World War I), 1941 (World War II), 1965 (Vietnam War), and 2001 (Operation Enduring Freedom) all graduated at the outset of major wars and the majority of their classmates deployed to the "tip of the spear" leading soldiers at the small-unit level. When George Brown graduated in June 1941, the Nazis occupied most of Europe and England stood alone.

The war clouds were looming for America, which meant that the Class of 1941 would soon see combat after Japan attacked Pearl Harbor December 7, 1941, and Hitler declared war on the United States December 11, 1941. George Brown would find himself on one of the most daring and costly air missions of the war, taking the lead of his air wing after his Commander was shot down. Thirty years later, he would lead the nations' military as the eighth Chairman of the Joint Chiefs of Staff during the waning years of the Vietnam War.

George Scratchley Brown was born August 17, 1918, in Montclair, New Jersey. His father, Brigadier General Thoburn Kaye Brown (USMA 1913), was a Cavalry Officer and instructor at West Point when he was born. George grew up as an "Army brat" and graduated high school in Fort Leavenworth, Kansas. He attended the University of Missouri for one year and enlisted in the Missouri National Guard before being accepted to West Point in 1937.

Commissioned in the Infantry he volunteered for flight school in the United States Army Air Corps, Brown was trained to fly the B–24 Liberator bomber. He married Alice Calhoun in 1942 before deploying overseas and they eventually raised three children. Flying out of Benghazi, Libya, as a Major and Executive Officer of the 93rd Bombardment Group, he participated in one of the most dangerous missions of the war, when he flew in Operation Tidal Wave. On August 1, 1943, the Air Corps mission was to bomb the oil fields of Ploesti, Romania, where the majority of German oil production was concentrated. One hundred seventy-seven B-24s attacked without fighter escort at low level against heavily defended targets with anti-aircraft and German fighters. Fifty-four of the 177 B-24s were shot down or crash-landed with the more than 600 crewmen lost. Five officers were awarded the Medal of Honor,

General George Scratchley Brown, USAF, USMA 1941

- **EIGHTH CHAIRMAN OF THE JOINT CHIEFS OF STAFF**
- **CHIEF OF STAFF, U.S. AIR FORCE**
- **COMMANDER AIR FORCE SYSTEMS COMMAND**
- **COMMANDER, 7TH AIR FORCE, MILITARY ASSISTANCE COMMAND, VIETNAM WAR**
- **DIRECTOR OF OPERATIONS, 5TH U.S. AIR FORCE, KOREAN WAR**
- **B–24 COMMAND PILOT WORLD WAR II**
- **SERVED IN WORLD WAR II, KOREAN WAR, AND VIETNAM WAR**
- **DISTINGUISHED SERVICE CROSS, SILVER STAR**

three of them posthumously. Brown, as the Executive Officer, took the lead of his formation after the Commander's aircraft was hit and forced to leave formation. Brown "was awarded the Distinguished Service Cross for extraordinary heroism in connection with military operations against an armed enemy while serving as Squadron Leader and Pilot of a B-24 Heavy Bomber in Headquarters, 93rd Bombardment Group (H), NINTH Air Force (Attached), while participating in a bombing mission on August 1, 1943, against the Ploesti Oil Refineries in Rumania."

During the Korean War, he served as Chief of Operations for the 5th Air Force out of Seoul,

Korea. In Vietnam, he commanded the 7th Air Force responsible for all bombing and air missions in Military Assistance Command-Vietnam (MAC-V) under General Creighton

FIFTY-FOUR OF THE 177 B-24S WERE SHOT DOWN OR CRASH-LANDED WITH THE MORE THAN 600 CREWMEN LOST.

Abrams (USMA 1936). In 1973, President Nixon named Brown Chief of Staff of the Air Force, and General Brown significantly supported the Israeli Air Force during the 1973 Yom Kippur War by sending in reinforce-

ments and supplies, which were desperately needed, without seeking approval from higher up. He was soon nominated by the President Nixon to become the eighth Chairman of the Joint Chiefs in 1974. In this role as Chairman, he served as the senior advisor to the President of the United States. General Brown advised Presidents Nixon, Ford, then Carter through some tumultuous times over four years. During his time as the Chairman, he advised the Presidents on the evacuation and inevitable fall of Saigon, the Ax Incident along the Demilitarized Zone (DMZ – where Major

Bonifas, USMA 1966, was killed), and the Panama Canal Treaty in 1977.

Diagnosed with prostrate cancer, he resigned from the Chairman role for health reasons and retired in June 1978. Five months after retiring, General Brown died of cancer on December 5, 1978. He is buried in Section 21 of Arlington National Cemetery near his friend General Creighton Abrams, whom he served under in Vietnam.

Official portrait in the Office of the Chairman, Joint Chiefs of Staff.

General Brown as Chairman of the Joint Chiefs of Staff with President Nixon.

>>> Spotlight

On August 1, 1943, Colonel Brown was the Executive Officer on a raid on the oil fields in Ploesti, Romania, with 177 B-24s. When the Commander's plane was shot down, Colonel Brown assumed command of the mission and led one of the most dangerous raids of the war. The raid departed Benghazi, Libya, and flew across the Mediterranean to attack the Romanian airfields and lost 53 B-24s with more than 600 airmen lost during the mission. Brown was awarded the Distinguished Service Cross for his leadership and valor, while five of his airmen were awarded the Medal of Honor, three of them posthumously.

Arlington National Cemetery.

B-24 Liberator over Ploesti, Romania.

The United States Army was battered and worn down after a 10-year war in Vietnam when Martin Dempsey and his classmates from the Class of 1974 were challenged to lead the Army back to full strength – at the peak of the Cold War, nevertheless. But Dempsey would accomplish that and more, including becoming a top-ranked officer for the United States military.

Born in Bayonne, New Jersey, Dempsey's family would move to Greenwood Lake, New York, when he was in the seventh grade. He attended John S. Burke Catholic High School in Goshen, where he met and started dating Deanie, his high-school sweetheart, whom he would eventually marry. He entered West Point in the summer of 1970 at the height of the unpopular Vietnam War, choosing the Academy over a full scholarship to Manhattan College. After graduating in June 1974, he married Deanie at West Point's Catholic Chapel and was commissioned as an Armor Officer and attended Armor Officer Basic and Airborne Schools. He was assigned to the 2nd Armored Cavalry Regiment in 1975, when he got his first taste of military leadership as Platoon Leader. He commanded an Armored Cavalry Troop in the 10th Cavalry at Fort

General Martin Dempsey, USMA 1974

- 18TH CHAIRMAN OF THE JOINT CHIEFS OF STAFF
- CHIEF OF STAFF, U.S. ARMY
- COMMANDER, TRAINING AND DOCTRINE COMMAND (TRADOC)
- COMMANDER, MULTI-NATIONAL SECURITY TRANSITION COMMAND, IRAQ
- COMMANDER, 1ST CAVALRY DIVISION, IRAQ
- COMMANDER, 3RD ARMORED CAVALRY REGIMENT (ACR)
- WEST POINT ENGLISH PROFESSOR

General Dempsey as the Chairman of the Joint Chiefs of Staff, 2011.

Colonel Dempsey as Commander of the 3rd Armored Cavalry Regiment.

Carson, Colorado, then attended Duke University to earn his master's of arts in English.

With graduate degree in hand, he returned to West Point to serve as an assistant professor in the Department of English and then attended the Command and General Staff College in Fort Leavenworth, Kansas. He was in Germany as the Cold War ended and the Soviet Union fell, but it didn't take long until rogue states took advantage of the void and Saddam Hussein invaded Kuwait. The then–Lieutenant Colonel Dempsey deployed as a Brigade Executive Officer in the 3rd Armored Division in 1991 in support of Operation Desert Shield/ Desert Storm and was part of the overwhelming defeat of Iraqi forces in 1991. After departing from Germany, he became the Armor Branch Chief at United States Army Personnel Command and, later, attended the National War College in Fort McNair, D.C., and was promoted to Colonel. He became the 67th Commander of the 3rd Armored Cavalry Regiment in 1996. After completing his Regimental Command, he was assigned to the Joint Staff as Assistant Deputy Director in the J-5 and as Special Assistant to the Chairman of the Joint Chiefs.

ON APRIL 11, 2011, PRESIDENT OBAMA APPOINTED DEMPSEY TO BECOME THE 37TH CHIEF OF STAFF OF THE U.S. ARMY, THEN, ONLY TWO MONTHS LATER, THE 18TH CHAIRMAN OF THE JOINT CHIEFS OF STAFF, A POSITION HE ASSUMED ON SEPTEMBER, 30, 2011.

Two weeks after 9/11 occurred, he returned to the Middle East as the Program Manager of the Saudi Arabian National Guard Mobilization Program and remained there for two years. He was promoted to Major General and, in 2003, took command of the 1st Armored Division in Baghdad, Iraq, for 14 months, as the United States military transitioned from direct action to counterinsurgency operations. He redeployed the division to Germany and completed his command, before returning to Iraq to train Iraqi Security Forces as Commanding General of Multi-National Security Transition Command (MNSTC) for 22 months. This was at the height of the insurgency, when training the Iraqi Army and police was the highest priority in the counterinsurgency plan. After returning from Iraq, he was promoted to Four-Star General and became the Deputy Commander and then Acting Commander of United States Central Command (CENTCOM), overseeing both the wars in Iraq and Afghanistan. He then was made Commanding General of United States Army Training and Doctrine Command (TRADOC).

On April 11, 2011, President Obama appointed Dempsey to become the 37th Chief of Staff of the United States Army, then, only two months later, the 18th Chairman of the Joint Chiefs of Staff, a position he assumed on September, 30, 2011. General Dempsey and Deanie have three children: Chris, Megan, and Caitlin, all of whom have served as Commissioned Officers in the Army, with two of them being West Point graduates. He is the seventh West Point graduate to become a Chairman of the Joint Chiefs, the first being General of the Army, Omar Bradley in 1950. He works with his classmates General David Petraeus (Director of the Central Intelligence Agency) and General Keith Alexander (who leads CyberCommand and the National Security Agency) – quite an accomplishment as no West Point class in history has ever held these three positions simultaneously.

The General Dempsey room at the Thayer Hotel was proudly dedicated by his West Point Class of 1974.

Cadet Dempsey leading USMA cadet formation.

Lieutenant Colonel Dempsey in Kuwait after Desert Storm successfully liberated Kuwait.

General Dempsey Room at the Thayer Hotel.

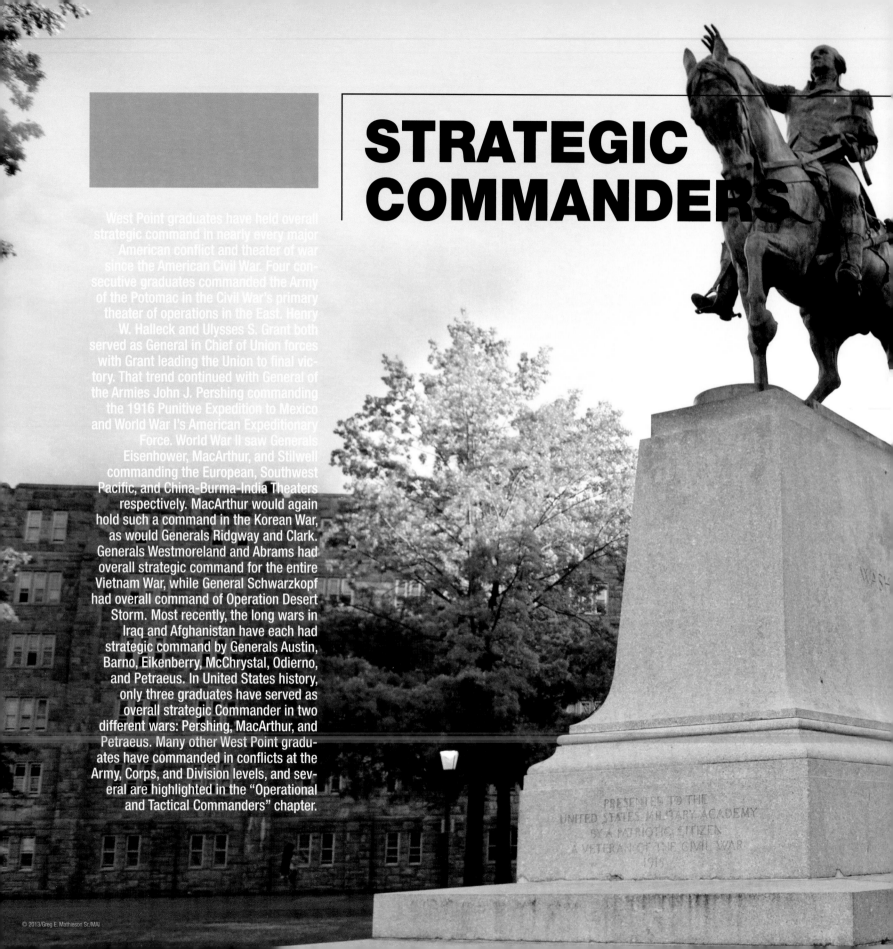

STRATEGIC COMMANDERS

West Point graduates have held overall strategic command in nearly every major American conflict and theater of war since the American Civil War. Four consecutive graduates commanded the Army of the Potomac in the Civil War's primary theater of operations in the East. Henry W. Halleck and Ulysses S. Grant both served as General in Chief of Union forces with Grant leading the Union to final victory. That trend continued with General of the Armies John J. Pershing commanding the 1916 Punitive Expedition to Mexico and World War I's American Expeditionary Force. World War II saw Generals Eisenhower, MacArthur, and Stilwell commanding the European, Southwest Pacific, and China-Burma-India Theaters respectively. MacArthur would again hold such a command in the Korean War, as would Generals Ridgway and Clark. Generals Westmoreland and Abrams had overall strategic command for the entire Vietnam War, while General Schwarzkopf had overall command of Operation Desert Storm. Most recently, the long wars in Iraq and Afghanistan have each had strategic command by Generals Austin, Barno, Eikenberry, McChrystal, Odierno, and Petraeus. In United States history, only three graduates have served as overall strategic Commander in two different wars: Pershing, MacArthur, and Petraeus. Many other West Point graduates have commanded in conflicts at the Army, Corps, and Division levels, and several are highlighted in the "Operational and Tactical Commanders" chapter.

PRESENTED TO THE
UNITED STATES MILITARY ACADEMY
BY A PATRIOTIC CITIZEN
A VETERAN OF THE CIVIL WAR
1916

> **"When we assumed the soldier, we did not lay aside the citizen.**
> *—General George Washington (Library of Congress. Washington Speech 26 June 1775.)*

> **"Duty, Honor, Country. Those three hallowed words reverently dictate what you ought to be, what you can be, what you will be."**
> *—General of the Army Douglas MacArthur, USMA 1903*

> **"By leadership we mean the art of getting someone else to do something that you want done because he wants to do it, not because your position of power can compel him to do it, or your position of authority.**
> *—President Dwight D. Eisenhower, USMA 1915*

West Point Graduates Who Have Served as Strategic Commanders of American Wars

War	Leader
Civil War Union Army	Major General George McClellan, USMA 1846 Major General Ambrose Burnside, USMA 1847 Major General Joseph Hooker, USMA 1837 Major General George Meade, USMA 1835 General Ulysses S. Grant, USMA 1843
Vera Cruz Expedition	Major General John J. Pershing, USMA 1886
World War I	General of the Armies John J. Pershing, USMA 1886
World War II	General of the Army Douglas MacArthur, USMA 1903 General of the Army Dwight D. Eisenhower, USMA 1915 General Joseph Stilwell, USMA 1904
Korean War	General of the Army Douglas MacArthur, USMA 1903 General James Van Fleet, USMA 1915 General Marc Clark, USMA 1917 General Matthew Ridgway, USMA 1917
Vietnam War	General William Westmoreland, USMA 1936 General Creighton Abrams, USMA 1936
Desert Storm	General H. Norman Schwarzkopf, USMA 1956
Kosovo War	General Wesley Clark, USMA 1966
Afghanistan War	Lieutenant General Karl Eikenberry, USMA 1973 Lieutenant General David Barno, USMA 1976 General Stanley McChrystal, USMA 1976 General David Petraeus, USMA 1974
Iraq War	General David Petraeus, USMA 1974 General Raymond Odierno, USMA 1976 General Lloyd Austin, USMA 1975

Perhaps the most controversial of West Point's antebellum graduates, George B. McClellan drew either uninhibited admiration or bitter derision from his peers and those left to scribe his legacy. During the Civil War, the officers and soldiers of the Army of the Potomac remained devoted to McClellan, even after his dismissal in 1862. History paints McClellan as an ineffective General for failing to reach Richmond during the Peninsula Campaign and then allowing Lee's Army to escape after Antietam. On the other hand, McClellan's peers held him in high regard. When asked to name his most capable opponent after the war, Robert E. Lee declared "McClellan, by all odds!" To be sure, McClellan possessed the traits and skills desired and admired in antebellum military leaders, and he rose accordingly through the ranks. Even so, his Civil War record remains a mix of failure, unfulfilled potential, and tragic inaction.

Born in Philadelphia, Pennsylvania, to a well-known doctor, McClellan entered West Point at the age of 15 in June 1842. Graduating second in the USMA Class of 1846, "Little Mac," as McClellan was sometimes called, served in the Mexican War as a Lieutenant in the Corps of Engineers. After the Mexican War, he returned to the Academy as an engineer instructor. There he furthered his study of strategy in Dennis Hart Mahan's Napoleon Club. After his West Point tour, McClellan's duties included surveying prospective routes through the Cascade Mountains for the transcontinental railroad and reconnoitering Santo Domingo as the United States considered annexing the Dominican Republic. In 1856, Secretary of War Jefferson Davis appointed McClellan to the Delafield Commission, a United States Army delegation sent to observe the Crimean War and bring back lessons learned.

By 1857, McClellan decided to try his hand at business, resigned from the Army and put his surveying and railroad expertise to use for the Illinois Central Railroad. From 1859 to 1861, McClellan earned a lucrative $10,000 a year (in 1859 dollars) as the President of the Ohio and Mississippi Railroad. Living in Cincinnati, Ohio, he supervised the railroad between Ohio and St. Louis, protecting the

Governor George McClellan, USMA 1846

- COMMANDER, UNION ARMY OF THE POTOMAC
- GOVERNOR, STATE OF NEW JERSEY, 1877–81
- COMMANDING GENERAL, ARMY OF THE POTOMAC, 1861–62
- PRESIDENT, OHIO & MISSISSIPPI RAILROAD
- MCCLELLAN STATUE IN FRONT OF PHILADELPHIA CITY HALL DEDICATED IN HIS HONOR
- 1864 DEMOCRATIC NOMINEE FOR U.S. PRESIDENCY – LOST TO LINCOLN IN THE GENERAL ELECTION
- CHIEF ENGINEER OF NEW YORK CITY DEPARTMENT OF DOCKS
- PROFESSOR, UNITED STATES MILITARY ACADEMY AT WEST POINT

McClellan Gate at Arlington National Cemetery.

>>> Spotlight

New Jersey, known as the "Garden State," was the third state to be admitted to the Union as part of the original 13 colonies on December 18, 1787. It is the 11th most populous state with more than nine million citizens. Major General George McClellan, after leading the Union Army during the Civil War, was elected 24th Governor of New Jersey and served from 1878 to 1881.

investments of New York businessmen William H. Aspinwall and Samuel Barlow. All the while, he continued to study and read about military tactics and strategy. On the eve of the Civil War, George McClellan had become one of the nation's most renowned military thinkers and successful railroad executives.

McClellan revealed his political inclinations as a conservative Democrat when he openly supported Stephen Douglas in the 1858 Senatorial election. He provided Douglas a private rail car to use for campaigning around Illinois. Apparently McClellan was not impressed by Lincoln's legal representation of the Illinois Central Railroad in the late 1850s. In spite of McClellan's pre-war opinion on the character and personality of Lincoln, he agreed to command the Army of the Potomac when the Commander in Chief called upon him in July of 1861.

McClellan's record as the Commander of the Army of the Potomac certainly failed to meet the leadership's expectations of an officer whose nickname was "Young Napoleon." For more than 15 months, Lincoln urged McClellan to crush the Confederacy by defeating Lee's Army of Northern Virginia and capturing Richmond. Under McClellan, the Army of the Potomac failed to accomplish either. The Peninsula Campaign stalled four miles outside Richmond, and Lee's Army escaped after the Battle of Antietam in September 1862. By November, Lincoln had had enough of McClellan's overly cautious approach to defeating the rebellion and relieved "Little Mac" of his command. McClellan returned to his home in Trenton, New Jersey, to consider his future.

While there were calls for McClellan to return to the field of battle during the remainder of the Civil War, he stayed in New Jersey preparing for a campaign as the 1864 Democratic Presidential nominee. In New York, the former Union Army Commander had a wellspring of democratic support, and became the favorite candidate of the Democrats, including both its "Peace" and pro-war factions. The young General not only had military star power (literally and figuratively), but he also possessed well-known opposition to the "radical" policies of Lincoln and the Republicans. Going into the November elections, the Democrats split their support between McClellan and Clement L. Vallandigham's peace platform, a position that McClellan did not endorse, even after winning the nomination. McClellan and the Democrats lost in landslide.

After McClellan lost his bid for the Presidency, he returned to the business world, seeking to become the President of the Morris and Essex Railroad in New Jersey. McClellan had hoped that the industrialist Abram Hewitt would negotiate with the board of directors to secure him the job, but the General's reputation had suffered greatly. According to Hewitt, the board of directors was not comfortable with McClellan as their company head for fear that it would jeopardize company relations with the government. McClellan then set off to tour Europe in January 1865.

During his European tour, McClellan traveled through Britain and the main continent. The highlight of his time abroad was meeting the great General Helmuth von Moltke, Chief of Staff of the Prussian Army. While in Europe, McClellan had been working for Edwin A. Stevens, looking for foreign buyers for the Stevens Battery, a doomed ocean-going ironclad more than 400 feet in length.

There were several offers soliciting McClellan for to lead companies or institutions. Most notably, the Board of Regents at the University of California offered McClellan $6,000 a year to become the President of the university. Settled comfortably in New Jersey, McClellan declined this and other lucrative offers that required him to relocate from the New York area. Not having any better prospects, he decided to become the Chief Engineer of New York City's Department of Docks in July 1870. By that November, General McClellan had proposed a series of uniform piers that would ring the shoreline of Manhattan. As Chief Engineer of the Docks, McClellan lacked the power to subdue the myriad of speculators and businessmen whose livelihoods depended upon New York's shipping and port activities.

WHEN MCCLELLAN DIED AT THE AGE OF 58, HE WAS ONE OF THE MOST CONTROVERSIAL FIGURES IN THE POSTBELLUM UNITED STATES.

In April 1873, McClellan left public service again for the private sector, resigning to start his own engineering company, Geo. B. McClellan & Co., Consulting Engineers and Accountants, where he focused on securing or insuring the investments of European clients into American railroads in an age of seemingly unbounded capitalism. Living in New Jersey, he remained active in the state's Democratic Party. In 1877, McClellan was nominated as the Democratic candidate for Governor, won, and served a single-term.

When McClellan died at the age of 58, he was one of the most controversial figures in the postbellum United States. Some portrayed him as a self-aggrandizing General whose political convictions and actions bordered on treason. Others, like Fitz John Porter and other veteran officers who had served under McClellan mourned the loss of a "soldier's General" who was loyal, capable, and wrongly sacked in the war. Given the arc of McClellan's life, "Little Mac" remains just as controversial still.

Written by: Lieutenant Colonel Jon Scott Logel, PhD (USA, Retired).

Major General McClellan Statue in front of Philadelphia City Hall.

Lincoln and McClellan at Antietam, October 4, 1862.

McClellan Statue in front of Philadelphia City Hall.

Photo: Mathew Brady/NARA

Major General Burnside.

Antietam Cannon at West Point.

Burnside Statue in Rhode Island.

© Thomas Eisfeller

Senator Ambrose Burnside, USMA 1847

- **U.S. SENATOR, STATE OF RHODE ISLAND, 1875–81**
- **GOVERNOR, STATE OF RHODE ISLAND, 1866–69**
- **COMMANDER, ARMY OF THE POTOMAC, 1862–63**
- **WOUNDED BY AN APACHE ARROW, 1850**
- **SERVED IN MEXICAN-AMERICAN WAR**
- **TREASURER, ILLINOIS CENTRAL RAILROAD**
- **MAJOR GENERAL AMBROSE BURNSIDE STATUE LOCATED AT CITY HALL PROVIDENCE, RHODE ISLAND**
- **FIRST PRESIDENT, NATIONAL RIFLE ASSOCIATION (NRA)**

"Trust to luck" was a proverb that Ambrose Burnside quoted from boyhood through his final days as United States Senator. He believed that even if he did his best, luck was necessary to be successful. Burnside learned early on that he needed to prepare thoroughly both in war and in peace, but he also recognized that chance played a role in any outcome of any human endeavor.

While he achieved his greatest military success during an amphibious assault on Roanoke Island and New Bern, North Carolina, in February of 1862, he was less fortunate leading the IX Corps at Antietam, and later, as Commander of the Army of the Potomac in at Fredericksburg. Ever the eternal optimist, Burnside remained devoted to the Union effort, faithfully leading the Army of the Ohio to capture Knoxville and then surviving the subsequent Confederate siege. In 1864, he once again commanded the IX Corps during Grant's Richmond campaign only to suffer more humiliation at the Battle of the Crater outside Petersburg. After the war, Burnside was able to move past his battlefield failures. He served three terms as Governor of Rhode Island and one as a Senator. Admired by many of his generation, General Burnside was the epitome of loyalty and remained a popular personality throughout his life. In spite of his tendency to trust his fellow man too much, Burnside was still able to recognize his own limitations and lead his troops to the best of his ability. Optimistic leadership in the face of multiple failures is what distinguished Burnside among his peers

>>> Spotlight

Rhode Island was one of the original 13 colonies and was the 13th to ratify the Constitution on May 29, 1790. It is currently the smallest state in the United States in size and ranked 43rd in overall population with more than 1,000,000 citizens. Major General Ambrose Burnside, after commanding the Union Army in 1862, was Rhode Island's Governor from 1866 to 1869 and then was elected as United States Senator in 1875 to 1881. He was the first West Point graduate to serve as a Senator from Rhode Island; the second was Jack Reed (USMA 1971), who has served in office since 1997.

Burnside Bridge at Antietam.

38. Among his classmates from the Class of 1847 were A.P. Hill and Egbert L. Viele. Commissioned in the Artillery, he and Viele departed the Military Academy and immediately set out to join Winfield Scott and the American Army in Mexico. By the time both young officers had arrived at Chapultepec in December that year, Burnside had gained a reputation as a poor card player prone to increasing the pot the worse his hand. As the newest Lieutenant in Mexico, Burnside was broke. Similar to U.S. Grant, money and business would prove to be a re-occurring vulnerability for Burnside.

HE SERVED THREE TERMS AS GOVERNOR OF RHODE ISLAND AND ONE AS A SENATOR. ADMIRED BY MANY OF HIS GENERATION, GENERAL BURNSIDE WAS THE EPITOME OF LOYALTY AND REMAINED A POPULAR PERSONALITY THROUGHOUT HIS LIFE.

Burnside's career followed a track similar to the other antebellum graduates with service in Mexico and East Coast forts, duty on the frontier, followed by resignation from the Army and attempts at civilian pursuits. In between his two stints at Fort Adams in Newport, Rhode Island, Lieutenant Burnside was ordered to report to "Bragg's Battery" at Las Vegas, New Mexico. There, he escorted the mail, protecting the mail trains against Apache attacks. In 1850, an Apache arrow wounded him during a skirmish, earning him an early reputation for being fearless in battle.

Perhaps, later in life, Burnside viewed his postings to Fort Adams as proof of trusting to luck for it was there that he met his wife and found a place to make his way as an entrepreneur. In 1852, he married Mary Bishop of Providence and established a breech-loading rifle factory at Bristol, Rhode Island. While he lobbied to sell his rifle to the War Department, Burnside became a Major General of the Rhode Island volunteer militia and served on the Board of Visitors to the United States Military Academy in 1856. By 1857, true to his trust in man and luck, Burnside was bankrupt after Secretary of War John B. Floyd reneged on a verbal agreement to purchase Burnside's rifles. This time, he turned to George B. McClellan, who was then President of the Illinois Central Railroad, where Burnside worked as treasurer until the outbreak of the Civil War.

During the Civil War, Burnside led the brigade of Rhode Island volunteers with Governor William Sprague at the Battle of First Bull Run. By the fall of 1861, he was training his Coast Division for the successful amphibious assault in North Carolina that effectively cut off the Confederate shipping to North Carolina during the war. At Roanoke Island, he led by example, navigating the flotilla and urging his men through the mud flats on the shore.

Two times President Lincoln offered Burnside the command of the Army of the Potomac when McClellan failed in the Peninsula Campaign of Spring and Summer 1862. Burnside declined those offers realizing that he lacked the capacity and experience to assume that level of responsibility. At Antietam in September 1862, Burnside substantiated his poor self-assessment by stalling his IX Corps at the now infamous "Burnside Bridge," and then substantiated it again at Fredericksburg as the commander of the Army of the Potomac – a position reluctantly placed upon him and reluctantly accepted by him – when he continually sent Union troops into the certain slaughter that awaited them in the assault at Marye's Heights.

Trusting to the end, Burnside declined to advocate for himself in the post battle debates that placed much of the blame for defeat squarely on him. Instead, he believed that history would eventually vindicate him for his wartime blemishes. As has been the case, save a biography or two, Burnside has been more commonly remembered for his facial hair – "sideburns" – than any of his wartime exploits and leadership.

In the end, though, Burnside's resilience in the face of great adversity remains a remarkable case of West Point instilled leadership. Many others would have never persevered through the financial duress or the battlefield defeats experienced by Ambrose Burnside. For the very trust to luck that led to much of his trials also empowered him to get through them.

Written by: Lieutenant Colonel Jon Scott Logel, PhD (USA, Retired).

in the Long Gray Line.

Born in Liberty, Indiana, to parents of Scottish ancestry, young Ambrose grew up doing farmwork and attending a one-room schoolhouse. Later the future Governor of Indiana, Samuel Bigger, tutored Burnside and saw the intellectual potential of the future officer. Initially Burnside pursued a career as a tailor, but though his father's political connections, Ambrose was able to secure an appointment to West Point in 1843.

As a cadet, Burnside flirted with expulsion from too many demerits. Although he was known to frequent Benny Havens and earned a "wild reputation" as a cadet, Burnside finished near the middle of his class of

Major General Joseph Hooker, USMA 1837

- **COMMANDER, ARMY OF THE POTOMAC, 1863**
- **SERVED AS A BRIGADE, DIVISION, CORPS, AND ARMY COMMANDER IN NEARLY EVERY ENGAGEMENT OF THE ARMY OF THE POTOMAC**
- **WOUNDED AT ANTIETAM AND CHANCELLORSVILLE**
- **SERVED IN SECOND SEMINOLE WAR AND MEXICAN-AMERICAN WAR**

When considering a "who's who" of top Civil War Generals, Major General Joseph Hooker is most likely not among them, let alone among any group of top American military leaders. Rightly or wrongly, Hooker's historical legacy primarily resides in his signature defeat at the Battle of Chancellorsville in April through May 1863 while commanding the Union's Army of the Potomac at a critical juncture of the war. History has often ascribed this defeat to Hooker's personal character flaws, such as drunkenness, a paralyzing loss of nerve, and a self-professed loss of confidence in the face of Confederate General Robert E. Lee.[1] Although the Union recovered from the defeat, Hooker, a man also frequently characterized as underminingly ambitious, morally flawed, and a braggart, never fully did. Perhaps another indicator of Hooker's historical popularity is that he has had only one primary biographer in contrast to the vast amounts of literature surrounding other Civil War contemporaries. Placing a spotlight on Chancellorsville as the sole measure of worthiness regarding Hooker's military career, however, certainly does him no justice. In particular, it fails to accurately reflect the

often overlooked service of a professional soldier who, over a span of 31 years, defined himself by bravely answering his nation's call to arms in nearly every conflict of his era.

Joseph Hooker's career modestly began as the Hadley, Massachusetts, native and grandson of a Revolutionary War Captain attended the United States Military Academy, graduated 29th out of 50 in the Class of 1837, and commissioned as a Second Lieutenant in the 1st United States Field Artillery. Although graduating in the lower-half of his class, Hooker's ranking is somewhat misleading considering the wealth of talent his class yielded as he and 21 of his classmates distinguished themselves in the Union and Confederate Armies during the Civil War.[2] In the immediate years following his commission, Hooker served in a variety of assignments around the country that included combat operations in Florida in the Second Seminole War, countering the Cherokee uprisings in the American southeast, and conducting peacekeeping operations along the U.S.-Canadian border in New England. By all accounts, Hooker performed commendably in these assignments and demonstrated

notable leadership and executive abilities.[3]

It was in the Mexican War, however, where First Lieutenant Hooker was able to showcase his broad range of abilities as both an administrator and combat leader. Again answering the nation's call to arms, Hooker served as the Chief of Staff for at least five different General Officers from 1846 to 1848 while taking part in the campaigns of both Zachary Taylor and Winfield Scott. In addition to his skillful management of the administrative details for his politically appointed Commanders, Hooker also led several combat missions. In his most notable action, Hooker took a regiment on short notice and stormed Chapultapec during the war's climactic battle outside of Mexico City. As a result of his actions in Mexico, Hooker earned three Brevet ranks for gallantry to Captain, Major, and Lieutenant Colonel – more than any of his service peers. Moreover, Hooker's Mexican War experience revealed a level of preparation and capability for command that was as great as any of his contemporaries for what was to lie ahead in the Civil War.[4]

After the Mexican War, Hooker was assigned as the Adjutant General in the Army's Pacific

Division in California, where he eventually resigned his commission in 1853 and experienced both failure and success during his eight-year military hiatus. He failed at farming and the timber business resulting in alledgedly unpaid debts to Henry W. Halleck and William T. Sherman – both West Point underclassmen of his and two of his Civil War Commanders – while succeeding as California militia Colonel and as a public servant. For the "personal" Hooker, still a bachelor, these years also formed his reputation as a drinker, gambler, and womanizer. With war looming, Hooker decided to return east and seek a commission, but he had to borrow money to make the trip.[5] Thus, Hooker brought both a wealth of professional military experience and a tainted personal reputation to the war.

Although Chancellorsville sealed Hooker's legacy, the reality is that his collective Civil War performance in terms of leadership, bravery, and command more accurately mirrored the successes of his earlier military career. "Fighting Joe," a nickname he disliked but one that stuck with him because of a journalistic error, did describe his character.[6]

>>> Spotlight

The Major General Joseph Hooker Equestrian Statue is located in front of the Massachusetts State House in Boston, Massachusetts. The State House was built in 1798. Hooker was born in Hadley, Massachusetts, and rose to command the Union Army of the Potomac during the Civil War.

As a Brigade, Division, and Corps Commander, he led his soldiers in the most intense stages of nearly every major engagement of the Army of the Potomac to include the Peninsula Campaign, Second Bull Run, Antietam, and Fredericksburg. It was these experiences and the high casualty rates associated with them that arguably influenced Hooker's cautious attitude and reliance on maneuver to defeat Lee at Chancellorsville rather than on attacking his entrenched enemy – a course of action that Hooker aggressively executed to gain the initiative early in the battle.[7]

HIS HORSE WAS SHOT FROM UNDER HIM DURING THE PENINSULA CAMPAIGN, AND HE WAS ALSO SHOT IN THE FOOT AT ANTIETAM, WHERE HE NEARLY PASSED OUT FROM THE LOSS OF BLOOD.

It is also hard to question Hooker's bravery and willingness, whether bravado or not, to put himself in harm's way and lead from the front. His horse was shot from under him during the Peninsula Campaign, and he was also shot in the foot at Antietam, where he nearly passed out from the loss of blood. Most notable, however, was his injury at a critical point in Chancellorsville when he was knocked unconscious by a Confederate artillery round that struck the porch of his headquarters and likely gave him a severe concussion. With Hooker drifting in and out of consciousness and none of his subordinates assertively assuming command, the Union Army lacked his leadership, lost the initiative, and ultimately lost the battle. It was also here where history may have easily confused his concussive symptoms from a serious head injury with the actions of a drunkard who suddenly lost confidence in himself.[8]

While commanding the Army of the Potomac, Hooker was extremely popular and administratively savvy. In less than five months, he rebuilt, reorganized, and restored the shattered morale of a devastated Army that was broken at Fredericksburg into what he boasted was "the finest Army on the Planet."[9] More importantly, Hooker so solidly transformed the Army that it not only weathered the storm of the Chancellorsville defeat, but also remained solidly in tact enough to survive and defeat Lee at Gettysburg.[10] Although Hooker was relieved on the eve of Gettysburg, his skillful maneuver of the Army helped set the conditions for the Union victory and eventually earned him recognition in a Congressional Resolution.[11]

Fighting Joe still proved to be an extremely resilient leader when he was re-assigned to Sherman's command in the west and made an immediate impact by leading multiple corps in victories at Lookout Mountain and during the heaviest fighting of the 1864 Atlanta Campaign as part of the Union's Army of the Tennessee. Following the death of Hooker's immediate Commander in Atlanta, however, Sherman passed him over for command of the Army of the Tennessee, even though Hooker was the senior-ranking officer and most-likely successor. In response, Hooker asked to be relieved as Corps Commander and Sherman honored his request. He then finished the war and his final years of service in various administrative commands until his retirement in October 1868.[12]

Hooker experienced additional hardships in the post-war years. At the age of 51, he finally married only to lose his wife three years later. He also suffered two debilitating strokes. Despite these hardships, however, Hooker focused intensely on veterans' issues that commemorated the soldiers, the Army, and the profession he loved – arguably his soldiers and the Army were his one true family. Like many of his peers, he also spent the remaining years of his life attempting to justify and shape his wartime legacy – an effort that was primarily unsuccessful. Joe Hooker died in October 1879 at the age of 65, never fully shaping that legacy and still remaining under the cloud of his Chancellorsville defeat. In hindsight, though, even if Hooker lost confidence in himself at Chancellorsville, Fighting Joe's body of work throughout his entire career certainly reveals that perhaps history need not be so quick to have lost confidence in him.

Major General George Gordon Meade was born December 31, 1815, in Cadiz, Spain, where his father ran a successful mercantile business, and grew up in Philadelphia and Washington, D.C. The fortunes of Meade's large and affluent family changed when the Spanish government jailed his father on dubious legal and monetary matters. When his father unexpectedly passed away, his mother sought an affordable education for her son. Meade wasn't even 16 when he entered the United States Military Academy in 1831 as one of the youngest cadets in his class. Although he accumulated a whopping 168 demerits by his first class year, he graduated 19 out of 54 cadets in his cohort.

Upon graduation in July 1835, Meade became a Brevet Second Lieutenant in the 3rd Artillery Regiment and served with the unit in Florida during the First Seminole Wars. Never healthy during his initial service, he resigned after his obligation was up and with help from his brother-in-law started work as an engineer for the United States government along the Florida coast and later the Mississippi Delta. For the next five years, he helped survey the national boundaries with Texas and Canada. He reentered Army service in 1842 as a Second Lieutenant in the Topographical Engineers, continuing his work along the Canadian border and later on along the Delaware coast until the outbreak of the Mexican War (1846–47). Meade served as a staff engineer for Major General Zachary Taylor through the Battles of Palo Alto, Resaca de la Palma, and Monterrey; for gallantry at the last battle, he received his promotion to Brevet First Lieutenant. He transferred to General Winfield Scott's Army and took part in the siege of Veracruz in March 1847, returning home shortly thereafter.

Meade stayed in the United States Army after Mexico and for the next several years served in various surveying posts in Florida, the East Coast, and the Great Lakes region. When the Civil War began, he sought a combat command and was appointed Brigadier General of volunteers for a Pennsylvania reserve brigade. He spent the first winter of the war with his unit camped in northern Virginia. After the Union Army of the Potomac kicked off its Peninsula Campaign in the spring of 1862, Meade's brigade found itself facing elements of the Army of Northern Virginia under General Robert E. Lee (USMA 1829). He saw intense action at the Battles of Mechanicsville, Gaines Mill, and Glendale during the Seven Days Campaign (June–July 1862). Meade was one of several Generals wounded at Glendale and took a leave of absence for nearly two months before returning to command during the Second Battle of Bull Run in late August 1862. As the Army of the Potomac shadowed Lee's Army into Maryland, Meade took over 3rd Division, I Corps. He fought in the Battle of South Mountain and temporarily assumed Corps command during the Battle of Antietam (September 17, 1862). Meade reverted back to division command through the disastrous Fredericksburg campaign, where his unit made the greatest gains during the attack against the Confederate defenders in and around the city. After Fredericksburg, Meade was briefly considered for Commanding General of the Army of the Potomac, but instead became Commander of V Corps and led his men through heavy fighting in the Battle of Chancellorsville. In the aftermath of Chancellorsville, President

> AT FIRST, HE THOUGHT THAT THE OFFICER WAKING HIM IN THE MIDDLE OF THE NIGHT WAS COMING TO EITHER RELIEVE OR ARREST HIM, NOT TO PROMOTE HIM.

Major General George G. Meade, USMA 1835

- COMMANDER, ARMY OF THE POTOMAC, 1863–65
- COMMANDER, V CORPS, 1863
- COMMANDER, 3RD DIVISION, I CORPS, 1862
- COMMANDER, PENNSYLVANIA RESERVE BRIGADE, 1961–62
- SERVED IN THE SEMINOLE WARS AND MEXICAN-AMERICAN WAR
- FORT MEADE, MARYLAND, NAMED IN HIS HONOR

Photo: NARA

Meade Statue at Gettysburg.

Abraham Lincoln decided to make a command change. Early on June 28, 1863, Meade, in the middle of pursuing Lee into Pennsylvania, found out that Lincoln had named him the new Commander of the Army of the Potomac. Given the track record of some officers in the Union Army to that point, Meade wrote his wife the next day that at first he thought that the officer waking him in the middle of the night was coming to either relieve or arrest him, not to promote him.

Meade showcased his steady presence and resolve in thwarting Lee's repeated assaults during the second and third days of the Battle of Gettysburg (July 1–3, 1863), the oft-claimed high tide of the Confederacy. He figured out his subordinates' strengths and used them to the Army's benefit and solicited input from his Commanders during the fight before taking a course of action. Nevertheless, Meade's decision to not swiftly pursue the Army of Northern Virginia south across the Potomac River frustrated Lincoln

and others. For the next eight months, Meade sparred off and on with Lee in piedmont Virginia, drawing criticism for the Mine Run campaign and the seeming stalemate in the eastern theater. In the spring of 1864, new Commanding General of the United States Army Lieutenant General Ulysses S. Grant (USMA 1843) joined Meade in the field with the Army of the Potomac. Despite the awkwardness of the situation, the two men became friends as Meade and Grant doggedly pursued Lee south toward Richmond during the Wilderness Campaign. As of June 1864, Meade had Lee's Army locked in a siege in and around Petersburg, Virginia. Meade's subordinates made slow but steady gains contracting the siege lines, effectively holding Lee and his Army in place as the Union made progress in the field against other Confederate armies to the west and south. When Lee evacuated Richmond in April 1865 and slipped west, Meade immediately followed, sending his Cavalry elements

ahead to block his opponent's path. Meade's Army surrounded Lee's in the vicinity of Appomattox Court House, Virginia, prompting the surrender of the symbolic heart of the Confederate cause.

Meade proudly rode at the head of his Army during the Grand Review in Washington, D.C., on May 23, 1865, and two years to the day of his taking command bid farewell to the disbanding Army of the Potomac. For much of his post–Civil War career, he commanded military departments in the east and south enforcing policies enacted under Reconstruction. He passed away in his beloved Philadelphia on November 6, 1872, at age 57. Meade is in many ways the forgotten Union General of the Civil War, overshadowed by Grant for most of his Army command and with few monographs on his life and career compared to other famous West Point graduates. Perhaps Meade's best and overarching quality as a Commander, as noted by Daniel Harvey Hill (USMA 1842),

was that he "was always in deadly earnest" when it came to fighting (Cleaves, xii). For someone who never planned on commanding an Army but was called upon by his country to do so, this trait indeed served him well.

Written by: Major Brit K. Erslev, PhD.

United States Army
Fort George G. Meade

Main Gate

Fort Meade, Maryland, named in Major General Meade's honor, is home to the National Security Agency.

Major General Meade Statue, U.S. Courthouse Washington, D.C.

Meade and his staff at Gettysburg.

>>> Spotlight

Fort Meade, Maryland, named after General George S. Meade, is home to the National Security Agency (NSA). NSA was formed in 1952 and is home to America's code-makers and code-breakers.

Major General George Meade.

Photo: NARA

General Pershing arriving in France in 1917.
Photo: AP

Photo: AP

General of the Armies John J. "Blackjack" Pershing, USMA 1886

- COMMANDER, PUNITIVE EXPEDITION TO MEXICO, 1916
- COMMANDER, U.S. FORCES, WORLD WAR I
- GENERAL OF THE ARMIES
- PERSHING BARRACKS AT WEST POINT NAMED IN HIS HONOR
- FOUNDER, RESERVE OFFICERS ASSOCIATION
- 10TH CHIEF OF STAFF, UNITED STATES ARMY

Photo: NARA

President Wilson and General Pershing.

Throughout America's rich military history, only John Joseph Pershing and George Washington are associated with the exclusive rank of "General of the Armies of the United States." Pershing, however, was the only one to ever hold the rank during his lifetime when he received the promotion following World War I and held it until his death on July 15, 1948. Unlike Pershing, Washington's rank came posthumously through a Congressional Joint Resolution in 1976 as part of America's Bicentennial celebration.[1] Pershing's elevation to the nation's highest military rank is a clear indication of his stellar service to the nation over a 38-year career spanning two different centuries and bridging the gap between post-Civil War and post-World War I America. During that period, Pershing fought in five separate conflicts from his time on the Frontier Army to his success as the Commander of the American Expeditionary Force (AEF) in World War I, served as a mentor to arguably the greatest generation of American generals to include George C. Marshall (VMI 1901), Douglas MacArthur (USMA 1903), and George S. Patton (USMA 1909), then culminated his career as the 10th Chief of Staff of the Army. Pershing ultimately emerged as the greatest military leader of his generation and arguably one of the greatest in American history. Unsurprisingly, he experienced tragedy throughout his career in the numerous Soldiers he lost in his various combat commands. Yet Pershing, himself decorated several times for valor, ironically would experience his greatest personal tragedy away from the battlefield when his wife and three daughters died in a house fire at the Presidio in San Francisco on August 27, 1915.[2]

Pershing was born on September 13, 1860, near Laclede, Missouri. He was the oldest of John and Ann Elizabeth Pershing's nine children – three of whom died as infants. He

General Pershing with President Franklin Delano Roosevelt, Arlington National Cemetery.

MGM-31 Pershing intermediate nuclear missiles named after General Pershing.

young Pershing.[4] Pershing graduated West Point on June 12, 1886. He ranked 30th out of 77 cadets and commissioned into the Cavalry.[5]

Pershing's early career put him at the forefront of the Army's frontier mission with his assignment to the 6th Cavalry Regiment. There, he fought with distinction in several campaigns against the Apache and Sioux Indians to include the aftermath of Wounded Knee. Among his most unique and rewarding frontier assignments was his command of a company of Sioux Scouts, in which Pershing further validated his own personal egalitarian notions of race. Upon leaving that command in 1891, a saddened Pershing had formed a very close bond with his scouts and noted that there existed "oneness to things and men."[6] He next became the Commandant of Cadets at the University of Nebraska – a school from where he also earned a law degree. In September 1895, he was again assigned to frontier duty, this time proudly commanding a cavalry troop of African-American "Buffalo Soldiers" in the famed 10th Cavalry Regiment where he earned his enduring moniker, "Black Jack." This nickname was intended to be derogatory and was given to him by prejudiced officers and cadets at West Point after he returned to the tactical staff because of both his service leading Buffalo Soldiers and his strict disciplinarian nature.[7]

When war broke out with Spain in April 1898, Pershing again returned to the 10th Cavalry Regiment as its quartermaster and deployed to Cuba where he was cited for gallantry under fire for actions at San Juan Hill, Kettle Hill, and during the siege of Santiago. His actions in support of those engagements also caught the eye of Colonel Theodore Roosevelt (who would eventually become President of the United States and also posthumously receive the Medal of Honor over a century later for his actions at San Juan Hill). Pershing too received a valor award for his gallantry in the Spanish-American War when he was awarded the Silver Star Citation and eventually the Silver Star Medal. Following the war, Pershing was responsible for supporting occupation forces in all the territories gained from Spain including Cuba, the Philippines, Guam, and Puerto Rico.[8] In 1899, war then broke out in the Philippines. Pershing, now a Captain, deployed there, participated in actions against the revolutionary Moros, and was again cited for bravery in combat along with receiving great praise for his pacification efforts around Lake Lanao. He remained in

the Philippines until returning home in June 1903 with a wealth of administrative and combat experience.[9]

At home, Pershing met and married Helen Warren, the daughter of sitting Wyoming Senator Francis E. Warren, the chairman of the US Military Appropriations Committee. Shortly after the marriage, Theodore Roosevelt, now President after the assassination of William McKinley, assigned Pershing to the politically appointed position of military attaché to Tokyo in March 1905 and as a military observer to the Russo-Japanese War. Pershing, newly wed to the daughter of a powerful Senator and in close favor of the President from their mutual service in the Spanish-American War, now had political connections at the highest levels. In 1905, Roosevelt then made the bold and controversial decision to promote Captain Pershing directly to Brigadier General – an effort he unsuccessfully attempted two years earlier – and vaulted Pershing over hundreds of other officers. While the promotion fueled rumors of nepotism, it was not unprecedented and was clearly indicative of Pershing's past performance and future potential.[10] Over the next several years, he and Helen had three daughters and a son as the family followed Pershing to various assignments to include a brief tour as an advisor in the Balkans in 1908 (the flashpoint that would spark World War I six years later), back to the Philippines as military commander of the Moro Province, and then brigade command at the Presidio in San Francisco. While at the Presidio, Pershing's brigade deployed to Fort Bliss, Texas in April 1914 to help ease tensions along the US-Mexican border caused by Mexican revolutionary general Francisco "Pancho" Villa. After a year at Fort Bliss, Pershing decided to move his family there when he received the horrific news that Helen and his three daughters had died

> ## AFTER WORLD WAR I, GENERAL PERSHING WAS A HERO, AND THE U.S. HAD BECOME A MAJOR PLAYER ON THE WORLD STAGE. CONGRESS PROMOTED HIM TO GENERAL OF THE ARMIES, A RANK NO LIVING GENERAL HAS EVER HELD BEFORE.

entered West Point in 1882 at the age of 22 after both serving as a teacher and earning a degree in Elementary Education. Part of that time included teaching African-America children at the Laclede Negro School where Pershing's progressive views on race relations made him a target of prejudice from both blacks and whites alike.[3] Much older than the average cadet when he arrived at West Point, Pershing's leadership qualities and maturity were evident and eventually

earned him the rare distinction of becoming both class president and First Captain despite an average cadet ranking. While First Captain, Pershing had the honor of regularly hosting dignitaries, among whom included frequent Academy visitor and one of Missouri's favorite native sons, Mark Twain, as well as the solemn privilege of leading the Cadet Honor Guard for the state funeral of President Ulysses S. Grant (USMA 1845) – an experience that profoundly touched the

in a fire at his Presidio quarters. Only his son Warren survived the fire. Despite this tragedy that would undoubtedly haunt Pershing for the rest of his life, he returned to Fort Bliss with his son Warren after burying his family and prepared his brigade for another operation.[11] Warren would eventually become an Army officer in World War II and serve on MacArthur's staff.[12]

The ever-resilient and dutiful Soldier, Pershing led his brigade on a punitive expedition into Mexico in March 1916 to capture Villa. This would be Pershing's fourth major combat action. Despite being ill-equipped, lacking a strong logistical structure, and receiving little support from the Mexican government, Pershing's force of nearly 5,000 Soldiers – to include a young George S. Patton – pursued Villa's forces for nearly a year. Pershing's expedition never succeeded in capturing Villa, but it was successful in stabilizing the border and breaking Villa's army. In February 1917, the expedition ended as Pershing, now a Major General, and his force returned to the US to face the impending involvement in Europe.[13]

After years of attempting to remain neutral since the outbreak of war in 1914, the US reluctantly entered World War I in April 1917 under President Woodrow Wilson. The leading contender to command the Allied Expeditionary Forces (AEF) was Major General Fredrick Funston, a Medal of Honor recipient from the Philippine-American War. In 1917, however, Funston suffered a fatal heart attack. After Funston's death, President Wilson selected Pershing to command the AEF over former Army Chief of Staff, Major General Leonard Wood, because of Pershing's better health, recent combat experience, and limited political ambitions.[14] Thus, Pershing now answered the nation's call to service in his fifth conflict and was charged with raising, equipping, training, and deploying an Army of millions in a limited amount of time as war raged on in Europe.

A gifted organizer and trainer, talented planner, tireless worker, and great judge of character – George C. Marshall was one of his top subordinates – Pershing built the AEF in under a year from a pre-war force of less than 130,000 to one exceeding 2,000,000. As the war devolved into one of stalemate and attrition, the Allies desperately needed fresh troops and looked to America for them. It is in this context that Pershing was able to secure his most strategically significant goal before placing American troops on the front line. He convinced the French and British

allies that the US would not amalgamate the AEF into the French and British Armies; rather, the US would have an autonomous sector of the Western Front under Pershing's command. Under this structure, Pershing directly led the AEF in the Aisne-Marne (July–August 1918), St. Mihiel (September 1917), and Meuse-Argonne (September-November 1918) Offensives. The AEF proved to be the tipping point in the Allies' favor and was a catalyst for the German surrender on November 11, 1918, that ended the war.[15] Despite its autonomy, the AEF still suffered very high casualties with nearly 116,000 soldiers killed in action and 230,000 wounded in 13 months of combat, while the entire conflict claimed more than 8.5 million lives.[16]

General Pershing returned to the US in July 1919 and Congress promoted him to his unprecedented rank of "General of the Armies." In his final assignment, Pershing served as the 10th Army Chief of Staff from July 1921 until retiring in September 1924. He remained active in retirement, but shunned politics and tried to maintain a level of privacy. Pershing formed the Reserve Officers Association (ROA) at the Willard Hotel in Washington, DC in 1922 and also served as the Chairman of the American Battle Monuments Commission (ABMC) from its formation in 1923 until his death in 1948. In 1932, Pershing won the Pulitzer Prize for History with his memoirs *My Experiences in the World War*.

Pershing spent his last years living at Walter Reed Hospital. In 1946, he secretly married Micheline Resco, a French woman he had met in France as the AEF commander during World War I, and the marriage remained a closely guarded secret for years. Almost two years later, at the age of 88, Pershing died in his sleep on July 14, 1948, after slipping into a coma.[17] He was given a State Funeral at Arlington National Cemetery and is buried among many of the Soldiers he led in World War I. His awards include the Distinguished Service Cross, Silver Star, and Purple Heart, along with more than 20 foreign awards and decorations. In addition to his lifetime of service, influence on a generation of military leaders, and his notable rank, Pershing's legacy also includes the M26 Pershing Tank, the Pershing Missile, Pershing Barracks at West Point, and the Thayer Hotel's Pershing Room all being named in his honor, along with many streets, squares, and schools across America.

Plaque on the outside of the Willard Hotel in Washington, D.C. dedicated to Pershing. Pershing Statue is nearby, 100 meters from the front door.

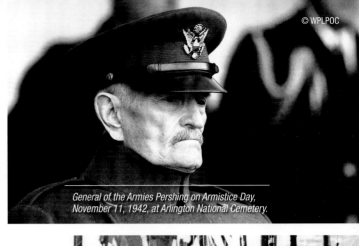

>>> Spotlight

RESERVE STRENGTH. RESERVE LIFE.

After World War I, General Pershing founded the Reserve Officer Association at the Willard Hotel in Washington, D.C.

General of the Armies Pershing on Armistice Day, November 11, 1942, at Arlington National Cemetery.

A plaque dedicated to General Pershing outside the Willard Intercontinental Hotel in Washington, D.C.

"TATES"

, FROM A N OR Y TIME."

L PROVIDE ENT AND

-TATES

STATES

JOHN J. PERSHING
GENERAL OF TH

1860
1948

General Pershing Statue across from Willard Hotel in Washington, D.C.

General Douglas MacArthur is one of West Point's most recognizable graduates and one of the great military leaders in American history. He is also a reminder of how the Constitution binds the military to civil authority. He was equal parts brilliant, courageous, articulate, prideful, arrogant, and stubborn. Graduating from West Point in 1903 as the top cadet in his class, he served nearly half a century in uniform, where he rose to become a Five-Star General of the Army, one of five men who accomplished this feat. One of the most decorated service members in American history and the most decorated among his Five-Star peers, MacArthur received the Medal of Honor, three Distinguished Service Crosses, seven Silver Stars, two Purple Hearts, and many foreign awards.[1]

His career was legendary but one that ended like a Shakespearean tragedy. His speeches, strategies, and leadership style – still taught at West Point today – reside in the shadow of his campaign to seek absolute victory in the Korean War.

Like Macbeth, MacArthur was in essence royalty – Army royalty. He grew up as an "Army brat." Not just any brat, though, he was the son of a national hero, Lieutenant General Arthur MacArthur, Jr., who received his Medal of Honor for heroic actions on Missionary Ridge in the Civil War and had also served in the Philippines. Though he did not commit regicide, it was the tragic death of his older brother Arthur III in 1923, from appendicitis at the age of 47, that placed Douglas at the head of the MacArthur hierarchy. Douglas MacArthur entered West Point in 1899, and throughout his four years there, his mother, like a doting queen, lived in the West Point Hotel on Trophy Point (predecessor to the Thayer Hotel).

He excelled as a cadet and rose to be the First Captain and first-ranked cadet academically in his class. He was also the manager of the fledging sport of football, only a year after the founder of Army football, Dennis Michie, had been killed on San Juan Hill.[2]

General of the Army Douglas MacArthur, USMA 1903

- **GENERAL OF THE ARMY**
- **MEDAL OF HONOR RECIPIENT**
- **SUPREME COMMANDER, SOUTHWEST PACIFIC THEATER OF WAR**
- **COMMANDER, UNITED NATIONS COMMAND, KOREAN WAR, 1950**
- **SUPERINTENDENT OF WEST POINT**
- **FIRST CAPTAIN AT WEST POINT**
- **ARMY FOOTBALL MANAGER**

General Douglas MacArthur wearing Five-Stars.

Brigadier General Douglas MacArthur, Superintendent West Point.

After graduating in 1903, he served as an Engineering Junior Officer and was then requested by his father, then a Major General, to be his Aide-de-Camp. Together they traveled the Far East, particularly the Philippines, where his father was already a hero. Douglas MacArthur first saw action when he was ambushed in the Philippines and killed two attackers. He then deployed to Mexico as part of the Vera Cruz expedition in 1914 under Major General John J. Pershing (USMA 1886).

MacArthur again distinguished himself under fire and personally killed several guerillas. There was no act of heroism in MacArthur's career that would equal this. Yet, his nomination for the Medal of Honor was not approved.[3]

As the United States entered a raging World War I in 1917 under General Pershing's command, a new division, the 42nd Division, was formed and MacArthur was chosen as the Chief of Staff. During the deployment, he also served as a Brigade Commander, then as Division Commander during combat and the occupation that followed. In World War I, he was wounded twice, gassed once, and was recognized for valor several times.

In 1921, he returned to West Point to lead the Academy as the Superintendent, where he implemented far-reaching reforms and expanded the Academy, including plans for the construction of a new hotel to replace the aging West Point Hotel. In 1928, he served as the Head of the United States Olympic Committee. In 1930, he was promoted to General and made the youngest and longest-serving Chief of Staff of the United States Army. In 1935, he went to the Philippines to serve as the United States Military Advisor. He actually retired from the United States Army in 1937 but chose to stay in Manila. He was hired by the Philippine government to build and train its Army and was given the rank of Field Marshal of the Philippine Defense Force. During this time, he also married Jean Faircloth (in 1937), and they had one child. With the Nazis occupying most of Europe and the Japanese gaining ground in

General MacArthur and staff watch Inchon Invasion, 1950.

Major General Westmoreland and General MacArthur walking into mess hall at West Point to give the "Duty, Honor, Country" speech 1962.

General MacArthur wades ashore in the Philippines fulfilling his "I shall return" promise.

MacArthur Statue, West Point.

the Pacific, he was recalled to active duty in July of 1941 and made Commander in Chief of the Armed Forces in the Far East.[4] This spoke volumes not only about MacArthur's leadership abilities, but also about the vital strategic location of the Philippines, where MacArthur was to be headquartered. He and his father were already heroes in the Philippines, and this new role only increased MacArthur's standing.

Hours after the Japanese attack on Pearl Harbor on December 7, 1941, they also attacked the Philippines. This was to be

MacArthur and Emperor Hirohito, September 27, 1945.

one of the low points of MacArthur's military career. Despite warning of a Japanese attack – or perhaps because of it – he abandoned the planned defense of Manila Bay and the Bataan Peninsula in favor of a hastily planned and ill-conceived defense of the beaches. His air cover was caught and destroyed on the ground, while his troops on the beaches were overextended, under-resourced, and overrun. MacArthur himself was ordered to leave the Philippines by President Franklin Roosevelt.[5] He and his family retreated to his new command in Australia to take charge of allied forces in the Southwest Pacific Theater; simultaneously, he abandoned General Jonathan Wainwright (USMA 1906) to a brutal and ultimately doomed defense of Manila Bay resembling the initial plan abandoned by MacArthur, but lacking the many resources MacArthur had squandered. Wainwright fought until captured and spent the remainder of the war in Japanese Prisoner of War camps.[6] Ironically, it would be for his retreat from the Philippines that MacArthur would be

awarded the Medal of Honor – making Arthur and Douglas MacArthur the first father-and-son Medal of Honor recipients.

In reality, the medal had more to do with Army Chief of Staff General George Marshall's desire to instill confidence in the American people after the initial Japanese onslaught than any real act of heroism.[7] MacArthur cannot be accused of seeking this award but he did refuse to accept responsibility for the fall of the Philippines. The forces remaining under General Wainwright fought until they ran out of food and ammunition and surrendered at Bataan in April 1942 and Corregidor in May 1942. They suffered under brutal Japanese torture as prisoners – to include the infamous Bataan Death March – and many were executed or died in captivity. Sadly, MacArthur blamed Wainwright for the loss of the Philippines and later unsuccessfully attempted to block Wainwright's Medal of Honor.[8] MacArthur left but ominously proclaimed, "I shall return." The public had a hero but his soldiers sometimes referred to him as "Dugout Doug" referencing his departure from the Philippines.[9]

After some intense, strategic-level debate, he successfully lobbied for a "Twin Drive" strategy in the Pacific. Admiral Chester Nimitz would pursue the Japanese Navy at sea through his "island hopping" campaign in the Central Pacific, and MacArthur, undeterred by the fall of the Philippines, designed and led the allied efforts against the Japanese across the Southwest Pacific with attacks in New Guinea, the Admiralty Islands, western New Britain, and the Solomon Islands, before successfully fulfilling his prophecy of returning to liberate the Philippines in 1944.[10]

MacArthur was promoted to General of the Army and received his fifth star in December of 1944. On September 2, 1945, he commanded the surrender ceremonies of the Japanese aboard the *USS Missouri* with Wainwright at his side, then commanded the occupation of Japan where he was the Military Governor. This was perhaps the crown jewel in his career. MacArthur was instrumental in the demobilization of the Japanese military forces, re-building of the economy, drafting of a constitution, and significant reforms for land redistribution, education, public health, and women's rights. His decision to retain Emperor Hirohito rather than try him for war crimes took moral courage and an acute understanding of the emperor's cultural significance to Japan – ultimately, it can be credited with greatly influencing Japan's recovery and its re-joining of the world community. His

generalship in destroying Japan the enemy and then his statesmanship in transforming Japan into one of the world's most peaceful and prosperous nations and strongest American allies rank among his greatest leadership accomplishments.[11]

Entering the twilight of his career, MacArthur still had one final yet tragic act in the drama of his life. In 1950, at the age of 70, North Korean forces invaded South Korea, and MacArthur was selected to lead allied efforts as the United Nations Supreme Commander.

At the time, it seemed as if this would be one last hurrah, one more time into the fray, the hero of the Pacific dealing a deadly blow to the new enemy – communism – on the world's stage in a most familiar place for him: the Far East. General MacArthur first defended the Pusan Perimeter, then led a most audacious and successful amphibious attack at the Port of Inchon in September 1950, which broke the back of North Korean forces. He then attacked north into the former North Korea in an effort to unite the country. He even publicly suggested that the United States attack staging areas across the border inside China, using nuclear weapons if necessary. President Harry Truman, however, did not want the Korean conflict to evolve into a general war with the Chinese, and ultimately into a possible nuclear confrontation with the Soviet Union.

Nevertheless, in November 1950, the Chinese crossed the border and attacked U.N. Forces en masse with far superior numbers, driving U.N. Forces all the way to Seoul.

War with China was an exponentially more dangerous escalation – tensions climbed to unprecedented heights between General MacArthur and President Truman. Unable to see the larger picture of global security in a new Cold War environment, one which required limiting wartime objectives, MacArthur was vocal and articulate in his advocacy of bringing the full might of the Armed Forces to bear against the Chinese, arguing that there was "no substitute for victory."[12] This strategic difference in opinion with President Truman and the rest of the American military senior leadership, progressed from disagreement to outright disobedience. MacArthur would go so far in his pursuit of victory that he attempted to segregate his oath to the Constitution from his oath to obey the orders of the President of the United States. On April 11, 1951, President Truman relieved the legendary General MacArthur of his command noting that his insubordination was a "direct

challenge" to the President's authority as Commander in Chief.[13] MacArthur magnified and extended the controversy by publicly supporting his position in speeches across the country and even attempting to enter the political arena. Ultimately, the event served to reinforce the Constitutionality of civil control of the military and as a public reminder that military personnel serve at the discretion of the President. Despite his personal flaws and the tragic ending to his career, MacArthur's lifelong contributions were not forgotten by his nation. When he returned to the United States for the first time since before World War II, he received a hero's welcome and a parade on 5th Avenue in New York City. He also gave a stirring address to Congress on April 19, 1951, proclaiming that "old soldiers never die, they just fade away."[14] MacArthur was undoubtedly a brilliant military strategist, leader, and orator. Many of his quotes are required knowledge that West Point cadets must still memorize verbatim. Perhaps his most memorable and inspiring speech was his May 12, 1962, Farewell Address to the Corps of Cadets, which contains his famous "Duty, Honor, Country" quote, after he received the prestigious Thayer Award.[15]

Gregory Peck portrayed him in the movie *MacArthur* in 1977, and countless books have been written about him, including William Manchester's 1978 biography *American Caesar*. The NCAA Division I Football Trophy is named after him as "The MacArthur Trophy," which was donated anonymously in 1959 to the NCAA and bears the famous MacArthur quote "There is no substitute for victory" upon it. At West Point, the MacArthur Statue, MacArthur Barracks, and MacArthur's Restaurant at the Historic Thayer Hotel are all named in his honor. In 1952, he accepted the role of Chairman of the Board of Remington Rand Corporation and lived in relative seclusion in the Waldorf Hotel in New York City until his death on April 5, 1964. He is buried in Norfolk, Virginia, at the MacArthur Memorial, a museum and research center dedicated to preserving the memory of General MacArthur. In the end, MacArthur remains one of America's greatest military figures, while his legacy certainly evokes a broad range of positive and negative critiques. One thing is for certain, though: MacArthur, the old soldier, will never fade away.

MacArthur signs Japanese Surrender Documents aboard the USS Missouri, September 2, 1945.

>>> Spotlight

In 1977, Gregory Peck portrayed MacArthur in the movie *MacArthur*. Several books have also been written about him, including William Manchester's 1978 biography *American Caesar*.

General MacArthur wades ashore in the Philippines, 1945.

General MacArthur receives ticker-tape parade in New York City, April 20, 1951.

General MacArthur delivering his May 12, 1962, "Duty, Honor, Country" speech to the Corps of Cadets.

"DUTY, HONOR, COUNTRY"

On May 12, 1962, MacArthur was awarded the Sylvanus Thayer Award at West Point, where he gave one of the most iconic speeches in American military history, known as the "Duty, Honor, Country" speech. Only two years later, in 1964, he died in Washington, D.C., and was buried in Norfolk, Virginia. His farewell speech to the Corps is considered one of the greatest speeches in American history:

General Westmoreland, General Grove, distinguished guests, and gentlemen of the Corps!

As I was leaving the hotel this morning, a doorman asked me, "Where are you bound for, General?" And when I replied, "West Point," he remarked, "Beautiful place. Have you ever been there before?"

No human being could fail to be deeply moved by such a tribute as this [Thayer Award]. Coming from a profession I have served so long, and a people I have loved so well, it fills me with an emotion I cannot express. But this award is not intended primarily to honor a personality, but to symbolize a great moral code – the code of conduct and chivalry of those who guard this beloved land of culture and ancient descent. That is the animation of this medallion. For all eyes and for all time, it is an expression of the ethics of the American soldier. That I should be integrated in this way with so noble an ideal arouses a sense of pride and yet of humility which will be with me always

Duty, Honor, Country: Those three hallowed words reverently dictate what you ought to be, what you can be, what you will be. They are your rallying points: to build courage when courage seems to fail; to regain faith when there seems to be little cause for faith; to create hope when hope becomes forlorn.

Unhappily, I possess neither that eloquence of diction, that poetry of imagination, nor that brilliance of metaphor to tell you all that they mean.

The unbelievers will say they are but words, but a slogan, but a flamboyant phrase. Every pedant, every demagogue, every cynic, every hypocrite, every troublemaker, and I am sorry to say, some others of an entirely different character, will try to downgrade them even to the extent of mockery and ridicule.

But these are some of the things they do. They build your basic character. They mold you for your future roles as the custodians of the nation's defense. They make you strong enough to know when you are weak, and brave enough to face yourself when you are afraid. They teach you to be proud and unbending in honest failure, but humble and gentle in success; not to substitute words for actions, not to seek the path of comfort, but to face the stress and spur of difficulty and challenge; to learn to stand up in the storm but to have compassion on those who fall; to master yourself before you seek to master others; to have a heart that is clean, a goal that is high; to learn to laugh, yet never forget how to weep; to reach into the future yet never neglect the past; to be serious yet never to take yourself too seriously; to be modest so that you will remember the simplicity of true greatness, the open mind of true wisdom, the meekness of true strength. They give you a temper of the will, a quality of the imagination, a vigor of the emotions, a freshness of the deep springs of life, a temperamental predominance of courage over timidity, of an appetite for adventure over love of ease. They create in your heart the sense of wonder, the unfailing hope of what next, and the joy and inspiration of life. They teach you in this way to be an officer and a gentleman.

And what sort of soldiers are those you are to lead? Are they reliable? Are they brave? Are they capable of victory? Their story is known to all of you. It is the story of the American man-at-arms. My estimate of him was formed on the battlefield many, many years ago, and has never changed. I regarded him then as I regard him now – as one of the world's noblest figures, not only as one of the finest military characters, but also as one of the most stainless. His name and fame are the birthright of every American citizen. In his youth and strength, his love and loyalty, he gave all that mortality can give.

He needs no eulogy from me or from any other man. He has written his own history and written it in red on his enemy's breast. But when I think of his patience under adversity, of his courage under fire, and of his modesty in vic-

tory, I am filled with an emotion of admiration I cannot put into words. He belongs to history as furnishing one of the greatest examples of successful patriotism. He belongs to posterity as the instructor of future generations in the principles of liberty and freedom. He belongs to the present, to us, by his virtues and by his achievements. In 20 campaigns, on a hundred battlefields, around a thousand campfires, I have witnessed that enduring fortitude, that patriotic self-abnegation, and that invincible determination which have carved his statue in the hearts of his people. From one end of the world to the other he has drained deep the chalice of courage.

As I listened to those songs [of the glee club], in memory's eye I could see those staggering columns of the First World War, bending under soggy packs, on many a weary march from dripping dusk to drizzling dawn, slogging ankle-deep through the mire of shell-shocked roads, to form grimly for the attack, blue-lipped, covered with sludge and mud, chilled by the wind and rain, driving home to their objective, and for many, to the judgment seat of God.

I do not know the dignity of their birth, but I do know the glory of their death. They died unquestioning, uncomplaining, with faith in their hearts, and on their lips the hope that we would go on to victory. Always, for them: Duty, Honor, Country; always their blood and sweat and tears, as we sought the way and the light and the truth.

And 20 years after, on the other side of the globe, again the filth of murky foxholes, the stench of ghostly trenches, the slime of dripping dugouts; those boiling suns of relentless heat, those torrential rains of devastating storms; the loneliness and utter desolation of jungle trails; the bitterness of long separation from those they loved and cherished; the deadly pestilence of tropical disease; the horror of stricken areas of war; their resolute and determined defense, their swift and sure attack, their indomitable purpose, their complete and decisive victory – always victory. Always through the bloody haze of their last reverberating shot, the vision of gaunt, ghastly men reverently following your password of: Duty, Honor, Country.

The code which those words perpetuate embraces the highest moral laws and will stand the test of any ethics or philosophies ever promulgated for the uplift of mankind. Its requirements are for the things that are right, and its restraints are from the things that are wrong.

The soldier, above all other men, is required

to practice the greatest act of religious training – sacrifice.

In battle and in the face of danger and death, he discloses those divine attributes which his Maker gave when he created man in his own image. No physical courage and no brute instinct can take the place of the Divine help which alone can sustain him.

However horrible the incidents of war may be, the soldier who is called upon to offer and to give his life for his country is the noblest development of mankind.

You now face a new world – a world of change. The thrust into outer space of the satellite, spheres, and missiles mark the beginning of another epoch in the long story of mankind. In the five or more billions of years the scientists tell us it has taken to form the earth, in the three or more billion years of development of the human race, there has never been a more abrupt or staggering evolution. We deal now not with things of this world alone, but with the illimitable distances and as yet unfathomed mysteries of the universe. We are reaching out for a new and boundless frontier.

We speak in strange terms: of harnessing the cosmic energy; of making winds and tides work for us; of creating unheard synthetic materials to supplement or even replace our old standard basics; to purify sea water for our drink; of mining ocean floors for new fields of wealth and food; of disease preventatives to expand life into the hundreds of years; of controlling the weather for a more equitable distribution of heat and cold, of rain and shine; of space ships to the moon; of the primary target in war, no longer limited to the Armed Forces of an enemy, but instead to include his civil populations; of ultimate conflict between a united human race and the sinister forces of some other planetary galaxy; of such dreams and fantasies as to make life the most exciting of all time.

And through all this welter of change and development, your mission remains fixed, determined, inviolable: it is to win our wars. Everything else in your professional career is but corollary to this vital dedication. All other public purposes, all other public projects, all other public needs, great or small, will find others for their accomplishment. But you are the ones who are trained to fight. Yours is the profession of arms, the will to win, the sure knowledge that in war there is no substitute for victory; that if you lose, the nation will be destroyed; that the very obsession of your

public service must be: Duty, Honor, Country.

Others will debate the controversial issues, national and international, which divide men's minds; but serene, calm, aloof, you stand as the Nation's war-guardian, as its lifeguard from the raging tides of international conflict, as its gladiator in the arena of battle. For a century and a half you have defended, guarded, and protected its hallowed traditions of liberty and freedom, of right and justice.

Let civilian voices argue the merits or demerits of our processes of government; whether our strength is being sapped by deficit financing, indulged in too long, by federal paternalism grown too mighty, by power groups grown too arrogant, by politics grown too corrupt, by crime grown too rampant, by morals grown too low, by taxes grown too high, by extremists grown too violent; whether our personal liberties are as thorough and complete as they should be. These great national problems are not for your professional participation or military solution. Your guidepost stands out like a ten-fold beacon in the night: Duty, Honor, Country.

You are the leaven which binds together the entire fabric of our national system of defense. From your ranks come the great Captains who hold the nation's destiny in their hands the moment the war tocsin sounds. The Long Gray Line has never failed us. Were you to do so, a million ghosts in olive drab, in brown khaki, in blue and gray, would rise from their white crosses thundering those magic words: Duty Honor, Country.

This does not mean that you are war mongers.

On the contrary, the soldier, above all other people, prays for peace, for he must suffer and bear the deepest wounds and scars of war.

But always in our ears ring the ominous words of Plato, that wisest of all philosophers: "Only the dead have seen the end of war."

The shadows are lengthening for me. The twilight is here. My days of old have vanished, tone and tint. They have gone glimmering through the dreams of things that were. Their memory is one of wondrous beauty, watered by tears, and coaxed and caressed by the smiles of yesterday. I listen vainly, but with thirsty ears, for the witching melody of faint bugles blowing reveille, of far drums beating the long roll. In my dreams I hear again the crash of guns, the rattle of musketry, the strange, mournful mutter of the battlefield.

But in the evening of my memory, always I come back to West Point.

Always there echoes and re-echoes: Duty, Honor, Country.

Today marks my final roll call with you, but I want you to know that when I cross the river my last conscious thoughts will be of The Corps, and The Corps, and The Corps.

MacArthur's Restaurant at the Thayer Hotel was proudly dedicated by the Thayer Leader Development Group.

The MacArthur Memorial in Norfolk, Virginia.

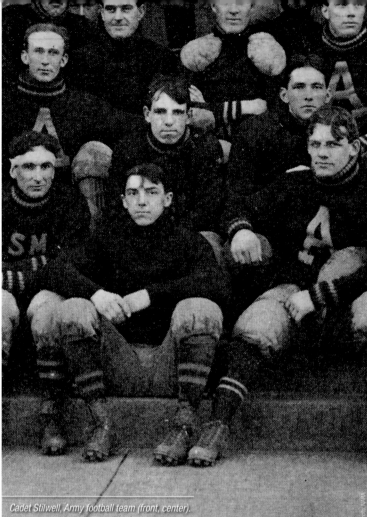

Cadet Stilwell, Army football team (front, center).

General Joseph Stilwell's gravesite at West Point.

General Joseph Stilwell, USMA 1904

- **COMMANDER, CHINA-BURMA-INDIA THEATER OF WAR, WORLD WAR II**
- **SERVED AS A STAFF INTELLIGENCE OFFICER FOR BOTH U.S. AND FRENCH FORCES IN WWI**
- **DEPUTY COMMANDER, 2ND INFANTRY DIVISION, AND U.S. III CORPS COMMANDER**
- **COMMANDER, THE 10TH U.S. ARMY BATTLE OF OKINAWA**
- **VETERAN OF THE PHILIPPINES INSURRECTION**
- **FOUNDED THE WEST POINT BASKETBALL TEAM/ARMY FOOTBALL PLAYER**
- **WEST POINT PROFESSOR, AND ASSISTANT FOOTBALL AND BASKETBALL COACH**

Few biographical studies are dedicated to Joseph Warren Stilwell, despite his centrality in U.S.-Chinese relations during the pivotal era of 1926 to 1945. During his 41 years of active service, including service in the Philippines Insurrection and both World Wars, "Vinegar Joe" played a unique role in the American Army as it transformed from the garrison force of the late-nineteenth century into the world's dominant military force.

Stilwell was born on March 19, 1883, in Yonkers, New York. He was named for his obstetrician, a family friend named for a martyr of the Battle of Bunker Hill.[1] Stilwell, called Warren by his family, excelled in both academics and in sports, but had a rebellious character, and his father arranged his appointment to West Point equally to develop Warren's self-discipline and his undeniable scholastic talents.[2] At the Academy, he continued to excel in academics, especially foreign languages, and is credited with introducing basketball to West Point. He graduated 32nd of 124 in the Class of 1904, though he was ranked ninth in his class in the area of "Military Efficiency."[3] He, like his famous classmate Leslie J. McNair, accepted a commission as a Second Lieutenant of Infantry. Other cadets with whom he shared his time at the Academy became the generation of leaders during World War II, including Douglas MacArthur (Class of 1903).

Stilwell's first assignment was in the Philippines, where he fought against the very Moro guerillas the United States had just liberated from Spain. After two years, he returned to West Point to the Department of Foreign Languages, where he taught Spanish and French. He married in 1910 and brought his wife with him to serve once again in the Philippines. Within a year, when revolution erupted in China, she returned to the States and he visited for the first time the country

>>> Spotlight

The November 13, 1944, *Time* magazine cover featured General Stilwell, Supreme Allied Commander of the China-Burma-India Theater of War, after a conflict between General Stilwell and General Chiang Kai-Shek resulted in President Roosevelt recalling General Stilwell to the United States.

Courtesy: Time, Inc.

Stilwell, second from left in rear row.

Despite the fact that by 1928, when he was once again promoted to Lieutenant Colonel, Stilwell was President of the United States Language School in China, he was predominantly functioning as an Intelligence Officer, gathering and reporting updates on the disposition of Chinese and Russian forces.[6] After four years of teaching tactics to Infantry Officers at Fort Benning, Georgia, and two more years of instruction in San Diego, Stilwell accepted an assignment as military attaché in China in 1935 as a full Colonel. He served in this position for four years. While most of America and the West focused upon the rise of Nazi power in Europe, Stilwell witnessed firsthand the spread of Japanese imperialism throughout the Far East. He also gained an appreciation for the implications of a cultural divide wider than any his peers in Europe would have to overcome in their theater of war.

Beginning in 1940, Stilwell, his talents recognized by General George Marshall, served as Deputy Commander of the 2nd Infantry Division, helped raise and train the 7th Infantry Division, and commanded III Corps. Early in 1942, he headed back to China to establish and command the American Army Forces, China, Burma, India (CBI). In August of 1944, he earned his fourth star.

Stilwell's famously gruff personality sometimes served him well among other Infantrymen, but it proved to be a serious impediment when working in his more diplomatic roles. He had a notorious dislike for Mountbatten's British forces, and he was often at odds with Chinese Generalissimo Chiang Kai-shek, under whom he served as Chief of Staff. Stilwell, ever the Infantrymen, favored a ground offensive aimed at retaking Burma from the Japanese. General Claire L. Chennault, who would later become Commander of the United States Air Force, presented a much more appealing plan of attack to the generalissimo: an air campaign. After the Japanese ran allied forces out of Burma, Stilwell was left with the difficult task of maintaining supply lines from India into China. His perseverance resulted in the famous Ledo Road that wove through difficult terrain in the jungles of Burma.

General Stilwell's many years as a language and tactics instructor were put to good use training Chinese forces in India, but he was operating under difficult constraints. He sought to exercise tight control of the Lend-Lease Program to combat Chinese inefficiencies and corruption, but the plan only put him more at odds with the leaders he was trying to help. After a poor Chinese performance against the Japanese in Operation Ichi-Go, Stilwell pressed President Roosevelt to urge Chiang Kai-shek to afford him more direct control of the Chinese Army. His plan backfired and resulted instead in his dismissal as Chiang's Chief of Staff and a return to the United States.

Stilwell served out the war among his beloved Infantrymen, commanding the Tenth Army after its previous Commander, General Simon Bolivar Buckner, died of wounds on Okinawa.[7] By this point, however, there were only weeks left in the war. He briefly served as military Governor of the Ryukus, but was soon recalled to Washington.

Stilwell was still serving in the active-duty Army when he died of stomach cancer on October 12, 1946. Though most remembered for his strong personality that gave rise to so many personal conflicts and led to his acerbic nickname, "Vinegar Joe," General Stilwell was an exceptionally competent officer, placed, because of his talents, in a role critical to United States victory in the East. Stilwell gained an appreciation for the complexities of Chinese culture that was without equal in the Allied Armed Forces. A difficult man given by his nation an even more difficult task, Stilwell rose to the challenge, prevented the collapse of China under the Japanese onslaught, and kept the Chinese fighting to the end of the war. Though his achievements are less heralded than the allied exploits in Europe and in the Pacific, Stilwell accomplished what few others could have even attempted.

> ## STILWELL ROSE TO THE CHALLENGE, PREVENTED THE COLLAPSE OF CHINA UNDER THE JAPANESE ONSLAUGHT, AND KEPT THE CHINESE FIGHTING TO THE END OF THE WAR.

Written by: Major Christian G. Teutsch, USMA 1997.

that would dominate the rest of his long career.[4] In 1912, Stilwell returned to West Point, at first to teach English and History, and later, Spanish. During this time he also coached the Academy's basketball and football teams.[5]

With the advent of the First World War, Stilwell served as Chief Intelligence Officer in IV Corps, where he contributed to the planning of the St. Mihiel Offensive. For a time, he also worked as an Intelligence Officer on the French XVII Corps staff at Verdun. By the end of the war, Stilwell had been promoted to Lieutenant Colonel and Brevetted a full Colonel, but when he returned to the United States in July 1919, he, as part of the reduction of the United States Army, was reduced in rank to Captain. A month later, at his own bequest, Stilwell began language training for service in China.

From 1920 to 1923, and from 1926 to 1929, Stilwell performed foreign service in China.

Mark Clark had an incredibly successful career as a combat leader serving in three of America's major twentieth-century conflicts: World War I, World War II, and the Korean War. He moved rapidly through the ranks, particularly in World War II, when he became America's youngest Four-Star General and later served as United Nations Commander during the Korean War.[2] Most critical accounts of Clark portray him as egotistical and overly concerned with publicity seeking and glory. Ironically, his most significant achievement, which deserved worldwide recognition, was overshadowed by other events and stole the glory that he allegedly sought, but arguably earned.

Clark was born May 1, 1896, at Madison Barracks in Sackets Harbor, New York. His father was a career Army Officer who was himself raised as a Protestant while Clark's mother, the daughter of Romanian immigrants, was Jewish. The family moved to Highland Park, Illinois, where his father was stationed at Fort Sheridan.

Clark entered West Point in 1913 as the youngest member of his class and graduated at age 21 with the Class of 1917.[3] He was commissioned in the Infantry and deployed to France with the 5th Infantry Division in World War I. Once in France, Clark was promoted twice in four months, commanded a battalion, and was seriously wounded by shrapnel from a German artillery shell during the Aisne-Marne Offensive, which forced him into staff duties the remainder of the war while recovering from his wounds.[4] Between the wars, Clark was part of the occupation forces in Germany, served with the Civilian Conservation Corps (CCC) at the height of the Great Depression, and attended various Army schools to include the Army War College, where he served as one of its instructors.[5] Clark's skills came to the attention of General George C. Marshall and General Dwight D. Eisenhower (USMA 1915), who would both take personal interest in Clark's professional development, ultimately helping him to skip the rank of Colonel, and propel him to become the youngest Three-Star and then the youngest Four-Star General in the Army.[6] His relationship with both Marshall and Eisenhower, although strained at times, would also serve him well in both World War II and the Korean War. Before Pearl Harbor, Clark was promoted to Brigadier General and served as Deputy Chief of Staff and then the Chief of Staff of the Army Ground Forces (AGF) under Lieutenant General Lesley McNair (USMA 1904), which was responsible for mobilizing, training, and equipping the massive build up of the United States Army.

Clark was next appointed by Eisenhower as the Deputy Commander of Operation Torch, the invasion of North Africa. He then had Clark lead a secret mission to meet with Vichy French leaders near Cherchell, Algeria, just prior to the invasion. Clark and future Chairman of the Joint Chiefs of Staff Brigadier General Lyman Lemnitzer (USMA 1920) met the Vichy leaders after being dropped ashore by a submarine and successfully negotiated an agreement with the Vichy French not to interfere with the allied landings. Shortly after this mission, Clark was promoted to Lieutenant General and placed in command of the United States 5th Army – the first United States Field Army to engage in combat in Europe – when he began planning for the invasion of Italy.[7]

As 5th Army Commander, Clark would lead his forces in the September 1943 amphibious invasion of mainland Italy at Salerno in the wake of the successful allied operations that drove Axis forces from both North Africa and Sicily. The United States reluctantly agreed with the decision to invade Italy in 1943 in the hopes that is would divert Axis resources away from the planned opening of a second front in France in 1944. On the other hand, the allies also had to ensure that the Italian campaign would not unintentionally divert too many allied resources away from the planned second front.[8] From Salerno to the end of the war in May 1945, Clark led American and allied forces through Italy as both 5th Army Commander and then 15th Army Group Commander. In its earliest stages, the Italian Campaign was at center stage of the effort in Europe and produced some of the war's bloodiest fighting among some of Europe's most inhospitable and mountainous terrain. Salerno, San Pietro, the Rapido River, Monte Cassino, and Anzio became synonymous with intense, gritty, and costly battles against an entrenched and determined enemy.

> CLARK DESERVES RECOGNITION AS ONE OF THE TOP AMERICA GENERALS IN EUROPE IN WORLD WAR II, ALONG WITH EISENHOWER, BRADLEY, AND PATTON.

General Mark Wayne Clark, USMA 1917

- COMMANDER, UNITED NATIONS FORCES, KOREAN WAR
- SIGNED THE CEASE-FIRE AGREEMENT ENDING THE KOREAN WAR, 1953
- ALLIED HIGH-COMMISSIONER FOR AUSTRIA
- COMMANDER, U.S. 6TH ARMY, PRESIDIO, SAN FRANCISCO, CALIFORNIA
- COMMANDER, U.S. 5TH ARMY AND 15TH ARMY GROUP, ITALIAN CAMPAIGN, WORLD WAR II
- LIBERATED ROME, ITALY, JUNE 4, 1944
- SERVED IN WORLD WAR I, WORLD WAR II, AND KOREAN WAR
- DISTINGUISHED SERVICE CROSS, PURPLE HEART
- PRESIDENT OF THE CITADEL AND BURIED AT THE CITADEL CEMETERY

President-Elect Eisenhower, General Clark, and Lieutenant General Van Fleet, Korea, December 1952.

Brigadier General Mark Clark and General Eisenhower, World War II.

In June 1944, with the German defenses split and a German Army potentially risking encirclement, Clark chose not to pursue the fleeing Germans; rather, he chose to seek the prize of entering and liberating Rome as a conquering hero. It is with this decision that Clark received much of his criticism by choosing the highly visible but strategically less-important objective of liberating Rome over pursuing and destroying the German Army to end the major fighting in Italy. On the other hand, Rome was the first major Axis capital to fall into allied hands and provided a much-needed psychological lift following the intense combat of the previous nine months. The news of Clark liberating Rome on June 4, 1944, should have given Clark the attention on the world stage that he apparently sought. As fate would have it, however, Clark did not receive that spotlight. Instead, unfortunately for Clark but fortunately for overall allied strategy, the evening of June 5, 1944, witnessed the long-awaited invasion of mainland Europe when allied paratroopers departed England for Normandy on the eve of the D-Day landings that followed on June 6th, which dominated the global headlines and validated Eisenhower's pre-invasion message to the Allied Expeditionary Force that "The eyes of the world are upon you."[9] Clark commented about the June 6th headlines that announced the opening of the second front as a result of the D-Day landings with, "How do you like that? They didn't even let us have the newspaper headlines for the fall of Rome for one day."[10] Arguably, one of Clark's greatest lifetime achievements as Rome's liberator was overshadowed by the invasion of Fortress Europe. Yet, for his leadership in liberating what British Prime Minister Winston Churchill called the "soft underbelly of Europe," Clark faced incredibly difficult circumstances as an allied secondary effort and deserves recognition as one of America's top World War II Commanders. In the end, Italy proved not to be so "soft," as the 608-day campaign cost roughly 312,000 allied casualties and uncertain German casualty figures estimated between 435,000 and 536,000.[11]

Clark's career continued to flourish after the surrender of both Italy and Germany. He was appointed as the High Commissioner of Austria at the end of the war and then returned to the United States to take command of the 6th Army in the Presidio at San Francisco, California. In 1951, President Harry Truman nominated Clark to become the first United States Ambassador to the Holy See (Vatican). As the liberator of Rome, Clark's nomination as Ambassador was particularly symbolic. Truman's attempt to open an official United States Embassy in the Vatican, a nation state, was highly controversial and met with great resistance, though. Most American groups did not oppose Clark's credentials (although some did because of Clark's Jewish lineage and Protestant upbringing); rather, they viewed this issue as violating the separation of church and state if the American government recognized the Catholic Church as a nation-state represented by the Vatican. As a result of the public backlash, President Truman removed Clark's name from consideration and did not pursue the issue. No United States President would attempt to assign an Ambassador to the Vatican until President Ronald Reagan successfully appointed William Wilson as the United States Ambassador to the Holy See in 1984 – this Ambassadorship has remained a permanent posting since.[12]

Truman then named General Clark to succeed General Matthew Ridgway, Clark's West Point classmate, as Commander of United Nations Forces in the Korean War in 1952. Clark was an advocate for increasing offensive operations but his requests were continuously declined. When Dwight D. Eisenhower, Clark's former Commander, was elected President in 1952, he immediately traveled to Korea as President-Elect in December 1952 to meet with General Clark and assess the war effort. Eisenhower wanted a peaceful settlement and advocated a cease-fire agreement, which Clark successfully negotiated and signed on July 27, 1953, ending hostilities in Korea with an armistice that currently remains in effect.[13]

Clark retired from the Army in 1953 after 36 years of service spanning three of America's greatest conflicts. A very capable Commander who was skilled in coalition warfare, Clark's role in World War II has often been overshadowed by more notable Commanders. Nonetheless, Clark's leadership was instrumental at every level in the overall allied victory as it was in every conflict he served. After his retirement, Clark was appointed as President of The Citadel in Charleston, South Carolina, where he served from 1954 to 1965.[14] General Clark died April 17, 1994, at age 87 and is buried at The Citadel.

Lieutenant General Clark and Lieutenant General Van Fleet, 1945.

Courtesy: Time, Inc.

>>> Spotlight

The July 7, 1952, *Time* magazine cover featured General Mark Clark with the caption: "The Korea Question: Win, Lose or Draw?" Just more than one year later, the war would end in a "draw," splitting Korea in half with democracy to the south and communism to the north as it remains to this day.

General Ridgeway's official photo.
Photo: NARA

General Ridgway in front of his
B-17, named after his wife, Penny.
Photo: AP

Photo: NARA

General Matthew B. Ridgway, USMA 1917

- **CHIEF OF STAFF U.S. ARMY**
- **SUPREME ALLIED COMMANDER, U.S. ARMY EUROPE (USAEUR)**
- **COMMANDING GENERAL UNITED NATIONS COMMAND, KOREAN WAR**
- **COMMANDING GENERAL, U.S. 8TH ARMY, KOREAN WAR**
- **COMMANDING GENERAL, 82ND AIRBORNE DIVISION, D-DAY**
- **PRESIDENTIAL MEDAL OF FREEDOM**

Photo: NARA

When historian Russell Weigley described strategies of annihilation as "characteristic of an American way in war," he could easily have employed General Matthew B. Ridgway as the poster boy for a thesis that is now widely accepted as gospel among scholars of American military history.[1] Matthew Ridgway's career spanned the four decades in which the United States – and its Army – grew to preeminence on the global stage. The Army relied heavily upon West Pointers to innovate and, most importantly, to lead during the daunt-

ing struggles of the mid-twentieth century. Among the hundreds of American Officers who wore stars during this coming-of-age for the Army, Matthew Ridgway embodied the essence of West Point leadership, as well as any of them. America has always expected its West Pointers to lead from the front and Ridgway was up to the task when he jumped into Normandy with his paratroopers of the 82nd Airborne Division on June 6, 1944. When he took charge of a faltering 8th Army in Korea only seven years later, General Ridgway cemented his place among the great

leaders in American history. Central to these feats was his deep personal faith in and adherence to what he called the "Cs"[3]: character, courage, and competence.[2] He applied these principles at every level of command, honed them in combat, and after retirement, preached them to political leaders and subsequent generations of military officers.

In a career full of highlights, his feat that most reflected the spirit of West Point – a can-do, no-quit spirit – came as the newly appointed Commander of the 8th Army in Korea in the winter of 1951. Ridgway took

the helm of a combined field Army reeling against a massive offensive by North Korean and Chinese troops. Communist forces had reversed the gains made by United Nations forces the previous year, driving the American-led coalition well south of Seoul. Most devastating, however, had been the damage to American morale along the front and American will back in the United States. After months of retrograde operations by the 8th Army, communist momentum seemed irreversible. As General Ridgway assumed command of the beleaguered Army, he

>>> Spotlight

The May 12, 1952, *Life* magazine cover featured General Ridgway after being named the Supreme Allied Commander of Europe.

Courtesy: Time Magazine

Ridgway's "3 Cs" offer a glimpse into the foundations of this remarkable resurgence of a field Army that had teetered so dangerously close to collapse. Touring the front and visiting subordinate Commanders during his first weeks in command of the 8th Army, he saw leaders and soldiers demoralized after months of retrograde operations and little hope of attaining "victory" against the oncoming waves of Chinese and North Korean troops. He instinctively rallied his men around the spirit of the offensive, sensing that flagging morale was the source of much of the field Army's malaise.[5] The ensuing turnaround saved the United Nations effort in Korea from total collapse. Character – in this case, the ability to convey a positive outlook in the face of overwhelming odds while demanding adherence to an offensive mindset – allowed the 8th Army and, later, the entire United Nations Command, to solidify its front lines, thus allowing political leaders to salvage acceptable terms for the termination of armed hostilities.

It helped that Ridgway, who had led his soldiers from the front from his very first days as a Rifle Company Commander along the Mexican border, was still willing to share some of the dangers of his riflemen on the front lines.[6] In his first days as 8th Army Commander, only miles from the forward line of contact, he personally stopped units that were fleeing from a new Chinese offensive. Personal courage and the second of Ridgway's "3 Cs" bought instant credibility among the soldiers of a field Army that had started to accept retreat as the word of the day. The men of the 8th Army would follow eagerly their courageous new leader.

The third of General Ridgway's "3 Cs" had been central to his ascent through the ranks. As he gained mastery of the tactical situation facing his subordinate units and the disposition of communist forces facing them across the peninsula, he was able to articulate the way forward. He understood the geopolitical context of the war he was fighting, just one example of the professional competence that garnered the confidence of President Truman, when the Commander in Chief relieved General of the Army Douglas MacArthur. Such competence produced prudent self-imposed limitations to the offensive spirit that characterized Ridgway's command of both 8th Army and as Supreme Commander, Far East. He thus provided the maneuver space for his political leaders to craft an acceptable negotiated settlement. Most importantly, it saved the men under his command from wanton, reckless

offensives that would have gained little toward the accomplishment such ambitious strategic objectives that his predecessor had established.

West Point exists for the singular purpose to provide the Nation with leaders of character to serve the common defense of the United States. This charter demands that graduates lead America's sons and daughters in combat with courage and competence. The core of West Point's mission, however, reaches deep into service beyond the military. Ideally, graduates will serve the Nation both in and out of uniform. Although General Ridgway is best remembered for his accomplishments in the Korean War, he continued to make enduring contributions to the common defense long after he hung up the uniform for the last time. Ridgway became an outspoken opponent of the Vietnam War, providing America's political leaders with insight that he had gained leading men in combat and managing the Army during the post-Korean War reorientation of the American defense establishment. For Ridgway, the American military experience in World War II, the nearly disastrous results of the first year of the Korean War, and the overzealous reliance on technological solutions that characterized the era of massive retaliation provided the context within which the retired General assessed American strategy during his country's tumultuous era of military involvement in Southeast Asia. His candor was a virtue, and while political leaders did not always follow his counsel, they trusted the source of the advice. Even into the final decades of the twentieth century, Matthew B. Ridgway, Class of 1917, served as a shining example of the West Point way of leadership.

"THERE WILL BE NO MORE DISCUSSION OF RETREAT. WE'RE GOING BACK!" SAID RIDGWAY.

Written by: Major Keith R. Walters, USMA 1997.

General Wainwright and General Van Fleet in Korea.

demanded a resumption of the offensive mind-set and a reinvigoration of a mythical "American Way of War." He issued the order: "There will be no more discussion of retreat. We're going back!"[3] He breathed the offensive spirit back into the 8th Army, transforming it by sheer force of will from a listless command all too accustomed to retreat, to a field Army that within a few short weeks, was able to stop the general communist advance and regain the initiative. Named operations of the 8th Army – Operation Ripper and Operation Killer –

conveyed the urgency of Ridgway's orders to resume the offensive and articulated to the lowest levels of his command the newfound vigor of the soldiers of the entire United Nations command. Ridgway implemented a strategy of attrition until his message could permeate the ranks of his resurgent 8th Army. Soon after, he would point that force toward a strategy of annihilation, albeit one of localized annihilation, treading within the political boundaries that Ridgway recognized as essential to containing the war to the Korean peninsula.[4]

General Westmoreland's
official photo.

President Johnson, General Westmoreland,
and South Vietnamese leader.

General William Westmoreland, USMA 1936

- CHIEF OF STAFF, U.S. ARMY
- COMMANDER, MILITARY ASSISTANCE COMMAND VIETNAM (MACV), 1964–68
- 187TH AIRBORNE REGIMENTAL COMBAT TEAM IN KOREA WAR, 1952–53
- CHIEF OF STAFF, 9TH INFANTRY DIVISION FRANCE, WORLD WAR II
- COMMANDER 34TH ARTILLERY BATTALION IN NORTH AFRICA AND SICILY
- SUPERINTENDENT, UNITED STATES MILITARY ACADEMY AT WEST POINT
- CADET FIRST CAPTAIN, CLASS OF 1936
- BOY SCOUTS OF AMERICA, EAGLE SCOUT

General William Westmoreland was the most prominent General during the Vietnam War, having served as Commander of the Military Assistance Command, Vietnam (MACV), from 1964 to 1968 and then as Chief of Staff of the United States Army from 1968 to 1972. As a Major General, he was the 45th Superintendent of the United States Military Academy from 1960 to 1960, among many other positions throughout his 36-year Army career. Like public opinion of the Vietnam War, assessments of General Westmoreland are complicated and mixed reflecting the challenges of command during the escalation of United States involvement in Vietnam. As Army Chief of Staff and after retirement, he was a passionate advocate for the recognition of the service and sacrifice of all those who served valiantly in Vietnam.

Westmoreland was born on March 26, 1914, and grew up in Spartanburg County, South Carolina, where he was an Eagle Scout at the age of 15 and graduated from Spartanburg

High School as the senior class President in 1931. After a year at The Citadel, the Military College of South Carolina, he received a Senatorial appointment to West Point with the Class of 1936. As a cadet, his handsome face, perfect posture, and fearless determination made a great impression on his classmates, one of whom gave him the nickname "Chief," even as a Plebe, thinking that Westmoreland would rise to great prominence in the future. At West Point, he did become the First Captain (the Cadet Commander of the Corps of Cadets), as well as being the Superintendent of Sunday School and the Vice President of his class. He graduated 112 out of his class of 276 and was commissioned as a Second Lieutenant in the artillery after General of the Armies John J. Pershing delivered the 1936 graduation address.

Lieutenant Westmoreland joined an Army with few resources, mediocre soldiers, and little focus, in spite of the advances that the German Army was making in the interwar

years. His first unit was the 18th Field Artillery at Fort Sill, Oklahoma, equipped with horse-drawn 75-millimeter guns, carrier pigeons, and Morse code for communications. From 1939 to 1941, he was assigned to the 8th Field Artillery in Hawaii, where he commanded Battery F of the 8th Artillery, then was the Battalion Operations Officer, even though he was only a First Lieutenant. In 1941, as the Army was beginning to mobilize, he transferred to the 9th Infantry Division at Fort Bragg, North Carolina, just as World War II started.

Westmoreland was given increasing responsibility rapidly during World War II, commanding the 34th Artillery Battalion in Casablanca in 1942, fighting his battalion alongside General Matt Ridgeway and General Maxwell Taylor in Sicily, then landing at Normandy in 1944 where he soon became the 9th Infantry Division's Chief of Staff. As victory in Europe was secured, he was promoted to Colonel and commanded the 60th Infantry during the postwar occupation of Germany. He later

commanded the 504th Parachute Infantry Regiment at Fort Bragg (1946–47) and the 187th Airborne Regimental Combat Team in Korea (1952–53). He had three Infantry commands and earned the Combat Infantryman's badge – all as an Artillery Officer! While in Korea, he also completed his 65th parachute jump, earning his master parachutist wings.

When he was at Fort Bragg, Westmoreland began dating Kitsy Van Deusen. They had met several years earlier at Fort Sill, when Kitsy's father was the Field Artillery School Executive Officer and Westmoreland was Scoutmaster of the Boy Scout Troop that included Kitsy's brother. After a six-month courtship, they were married at St. John's Church, in Fayetteville, North Carolina, and later had three children: Katherine Stevens Westmoreland, James Ripley Westmoreland II, and Margaret Childs Westmoreland.

After more than four years of Pentagon assignments and promotion to Major General, Westmoreland commanded the 101st

>>> Spotlight

In 1965, General Westmoreland was named *Time* magazine's "Man of the Year," reflecting the hopes of the nation at that time that he could effectively command the war in Vietnam to a successful conclusion.

General Westmoreland visits cadets as U.S. Army Chief of Staff.

Westmoreland family at Trophy Point.

General Westmoreland's gravesite at West Point Cemetery.

HE WAS A PASSIONATE ADVOCATE FOR THE RECOGNITION OF THE SERVICE AND SACRIFICE OF ALL THOSE WHO SERVED VALIANTLY IN VIETNAM.

Airborne Division at Fort Campbell, Kentucky, from 1958 to 1960. Although he briefly taught at Command and General Staff College and the Army War College, because of rapid promotions during World War II, he never attended any formal military schools after West Point. Nevertheless, in 1960, he was appointed as Superintendent of West Point by Chief of Staff of the Army General Lyman Lemnitzer. While Superintendent, Westmoreland hosted both General MacArthur's now famous "Duty, Honor, Country" speech and President Kennedy's 1962 graduation address. He also began the process to increase the size of the

Corps of Cadets from 2,500 to 4,400 so that West Point would be the same size as the Naval Academy.

After only one year as a Three-Star General and Commander of XVIII Airborne Corps, Westmoreland was sent to Vietnam, first as Deputy Commander, then he assumed command of Military Assistance Command, Vietnam, on June 20, 1964, with promotion to the rank of Four-Star General. For the next four years, he supervised the buildup of United States forces in Vietnam from 16,000 to 535,000 by 1968.

Critics of Westmoreland fault him for fighting the Vietnam War using attrition-oriented tactics and relying on the heavy use of artillery, air-dropped bombs, and large conventional forces against the North Vietnamese Army. His estimates of progress in Vietnam became increasingly criticized as being overly positive. This was especially true after the "Tet Offensive" in January 1968, which was strategically important in convincing the

public that the United States could not win in Vietnam. Lewis Sorley (USMA 1956) captures this critique succinctly in his book title, *Westmoreland: The General Who Lost Vietnam*.

Westmoreland would maintain that the United States did not lose any major conventional battles and even the Tet Offensive was a military defeat for the North Vietnamese. The hundreds of thousands of North Vietnamese who were killed reflect the success that United States forces had been having and could have been more effective if President Johnson had permitted further expansion of the war. Ultimately, Westmoreland believed that, in the end, the United States failed to fulfill its commitment to South Vietnam. As great as the loses may have been, the 10 years of war in Vietnam prevented further communist expansion throughout Asia and demonstrated United States resolve at a critical period during the Cold War.

After four years in Vietnam, General Westmoreland relinquished command to his

West Point classmate, General Creighton Abrams, and became the 25th Chief of Staff of the United States Army on July 3, 1968. As Chief of Staff, he supported the war in Vietnam with personnel, material, and speeches throughout the nation. He also presided over the preparation for the end of conscription and the implementation of the All Volunteer Force, which was directed by President Richard Nixon. Although General Westmoreland was not personally in favor of an All Volunteer Force, he began the process that substantially changed the Army by improving training, enhancing respect for soldiers, and improving leadership that helped the Army recover after Vietnam.

General Westmoreland received the Distinguished Graduate Award from the West Point Association of Graduates in 1996 and died in Charleston, South Carolina, on July 18, 2005, at the age of 91.

Written by: Brigadier General Michael J. Meese, PhD (USA, Retired), USMA 1981.

General Abrams, Army Chief of Staff.

General Abrams at West Point, 1972.

General Creighton Abrams, USMA 1936

- CHIEF OF STAFF, U.S. ARMY
- VICE CHIEF OF STAFF U.S. ARMY
- COMMANDER, MILITARY ASSISTANCE COMMAND, VIETNAM (MACV)
- COMMANDER, 2ND ARMORED CAVALRY REGIMENT
- COMMANDER, 37TH TANK BATTALION, WORLD WAR II
- ARMY FOOTBALL PLAYER
- TWO DISTINGUISHED SERVICE CROSSES, TWO SILVER STARS, ONE BRONZE STAR MEDAL
- ABRAMS M-1 SERIES OF TANKS NAMED IN HIS HONOR MANUFACTURED BY GENERAL DYNAMICS

★★★★

M1 Abrams Tank
Desert Storm, 1991

Lieutenant Colonel Abrams entering Bastogne,
January 2, 1945, under General George S. Patton.

General Abrams and Colonel George S. Patton
(USMA 1946), son of General Patton, Vietnam, 1968.

>>> Spotlight

General Abrams was featured on three *Time* magazine covers: in October 1961, as 3rd Armored Division Commander defending against the Soviets; in April 1968 (pictured here), as he was taking command of MACV; and in February 1971, as the nation was reevaluating war strategy in Vietnam.

Courtesy: Time, Inc.

General Creighton Abrams was one of the most-popular and well-respected Generals of his generation, having served with distinction as Commander of the 37th Tank Battalion in World War II, as Commander Military Assistance Command, Vietnam (MACV) from 1968 to 1972, and as Chief of Staff of the Army from 1972 until his death in 1974. Abrams was heralded for his concern for soldiers, emphasis on combat readiness, and insistence on personal integrity. In recognition of General Abrams, the Army named its new main battle tank the M1 Abrams Tank.

Abrams was born on September 15, 1914, in Springfield, Massachusetts, and grew up in rural Agawam, Massachusetts, playing football, as well as being elected class President and most likely to succeed by his high-school classmates. Finishing fourth in his high-school class, he earned a Congressional appointment to West Point in 1932. At West Point, as a stocky five-foot nine-inch cadet, he was not a starting player but earned a varsity letter on the Army football team because of his "guts and scrappiness." His classmates wrote a fitting prelude to his 38 years in the Army: "Whenever you find Abe, you'll find action." Graduating 185 out of 276 in his class, Abrams was commissioned in the Cavalry.

Lieutenant Abrams's first assignment was with the 7th Cavalry Regiment in the 1st Cavalry Division at Fort Bliss, Texas, from 1936 to 1940. Although his unit was under strength in material, personnel, and funding, Abrams learned much about leadership as a Horse Cavalry and Division Staff Officer. He also recognized, before many others, that the days of the Horse Cavalry were numbered, but the effective application of Cavalry tactics to the new "untried armor machines" would be essential to the Army's success in the impending World War.

In 1941, Abrams was assigned to the 37th Armored Regiment as part of the newly acti-vated 4th Armored Division in Pine Camp, New York (later renamed Fort Drum). On September 10, 1943, he assumed command of the 37th Tank Battalion. After many exercises to train and refine the newly developed tactics of armored warfare, Abrams and his battalion deployed to England in January 1944.

With his head emerged from his tank turret and usually seen chomping on a cigar, Colonel Abrams led the 37th Tank Battalion as they fought decisively in the lead of the 4th Armored Division's Combat Command A (led by General Bruce Clarke) across France. In December 26, 1944, in the Battle of the Bulge, Abrams's unit punched through enemy lines to provide relief for the 101st Airborne in Bastogne. In 1945, he inspired his men from the front, leading his battalion through Germany and into Czechoslovakia, link-ing up with Russian forces. For his heroism in combat, he received two Distinguished Service Crosses, two Silver Stars, and a Bronze Star for Valor. At the end of World War II, General George Patton said, "I'm supposed to be the best Tank Commander in the Army, but I have one peer – Abe Abrams. He's the world's champion."

After the war, Abrams was hand-picked to be the Chief of the Tactics of the Armor School at Fort Knox, Kentucky (1946–49), and later served as its Chief of Staff (1954–56). He commanded the 63rd Tank Battalion and 2nd Armored Cavalry Regiment in Germany (1949–52) as NATO was being established and then went to Korea where he was the Chief of Staff of three different Army Corps (I, IX, and X Corps). He also attended the Army Command and General Staff College (1949) and the Army War College (1953).

In his first General Officer's job, Abrams worked from 1956 to 1959 with the Army Reserve and National Guard, developing rela-tionships that would serve him well as Chief of Staff of the Army. In 1960, he was promoted to Major General and command of the 3rd Armored Division. He had responsibility for the defense of the vital Fulda Gap, which became even more important during the Berlin crisis of 1961.

Abrams returned to Washington to serve in the Army's operations staff (1962–63), moved back to Germany to command V Corps (1963–64) as a Lieutenant General for just one year, then became Vice Chief of Staff of the Army from 1964 to 1967. In April 1967, President Johnson directed that General Abrams become the Deputy Commander of MACV, where he worked for his West Point classmate General William Westmoreland for a year before succeeding him in 1968.

As MACV Commander, Abrams held the line militarily while the United States withdrew most forces and turned over military respon-sibility to the South Vietnamese. He shifted American strategy from search and destroy operations to a population-centric counter-insurgency strategy, which built up the Army of the Republic of Vietnam (ARVN). In spite of substantial American troop reductions, from 543,000 in 1968 to 49,000 in 1972, Abrams continued to pressure the North Vietnamese Army throughout Vietnam and by attacking supply lines in Cambodia and Laos. Although they were ultimately defeated after the United States withdrawal, the success of the ARVN training was reflected in their effective counter to the North Vietnamese Easter Offensive in 1972.

ABRAMS WAS HERALDED FOR HIS CONCERN FOR SOLDIERS, EMPHASIS ON COMBAT READINESS, AND INSIS-TENCE ON PERSONAL INTEGRITY.

In 1972, General Abrams departed Vietnam and returned to Washington to become the 26th Chief of Staff of the Army (C.S.A.). Because of delays in Abrams's confirma-tion, after General Westmoreland left the C.S.A. office in June, General Bruce Palmer, Jr., was the Acting C.S.A. until General Abrams was sworn in on October 12, 1972. It was the only time in history that three West Point classmates (all from the Class of 1936) succeeded each other in any Four-Star position.

As Chief of Staff of the Army, Abrams imple-mented a bold vision for the Army. That vision was driven by a report he commissioned, the Astarita Report, which provided the intellectual foundation for Army strategy. He redesigned the Army's force structure, growing the Army to 16 divisions using "roundup" brigades from the National Guard and greater reliance on the Army Reserve. Faced with limited acquisition budgets, he concentrated Army moderniza-tion on only five weapon systems – the M1 Tank (later named the Abrams), the Bradley Fighting Vehicle, the Blackhawk and Apache Helicopters, and the Patriot Missile system. All were critical to deter the Soviets in the Cold War, were vital to the Army's rapid success in Iraq in 1990 to 1991, and have been the mainstay of United States Forces for more than three decades.

General Abrams was in a unique and critical position to provide a vision for the Army of the future that was relevant to the international environment and acceptable to the political leaders in the Pentagon and Congress. It was largely based on his instincts, background, and experience; and was influenced by his personal contact with soldiers throughout the Army. It was a forceful vision for what the Army could be and what it had to be to maintain its relevance after the Vietnam War. Tragically, General Abrams died on September 4, 1974, after battling lung cancer. He had been Chief of Staff for less than two years.

General Abrams's family reflects his close connection to the Army. He began dating Julia Harvey in his Yearling year at West Point, when she was attending Vassar College. They were married soon after his graduation on August 30, 1936, and they had three sons and three daughters. All three sons became General Officers: Brigadier General (Retired) Creighton Abrams III, General (Retired) John Abrams, and Major General Robert Abrams (USMA 1982). The Abrams's daughters – Noel, Jeanne, and Elizabeth – all married Army officers.

Written by: Brigadier General Michael J. Meese, PhD (USA, Retired), USMA 1981.

An M1A1 Abrams Tank in the Kuwaiti Desert 1990 named in honor of General Creighton Abrams is built by General Dynamics

In the early hours of Operation Desert Storm, stationed alongside his troops in the cold winter desert of the Arabian Peninsula, General H. Norman Schwarzkopf anxiously awaited the phone call that would assure him of the safe return of the pilots he had sent into the first phase of the battle on January 17, 1991. Filled with a sense of duty to his nation and to his soldiers, he did not take for granted the young lives he was directing into combat. The phone call from his Air Force Commander came soon. To great relief, all the American pilots were coming back unharmed from the first mission.

Recognized long before his illustrious Gulf War victory as a man of great character and dedication, H. Norman Schwarzkopf adopted the principles of "Duty, Honor, Country" as the values by which he has lived his entire life. He emphasized this fact by noting in his autobiography that "My father's saber was a sacred thing in our family. We called it his West Point sword, because he'd gotten it the year he graduated, in 1917. 'Duty, Honor, Country,' the West Point motto, was his creed, and it became mine"[1]

His father served in World War I and was wounded in a gas attack. During World War II, he was assigned to Iran and then after the fall of Germany was assigned as Provost Marshal in Germany, retiring as a Brigadier General. In his formative years, Schwarzkopf, Jr., moved with his military family to Tehran in 1946 where his father was commissioned to help organize the Iranian police force. Iran was followed by a year in Switzerland for schooling, then Frankfurt, Heidelberg, and Rome during which time he became fluent in German and French.

After graduating from high school at the Valley Forge Military Academy, Schwarzkopf followed in the footsteps of his father by attending the United States Military Academy at West Point. At West Point, he played

General Norman Schwarzkopf, USMA 1956

- **SUPREME ALLIED COMMANDER, OPERATION DESERT SHIELD/DESERT STORM**
- **COMMANDER, CENTRAL COMMAND (CENTCOM)**
- **GROUND FORCE COMMANDER, OPERATION URGENT FURY (GRENADA)**
- **THREE SILVER STARS, PURPLE HEART**
- **TWO TOURS VIETNAM WAR**
- **ADD PRESIDENTIAL MEDAL OF FREEDOM**
- **ARMY FOOTBALL PLAYER**

Lieutenant General Schwarzkopf's official photo.

Cadet Schwarzkopf with West Point Professor.

>>> Spotlight

Time magazine featured General H. Norman Schwarzkopf (USMA 1956) on the February 4, 1991, cover, during the bombing campaign of Operation Desert Storm. Three weeks later, on February 24, 1991, the General Schwarzkopf ordered the ground invasion that would begin and end on February 28, 1991, successfully liberating Kuwait from Saddam Hussein's Iraqi Army.

football, ran track, and sang with the choir before being commissioned in 1956 as an Infantry Second Lieutenant with a degree in mechanical engineering.

The common narrative that appears from his time at West Point tells of a man destined to be a remarkable leader with an undeniable love of country. According to what is now a legendary West Point account, Schwarzkopf, as a cadet, is said to have predicted for himself a future as a commander in a

decisive war that would change the course of history. Little did anyone know then, that the 1991 Gulf War would be that war, and in fact, reshape the fate of the U.S.–Middle East relationship by ushering in a new era of American influence in the region.

After a few years in the Army, with several military assignments at home and in Germany, and armed with a master's degree in Guided Missile Engineering from the University of Southern California,

Schwarzkopf returned to West Point as an engineering instructor in 1965, but that would be a short tour. He volunteered for duty in Vietnam that same year in a desire to serve alongside his peers.

Celebrated for being loyal to his soldiers, Lieutenant Colonel Schwarzkopf demonstrated great leadership in Vietnam that would earn him three Silver Stars and cement his reputation as a successful Combat Commander and committed leader

to his soldiers. In one tragically memorable incident during his second tour in Vietnam, he learned that the soldiers under his command were trapped in a minefield. Upon arriving at the location, he found his Artillery Liaison Officer severely maimed while another three of his men were killed in front of him. Schwarzkopf crawled through the minefield toward a wounded Private whose leg had just been shattered by a mine explosion. He himself injured in an explosion, Colonel Schwarzkopf moved the survivors back to the helicopter and returned home to receive his third Silver Star, angry and unsure about the Administration's conduct of this war that had claimed so many American lives.

For the next 15 years, the man affectionately known as "The Bear" for his overwhelming physical presence and fatherly demeanor, attended the United States Army War College, served as Deputy Commander of United States Forces in Alaska, and as Assistant Division Commander in West Germany. In 1983, under the directive of President Ronald Reagan, United States forces were sent to liberate the Caribbean island of Grenada after a communist coup. Schwarzkopf was named Deputy Task Force Commander and overall Ground Forces Commander in the 1983 United States operations in Grenada as a Major General. United States forces successfully liberated the island of Grenada.

Within two years of his promotion to Lieutenant General in 1986, Schwarzkopf received his fourth star and became Commanding General of United States Central Command (CENTCOM). In 1989, he led a CENTCOM exercise centered on a hypothetical invasion of the Gulf oil fields by Iraq, beginning with the annexation of Kuwait, a year before that very same hypothetical scenario came to life.

On August 2, 1990, Iraqi forces under Saddam Hussein invaded Kuwait to seize the oil fields of Kuwait and the port at Basra. The Emir of Kuwait, Sheikh Jaber Al Ahmad Al-Sabah, met with Secretary of Defense Richard Cheney to request American military support immediately following the invasion. President George H. W. Bush publicly condemned the offensive and entrusted the CENTCOM Commander in Chief to assume full command over the war effort to liberate Kuwait. Schwarzkopf worked closely with the Kuwaiti leadership in exile in Taif, Saudi Arabia, that fostered long-standing ties with his Kuwaiti counterparts.

General Schwarzkopf with Shiekh Saad Al-Sabah, Crown Prince of Kuwait, shortly after the liberation of Kuwait.

General Schwarzkopf briefing Operation Desert Storm, February 27, 1991.

General Schwarzkopf speaking before joint session of Congress after Desert Storm, May 8, 1991.

As CENTCOM Commander, General Schwarzkopf then assembled and directed one of the most comprehensive and effective military coalitions and campaigns in modern history. The mobilization of 750,000 coalition forces from 34 nations, including 541,000 Americans, for Operation Desert Storm was one of the most challenging strategic and logistical operations at that time, earning Schwarzkopf accolades from around the world as a true American Hero and the now famous moniker of "Stormin' Norman."

Yet the decision to engage American and coalition lives in this war did not come lightly to the architect of Desert Storm. The General had no doubt as to the readiness of his military or of the humanitarian legiti-macy and strategic objectives of this swift involvement, but he did not take lightly the decision to invade. United States casualties were expected to be high, with estimates as high as 20,000 casualties in order to liberate Kuwait. A humanitarian at heart, he knew the right time to enter into this conflict was immediate, saying, "If you were somebody who was in Kuwait and you were seeing your children tortured, and your wives raped, and the terrible things that were going on to the people in Kuwait, was it okay to wait for them?"[2]

On November 29, 1990, U.N. Security Council Resolution 678 authorized the use of all necessary means to expel Iraqi forces from Kuwait's sovereign land. Spearheaded by the United States and with outstanding inter-national support and assistance, the war to liberate Kuwait was put into motion.

The Iraqi Army had just recently waged a 10-year war with Iran and its military capabilities were well documented. General Schwarzkopf had studied the Iraqis in their Iranian battles and knew well enough what their strengths and weaknesses were, and accordingly, devised a plan to capital-ize on the supremacy of the American air power and superior technological advan-tage over an adversary who possessed the world's fourth largest Army. The first United States–led aerial strikes against Saddam Hussein's military and political headquarters in Baghdad began on January 17, 1991, with unprecedented technical precision and significant safeguarding of civilian welfare. Army AH-64 Apache attack helicopters led the attack, hitting Iraqi air defense systems deep within Kuwait and Iraq, followed by massive fixed wing bombers of all configurations. The 30-nation coalition, backed militar-ily, politically, and financially by 34 countries around the world, was united under the main objec-tive to liberate the State of Kuwait from Iraq's unprovoked aggression.

HE LOVED HIS FAMILY, AND HE LOVED HIS TROOPS, AND THEY LOVED HIM – PERIOD.

Schwarzkopf with King Fahd of Saudi Arabia, inspecting U.S. Troops, January 6, 1991.

President Bush awards General Schwarzkopf with Presidential Medal of Freedom, July 4, 1991.

Operation Desert Storm's early and expert air attacks proved devastating to Iraqi communication stations and warning radar installations on the ground. The attacks also gave the coalition immediate air superiority, restricting the Iraqis to vulnerable ground positions, and exposing their critical Republican Guard units. After 40 days of air attacks, the ground invasion began on February 23, 1991, with VII Corps (led by Lieutenant General Fred Franks, USMA 1959) conducting a massive "Left Hook" that outmaneuvered Iraqi forces who then surrendered after less than 100 hours of ground combat. The victory was so complete that coalition forces killed an estimated 100,000 Iraqi forces with the loss of 145 American soldiers Killed In Action.

Under Schwarzkopf's leadership, the coalition had perfectly implemented the plan that he had developed well before the Iraqi invasion. While the liberation was planned and executed perfectly, the post-conflict objectives had not been well-planned. Schwarzkopf and his staff had not prepared for the cease-fire negotiations, which he would later lament. The talks were held in the southeastern Iraqi town of Safwan near the Kuwaiti border, where General Schwarzkopf met with the Iraqi Lieutenant General Sultan Hashim Ahmad to discuss the terms for a cease-fire that were neither developed nor reviewed by Washington, agreeing to Iraqi requests to continue to fly their armored helicopters within their borders. These armored helicopters would later be infamously used

to put a brutal end to Kurdish and Shiite uprisings against Saddam Hussein – ironically, uprisings that were publicly called for by President H.W. Bush.

Schwarzkopf and the soldiers of the coalition returned home heroes, having successfully liberated Kuwait and achieving all of the U.N. objectives in Operation Desert Storm.

General Schwarzkopf received the Presidential Medal of Freedom, addressed a joint session of Congress, and was awarded decorations from Kuwait, Saudi Arabia, United Arab Emirates, Qatar, Great Britain, and several other countries of the coalition.

In his autobiography, *It Doesn't Take a Hero*, Schwarzkopf summarized his own life in a

way that most soldiers who served with him would claim most appropriate:

"A man does not get to write his own epitaph. But if I were to write mine it would say the following: He loved his family, and he loved his troops, and they loved him – period." This sentiment, however, went far beyond Schwarzkopf's family and troops after his death on December 27, 2012, at the age of 78. In the wake of his passing, the outpouring of sentiments lauding Schwarzkopf validated that he was not only loved by his family and troops, but by a grateful nation, as well.

Written by: Captain Sabah al Sabah, USMA 2007, Kuwait Army.

Schwarzkopf with Kuwaiti Commander-in-Chief Jabar Al Sabah, March 3, 1991, at Captured Iraqi Airfield at Safwan, Iraq.

Schwarzkopf negotiating Iraqi surrender, March 3, 1991.

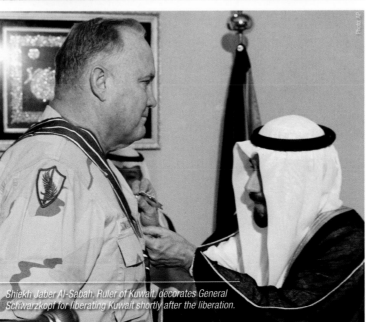

Shiekh Jaber Al-Sabah, Ruler of Kuwait, decorates General Schwarzkopf for liberating Kuwait shortly after the liberation.

Queen Elizabeth II awards General Schwarzkopf medal and Honorary Knighthood, May 20, 1991, in Tamp.

Rising from the humblest of beginnings as the son of a single mother who worked as a secretary in Little Rock, Arkansas, General Wesley Clark has distinguished himself over the past 46 years as an academic and combat leader and a public servant. A graduate of West Point and a Rhodes Scholar, he led both American soldiers (at the Company, Battalion, Brigade, and Division levels) and NATO to victory in its first-ever combat action as Supreme Allied Commander, saving one and a half million Albanians from ethnic cleansing and helping to create the free country of Kosovo. He was drafted to run as a candidate for the Democratic nomination in 2004 and is a frequent commentator on CNN. In light of these accomplishments, Clark claims that West Point prepared him to lead at the highest levels, as well as providing him with an education and opportunities he never imagined.

Clark was born December 23, 1944, in Chicago to Veneta and Benjamin Kanne. After his father passed away in 1948, his mother decided to relocate the two of them back to Little Rock, Arkansas, to live with her grandmother. Eventually, Veneta remarried an Arkansas state worker, Victor Clark, and both he and his mother assumed the Clark last name while keeping Kanne as his middle name. Clark grew up in the Little Rock public school system, but in 1959, with desegregation providing a violent atmosphere, he was sent to Castle Heights Military Academy in Lebanon, Tennessee, for one year. After the violence subsided, he returned and became Captain of the state championship–winning swim team, participated in the state championship debate team, and eventually graduated first in his class at Hall High School. Although he had scholarships to Duke University, Georgia Tech, and an offer from Harvard University, he immediately decided to attend West Point after hearing a cadet speak about the Academy at Boys' State.

While at West Point, he excelled in many areas – particularly in math and science – and he fully intended on becoming a theoretical physicist. A well-rounded individual, Clark joined the SCUBA club and was a member of the swimming and dive team, as well as the debate team competing at the national level. During his freshman and sophomore years, he also took Russian language classes and went to the Soviet Union for two weeks before the start of his junior year with a number of his classmates. He and his classmates happened to be in Leningrad during the Gulf of Tonkin crisis in August 1964, which escalated the prominence of the conflict in Vietnam. When he returned to West Point, his cadet training, in most areas, focused primarily on Vietnam, and his class knew that was where many of its members would be going upon graduation. The course of Clark's immediate future would change one night during his sophomore year when he was selected, along with three other cadets, to go to Thayer Hall where four Army Officers, all former Rhodes Scholars and graduates from the West Point (Classes of 1952, 1953, 1954, and 1955), told the cadets that they each had the potential to become Rhodes Scholars. Ironically, only one of the four cadets was familiar with the scholarship, and it was not Clark. Most of the Rhodes Scholars were also Armor Officers. It was through this interaction, then, that Clark changed his concentration

DURING THE ATTACK, CAPTAIN CLARK WAS HIT BY FOUR AK-47 ROUNDS AND NEARLY DIED.

General Wesley Clark, USMA 1966

- RHODES SCHOLAR/#1 IN WEST POINT CLASS OF 1966
- WHITE HOUSE FELLOW
- NATO COMMANDER IN FIRST NATO COMBAT ACTION
- U.S. PRESIDENTIAL DEMOCRATIC CANDIDATE IN 2004 ELECTION
- SILVER STAR AND PURPLE HEART, VIETNAM
- PRESIDENTIAL MEDAL OF FREEDOM

Clark working NATO strategy at headquarters with Secretary General Solana during the Kosovo Campaign, March 1999.

to National Security within the Department of Social Sciences, competed for, and won a Rhodes Scholarship. He then followed his mentors' leads by selecting the Armor branch.

As a cadet, Clark remembers walking out of military art class and running into his Tactical Officer who asked him how classes were going. Clark replied that they were studying Napoleon, telling the officer, "I think I can understand how he did it." Today, Clark still remembers how the officer responded: "Mr. Clark, you need to learn to command a company before you can command an Army." Nearly 50 years later, Clark would also accomplish that with exceptional skill.

After graduation, Second Lieutenant Clark attended Airborne School and then headed to London to attend Oxford University for two years. The late 1960s were interesting times with protests over Vietnam, a roaring

economy, and The Beatles and Rolling Stones dominating the scene. Rhodes Scholars typically gave many speeches around England, and Clark was the last American Rhodes Scholar in the 1960s to speak favorably of the United States policy in Vietnam. He spent considerable time at those events debating with communists, draft dodgers, and anti-war protestors.

In 1968, Captain Clark returned to the Army and to Fort Knox, where he commanded an Armor company for a few months. He then deployed to Vietnam as an individual replacement in a division headquarters, preparing presentations and conducting briefings. He finally received command of A Company 1/16th Infantry Regiment – a mechanized Infantry company. He was in command for two months, when he was leading a platoon-sized, dismounted patrol. At the time, they did not have a Platoon Leader

because Clark had relieved him for submitting false position reports. The dismounted patrol's mission was to set up an ambush but engaged the enemy before reaching the ambush site. Neither side suffered casualties as the enemy disengaged. Clark led his patrol in pursuit of the VC unit, found the enemy base camp, and attacked it. During the attack, Captain Clark was hit by four AK-47 rounds and nearly died. He was medically evacuated to Saigon, then to Japan, and finally to Valley Forge Medical Center in Pennsylvania, where he recovered from his wounds. He received the Silver Star and Purple Heart for his heroic actions leading his unit against the enemy, and, although, he was an Armor Officer, was also awarded the Combat Infantryman Badge.

He returned to Fort Knox and took command of his third armor company in 6-32 Armor, which he commanded for five months before attending the Armor Advanced Course.

He returned to West Point to teach in the Department of Social Sciences from 1971 to 1974. He then commanded at the Battalion, Brigade, and Division levels, leading 1-77 Armor at Colorado's Fort Carson from 1980 to 1982; 3rd Brigade, 4th Infantry Division at Fort Carson from 1986 to 1988; and finally 1st Cavalry Division at Fort Hood, Texas, from 1992 to 1994.

In addition to having more command and troop time than most officers (9 years in an 11-year period from 1980 to 1992), he also had four unique staff jobs that he considers essential to his successful career. His first was as speechwriter from 1978 to 1979 to General Alexander Haig, NATO Commander. He then served in the Pentagon from 1983 to 1984 where he formed the Army Studies Group under the Army Chief of Staff and Vice Chief of Staff. Next, as a Brigadier General, he was deputy Chief of Staff for the Commander,

Freedom assured, Kosovars throng to welcome General Clark in the streets of Pristina, July 1999.

General Clark and President Clinton with NATO Secretary General Solana at NATO headquarters, May 1999.
Photo: AP

>>> Spotlight

Written by General Wesley Clark and his West Point classmate Tom Carhart, *A Time to Lead* was published six years after retirement from the Army and two years after leaving the Presidential race. This book gives perspective on the life of General Wesley Clark, from lessons at West Point, Oxford, Vietnam, working as a Major for General Alexander Haig, a year as a White House Fellow, and in various command and staff jobs throughout his career, culminating in command of NATO's first major military action in the Balkans that helped stop the ethnic cleansing that threatened a million and a half civilians. The book validates all the lessons from West Point that General Clark credits as the foundation for a lifetime of service to the nation.

Book Cover Courtesy: Wesley Clark

Photo: AP

General Clark addressing the Democratic National Convention, Boston, July, 2004.

Training, and Doctrine Command (TRADOC) in 1991. Lastly, as a Lieutenant General, he was the Chairman of the Joint Chiefs of Staff's Director of Strategic Plans (J-5) at the Pentagon from 1994 to 1995.

As the Director of Strategic Plans, he helped negotiate the Bosnian Peace Agreement (known as the Dayton Accords), helped plan the movement of the United States Southern Command (SOUTHCOM) Headquarters from Panama to Miami, and put together and executed the invasion of Haiti. He also helped write the national military strategy and Joint 2010 vision, which guided the evolution of the Armed Forces. Promoted to General in 1996, he then took command of SOUTHCOM and was responsible for all United States military forces and strategy throughout Central and South America.

In 1997, General Clark was appointed Commanding General of NATO forces. The day he took command was also the first day NATO forces captured Serbian war criminal Goran Jelisic in Bosnia in accordance with the Dayton Accords. The Serbs immediately turned hostile. Clark had spent a lot of time focused on the Balkans and was familiar with all the major players – Bosnians, Serbs, Croats, and NATO. Now as the new NATO Commander, General Clark was responsible for implementing the Dayton Accords that he had helped negotiate, but the Serbs passively and actively resisted. Clark implemented a strategy he described as "using forces without using force" and outmaneuvered the Serbs politically on the ground to capture war criminals and reduce their freedom of movement. In March 1998, a fight broke out between Serbian military police and Albanian nationalists in Kosovo. Clark then requested and received approval from NATO members to execute a series of war planning exercises in response to the outbreak of violence in Kosovo.

Coincidentally, previously, in 1975 as a Command and General Staff College student at Fort Leavenworth, Kansas, then-Major Clark focused his thesis on lessons learned from American contingency operations up to 1975. Twenty-three years later, General Clark was able to draw upon and implement lessons learned from his thesis. While the Serbs continued to defy the Dayton Accords and kill Albanians in ethnic cleansing, Clark made three trips to Belgrade to personally negotiate with Serbian Leader, Slobodan Milosovic, and warned him that if he did not comply with the Dayton Accords, NATO would retaliate.

On March 25, 1999, General Clark initiated the bombing campaign – focusing initially on selected targets within Kosovo and then expanding throughout the former Yugoslavia. The campaign started with 300 aircraft and eventually increased to 1,000. In support of the air campaign, Clark readied 30,000 NATO ground troops for an invasion with plans to commit up to six divisions to a

General Clark debates Howard Dean in the 2004 Presidential Debates.

General Clark receiving the Presidential Medal of Freedom from President Clinton.

General Clark testifying before the Senate.

ground campaign. After 77 days of the air campaign, however, Milosovic conceded to withdraw his forces and allow Albanians to return to Kosovo under the protection of a NATO occupying force. This was NATO's first major combat operation and one that was successful through the excellent combination of airpower, the ability to mass forces and plan for a ground invasion, and the skillful art of diplomacy.

Clark was a key leader in the success of this unusual coalition – NATO forces engaged in combat under Clark along with diplomatic support from Finland and Russia – mainly due to his skillful military leadership and diplomacy.

As a result, he received the Presidential

Medal of Freedom in 2000. After 34 years of military service, General Clark eventually retired in 2000 and took several board positions, became a regular commentator on CNN, and focused on learning the investment banking business with Stephens Investment Banking firm.

Following the attacks of September 11th and the wars in Afghanistan and Iraq, Clark was a regular guest on CNN and a nationally recognized leader. Congress also asked for him to testify on his opinion of the two conflicts. In general, Clark supported action in Afghanistan, but was an outspoken critic against the invasion of Iraq. At that time, he also drew the attention of several prominent Democrats and was asked to meet with

President Jimmy Carter, who suggested that Clark run for President in 2004. Clark was realistic, saying in 2003 that he was unprepared for the 2004 Presidential race since he did not have a war chest, did not have a national organization, and had no experience in politics. Still, 60 "blue dog" Democrats from Congress requested that he run, and he was "drafted" to start his campaign in mid-September 2003. Despite the extremely late start, Clark made an impressive run as he visited 30 states and raised $23 million in his first three months. He also competed in several state primaries, winning Oklahoma; placing second in New Mexico, Arkansas, and North Dakota; and third in New Hampshire. Following a series of John Kerry victories over two consecutive

weeks and a lack of funds, Clark decided to withdraw from the race, but considers it a wonderful experience.

In looking back on the five decades since taking the oath on the Plain in July 1962, Clark is awed by the preparation he received while at West Point, as well as the opportunities and jobs afforded him for having succeeded at West Point. His simple advice in how to be successful and be promoted in the military? "Just do your job, and give it 100%."

General Clark with Secretary of State Hillary Clinton.

General Clark with President Obama.

Promotion to Lieutenant General aboard
USS Port Royal *at Pearl Harbor in 2005.*

Courtesy: LTG Eikenberry

Ambassador Karl Eikenberry, USMA 1973

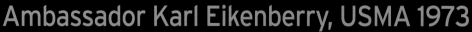

- **U.S. AMBASSADOR TO AFGHANISTAN**
- **COMMANDING GENERAL AFGHANISTAN WAR**
- **NATIONAL SECURITY FELLOW AT THE KENNEDY SCHOOL OF GOVERNMENT AT HARVARD UNIVERSITY**
- **DEPUTY CHAIRMAN OF THE NORTH ATLANTIC TREATY ORGANIZATION (NATO)**
- **COMMANDED AIRBORNE, MECHANIZED, LIGHT INFANTRY, AND RANGER UNITS**

As the fires burned in the Pentagon on September 11th, Major General Bob Wood (USMA 1972) was trapped in his office that was filling with smoke. Brigadier General Karl Eikenberry, who was in the next room when the plane hit the building, forced the door open and rescued Major General Wood. The attacks had been formulated and led by terrorists operating in Afghanistan, and as fate would have it, Eikenberry would later travel 7,000 miles from ground zero at the Pentagon to the source of the terrorism in Afghanistan. He would serve three tours (five years) in Afghanistan over the next decade, including one tour as Commander and one as the United States Ambassador to Afghanistan. He was one of the first of many Americans to perform an act of bravery on September 11th, and he would spend more

time in Afghanistan leading the American war effort and our courageous soldiers than any other General Officer over the next decade.

Eikenberry graduated from high school in North Carolina and entered West Point in 1969 at the height of the Vietnam War. His roommate for three years was John Abizaid, who would later rise to become a Four-Star General and Commander of United States Central Command (CENTCOM). Second Lieutenant Eikenberry graduated eighth in his class in 1973 and was commissioned in the Infantry. His class had attended West Point while the war raged, expecting to deploy to combat in Vietnam after graduation, but the conflict officially ended in March 1973. As a result, they entered an Army that was tired and demoralized and had to rebuild it. The last conscripts entered service in June 30,

1973, as the draft was eliminated in favor of an all-volunteer military. Joining the military was very unpopular post-Vietnam, and in order to recruit, standards had to be lowered. These were some of the most difficult years to serve in the Army, but Eikenberry and his classmates helped rebuild the Army over the next several decades.

The war in Vietnam had been fought as an extension of the Cold War and the battle against communism. After the loss of Vietnam, the focus of the Army was still on containing communism. Eikenberry chose the Infantry branch and had his pick of assignments being at the top of his class. After graduating from Airborne and Ranger schools, he deployed to Korea with the 1st of the 17th Infantry near the Demilitarized Zone (DMZ) – the most challenging assignment

he could find. The DMZ was still considered a combat zone, and patrols occasionally exchanged fire with the North Koreans. Not long after Eikenberry left Korea, two American Army Officers were brutally murdered by a North Korean Officer in plain sight (including Major Art Bonifas, USMA 1966), an incident that became internationally known.

Later, in 1984, when then Major Eikenberry was the Deputy Commander of the U.N. Security Force in Panmunjom, Korea (the same unit as Major Bonifas served in), his unit sharply defeated a North Korean guard force that crossed the demarcation line in pursuit of a Soviet defector, a day on which his forces recalled the loss of Major Bonifas and his fellow officer.

On NATO maneuvers in 1989.

With Afghan leaders in Helmand Province as U.S. Ambassador in 2010.

Courtesy LTG Eikenberry

After his first assignment in Korea, Eikenberry was selected to join the newly formed 1st Ranger Battalion at Fort Stewart, Georgia, an elite, handpicked unit estab-

BRIGADIER GENERAL KARL EIKENBERRY, WHO WAS IN THE NEXT ROOM WHEN THE PLANE HIT THE BUILDING, FORCED THE DOOR OPEN AND RESCUED MAJOR GENERAL WOOD.

lished to rebuild the discipline and training standards depleted over the course of the Vietnam War and transition to an all-volunteer force. Over the next three decades, drawing upon his foundational experiences from his West Point and Ranger days, Eikenberry led troops in Airborne,

Mechanized, Light Infantry, and Ranger units. He was Deputy Commander of an Airborne battalion in Vicenza, Italy, when the Berlin Wall came down, and the enemy that our Army had trained to repel and defeat suddenly faded away without a shot being fired. However, the void was filled quickly when Saddam Hussein invaded Kuwait the next year and the Middle East became the national security focus of the United States for the next several decades.

Eikenberry had graduated at the top of his class at West Point and thrived as a student. He received two master's degrees

from Harvard and Stanford in Asian studies and political science respectively and earned an advanced degree in history from Nanjing University in China. He was fluent in Mandarin-Chinese and was a National Security Fellow at the Kennedy School of government at Harvard. He served as the Defense and Assistant Army Attaché during two tours in Beijing, China.

When the terrorists attacked the Twin Towers and the Pentagon, Brigadier General Eikenberry was in the Strategy, Plans, and Policy Directorate of the Office of the Army Chief of Staff. One year later, he was sent to Afghanistan as the Chief of the Office of Military Cooperation tasked with helping establish and build the new Afghan National Army and coordinating Afghan security sector

Courtesy LTG Eikenberry

Speaking with President Obama at the Lisbon NATO Summit in 2010.

reform. While he was serving in Afghanistan in March 2003, Operation Iraqi Freedom and the invasion of Iraq started.

In May 2005, after serving as the first Army Director for Strategic Planning and Policy (J-5) in the history of United States Pacific Command in Camp Smith, Hawaii, Major General Eikenberry was promoted to Lieutenant General. Replacing Lieutenant General David Barno (USMA 1976), Eikenberry took command of the war in Afghanistan as Commander of Combined Forces Command – Afghanistan (CFC-A). While Eikenberry commanded in Afghanistan, he reported to his friend and former West Point roommate General John Abizaid, Commander of United States Central Command. By this time, the war in Iraq had turned into a full-scale counterinsurgency and the country was on the brink of a civil war. The total number of troops in Afghanistan was 20,000, while more than 140,000 were deployed to Iraq. The United States was conducting counterinsurgency operations in Afghanistan while trying to build a functioning government, field Afghan Army and Police, provide critically needed social services, and jump-start a broken economy – all with limited resources. Eikenberry focused on constructing critical infrastructure and a legitimate government in a "whole of nation" approach while strengthening Afghanistan's security forces, attacking Taliban elements, setting conditions for transition to NATO to command the Afghan Theater, and focusing attention on enemy sanctuary in Pakistan.

Subsequent to his command in Afghanistan, Lieutenant General Eikenberry was assigned to be the Deputy Chairman of the North Atlantic Treaty Organization (NATO) in Brussels, Belgium. He retired from active duty in April 2009 and was appointed the United States Ambassador to Afghanistan one day later.

U.S. Coalition Commander
in Afghanistan in 2006.

Courtesy: LTG Eikenberry

>>> Spotlight

Karl Eikenberry is the William J. Perry Fellow in International Security Studies at the Freeman Spogli Institute for International Studies (FSI), which is Stanford University's primary center for innovative research on major international issues and challenges. FSI builds on Stanford's intellectual strengths and rigorous academic standards through interdisciplinary research conducted by its university-wide faculty, researchers, and visiting scholars.

By the time of his third tour in Afghanistan, the regional situation had changed considerably, and the United States government's main effort was now turning from Iraq back to Afghanistan. Since the "surge" in Iraq had proven successful and violence was down significantly, the United States began to withdraw its forces. Violence in Afghanistan, on the other hand, had steadily increased as the Taliban had consolidated in Pakistan and had returned to Afghanistan to terror-ize the population. While troop levels were declining in Iraq, they were steadily increasing in Afghanistan reaching to more than 50,000 in 2009. Since his deployments had kept him away from home for many years, Eikenberry requested and was approved, to bring his wife, Ching, to Afghanistan during his Ambassadorship. She worked for USAID under the Eligible Family Member Program and accompanied him on most of his frequent travel around the country acting as a bridge to the Afghan women.

With a new President taking office in January 2009, the war aims and strategy were in question and thoroughly debated at the White House and in the halls of Congress. President Obama chose to increase troop levels, making the announcement at West Point in December 2009 on a nationally televised announcement at Eisenhower Hall. Ambassador Eikenberry served in Afghanistan at the same time as two other West Point graduates, General McChrystal (USMA 1976) and General Petraeus (USMA 1974), commanded the war.

After leaving Afghanistan, Ambassador Eikenberry became the Frank E. and Arthur W. Payne Distinguished Lecturer at the Freeman Spogli Institute for International Studies at Stanford University.

Speaking at the Austrian Defense Academy as the NATO Deputy Chairman of the Military Committee in 2008.

Courtesy: LTG Eikenberry

With U.S. Army CH-47 crew and Pakistan Army Liaison Officer during Kashmir earthquake disaster relief operation in 2005.

With Pashtun tribal elders in Afghanistan when serving as Ambassador in 2009.

General Tommy Franks, CENTCOM Commander, with Major General Eikenberry.

Courtesy: LTG Eikenberry

One of the most distinguished West Point graduates of his generation, David Howell Petraeus – who grew up just a few miles from West Point in the town of Cornwall-on-Hudson – has dedicated his life to public service. Upon retiring from the United States Army on August 30, 2011, after a distinguished 37-year career, Petraeus was sworn in as the 20th Director of the Central Intelligence Agency on September 6, 2011, as the first West Point graduate to lead the Agency. He served as CIA Director until November 9, 2012. The legacy of General Petraeus was forged in the conflicts that the United States faced in the years following the attacks of September 11, 2001. In both theory and practice, General Petraeus has defined counterinsurgency strategy and tactics for the modern military.

Prior to his selection as Director of CIA by President Barack Obama, General Petraeus served as Commander, NATO International Security Assistance Force and Commander, U.S.-Afghanistan from July 4, 2010 to July 18, 2011. Prior to his Afghanistan command, he was the Commander of United States Central Command (CENTCOM), where he had served since October 2008; prior to CENTCOM, he served for more than 19 months as the Commanding General of the Multi-National Force-Iraq, overseeing the execution of the surge and implementing the counterinsurgency concepts he helped develop and promulgate throughout the military.

As the Commander of the Iraq War in 2007 and 2008, General Petraeus provided the leadership that turned around a war that many had thought was lost, and, in doing so, earned his place in American military history. Despite mounting United States casualties, declining public support, and a Sunni-Shiite civil war that threatened to tear Iraq apart, General Petraeus implemented a "surge" pushing thousands of United States troops, along with their Iraqi counterparts, into the cities to protect the population. He led by example, often exposing himself by visiting

General David Petraeus, USMA 1974

- **COMMANDING GENERAL OF ALL U.S. AND COALITION FORCES IN BOTH THE IRAQ AND AFGHANISTAN WARS**
- **PRINCETON UNIVERSITY WOODROW WILSON SCHOOL OF PUBLIC AND INTERNATIONAL AFFAIRS MPA AND PHD**
- **COMMANDING GENERAL, MULTI-NATIONAL SECURITY TRANSITION COMMAND-IRAQ (MNSTC-I)**
- **COMMANDING GENERAL, U.S. CENTRAL COMMAND (CENTCOM)**
- **COMMANDING GENERAL, 101ST AIRBORNE DIVISION (AIR ASSAULT) IRAQ**
- **DIRECTOR OF THE CENTRAL INTELLIGENCE AGENCY (CIA)**
- **ARMY SOCCER PLAYER**
- **BUSINESS EXECUTIVES FOR NATIONAL SECURITY (BENS) ANNUAL EISENHOWER AWARD RECIPIENT**

Director Petraeus's official CIA photo.

General Petraeus circulating among the Iraqi population 2007.

villages and cities to provide inspiration for Americans and Iraqis. By gaining support from multiple stakeholders, he effectively implemented a comprehensive counterinsurgency strategy, which included aggressive support for reconciliation, development of Iraqi forces, and improvements in civilian governance and development. In seemingly record time, the war turned around, violence dropped drastically, and a cohesive, yet imperfect central government of Iraq and a Iraqi Security Forces were able to control the country. This set conditions for the suc-cessful United States withdrawal three years later. He often says "the role of a leader is to get the 'big ideas' right." The "surge" was a big, highly controversial idea, but he got it right owed to effective implementation by he and brave United States, Iraqi, and coalition soldiers.

General Petraeus also commanded the United States Army Combined Arms Center and Fort Leavenworth, during which time he oversaw the development of the Army/Marine Corps Counterinsurgency Field Manual and corresponding changes to Army training and leader development. He spoke often of the importance of the "Engine of Change" to transform the Army to ensure that it stayed up-to-date with the latest developments. More than 20 years earlier at Fort Leavenworth, he had earned the coveted General George C. Marshall award as the top graduate of the United States Army Command and General Staff College Class of 1983.

Prior to Fort Leavenworth, he served for more than 15 months as the first Commander of both the Multi-National Security Transition Command-Iraq and the NATO Training Mission-Iraq, directing the "Train and Equip" mission. That deployment to Iraq followed his command of the 101st Airborne Division (Air Assault), during which he led the "Screaming Eagles" during the fight to Baghdad and throughout the first year of Operation Iraqi Freedom. The 101st Airborne Division was alerted in February 2003, moved all their equipment and personnel to the Middle East in little more than a month, then fought decisively as coalition forces defeated Saddam Hussein's Army in April 2003. When fighting broke out in Mosul (Northern Iraq), Petraeus's division conducted the longest air assault in Army history and reestablished security in the northern provinces of Iraq. Petraeus was noted for developing the process to select local leaders and for implement-ing a comprehensive approach to security, including development and governance in Northern Iraq.

General Petraeus's command of the 101st followed a year deployed on Operation Joint Forge in Bosnia, where he was the Assistant Chief of Staff for Operations of the NATO Stabilization Force. Petraeus was in Bosnia on September 11, 2001, and became the Deputy Commander of the United States Joint Counter-Terrorism Task Force-Bosnia, which coordinated United States actions to counter terrorists in Bosnia. He was instrumental in pulling together all instru-ments of national power as an example of the way that interagency coordination can significantly support effective actions against terrorists. Prior to his tour in Bosnia, he spent two years at Fort Bragg, North Carolina, serving first as the Assistant Division Commander for Operations of the 82nd Airborne Division and then as the Chief of Staff of XVIII Airborne Corps.

In addition to his commands as a General Officer, Petraeus held leadership positions in airborne, mechanized, and air assault Infantry units in Europe, the United States, and the Middle East, including command of a company in the 24th Infantry Division, a Battalion in the 101st Airborne Division (Air Assault), and a brigade in the 82nd Airborne Division. He also held a number of staff assignments: Aide to the Chief of Staff of the Army; Battalion, Brigade, and Division Operations Officer; Military Assistant to the Supreme Allied Commander-Europe; Chief of Operations of the United Nations Force in Haiti; and Executive Assistant to the Chairman of the Joint Chiefs of Staff.

General Petraeus was commissioned in the Infantry upon graduation as a "distinguished cadet" from West Point in 1974. During his time there, Petraeus was a member of the soccer team and ski team and honed his lifelong dedication to physical fitness, in addition to graduating near the top of his class and serv-ing as a Cadet Captain on the brigade staff. His dedication to intellectual pursuits continued throughout his military career. He subsequently earned MPA and PhD degrees in international relations from Princeton University's Woodrow Wilson School of Public and International Affairs, and he later served as an assistant profes-sor of International Relations at the United States Military Academy. He also completed a fellowship at Georgetown University.

In 2005, he was recognized by the *U.S. News & World Report* as one of "America's 25 Best Leaders," and in 2007, he was one of four runners-up for *Time* magazine's "Person of the Year." In 2009, he was selected by *Foreign Policy* magazine as one of the "World's Top 100 Public Intellectuals" and by *Esquire* magazine as one of the "75 Most Influential People of the 21st Century." Most recently, General Petraeus was awarded the 2010 James Madison Medal by Princeton University and was named as one of the "100 Most Influential People in the World" by *Time* magazine in 2011.

General Petraeus is married to the former Holly Knowlton, a graduate of Dickinson College and the daughter of Army General William A. Knowlton, who was the Superintendent of West Point when they met. They have a daughter and a son, Anne and Stephen.

> ## "GOOD LEADERS GET THE BIG IDEAS RIGHT," SAYS GENERAL PETRAEUS.

General Petraeus with President Bush, 2007.

General Petraeus with Iraqi Generals.

Petraeus with President Obama in the White House, 2009.

Photo: White House

Secretary Gates with Director Petraeus.

>>> Spotlight

General Petraeus earned his master's in Public Administration (1985) and PhD in International Relations (1987) from the Princeton University Woodrow Wilson School of Public & International Affairs, where the motto is "Princeton in the Nation's service, in the service of all nations."

Courtesy: Princeton University

Dave and Holly Petraeus, Princeton Graduation.

Courtesy: General Petraeus

Second Lieutenant Petraeus as Ranger School Honor Graduate, 1975.

Dave and Holly Knowlton, West Point Graduation, 1974.

Photo: AP

General Petraeus with President Obama flying over Iraq.

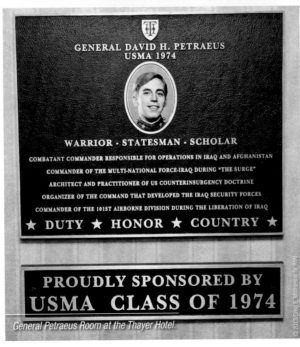

GENERAL DAVID H. PETRAEUS
USMA 1974

WARRIOR · STATESMAN · SCHOLAR

COMBATANT COMMANDER RESPONSIBLE FOR OPERATIONS IN IRAQ AND AFGHANISTAN

COMMANDER OF THE MULTI-NATIONAL FORCE-IRAQ DURING "THE SURGE"

ARCHITECT AND PRACTITIONER OF US COUNTERINSURGENCY DOCTRINE

ORGANIZER OF THE COMMAND THAT DEVELOPED THE IRAQ SECURITY FORCES

COMMANDER OF THE 101ST AIRBORNE DIVISION DURING THE LIBERATION OF IRAQ

★ DUTY ★ HONOR ★ COUNTRY ★

PROUDLY SPONSORED BY
USMA CLASS OF 1974

General Petraeus Room at the Thayer Hotel.

General Petraeus in the field with soldiers in Iraq.

Describing the Afghan mission to reporters, Kabul, 2004.

Change of command ceremony at Bagram Airbase, Afghanistan, March 2005.

>>> Spotli

Lieute
Amer
natio

Center for a
New American
Security

Courtesy: Ce

Lieutenant General Dave Barno, USMA 1976

- **COMMANDING GENERAL, AFGHANISTAN WAR, 2003-2005**
- **SENIOR ADVISOR, CENTER FOR THE NEW AMERICAN SECURITIES (CNAS)**
- **MASTER OF ARTS, NATIONAL SECURITY STUDIES, GEORGETOWN UNIVERSITY**
- **COMMANDER, 2ND RANGER BATTALION, 75TH RANGER REGIMENT**
- **MEMBER, COUNCIL OF FOREIGN RELATIONS AND INTERNATIONAL INSTITUTE OF STRATEGIC STUDIES**

I n October 1983, Captain Dave Barno led a rifle company with the 1st Ranger Battalion in Operation Urgent Fury, the invasion of Grenada. Six years later on December 20, 1989, as part of 2nd Ranger Battalion, Major Barno stepped out of a C-130 at 500 feet and parachuted under fire into the darkness of Rio Hato Airfield at the opening of Operation Just Cause, the United States invasion of Panama. Less than 14 years later in November 2003, Lieutenant General Barno was the first member of the Class of 1976 to receive his third star when he was promoted Lieutenant General and

took command of the war in Afghanistan where he served as overall commander from late 2003 to mid-2005. Barno, in his third conflict leading American Soldiers in combat, became part of an exclusive group of West Point graduates who have commanded an entire wartime theater of operations.

David W. Barno was born July 5, 1954, and grew up in Endicott, New York. He attended Union-Endicott High School and graduated in 1972. He then entered West Point as part of America's bicentennial Class of 1976. While Barno graduated 117th in his class, he was most noted for his devotion to his steady

girlfriend, Susan, who would later become his wife, and his desire to become an officer and serve in the United States Army. He was drawn to military activities while at the Academy, earning a coveted cadet slot to the US Army Ranger School at age 19 and completing it with honors. Shortly after graduation, he married Susan and began an exciting career that centered on both his family and his service as an Infantry officer in the most highly challenging assignments.

Following his completion of Airborne and the Infantry Officer's Basic courses, Barno joined the 1st Battalion, 27th Infantry Regiment "Wolfhounds" of the 25th Infantry Division in

Schofield Barracks, Hawaii. He served as a rifle platoon leader, weapons platoon leader, scout platoon leader, and the battalion's assistant operations officer before taking command of Company A from 1979 to 1981. His impressive company grade performance to that point in his career then earned him an assignment to the elite 1st Battalion 75th Ranger Regiment where he briefly served as the battalion supply officer (S-4) before taking his second company command of C Company. Shortly after taking command, President Ronald Reagan ordered the invasion of the small Caribbean Island of Grenada in October 1983 after a Cuban-backed

Lieutenant General Barno briefing Vice President Dick Cheney and Secretary Rumsfeld at Bagram Airbase, Afghanistan, 2004.

Discussing operations with Secretary of State Condoleeza Rice during her 2005 visit to Kabul.

Dave Barno watching a 1999 airpower demonstration in the Capstone Course.

Fall parade season, 1975, Commander of Company F-3, USCC.

David W. Barno (USA Retired), is a Senior Advisor and Senior Fellow at the Center for a New ... in Washington, D.C. The mission of CNAS is to develop strong, pragmatic and principled ... defense policies while developing the national security leaders of today and tomorrow.

the ground and with supporting attack aircraft, the assault force secured the airfield and surrounding military base by daylight. Barno's battalion suffered two killed and several injured or wounded in the fight.

Across the Panamanian isthmus, airborne forces, ground forces, and helicopters conducted 27 simultaneous attacks against key PDF objectives in an impressive display of coordinated combat power-projection. By daybreak, US forces had seized most of the country's key objectives. General Manuel Noriega eventually surrendered and operations ceased on January 12, 1990. In the operation, the United States lost 23 killed in action and 324 wounded. Barno once again served a key role in a second American combat operation.

After a tour as Aide-de-Camp to the commander of the Army's Training and Doctrine Command, Barno was promoted to Lieutenant Colonel and assumed command of another elite combat unit, the 82nd Airborne Division's 3rd Battalion, 505th Parachute Infantry Regiment. Following his extremely successful command in the 82nd Airborne Division, Barno received the rare privilege of a second battalion command position and returned to the 2nd Ranger Battalion at Fort Lewis, which was coincidentally preparing for another potential combat mission – this time in Somalia. As commander, Barno prepared and rehearsed his battalion for possible deployments to both Somalia and Haiti.

Barno's next series of assignments and promotions were rapidly paced and clearly prepared him for his eventual theater command in Afghanistan. He graduated from the US Army War College, was promoted to Colonel, and selected for command of a multi-functional support brigade at Fort Polk, Louisiana. He then led a joint task force training program at US Atlantic Command in Norfolk, Virginia, to train deployable combat headquarters elements. He was then promoted to Brigadier General in 2000 and returned to Hawaii, this time as the Assistant Division Commander of the 25th Infantry Division and later also served as Deputy Director of Operations, United States Pacific Command.

In late 2002, Barno, now a Major General, commanded the Army's largest Initial Entry Training base at Fort Jackson, South Carolina. While in command, he was also charged with the unique mission of forming a training task force to deploy overseas and train Iraqi exiles for potential service with United States combat units should hostilities break out with Iraq. From January 2003 to April 2003, the month following the invasion of Iraq, Task Force Warrior conducted training at Taszar Air Base in Hungary preparing Iraqi expatriates to join US units in Iraq and provide regional and cultural expertise. Soon after completing this complex mission, Barno was selected to direct the Army Chief of Staff's Warrior Ethos Task Force where he became the principal creator and author of the Army's new Warrior Ethos. By late summer of 2003, Barno established a new, three-star level coalition headquarters in Kabul, Afghanistan. He was promoted to Lieutenant General and in this role, led all US and coalition military operations across the war-torn country. For nineteen months, LTG Barno commanded over 20,000 US and coalition forces in Operation Enduring Freedom. Leveraging experiences from his variety of previous command and staff assignments, Barno was responsible for a complex political-military mission that spanned four countries and required him to develop a highly innovative counter-insurgency strategy throughout Afghanistan and in close partnership with all coalition nations. Beyond simply commanding and directing military forces, Barno's strategy required coordinated efforts with a myriad of US and international political and military organizations to include the US State Department, the United Nations, NATO, the Afghanistan government, and the governments of Afghanistan's neighboring countries. Such a complex strategy could only be conceived, implemented, and executed by an experienced leader like Barno. In 2006, Barno retired after serving his nation and leading Soldiers for 30 years. He continues to provide service to the nation with thoughtful policy analysis and recommendations as a Senior Advisor and Senior Fellow at the Center for a New American Security in Washington, D.C. He and Susan have three children, including two sons who are active-duty Army officers and a daughter who works for the Department of Energy.

MAJOR DAVE BARNO STEPPED OUT OF A C-130 AT 500 FEET AND PARACHUTED INTO THE DARKNESS OF RIO HATO AIRFIELD UNDER FIRE, OPENING OPERATION JUST CAUSE, THE U.S. INVASION OF PANAMA.

military coup overthrew the government and threatened the security of the region, as well as the safety of hundreds United States students on the island. With less than 96 hours notice, Barno's company, along with the rest of his battalion, the 2nd Ranger Battalion, and other precision special operations units led the invasion on October 25, 1983.

This short-noticed deployment of a joint US task force that included the Ranger battalions, several special operations elements, the 82nd Airborne Division, and a US Marine task force successfully achieved all key objectives in only three days – not least among them the rescue of the US students. After several weeks of consolidation to secure the island, Grenada's democratic government was restored. During the operation, the United States suffered 19 Americans killed in action and 116 wounded in what was the first major combat engagement since the Vietnam War. Following his assignment in the 1st Ranger Battalion, Barno

next attended Georgetown University where he earned a master's degree in National Security Studies while serving in Washington, DC, and then attended the US Army Command and General Staff College.

Barno's next assignment saw him return to the special operations community in 1988 as the operations officer (S-3) of the 2nd Ranger Battalion at Fort Lewis, Washington. On December 20, 1989, the United States again responded to a crisis in Latin America and launched the invasion of Panama in Operation Just Cause. As his battalion's operations officer, Barno had been a key part of planning the mission months before the actual invasion. At 0100 hours on December 20, Major Barno parachuted into the heavily defended Panamanian airfield at Rio Hato. Several companies of the Panamanian Defense Force (PDF) opened fire on the US force, striking eleven of fifteen aircraft. The Rangers immediately engaged the enemy upon landing on

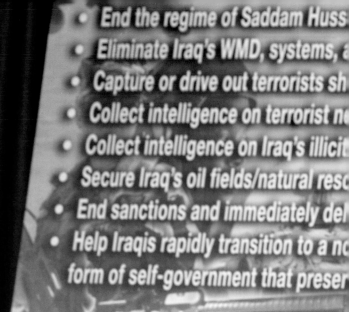

- End the regime of Saddam Huss
- Eliminate Iraq's WMD, systems, a
- Capture or drive out terrorists sh
- Collect intelligence on terrorist ne
- Collect intelligence on Iraq's illicit
- Secure Iraq's oil fields/natural reso
- End sanctions and immediately del
- Help Iraqis rapidly transition to a no form of self-government that preser

Courtesy: General McChrystal

General Stanley McChrystal, USMA 1976

- **COMMANDING GENERAL, AFGHANISTAN WAR**
- **SENIOR FELLOW JACKSON INSTITUTE FOR GLOBAL AFFAIRS YALE UNIVERSITY**
- **COMMANDER, JOINT SPECIAL OPERATIONS COMMAND (JSOC)**
- **DIRECTOR OF THE JOINT STAFF**
- **COMMANDER, 75TH RANGER REGIMENT**

Photo: NARA

Photo: AP

JSOC, Afghanistan, 2003

Area tours as a cadet.

>>> Spotlight

YALE UNIVERSITY

General McChrystal is a Senior Fellow at the Jackson Institute for Global Affairs at Yale University in New Haven, Connecticut. McChrystal teaches one course on leadership and another in the "Gateway to Global Affairs" course. Yale University was founded in 1701 and is the third-oldest university in the United States. Yale University it a top-tier university and has approximately 11,000 students in the undergraduate (Yale College), graduate, and professional schools.

General McChrystal, CDR ISAF, Senate Testimony, December 8, 2009.

General McChrystal and wife, Ann at his retirement, July 23, 2010.

Every generation produces leaders who, by ethos and habit, "lead from the front," as John Buford did outside the town at Gettysburg and Jim Gavin did over the skies of Normandy. For the wars in Iraq and Afghanistan, Stanley McChrystal stands out as such a General. For more than 34 years, Stan led by example. This 1976 West Point graduate spent most of his career in the United States Special Operations before leading more than 100,000 coalition troops in the war in Afghanistan as the Commander of International Security Assistance Forces (ISAF). For nearly a decade after 9/11, McChrystal led soldiers in combat around the world, helping target America's most dangerous enemies and innovate new ways of fighting the complex War on Terror.

McChrystal was born August 14, 1954, at Fort Leavenworth, Kansas, to an Army family. His father, Major General Herbert McChrystal, was a 1945 West Point graduate and decorated combat leader who led Infantry soldiers in both Korea and Vietnam, receiving four Silver Stars, a Bronze Star for Valor, and two Combat Infantryman Badges.

The summer of 1972 was a low point for the United States Army. The Vietnam War had cost more than 58,000 American lives and the public approval of the military was at a low. With the draft soon to be eliminated, recruiting was a challenge. That summer, McChrystal entered West Point and took the oath with a class that would be charged with re-building a deteriorated Army. That class, USMA 1976, would produce at least 33 General Officers and have more graduates take command of a theater of war than any other in history – even more than the famous Class of 1915, which included such legendary graduates as Eisenhower, Bradley, and Van Fleet. McChrystal would enter as a Plebe with Ray Odierno, Dave Barno, Dave Rodriguez, Frank Helmick, among others.

McChrystal fit right in when he entered West Point. He made lifelong friends and adapted to the environment – particularly field training exercises. He had an almost instinctive desire to conduct raids against the enemy. In his Yearling year, he joined a group of cadets in a mock raid against Grant Hall using rolled-up socks for hand grenades and unloaded automatic weapons. While the stunt ended up getting him in trouble, the raid left an indelible impression on his classmates and the 1976 Howitzer (yearbook) included this entry in McChrystal's

bio: "Competitiveness, dedication, and desire made 'Mac' the friend we know and respect...inherent in his success was the infamous Grant Hall raid." That young cadet's forces would later oversee complex real-world raids.

Second Lieutenant McChrystal attended Infantry Officer Basic, Airborne, and Ranger schools, then joined the famed 82nd Airborne Division. After serving as an Infantry Platoon Leader and Company Executive Officer in the 82nd, he chose to join the Special Forces and attended Special Forces course at Fort Bragg, North Carolina. This was prior to Special Forces having its own branch, so he remained an Infantry Branch Officer and led a Special Forces (Green Beret) "A Team" for two years in the 7th Special Forces Group. He returned to the conventional Infantry to lead an Infantry company in the 24th Infantry Division, before taking command of a company in the 75th Ranger Regiment. In all of these roles, he loved to be in the field, training, leading soldiers, preparing for wars they hoped they would never fight, but being prepared to do so at a moment's notice.

His first combat deployment would come shortly after leaving command of the Ranger company, after Saddam Hussein invaded Kuwait. Major McChrystal served as an Operations Officer (J-3) in Joint Special Operations Command during Operations Desert Shield and Desert Storm. In that role, he was in a critical position to plan and execute all the missions conducted by Army Special Operations from August 1990 through February 1991.

After Desert Storm, Stan was promoted to Lieutenant Colonel and took command of a battalion in the 82nd Airborne Division in 1992. By 1997, Colonel McChrystal was

MCCHRYSTAL TOOK COMMAND OF JOINT SPECIAL OPERATIONS COMMAND (JSOC). IN THIS ROLE, HE THRIVED AND BECAME A LEGEND. HE WOULD OFTEN PERSONALLY PARTICIPATE IN PATROLS AND RAIDS – A TRUE FIGHTING GENERAL.

widely regarded as one of the rising stars in the Army. He was known as a thoughtful, soft spoken, incredibly fit, hard-charging officer who rarely slept and only ate once a day. He was selected to take the most prestigious command for a Colonel: the 75th Ranger Regiment.

After the attacks of September 11th, Brigadier General McChrystal was the Chief of Staff Combined Joint Task Force 180 in Afghanistan. In 2003, he took command of Joint Special Operations Command (JSOC). In this role, he thrived and became a legend. He would often personally participate in patrols and raids – a true fighting General. Most of the Special Operations's successes remain classified, but a few were too public to keep classified, such as the capture of Saddam Hussein and the killing of the terrorist Abu Musab al-Zarqawi. By the time Lieutenant General McChrystal left command of JSOC in 2008, the war in Iraq had turned the corner and the surge was showing signs of success.

In 2009, General McChrystal was asked by President Obama to lead the eight-year-old war in Afghanistan, which had become a complicated insurgency. General McChrystal took command and brought the offensive against the enemy, recommending that the President increase troops in order to protect the population and secure nascent gains, which was approved. After more than a year in command, a politically charged article was published. Rather than make a public spectacle and showing selfless leadership, General McChrystal submitted his resignation and retired after 34 years of service, at the permanent rank of Four-Star General.

Soon after his retirement, McChrystal was asked by the White House to work with the First Lady to cochair a White House Commission on Military Families, called "Joining Forces." He also teaches leadership courses at the Jackson Institute at Yale University and is the Co-Founder of the McChrystal Group.

In addition to his military schooling, General McChrystal received two master's degrees and was a military fellow at both Harvard University and the Council of Foreign Relations in New York City. He and his wife, Annie, live in Alexandria, Virginia.

Chief of Staff of the Army General Ray Odierno greets troops on a visit to Afghanistan.

Cadet Odierno in formation at West Point.

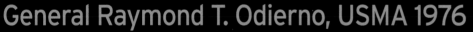

General Odierno with Cadets on the Plain at West Point.

General Raymond T. Odierno, USMA 1976

- **CHIEF OF STAFF U.S. ARMY**
- **COMMANDING GENERAL, MULTI-NATIONAL FORCES, IRAQ**
- **COMMANDING GENERAL, MULTI-NATIONAL CORPS, IRAQ**
- **COMMANDING GENERAL, 4TH INFANTRY DIVISION, IRAQ**
- **COMMANDING GENERAL, U.S. JOINT FORCES COMMAND**
- **ARMY FOOTBALL PLAYER**
- **BUSINESS EXECUTIVES FOR NATIONAL SECURITY (BENS) ANNUAL EISENHOWER AWARD RECIPIENT**

General Ray Odierno is the 38th Chief of Staff of the United States Army and one of America's greatest combat commanders. He has had significant combat command time as a General Officer. General Odierno commanded in combat in Iraq at the Division, Corps, and Theater level.

Born September 8, 1954, and raised in Rockaway, New Jersey, he attended public school at Morris Hills High School. He entered West Point in 1972 at the end of the Vietnam War, when joining the military was highly unpopular, with the goal of playing football, serving his five years in the Army, then becoming a civilian. However, he found he had a passion and love for the Army and just kept serving. Three decades later,

he and several of his classmates would rise to become Generals and bravely lead American soldiers through the wars in Iraq and Afghanistan – including West Point classmates General Stanley McChrystal, General David Rodriguez, and Lieutenant General David Barno – who all commanded the war in Afghanistan at the Theater or Operational levels.

Originally recruited to play football, Odierno injured both of his knees in his first two years and could no longer play. He played on the Army baseball team and lettered as a pitcher, playing on Doubleday Field (named after Major General Abner Doubleday, USMA 1842).

After graduating with an engineering degree

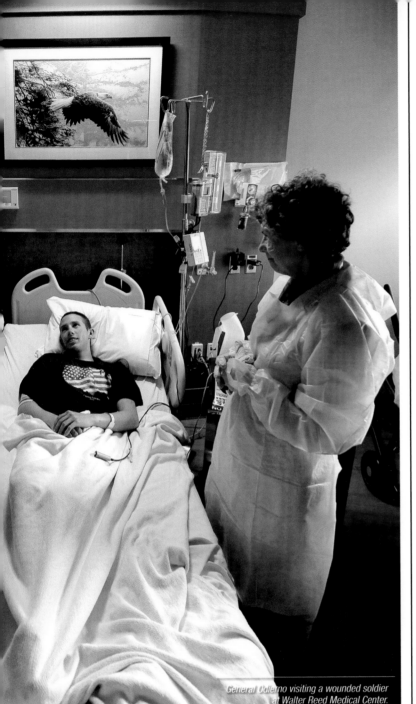

General Odierno visiting a wounded soldier at Walter Reed Medical Center.

deployment as a General Officer was in April 1999 to Albania, where he served as the Deputy Commanding General for Ground Operations of Task Force Hawk. His next combat tour came when he led a division in combat as Major General Odierno, Commanding General of the 4th Infantry Division in 2003.

The 4th Infantry Division was rerouted from the planned northern invasion route via Turkey to a southern route through Kuwait. When the division arrived in Iraq for Operation Iraqi Freedom in April, Baghdad had fallen, so they pressed north to Tikrit, Samarra, Baqubah, and Kirkuk, ultimately assuming responsibility for six of Iraq's 18 provinces, including Salah ad-Din, At-Tamin/Kirkuk, Diyala, Dahouk, Arbil, and As-Sulaymaniyyah. Odierno quickly transitioned the division from conventional kinetic offensive operations to post-conflict offensive operations based out of Tikrit, focused on eliminating pockets of resistance and deliberately targeting anti-Iraqi and anti-U.S. fighters as they began seeding an insurgency. A Sunni insurgency took root in late 2003 and early 2004, and the 4th Infantry Division and United States Army were now engaged in a type of warfare not anticipated or seen since Vietnam. Adapting to this new operational environment and fighting method took time and was enabled by inspiring and innovative leaders throughout the force, led by officers like Odierno, not afraid to adapt and learn, and determined to accomplish the mission. The highlight of the 4th Infantry Division deployment occurred in December 2003, when they captured Iraqi dictator Saddam Hussein near his hometown of Tikrit (north of Baghdad) hiding in a "spider hole." Hussein was later hung by an Iraqi government tribunal for crimes against the Iraqi people. The division re-deployed back to the United States in April 2004 with the loss of 81 soldiers Killed In Action and hundreds wounded.

As both a commander and a father, Odierno understands the risks and sacrifices of war, especially as he comes from a military family. His father served in World War II and inspired Odierno to enter West Point in 1972. As with many other war-fighting commanders (Grant, Pershing, Eisenhower, Van Fleet, Barno, Rodriguez, and Petraeus), General Odierno has a son, Anthony (Tony), who chose to join the Army and graduated from West Point in 2001. He was commissioned as an Infantry Officer. In August 2004, just after Odierno, left Tikrit with the 4th Infantry Division, Tony, a First Lieutenant,

was leading soldiers south of Baghdad when his Humvee was hit by a rocket propelled grenade, killing one soldier and wounding Tony. Tony woke up in Walter Reed Hospital days later missing his left arm. Captain Tony Odierno, now medically retired, is a successful executive with the New York Yankees, as well as a member of the Board of Directors for the Wounded Warrior Project.

In December 2006, General Odierno returned to Iraq as the Corps Commander to a much different situation on the ground than when he left in 2004. Al Qaeda had effectively attacked both Sunni and Shiite and baited them into a virtual civil war with mass killings on both sides. The population was held hostage in between the battling tribal, ethnic forces, and Al Qaeda. President Bush chose to increase the commitment in what would be called "the surge," appointing General David Petraeus as the leader of the Multi-National Force-Iraq (MNF-I),

"THE STRENGTH OF OUR NATION IS OUR ARMY, THE STRENGTH OF OUR ARMY IS OUR SOLDIERS, THE STRENGTH OF OUR SOLDIERS IS OUR FAMILIES, THIS IS WHAT MAKES US ARMY STRONG!" SAYS GENERAL ODIERNO.

while Lieutenant General Odierno led, orchestrated, and effectively implemented the strategy on the ground as Commander of MNC-I. Lieutenant General Odierno became known as the operational architect of the surge, creating and implementing a counterinsurgency strategy that pushed United States troops out and amongst the population with a purpose of protecting the people. After a yearlong brutal battle with increasing United States casualties, the Iraqi population rose to the task with their United States partners, turned on the insurgents, and supported the Iraqi Army, police, and government. Violence rapidly subsided, setting conditions for a transition to stable operations and eventual successful United States withdrawal three years later. In September 2008, General Petraeus was appointed to command United States Central Command, and Odierno was promoted to General and given command of MNC-I to replace Petraeus.

General Odierno commanded MNF-I

in 1976, Second Lieutenant Odierno was commissioned in the Field Artillery and was first assigned to United States Army Europe during the Cold War. He led artillery units from the Platoon level to the Brigade level (Division Artillery) in the United States and in Europe. He received two master's degrees: one from North Carolina State University in nuclear effects engineering and the other

from the Naval War College in national security and strategic studies. In 2010, he received an honorary doctorate degree from North Carolina State University. He is also a graduate of the Army War College.

He first saw combat as a Division Artillery Executive Officer in Operation Desert Storm in February 1991. His first operational

Chief of Staff of the Army General Ray Odierno observes troops during a training exercise at the Joint Readiness Training Center with Colonel Bill Burleson (USMA 1988) in 2012

Photo: D.O.D

As the operational architect of "the surge" in Iraq, Lieutenant General Odierno engages with Iraqi Sheiks.

(subsequently renamed USF-I) for two years from September 2008 to September 2010, during which time the security of Iraq's cities was transferred to the Iraqi Army and police. He transferred command to General Lloyd Austin (USMA 1975) in September 2010, after 25 consecutive months of command in Iraq and rotated home to assume command of United States Joint Forces Command at Norfolk, Virginia. He commanded soldiers in

Iraq for nearly four straight years through some of the toughest leadership challenges of a generation.

Standing at 6 foot 5 and 260 pounds with a shaved head, Odierno is both intimidating and inspirational to his soldiers. He is a soldier's soldier, and it is obvious that he genuinely loves being around the men and women who voluntarily serve in the United States

Army. His leadership style is reminiscent of General of the Army Omar Bradley, another General Officer described with the same attributes. Odierno is relatively soft spoken in public, but with a good sense of humor. His appearance on live television in Iraq in front of a thrilled audience of soldiers on Comedy Central's *The Colbert Report* as the Commander of Iraq in 2009 was illustrious of both his leadership style and his personality.

President Barack Obama appeared on video teleconference and ordered General Odierno to shave the head of Steven Colbert, which he did, to the delight of the soldiers and the American public.

In 2010, he was nominated and confirmed as Commander, United States Joint Forces Command. He took command following his return from Iraq in October, and Secretary

>>> Spotlight

General Odierno is the 38th Chief of Staff of the United States Army since the position was created in 1903. Prior to 1903, the position was called the Commanding General of the U.S. Army. The Chief of Staff prior to General Odierno was General Martin Dempsey (USMA 1974), who was appointed to Chairman of the Joint Chiefs of Staff by President Obama in 2011. The flag of the Chief of Staff is seen here.

Major General Odierno, then 4th Infantry Division Commander, discusses the capture of Saddam Hussein.

General Odierno appears on The Colbert Report *as the new Chief of Staff of the Army.*

Robert Gates gave him the responsibility to close down the combatant command.

In 2011, President Obama appointed Army Chief of Staff General Martin Dempsey (USMA 1974) as the Chairman of the Joint Chiefs of Staff and appointed General Odierno to succeed him as the 38th Chief of Staff of the United States Army.

In 2009, the *U.S. News & World Report* listed General Odierno as one of "America's Best Leaders." He was inducted in the Morris Hills District Hall of Fame in 2006. In 2008, General Odierno was awarded the United States Department of State's highest award: the Distinguished Service Medal. He was the 2009 recipient of the Naval War College Distinguished Graduate Leadership award for his strategic leadership and insight. General Odierno has been recognized by a diverse range of organizations over the past several years, such as The Council on Foreign Relations, The Institute of World Politics, World Affairs Councils, National Committee on American Foreign Policy, The Union Leagues of New York and Philadelphia, The Ends of the Earth Club, The Links Club, and New York University's Stern School of Business. His impact was felt internationally, as demonstrated by the President of Romania presenting him with the Romanian Order of Military Merit.

General Odierno is married to his high-school sweetheart, Linda. They have three children – Tony, Katie, and Mike – plus three grandchildren.

Iraq End of Operations Ceremony, December 21, 2011, conducted at Andrews Air Force Base, Maryland.

MG Lloyd J. Austin III assumes command of 10th Mountain Division in 2003.

General Lloyd Austin III, USMA 1975

- **COMMANDER, U.S. CENTRAL COMMAND (CENTCOM)**
- **VICE CHIEF OF STAFF, U.S. ARMY (VCSA)**
- **COMMANDING GENERAL, IRAQ WAR**
- **COMMANDING GENERAL, XVIII CORPS**
- **COMMANDING GENERAL, 10TH MOUNTAIN DIVISION (LIGHT)**
- **SILVER STAR RECIPIENT**

General Lloyd Austin is the Commander of United States Central Command (CENTCOM) and one of the foremost Combat Commanders of the Iraq and Afghanistan conflicts. General Austin has been a proven leader throughout his life and career in the United States Army. He has also been a trailblazer, achieving a number of "firsts" to include becoming the first African-American Vice Chief of Staff of the Army (VCSA), as well as the first African-American General Officer in history to command an entire theater of war.

General Austin was born in Mobile, Alabama, and raised in Thomasville, Georgia. He was just 11 years old when the Civil Rights Act of 1964 banned segregation. Seven years later, he entered the United States Military Academy at West Point as a Plebe, 94 years after the first African-American graduate, Henry O. Flipper, also a native of Thomasville, Georgia, received his diploma and commission as an officer in the United States Army.

Austin joined the military, in part, because he was inspired by uncles, cousins, and other relatives who also served. Some of them fought in Vietnam, and they would come home from training or yearlong tours overseas, and he looked up to them and admired them and he wanted to follow in their footsteps. While a cadet at West Point, Austin played rugby and was also a triple jumper on the track team.

After graduating in 1975, Second Lieutenant Austin was commissioned in the Infantry. He completed Airborne and Ranger Schools before heading to Germany and his initial assignment with the 3rd Infantry Division (Mechanized) as a Rifle Platoon Leader and later as a Scout Platoon Leader in 1st Battalion, 7th Infantry.

Austin spent much of his career assigned to the 10th Mountain Division (Light). Division at Fort Bragg, North Carolina, where he commanded at the Company, Battalion, Brigade, and Division levels. He also served as the 10th Mountain Division (Light) Division's Operations Officer in G3. He earned two master's degrees: one from Auburn University in education and the other from Webster University in business management. He is also a graduate of the Army War College. After completing his studies at Auburn, Austin was assigned to West Point, where he served as a Company Tactical Officer.

Brigadier General Austin was serving as the Assistant Division Commander for Maneuver for the 3rd Infantry Division (Mechanized) at Fort Stewart, Georgia, on September 11, 2001, a position he held for the next 21 months. As the ADC(M), he played a key role in the planning effort in support of Operation Iraqi Freedom. He ultimately helped spearhead the division's invasion of Iraq in March of 2003. In doing so, he became the first African-American to lead a division-size element into war. The assault into Baghdad was, as expected, a bloody battle. Austin was awarded the Silver Star, our nation's third-highest award for valor as a result of his actions during the invasion. In part, his award citation reads, "[Brigadier General Austin] continually placed himself and the division tactical operations center at the key point of the battle to provide command and control to the division on a fast-paced and violent battlefield. [His] gallantry in combat and relentless determination to defeat the enemy reflect great credit upon himself, the 3rd Infantry Division, and the United States Army."

After the invasion and liberation of Iraq, Austin was promoted to Major General and he subsequently took command of the 10th Mountain Division (Light Infantry), with duty as Commander, Combined Joint Task Force-180, Operation Enduring Freedom, Afghanistan. He is one of few General Officers to command in both Iraq and Afghanistan, and he is the first African-American to serve as a United States Army Division Commander in combat. During that deployment, General Austin worked tirelessly to help bring stability to the country of Afghanistan, and he oversaw efforts to develop the Afghan military and police forces.

Austin next served as Chief of Staff for General Abizaid (USMA 1973) at United States Central Command in Tampa, Florida. More than three decades earlier, then–Cadet Abizaid had been Austin's squad leader in Company G-1 at West Point. On December 8, 2006, Austin was promoted to the rank of Lieutenant General, and he assumed command of the XVIII Airborne Corps at Fort Bragg, North Carolina. Then, in February of 2008, he became the second-highest-ranking commander in Iraq, taking command of Multi-National Corps-Iraq (MNC-I), replacing Lieutenant General Raymond Odierno (USMA 1976). General Austin, in so doing, became the first African-American General Officer ever to command a Corps in combat. As Commander of MNC-I, Austin directed the operations of approximately 160,000 joint and Coalition Forces from more than 20 countries. He did so during a tumultuous period that included Prime Minister Nuri Kamal el-Maliki's push to wrest control of the key port city of Basra from Sadrist militias, a unilateral operation mounted by the Iraqi Security Forces.

However, early on the offensive stalled when Iraqi forces faced heavy resistance from the Mahdi Army inside the city of Basra. The Iraqi forces were under significant duress, Iraqi

LTG Austin, XVIII Airborne Corps commander, returns to Pope Air Force Base, North Carolina, in 2009 following a 15-month tour in Iraq.

Photo: DoD

>>> Spotlight

The Silver Star is the third-highest award for valor awarded to members of the United States military for distinguished gallantry in action against an enemy of the United States or while serving with friendly forces against an opposing enemy force. The Silver Star is the successor decoration to the Citation Star, which was established by an Act of Congress on July 9, 1918. On July 19, 1932, the Secretary of War approved the Silver Star to replace the Citation Star, including retroactively. The original Citation Star is incorporated into the center of the Silver Star, and the ribbon for the Silver Star is based closely on the Certificate of Merit Medal.

© 2013/Greg E. Mathieson Sr./MAI

General Austin, Vice Chief of Staff, Army (VCSA), presiding over a ribbon-cutting ceremony for the Fisher House at Fort Belvoir, Virginia.

Photo: DOD

General Austin, VCSA, visits troops.

---

senior leaders to include Prime Minister Maliki, and the members of his Cabinet were trapped in an increasingly precarious situation in the heart of Basra. Seeing an opportunity, General Austin made the decision to maneuver forces to support them on the ground. In the end, this joint U.S.-Iraqi endeavor, referred to as the "Charge of the Knights," stabilized previously contested parts of Iraq and enabled Maliki to garner much-needed political support for his newly established, democratically elected government.

THE ASSAULT INTO BAGHDAD WAS, AS EXPECTED, A BLOODY BATTLE. AUSTIN WAS AWARDED THE SILVER STAR, OUR NATIONS'S THIRD-HIGHEST AWARD FOR VALOR AS A RESULT OF HIS ACTIONS DURING THE INVASION.

As Commander of MNC-I, then–Lieutenant General Austin led positive change in Iraq while effectively expanding partnering efforts with the Iraqi forces. Over the course of 18 months, United States and Coalition Forces severely weakened militias and insurgents throughout Iraq, capitalizing on the gains achieved through the surge in forces. This ultimately relieved pressure on the Iraqi government, thus enabling Maliki the opportunity to build capacity and strengthen key institutions.

In August of 2009, Austin relinquished command of XVIII Airborne Corps, and he assumed the position as Director of the Joint Staff at the Pentagon in Washington, D.C. Then, in September of 2010, he was promoted to the rank of General, becoming the Army's 200th Four-Star General Officer and the sixth African-American in the United States Army to achieve the rank of General. He assumed the position of Commanding General of United States Forces Iraq (USF-I), likewise becoming the first African-American in history to command an entire theater of war. In doing so, he joined a very distinguished group of West Point graduates that includes Generals Grant, Pershing, MacArthur, Eisenhower, Ridgeway, Clark, Westmoreland, Abrams, Schwarzkopf, Petraeus, Odierno, and McChrystal.

During that 15-month deployment, General Austin focused efforts necessarily on the continued development of the Iraqi Security Forces while simultaneously coordinating the transition of missions and the retrograde of people and equipment back from theater after nearly a decade of war. It was a herculean effort, historic in scale and well executed by United States forces in a remarkably short period of time. The overall effort required the transfer of hundreds of bases and infrastructure to the Iraqis and the removal of thousands of troops and millions of pieces of equipment from Iraq. At the same time, United States forces continued to defend against attacks by a hostile enemy determined to hinder progress.

On December 15, 2011, General Austin, together with Defense Secretary Leon E. Panetta and General Martin E. Dempsey, Chairman of the Joint Chiefs of Staff, led a flag casing ceremony at the former Sather Air Base in Baghdad marking the end of Operation New Dawn and thus the end of the United States military mission in Iraq. General Austin's efforts and the efforts of the servicemen and women he led were critical to the success of United States and Coalition forces and the enduring stability, security, and prosperity of Iraq. Together, they set the conditions for a continued strong partnership between the two nations.

On December 18, 2011, General Austin

transmitted the final assessment to Secretary of Defense Panetta, General Dempsey, and General Mattis, Commander of United States Central Command, declaring the completion of the transfer of mission to the government of Iraq or United States Mission-Iraq and the successful reposture of all USF-I personnel and equipment out of Iraq. This message essentially ended Operation New Dawn. In part, it stated, "Through the commitment and sacrifice of all those who have served in Iraq and the thousands who have made the ultimate sacrifice, Iraq is now a sovereign nation, free from the bonds of tyranny. Iraq has the opportunity to emerge as a secure and self-reliant leader in the region. It is now incumbent upon the people of Iraq to take advantage of this opportunity."

In 2003, at the start of the war, General Lloyd J. Austin III was a One-Star General, bravely leading American's soldiers in the invasion of Iraq. Eight years later, as a Four-Star General, he successfully directed the completion of the mission in Iraq and the full withdrawal of United States forces. You might say he was the first one in and the last one out.

General Austin is married to his bride of 31 years, Charlene.

General Austin, VCSA, greeting President Obama during a visit to Fort Bliss, Texas.

Gen. Austin, US Force-Iraq commander, receives a briefing from MG Tony Cucolo, 3rd Infantry Division commander in Iraq.

General Austin and President Obama during an Iraq delegation visit to Arlington National Cemetery.

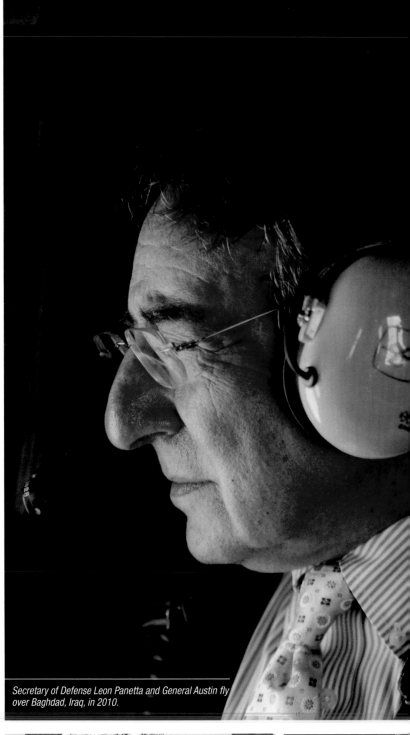
Secretary of Defense Leon Panetta and General Austin fly over Baghdad, Iraq, in 2010.

U.S. Ambassador to Iraq James Jeffrey and General Austin lead the DoS/DoD mission in Iraq.

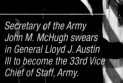
Secretary of the Army John M. McHugh swears in General Lloyd J. Austin III to become the 33rd Vice Chief of Staff, Army.

General Austin and his wife, Charlene attending a holiday reception at the home of Chief of Staff of the Army, General Raymond Odierno.

General Austin and his wife, Charlene, speaking at an Auburn University event, October 2012.

General Austin and his wife, Charlene, attending a White House event along with their good friends Secretary Lute and his spouse, Jane.

OPERATIONAL AND TACTICAL COMMANDERS

The previous chapter highlighted West Point graduates who have led the nation as overall strategic commanders during times of conflict. There are also thousands of West Point graduates deserving recognition who have commanded forces in times of conflict at every level from company command through Army-level command. These are only a few of the graduates who courageously led soldiers in every American conflict since the War of 1812.

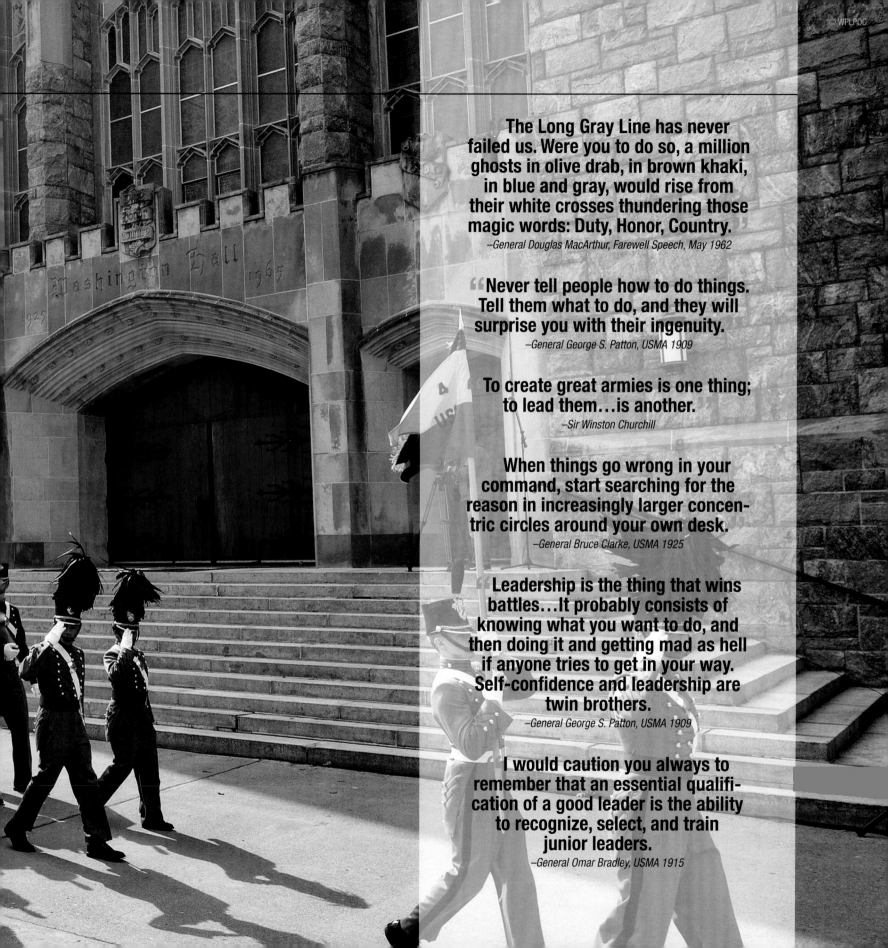

The Long Gray Line has never failed us. Were you to do so, a million ghosts in olive drab, in brown khaki, in blue and gray, would rise from their white crosses thundering those magic words: Duty, Honor, Country.

–General Douglas MacArthur, Farewell Speech, May 1962

"Never tell people how to do things. Tell them what to do, and they will surprise you with their ingenuity.

–General George S. Patton, USMA 1909

To create great armies is one thing; to lead them…is another.

–Sir Winston Churchill

When things go wrong in your command, start searching for the reason in increasingly larger concentric circles around your own desk.

–General Bruce Clarke, USMA 1925

Leadership is the thing that wins battles…It probably consists of knowing what you want to do, and then doing it and getting mad as hell if anyone tries to get in your way. Self-confidence and leadership are twin brothers.

–General George S. Patton, USMA 1909

I would caution you always to remember that an essential qualification of a good leader is the ability to recognize, select, and train junior leaders.

–General Omar Bradley, USMA 1915

In B.H. Liddell Hart's forward to William Tecumseh Sherman's memoirs, he writes that Sherman was the "most original of the many remarkable military leaders who emerged" in the Civil War. Hart goes so far as to call Sherman a genius.[1] While genius is perhaps a stretch of words, there can be no doubt that William Tecumseh Sherman was one of the most extraordinary Generals of the Civil War. It was not genius that made Sherman so extraordinary. In reality, his most extraordinary trait was his simplicity. In truth, the military genius of William T. Sherman lay in his willingness to take extraordinary measures that were by no means unprecedented but to that date and time unmatched in their speed and scope.

Sherman was born in 1820 in Lancaster, Ohio. He went to West Point at 16 and graduated in 1840. Prior to the Civil War, he was stationed at Fort Moultrie, South Carolina, then deployed to California for the War with Mexico in 1846, where he stayed through the Gold Rush and ensuing establishment of San Francisco.[2] During the Gold Rush, Sherman experienced a great deal of difficulty with desertion and theft as gold fever swept everyone. He also profited $1,500 through supplying a store with two other officers at $500 a piece in investment.[3] He turned a fair profit, investing in land lots in Sacramento City, clearing $6,000 in two months of work. It

was no wonder desertion was such a problem for Sherman as he reported that men could command $16 a day for wages during the rush while soldiers regularly got $8 a month with $0.20 for extra duty. Sherman recalled that there really was not much talk of slavery in California from Southern Commanders.[4] Little did he know how big of an issue slavery would become.

In 1850, Sherman was promoted to Captain and married Ellen Ewing, whose parents had raised him after his father's death in 1829.[5] After that, he spent time in Louisiana from 1859 to 1861. It was here that he was first pressed on the issue slavery on account of his brother being perceived and abolitionists by the Governor. He felt slavery was inherited and nobody's fault. He also felt that house slavery was fine as they were well treated but had pause about the second state of slavery, "field-hands was different" depending on the temper of masters. "Were I a citizen of LA, and a member of the Legislature, I would deem it wise to bring the legal condition of the slaves more near the status of human beings under all Christian and civilized governments," he said. He had two major proposals on how to improve the system: First was to forbid the separation of families; second was the repeal of penalties for teaching reading and writing. He believed this actually increased the value of a slave based on

services rendered, which really ignores what field hands needed to be capable of doing. He had witnessed an educated slave in California become educated and sufficient enough to buy his and his family's freedom. Like many others, he underestimated the institutional issue of slavery. He certainly understood that "all their wealth" was tied in slaves so they liked the idea of increasing that wealth.[6]

Sherman recalled that the "election of Lincoln fell upon us like a clap of thunder," He was not much consulted about secession, though his opinion that "secession was treason, was war" he felt was well known.[7] Sherman was very well read and informed on his opinions and proves in his memoirs to be extremely thoughtful and intelligent in his views. In a particularly astute instance, Sherman tried to advise the Governor, in his role as Superintendent of Louisiana State Learning & Military Academy, that the arms of the arsenal at Baton Rouge be secured and removed. The

arms would indeed be seized by Southerners and scattered on January 10, 1861, secession 25th and 26th.[8] Interestingly enough, Sherman himself turned the arms over to the Governor of Louisiana – ironic, considering that Sherman felt that the crisis had been "brought about by politicians, and, as it was laid upon us, they 'might fight it out.'"[9]

With the advent of the Civil War, Sherman saw his first real military action at the First Battle of Bull Run, a disaster for the Union but hardly a victory for the South. Though an honest man, Sherman felt that the "truth is not always palatable and should not always be told."[10] Sherman's report of the First Battle of Bull Run is perhaps one of the most illuminating and honest of any that exists.

Though the North was overwhelmed with mortification and shame, the South really had not much to boast of, for in the three or four hours of fighting their organization was so broken up that they did not and could not

SHERMAN'S MARCH TO THE SEA BECAME HIS DEFINING MOMENT – AN ALL-OR-NOTHING SPRINT TO THE COAST IN WHICH SHERMAN ABANDONED THE PURSUIT OF CONFEDERATE FORCES IN FAVOR OF THE DESTRUCTION OF CONFEDERATE RESOURCES AND VITAL LINES OF COMMUNICATION AND SUPPLY.

General William Tecumseh Sherman, USMA 1840

- **COMMANDER, "SHERMAN'S MARCH TO THE SEA" CIVIL WAR**
- **UNION GENERAL**
- **COMMANDED ATLANTA CAMPAIGN**
- **M-4 WORLD WAR II SHERMAN TANK NAMED IN HIS HONOR**

Sherman and his soldiers with artillery in Atlanta.

Sherman Statue in Washington, D.C.

Photo: NARA

follow our Army when it was known to be in a state of disgraceful and causeless flight. It is easy to criticize a battle after it is over, but all now admit that none others, equally raw in war, could have done better than we did at Bull Run; and the lesson of that battle should not be lost on a people like ours.[11]

The truth, as Sherman saw it, was that the Union Army had "good organization, good men, but no cohesion, no real discipline, no respect for authority, no real knowledge of war." Sherman lost 111 men, killed 205, wounded 293, missing 609 casualties during the battle. Things were not looking much better afterward as one of his Captains tried to leave after his three-month term for New York to return to his law practice and did this in a public manner, leaving General Sherman to respond:

"Captain, this question of your term of service has been submitted to the rightful authority, and the decision has been published in orders. You are a soldier, and must submit to orders till you are properly discharged. If you attempt to leave without orders it will be mutiny, and I will shoot you like a dog! Go back into the fort now, instantly, and don't dare to leave without my consent."[12]

Sherman was just beginning to understand the truth and the terrible hardships that would be necessary to win the war. A disciplinarian to his men he would evolve into a disciplinarian for the South for the sake of his men.

Though he recalled it as a relatively ordered event, the Battle of Shiloh was anything but. Afterward, Sherman nearly fell into despair over his "failures." James McDonough reports things differently than Sherman, who reported the killing of his orderly Halliday as almost routine in his memoirs.[13] McDonough reported that Sherman exclaimed, "My God, we are attacked!" after having earlier been dismissive of reports of Confederate activity against his lines.[14] War was becoming an unbearable burden for Sherman as the losses of men mounted.

Even after the Siege of Vicksburg was complete, Sherman recalls in a letter that shows he understood that the war was far from over. Sherman did indeed have an eye for its outcome and began there to realize that something along the lines of his march from Atlanta would be necessary in order to subdue the South.[15] His time in Louisiana and in South Carolina, combined with the dreadful campaigns in the West and monotonous losses of life, had served to convince Sherman that a reckoning, of not just the Southern Armies, but also the Southern people, would be necessary in order to bring about a reconstruction of the South into the United States.

Sherman's March to the Sea became his defining moment. An all-or-nothing sprint to the coast in which Sherman abandoned the pursuit of Confederate forces in favor of the destruction of Confederate resources and vital lines of communication and supply. Sherman was not unique in the totality of his service, but he was indeed in rare company. Sherman's combat record service stretched from commanding the principle union feint at the Bull Run Bridge during the First Battle of Manassas on the first day of the War in 1861 and was personally responsible for choosing a course of action that significantly contributed to the prosecution of the defeat of the Confederacy four years later in 1865. Whether or not an accurate count of the number of men Sherman had lost to war under his command can be achieved is irrelevant to the likely fact that Sherman new that number. Sherman's march was decried as barbarous by many in the South and celebrated as the dawn of a new form of warfare by many historians. In Sherman's mind, this was an act of mercy that would ultimately save lives. Sherman had resigned himself to the fact that, "War is cruelty. There's no use trying to reform it. The crueler it is, the sooner it will be over." This is actually a paraphrase from a letter to the Mayor of Atlanta. A more contextual look at the letter reveals more of Sherman's feelings:

"You cannot qualify war in harsher terms than I will. War is cruelty, and you cannot refine it;

and those who brought war into our country deserve all the curses and maledictions a people can pour out. I know I had no hand in making this war, and I know I will make more sacrifices to-day than any of you to secure peace. But you cannot have peace and a division of our country. If the United States submits to a division now, it will not stop, but will go on until we reap the fate of Mexico, which is eternal war [...] I want peace, and believe it can only be reached through union and war, and I will ever conduct war with a view to perfect and early success. But, my dear sirs, when peace does come, you may call on me for anything. Then will I share with you the last cracker, and watch with you to shield your homes and families against danger from every quarter."[16]

For Sherman, it became simple. The battering of Armies against each other in the field had failed to achieve any tangible results after four long and hard fought years. Each battle brought more and more death to both Confederate and Union soldiers alike. If, as Sherman believed, this was had been brought upon by politicians, and they had might, as well fight it out. Then finally in this letter and in his operational strategy, Sherman put his theory to test in 1864 with compelling results.

Written by: Major Paul N. Belmont.

Sherman on horseback.

Sherman Statue in Central Park, New York City.

>>> Spotlight

The M4 Sherman tank was named after Major General William Sherman (USMA 1840). Approximately 49,000 Sherman tanks were produced and saw service during World War II. Each tank weighed 30 tons, had a crew of five, 75 mm main gun, and weighed 30 tons.

Thomas Circle in Washington, D.C.

Brigadier General Thomas.

Major General George Henry Thomas, USMA 1840

- NICKNAMED "THE ROCK OF CHICKAMAGUA"
- COMMANDER ARMY OF THE CUMBERLAND
- LED UNION VICTORY AT BATTLE OF NASHVILLE
- THOMAS CIRCLE IN WASHINGTON, D.C., NAMED IN HIS HONOR

In the pantheon of Civil War leaders, George Henry Thomas remains a relative unknown. He never obtained the status of a Grant, Sherman, or even a Sheridan, despite a consistently successful record and distinguished service in several key campaigns. Partly this is because he died shortly after the conflict, while the other Union Commanders went on to write memoirs and have distinguished post-war careers. Part of it also may be because Thomas, a Virginian by birth, elected to fight for the Union when so many of his peers served the Confederacy.

Thomas grew up in a slaveholding family in Southampton County, Virginia. His early years were uneventful, except for the time in 1831, when his family had to flee their plantation briefly to escape Nat Turner's rebellion. His first year at West Point, Thomas roomed with a young William T. Sherman, and though he struggled initially with academics, his superiors recognized his mature bearing by giving him cadet leadership roles starting in his second year. His diligent studies ultimately allowed him to rank high enough in his class to branch into the artillery.[1]

Shortly after graduation, the Army assigned Thomas to Florida, which was in the midst

>>> Spotlight

Thomas Circle is a traffic circle located in Washington, D.C., northwest at the intersection of 14th and M Street. The Equestrian Statue of Major General George H. Thomas was created by John Quincy Adams Ward was erected in 1879.

Thomas Statue on Thomas Circle at K Street and 14th Street, NW, Washington, D.C.

of the Seminole Wars. He served efficiently in a variety of administrative tasks and received a promotion for his role in a successful raid against the Seminoles. His superiors praised his calmness, efficiency, and gallantry. During the Mexican War of 1846 to 1848, Thomas again distinguished himself for his service with Zachary Taylor in the battles of Monterrey and Buena Vista, eventually receiving a Brevet promotion to Major.[2] In addition to receiving valuable combat experience from his time in Florida and Mexico, Thomas also learned about the critical need to coordinate adequate logistics and insure the proper discipline of volunteer soldiers.[3]

In 1860 and 1861, while many of his peers, superiors, and subordinates resigned to join the Confederacy, Thomas maintained his loyalty to his oath, rather than his home state. After Virginia's Governor offered him an important state position, Thomas replied, "That it is not my wish to leave the service of the United States as long as it is honorable for me to remain in it." When asked to explain his decision, Thomas reportedly argued that oath-bound Army officers had no right to resign for purposes of secession, especially those who owed their livelihood and position to a government-provided West Point education. Thomas's sisters never forgave him for his decision, and none of his family would attend his funeral in 1870.[4]

Many factors shaped Thomas's leadership style. He was known for his sense of honor, antipathy to politics, and loyalty (sometimes to a fault) to senior commanders.[5] He also showed an interest in tactical innovations, such as the battlefield telegraph and repeating carbine.[6] His tactical caution and focus on training and adequate logistics led some to accuse him of the "slows," but his devotion to his soldiers meant he was one of the most beloved Union Commanders.[7]

Thomas first made a name for himself in the Civil War in January 1862 at the Battle of Mill Springs in southern Kentucky, where his force successfully routed a Confederate incursion back into Tennessee. Though this was a minor engagement, with only around 4,000 to a side, it was one of the first Union victories since the setback at First Manassas and drew widespread media attention.[8] Thomas served capably in the hard-fought Union victory at Stones River in Tennessee almost a year later, but his next critical role was in the Battle of Chickamauga in September 1863. Early on the second day of the battle, a communication breakdown between Thomas and his superior, William Rosecrans, contributed to the success of a Confederate breakthrough that threatened the entire Union position. While Rosecrans and the rest of the Union Army of the Cumberland retreated in disarray towards Chattanooga, Thomas directed two brigades in a masterful defense against the attacking Confederates, saving the Union force from greater disaster. For his calm, unperturbed leadership in a time of crisis, Thomas became known as "the Rock of Chickamauga."[9]

In October 1863, Thomas replaced Rosecrans in command of the Army of the Cumberland besieged by the Confederates in Chattanooga. In November, Ulysses S. Grant coordinated a counteroffensive, and Thomas's Army captured Missionary Ridge. Aside from its overall contribution to the Union victory in the Battle of Chattanooga, historians point out that this was one of the very few times in the War that a frontal assault against defenders entrenched on a hill was successful.[10]

When Grant assumed overall command of Union forces, Thomas and his 60,000-man Army remained under the command of Thomas's old roommate, Sherman, for the campaign against Atlanta. Despite occasional complaints by his commander that Thomas was "dreadfully slow," the Rock of Chickamauga performed admirably.[11] In the Battle of Kennesaw Mountain in June 1864, Thomas was instrumental in convincing Sherman to end the futile assaults on the Confederates' heavily entrenched positions. The next month, his Army defeated an attempt by the new Confederate Commander in Georgia, John B. Hood, to halt the Union advance at Peachtree Creek. By September, Atlanta had fallen to Sherman's forces.[12]

THOMAS, A VIRGINIAN BY BIRTH, ELECTED TO FIGHT FOR THE UNION WHEN SO MANY OF HIS PEERS SERVED THE CONFEDERACY.

Thomas then assumed command of the 55,000 Union soldiers defending Tennessee while Sherman launched his famous "March to the Sea." As Sherman ravaged across Georgia, Hood launched a campaign into Tennessee. After a battle with one of Thomas's subordinates in the town of Franklin, Hood's Army of the Tennessee closed on Nashville. Thomas's cautious response to Hood's invasion led Grant to consider relieving him, but on December 13, 1864, Thomas launched the Battle of Nashville with what historians call an "almost perfectly coordinated maneuver, reminiscent of Frederick the Great." An intricate series of feints, cannonades, and attacks designed to envelop Hood's forces was slowed by the mud of that cold winter morning, but Thomas inflicted massive casualties on Hood's force before it retreated in disarray.[13] It was his greatest moment as a Field Commander and one of the most dramatic Union victories of the War.

Buford Statue at Gettysburg.

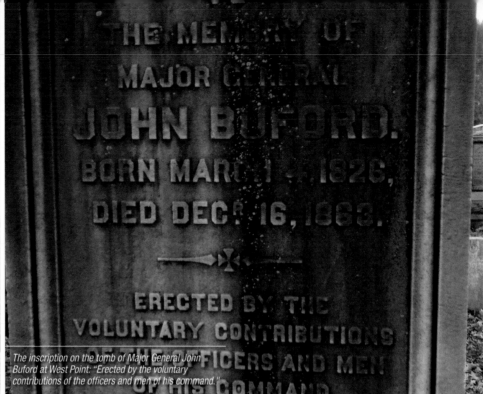

The inscription on the tomb of Major General John Buford at West Point: "Erected by the voluntary contributions of the officers and men of his command."

Buford Grave at West Point Ceme

Major General John Buford, USMA 1848

- **HERO OF THE BATTLE OF GETTYSBURG**
- **BUFORD STATUE AT GETTYSBURG ERECTED IN HIS HONOR**
- **DIED OF TYPHOID FEVER, DECEMBER 16, 1863**
- **BURIED AT WEST POINT CEMETERY**

Of the many battles fought during the American Civil War, Gettysburg more than any other would leave an indelible mark on the collective conscious of the American people. Of the many pivotal aspects of this battle, John Buford's decision to hold the high ground in the face of a superior Confederate force ranks among the most important. In 1875, in one of the first widely published accounts of the Battle of Gettysburg, the Comte de Paris wrote:

"[General Buford] boldly resolved to risk everything in order to allow... [Reynolds] time to reach Gettysburg in advance of the Confederate Army. This first inspiration of a Cavalry Officer and true soldier decided in every respect the fate of the campaign."

On the morning of the 1st of July 1863, Brigadier General John Buford, Jr., sat atop his horse, Grey Eagle, as he led his soldiers into the little known town of Gettysburg. Buford's 1st Division of the Cavalry Corps was the first element of the Union's Army of the Potomac to arrive on the scene of what would be the perhaps the most significant battle of the American Civil War. Buford was a career Cavalry Officer; indeed, Cavalry was in his blood as his grandfather, Simeon Buford, had served as a Cavalryman in the American Revolution under the command of Henry "Light-Horse Harry" Lee (the father of Robert E. Lee). On this early July day, John Buford was screening the advance of the Union Army as it moved through southern Pennsylvania.

Buford had encountered elements of Pettigrew's Brigade the day prior and information obtained from captured Confederate soldiers confirmed that he was facing a major portion of the Confederate Army. Nonetheless, when Buford moved in to the town of Gettysburg, he understood almost instinctively that he must retain control of this terrain. The value of this small town, situated at the convergence of almost a dozen different roads, and the high ground surrounding it was immediately obvious to him. Buford, with only two Brigades of Cavalry and a single artillery battery at his disposal, also knew that the task of holding this ground would not be an easy one. As he told one of his Brigade Commanders, "the enemy will attack us in the morning...and we shall have to fight like devils to maintain ourselves until the arrival of the Infantry."

At 7:30 on the morning of July 1st, forward elements of Buford's division made contact with the Confederate force now advancing toward Gettysburg. Buford immediately began to develop the situation, ordering a force from Gamble's brigade to reinforce the forward elements along McPherson's Ridge on the Chambersburg pike. This initial engagement by Buford's Cavalry forced the advancing Confederate column to transition from a travel formation into line formation; this process itself would take several minutes to accomplish and would also slow all subsequent movement of the Confederate Infantry. Fighting then withdrawing from one ridge to the next, Buford's Cavalry troopers conducted a series of successful delaying actions against the much larger Confederate force. Rather than advancing swiftly into the town of Gettysburg, Lee now found himself with 50,000 troops bottled up on the Chambersburg pike. The stubborn defense of Buford and his Cavalry Division ultimately prevented the Confederate column from entering the town of Gettysburg before the first elements of the Union 1st Corps arrived on the battlefield.

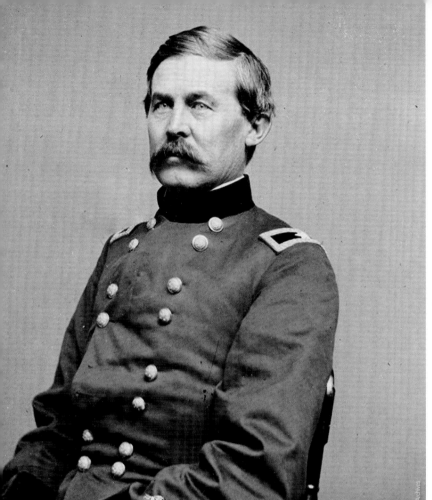

>>> Spotlight

Gettysburg National Park is located 40 miles southwest of Harrisburg, Pennsylvania, and is open to the public. The Battle of Gettysburg was fought from July 1 to 3, 1863, and was one of the bloodiest battles of the Civil War with 51,000 casualties and a Union victory. It is one of the most frequently visited battlefields and the best restored parks in the United States. Gettysburg is often considered the turning point in the war and was the site of President Lincoln's Gettysburg Address on November 19, 1863, which is considered one of the greatest speeches in American history. Major General Buford is crediting with bravely securing the key ground at the outset of the battle that helped the Union win the Battle of Gettysburg and eventually restored the United States of America as we know it today.

Battle Monument at West Point, Gettysburg Cannon.

Brigadier General Buford and his staff.

Over the ensuing days of battle, the Confederate forces attempted to turn the northern and southern flanks of the Union position. In every case, the terrain that

TODAY, A MONUMENT TO GENERAL BUFORD STANDS ON MCPHERSON'S RIDGE, THE SITE WHERE HIS DISMOUNTED CAVALRY TROOPERS BLUNTED THE INITIAL ADVANCE OF MULTIPLE CORPS OF CONFEDERATE INFANTRY.

Buford had retained for the Union provided a tactical advantage to the Union force and the Confederate assaults were repulsed or achieved limited results. On the third day of the battle, General Lee concentrated his forces for an attack on the center of the Union line on Cemetery Ridge. At 3 p.m., the Confederate

Infantry of Longstreet's Corps stepped out of the trees along Seminary Ridge and began their advance on the Union II Corps. This was to be final Confederate offensive of the campaign. This final attack would become known as "Pickett's Charge" for the soldiers from Major General George Pickett's Division who – briefly – succeeded in piercing the Union defensive line on Cemetery Ridge. This last assault of the Gettysburg campaign has since come to be known as the "high water mark of the Confederacy."

By July 4, 1863, the Confederate Army began their withdrawal from the battlefield at Gettysburg. This would be the last time a major element of the Confederate Army

would venture into the Union. General Robert E. Lee had led his forces north in hopes of taking pressure off of his native Virginia while threatening the Union capitol in Washington and possibly forcing an early end to the conflict. This sojourn into Pennsylvania did not produce the results Lee had sought; indeed, this campaign would come to be seen as the beginning of the demise of Lee's Army of Northern Virginia.

Following Gettysburg, General Buford continued to lead the 1st Division until November, when he was stricken with typhoid fever during the Rappahannock campaign; sadly, this would claim his life before the end of the year. Before Buford's death, President Lincoln wrote: "I am informed that General Buford will not survive the day. It suggests itself to me that he be made Major General for distinguished and meritorious service at the Battle

of Gettysburg." Buford died on December 16th, moments after learning of his promotion to Major General. Today, a monument to General Buford stands on McPherson's Ridge, the site where his dismounted Cavalry troopers blunted the initial advance of multiple corps of Confederate Infantry. The judgment of this savvy Cavalry Commander set the stage for what many consider the most important battle of the war. By securing the key terrain on the battlefield for the Union Army of the Potomac, John Buford made what is arguably the single-most important contribution of any commander in securing the Union victory in this campaign. Following his death, General Buford's body was laid to rest in the cemetery at West Point.

Written by: Lieutenant Colonel Craig Morrow, PhD, USMA 1991.

Sheridan Square in Washington, D.C.

General Philip Henry Sheridan, USMA 1853

- GENERAL IN CHIEF, U.S. ARMY
- COMMANDER, DEPARTMENT OF THE MISSOURI DURING THE INDIAN WARS
- RECONSTRUCTION MILITARY GOVERNOR, TEXAS, AND LOUISIANA
- COMMANDER, ARMY OF THE SHENANDOAH
- COMMANDER, CAVALRY CORP, ARMY OF THE POTOMAC
- NINTH PRESIDENT, NATIONAL RIFLE ASSOCIATION (NRA)

Philip Henry Sheridan is perhaps one of the most compelling men ever to bear the title General. So rarely is a soldier remembered as such a hero and such a villain. According to his personal memoirs, Philip Henry Sheridan was born in Albany on March 6, 1831, to John and Mary. His parents had moved to Albany from County Cavan, Ireland, the previous year to "try their fortunes in the new world."[1] Sheridan recalls growing up in a rather normal life of school and home until the age of 14 when, other than "self study," he left school and began working in a country store until he received his appointment to West Point in 1848. There would have been nothing exceptional about this episode if not for the fact that it was one of his customers, Congressman Thomas Ritchey, being responsible for granting young Philip his appointment.[2] According to Roy

Morris's biography, Sheridan had lied about his age to get into the Academy.[3]

Sheridan's time at the Academy was not an exceptional one. He was forced to leave the Academy on account of poor grades in the fall of 1851, leaving behind notable classmates, the later Generals Slocum, Stanley, Woods, Kautz, and Crook.[4] He would eventually return to West Point in 1852 and subsequently finish his cadet career in June of 1853, along with several notable Generals of the Grand Army of the Republic: Generals James B. McPherson, John M. Schofield, Joshua W. Sill among them, and a notable Confederate Commander, General John B. Hood.[5] In all, it was quite a wealth of talent in which Sheridan would find himself ascending with and against during his Army career despite a humble ranking of 32nd of 52 cadets in the Class of 1853. The

Superintendent of West Point at his graduation was none other than Robert E. Lee.

As a young officer, Sheridan had a well-rounded and -traveled career serving with the 1st United States Infantry Regiment in Texas, and the 4th Infantry in California and in the Pacific Northwest. It was during his travels to Texas that Sheridan would first acquaint himself with the Ohio and Mississippi Rivers along whose banks and valleys he would later rise to prominence during the Civil War.[6] He conducted standard survey missions for the United States Army in 1855 but saw his first action during the Yakima and Rogue River Wars in 1857.[7] Morris's biography adds to Sheridan's own account of his life during this time with an Indian woman named Sidnayoh (aka Frances).

The Civil War was and always will be the

most memorable and distinguished period of Philip Sheridan's career. Despite some successes and adventures, there was little room for advancement in the Army in the Pacific northwest and his service there would not have stacked up well against the "heroes" of the Mexican War who preceded him out of the Academy. Sheridan would not be promoted to First Lieutenant until March of 1861, just months before the outbreak of hostilities during the Civil War and would subsequently receive a second promotion to Captain after Fort Sumter that May.[8] His first service was under General Henry W. Halleck in the Mississippi Valley, where he worked his way up from a Commissary Officer to Quartermaster General.[9] Sheridan recalls turning his success at audits needed in the wake of General John C. Fremont's Command into a case he himself made to

>>> Spotlight

On the eve of the Battle of Stones River, West Point friends and classmates Brigadier General Sheridan and Brigadier General Sill met at a strategy meeting to prepare for the bloodiest battle of the Civil War. Sill accidentally left wearing Sheridan's frock instead of his own. The next day during the battle, Joshua Sill was killed wearing Sheridan's frock. The frock, originally owned by Sill, was kept in Sheridan's memorabilia where it remained until the late 1940s when Major Richard Douglas, a Sill descendant, was given the coat by one of Sheridan's nieces (who also gave Douglas one of Sheridan's Major General's frock coats). Douglas then returned to Chillicothe with both coats and donated them to the Ross County Historical Society where they remain today. In 1869, Sheridan would name an outpost in the Oklahoma hills after his friend, called Fort Sill. Fort Sill grew from a remote outpost in Indian country into the home of the artillery. His name is now immortalized in Army history through the fort that one classmate named in honor of another.

Photo: Ross County Historical Society

Sheridan Grave in front of Arlington House, Robert E. Lee's former home, now Arlington National Cemetery.

ful Cavalry raids on Confederate supplies Sheridan found himself dogging General John Gordon's Brigade near Yellow Tavern. It was during this pursuit that Sheridan would first succeed at the mythic. Thanks in large part to a desperate charge by George Custer, Sheridan's forces succeeded in capturing a number of prisoners; however, it was the casualties who would begin to render him both famous and infamous all at once. For in the aftermath of May 11, 1864, against Gordon's Brigade, Sheridan's Cavalry found itself the slayers of two of the Confederacies brightest and most invincible stars as John B. Gordon was left defeated and wounded and J.E.B. Stuart fell, mortally wounded.[15]

It would be not long before Sheridan would permanently cement his reputation as both hero and butcher when he would take command of Union Forces at Washington, D.C., and begin his dogged pursuit of General Jubal Early from D.C. back to and up the Shenandoah Valley after assuming Command from General David Hunter. It was here in the valley that Sheridan would be remembered as a butcher by the South and a savior by the North. Sheridan himself might disagree on both counts. David Hunter's campaign in the Shenandoah is perhaps wrongly remembered by history as a failure which was salvaged by Philip Sheridan's brilliant and dogged pursuit of Jubal Early's forces up the Shenandoah. Interestingly, Sheridan himself remembers and records Hunter's march to Lynchburg as a success.[16] Unfortunately for David Hunter, he was unable to exploit his success at Lynchburg and out of supplies and ammunition was forced to withdraw through West Virginia. This opened the door for Jubal Early to march on Washington, D.C., which resulted in Sheridan's summoning to repel him. It is true that David Hunter failed to sustain his momentum in the Shenandoah and break out of Lynchburg to come east. It is often forgotten that by the time Hunter had reached Lynchburg he had far exceeded the orders of U.S. Grant to divert forces from Richmond to the west and, "if even for a day or two," occupy those forces so that Grant might exploit their absence.

It is arguable that it was not Hunter who failed at Lynchburg, but Sheridan who failed to meet him there. Lost in the great exploits of Philip Sheridan is one of his biggest failures. Hunter was forced to withdraw from Lynchburg due to the Confederates receiving reinforcements via rail throughout the night and creating an untenable situation for Hunter. Critics have suggested that

Hunter might have exploited his initiative better but regardless. Hunter's eventual orders had been to link up with Sheridan's Calvary in Charlottesville; however, Sheridan had been repulsed several days prior to the battle of Lynchburg, fought from June 17 to 18, 1864, and at the Battle of Trevilian Station, fought from June 11 to 12, 1864. Sheridan makes an excuse for giving up the fight at Trevilian Station that Hunter, in moving on Lynchburg from Lexington and not Charlottesville, was moving "away from me" and used this to break off of his engagement. A simple understanding of Shenandoah Valley geography might argue that the quickest way to Charlottesville from Lexington could be Lynchburg. If Sheridan had secured the rail lines at Trevilian, he could have easily reached Hunter's forces by rail or on horse. In reality, it was Sheridan who gave up on Hunter, not Hunter who gave up on Sheridan. Regardless, history would record Sheridan as the butcher of the Valley of Virginia and Hunter a failure. It is interesting that Sheridan, at the end of his life in writing his memoir, published in the year of his death at 57 years old in 1888, would separate the events of days or a week by chapters and hundreds of pages making himself more hero of the Shenandoah and less the goat. It seems that history does indeed go to the last victor.

In the aftermath of the war, Sheridan certainly benefited from his wartime success. He served as both military Governor of Texas and Louisiana during Reconstruction, then as Commander of the Department of the Missouri to help "pacify" the Great Plains during America's continued westward expansion. Sheridan also experienced a myriad of other diverse assignments and positions, such as an observer in the Franco-Prussian War in 1870, the coordinator for military relief efforts following the Great Chicago Fire, and the ninth President of the National Rifle Association. He reached the pinnacle of success when he succeeded Sherman as the Commanding General, United States Army in 1883. Sheridan died in 1888 and was buried at Arlington National Cemetery. Ironically, he rests directly in front of Arlington House, the former home of his Superintendent and later enemy Commander – Robert E. Lee. Sheridan has been memorialized in many ways to include through the naming of Fort Sheridan, Illinois, and the M551 Sheridan tank.

Written by: Major Paul N. Belmont.

Halleck for the promotion.[10] It was working in Halleck's headquarters where Sheridan would meet his greatest benefactor, William Tecumseh Sherman, who offered Sheridan an Infantry regiment during the siege of Corinth. This fell through, but thanks to some "political help," Sheridan would instead receive a Calvary Command.[11]

Calvary would be where Sheridan would earn his stripes in the shape of stars. He commanded a small Brigade, which included his regiment at the

IT WAS HERE IN THE VALLEY THAT SHERIDAN WOULD BE REMEMBERED AS A BUTCHER BY THE SOUTH AND A SAVIOR BY THE NORTH.

Battle of Booneville, where he held back a large Confederate Cavalry attack meant to envelop the Union Flank. This impressed General William S. Rosecrans enough to recommend Sheridan for promotion to Brigadier General.[12]

Sheridan continued to serve with distinction through Louisville, Bowling Green, Murfreesboro, and eventually Stone's River culminating in his promotion to Major General in January of 1863.[13] His successes as part of the well-known exploits of U.S. Grant's command would culminate with his promotion to Commander of the Calvary Corps of the Army of the Potomac during the Overland Campaign in Virginia under General George G. Meade.[14]

His record in Virginia set in stone the polarizing memory of him as both hero and villain. In addition to several success-

obert Edward Lee was born on January 19, 1807, in Stratford, Virginia. He was the fourth of five children of "Light Horse" Harry and Ann Lee. His father, an American Revolutionary War hero of some ignominy and one-time Virginia Governor, undoubtedly left an indelible mark on young Lee that would last long past the few early years that Harry acted as a father.[1] Harry, in fact, was in many ways the opposite of his youngest son. A vehement Federalist, argumentative and unscrupulous, continually in debt and twice in jail, the father was forced into self-imposed exile in Barbados when Lee was only 6 years old. After five years, Harry attempted to return to the family he had left in Virginia but died of illness in Georgia while making the journey.[2] Lee, who apparently inherited his mother's humility and temperament, was, however, destined to share his father's occupation. In 1825, he entered West Point with the personal endorsement of then-Senator and notorious states' rights advocate John C. Calhoun.[3]

Lee was, by all accounts, an excellent scholar and cadet, excelling in math and engineering, and graduating second of 46 in the Class in 1829 at the height of the Thayer superintendency. His most notable classmate was Joseph E. Johnston – future fellow Confederate General – but Lee shared his time at the Academy with numerous other prominent future Civil War personalities, both Union and Confederate, including Albert S. Johnston, Samuel P. Heintzelman, Jefferson Davis, Leonidas Polk, and John B. Magruder. Upon graduation, Lee was commissioned into the prestigious United States Army Corps of Engineers and began his Army career with a post in Savannah, Georgia. In 1831, he married Mary Custis, wealthy heiress of Arlington, Virginia, the only surviving child of President George Washington's adopted son.

Lee spent the first decade and a half of his professional career leading increasingly visible engineering projects in Savannah,

PRESIDENT DWIGHT D. EISENHOWER COMMENTED THAT "TAKEN ALL TOGETHER, [LEE] WAS NOBLE AS A LEADER AND AS A MAN, AND UNSULLIED AS I READ THE PAGES OF OUR HISTORY."

Fort Monroe, St. Louis, and New York Harbor. During this last assignment, his involvement at West Point rematerialized, and there and in Washington, he came to know the Commanding General of the Army, Major General Winfield Scott.[4] Soon after, Lee had his first taste of battle serving under Scott in Mexico, where he distinguished himself through valor at Vera Cruz and Chapultepec. During this time, he was on staff as both

Engineer and Inspector General, and worked with Joe Johnston, George McClellan, P.G.T. Beauregard, and George Meade.[5]

After brief engineering assignments in Florida and Maryland, on September 1, 1850, Lee began duty at West Point as the Academy's Superintendent. While in that position, he instituted stricter academic and disciplinary policies in an effort to improve the quality of the cadets' preparation for service to the nation. He also dedicated himself to the study of Napoleon and other Great Captains in the extensive Academy library.[6] The new Superintendent took his charge of the cadets very personally, so much so that Jefferson Davis, then United States Secretary of War, remarked upon the many gray hairs Lee was gaining from his excessive "sympathy with young people."[7] Lee's first command showed

General Robert E. Lee, C.S.A., USMA 1829
- **GENERAL IN CHIEF, CONFEDERATE ARMY**
- **WASHINGTON & LEE UNIVERSITY NAMED IN HIS HONOR**
- **SUPERINTENDENT, WEST POINT**
- **LEE BARRACKS AT WEST POINT NAMED IN HIS HONOR**

Courtesy CSA

Robert E. Lee Monument on Monument Avenue, Richmond, Virginia.

Robert E. Lee Equestrian Statue at Antietam Battlefield.

him to be a caring and charismatic leader.

In 1856, Lee moved back to St. Louis to begin duties as second-in-command of the 2nd Cavalry Regiment under Albert Sydney Johnston. There, his subordinates included George H. Thomas, E. Kirby Smith, and John Bell Hood.[8] On October 18, 1859, Lee commanded a detachment of Marines in the apprehension of John Brown when the abolitionist seized the United States armory at Harpers Ferry. His aide for the action was the young J.E.B. Stuart.

On April 18, 1861, Lee, then a Colonel, was offered the rank of Major General and command of the Union Army. He declined. The next day, Virginia seceded, and on the following, Lee resigned from the United States Army, though he had no desire to fight against the Army and nation he had served so honorably for more than 30 years.[9] On April 21st, Lee accepted the rank of Major

General and command of "the military and naval forces of Virginia."[10] His command lasted only six weeks, after which Virginia joined the Confederate States of America, which absorbed the state's Army. Lee, now a Confederate General, became military advisor to the Confederacy's President, longtime friend Jefferson Davis.[11] One year later, when Joe Johnston fell at the Battle of Seven Pines, Lee took command of the men he then called the Army of Northern Virginia.

Over the course of the next year, Lee defeated the Union Army of the Potomac four times under four opposing commanders. Lee foiled his old compatriot, McClellan, in the Peninsula Campaign; he overwhelmed Pope at Second Manassas;[12] he definitively repelled Burnside at Fredericksburg; and, he decisively outmaneuvered Hooker at Chancellorsville, the battle that would come to be known as "Lee's Austerlitz." During this time, Lee acted in accordance with his

firm belief that the only way to defeat the Union Army was to force it to attack him on ground that favored the defender. He was, however, either unable or unwilling to adhere to this strategy at the Battle of Gettysburg, a defeat from which the Confederacy would never recover. For his victory over Lee, Union General and friend George Meade would keep his command of the previously winless Army of the Potomac for the rest of the war.

Lee spent the two remaining years of the Civil War defending Richmond with an ever-weakening Army, against relentless attacks from increasingly strengthened Union advances personally directed by U.S. Grant. When Lee surrendered to Grant at Appomattox Courthouse on April 9, 1865, the Confederacy did not survive many days longer. Lee's name had become synonymous with chivalry, particularly in the South, and he used his notoriety to encourage his fellow Southerners to rejoin the United States

as loyal citizens.[13] Lee, however, was not finally granted United States citizenship until President Ford issued an executive order in 1975.[14] During his last years, he avoided political life and served enthusiastically as President of Washington College. He died on October 12, 1870.

Lee, one of the most capable Generals the United States Army has ever had to face in battle, is remembered most for his courage, humility, and personal honor. He has been immortalized on the granite of Stone Mountain, the stained glass, buildings, and roads at his beloved West Point, and in countless memorials, films, and histories. Son of a Founding Father, his legacy is the personification of the growing pains of nineteenth-century America.

Written by: Major Christian G. Teutsch, USMA 1997

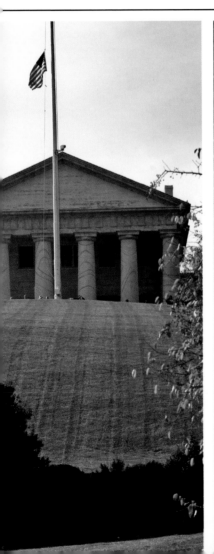

Lee on his back porch in Richmond, Virginia, 1865, after the Civil War.

Robert E. Lee after Appomattox, April 1865, on his back porch with his son, Major General Washington Custis Lee, and to the right is Colonel Walter Tayler (Matthew Brady photo).

General John Bell Hood, C.S.A., USMA 1853

- FORT HOOD, TEXAS, THE LARGEST ARMORED POST IN THE U.S. ARMY, NAMED IN HIS HONOR
- CONFEDERATE CORPS COMMANDER, DIVISION COMMANDER, AND BRIGADE COMMANDER
- WOUNDED BY AN INDIAN ARROW, 1857; SHOT IN ARM AT GETTYSBURG; LOST LEG AT CHICKAMAUGA
- AUTHORED MEMOIRS ENTITLED *ADVANCE AND RETREAT*

Courtesy: CSA

Photo: NARA

John Bell Hood, the youngest son of a physician, was born on June 29, 183,1 in Owingsville, Kentucky. He was raised mainly by his mother as his father was often absent teaching and writing books about experimental medicine. Perhaps inspired by stories about family members in the Revolutionary War, he expressed an interest in the military; following nomination by his uncle, he enrolled at West Point on July 1, 1849. His classmates were future fellow Civil War Generals and opponents John Schofield, Philip Sheridan, and James McPherson. During his first class year, he made an auspicious first acquaintance with Lieutenant Colonel Robert E. Lee, the new Superintendent and later a big supporter of Hood, who found Cadet Lieutenant Hood guilty of being absent from quarters and stripped him of his rank. Not the best student – he finished last in the graduating members of his class in ethics – he accumulated a whopping 196 demerits in his first class year, settling in at number 44 out of 52 cadets.

Hood graduated on July 1, 1853, as a Brevet Second Lieutenant of Infantry. His first posting was at Fort Columbus, New York, but after one year, he moved west where he was assigned to various scouting and escort parties in California and Texas. As of 1855, he was a member of the new 2nd Cavalry Regiment commanded by Colonel Albert Sidney Johnston and whose second-in-command was Lee. While leading a 25-man patrol near Devil's Run in July 1857, he sustained an arrow wound to the left hand during a skirmish with Comanche and Lipan Indians. For the remainder of his time in the United States Army, Hood stayed in Texas, taking a leave of absence (and declining appointment as Chief of Cavalry at USMA) before resigning from service in April 1861 to join the Confederate Army.

Because Kentucky stayed in the Union, Hood entered Confederate service as a First Lieutenant representing Texas, the state with which he would become forever associated during the Civil War. He first served as a Cavalry Commander for Colonel John B. Magruder on the Virginia Peninsula and rapidly rose in rank to Colonel by late 1861. In the process, he organized the 4th Texas Infantry Regiment, and by spring of 1862, took command of the Texas Brigade in General Joseph Johnston's Army in northern Virginia. Hood led his Brigade through the Battles of Eltham's Landing, Seven Pines, and the Seven Days, earning a reputation for aggressiveness and tactical prowess. He moved up to division command in Lieutenant General James Longstreet's corps in time for the Second Battle of Bull Run. Although Hood was placed under arrest for a dispute with another officer, Lee kept him in command during the Maryland Campaign of September 1862, when he reinforced Confederate units at South Mountain and counterattacked elements of the Union I Corps at the Battle of Antietam, suffering high casualties.

Promoted to Major General after Antietam, Hood led his division from Fredericksburg through Gettysburg, where during his attack against the Union left in the vicinity of Little Round Top on July 2, 1863, he was shot in the left arm. He stayed with Longstreet's command and transferred to the western theater, where in September 1863, he led a corps at the Battle of Chickamauga, losing his right leg to a gunshot wound. Hood was promoted to Lieutenant General and remained with the Army of Tennessee, eventually attaining the temporary rank of General and taking over the Army from Johnston during the Atlanta Campaign in the summer of 1864. Placed in command because of his fighting reputation, Hood proceeded to repeatedly attack General William T. Sherman's Union Army, which included subordinates McPherson and Schofield. In an attempt to annihilate separate Federal corps in sequentially planned attacks, he lost many men and was forced to evacuate Atlanta. He tried to lure Sherman after him into Tennessee by threatening the Federal supply lines, but his opponent instead turned toward the Atlantic and detailed Schofield to deal with Hood. Hood marched on Franklin and Nashville in November and December to destroy Schofield's corps and besiege General George Thomas's Army, but instead lost more manpower in repeated attacks against his old colleagues, forcing the retreat of what remained of his Army toward Mississippi. He requested removal from command in January 1865, demoralized by his inability to see his vision through and hurt by accusations that he had squandered the Confederacy's main western Army.

> HOOD ATTAINED THE TEMPORARY RANK OF GENERAL AND TOOK OVER THE ARMY FROM JOHNSTON DURING THE ATLANTA CAMPAIGN IN THE SUMMER OF 1864.

En route to his next assignment, he was arrested and paroled by Union forces near Natchez, Mississippi, in May 1865.

Still a young man at the end of the Civil War, Hood started a second career in cotton brokerage and insurance and settled in New Orleans. Having suffered through a failed romance with a southern belle during the war, he finally found happiness with a local woman; they married in 1868 and had 11 children, including three sets of twins. Although he prospered in his family and financial life, he still harbored resentment toward Johnston, who had retaken command of the Army of Tennessee in 1865. A good portion of Hood's memoirs, *Advance and Retreat*, consists of verbal attacks against Johnston and a defense of his own performance during the Atlanta Campaign. Surviving the yellow fever epidemic of 1878 in New Orleans, Hood's business failed because of the decreased activity in the city. Tragically, his wife and oldest daughter caught a surviving strain of the sickness the following year, and he followed them in death on August 30, 1879, at only 48 years of age. A county in Texas is named after him, as is "The Great Place," Fort Hood, the former World War II tank destroyer training center. Fittingly for the former Cavalryman, Fort Hood remains the largest armored post in the United States Army. Hood enjoyed one of the most meteoric rises in any wartime Army, excelling at tactical command and inspiring extreme loyalty from his men, but he could not make a successful transition to corps and higher command, failing to fully grasp the strategic implications of his actions in the Civil War's western theater.

Written by: Major Brit K. Erslev, PhD.

Most Americans, even those who are not familiar with the Civil War, can usually name two events from that war: the first is the Battle of Gettysburg; the second is Pickett's Charge. While many of these people may know little or nothing about the ill-fated charge, or even make the connection that Pickett's Charge took place during the Battle of Gettysburg, the charge itself has etched itself in the collective minds of America. Consequently, George Pickett, whose military career spanned nearly 20 years (both in the United States Army and Confederate States Army), will forever be remembered for the events that took place on a single day in July 1863.

George Pickett was born into a well-respected family in Richmond, Virginia. After studying law at a very early age, Pickett attended West Point and graduated in 1846. Although he was a very likeable young man, he was a poor student and graduated last in his class of 59 cadets. However, after graduating from West Point, Pickett served as an Officer in the Mexican-American War (1846–48), where he returned as a hero after raising the American flag over a captured castle during the Battle of Chapultepec.

When his home state of Virginia seceded from the Union, George Pickett resigned his commission to join the Confederate Army. Within two years, he was promoted to Brigadier General and given command of a Brigade, where he served with distinction during the 1862 Peninsula Campaign at the Battles of Williamsburg and Seven Pines fighting against his more academically successful classmate and Commander of the Union Army of the Potomac, George B. McClellan, who graduated second in their class. During the Battle of Seven Pines, Pickett was severely wounded and was not able to rejoin his unit for four months.

During the Battle of Gettysburg (July 1–3, 1863), Pickett, who was now a Division Commander in General James Longstreet's corps, and his unit arrived late, missing the first two days of battle. On the third day, Confederate General Robert E. Lee decided to mount an attack in the center of the Union line with Longstreet's corps and chose Pickett's fresh division to lead the attack. Lee believed that the Union center would be the weakest in its defensive position and would break under a determined assault. Following a massive artillery bombardment – arguably the largest bombardment of the war – that was designed to weaken the center of the Union line on Cemetery Ridge, Pickett's division advanced toward Union position. Unfortunately for Pickett and his division, the artillery bombardment was ineffective as most the rounds either detonated early or shot over their intended targets. As a result, the Union defenses and artillery remained virtually untouched and able to engage Pickett's division as it crossed over a mile of open ground. The attack ended in a complete disaster. More than 50 percent of Pickett's men, including all of his Brigade Commanders, were killed, wounded, or captured. Pickett assumed the historical blame for the failure of Pickett's Charge, and he would remain bitter about the loss, and toward General Lee in particular, until his death. While much of history has assigned that blame to Pickett, the fateful attack on July 3, 1863, can more accurately be characterized as "Longstreet's Assault" with Lee and Longstreet bearing as much, if not more responsibility for its failure than Pickett.

After Gettysburg, Pickett was given a command in North Carolina. When Pickett failed to capture New Bern, North Carolina, he ordered the hanging of 22 prisoners found to be former Confederate soldiers who changed their allegiances. This action resulted in an investigation of war crimes against Pickett at the conclusion of the war.

Pickett returned to Virginia and experienced his final major engagement during the war that ended in his defeat at Five Forks in April 1865. This defeat prompted Lee to abandon his defenses at Petersburg and contributed to Lee's decision to surrender at Appomattox Court House only a few days later.

After the surrender, Pickett and his family fled to Canada to avoid prosecution of his alleged war crimes. However, after receiving a letter of support from Union Army Commander General Ulysses S. Grant, Pickett returned to Virginia, received a pardon, and spent his remaining years as a farmer and insurance agent until he died of scarlet fever in July 1875. Fort Pickett, a Virginia National Guard training base in Blackstone, Virginia, is named in his honor.

> **GEORGE PICKETT, WHOSE MILITARY CAREER SPANNED NEARLY 20 YEARS (BOTH IN THE UNITED STATES ARMY AND CONFEDERATE STATES ARMY), WILL FOREVER BE REMEMBERED FOR THE EVENTS THAT TOOK PLACE ON A SINGLE DAY IN JULY 1863.**

Major General George Pickett, C.S.A., USMA 1846

- FORT PICKETT IN BLACKSTONE, VIRGINIA, NAMED IN HIS HONOR
- COMMANDED THE UNSUCCESSFUL ASSAULT AGAINST UNION FORCES AT GETTYSBURG
- CONFEDERATE BRIGADE AND DIVISION COMMANDER IN THE CIVIL WAR
- FOUGHT IN THE MEXICAN WAR, 1846–48
- BURIED IN HOLLYWOOD CEMETERY, RICHMOND, VIRGINIA

Courtesy: CSA

Photo: NARA

Pickett Tombstone, Hollywood Cemetery, Richmond, Virginia.

2013/Greg E. Mathieson Sr./MAI

Photo: NARA

General Braxton Bragg, C.S.A., USMA 1837

- COMMANDER, THE CONFEDERATE ARMY OF TENNESSEE
- MILITARY ADVISER TO THE CONFEDERATE PRESIDENT JEFFERSON DAVIS
- FORT BRAGG, NORTH CAROLINA, DEDICATED IN HONOR OF MAJOR GENERAL BRAGG, C.C.S.A.
- GRADUATED WEST POINT AT THE AGE OF 20

Photo: NARA

Fort Bragg Home Of The Airborne And Special Operations Forces

Photo: AP

Braxton Bragg, a native of North Carolina, entered West Point at the age of 16. Graduating fifth out of a class of 50 in 1837, Bragg was commissioned into the artillery. Over the course of his 19 years of service prior to the Civil War, Bragg was Brevetted to the rank of Lieutenant Colonel, though he never actually exceeded the rank of Captain while in the United States Regular Army.

In addition to his service in the Second Seminole War, Bragg's most notable actions came during his service in the Mexican-American War, particularly during the Battle of Buena Vista. In February 1847, Colonel (and future Confederate President) Jefferson Davis's (USMA 1828) troops refused to retreat while facing a Mexican advance. Bragg's artillery battery provided vital support to Davis, which allowed his men to reorganize. The events of the battle led to mutual admiration between Davis and Bragg, an admiration that would provide him command opportunities for the Confederacy during the Civil War. After a series of posts in the Indian Territory of present-day Oklahoma, he resigned from the United States Army in 1856 and moved to Louisiana to become a sugar plantation owner.

At the outbreak of the Civil War, Bragg was a Colonel in the Louisiana Militia. The Governor of Louisiana appointed him to the state military board charged with building an Army to support the Confederacy. Despite the fact that he opposed secession, Bragg took the position. He became a Corps Commander and received praise following the Battle of Shiloh in April 1862. Davis promoted him to full General of the Confederacy and named him Commander the Army of Mississippi (later known as the Army of Tennessee). After the Army of Mississippi was forced to evacuate Chattanooga, Tennessee, Bragg counterattacked and defeated the Union Army of the Cumberland at the Battle of Chickamauga in September 1863 — the Union's worst defeat in the Civil War's Western Theater, the only major Confederate victory in that theater, and war's second costliest battle in terms of casualties. In his final action as a commander, Bragg's Army was routed by Major General Ulysses S. Grant (USMA 1843) in the Battle of Chattanooga in November 1863.

Bragg established a reputation as a strict disciplinarian, but also as an officer willing to publicly argue with and criticize his superior officers. He was known to have fought against his uncooperative subordinates as much as he fought against the enemy. There were multiple attempts to have him replaced as Army Commander, but suitable replacements were in short supply. Following his defeat at Chattanooga and his retreat into Georgia, Bragg resigned his command. Although never able to relieve his longtime friend, Davis accepted Bragg's resignation and made Bragg his Chief Military Advisor responsible for the general administrative and logistical operations of the Confederacy. Bragg's wartime legacy has received mixed reviews from historians who point to varying degrees of command and administrative strengths.

FORT BRAGG, NORTH CAROLINA, THE HOME TO OUR AIRBORNE AND SPECIAL FORCES, BEARS THE NAME OF THIS FORMER CONFEDERATE GENERAL.

At the age of 59, Bragg died suddenly in Galveston, Texas, from a condition of the cerebral blood vessels. He is buried in Mobile, Alabama. In 1918, Camp Bragg, North Carolina, named after Bragg, was established as a World War I artillery training ground. It became Fort Bragg four years later and is currently the "Home of the Airborne" with the XVIII Airborne Corps, the 82nd Airborne Division, and the United States Army Special Operations Command stationed there.

Written by: Lieutenant Colonel Todd Gile (USA, Retired), USMA 1986.

Frank Dow Merrill was born December 4, 1903, in Woodville, Massachusetts. Merrill enlisted at 17 and was deployed to Haiti and Panama while reaching the rank of Sergeant before gaining admission to West Point in 1925. Older than many of his classmates, he graduated at age 25, along with Jim Gavin, who would go on to lead the 82nd Airborne Division in World War II. Upon graduation, he was commissioned in the Cavalry, but would first earn a B.S. in Military Engineering from Massachusetts Institute of Technology in 1932[1], before reporting to the Cavalry School at Fort Riley, Kansas.

In 1938, Merrill became the Military Attaché in Tokyo, where he studied the Japanese language and ultimately join General Douglas MacArthur's staff in the Philippines in 1941 as a Military Intelligence Officer. At the time of the attack on Pearl Harbor, Merrill was in Rangoon, Burma, and he remained in Burma after the Japanese invasion. He became a Liaison Officer with the British forces – reporting to General Joseph Stilwell. He became Stilwell's Operations Officer in 1942.

At the Quebec Conference in 1943, President Roosevelt, Prime Minister Churchill, and other allied leaders decided that an American Long Range Penetration Mission behind the Japanese Lines in Burma was needed to destroy the Japanese supply lines and communications and to disrupt enemy forces in order to reopen the much needed Burma Road. The unit was officially designated as the 5307th Composite Unit (Provisional) – Code Name: GALAHAD.[2]

General Merrill became the Commander of this new United States Army special forces unit patterned after the Chindits – British Long Range Jungle Penetration groups that harassed Japanese forces in Burma. As the three battalions of the 5307th deployed into Burma in February 1944, "Merrill's Marauders" became immortalized themselves as the first American Infantrymen to fight on the Asiatic mainland. Colonel Charles Hunter, the Senior Officer and West Point classmate under Merrill, described his Commanding Officer as "rather tall, he was by no means a rugged individual, being narrow of chest and rather thin. His features were sharp but his nature ebullient, affable and confident."[3]

The first Marauder campaign took place in late February 1944, when they attacked the Japanese 18th Division at Walawbum. In five months of combat in Burma, the Marauders covered 750 miles of the harshest jungle terrain in the world. They fought five major campaigns – WALAWBUM, SHADUZUP, INKANGAHTAWNG, NHPUM GA, and MYITKYINA – and 30 minor engagements. Their final mission behind Japanese lines resulted in the capture of Myitkyina Airfield, the only all-weather airfield in Northern Burma. As a result of the mission, the Marauders suffered 272 killed, 955 wounded, and 980 evacuated for illness and disease. The casualties included General Merrill himself, who had refused early evacuation and suffered a heart attack.[4]

Following World War II, General Merrill served as Chief of Staff of the Western Defense Command, and later the Chief of Staff of the 6th Army at the Presidio in San Francisco under General Mark Clark (USMA 1917). General Merrill's awards and decorations include the Distinguished Service Medal, Purple Heart, Bronze Star, two Legion of Merits, and Combat Infantryman's Badge.

Major General Merrill was medically retired in 1948 and moved with his wife and two sons to New Hampshire. He served as the Commissioner of New Hampshire Public Works & Highways from 1949 to 1955 and was elected President of the American Association of State Highway and Transportation Officials at their annual conference in New Orleans in 1955. Unfortunately, he died of a heart attack two days later on December 11, 1955, at age 52 and was laid to rest at the West Point Cemetery. Jeff Chandler played Merrill in the 1962 movie *Merrill's Marauders* but never saw the movie himself; Chandler died of a staph infection contracted during the filming in the Philippines before the film was completed. Camp Frank Merrill was named in Merrill's honor and is the home of the 5th Ranger Battalion and Mountain Training Phase of Ranger School training in Dahlonega, Georgia. Major General Merrill was inducted in to the Ranger Hall of Fame in 1992.

Written by: Lieutenant Colonel Todd Gile (USA, Retired), USMA 1986.

JEFF CHANDLER PLAYED MERRILL IN *MERRILL'S MARAUDERS*, BUT CHANDLER DIED JUST AFTER FILMING AND NEVER SAW THE MOVIE HIMSELF.

Major General Frank Dow Merrill, USMA 1929

- COMMANDING GENERAL, 5307TH COMPOSITE UNIT (PROVISIONAL) KNOWN AS "MERRILL'S MARAUDERS"
- CHIEF OF STAFF, THE WESTERN DEFENSE COMMAND
- CHIEF OF STAFF, THE U.S. 6TH ARMY IN SAN FRANCISCO
- DISTINGUISHED SERVICE MEDAL, PURPLE HEART, BRONZE STAR, LEGION OF MERIT (TWO), AND COMBAT INFANTRYMAN'S BADGE
- COMMISSIONER, NEW HAMPSHIRE PUBLIC WORKS AND HIGHWAYS, 1949–55
- ELECTED PRESIDENT OF THE AMERICAN ASSOCIATION OF STATE HIGHWAY AND TRANSPORTATION OFFICIALS, 1955
- BURIED AT THE WEST POINT CEMETERY

General George S. Patton, USMA 1909

- **COMMANDING GENERAL, U.S. 3RD ARMY, WORLD WAR II**
- **PATTON TANK NAMED IN HIS HONOR**
- **U.S. OLYMPIAN**
- **PATTON STATUE AT WEST POINT DEDICATED IN HIS HONOR**
- **TWO DISTINGUISHED SERVICE CROSSES, TWO SILVER STARS, PURPLE HEART**

George S. Patton is one of the most colorful leaders in American military history. He was a fierce soldier, who led from the front as both a Junior Officer and as a General Officer. He was the most feared and respected Allied General by the Nazis, and even his fictitious Army (intended to fool the Germans) was enough to affect the landings at D-Day in favor of the allies. Patton was contentious, aggressive, ornery, and egotistical – and the American public loved him for that.

Patton's grandfather and father had both attended Virginia Military Institute (VMI). His grandfather was killed as a Confederate Colonel in the Battle of Opequon. Like his family, Patton attended VMI in 1904 for one year before being accepted to West Point, from which he graduated in 1909. He was an outstanding athlete and won a position on the United States Olympic team in Stockholm in the first modern pentath-

lon, finishing fifth overall.

In 1916, Patton served in the Punitive Expedition into Mexico in pursuit of the guerrilla Pancho Villa. He served as an aide to Brigadier General John J. Pershing (USMA 1886). After Pancho Villa's forces crossed into New Mexico and killed several Americans, Patton led the first armored assault with a convoy of armored cars. Patton himself killed one of the guerillas with his pistol and earned the respect of Pershing and the American public. His aggressive leadership style and his willingness to take risks and personally attack and kill the enemy gained the respect of both allies and enemies and became part of Patton's brand.

World War I had started in 1914, but the United States had avoided entry into the war until April 1917. Pershing was promoted to a Four-Star General and was given com-

mand of the American Expeditionary Forces (AEF). Pershing chose George C. Marshall as his Chief of Staff and promoted Patton to Captain, assigning him to establish the Light Tank Training School in France. Patton was promoted to Major, Lieutenant Colonel, then Colonel in short order. He commanded armored forces at the Battle of Saint Mihiel and the Meuse-Argonne Offensive. He was wounded in an attack on September 26, 1918. He received the Distinguished Service Cross and Purple Heart. The war ended before he recovered from his wounds.

Soon after returning to the United States to Camp Meade, his rank reverted back to Captain. Patton and Dwight D. Eisenhower (USMA 1915) formed a relationship that would last the remainder of their lives. Patton was an advocate for building up United States armored forces for the entire two decades between wars. When the buildup for World

War II began, Patton was a natural choice to lead armored units. He was given command of 2nd Brigade, of the 2nd Armored Division. By the time the United States entered World War II, Patton was a Major General and the Division Commander of 2nd Armored Division. He led the division in Operation Torch – the invasion of North Africa – in November 1942. He commanded the Western Task Force that battled French Vichy fighters in and around Casablanca. The 2nd Armored Division liberated Casablanca in two days. After the German Afrika Korps defeated United States forces at the Battle of Kasserine Pass, Eisenhower relieved Lieutenant General Fredenhall and promoted Patton to the position. He gave Patton command of II Corps, in which he chose Major General Omar Bradley (USMA 1915) as his Deputy Corps Commander. Patton's II Corps defeated Rommel's Afrika Korps.

>>> Spotlight

The M46, M47, M48, and M60 Patton tanks were named after General George S. Patton (USMA 1909) and saw service from the Korean War, Vietnam War, and Desert Storm and are still used by foreign militaries. The United States military replaced the Patton Tank with the Abrams Tank beginning in 1980. Approximately 37,000 Patton tanks were built between 1950 and 1987, weighed approximately 50 tons, had a crew of four, a 105-mm main gun, and was made by Chrysler.

Eisenhower, Patton waving, and Bradley with C-47 in background.

Patton and Montgomery.

Patton was then given command of the 7th Army for the invasion of Sicily, where they successfully invaded and occupied Sicily, but the German and Italian Armies largely escaped back to mainland Italy. It was during this Sicily campaign that Patton's career nearly ended, when he slapped two soldiers, who were hospitalized for battle fatigue — what is now known as post-traumatic stress disorder (PTSD). The incident reached the American press and Eisenhower temporarily removed him from his command.

PATTON WAS CONTENTIOUS, AGGRESSIVE, ORNERY, AND EGOTISTICAL — AND THE AMERICAN PUBLIC LOVED HIM FOR THAT.

Patton made an official retraction and apology to the soldiers.

While the allies were preparing for the Normandy invasion, Major General Bradley was promoted to Lieutenant General and given command of the ground invasion of Normandy. Patton, meanwhile, stayed in Sicily and was given command of the fictitious 1st United States Army Group, intended to mislead the Germans, who believed Patton would command the invasion of France. The diversion successfully deceived the Germans into thinking Normandy was only a feint, while they waited for Patton's invasion of Calais.

After the successful invasion of Normandy on June 6, 1944, Patton was given command of the 3rd Army in France on the far eastern flank of the allied advance. In addition to being one of the first General Officers to rapidly adopt the use of armored forces,

Patton also showed the ability to implement advances in both tactical airpower and logistical innovations. The 3rd Army moved rapidly across France, employing these new strategies and tactics until they literally ran out of fuel in September 1944.

On December 16, 1944, massive German armored forces formed a surprise attack that became known as The Battle of the Bulge. They advanced rapidly, overrunning large numbers of United States divisions that were unprepared for such an attack. The 101st Airborne was rushed forward to the major crossroads at Bastogne, and they were quickly surrounded. Patton saw the battle as an opportunity where the Germans had stuck their neck out, so he ordered six divisions to attack toward Bastogne from the south. The 3rd Army advanced across a broad front and relieved the beleaguered forces at Bastogne. This was the largest battle that the

United States Army had ever fought, suffering more than 80,000 casualties out of 800,000 soldiers. It was Patton's finest hour, and his bold and aggressive leadership had passed throughout the chain of command to mobilize an entire Army in the middle of winter to counterattack along a broad front. He was promoted to a Four-Star General in April 1945, just prior to the end of the war.

General Patton died as a result of injuries sustained in a car accident in Germany in December 1945. He is buried at the head of the Luxembourg American Cemetery (a United States military cemetery) with his men from the 3rd Army. Actor George C. Scott played Patton in the blockbuster movie *Patton* in 1968, which he won the Academy Award for "Best Actor" in 1970, but refused to attend the awards ceremony. His reasoning: He "did not do him justice."

General George S. Patton Statue at West Point.

Photo: AP

>>> Spotlight

Actor George C. Scott played Patton in the blockbuster movie *Patton* in 1968, which he won the Academy Award for "Best Actor" in 1970.

Patton with a soldier at Messina, Italy.

Eisenhower and Patton.

Patton, Bradley, and Eisenhower viewing concentration camp victims, 1945.

Patton and Eisenhower.

The General McAuliffe Room at the Thayer Hotel.

General Anthony McAuliffe, USMA 1919

- IN RESPONSE TO GERMAN REQUEST OF SURRENDER AT BASTOGNE, HE REPLIED, "NUTS!"
- DIVISION ARTILLERY COMMANDER, 101ST AIRBORNE DIVISION ON D-DAY
- ACTING DIVISION COMMANDER, 101ST AIRBORNE DIVISION DURING BATTLE OF THE BULGE, BASTOGNE
- COMMANDER, U.S. ARMY EUROPE

McAuliffe as Commander 103rd Infantry Division, May 24, 1945.

Patton and McAuliffe, January 15, 1945.

It seems hard to believe that after a lifetime of service to a nation, a person can be universally synonymous with just one word; Anthony McAuliffe will always be remembered and associated with the word: "Nuts!" But McAuliffe – a man who joined the paratroopers when it was just a novel concept, led America's Army in combat in one of its biggest battles, and rose to command all of the United States Army European Forces –

OUTNUMBERED AND UNDER-SUPPLIED, THE 101ST AIRBORNE FOUGHT DAY AND NIGHT. WHEN THE GERMAN COMMANDER SENT IN A TEAM UNDER A WHITE FLAG TO REQUEST THE 101ST SURRENDER, THE ACTING DIVISION COMMANDER BRIGADIER GENERAL MCAULIFFE'S INITIAL REACTION WAS "NUTS!"

probably wouldn't want it any other way. It wasn't his state of mind that the single word refers to, but his gut reaction as a soldier, immortalizing himself in American military history. It is a word that spoke volumes about not only the character of the man that was McAuliffe, but the men who made up the 101st Airborne Division, aka "the Screaming Eagles," in World War II.

Anthony McAuliffe was born in Washington, D.C., in 1898. He started college at West Virginia University in 1916 and then entered West Point in June 1917. Because of World War I, the class had a shortened time, and he graduated in November 1918 to deploy to the France to fight in what was then called "The Great War." However, before they deployed, Germany surrendered and McAuliffe's class was ordered back to West Point to finish their full amount of schooling, officially graduating in 1922. They missed the "war to end all wars," but nearly 20 years after their second graduation, the Class of 1922 found themselves fighting the second Great War, World War II.

Between the wars, McAuliffe's rose through the ranks and entered World War II as a Colonel. He parachuted into Normandy as the Commander of Division Artillery for the 101st Airborne and, later, landed by glider in Operation Market Garden during the invasion of Holland. He'll forever be known for his leadership at a critical moment during the biggest battle the United States Army had ever fought in World War II: The Battle of the Bulge, where he rose to the occasion and commanded the brave paratroopers of the 101st Airborne Division, while surrounded by Germans.

The Battle of the Bulge started December 16, 1944, and caught the allies completely by surprise. As most of the United States Army retreated from the surprise attack of 44 German divisions, one unit, the 101st Airborne, was rushed forward by trucks to defend the town of Bastogne, which was a vital intersection for both the allies and the Germans. Soon surrounded by superior numbers of German armor units, the 101st paratroopers sardonically joked that that was exactly what they trained for: to be surrounded by the enemy. With cloud cover preventing allied air support, the 101st Airborne was attacked by Armor, Artillery, and Infantry Divisions. Outnumbered and undersupplied, they fought day and night. When the German Commander sent in a team under a white flag to request the 101st surrender, the Acting Division Commander Brigadier General McAuliffe's initial reaction was "Nuts!"

His staff convinced him to go with his initial reaction, so his exact reply was: "to the German Commander from the American Commander: Nuts!" He said it brazenly defiant, but also slightly with a sense of gallows humor as 101st soldiers were dying by the hour. When the battle was finally won (Patton's 3rd Army attacked the German flank and came to relieve

the 101st), and the heroes of Bastogne and their sacrifice was recognized, his defiant reaction echoed around the free world. The family of General McAuliffe provided a copy of the German request, which is now displayed in the McAuliffe Room at the Thayer Hotel.

After the Battle of the Bulge, McAuliffe was promoted to Major General and was given his own division, the 103rd Infantry Division, which he commanded throughout the remainder of the war. After the war, he held many positions, rising up to command the Chemical Corps, Army G-1, Commander of 7th Army, and eventually Commander in Chief of United States Army Europe. He retired in 1956.

The new headquarters of the 101st Airborne Division at Fort Campbell in Kentucky is dedicated in his honor. The Alumni Association of the 101st Airborne is appropriately called The McAuliffe Chapter, honoring McAuliffe and the soldiers of the 101st Airborne, many of them who made the ultimate sacrifice for our country in World War II, Korea, Vietnam, Iraq, Afghanistan, and still continue to defend America as the men and women of the Screaming Eagles.

The General McAuliffe Room at the Thayer Hotel is proudly dedicated by Edward and Lydia Knapp.

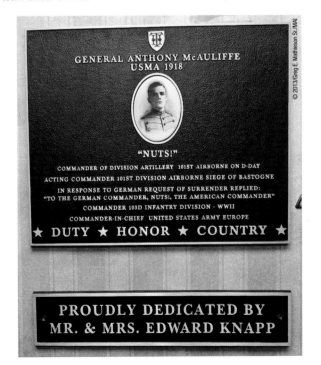

GENERAL ANTHONY McAULIFFE
USMA 1918

"NUTS!"

COMMANDER OF DIVISION ARTILLERY 101ST AIRBORNE ON D-DAY
ACTING COMMANDER 101ST DIVISION AIRBORNE SIEGE OF BASTOGNE
IN RESPONSE TO GERMAN REQUEST OF SURRENDER REPLIED:
"TO THE GERMAN COMMANDER, NUTS!, THE AMERICAN COMMANDER"
COMMANDER 103D INFANTRY DIVISION · WWII
COMMANDER-IN-CHIEF UNITED STATES ARMY EUROPE

★ DUTY ★ HONOR ★ COUNTRY ★

PROUDLY DEDICATED BY
MR. & MRS. EDWARD KNAPP

© 2013/Greg E. Mathieson Sr./MAI

Brigadier General McAuliffe observing training prior to the invasion.

In 2005, Hollywood immortalized the late Colonel Henry Mucci and his soldiers when Benjamin Bratt portrayed Mucci in the movie *The Great Raid*, which was based on the Hampton Sides bestselling book *The Ghost Soldiers*. The movie accurately portrayed one of the greatest raids in United States military history – a raid that remains a textbook Ranger operation for skillfully using intense preparation, surprise, and speed, while accomplishing a mission against a much larger enemy force deep behind enemy lines.[2] The January 1945 raid to rescue more than 500 American and Allied Prisoners of War (POWs) held in the Japanese POW camp near Cabanatuan, Philippines, was as risky as it was audacious, yet its overwhelming success defined Mucci's career as a combat leader.

Mucci was born and raised in Bridgeport, Connecticut, where a highway now bears his name as the local hero. He graduated with the West Point Class of 1936 and commissioned into the Infantry. A Pearl Harbor survivor, Mucci would spend the entire war in the Pacific. He was tough, ambitious, and brave. His soldiers universally loved and respected him – and he felt the same way for them.[3] He even received the soldiers' medal for swimming a quarter mile in uniform to rescue a drowning soldier during training.[4]

In 1943, Lieutenant Colonel Mucci took command of the 98th Field Artillery Battalion, a mule-drawn pack-artillery unit assigned to New Guinea. By January 1944, however, the battalion was re-designated as the 6th Ranger Battalion and officially activated in September 1944. The battalion was configured similarly to Colonel William O. Darby's (USMA 1933) 1st Ranger Battalion, which had been fighting in Italy since 1943. Although it would be short-lived and deactivated December 30, 1945, the 6th Ranger Battalion left a legacy worthy of the Ranger name.[5] Through Mucci's sheer determination and leadership, he rapidly transformed the unit by reducing its size from 1,000 to only 500, all of whom were volunteers; establishing an intense training camp in New Guinea, where he pushed his men to their extreme physical and mental limits; and personally leading, supervising, and participating in every aspect of their training.

Working closely with conventional forces and Filipino guerrillas, Mucci's Rangers conducted various missions that set the conditions for the successful Allied invasion to retake the Philippines in October 1944. As American forces liberated the islands, intelligence reports also confirmed the existence of large groups of allied POWs, specifically those who had been taken at Bataan in early 1942 during the beginning of the war. Since that humiliating defeat at the hands of the Japanese, the fate of those prisoners had long haunted the nation. Growing knowledge of the Bataan Death March and the atrocities being committed by the Japanese against American prisoners had long since fueled the intensity and rage with which America fought against Japan. Now, intelligence reports of Japanese directives to kill POWs in the wake of the American invasion, spurred Mucci's Rangers into action.[6]

Following the United States 6th Army's unopposed landing on the main island of Luzon in January 1945, Mucci was ordered to raid and liberate the POWs at Cabanatuan. Personally leading a force of about 130 Rangers and 200 Filipino guerrillas, Mucci's force moved more than 30 miles behind enemy lines to execute the raid on January 30, 1945. It was so well prepared and trained that within half an hour, the Rangers had destroyed the installation, killed more than 200 Japanese guards, rescued more than 500 prisoners, and returned to friendly lines

BENJAMIN BRATT PLAYED MUCCI IN THE MOVIE *THE GREAT RAID*.

Colonel Henry Andrews Mucci, USMA 1936

- PEARL HARBOR SURVIVOR
- ORGANIZED, TRAINED, AND COMMANDED 6TH RANGER BATTALION
- LED THE HISTORIC RAID ON CABANATUAN, PHILIPPINES, SUCCESSFULLY RESCUING 511 POWS
- ROUTE 25 IN CONNECTICUT NAMED "COLONEL HENRY A. MUCCI HIGHWAY" IN HIS HONOR
- ACTOR BENJAMIN BRATT PORTRAYED MUCCI IN THE 2005 MIRAMAX FILM *THE GREAT RAID*
- DISTINGUISHED SERVICE CROSS, SILVER STAR, SOLDIERS MEDAL, BRONZE STAR MEDAL (TWO), PURPLE HEART, COMBAT INFANTRYMAN BADGE[1]
- MEMBER OF THE RANGER HALL OF FAME

the next day despite strong resistance while only suffering two dead and seven wounded among both liberators and prisoners – nothing short of amazing.[7]

Mucci's feat of liberating the POWs was celebrated by United States forces, allied journalists, and the American public as intensely as the fall of Bataan and the Philippines – the reason why the prisoners existed in the first place – had been mourned nearly three years earlier. Colonel Mucci received the Distinguished Service Cross (DSC) for his heroic actions during this raid. When presenting the award, General Douglas MacArthur praised Mucci and considered the raid "magnificent," and that it "reflected extraordinary credit to all concerned."[8] The DSC citation read:

"...for extraordinary heroism in connection with military operations against an armed enemy while serving with the 6th Ranger Infantry Battalion, in action against enemy forces on 30 January 1945, during the rescue of Allied Prisoners of War from the Cabanatuan Prison Camp in the Philippine Islands. Colonel Mucci was charged with the rescue of several hundred Americans held prisoner by the enemy. It was believed that the enemy would kill or remove the prisoners when our attack was launched in that area. Colonel Mucci promptly assembled a rescue team composed of Ranger Infantry, Scouts, guerrillas and Filipino volunteers. On 28 January, he secured guides, and moved to rendezvous with the Scouts, who reported that three thousand enemy, with some tanks, were in the stockade area. He ordered the attack at dark on 30 January. The attack was launched, and within five minutes the Rangers and Scouts entered the camp, and killed the guards. Ten minutes later all prisoners were out of the camp, and were being taken to carts previously assembled. En route, our troops encountered a force about eight hundred enemy, attacked and killed three hundred. Eight enemy tanks attacking the convoy were held off by a quickly established roadblock. The convoy proceeded through the enemy-held area and completed the evacuation of the released prisoners. Colonel Mucci's gallant leadership, superior professional ability and outstanding personal courage contributed immeasurably to the brilliantly executed rescue of American imprisoned by the enemy. Lieutenant Colonel Mucci's intrepid leadership, personal bravery and zealous devotion to duty exemplify the highest traditions of the military forces of the United States and reflect great credit upon himself, his unit, and the United States Army."

Mucci and the raiders were ecstatic and proud to have saved their comrades and countrymen. Many of the Ranger raiders were sent back to the United States to participate in a war bond drive, including the Company Commander, Captain Robert Prince. Prince, who was portrayed in *The Great Raid* by actor James Franco, was asked about the mission in April 1945 while on leave in the United States. He commented that "People everywhere thank me. I think the thanks should go the other way. I'll be grateful the rest of my life that I had a chance to do something in this war that was not destructive. Nothing for me can ever compare with the satisfaction I got from freeing those men."[9] Prince died in 2009, but lived long enough to see his unit's actions accurately depicted in Director John Dahl's film. Mucci, unfortunately, did not. After leaving the Army as a Colonel in 1947, he lived an extremely active life in the auto and oil industries. Moreover, just as he lived his life like a Ranger, he died like one. On April 20, 1997, at age 86, he passed away from complications resulting from a fractured hip while surfing near his home in Melbourne, Florida, and is buried in the West Point Cemetery.[10]

Written by: Frank Flowers, USMA 1986.

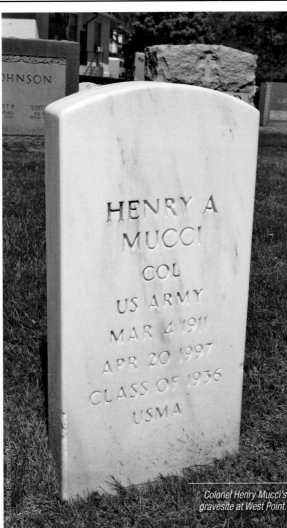

Colonel Henry Mucci's gravesite at West Point.

Benjamin Bratt as Colonel Mucci in The Great Raid.

Harold Moore served during World War II, the Korean War, and Vietnam, and rose to the top ranks of the United States Army to achieve the rank of Lieutenant General. He will forever be immortalized for his heroic leadership as the Commander of 1st Battalion, 7th Cavalry Regiment in the first major battle, Battle of the Ia Drang Valley, of the Vietnam War. The battle was documented in a book he co-authored, titled *We Were Soldiers Once…and Young*, which was later made into the Hollywood movie, *We Were Soldiers*, in which Moore was played by Mel Gibson.

Moore grew up in Kentucky, but moved to Washington, D.C., during high school with the intent to attend West Point. He attended George Washington University for two years, before securing his appointment to West Point. When he entered West Point in June 1942, the United States was at the beginning of World War II. His class would graduate just after Victory in Europe Day (VE Day) in June 1945 and be handed their diplomas by the legendary General of the Army Omar Bradley. Moore was commissioned in the Infantry and shipped off to the Pacific, arriving just after Victory over Japan Day (VJ Day). Though he missed serving in action in World War II, he would later serve in significant combat operations in both the Korean War and the Vietnam War.

After serving in the occupation of Japan from 1945 to 1948, Moore returned to the United States to serve with the 82nd Airborne Division for three years at Fort Bragg, North Carolina. His chance for combat came in 1952 in the Korean War, where he was a Company Commander in the 17th Infantry Regiment of the 7th Infantry Division and then with a heavy mortar company in the same Regiment. He was awarded three bronze star medals – two for valor and his first Combat Infantryman Badge.

In 1953, he returned to West Point to teach Infantry tactics to cadets for two years before attending the Command and General Staff College (CGSC) in Fort Leavenworth, Kansas. His next assignment was to help prepare him for Vietnam, as he was assigned to the Office of the Chief of Research and Development to develop new airborne and air assault equipment, tactics, and procedures. After graduating from CGSC, he deployed to Oslo, Norway, to the Headquarters of Allied Forces Northern Europe. After attending the National War College and receiving a master's degree from George Washington University (both located in D.C.), he was finally given his own battalion command with the 11th Air Assault Division, which was re-designated the 1st Cavalry Division, then deployed to Vietnam.

The Battle of Ia Drang Valley took place in November 1965 as the first of 300,000 regular Army American troops were being deployed to

> **MOORE AND HIS SOLDIERS FOUGHT A BRUTAL BATTLE THAT INCLUDED HAND-TO-HAND COMBAT AND RESULTED IN THE MAJORITY OF THE BATTALION BEING KILLED OR WOUNDED.**

Lieutenant General Harold Moore, Jr., USMA 1945

- **COMMANDER, U.S. ARMY TRAINING CENTER**
- **COMMANDER, 7TH INFANTRY DIVISION**
- **COMMANDER, 1ST BATTALION, 7TH CAVALRY, 1ST CAVALRY DIVISION, IA DRANG VALLEY, FIRST MAJOR BATTLE OF THE VIETNAM WAR**
- **MEL GIBSON PLAYED LIEUTENANT COLONEL MOORE IN *WE WERE SOLDIERS***
- **DISTINGUISHED SERVICE CROSS, COMBAT INFANTRYMAN BADGE**

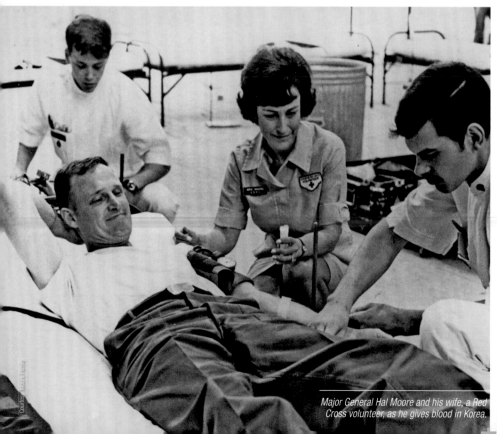

Major General Hal Moore and his wife, a Red Cross volunteer, as he gives blood in Korea.

Mel Gibson as Lieutenant Colonel Hal Moore in We Were soldiers.

defend South Vietnam against the communist Viet Cong guerillas and the North Vietnamese Army (NVA). The enemy was located in a very difficult area to reach, which tested the new American air mobility strategy. The 3rd Brigade, 7th Cavalry was sent into the area on a search and destroy mission. Moore led the 400 men of the 1st Battalion into the landing zones, but soon found them encircled by superior enemy forces of more than 2,000 NVA soldiers. The battle that ensued was fought by a smaller United States force, using superior airpower to defend itself against an enemy intent on overrunning and decimating the American battalion.

Vietnamese Commanders intended to destroy the American political commitment by decimating a battalion in the field. Over the course of three days, Moore and his soldiers fought a brutal battle that included hand-to-hand combat and resulted in the majority of the battalion being killed or wounded, but they continued to throw back the enemy until reinforcements finally arrived. Both sides claimed victory – the United States proved that air mobility and firepower, combined with superior Infantry tactics, could defeat large enemy units; the NVA claimed victory and success by getting so close to limit the benefits of United States superior firepower from artillery and airpower. These strategies and tactics dictated the next eight years of battle between the United States and NVA.

Moore and reporter Joe Galloway, who was imbedded with his battalion, later chronicled the events of that battle. The United States reported 234 of their men were Killed In Action and 250 wounded, but estimated that at least 1,500 of the enemy were killed. Moore was awarded the Distinguished Service Cross, while Joe Galloway was the only civilian in the Vietnam War to receive the Bronze Star for Valor. Three Medals of Honor were awarded – two for helicopter pilots, who continuously braved enemy fire, and one for Second Lieutenant Walter Marm for his actions at Ia Drang's Landing Zone X-Ray.

After Vietnam, Moore rotated to Korea as the Chief of Staff of the 8th Army and then the Commanding General of the 7th Infantry Division. He returned to the United States to Fort Ord, California, as Commanding General of the United States Army Training Center. His final assignments were as the Commanding General of the Military Personnel Center (MILPERCEN) and Deputy Chief of Staff for Personnel, where he was instrumental in integrating the first class of women into West Point.

In 1977, he retired and moved his family to Crested Butte, Colorado, where he became the Executive Vice President of Crested Butte Mountain Ski Area. He and his wife, Julia, raised five children, two of whom were career Army Officers. In 2003, he was awarded the prestigious West Point Distinguished Graduate Award. On December 3, 2011, the Lieutenant General Hal Moore Room at the Thayer Hotel at West Point was dedicated in his honor by Ed and Lydia Knapp on behalf of the grateful members of the McAuliffe Chapter of the 101st Airborne (Air Assault) Division reunion.

The Hal Moore Room at the Thayer Hotel was dedicated by the Moore family.

Lieutenant General Hal Moore dressed in full dress blue uniform at the Thayer Hotel at age 90.

The Moore family (David is in West Point dress gray uniform).

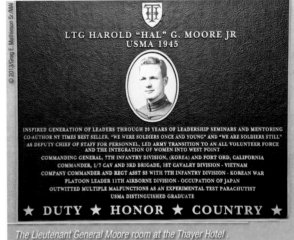

LTG HAROLD "HAL" G. MOORE JR
USMA 1945

INSPIRED GENERATION OF LEADERS THROUGH 20 YEARS OF LEADERSHIP SEMINARS AND MENTORING
CO-AUTHOR NY TIMES BEST SELLER, "WE WERE SOLDIERS ONCE AND YOUNG" AND "WE ARE SOLDIERS STILL"
AS DEPUTY CHIEF OF STAFF FOR PERSONNEL, LED ARMY TRANSITION TO AN ALL VOLUNTEER FORCE
AND THE INTEGRATION OF WOMEN INTO WEST POINT
COMMANDING GENERAL, 7TH INFANTRY DIVISION, (KOREA) AND FORT ORD, CALIFORNIA
COMMANDER, 1/7 CAV AND 3RD BRIGADE, 1ST CAVALRY DIVISION - VIETNAM
COMPANY COMMANDER AND REGT ASST S3 WITH 7TH INFANTRY DIVISION - KOREAN WAR
PLATOON LEADER 11TH AIRBORNE DIVISION - OCCUPATION OF JAPAN
OUTWITTED MULTIPLE MALFUNCTIONS AS AN EXPERIMENTAL TEST PARACHUTIST
USMA DISTINGUISHED GRADUATE

★ DUTY ★ HONOR ★ COUNTRY ★

The Lieutenant General Moore room at the Thayer Hotel.

>>> Spotlight

Photo Courtesy: Moore Family

Moore co-authored a book that documented Vietnam's first major battle, the Battle of the Ia Drang Valley, which he led as the Commander. The book with correspondent Joe Galloway, titled *We Were Soldiers Once…and Young*, was later made into the Hollywood movie, *We Were Soldiers*, in which Moore was played by Mel Gibson.

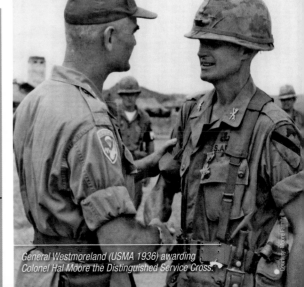

General Westmoreland (USMA 1936) awarding Colonel Hal Moore the Distinguished Service Cross.

General Downing leading the Khobar Tower bombing.

General Wayne Allan Downing, USMA 1962

- COMMANDER, U.S. SPECIAL OPERATIONS COMMAND (USSOCOM)
- COMMANDER, U.S. ARMY SPECIAL OPERATIONS COMMAND (USASOC)
- COMMANDER, JOINT SPECIAL OPERATIONS COMMAND (JSOC), U.S. SPECIAL OPERATIONS COMMAND
- COMMANDER, 75TH RANGER REGIMENT (AIRBORNE)
- COMBAT INFANTRYMAN BADGE, MILITARY FREE FALL JUMPMASTER BADGE, MASTER PARACHUTE BADGE, RANGER TAB, AND PATHFINDER BADGE
- SILVER STAR (TWO), SOLDIER'S MEDAL, BRONZE STAR FOR VALOR (TWO), PURPLE HEART, AIR MEDAL FOR VALOR (THREE), ARMY COMMENDATION MEDAL FOR VALOR (THREE)
- BURIED AT THE WEST POINT CEMETERY

Wayne Allan Downing was born in Peoria, Illinois, on May 10, 1940. A member of the West Point Class of 1962, General Downing's career in both the military and following his retirement brought extraordinary credit to the United States Military Academy and the Nation. A leader through the ranks of the Special Operations Community and as a national security expert following his retirement, General Downing's career epitomized the phrase "lifetime of service to the Nation" and exemplified the ideals of the Military Academy – "Duty, Honor, Country."

As the future Commander of all United States Military Special Operations Forces, it is little wonder that Downing began taking part in clandestine missions as a Plebe at West Point in 1958. Stories relayed by his company H-2 Cadet classmates tell of Downing, along with classmates Tom Kling, Tony Leatham, and Steve Ellis, mounting an unsuccessful mission to leave post during the Christmas holiday. Unfortunately, the Officer-in-Charge (OC) caught wind of the operation and was able to thwart their planned escape as they left the cadet barracks. While most of the

coconspirators would ultimately receive considerable punishment in terms of demerits and area tours, Downing's quick thinking and decisive action left him in his own bed, albeit without the civilian clothes he had acquired for the mission, pretending to be asleep and ultimately avoiding detection by the OC. Downing, however, failed to learn a lesson from his brush with severe discipline. Four weeks later, he and classmate Charlie Shaw "had the book thrown at them," resulting in many hours on the area for skipping chapel (which was mandatory at West Point

until 1972). Downing later recounted, "King Hussein (Jordan) rescued us two or three weeks later with a general amnesty. Years later, I met the King and told him the story and he loved it. Whenever I would meet him afterward, he would ask me to tell the amnesty tale to whomever was around."[1]

The Tactical Officer of Cadet Company H-2 – Lieutenant General Richard G. Trefry (USMA 1950) who earned the 2006 General Creighton W. Abrams Medal for exceptional service to the United States Army, was told by the Commandant of Cadets at West Point

>>> Spotlight

On October 28, 2008, the city of Peoria, Illinois, renamed its airport the General Wayne A. Downing Peoria International Airport in honor of the legendary hero who grew up in their community. An 11-foot-tall bronze statue of General Downing was unveiled at the airport with Downing in combat gear and M-16. At the base of the statue an inscription reads "Rangers Lead the Way." The statue was commissioned by his friend Mr. H. Ross Perot.

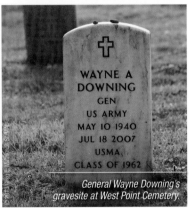

General Downing's funeral services were held at the West Point Chapel, and he was laid to rest in the West Point Cemetery.

WAYNE A DOWNING
GEN
US ARMY
MAY 10 1940
JUL 18 2007
USMA
CLASS OF 1962

General Wayne Downing's gravesite at West Point Cemetery.

from Tulane University prior to an assignment as a Senior Operations Research/Systems Analyst in the Office of the Secretary of Defense.

General Downing's extensive experience with the United States Army Rangers began as the Operations Officer (S-3) and Executive Officer (XO) of 1st Battalion, 75th Ranger Regiment at Fort Stewart, Georgia, from 1975 to 1976, when he was a Major. He would later command the 2nd Battalion, 75th Ranger Regiment and ultimately would serve as the 3rd Commander of the 75th Ranger Regiment as a Colonel from 1984 to 1985. During his tour as the Regimental Commander, the activation of the 3rd Ranger Battalion and its integration into the regiment, which would also include the previously independent 1st and 2nd Ranger Battalions, marked the new era of the Ranger Regiment. In 1999, General Downing was inducted in to the Ranger Hall of Fame.[2] His induction was based on his recognition as the first commander of the modern era and, under his leadership, the 75th Ranger Regiment became the world's premier Infantry unit.

In 1989, General Downing became the Commanding General of the Joint Special Operations Command (JSOC) at Fort Bragg, North Carolina. Immediately following his assumption of command, he led the Special Operations units that helped liberate Panama during Operation Just Cause. The following year, General Downing commanded the Special Operations Forces during Operation Desert Storm that infiltrated Iraq in order to reduce the Iraqi ballistic missile threat (SCUDS). Following Desert Storm, General Downing became the Commander of United States Army Special Operations Command (USASOC) at Fort Bragg that included all of the Army's special operators: Ranger, Civil Affairs, Army Special Operations Aviation, Psychological Operations, and Special Operations forces.

General Downing's final command was the Commander of the United States Special Operations Command (USSOCOM) from 1993 until his retirement in 1996. As CINC USSOCOM, he was responsible for training, equipping, and deploying the 47,000 special operators from the Army, Navy, and Air Force in support of United States foreign policy objectives and the Global Combatant Commanders.

General Downing retired as the Commander of the United States Special Operations Command, having served 34 years in the United States Army. Following his retirement, General Downing directed the 1996 Khobar Towers Commission and served as a Commissioner on the 2000 National Commission on Terrorism. In 2001, General Downing was asked by President George W. Bush to serve in the White House as National Director and Deputy National Security Advisor for Combating Terrorism. In this position, he was responsible for coordinating the diplomatic, law enforcement, intelligence, financial, and military aspects of the war on terrorism. Finally, in 2003, General Downing was appointed as the first Distinguished Chair of the Combating Terrorism Center (CTC) at West Point until his sudden and untimely death in 2007. On October 10, 2008, the Greater Peoria Airport was renamed "General Wayne A. Downing Peoria International Airport" during a groundbreaking ceremony in honor of the late General Downing. His friend H. Ross Perot, Sr., donated the bronze statue of General Downing that stands vigilant on patrol in front of the airport.

Downing served our country in the highest levels of command and in the critical positions during three decades of our nation's wars. He was considered to be a decisive, courageous, forceful, and caring leader known in particular for his unwavering determination to accomplish any mission assigned and provide his soldiers the best possible support. Following his retirement, General Downing repeatedly answered the call of public service. He was one of our nation's foremost advisors and experts on fighting the war on global terrorism. Accordingly, the Association of Graduates of the United States Military Academy presented the 2006 Distinguished Graduate Award to Wayne A. Downing.[3]

> AS CINC USSOCOM, HE WAS RESPONSIBLE FOR TRAINING, EQUIPPING, AND DEPLOYING THE 47,000 SPECIAL OPERATORS FROM THE ARMY, NAVY, AND AIR FORCE IN SUPPORT OF U.S. FOREIGN POLICY OBJECTIVES AND THE GLOBAL COMBATANT COMMANDERS.

that taking charge of H-2 in 1959 could be "a career-ending event." By graduation in 1962, the company was taking honors as best company in the Corps. In addition to Downing, H-2 would also start the careers of Lieutenant General Dennis Benchoff and Lieutenant General Robert Ord. A considerable achievement for what was earlier considered the worst company in the Corps.

Downing was granted an appointment to West Point as a result of being the son of a deceased World War II veteran, Private First Class Francis Wayne "Bud" Downing, killed in March 1945 in Germany with the 9th Armored Division. Following graduation, assignments in Okinawa and with the 173rd Airborne Brigade in Vietnam, Captain Downing became an instructor at the Infantry School at Fort Benning and a Company Commander in the 1st Training Brigade in the Infantry Training Center. His second tour in Vietnam from 1968 to 1970 would include command of A Company, 2nd Battalion, 14th Infantry Regiment, 25th Infantry Division and Operations Officer (S-3) at both the Battalion and Brigade level of 2nd Brigade, 25th Infantry Division. In 1971, Major Downing earned a master's in Business Administration (MBA)

At Yankee stadium, first pitch activities

July 2007 as Dep SOCOM

Lieutenant General Frank Kearney, USMA 1976

- DEPUTY DIRECTOR, US NATIONAL COUNTER TERRORISM CENTER (NCTC)
- DEPUTY COMMANDER, US SPECIAL OPERATIONS COMMAND (USSOCOM)
- COMMANDER, SPECIAL OPERATIONS COMMAND CENTRAL, US CENTRAL COMMAND (SOCCENT)
- ASSISTANT COMMANDER, JOINT SPECIAL OPERATIONS COMMAND (JSOC)
- ASSISTANT DIVISION COMMANDER, 24TH INFANTRY DIVISION
- CHIEF, JOINT MILITARY COMMISSION, TUZLA, BOSNIA
- COMMANDER, SETAF INFANTRY, BRIGADE, VICENZA, ITALY (BOSNIA, KOSOVO)
- COMMANDER, 3RD RANGER BATTALION, FORT BENNING GEORGIA
- COMMANDER, 1ST BATTALION, 501ST AIRBORNE BRIGADE, ALASKA
- OPERATIONS OFFICER, 3RD RANGER BATTALION, INVASION OF PANAMA
- TACTICAL OFFICER, COMPANY F-3, US CORPS OF CADETS WEST POINT
- COMPANY COMMANDER, A CO, 2ND RANGER BATTALION, INVASION OF GRENADA
- COMPANY COMMANDER, 4TH INFANTRY DIVISION

Frank Kearney is a West Point graduate who led special operations soldiers for three decades in nearly every conflict the United States has undertaken since the invasion of Grenada. As a young Captain, Kearney led a Ranger company parachuting into the dawn hours of Grenada so low that they didn't carry reserve parachutes. As a Major, he jumped into Rio Hato Airfield in Panama as the Operations Officer of 3rd Ranger Battalion. As a Colonel, he served as the Chief of the Joint Military Commission in Bosnian pursuing persons indicted for war criminals. After the attacks of September 11th, as a Brigadier General, he served as Deputy Commander of Joint Special Operations Command (JSOC) and planned the initial special operations attacks into both Afghanistan in 2001 and then the invasion of Iraq in 2003. As a Major General, he commanded all theater special operations troops in the CENTCOM area of operations that included Iraq, Afghanistan, Yemen, Lebanon, and other operations from 2005–2007. He served as Deputy Commander of US Special Operations Command from 2007–2010.

Kearney's career, and his life, has been unconventional. The second of six children, he grew up in Newburgh, New York, in a family with little money and little hope for a college education. That was at a time when race riots defined the city of Newburgh's reputation. His senior year in high school, near the end of the Vietnam War, the popularity of the American military among the public was at an all time low. The Kearney family had little money with eight mouths to feed. Yet Kearney was determined to pursue a military path, in large part due to financial reasons. He applied only to West Point with barely enough money scraped up to pay for the SAT and application forms. His guidance counselor, unsupportive of the military, asked Kearney why he would even apply to West Point. Kearney's plan was

>>> Spotlight

LTG Kearney served as the Deputy Director of the US National Counterterrorism Center. Their mission is to "Lead our nation's effort to combat terrorism at home and abroad by analyzing the threat, sharing information with our partners, and integrating all instruments of national power to ensure unity of effort."

www.nctc.org

Retirement Ceremony, 4 Nov 2011 at NCTC

a lifetime Rugby player. His junior year at West Point Kearney met Betty-Sue, a student at Ladycliff College (the all-female school previously located in what is now the West Point Museum. Ladycliff closed in 1980). They married shortly after graduation in July 1976 and would have two sons, Sean and Daniel. Kearney chose the Infantry branch and selected the 4th Infantry Division at Ft. Carson, mostly out of quality of life decision for he and Betty-Sue. As fate would have it, the 4th Infantry Division, the rapid deployment heavy division, was understrength during the oil embargo with little funding for training, but it would nonetheless turn out to be a good career choice. Kearney served as an Infantry Platoon Leader, Scout Platoon Leader, Battalion Motor Officer and then was chosen as a Company Commander as one of a few First Lieutenant's in the division to command prior to attending the Advanced Course. This command as a First Lieutenant changed his fate, as he was selected to attend the Armor Advanced Course and then selected to join the 2nd Ranger Battalion in 1980. By 1983 Kearney was Company Commander of A Company, 2nd Ranger Battalion, with 160 Airborne-Rangers under his command. Ranger commands are only granted to officers who have first commanded a conventional unit of the same size, so the command at Ft. Carson had fortuitously prepared him well for the Ranger command.

Kearney's first combat experience in 1983 and his last combat experience 27 years later in 2010 would exemplify a generation of progress and maturation for the United States Special Operations Community. When President Ronald Reagan ordered the invasion of Grenada due to a Marxist coup in order to liberate American medical students at the University of Grenada, little was known about the Island, and a hasty invasion was ordered. It was a joint operation of Army, Navy, Air Force, and Marines. Among the special operations groups involved in the invasion included Rangers, SEALS, and DELTA. The hasty invasion had poor planning and confusion reigned. There had been no military maps of the island and commanders were forced to use tourist maps. Yet even without a well-planned invasion, the soldiers were well trained to operate in small teams, and despite the confusion, the soldiers in small two and three man ad hoc teams, won the day. Kearney lost three of his Rangers killed in action and seven wounded. At the time the two Ranger Battalions each operated independently with no higher headquarters. Out of the chaos of Grenada, was created

the 75th Ranger Regimental Headquarters and the 3d Ranger Battalion to ensure future Ranger operations were well planned and executed at the Regimental level. This change would serve the battalions well in the future.

After completing his command Captain Kearney attended graduate school at the University of South Carolina, en route to West Point. At West Point he served as a Tactical Officer for Cadet Company F-3 and coached the intercollegiate Rugby team. In this role as a mentor and advisor of cadets, he met many who would later serve in Special Operations with him, and who would go on to great leadership positions including Brigadier General Erik Kurilla, Colonel Brian Mennes and Colonel Dan Walwrath. Kearney was only one of two officers at West Point with recent combat experience and he was well known for it by the cadets. In 1988 Major Kearney left West Point for CGSC and then to return to the Rangers in 1989 where he served as the Operations and a Plans Officer for the 3rd Ranger Battalion. It was in this role that he was responsible for planning the battalion's role in the invasion of Panama.

AFTER RETIRING FROM THE ARMY, KEARNEY HAS FOCUSED HIS EFFORTS ON TRAINING CORPORATE LEADERS USING THE LEADERSHIP PRINCIPLES TAUGHT AT WEST POINT AND PRACTICED OVER HIS THIRTY-FIVE YEARS IN UNIFORM

On December 20, 1989, under the directive of President George H.W. Bush, the United States invaded Panama with the intent to ouster Panamanian dictator Manuel Noriega in Operation Just Cause. The entire 75th Ranger Regiment parachuted in to secure two airfields with 23 C-130s and 7 C141s simultaneously, while the 82nd Airborne would follow on and jump on the Omar Torrijos/Tocumen airfield hours later. Major Kearney, on his second combat jump, parachuted into Rio Hato Airfield in a classic Ranger mission to take down an airfield. The invasion force hit 40 targets simultaneously throughout Panama within seconds of each other. The difference between Grenada and Panama was stark in the planning.

to enlist in the Army if he wasn't accepted to West Point. He was indeed accepted, and in the end he was the only one of six siblings to graduate from college and later graduate school.

Kearney remembers feeling goose bumps the first time he ever put on a cadet uniform in July 1972: He had found his home and would not take off the uniform until retiring 39.5 years later. Among the classmates who joined the Long Gray Line with him on

July 2, 1972, would rise many of the great leaders who would help revive and lead the US Army 30 years later, including General Raymond Odierno, General Stan McChrystal, Lieutenant General David Barno, General Dave Rodriguez, LTG Frank Helmick, LTG Guy Swan, LTG Mike Barbero and Lieutenant General Keith Walker, and many others.

As a very skinny cadet, Kearney was a high jumper as a plebe on the Army track team. Years later he would gain weight and become

Company Commander,
Company G-2, USCC

Wedding 10 July 1976,
Amsterdam NY, Frank and
Betty-Sue Kearney

1LT Dan Kearney and BG Kearney, Mosul
Iraq, Christmas 2004, Commander
JIATF-FRE

It was also here that the model was proven successful that it isn't necessary to kill people to win the battle. In order to transition the country back to the Panamanian people as quickly as possible, major infrastructure was not attacked. The Noriega regime was decapitated and the country was quickly transitioned back to the peaceful Panamanian people while achieving US national security objectives. Kearney had been responsible for planning the 3d Ranger Battalion's entire operation. This would be a trend throughout his career, he was most often assigned as a commander or in Operations (planning)- two roles that often are the most competitive and that result in continued responsibility.

The unit returned from combat within a month of parachuting into Rio Hato. He remained in the battalion operations section and as the battalions XO until 1992 when he moved from 3rd Ranger Battalion to the 75th Ranger Headquarters as a newly promoted Lieutenant Colonel reporting into then Colonel David Grange. Tragically, the 3rd Ranger Battalion Commander LTC John T. Keneally (posthumously promoted to Colonel) was killed in an aircraft crash in training on 29 October 1992. Kearney was assigned by Colonel Grange as the interim battalion commander for four months. Normally, command of a Ranger unit requires command of a similar size regular army unit first, so this was an unfortunate and tragic situation, but allowed Kearney to take command for four months of 3rd Ranger Battalion. Several of his platoon leaders were his former cadets from West Point: Kurilla, Walrath and Mennes. Grange was the first of four commanders that Kearney in assessing his career considers his mentor, the other later mentors being General Buck Kernan, Lieutenant General Dell Dailey, General Doug Brown.

In March 1993, Kearney moved the family to Alaska to take permanent command of his battalion in the 1st of the 501st Airborne Regiment. While in Alaska, the 3rd Ranger Battalion and TF Ranger suffered the tragic loss of 19 soldiers in Mogadishu, Somalia in what would later be referred to as "Black Hawk Down" for the movie that was later made about the mission. Kearney returned to Ft. Benning to again take command of the 3rd Ranger Battalion. He had been assigned to the battalion as the Operations Officer in the invasion of Panama, the interim Commander prior to Mogadishu, and now he returned to lead the unit through the healing process after the tragic mission. One lesson he soon learned about healing, was that a new mission took the men's minds off of the previous one. No sooner had he taken command that the battalion started planning for the invasion of Haiti, which helped them recover from Somalia. 3rd Ranger Battalion was rigged and loaded on aircraft at Hunter Army Airfield in Savannah, Georgia but did not take off. General Wayne Downing came to LTC Kearney's aircraft and let him know the operation was on hold and the invasion was cancelled. Their aircraft landed on a secure airfield in Haiti without hostile fire and helped secure a peaceful government transition on the Island.

After completing a successful battalion command Kearney attended the Army War College in Carlisle Pennsylvania from 1996-1997. He then headed to northern Italy to command the SETAF Infantry Brigade (Airborne) which was later reflagged as the 173d Airborne Brigade and was promoted to Colonel by Major General David Grange while serving with him in Bosnia, Major Erik Kurilla served as Kearney's Brigade Operations Officer.

Kearney returned to the United States in March 2000 to the Joint Special Operations Command (JSOC). In this role he helped run "Operation Top Off" which was a major train-

Exercise Leatherneck Ranger, 29 Palms CA, Nov 1992 as Interim Commander 3rd Ranger Battalion with Major (now LTG) Mike Ferriter (S3)

With Yankee Catcher Francisco Cervelli 1st Pitch June 2010

ing exercise with secretary and Cabinet-level officials training for a major Weapons of Mass Destruction (WMD) attack. The exercise found the United States woefully unprepared for such a large-scale disaster.

When September 11th actually did occur, his JSOC was in the Balkans. It would take over a week for them to successfully re-enter the United States due to all aircraft, including the nations A-teams, grounded. Promoted to Brigadier General 1 Oct 2003, Kearney was responsible for planning the joint special operations attack against the Taliban in October 2001 that successfully demonstrated US attack capabilities deep in Afghanistan using Special Operations forces and inter-agency partners working together with major air support. Kearney remained in Afghanistan through Operations in Tora Bora, the initial operation intended to capture or kill Osama Bin Laden and his top Lieutenants. Bin Laden escaped into Pakistan and was finally killed

by Special Operations in 2012.

Returning from Afghanistan to JSOC, COL Promotable Kearney began planning the invasion of Iraq in earnest as the Assistant Commander of JSOC under JSOC Commander Major General Dell Dailey. Kearney was in and out of Iraq from March-June 2003 during the kinetic phases of Operation Iraqi Freedom. JSOC headquarters meanwhile, had grown from a previously sized unit of 200-300 people (when they largely were involved in hostage rescue and reactive missions) and now had grown to in excess of 1000 people coordinating Joint Special Operations mission globally to identify and disrupt terrorist networks around the world.

Soon after arriving as the JSOC Operations Officer, J3, a new commander MG Dell Dailey took command from MG Doug Brown.

In 2004 Brigadier General Kearney moved to Ft. Leavenworth to become the Assistant

Division Commander of 24th Infantry Division, which was largely a mobilization platform to help deploying units. In this role, he unfortunately was often required to notify families in the region of the loss of their loved one in Iraq or Afghanistan and attended funerals as the ranking officer, an honorable and important, yet dreaded role.

One of Frank and Betty-Sue's son's, Sean, became a very successful accountant in New York City and Charlotte. The other son, Dan, chose to follow his father's profession of arms. Dan became a very well known figure in the military community as the company Commander in the documentary "Restrepo" about a platoon in Afghanistan. From 2002-2012 Dan deployed as an infantry officer two times with conventional forces and multiple times with Ranger units and his dad, LTG Kearney often visited him in the combat zone. The son Captain Kearney led his soldiers in several intense combat operations. Several

of his soldiers were killed and wounded in both Iraq and Afghanistan. One of his soldiers, Sergeant Sal Giunta, would be awarded the Medal of Honor for his actions after being nominated for this award by Captain Kearney.

Throughout his career Frank Kearney has considered developing leaders as one of his primary responsibilities and skill sets. After retiring from the Army, he has focused his efforts on training corporate leaders using the leadership principles taught at West Point and practiced over his thirty-five years in uniform. He joined the Thayer Leader Development Group at West Point as a Senior Advisor and frequently leads C-level executives from global corporations through their leadership training at the Thayer Hotel.

Courtesy: Lee Van Arsdale

Lee (in brown jacket) advising on the set of Black Hawk Down.

Courtesy: Lee Van Arsdale

Colonel Lee Van Arsdale, USMA 1974

- **25 YEARS LEADING SPECIAL OPERATIONS TROOPS**
- **SQUADRON COMMANDER, 1ST SPECIAL FORCES OPERATIONS DETACHMENT, DELTA (SFOD-D)**
- **FOUGHT IN BATTLE OF MOGADISHU AND INVASION OF PANAMA**
- **MILITARY ADVISOR TO THE MOVIE *BLACK HAWK DOWN***
- **CHIEF EXECUTIVE OFFICER, TRIPLE CANOPY**
- **BOY SCOUTS OF AMERICA, YOUTH MEMBER**
- **SILVER STAR, PURPLE HEART**
- **BOARD OF ADVISORS, THAYER LEADER DEVELOPMENT GROUP**

Photo: NARA

© Dan Rice

Lee Van Arsdale with USMA 1974 classmates at the Thayer Hotel's dedication of the Colonel Lee Van Arsdale Room.

Successful Big Horn Sheep Hunt, 2012.
Courtesy: Lee Van Arsdale

© 2013 Greg E. Mathieson Sr./MAI

The Van Arsdale Room at the Thayer Hotel.

>>> Spotlight

The 2001 film *Black Hawk Down* chronicled the October 1993 mission to capture two of Mohammad Farrah Aidid's Lieutenants. Van Arsdale was one of the military advisors in the filming of the movie.

Courtesy: of Paramount Pictures

Courtesy: Lee Van Arsdale

Lee Van Arsdale was born to lead Special Operations soldiers in unconventional warfare. Although he loved his alma mater, he never needed a West Point ring on his finger or a rank on his collar to motivate him to guide his men – and he rarely wore either. The son of a career Army Sergeant Major, he took personal pride in the fact that the NCOs of the military's most elite Special Operations unit often said he led more like an NCO than an officer. He was unorthodox and unconventional, and people naturally liked, respected, and followed him in everything he did.

The Army nearly lost one of its best leaders to the private sector in 1979, when Van Arsdale left the Army after serving five-and-a-half years in the Infantry in the 101st Airborne Division and the 10th Special Forces Group. However, after a brief stint in the private sector, he found he missed being a Soldier and returned to the Army in 1983 to serve in the 172nd Light Infantry Brigade in Alaska. From there he went to the 1st Special Forces Operational Detachment–Delta assessment and selection course, and was accepted to serve in the Delta Force in 1985. He spent the next 14 years leading some of the most elite soldiers in the American military.

DUE TO THE NATURE OF THE WORK, MOST OF VAN ARSDALE'S TIME AND ACCOMPLISHMENTS IN SPECIAL OPERATIONS WILL BE KNOWN ONLY TO HIS COMRADES. BUT A FEW MOMENTS IN AMERICAN HISTORY WERE TOO HIGHLY VISIBLE TO BE KEPT SECRET.

Born in 1952, after his father had returned from World War II and Korea, Van Arsdale has led a life that has been both contrarian in his actions and in his timing. After growing up as an "Army brat" on bases around the world, Van Arsdale entered West Point in July 1970 at a time when joining the military was most unpopular, as much of the American public had grown weary of the Vietnam War. He was a tight end on the Army football team, but only during his senior year, after having been denied the medical pass required his first three years. However, not wanting to graduate without having played Army football, he simply went out for the team as a senior, the coaches assumed he had the medical pass. Near graduation, the commissioning physician informed Van Arsdale that he could not be commissioned into the Infantry due to knee injuries – shattering his dream. After "misappropriating" that paperwork, he was commissioned in the Infantry. He graduated from Infantry Basic, Airborne, and Ranger School (in which he was an Honor Graduate), then went on to lead Infantry and Special Operations soldiers for the next 25 years.

He and his soldiers distinguished themselves in actions around the world. Due to the nature of the work, most of his time and accomplishments in Special Operations will be known only to his comrades. But a few moments in American history were too highly visible to be kept secret. During the invasion of Panama in 1989, his SFOD Assault Troop executed more than 20 raids en route to apprehending the dictator Manual Noriega, whom Major Van Arsdale personally held while Noriega was handcuffed by SGM Tommy Corbett and Master Sergeant Kevin Connell.

In 1993, during the U.N. peacekeeping operation in the failed state of Somalia, Van Arsdale was serving in the Task Force Ranger Joint Operations Center, while his former squadron conducted several raids. On October 3, 1993, in what would be later referred to as Black Hawk Down, Task Force Ranger embarked on a mission to capture two of Mohammad Farrah Aidid's Lieutenants. (Aidid was the leader of a clan militia that had killed 22 Pakistani coalition troops the previous June, and Task Force Ranger was deployed to kill or capture Aidid and his leadership.)

In the battle that ensued that night, two Black Hawk helicopters were shot down and 17 American soldiers were Killed In Action. Van Arsdale was not on the original mission, but after the first Black Hawk went down he led the rescue effort from the airport to crash site #1. While the mission was accomplished and Aidid's militia was all but eliminated, the American public was unprepared for combat deaths in Somalia, and the Task Force was redeployed two weeks later. Two days after the battle, the Squadron Commander was injured in a mortar attack, and Van Arsdale was selected to return to his old squadron as the Commander. Much of what happened that night, but not all, was chronicled in the book and later the 2001 movie *Black Hawk Down* in which Van Arsdale was one of three military advisors.

After the battle, many of those on the mission felt that Van Arsdale should be awarded the Congressional Medal of Honor. The families of the returning soldiers had heard the stories of the battle and together visited Task Force Ranger Commander General Bill Garrison to request he be nominated for the medal. His two soldiers, Sergeant First Class Randy Shughart and MSG Gary Gordon, both did in fact receive the Medal of Honor posthumously for their actions, which were presented to their families on May 23, 1994, by President Clinton at the White House. For his actions, Van Arsdale was awarded the Silver Star and the Purple Heart.

He was promoted to Colonel and spent his last two years in the Army at the Pentagon in the Office of the Secretary of Defense as Counterterrorism and Special Projects Branch Chief. He was medically retired in 1999 after 25 years, but his impact on America's wars was far from over. In 2005, after the war in Iraq had turned to a full blown insurgency, the United States government began outsourcing security on a large scale. Van Arsdale became Chief Executive Officer of Triple Canopy and led that company from 2005 to 2009, in which time it quadrupled sales, more than doubled profitability, and expanded the number of employees from 1,000 to 6,000. When he retired in 2009, Triple Canopy was the largest American security company in Iraq and was known for quiet professionalism at a time when competitors were riddled in controversy.

After retiring from Triple Canopy, Van Arsdale became a partner in SunDial Capital Partners and helped successfully launch the first solar-powered micro-grids to Special Operations units in Afghanistan.

In 1977, Van Arsdale married Marilee and together they raised three sons, Luke, Nathan, and Paul. He received a master's degree from the University of Colorado and was inducted into Mensa. In 2009, he and his wife retired to a mountain home west of Colorado Springs, close to where he had attended high school prior to entering West Point nearly 40 years earlier.

The Lee Van Arsdale Room at the Thayer Hotel was proudly dedicated by SunDial Capital Partners.

Special Operations team in civilian clothes overseas, mid-1980s.

In an unnamed jungle conducting Special Operations missions.

Lieutenant General Buster Hagenbeck served 39 years in the Army, leading soldiers through the Vietnam era, the Cold War, the Invasion of Grenada, and culminating in leading the largest conventional action since Vietnam in Operation Anaconda in 2001 to 2002 in Afghanistan. After a career spent traveling the world in the service of his country, there are four themes that are consistent themes in his life: family, West Point, Florida State, and football.

Hagenbeck was born in Rabat, Morocco, on November 25, 1949. His father, Carl, was serving overseas as an enlisted sailor overflying Eastern Europe. Carl had served aboard the legendary aircraft carrier *USS Enterprise* throughout World War II, from March 1941 through March 1945. He was aboard the *USS Enterprise* when she arrived at Pearl Harbor on December 8th while the fleet was still in flames after the Japanese attack on December 7th. He served aboard the *Enterprise* during the Battle of Midway, Guadalcanal, and Leyte Gulf on the most decorated ship in World War II with 20 battle stars.

"Buster" Hagenbeck grew up in Jacksonville, Florida, with his two sisters, Carla and Robin, and younger brother, Casey. He played baseball and football for three years and served as a Class Officer throughout his time at Forrest High School in Jacksonville, Florida. He fell in love with a girl who lived a few blocks away, Judy, whom he would date during college and marry upon graduation. Growing up in Jacksonville, he had always dreamed of playing football at Florida State University. An avid athlete, he had walk-on offers from Arkansas and Florida State Universities, but was also accepted to both West Point and Annapolis with an "at large" nomination from Senator William Fulbright of Arkansas. The Vietnam War was waging and Hagenbeck was torn: He wanted to enlist to serve in Vietnam and then go to college on the GI Bill. His father preferred Hagenbeck earn a commission, so West Point was the perfect solution.

Hagenbeck entered West Point in July 1967 and played sprint football (150 pound) as a strong safety and returning punts. He also played rugby. Like all cadets at that time,

he majored in engineering, but he chose his field of study in National Security and Public

OPERATION ANACONDA IN MARCH 2002 WAS THE LARGEST CONVENTIONAL FIGHT SINCE VIETNAM. IT UNDERSCORED CENTRALIZED PLANNING, DECENTRALIZED EXECUTION – THE FIGHT WAS LED BY WELL-TRAINED JUNIOR OFFICERS AND SERGEANTS WHO WERE PHYSICALLY AND MENTALLY TOUGH.

Affairs. The Class of 1971 attended West Point at the height of the Vietnam War (from 1967 to 1971) and there seemed to be several burials every week for graduates Killed In Action, which had a big impact on Hagenbeck and his fellow cadets. Despite the casualties, Hagenbeck and most of his classmates volunteered to deploy to Vietnam upon graduation, but only a few actually deployed to that conflict. The United States was withdrawing and only a few logisticians and support

personnel deployed in the waning months of the war; most who joined the combat arms did not deploy.

Hagenbeck attended the basic Infantry courses at Fort Benning before deploying to Hawaii with the 25th Infantry Division where he served as a Platoon Leader, Executive Officer, and Company Commander. After attending the Advanced Course, Captain Hagenbeck was accepted to attend graduate school at Florida State University, where he had been offered a football walk-on opportunity 10 years earlier. He returned home to Florida where he and Judy had grown up to attend graduate school. While at graduate school, Hagenbeck coached football and served on the staff of the Florida State Seminole football team as an Assistant Coach under future Hall of Fame Coach Bobby Bowden. He received an

Lieutenant General Franklin L. Hagenbeck, USMA 1971

- **COMMANDING GENERAL, TASK FORCE 180, AFGHANISTAN WAR**
- **SUPERINTENDENT, WEST POINT**
- **COMMANDING GENERAL 10TH MOUNTAIN DIVISION**
- **G-1, DEPUTY CHIEF OF STAFF FOR PERSONNEL, DEPARTMENT OF THE ARMY**
- **ASSISTANT DIVISION COMMANDER FOR OPERATIONS; 101ST AIRBORNE (AIR ASSAULT) DIVISION**

Brigadier General Hagenbeck 101st Parachute operation in Belgium, 1999.

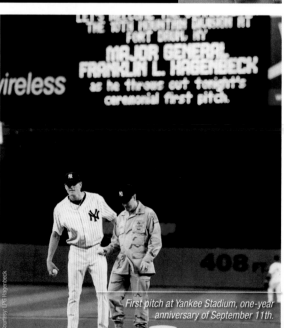

First pitch at Yankee Stadium, one-year anniversary of September 11th.

master's in Business Administration from LIU in 1980.

In 1981, Major Hagenbeck was assigned to Fort Bragg, North Carolina. President Reagan ordered the 82nd Airborne Division to liberate the Island of Grenada in October 1983, and Hagenbeck deployed as the division's liaison to Special Operations. In 1984, he attended Command and General Staff College, followed by an assignment to the Australian Infantry Center in Singleton, Australia. He returned to Washington, D.C., as an Infantry Branch Officer from 1987 to 1988. Lieutenant Colonel Hagenbeck received his battalion command in 1989 as Commander 1/87th Infantry 10th Mountain Division. He was promoted to Colonel and commanded 3rd Training Brigade from 1993 to 1995 at Fort Leonard Wood, Missouri. Promoted to Brigadier General, he became the Assistant Division Commander for Operations (ADC-O) of the 101st Airborne, Division from 1998 to 1999, followed by a two-year assignment on the Joint Staff in the Pentagon.

Major General Hagenbeck took command of the 10th Mountain Division in 2001, five weeks before the attacks of September 11th. Subsequently, the Army mobilized to attack the Taliban and Al Qaeda in Afghanistan. In October 2001, Major General Hagenbeck deployed one of his battalions (the 1-87th Infantry Battalion) to provide force protection for Special Operations Forces in Afghanistan. In November 2001, Major General Hagenbeck traveled to Afghanistan and Pakistan with Army Chief of Staff General Shinseki (USMA 1965). En route back to the United States, General Shinseki ordered the headquarters element of 10th Mountain Division to deploy within 72 hours in support of Operation Enduring Freedom and what would become a 10,000-person conventional force that would later include nine coalition countries and some special operations. The headquarters became "Coalition Task Force (CTF) Mountain," and in mid-2002, it expanded to "Coalition Joint Task Force (CJTF) 180."

"Entering Afghanistan in the fall of 2001 was like going back to biblical times – no reliable running water, electricity, communications, road networks. Very difficult terrain and extreme weather conditions. Operation Anaconda in March 2002 was the largest conventional fight since Vietnam. It underscored centralized planning, decentralized execution – the fight was led by well-trained Junior Officers and Sergeants who were physically and mentally tough," said Hagenbeck. The 10th Mountain Division would be the first of many divisions to deploy over the next decade to Afghanistan to fight extremists and help bring Afghanistan into the world community with roads, communications, and improved centralized governance.

In 2006, Lieutenant General Hagenbeck became the Superintendent of West Point to prepare the next generation of our nation's leaders after having served himself for nearly four decades. As he looks back on his times at West Point he thinks of General Powell's description that "West Point is the wellspring of our profession." From 2006 to 2010, while America was at war in both Iraq and Afghanistan, cadets continued to volunteer to join the Long Gray Line and West Point was able to continue to attract the best men and women from across the country. In 2009, under Hagenbeck's leadership after eight years of continuous war and casualties, *Forbes Magazine* ranked West Point as the "#1 University in the United States."

Hagenbeck retired in 2010 and serves on several for-profit and non-profit boards.

He works with corporate America to train executives using the principles that helped build the United States Army from the broken Army of 1971 to the greatest fighting force in the world. "Everything starts and ends with leadership. It begins with competency and caring built upon a foundation of integrity and trust," says Hagenbeck.

Lieutenant General and Mrs. Hagenbeck have two children – a son Kelly and a daughter Leeann – and four grandchildren.

Lieutenant General Hagenbeck's official superintendent portrait.

Operation Bright Star with 82nd Airborne Division, 1982.

Lieutenant General and Mrs. Hagenbeck, Founder's Day, 2007.

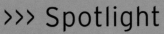

>>> Spotlight

Lieutenant General Hagenbeck was born and raised in Jacksonville, Florida. He received a master's degree from Florida State University (FSU), served as an assistant coach of the FSU football team, and now serves on the Board of Governors for the College of Human Sciences of the University. FSU is a top-tier undergraduate and graduate university with more than 40,000 students located in Tallahassee, Florida. Lieutenant General Hagenbeck has been selected as one of the "Top 100 FSU Graduates."

Logo Courtesy: Florida State University

President Obama and Lieutenant General Hagenbeck, May 22, 2010, USMA graduation.

Fred Franks's life story serves as an amazing parallel to the story of the United States Army, from when it was badly beaten down after Vietnam to its triumph in Desert Storm. Like the United States Army, after being seriously wounded in Vietnam, he faced a challenging recovery over many years. That is, until he fully rebounded, leading United States forces to crush the third-largest Army in the world in 1991.

Franks was born in West Lawn, Pennsylvania, where he attended local schools and graduated from Wilson High School in 1954. He attended West Point and graduated June 3, 1959, from Airborne and Ranger Schools and was commissioned as an Armor Officer. He received multiple assignments in both the 3rd and 11th Armored Cavalry Units, then was deployed to Vietnam in 1969. But not before he married his sweetheart, Denise, in 1959 and had a daughter, Marjorie, in 1961. He

and Denise have been married for more than 50 years.

As a Major, Franks served in Vietnam as Operations Officer (S-3) 2nd Squadron, 11th Armored Cavalry Regiment. During the invasion of Cambodia on May 5, 1970, a North Vietnamese grenade seriously wounded him near Snuol, Cambodia. After being evacuated, he endured multiple surgeries, which ended in amputating his left leg below the knee at Valley Forge General Hospital in January

1971. There he remained from May 1970 to February 1972 to recover and rehabilitate with a prosthetic leg, until he was able to return to active duty in February 1972.

The United States Army was badly battered after Vietnam, and the 1970s were a difficult time for both the United States Army and the Franks's family. He and his family still refer to that time as "the Valley Forge Experience," after how beaten down the Continental Army had been at the beginning of a six-month

General Fred Franks, USMA 1959

- **COMMANDING GENERAL, VII CORPS OPERATION DESERT STORM**
- **COMMANDING GENERAL, TRADOC**
- **TEAM CAPTAIN, ARMY BASEBALL**
- **NINTH CHAIRMAN OF THE BATTLE MONUMENTS COMMISSION (ABMC)**
- **CHAIRMAN, U.S. ARMY AMPUTEE ADVISORY BOARD**
- **CHAIR, SIMON CENTER FOR PROFESSIONAL MILITARY ETHIC AT WEST POINT**
- **WEST POINT DISTINGUISHED GRADUATE AWARD**

General Franks's official photo.

1959 Army Baseball Captain.

>>> Spotlight

Into the Storm: A Study in Command, a book authored by General Franks and Tom Clancy, became a *New York Times* best seller.

Courtesy: Fred Franks

encampment during the winter of 1778 to 1779, yet they emerged highly trained, confident, and ready fight. Likewise, Franks and the modern Army rebuilt, re-armed, and emerged stronger than ever. During the next 18 years, from early 1975 to 1984, Franks commanded Armored Cavalry units at the squadron in the 3rd Armored Cavalry Regiment and the Regimental level of the 11th Armored Cavalry Regiments. He received two master's degrees from Columbia University and graduated from the National War College. Then, in the 1980s, President Reagan expanded the Army, modernizing it to fight the next war.

In August 1990, 20 years after being wounded in Cambodia, Franks was commanding the VII Corps in Germany when Saddam Hussein's forces invaded Kuwait. In 1991, the world held its breath as it prepared for the impending war with Iraq. Allied forces, overwhelmingly American, stood on the border of Saudi Arabia, preparing to invade and liberate Kuwait from the Iraqis who had invaded it six months earlier. Allied aircrews pounded Iraqi forces 24 hours a day throughout Kuwait and Iraq for five weeks, starting January 17, 1991. Many air forces were shot down and several were killed or taken prisoner. The American public was told to expect up to 20,000 casualties to liberate Kuwait from Saddam Hussein's Army, which, at the time, was the third-largest Army in the world.

At the order of President George H.W. Bush, the ground invasion began on February 24, 1991, as allied armored forces launched the largest invasion since Normandy. In what became known as the "Left Hook," United States forces spearheaded the invasion of Iraq and enveloped the Iraqi forces still in Kuwait. In 89 hours, the VII Corps of United States and British forces, led by Lieutenant General Franks, accomplished the impossible: attacking more than 250 kilometers with four United States divisions and one British armored corps across the desert, linking up with the XVIII Airborne, then crushing the Iraqi forces and liberating Kuwait. The entire ground war lasted less than four days with 187 American servicemen Killed In Action. Franks had overcome incredible odds and had battled adversity to achieve this command.

He concluded his active service as Commanding General Training and Doctrine Command (TRADOC) from 1991 to 1994, when he was responsible for the United States Army's school system, for formulating concepts and requirements for future land warfare, and for publishing the first post–Cold War Army war fighting doctrine.

After retiring, Franks actively supported military and veterans causes. President George W. Bush appointed him to serve as the ninth Chairman on the American Battle Monuments Commission (ABMC), doing so from January 2005 through January 2009. Franks was also appointed to serve on the Defense Health Board and chaired the United States Army Amputee Advisory Board. Currently, he serves as a senior advisor with the Veterans Outreach for the Red Sox Foundation and Massachusetts General Home Base Program, which serves the needs of veterans and their families for post-traumatic stress disorder (PTSD) and traumatic brain injury (TBI).

He serves as the Class of 1966 Chair in the Simon Center for the Professional Military Ethic at West Point, where he teaches battle command and serves as a mentor to the United States Army's current Profession of Arms. He co-authored a *New York Times* best seller with Tom Clancy, called *Into the Storm: A Study in Command*. He received four awards for valor, two Purple Hearts, numerous military awards for service, and individual decorations and awards from France, Germany, Spain, and his native Pennsylvania. In May 2000, the West Point Association of Graduates named him a Distinguished Graduate of West Point. In May 2008, he was inducted in to the Fort Leavenworth Hall of Fame.

IN 89 HOURS, THE VII CORPS OF U.S. AND BRITISH FORCES, LED BY LIEUTENANT GENERAL FRANKS, ACCOMPLISHED THE IMPOSSIBLE: ATTACKING MORE THAN 250 KILOMETERS WITH FOUR U.S. DIVISIONS AND ONE BRITISH ARMORED CORPS, THEN CRUSHING THE IRAQI FORCES AND LIBERATING KUWAIT.

Promotion to General, by Army Chief of Staff Gordon Sullivan, with wife, Denise, August 1991.

Desert Storm February 25, 1991, planning meeting for continuation of attack.

General Franks Guest Room at the Thayer Hotel.

The General Fred Franks Room at the Thayer Hotel was proudly dedicated by the Osh Kosh Corporation.

General Sheik Mohammad Bin Zayed Alnahyan, Abu Dhabi Crown Prince, greets General Abizaid in Abu Dhabi July 20, 2005.

General John Philip Abizaid, USMA 1973

- **LONGEST-SERVING U.S. CENTRAL COMMAND (CENTCOM) COMMANDER, 2003–07**
- **COMMANDED 1ST INFANTRY DIVISION AS THE INITIAL GROUND FORCE IN KOSOVO**
- **DIRECTOR OF PLANS AND POLICY (J-5) AND DIRECTOR OF THE JOINT STAFF ON AND AFTER 9/11**
- **66TH COMMANDANT OF CADETS, 1997–99**
- **COMMANDED A RANGER COMPANY THAT PARACHUTED INTO GRENADA**
- **FIRST OLMSTED SCHOLAR TO STUDY IN AN ARAB COUNTRY**
- **WEST POINT DISTINGUISHED CADET AND DISTINGUISHED GRADUATE AWARD**
- **BOY SCOUTS OF AMERICA, YOUTH MEMBER**

General John P. Abizaid is one of his generation's most intelligent and influential West Point graduates who stands out both for his leadership in numerous combat theaters and his deep knowledge of the Middle East. He commanded units at every level from Platoon to Combatant Command serving in Jordan, Grenada, Lebanon, Iraq, Bosnia, Kosovo, and throughout the Middle East as he concluded his 34-year Army career in 2007 as the longest-serving Commander of

United States Central Command. Abizaid was an exceptional leader and Middle East expert who unfailingly provided his candid, blunt, and well-informed analysis to improve United States national security policy. After retirement, he has continued to serve as the Distinguished Chair in the Combating Terrorism Center at West Point, with the Hoover Institution at Stanford, and in other important roles.

Abizaid was born on April 1, 1951, in Redwood City, California and grew up in Coleville,

California, a small high desert town at the base of the Sierra Nevada mountains. After his mother died of cancer when he was 10, he was raised by his father, who had served as a machinist in the Navy during World War II. From his father, Abizaid learned a great respect for service, camaraderie, and the opportunity that the military could provide. He studied hard in high school and was admitted to West Point at the height of the Vietnam War as a member of the United States Military Academy Class of 1973.

Cadet Abizaid was more inclined to succeed in languages, history, and social sciences than he was in math or engineering, but his determination and hard work paid off. He finished 42nd out of 944 in his class and was an exceptional history student. His senior thesis, "Great Power Diplomacy and the Bosnian Crisis of 1908–09," was a graduate-level 133-page tome, including extensive citations of Austrian, German, and British original documents. The thesis is still in use by West Point both for its historical

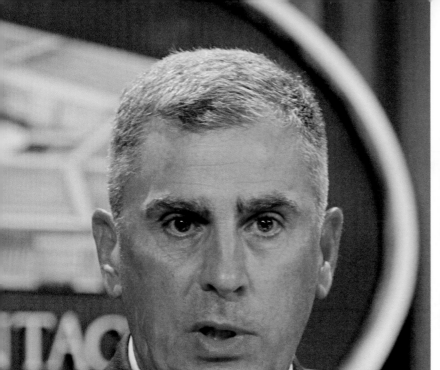

ABIZAID

General Abizaid talks with reporters at the Pentagon, July 16, 2003. Abizaid said Iraqi insurgents are increasingly organized and are waging a "classical guerilla-type" campaign against American forces.

>>> Spotlight

In the movie *Heartbreak Ridge*, Clint Eastwood portrays General Abizaid's decisive action after he parachuted into Grenada in command of a Ranger Company. Then, Captain Abizaid ordered a Sergeant to hot-wire a bulldozer and charge at Cuban fighters with the blade raised, while Abizaid and his Rangers advanced behind it.

General Abizaid takes command of CENTCOM from General Tommy Franks, July 7, 2003, in Tampa, Florida.

contribution and as a model for today's cadets. Beyond academics, Abizaid was well respected by his classmates, who called him the "Mad Arab," owing to his Lebanese heritage. In his senior year, he commanded Company G-1 was commissioned in the Infantry.

After graduation, he married Kathy (his home-town sweetheart from Coleville), completed his Infantry schooling, and reported to 1st Battalion, 504th Parachute Infantry Regiment at Fort Bragg. He excelled as a Rifle and

Scout Platoon Leader and was selected for the Rangers, with his initial assignment with the 2nd Battalion, 75th Ranger Regiment in Fort Lewis, Washington. While serving as Headquarters Company Commander, Abizaid was selected as an Olmsted Scholar – a distinction for only a handful of officers from all services – and he was the first Olmsted Scholar to study in an Arab country. He and his family spent two years in Jordan, studying at the University of Amman and traveling

throughout the Middle East. This challenging assignment at a critical time was critical to General Abizaid's personal and professional development and served him well throughout his career. He built on this experience earning a M.A. from Harvard, and later completing the Armed Forces Staff College and a war college fellowship at Stanford's Hoover Institution.

An Olmsted Scholarship might derail the careers of other officers, but not Captain Abizaid. He soon took command of A Company,

1st Battalion, 75th Rangers, with whom he parachuted into combat during Operation Urgent Fury in Grenada in 1983. Soon after Grenada, he worked for General Max Thurman, the Army Vice Chief of Staff, then spent a year with the United Nations Observer Group in Lebanon. In 1986, he joined the 3rd Battalion, 325th Infantry in Vicenza, Italy, eventually taking command of the battalion. In 1991, he deployed his battalion to Iraq during Operation Provide Comfort, protecting the Kurdish popu-

General Abizaid in Fallujah, Iraq, February 12, 2004, moments after an explosion nearby.

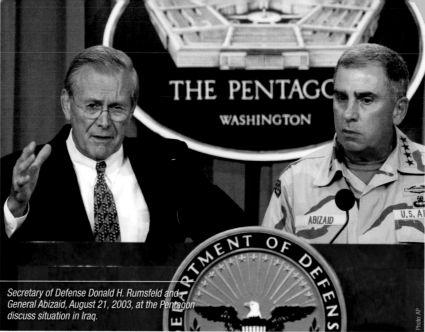

Secretary of Defense Donald H. Rumsfeld and General Abizaid, August 21, 2003, at the Pentagon discuss situation in Iraq.

Defense Secretary Robert Gates (left) is greeted at the aircraft by General Abizaid and General Casey in Baghdad, Iraq, December 20, 2006.

lation in Northern Iraq after Desert Storm.

He later commanded 1st Brigade, 82nd Airborne at Fort Bragg and was the Assistant Division Commander (Maneuver) for the 1st Armored Division as the division formed part of the NATO Stabilization Force in Bosnia. He would later return to the Balkans as the Commanding General of the 1st Infantry Division, the "Big Red One," commanding the initial ground deployment into Kosovo.

While serving as the 66th Commandant of

Cadets at West Point from 1997 to 1999, Brigadier General Abizaid improved the military program, reduced hazing rituals, emphasized realistic military training, and improved cadet leadership development.

His key assignments working with the Joint Chiefs of Staff included service as the Executive Assistant to the Chairman of the Joint Chiefs, Director of Plans and Policy (J-5), and Director of the Joint Staff. In the latter two positions, he coordinated the interagency and

international response after the September 11, 2001, attacks, including supervising day-to-day operations and military advice for the Joint Chiefs of Staff Chairman and the Secretary

ABIZAID WAS AN EXCEPTIONAL LEADER AND MIDDLE EAST EXPERT WHO UNFAILINGLY PROVIDED HIS CANDID, BLUNT, AND WELL-INFORMED ANALYSIS TO IMPROVE U.S. NATIONAL SECURITY POLICY.

of Defense. Based on his success in these positions, Abizaid was selected as the Deputy Commander and then as the Commander of United States Central Command (CENTCOM) from 2003 to 2007.

As the CENTCOM Commander, Abizaid bluntly and accurately described the challenges America faced, based on his observations and experience in the Middle

General Abizaid meets Pakistan's President General Pervez Musharraf at President House in Islamabad, Pakistan, on January 10, 2005.

Egyptian Minister of Defense and Military Production Field Marshall Mohammed Hussein Tantawi talks to General Abizaid, September 15, 2005.

Afghan President Hamid Karzai meets with General Abizaid in the Presidential palace in Kabul, November 26, 2004.

East. At the outset of the Iraq War, when some downplayed the insurgency, he was the first to correctly describe it as a guerilla-type campaign, thereby realistically preparing soldiers, leaders, and the American public. He recognized the protracted nature of the conflict and coined the term "The Long War" to capture the persistent conflict against religious-inspired extremists. Soldiers, military commanders, and thoughtful policymakers always respected and appreciated General Abizaid for not only being

wise enough to understand complex problems, but also having the moral courage to plainly speak the truth.

Throughout his 54 months as CENTCOM Commander and Deputy, General Abizaid effectively coordinated military strategy and joint operations across the Middle East, the Horn of Africa, and Central Asia. He assiduously worked to promote counterterrorist and counterinsurgency capabilities to help the nations of the region help themselves, improving security

for the United States and the world.

Since retiring, he has continued contributions to the nation and especially to the Corps of Cadets as the Distinguished Chair in the Combating Terrorism Center (CTC) at West Point. In this capacity, he has taught a section of cadets, provided dozens of guest lectures, improved the quality of published reports, and provided critical advice for Academy leaders. As Chair, he shaped the publication and wrote the forward the CTC's path-breaking report

on Osama bin Laden's documents seized during the Abbotabad raid. General Abizaid's significant, positive impact on the nation was recognized when West Point designated him as a Distinguished Graduate in 2009.

Written by: Brigadier General Michael J. Meese, PhD (USA, Retired), USMA 1981.

The 75th Ranger Regiment is one of the most prestigious units in the United States Army comprised of all United States Army Rangers. It remains one of the only units in the Army that has been in continuous combat since October 19, 2001, and still so as of the writing of this book. In 2009, Colonel Erik Kurilla took command of this elite Special Operations unit, joining the list of distinguished commanders, including several who were West Point graduates, such as Wayne Downing (USMA 1962) and Stanley McChrystal (USMA 1976), both of whom also commanded the 2nd Ranger Battalion.

Erik Kurilla was raised in Elk River, Minnesota, and graduated from Saint John's Preparatory School in Collegeville,

Minnesota, where he played baseball and football. He played Rugby at West Point and graduated in the top five percent of his class academically as a "star man" with a degree in Aerospace Engineering. He chose the Infantry Branch and his first assignment was in the 82nd Airborne Division. At that time, in 1988, the United States had not been involved in significant combat operations since the Vietnam War had ended 15 years earlier (1973) and the Cold War seemed to be warming between United States and Soviet leaders Reagan and Gorbachev. Thus, significant combat operations seem less likely – or so the conventional thinking at the time went. However, folklore at West Point holds that if it rains upon the class graduation, that class is destined for war. Ominously, it not only rained, but it poured

throughout the entire 1988 West Point graduation from start to finish. Vice President George H.W. Bush handed Kurilla and each member of the class their diplomas, and they departed West Point to join the Cold War Army.

The Cold War ended nearly one year later without a shot being fired as the Wall came down and the Soviet Union dissolved. Unfortunately, with a peaceful end of the Cold War, the world became less stable instead of more stable, and the United States as the only Super Power would find itself in recurring combat operations for decades to come. It took only 18 months after graduation before Kurilla would parachute into Panama as a Rifle Platoon Leader during Operation Just Cause. Kurilla would

himself be involved in almost every major conflict in which the United States participated: Panama (1989), Desert Shield/Desert Storm (1990–91), Haiti (1994), multiple missions in Kosovo, Bosnia, and Macedonia (1999–2002), and multiple deployments to Iraq and Afghanistan, including deployments that covered every year over 10 years, from 2004 to 2013.

At the peak of the Iraq War in 2004, Kurilla deployed his Infantry Battalion to Mosul, one of the most dangerous cities in Iraq. Over the course of the next year, his soldiers would have contact with the enemy nearly daily. The Stryker battalion "Deuce Four" of roughly 800 soldiers took 187 casualties killed or wounded and the Iraqi security forces that they were leading would be

Brigadier General Michael "Erik" Kurilla, USMA 1988

- ASSISTANT COMMANDER, JOINT SPECIAL OPERATIONS COMMAND (JSOC)
- DIRECTOR OF OPERATIONS, JOINT SPECIAL OPERATIONS COMMAND (JSOC)
- COMMANDER, 75TH RANGER REGIMENT
- COMMANDER, 2ND RANGER BATTALION
- COMMANDER, 1ST BATTALION, 24TH INFANTRY DIVISION "DEUCE FOUR" (STRYKER)
- COMPANY COMMANDER, 3RD RANGER BATTALION
- COMPANY COMMANDER, 2ND INFANTRY DIVISION, KOREA
- RIFLE PLATOON LEADER, 3RD RANGER BATTALION AND 82ND AIRBORNE DIVISION

Photo: DOD

KURILLA

Lieutenant Colonel Kurilla and Sergeant First Class Bowman leading soldiers after 1 of 55 car bombs hit their patrol.

>>> Spotlight

"The 75th Ranger Regiment remains the most elite Infantry force in the world. As the Army's premier special operations raid force with more than 10 years of continuous combat experience, the Ranger Regiment must carry on its tradition as a standard bearer for discipline and excellence. It must continue to link our Army's brigade combat teams and special operations forces by mitigating its best leaders, training, equipment, and warrior ethos to the operational force in unified land operations while actively collaborating with the Army's Centers of Excellence to further this end. Finally, the 75th Ranger Regiment will stand ready to execute the most difficult joint special operations and forcible entry missions required by our nation." – General Raymond Odierno, United States Army Chief of Staff, January 2012

Courtesy: D.O.D.

equally bloodied in trying to bring security to the fledgling democracy. Kurilla received a minor wound during a complex ambush in December 2004, which was a prelude of what was to come. Kurilla led the battalion for nearly a year until he himself left on a stretcher in August 2005 with three gunshots from an AK-47 as the battalion's last casualty.

Counterinsurgency operations in Iraq were extremely complicated, fluid, and a learning process. It was a war fought at the Battalion level and below and included direct combat with insurgents, training, and equipping Iraqi-friendly security forces, and winning the confidence of the public both in the United States and Iraq. Usually these missions/lessons occurred all at once at the

Battalion level. United States forces not only needed to kill or capture the enemy, and not only build up the security forces, but they needed to win the confidence of the Iraqi community. Embedded reporters were an essential component to getting the truth out to the public, and few – if any – reporters in American history have spent more time in combat than a reporter named Michael Yon. Yon was willing to go on patrol in the streets of Mosul for months at a time, following the brave soldiers of Kurilla's Stryker Battalion. Yon recorded Kurilla's soldiers building trust and confidence with the local Iraqis to stand up to the terrorists. Yon's photo of Major Mark Beiger, one of Kurilla's Staff Officers holding a wounded Iraqi infant who had been wounded by a terrorist car bomb (and later died), made front-page news

around the world, helping to expose the terrorists' motives of targeting children and thus helping the Iraqi community bond around the United States and local Iraqi security forces, which eventually helped bring a form of stabilization to Iraq.

> **"KURILLA WAS RUNNING WHEN HE WAS SHOT, BUT HE DIDN'T SEEM TO MISS A STRIDE; HE DID A CRAZY JUDO ROLL AND CAME UP SHOOTING," WROTE MICHAEL YON.**

On one of the last patrols of their one-year deployment, on August 19, 2005, Kurilla was leading the Infantry battalion in downtown Mosul. There was enemy contact a block away, and he and his soldiers were running to link up with another element. Yon was slightly behind Kurilla running, snapping photos with a high-speed shutter, when a burst from an AK-47 hit Kurilla three times, twice in each leg and once in his arm. Yon's dispatches were widely read:

"Three bullets reach flesh: One snaps his thigh bone in half. Both legs and an arm are shot. Kurilla was running when he was shot, but he didn't seem to miss a stride; he did a crazy judo roll and came up shooting. BamBamBamBam! Bullets were hitting all around Kurilla. And then help arrived in the form of one man: Command Sergeant Major (CSM) Prosser. Prosser ran around the corner, passed the two young soldiers who were crouched low, then by me and right to the shop, where he started firing at men inside. A man (insurgent) came forward, trying to shoot Kurilla with a pistol, apparently realizing his only escape was by fighting his way out, or dying in the process. Kurilla was aiming at the doorway waiting for him to come out. Had Prosser not come at that precise moment, who knows what the outcome might have been. Prosser shot the man at least four times with his M4 rifle. But the American M4 rifles are weak – after Prosser landed three nearly point blank shots in the man's abdomen, hitting him in the groin with a fourth, the man just staggered back, regrouped and tried to shoot Prosser. Prosser's M4 went 'black' (no more bullets). A shooter inside was also having problems with his pistol, but there was no time to reload. Prosser threw down his empty M4, ran into

the shop and tackled the man."

After hand-to-hand combat, Prosser subdued and captured the insurgent who would later die of his wounds at the combat hospital in a bed right next to Kurilla. CSM Robert Prosser was awarded the Silver Star for risking his life to save his commander. Kurilla beams when he talks about the valor, courage, and selfless service of the soldiers he has led, including Sergeant First Class Leroy Petry from 2nd Ranger Battalion who received the Medal of Honor for his actions in Afghanistan and remains one of the only active-duty Medal of Honor recipients.

After an incredibly difficult physical rehabilitation recovering from his wounds (he still has a titanium femur to this day), Lieutenant Colonel Kurilla took command in 2006 of the legendary 2nd Ranger Battalion (which started its history by conducting one of the most daring assaults of World War II when it scaled the cliffs on Point Du Hoc on D-Day). After a year at the National War College in Washington, D.C., Kurilla took command of the entire 75th Ranger Regiment in 2009. While the missions of the Rangers remain classified, during his more than four years as Commander of 2nd Ranger Battalion and the 75th Ranger Regiment, Kurilla would spend the vast majority of his time commanding Special Operations Forces in Iraq and Afghanistan.

On February 1, 2013, Erik Kurilla became one of the first of four members of the Class of 1988 to be promoted to Brigadier General when Lieutenant General Joseph Votel (USMA 1980), Commander of Joint Special Operations Command, pinned on Erik Kurilla's star as the new Assistant Commanding General of Joint Special Operations Command (JSOC). Kurilla would wear the stars passed to him from General (Retired) Montgomery Meigs (USMA 1967) and Lieutenant General (Retired) Frank Kearney (USMA 1976), both of whom were instrumental in coaching, teaching, and mentoring Kurilla throughout his career.

Lieutenant Colonel Kurilla returns fire after being shot three times Mosul, Iraq, 2005.

Kurilla, Medal of Honor Recipient Sergeant First Class Petry, and Admiral McRaven.

Photo: DOD

Lieutenant General in command of 3rd Army/U.S. Army Central, 2011 to present.

Colonel Brooks conducting a joint press conference in Kosovo as a Brigade Commander in 2001. Brooks was in Kosovo on September 11, 2001 trying to rebuild a destroyed village that had been home to a mixed ethnic population.

Photo: DOD

General of the Army Omar Bradley with Brooks in front of the statue of Colonel Sylvanus Thayer, 1980.

Receiving an Honorary Doctor of Laws, along with brother Brigadier General Leo Brooks in 2005 (left to right: Brigadier General Vincent Brooks, spouse Carol, father Major Leo Brooks, sister – and only real lawyer in the family – Marquita Brooks, mother Naomi, sister-in-law Ellyn, and brother Brigadier General Leo Brooks USMA 1979.

Courtesy: Vincent Brooks

Photo: NARA

General Vincent K. Brooks, USMA 1980

- **FIRST AFRICAN-AMERICAN CADET FIRST CAPTAIN**
- **COMMANDED AT COMPANY, BATTALION, BRIGADE, DIVISION, ARMY LEVELS**
- **COMMANDER ARCENT AND 3RD ARMY**
- **U.S. CENTRAL COMMAND SPOKESMAN DURING INVASION OF IRAQ IN OPERATION IRAQI FREEDOM**
- **ARMY BASKETBALL PLAYER**
- **COMMANDER, U.S. ARMY PACIFIC COMMAND**

★★★★

On May 28, 1980, the famous West Point Class of 1980 assembled in Michie Stadium for graduation. That day was a seminal event in the history of the United States Military Academy and was widely publicized for two major reasons. For the first time in history, 62 women were graduating from West Point, and the highest-ranked cadet in the Corps of Cadets, Vincent Brooks, was to be the first African-American First Captain in West Point history. Brooks faced

a tremendous amount of media coverage for both his own accomplishments and that of his classmates in this groundbreaking class, and he performed superbly in the public spotlight. Twenty-three years after graduation, the American public would again see Brooks – this time as a One-Star Brigadier General public spokesperson for Central Command during the invasion of Iraq in March 2003, and again, he performed superbly in the public spotlight.

Brooks was born in Anchorage, Alaska, to a military family. His father, Leo Brooks, was an Army Major General who had obtained his commission through ROTC at Virginia State in 1954, and his mother was an educator. Brooks, his older brother, Leo, and his sister, Marquita, grew up as "military brats" on various military posts around the world. Brooks attended two years of Thomas Jefferson High School in Alexandria, Virginia, before attending Jesuit High School in Carmichael,

California, for his junior and senior years. Brooks was recruited to play basketball at West Point by Army Head Coach Mike Krzyzewski (USMA 1969), who would go on to become the winningest coach in NCAA history (including 20 wins at West Point with Cadet Brooks on the team.) Brooks originally wanted to become a doctor, but when his brother entered West Point in 1975 and returned home for Christmas during his Plebe year, Brooks saw the changes that

>>> Spotlight

Brooks holds many "firsts" at West Point and in the Army: He was the first African-American First Captain at West Point; he was the leader of the first class at West Point to include women; he is a member of the first family to have three African-American General Officers in two generations.

Number 44, Plebe on the 1976–77 season Army varsity basketball team under Coach Krzyzewski (USMA 1969, Coach K is on the far left).

under pressure and very popular with his classmates and faculty. Brooks joined the ranks of famous First Captains, including Pershing (1886), MacArthur (1903), Wainwright (1906), Westmoreland (1936), and Dawkins (1959).

African-Americans had been attending West Point for more than 100 years and by 1979 were fully accepted and integrated into the Corps. The first African-Americans to graduate from West Point had been trailblazers who lived lonely lives, often being silenced by their classmates and living alone for their four years, including Henry O. Flipper (USMA 1877), Colonel Charles Young (1889), and General Benjamin O. Davis, Jr. (USMA 1936). By the time the military was integrated in 1947 by President Truman, West Point had already done so many decades prior. Even so, in 1979, when Brooks was named First Captain of the Class of 1980, he still received anonymous hate mail from the public because of the color of his skin (although the amount was far less than expected). By being named First Captain, Brooks helped complete the journey that former slave Henry O. Flipper had started more than 100 years earlier and would forever show Americans that African-Americans could succeed in any capacity at West Point. At the conclusion of the ceremony, Brooks ordered "Class dismissed!" and the class threw their hats in the air and joined the Army as Second Lieutenants.

Upon graduation, Second Lieutenant Brooks was commissioned in the Infantry, graduated from Ranger School (while a cadet) and Airborne School, and chose the 82nd Airborne as his first assignment. He would command at every level from company through Army. All of his commands were forward deployed with two Company Commands in Germany during the Cold War, Battalion Command south of the Demilitarized Zone (DMZ) in Korea from 1996 to 1998, Brigade Command in 2001 in Kosovo, Division Command as the 1st Infantry Division Commander in Operations Iraqi Freedom and New Dawn in 2010, and Army Command of ARCENT/3rd Army Middle East and Central Asia from 2011 to the present.

Brooks holds many firsts at West Point and in the Army: He was the first African-American First Captain at West Point; he was the leader of the first class at West Point to include women; he is a member of the first family to have three African-American General Officers in two generations (his father was an Army Major General and

brother was an Army Brigadier General and former Commandant of Cadets at West Point); in 2002, he was the first member of the Class of 1980 to be promoted to Brigadier General.

The Iraq War lasted for more than eight years, and Brooks was involved from the beginning through the end.

To the public, he was the face of the original invasion as the USCENTCOM Chief Operations Spokesperson in 2003 at the start of Operation Iraqi Freedom. He was described by one journalist from a major international cable news organization as "the only U.S. government official regularly talking to the international audience…" He then served as Deputy Commanding General of the main effort (Multi-National Division-Baghdad) during the "Surge" from November 2006 to December 2007. In 2010, he served as the United States Commander of the nine Southern Iraq provinces, and, in December 2011, he commanded ARCENT and 3rd Army until 2013 when he was promoted to Four-Star General and took command of the Army Pacific Command.

> **BY BEING NAMED FIRST CAPTAIN, BROOKS HELPED COMPLETE THE JOURNEY THAT THE FORMER SLAVE HENRY O. FLIPPER HAD STARTED MORE THAN 100 YEARS EARLIER.**

His wife, Carol, is also from a military family (her father was an Army Colonel). They met while their parents were both stationed at Fort Lee, Virginia, in 1980, while Brooks was a new Second Lieutenant on Christmas leave before reporting to his first unit at Fort Bragg a month later. They were married two years later during their first assignment with the 82nd Airborne, Fort Bragg, North Carolina.

the Military Academy had on his brother and decided to follow him to West Point to become an Army Officer.

The Class of 1980 faced challenges that no other class had faced in the past. One-hundred-and-nineteen women entered with the class on R-Day in 1976 and only 62 would graduate four years later. The challenges faced by the class were unique, adding women was a logistical challenge (adding bathrooms, additional phys ed

classes, etc.), but more importantly required a major cultural change to a previously male-dominated environment. The Class of 1980, both male and female, would be more sensitive to all-minority issues because of the challenges, pressures, and experiences that they all faced in this integration process.

When it came time to pick the Cadet First Captain, Brooks was the natural pick. He had been an Army basketball player, making varsity in his Plebe year. He was very calm

ARMY MEDAL OF HONOR

During the American Civil War, Congress created the Medal of Honor on February 17, 1862, for those who distinguished themselves in battle. President Abraham Lincoln signed the bill into law on July 12, 1862, and the Army Medal of Honor became official. Since then, the Medal of Honor has become America's highest award for military valor for those who have performed acts of such conspicuous gallantry, so much that they rise "above and beyond the call of duty." In short, there is no higher symbol of American heroism. Eighty-three West Point graduates or former cadets have received the Medal of Honor, four of whom are highlighted in this chapter.

Realizing the hopelessness of the situation, the bail-out order was given. Without regard for his personal safety, he gallantly remained alone at the controls to afford all other crew members an opportunity to escape. Still another attack exploded gasoline tanks in the right wing, and the bomber plunged earthward, carrying General Castle to his death.

—Medal of Honor citation for recipient Brigadier General Frederick Castle, USMA 1930, B-17 Wing Commander

The enemy was unable to break his indomitable will, his faith in God, and his trust in the United States of America. Captain Versace, an American fighting man who epitomized the principles of his country and the Code of Conduct, was executed by the Viet Cong on September 26, 1965.

—Medal of Honor citation for recipient Captain Humbert "Rocky" Versace, USMA 1959

Captain Foley moved to personally direct this critical phase of the battle. Leading the renewed effort, he was blown off his feet and wounded by an enemy grenade. Despite his painful wounds, he refused medical aid and persevered in the forefront of the attack on the enemy redoubt. He led the assault on several enemy gun emplacements and, single-handedly, destroyed three such positions.

—Medal of Honor citation for recipient Lieutenant General Robert Foley, USMA 1963

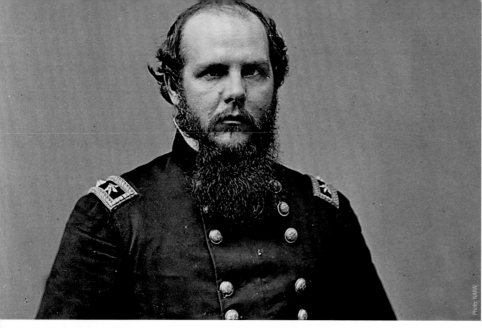

Lieutenant General John McAllister Schofield, USMA 1853

- COMMANDING GENERAL, U.S. ARMY, 1888–95
- 19TH SUPERINTENDENT, UNITED STATES MILITARY ACADEMY, 1876–81
- ADVOCATE FOR U.S./ ESTABLISHMENT OF A NAVAL PORT AT PEARL HARBOR
- INTERIM SECRETARY OF WAR DURING PRESIDENT ANDREW JOHNSON'S ADMINISTRATION, 1868–69
- SPECIAL U.S. EMISSARY TO FRANCE, 1865–66
- UNION DIVISION, DEPARTMENT, AND CORPS COMMANDER DURING THE CIVIL WAR, 1861–65
- MEDAL OF HONOR RECIPIENT, AMERICAN CIVIL WAR DURING THE BATTLE OF WILSON'S CREEK, 1861
- SCHOFIELD BARRACKS IN HAWAII NAMED IN HIS HONOR

>>> Spotlight

Schofield's Definition of Discipline

The discipline which makes the soldiers of a free country reliable in battle is not to be gained by harsh or tyrannical treatment. On the contrary, such treatment is far more likely to destroy than to make an Army. It is possible to impart instruction and to give commands in such a manner and such a tone of voice to inspire in the soldier no feeling but an intense desire to obey, while the opposite manner and tone of voice cannot fail to excite strong resentment and a desire to disobey. The one mode or the other of dealing with subordinates springs from a corresponding spirit in the breast of the commander. He who feels the respect which is due to others cannot fail to inspire in them regard for himself, while he who feels, and hence manifests, disrespect toward others, especially his inferiors, cannot fail to inspire hatred against himself.

Major General John M. Schofield
Address to the Corps of Cadets, August 11, 1879

5TH INFANTRY DIVISION

Among the esteemed list of West Point graduates who became iconic leaders in the military, industry, politics, diplomacy, scholarship, and philanthropy, a surprising few have had their statements canonized as part of the institution's heritage. John M. Schofield is one of them. In his August 11, 1879, address to the Corps of Cadets as a response to the upper-class hazing and maltreatment of new cadets, Major General Schofield, the 19th Superintendent of the United States Military Academy, asserted:

"The discipline which makes the soldiers of a free country reliable in battle is not to be gained by harsh or tyrannical treatment. On the contrary, such treatment is far more likely to destroy than to make an Army. It is possible to impart instruction and to give commands in such a manner and such a tone of voice to inspire in the soldier no feeling but an intense desire to obey, while the opposite manner and tone of voice cannot fail to excite strong resentment and a desire to disobey. The one mode or the other of dealing with subordinates springs from a corresponding spirit in the breast of the commander. He who feels the respect which is due to others cannot fail to inspire in them regard for himself, while he who feels, and hence manifests, disrespect toward others, especially his inferiors, cannot fail to inspire hatred against himself."[1]

His definition of discipline has become a tenet of leader development at West Point, where cadets must still memorize the quote verbatim. Yet, while Schofield's definition of discipline was originally given in a military context, it has grown more universal in its application by transcending the Academy and serving to inform senior-subordinate interactions in countless other areas of the military and civilian worlds alike. So it is not surprising at all that West Point, the world's premier leadership institution, values such a commentary and that it is so well known. What is surprising, however, is that Schofield's 42-year career of distinguished military and public service to the nation is virtually unknown.

Born on September 29, 1831, in Gerry, New York, Schofield entered West Point via the state of Illinois, graduated seventh out of 52 cadets in the USMA Class of 1853, and commissioned into the artillery.[2] Like many of his contemporaries and classmates, Schofield's career saw a meteoric rise during the American Civil War, when he achieved the rank of Brevet Major General by the war's end. His initial assignment in the war was as a Major in the 1st Missouri Volunteer Infantry, where he was awarded the Medal of Honor for his actions at the Battle of Wilson's Creek, Missouri, on August 10, 1861 – he would not receive the Medal of Honor until July 2, 1892. Schofield then successfully commanded at the Division, Department, and Corps levels seeing major action in Missouri, the Atlanta Campaign, the Battle of Nashville, the Battle of Franklin, and at Durham Station, North Carolina, where Confederate General Joseph E. Johnston surrendered some of the last remnants of the Confederate Army. By all accounts, his Senior Commanders during the war viewed the unassuming Schofield as a professional and skilled combat leader, administrator, and trusted advisor, as well as intellectually gifted and politically astute, which served him well for the rest of his career.[3]

Schofield's career after the Civil War placed him at the center of reconstructing the nation, regularly confronted him with the challenges to proper civil-military relations – particularly with reconstruction as the greatest civil-military crisis in American history, and presented him with the growing pains associated with professionalizing the United States Army. His first post-war assignment in 1865 to 1866 had international implications. He served as an American diplomatic emissary to France. It was here that Schofield successfully persuaded the French to remove troops from Mexico it had stationed there during the American Civil War in violation of the Monroe Doctrine. Schofield then oversaw Reconstruction in Virginia as Commander, Department of the Potomac from 1866 to 1868 with a systematic and well-developed plan that was impartial and absent of personal biases he may have held toward the defeated population or freed slaves. His primary concern was to readmit Virginia quickly and fairly, but also in line with civilian policymakers. Schofield firmly believed that it was his duty to carry out national policy in his role as a military commander and not to create, alter, or ignore it as other military commanders did.[4] In 1868 to 1869, he then served as Interim Secretary of War for the remainder of President Andrew Johnson's troubled administration following Johnson's impeachment. Schofield resigned that post upon the election of his former Civil War Commander, President Ulysses S. Grant.

Schofield next held a variety of Army-level commands from 1869 to 1886 that included twice as Commander, Division of the Pacific. It was while in this command that he realized the strategic potential of the Hawaiian Islands and most notably and successfully recommended to President Grant that the United States establish a naval port at Pearl Harbor. Also nested within this period was Schofield's assignment as West Point Superintendent, where he espoused his famous definition of discipline. In his final assignment, Schofield served as Commanding General of the United States Army from 1888 to 1895. It was here that he confirmed his belief that the Army could only succeed as a legitimate professional force with the active support and approval of political institutions, such as Congress and the Secretary of War. By fostering a solid relationship with these institutions and gaining their support and approval, Schofield successfully pursued policies in key areas to include personnel management, training, education, pay, and promotions, all of which helped reform and continue to professionalize the Army while emphasizing the concept of civilian supremacy over the military. Even after Schofield retired in 1895 at the rank of Lieutenant General, civilian leaders in subsequent administrations sought his advice on civil-military relations and the continued professionalization of the Army until his death in 1906.[5]

In looking back over his career, Schofield's political balance and exercise of proper civil-military relations are particularly telling in the fact that he earned the trust of the multitude of leaders under whom he served regardless of their vastly different political and philosophical outlooks. This was an especially daunting accomplishment in the latter half of the nineteenth century during the politically charged, economically challenging, and socially divisive eras of Reconstruction and post-Reconstruction America.[6] Although Schofield never codified his definition of discipline until his August 1879 address to the Corps, his successful body of work serving the nation in a variety of positions clearly indicates that he regularly practiced what he eventually preached. So perhaps it is now time that history defines Lieutenant General John M. Schofield by his impressive career as much as it has by his definition of discipline.

HIS DEFINITION OF DISCIPLINE HAS BECOME A TENET OF LEADER DEVELOPMENT AT WEST POINT, WHERE CADETS MUST STILL MEMORIZE THE QUOTE VERBATIM.

enry Algernon DuPont was born July 30, 1838, at Eleutherian Mills and hailed from Winterthur, Delaware. Even without service in the Civil War, the name Henry DuPont likely would have been important to its outcome. DuPont was named after his father, Henry, who had inherited the family business in Delaware, the E.I. DuPont de Nemours and Company, from his father, Eleuthere Irenee DuPont, when he was in his early 30s. The business made powder and explosives, mostly for mining, but would be critical to the Union War effort.[1] The younger DuPont was a driven young man, whose family's wealth combined with his own diligence and talents that likely would have succeeded greatly in life and risen to prominence in American society even without the accolades he received as a young officer during the Civil War.

DuPont was a talented student and scholar and had attended the University of Pennsylvania in 1855. After a year there, he decided to follow in the elder DuPont's footsteps receiving an appointment to the United States Military Academy, where he matriculated in the summer of 1856. Young DuPont was a diligent and talented student and would eventually graduate at the top of his class in May of 1861 right at the outset of the Civil War.[2]

DuPont left more than a good reputation behind from his time at West Point in the form of a mountain of correspondence, which helps to build a unique perspective of West Point. His correspondence was varied in that he routinely wrote to several members of his family, including his mother, father, aunt, and siblings. This varied audience also provides a diverse perspective of the years leading up to the Civil War and his feelings on the war. DuPont was unique among his cadet peers at West Point being not only one of the top minds in his class, but also having access to a perspective of the world outside West Point that involved more than just the mundane and routine at West Point. As a top cadet and child of privilege, DuPont was often privy to the inner workings of the government and the higher levels of the Army. His status also afforded him access to not only senior officials at West Point, but also to being availed audiences with professors, the Superintendent, and even the Secretary of War and eventual President of the Confederacy, Jefferson Davis, as well as correspondence with his father who was well connected in both state and national politics.[3] As such, DuPont's gaze was often wider than the barracks walls around him as the country began to unravel. In October and November of 1859, DuPont began forming opinions about governance and politics as he kept a close eye on John Brown's raid at Harpers Ferry and the Republican responses to it, as well as trying to get his father to disclose the happenings of the appropriations committee in torpedoing the short-lived and much-hated five-year curriculum implemented by Jefferson Davis as Secretary of War.[4] While many of his peers seemed surprised and shocked by the advent of war, DuPont had a very sober read on the situation after the 1860 elections and had already developed some decided and informed positions on the course of the country and secession. He reported to his mother in November of 1860 that the elections had turned out as he thought they would. He correctly read the situation that despite his disagreement with secession on the grounds of Lincoln's election, he believed that things had "gone too far to retrace their steps and unless some concessions [were] made," secession was likely for many states.[5]

Interestingly, his father was a Whig who did not vote for Lincoln in 1860. When Democrats began to secede, he became a Republican and with the state under Democratic rule after many Republicans had volunteered and were away, he used

Senator Henry Algernon DuPont, USMA 1861

- **U.S. SENATOR, STATE OF DELAWARE**
- **MEDAL OF HONOR RECIPIENT**
- **PRESIDENT, WILMINGTON & NORTHERN RAILROAD COMPANY**
- **GRADUATED FIRST IN THE CLASS OF 1861**

>>> Spotlight

DECEMBER 7, 1787

Delaware, one of the original 13 colonies, was the first state to ratify the Constitution in December 7, 1787, and is considered "The First State." During the War of 1812, the "Star Spangled Banner" was written by Francis Scott Keys in 1814, while he was a Prisoner of War held in a British warship, while watching the bombardment of Fort McHenry in Baltimore Harbor. The DuPont Corporation was founded in Delaware in 1802, the same year that West Point was founded. DuPont Corporation is based in Wilmington, Delaware, is a Fortune 100 company and one of the most respected companies in America. Henry DuPont, a member of the family that founded and ran DuPont, graduated from West Point in 1861, received the Medal of Honor for his actions at Battle of Cedar Creek and was elected United States Senator from Delaware and served from 1906 to 1917.

the military to suppress the potential for the secession of Delaware.[6] In a biography written by young DuPont about his father, he showed his true feelings on secession referring to even northern Democrats in Delaware as "disloyal" and spent some time arguing vehemently against the case for the legality of secession in Delaware and in the South in general.[7] As it became clear that war was a reality, DuPont reported to his mother that the Civil War was the "worst thing" he could conceive of and predicted a very "gloomy future." He felt that every man had the right to make up his own mind on secession but grew weary while at West Point of "blood thirsty speeches by cadets." While he respected his classmates' decisions to join the Southern cause, he eventually came to believe that someone "must stand against the fire-eaters in the cotton states." Interestingly, DuPont did not think that Lincoln was the man for the job and openly wished that Seward, Lincoln's Secretary of State, were President.[8]

Upon graduating from West Point in May of 1861, DuPont was commissioned Second Lieutenant in the Corps of Engineers and went to work drilling volunteers in Washington, D.C., from May to July. He was promoted to First Lieutenant in the 5th Artillery on May 14, 1861. He would serve several years away from the "active" front until he joined the Department of West Virginia as part of General Franz Sigel's expedition into the Valley of Virginia, where he was made a Captain of Artillery on March 24, 1864.[9] At this point, serving under the inept General Franz Sigel, DuPont made a name for himself as an officer.

The Battle of New Market is infamous in the Civil War. It was here that a superior force under General Franz Sigel was repelled by the forces of General John C. Breckenridge. In his own history of the battle, DuPont correctly points out that it was of "comparatively little importance, either with respect to numbers engaged or the results attained." However, the battle has endured in fame for three basic reasons. First, the battle of New Market "has always aroused a special interest in Virginia, largely due to the fact that the youthful cadets of the Virginia Military Institute had participated so valiantly in that engagement."[10] This is as true today as it was when DuPont wrote the words in 1923. Second, even without the mythology and reality of the Keydets mucking across the Field of Lost Shoes to break the center of Siegel's line, this famous battle remains "infamous" in military history as a study

of properly versus improperly employed generalship on the battlefield. Breckenridge and the Confederates did almost everything right, while Sigel and the Union did almost everything wrong. Finally, despite the debacle of command under Franz Sigel, the Department of West Virginia force was saved during its flight by the cool and competent actions of then Captain Henry A. DuPont.

The Battle of New Market suffered from poor planning by Franz Sigel, over-cautiousness in leaving significant amounts of his forces behind and in no position to provide relief or support, poor planning in not bringing all of the artillery he had available to him into the direct action of the fight, and sheer incompetence in failing to realize, despite commanding decisive high ground and an advantage of 1,500 troops, that he had allowed his right flank, which should have been protected by drastically steep terrain from any envelopment, to actually be enveloped and turned by a confused and mixed up Confederate force.[11]

HAILING FROM ONE OF AMERICA'S WEALTHIEST FAMILIES- HENRY DUPONT EXCELLED AT EVERYTHING HE DID – IN THE CLASSROOM, ON THE BATTLEFIELD, IN THE BOARDROOM, AND IN THE HALLS OF CONGRESS.

Sigel's whole force would have been lost if it were not for DuPont's competent and valiant actions. Ironically, his valor was first emphasized by an article in the *Journal of the Military Service Institution* written by the Cadet Captain of Company D of the Virginia Military Institute battalion. The retreat and withdrawal had been mischaracterized in Sigel's own report and DuPont's role left out entirely. In short, Captain DuPont, completely on his own initiative, conducted a masterful artillery defense by harassing the pursuing Confederate force under constant fire from his guns which he kept in action by bounding them in retreat. Through brilliant artillery tactics and the holding and subsequent destruction of the bridge over the Shenandoah River, DuPont succeeded in halting a dogged Confederate pursuit, which would have crushed the forces Sigel had

brought to the battle and likely exploited that pursuit to further engage and overwhelm the reserves which Sigel had left in the vicinity of Woodstock and Strasbourg to the north along the Valley Pike.

Sigel had been relieved and replaced by General David Hunter. DuPont was then brevetted to Major in September of 1864 after having his horse shot out from under him at Winchester and promoted to the Chief of Artillery for the Department of West Virginia. He was then brevetted again to Lieutenant Colonel in October of 1864.[12] His second brevet came for actions at the Battle of Cedar Creek. There, Major DuPont succeeded once again in saving Union forces from disaster. Despite Confederates achieving tactical surprise, DuPont managed to engage his guns and hold the flank for the Union Army, as well as establish a rally point with which the Union established a successful counterattack. When it had been determined exactly how much danger the Union had been in at Cedar Creek, DuPont was also awarded the Medal of Honor.[13]

DuPont would later see action in the final campaigns to take Richmond and serve on the occupation force there from 1866 to 1868. He resigned his commission on the 1st of March 1875 and returned to oversee his family business of powder manufacturing in Winterthur, Delaware. He also continued his service to his country. He refused an appointment from President William McKinley, whom he had served with in the Civil War, to be a minister to Russia in 1897. He was elected to the United States Senate from Delaware in 1906 and subsequently re-elected in 1911 serving to the end of his second term in 1917. He notably served as member and chair of the Committee on Military Affairs from 1911 to 1913, making a point to stand against hazing at the Military Academy. In a grand gesture of reconciliation, DuPont successfully introduced a bill in the Senate in April of 1913, which paid for the loss of property VMI had experienced as a result of General David Hunter's order to have it destroyed during his 1864 Valley Campaign – an order that ironically had been the responsibility of Hunter's Chief of Artillery, Henry DuPont, to carry out.[14] DuPont died on December 31, 1927, at the age of 88.

Written by: Major Paul N. Belmont.

Captain Rocky Versace epitomizes all that West Point stands for and all that is meant by "Duty, Honor, Country." Versace was a Special Forces Officer who was executed by the Viet Cong as a Prisoner of War because he would not break under torture. He provided a great example of courage leadership under the harshest circumstances until his death. The enemy simply could not break this graduate of West Point, and so they executed him.

Versace was "short" on his second consecutive tour in Vietnam after having served for 18 months with the 5th Special Forces as an advisor to the South Vietnamese Army. Upon completion of this tour, Versace had been planning to leave the Army to join the seminary to return to help Vietnamese children. Instead, in his last month in South Vietnam, his unit was attacked, he was wounded, but continued to fight until his unit was overrun. He was taken prisoner by Viet Cong forces in South Vietnam and underwent some of the most horrific conditions, including starvation,

physical, and psychological torture.

Versace was born in Honolulu, Hawaii, on July 2, 1937. His father was an Army Colonel, and Versace grew up as an "Army brat," living on military bases and attending high school in both Alexandria and Norfolk, Virginia. He attended West Point from 1955 to 1959 and was commissioned in the Armor Branch. After graduating from Ranger and Airborne Schools, he served in Korea in the 1st Cavalry Division. He then returned stateside to serve in the 3rd Infantry Division (Old Guard) in Washington, D.C.

Under President Kennedy, advisors were being sent to Vietnam in the early 1960s, and Versace volunteered for duty there. Prior to deployment, he attended Vietnamese language school and Military Assistance Institute. In May 1962, he began his tour as an advisor in Vietnam. In May 1963, he extended his tour by six months. On October 23, 1963, while acting as an Intelligence Officer for 5th Special Forces, his South Vietnamese unit was ambushed by Viet Cong forces. Although

wounded, Captain Versace fought a withdrawing action, providing cover so that his unit could withdraw. He and two other Americans, First Lieutenant James "Nick" Rowe and Sergeant Daniel Pitzer, were taken prisoner. Although wounded and weakened, he resisted captivity and lived by the Code of Conduct from the outset. He attempted escape four times and was seen by the other prisoners as continually resisting the captors, insulting them in their native Vietnamese and also in French.

Over the course of 23 months, he never broke, despite repeated torture and abuse. His physical appearance witnessed by his two fellow prisoners showed that while his body was being broken, his spirit could not. He was finally separated from his other prisoners. The last time they heard his voice, he was singing "God Bless America," giving inspiration to his fellow prisoners and displaying incredible courage in the face of unbearable torture. On September 25, 1965, on "Liberation Radio," the North Vietnamese announced they had

executed Captain Versace.

His fellow prisoner, Lieutenant Rowe, was a prisoner for five years until he managed to escape when he overpowered a guard. Rowe was the only POW during Vietnam to successfully escape captivity. He later documented Versace's story in the book *Five Years to Freedom* and personally appealed to President Nixon to award Versace with the Medal of Honor for his actions before and during captivity. President Nixon assured Major Rowe that he would do so. Both Rowe and Pitzer were the founders of the United States Army SERE (Survival, Evasion, Resistance, Escape) program at Fort Bragg, North Carolina, based on their own experiences and witnessing Captain Versace's leadership and example before and during captivity.

Colonel Rowe himself was Killed In Action when insurgents in the Philippines assassinated him in 1988. Versace was nominated for the Congressional Medal of Honor in 1969, but the award was downgraded to the Silver

Captain Humbert "Rocky" Versace, USMA 1959

- **MEDAL OF HONOR (POSTHUMOUS)**
- **VIETNAM PRISONER OF WAR**
- **EXECUTED BY VIET CONG**
- **VERSACE PLAZA, ALEXANDRIA, VIRGINIA, NAMED IN HIS HONOR**
- **U.S. ARMY SPECIAL FORCES (GREEN BERET)**

President George H. W. Bush presents Steve Versace, brother of Captain Versace, with the Medal of Honor, July 8, 2002, at the White House.

Rocky Versace with Vietnamese children, statue erected in Alexandria, Virginia.

Star, even though President Nixon personally committed to assisting Captain Rowe with getting the award for Versace. In 2002, the "Friends of Rocky" were finally successful in getting him the well-deserved award for valor above and beyond the call of duty. Despite the fact that the only two witnesses and the nominee were all now deceased, the evidence of his heroism was overwhelming.

On July 8, 2002, President George W. Bush awarded Captain Versace the posthumous Congressional Medal of Honor. Citation:

"For conspicuous gallantry and intrepidity at the risk of his life above and beyond the call of duty while a Prisoner of War during the period of October 29, 1963, to September 26, 1965, in the Republic of Vietnam. While accompanying a Civilian Irregular Defense Group patrol engaged in combat operations in Thoi Binh District, An Xuyen Province, Republic of Vietnam on October 29, 1963, Captain Versace and the CIDG assault force were caught in an ambush from intense mortar, automatic weap- ons, and small arms fire from elements of a reinforced enemy Main Force battalion. As the battle raged, Captain Versace fought valiantly

THE LAST TIME THEY HEARD HIS VOICE, HE WAS SINGING "GOD BLESS AMERICA," GIVING INSPIRATION TO HIS FELLOW PRISONERS AND DISPLAYING INCREDIBLE COURAGE IN THE FACE OF UNBEARABLE TORTURE.

and encouraged his CIDG patrol to return fire against overwhelming enemy forces. He provided covering fire from an exposed position to enable friendly forces to withdraw from the killing zone *when it was apparent that their position would be overrun, and was severely wounded in the* knee and back from automatic weapons fire and shrapnel. He stubbornly resisted capture with the last full measure of his strength and ammunition. Taken prisoner by the Viet Cong, he demonstrated exceptional leadership and resolute adherence to the tenets of the Code of Conduct from the time he entered into a Prisoner of War status. Captain Versace assumed command of his fellow American prisoners, and despite being kept locked in irons in an isolation box, raised their morale by singing messages to popular songs of the day, and leaving inspiring messages at the latrine. Within three weeks of captivity, and despite the severity of his untreated wounds, he attempted the first of four escape attempts by dragging himself on his hands and knees out of the camp through dense swamp and forbidding vegetation to freedom. Crawling at a very slow pace due to his weakened condition, the guards quickly discovered him outside the camp and recaptured him. Captain Versace scorned the enemy's exhaustive interrogation and indoctrination efforts, and inspired his fellow prisoners to resist to the best of their ability. When he used his Vietnamese language skills to protest improper treatment of the American prisoners by the guards, he was put into leg irons and gagged to keep his protestations out of earshot of the other American prisoners in the camp. The last time that any of his fellow prisoners heard from him, Captain Versace was singing God Bless America at the top of his voice from his isolation box. Unable to break his indomitable will, his faith in God, and his trust in the United States of America and his fellow prisoners, Captain Versace was executed by the Viet Cong on September 26, 1965. Captain Versace's extraordinary heroism, self-sacrifice, and personal bravery involving conspicuous risk of life above and beyond the call of duty were in keeping with the highest traditions of the United States Army, and reflect great credit to himself and the United States Armed Forces."*

Captain Versace receiving the Combat Infantryman Badge with his parents.

Cadet Rocky Versace with his family, 1962.

>>> Spotlight

The National League of Families of American Prisoners and Missing in Southeast Asia has the sole purpose of obtaining the release of all prisoners and the fullest possible accounting for the missing and repatriation of all recoverable remains of those who died serving our nation during the Vietnam War. Captain Versace's remains have not yet been recovered.

Lieutenant General Robert F. Foley, USMA 1963

- **MEDAL OF HONOR RECIPIENT**
- **COMMANDING GENERAL, 5TH U.S. ARMY**
- **WEST POINT COMMANDANT OF CADETS**
- **CAPTAIN, ARMY BASKETBALL, 1962–63**
- **COMMANDER, 2ND BRIGADE, 3RD INFANTRY DIVISION**
- **WEST POINT DISTINGUISHED GRADUATE AWARD**
- **DIRECTOR, ARMY EMERGENCY RELIEF (AER)**

Lieutenant General Bob Foley served on active duty for 37 years, retiring in 2000 as Commanding General of 5th United States Army at Fort Sam Houston, Texas. His West Point experience includes time as a Cadet, Company Tactical Officer, and Commandant of Cadets. He received the Congressional Medal of Honor – our nation's highest award for his actions in November 1966 while serving as an Infantry Rifle Company Commander during the War in Vietnam.

Foley was born and raised in Newton, Massachusetts. His parents owned a restaurant, and the family moved to Belmont, Massachusetts, when he was 14. He attended Belmont High School and at six-foot seven-inches was Captain of the 1958–59 basketball team. At West Point, he was Captain of the 1962–63 Army basketball team and was selected as a member of the 1963 Eastern All-Stars.

After graduation, he attended the Infantry Officer Basic Course at Fort Benning, Georgia, followed by Airborne and Ranger School. Second Lieutenant Foley's first assignment was as Rifle Platoon Leader in Bravo Company, 2nd Battalion, 27th Infantry in the 25th Infantry Division, Schofield Barracks, Hawaii. When the 25th ID deployed to Vietnam in 1966, Foley was the Battalion Heavy Mortar Platoon Leader. With only three years of service and at 25 years of age, he was selected to take command of Alpha Company. Foley was told he was given command because of his observations about the lack of bold, aggressive leadership on the part of Company Commanders during search and destroy missions. In a few short months, Captain Foley would be given the opportunity to prove his leadership abilities in combat.

In early November 1966, Captain Foley's company returned from a 10-day "search-

>>> Spotlight

On May 1, 1968, Captain Robert F. Foley receives the Medal of Honor from President Lyndon B. Johnson, along with Private First Class John F. Baker, Jr., who received his Medal of Honor for his actions during the same battle.

Presenting diploma to son, Dave, at graduation exercises, May 28, 1994.

they could not use close air support (CAS) or indirect fires. The VC had cut waist-high fields of fire through the jungle in front of their hardened bunkers that were impossible to see standing up. It was not until some of his soldiers were crouching down that they found these crossing lanes of fire. Foley's unit immediately came under fire. In the ensuing battle that lasted more than five hours, Captain Foley was wounded by a grenade but continued to fight, taking out several enemy bunkers single-handedly. Due to his heroic leadership and the bravery of his troops, the besieged company was rescued and successfully exited the area.

"THE INCULCATION OF HONOR AND RESPECT CONTRIBUTES IMMEASURABLY TO DEVELOPING LEADERS OF CHARACTER AND COLLECTIVELY SUSTAINS THE KIND OF TRUST AND COHESION REALIZED BY ONLY THE MOST SUCCESSFUL ORGANIZATIONS," SAYS LIEUTENANT GENERAL FOLEY.

There were several lessons learned as a result of this action regarding leadership at the Company level:

1. Leaders must lead from the front.

2. Situations change rapidly and leaders must make quick decisions on the battlefield.

3. You may have to fight with only what you carry with you into battle.

Equally as important, Captain Foley took away from his tour as Company Commander a deep appreciation for the need to instill respect in the unit culture. Foley kept asking himself, "What is it that motivates these terrific young soldiers to do what they must on the battlefield day after day?" While he knew that discipline, teamwork, training, and leadership were a part of the equation, he found that the most compelling reason was the caring, compassion and respect that soldiers have for their buddies, their comrades. They would do anything to prevent their fellow soldiers from being killed or wounded.

It wasn't until after Captain Foley had already departed Vietnam in December

1966 that he and another soldier from his company, Private First Class John F. Baker, were both nominated for the Medal of Honor. In 1968, a classmate, Captain Jay Westermeier, working in the awards branch at the Pentagon came to Foley's apartment in Alexandria, Virginia, and notified him that he was going to receive the Medal of Honor. On May 1, 1968, President Lyndon Johnson awarded both Captain Robert F. Foley and Private First Class John F. Baker the Medal of Honor for their actions in the same battle.

Captain Foley's Medal of Honor citation reads:

"For conspicuous gallantry and intrepidity in action at the risk of his life above and beyond the call of duty. Captain Foley's company was ordered to extricate another company of the battalion. Moving through the dense jungle to aid the besieged unit, Company A encountered a strong enemy force occupying well concealed, defensive positions, and the company's leading element quickly sustained several casualties. Captain Foley immediately ran forward to the scene of the most intense action to direct the company's efforts. Deploying 1 platoon on the flank, he led the other 2 platoons in an attack on the enemy in the face of intense fire. During this action both radio operators accompanying him were wounded. At grave risk to himself he defied the enemy's murderous fire, and helped the wounded operators to a position where they could receive medical care. As he moved forward again 1 of his machine gun crews was wounded. Seizing the weapon, he charged forward firing the machine gun, shouting orders and rallying his men, thus maintaining the momentum of the attack. Under increasingly heavy enemy fire he ordered his assistant to take cover and, alone, Captain Foley continued to advance firing the machine gun until the wounded had been evacuated and the attack in this area could be resumed. When movement on the other flank was halted by the enemy's fanatical defense, Captain Foley moved to personally direct this critical phase of the battle. Leading the renewed effort he was blown off his feet and wounded by an enemy grenade. Despite his painful wounds he refused medical aid and persevered in the forefront of the attack on the enemy redoubt. He led the assault on several enemy gun emplacements and, single-handedly, destroyed 3 such positions. His outstanding personal leadership under intense enemy fire during the fierce battle, which lasted for several hours, inspired his

and-destroy" operation looking forward to some much earned rest and recovery. However, the next morning, he was notified that Charlie Company, 2/27 was in a tough firefight. The Battalion Commander, Company Commander, and many of the other leaders had been killed or wounded. Charlie Company was surrounded by the enemy and Alpha Company had to "get them out." Captain Foley quickly gathered his company together and told them that their fellow Wolfhounds were in trouble,

and they had to get back in action. That same afternoon Alpha Company flew from Cu Chi to Dau Tieng, where Captain Foley received his mission to attack the fortified VC complex, extract Charlie Company, and lead them out of the jungle.

The challenges confronting Foley's relief element were significant. Visibility was limited to five to 10 meters due to dense jungle undergrowth and triple canopy trees. Due to the proximity of Charlie Company,

men to heroic efforts and was instrumental in the ultimate success of the operation. Captain Foley's magnificent courage, selfless concern for his men and professional skill reflect the utmost credit upon himself and the United States Army.'"

In 1969, he returned to West Point as a Tactical Officer for Company E–3. While at West Point, he attended graduate school at Farleigh Dickinson University, where he graduated cum laude and received his master's in Business Administration. In 1967, he met Julie T. Languasco. They were married on September 27, 1969, at the Catholic Chapel at West Point by Father Edwin F. O'Brien, who is now a Cardinal serving in the Vatican in Rome.

They have three children: Mark is a graduate of the Air Force Academy, Class of 1995; David is a graduate of West Point, Class of 1994; and their daughter, Sara, is married to William D. Edwards a West Point graduate, Class of 1998.

Foley commanded 1st Battalion, 4th Infantry, and 2nd Brigade in the 3rd Infantry Division and was Assistant Division Commander in the 2nd Infantry Division, yet his most rewarding and most enjoyable assignment was his tour of duty as Commandant of Cadets.

Foley and his wife, Julie, loved every moment of their involvement with the Corps of Cadets. During his tenure as Commandant, he instituted the Consideration of Others (now called Respect) Program complete with Respect Captain, Company Respect Representatives, and a Respect education program. This was modeled after the Honor Code and System and is a mainstay of the Honor and Respect curriculum at West Point today. With his experience as a Rifle Company Commander in Vietnam, Foley became convinced that respect is not only an essential ingredient in the warrior ethic but is also consistent with West Point traditional values as manifested

by Major John M. Schofield, during his address to the Corps of Cadets on August 11, 1879, when he said in part, "He who feels the respect which is due to others cannot fail to inspire in them regard for himself..."

In Foley's own words, "The inculcation of Honor and Respect contributes immeasurably to developing leaders of character and collectively sustains the kind of trust and cohesion realized by only the most successful organizations."

Foley received the 2004 Fairleigh Dickinson University Pinnacle award, was selected as a 2009 USMA Distinguished Graduate, received the Military Order of the World Wars 2010 Distinguished Service Award, and is a recipient of the 2012 Doughboy Award.

After retiring from active duty in 2000, Lieutenant General Foley became President of Marion Military Institute in Marion, Alabama. In 2005, he became the Director

for Army Emergency Relief, a non-profit institution that has existed since 1942 for the sole purpose of providing financial assistance to soldiers and their families.

Brigadier General Richard G. Stilwell, Commandant of Cadets with Coach George Hunter, Army Men's Basketball Coach, presenting award to Cadet Foley.

President of Italy Oscar Luigi Scalfaro with Major General Foley laying wreath at the Tomb of the Unknowns, Arlington National Cemetery.

Rank and organization: Captain, U.S. Army, Company A, 2nd Battalion, 27th Infantry, 25th Infantry Division.

Place and date: Near Quan Dau Tieng, Republic of Vietnam, November 5, 1966.

Entered service at: Newton, Massachusetts.

Born: May 30, 1941, Newton, Massachusetts.

Citation: For conspicuous gallantry and intrepidity in action at the risk of his life above and beyond the call of duty. Captain Foley's company was ordered to extricate another company of the battalion. Moving through the dense jungle to aid the besieged unit, Company A encountered a strong enemy force occupying well concealed, defensive positions, and the company's leading element quickly sustained several casualties. Captain Foley immediately ran forward to the scene of the most intense action to direct the company's efforts. Deploying one platoon on the flank, he led the other two platoons in an attack on the enemy in the face of intense fire. During this action, both radio operators accompanying him were wounded. At grave risk to himself, he defied the enemy's murderous fire and helped the wounded operators to a position where they could receive medical care. As he moved forward again, one of his machine gun crews was wounded. Seizing the weapon, he charged forward firing the machine gun, shouting orders and rallying his men, thus maintaining the momentum of the attack. Under increasingly heavy enemy fire he ordered his assistant to take cover and, alone, Captain Foley continued to advance firing the machine gun until the wounded had been evacuated and the attack in this area could be resumed. When movement on the other flank was halted by the enemy's fanatical defense, Captain Foley moved to personally direct this critical phase of the battle. Leading the renewed effort, he was blown off his feet and wounded by an enemy grenade. Despite his painful wounds, he refused medical aid and persevered in the forefront of the attack on the enemy redoubt. He led the assault on several enemy gun emplacements and single-handedly, destroyed three such positions. His outstanding personal leadership under intense enemy fire during the fierce battle, which lasted for several hours, inspired his men to heroic efforts and was instrumental in the ultimate success of the operation. Captain Foley's magnificent courage, selfless concern for his men, and professional skill reflect the utmost credit upon himself and the United States Army.

Captain Robert F. Foley and Sergeant John F. Baker receiving Medal of Honor from President Lyndon B. Johnson, May 1, 1968, at the White House.

Paul "Buddy" Bucha was an All-American Swimmer at West Point, graduated at the top of his West Point class, received his master's in Business Administration from Stanford, and was awarded the Medal of Honor for actions in Vietnam in 1968. He is an American hero who works tirelessly to support soldiers and veterans causes while leading his international consulting business for the past 30 years.

Buddy was born August 1, 1943, in Washington, D.C., and grew up as an "Army brat" at bases around the world in Japan, Germany, and throughout the United States. His father was American Army Officer Colonel Paul A. Bucha, who himself lead an amazing career. A typical "Army brat," Buddy lived in four cities before the first grade. He attended grades one, two, and three in Heidelberg, Germany, then returned to Indianapolis for his fourth through eighth grades. The family then moved to Japan. A national age group champion swimmer while in Indianapolis, he swam against college students while in Japan in an outdoor pool during spring and summers, including gold medal Olympic swimmers. The remainder of the year he played football, basketball, and baseball. His dad would give him $50 each time his swim times broke an American national age group record, which was frequently. When he returned to the United States, he entered Horton Watkins High School in Ladue, Missouri, one of the highest per capita income areas of the nation. Buddy's swim times in his freshman and sophomore years in Japan would have qualified him for All-American High School recognition, and the director of athletics at Ladue immediately recognized Bucha's potential in swimming. Bucha soon became captain of the swim team, a High School All-American swimmer, and led his high school to become Missouri State Champions.

Recruited by several top colleges, Buddy was intent on attending Yale University. He and his father drove from Missouri to Connecticut

Captain Paul "Buddy" Bucha, USMA 1965

- **MEDAL OF HONOR RECIPIENT**
- **ALL-AMERICAN NCAA SWIMMER**
- **RANGER HALL OF FAME**
- **STANFORD UNIVERSITY, MASTER'S IN BUSINESS ADMINISTRATION**
- **ASSISTANT PROFESSOR OF SOCIAL SCIENCES, WEST POINT**
- **PRESIDENT, PAUL W. BUCHA & COMPANY**
- **BOY SCOUTS OF AMERICA, YOUTH MEMBER**

>>> Spotlight

"The Medal of Honor is proof that ordinary men and women have within them the potential to challenge fate as they understand it to be and literally change the course of history. It only requires the courage to try."
—Paul Bucha

to visit Yale during his junior year of high school, and en route, his father asked if he wanted to visit West Point. They met with West Point Swim Coach Jack Ryan at the historic Thayer Hotel in 1960. The coach explained that he had already received acceptances from eight High School All-American swimmers and asked Buddy if he wanted to join the great team that was forming. Having been turned down by his local Congressman, Buddy applied directly to President John F. Kennedy and received a Presidential nomination.

At West Point, he lettered all four years in Swimming and was an All-American NCAA swimmer. He graduated 18th in his class academically and second militarily. At the time, the top five percent of each class could attend graduate school immediately after graduation, paid by the government with full salary as an officer, as long as they were accepted to grad school. Buddy was accepted by Harvard and Stanford, and chose Stanford. At Stanford Graduate School of Business (GSB), besides his studies, he helped coach the Stanford swim team, taught SCUBA and surfing, and was Chairman of the Stanford GSB Administrative Committee. During his summer break, he had 92 days leave and elected to attend Airborne and Ranger Schools.

First Lieutenant Bucha graduated from Stanford with his master's in Business Administration and finally entered the regular Army at Fort Campbell, Kentucky, where he was assigned to the 101st Airborne Division. Having fallen behind his class due to his grad school time, he was anxious to get a Platoon Leader position – which he did, but only for four weeks. Soon after arrival, the 101st expanded each battalion from three line companies to four, and was the last division in the Army to do so. This created additional Company Commander positions and the division was short on qualified Captains. Bucha was given command of Delta Company, 3rd Battalion, 3rd Brigade, and as the Commander, he was the first and only member of the company. Slowly he built up the company, with many members of the company actually coming from the stockades of the 101st Airborne and 82nd Airborne, and he was proud of the team that they built. They trained hard and realistically to get ready for combat.

IT WAS DURING THIS BATTLE THAT THE COMPANY LOST 11 KILLED IN ACTION AND 64 WOUNDED OUT OF A 90-PERCENT CASUALTY RATE.

The 101st deployed to Vietnam in 1968. Bucha's company was often detached and spent most of its time in the field as a special unit. During the Tet Offensive, his company was sent to pursue fleeing North Vietnamese Army (NVA) units after they had lost battles attacking large cities and bases. It was in the pursuit of these fleeing NVA units when Bucha's 89 soldiers battled an NVA battalion. It was during this battle that the company lost 11 Killed In Action and 64 wounded out of 89 – a 90 percent casualty rate. The battle lasted for three days and was the biggest battle in Vietnam that day, so the battalion, brigade, and even General Westmoreland himself was on the net calling in support. Westmoreland knew Bucha personally from his time as Superintendent at West Point. Bucha led the unit for three days, calling in fire, attacking enemy positions, and motivating his troops even after being wounded himself. There were many heroes in that battle, but one stood out above the rest, the company's medic Dennis Moore whom Bucha recommended for the Medal of Honor. In the days following the battle, Ray Coffee of the *Chicago Sun Times* heard about the battle and the history of the soldiers in the unit. The *Sun Times* published an article about the "Clerks and

Bucha at West Point with Color Guard in front of Washington Statue.

Jerks" of Delta Company, 3/187 Airborne, and the courage of this infamous unit in the three-day and -night battle that left a North Vietnamese battalion decimated on the battlefield.

After returning to the United States, Bucha attended the Armor Advanced Course at Fort Knox,and while there, he was notified that he was going to receive the Distinguished Service Cross (DSC) for his actions in that battle in 1968. After completing the advanced course, he thought he would be returning to Vietnam, but the Branch Officer told him he could not return to Vietnam, though at the time, the officer would not state clearly why Bucha could not return to Vietnam. Since he already had his graduate degree, even though he was a young Captain, he was assigned to West Point as an instructor in the Social Sciences department. It was at West Point that Bucha was informed that he was being awarded the Medal of Honor, his first question was "for what?" Bucha initially wanted to turn down the award since he didn't believe he had earned it, but was convinced by an NCO that the award was not only for himself, but it was, on the contrary, an award for all of the men who had fought in the battle.

President Nixon awarded the Medal of Honor to Captain Bucha in May 1970, along with Bob Kerry (later Senator) and Jay Vargas, who became lifelong friends. This was Bucha's first visit to the White House and first time meeting a United States President – his revelation that day was that he found he was not in awe of "the man" who was President. He realized that he was more inspired being in front of soldiers than being in front of a United States President. To this day, after meeting eight Presidents, he finds standing in front of soldiers to far more awe-inspiring after all they have offered their lives for the nation.

Speaking as a recipient of our nations' highest award, Bucha modestly believes that the adulation of valor awards is often misplaced. He often tells young cadets and soldiers that if one meets a leader, and from his or her decorations, you can see they have been every where and served in all the hot spots, but no medals for valor have been received, stop because you may have met perfection in leadership personified. After all, the objective is to lead, accomplish the mission, and return for the next assignment – no valor required. He, to this day, seems uncomfortable that he received the medal, but his medic who he recommended for it received the DSC. Bucha has found that being awarded the Medal of Honor has given him the platform to represent the military and veterans. With this platform, he tries to do as much as he can for our troops. There is always the sense of guilt – how can one be awarded the Medal of Honor when there are 11 names on a black polished wall in Washington, D.C., who lost their lives and with that all that they might have been, under your command?

His personal story, and his reconciling his own feelings about the actions of that battle in 1968, are the reason Bucha's focus now is to help soldiers address the issues related to post-traumatic stress that he himself has experienced. His belief is that leaders should be more willing to admit to experiencing post-traumatic stress (PTS) and differentiating it from post-traumatic stress disorder (PTSD). PTSD is a clinical diagnosis of a condition whose symptoms are seen and measured and for which a protocol exists for treatment. Before the symptoms manifest themselves, it is PTS, the time after a traumatically stressful event, whether in the military or civilian world. To suggest there is a "disorder" before a diagnosis has been completed creates a stigma to a condition that so many have and that requires counseling in order to be prepared should the symptoms manifest themselves. As one of the few living recipients of the Medal of Honor, his opinion and his willingness to discuss this difficult topic have helped other soldiers address their own issues from their own battles.

Bucha left the Army in 1972 to pursue a business career and worked as a officer for Ross Perot's Electronic Data Systems Corporation and EDS World for seven years in Iran and France. In 1980, Bucha started his own consultant business in international trade and real estate. Over the past 30 years, he has built Paul W. Bucha & Company and served as a consultant and advisor to several very successful enterprises. Buddy Bucha has four children, five grandchildren, and is married to Cynthia Carter Bell of Cornwall, New York.

Bucha and his medic treating a wounded soldier.

UH-1 Huey Helicopter taking away casualties from Captain Bucha's company.

Photo: NARA

Rank and organization: Captain, U.S. Army, Company D, 3rd Battalion. 187th Infantry, 3rd Brigade, 101st Airborne Division.

Place and date: Near Phuoc Vinh, Binh Duong Province, Republic of Vietnam, March 16–19, 1968.

Entered service at: United States Military Academy, West Point, New York.

Born: August 1, 1943, Washington, D.C.

Citation: For conspicuous gallantry and intrepidity in action at the risk of his life above and beyond the call of duty. Captain Bucha distinguished himself while serving as Commanding Officer, Company D, on a reconnaissance-in-force mission against enemy forces near Phuoc Vinh. The company was inserted by helicopter into the suspected enemy stronghold to locate and destroy the enemy. During this period, Captain Bucha aggressively and courageously led his men in the destruction of enemy fortifications and base areas and eliminated scattered resistance impeding the advance of the company. On March 18th, while advancing to contact, the lead elements of the company became engaged by the heavy automatic weapon, heavy machine gun, rocket propelled grenade, claymore mine and small-arms fire of an estimated battalion-size force. Captain Bucha, with complete disregard for his safety, moved to the threatened area to direct the defense and ordered reinforcements to the aid of the lead element. Seeing that his men were pinned down by heavy machine gun fire from a concealed bunker located some 40 meters to the front of the positions, Captain Bucha crawled through the hail of fire to single-handedly destroy the bunker with grenades. During this heroic action, Captain Bucha received a painful shrapnel wound. Returning to the perimeter, he observed that his unit could not hold its position and repel the human wave assaults launched by the determined enemy. Captain Bucha ordered the withdrawal of the unit elements and covered the withdrawal to positions of a company perimeter from which he could direct fire upon the charging enemy. When one friendly element retrieving casualties was ambushed and cut off from the perimeter, Captain Bucha ordered them to feign death and he directed artillery fire around them. During the night, Captain Bucha moved throughout the position, distributing ammunition, providing encouragement and insuring the integrity of the defense. He directed artillery, helicopter gunship, and Air Force gunship fire on the enemy strong points and attacking forces, marking the positions with smoke grenades. Using flashlights in complete view of enemy snipers, he directed the medical evacuation of three air-ambulance loads of seriously wounded personnel and the helicopter supply of his company. At daybreak, Captain Bucha led a rescue party to recover the dead and wounded members of the ambushed element. During the period of intensive combat, Captain Bucha, by his extraordinary heroism, inspirational example, outstanding leadership, and professional competence, led his company in the decimation of a superior enemy force, which left 156 dead on the battlefield. His bravery and gallantry at the risk of his life are in the highest traditions of the military service, Captain Bucha has reflected great credit on himself, his unit, and the United States Army.

Courtesy Paul Bucha

Courtesy Paul Bucha

Captain Bucha calling in fire.

Courtesy Paul Bucha

Second Lieutenant Alexander R. Nininger, USMA 1941

- **MEDAL OF HONOR RECIPIENT (POSTHUMOUS)**
- **KILLED IN ACTION BATAAN, PHILIPPINES**
- **THE PRESTIGIOUS NININGER AWARD AT WEST POINT NAMED IN HIS HONOR TO BE AWARDED TO ONE WEST POINT GRADUATE PER YEAR FOR VALOR**
- **57TH INFANTRY (PHILIPPINE SCOUTS), BATAAN, P.I., JANUARY 12, 1942**

Nininger Plaque in Cullum Hall, West Point.

For conspicuous gallantry and intrepidity above and beyond the call of duty in action with the enemy near Abucay, Bataan, Philippine Islands, on January 12, 1942. This officer, though assigned to another company not then engaged in combat, voluntarily attached himself to Company K, same regiment, while that unit was being attacked by enemy force superior in firepower. Enemy snipers in trees and foxholes had stopped a counterattack to regain part of position. In hand-to-hand fighting that followed, Second Lieutenant Nininger repeatedly forced his way to and into the hostile position. Though exposed to heavy enemy fire, he continued to attack with rifle and hand grenades and succeeded in destroying several enemy groups in foxholes and enemy snipers. Although wounded three times, he continued his attacks until he was killed after pushing alone far within the enemy position. When his body was found after recapture of the position, one enemy officer and two enemy soldiers lay dead around him.

Brigadier General Frederick Walker Castle, USMA 1930

- **MEDAL OF HONOR (POSTHUMOUS)**
- **COMMANDING GENERAL, 4TH BOMB WING**
- **B-17 PILOT**
- **KILLED IN ACTION LEADING AIR WING, DECEMBER 24, 1944, DURING BATTLE OF THE BULGE**
- **BURIED IN AMERICAN NATIONAL CEMETERY BELGIUM**

Castle's gravesite in American Military Cemetery, Belgium.

He was Air Commander and leader of more than 2,000 heavy bombers in a strike against German airfields on December 24, 1944. En route to the target, the failure of one engine forced him to relinquish his place at the head of the formation. In order not to endanger friendly troops on the ground below, he refused to jettison his bombs to gain speed maneuverability. His lagging, unescorted aircraft became the target of numerous enemy fighters that ripped the left wing with cannon shells, set the oxyGeneral system afire, and wounded two members of the crew. Repeated attacks started fires in two engines, leaving the Flying Fortress in imminent danger of exploding. Realizing the hopelessness of the situation, the bailout order was given. Without regard for his personal safety, he gallantly remained alone at the controls to afford all other crew members an opportunity to escape. Still another attack exploded gasoline tanks in the right wing, and the bomber plunged earthward, carrying General Castle to his death. His intrepidity and willing sacrifice of his life to save members of the crew were in keeping with the highest traditions of the military service.

First Lieutenant Samuel Streit Coursen, USMA 1949

- **MEDAL OF HONOR (POSTHUMOUS)**
- **KILLED IN ACTION NEAR KAESONG, KOREA, OCTOBER 12, 1950**
- **MEDAL OF HONOR, COMBAT INFANTRYMAN BADGE, PURPLE HEART**

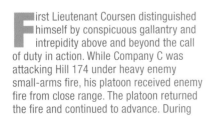

First Lieutenant Coursen distinguished himself by conspicuous gallantry and intrepidity above and beyond the call of duty in action. While Company C was attacking Hill 174 under heavy enemy small-arms fire, his platoon received enemy fire from close range. The platoon returned the fire and continued to advance. During this phase, one of his men moved into a well-camouflaged emplacement, which was thought to be unoccupied, and was wounded by the enemy who were hidden within the emplacement. Seeing the soldier in difficulty he rushed to the man's aid and, without regard for his personal safety, engaged the enemy in hand-to-hand combat in an effort to protect his wounded comrade until he himself was killed. When his body was recovered after the battle, seven enemy dead were found in the emplacement. As the result of First Lieutenant Coursen's violent struggle several of the enemies' heads had been crushed with his rifle. His aggressive and intrepid actions saved the life of the wounded man, eliminated the main position of the enemy roadblock, and greatly inspired the men in his command. First Lieutenant Coursen's extraordinary heroism and intrepidity reflect the highest credit on himself and are in keeping with the honored traditions of the military service.

Lieutenant Colonel Andre C. Lucas, USMA 1954

- **MEDAL OF HONOR (POSTHUMOUS)**
- **COMMANDER, 1ST BATTALION, 34TH INFANTRY REGIMENT, GERMANY, 1968–69**
- **COMMANDER, 2ND BATTALION, 506TH AIRBORNE REGIMENT, 101ST AIRBORNE DIVISION, REPUBLIC OF VIETNAM, 1969–70**
- **TACTICAL OFFICER, WEST POINT, 1961–63**
- **KILLED IN ACTION, FIREBASE RIPCORD, JULY 23, 1970**

Lieutenant Colonel Lucas distinguished himself by extraordinary heroism while serving as the Commanding Officer of the 2nd Battalion. Although the fire base was constantly subjected to heavy attacks by a numerically superior enemy force throughout this period, Lieutenant Colonel Lucas, forsaking his own safety, performed numerous acts of extraordinary valor in directing the defense of the allied position. On one occasion, he flew in a helicopter at treetop level above an entrenched enemy directing the fire of one of his companies for more than three hours. Even though his helicopter was heavily damaged by enemy fire, he remained in an exposed position until the company expended its supply of grenades. He then transferred to another helicopter, dropped critically needed grenades to the troops, and resumed his perilous mission of directing fire on the enemy. These courageous actions by Lieutenant Colonel Lucas prevented the company from being encircled and destroyed by a larger enemy force. On another occasion, Lieutenant Colonel Lucas attempted to rescue a crewman trapped in a burning helicopter. As the flames in the aircraft spread, and enemy fire became intense, Lieutenant Colonel Lucas ordered all members of the rescue party to safety. Then, at great personal risk, he continued the rescue effort amid concentrated enemy mortar fire, intense heat, and exploding ammunition until the aircraft was completely engulfed in flames. Lieutenant Colonel Lucas was mortally wounded while directing the successful withdrawal of his battalion from the fire base. His actions throughout this extended period inspired his men to heroic efforts and were instrumental in saving the lives of many of his fellow soldiers while inflicting heavy casualties on the enemy. Lieutenant Colonel Lucas's conspicuous gallantry and intrepidity in action, at the cost of his own life, were in keeping with the highest traditions of the military service and reflect great credit on him, his unit and the United States Army.

First Lieutenant Richard Thomas Shea, Jr., USMA 1952

- **MEDAL OF HONOR (POSTHUMOUS)**
- **SHEA STADIUM AT WEST POINT DEDICATED IN HIS HONOR**
- **17TH INFANTRY REGIMENT, 7TH INFANTRY DIVISION, KOREA**
- **KILLED IN ACTION, JULY 8, 1953, KOREAN WAR**
- **MEDAL OF HONOR, PURPLE HEART, COMBAT INFANTRYMAN BADGE**

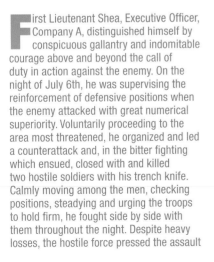

First Lieutenant Shea, Executive Officer, Company A, distinguished himself by conspicuous gallantry and indomitable courage above and beyond the call of duty in action against the enemy. On the night of July 6th, he was supervising the reinforcement of defensive positions when the enemy attacked with great numerical superiority. Voluntarily proceeding to the area most threatened, he organized and led a counterattack and, in the bitter fighting which ensued, closed with and killed two hostile soldiers with his trench knife. Calmly moving among the men, checking positions, steadying and urging the troops to hold firm, he fought side by side with them throughout the night. Despite heavy losses, the hostile force pressed the assault with determination, and at dawn, made an all-out attempt to overrun friendly elements. Charging forward to meet the challenge, First Lieutenant Shea and his gallant men drove back the hostile troops. Elements of Company G joined the defense on the afternoon of July 7th, having lost key personnel through casualties. Immediately integrating these troops into his unit, First Lieutenant Shea rallied a group of 20 men and again charged the enemy. Although wounded in this action, he refused evacuation and continued to lead the counterattack. When the assaulting element was pinned down by heavy machine gun fire, he personally rushed the emplacement and, firing his carbine and lobbing grenades with deadly accuracy, neutralized the weapon and killed three of the enemies. With forceful leadership and by his heroic example, First Lieutenant Shea coordinated and directed a holding action throughout the night and the following morning. On July 8th, the enemy attacked again. Despite additional wounds, he launched a determined counterattack and was last seen in close hand-to-hand combat with the enemy. First Lieutenant Shea's inspirational leadership and unflinching courage set an illustrious example of valor to the men of his regiment, reflecting lasting glory upon himself and upholding the noble traditions of the military service.

Shea Stadium at West Point, named in his honor.

First Lieutenant Frank Stanley Reasoner, USMC, USMA 1962

- **MEDAL OF HONOR (POSTHUMOUS)**
- **3RD RECONNAISSANCE BATTALION, USMC**
- **KILLED IN ACTION VIETNAM, JULY 12, 1965**
- **NAVY MEDAL OF HONOR, PURPLE HEART**

Navy Medal of Honor.

For conspicuous gallantry and intrepidity at the risk of his life above and beyond the call of duty. The reconnaissance patrol led by First Lieutenant Reasoner had deeply penetrated heavily controlled enemy territory when it came under extremely heavy fire from an estimated 50 to 100 Viet Cong insurgents. Accompanying the advance party and the point that consisted of five men, he immediately deployed his men for an assault after the Viet Cong had opened fire from numerous concealed positions. Boldly shouting encouragement and virtually isolated from the main body, he organized a base of fire for an assault on the enemy positions. The slashing fury of the Viet Cong machine gun and automatic weapons fire made it impossible for the main body to move forward. Repeatedly exposing himself to the devastating attack he skillfully provided covering fire, killing at least two Viet Cong and effectively silencing an automatic weapons position in a valiant attempt to effect evacuation of a wounded man. As casualties began to mount, his radio operator was wounded and First Lieutenant Reasoner immediately moved to his side and tended his wounds. When the radio operator was hit a second time while attempting to reach a covered position, First Lieutenant Reasoner courageously running to his aid through the grazing machine gun fire fell mortally wounded. His indomitable fighting spirit, valiant leadership, and unflinching devotion to duty provided the inspiration that was to enable the patrol to complete its mission without further casualties. In the face of almost certain death, he gallantly gave his life in the service of his country. His actions upheld the highest traditions of the Marine Corps and the United States Naval Service.

Colonel William Atkinson Jones, III, USAF, USMA 1945

- **AIR FORCE MEDAL OF HONOR RECEIVED FOR VALOROUS RESCUE OF DOWNED PILOT, 1968, VIETNAM**
- **COMMANDER, 602ND SPECIAL OPERATIONS SQUADRON, THAILAND**
- **MASTER'S IN INTERNATIONAL RELATIONS GEORGETOWN UNIVERSITY**
- **AIR WAR COLLEGE**
- **DIED IN AIR CRASH WOODBRIDGE, VIRGINIA, NOVEMBER 15, 1969**
- **AIR FORCE MEDAL OF HONOR AWARDED TO HIS WIDOW POSTHUMOUSLY, 1970**

The Air Force Medal of Honor.

For conspicuous gallantry and intrepidity in action at the risk of his life above and beyond the call of duty. Colonel Jones distinguished himself as the pilot of an A-1H Skyraider aircraft near Dong Hoi, North Vietnam. On that day, as the on-scene commander in the attempted rescue of a downed United States pilot, Colonel Jones's aircraft was repeatedly hit by heavy and accurate anti-aircraft fire. On one of his low passes, Colonel Jones felt an explosion beneath his aircraft and his cockpit rapidly filled with smoke. With complete disregard of the possibility that his aircraft might still be burning, he unhesitatingly continued his search for the downed pilot. On this pass, he sighted the survivor and a multiple-barrel gun position firing at him from near the top of a karst formation. He could not attack the gun position on that pass for fear he would endanger the downed pilot. Leaving himself exposed to the gun position, Colonel Jones attacked the position with cannon and rocket fire on two successive passes. On his second pass, the aircraft was hit with multiple rounds of automatic weapons fire. One round impacted the Yankee Extraction System rocket mounted directly behind the headrest, igniting the rocket. His aircraft was observed to burst into flames in the center fuselage section, with flame engulfing the cockpit area. He pulled the extraction handle, jettisoning the canopy. The influx of fresh air made the fire burn with greater intensity for a few moments, but since the rocket motor had already burned, the extraction system did not pull Colonel Jones from the aircraft. Despite searing pains from severe burns sustained on his arms, hand, neck, shoulders, and face, Colonel Jones pulled his aircraft into a climb and attempted to transmit the location of the downed pilot and the enemy gun position to the other aircraft in the area. His calls were blocked by other aircraft transmissions repeatedly directing him to bail out and within seconds his transmitters were disabled and he could receive only on one channel. Completely disregarding his injuries, he elected to fly his crippled aircraft back to his base and pass on essential information for the rescue rather than bailout. Colonel Jones successfully landed his heavily damaged aircraft and passed the information to a Debriefing Officer while on the operating table. As a result of his heroic actions and complete disregard for his personal safety, the downed pilot was rescued later in the day. Colonel Jones's profound concern for his fellow man at the risk of his life, above and beyond the call of duty, are in keeping with the highest traditions of the United States Air Force and reflect great credit upon himself and the Armed Forces of this country.

General of the Army Douglas MacArthur, USMA 1903

- **GENERAL OF THE ARMY**
- **MEDAL OF HONOR RECIPIENT**
- **SUPREME COMMANDER, SOUTHWEST PACIFIC THEATER OF WAR, WORLD WAR II**
- **COMMANDER, UNITED NATIONS COMMAND, KOREAN WAR, 1950**
- **SUPERINTENDENT. WEST POINT**
- **FIRST CAPTAIN, WEST POINT**
- **ARMY FOOTBALL MANAGER**

For conspicuous leadership in preparing the Philippine Islands to resist conquest, for gallantry and intrepidity above and beyond the call of duty in action against invading Japanese forces, and for the heroic conduct of defensive and offensive operations on the Bataan Peninsula. He mobilized, trained, and led an Army that has received world acclaim for its gallant defense against a tremendous superiority of enemy forces in men and arms. His utter disregard of personal danger under heavy fire and aerial bombardment, his calm judgment in each crisis, inspired his troops, galvanized the spirit of resistance of the Filipino people, and confirmed the faith of the American people in their Armed Forces.

General Leon William Johnson, USAF, USMA 1926

- **MEDAL OF HONOR, SILVER STAR**
- **COMMANDING GENERAL, 14TH COMBAT BOMBER WING**
- **COMMANDING GENERAL, 3RD AIR FORCE, 1948–52**
- **PLOESTI RAID, 1943**
- **COMMANDING GENERAL, CONAC, 1952**

For conspicuous gallantry in action and intrepidity at the risk of his life above and beyond the call of duty on August 1, 1943. Colonel Johnson, as Commanding Officer of a heavy bombardment group, let the formation of the aircraft of his organization constituting the fourth element of the mass low-level bombing attack of the 9th United States Air Force against the vitally important enemy target of the Ploesti oil refineries. While proceeding to the target on this 2,400-mile flight, his element became separated from the leading elements of the mass formation in maintaining the formation of the unit while avoiding dangerous cumulous cloud conditions encountered over mountainous territory. Though temporarily lost, he reestablished contact with the third element and continued on the mission with this reduced force to the prearranged point of attack, where it was discovered that the target assigned to Colonel Johnson's group had been attacked and damaged by a preceding element. Though having lost the element of surprise upon which the safety and success of such a daring form of mission in heavy bombardment aircraft so strongly depended, Colonel Johnson elected to carry out his planned low-level attack despite the thoroughly alerted defenses, the destructive antiaircraft fire, enemy fighter airplanes, the imminent danger of exploding delayed action bombs from the previous element, of oil fires and explosions, and of intense smoke obscuring the target. By his gallant courage, brilliant leadership, and superior flying skill, Colonel Johnson so led his formation as to destroy totally the important refining plants and installations that were the object of his mission. Colonel Johnson's personal contribution to the success of this historic raid, and the conspicuous gallantry in action, and intrepidity at the risk of his life above and beyond the call of duty demonstrated by him on this occasion constitute such deeds of valor and distinguished service as have during our Nation's history formed the finest traditions of our Armed Forces.

Colonel Demas Thurlow Craw, USMA 1924

- MEDAL OF HONOR (POSTHUMOUS), PURPLE HEART
- KILLED IN ACTION, NOVEMBER 8, 1942, LYAUTEY MOROCCO DURING ASSAULT LANDING OPERATION TORCH

For conspicuous gallantry and intrepidity in action above and beyond the call of duty. On November 8, 1942, near Port Lyautey, French Morocco, Colonel Craw volunteered to accompany the leading wave of assault boats to the shore and pass through the enemy lines to locate the French Commander with a view to suspending hostilities. This request was first refused as being too dangerous but upon the officer's insistence that he was qualified to undertake and accomplish the mission he was allowed to go. Encountering heavy fire while in the landing boat and unable to dock in the river because of shell fire from shore batteries, Colonel Craw, accompanied by one officer and one soldier, succeeded in landing on the beach at Mehdia Plage under constant low-level strafing from three enemy planes. Riding in a bantam truck toward French headquarters, progress of the party was hindered by fire from our own naval guns. Nearing Port Lyautey, Colonel Craw was instantly killed by a sustained burst of machine gun fire at point-blank range from a concealed position near the road.

Colonel William Hale Wilbur, USMA 1949

- MEDAL OF HONOR (POSTHUMOUS), PURPLE HEART
- WORLD WAR II VETERAN
- 1ST CAVALRY DIVISION
- KILLED IN ACTION, KOREAN WAR, SEPTEMBER 6, 1950

For conspicuous gallantry and intrepidity in action above and beyond the call of duty. Colonel Wilbur prepared the plan for making contact with French Commanders in Casablanca and obtaining an armistice to prevent unnecessary bloodshed. On November 8, 1942, he landed at Fedala with the leading assault waves where opposition had developed into a firm and continuous defensive line across his route of advance. Commandeering a vehicle, he was driven toward the hostile defenses under incessant fire, finally locating a French Officer who accorded him passage through the forward positions. He then proceeded in total darkness through 16 miles of enemy-occupied country intermittently subjected to heavy bursts of fire and accomplished his mission by delivering his letters to appropriate French officials in Casablanca. Returning toward his command, Colonel Wilbur detected a hostile battery firing effectively on our troops. He took charge of a platoon of American tanks and personally led them in an attack and capture of the battery. From the moment of landing until the cessation of hostile resistance, Colonel Wilbur's conduct was voluntary and exemplary in its coolness and daring.

Lieutenant Colonel Emory Jenison Pike, USMA 1901

- MEDAL OF HONOR (POSTHUMOUS)
- CUBA, 1907–08
- PHILIPPINES, 1905–06
- COMMANDER, 321 MACHINE GUN BATTALION, FRANCE, WORLD WAR I
- KILLED IN ACTION NEAR VANDIERES, FRANCE, SEPTEMBER 16, 1918

Having gone forward to reconnoiter new machine gun positions, Lieutenant Colonel Pike offered his assistance in reorganizing advance Infantry units that had become disorganized during a heavy artillery shelling. He succeeded in locating only about 20 men, but with these he advanced and when later joined by several Infantry platoons rendered inestimable service in establishing outposts, encouraging all by his cheeriness, in spite of the extreme danger of the situation. When a shell had wounded one of the men in the outpost, Lieutenant Colonel Pike immediately went to his aid and was severely wounded himself when another shell burst in the same place. While waiting to be brought to the rear, Lieutenant Colonel Pike continued in command, still retaining his jovial manner of encouragement, directing the reorganization until the position could be held. The entire operation was carried on under terrific bombardment, and the example of courage and devotion to duty, as set by Lieutenant Colonel Pike, established the landing until the cessation of hostile resistance, Colonel Wilbur's conduct was voluntary and exemplary in its coolness and daring.

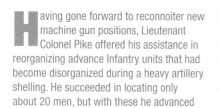

Before coming to West Point, Oliver Otis Howard had been educated at Bowdoin College in his home state of Maine. In 1854, he graduated from West Point ranked number four of the 36 cadets in his class. Three years later, Howard returned to West Point teach mathematics and remained until the commencement of the Civil War.

Before coming to West Point, Oliver Otis Howard had been educated at Bowdoin College in his home state of Maine. In 1854, he graduated from West Point ranked number four of the 36 cadets in his class. Three years later, Howard returned to West Point teach mathematics and remained until the commencement of the Civil War.

On the outbreak of the war, Howard was appointed Colonel of the Third Maine Volunteers. He fought in numerous battle and campaigns during the war, including Bull Run, the Peninsular Campaign, Antietam, Fredericksburg, Chancellorsville, and Gettysburg. During the battle at Fair Oaks in May of 1862, Howard was shot twice in his right arm. His arm would need to be amputated but his actions at Fair Oaks would earn him the Medal of Honor.

After the war President Andrew Johnson appointed Howard to be the commissioner of the Bureau of Refugees, Freedmen, and Abandoned Lands. In this capacity, he was tasked to provide food, clothing, and medical care for former slaves. Howard drew the ire of both Southern and Northern whites. Most Southerners did not favor the programs to pay the newly freed slaves a wage set by Howard's Bureau; many Northerners felt that the former slaveholders should pay the entire cost of integrating the freedmen into society. Howard pushed forward, driven by his belief in racial equality. He commented publicly that "I never could detect the shadow of a reason why the color of the skin should impair the right to life, liberty, and the pursuit of happiness."[1] He also believed that education was the only avenue through which former slaves could make lasting progress in society. In 1867, with the support of Radical Republicans in Congress, he established a university in Washington, D.C., devoted to the education of freedmen. The school, Howard University, was named in his honor and he served as its President from 1869 until he was dispatched by the Army to serve in the Indian Wars.

In 1872, General Howard was sent to meet with Cochise, leader of the Chiricahua Apache who had been waging war with American settlers in the Arizona Territory over the preceding decade. An unarmed Howard met with Cochise, promising a reservation of their choosing he secured a peace agreement with Chiricahua. Howard was criticized by military officers and other government officials for what they believed to be an overly generous agreement. An executive order upheld the agreement, setting aside much of the southeastern corner of Arizona as a Chiricahua reservation for Cochise and his people.[2]

In 1880, Cadet Johnson C. Whittaker, an African-American, was found bound, bleeding, and unconscious on the floor of the barracks at West Point. The event stirred great emotion for and against Cadet Whittaker with some people claiming this was the result of a brutal hazing and other claiming Whittaker's injuries were self-inflicted.[3] President Hayes felt that General Howard would be the right officer to settle the Whittaker case.[4] Howard returned to West Point as the 20th Superintendent of the Military Academy from 1881 through 1882. Howard's military career continued with him assuming command of the Department of the Platte and the Military Division of the East. Howard retired from the Army in 1894 but continued to be an active scholar and educator, publishing a number of books and founding Lincoln Memorial University in Tennessee for the education of the "mountain whites."[5] In 1909, Major General Howard's long life of service to mankind ended and he was buried near his home in Burlington, Vermont. After his death, General Howard's significant contributions to American life were recognized by his inclusion in the Dictionary of American Biography.

Written by: Lieutenant Colonel Craig Morrow, PhD, USMA 1991.

> "I NEVER COULD DETECT THE SHADOW OF A REASON WHY THE COLOR OF THE SKIN SHOULD IMPAIR THE RIGHT TO LIFE, LIBERTY, AND THE PURSUIT OF HAPPINESS," SAID HOWARD.

Major General Oliver Otis Howard, USMA 1854

- FOUNDER AND PRESIDENT, HOWARD UNIVERSITY IN WASHINGTON, D.C.
- FOUNDER, MEMORIAL UNIVERSITY IN TENNESSEE
- SUPERINTENDENT, WEST POINT
- COMMISSIONER OF THE BUREAU OF REFUGEES, FREEDMEN, AND ABANDONED LANDS
- MEDAL OF HONOR RECIPIENT FOR ACTIONS AT THE BATTLE OF FAIR OAKS, 1862
- NEGOTIATED PEACE AGREEMENT WITH THE CHIRICAHUA APACHE IN ARIZONA, 1872

Howard University.

Major General Howard Equestrian Statue at Gettysburg National Battlefield.

Courtesy: Thomas Eishen of Gettysburg Photographs

Major General Howard and Nez Perce leader Chief Joseph in 1904 at the Carlisle Indian School in Pennsylvania (now home to the Army War College).

Photo: NARA

General MacArthur embraces an emaciated General Wainwright shortly after his release from Japanese POW Camp.

Major General Wainwright Philippines, March 1942.

General Jonathan Wainwright, USMA 1906

- MEDAL OF HONOR
- COMMANDER, ALLIED FORCES PHILIPPINES
- PRISONER OF WAR
- FORT WAINWRIGHT, ALASKA, NAMED IN HIS HONOR
- CADET FIRST CAPTAIN

★ ★ ★ ★

In the most widely circulated photograph of General Jonathan Wainwright, General of the Army Douglas MacArthur has an arm draped around an emaciated Wainwright, who, only days before, had been the ranking American Prisoner of War held in Japanese captivity. That photograph portrays both triumph and tragedy: It is triumphant in its depiction of a loyal Field Commander's reunion with his Theater Commander; the photo is tragic in that three long years of

captivity had reduced Jonathan Wainwright, a proud soldier, an officer who dedicated his career to the men under his command, to a foil amid the victorious prose and raucous celebrations following the Japanese surrender. Never forgotten by his superiors or by his country, Wainwright had faded from the American conscience as newsreels celebrated the cross-Pacific advances of MacArthur and Nimitz. Through that indelible image that ran in newspapers across the

world, Wainwright symbolized the triumph of will and the brutality of the Pacific War. His story, though tragic in his ultimately futile defense of Bataan and Corregidor, is one of a career of unflinching dedication to his men, a true testament to the leadership principles he learned at West Point and honed during a distinguished military career.

Senior Field Commanders of any era can learn from the experience of Jonathan

Wainwright in the Philippines on the eve of World War II. With war between the United States and Japan looming in the fall of 1941, Wainwright raced against time to prepare the Philippine Division – a force comprised largely of poorly trained and ill-equipped Filipino soldiers – to defend the strategic archipelago from Japanese advances. The task was onerous. With only one squadron of well-trained American troops forming the nucleus of his force, he set out to

>>> Spotlight

In 1939, an Air Force base was built near Fairbanks, Alaska, and called Ladd Field. It was transferred to the Army in 1961 and re-designated Fort Wainwright in honor of General Wainwright (USMA 1906). In 2006, the 1st Brigade, 25th Infantry Division was transferred to Fort Wainwright and remains an active-duty brigade at Fort Wainwright.

Photo Courtesy: Fort Wainwright PAO

Major General Wainwright and General MacArthur, Philippines, 1941.

state of readiness of Philippine defenses.[2] While MacArthur inflated his assessments in reports to Washington, Wainwright had no choice but to drive forward and prepare to operate with the forces and equipment on hand. He knew that his men would have to bear the complete burden of defending the archipelago and the honor of General MacArthur. Wainwright saluted and continued his mission.

When war came to the Philippines on December 8, 1941, the Japanese gained immediate air and naval superiority in advance of their amphibious landings against Luzon. When the Japanese launched a series of amphibious landings in late December, General Wainwright's North Luzon Force fought a valiant delaying operation, ultimately ceding most of northern Luzon to the Japanese while tenaciously defending the Bataan peninsula. Wainwright personally admonished his ill-equipped and demoralized men to hold the line. He was leading his command by example and from the front, much as he had done as a young Cavalry Lieutenant in the Philippines, two short years after graduating from West Point. General Wainwright's personal courage during the months of close fighting in Bataan was a source of inspiration to the men under his command, but his outward enthusiasm belied a sense of foreboding that the campaign would end in disaster. When President Roosevelt ordered MacArthur to depart the Philippines for Australia, Wainwright assumed command and began the last stand of American and Filipino forces on the small island of Corregidor. Even if the morale of he and his men was evaporating by the moment, the last stand of Wainwright and his men inspired an American public that had little to cheer for in the winter and spring of 1942.

General Wainwright's candor in assessing the forces at his disposal prior to the outbreak of war was commendable and his skillful employment of his ill-trained and poorly equipped force slowed the pace of Japanese conquest in the South Pacific, but historians will longer remember the virtues he demonstrated during his seemingly interminable years of brutal captivity as a Prisoner of War. As his Japanese captors moved he and his fellow prisoners from Luzon to Taiwan to Manchuria, General Wainwright endured the same privations that his subordinates suffered.[3] During more than three years in captivity, he held tight to his responsibilities – his duty – to continue

to lead his fellow American and British prisoners by example. He suffered some serious physical abuse by his Japanese captors, never requesting special treatment commensurate with his rank and status as the senior American prisoner. Even through the darkest days, weeks, and months of his ordeal, Jonathan Wainwright remained true to his reputation as a soldier's General.

At the end of a career distinguished by his sincere love of his men, President Harry Truman awarded him with the Congressional Medal of Honor. The citation highlighted General Wainwright's unwavering commitment to the well-being of his soldiers, from the defense of Bataan and Corregidor, through his ordeal as a Prisoner of War. The Medal of Honor Citation provided an appropriate summary of Jonathan Wainwright's career:

> ## EVEN THROUGH THE DARKEST DAYS, WEEKS, AND MONTHS OF HIS ORDEAL, JONATHAN WAINWRIGHT REMAINED TRUE TO HIS REPUTATION AS A SOLDIER'S GENERAL.

"Distinguished himself by intrepid and determined leadership against greatly superior enemy forces. At the repeated risk of life above and beyond the call of duty in his position, he frequented the firing line of his troops where his presence provided the example and incentive that helped make the gallant efforts of these men possible. The final stand on beleaguered Corregidor, for which he was in an important measure personally responsible, commanded the admiration of the Nation's allies. It reflected the high morale of American arms in the face of overwhelming odds. His courage and resolution were a vitally needed inspiration to the then sorely pressed freedom-loving peoples of the world."[4]

It was a fitting conclusion to this warrior's career and an honor that truly reflected General Jonathan Wainwright's half century of service to his country.

Written by: Major Keith R. Walters, USMA 1997.

---

train a force that would assume complete responsibility for defense of the Philippines by 1946. A dire lack of equipment, however, limited training opportunities to individual drills. There would be very few opportunities for unit maneuvers at any level, even as the Imperial Japanese Army made final preparations for the conquest of the Philippines. Equally troublesome to General Wainwright was the absence of a sense of urgency from his commander, General

Douglas MacArthur, even after the War Department warned in August 1941 of the increasing likelihood of war.[1] As Wainwright assumed command of the decisive North Luzon Force in late-November, he found his command – the force tasked with defending the most likely landing beaches on Luzon – in a pitiful state of readiness. His candid assessments of the posture of his field force fell unheeded as MacArthur informed General George Marshall of the splendid

West Point's primary mission is to develop Commissioned Officers of character who will lead the nation's military. West Point has unfailingly succeeded in that mission, particularly in times of conflict, as graduates have led American forces in combat in every American conflict since the War of 1812. In doing so, West Point graduates have suffered many thousands of casualties in these conflicts, with more than 1,200 making the ultimate sacrifice. The table to the right shows the total number of Americans killed in each conflict, as well as the number of those who were West Point graduates. The total killed in the Indian Wars is not well documented but is estimated at approximately 70 graduates. While this book cannot profile every one of those graduates, this chapter will highlight a few. It will also highlight one graduate killed in the World Trade Center by the terrorist attacks on September 11, 2001. Those terrorist attacks, in turn, placed thousands of West Point graduates on the battlefields in Afghanistan and Iraq, where they would all lead American Soldiers and many would make the ultimate sacrifice in doing so.

LONG GRAY LINE MEMBERS WHO MADE THE ULTIMATE SACRIFICE

> **"It is foolish and wrong to mourn the men who died. Rather, we should thank God that such men lived."**
>
> *–General George S. Patton, USMA 1909*

> **"The most terrible job in warfare is to be a Second Lieutenant leading a platoon when you are on the battlefield."**
>
> *–General of the Army Dwight D. Eisenhower, USMA 1915*

> **"The soldier above all other people prays for peace, for he must suffer and bear the deepest wounds and scars of war. But always in our ears ring the ominous words of Plato, that wisest of all philosophers: 'Only the dead have seen the end of war.'"**
>
> *–General of the Army Douglas MacArthur, USMA 1903*

WEST POINT WARTIME KILLED

War	U.S. Killed	West Point Graduate Killed
Revolutionary War (1775–83)	4,435	–
War of 1812 (1812–14)	2,260	6
Indian Wars (1789–1918)	2,700	unknown
Mexican-American War (1846–48)	1,507	48
Civil War* (1861–65)	623,026	105
Spanish-American War (1898)	2,446	16
Philippine War (1898–1902)	4,196	22
World War I (1917–18)	116,708	32
World War II (1941–45)	407,316	487
Korean War (1950–53)	36,574	157
Vietnam War (1964–73)	58,200	273
Invasion of Grenada (1983)	19	–
Invasion of Panama (1989)	23	–
Persian Gulf War (1991)	145	1
Somalia (1992–93)	43	–
September 11 (2001)	2,996	1
Afghanistan (2001–present)	1,532	34
Iraq (2003–11)	4,452	58
Philippines (Operation Enduring Freedom)	2	2
Totals	1,268,578	1,231

*This includes both Union and Confederate Killed In Action.

AOG Register of Graduates, www.westpointaog.org

Leonidas Polk was born into a life of privilege and military prominence. During the American Revolution, his grandfather had served with Washington and Greene and escorted the Liberty Bell. His father had served with partisan leaders like Thomas Sumter and Francis Marion.[1] From an early age, he seemed destined for military greatness, but he instead became one of the most controversial figures in American history.

Born in 1806, Polk attended the University of North Carolina before enrolling at West Point, where he roomed with his eventual Civil War Commander Albert Sydney Johnston. Although he did quite well at the Academy, Polk gradually became more involved in spiritual affairs. While on post-graduation furlough in 1827, he submitted his resignation and enrolled in a seminary in Virginia. Following his ordination as an Episcopal minister in 1830, he served at churches throughout the South, while also managing extensive plantation estates. In 1841, he became the first Episcopal Bishop of Louisiana.[2]

Bishop Polk worked throughout the 1850s to convince the Episcopal leadership to create a Southern academic institution on par with Harvard or Yale to train religious ministers. The development of this school was especially important, he argued, because of the growing sectional tension in the nation. Ultimately, he convinced the leadership to select his favored spot in south-central Tennessee for this University of the South, which opened its doors in 1860.[3] National events, however, would soon draw the Bishop away from his pet project.

As sectional tensions flared, Polk emerged a decisive advocate of the Southern cause. In the winter and spring of 1860 to 1861, he worked to effect the secession of his diocese from the national Episcopal organization. He then traveled to Virginia to minister to Confederate soldiers from Louisiana and Tennessee.[4] While there, he made the momentous decision to accept Confederate President Jefferson Davis's offer of a General's commission, even though he had not studied or thought about military science since his graduation 34 years earlier.[5]

Despite this, Polk's bearing, education, and social prominence seemed to make him an ideal commander, and he was assigned to Western Tennessee. Once there, however, he made one of the costliest Confederate mistakes of the war. At the outset, both the Union and Confederacy chose to honor the wishes of Kentucky, a slave state bordering on the free North, to remain neutral in the growing conflict. Fearing (correctly) that Union forces might be intent on occupying the strategic Ohio River town of Columbus, however, Polk took the initiative to seize the town in September 1861. Polk's decision had huge strategic implications: In response to his incursion, the state government of Kentucky cast its lot with the Union.[6] While Polk fortified Columbus, a young Union General named Ulysses Grant first gained prominence probing those defenses at Belmont, Missouri.[7] Polk was so fixated on his massive bastion that he did nothing while Grant captured Forts Henry and Donaldson, opening central Tennessee to Union forces.[8]

In early 1862, Johnston, now overall Confederate Commander of the Western theater, ordered Polk's forces to join him in an attempt to destroy Grant's Army in Tennessee. At the ensuing Battle of Shiloh, the Confederate units became intermingled and timely Union reinforcements turned the Confederates' surprise attack into a costly defeat. Polk's roommate, Johnston, was

Lieutenant General Leonidas Polk, C.S.A., USMA 1827

- FORT POLK, LOUISIANA, NAMED IN HIS HONOR
- CONFEDERATE ARMY CORPS COMMANDER
- KILLED IN ACTION DURING THE BATTLE OF ATLANTA
- FIRST EPISCOPAL BISHOP OF LOUISIANA
- INSPIRED THE FOUNDING OF THE UNIVERSITY OF THE SOUTH IN SEWANEE, TENNESSEE

Courtesy: CSA

Front gate at Fort Polk, Louisiana, named after Leonidas Polk.

© 2013/Greg E. Mathieson Sr/MAI

among the casualties.[9]

In the ensuing Confederate campaign back into Kentucky under Braxton Bragg (the new overall commander in the West), Polk almost met the same fate. At the Battle of Perryville in October, a confused Union Officer accidentally reported to Polk, who made him a prisoner. Later that day, Polk rode up to admonish an officer for firing on friendly troops only to realize that he was addressing the Commander of an Indiana unit. Polk

SHERMAN SAW THE GROUP WITH A SPYGLASS AND ORDERED HIS ARTILLERY CREW TO FIRE ON THEM, AND ONE OF THE SHELLS HIT POLK IN THE CHEST, KILLING HIM INSTANTLY.

haughtily bluffed his way out of his predicament before riding away to safety. During the campaign, Polk's tendency to autonomy began to grate on Bragg, especially when Polk disobeyed specific orders in the run-up to Perryville.[10] Bragg's irascible personality likely did not help matters much, and after the hard-fought, inconclusive Battle of Stones River at the beginning of 1863, Polk joined the chorus of subordinates calling for Davis to relieve Bragg.[11]

Tensions continued to mount between the two. After days of hard fighting in the Battle of Chickamauga in September 1863, Bragg planned to destroy the Union Army of the Cumberland with an elaborate echelon attack. Polk started his attack several hours late, resulting in a failed frontal assault. Elsewhere, however, Confederate forces exploited a Union mistake in positioning units and broke through the line.[12] As Union forces collapsed, one of Polk's subordinates urged his soldiers to "give 'em hell." Polk echoed his sentiments, but, ever the bishop, simply added, "Give 'em what General Cheatham says, boys!"[13] Despite this hard-fought victory, Polk's lackadaisical attack was the final straw, and Bragg suspended him.[14]

Davis transferred Polk to command of forces in Alabama and Mississippi. Polk made his headquarters in Meridian, Mississippi, until Union General William Sherman launched a large-scale raid in February 1864, expelling Polk's forces from the town.[15] In the spring, Polk was directed to shift his forces to Georgia as Sherman began his campaign against Atlanta. In June of 1864, Polk was gathered with his commander on a hill observing the Union advance. Sherman saw the group with a spyglass and ordered his artillery crew to fire on them, and one of the shells hit Polk in the chest, killing him instantly.[16]

In command, Polk exuded confidence, but his imperious nature and autonomy led to problems on and off the battlefield. One observer noted that "Polk had probably been a bishop too long to be a successful subordinate."[17] Then again, President Davis once called his corps "the best appointed troops he had seen."[18] While his military record is dubious at best, Polk's religious efforts doubtless touched many lives, and his emphasis on improving the Southern ministry left a legacy to this day. His beloved University of the South in Sewanee, Tennessee, continues to be one of the nation's finest liberal arts colleges.[19]

Written by: Major Joseph C. Scott.

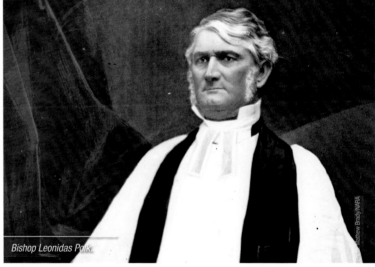
Bishop Leonidas Polk.

Battle Monument at West Point, cannon commemorating the Battle of Atlanta.

>>> Spotlight

The Louisiana Purchase was made in 1803 by President Thomas Jefferson and doubled the size of the United States. Louisiana received statehood in 1813 as the 18th state and succeeded from the United States to join the Confederate States of America in 1861. Camp Polk construction began in 1941, and the camp opened and closed several times after World War II. It was made Fort Polk in the 1950s and became home to the Joint Readiness Training Center (JRTC) in 1993.

Sedgwick Statue at West Point.

Major General John Sedgwick, USMA 1837

- **COMMANDED THE II CORPS, THE IX CORPS, AND THE VI CORPS OF THE ARMY OF THE POTOMAC**
- **ASSISTANT INSPECTOR GENERAL, MILITARY DEPARTMENT OF WASHINGTON**
- **KILLED IN ACTION DURING THE BATTLE OF SPOTSYLVANIA COURT HOUSE, MAY 1864**
- **SERVED IN MEXICAN-AMERICAN WAR AND SEMINOLE WARS**
- **WOUNDED THREE SEPARATE TIMES AT THE BATTLE OF ANTIETAM**
- **SEDGWICK STATUE AT WEST POINT DEDICATED IN HIS HONOR OVERLOOKING BATTLE MONUMENT**

Major General John Sedgwick was born on September 13, 1813, in Cornwall, Connecticut, and died on the battlefield in Spotsylvania County, Virginia, on May 9, 1864. Over his 27 years as a regular Army Officer, Sedgwick fought in three of America's major wars. At the time of his death, Sedgwick was the highest-ranking Union casualty in the Civil War.

John Sedgwick reported to West Point in 1833 and joined the Class of 1837. Upon graduation, he was commissioned into the artillery and experienced his first combat in the Seminole War. He then fought in the Mexican-American War from 1846 to 1848, when he earned two Brevet promotions. After returning from Mexico,

he became a Calvary Officer and served in various campaigns against Native Americans in the West until the start of the Civil War.

Colonel Sedgwick served as the Inspector General of the Military Department of Washington at the beginning of the Civil War. He was quickly promoted to Brigadier General and commanded the 2nd Division, II Corps, of the Army of the Potomac, where he fought and was wounded at the Battle of Glendale in the 1862 Peninsula Campaign. During the Battle of Antietam, Major General Sedgwick was again wounded on three separate occasions while engaged with Confederate forces under the command of Major General Thomas "Stonewall" Jackson (USMA 1846).

Sedgwick returned to action from his wounds as a Corps Commander for the Army of the Potomac's VI Corps during the Battle of Chancellorsville in April through May 1863, and would command that corps until his death. In his final battle, the Battle of Spotsylvania

SEDGWICK WAS THE HIGHEST-RANKING OFFICER TO BE KILLED IN ACTION LEADING UNION TROOPS. HIS STATUE STANDS ON THE PLAIN, SYMBOLICALLY OVERLOOKING BATTLE MONUMENT THAT MEMORIALIZES THE NAMES OF EVERY REGULAR ARMY UNION SOLDIER KILLED IN ACTION, INCLUDING HIS OWN NAME.

Courthouse, Sedgwick's corps supported General Ulysses S. Grant's (USMA 1843) Overland Campaign in Virginia. While Sedgwick personally inspected artillery emplacements in the midst of the battle on May 9, 1864, Confederate sharpshooters caused members of his staff and artillerymen to seek cover. Sedgwick allegedly commented on his staff's actions by asking, "What? Men dodging this way for single bullets? What will you do when they open fire along the whole line?" His men

The spurs on Major General Sedgwick Statue at West Point.

>>> Spotlight

Sedgwick Monument is located on the Plain at West Point across the street from Battle Monument. It was sculpted by Launt Thompson and dedicated in 1868 by Major General Sedgwick's officers and men after he was Killed In Action at the Battle of Spotsylvania in 1864. Tradition at West Point holds that any cadet failing an academic class go to the monument at midnight before an exam, dressed in full dress gray under arms, to spin the spurs on the statue to gain good luck to pass the exam. The spurs are functioning and pictured here. Many graduates attribute their success to adhering to this time-honored tradition.

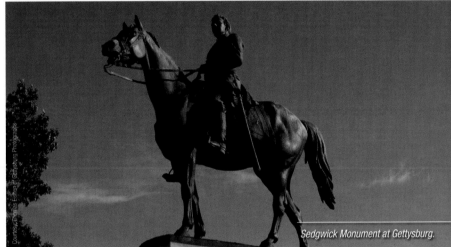

Sedgwick Monument at Gettysburg.

continued to flinch, however, prompting him to further comment, "I'm ashamed of you, dodging that way. They couldn't hit an elephant at this distance."[1] Ironically, shortly after uttering these prophetic words, he was fatally shot in his eye.[2] Sedgwick's death accounted for one of nearly 32,000 casualties from Spotsylvania Court House – the costliest battle of the Overland Campaign and one of the top five casualty-producing battles of the Civil War.

By all accounts, Sedgwick was well liked by his soldiers, who referred to him as "Uncle John." His death on the battlefield was tragic to leaders on both sides. Confederate General Robert E. Lee (USMA 1829) was saddened by the loss of an old friend. Grant further charac-

terized Sedgwick as one who "was never at fault when serious work was to be done" and told his staff that the loss of Sedgwick was worse than that of an entire division. Upon hearing of his death, Grant repeatedly asked, "Is he really dead?"[3]

Major General Sedgwick was buried near his Connecticut birthplace. There are numerous memorials throughout the country dedicated to his memory to include a statue honoring him and the VI Corps at Gettysburg National Military Park and his most famous memorial, the Sedgwick Monument, located on the Plain at West Point. Officers and soldiers of the VI Corps erected the monument to honor Sedgwick and his death at the Battle of Spotsylvania Court

House.[4] Originally, the monument was located on the northwest edge of the Plain, but was later relocated to its current location directly across Washington Road from the Battle Monument. In this fitting location, Sedgwick now faces the names of the 188 officers and 2,042 men of the Union's Regular Army etched in the Battle Monument who were killed during the Civil War, including his own.[5] More than a testament to Sedgwick's legacy as a Civil War Commander, his monument has also rooted itself in West Point tradition. As all cadets know, and many have tested, Academy lore states that the Sedgwick Monument can help cadets deficient in academics to pass their final exams. The night before a particular term-end examination, the deficient cadet must

go to the monument at midnight, in full dress uniform under arms, and spin the rowels on the monument's spurs to bring that cadet good luck when taking the exam. Thus, through the simple tradition surrounding Sedgwick's monument, current cadets are able to associate themselves with a noted alumnus from nearly two centuries ago, exemplifying the strength and continuity of the Long Gray Line.

Written by: Lieutenant Colonel Todd Gile (USA, Retired), USMA 1986.

Thomas Jonathan "Stonewall" Jackson was born on January 21, 1824, in then Clarksburg, Virginia, now West Virginia.[1] His father died when he was 3, and at 6, he was raised by his Uncle Cummins, who died in the Gold Rush.[2] Thomas Jackson is remembered as one of the brilliant commanders of the Civil War who often drove his men to accomplish seemingly impossible tasks. His nickname, "Stonewall," earned through a dubious quote from General Bee at the 1st Battle of Manassas, has become his permanent calling card. John B. Gordon remembers Stonewall Jackson in an intro to his memoirs as deserving of his reputation for being resolute but perhaps undeserving of images of a coldness or hardness of heart.

That he did, on his forced marches, tax to the utmost the strength and physical endurance of his men is undoubtedly true, but his object was to achieve results by surprises if possible, rather than through hotly contested and bloody battles where the enemy was fully prepared "…[Jackson] hurled his whole Army like a thunderbolt against the opposing lines...the victory was won at the least possible cost of blood and life to his Army."[3]

John Gordon here calls to mind Jackson's victory at the First Battle of Bull Run, where his moniker "Stonewall" was coined. Jackson arrived on the scene late in the battle and indeed held his forces back until the decisive moment. While Brigadier General Bernard Elliot Bee sat in a slaughter pen against the high tide of the Union effort with little hope of victory he recalled "there stood Jackson...like a 'stone wall.'"[4] This description from a man in desperate need of relief on the battlefield looking upon Jackson willing to sacrifice Bee's forces for the greater battle was likely not likely intended to be flattering one. In reality, this was a calculated move but not one taken lightly. "He had at times the aspect of an austere man; but it was only the sem-

Lieutenant General Thomas Jonathan "Stonewall" Jackson, C.S.A., USMA 1846

- CONFEDERATE CORPS COMMANDER
- PROMOTED TO BREVET MAJOR IN THE MEXICAN-AMERICAN WAR
- INSTRUCTOR AT VIRGINIA MILITARY INSTITUTE (VMI) PRIOR TO THE CIVIL WAR
- FATALLY WOUNDED BY FRIENDLY FIRE AT THE BATTLE OF CHANCELLORSVILLE
- *USS STONEWALL JACKSON* NUCLEAR SUBMARINE NAMED IN HIS HONOR
- JACKSON MEMORIAL HALL AT VIRGINIA MILITARY INSTITUTE (VMI) NAMED IN HIS HONOR
- IMMORTALIZED, ALONG WITH JEFFERSON DAVIS AND ROBERT E. LEE, ON THE STONE CARVING AT STONE MOUNTAIN, GEORGIA

Courtesy CSA

Photo: NARA

Stonewall Jackson Equestrian Statue in Clarksburg, West Virginia.

>>> Spotlight

Photo: AP

The *USS Stonewall Jackson* (SSBN-634) was a nuclear powered James Madison–class submarine was launched on November 30, 1963. She served in the fleet for more than 30 years until being decommissioned on February 9, 1995. It was the third United States Navy ship named after the Confederate General.

blance and not the substance of severity...his nature was gentle, emotional, and affectionate."[5] In this instance, Jackson merely saw the military necessity in holding a significant position at the Manassas battlefield waiting for the Union Army to attack him from his position of strength.

Resolve was likely Jackson's greatest trait. He achieved success in his young life despite the disadvantage of having lost both his parents. Resolve more than anything

else was responsible for his acceptance to and success at the United States Military Academy. At the age of 18, Jackson was accepted to the United States Military Academy at West Point, New York, where he matriculated in 1842. His schooling to that point might kindly be considered inadequate. Young Thomas had difficulty with the entrance examinations and began his studies at the bottom of his class. His second wife, Anna, recalled that Mr. Hays, who appointed

Jackson to the USMA, gave a "testimony to his excellent character and courageous spirit and asking that due allowance be made for his limited education...the authorities were very lenient in their examination and he was admitted."[6] Jackson himself recalled to his wife that "It was all he could do to pass his first examination" in algebra. It was indeed his resolve to succeed, not any innate ability or preparation that left a lasting impression on his peers and teachers. His friend and

roommate, George Stoneman, recalled that "if we had to stay [at West Point] another year 'old Jack' would be at the edge of the class...others were smarter but none... more absolutely possessed the respect and confidence of all."[7] Jackson himself admitted that he "studied *very hard* for what he got at West Point" and expected to be dismissed and prepared to explain that "If [*his peers*] had been there and found it as hard as he did, they would have failed too."[8] Jackson simply resolved to become one of the hardest-working cadets at the Academy. He moved steadily up the academic rankings eventually ranking graduated 17th out of 70 students in the Class of 1846.[9] This was also among some vaunted company. Stoneman himself became a Union Calvary General and Governor of California. Also in his cohort from 1842 to 1846 were George B. McClellan, A.P. Hill, George Picket, and Maury.[10]

JACKSON WAS ACCIDENTALLY SHOT BY HIS OWN CONFEDERATE PICKETS ON MAY 2, 1863. HE SURVIVED WITH THE LOSS OF AN ARM TO AMPUTATION; HOWEVER, HE DIED OF PNEUMONIA CONTRACTED DURING HIS RECOVERY EIGHT DAYS LATER.

That Jackson's success was gained through resolve is further backed up through his a small black book in which Jackson developed for himself many maxims that he certainly lived out. The most famous, now inscribed above Jackson Arch at the Virginia Military Institute and a favorite motto of many a class there, was "You may be whatever you resolve to be." Several others shed greater light on the character which Jackson formed for himself at West Point, including "Let your principle object be the discharge of duty. Endeavor to be at peace with all men. Sacrifice your life rather than your word. Endeavor to do well everything which you undertake. Temperance, Silence. Resolve to perform what you ought; perform without fail what you resolve-Frugality, Industry, Sincerity, Justice, Moderation, Cleanliness, Tranquility." Clearly perceived in Jackson's writing was his belief that mastery of self was the key to mastery of life. Quite the philosopher Jackson also developed what he

Stonewall Jackson Monument on Monument Avenue, Richmond, Virginia.

STONEWALL JACKSON

Casualties at Antietam, 1862.

believed should be the motives to all action: [1] "Regard your own happiness. [2] Regard for the family to which you belong. [3] Strive to attain a very great elevation of character. [4] Fix upon a high standard of action and character. [11] Jackson also demonstrated a conscious desire to hold things close to the vest in his book and to be careful about with whom he chose to share himself completely with. Writing about choice of friends Jackson wrote that:

"It is not desirable to have a large number of intimate friends; you may have many acquaintances, but few intimate friends. If you have one who is what he should be, you are comparatively happy. That friendship may be at once fond and lasting, there must not only be equal virtue in each, but virtue of the same kind: not only the same end must be proposed, but the same means must be approved."[12]

This particular maxim was perhaps most evident in its validation with his relationship with Robert E. Lee. Their success was clearly linked to their ability to work with and trust each other. Lee's rise and fall as a General seem directly proportional the intertwining of his Confederate career with Thomas Jackson.

After graduating from West Point in 1846, Jackson soon found himself on the front lines of the Mexican-American War from 1846 to 1848. His conduct ultimately resulted in a regular promotion to First Lieutenant, as well as two Brevet promotions to Captain and Major. Jackson several times distinguished himself as an artilleryman during the war. Jackson was promoted to Captain when his commander, Captain Magruder, lost his First Lieutenant at Cherubusco. Magruder reported that as a commander of the second section of the battery Lieutenant Jackson had, "In a

few moments opened fire upon the enemy's works from a position to the right and kept it up with great briskness and effect. His conduct was equally conspicuous the whole day and I cannot too highly commend him to the Major General's favorable consideration."[13] Young Thomas Jackson had become one of the bright stars within the ranks of Junior Officers during the Mexican-American War.

Following the war, Jackson returned to Virginia, and in the spring of 1851, became the "professor of Natural and Experimental Philosophy and Artillery at the Virginia Military Institute, a position to which he was elected unanimously.[14] Right off the bat, though, Jackson showed why his nickname at VMI was not "Stonewall" but "Tom Fool." Jackson was practically in his death bed, and he could not fulfill the duties of the post when he received it. However, in one of his

famous demonstrations of his Presbyterian faith, Jackson believed it was providence. He recalled to a friend who questioned the prudence of this that based on the sign of providence, he simply resolved to get better "and you can see that I am." In actuality, this predated his becoming a Presbyterian but showed a natural fit for Jackson in the Presbyterian Church in Lexington.

Jackson was actually married twice in Lexington. His first was to Elinor Junkit, daughter of the concurrent President of Washington College who died in childbirth and lost the child. He then married Anna in 1857. The late 1850s were tumultuous times for Jackson both personally and professionally. Not only had he lost a wife and child, but the nation began to crumble around him. Jackson was called into duty to help with the John Brown Raid. Jackson was deeply

Monument at Hollywood Cemetery in Richmond, Virginia. "Fate Denied Them Victory But Gave Them A Glorious Immortality."

Lieutenant General Stonewall Jackson Equestrian Statue Battle of Bull Run.

troubled by this going so far as to send up a petition that he might be saved.[15] Jackson was surprised about secession and described himself as Union man, firmly states rights, who believed it was better to "fight from within."[16] He believed that war itself "is the sum of all evils" and hoped to avoid it.[17]

One of the great irony's of Jackson's career is in the mingling of his personal faith and the outcome of the war and his own life. It is likely that Jackson might likely have accepted his own death and the consequences of the war rather easily. He was troubled by slavery, even if he did accept it as biblical and owned several slaves inherited through his marriage. Though he hated war and questioned its necessity – "Why should Christians be disturbed about the dissolution of the Union?" – Jackson indeed felt that war could come only by God's permission and will

only be permitted if for His people's good: "…I cannot see how *we* should be distressed about such things, whatever be their consequences…The mighty ruler of the nations saw fit to give victory to the strong arm of power, and He makes no mistakes….It was in mercy that He who knew the end from the beginning did not lift the veil."[18]

Indeed that veil was the eventual defeat of the Confederacy many argue due to the very absence of Stonewall Jackson. After a brilliant campaign in the Valley of Virginia in 1862 the mere threat of Jackson, despite his lack of decisive action, helped bring about a stunning defeat of McClellan's forces during the seven-day battles. It was at the high tide of the Confederate Military success and Jackson's most brilliant maneuver at the battle of Chancellorsville that Jackson was accidentally shot by his own Confederate

pickets on May 2, 1863. He survived with the loss of an arm to amputation; however, he died of pneumonia contracted during his recovery eight days later.[19] John Gordon recalled that "General Jackson's unostentatious, sincere and deeply rooted religious faith should be treated as his noblest and crowning characteristic. His trust in God and reliance upon an overruling Providence permeated his thought and guided his actions at all times and in all stations." It seemed that whether Jackson was at home, in school, teaching, praying, planning, or fighting "his sublime faith never faltered."[20] In Jackson's own eyes his death, treated by many as such a crushing blow to the confederacy, one from which Lee could not recover from personally or replace on the battlefield, would indeed be the providence of God. The Confederacy was never again able to capture the initia-

tive in the Civil War. Lee's campaign into Pennsylvania would have been advocated by Jackson, but his absence was felt at the Battle of Gettysburg and the rest was history. It is hard to study the rest of Lee's Civil War career without encountering the shadow of Jackson in plans, successes, and failures, with both historians and peers constantly asking "what if." John Gordon was prophetic when he wrote that Stonewall Jackson "will undoubtedly be accorded in history a commanding position among the great Generals of the world."[21]

Written by: Major Paul N. Belmont.

A 90-foot-tall pyramid built to honor the Confederate dead was erected in 1868 in Hollywood Cemetery, Richmond, Virginia.

Lieutenant General Ambrose Powell Hill, Jr., C.S.A., USMA 1847

- FORT A.P. HILL, VIRGINIA, NAMED IN HIS HONOR
- CONFEDERATE CORPS COMMANDER
- KILLED IN ACTION DURING THE LAST WEEK OF THE CIVIL WAR DURING 3RD BATTLE OF PETERSBURG
- COMMANDER, THE CONFEDERATE "LIGHT DIVISION"
- BRIGADE COMMANDER, ARMY OF NORTHERN VIRGINIA
- *SS. A.P. HILL* LIBERTY SHIP NAMED IN HIS HONOR DURING WORLD WAR II
- BURIED IN RICHMOND, VIRGINIA, UNDER THE A.P. HILL MONUMENT AT LABURNUM AVENUE AND HERMITAGE ROAD

Courtesy: CSA

>>> Spotlight

Fort A.P. Hill was founded on June 11, 1941, as a 60,000-acre United States Army training facility to prepare four million soldiers for a two-front war in the Pacific and European Theaters of War. Active duty, Reserve, and National Guard units, as well as several other United States agencies, currently use Fort A.P. Hill. The installation was named after Virginian and Confederate Lieutenant General A.P. Hill who was killed a week before Robert E. Lee surrendered at Appomattox. Two weeks after Appomattox John Wilkes Booth assassinated President Lincoln. Booth was himself killed at the Garrett Farmhouse, which was located just outside the current borders of Fort A.P. Hill.

Photo: NARA

Ambrose Powell Hill, Jr., was referred to as A.P. Hill in order to differentiate him from another Confederate General, D.H. Hill. However, he was called "Powell" by his family and "Little Powell" by his troops (due to his small physical stature). He was born in Culpeper, Virginia, the seventh and youngest child of Thomas and Fannie Russell Baptist Hill. Powell was named for his uncle, Ambrose Powell Hill, who served in both houses of the Virginia legislature and Captain Ambrose Powell, an Indian fighter, explorer, legislature, and a close friend of President James Madison.[1]

A.P. Hill started his military career with the West Point Class of 1846. He made friends with many future Generals who would serve on both sides of the Civil War, including Darius N. Couch, George Pickett, George Stoneman, and George B. McClellan, who became his roommate. Another classmate, Thomas "Stonewall" Jackson, was to become Hill's future commander. Their tumultuous relationship, which would continue throughout the Civil War, began when they were cadets. Hill had a higher social status than Jackson in Virginia and put a greater emphasis on having a good time in his off-hours. Jackson, by contrast, was a very religious man and scorned Hill's levity. Upon Hill's return from a furlough before his third year at West Point, Hill contracted gonorrhea. The resulting medical complications required Hill to repeat his third year, postponing his West Point graduation until Class of 1847.[2]

After graduating 15th in a class of 38 students, Hill was assigned to various relatively insignificant positions, participating in only very minor skirmishes during the Mexican-American War and the Seminole War. He did, however, become engaged to Ellen B. Marcy, the future wife of Hill's former roommate George B. McClellan. Ellen broke off the engagement after receiving pressure from her parents. Although Hill claimed no hard feelings toward McClellan, rumors during the war claimed that Hill fought with more tenacity if he knew McClellan was present with the opposing Army.[3]

Just before the outbreak of the Civil War, Hill resigned his commission in the United States Army. After Virginia seceded, he was appointed Colonel of the 13th Virginia Infantry Regiment. Although Hill was not involved in any major battles, he was promoted to Brigadier General on February 26, 1862, and given command of a brigade in the Confederate Army of the Potomac, shortly thereafter named the Army of Northern Virginia.[4]

As a Brigade Commander, Hill performed well during the Battle of Williamsburg. He was promoted to Major General and given command of a division. This division would be known as The Light Division. Although this was the largest division in all of the Confederate Army, Hill began using this nickname for his division to establish a reputation for being fast and agile. One of Hill's soldiers wrote after the war, "The nickname was applicable, for we often marched without coats, blankets, knapsacks, or other burdens except our arms and haversacks, which were never heavy and sometimes empty."[5]

Hill launched multiple attacks during the Seven Days Battles, including Mechanicsville. After the campaign, Hill became involved with a dispute with General Longstreet over

> **"DAMN YOU, IF YOU WILL NOT FOLLOW ME, I'LL DIE ALONE!" SAID HILL.**

a series of newspaper articles that appeared in a Richmond newspaper. Their relationship became so antagonistic, that Longstreet had Hill arrested. Hill subsequently challenged Longstreet to a duel. The duel never occurred, but General Robert E. Lee decided to send Hill and his division to reinforce General "Stonewall" Jackson.[6]

During the Battle of Fredericksburg in December 1862, two of Hill's brigades were decimated, along with most of a third brigade. Hill's division suffered more than 2,000 casualties, which accounted for more than two-thirds of all casualties in Jackson's Corps during the battle.[7] Hill was criticized for leaving a gap in his troop line, in spite of warnings by his subordinate commanders. To complicate matters more, there were reports that Hill was also absent from his division, and there is no record of where he was during the battle.[8]

After being assigned to Jackson's 2nd Corps, the animosity between these two former classmates continued. Hill and Jackson argued several times during the Northern Virginia Campaign and the 1862 Maryland Campaign. During the invasion of Maryland, Jackson had Hill arrested and charged with eight counts of dereliction of duty.[9] During the break after the Battle of Fredericksburg, Hill repeatedly requested that Lee set up a court of inquiry, but General Lee felt that doing so would be a detriment to the Corps and refused Hill's request.[10] Throughout the war, the feud between Hill and Jackson would escalate during lulls in battle, but would immediately subside when battle started.

This pattern lasted until Jackson was injured during the Battle of Chancellorsville in May 1863. Hill temporarily took command of the Corps when Jackson was removed from the battlefield.[11]

After Jackson died of pneumonia in May 1863, Hill was promoted to Lieutenant General and was given command of Lee's 3rd Corps. Hill commanded this Corps during the famous campaign of Gettysburg of 1863. Of the three Infantry corps participating in the Gettysburg Campaign, Hill's corps suffered the largest number of casualties, which prompted Lee to order a retreat back to Virginia.[12]

Only seven days before Lee's surrender at Appomattox Court House, Hill was shot and killed by a Union soldier during the 3rd Battle of Petersburg. Although his family wanted him buried in Richmond, the occupation of Union soldiers prevented his burial. Hill's body was, however, relocated in 1892 to Richmond and buried under a monument to A.P. Hill, funded by former officers under his command.[13] This monument is the only one of its type in Richmond under which the subject individual is actually interred.[14]

Written by: Frank Flowers, USMA 1986.

Statue of General A.P. Hill in Richmond, Virginia, traffic circle where Hill is buried.

A.P. HILL

Major General McPherson was killed at the Battle of Atlanta. This cannon memorializes the Battle of Atlanta on Battle Monument, West Point.

Major General James Birdseye McPherson, USMA 1853

- **SECOND-HIGHEST-RANKING UNION OFFICER KILLED IN ACTION DURING THE CIVIL WAR**
- **COMMANDING GENERAL OF THE UNION VICTORY IN THE BATTLE OF VICKSBURG**
- **KILLED IN ACTION BATTLE OF ATLANTA, JULY 22, 1864, AT AGE 35**
- **ENGINEER, ALCATRAZ ISLAND, SAN FRANCISCO**
- **GRADUATED FIRST IN THE WEST POINT, CLASS OF 1853**
- **MCPHERSON EQUESTRIAN STATUE ERECTED IN MCPHERSON SQUARE IN HIS HONOR, WASHINGTON, D.C.**
- **FORMER FORT MCPHERSON, GEORGIA, NAMED IN HIS HONOR**

Graduating first in his class of 52 cadets from the West Point Class of 1853, James McPherson distinguished himself significantly over the course of a relatively brief military career. Born on November 14, 1828, to pioneer farmers in Sandusky County, Ohio, he overcame his modest beginnings and childhood hardship to attain high rank and significant fame.[1] He is best remembered for two significant events of the American Civil War: one fortunate and the other not. As Commanding General of XVII Corps during the Battle of Vicksburg from January to July 4, 1863, Generals William T. Sherman and Ulysses S. Grant cited McPherson for his inspired leader-

"I WILL RECORD THE DEATH OF MY CLASSMATE AND BOYHOOD FRIEND, GENERAL JAMES B. MCPHERSON, THE ANNOUNCEMENT OF WHICH CAUSED ME SINCERE SORROW," SAID CONFEDERATE LIEUTENANT GENERAL JOHN BELL HOOD, MCPHERSON'S CLASSMATE.

ship that contributed directly to the Union victory. Unfortunately, McPherson was killed by Confederate small arms fire during the Battle of Atlanta on July 22, 1864, giving him the unwelcome distinction of being the second-highest Union Officer killed during the Civil War.

Following graduation from West Point in 1853 and commissioned into the Engineer Branch, McPherson remained an extra year at the Academy to serve as an instructor, a common practice for high-ranking graduates. He then served in New York City followed by a tour of duty as an engineer on Alcatraz Island in San Francisco Bay, California Territory, in 1854, with a series of harbor defense duties until the eve of the Civil War in 1861.[2] Campaigning for and receiving active troop service at the start of the Civil War, he served briefly as the Aide-de-Camp to Union Commanding General Henry Halleck from December 1861 until being appointed General Grant's Chief of Engineers at the start of Forts Henry and Donelson Campaign in February 1862.[3] The following months

>>> Spotlight

McPherson Square is located in northwest Washington, D.C. The Equestrian Statue of Major General McPherson was created by Louis Rebisso and erected in 1876. Just down the street behind McPherson is Thomas Circle named after Major General George Henry Thomas "The Rock of Chickamagua."

McPherson Square with Thomas Circle in the distance to his rear, Washington, D.C.

2013/Greg E Mathieson Sr/MAI

witnessed extended and inspired leadership in the western theater, most notably in April 1862 at the Battle of Shiloh, where he served with great distinction.[4] Promoted to Brigadier General of volunteers in May, he then became military superintendent of West Tennessee railroads in October 1862.

McPherson's greatest fame undoubtedly came during the Battle of Vicksburg, arguably the pivotal battle of the entire Civil War. During the lengthy campaign, General Sherman, McPherson's Commanding General, rejected McPherson's request for a leave of absence to get married. Clearly Sherman's apparent harshness was justified because McPherson's corps and the General's capable leadership proved instrumental to the Union victory on July 4, 1863. Promotion to command Sherman's former command, the Army of the Tennessee followed in March 1864, but his days in high command were numbered. With modest performances at Dalton and Resaca in May 1864, and Kennesaw Mountain in June 1864, his career and life were ended during the Battle of Atlanta on July 22, 1864. When surprised by Confederate soldiers he attempted to escape and was shot while trying to escape.[5]

Fittingly, Fort McPherson in Atlanta, Georgia, was named in his honor and served as an active-duty post for 126 years prior to its recent 2011 closure.

Respected and loved by classmates on both sides of the Civil War, he was renowned for his strong sense of duty, impeccable leadership, charm, intelligence, and compassion. Although such a powerfully unique combination of attributes is rare at any time, it was especially lacking in too many cases during the American Civil War. There are few West Point graduates of the Civil War who better exemplify the concepts of "Duty, Honor, Country" than Major General James Birdseye McPherson. Perhaps nothing better captures his legacy than his entry in the *Register of Graduates*: "Brilliant skillful beloved commander: Honored by his Army with equestrian statue in Washington."[6]

Written by: Colonel Kevin W. Farrell, PhD (USA, Retired), USMA 1986.

Fort Sill, Oklahoma, has long been well known in the United States as the home of the Field Artillery. The story of how and for whom Fort Sill was named, however, is lesser known.

Joshua W. Sill was born December 6, 1831, in Chillicothe, Ohio. His father was a lawyer and home schooled Joshua in Chillicothe. In 1849, Sill was appointed to West Point and graduated in 1853, third in his class of 52.[1] Less than a decade later, his class would be divided between North and South while fighting in the Civil War – many of them would gain fame while many others lost their lives, including Sill. Among his classmates that set their fate with the South was Sill's good friend, Confederate General John Bell Hood, along with other classmates who died for the Confederacy to include Rueben Ross, Lucius Rich, and John Bowen (died as a Prisoner of War). On the other hand, Sill, along with many of his other classmates, maintained their loyalty to the Union and would also gain fame in the war. Generals Philip Sheridan and John Schofield experienced great success – both would also eventually be Commanding Generals of the United States Army in the post-war period. Likewise, Major General James McPherson, who graduated first in the class, was one of the most promising

Union Commanders before he was killed at the Battle of Atlanta in July 1864 – the second-highest-ranking Union Officer killed in the war.

Upon graduation, Sill was originally commissioned in the Ordnance Corps and assigned to the Watervliet Arsenal in Troy, New York. He then returned to West Point as a professor from 1854 to 1857. Just prior to the war, he resigned his commission in January 1861 to teach mathematics at the Collegiate and Polytechnic Institute in Brooklyn, New York.

SILL WAS WEARING HIS FRIEND SHERIDAN'S OVERCOAT WHEN HE WAS KILLED IN ACTION AT STONES RIVER. LATER, AS GENERAL IN-CHIEF, SHERIDAN WOULD NAME AN OUTPOST IN HIS FRIEND'S NAME: FORT SILL.

When hostilities broke out at Fort Sumter in April 1861, however, Sill, like many West Point graduates, volunteered to re-join the military. He was commissioned as a Colonel and initially assigned as the Assistant Adjutant General of the State of Ohio. In less than a year, he ascended to Brigade Commander in the Army of the Ohio, was promoted to Brigadier General and given a

temporary division command, and finally assigned as a Brigade Commander in the Army of the Cumberland, reporting to his friend and classmate Brigadier General Philip Sheridan.

In December 1862, Sill and Sheridan were together leading the Union Army of the Cumberland in Tennessee in pursuit of the Major General Braxton Bragg's Confederate Army of Tennessee. On the eve of the Battle of Stones River, Sheridan held a conference with his subordinate commanders. At that time, Sill and Sheridan were both Brigadier Generals (denoted by a single star on their epaulets) and both relatively small in stature at about five feet, five inches tall.[2] When the meeting ended, Sill accidentally mistook Sheridan's frock coat for his own and left wearing Sheridan's jacket. The next day, New Year's Eve Day, December 31, 1862, Sill was leading his soldiers against a Confederate assault when he was shot in the head and killed. After the battle, Sill was initially buried by the Confederates in a small graveyard near the battlefield but was later moved to

Grandview Cemetery in his Chillicothe, Ohio, hometown.[3]

Sheridan was saddened by the loss of his friend, classmate, and subordinate. Upon realizing that he had Sill's jacket, Sheridan returned the jacket with his sympathies to the Sill family. That jacket now resides with the Ross County Historical Society in Chillicothe.

In 1869, seven years after Sill's death at Stones River and four years after the Civil War ended, General Sheridan led the Department of Missouri in pacifying Native American tribes in the west. In support of that mission, he established a fort in the Wichita Mountains of Oklahoma and named it in honor Sill. Today, Fort Sill is one of the largest bases in the United States Army, home to the Field Artillery and Air Defense Artillery, and a National Historic Landmark. Perhaps as important, it reflects General Sheridan's views on the camaraderie of military service and the brotherhood of arms as he never forgot the sacrifice of his friend and classmate Joshua Sill.

Brigadier General Joshua W. Sill, USMA 1837

- FORT SILL, OKLAHOMA, NAMED IN HIS HONOR
- KILLED IN ACTION BATTLE OF STONES RIVER, TENNESSEE, AT AGE 31
- BRIGADE COMMANDER, ARMY OF THE CUMBERLAND
- ASSISTANT ADJUTANT GENERAL, STATE OF OHIO
- WEST POINT PROFESSOR

Front gate at Fort Sill, Oklahoma.

Monument for Brigadier General Sill located at Fort Sill, Oklahoma.

>>> Spotlight

Oklahoma was admitted as a state on November 16, 1904, as the 46th United States state. Fort Sill was founded in 1869 by Major General Philip Sheridan, who named the fort after his friend Brigadier General Joshua Sill, who was Killed In Action as a Union General in the Battle of Stones River on December 31, 1862, as a Brigadier General (while wearing Sheridan's Union jacket that they accidentally mixed up prior to the battle). Fort Sill is the home of the Field Artillery located in Lawton, Oklahoma, 85 miles south of Oklahoma City.

Lesley J. McNair was born on May 25, 1883, in Verndale, Minnesota. He graduated 11th in his class of 124 cadets from West Point in 1904 and was commissioned in the Field Artillery. Over the next four decades, he served in Mexico, on the battlefields of France in World War I with the 1st Infantry Division, and again returned to Europe, as well as North Africa, during World War II. Wounded in Tunisia during the North Africa Campaign and then killed in France in July 1944, McNair's death revealed war's indiscriminant nature as even the highest-ranking leaders gave the ultimate sacrifice. Particularly telling in McNair's case was the fact that he was not commanding operational forces at the time; rather, he was observing firsthand on the front lines soldiers who had prepared for war under the training component of the Army of the United States, the United States Army Ground Forces, which McNair commanded.

As the United States prepared for and then entered World War II, McNair was an engine behind the war effort in terms of preparing soldiers. Before the war, he was the Commandant of the United States Army Command and General Staff College and instituted many curriculum and training changes that would prepare graduates for the challenges they would face. Following a tour as Chief of Staff, General Headquarters of the United States Army, McNair was promoted to Lieutenant General and named Commander of United States Ground Forces in 1942. Under his leadership, the Army organized, trained, and deployed unprecedented millions of soldiers and staffs to fight in North Africa, Europe, and the Pacific. On December 28, 1942, McNair's monumental task and efforts were lauded as he appeared on the cover of *Time* magazine and called "McNair, Trainer of Troops."

Following the successful Allied invasion of Normandy on D-Day, June 6, 1944, United States forces remained bogged down in the hedgerow country of northern France as they battled well-entrenched Nazi forces. Lieutenant General Omar Bradley, the United States 1st Army Commander, planned a breakout from the hedgerow country as part of Operation Cobra. The plan envisioned a massive aerial bombardment of Nazi forces by the United States 8th Air Force with more than 2,400 heavy, medium, and fighter bombers followed by a ground attack to break through the German lines. McNair was visiting United States troops on the front line near Saint Lo, France, just prior to the operation. Unfortunately, however, coordination for close air support was still developing. Instead of aircraft flying parallel to the Allied lines, they flew perpendicular to the lines from the rear to the front. A large number of bombs fell short on allied troops, including Lieutenant General McNair, who was killed on July 25, 1944, in a foxhole alongside 110 other United States soldiers he had prepared for war; more than 500 others were wounded. Despite the disastrous friendly fire casualties, the bombing shattered the German forces as designed and United States troops successfully broke out, pouring more than 100,000 troops through a five-mile gap in the German lines. Tragically, McNair's only son, Colonel Douglas C. McNair (USMA 1928), was killed on Guam 11 days later on August 6, 1944, while serving as the Chief of Staff the 77th Infantry Division.

In the end, McNair never experienced the victorious conclusion of World War II, a victory of which he was a key architect. Despite criticisms directed against him for executing a limited and hurried initial entry training program and for the individual replacement system, both of which resulted in a steep learning curve for United States soldiers early in the war against seasoned Axis troops, McNair continually delivered the necessary manpower demanded by the operational environment. He was eventually promoted posthumously to General in 1954. Interestingly, his gravesite in the Normandy American Cemetery was inscribed with the rank of Lieutenant General until 2010, when it was discovered that the change had never been made. He is now the highest-ranking soldier buried in the Normandy American Cemetery. In Washington, D.C., Fort Lesley J. McNair, Headquarters for the United States Army Military District of Washington, is fittingly named in his honor.

General Lesley James McNair, USMA 1904

- HIGHEST-RANKING OFFICER KILLED IN EUROPEAN THEATER OF WAR WORLD WAR II
- POSTHUMOUSLY PROMOTED TO FOUR-STAR GENERAL
- SERVED IN PUNITIVE EXPEDITION TO MEXICO, WORLD WAR I, AND WORLD WAR II
- COMMANDING GENERAL, ARMY GROUND FORCES, WORLD WAR II
- DISTINGUISHED SERVICE MEDAL (TWO), PURPLE HEART (TWO)
- BURIED AT THE NORMANDY AMERICAN CEMETERY
- FORT LESLEY J. MCNAIR IN WASHINGTON, D.C., NAMED IN HIS HONOR

Fort McNair front gate, Washington, D.C.

Emory Thomas said it best when he stated that James Ewell Brown Stuart "lives in the American memory more as antique metaphor than as man – as figure of speech rather than flesh and blood."[1] In truth, J.E.B. Stuart was in many ways a living metaphor. Born a Virginian to a prominent family, a grandson of the Revolutionary War, a writer of bad poetry who appreciated beauty in nature and people, it is perhaps no surprise that Stuart earned the nickname "beauty." Stuart apparently received his appointment to West Point in 1850 from Thomas Averett who had defeated his father Archibald Stuart for

his Congressional seat in 1848. Fitz Lee said the nickname "beauty was use to describe his 'personal comeliness' in inverse ratio to the term employed."[2] Apparently Stuart could sing well but the name most likely had to do with his many "scraps" with fellow cadets at West Point.[3] Stuart graduated from West Point 1854 and served in Corpus Cristi Texas and Kansas with the United States Army.[4] Prior to the outbreak of the Civil War, he had become a veteran of frontier conflict. He had seen action against Native Americans and during the violence of Bleeding Kansas. Stuart also played a pivotal role in the

capture of John Brown at Harpers Ferry, where he also served under Robert E. Lee for the first time as a Military Officer. Stuart had attended the Academy during Lee's term as Superintendent.[5] Like many of his peers, Stuart resigned his commission when his home state of Virginia seceded. Like many others, Stuart didn't believe that the Civil War would actually happen. Stuart was certain to take action regardless of what Virginia decided. Eager to fight and lead he covered all his bets. He wrote letters to the new Secretary of War Stanton, Governor Letcher of Virginia, and to Jefferson Davis, letting all

of them know of his willingness to serve and command ably.[6] The cause itself seemed secondary to the possibility for glory achieved in battle.

With the secession of Virginia Stuart found himself under the command of Stonewall Jackson in the Shenandoah Valley. Even at this early stage in his career there was, as seems to always be with Stuart, some controversy. Stuart's commission had been as a Colonel of Infantry but Jackson saw his potential and experience as a Cavalryman. However, the local politics surrounding Turner Ashby impeded this from happening. Ashby, like

Major General James "J.E.B." Stuart, C.S.A., USMA 1854

- **CONFEDERATE CORPS COMMANDER**
- **KILLED IN ACTION**
- **M-3 STUART TANK (WWII) NAMED IN HIS HONOR**

Courtesy: CSA

Photo: NARA

© 2013/Greg E. Mathieson Sr/MAI

J.E.B. Stuart Monument on Monument Avenue, Richmond, Virginia.

>>> Spotlight

M-3 Stuart Light Tank, the light tank of United States and British forces in World War II, was called the Stuart Tank after Confederate Major General J.E.B. Stuart. More than 16,000 Stuart Tanks were produced. Each tank had a crew of four and weighed 16 tons.

Stuart, might also be described as somewhat of a prima donna. A native of the Valley of Virginia, Ashby had helped raise many of the soldiers under Jackson and fancied the Cavalry position for his own. After some amount of complaining and jockeying Ashby, not Stuart, became a less than adequate Commander of Jackson's Cavalry.[7] After Ashby's death, Stuart received increasingly important Cavalry commands within the Army of Northern Virginia and played a large role in Lee's campaigns until he, too, was Killed In Action on May 12, 1864. Many were impressed but others thought "he was some sort of damned fool."[8] Stuart's reputation was equal parts brilliance, audacity, risk, and controversy. He is perhaps most famous for his circumnavigation of the Army of the Potomac during the Peninsular, Maryland, and Pennsylvania campaigns. The first brought the greatest amount of fame and success to Stuart and each subsequent repetition of this feat was met with an inverse relation of praise, success, and fame to himself and embarrassment to the north.

Stuart's career can be summed up however in three big moments: his ride around McClellan in 1862, his successful relief of Jackson at Chancellorsville, and his "absence" at the Battle of Gettysburg. Stuart's ride around McClellan was executed from June 12 to 15, 1862. According to Robin's report, "The Southern papers were filled with accounts of the expedition, none accurate and most of them marvelous." This was the moment that put Stuart on the map forever. His ride was celebrated but its accomplishment is perhaps exaggerated. While Stuart certainly provided good intelligence, it did not turn into a real gain for the confederacy due to the failure of Jackson to capitalize. One of the most celebrated moments of this ride was Stuart engaging the Union forces at Evelington Heights. On July 3rd, Stuart was able to loose fire upon the Union forces there from a commanding position but one in which he was incapable of keeping tenable due to the size of his forces. The problem with this stunt was that there was no immediate support from Jackson or Longstreet, and it resulted in the Union Army shoring up its lines. The fact is that Jackson himself was too slow in crossing a tributary of the James River and Stuart's action could not be developed. A question remains if it was Jackson, who was certainly uncharacteristically slow in his advance, was to blame for this or if Stuart was simply to quick in exposing his advantage with no ability to capitalize on it. The reality is that a moment was missed to severely cripple the Army of the Potomac and achieve a much greater operational victory over the tactical and moral one that was achieved. Without the benefit of hindsight the Peninsular campaign was viewed as a massive success for the Confederate cause and Stuart became a shining star in the ranks of Lee's Army of Northern Virginia.

Perhaps J.E.B. Stuart's best moment is one which is the least celebrated or understood. While the tremendous Confederate victory at Chancellorsville is remembered as belonging to Stonewall Jackson, the fact is that it could not have been achieved without the brilliant leadership and ability of General Stuart who reverted for the last time in the war to a Commander of Infantry. Stuart relieved a wounded Jackson when A.P. Hill ceded the command of Jackson's corps to him. He had only the most basic orders from Lee to simply prosecute the initiative which Jackson had seized. Stuart showed in this battle an ability to integrate many parts of an Army using Calvary, Artillery, and Infantry together to achieve stunning results at Hazel Grove.[9] In this instance, Stuart showed a natural ability to combine Infantry and artillery and prosecute a battle with them in short proximity, something that eluded almost all Commanders in the Civil War due to the range and effectiveness of rifled muskets. While Stuart's success in this type of combined arms action was not widely noted, similar plan failed spectacularly and famously during Picket's Charge that may have been an attempt by Lee to replicate Stuart's success one month prior at the Battle of Chancellorsville.

Despite these two massive successes, there will always remain Stuart's stunning failure at the Battle of Gettysburg. Again attempting to replicate his ride around McClellan, Stuart lost all contact with Lee, a cardinal sin of Cavalry operations. Stuart's leaving Lee blind bears perhaps the greatest responsibility for their being a battle in the first place and certainly played a significant role in its poor development by the Confederates on July 1, 1863. Stuart and his Cavalry were also not on hand to assist with the second day of the battle in which Union Cavalry was inexplicably absent. Finally on the 3rd of July and third day of the battle, Stuart was thwarted by George Custer and Pickett could not replicate Stuart's own feat of a direct assault of Union lines at the Battle of Chancellorsville.

After its defeat at Gettysburg, Lee's Army found itself constantly on the run and would never again posses and operational initiative. During U.S. Grant's 1864 Overland Campaign, Philip Sheridan's Cavalry launched an offensive to defeat Stuart. After such an audacious and conspicuous career Stuart was mortally wounded at the rather inconsequential Battle of Yellow Tavern.

Written by: Major Paul N. Belmont.

> STUART'S CAREER CAN BE SUMMED UP HOWEVER IN THREE BIG MOMENTS: HIS RIDE AROUND MCCLELLAN IN 1862, HIS SUCCESSFUL RELIEF OF JACKSON AT CHANCELLORSVILLE, AND HIS "ABSENCE" AT THE BATTLE OF GETTYSBURG.

J.E.B. Stuart's gravesite in Hollywood Cemetery, Richmond, Virginia.

Bronze Buffalo head on Custer tombstone, West Point Cemetery.

Lieutenant Colonel George Armstrong Custer, USMA 1861

- BREVET BRIGADIER GENERAL BY AGE 24
- PROMOTED TO BREVET MAJOR GENERAL DURING THE CIVIL WAR
- 11 HORSES SHOT OUT FROM UNDER HIM DURING THE CIVIL WAR
- ANNIHILATED WITH HIS ENTIRE 7TH CAVALRY COMMAND AT LITTLE BIG HORN
- LAST IN HIS CLASS AT WEST POINT
- BURIED AT THE WEST POINT CEMETERY

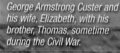

George Armstrong Custer and his wife, Elizabeth, with his brother, Thomas, sometime during the Civil War.

One would be hard-pressed to find an officer more defined by one bad day than George Armstrong Custer. Prior to his defeat at the Little Bighorn, however, he had established himself as one of the best-known Army Officers in the nation. His daring, innovation, and romantic flair had emblazoned him in the popular consciousness, but it would be these very qualities that would spell doom for his command on that fateful day in 1876.

Custer grew up in Ohio and Michigan, and briefly served as a teacher before entering West Point, where his poor academic performance and indiscipline became infamously legendary. He was intelligent, and his outgoing nature and natural leadership ability made him quite popular among his fellow cadets, but his frequent brushes with authority and regulations kept him at the bottom of his class.[1]

Despite this, he managed to graduate in 1861, and three days after leaving West Point saw action in the First Battle of Bull Run. Immediately thrust into a position of leadership, he earned a citation for bravery.[2] Custer was an egregious self-publicist, but even his detractors acknowledge that his reputation for bravery and tactical ingenuity was well earned.[3] His eagerness to place himself in

HIS DARING, INNOVATION, AND ROMANTIC FLAIR HAD EMBLAZONED HIM IN THE POPULAR CONSCIOUSNESS, BUT IT WOULD BE THESE VERY QUALITIES THAT WOULD SPELL DOOM FOR HIS COMMAND ON THAT FATEFUL DAY IN 1876.

the center of the action – and the spotlight – earned him the admiration of his superiors, his subordinates, and his nation, but it also sometimes earned him the resentment of peers.[4]

Following his first taste of combat, Custer became an Aide-de-Camp for the new Union Commander, George McClellan, and served in a staff role throughout McClellan's ill-fated 1862 Peninsula Campaign, even participating in balloon reconnaissance missions.[5] But Custer's leadership and tactical abilities could not be kept from the battlefield for long.

By the following summer, his reputation and experience had earned him a spot commanding a brigade of Cavalry. His brigade first saw serious action on the third day of Gettysburg in a sharp clash east of the main battle. As Confederate Cavalry charged the Union Cavalry in an attempt to gain the rear of the Army of the Potomac during Pickett's Charge, Custer led a Michigan Cavalry regiment in a counter-attack, screaming, "Come on, you Wolverines!" Forty minutes of hard

fighting resulted in a tactical draw, but the Confederates' plans had been thwarted. More than 80 percent of the Union casualties in the skirmish came from Custer's soldiers.[6]

Custer's brigade continued to serve in the Virginia Theater the following year, fighting in Ulysses Grant's overland campaign against the Army of Northern Virginia. Later, it supported General Philip Sheridan's efforts to subdue the Shenandoah Valley. Custer's command played a critical role holding the line almost alone against Jubal Early's forces in the Battle of Cedar Creek, before Union reinforcements crushed the Confederates.[7]

By the end of 1864, three years out of West Point, Custer had risen to command of a Cavalry Division and, because of his success at Cedar Creek, had earned a Brevet promotion to Major General. In the spring of 1865, the "Boy General" led yet another massive Cavalry charge at the Battle of Five Forks. The Union victory brought an end to

>>> Spotlight

Little Big Horn Battlefield in Montana is managed by the National Parks Service and memorializes the soldiers of the 7th Cavalry and the Sioux and Cheyenne who fought to preserve their way of life. Lieutenant Colonel Custer and 262 other soldiers were killed in one of the last battles of the Indian Wars.

Custer's gravesite at West Point Cemetery.

Plaque on Custer's gravesite.

the siege of Petersburg.[8] A few days later, his command helped seal the fate of the Army of Northern Virginia by seizing railroad trains meant to supply Lee's Army as it fled toward Appomattox.[9]

Because of his prominent role in so many important battles (and because of his knack for self-promotion), Custer ended the war as one of the North's great celebrities. Now assigned the rank of Lieutenant Colonel in the Regular Army, he was ordered to the frontier for the Army's next great campaign: the effort to subdue American Indian resistance to White expansion on the Great Plains. In these campaigns, his bravado and dash would once again bring him widespread fame and ultimately cost him his life.

By 1867, conflict between native tribes in Kansas and Indian territory was threatening white settlers, and Custer's old boss Sheridan ordered a campaign to stabilize the area.[10] Efforts to bring the elusive tribes to

battle proved futile, so Custer developed a plan to launch a winter campaign to catch and defeat the hostile groups in their winter encampments.[11] The result was the controversial Battle of Washita.

In November of 1868, Custer's forces followed a trail of Indians through "terrible snow storms" to a village of Cheyenne, Arapahoe, and Sioux on the Washita River. Four columns of Cavalrymen mounted a simultaneous surprise offensive into the village, killing dozens of warriors (along with "some of the squaws and a few of the children") and wounding and capturing others.[12] The Army heralded the success, but some began to question whether Custer's great victory was tainted. Custer's rivals within the command muttered dark imprecations about the possible abandonment of some fallen Cavalrymen, and others called Custer's "battle" a massacre, questioning the valor in a dead-of-winter sneak attack on a village full of women and children.[13] The controversy over what actually

happened continues to this day.

It was, of course, Custer's next large scale Indian campaign that would be his most famous, his most controversial, and his last. In 1876, the United States Army mounted a theater-wide effort to bring the tribes of the upper Great Plains to heel, converging three columns of Cavalrymen in Montana Territory.[14] In Custer's part of the action, all the characteristics that made him inspiring and successful – the bravado, the drive, and the rapid mobility – would ultimately cost the lives of 200 men of the 7th United States Cavalry, along with their dashing commander.

Just as in his successful attack at the Washita, Custer rapidly pursued the renegade tribes in an attempt to bring them to battle. As he approached the Indians along the Little Bighorn, he again divided his command, preparing for a surprise assault on the village before the Indians could make their escape. This time, however, there were thousands of

Plains Indians, and they had no intention of fleeing. Instead, they surrounded and annihilated Custer's battalion.[15] Custer's bad day had cost him life and, perhaps, his legacy.

Written by: Major Joseph C. Scott.

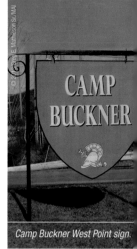

Camp Buckner West Point sign.

General Simon Bolivar Buckner, Jr., USMA 1908

- **HIGHEST-RANKING OFFICER KILLED IN ACTION BY ENEMY FIRE DURING WWII (POSTHUMOUSLY PROMOTED TO FOUR-STAR GENERAL)**
- **COMMANDING GENERAL 10TH U.S. ARMY, BATTLE OF OKINAWA, 1944–45**
- **COMMANDANT OF CADETS, UNITED STATES MILITARY ACADEMY AT WEST POINT, 1933–36**
- **SON OF SIMON BOLIVAR BUCKNER, SR., USMA 1844, CONFEDERATE GENERAL AND GOVERNOR OF KENTUCKY**
- **FORT BUCKNER, AN ARMY SUB-POST OF THE MARINE CORPS'S CAMP FOSTER ON OKINAWA, IS HOME TO THE 58TH SIGNAL BATTALION AND INCLUDES A SMALL MEMORIAL TO ITS NAMESAKE**
- **WEST POINT'S CAMP BUCKNER DEDICATED IN HIS HONOR**

General Simon Bolivar Buckner, Jr., was the son of Confederate Lieutenant General Simon Bolivar Buckner, Sr., (USMA 1844) who was later Governor of Kentucky and candidate for United States Vice President in 1896. General Buckner, Jr., grew up in the rural area of Munfordville, Kentucky, and attended Virginia Military Institute (VMI) before being appointed to join the West Point Class of 1908.

After World War I, he served two tours of duty in the Philippines and then returned to West

Point as an associate professor (1919–23) and later as Commandant of Cadets (1933–36). As Commandant, Buckner was known as being fair but very tough and demanding. He was known for confiscating cadets' after-shave lotion, saying, "If you're going to be a man, you've got to smell like a man."[1]

Buckner would participate in two critical battles during World War II: the first during the Battle of Midway in June 1942; then during the last major land battle of World War II at the Battle of Okinawa from April to June

1945. Following his promotion to Brigadier General in 1940, Buckner was assigned as Commanding General of the Alaska Defense Command. While he was in this command, the Japanese bombed Dutch Harbor, Alaska on June 3, 1942, as a diversionary attack during the initial stages of the Battle of Midway and then followed up with invasions of the Aleutian Islands of Attu and Kiska. The Battle of Midway would prove to be a major turning point in the Pacific Theater of Operations as United States Naval Forces,

after breaking the Japanese codes, did not fall for the diversion and instead surprised the invading Japanese fleet near Midway Island. In the aftermath of the battle, the United States sunk four Japanese aircraft carriers and turned back the invasion while losing one carrier of its own, the *USS Yorktown*. In May 1943, Buckner ordered the attack to re-take Attu, which was eventually liberated by the end of May. When the United States invaded Kiska in August 1943 to re-take the island, the American forces found that the Japanese

>>> Spotlight

Camp Buckner West Point was dedicated in honor of General Buckner in 1946. All cadets receive military training at Camp Buckner during their Yearling years with instruction being provided by Firsties, as well as an active-duty Infantry battalion.

© John Vigna

Lieutenant General Buckner seconds before being killed by a mortar, Okinawa, Japan.

psychological blow to the Japanese as the ground war would now enter Japanese soil.

By April 1945, German resistance in the European Campaign was on the verge of collapse, but the Empire of Japan continued to defiantly resist American advances across the Pacific. As American forces drew closer to the mainland of Japan, the ferociousness of the fighting escalated as Japanese forces no longer considered surrender an option and were intent on preventing any foreign force from invading Japan. Thus, the strategic importance of Okinawa became clear.

Commencing the invasion on April 1, 1945, the 82-day-long battle lasted until late June and resulted in the most casualties of any battle in the Pacific Theater of Operations. Casualties totaled more than 38,000 Americans wounded and 12,000 killed or missing, more than 107,000 Japanese and Okinawan conscripts killed, and perhaps 100,000 Okinawan civilians who perished in the battle or committed suicide rather than fall into the hands of the Americans. In fact, more people died during the Battle of Okinawa than all those killed during the atomic bombings of Hiroshima and Nagasaki. Not surprisingly, the cost of this battle in terms of lives, time, and material, foreshadowed what any potential invasion of mainland Japan would cost, and arguably weighed heavily in the decision to use the atomic bomb against Japan just six weeks later.[2] Military advisors cautioned President Harry Truman that an invasion of mainland Japan would result in an estimated 500,000 to one million American casualties.[3] Truman eventually ordered the use of the atomic bombs to convince the Japanese that unconditional surrender was their only option.

As a Commander, General Buckner was known for "leading from the front" and was a frequent visitor to his most forward lines. On June 18, 1945, Buckner had arrived in his command Jeep, which was flying its standard Three-Star flag, to inspect a forward observation post. A nearby marine outpost sent a message to Buckner's position that in addition to the stars on the Jeep, the General's bright stars on his helmet were clearly visible. Buckner quickly replaced his helmet with a less-conspicuous helmet without stars; however, a Japanese artillery position had already observed General Buckner and fired upon his position and mortally wounded him as shrapnel tore into his chest.[4]

On August 6, 1945, the B-29 *Enola Gay* dropped the first atomic bomb on Hiroshima, followed by *Boxcar*, which dropped the

second atomic bomb on Nagasaki on August 9, 1945. On August 15, 1945, Japan accepted unconditional surrender terms signaling Victory over Japan Day (VJ Day). President Truman, who hailed from the state of Missouri, chose the *USS Missouri* as the location to sign the official unconditional surrender instrument on September 2, 1945, instead of Admiral William F. Halsey's flagship, the *USS Wisconsin*. General Douglas MacArthur (USMA 1903), with Halsey and General Jonathan M. Wainwright (USMA 1906) in attendance, would lead the official surrender ceremonies aboard the *USS Missouri* to end World War II.[5]

Simon Bolivar Buckner, Jr., is interred in the family plot at Frankfort Cemetery in Frankfort, Kentucky. Buckner was posthumously promoted to the rank of Four-Star General on July 19, 1954, by a Special Act of Congress (Public Law 83–508), making him the highest-ranking officer killed by enemy fire in World War II. Buckner's son, William Claiborne Buckner, entered West Point in 1944 and had just completed Plebe year at West Point when his father was killed on Okinawa while likely training on what would later be dedicated Camp Buckner in his father's honor. The Buckner family history is an incredible story of both the Long Gray Line and the nation, spanning three generations and more than 100 years of military history. The grandfather, Simon, Sr., was a Confederate Civil War General and later post-war Governor of Kentucky during Reconstruction and reconciliation; 80 years later, his son, Simon, Jr., was the highest-ranking officer killed in World War II; and the grandson, William, served in the Cold War in Europe. In 1946, Major General Maxwell Taylor (USMA 1922), the Superintendent of West Point, dedicated the cadet summer training facilities in honor of General Simon Bolivar Buckner, Jr., designating it Camp Buckner, West Point. In a fitting tribute to his father's legacy, Cadet William Buckner attended the dedication ceremony.

Written by: Frank Flowers, USMA 1986.

> **AS A COMMANDER, GENERAL BUCKNER WAS KNOWN FOR "LEADING FROM THE FRONT" AND WAS A FREQUENT VISITOR TO HIS FRONT LINES.**

had abandoned the island. The United States then put the Japanese on the defensive in the Pacific as it executed an "island hopping" strategy through the Central and Southwest Pacific towards Japan.

In July 1944, Buckner was promoted to Lieutenant General and sent to Hawaii to organize the United States 10th Army, which consisted of both United States Army and United States Marine Corps units. His initial mission was to prepare for the invasion of Taiwan. This mission was canceled and the 10th Army was given the new mission of preparing for the Battle of Okinawa (Operation Iceberg).

Strategically located some 400 miles south of the Japanese mainland, Okinawa is the southernmost portion of Japan. Possession of Okinawa would enable the Allies to cut Japan's sea lines of communication and isolate it from its vital sources of raw materials in the south. Okinawa would also provide the main staging area for any potential invasion of Japan with its numerous harbors, anchorages, and airfields. Just as important, successfully invading Okinawa would be a

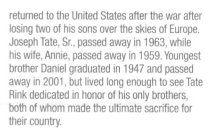

Lieutenant Colonel Joseph Scranton Tate, USMA 1941
Captain Frederic Homer Sergeant Tate, USMA 1942

- TATE HOCKEY RINK AT WEST POINT NAMED IN THEIR HONOR
- FREDERIC TATE WAS ARMY HOCKEY TEAM CAPTAIN, 1941–42
- BOTH TATE BROTHERS WERE ARMY HOCKEY PLAYERS KILLED IN ACTION AS U.S. ARMY AIR CORPS PILOTS DURING WORLD WAR II

In the middle of World War II, Daniel Tate entered West Point in 1943 as a member of the Class of 1947. With his entry, Daniel Tate became the fifth Tate family member to join the Long Gray Line. His grandfather and namesake, Daniel Lyle Tate (USMA 1880), father Joseph Tate (USMA 1917), and only two brothers, Lieutenant Colonel Joseph S. Tate, Jr., (USMA 1941) and Captain Frederic Tate (USMA 1942), were all West Point graduates.[1] At the time, young Daniel entered West Point in 1943, his father and two brothers fighting the war in Europe and sadly, only one would return alive.

His father was a field artilleryman and both of his brothers were pilots in the Army Air Corps. His brothers also played three varsity sports at West Point – both played varsity

Hockey – Frederic even captained the 1942 Army Hockey team. Joseph, the oldest brother, was the command pilot of a B-24 Liberator with a 10-member crew. He had survived the disastrous Ploesti, Romania oil field raids of Operation Tidal Wave in August 1943 where he had been awarded the Silver Star and Purple Heart as a member of the 328th Bomber Squadron, 93rd Bomber Group, 8th United States Air Force. Frederic was a fighter pilot in a single engine P-47 Thunderbolt with the 387th Fighter Squadron, 365th Fighter Group, 9th Tactical Air Corps.

Lieutenant Colonel Joseph Tate, Jr., became the first casualty of the Tate family when he was declared Missing in Action (MIA) after his B-24 was shot down on a mission over Osnabruck,

Germany, on December 23, 1943, yet the family remained hopeful that he had survived to become a Prisoner of War. Following the June 6, 1944, D-Day landings at Normandy, Colonel Joseph Tate, Sr., took Command of the 411th Field Artillery Group as it fought across Europe, Captain Frederic Tate flew missions in his P-47 out of the newly established airfields in France, while Joseph, Jr., remained MIA somewhere in Germany. Tragedy again struck the Tate family on September 20, 1944, when Captain Frederic Tate was Killed In Action (KIA) flying his P-47 on a combat mission over Vigneulles, France. When the war in Europe ended in May 1945, Joseph, Jr., was unfortunately still missing and officially declared KIA on September 9, 1945, just days after the Japanese surrender signaled the end of World War II. Colonel Joseph Tate, Sr.,

returned to the United States after the war after losing two of his sons over the skies of Europe. Joseph Tate, Sr., passed away in 1963, while his wife, Annie, passed away in 1959. Youngest brother Daniel graduated in 1947 and passed away in 2001, but lived long enough to see Tate Rink dedicated in honor of his only brothers, both of whom made the ultimate sacrifice for their country.

Tate Rink, with its 2,648-seat capacity, has been the home of Army Hockey since October 1985 and is located in the Holleder Sports Center, across the street from Michie Stadium – all facilities named in honor of West Point graduates and athletes who have made the ultimate sacrifice.[2]

GILLIS FIELD HOUSE AT WEST POINT

Major William Graham Gillis, Jr., USMA 1941

- **GILLIS FIELD HOUSE AT WEST POINT NAMED IN HIS HONOR**
- **TEAM CAPTAIN, ARMY FOOTBALL, 1940, THREE-TIME LETTERMAN ARMY TRACK**
- **DISTINGUISHED SERVICE CROSS, SILVER STAR, BRONZE STAR MEDAL, TWO PURPLE HEARTS**
- **KILLED IN ACTION, OCTOBER 10, 1944, IN GREMERCY FOREST FRANCE**

The Gillis Field House at West Point is a large world-class track and field structure located below Eisenhower Hall near the western bank of the Hudson River. Visitors to the Academy are often amused to see the highly visible "BEAT AIR FORCE" sign painted on its massive roof. The beautiful facility is regularly the home to intercollegiate and state high school track meets, volleyball matches, myriad other sports, and was the home to Army men's basketball from 1938 to 1985. The facility's name honors Major William G. Gillis and is a constant reminder of West Point's underlying mission in preparing cadets for service to the nation in both times of peace and war, and that its graduates might have to give the ultimate sacrifice in that service.

William Gillis entered West Point in 1937 during the Great Depression. At the beginning of his junior year, Adolf Hitler's Nazi forces invaded Poland on September 1, 1939, and by the end of his senior year, the Nazis occupied most of Europe with only Great Britain remaining free. Shortly after Gillis's graduation in 1941 the Japanese attacked Pearl Harbor, Hitler declared war on the United States, and America became embroiled in World War II before the year's end. During his four years at West Point, Gillis had clearly prepared himself for serving his nation in time of war by honing his leadership skills and his physical abilities – particularly on the "fields of friendly strife." Gillis was a three-time letterman and Captain of the Army football team, as well as a three-time hurdler on the Army track team. During his sophomore year, Gillis competed in the

high and low hurdles in the newly opened field house that now bears his name. Upon graduation, Gillis chose the Infantry Branch because like his West Point experience, he wanted to continue leading from the front. Before he deployed to Europe, he married the former Lenore Riley Mudge.

On October 1, 1944, Major Gillis gave the ultimate sacrifice in service to his nation. He was Killed In Action at the age of 26 while commanding 1st Battalion, 320th Infantry Regiment, 35th Infantry Division during operations in France's Gremercy Forest. In that action, Gillis was posthumously awarded the Distinguished Service Cross – the nation's second-highest valor award. He was also awarded the Silver Star, two Purple Hearts, and several foreign awards during his war-

time service. It is fitting that the field house in which he once competed as a cadet now bears his name: Gillis Field House. Moreover, it also serves as a daily reminder that within its walls, Gillis Field House continues to develop and prepare cadets on those "fields of friendly strife," in the event they have to lead soldiers upon other fields, on other days in service to the nation.

Gillis Field House at West Point.

First Lieutenant Edward Charles Christl, Jr., USMA 1944

- CHRISTL BASKETBALL ARENA AT WEST POINT NAMED IN HIS HONOR
- DISTINGUISHED SERVICE CROSS, PURPLE HEART
- ARMY BASKETBALL TEAM CAPTAIN, 1943–44
- KILLED IN ACTION, AUSTRIA, MAY 4, 1945

The Christl Arena at West Point is a 5,043-seat, world-class basketball facility housed in the Holleder Center and home to the Army men's and women's Division I basketball teams. It has hosted a myriad of events ranging from intercollegiate basketball games and tournaments, volleyball matches, and gymnastics meets to high school sports competitions, camps, and clinics.

The arena is named in honor of First Lieutenant Edward C. Christl, Class of 1944, who was Killed In Action leading soldiers during the waning days of World War II. Christl had been a four-year letterman on the Army basketball team and elected team Captain during his senior year. That year, he led Army to an undefeated 15–0 season while playing in the Army Field House (now known as Gillis Field House). Graduating on June 6, 1944, D-Day, Christl was commissioned as a Field Artillery Officer and assigned as a forward observer in the 65th Infantry Division. Landing in Le Havre, France, in January 1945, Christl and his division saw their first action in March 1945 during the Rhineland Campaign as the Allies advanced into the heart of Nazi Germany on two fronts. The Americans and the British attacked through Germany and Austria from the West, while the Soviets attacked and took Berlin from the East. With Adolph Hitler's suicide on April 30, 1945, in his Berlin bunker, the end of the World War II in Europe was only days away. Many German units surrendered, but pockets of fanatical German resistance remained. During an engagement with one of those resisting units at Erferding, Austria on May 4, 1945, First Lieutenant Christl was killed leading troops in an assault against the strongly defended town. Tragically, his death occurred three days before Germany surrendered. For his heroic leadership and sacrifice, First Lieutenant Christl was posthumously awarded the nation's second-highest valor award – the Distinguished Service Cross. Although he is honored daily with an athletic arena bearing his name and housing his favorite sport, his Distinguished Service Cross citation best captures the true description of Christl's character and leadership. The citation reads:

"The President of the United States of America, authorized by Act of Congress, July 9, 1918, takes pride in presenting the Distinguished Service Cross (Posthumously) to First Lieutenant (Field Artillery) Edward Charles Christl, Jr. United States Army, for extraordinary heroism in connection with military operations against an armed enemy while serving with Headquarters, 868th Field Artillery Battalion, 65th Infantry Division, in action against enemy forces on 4 May 1945, in Austria. During an attack on Eferding, Austria, our troops met fierce resistance from German SS troops. Lieutenant Christl, although an artillery forward observer, heroically volunteered to lead an Infantry squad into the bitterly defended town. With utter disregard for his own safety, he exposed himself to intense hostile automatic weapons fire and led his men in the successful accomplishment of their mission. Lieutenant Christl was killed in this action. His intrepid actions, personal bravery and zealous devotion to duty at the cost of his life, exemplify the highest traditions of the military forces of the United States and reflect great credit upon himself, the 65th Infantry Division, and the United States Army."

Captain Carl Robert Arvin, USMA 1965

- **ARVIN GYMNASIUM AT WEST POINT DEDICATED IN HIS HONOR**
- **KILLED IN ACTION IN VIETNAM, OCTOBER 8, 1967**
- **FIRST CAPTAIN, CLASS OF 1965**
- **SILVER STAR (TWO), PURPLE HEART (TWO), COMBAT INFANTRYMAN BADGE**
- **CAPTAIN, ARMY WRESTLING CAPTAIN, 1964–65**

Captain Arvin plaque in the entrance to Arvin Gymnasium at West Point.

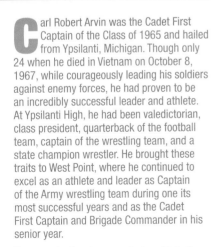

Carl Robert Arvin was the Cadet First Captain of the Class of 1965 and hailed from Ypsilanti, Michigan. Though only 24 when he died in Vietnam on October 8, 1967, while courageously leading his soldiers against enemy forces, he had proven to be an incredibly successful leader and athlete. At Ypsilanti High, he had been valedictorian, class president, quarterback of the football team, captain of the wrestling team, and a state champion wrestler. He brought these traits to West Point, where he continued to excel as an athlete and leader as Captain of the Army wrestling team during one its most successful years and as the Cadet First Captain and Brigade Commander in his senior year.

Upon graduation, he commissioned into the Infantry and received an assignment with the 82nd Airborne Division. Following Airborne and Ranger Schools, he served briefly as a Platoon Leader, Executive Officer, then as a very young Company Commander. During that time, he returned home to Ypsilanti to marry Merry Lynn Montonye on July 30, 1966, then returned to Fort Bragg to serve as Aide-de-Camp to the Assistant Division Commander of the 82nd Airborne Division.

First Lieutenant Arvin arrived in Vietnam in May 1967 and was assigned as an advisor to the 7th Vietnamese Airborne Battalion. The unit saw combat consistently and Arvin was awarded the Silver Star and Purple Heart for his courageous leadership for actions on September 5, 1967. One month later, after recovering from his wounds, Arvin insisted on returning to duty and on October 8, 1967, he was again leading his unit in heavy combat against a much larger enemy when he was Killed In Action. For his selfless sacrifice, Arvin was posthumously promoted to Captain, awarded the Silver Star, and is buried at the West Point Cemetery.

His courageous leadership was immortalized at West Point when the Academy named the cadet gymnasium in his honor on February 25, 1989, as the Arvin Cadet Physical Development Center. The 495,100-square-foot facility hosts some of the best athletic and training of any university in the United States with nine basketball courts, six racquetball courts, a state-of-the-art weight room, a rock-climbing wall, boxing rooms, a world-class wrestling facility, an Olympic-sized pool with diving platforms, an intramural pool, and a combat water survival lab. Constructed and renovated between 1910 and 2005, the facility actually consists of six separate buildings with dozens of floor levels. Every day cadets are reminded of Captain Arvin's leadership and sacrifice as they enter the Arvin Gymnasium. Intercollegiate athletes and guests also realize that the cadets they compete against are following Captain Arvin's example and will soon become Commissioned Officers who will lead American soldiers in the service of their country.

Holleder Center at West Point.

Major Donald Holleder, USMA 1956

- HOLLEDER CENTER AT WEST POINT NAMED IN HIS HONOR
- DISTINGUISHED SERVICE CROSS, BRONZE STAR MEDAL (FOUR), PURPLE HEART, COMBAT INFANTRYMAN BADGE
- KILLED IN ACTION, VIETNAM WAR
- COLLEGE FOOTBALL HALL OF FAME INDUCTEE, 1985
- ALL-AMERICAN ARMY FOOTBALL PLAYER DRAFTED BY THE NEW YORK GIANTS

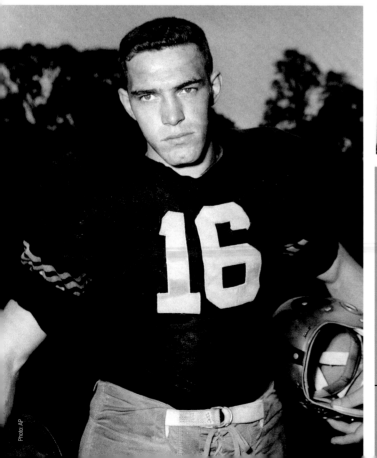

>>> Spotlight

The Holleder Center opened in 1985 and is home to the West Point basketball and hockey teams, which are housed in the Christl Arena and Tate Rinks respectively. Each of these names — Holleder, Christl, and Tate — represent West Point student-athletes who were team Captains of their respective Army teams (football, basketball, and hockey) and who later made the ultimate sacrifice for their country as Army officers. The 131,000-square-foot building includes a 2,650-seat hockey arena (Tate Rink) and a 5,043-seat basketball arena (Christl Arena) and cost $16 million to construct from 1982 to 1985.

Photo © 2013/Greg E. Mathieson Sr./MAI

Photo: AP

FRIENDLY STRIFE.
EDS THAT. UPON
N OTHER DAYS.
UITS OF VICTORY.

DOUGLAS MACARTHUR – USMA CLASS

Following a stunning 14–6 victory over a heavily favored Navy team in December 1955, General Douglas MacArthur was so overwhelmed he sent the following message, "No victory the Army has won in its long years of fierce football struggles has ever reflected a greater spirit of raw courage, of invincible determination, of masterful strategic planning and resolute practical execution."[1] All-American end-turned-quarterback Don Holleder had envisioned such a victory just one day earlier. Holleder boldly told his head coach, Colonel Earl "Red" Blaik, he would not have to take the lonely walk to the center of the field to congratulate the opposing head coach on Navy's victory when he emphatically asserted in front of the team, "Colonel, you will not have to make that walk!"[2] Holleder made good on his promise.

Donald Walter Holleder was born in Buffalo, New York, on August 3, 1934. When Holleder was 13, he and his family moved to Irondequoit, New York, where he attended high school at Aquinas Institute in Rochester. He was heavily recruited to play collegiate football out of high school and chose West Point largely because of the many conversations he had with his recruiting coach, Coach Vince Lombardi (who would later lead the Green Bay Packers to two Super Bowl victories and have the Super Bowl trophy named in his honor as the Lombardi Trophy).

After an extremely successful junior campaign, Holleder was one of three cadets named to the All-American team, along with halfback Tommie Bell and offensive guard Ralph Chesnauskas. Holleder piled up impressive stats as he led the team in receptions (17), receiving yards (495), yards per catch (29.1), and receiving touchdowns (5). Along with being a mainstay on offense, Holleder used his speed and his six-foot one-inch, 200-pound frame, to his advantage as a standout at safety on defense.

Barring injury, Don Holleder was heavily favored for a repeat performance as an All-American in his senior season; however, with the graduation of Army's quarterback Pete Vann in 1955, the cupboards were bare behind center. Coach Blaik had to be innovative and decided to take an enormous risk by moving his best athlete, Holleder, to quarterback. Blaik noted in his 1960 biography that "Holleder was a natural athlete, big, strong, quick, smart, aggressive, a competitor," while also adding "I knew he could learn to handle the ball well and to call the plays properly. Most important, I knew

that he would provide bright, aggressive, inspirational leadership."[3] Fans, players, and the press were mixed in their reception of the bold move. Jim Shelton, a former player from the University of Delaware, gridiron opponent of Holleder, and a retired Army Major recalled, "He couldn't throw…he would roll left or roll right and run it himself. But he was a load to bring down. Tackling him was like trying to tackle a horse. And after you did, he got up kicking and swinging."[4] Further complicating the position switch, Holleder suffered a broken ankle in the first week of spring football and put his transition behind schedule.

Validating Coach Blaik's bold move, the 1955 season started with two lopsided victories over Furman and Penn State. After two lopsided losses to Michigan and Syracuse that followed, however, the initial optimism turned into despair. To make matters worse, Army only managed to score two total points in both contests because of a lack of offensive execution and multiple turnovers, many of which were made by Holleder. Despite these setbacks, Coach Blaik was resolute in his decision and reassured Holleder that "I am coaching this Army team…and you are my quarterback!"[5]

ON A DAY WHEN ACTS OF HEROISM WERE THE RULE, RATHER THAN THE EXCEPTION, HIS STOOD OUT.

Entering the 1956 Army-Navy game, the Army team, unranked with a 5–3 record, faced the 11th-ranked Navy squad as a heavy underdog. Navy excited its fans early by orchestrating a 76-yard opening drive, jumping to a 6–0 lead. Navy threatened to put the game away early with two more long drives, but the cadets' defense stopped both of them at the Army 20-yard line. Holleder, playing both ways, had a hand in both stops. First, when he hit a Navy receiver so hard he dropped a fourth-down pass, and second when he recovered a Navy fumble. Army eventually rallied to a 14–6 come-from-behind victory and made good on Holleder's promise. Holleder had even appeared on the November 28, 1955, cover of *Sports Illustrated* magazine in a much-anticipated preview of the game. At the season's end, Holleder was awarded the annual Swede Nelson Award for Sportsmanship, which was likely influenced by his unselfishness in giving up the possibility of being a two-time All-American end in order to play

quarterback where his team needed him.

In further recognition of Holleder's talents, the New York Giants drafted him in the eighth round of the 1956 National Football League draft, but Holleder chose to pursue his Army career rather than to play professional football.

After graduating from West Point and commissioning in the Infantry, Lieutenant Holleder was assigned to the 25th Infantry Division in Schofield Barracks, Hawaii. He returned to West Point from 1959 to 1962 for a brief stint as an assistant football coach. He next deployed to Korea for a year with the 31st Infantry Regiment, 7th Infantry Division where he commanded a rifle company. He redeployed to Fort Monroe, Virginia, with an initial assignment as Aide-de-Camp to the Deputy Commanding General of the Continental Army Command; however, with the war in Vietnam waging, Holleder persistently lobbied to lead soldiers in combat and was soon sent overseas.

Unsurprisingly, it was not very long into his tour that Holleder, now a Major, found himself in the thick of the fight. On October 17, 1967, he was flying a combat mission in a helicopter northeast of Saigon above the intense Battle of Ong Thanh as Operations Officer of an Infantry Battalion in the 28th Infantry Regiment, 1st Infantry Division. It was also on that day that Tom Hinger, a combat medic, witnessed Don Holleder's true heroism and ultimately his untimely death as Holleder led three volunteers to assist 142 soldiers being fired on by 1,400 enemy troops protected by underground bunkers.[6] Holleder died in Hinger's arms, but Hinger's personal account of the incident provides a riveting tribute:

"Major Holleder overflew the area and saw a whole lot of Viet Cong and many American soldiers, most wounded, trying to make their way out of the ambush area. He landed and headed straight into the jungle, gathering a few soldiers to help him go get the wounded. A sniper's shot killed him before he could get very far. He was a risk-taker who put the common good ahead of himself, whether it was in giving up a position in which he had excelled or putting himself in harm's way in an attempt to save the lives of his men. My contact with Major Holleder was very brief and occurred just before he was killed, but I have never forgotten him and the sacrifice he made. On a day when acts of heroism were the rule, rather than the exception, his stood out."[7]

A selfless leader in every respect who

exemplified West Point's motto of "Duty, Honor, Country," Holleder departed this Earth at the too young age of 33, leaving behind a wife and four children. Coach Red Blaik and Coach Vince Lombardi both attended Holleder's funeral at Arlington National Cemetery.

For his actions that day, Holleder was posthumously awarded the Silver Star. More than 44 years later, however, Holleder's award was upgraded to the Army's second-highest valor award – the Distinguished Service Cross – on April 27, 2012, to more accurately reflect Holleder's heroism noted in his citation:

"When the intense sniper fire impeded the evacuation of the wounded, Maj. Holleder unhesitatingly moved forward to reconnoiter the evacuation route," the citation stated. "He refused to seek cover from the deadly volleys of insurgent sniper fire and continued to assess the enemy situation until he was mortally wounded from the heavy ground fire. His tremendous courage and poise in the face of overwhelming odds had a stabilizing effect on his men and was instrumental in saving many lives."[8]

Today, the Holleder Center fittingly sits alongside Michie Stadium as a tribute to Holleder's selfless life and career. The Holleder Center plays host to Army Basketball (Christl Arena) – which Holleder also played while at West Point – and Army Hockey (Tate Rink). It is an enduring tribute to Holleder, who as much as any graduate has, represents the values that have made the United States Military Academy, and the nation its cadets are sworn to defend, truly great.

Written by: Steve Chaloult, USMA 1992, and Greg Oliver.

Courtesy: Sports Illustrated

Coach Blaik in the locker room with Holleder (#16) after the 1955 Army-Navy 14–6 victory.

© WPLPOC

At the outbreak of the Second World War, then Lieutenant Colonel William Orlando Darby was stationed in Northern Ireland training with his artillery unit. While there, he had the privilege of observing British Commando training and straight away developed a deep interest and affection for special operations. It came as no surprise that when the United States Army decided to create its own commando unit, Darby, who had already distinguished himself as an accomplished commander, immediately volunteered and was placed in charge of the unit's formation. Darby called for volunteers by placing notices on the bulletin boards of the 34th Infantry Division, the 1st Armored Division and other units training in Northern Ireland. He personally selected the all of the officers for the new organization; these officers then assisted him in the selection of the Sergeants and enlisted men. Energetic and tough from years of playing sports as a youth, Darby sought smart, athletic men in superior physical condition. Word spread rapidly about the new unit's formation and volunteers poured in from every division in the Army, but most of them came from the units training in Northern Ireland and Scotland. These volunteers ranged in age from 17 to 35 years and "included a former lion tamer and a full-blooded Sioux Indian."[1] Disparate as they seemed, they all shared several traits. They were intelligent, possessed exceptional physical stamina and all carried an intense desire to engage with the enemy.

Although originally commissioned as a Field Artillery Officer, Darby immersed himself and his volunteers in an intense training regimen with the British Commandos. The instruction consisted of advanced light Infantry tactics, commando operations, and long-range night patrols. These patrols – forced marches on foot of up to 20 miles or more over rough terrain – were designed to weed out the weak and fortify the strong. Consequently, the new unit felt an affinity for the elite militias of colonial America and the American Revolution, where highly skilled frontiersmen would report on that night's patrol by first stating how far it "ranged." The United States Army henceforth designated the new commando unit as the 1st Ranger Battalion. Darby understood that the more intense and realistic the training, the more prepared his volunteers would be for the highly dangerous missions they would be tasked to perform. Thus, "Darby's Rangers" as they were now known, received training in hand-to-hand combat, multiple small arms engagement, obstacle courses, night operations, and small boat patrolling. Live ammunition and grenades were often used in these exercises, which resulted in plenty of injuries due to the extremely tough yet authentic training conditions.

Within a few short months, Darby's Rangers received their first and arguably one of their most dangerous missions. The 1st Ranger Battalion was tasked to spearhead the invasion of French North Africa, code named Operation Torch. Critical to the Allied invasion of North Africa would be the successful landing of the United States 1st Infantry Division at Arzew harbor. During the early hours of November 8, 1942, two companies of Darby's Rangers stealthily passed through a boom blocking the entrance to the inner harbor of Arzew and silently advanced on Fort de la Pointe. Under cover of darkness, the two Ranger units climbed over a seawall and cut through barbed wire catching the enemy by surprise. The raiders assaulted from opposite directions and in less than an hour, had seized the fort, along with 60 prisoners. Meanwhile, the other four companies of the battalion, under command of now 31-year-old Lieutenant Colonel Darby, landed near Cap Carbon. Darby and his men silently climbed a ravine to reach Batterie du Nord, which overlooked the harbor. Darby's superior understanding of commando operations and skillful use of the Ranger's four 81-mm mortars allowed his unit to surprise and overwhelm a larger defensive force. Again, the Rangers proved themselves worthy when they captured the battery and 60 additional prisoners.[2] Darby's emphasis on realistic and intensive training, along with his astute planning and brilliant leadership, allowed the Rangers to successfully capture and occupy the two forts at the harbor's entrance, thus securing the landing site for the 1st Infantry Division.

With Operation Touch now underway, the American Field Commanders were focused on convention battlefield operations and with no doctrine or widespread understanding of seaborne commando raids, many months passed before the 1st Ranger Battalion received its next mission. Then, in early February, Lieutenant General Dwight D. Eisenhower attached Darby's Rangers to Major General Lloyd R. Fredendall's II Corps in Tunisia to "gather intelligence and mislead the enemy regarding Allied strength and intentions."[3] Darby led his Rangers on a series of raids against Italo-German lines, striking first at the Italian outpost at Sened from February 10 to 11, 1943. The mission was the epitome of a Ranger commando operation. Three companies of Darby's Rangers patrolled across more than eight miles of rugged terrain to reach a point from which they could stealthily observe the enemy positions. Understanding the value of battlefield intelligence, Darby commanded his Rangers to stay hidden and reconnoiter the outposts for the entire day, making note of the enemy's routines, guard shifts, and patrols. About midnight on the following night, Darby, using small colored lights to maintain attack formation, covertly advanced upon the enemy. The commandos slipped to within a couple hundred meters of the enemy position before the Italians spotted them approaching and opened fire. Undeterred, the raiders rapidly closed the distance and at about 50 meters from the garrison, launched a ferocious bayonet assault. In less than half an hour, Darby's Rangers breached the fortification and swarmed the enemy stronghold, killing 50 of its 66 defenders.

Darby received the Silver Star for his actions in 1943 and later commanded the United States 10th Mountain Division when its commander, Brigadier General Robinson E. Duff, was wounded. On April 23, 1945, while issuing orders for the attack on Trento, Italy, a German 88-mm shell landed near Darby killing him instantly. He was posthumously promoted to Brigadier General; he was 34 at the time of his death. In 1952, the United States Army named Camp Darby, Italy in his honor. The influence of General Darby is still evident in the United States Army more than half a century after his death. As a strong advocate for the formation of elite special operations units, he is directly responsible for the establishment of the Ranger Regiment that exists in the United States Army today.

Written by: David J. Walker, USMA 1991.

Brigadier General William O. Darby, USMA 1933

- **"FATHER OF THE MODERN RANGERS"**
- **FOUNDER AND COMMANDER, 1ST RANGER BATTALION**
- **KILLED IN ACTION, ITALY, APRIL 23, 1945**
- **CAMP DARBY, ITALY, NAMED IN HIS HONOR**
- **PROMOTED TO BRIGADIER GENERAL (POSTHUMOUSLY)**
- **1958 MOVIE *DARBY'S RANGERS* STARRED JAMES GARDNER, WHO PORTRAYED DARBY**
- **CAMP DARBY AT FORT BENNING, GEORGIA, NAMED IN HIS HONOR AND HOSTS THE FIRST PHASE OF U.S. ARMY RANGER SCHOOL**
- **DISTINGUISHED SERVICE CROSS (TWO), SILVER STAR, BRONZE STAR MEDAL, PURPLE HEART (THREE)**

Currently, more than 8,000 souls have a final resting place at the United States Military Academy's cemetery. Among them are 24 Medal of Honor recipients; 25 West Point superintendents; military and civilian leaders from every American war; and distinguished academics, engineers, soldiers, athletes, and family members. A walk among the headstones of this hallowed ground provides a distinct snapshot of the entire breadth of America's storied past. One headstone in particular that symbolizes a very unique part of this story is that of Colonel David Daniel "Mickey" Marcus. One of the most visited graves, Marcus's headstone bears two notable characteristics, a large volume of small rocks continually covering its top surface – a customary Jewish symbol of remembrance and respect for the deceased – and a short inscription reading "A Soldier For All Humanity."[1] While honoring his legacy – one that includes being the only soldier killed fighting under a foreign flag – these characteristics also speak volumes about the life Marcus spent

seeking justice in the service of both his nation and others.[2]

Mickey Marcus was born in New York City on February 22, 1901, the fifth child of immigrant parents from Romania who had escaped the Jewish pogroms of Eastern Europe. While growing up in Brooklyn, he learned to box in order to defend both himself and elderly members of his neighborhood from the anti-Semitism of local bullies. These experiences were likely the foundation for his strong, lifelong commitment to justice. In high school, Marcus was a superior performer as a four-sport athlete and student, attributes that earned him an appointment to West Point's Class of 1924 and led him down a military path that surprised his family.[3] While at West Point, he excelled as a scholar, leader, and athlete, winning an intercollegiate boxing championship, receiving an Olympic tryout for gymnastics, and declining a Rhodes Scholarship in order to stay near his future wife. After serving his commitment as an Infantry Officer, Marcus resigned his commission in 1926 to study his true passion of law.[4]

During his military hiatus, Marcus built an impressive reputation for seeking justice as a lawyer and administrator. He served in the United States District Attorney's New York office and for the United States Treasury Department, where he battled many levels of

THE PROVISIONAL GOVERNMENT PROMOTED MARCUS TO BRIGADIER GENERAL ON MAY 28, 1948, MAKING HIM ISRAEL'S FIRST GENERAL AND THE FIRST GENERAL OF A JEWISH ARMY SINCE JUDAH MACCABBEE IN 164 BCE.

Prohibition-era corruption. His successes led to New York City Mayor Fiorello La Guardia appointing Marcus to Deputy Commissioner of Corrections in order to confront corruption within the city's prison system. By 1939, Marcus's reputation undoubtedly set him on the path for a promising political career, but events in Europe redirected that path.[5]

Like many of his classmates and contemporaries, Marcus recognized the threat posed by Nazi Germany. He rejoined the Army in 1939 as a Lieutenant Colonel,

but this time as a Judge Advocate attorney based on his civilian experience. Realizing his breadth of talent as both a war fighter and lawyer, however, the Army used Marcus for a variety of missions during his World War II service while also promoting him to Colonel. From training soldiers at Ranger School in Hawaii to jumping with the 101st Airborne Division in support of the D-Day invasion, he was one of only two soldiers that day who had never parachuted from a plane – Marcus proved to be a skilled and fearless war fighter. As an attorney and administrator, his counsel was invaluable in many areas. He helped implement the wartime occupation of France, drafted the surrender terms for Italy and Germany, provided key counsel at several wartime conferences to include Teheran, Cairo, and Yalta, and

Colonel David "Mickey" Marcus, USMA 1924

- **FIRST GENERAL OFFICER OF THE MODERN ISRAELI ARMY**
- **ASSISTANT U.S. ATTORNEY, NEW YORK**
- **HELPED DRAFT THE SURRENDER TERMS FOR ITALY AND GERMANY**
- **CHIEF OF WAR CRIMES TRIBUNAL NUREMBERG WAR TRIALS**
- *CAST A GIANT SHADOW* **STARRING KIRK DOUGLAS AND JOHN WAYNE PORTRAYED MARCUS'S LIFE**
- **ONLY PERSON BURIED IN THE WEST POINT CEMETERY WHO FOUGHT UNDER A FOREIGN FLAG**

John Wayne and Kirk Douglas in Cast a Giant Shadow

served on the United States Occupation Staff in Germany. Arguably the single-most important mission of his wartime service – one that undoubtedly highlighted Marcus's quest for justice – was as the Pentagon's War Crimes Division Chief, where he was responsible for selecting hundreds of judges, prosecutors, and other participants for the Nuremberg trials. It was here where Marcus saw firsthand the horrors of the Nazi concentration camps and the toll that the war had taken on the civilian population.[6]

Marcus returned to civilian life in 1947 despite the Army's offer to promote him to Brigadier General. His experiences in World War II and with its aftermath, however, whetted his interest in the November 1947 U.N. decision to partition Palestine and allow the formation of a Jewish nation, particularly in light of the fierce Arab resistance to the resolution. Approached various times by members of the Provisional Jewish government and its underground Army, the Haganah, Marcus was seen as the right man to help build a fledgling Israeli Army

where inexperience left a massive void that only foreign volunteers could fill. So Mickey Marcus volunteered and filled that void.[7] A reluctant United States War Department approved Marcus's decision as long as he hid his identity, which he did under the alias of "Michael Stone."[8]

Arriving in Tel Aviv in January 1948 and offering his advisory services without pay, Marcus had an immediate impact on the Israeli Army. Drawing from his previous wartime and administrative experiences, Marcus helped build an effective Army in a very short period. He wrote doctrine and had manuals translated, he organized training schools for soldiers and officers, and above all, he instilled confidence, discipline, and spirit within the young Army.[9] His efforts immediately won the confidence of the provisional government leadership. So much so that following the Arab siege of Jerusalem and the Israeli declaration as an independent state on May 14, 1948, the provisional government promoted Marcus to Brigadier General on May 28, 1948,

making him Israel's first General and the first General of a Jewish Army since Judah Maccabbee in 164 BCE.[10]

Within two weeks, Marcus's leadership on the Jerusalem front proved a critical factor in breaking the siege and setting the conditions for a United Nations cease fire. Tragically, six hours before the cease fire went into effect on the morning of June 11, 1948, Marcus was shot and killed by an Israeli sentry who mistook him for an enemy, while Marcus was inspecting the defensive perimeter. Thus, Marcus arguably became the last Israeli casualty of the initial fighting on the Jerusalem front,[11] not, however, before the possibility of an independent Israel became a reality. Marcus's body was then flown back to the United States and to West Point, where he had asked to be buried. Numerous dignitaries – Thomas E. Dewey, General Maxwell D. Taylor, Henry Morgenthau, Jr., and Moshe Dayan among them – attended his funeral, providing a further testimonial to the honor, respect, and admiration he gained throughout his life.[12]

In his lifelong pursuit of justice, Mickey Marcus unquestionably lived the West Point code of "Duty, Honor, Country," in addition to other critical Army values not yet codified, such as selfless service and loyalty. With his life's example, Marcus transcended commitment to the nation and applied it to the world. In essence, Marcus took the code of "Duty, Honor, Country," and elevated it to "Duty, Honor, Humanity," truly justifying his epitaph of "A Soldier For All Humanity."

The Colonel Marcus Room at the Thayer Hotel is proudly dedicated by Tawani Enterprises and Squadron Capital.

Mickey Marcus Monument near Abu Ghosh, Israel, where he fell.

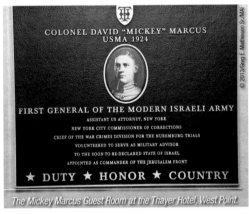

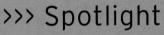

The Mickey Marcus Guest Room at the Thayer Hotel, West Point.

>>> Spotlight

The State of Israel was founded May 14, 1948, when Ben Gurian read the declaration establishing the State of Israel. The United States was the first superpower to recognize the State of Israel the same day. The Arab states of Egypt, Syria, Lebanon, Iraq, and Jordan attacked Israel the next day on May 15, 1948. Mickey Marcus, the first modern General Officer of the newly formed Israeli Army, was killed in the combat zone only four weeks later on June 10, 1948. He is buried at the West Point Cemetery and is the only soldier buried in the cemetery killed fighting under a foreign flag.

Courtesy: State of Israel

Colonel Daniel Mickey Marcus's gravesite at West Point Cemetery.

From 1950 to 1953, the United States tragically lost 36,574 soldiers defending South Korea against North Korean and Chinese Communist forces during the Korean War. In this first major armed conflict of the Cold War, the United States, with the support of the United Nations, affirmed its resolve to support nations facing the threat of communist aggression. Although he was also Killed In Action in Korea, Major Arthur G. Bonifas did not die during the Korean War; rather, he ironically died 23 years later in 1976 after hostilities ended in Korea with an uneasy cease-fire as he was trying to maintain the peace.

While the Korean War culminated in July 1953 with an armistice, it still has never officially ended. North and South Korea remain divided by a tenuous area known as the de-militarized zone (DMZ), separating the two Koreas. United States, South Korean, and North Korean forces still regularly patrol the DMZ, adding to the uneasy tension that has existed since 1953 and still giving the DMZ the aura of a combat zone. Despite this 60-year armistice, the cease-fire has been intermittently broken leading to the deaths of more than 1,000 South Koreans, 600 North Koreans, and nearly 50 American service members in the vigilant defense of South Korea against North Korea.[1] In a visual testament to what American soldiers continue to defend, South Korea has prospered since the war, transitioning from a primarily agrarian society in 1953, to one of the most technologically advanced and economically successful countries in the world. It also stands as a true political success story with a thriving democracy. In contrast, North Korea remains one of the last, isolated bastions of communism in the world, the polar opposite of its southern neighbor in terms of political freedom and economic success. It was in the preservation of these freedoms represented by South Korea for which Bonifas ultimately gave his life 23 years after the war.

Arthur G. Bonifas was born in Omaha, Nebraska, on April 22, 1943, to Raymond and Thelma Bonifas. He entered West Point in July 1962 after a year at Creighton University. At West Point, he was a member of the water polo and scuba clubs. Bonifas met the love

THE CEASE-FIRE HAS BEEN INTERMITTENTLY BROKEN LEADING TO THE DEATHS OF MORE THAN 1,000 SOUTH KOREANS, 600 NORTH KOREANS, AND NEARLY 50 AMERICAN SERVICE MEMBERS IN THE VIGILANT DEFENSE OF SOUTH KOREA AGAINST NORTH KOREA.

of his life, Marcia McGuire, during Plebe year, and they dated throughout his time at West Point. He proposed while still a cadet and gave Marcia a miniature class ring as her engagement ring. Bonifas graduated with the Class of 1966, and he and Marcia were married on April 29, 1967. Their three children

were born at each major stage of their Army career: Beth (who eventually would become and Army nurse) was born during their first assignment at Fort Benning, Georgia; Brian was born while Bonifas attended the Advanced Course at Fort Sill, Oklahoma; and

Megan was born at West Point when Bonifas had returned as a member of the faculty.

After his West Point graduation and commissioning in the Field Artillery, Bonifas attended the Field Artillery Officer Basic course, then graduated from both Airborne and Ranger Schools. In his first assignment at Fort Benning, he commanded a battery in the 2nd Battalion, 10th Field Artillery Regiment. His second assignment took him to the war in Vietnam where he commanded a battery in the 5th

Major Arthur Bonifas, USMA 1966

- KILLED IN ACTION IN THE DEMILITARIZED ZONE (DMZ) IN KOREA
- CAMP BONIFAS KOREA NAMED IN HIS HONOR
- BATTERY COMMANDER, VIETNAM WAR
- MASTER'S OF SCIENCE, SYRACUSE UNIVERSITY
- WEST POINT PROFESSOR OF MATHEMATICS

U.S. soldiers lay a wreath at the Barrett-Bonifas Ceremony, where they were murdered.

Photo: AP

Battalion, 16th Field Artillery Regiment, then served as that battalion's adjutant (S-1). After completing his tour in Vietnam, he returned to attend graduate school, where he received a master's degree at Syracuse University, and was then assigned to West Point, where he served as a professor in the Mathematics Department. He then deployed in 1975 on his final and fateful assignment as an Officer in the United Nations Command along the DMZ in South Korea.

Captain Bonifas was one of the millions of Americans who has served in South Korea since the cease-fire of 1953 in order to ensure that South Korea remains free. In 1976, he was assigned as a Company Commander at the Joint Security Agency Panmunjom, South Korea, and was only three days away from returning to his family in the United States. His bags were already packed and his wife was preparing his homecoming party. As he was transitioning with the Inbound Commander, an incident

occurred on August 18, 1976, that became an international crisis. The incident involved a confrontation between North Korean and United Nations forces regarding a single Normandy poplar tree. U.N. forces wanted the tree pruned because it obscured the U.N. observers' view of the Bridge of No Return in the DMZ. Captain Bonifas and another officer, First Lieutenant Mark T. Barrett, were supervising a joint U.S.–South Korean detail to prune the tree when North Korean soldiers entered the DMZ and confronted Bonifas's detail. In an event caught on film, a North Korean Officer with a much larger force of North Korean soldiers attacked Bonifas and his group from behind with axes and clubs. Bonifas was unable to defend himself as he was beaten to death without provocation. The North Koreans then dragged Lieutenant Barrett into a ravine where they executed him. Along with the murders of Bonifas and Barrett, the incident resulted in the injury to four United States and five South Korean soldiers. This incident also nearly escalated

into a full-scale war as United States forces were placed on high alert in one of the most tense situations of the Cold War. In a symbolic response, General Richard G. Stilwell, 8th Army Commander in Korea, authorized a show of force in the DMZ by having the entire tree removed by a large combat force. The removal occurred without incident and U.S.–North Korean tensions decreased shortly afterward.[2]

At the time of his death, Bonifas was on the promotion list and was promoted posthumously to the rank of Major while being added to the list of the Class of 1966 graduates who gave their lives in service to the nation. The Class of 1966 suffered the highest casualty rate of any West Point class to serve in Vietnam with 30 of its members being Killed In Action. Although not killed in Vietnam, Bonifas is the only Class of 1966 graduate Killed In Action outside of Vietnam. As a result of this tragic event, Marcia Bonifas was suddenly widowed with three children. She

eventually raised them in Colorado Springs and in the suburbs of Washington, D.C., where she pursued a career in assisting soldiers and their families with Tricare. Pulitzer Prize–winning journalist, historian, and author Rick Atkinson documented the Bonifas story, along with the rest of the West Point Class of 1966, in his book *The Long Gray Line*.[3]

Bonifas was standing vigilantly at his post while carrying out his duty in South Korea as so many others have done for the past 60 years when enemy forces killed him. He returned home and was laid to rest in the West Point Cemetery. The base where Major Bonifas and Lieutenant Barrett were killed is now named "Camp Bonifas" in his honor, and each year, on August 18th, there is a memorial ceremony that honors their sacrifice to the nation.

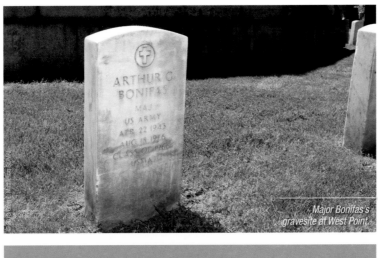

Major Bonifas's gravesite at West Point.

>>> Spotlight

Camp Bonifas, South Korea was the base camp of the U.N. Command Security Force-Joint Security Area (UNCSF-JSA), which transferred control to the South Korean Army in 2004. It was originally named Camp Kitty Hawk but was renamed Camp Bonifas in 1986, 10 years after Captain Arthur Bonifas was killed along the DMZ. For more than half a century, the UNCSF-JSA was the most forward deployed unit in the world standing against communist forces.

Captain Arthur Bonifas's official photo.

Photo: AP

Nick Rowe is a legend in the United States Army Special Forces community. He was born in McAllen, Texas, on February 8, 1938, and entered West Point in 1956 as a member of the Class of 1960. In 1963, Rowe was captured by Viet Cong forces and spent five years as a Prisoner of War before escaping. Twenty years later, communist insurgents in the Philippines assassinated him in 1989, but his legacy endures to this day.[2] All Special

Forces soldiers are taught lessons from Rowe's personal experiences through the training program that he established after escaping captivity. Appropriately, many of these lessons are taught at Fort Bragg, North Carolina's Rowe Training Facility. He valiantly fought communism, first in the 1960s in Vietnam and then in the Philippines in the 1980s, where he made the ultimate sacrifice for his country.

After graduating from West Point in 1960,

Rowe was commissioned in the Field Artillery and assigned to the 82nd Airborne Division at Fort Bragg. He joined the Special Forces and arrived in Vietnam in 1963 as the Executive Officer of Detachment A-23, 5th Special Forces Group, which was commanded by Captain Humbert "Rocky" Versace (USMA 1959). On October 29, 1963, after three months in country working with South Vietnamese forces, his base was attacked and overrun by a superior

enemy force. First Lieutenant Rowe, Captain Versace, and Sergeant First Class Dan Pitzer were taken prisoner. For five years, Rowe was fed minimal rations – resorting to catching and eating rats and insects while exercising other survival techniques that he learned out of necessity. Captain Versace, the Ranking Officer, bravely resisted his captors and refused to break under intense torture until he was executed by his captors in September 1965. Sergeant First Class

Colonel James Nicholas "Nick" Rowe, USMA 1960

- **DEVELOPED THE SURVIVAL, EVASION, RESISTANCE, AND ESCAPE (SERE) COURSE AT FORT BRAGG, NORTH CAROLINA**
- **CHIEF OF THE ARMY DIVISION OF THE JOINT U.S. MILITARY ADVISORY GROUP (JUSMAG)**
- **ASSASSINATED BY COMMUNIST INSURGENTS IN THE PHILIPPINES, 1989**
- **SURVIVED FIVE YEARS AS A PRISONER OF WAR IN VIETNAM AND SUCCESSFULLY ESCAPED**
- **SILVER STAR, BRONZE STAR WITH VALOR (TWO), PURPLE HEART (TWO)**
- **BURIED AT ARLINGTON NATIONAL CEMETERY**

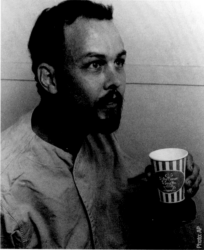

Rowe standing next to a mock-up of his cage in Vietnam.

>>> Spotlight

FIVE YEARS TO FREEDOM

A Young American's Own Story of Defiance, Survival and Courageous Escape from the Viet Cong After More Than Five Years as a Prisoner of War.

Courtesy: James N. Rowe

Five Years to Freedom was written by Rowe in 1971 about his five years as a Prisoner of War in Vietnam. It is required reading for students and instructors at Survival, Evasion, Resistance, and Escape School.

Pitzer survived four years of horrible conditions before he was released back to United States forces in 1967.

Rowe made several attempts to escape. Finally, on New Year's Eve day, December 31, 1968, his captors ordered his execution as they had done to Captain Versace previously. During a B-52 carpet-bombing mission near the area where Rowe was being held, however, Rowe took advantage of the chaos of the bombing, overpowered

Rowe with his parents at his homecoming parade in Texas.

Rowe being interviewed after his escape from a Prisoner of War camp, 1969.

his captors, and fled to an opening where United States helicopter pilots spotted him and rescued him. Rowe and Versace were each awarded the Silver Star for their actions. Rowe's citation reads:

"Major James N. Rowe, Artillery, United States Army, distinguished himself by outstanding gallantry in action on 31 December 1968 while a prisoner of the Viet Cong in the U Minh Forest of South Vietnam. During the period 22 to 31 December 1968, after more than five years in Viet Cong prison camps, Major Rowe was forced by his captors to move at least twice daily to avoid friendly air strikes. On 31 December at approximately 0900 hours, two helicopter gunships began firing into an area approximately 300 meters from his location. The guard detail consisted of one Viet Cong cadreman and five guards, one of whom was assigned to remain with Major Rowe at all times. The guard detail, while monitoring a radio, learned that South Vietnamese Infantrymen were searching the terrain nearby. Becoming frightened, the guard moved Major Rowe into a large field of reeds, hoping to evade the Infantry force. Major Rowe realized that if he were to escape, he must first get away from some of his guards, so he tricked them into splitting into smaller groups in order to exfiltrate the area. Major Rowe persuaded his one remaining guard that they were being surrounded and kept him moving in a circle through the dense underbrush. While doing so, Major Rowe was able to remove the magazine from the weapon slung across his guard's back. Finding a club, he overpowered the guard, knocking him unconscious, seized his radio, and moved 200 meters into a grassy area. At great personal risk he quickly cleared a section and signaled one of the circling helicopters which landed and picked him up. His first action after rescue was to request permission to re-enter the area with combat troops and to continue the fight based upon his intimate knowledge of the area. Major Rowe's burning determination to escape, undiminished after five years of intimidation and deprivation, his clearheadedness in formulating an effective plan, and his audacity in executing it successfully, reflect the highest credit on his professionalism and extraordinary courage and are in keeping with the highest traditions of the military service."[3]

Upon his return to the United States, Rowe met with President Richard Nixon at the White House and told of his story and that

of Captain Versace. The *Washington Post* documented the meeting with President Nixon years later:

"The President wasn't prepared – I don't think anyone was – for what we were about to hear," said retired Colonel Ray Nutter, an Army Congressional liaison Officer who accompanied Rowe to the meeting. Rowe spoke for more than an hour, describing the prisoners' treatment and Versace's resistance. When it ended, Nixon, visibly moved, stood and hugged Rowe, Nutter said. Rowe told the President that Versace deserved the Medal of Honor. Nixon turned and told the liaison Officers to 'make damn sure' it happened."[4]

Despite Nixon's verbal endorsement, Rowe's Medal of Honor nomination for Captain Versace was downgraded to a Silver Star.

ON NEW YEAR'S EVE 1968, AFTER MORE THAN FIVE YEARS AS A PRISONER OF WAR, ROWE OVERPOWERED A VIET CONG GUARD AND ESCAPED.

In 1971, Rowe published the book, *Five Years to Freedom*, recounting his ordeal in the jungles of Vietnam and also documenting Versace's extraordinary leadership and heroism in the POW camp. Although Rowe retired from the Army in 1978, he continued to work diligently, but unsuccessfully, to have Captain Versace's award upgraded to the Medal of Honor for his valor.

In 1981, Rowe returned to active duty as a Lieutenant Colonel. At that time, the United States Army Special Forces School at Fort Bragg also recognized the need to establish a program teaching Survival, Evasion, Resistance, and Escape (SERE) techniques – and there was no better officer to lead the development of this program than Rowe. Based on his own personal experiences, as well as those of Sergeant First Class Pitzer, who joined Rowe as a civilian contractor at the school, they developed a world-class program to prepare soldiers for possible capture so they would not have to learn survival techniques "on the job" as Rowe, Pitzer, and Versace had been forced to do as prisoners.

In April 1987, Special Forces became an independent officer branch and Rowe

traded in his crossed cannons of the Field Artillery for the new Special Forces Branch insignia of the crossed arrows. Rowe was promoted to Colonel and assigned to the Philippines as the Chief of the Army Division of the Joint United States Military Advisory Group (JUSMAG). In this capacity, he was charged with providing counterinsurgency training for the Armed Forces of the Philippines who were fighting against communist forces under the New People's Army (NPA).

While driving to work in Manila in an armored limousine, NPA insurgents attacked Colonel Rowe's vehicle. Several rounds passed through a small vent, hit Colonel Rowe in the head, and killed him instantly. He became the first officer Killed In Action within the new Special Forces Branch.[5]

Rowe was buried on May 2, 1989, in Section 48 of Arlington National Cemetery. Inscribed on his gravestone at Arlington National Cemetery are the words from a poem he wrote in 1964 while in captivity:

So look up ahead at times to come,

despair is not for us.

We have a world and more to see,

while this remains behind.[6]

The SERE school he developed at Fort Bragg now bears his name: the Rowe Training Facility. His legacy lives on through the lessons that will help soldiers survive in combat and captivity against future enemies of the United States. The obstacle course at Camp Mackall, a sub-post of Fort Bragg, is one of the most difficult courses in the Army and is referred to as the "Nasty Nick" in his honor.[7]

Rowe's initial efforts to recognize his fellow West Point graduate and late commander's valor were not in vain. On July 8, 2002, President George W. Bush awarded Captain Rocky Versace's family with the Medal of Honor posthumously for the valor and sacrifice that cost Versace his life in Vietnam, but whose memory and actions were kept alive by Rowe and documented in *Five Years to Freedom*.

Written by: Lieutenant Colonel Todd Gile (USA, Retired), USMA 1986.

Lieutenant Doug Gurian in dress blues.

Doug and Tyler, Fire Island, 2000.

Susan and Doug Gurian's wedding in 1992.

Doug Gurian, USMA 1986

- KILLED BY TERRORISTS IN THE WORLD TRADE CENTER, SEPTEMBER 11, 2001
- ARMY BASEBALL PLAYER, PITCHER
- AIR DEFENSE ARTILLERY OFFICER

On September 11, 2001, Doug Gurian, age 38, said good-bye to his wife, Susan, and children, Tyler (7) and Eva (4), and left his home in Tenafly, New Jersey, bound for a technology conference at Windows on the World, the famous restaurant on the top two floors of the North Tower of the World Trade Center.

Gurian had previously worked for Cantor Fitzgerald in the World Trade Center but had recently changed jobs and was working in Midtown for a firm called Radianz. As fate would have it, he was returning to the North Tower for the conference.

Gurian was born and raised in New York City and attended Horace Mann School. He entered West Point in 1982. At 6 foot 1 inch, with a 90-mile-per-hour fastball, he was a star pitcher on the Army baseball team. He was well liked and made lifelong friends. Upon graduation, he chose the Air Defense Artillery Branch and served a tour in Germany before leaving the Army in

1990. He had met Susan on a blind date in 1990 and they married in 1992. They were blessed with two healthy children and were living the life of the all-American family with a home in the suburbs and summer vacations on Fire Island.

That morning, terrorists hijacked four commercial airplanes. Two crashed into the World Trade Centers, one into the Pentagon, and another into a field in Pennsylvania. Gurian and 2,996 other innocent individuals had their lives cut short by these unspeakable acts of terrorism. Gurian was the first member of the Long Gray Line to die in the War on Terror, but he would not be the last.

President George W. Bush, in response to these unprecedented and unprovoked attacks, ordered immediate military action. Thus began a long war called Operation Enduring Freedom in Afghanistan and elsewhere. Many soldiers and West Point graduates made the ultimate sacrifice.

Gurian's friend and classmate, Colonel John McHugh, age 48, who would be the highest-ranking West Point graduate killed by enemy forces, died from injuries received from a Taliban car bomb in 2010.

The New York Times published obituaries for every one of the victims of 9/11. The last paragraph of Gurian's obituary read, "Mr. Gurian loved his children, Tyler (7) and Eva (4), most of all, his wife said. Eva is too

GURIAN AND 2,996 OTHER INNOCENT INDIVIDUALS HAD THEIR LIVES CUT SHORT BY THESE UNSPEAKABLE ACTS OF TERRORISM. GURIAN WAS THE FIRST MEMBER OF THE LONG GRAY LINE TO DIE IN THE WAR ON TERROR, BUT HE WOULD NOT BE THE LAST.

young to understand what happened to her Dad, but Tyler told his mother, 'I just don't feel I'll ever be happy again.'"

On the 10th anniversary of 9/11 in 2011, Gurian's family, classmates, and loved ones still felt the pain of his loss, while they also remembered and celebrated his life.

Gurian and Susan's little girl, Eva, is now 14 and attending high school. Her post on Facebook sent as "Dear Daddy" on September 11, 2011, went viral around the country and would speak for the nation as we mourned the victims and remembered their families. He would certainly be proud of her.

"Dear Daddy,

So much has happened since you've been gone. I went to EMS for middle school, just like you did, and I won a scholastic award for my essay about you. I started high school a few days ago. I go to Holy

Firefighters at the World Trade Center, September 12, 2001.

>>> Spotlight

On September 11, 2001, terrorists hijacked four aircraft and used them to attack the World Trade Centers and the Pentagon. Doug Gurian and thousands of other innocent people were murdered. Terrorists had been attacking the United States in the Middle East, Africa, and in the United States for three decades, culminating in the catastrophic attacks of September 11, 2001. After 9/11 the United States would attack terrorists in their staging areas of Afghanistan and then preemptively attack Iraq after dictator Saddam Hussein failed to comply with United Nations's resolutions. Gurian's friends and classmates would lead soldiers around the world after 9/11 in uniform, in United States agencies, and as contractors supporting the military.

Gurian wedding party (left to right): Mike Spingler, Doug Gurian, Dave Urban, Scott Poirer, Jim Belanger, Dan Charron, and John Olvey (died December 2011).

Angels, but you know that because you were there with me on my first day. I made it into mostly high honors or honors classes. I also run cross-country now, just like mommy, and I'm very strong, just like you. We still go skiing in Utah a lot, just like you taught me, although I've become a better skier than I was when I was little, but you already know that. I have a lot of great friends, too. I know that you would love them, and they would love you, too, if they ever get the chance to meet you. We still spend a lot of time on Fire Island and around the baseball field, on which you were one of the greatest players ever. We recently had the over/under softball game in honor of you and one of your best friends, Doug Gardner. I hope you enjoyed watching the game and watching the overs win. Do you remember the ocean on Fire Island? Do you miss it? I usually don't go in because it scares me a little bit, but every time I see it, I think of you. I know

how much you loved it.

I miss every moment I ever spent with you. Ten years later, the pain doesn't go away, it doesn't lessen, it doesn't fade. It still hurts like it was yesterday. Because I was so young, I don't remember everything. From what I hear, you were the greatest father, and person, anyone could ever ask for. I've heard just about every story of you out there, and just about every one made me laugh. They say I look so much like you, and I could not be prouder. I still try to make you proud of me every day, and I know you're always with me every step I take. I miss you and think about you each and every day. Everywhere I go, something or someone reminds me of you, and it brightens my day a little bit. They say you're in a good place now, with angels watching over you, and you're my angel. I know you would be proud of me. I know you don't want me

to cry, Daddy. But sometimes I just can't help it. My life won't ever be the same. I won't ever be able to move on, but I know that I can move forward, and that will make all the difference. That is what will make you proud.

Love, your little girl"

Rest in peace, Doug.

Tyler and Eva Gurian.

Hollywood has typically depicted military leaders as stone-faced, steely eyed men who never turn off the switch from high-intensity to light-hearted and compassionate.

Apparently, Hollywood never met Colonel John McHugh.

McHugh, a member of West Point's Class of 1986, was one of the highest-ranking officers to lose his life in the war in Afghanistan when a suicide bomber in a pickup truck killed McHugh and 18 others on May 18, 2010. To the end, McHugh was described as friendly, full of love and laughter, the antithesis of the stereotypical Army Officer.

"What I remember about Johnny Mac is that smiling face," recalls Bob Eisinminger, West Point Class of 1988. "Don't get me wrong, he knew when he had to get serious when guys needed to be put in line, but more than anything, I remember his smile."

Eisinminger not only knew McHugh as his superior at West Point; he knew him as the goalkeeper and Captain of the Army soccer team. The goalkeeper is not only a soccer team's last line of defense; he's the man charged with organizing the players in front of him, barking at them about positioning, imploring them and, at times, chastising them. It is hard enough for the keeper of an ordinary soccer team to handle this task, but to take on this job while playing behind future military officers requires something extra.

"John was named Captain in the spring of 1985, as he finished up junior year," says Aaron Kuzemka, a defender from the Class of 1988. "To that point in his career, he'd never even been the starting keeper, but it was a no-brainer that he be our Captain based on his work ethic, enthusiasm, and the respect he had from everyone on the team. I can still hear his voice, telling us to mark our men tighter or to push up the field. He wasn't afraid to get in our face during games, but then on the bus ride home or in the locker room, he'd be smiling, making us all laugh about something that happened during the game."

That McHugh was able to be a leader among leaders surprised no one who grew up with him. At James Caldwell High School in Caldwell, New Jersey, McHugh was not only the goalkeeper on a team that made it to the state finals; he was the catcher on a baseball team that won the prestigious Greater Newark Tournament. He was also known as an altar boy at St. Aloysius Church and diligent caddie at Essex Fells Country Club.

"MY DAD WOULD HAVE BEEN JUST AS HONORED TO KNOW OUR U.S. NATIONAL TEAM UNDERSTANDS THAT THE REASON THEY GET TO STAY ON THE FIELD IS BECAUSE OF PEOPLE LIKE HIM," SAID KELLY MCHUGH.

"The play that brings it all together for me occurred in his freshman year in high school," says McHugh's older brother, Jim. "John was playing at perennial baseball powerhouse Seton Hall Prep in ninth grade. There was a play at the plate and the runner going home collided with John, trying to dislodge the ball. The runner's helmet hit John just below the eye, opening quite a gash on his left cheek. John held onto the ball and the runner was called out. Bleeding from the cut on his face, John handed the ball back to the umpire and walked off the field, not saying a word. That play defined the type of leader he was."

In his hometown, everyone knew "Mac," the freckle-faced clean-cut kid who was always looking for a game, always ready to round up the gang and play ball.

"Whether in the classroom, on the playing field, or in more intimate settings with his many friends," said childhood friend Tom Beusse, now the publisher of *USA Today*. "We marveled at his constant energy, his persistent smile, his infectious laugh, his unmatched work ethic, and his incredible abil-

Colonel John McHugh, USMA 1986

- **KILLED IN ACTION, AFGHANISTAN, 2010**
- **ARMY SOCCER, CAPTAIN AND GOALIE**
- **ARMY UH-60 BLACK HAWK PILOT**
- **COMMANDER 1ST BATTALION, 11TH AVIATION REGIMENT**

The McHugh Family (left to right): Kristen, Kelly, Colonel McHugh, Maggie, Connie, David, Michael, and his wife, Angela, in 2008.

ity to lead. He had unwavering principles."

Discussions with then–West Point soccer coach Joe Chiavaro started McHugh's interest in attending West Point and led to the Honorable Joseph Minish from New Jersey recommending McHugh's appointment. He entered the Long Gray Line the summer of 1982. He entered West Point with little appreciation of military history but once he got there, he was hooked. The code of "Duty, Honor, and Country" was a similar philosophy to the team play he embraced as a soccer and baseball player. The worst part of his experience at West Point was probably the last week or so of basic training the summer of 1982.

"He got over it once soccer started," recalls classmate Jim DiOrio, who had grown up playing American Legion baseball with McHugh for Caldwell Post 185. "And soon after that, he was the go-to guy for a lot of our class. I had a moment early on where I was questioning myself, and he said to me, quietly, 'Meet me later at the chapel.' When we got there, he said he sensed I was

lacking confidence. He said, 'Look around, Jimmy. You belong here. You are meant to be here.' I never questioned myself again."

A year after his graduation from West Point, McHugh married Connie Jensen, a high-school classmate he had begun dating while at West Point. Together they had five children, a son followed by three daughters and one more son. A few months before his life was taken in Afghanistan, McHugh had become a grandfather. Having grown up in a close-knit family of five children, McHugh was determined to never let his career in the Army interfere with his number-one priority, which was to be a devoted husband and father.

McHugh was a helicopter pilot originally assigned to the Army aviation school at Fort Rucker, Alabama. As part of the VII Corps, 2nd Armored Cavalry Regiment, McHugh's unit helped block the return of the Republican Guard to Baghdad during Operation Desert Storm. He was stationed in Germany twice, as well as at 4th Infantry Division, Fort Carson, Colorado; and at Fort

Irwin, California; Fort Leavenworth, Kansas; and at the Army War College in Carlisle, Pennsylvania. He commanded the 1st Battalion, 11th Aviation Regiment at Fort Rucker, Alabama. Along the way, he coached his kids in soccer and told his daughter, Kelly, once he retired from the Army, he would be a full-time coach.

"As a coach, he was really quiet," said Kelly. "He'd never yell, but you knew what he expected from you. Everyone he ever coached loved having him as a coach – all my friends would list him as their favorite."

Shortly before he got the call to return to Afghanistan on a transitional mission, McHugh took a goal-keeping class, pushing his 47-year-old body to the limit for a few days. He joked with friends that he could barely walk after the course, but it was worth it. He was gearing up to watch the United States national team play in the 2010 World Cup as the team was coached by Bob Bradley, a family friend from New Jersey.

When McHugh's life was taken, Bradley

spoke to his team about the Colonel, telling them, "You think what it means to represent your country, you think about obviously how important the soccer is, but how it's not even close to what it means to be somewhere else in the world defending everything."

Said Kelly, "My dad would have been just as honored to know our United States national team understands that the reason they get to stay on the field is because of people like him."

In eulogizing her dad, Kelly said, "There are four things my dad loved: God, his family and friends, his country, and soccer."

Fittingly, the congregation smiled in McHugh's honor.

Written by: Jeff Bradley.

Army Soccer Captain Cadet John McHugh, 1985.

McHugh and son, David, July 4, 2009.

Colonel McHugh with wife, Connie, in Carlisle, Pennsylvania, after receiving the MOAA Writing Award.

>>> Spotlight

JOHNNY MAC MEMORIAL FOUNDATION

Since 2011, the Johnny McHugh Foundation has hosted an annual May golf tournament as a memorial to "Johnny Mac" and as a gathering for all of those who loved him so much.

Second Lieutenant Donnie Tillar's Flight School photo.

Tillar, age 13, fishing with his grandfather.

DONALDSON
PRESTON
TILLAR, II

FIRST LIEUTENANT
1ST INFANTRY DIVISION (MEC
CLASS OF 1988
BORN MAY 13, 1965

KILLED IN ACTION
FEBRUARY 27, 1991
WHEN HIS UH-60 BLACKHA
HELICOPTER WAS SHOT DO
OVER IRAQ DURING
OPERATION DESERT STOR

ERECTED BY HIS CLASSMA

Plaque in Cullum Hall dedicated by his classmates.

First Lieutenant Donaldson P. Tillar, III, USMA 1988

- **UH-60 BLACK HAWK PILOT**
- **KILLED IN ACTION, OPERATION DESERT STORM**
- **ARMY LACROSSE PLAYER**
- **FIRST COACH OF KANSAS STATE UNIVERSITY LACROSSE TEAM**
- **DONNIE TILLAR LACROSSE CLASSIC HELD AT KANSAS STATE UNIVERSITY ANNUALLY IN HIS HONOR**

Donaldson (Donnie to his family and friends) Tillar is the son of Colonel (USA, Retired) and Mrs. Donaldson P. Tillar, Jr., (USMA 1959) and the grandson of Mr. and Mrs. Donaldson P. Tillar of Emporia, Virginia. As an "Army brat," he was born at Fort Sill, Oklahoma, and lived in Torrance, California; Montgomery, Alabama; Quantico, Virginia; Honolulu, Hawaii; Springfield, Virginia; and West Point, New York. He graduated from James I O'Neill High School in Highland Falls, New York, and attended Virginia Tech, as well as West Point. At West Point, he was a varsity lacrosse player and a dean's list cadet.

Tillar graduated from the Academy in 1988 after returning in 1987 from a year's study and cadetship at Virginia Tech and was commissioned into the Aviation Branch. Upon completion of the Officer Basic Course, Flight School, and Black Hawk helicopter qualification at Fort Rucker, Alabama, he reported for duty in the 1st Infantry Division (The Big Red One) at Fort Riley, Kansas. He was assigned duties as the division's quick-fix Platoon Leader and, later, Company Executive Officer. During this assignment, Tillar also coached the Kansas State University lacrosse club, establishing a "tradition," where former Army lacrosse players stationed at Fort Riley, coach lacrosse at Kansas State.

Tillar was killed in a helicopter crash, along with eight other soldiers, due to enemy anti-aircraft fire in Iraq on the last day of Operation Desert Storm. His body was recovered and returned to the United States in March 1991. He was buried, next to his grandfather, with full military honors in the cemetery in Emporia, Virginia, on March 16, 1991. Decorations for his brief service include the Purple Heart, Bronze Star, and Air Medal. He is survived by his parents and two sisters, Katherine Elizabeth and

>>> Spotlight

This photo of Tillar and several of his best friends at Dave Ebrecht's wedding was taken at Trophy Point, West Point.

First Lieutenant Tillar was posthumously awarded the Bronze Star Medal and Purple Heart.

Tillar in the desert during Operation Desert Storm.

Army lacrosse team.

as we drove more than 100 miles back to Fort Rucker, we could not help but feel that we had forgotten something. Unfortunately, we forgot Donnie. Knowing that it would take him hours to hitch a ride home, we waited in fear that he was going to whip our hides. And he did. But then he laughed. He laughed because what was important to him was not our gross mistake, but our friendships. Friendships that this, and other more trying situations, strengthened instead of weakened.

A product of his happiness was the abundant sense of pride and patriotism that was uniquely Donnie's. No one was prouder of what they did than Donnie. We teased him, as good friends always do, but deep inside we were all just a little bit envious. His selfless service and devotion to duty were always the example for us to follow. Had Donnie known what would happen to him, he would have gone anyway, because that is how strongly he believed in what he was doing.

HAD DONNIE KNOWN WHAT WOULD HAPPEN TO HIM, HE WOULD HAVE GONE ANYWAY.

There is nothing that I, or anyone else, can say to ease our sadness. The healing will come from within ourselves. It comes from all the great memories and it comes from encouraging some of Donnie's kindness, enthusiasm, and love into our own lives. Do not worry, Donnie; you will continue to inspire us, and you will remain in our hearts forever."

Frances Leilani.

During funeral services at the First Presbyterian Church of Emporia, Tillar's classmate and flight school roommate, Sean Deller (USMA 1988), rose and delivered the following eulogy:

"It is often said that someone 'lived life to the fullest,' but never was it more appropriate than now. However Donnie touched the lives of his family and friends, he inevitably left that impression. It takes a special kind of person to do that, and it takes a very fortunate person to have the loving family, friends, and talent to make it possible. Donnie had all that, and he appreciated it. He was grateful because he knew that there were too many people in the world whose lives would never be as happy as his.

And happy he was. Our photo albums are full of Donnie's smiling pictures. His list of achievements is long, but what really matters is the happiness, the happiness that

he lived off of and then returned to us in greater amounts than he took. He taught us how to water ski, how to ride a motorcycle, how to play lacrosse and soccer. He encouraged us to live.

Donnie was the Captain of our weekly ritual to pick a place on the map and bring a party to it. Every weekend, he led the exodus from West Point or Fort Rucker or Fort Riley to go somewhere to enjoy old friends and make new ones. After one enjoyable weekend,

Paul John Finken and twin brother, Peter, were born on July 31, 1966, the youngest of 10 children to Edna and Charles Finken in the Midwestern farm town of Manning, Iowa. In this family, Finken learned and lived principles he modeled throughout his life: hard work, perseverance, respect for others, and most of all, love. During his youth, Finken developed his love for life, family, friends, and the outdoors in everything he did – delivering papers, doing farmwork, mowing lawns, and shoveling snow.

As a high-school student athlete, Finken wrestled varsity for four years and stayed in shape by running cross-country. On weekends, he worked for his father's business or his community. In Boy Scouts, he learned leadership and earned the rank of Eagle Scout. Graduating from Harlan High School in 1984, his enrollment into West Point was delayed one year as he obtained a medical waiver for his limited hearing – a result of his avid passion, pheasant hunting on his father's farm. After attending Iowa State University,

his persistence paid off and he entered USMA in 1985. He made the West Point wrestling team as a walk-on. Ever the prankster, Finken consistently found new ways to make fun out of the mundane. Between his studies, athletics, and military training, he met his future wife and lifelong love, Jackie. They courted and were married in Earling, Iowa, on October 10, 1992.

Graduating in May 1989 and commissioned Infantry, Finken completed Ranger and Air Assault School prior to his first duty assign-

ment in Fairbanks, Alaska. This initial assignment fueled his passion for the outdoors as he hunted and fished whenever possible in the Alaskan wilderness.

He started his life as a husband and father, the same he way lived his youth – committed to loving his family and respecting all. His military journey took him to Europe, where he commanded a company in the Bosnian/ Herzegovinian conflict. After obtaining a master's degree in Operations Research from the Naval Post-Graduate School, his next

Lieutenant Colonel Paul John Finken, USMA 1989

- KILLED IN ACTION, IRAQ WAR
- WEST POINT WRESTLING TEAM
- RANGER, AIRBORNE, AIR ASSAULT, AND PATHFINDER QUALIFIED
- MILITARY IN TRANSITION TRAINING COMMANDER, 101ST AIRBORNE DIVISION
- BRONZE STAR (TWO), PURPLE HEART, COMBAT INFANTRYMAN BADGE, EXPERT INFANTRY BADGE
- TRADOC ANALYSIS CENTER (TRAC) LIEUTENANT COLONEL FINKEN MEMORIAL AWARD ESTABLISHED IN 2009
- BOY SCOUTS OF AMERICA, EAGLE SCOUT

The Finken family.

>>> Spotlight

In 2009, the United States Army Training and Doctrine Command Analysis Center established the Lieutenant Colonel Paul Finken memorial award in his honor. Lieutenant Colonel Finken was a TRAC combat analyst. The annual award recognizes the TRAC military officer who best embodies the exemplary analytic skills, commitment to excellence, selfless service, and support to the community, in the spirit set by Lieutenant Colonel Finken. This was one of two academic institutions (Iowa State University is the other) that honored Lieutenant Colonel Finken for his service and commitment to his country with lasting memorials to his selfless leadership.

stop was to Fort Leavenworth, Kansas. His last military assignment was with the 101st Airborne Division.

After serving in various units and roles within the 101st Battalion Executive Officer and then Battalion Adjutant (S-3), Finken's final assignment was to the Headquarters and Headquarters Company, 506th Infantry Regiment. Again, Finken overcame adversity, being tasked to lead a "newly designed unit" – a Military Transition Team (or MiTT) whose mission was training the Iraqi Army. Only months before their scheduled deploy-ment and initially only supplied with a desk, Finken dug deep and leveraged his lifelong principles: hard work, perseverance, and respect for others. He interviewed all possible soldiers being sent his way, ensured they were a fit for his team, and challenged them. Most importantly, he trained and developed them through his words and actions on these principles. He focused on physical, mental, and military training – crucial elements to bring soldiers home safe. He conducted plyo-metric and fitness training while in theater (achieving a personal fitness best only weeks before his death by benching 250 pounds), sought out extra firearms ranges before and during deployment so everyone could handle weapons in the face of enemy fire. This final assignment exemplified Finken's strong leadership abilities and maybe his greatest achievement, taking soldiers and equip-ments from various units throughout the division (similar to a real-life version of the *Dirty Dozen* movie), training, developing, and leading them into a cohesive combat team to train Iraqi's military (officers and enlisted) in military fundamentals: discipline, hard work, training, and respect.

During Finken's last mission and one week before his scheduled return home, a roadside bomb (Improvised Explosive Device) killed him, Staff Sergeant Joseph A. Gage, 28, of Modesto, California; and Lieutenant Colonel Eric J. Kruger, 40, of Garland, Texas.

Finken's love returned to him in death through the thousands who came and paid him respect in his hometown. The Captain of the Nebraska Patriot Guard Riders, Dave "DC" Charles, who escorted Finken throughout his burial, wrote in an article to the editor of the *Harlan Tribune* his thoughts entitled "Hero":

"…When I was growing up, it was instilled in me what great men were. They were conquerors, artists, philosophers, inventors, and the like that long after they were gone, their memory lived on with their accomplish-ments. As time went on in my life, these things gradually changed…this weekend… those prerequisites for greatness…taught to me in a town much like your own… were shattered.

Myself and a baker's dozen of others escorted Lieutenant Colonel Finken home from Omaha's airport Thursday evening. Something told me I should see this man home completely and stayed for the next two days to honor him during visitations and his funeral. During those eight hours Friday and the funeral on Saturday, what I witnessed changed my definition of greatness. I watched hundreds of people stream by me on both of those days, each with a mission of their own…To pay their last respects and to say goodbye to someone special. In each of those faces I saw someone touched, literally touched by the actions and life of this man. In all of my missions, over all of the miles, I can honestly say, I have never experienced this sense of loss. In a town of 450ish, I saw hundreds waiting for Finken's arrival Friday evening to the church on the Earling, Iowa, hillside. Upon arrival, and his being taken into the church (where he was baptized, married, and his daughters baptized), they stood, in the freezing cold, absolutely silent, to enter the church. As the first group waited to enter, you could have heard a pin drop on that frosty night, even though we were outside. Not a whisper, not even a baby crying. They were all focused on one thing: Paul J. Finken.

This was when my mind changed about greatness. Those things taught to me, are forever erased as a requirements for such a distinction. You see, I never knew George Washington, or Aristotle, or an Emperor, and you know I didn't even know Finken before Friday. But through the thousands of eyes, the words, the tears, and my purely positive interaction with those in this small Iowa town, he has touched me, as well. I have to think just how much he would have affected me had I truly known him. This is my new threshold for my 'greatness' pedestal. For Earling, Iowa, you have your own hero, one who has changed the lives of many, well past your own. Be proud, be very proud. I am honored to have been among those asked to pay our respects and to honor this great man."

PAUL'S FUNERAL SERVICE OCCURRED ON THE 11TH HOUR, 11TH DAY, AND 11TH MONTH IN 2006 – VETERAN'S DAY.

Finken's funeral service occurred on the 11th hour, 11th day, and 11th month in 2006 – Veteran's Day. Finken – a father, husband, brother, classmate, soldier, friend, and leader – was buried next to parents Charles and Edna, and brother John. Finken's siblings and families were all present: Steve, Alan, Rich, Dave, Jean, Mark, Joan, and Peter – shar-ing tears and laughs while recalling times he made them smile. Many others came – elementary, high school, and West Point classmates; soldiers he served with and lead; neighbors and friends – each honoring him in their own personal way for his service and dedication to country.

Most importantly, Finken's love for life, friends, and family are visible in life's supreme treasures he was responsible for: his devoted wife, Jackie, and three beautiful daughters, Emilie, Caroline, and Julia. They live today committed to Finken's memory, living life without someone special but touched by his love.

Cadet Paul Finken and his classmates in front of the World Trade Center.

Second Lieutenant Finken receives his Lieutenant rank from his parents.

The Hines family never thought that they would lose their eldest son, Derek, in Afghanistan. Derek's father, Steve, a Massachusetts State Trooper, said that his son repeatedly comforted him: "Dad, I'm OK. Don't worry about me." So Steve tried not to worry, only looking forward to the day Derek would come home his mission complete. But he never did. First Lieutenant Derek Hines was Killed In Action on September 1, 2005, in Baylough, Afghanistan.

From an early age, Derek was curious and athletic, if somewhat accident prone. Steve recalls a fall in the doctor's office: stitches. Slipping off the stage during a school play: stitches. These left him, and Derek was soon setting an example to follow for his sister and two younger brothers in both sports and academics.

Derek's decision to attend St. John's Prep for high school was welcomed by his parents, though they worried about him making the jump to this very challenging academic environment. At the first parent-teacher conference, Steve recalls being shocked

as Hines's French teacher called Hines a model student.

His parents had no worries about Hines athletically. Hines excelled at lacrosse and ice hockey, never letting his smaller physical size be an issue. Perhaps more importantly it is here where he first manifested his talents as a leader being selected as captain of the lacrosse team.

More challenges awaited Hines at West Point. Listed at a generous five foot eight inches in the West Point hockey program, Hines was one of the smallest forwards in all of Division 1 hockey. Hines never gave this fact a single thought, making the varsity his freshman year. His dad, Steve, recalled, "I remember Hines's first college hockey game in Minnesota, against Bemidji State, as though it were yesterday. He scored on his first shot on net, though he soon found out they weren't all going to be that easy."

What coaches, teammates, and fans noticed most about Hines was his tireless work ethic. On the ice, Hines was kinetic energy, constantly in motion, constantly badger-

ing the opposition, and never passing on a chance to hit an opponent regardless size. He even had a fan club made up of local kids who cheered exuberantly by banging Heinz ketchup bottles against the glass anytime Hines scored or made a big hit. Win or lose, he would meet up with these kids and pass out sticks, autographs, or simply a high-five. Hines culminated his hockey career as a team captain.

All the while, Hines's mother, Sue, worried about what would happen post-commissioning. She asked Steve, "Aren't you worried about him having to go to war after he graduates?" Shortly after classes began in Hines's junior year of September 2001, the Twin Towers collapsed a scant 50 miles to the south. It was now certain that Hines's West Point class would go to war.

After graduating, Hines was commissioned in the Field Artillery and competed for a coveted slot to Ranger School, arguably the Army's most difficult non-wartime challenge. Hines earned his Ranger Tab, and he and his new unit the 173rd Airborne Brigade

Combat Team rotated into Afghanistan. Hines's primary job was to direct artillery support for an Infantry Company, a 100-man unit of riflemen. Hines's additional responsibilities included civil affairs missions, such as helping plan and build police stations, schools, and hospitals. His journal entries show a caring and introspective leader genuinely concerned with helping out the Afghani people. One entry made short after his arrival in Afghanistan noted his satisfaction with plans being made to start building a school: "Today I felt good because my work benefited the future of the Afghani education."

"COURAGE. I DO NOT KNOW IF THIS QUALITY EXISTS IN ME, BUT I HOPE WHEN THE TIME COMES I WILL RESPOND," WROTE HINES.

Hurried calls home were sparse with detail; instead, Hines was more focused on making

First Lieutenant Derek Steven Hines, USMA 2003

- KILLED IN ACTION, AFGHANISTAN WAR, AGE 25
- ARMY HOCKEY TEAM, CAPTAIN
- AIRBORNE AND RANGER QUALIFIED
- FIRE SUPPORT OFFICER, 173RD AIRBORNE REGIMENT

requests for toys and school supplies for his new fan club composed of the local Afghani children. However, as incremental gains were made in improving infrastructure, the reality of the situation emerged. Terrorists were plentiful and intent on inflicting damage to the American soldiers. Hines wondered how he would respond to this threat. A journal entry read, "Courage. I do not know if this quality exists in me, but I hope when the time comes, I will respond."

Hines's question about courage was soon answered a few weeks later during a routine patrol. His convoy was ambushed and his 0.50 caliber machine gunner was wounded. Hines quickly replaced him on the 0.50 cal while leading the counterattack. Several soldiers were wounded, including Hines who was hit by shrapnel. Hines had won even more respect from his peers and subordinates and his Company Commander Captain Mike Kloepper would remember, "It was also immediately apparent that I had an Army hockey player on my hands. Supremely competitive, absolutely fit, exceptionally intelligent, with a work ethic that

was unmatched."

As Hines's confidence and awareness grew, he felt a need to describe his observations to everyone back home. A July letter to the *Newburyport Times* was a sober commentary on his experiences. He felt a need to emphasize to the public that while there were community successes, the Army was facing a determined, lethal enemy daily.

Taliban attacks increased throughout the summer with one of their favorite tactics being planting roadside bombs. In mid-August, Hines's convoy fell prey to one. Four soldiers in the lead vehicle lost their lives. Hines was first on the scene and helped pull their torn bodies from the wreckage.

Ten days later, intelligence reported that the Taliban Commander responsible for the attack was hiding in a nearby house. As Hines's unit took up positions outside the house, two men suddenly emerged from the front door firing their weapons. The American response was swift, killing both Taliban members. One soldier was wounded, but it was a mortal wound. First Lieutenant

Hines was Killed In Action in Baylough, Afghanistan on September 1, 2005. For his service in Afghanistan, he was awarded two Purple Hearts and the Bronze Star with valor device.

At Derek's funeral, his dad, Steve, observed, "After I received the news of Derek's death, I was angry at the world, the Army, the President, the war, even myself for letting him attend West Point. I quickly realized that to take this stance would minimize all that Derek believed in and all that he accomplished in his life because he truly believed in his mission that he was making the world a better place."

In 2007, Steve Hines accepted the NCAA's Award of Valor on behalf of Derek. This award goes to "a former NCAA varsity student-athlete who when confronted with a situation involving personal danger, averted or minimized potential disaster by courageous action or noteworthy bravery." At West Point each year, the hockey program now gives a Derek Hines Award to "recognize a person who has displayed an extraordinary amount of support to the program. Like

Hines, this person cares more about giving than receiving." And the Derek Hines Unsung Hero Award is given annually by a committee of college hockey coaches to a Division 1 hockey player who was a "consummate team player and team builder."

Hines's legacy of helping people lives on through his family's work in the Derek Hines Soldiers Assistance Fund, raising money to provide financial assistance to Massachusetts's soldiers, and their families, who have incurred serious, career-ending, and life-altering injuries while on active duty.

As Captain Kloepper remarked, "Derek Hines, I can honestly say, was a true and loyal friend to every person he met, and with a friendship that transcended rank and position, he was equally comfortable sitting with his Battalion Commander as he was the newest soldier to the company, showing each a genuine respect that was hard to turn away from."

Written by: Richie Sheridan, USMA 1990.

>>> Spotlight

Hundreds of servicemen stand in formation as the body of First Lieutenant Derek Hines passes and is loaded onto the C-17 Globemaster III for transport home to his family and his final resting place. This photo was taken by Lieutenant Colonel Kevin Bigelman USMA 1993 at Kandahar Air Force Base Afghanistan. Only later did Lieutenant Colonel Bigelman discover that the ceremony he captured on film was being held for First Lieutenant Derek Hines, whom he knew from his time as an Associate Professor at West Point. Every time a service-member is Killed In Action, the military makes every effort to honor the life and sacrifice of that soldier the entire way home until and even after burial. The flag-draped coffin receives official ceremonies starting in the field and all the way back home to Dover Air Force Base, where the families meet their fallen hero and then on to their chosen cemetery. Every time a fallen soldier leaves from Bagram Air Force Base, all personnel are requested to line the roads and the airfield, where they all salute the flag draped coffin as it passes.

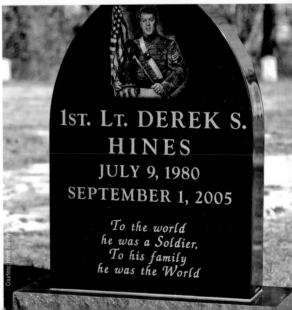

1st. Lt. DEREK S. HINES
JULY 9, 1980
SEPTEMBER 1, 2005

*To the world
he was a Soldier.
To his family
he was the World*

Some men live long lives, marking time to the monotonous beat of the daily humdrum, decaying in quiet desperation as they search for meaning and fulfillment, yet lacking the fortitude to strike the comfortable tents of familiarity and fearlessly pursue their dreams. John Ryan Dennison did not suffer from this malady. At age 24, Dennison departed this world at full speed, eyes fixed on his objective, far from the comforts of home.

Dennison wouldn't have felt cheated. In his final journal entry before deploying to Iraq, he wrote, "I am so very thankful that God has blessed me with so much! If catastrophe strikes in Iraq, I will still feel blessed because I have lived the equivalent of four-men's lives in my short 24 years on this planet. I owe it all to God, my Father. He blessed me with wonderful friends, family, and parents to adopt me! And most of all with my beautiful wife, my companion, my very best friend. I pray that I will remain vigilant and faithful as any disciple of Christ should be during a tour in the wilderness. Thank you God for all your blessings."

"Still blessed." That's us, actually. And these blessings began on February 22, 1982, the day Dennison was born, at Landstuhl Army Medical Center, Germany. Jack and Shannon Dennison adopted him at age of two months, and he became the oldest of three children in a family with a strong record of military service.

Dennison had no brake – only accelerator – as he navigated through his childhood and adolescence, seeking new experiences and more difficult challenges along the way. Any who were fortunate enough to call themselves fellow passengers on Dennison's journey, even at this early stage, could certainly attest to his intense passion for life. As a rare teen, Dennison was even passionate about reading, keeping books by great authors like Tolstoy by his bed.

The rest of Dennison's community became familiar with his drive and determination in high school, where he earned a starting job as an undersized offensive guard on a football team that won two consecutive state championships, and he also placed second at the state wrestling tournament. Dennison's prowess was not limited to athletics, however; he also received balanced recognition for his academic performance, leadership, and community service, earning induction into the National Honor Society, representing his school at Boys State, and volunteering as a Big Brother.

Given his high-school success, Dennison had countless post-graduation opportunities open to him; however, when he received an appointment to the United States Military Academy at West Point, New York, the combination of disparate challenges and the occasion to follow in his parents' military boot-steps was too attractive to forgo. Dennison matriculated to West Point in the

Captain John Ryan Dennison, USMA 2004

- KILLED IN ACTION, IRAQ WAR
- BLACK KNIGHT PARACHUTE TEAM CAPTAIN
- JUMP MASTER, SAPPER, AND RANGER QUALIFIED
- PLATOON LEADER 5-73 CAV, 3RD BRIGADE COMBAT TEAM, 82ND AIRBORNE DIVISION
- BOY SCOUTS OF AMERICA, YOUTH MEMBER

Dennison overlooking the Iraq-Iranian border, September 2006.

>>> Spotlight

The Bronze Star Medal was established by President Franklin Delano Roosevelt on February 4, 1944, retroactive to December 7, 1941. The medal was conceived by Colonel Russell P. "Red" Reeder (USMA 1926) in 1943 for a new award that small-unit ground commanders could award quickly in the field to reward combat soldiers that were in the line for long periods, doing their job in a dedicated, meritorious manner or for acts of heroism in ground combat. Originally conceived as the "Ground Medal," the name was changed to "Bronze Star Medal" and approved by the President. The first valor devices were authorized in 1944 as an attachment to the Bronze Star Medal and are identified as a "V" device. The Bronze Star with "V" for valor ranks fourth after the Silver Star Medal for valor against enemies of the United States.

Photo © 2013/Greg E. Mathieson Sr./MAI

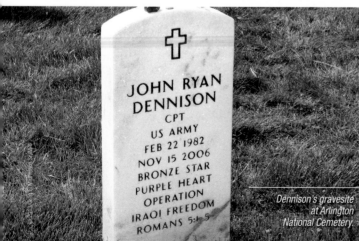

JOHN RYAN
DENNISON
CPT
US ARMY
FEB 22 1982
NOV 15 2006
BRONZE STAR
PURPLE HEART
OPERATION
IRAQI FREEDOM
ROMANS 5:4-5

Dennison's gravesite at Arlington National Cemetery.

summer of 2000, the genesis of his training to become a soldier and an Army Officer.

It generally proves difficult for a single light to shine distinctively in a room full of lights. West Point is such a room, populated by some of the brightest lights from across America. And yet Dennison achieved such distinction, although he was never one to distance himself from his peers as an end unto itself. He excelled in the classroom, earning recognition as a Superintendent's Award Recipient en route to earning his Bachelor of Science degree in International Relations. He excelled physically, becoming one of the highest-ranked cadets in his class in the fitness category, while also earning his Sapper Tab from the Engineer Branch's pre-

mier leadership school. And he excelled as a leader, rising to become the Team Captain of the West Point Parachute Team — one of the most selective and demanding teams at the Academy.

Dennison encountered two life-changing experiences while at West Point. He was just beginning his second year as a cadet when terrorists attacked our nation on September 11, 2001. During skydiving practice, in the days immediately after the World Trade Center fell, he could see in the distance the dust and smoke still emanating from Ground Zero. This tremendous national tragedy profoundly affected Dennison.

As much as that event weighed on

Dennison's heart, his heart sustained an impact greater still — when he met his future wife, Haley, a fellow cadet from the West Point Class of 2004. Dennison was absolutely head over heels for Haley. His classmate, Erik Wright, recalled accompanying Dennison to women's basketball games at West Point and observing how fixated Dennison's attention was on Haley's action on the court. Jack Morrow, another classmate, observed that Haley's influence stimulated Dennison to attend bible studies and to seek to better know God. They were married on July 17, 2004, just a few months after their graduation from West Point.

Only one branch of the Army would suit Dennison: the Infantry. He wanted to feel enemy soil give way beneath his boot; he sought the ultimate challenge of leading soldiers against a determined foe in ground combat. As such, he attended and graduated from the Infantry Officer Basic Course and Ranger School before joining his platoon at Fort Bragg, North Carolina, in 3rd Brigade of the storied 82nd Airborne Division. While stationed at Fort Bragg, Dennison would continue his record of graduating from rigorous Army courses by completing requirements to be qualified as a parachute Jump Master. In September 2005, Dennison deployed with his unit, the 3rd Battalion, 505th Parachute Infantry Regiment, to New Orleans, Louisiana, to provide support for victims of Hurricane Katrina. While this was not exactly the mission Dennison had envisioned undertaking as a Platoon Leader, he got his wish nearly a year later, five years after the attacks of September 11, 2001.

In August 2006, Dennison again deployed with his unit, this time to Kuwait, and by September, they were firmly ensconced in their assigned area of responsibility, a 200-kilometer stretch along the border of Iraq and Iran. This region had not seen United States presence in more than a year, a fact that became clear when local air reconnaissance assets found an enormous cache of munitions, bomb-making materials, and miscellaneous documents tying the cache to terrorists. After this tremendous discovery near the village of Turki, Dennison's unit spearheaded a three-month period of offensive operations, dubbed Operation Turki Bowl, operations for which the unit would later receive the Presidential Unit Citation — the most prestigious award that can be given to a combat unit. The insurgents in the Turki area were disciplined, well trained in tactics and marksmanship, and intentionally targeted the unit's leaders,

according to Major Brett Sylvia, the squadron's Operations Officer.

And so it happened, on November 15, 2006, near the birthplace of human life, that one who lived his life to the fullest gave it up — while leading his platoon in ground combat against a determined foe, with enemy soil giving way beneath his boot.

Dennison was posthumously promoted from First Lieutenant to Captain, and he was awarded the Bronze Star and Purple Heart. More important than medals, however, was the praise he received for being a highly effective and charismatic leader, sentiments shared by his subordinates, peers, and superiors. Colonel Brian Owens, former Commander of the 3rd Brigade Combat Team, said that Dennison "was a superb young officer and warrior. He led from the front in all that he did." Colonel Andrew Poppas, Dennison's Squadron Commander, referred to Dennison as the "Gold Standard of the 82nd." First Lieutenant Robert Moore, the squadron's rear detachment Commander and a friend of Dennison's, was impressed with how much he cared about his

"IF CATASTROPHE STRIKES IN IRAQ, I WILL STILL FEEL BLESSED BECAUSE I HAVE LIVED THE EQUIVALENT OF FOUR MEN'S LIVES IN MY SHORT 24 YEARS ON THIS PLANET," SAID DENNISON.

men. "If they didn't have enough to eat, he gave them what he had. If they were tired he let them sleep and he stayed up. His paratroopers were his brothers and he loved and respected them."

John Ryan Dennison poured his heart and soul into every task he encountered, always testing his own limits in order to experience all of life — its peaks and pains, its successes and shortfalls. And yet he poured his heart and soul more fully into those he loved — his family, his friends, and his soldiers. They are all still blessed.

Haley and Ryan at an Army Football game after Ryan jumped onto the 50-yard line, October 2003.

Haley and Ryan celebrating on their wedding day, July 17, 2004.

Jack and Shannon Dennison pinning Ryan's Second Lieutenant bars at his Commissioning Ceremony, May 2004.

THE TRAILBLAZERS

West Point has produced graduates who have been literal and figurative trailblazers in many areas. As the nation's first engineer school, West Point graduates have been critical in developing the expanding nation through leading exploration of the West, building and leading railroads, and founding universities. West Point has also produced graduates who have led the efforts of some of the world's great engineering and scientific marvels to include construction of the Panama Canal and the Pentagon, and the development of the atomic bomb through the Manhattan Project. At the same time, West Point has also been at the forefront of social change. The first Jewish cadet graduated in West Point's first graduating class in 1802. The first Native-American cadet graduated in 1824 in the earliest stages of America's westward expansion. Soon after the Civil War, West Point began accepting African-American cadets, with the first graduating in 1877. The first class with women entered in 1976. This chapter highlights only a few of the West Point trailblazing graduates.

The Panama Canal, one of the American Society of Civil Engineers's "Engineering Marvels of the World," built by Major General George W. Goethals, USMA 1880.

"The man we honor today was an extraordinary American. Henry Flipper did all his country asked him to do. Though born a slave in Georgia, he was proud to serve America: the first African-American graduate of West Point; the first African-American commissioned officer in the regular United States Army."

–President William Jefferson Clinton

"My own opinion was that blacks could best overcome racist attitudes through achievements, even though those achievements had to take place within the hateful environment of segregation.

–General Benjamin O. Davis, Jr., USMA 1936, Commander of the Tuskegee Airmen

"There are two rules to life. Rule number one: Don't quit. Rule number two: Refer back to rule number one.

–Brigadier General Rebecca Halstead, USMA 1981, the first female West Point graduate to become a General Officer

"I have come to accept my role as part of a social experiment. I hope that one day I'll be part of a conclusive body of evidence that says something intelligent about women in combat."

–Andrea Lee Hollen, USMA 1980, Rhodes Scholar and the first female graduate of West Point

"I never thought of myself as setting a precedent. Everybody else thought about it a lot."

–Colonel Kristin Baker, USMA 1990, the first female Cadet First Captain at West Point

"[Henry O. Flipper] was my inspiration during the lonely times of being the Cadet Brigade Commander."

–General Vincent Brooks, USMA 1980, the first African-American Cadet First Captain

President Bill Clinton honors Henry O. Flipper.

Henry O. Flipper, USMA 1877

- **BORN A SLAVE IN GEORGIA**
- **FIRST AFRICAN-AMERICAN GRADUATE OF WEST POINT**
- **FIRST AFRICAN-AMERICAN OFFICER IN THE U.S. ARMY**
- **SERVED WITH 10TH CAVALRY (BUFFALO SOLDIERS) IN THE INDIAN WARS**
- **APPOINTED AS SPECIAL AGENT OF THE U.S. DEPARTMENT OF JUSTICE**
- **ASSISTANT TO THE SECRETARY OF THE INTERIOR**

First African-American graduate of West Point.

Bust of Flipper at Fort Leavenworth.

>>> Spotlight

The ditch that Flipper designed while at Fort Sill was designated a National Historic Landmark in 1977 as is known as "Flipper's Ditch."

HONORING AN AMERICAN HERO

Henry O. Flipper is now a celebrated icon at West Point as the first African-American graduate. But the roller coaster life he lived was far from glamorous; it was fraught with challenges, racism, discrimination, and scandal. But it was also a life of achievement, pride, and success. In hindsight, he was a heroic leader who broke down racial barriers. Yet, he died having been found guilty of "conduct unbecoming an officer and a gentleman." Although he fought for more than half a century to clear his name while he was alive, he was unsuccessful in doing so. However, ever resilient, even in death he overcame adversity; more than a century later, after being found guilty of his charge, he was posthumously pardoned by President Clinton in 1999 and is now a heroic icon of West Point history.

Born as a slave in Georgia on March 21, 1826, Flipper was schooled in another slave's home until he started attending missionary school at age 8. After President Lincoln issued the Emancipation Proclamation in 1863, slaves in the North were freed, but in the South, Flipper remained a slave until 1865. In 1869, he was one of the first to attend the newly founded Atlanta University, and the fourth black cadet to enter West Point (on July 1, 1873). The first three did not graduate, and the challenges he faced as the sole black cadet would be daunting. He faced incredible prejudice in an Academy still divided between North and South working toward post–Civil War reconciliation after a war that was in part fought over the slavery issue. Despite West Point's efforts to integrate blacks into the Academy, the United States was still a society where segregation was the law and blacks did not have full privileges of an American citizen. There was still an atmosphere of prejudice at the Academy, and Flipper was silenced by many of his classmates who refused to speak with a black cadet. Despite the challenging environment, in 1877, he graduated 50th in his class of 76 cadets and was commissioned as an officer – the first black officer in the United States Army.

He fulfilled his personal dream when he was assigned as a Second Lieutenant in Troop A of the 10th Cavalry assigned to Fort Sill, Oklahoma, leading black soldiers in one of two Cavalry Regiments called "Buffalo Soldiers." In 1879, he was in temporary command of Troop G as Acting Commander. While at Fort Sill, he was responsible for designing and building a ditch to resolve a drainage problem that was causing a malaria outbreak from stagnant water. The engineering project was so successful, the ditch he designed and built bore his name and was designated a National Historic Landmark in 1977 as "Flipper's Ditch."

In May 1880, his unit was assigned to Fort Concho, Texas, in pursuit of the Apache Chief Victorio. In the spring of 1881, Flipper was acting as quartermaster when an event occurred that would change his life. The details of the events still remain unclear even years later. Money was missing from commissary funds, which Flipper discovered and was personally investigating. His new commander had created a challenging and racially charged climate as Lieutenant Flipper was the only black officer in the Army at the time. While investigating the whereabouts of the funds, Flipper lied to his commander in order to buy more time to discover the reason for the loss or the whereabouts of the funds. He was court-martialed for embezzlement and "conduct unbecoming of an officer." The embezzlement charge was dropped for a lack of evidence, but he was still discharged from the Army for having lied to his commander. He was the first officer in the history of the Army to be charged with conduct unbecoming.

He spent the rest of his life trying to clear his name, although all of his efforts were unsuccessful. He owned his own company for a short time, worked as a translator for the Senate and a special assistant for the Justice Department. He died at age 84, in 1940, never knowing that his name would one day be cleared. During the Civil Rights movement of the 1960s, his records were reviewed, and the Army officially evaluated his case in 1976. The evaluation determined that although Flipper had lied, the dismissal was too severe, and he was given an honorable discharge effective June 30, 1882. In 1999, President Clinton pardoned Flipper, restoring his name to the honorable status well earned by an American hero who blazed a trail in history to help end discrimination and reduce racism after the American Civil War.

Even though West Point and the Army were far ahead of society in integrating African-Americans at that time, it was still a very discriminatory and racially charged environment. It is hard to imagine the struggles, racism, and discrimination that Flipper overcame to graduate from West Point in 1877. Every year, on the date of his birth, March 21st, all cadets celebrate "Henry O. Flipper Day." His bust is displayed in West Point's Jefferson Library in the Haig Room, deservedly beside other iconic statues and busts of West Point legends: Eisenhower, MacArthur, Bradley, Pershing, Patton, and Schwarzkopf. He is remembered as an American hero, who helped break down racial barriers.

FLIPPER WAS SILENCED BY MANY OF HIS CLASSMATES WHO REFUSED TO SPEAK WITH A BLACK CADET. DESPITE THE CHALLENGING ENVIRONMENT, IN 1877, HE GRADUATED AND WAS COMMISSIONED AS AN OFFICER – THE FIRST BLACK OFFICER IN THE UNITED STATES ARMY.

The Henry O. Flipper Room at the Thayer Hotel was dedicated by the family of Thomas Morgan (USMA 1983) in honor of his late wife, Vanessa Morgan.

Henry O. Flipper Room at the Thayer Hotel.

In contemporary American military doctrine, soldiers are taught to understand the concept of "commander's intent" while executing missions. Field Manual 3-0, *Operations*, one of the Army's key doctrinal manuals, defines commander's intent as "a clear, concise statement of what the force must do and the conditions the force must establish with respect to the enemy, terrain, and civil considerations that represent the desired end state."[1] Thus, the commander's intent is a guide for soldiers at all levels in carrying out missions with a distinct goal of encouraging individual initiative and freedom of action in the absence of direct supervision.[2] Andrew S. Rowan and his mission to Cuba in 1898 became the consummate example of this concept, and more than a century later, Rowan's story still remains as relevant today to military and business leaders alike as it did then.

Born in Virginia to John Rowan and Virginia Summers, Rowan entered West Point in 1877 and graduated in 1881. He served on the American frontier for many years. In 1898, as war was looming between the United States and Spain, President William McKinley sought to connect with Cuban rebels who were fighting for their independence from Spain. One of those rebel leaders was Calixto Garcia, who McKinley pursued as a potential ally in the event America went to war with Spain. McKinley asked War Department Information Chief, Colonel Arthur L. Wagner (USMA 1875), to recommend an officer to send to Cuba and meet with Garcia. Wagner recommended then-Lieutenant Rowan for the mission, and McKinley agreed.

Colonel Wagner next gave Rowan a letter that President McKinley wrote to Garcia and issued Rowan the general mission to deliver that letter to Garcia. Wagner did not tell Rowan how to deliver the message, nor did Rowan ask why or how. Rowan simply knew the message was important and that he must deliver it to Garcia. Rowan then departed that night, sailing for Cuba by way of Jamaica, in order to carry out his mission.

Rowan faced significant challenges and dangers from both sides. Had the Spanish captured him, he likely would have been executed as a spy. Had he delivered the message but Garcia chosen to work with the Spanish instead, he could have been killed by Garcia's rebel Army. Moreover, he had no communications or logistical support of any kind. In spite of these obstacles, however, he understood his commander's intent – to get the message to Garcia. Nine days later, Rowan made contact with Garcia, delivered the message, and secured Garcia's support for the United States. Three of Garcia's soldiers then accompanied Rowan on the arduous and dangerous return trip to the United States where they provided necessary information in return for the aid and support they needed in fighting against the Spanish.

Upon his return to the United States, Rowan received the thanks and praise of President McKinley and was eventually awarded the Distinguished Service Cross for his valor in Cuba. The citation notes:

"At the outbreak of the Spanish-American campaign, Lieutenant Rowan, under disguise, entered the enemy lines in Oriente, crossed the island of Cuba, and not only succeeded in delivering a message to General Garcia, but secured secret information relative to existing military conditions in that region of such great value that it had an important bearing on the quick ending of the struggle and the complete success of the United States Army."

Rowan eventually served with the 6th United States Volunteer "Immunes" Infantry Regiment in Cuba after America's entry in the Spanish-American War, the 19th Infantry Regiment in the Philippines, where he was awarded the Silver Star, then retired in 1909 after 28 years of service.

With nothing more than the simple commander's intent of delivering a letter to Calixto Garcia, Rowan used his initiative to accomplish a complex and dangerous mission – the success of which was instrumental to the outcome of the Spanish-American War. The press lauded Rowan's bravery, while American author and philosopher, Elbert Hubbard, published a short story entitled *Message to Garcia* to honor the event. Since then, the story has been translated into dozens of languages and has become an international best seller – one of the top-selling books in history.[3] Applicable to both military and business leaders alike, *Message to Garcia*, like the contemporary doctrinal concept of "commander's intent," has become synonymous with initiative, duty, and responsibility.

> **MORE THAN A CENTURY LATER, ROWAN'S STORY STILL REMAINS AS RELEVANT TODAY TO MILITARY AND BUSINESS LEADERS ALIKE AS IT DID THEN.**

Lieutenant Colonel Andrew S. Rowan, USMA 1881

- INSPIRATION FOR THE INTERNATIONALLY BEST-SELLING STORY *MESSAGE TO GARCIA*
- AWARDED DISTINGUISHED SERVICE CROSS FOR VALOR IN CUBA DURING SPANISH-AMERICAN WAR
- FIRST AMERICAN OFFICER TO ARRIVE IN CUBA, 1898
- SERVED ON AMERICAN FRONTIER DUTY, 1881–89
- WOUNDED SERVING IN THE PHILIPPINE INSURGENCY
- BURIED IN ARLINGTON NATIONAL CEMETERY

Monument to Spanish-American War Casualties in Central Park, New York City.

IN MEMORY OF THE OFFICERS AND ENLISTED MEN OF THE ARMIES OF THE UNITED STATES WHO GAVE THEIR LIVES IN THE SPANISH-AMERICAN WAR 1898 – 1899. ERECTED BY THE DAUGHTERS OF THE REVOLUTION OF THE STATE OF NEW YORK

General Robinson.

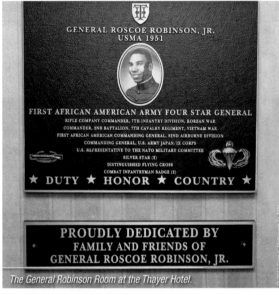

GENERAL ROSCOE ROBINSON, JR.
USMA 1951

FIRST AFRICAN AMERICAN ARMY FOUR STAR GENERAL

RIFLE COMPANY COMMANDER, 7TH INFANTRY DIVISION, KOREAN WAR
COMMANDER, 2ND BATTALION, 7TH CAVALRY REGIMENT, VIETNAM WAR
FIRST AFRICAN AMERICAN COMMANDING GENERAL, 82ND AIRBORNE DIVISION
COMMANDING GENERAL, U.S. ARMY JAPAN/IX CORPS
U.S. REPRESENTATIVE TO THE NATO MILITARY COMMITTEE
SILVER STAR (2)
DISTINGUISHED FLYING CROSS
COMBAT INFANTRYMAN BADGE (2)

★ DUTY ★ HONOR ★ COUNTRY ★

PROUDLY DEDICATED BY
FAMILY AND FRIENDS OF
GENERAL ROSCOE ROBINSON, JR.

The General Robinson Room at the Thayer Hotel.

General Roscoe Robinson, Jr., USMA 1951

- **FIRST AFRICAN-AMERICAN ARMY FOUR-STAR GENERAL**
- **U.S. REPRESENTATIVE TO NATO COMMITTEE**
- **COMMANDING GENERAL U.S. ARMY JAPAN/IX CORPS**
- **FIRST AFRICAN-AMERICAN COMMANDER, 82ND AIRBORNE DIVISION**
- **COMMANDER, 2ND BATTALION, 7TH CAVALRY REGIMENT, VIETNAM WAR**
- **RIFLE COMPANY COMMANDER, 7TH INFANTRY DIVISION, KOREAN WAR**
- **SILVER STAR (TWO), COMBAT INFANTRYMAN BADGE**

★ ★ ★ ★

Roscoe Robinson was the first African-American Four-Star General in the history of the United States Army. He was born in St. Louis, Missouri, on October 11, 1928, during segregation. He was a trailblazer, a leader, and an inspiration to the soldiers who followed him in combat – especially the generations of African-Americans who came after him. He had significant command time in combat as both a Company Commander in Korea and later

as a Battalion Commander Vietnam. He was renowned to his classmates, soldiers, and NCOs as being a great leader who people loved and followed.

During the early years of World War II, while in the Boy Scouts, Robinson developed a clear sense of patriotism, readily participating in such home-front efforts as collecting aluminum cans for recycling as part of the war effort. He entered Charles Sumner High School, the first high school for blacks

west of the Mississippi River, in 1942. He graduated from high school on January 21, 1946, as salutatorian, the second-highest academically ranked student in his class and class president. Determined to proceed with his academic career, Robinson enrolled for one semester in the all-black Stowe College. Then, in the summer of 1946, he was accepted to Saint Louis University.

Entering Saint Louis University was a historic event, as it was only two years

after the Jesuit institution became the first school on any level in Saint Louis to admit African-American students. With racial integration at Saint Louis University still in its infancy, Robinson entered the school as an undergraduate with the intent of pursuing a degree in industrial engineering. Then, in his second semester, Robinson received a telephone call Principal George Dennis Brantley of Sumner High School, informing him that Brantley planned to nominate him

Bust of General Robinson located at Fort Leavenworth, Kansas, near the Buffalo Soldiers Monument.

respect for the Academy, and the lifelong camaraderie of his classmates. His graduating class also included four other African-Americans, which, at that time, was the largest number of African-American cadets ever to graduate from the Academy.

He graduated with the Class of 1951 and was commissioned in the Infantry. He went on to lead every size unit from a Platoon to an Army. His first assignment was with the 11th Airborne Division as a Platoon Leader. He saw his first combat in 1952, as a Rifle Company Commander with the 7th Infantry Division in the Korean War, where he was awarded the Bronze Star. Robinson returned to the United States, became an instructor at Airborne School, then served a year in Africa as a military liaison with the United States mission in Liberia.

He attended D.C.'s National War College and then received his master's in international relations from the University of Pittsburgh. In 1968, Robinson again commanded in combat, this time as a Battalion Commander for the 27th Cavalry in Vietnam, where he excelled in a time of significant and intense combat operations during the peak of war. He received two Silver Stars and a Distinguished Flying Cross for his leadership under fire. He then served in Vietnam on the staff of the 1st Cavalry Division.

After leaving Vietnam, he became the Executive Officer to Commander in Chief, Pacific Command (CINCPAC) in Hawaii and then went to Fort Bragg in North Carolina as a Brigade Commander with the 82nd Airborne Division. He returned to the Pacific as the Commander of United States Army Forces in Okinawa before deploying back to Fort Bragg. In 1976, he became Commanding General of his beloved and famed 82nd Airborne Division. His final command was back to the Pacific at Camp Zama, Japan, where he was the Commander of United States Army Japan and IX Corps. His final assignment in the Army was in Europe as a Four-Star General where he served as the United States Military Representative to the North Atlantic Treaty Organization.

He married Mildred Sims in 1952 at Fort Campbell, Kentucky. They had two children, Bruce and Carol, who had three and two children of their own, respectively. Bruce served as an officer in the Army.

After retiring from the Army in 1986, Robinson served on several corporate boards, including Northwest Airlines and was a trustee for the West Point Association of Graduates. He was asked to sit on several committees for the Department of the Army, in order to take advantage of his talents and experience. He then went to battle again, one last time, this time with leukemia.

In May 1993, General Robinson was awarded the Distinguished Graduate Award from West Point. He had been fighting leukemia for nearly 18 months, receiving the award from a wheelchair, but he stood at straight at attention one last time on the Plain at West Point for the playing of the National Anthem. He passed away two months later on July 22, 1993, and was laid to rest at Arlington National Cemetery. In April 2000, the South Auditorium at Thayer Hall was named in honor of him as "General Roscoe Robinson, Jr. Auditorium."

His awards include the Distinguished Service Medal, two Silver Stars, three Legion of Merits, the Distinguished Flying Cross, the Bronze Star, and the two Combat Infantryman Badges.

It is impossible to appreciate all the challenges that Roscoe Robinson overcame as an African-American growing up in America under segregation. But he took it all in stride, always with a smile on his face and a positive attitude, and considered himself to be very fortunate. The United States Army is fortunate to have had a leader of such character who helped break down racial barriers and led soldiers of all races, color, and religions. In peacetime and under fire in combat, he proved he was a leader worthy of following.

> **IT IS IMPOSSIBLE TO APPRECIATE ALL THE CHALLENGES THAT ROSCOE ROBINSON OVERCAME AS AN AFRICAN-AMERICAN GROWING UP IN AMERICA UNDER SEGREGATION. BUT HE TOOK IT ALL IN STRIDE, ALWAYS WITH A SMILE ON HIS FACE AND A POSITIVE ATTITUDE.**

to the United States Military Academy at West Point.

Having watched Robinson's development as a young man, when the families were neighbors, and having observed his outstanding performance as a scholar and leader at Sumner, Brantley was convinced that Robinson would be successful at the Academy. After some rigorous physical and academic tests, Robinson was selected over another local candidate. He began an academic career that would lay the foundation for his eventual prominence as a military hero.

In the summer of 1947, Robinson entered the United States Military Academy at West Point, where he was one of a small number of African-Americans admitted. Robinson took away many things from West Point: a first-rate education (graduating with a bachelor's of science in engineering), leadership skills, a love for athletics, a deep

The General Robinson Room at the Thayer Hotel is proudly dedicated by his friends and family.

Thank you for the inspiration and guidance you have provided over the course of the last three years and the last semester for me in particular.

I wish you and Mrs. Gorden only the best in Hawaii and wherever fortune may take you.

Kristin M. Baker
'89 CPT USCC
Class of...

Major General Gorden receiving cadet saber from Cadet First Captain Kristin Baker at his last parade as Commandant.

Major General Frederick A. Gorden, USMA 1962

- FIRST AFRICAN-AMERICAN COMMANDANT OF CADETS AT WEST POINT
- ARMY CHIEF OF PUBLIC AFFAIRS
- COMMANDING GENERAL, 25TH INFANTRY DIVISION (LIGHT)
- COMMANDER, 7TH INFANTRY DIVISION (LIGHT) ARTILLERY
- COMMANDER, 1ST BATTALION, 8TH FIELD ARTILLERY REGIMENT
- MASTER'S OF ARTS, MIDDLEBURY COLLEGE
- WEST POINT ASSISTANT PROFESSOR DEPARTMENT OF FOREIGN LANGUAGES
- ARMY PLEBE BASKETBALL; ARMY MEN'S B-SQUAD CROSS-COUNTRY (THREE); ARMY MEN'S TRACK AND FIELD LETTERMAN (FOUR)

In 1987, President Ronald Reagan spoke at West Point:

"The only black cadet in his class, today General Gorden has come back to West Point as Commandant, setting an example for you, and indeed for all young Americans, of what hard work and devotion to duty can achieve. These last two names I mentioned, General Gorden and General MacArthur, call to mind a special moment in the history of this Academy. For it was 25 years ago that General of the Army Douglas MacArthur stood in this spot and addressed the cadets of West Point. And General Gorden, at the time Cadet Gorden, was sitting where you are today. It was a moment Cadet Gorden would never forget. Just days from graduation, he looked around this mess hall and saw war-hardened officers moved to tears by the power of MacArthur's words: 'The Long Gray Line has never failed us.' He said, 'Were you to do so, a million ghosts would rise from their white crosses, thundering those magic words: Duty, Honor, Country.'"

Fred Gorden born February 22, 1940, at the end of the Great Depression and was raised in Atlanta, Georgia, while the South was still racially segregated. His mother, Mary Ethel, had four children, but since her oldest sister, Gertrude, had no children after eight years of marriage, they agreed on a unique arrangement to have the sister raise the fourth child. Thus Gorden was raised by his Aunt Gert and Uncle Bo – whose given name, Augustus, was also Gorden's middle name – just one street over from his biological parents and his siblings. In the fifth grade, his aunt and uncle's marriage broke up, and she moved from Atlanta to Michigan with Gorden following her shortly after the move. After graduating from high school, he attended a year of junior college and knew little about West Point other than the popular weekly television show during the 1950s called *The West Point Story*. Recommended by officials of his high school,

Gorden was approached by a local lawyer who was recruiting for West Point. He recommended Gorden to their Congressman as having the competitive potential to attend the Academy. In late May 1958, he went to West Point by bus at his own expense and took the various medical, physical, and college board entrance exams. In mid-June, he received a telegram saying, in essence, "Congratulations you are my appointee to West Point, you need to be there the 1st of July." Attending junior college on scholarship and facing financial uncertainty about being able to pursue studies at Wayne State University as an architectural engineer, Gorden saw the paid high-quality education as an amazing opportunity but knew little about West Point or the Army and the direction his entire life had just taken.

On his first day at West Point, after going through some traditional hazing learning how to report to upper-class cadets, he found himself in his room looking out over North

Area watching other new cadets undergo what he had just experienced and wondering what he had gotten himself into. He remembers also looking at the upper-class cadets and realizing that they too had undergone the same indoctrinating experiences themselves just a year or so earlier. He found strength in knowing that others had gone before him, both white and black cadets. He soon discovered that his Platoon Sergeant Wilbourne Kelley III (USMA 1959) was an African-American, also from Michigan, and another upperclassman nearby was Ira Dorsey (USMA 1960). For a while, Gorden thought he was the only African-American cadet in his class but found that there was one other, Sinclair Parks, when classes started in the fall. Parks, unfortunately, left after first semester, leaving Gorden as the only African-American in a class of more than 800 cadets.

As a Plebe, he found humor in the fact that he received his draft notice while wearing a uniform. Despite the challenges of being

Major General Gorden with South African President Nelson Mandela.

President Reagan visit to West Point, October 1987.

FRED GORDEN FOUND INSPIRATION FROM OTHERS THAT MOTIVATED HIM TO HIMSELF BE A PIONEER, BREAKING DOWN BARRIERS AND LEADING MEN AND WOMEN IN A VARIETY OF ROLES AROUND THE WORLD.

As a first classman and senior black cadet in the Corps, he often represented the Academy

a cadet, he found solace in sports and clubs. He played basketball as a Plebe and lettered on the track team as a high jumper, triple jumper, and occasionally long jumping. He joined the cadet choir and glee club, which often allowed him to leave the Academy on additional trips.

before African-American audiences honoring such predecessor black Academy graduates as Henry Flipper and Charles Young.

As graduation neared, Gorden's class lived through several surreal experiences. On May 12, 1962, Cadet Gorden was chosen to be part of the Honor Guard for General MacArthur's speech when he received the Sylvanus Thayer Award and gave what is now considered one of the greatest speeches in American history that President Reagan later spoke of in 1987. One month later on June 6, 1962, President John F. Kennedy provided the commencement speech for the Class of 1962 and prophetically emphasized the future combat that they would experience in Vietnam:

"This is another type of war, new in its intensity, ancient in its origin – war by guerrillas, subversives, insurgents, assassins, war by ambush instead of by combat; by infiltration, instead of aggression, seeking victory by eroding and exhausting the enemy instead of engaging him."

President Kennedy drove that day at West Point in his Lincoln Continental Presidential convertible with Superintendent Major General Westmoreland (photo on page 80) and tragically, would himself be shot by an assassin only 18 months later in Dallas in that same vehicle.

Languages had always come easy to Gorden, who first studied Latin and then Spanish in high school and at West Point. He soon found his language skills to be extremely beneficial to his career and was considering a foreign area officer career. When he graduated 221 out of his class of 601, he had many choices available to him and he chose Panama, where he was assigned to a battery of the 22nd Field Artillery organic to the 193rd Infantry Brigade. He attended Field Artillery Officer Basic, Airborne, and Ranger Schools before heading to Panama. More than

one-third of the soldiers in the unit were of Hispanic origin, mostly from Puerto Rico, who naturally gravitated to assignment locations with native culture influences. Whenever VIPs would visit from Central and South America, Gorden always found himself chosen to escort the Spanish speaking VIPs. His love for light Infantry grew to match his Spanish language facility, and these would become his focus over the next three decades. Light Infantry and language skills were essential in his first assignment and would turn out to be the focus of his 35-year career.

It was during this first tour that he experienced his first international incident when the country became inflamed after an incident inside the Canal Zone at Balboa High School over a flag incident, when an American flag was flown and the Panamanian flag was not flown in accordance with protocol. In January 1964, riots broke out across Panama and protesters attacked and fired on American troops. Gorden, his wife, Marcia, and their

Major General Gorden and General Colin Powell

Major General and Mrs. Gorden with President William Jefferson Clinton and Emperor Akihito of Japan.

Cadet Gorden receiving his diploma from Major General William West, Moreland 1962.

eight-month-old daughter were living on the local economy and were trapped and couldn't return to base for several days in a dangerous and volatile situation. The excitement and lively debates of the international stage intrigued him. He and his wife chose to return to the United States via a cruise ship to New York, where he stopped at West Point to get some career counseling en route to the Field Artillery Advanced Course, which would later help him return to West Point as a professor.

The keynote address at his Field Artillery advanced course was General Creighton Abrams, who impressed Gorden greatly. Deployments to Vietnam were increasing as General Westmoreland was rapidly increasing United States troop strength, and Gorden's first choice for assignments upon graduation was Vietnam, where he deployed in 1967. Originally assigned to a headquarters unit,

he actively worked to get down to a field artillery battery with troops. He was assigned to the 320th Field Artillery, 1st Brigade, 101st Airborne Division, with the brigade in Vietnam operating separate from the division back at Fort Campbell at the time. He was First Battalion Assistant S-3 Fire Direction Officer, then Liaison (fire support) Officer with two Infantry battalions and then worked his way down to a battery command. It was in this role as a Battery Commander that he was awarded the Bronze Star for Valor for his battery defense performance during a mortar, recoilless rifle and small arms attack.

The trip to West Point to get career counseling prior to deploying to Vietnam paid off. For his follow-on assignment after leaving Vietnam, he was selected to teach at West Point in the language department, and the Army sent him to Middlebury College in

Vermont to receive his master's degree in Spanish language, literature, and civilization, which included an immersion in Spain for a year. Back at West Point, the Gordens enjoyed being with cadets and opened their home to cadets, their dates, and other guests, especially those on the track team for which Gorden served as Officer Representative.

After three years at West Point, staff college, a Field Artillery Branch assignment, and with the Vietnam War ended, Major Gorden deployed for a one-year hardship tour in Korea, where he served as Battalion Executive Officer. Promoted to Lieutenant Colonel, he was made Special Assistant to the Division Artillery Commander after a short time as the Interim Battalion Commander. After Korea, he transferred intra-theater to Hawaii to the 25th Infantry Division (Light) under Major General Willard Scott and was

assigned as the Division Artillery Operations Officer (S-3) and later as a Battalion Commander. With the end of the war in Vietnam also came steep force reductions, the end of the draft, and the beginning of the all-volunteer Army in 1973. Among the many leadership challenges, Gorden recalls, were those related to manpower shortfalls in both quantity and quality. It was also a period during which a swirl of anti-war sentiment embroiled the country. Frustrations among Junior Officers were high as the Army non-commissioned officer corps underwent rebuilding, thus presenting formidable challenges to keeping them in uniform. Often recalled as the "Hollow Army," Gorden recalls the period as being the most resource-constrained, readiness-imperiled environment of any during his service. Still, he relished the responsibility of assuring that he and his sol-

>>> Spotlight

Major General Gorden served as a Senior Vice President with USAA after retiring from the Army. USAA provides insurance, banking, investment, and retirement products and services to 9.3 million members of the United States military and their families. Known for its legendary commitment to its members, USAA is consistently recognized for outstanding service, employee well-being, and financial strength. USAA membership is open to all who are serving or have honorably served our nation in the United States military – and their eligible family members.

Courtesy: USAA

Photo: NARA

His former commander, now–Lieutenant General Willard Scott had become the Superintendent of West Point in 1984, and was a fellow Redleg and mentor. He supported the nomination of Brigadier General Gorden as a potential Commandant of Cadets. In 1987, endorsed by then–Superintendent Lieutenant General Dave Palmer, Brigadier General Fred Gorden was selected as the 61st Commandant of Cadets, and the first African-American Commandant of Cadets. In fact, he was also the first African-American General Officer ever assigned to West Point, and also the first African-American assigned to Foreign Languages – neither of which he realized at the time. These significant milestones and accomplishments notwithstanding, his main focus was on leading all of the 4,400 cadets and the officers, non-commissioned officers and soldiers of West Point, regardless of color. In doing so, his leadership also gave inspiration to others who would follow and who, as new Cadet Gorden had years earlier, rationalized to themselves: "If someone else has done this before me, I can do it too," thereby giving themselves the confidence to overcome challenges and strive for success.

Having been born during the Depression and raised in the segregated South, Gorden helped break racial barriers as a leader in the Army. As the commandant of Cadets, he helped break down gender barriers by selecting Kristin Baker as the First Cadet Brigade Commander or First Captain of the Class of 1990. At the graduation of 1990, the commencement address was testimony to how far the Army had come in both racial and gender equality in a full meritocracy. General Colin Powell, the first African-American Chairman of the Joint Chiefs of Staff, presented Kristin Baker her diploma and delivered the commencement. Just a few months earlier, Gorden had been promoted to Two-Star Major General and headed off to Hawaii to take command of the 25th Infantry Division (Light). It was in this role leading assigned and attached non-divisional soldiers operating across the Pacific theater that brought all of Gorden's skills together. He loved light Infantry and the 25th was the most internationally deployed division of all light Infantry Divisions working with the militaries of all our Pacific allies, such as Korea, Japan, Thailand, Australia, Philippines, and others in that vast region.

His last assignments were in Washington, D.C. As Commanding General, Military District of Washington, he was frequently the Ranking Officer responsible for escorting dignitaries. He escorted the Nixon family to the funeral of President Nixon. He escorted South African President Nelson Mandela to the Tomb of the Unknown Soldier at Arlington National Cemetery. When President Clinton found that the former commander of the Tuskegee Airmen Lieutenant General Benjamin O. Davis (USMA 1936) had not been promoted to full General no doubt due to matters of race, he promoted him in 1996, 30 years after he had retired. Major General Gorden escorted General Davis to the ceremony, and they became close friends until his death in 2002. While we celebrate many of these pioneers, it is often hard to imagine the challenges they faced at the time. General Davis described to Gorden, as he also does in his autobiography, that he had not returned to West Point from 1936 until 1987, the painful memories of being ostracized for four years at West Point as the fourth African-American graduate made returning to West Point undesirable. Major General Gorden closed his career in 1996, retiring as Army Chief of Public Affairs.

Gorden found inspiration from others that motivated him to himself be a pioneer, breaking down barriers and leading men and women in a variety of roles around the world. Many others would follow his leadership, including one of the Tactical Officers whom Gorden led as Commandant – then-Major Lloyd Austin would rise to Four-Star General and command the war in Iraq and the serve as the first African-American Vice Chief of Staff of the Army and then Central Command Commander (CENTCOM). The institutions of America had changed significantly since Gorden was born during the Great Depression and raised in a segregated South. The American military had led much of that progress with pioneers, such as Gorden bravely pushing the limits to ensure fealty to America's creed that "all men are created equal."[2]

diers would live up to the reputation gained during Korea as the "automatic eighth" if called to do so.

In 1980, Lieutenant Colonel Gorden was assigned to the Pentagon in the Office of Legislative Affairs, where he had the unique perspective to see the legislative branch working with the military during the Reagan years as the Army turned the corner and rebuilt after the Hollow Army years.

During the Reagan build-up, a new emphasis was put on light Infantry Divisions after Chief of Staff John Wickham drafted a new strategy to build light divisions to confront low-intensity conflicts. Gorden was promoted to Colonel and charged with building the new Division Artillery for the newly configured 7th Infantry Division (Light) out of Fort Ord, in Monterey, California. This role required his leadership and strategic perspective as the role of artillery in the new light divisions

was highly debated, which would dictate the mobility of the entire division. The artillery force development community wanted heavy artillery, while Gorden believed mobility and the need to be "light" were key to rapid deployability. In the end, the Chief of Staff of the Army approved equipping light division artillery battalions with 105-mm artillery versus 155-mm heavy artillery, thus setting the precedent that would be followed by the 7th, 10th, and 25th light Infantry Divisions for the next three decades. Promoted to Brigadier General after his successful command, his career was again influenced by his language skills when he was assigned as Director of the Inter-American Region, International Security Affairs, Department of Defense. This was followed by another short assignment in Monterey at the 7th Infantry Division as Assistant Division Commander for eight months.

The MG Fred Gorden Room at the Thayer Hotel is proudly dedicated by USAA.

The 62 female graduates of the first class with women in the Class of 1980.

Andrea Lee Hollen, USMA 1980

• FIRST FEMALE GRADUATE OF WEST POINT
• FIRST WEST POINT FEMALE RHODES SCHOLAR
• COMMANDER, A COMPANY, 123RD SIGNAL BATTALION, WUERZBURG, GERMANY
• DIRECTOR OF ANALYTICS AND RESEARCH, CASE COMMONS
• OXFORD UNIVERSITY, BACHELOR OF ARTS IN MODERN HISTORY AND MODERN LANGUAGES
• MASTER OF PUBLIC ADMINISTRATION, NEW YORK UNIVERSITY

Cadet Andrea Lee Hollen receives her diploma from West Point as the first female graduate in Academy history, May 1980.

>>> Spotlight

Hollen has a passion for social entrepreneurship. Social entrepreneurs create and scale ventures that solve pressing social problems in groundbreaking ways, in settings where government programs and commercial business models may have failed. Social ventures typically apply innovative financial instruments, such as social impact bonds and micro-loans, to create new markets for products that improve outcomes for underserved populations. Examples of such products include sanitation technologies that are widely affordable in developing countries. Looking beyond traditional community activism, social entrepreneurs may work in concert with government leaders to improve public service delivery by breaking down the barriers to the flow of ideas and capital across sectors.

LEADERSHIP ACHIEVEMENT
FIRST FEMALE GRADUATE OF WEST POINT

The first female cadets in basic training, 1976.

Three days after the American Bicentennial, on July 7, 1976, history was made when 119 brave young women entered the previously all-male bastion at West Point. One-hundred-eighteen of those young women had completed their senior year in high school. One unique new cadet, Andrea Lee Hollen, went directly from junior year in high school to West Point. Apparently she didn't need to complete senior year to compete at the collegiate level; she graduated as a Rhodes Scholar and first out of the 62 female classmates who completed the journey becoming the first female West Point graduates in June 1980.

She's so proud of her entire class, both male and female, that she is reluctant to talk about her own accomplishments ahead of her classmates. When asked about being the first female to graduate in West Point history, even 30 years after graduation, she still believes she deserves no more attention than any of the other 61 classmates who graduated with her. Nonetheless, there is only one woman who graduated first from West Point and Hollen is that person. For Hollen, she looks back and realizes, like many of the males who have entered West Point, that she naively had no idea what she was getting into when she applied to West Point – and that was probably best in hindsight.

THIRTY YEARS LATER AND INDEED THANKS TO THE CLASS OF 1980'S LEADERSHIP, HOLLEN'S HOPES HAVE BEEN VALIDATED AND THE CONCLUSIVE BODY OF EVIDENCE DOES SAY SOMETHING INTELLIGENT ABOUT WOMEN IN COMBAT.

Hollen grew up in Altoona, a small town in western Pennsylvania. Her dad, Andrew, was a cameraman and engineer at a local television station and her mom, Grayce Ann, worked as a secretary at a bank. Hollen was self-described as being very introverted, conservative, and patriotic in high school. She was an exceptional student, very involved in music and academic clubs, and had already been accepted to Georgetown premed as a junior in high school. She

applied to West Point because she wanted to serve her country, but hadn't thought through the challenges of being in the first class with women. Her parents were supportive but not thrilled to see their daughter enter with the first class of women at West Point. She was the first in her family to attend college.

Hollen was caught off guard by the hostility her female classmates faced immediately upon entering West Point. The first day at West Point is a shock to any male or female, but there was a widespread belief among the men that women should not be at the Academy, in part because they were taking up slots intended for Combat Officers (men). And be they upperclassmen or faculty, most openly expressed their opinions. Their arguments ranged from concerns about physical prowess (the number of push-ups and pull-ups required) to the deep conviction that our national security was at risk. As she looks back, she is appreciative of the men who were principled in their opposition to the policy yet insisted on treating the women as individuals and with respect. Unfortunately, many others did not act so objectively and professionally. The challenges of admitting women were daunting and all encompassing – cultural, administrative, logistical – and led to mundane and comical challenges, such as having male upperclassmen trying to teach Plebe females how to properly fold a bra. West Point was a shock to Hollen's system. The women at West Point were a shock to West Point.

During high school, Hollen was more of a Latin club, orchestra, and Junior Academy of science type than an athlete, and the indoor obstacle course and other physical challenges at West Point proved humbling, but she persevered. She found the academic rigor, however, soothing. Academics became her respite.

Like all cadets who didn't play an intercollegiate sport, Hollen was required to participate in intramurals and an upperclassman assigned her to the triathlon team. To everyone's amazement, she could shoot pistols extremely well. And soon, the guys who put her on the intramural team changed their approach from trying to test her, push her, or perhaps force her out, to trying to recruit her to compete on the West Point Corps Squad (intercollegiate) Pistol Team. She made the team and competed through her Plebe and Yearling years. Cow year, she had the honor of being an exchange student for one semester at the United States Air Force Academy, which she affectionately describes as the "United States Air Force Resort." Apparently, she picked up some bad habits after a semester at USAFA. When she returned to West Point, she received more demerits than at any other time in her cadet career.

Hollen chose American History as her academic concentration and chose her electives in Electrical Engineering, which she oddly loved. With outstanding grades, Hollen was invited to compete for a Rhodes Scholarship. While she claims that her scholarship was more about "being in the right place at the right time," her classmates claim she was brilliant and humble, and more than deserving. She was the only female cadet invited to compete for the scholarship. The Rhodes Scholarship committee in Pennsylvania who interviewed her had never seen a female cadet before (obviously), and she says that they had more probing questions about being a female at West Point than they had about current affairs. She was stunned and honored to be told shortly after the interview that she was being awarded a Rhodes Scholarship.

Her class, both males and females alike, had persevered through a unique cadet experience being the first coed class, one that had brought them together as classmates. Firstie year, they made history again when their classmate Vincent Brooks was named the first African-American Cadet First Captain – the highest-ranking cadet in the Corps of Cadets. The Class of 1980 had broken another milestone in West Point history.

Hollen chose the Signal Corps as her branch because her Electrical Engineering professors had been thoughtful and inspiring mentors and were Signal Officers. Her dad had always messed around with old radios and amplifiers, and the more she learned about the branch, she felt it was in her blood.

When graduation came in May 1980, the media spotlight was on the class and particularly the females and Vincent Brooks. In a *People Magazine* article in April 1980, Hollen stated, "I didn't come with any crusading attitude about being a woman… But I have come to accept my role as part of a social experiment. I hope that one day I'll be part of a conclusive body of evidence that says something intelligent about women in combat."[1]

Thirty years later and indeed thanks to the Class of 1980's leadership, Hollen's hopes have been validated and the conclusive body of evidence does say something intelligent about women in combat. Female graduates have led soldiers in combat in Grenada, Panama, Desert Storm, Afghanistan, Iraq, and elsewhere to great acclaim, indeed females, such as Laura Walker (USMA 2003) and Emily Perez (USMA 2005), have unfortunately made the ultimate sacrifice for our country bravely leading soldiers in combat.

Once in England, Hollen found Oxford University disorientingly unstructured. Students could pick and choose when to go to classes or lectures, and could graduate by passing marathon final exams. Succeeding required exceptional self-discipline. Hollen most enjoyed the intensive tutorials with world-class professors, such as the distinguished military historian Sir Michael Howard. While at Oxford, she became active in the university's Officer Training Corps (similar to American ROTC), which allowed her to sharpen her military skills, work with British Royal Signals equipment, and enjoy field exercises in the Black Mountains of Wales, where she learned tactics from the Ghurkas.

After graduating from Oxford, Hollen returned to the Army and attended Airborne School and a Signal Corps course at Fort Sill before deploying to her first assignment in Kitzingen, Germany with 3rd Infantry Division. She arrived as a First Lieutenant, yet, because she had spent two years at Oxford, she hadn't really had the experiences that most Second Lieutenants had at that point, so she had to climb a steep learning curve to catch up with her year group. She was assigned to the Division Artillery of the 3rd Infantry Division as the Signal Platoon Leader. Her duties included managing the codes to unlock tactical nuclear weapons. She was promoted to Captain and went on to command Alpha Company, 123rd Signal Battalion. Thirty years later, she still believes the greatest privilege of her life was leading soldiers, and she is appreciative of the dedicated soldiers and non-commissioned officers under her command. She found teaching – and all the learning and re-thinking that goes with it – to be the most rewarding aspect of leadership.

Hollen returned to the United States to attend her branch advanced course (which is usually required before receiving a command which she already had achieved). For her next assignment, she was chosen for an elite

General of the Army Omar Bradley, the last living Five-Star General, visits West Point in spring of 1976 with the first class of female cadets in formation behind him.

Cadet Andrea Lee Hollen as a Plebe in classroom.

role in the White House Communications Agency. Before being assigned to the White House, she was accepted and attended graduate school in University of Colorado. While at CU, she was required to undergo all the special security clearances required for a White House assignment. It was during this rigorous clearance process that she found herself in a personal dilemma. She had recently acknowledged her gay identity, and therefore either had to lie about it or risk the clearance required to work in the White House. She decided that she simply could not lie to obtain the clearance, nor could she systematically dissemble her way through the rest of her career. So she chose to submit her unqualified resignation. This was a traumatic experience, walking away from the military family and soldiers she loved; she went through all the stages of grieving after leaving the military, which she will always regard as her true calling.

Once she was a civilian, Hollen worked as an Information Technology consultant across a range of industries. After serving two terms as a city planning commissioner, she found her passion in technology for state and local government, with a focus on municipal utilities, infrastructure and economic develop-

ment. Outside of leading soldiers, this was the most rewarding work she had every undertaken. She saw opportunities to better integrate Human Services delivery with economic and workforce development, and wondered if social enterprise – with the ability to blend donated and invested capital and form innovative public-private partnerships – held promise. After moving back east to be near her parents, she became a Graduate Fellow in New York University's Reynolds Program in Social Entrepreneurship.

Through the Reynolds Program, she met Kathleen Feely, the Vice President for Innovations at the Annie E. Casey Foundation. Feely had recently seen her daughter's Facebook page and had resolved to make such cutting-edge software available to frontline Human Services workers, beginning with Child Welfare agencies. The result was Casebook, a family-centric case management system based on a social networking platform. Developed by Case Commons, a startup non-profit social venture, Casebook is now live as Indiana's Child Welfare system of record. Hollen is Case Commons's Director of Analytics and Research and is working with a gifted team on building analytical tools, such as

exploratory data visualization, into Casebook. She is excited to be part of Case Commons's efforts to take the company's ideas to scale by forming partnerships with other states and cities. Hollen hopes that, through sharing this profile, she might encourage young people to pursue public service through social entrepreneurship.

Shortly after leaving the service, Hollen became a founding board member of the Servicemembers Legal Defense Network (SLDN, now OutServe-SLDN), which worked to end "Don't Ask, Don't Tell" and provide legal support to service members facing harassment or discharge under that policy. She served on the SLDN board for seven years, stepping down to focus on her duties as a planning commissioner. She is glad that the "Don't Ask, Don't Tell" policy has been eliminated since she believes it was a "tragically misguided" policy from the beginning, because of how it codified deception and underestimated the remarkable ability of soldiers to pull together to accomplish the mission, regardless of their differences. She believes there is still much work to be done to ensure full inclusion for LGBTQ servicemembers, veterans and their families.

As she looks back on her class at West Point, she is immensely proud of all that her classmates have achieved across so many areas of the American experience, including military service, government, politics, business, athletics, and community activism. She admires not only their leadership ability, but also their impact as change-makers.

She's in awe of so many of them, including and not limited to General Vincent Brooks; Lieutenant General Dave Perkins; Brigadier General Anne Macdonald; Congressman John Shimkus; Sue Fulton, who led Knights Out and now serves as a member of the West Point Board of Visitors; and Marene Allison, a corporate executive and founding member and the President of West Point Women.

Hollen is still reluctant to be recognized for being the first female graduate of West Point, because, as she repeatedly says, with selfless leadership, "I never would have survived without my classmates."[2]

Captain Hollen and Lieutenant Roberts in Germany.

Major (Retired) Priscilla "Pat" Walker Locke, USMA 1980

- FIRST AFRICAN-AMERICAN FEMALE GRADUATE OF WEST POINT (BY ORDER OF MERIT)
- CO-CAPTAIN ARMY WOMEN'S GYMNASTICS TEAM
- ENLISTED IN THE ARMY AT AGE 17
- RAISED IN POVERTY IN THE PROJECTS OF DETROIT / LIVED THROUGH THE "RACE RIOTS"

>>> Spotlight

When Sarah entered West point as a new Cadet in 2011, she and her mother Pat made history by becoming the first mother-daughter legacies of West point. Pat (USMA 1980) and Sarah (USMA 2015) are two of more than 400 African-American females who have attended West point since Pat first entered in 1976. As of 2013, 372 African-American females have graduated from West point.

Growing up in the extreme poverty of inner-city Detroit, Priscilla "Pat" Walker-Locke was determined to better herself through education and service to the nation. Locke credits her West Point experience and education with "saving her life" by affording her the chance to overcome the challenges of her childhood; and today, she continues to serve as a role model to both women and minorities.

Locke grew up in the projects of Detroit, living in her grandmother's apartment, which she shared with her mother – who was only 15 when she gave birth to Pat – and many other family members. During Detroit's 1967 race

riots, Locke, who was 10 years old at the time, had her first exposure to the United States Army. Soldiers of the 82nd Airborne Division were deployed there in order to stabilize the city. Locke remembers a young paratrooper who walked her and her friends through the streets of Detroit to ensure that they could travel safely. In 1973, Locke was 17 when she saw a sign in an Army recruiting station that read, "Join the People who've joined the Army." The Sergeant on duty had just closed the station for the evening but allowed her to sleep in the inner foyer until he returned in the morning. That next day, Locke was on a plane headed to basic training at Fort Jackson, South Carolina. Incredibly, upon her arrival, she spotted the same Soldier from the 82nd Airborne Division who had helped guide her and her friends safely through the race riots. This once ally and protector of a scared 10-year-old girl, was now an intimidating drill sergeant who was intent on transforming Locke into a professional Soldier. After basic training, Private Walker was assigned to Fort Polk, Louisiana.

In 1975, Congress authorized the admission of women to the service academies for classes entering in 1976. In the wake of this decision, the Army scrambled to find qualified female applicants. Locke was identified as one and joined 19 other enlisted women to attend the United States Military Academy Preparatory School (USMAPS) at Ft. Monmouth, New Jersey. Of the 20 women entering USMAPs in January 1976, only six entered West Point – Locke was one of them.

On July 7, 1976, the Corps of Cadets received its first-ever female members when 119 women entered as part of the Class of 1980. Lieutenant General Sidney Berry (USMA 1948), the Superintendent at the time, had publicly contemplated resignation over the policy. When women were admitted, he did not in fact resign, but his statements – which he later retracted with regret – had created a command climate that was openly hostile to the incoming females.[1] Some alumni, faculty, and the upper classes acted on that hostility claiming that it was a "disgrace" for women to be at the Academy and that it was ironically their "duty" to run out as many females as possible.[2] Most of the female cadets had come from middle to upper middle-class backgrounds and had stable families. Other than Joy Dallas, the only other African-American female cadet, Locke initially found that she had little in common with her female classmates.

Despite the challenges of cadet life, Locke understood that her West Point education and experience was the greatest opportunity of her life and she never once thought about quitting.

Locke did, however, experience open hostility from a small number of faculty members. In one instance, a paper she prepared and was authorized to submit for two different subjects received a "B" from one professor, while another professor (who had made it evident that he wanted to see her out of the Academy), gave the paper an "F." Once his intent was publicly identified, her professor retracted the failing grade.

Like Henry O. Flipper, Benjamin O. Davis, Roscoe Robinson, and other pioneering African-American cadets before them, Locke and Dallas were breaking the gender barrier as well. The other 117 female cadets were white women who could at a minimum relate to each other and the vast majority of white male cadets. Locke and her first-semester roommate, Danna Maller, had little in common and did not speak for the first three weeks. Attempting to break the ice, Maller reached out noting she could relate to Locke's status as a minority since she too was a minority as a Jewish cadet. Locke burst out laughing and the two connected, beginning a friendship that continues to this day.

Always an athlete, Locke became a member of the newly formed women's gymnastics team and was eventually selected as Co-Captain along with her classmate Kathy Snook. As a Plebe, Locke once found herself alone in a tunnel with an upperclassman who unsuccessfully tried to physically haze her since there were no witnesses. She never reported him, and to this day, Locke believes this to be a "trivial" incident that she and other females had to experience in order to pave the way for other women, and in no way reflects on the values of West Point, which she holds in the absolute highest regard.

Along with the entry of women to the Academy in 1976, West Point also faced a major cheating scandal that same year leading to the dismissal of several members of the Class of 1977. This scandal exacerbated an already hostile, and sometimes toxic environment. In 1977, Berry retired and was followed by LTG Andrew J. Goodpaster (USMA 1939). The highly respected Goodpaster had recently retired as a four star general yet he voluntarily returned to active duty at a lower rank in order to serve as the 51st Superintendent and to help West Point both recover from the cheating scandal and facilitate the integration of women. His selfless leadership was inspirational and directed the Academy through a difficult time.

In 1980, 62 females completed their journey as West Point's first female graduates – among them were Pat Locke and Joy Dallas.

Locke's journey was even honored as she was awarded the Key to the City of Detroit. While Andrea Lee Hollen holds the distinction as the first female graduate by order of merit (class rank), Locke is the first African-American female graduate by that same metric. Commissioned into the Air Defense Artillery, a combat arms branch open to women, Locke also selected Fort Bliss, Texas as her first assignment.

While on a field training exercise at Fort Bliss, she met her eventual husband Mike Locke, also an Army officer, and they were married in 1987. Unfortunately, Locke had suffered serious injuries in 1983 when she fell from a building. Her immediate injuries included bilateral detached retinas, which were surgically repaired, and spinal damage, which would manifest its severity over the next several years. It was these longer-term injuries causing damage to her back, neck, and spinal cord, however, which would eventually force her to medically retire as a major-promotable in 1995 with 100% disability. They would not, however, hamper her desire to help those less-fortunate around her.

LOCKE'S EFFORTS AND OUTREACH CONTINUE AS SHE ACTIVELY ENGAGES MEMBERS OF UNDER-SERVED AND UNDER-REPRESENTED COMMUNITIES

As her husband rose to the rank of colonel and commanded a brigade, Locke continued to serve the Army family as the head of his unit's family readiness groups and as an Army Family Team Building master trainer. On January 9, 1993, Pat and Mike gave birth to their daughter, Sarah. Eighteen years later, Sarah entered West Point as a member of the Class of 2015, making her the first daughter of an African-American female graduate to attend West Point. As of 2013, more than 372 African-American females have graduated from West Point. Locke's efforts and outreach continue as she actively engages members of under-served and under-represented communities so that one day each of them may also have the same opportunity she did to become leaders of character.

Brigadier General Halstead's official photo.

Brigadier General (Retired) Halstead.

Brigadier General Rebecca Halstead, USMA 1981

- **FIRST FEMALE WEST POINT GRADUATE TO BE PROMOTED TO GENERAL OFFICER**
- **COMMANDING GENERAL, U.S. ARMY ORDNANCE CENTER AND SCHOOLS**
- **COMMANDING GENERAL, 3RD CORPS SUPPORT COMMAND, IRAQ**
- **COMMANDER, 10TH MOUNTAIN DIVISION SUPPORT COMMAND, AFGHANISTAN**
- **COMMANDER, 325TH FORWARD SUPPORT BATTALION, 25TH INFANTRY DIVISION**

In 2004, Rebecca "Becky" Stevens Halstead became the first female graduate of West Point to rise to the rank of General Officer in the United States Army. Halstead was amongst the first of the female trailblazers in a historically male institution, entering West Point in 1977 as a member of the second class to include women.

Halstead was born March 26, 1959, and was raised in Willseyville, New York. She graduated from Candor Central, the local high school, and received her Congressional appointment to West Point in 1977. She entered West Point in July with 103 other women and more than 900 men. As a cadet, she played on the women's volleyball, softball, and handball teams. She was also the team manager for women's basketball and swimming. Following graduation on May 27, 1981, Halstead was commissioned in the Ordnance Corps. Her assignments included Vicenza, Italy; Fort Lewis, Washington; Fort Campbell, Kentucky; Schofield Barracks, Hawaii; Fort Drum, New York; and Afghanistan and Uzbekistan.

Along with her entire class, Halstead experienced a memorable and historic last semester at West Point. In her Firstie year, on January 20, 1981, Ronald Reagan was inaugurated as our nation's 40th President – the same day United States hostages were released from Iran following 444 days of captivity. President Reagan, who actually starred in the movie *The Long Gray Line*, a film based on the life of a real West Point cadet, had always loved West Point. His heartfelt decision that the former hostages should be welcomed back and reintegrated at West Point, spending their first three nights in the United States at the historic Thayer Hotel, served to add another page to the West Point legacy and spoke to his high regard for the institution.

Halstead had stood alongside the hundreds of her fellow cadets, who lined the street to form a welcoming wall of gray to celebrate the arrival of the freed hostages as they and their families were bussed across the hallowed grounds of West Point. The event held a special significance for Halstead as one of the Senior Officers held in captivity, Commander Don Sharer, and his family were also personal friends of the Halstead family. She was honored to escort them into the cadet mess hall on the evening of January 25, 1981, where they, along with the other hostages, were greeted by a thunderous roar of cadets wildly cheering and banging their silverware on their plates.

It was a turning point in Halstead's cadet career as she expressed in a letter to her parents after the historic event:

"The famous, hallowed words of General Douglas MacArthur, 'Duty, Honor and Country' had new life breathed into them tonight as we honored the hostages and their families in the cadet mess hall. I met Commander Sharer and his family at the steps of the mess hall. I gave them both big hugs and kisses. Everyone was crying. I shook Commander Sharer's hand, stepped back, saluted, and said, 'Welcome home, sir!' He smiled and replied with, 'It's great to be home!' As we walked into the mess hall, the cheering was overwhelming. The excitement, concern, and patriotism were omnipresent! As the glee club sang our national anthem, it gave me chills and made me feel proud to be standing at attention and being a part of the greatest Academy in the United States and the greatest country in the world. I have never felt greater. The whole experience added so much to my cadet career and my purpose in life!"

Just two months later, on March 30th, President Reagan would be shot in an assassination attempt. The attempt on his life did not deter the beloved President, who personally attended and delivered the emotional commencement speech for Halstead's

Halstead Room Dedication at Thayer Hotel.

Halstead receiving West Point Diploma, 1981.

HALSTEAD IMMORTALIZED HERSELF AS ONE OF THE FIRST WOMEN TO ENTER THE ACADEMY AND AS THE FIRST WOMAN GRADUATE TO BECOME A GENERAL OFFICER.

graduating class, "Strength As One, '81."

From this historic and dramatic start to her Army career, Second Lieutenant Halstead herself made history 22 years later, when she was announced for selection to Brigadier General in January 2003. With her selection for promotion, Halstead became the first female West Point graduate to achieve the rank of General Officer. During 2003, she served as the Deputy Commanding General for the 21st Theater Support Command in Germany, as

a promotable Colonel. She was responsible for overseeing logistics for the largest movement of equipment in and out of Europe (in support of the wars in Iraq and Afghanistan) since WWII.

Halstead pinned on her star for Brigadier General in 2004 and became the Commanding General of the 3rd Corps Support Command (3rd COSCOM) in V Corps, United States Army Europe, Germany. In 2005, she deployed her command to Operation Iraqi Freedom and became the first female Commanding General in our nation's history to lead America's sons and daughters in combat operations at the strategic level. Halstead led 20,000 soldiers and 5,000 civilians in the Iraq combat theater of operations from 2005 to 2006. Her 200-plus company-sized units provided distribution logistics (supply, maintenance, ammunition, water, fuel, and medical supplies) for the 250,000 men and women serving in Iraq. After

commanding in Iraq, Halstead returned to the United States in 2006 and became the first female Chief of Ordnance and served as the Commanding General for the Army's Ordnance Center and Schools.

Halstead retired in 2008 after 27 years of service to our nation. At the time of her retirement, she had achieved the highest rank by a female West Point graduate. In 2010, she started her own company, STEADFAST Leadership, specializing in motivational speaking and leadership training. In the course of three decades of service to her country, she immortalized herself not only as one of the first women to enter the Academy, but through the remarkable accomplishment of becoming the first woman graduate to become a General Officer. The nation has changed considerably, and Halstead, along with her classmates, paved a new path for both women and men of future generations. From Cadet to General Officer, she inspired

all those she served with and has become an iconic figure in the history of the Long Gray Line.

The Brigadier General Halstead Room at the Thayer Hotel is proudly dedicated by the Foundation for Chiropractic Progress.

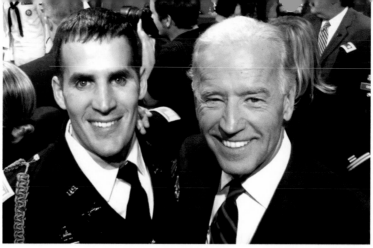

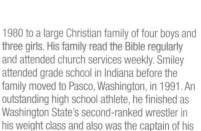

Captain Smiley receiving the Purple Heart. His brother is leaning over him. His wife's hand is on his shoulder

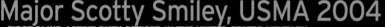

1LT Smiley with Iraqi children in Mosul in front of his Stryker Armored Vehicle

Major Scotty Smiley, USMA 2004

- **FIRST BLIND ACTIVE DUTY OFFICER IN THE UNITED STATES MILITARY**
- **ASSISTANT PROFESSOR OF MILITARY SCIENCE, GONZAGA UNIVERSITY**
- **INSTRUCTOR, BEHAVIORAL SCIENCES & LEADERSHIP DEPARTMENT, WEST POINT**
- **COMPANY COMMANDER, WARRIOR TRANSITION UNIT, WEST POINT**
- **BLINDED BY A SUICIDE CAR BOMBER IN MOSUL, IRAQ 6 APRIL 2005**
- **PLATOON LEADER, A COMPANY, 1-24 INFANTRY REGIMENT, 1ST BRIGADE, 25TH INFANTRY DIVISION, MOSUL, IRAQ**
- **MASTERS IN BUSINESS ADMINISTRATION, FUQUA SCHOOL OF BUSINESS, DUKE UNIVERSITY**
- **AUTHOR OF HOPE UNSEEN: THE STORY OF THE FIRST BLIND ACTIVE DUTY OFFICER**
- **COMBAT INFANTRYMAN BADGE, COMBAT DIVER QUALIFICATION COURSE BADGE, AIRBORNE BADGE, RANGER TAB, BRONZE STAR MEDAL, PURPLE HEART**

Major Scott Smiley is the first blind Soldier ever to have commanded a unit in the history of the United States Military – an accomplishment for which he is incredibly proud, yet one for which he soberly concedes that no one should ever aspire to achieve. Fittingly, the name tag "Smiley" adorning his uniform not only indicates his name, it also reflects the incredibly positive attitude and character of one of this generation's most inspirational leaders who has bravely led

Soldiers in combat, was seriously wounded, and has overcome tremendous adversity. As a result, Major Smiley leads a wonderful life with a beautiful family, and continues to serve the nation while inspiring future combat leaders. Though he himself cannot see it, Smiley brings a smile to the face of all who meet him because of his positive attitude and inspirational leadership.

When Smiley arrived at Fort Lewis, Washington for his first assignment, his Battalion Commander, Lieutenant Colonel Erik Kurilla

(USMA 1988), looked at Smiley's left shoulder to see if he had earned his Ranger Tab. Smiley indeed had before he arrived and Kurilla immediately gave responsibility of a 45-man infantry platoon to Second Lieutenant Smiley. It was this platoon that 2LT Smiley would take to war, and although it would unfortunately be the last combat unit he would ever see himself lead, it would fortunately not be the last Army unit that would see him lead.

Scott Smiley was born in Warsaw, Indiana, in

1980 to a large Christian family of four boys and three girls. His family read the Bible regularly and attended church services weekly. Smiley attended grade school in Indiana before the family moved to Pasco, Washington, in 1991. An outstanding high school athlete, he finished as Washington State's second-ranked wrestler in his weight class and also was the captain of his high school's state championship football team.

After receiving scholarships to several northwestern US universities, Smiley was accepted

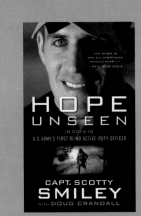

>>> Spotlight

Since releasing the *Hope Unseen* book in 2010, Scotty Smiley, Active Duty Army Office, Decorated War Veteran and Father, has been speaking to corporations, educators and church groups sharing his message of optimism and perseverance.

found himself failing both Freshman English and History. It was then Smiley realized he had to make some tough choices regarding athletics and academics or risk failing out of the Academy. After thinking and praying about his choices, he gave up wrestling in order to concentrate on academics. Nevertheless, Smiley was able to capitalize on his excellent physical abilities through his military training at the Academy. As a junior, he attended both the Army's demanding Combat Divers' Course and Airborne School, and then spent a summer with the 1st Special Forces Group at Ft. Lewis, Washington.

At this time in his life, Smiley envisioned that he would only serve five years in the Army, earn his MBA at graduate school, then enter the business world. It was during his junior year, however, that everything would change when the United States was attacked on September 11th 2001. The sight of the billowing smoke from the collapsed Twin Towers led to a realization that those attacks could have just as easily targeted any place in the United States to include his Washington home or West Point. The attacks were also an ominous sign to the Corps of Cadets as its members realized they would soon be heading to "the sound of the guns." In retrospect of those transformational days, Smiley concluded that he and his classmates matured very quickly during their final two years as cadets as they regularly received briefings from combat veterans returning from action in Afghanistan, the Philippines, and elsewhere against terrorist organizations. They were also confronted with their own mortality and understood that they would soon be risking their lives for their country and leading Soldiers in harm's way. For Smiley and the Class of 2003, Combat was no longer a hypothetical situation or academic exercise; it was a reality. Smiley would also make another momentous decision as a cadet when he proposed to Tiffany during Christmas break of his senior year. She accepted and they eventually married in December 2003.

Following his graduation and commissioning into the Infantry branch in 2003, he attended the Infantry Officer's Basic Course at Ft. Benning, Georgia, and then winter Ranger School from January to March 2004 after his and Tiffany's wedding. When the Smileys arrived at Fort Lewis, Washington, in April of 2004, the war in Afghanistan was already entering its third year, and combat operations in Iraq had begun a year earlier following the US invasion in March 2003. It was at Fort Lewis where LTC Kurilla (who would later be promoted to Brigadier General) assigned Smiley as the platoon leader. Coincidentally, both Smiley and

Kurilla would eventually leave the battlefield on bloodied gurneys after being severely wounded while leading their Soldiers in combat.

After six months as a platoon leader at Fort Lewis, Smiley's battalion deployed to the city of Mosul, Iraq, in October 2004. At that stage of the war, Mosul was one of Iraq's most dangerous cities due to the growing insurgency. Shortly after his arrival, a suicide bomber disguised as an Iraqi soldier blew himself up in the mess hall in Mosul, killing 14 US soldiers, four US contractors, and four Iraqi soldiers. Several of members of Smiley's platoon were seriously wounded in the attack. The battalion patrolled the streets of Mosul daily and was in constant contact with the enemy. He and his platoon regularly experienced improvised explosive devices (IEDs) and vehicle-borne improvised explosive devices (VBIEDs) – or suicide car bombers.

> **SMILEY'S FIRST REGRET WAS THAT HE WOULD NEVER SEE HIS BEAUTIFUL WIFE TIFFANY AGAIN – HE WOULD NEVER SEE ANYTHING AGAIN. EVER.**

It was six months into his deployment and in this setting that Smiley vividly recalled the day his life changed forever. On April 6, 2005, he was leading his Soldiers on a patrol and spotted a suspicious-looking vehicle. His Company Commander, Captain Jeff Van Antwerp, was with him on the patrol. The rear end of the suspicious vehicle was visibly lower than the front (indicating that it was weighted down with explosives) while it was occupied by a sole male driver who was freshly shaven (a Muslim ritual before death). Smiley cordoned off the vehicle and remained standing in the commander's hatch of his Stryker armored vehicle only 25 meters from the cordoned vehicle. Following the rules of engagement, Smiley next fired two warning rounds into the front of the vehicle with his M-4 rifle and yelled in Arabic for the man to exit the vehicle, which the man refused to do. While standing in the commander's hatch of his Stryker, Smiley's body was largely protected but his head was exposed so he could observe the driver and the vehicle. At this point, while looking directly into the eyes of the driver, the suicide driver detonated his vehicle, which tragically was the last thing Smiley would ever see.

The next thing Smiley remembered was waking up in Walter Reed Medical Center several weeks later with both Tiffany and his brother holding his hands. Shrapnel had penetrated

at both West Point and the United States Air Force Academy. He was most attracted to West Point because of the extensive focus on leader development he had seen in both West Point's marketing materials and that was reinforced through his interaction with members of the Long Gray Line he had met during the admissions process. Additionally, Scott's older brother Neal was a second-class cadet (junior) at West Point, so Scott had intimate knowledge of the cadet experience from his brother.

Smiley accepted the appointment to West Point and left both his family and his high school girlfriend, Tiffany, to enter West Point on June 28, 1999, as part of the Class of 2003. As a cadet, he tried out for the Army football team only to be cut just prior to the first game of the season. Undeterred and ever determined to play an intercollegiate sport, Smiley tried out for and earned a place on the Army wrestling team. Despite his 3.93 grade point average in high school, however, he was humbled by West Point's rigorous academic load and soon

CPT Smiley Teaching at West Point

both eyes, part of his head was missing around the eye socket, and his left eye had been removed. He was told he would never see again. The left side of his brain had also been hit causing paralysis on the right side of his body. The pain, suffering, confusion, regret, and loss, all were the beginning of a long healing process that would test the limits of his emotional, physical, and spiritual strength. His first regret was that he would never see his beautiful wife Tiffany again – he would never see anything again. Ever.

Many of his life's dreams for the future were now shattered, and each time he would realize this he experienced more mental anguish. His first impulse was to think about returning to his Soldiers, which he knew he would never do. He would never join a Ranger battalion as he had hoped. He saw only a future life of absolute despair.

Over time, it was through the love and strength of Tiffany, his family, and the power of prayer that he was able to heal mentally, physically, and spiritually. The loss of his dreams was

similar to the loss of a loved one. Smiley had to experience his own grieving process in order to accept his physical challenges, while also setting new goals and pursuing new dreams for the future. He could let his circumstances defeat him, or he could use this tragic, life-changing event as an opportunity to inspire those around him in every way. Smiley chose the latter.

Physically, his paralysis fortunately subsided and he started to recover feeling in the right side of his body. Learning to walk again would soon follow. Emotionally and spiritually, he also knew that he had to reconcile his feelings about the suicide bomber. Smiley learned to forgive the bomber for the pain he had caused, which was a critical step toward his own emotional and spiritual healing.

Smiley then went to the Blind Rehabilitation Center in Palo Alto, California, where he continued his remarkable recovery. He learned how to walk, how to operate a computer for the blind, and countless other mundane tasks, such as cooking and dressing that people with

vision take for granted. As part of his physical rehabilitation, Smiley received a new portion of his skull on October 31s 2005, and later he received new eyes. Smiley's appearance gradually returned to what he had looked like prior to the attack, and with the return of his physical appearance and abilities – although he could not physically see the changes – came an enormous return of his morale and confidence. In fact, his physical appearance was so complete that he found joy and a sense of accomplishment at one point when a superior officer corrected Smiley for not saluting, only for that superior officer later to realize regretfully that he had corrected a blind man for not recognizing his rank.

Throughout the recovery process, Scott and Tiffany began to envision new dreams for themselves and their future together. They first and foremost thanked God for the gift of his life and then planned a family together. Since then, they have been blessed with three healthy children over the next five years: Grady Douglas in 2007, Graham Elliott in 2009, and Baylor Scott in 2012.

Facing a medical retirement from the Army, Smiley pursued his next dream of remaining in the Army so he could continue serving the nation and Soldiers he loved. In doing so, Smiley discovered a very specific regulation that allowed disabled soldiers to remain on active duty. However, his chances were slim as this process had never been approved for a blind soldier. Smiley would have to break new ground in the 232-year history of the United States Army. Fortunately, Lieutenant General Robert L. Van Antwerp (USMA 1972, commander of the US Army Accessions Command, and father of Smiley's company commander who had been on patrol with him that fateful day in Iraq) led Smiley through the Medical Evaluation Board process at Fort Monroe, Virginia. The board decided to retain Smiley on active duty making him the first blind officer in US Army history. He spent more than a year in Accessions Command in the Operations Center and travelled across the US with LTG Van Antwerp inspecting training bases. His assignment there culminated in him winning the award as the 2007 Army Times Soldier of

Scott holding 2nd son Graham Elliott on the apron at West Point.

MAJOR SCOTTY SMILEY'S LEADERSHIP POSITIONS AND AWARDS:

- Recipient of the General Douglas MacArthur Leadership Award
- Excellence in Sports Performance Yearly (ESPY), 2008
- Christopher Award
- Father of the Year Award
- Army Times, Soldier of the Year
- Honorary PhD, Mount Saint Mary's, Newburgh New York

the Year.

With LTG Van Antwerp's support, Smiley was then selected to teach leadership at West Point in the Department of Behavioral Sciences and Leadership (BS&L). Prior to teaching, he attended Army-funded graduate school at Duke University's Fuqua School of Business where he earned his Master of Business Administration (MBA). While at Duke, legendary basketball coach Mike Krzyzewski (USMA 1969) formed a friendship with Smiley and often asked him to speak before the Duke and USA Olympic basketball teams. Krzyzewski became a mentor to Smiley, encouraging him not to consider his physical challenges an embarrassment; rather, he encouraged Smiley to proudly embrace them as the sacrifice he made in serving the nation. In addition, Krzyzewski also encouraged Smiley to proudly accept the rare, but occasional, advantages for all of the sacrifices that he had made and continues to make. For instance, one such rare advantage included courtside seats at Duke Basketball games, seats for which Duke graduate students

normally endure a heavy dose of traditional forms of hazing. Smiley had already endured far more than the other graduate students to earn these prestigious seats.

Smiley then returned to West Point to teach cadets in the Leadership Department and cadets loved him as an instructor. After one semester of teaching, the Army asked Smiley to Command the Warrior Transition Unit (WTU) located at West Point, New York. The Army specifically established WTUs to support wounded Soldiers who require lengthy rehabilitative care and complex medical management. This assignment seemed tailor-made for Smiley. He discussed this opportunity with Tiffany, and after praying about it, they both knew that Scott could have the most positive impact on the Army in this command assignment. Thus, Smiley not only was the first blind Soldier to serve on active duty in the US Army, he also became its first blind company commander. As commander, Smiley led with vigor and inspiration knowing that God had planned his life for this purpose. While in command, he was also nominated for the General Douglas

MacArthur Leadership Award, which recognizes outstanding Company Grade Officers across the Army, and was the United States Military Academy's 2010 award winner.

As Smiley healed he realized that he still had lessons to teach to young cadets and Soldiers, lessons the average officer would have trouble teaching because they had never experienced what he had. Through his unyielding faith, with the support of his family, and through pure determination and perseverance, Smiley experienced and overcame hurdles that likely would have been insurmountable to most people. He then believed he could articulate those lessons that may help save the lives of cadets and their Soldiers in the future. In 2010, Smiley, who had once been failing English at West Point, published *Hope Unseen: The Story of the US Army's First Blind Active-Duty Officer*, an award-winning book about his and Tiffany's inspirational journey to overcome the adversity associated with such a devastating combat injury.

In 2011, he attended the Infantry Advanced

Course at Ft. Benning and then was selected to teach Military Science at Gonzaga University in Spokane, Washington. This assignment was a wonderful and rewarding return to his and Tiffany's home state after a trying, eight-year journey that took them to their first assignment at Fort Lewis, Washington; through the streets of Mosul, Iraq; to Walter Reed Medical Center in Washington, DC, and rehabilitation in Palo Alto, California; to Fort Monroe, Virginia; graduate school at Durham, North Carolina; the faculty and command at West Point, New York; and finally to school at Fort Benning, Georgia. They are now surrounded by family and friends who will certainly add to the Smiley's quality of life. Perhaps most importantly for Major Scott Smiley, however, is that he can continue to realize his dream and vision of serving his nation through educating and inspiring the next generation of Army leaders – a vision clearly seen by everyone, especially Scotty.

Montgomery C. Meigs helped lead our Army through some uncertain times. A decorated combat veteran, he commanded troops in Vietnam, Desert Storm, and in peace enforcement in Bosnia.

Meigs's father, Lieutenant Colonel Montgomery C. Meigs (USMA 1940), was Killed In Action in France at age 25 commanding the 23rd Tank Battalion. Raised in a family with a strong Naval tradition, Meigs followed his father and his three-time great uncle – the original Montgomery C. Meigs (USMA 1836), Quartermaster General of the Union Army – into the military.

Graduating from West Point in 1967, he joined the Armor Branch. After Ranger School and reporting to 3rd Armor Division in Germany, Meigs served for a year as an Armored Cavalry Troop Commander and then headed to Vietnam. A week after reporting to 3rd Squadron 5th Cavalry, he found himself in the Ashau Valley commanding Troop A. Ranging all over the northern provinces of Vietnam provided multiple opportunities for "tactical learning."

He later served as Aide-de-Camp to Brigadier

General George S. Patton, the son of the legendary World War II Commander. Patton had a huge impact on Meigs's determination to remain in the Army. Stern, often volatile, Patton possessed a deft personal touch with soldiers and a cagey, discerning sense of initiative and "educated audacity." He imbued a rough-hewn, hands-on, soldier-focused kind of leadership. Patton's teachings were invaluable to Meigs throughout his career, but especially in his next assignment, to command a 3rd Cavalry troop in Germany in the "Hollow Army" of 1974. Penetrated by three drug rings, undisciplined, and manned by soldiers with a "don't mean nuthin'" mentality, Troop A, 1-1 Cavalry took almost 18 months to turn around.

Meigs next pursued a doctorate in history, a course of study that helped to define his later successes as a General Officer. Two years on the faculty of the United States Military Academy and a year at MIT as a Council on Foreign Relations International Affairs Fellow gave Meigs time to finish his dissertation on the management of the atomic bomb development in WWII. Later, as a student at the National War College, he published a book

on submarine warfare in World War II. These experiences helped him to refine his ideas on technological innovation.

In 1990, as Commander of 2nd (Iron Brigade), 1st Armored Division, Meigs deployed to

IN 2009, HE ACCEPTED THE POSITION OF PRESIDENT AND CHIEF EXECUTIVE OFFICER OF BUSINESS EXECUTIVES FOR NATIONAL SECURITY. THE WASHINGTON, D.C.–BASED NON-PROFIT BRINGS CORPORATE EXECUTIVES TOGETHER TO APPLY BEST BUSINESS PRACTICE TO HELP GOVERNMENT SOLVE SOME OF ITS TOUGHEST CHALLENGES IN NATIONAL SECURITY.

Saudi Arabia for Desert Storm. On day three of the campaign, the brigade attacked Iraqi units newly deployed to protect the Basra-Kuwait City road. In the Battle of Medina Ridge in less than 30 minutes, the Iron Brigade destroyed the Republican Guard's B Brigade of the Medina and elements of the Adnan Division. For its service in Desert

Storm, the Iron Brigade received the Valorous Unit Award.

From 1995 to 1997, Meigs commanded 3rd Infantry Division and, at mid-tour, supervised its reorganization to 1st Infantry. Over his second year of command, the Big Red One rotated more than 12,000 troops through two tours in the northern sector in Bosnia as part of the NATO effort to enforce the Dayton Peace Treaty. The division managed a number of violent demonstrations and confrontations with Bosnian Serb forces and operated in undeveloped country in severe winter weather without losing a single soldier.

A tour as Commandant of the Army's Staff College followed division command. During this assignment, Meigs introduced case study methods into the college's leadership

General Montgomery C. Meigs, USMA 1967

- CHIEF EXECUTIVE OFFICER, BUSINESS EXECUTIVES FOR NATIONAL SECURITY (BENS)
- COMMANDER, JOINT IMPROVISED EXPLOSIVE DEVICE DEFEAT ORGANIZATION (JIEDDO)
- SERVED IN VIETNAM, DESERT STORM, AND BOSNIA-HERZOGOVINIA
- BRONZE STAR FOR VALOR, PURPLE HEART

Having just become Director of the Joint Improvised Explosive Device Defeat Organization (JIEDDO), this was the first briefing with President George W. Bush, Secretary of Defense Donald Rumsfeld, and Joint Chiefs of Staff Chairman General Peter Pace in January 2006.

instruction and helped write a new leadership manual for the Army termed by Frances Hesselbein, then-Director of the Peter F. Drucker Foundation – the best of its kind.

Promoted to General in 1998, Meigs returned to Germany to command United States Army Europe (USAREUR.) Between 1998 and 1999, he also served as Commander of SFOR, NATO's Stabilization Force in Bosnia. In 1999, to stop the Serbs' ethnic cleansing of Kosovo, NATO conducted an air campaign against their forces. Throughout this operation, while ensuring a safe and secure environment, SFOR kept the ethnic cleansing and fighting in Kosovo from spilling over into Bosnia. Simultaneously, SFOR continued to pry open barriers to freedom of movement and resettlement.

Meigs's interest in operational innovation continued during this tour in USAREUR. In 1994, he supported peacekeepers patrolling the Macedonian-Kosovo border. Tracking patrols to ensure they did not inadvertently cross any one of the three borders between these countries posed a daily challenge. Upon arrival in USAREUR in 1998, in conjunction with his duties in Bosnia, Meigs developed

a requirement for a unit-tracking system and provided the necessary resources and command support. In less than a year, USAREUR fielded "Blue Force Tracker," a vehicle and unit-tracking communications system that allowed continuous location within and between units on the move. As the clock wound down to D-Day for the invasion of Iraq, Blue Force Tracker went viral and became a critical tool for maintaining situational awareness for Army and Marine ground forces.

Other innovations that Meigs initiated included fully instrumented opposed-force training in Poland and, in 2002, the opening of a rail-based line of communication through Russia to support NATO operations in Afghanistan. Meigs also supervised the modernization and training of V Corps elements that deployed on Iraqi Freedom, the invasion of Iraq. They included the capability for the Corps Commander of V Corps during the offensive into Iraq, to command his entire formation on the move from a command post of two modified Bradley Fighting Vehicles.

Meigs retired from active service in 2003 expecting to teach in graduate schools on

topics in national security affairs. In 2004, the United States and NATO confronted expanding insurgencies in Southwest Asia. With explosive materials readily available in Iraq and Afghanistan and technologies spawned in the information age, Improvised Explosive Devices (IEDs) became the weapon of choice, eventually causing more than half the casualties in the campaign.

In December 2005, Secretary of Defense Donald Rumsfeld appointed Meigs to lead the Joint IED Defeat Organization (JIEDDO), the organization assigned the mission of reducing the effectiveness of IEDs. Under Meigs's leadership, JIEDDO identified three major lines of effort: attack the network, train the force, and defeat the device. On his watch, JIEDDO increased intelligence fusion available to brigades and battalions, fostered extended discovery of new counter-IED technology, fielded one new family of jammers and initiated development of another. JIEDDO also invested in intensifying service training in mission rehearsals and developed and deployed equipment to find and destroy IEDs in place. These efforts helped reduce casualties of IEDs by a factor of six.

Meigs then returned to teaching, but in 2009, he accepted the position of President and Chief Executive Officer of Business Executives for National Security. The Washington, D.C. – based non-profit, non-partisan organization brings corporate executives together to apply best business practices to help government solve some of its toughest challenges in national security.

Meigs has been awarded the Bronze Star for Valor, the Purple Heart, the Department of Defense Medal for Distinguished Public Service, the Defense Distinguished Service Medal, and the German Federal Republic's Honor Award for Distinguished Service with Star. He is also an officer of the French Legion of Honor.

The General Meigs Room at the Thayer Hotel is proudly dedicated by USAA.

Commander SFOR's first visit to Srebrenica, Bosnia, just after assuming command in November 1998.

Commander 2nd Brigade, 1st Armored Division, Desert Storm, the night before the Battle at Medina Ridge, in position and ready to go in M1-A1 tank, HQ-66, in February 1991.

Courtesy: General Meigs

>>> Spotlight

Business **Executives** for **National Security**

Change Do Act Solve Work Team Drive

Founded in 1982, BENS has served as the primary channel through which senior American business leaders contribute special experience and talent to help build a more secure nation – pro bono. With regional offices across the country and from its headquarters in Washington, D.C., the membership has earned the trust and respect of leaders in government. BENS believes that the defining strengths of the American private sector – ingenuity, innovation, and efficiency – should be applied to our nation's security, by working with government partners to develop creative, new approaches to deal with the challenges we face today.

Courtesy: BENS

Executive Officer of 2nd Armored Cavalry conducting a tour of the FRG/GDR border in summer 1983 (Iron Curtain).

Courtesy, Admiral Shelton

Plebe year, 1963, H-1.

Shelton with Seabees in Somalia.

Courtesy, Admiral Shelton

Rear Admiral Michael W. Shelton, USN, USMA 1967

- **ONLY WEST POINT GRADUATE TO EVER BECOME A U.S. NAVY FLAG OFFICER**
- **CIVIL ENGINEER CORPS, U.S. NAVY**
- **FATHER OF THE MODERN SEABEES, FOUNDER 1ST NAVAL CONSTRUCTION DIVISION**
- **TWO TOURS OF DUTY IN VIETNAM**
- **BOY SCOUTS OF AMERICA, EAGLE SCOUT**

Tet 1968, Danang , Republic of Vietnam.

Photo: DOD

Shelton's official photo, 2001.

>>> Spotlight

EMCOR®
Build. Power. Service. Protect.

EMCOR Group, Inc. (NYSE: EME) is a Fortune 500 company with estimated 2012 revenues of approximately $6.4 billion and a leader in mechanical and electrical construction, energy infrastructure, and facilities services. EMCOR provides critical infrastructure systems, giving life to new structures and sustaining life in existing ones by planning, installing, operating, maintaining, and protecting the sophisticated and dynamic systems that create facility environments – such as electrical, mechanical, lighting, air-conditioning, heating, security, fire protection, and power generation systems – in virtually every sector of the economy and for a diverse range of businesses, organizations, and government.

Beast Barracks Detail, 1966.

Mike Shelton is the only West Point graduate to ever become a Flag Officer in the United States Navy. He brought West Point leadership to the United States Navy Seabees. After graduating from West Point, Shelton led Seabees, commanding at every level from Platoon through Battalion, Regiment, Brigade (the Navy division equivalent at that time) in combat, and contingency operations around the world and reorganized them for the twenty-first century.

Shelton grew up as a "Navy brat," traveling worldwide. His father retired as a Navy Master Chief (E-9) after a 31-year career that included combat at Pearl Harbor, Midway, off Guadalcanal, and during the Korean War. Shelton's father had always wanted him to go to the Naval Academy, but Shelton failed the eye test during his entrance exam to USNA. Fortunately, he passed the eye test for West Point and chose that path.

During Shelton's cadet career, he had the unique distinction of possibly being the only cadet in history to be ever written up by an officer for being "apparently asleep while marching to breakfast," which resulted in marching the area (penalty tours in full uniform with rifle) in February of his second year. The "offense" happened on a bitterly cold day when cadets were allowed to turn up their overcoat collars, but a Major did not like the fact that Shelton's cap had slipped down on his forehead, making it look to him like he was sleeping, despite the impossibility of the task.

While at West Point, Shelton's goal was to graduate and join the Corps of Engineers, but he did not have the class rank to get to fulfill his ambition. But when he discovered a regulation that allowed West Point graduates to join any service that their father had served in (if they had served a full career), his Master Chief father vectored him to the Navy Civil Engineer Corps (Seabees), offering him the battalion of his choice in Vietnam. So, after graduation (plus two years of graduate school upon return), Shelton chose the Seabees.

The Class of 1967 had entered West Point in 1963 as United States advisors were being deployed to Vietnam. By the time they graduated on June 7, 1967, the United States had 500,000 troops in Vietnam, and one of Shelton's Beast Barracks squad leaders, Doug Davis (USMA 1965), had been KIA. Commissioned an Ensign, Shelton was the first member of the class to be deployed to Vietnam arriving on October 25, 1967, to join Naval Mobile Construction Battalion 9

outside Danang in I Corps. In 1968, the Viet Cong conducted surprise attacks all across Vietnam. Ensign Shelton saw combat in the TET offensive. His first Army classmates joined him in the reinforcing brigade from the Airborne. He passed that brigade in a convoy headed north shortly before the first classmate, Jim Adams, was KIA, followed by Ron Frazer and John Brown. The Class of 1967 would lose a total of 29 classmates (five percent of their class) in Vietnam, three of them had been Shelton's roommates: Ron Frazer, John Brown, and Dan Neuberger.

Shelton was one of the first in the class to return to Vietnam for a second tour when he deployed in 1970 with MACV Studies and Observation Group (SOG, which was the cover name for the Special Operations Force command during the war). As a Navy Lieutenant, Shelton, an E-8, and 140 Vietnamese constructed and maintained camps for the Navy SEALs, Army Long Range Patrols, Marine Recon, and SOG elements in I Corps. Shelton watched the last Marine/Seabees units leave Vietnam in 1971, as his unit did classified missions that earned him a Presidential Unit Citation.

In what would, in hindsight, be closure on the Vietnam War, Lieutenant Shelton assumed his assignment as Operations Officer, S-3, of Naval Mobile Construction Battalion 4 in Guam in April 1975, the day before they were tasked to construct and maintain a camp at Orote Point for 50,000 Vietnamese evacuees after the fall of Saigon. As a result of performance, the battalion won the Petlier Award as the best construction battalion in the Navy and a Navy Meritorious Unit Award.

Commander Shelton assumed command of Amphibious Construction Battalion 2 in 1983 just as they were tasked to develop the operational doctrine for the loading and unloading (at sea) of the Maritime Preposition Ship Squadron. The squadron was the key strategic logistics force for supporting a Marines brigade in contingencies while serving as the test platform for the next generation logistics system designed to off-load containers/POL at sea.

October 1983 was the most active month for the Department of Defense since the Vietnam War – with operations in the Middle East and Central America – and Shelton's battalion was involved in both major operations. On October 23, 1983, the Marine Corps suffered its worst loss in a single day since the Battle of Iwo Jima. The 24th Marine Amphibious Unit (24th MAU), with Shelton's Seabees attached, was attacked by a suicide truck

bomb driven into the barracks and detonated in Beirut with the loss of 241 United States servicemen. His men performed rescue operations there, while simultaneously, two days later, the United States invaded the Caribbean island of Grenada to rescue some American medical students and to overturn a communist coup with another detachment from the battalion participating. The battalion's performance during his command earned it an individual Joint Service Meritorious Unit Award (first ever awarded to a Seabee battalion) and a Navy Meritorious Unit Award.

In 1992, Captain Shelton was selected to integrate active and reserve Seabee units into the operational brigade within the Atlantic fleet as the first test case for such a unit in the Navy. This was a result of poor "lessons learned" on active/reserve integration in Desert Storm. He had additional duty as the commander of a newly commissioned operational regiment. The "culture war" was successfully resolved and served as the basis for a larger later restructuring of the Seabees.

Shelton was promoted to Rear Admiral (Lower Half) in 1995. His 1967 class contained the largest group of USNA engineers since World War II, but Shelton was the only one from this group to be promoted to Two-Stars – the highest Navy engineer rank when he was promoted in 1998. He was the only member of his class of engineers to be promoted to Flag rank.

Rear Admiral Shelton became the "Father of the Modern Seabees" by conceiving and winning approval from the Chief of Naval Operations, Admiral Vern Clark, to stand up a Seabee Division, 1st Naval Construction Division, comprised of ALL the Seabee units (active and reserve) in the Navy under a Two-Star Command to support Marine and Joint contingency construction efforts in 2001. Achieving this task required fighting and winning programmatic budget battles within the Navy and Pentagon to outfit and recapitalize this unit. This unit was stood up in time to support the invasion of Iraq in 2003 and won a Presidential Unit Award for its outstanding performance in support of all the Armed Forces. Shelton retired in October 2001 and is currently chairman of EMCOR Government Services.

22nd Construction Regiment COC.

Camp Hoover I Corps RVN, 1967.

Photo: NARA

Cadet First Captain John Tien, 1987.

Courtesy Colonel Tien

Lieutenant Colonel Tien with Iraqi "Sons of Iraq" Ramadi, Iraq 2007.

Photo: White House

President Bush and Colonel Tien in the Oval Office, January 2009.

President Obama and Colonel Tien in the Oval Office, August 2010.

Colonel John Tien, USMA 1987

- **FIRST ASIAN-AMERICAN CADET FIRST CAPTAIN**
- **RHODES SCHOLAR**
- **WHITE HOUSE FELLOW**
- **OPERATION IRAQI FREEDOM BATTALION COMMANDER**
- **NATIONAL SECURITY COUNCIL STAFF (IRAQ, AFGHANISTAN, PAKISTAN), THE WHITE HOUSE**

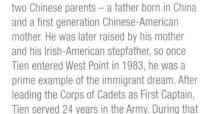

Photo: NARA

In August 1986, John Tien became the first Cadet First Captain of Asian descent. He was born in New Haven, Connecticut, to two Chinese parents – a father born in China and a first generation Chinese-American mother. He was later raised by his mother and his Irish-American stepfather, so once Tien entered West Point in 1983, he was a prime example of the immigrant dream. After leading the Corps of Cadets as First Captain, Tien served 24 years in the Army. During that time, he distinguished himself as both a soldier and a scholar, shaping United States policy at critical times in Iraq, Afghanistan, and Pakistan as an advisor to both President Bush and President Obama.

As a cadet, Tien earned four very exclusive distinctions: First Captain, Rhodes Scholar, and Starman (for those in the top five percent for academic ranking). His fourth distinction was less formal, but even more important: He was a member of the unofficial "Two Percent Club," for cadets who entered and graduated from the Academy with the same girlfriend. That girlfriend, Tracy Franklin, married Tien one year after graduation and served alongside him for 24 years in the Army and 12 different household moves, while raising two daughters.

In retrospect, Tien can trace much of his leadership ethos back to the lessons he learned as a First Captain – particularly from his interactions with classmates and officer and non-commissioned officer mentors. For instance: He remembers the Commandant of Cadets Brigadier General Peter Boylan telling him at the start of the academic year, "John, being a leader means you must always be there for your troops even in their toughest hours, and it's then that they may need you to be both their cheerleader and their Platoon Leader." Although far different than leading football cheers at Michie Stadium or giving speeches in South Auditorium, 20 years later and under much more serious conditions,

LEADERSHIP ACHIEVEMENT
FIRST ASIAN-AMERICAN CADET FIRST CAPTAIN

>>> Spotlight

Citi, the leading global bank, has approximately 200 million customer accounts and does business in more than 160 countries and jurisdictions. Citi provides consumers, corporations, governments, and institutions with a broad range of financial products and services, including consumer banking and credit, corporate and investment banking, securities brokerage, transaction services, and wealth management.

Courtesy: Citi

Tien's experiences as a First Captain helped him stand again in front of more than thousand soldiers. This time, it was at Camp Arifjan in Kuwait, where he told them why and how they were about to deploy north to Iraq in the midst of what would later be considered the height of the Iraq War.

At Oxford, Tien studied philosophy, politics, and economics, learning everything he could about why nations went to war and why their citizens volunteered to join those battles.

Debating with students from all over the world – like whether Mikhail Gorbachev was indeed intent on redefining the Cold War landscape – was a timely prelude to Tien's first tactical assignment in southern Germany. Within one month of Tien leaving Oxford and his study of Soviet politics, he led his Germany-based Abrams tank platoon on its last-ever border patrol along the West German–Czechoslovakia border. Two months later on November 10, 1989, the Berlin Wall fell, ending the 45-year-old Cold War.

More than a year later, Tien's platoon (VII Corps's most left-flank battalion) became one of the most western and eventually northern deployed United States military units in Operation Desert Storm. The VII Corps wheeled around Kuwait in its famous "Left Hook" maneuver led by General Fred Franks (USMA 1959). As the initial phase of the ground war ended on February 28, 1991, Tien was working on plotting latitude and longitude grids – his generation's version of a global positioning system – to lead the battalion toward Baghdad. His Battalion Commander told him the war was over and their new mission was now to oversee the burning oil fields near Basra. Tien followed his Germany assignment with two company command tours at Fort Hood, a teaching assignment in West Point's Department of Social Sciences, a White House Fellowship in the Clinton Administration, and a four-year field grade tour at the National Training Center at Fort Irwin, California.

Fifteen years after he turned his Scout Platoon south toward Basra versus north toward Baghdad, Tien led his 1,100-soldier-combined arms battalion, Task Force 2-37th Armor, to the northwest corner of Iraq. They were to stabilize and secure the strategic city of Tal Afar that sat astride the Al-Qaeda infiltration routes from Syria. Nine months later, in October 2006, Tien and his unit helped transform Tal Afar from being one of the most dangerous cities in Iraq to one of the very first to be transitioned not just to Iraqi Army Officers, but also to Iraqi civilian leaders. Tien and his battalion then rejoined their parent brigade, 1st Brigade 1st Armored Division, in Al Anbar Province where Task Force 2-37 Armor assumed responsibility for all areas in Ramadi north of the Euphrates River. In Ramadi, Tien and his battalion partnered with Sunni Sheiks, such as Sheik Jabbar and the al Fahad tribe, creating one of the first "Sons of Iraq" units. These units were small neighborhood coalitions of Sunni military-aged males, who had turned against Al-Qaeda. These units were the force that fueled the Al Anbar Awakening and the eventual overall stabilization of Iraq. In the 2007 State of the Union Address, President George W. Bush said, "And, in Anbar province – where Al Qaeda terrorists have gathered and local forces have begun showing a willingness to fight them – we are sending an additional 4,000 United States Marines with orders to find the terrorists and clear them out."

While Tien was an Army War College Fellow at the Harvard Kennedy School, Deputy National Security Advisor Lieutenant General Doug Lute (USMA 1975) asked him to join the National Security Council Staff as a director for Iraq policy. With Iraq stabilizing and the situation in Afghanistan worsening, Tien was given the task to develop the policy that would shift America's wartime emphasis from Iraq to Afghanistan. On September 9, 2008, Tien accompanied President Bush to the National Defense University where the President announced the first-ever reallocation of forces during the administration from Iraq to Afghanistan. In June 2009, the Obama administration named Tien as its first NSC senior director for Afghanistan and Pakistan, and, in the fall of that year, General Lute, Tien, and their Afghanistan-Pakistan policy team conducted the first policy review for President Obama. That review was later described in detail by Bob Woodward in his book *Obama's Wars*, including a chapter devoted to Tien's significant policy role during one of the pivotal Oval Office meetings in late November 2009. On December 1, 2009, Tien flew on *Air Force One* with President Obama to West Point, where the President announced his policy to significantly increase America's level of effort in Afghanistan and against Al Qaeda.

IN RAMADI, TIEN AND HIS BATTALION PARTNERED WITH SUNNI SHEIKS, SUCH AS SHEIK JABBAR AND THE AL FAHAD TRIBE, CREATING ONE OF THE FIRST "SONS OF IRAQ" UNITS.

On June 1, 2011, Tien retired from the United States Army and departed the White House after three years on the NSC staff and a career that included three combat tours in Iraq; 24 years of having the honor to serve with America's soldiers and their families; and, with his wife, raising two daughters, Amanda and Rebecca. He joined Citigroup in August 2011 as a Managing Director in their Global Consumer Operations and Technology organization. He was also named the national co-head of their Citi Military Veterans Initiative, helping military veterans and their families both in and outside of the company. John also serves on the board of the veterans non-profit organization, The Mission Continues, which empowers post-9/11 veterans to transition from military service to positions of community service leadership in America.

On December 19, 1989, President George H.W. Bush ordered the invasion of Panama to oust dictator Manuel Noriega from power. In the ensuing battle, Sergeant Delaney Gibbs from the 7th Infantry Division (Light) was Killed In Action. He left behind a pregnant wife who gave birth to a daughter in March 1990, named Delaney in her father's memory. Second Lieutenant David Kim was serving in the same Infantry Battalion as Sergeant Gibbs.

After completing his commitment, Kim went on to a successful business career, yet he always remembered the Sergeant who didn't come home and the daughter who would never meet her father. It was in Sergeant Gibbs's memory and the daughter he left behind that Kim and his wife, Cynthia, founded Children of Fallen Patriots (CFPF) to provide scholarships to military children who have lost a parent in the line of duty. CFPF has awarded more than $4.6 million and supported more than 300 children since 2003.

Kim was born April 21, 1966, and raised in Springfield, Virginia. His father was Korean and learned English in college. During the Korean War, his father worked as an interpreter for the American Army in Korea and was captured by the Chinese during the Thanksgiving offensive of 1950. He was held as a Prisoner of War and marched north with the American prisoners. Since he was technically a civilian, the Chinese released him, and he headed south and worked for the Americans again. He immigrated to the United States in the late 1950s, attended the University of Michigan graduate school of journalism, and became a science journalist at Cornell University. Kim was born 1966 and raised in Springfield, Virginia, and ironically, attended Robert E. Lee High School. Although no one is his family had ever been a career soldier, many had served in the military. Kim's grandmother's grandfather, Private John Thomas Dixon, served in the Army of Northern Virginia and was wounded during Pickett's Charge. Kim's grandfather was a history professor who lived near Gettysburg and frequently took Kim, his sister, and their cousins to tour Gettysburg, where they heard many stories of West Point graduates. Kim's parents divorced and his mother, an orchestra schoolteacher, worked three jobs to raise Kim and his sister.

At Robert E. Lee High School, Kim was President of the National Honor Society and lettered in football as a defensive end. Growing up with a patriotic family, the opportunity to attend West Point was a dream come true and he entered West Point on July 2, 1984. The core curriculum in 1988 was heavily math, science, and engineering, and for his electives, Kim chose to pursue a concentration in East Asian studies, believing that China was growing in influence as a world power. He was selected as a Cadet Battalion Commander his senior year and graduated 13th out of 960. Kim chose the Field Artillery Branch because it was both combat arms, but also was heavily math based, and required a sound strategic understanding of the entire battlefield. After officer basic training at Fort Sill, Kim competed and won a slot to attend the challenging Ranger School.

He graduated Ranger School in February 1989, was awarded the Ranger Tab, then was posted to Fort Ord in Monterey, California. His battalion was moved to Panama in early October in order to guard United States citizens living in the canal zone so they were already on the ground when the invasion started. Second Lieutenant Kim was a Fire Support Officer for C Company, 4-17th Infantry, and had six soldiers supporting the company. C Company attacked the Panamanian Marines in Coco Solo Naval Station on the north coast of Panama near Colon. After the successful liberation of Panama and the ouster of Manuel Noriega, the 7th Infantry returned to Fort Ord. In 1991, after the end of the Cold War, the Army was downsizing significantly and Kim chose to leave the military to pursue a civilian career. Knowing he had no business experience and having had no exposure growing up (since his mother was a schoolteacher and his father a journalist), he decided he should get a formal business education. He was thrilled to be accepted into the Harvard Business School (HBS) and moved from California to Boston.

In 1991, Kim attended his best friend's wedding in Virginia Beach and met the sister of the bride, Cynthia Lotuaco, and it was love at first sight. They married in 1997 and have four children: Whit (born 1998), Seth (2000), and Molly and Elyse (twins born 2002). At Harvard, Kim was the cochairman of the student Honor Committee that led the student body process to adopt the first-ever student honor code at HBS, modeled after

HE ALWAYS REMEMBERED THE SERGEANT WHO DIDN'T COME HOME AND THE DAUGHTER WHO WOULD NEVER MEET HER FATHER.

David Y. Kim, USMA 1988

- **FOUNDER, CHILDREN OF FALLEN PATRIOTS FOUNDATION (CFPF)**
- **PARTNER, APAX PARTNERS**
- **HARVARD BUSINESS SCHOOL, MASTER'S IN BUSINESS ADMINISTRATION**
- **OPERATION JUST CAUSE (PANAMA) VETERAN**
- **AIRBORNE-RANGER QUALIFIED**

HERE RESTS IN HONORED GLORY AN AMERICAN SOLDIER KNOWN BUT TO GOD

An Old Guard soldier marches in front of the Tomb of the Unknown soldier in Arlington National Cemetery.

the West Point Honor Code. He graduated with second-year academic honors. At graduation, Kim chose to begin his career in private equity.

He started at Butler Capital Corporation, and in 2000, he joined Apax where he eventually was promoted to partner. In 2009, he was promoted to co-head Investor Relations (IR) where he could leverage his deep deal experience and explain all aspects of the $35-billion private equity firm. Kim is responsible for North and South America, covering nearly half of the $35 billion in total funds raised.

In 2002, after the attacks of September 11th and with the United States at war in Afghanistan, Kim felt a need to do something to support the soldiers heading into combat. As he thought back to his own combat experience, he naturally thought of Sergeant Gibbs and the daughter he left behind. Kim and Cynthia founded Children of Fallen Patriots, recruited a board of directors and started raising funds. One of the first children they helped was Delaney Gibbs. One child became 10, and 10 became 100, and the fund grew, as sadly, so did the number of children who have been left behind as casualties mounted in Iraq and Afghanistan.

Kim set up the foundation very creatively, knowing that he wanted donor funds to go directly to the children. He and the board contributed personal funds to cover all expenses so that all the funds contributed by donors went directly to children. As the foundation grew and the expenses increased, members of the board continued to support the foundation in the same spirit. The board pays for all the expenses of the foundation so 100 percent of the funds donated by charitable Americans go directly to the children. More than $4.6 million has been distributed to more than 300 children to support their college tuition, books, and expenses. But numbers are impersonal, cold, and don't tell the story of the life; the tragedy and the hopes of each of these individual children after they have lost a parent. Kim's wife serves as the volunteer Program Director and she, along with the programs staff personally form a relationship with each of the children they support. This emotional support is just as beneficial to the children as the funds.

One of the recent team members who joined the foundation, sadly has also been one of the children supported by CFPF. Tabitha Bonilla married an Army pilot, and her father was also a soldier, a non-commissioned officer with 1st Cavalry. Tragically, in 2005,

her husband's helicopter crashed in Iraq, killing him.[11] Months earlier, her father was Killed In Action by an IED. Within 11 months, she had lost her father and then her husband in combat. The foundation helped her with college and paid her tuition and expenses. She graduated from Campbell University in 2008. Having seen how the foundation helps children through some of the most difficult times, not only with funds but with counseling, listening and support, she believed it was her calling to do the same for other children of fallen patriots, and she joined full time in 2011 working directly with children to provide them scholarships.

Not only does the foundation help the children who have been left behind; it also gives inspiration and comfort to those serving, knowing that the American public is behind them and will help their children if the worst is to occur. At the annual CFPF dinner in 2012 in Greenwich, Connecticut, Kim's classmate Colonel Brian Mennes (USMA 1988) gave an emotional keynote address at the dinner, thanking the crowd for supporting the children of those who did not return. Having just returned from Afghanistan a few weeks earlier as a Brigade Commander, Colonel Mennes had lost 16 soldiers Killed In Action, he sincerely

thanked the attendees for remembering his soldiers who had made the ultimate sacrifice and for doing all they could to ensure the children of those soldiers would be taken care of and sent to college.

In the spirit of the tomb of the unknown, Kim and Cynthia have ensured that we will never forget the soldiers who have made the ultimate sacrifice – or their children.

David and Cynthia Kim awarding the Patriot's Award to General Raymond Odierno.

Tabitha Bonilla, CFPF grantee and Program Manager.

Apax PARTNERS

>>> Spotlight

Apax Partners is a leading global private equity firm with approximately $35 billion of assets under advisement. The firm has a global network of nine offices in three continents and employs more than 300 people. Apax invests in five sectors: Financial & Business Services, Healthcare, Media, Retail & Consumer, Tech & Telecom. Apax portfolio companies employ more than 270,000 people and have an enterprise value of nearly $100 billion.

Courtesy: Apax

Children of the Fallen Patriots logo.

FALLEN PATRIOTS

Kristin Baker became the first female First Captain in West Point history when she was selected to be the "First Captain of the Class of 1990." She was a trailblazer and a leader at West Point, and has led soldiers in the Army for 21 years, rising to her current rank as Colonel.

The first class of females had entered West Point in 1976 – only 10 years prior to Baker's. Over those 10 years, female cadets had bravely battled to be accepted in the previously male-dominated institution and progressively gained higher positions within the Corps of Cadets. With the appointment of

Baker to First Captain, female cadets have now held roles at every level in the Corps of Cadets and the Army. Thanks to trailblazers like Baker, Andrea Lee Hollen (first female graduate from West Point), and Rebecca Halstead (first female graduate to become a General Officer) who set the example, incoming female cadets know West Point and the Army is a meritocracy and their opportunities are unlimited.

Baker was born into an Army family in Dickinson, North Dakota, on May 23, 1968. Her father, Colonel Bob Baker, graduated from West Point in 1966 and served 30

years on active duty. Baker grew up as an "Army brat" as their family had moved to various Army posts in the United States and Germany.

Baker entered West Point in 1986 and thrived. She lettered on the Army soccer team and was a member of the Army ski team. While she was at West Point, the Army was preparing to fight the Cold War to defend Western Europe against the Soviet Union and her satellite countries on the plains of Europe. Military training revolved largely around large-scale armored battles against state actors. President Ronald

Reagan visited West Point in Baker's Yearling year in 1987 to announce the Intermediate Nuclear Freeze (INF). He stood in West Berlin in front of the Brandenburg Gate in June 1987 and challenged the Soviet leader to "Tear down this wall, Mr. Gorbachev!" Everything the Class of 1990 was preparing for centered on defending Europe against the Soviet threat.

In the summer of 1989, Baker was selected to become the first detail Brigade Commander of the Cadet Basic Training (CBT, commonly called "Beast Barracks") for the incoming Class of 1993. Her position

Colonel Kristin Baker, USMA 1990

- **FIRST FEMALE CADET FIRST CAPTAIN**
- **V CORPS SENIOR INTELLIGENCE OFFICER (G-2)**
- **CHIEF OF THE OPERATIONS DIVISION, U.S. ARMY PACIFIC COMMAND JOINT INTELLIGENCE OPERATIONS CENTER**
- **COMMANDER, C COMPANY, 302ND MI BATTALION (BOSNIA)**
- **ARMY SOCCER PLAYER (FOUR) AND ARMY SKI TEAM (FOUR)**

Colonel Baker with her husband Army Colonel Mark Kjorness, and their three daughters, Ashley, Brenna, and Cassie.

Baker receives diploma from General Colin Powell.

Cadet First Captain Kristin Baker, 1990.

was previously called "the King of Beast," so as the first female in this role, her title thus changed to the "Queen of Beast." In October 1989, she was selected by the Superintendent Lieutenant General David Palmer to become the First Captain for the Class of 1990. This groundbreaking announcement put her in the company of other Cadet First Captains, such as Pershing (USMA 1886), MacArthur (USMA 1903), Wainwright (USMA 1906), Westmoreland (USMA 1936), and Dawkins (1959).

Baker's Firstie year saw the collapse of the Iron Curtain as the Berlin Wall came down in November 1989, and suddenly, the Soviet Union and her satellites no longer existed. The Army's mission and very existence was in flux in an uncertain world. At graduation on May 31, 1990, the Chairman of the Joint Chiefs, General Colin Powell, gave the commencement speech. He recognized Baker's accomplishment as the leader of the class and commented that they had a running joke between them, since both their promotions had been announced the same day in October 1989 (when she was announced as the 1st Captain of West Point Class of 1990, he was announced as the Chairman of the Joint Chiefs). When addressing the future the class should prepare for, General Powell said the "prospect of a world war is no longer a fear, although the world is still troubled." Nevertheless, he added, "the prospect of peace is now more than a dream." He ominously warned against "dismantling our Armed Forces when danger seems to be gone."

Baker had graduated at the top of her class (27th out of 931) with a Bachelor of Science degree in Engineering Psychology. As Cadet First Captain, Second Lieutenant Baker was afforded the honor of dismissing the class at graduation, which signals the tossing of the hats. "Class dismissed!" she ordered, and the Class of 1990 joined the Army as Second Lieutenants as they tossed their cadet hats into the air. Sixty-two days later, Saddam Hussein's Iraqi Army invaded Kuwait and the post–Cold War period of global uncertainty had begun. The Class of 1990 headed off to Officer Basic and many joined their units in the desert of Saudi Arabia in preparation for Operation Desert Storm and the liberation of Kuwait. Soon many would be in combat, leading soldiers as they had been trained to do so for the last four years at West Point. The Class of 1990 had graduated after the Cold War, but spent their careers at war in Kuwait, Iraq, Somalia, Bosnia, Afghanistan, Philippines, and elsewhere – none of the places that they had prepared for as cadets.

Baker attended Military Intelligence Officer Basic at Fort Huachuca, Arizona, in the summer of 1990 and then deployed to Germany for her first assignment. She began her career serving as an Intelligence Platoon Leader and Operations Officer for C Company, 302nd MI Battalion in Mainz-Finthen, Germany. As a First Lieutenant, she deployed to the Middle East as a Patriot Missile Battalion Intelligence Officer while assigned to 6-43 Air Defense Artillery Battalion, 69th Air Defense Brigade, Ansbach, Germany.

Baker married fellow Army Officer Mark Kjorness in Dickinson, North Dakota, on July 2, 1993, and had three daughters – Cassie, Ashley, and Brenna. Together they have deployed around the world with their family, since their first daughter was born in 1998.

Following the Intelligence Advanced Course, Captain Baker was assigned to Fort Hood, Texas, where she served as a Collection Manager and Intelligence Plans Officer while assigned to the 205th MI Brigade, III Corps Headquarters. She deployed to Bosnia as Commander, C Company, 302nd MI Battalion during Operation Joint Endeavor and was assigned to 4th Brigade, 1st Cavalry Division, where she served as an Aviation Brigade Intelligence Officer.

Colonel Baker was then assigned to Human Resources Command in Washington, D.C., where she served as a Distribution Officer and Branch Manager for Army Intelligence Officers. Following Army Command and General Staff College, Colonel Baker was transferred to Germany, where she spent three years as Chief of the Combating Terrorism Branch, United States Army Europe, and a year as the Executive Officer to the Senior Army Intelligence Officer for all of Europe. She then served as the Chief of the Operations Division, United States Army Pacific Command Joint Intelligence Operations Center, where she led 130 joint service members and civilians who provided intelligence support to Pacific Command operations.

Colonel Baker is currently the V Corps G2, or Senior Intelligence Officer, in Wiesbaden, Germany, where she continues to lead American soldiers in an uncertain world.

IN THE SUMMER OF 1989, BAKER WAS SELECTED TO BECOME THE FIRST DETAIL BRIGADE COMMANDER OF THE CADET BASIC TRAINING (CBT, COMMONLY CALLED "BEAST BARRACKS"). HER POSITION WAS PREVI-OUSLY CALLED "THE KING OF BEAST," SO AS THE FIRST FEMALE IN THIS ROLE, HER TITLE THUS CHANGED TO THE "QUEEN OF BEAST."

Colonel Baker thanking her fellow soldiers for their support at her promotion to Colonel.

Cadet Baker with President Ronald Reagan at his Sylvanus Thayer Award presentation.

At key moments throughout its history, the United States has been fortunate to have the right leader – someone with an ideal combination of rare talent and strong character – rise to a position of great responsibility in public service. With General Keith B. Alexander serving as the first Commander of United States Cyber Command and the Director of the National Security Agency (NSA), Americans are again experiencing this auspicious state of affairs. A visionary technologist, innovative trailblazer, and inspirational leader, Alexander will undoubtedly be seen by history as an important figure who helped the country recognize and navigate its recently acquired dependence on cyberspace as a place where wealth is made and stored, essential services are delivered, and vital national security functions are performed. Ever the voice of optimism about technological possibilities, Alexander is already seen as a crucial partner to those in government, academia, the private sector, and the governments of United States allies who seek to advance the frontiers of information technology while mitigating the attendant risks.

General Alexander's path to becoming the United States Army's first and only Four-Star Intelligence Officer began with a college choice. Born on December 2, 1951, to parents Charlotte and Donald, Alexander grew up in Syracuse, New York, where he attended Westhill High School. Although he earned scholarships to Purdue and Syracuse, he decided to accept an appointment to the United States Military Academy at West Point. Attracted by the opportunities and challenges the Academy offered – and undeterred by the associated service commitment – he began a cadet career that he remembers

General Keith Alexander, USMA 1974

- **COMMANDER, U.S. CYBER COMMAND**
- **DIRECTOR, NATIONAL SECURITY AGENCY**
- **TRANSFORMATIONAL LEADER**
- **CYBERSPACE PIONEER**
- **BOY SCOUTS OF AMERICA, YOUTH MEMBER AND SENIOR ASSISTANT SCOUT MASTER**

Photo: NARA

Courtesy: General Alexander

General Keith Alexander and Mr. John "Chris" Inglis, Deputy Director, National Security Agency.

Courtesy: General Alexander

General Alexander with Dr. James Miller, Undersecretary of Defense for Policy, testifying before Congress.

>>> Spotlight

Activated in 2010 and headquartered at Fort Meade, Maryland, United States Cyber Command operates and defends Department of Defense (DoD) information networks. Also headquartered at Fort Meade, the National Security Agency and Central Security Service protect United States national security systems and produce foreign signals intelligence information.

Courtesy: Fort Meade PAO

Courtesy: General Alexander

most fondly for the deep camaraderie he enjoyed with fellow members of the Corps of Cadets. Commissioned to become a Military Intelligence (MI) Officer after an initial period of service in the Armor Corps, he began a career that was punctuated early and often with exceptional accomplishments.

Alexander first revealed his potential as a change agent when he was assigned to the 525th MI Group at Fort Bragg, North Carolina, as a young Captain in February 1979. In addition to his duties as the Electronic Warfare Officer, he was also the Special Security Officer – a position that gave him the ability to send official message traffic. Knowing of the desire of the Group Commander, then-Colonel Sidney Weinstein, to acquire new capabilities, he used his message sending authority to convene appropriate Representatives from the Army staff and hosted them for a meeting at Fort Bragg. Having done the analysis on the requirements, Alexander laid them out and requested support. The meeting was a success; on his own initiative, Alexander obtained the people, equipment, and money needed to establish a new organization that would better enable the XVIII Airborne Corps to benefit from national intelligence capabilities. To his credit, Weinstein overcame his initial reaction to the irregularities in Alexander's process – there are normally several echelons between a Captain at Fort Bragg and the Army staff in the Pentagon – and appointed Alexander to stand up the unit as its first Company Commander.

As his career in Army intelligence progressed, Alexander's contributions continued to be marked by a similar combination of vision, initiative, collaboration, empowering leadership, and hard work. Outstanding examples distinguish his service as a commander at various echelons. After he assumed command of the 204th MI Battalion in Germany in 1991, it became quickly apparent to him that the unit was ill suited to respond effectively to changes in communications technology, as well as new strategic requirements created by the emerging post–Cold War world. While most Battalion Commanders are capable of identifying capability shortfalls, few succeed – as Alexander did – in wholly transforming their units through new equipment acquisitions and other operational changes. In the mid-1990s, as the Commander of the 525th MI Brigade at Fort Bragg, North Carolina, he had a similarly outsized impact on the capabilities of the XVIII Airborne Corps as he leveraged automation to improve real-time intelligence, enhance the integration of intelligence and operations, and enable operational and planning visualizations for the Corps and its subordinate commands.

To Alexander, improving intelligence and exploiting every advance in technology are such critical activities because they further mission accomplishment and ultimately save lives. As the 1st Armored Division G2 (Intelligence) during the Persian Gulf War of 1991, he was respected by his commander, then–Major General Ron Griffith, as much for his deep knowledge of war-fighting doctrine as for his mastery of intelligence and his ability to exploit new technologies. Griffith recalls that Alexander, who had forged a superb partnership with the Division G3 (Operations), "had as much input into the operational plan as anyone because he knew where the enemy was and how he was acting and reacting." In Griffith's view, "no one in the division enjoyed a greater reputation for competence" among the division's senior leaders and commanders. In 2004 and 2005, when responsible for all of Army MI as the Army G2, Alexander led the effort to field an integrated operational and intelligence solution, called Joint Intelligence

Major General Ronald Griffith, Commanding General of the 1st Armored Division, flanked on his right by his G3 (Operations) Lieutenant Colonel Tom Strauss and on his left by his G2 (Intelligence) Lieutenant Colonel Alexander during Operation Desert Storm.

Operational Capabilities-Iraq (JIOC-I), that improved situational awareness and better enabled planning. In the words of one commander in Iraq, he "could spend more time fighting the enemy" as opposed to "fighting for information" because of JIOC-I.

Underpinning his success in all of these endeavors has been Alexander's ability to communicate complex material effectively to all audiences. He is one of the rare individuals who can answer questions ranging from the highly technical to the operational, from the details of wiring diagrams to the nuances of policy, with equal facility. These strengths were already apparent early in his career when, as a Captain in 1984, he led a six-month study for the Army's Vice Chief of Staff, General Max Thurman, which detailed the Army's intelligence capabilities and identified gaps against the Soviet threat. Later,

as a Major in 1986, he created the first Army Intelligence Master Plan, laying out for Lieutenant General Sidney Weinstein (who had by then become the Army's senior Intelligence Officer), a master plan for the Army's intelligence capabilities for the next 15 years. Good ideas are critical, but it takes effective and persuasive communication to enable them to be approved, funded, and implemented.

Since Alexander's confirmation to become the 16th Director of the NSA in 2005, his talents and visionary leadership have been given an even larger stage. As a technologist, he is constantly moving the bar – at times, even conceiving potential solutions to the point that all that remains is the associated engineering implementation. As an innovator, he has dramatically improved the provision of actionable intelligence to counterterrorism operations and to deployed military forces, ensuring

unprecedented levels of support to current operations and targeting in places, such as Iraq and Afghanistan. The Agency has never been more successful, in either its information assurance or its foreign intelligence missions, than it has been under his leadership.

The nature of intelligence work is that accomplishments are rarely known until decades have elapsed; however, one example begins to reveal the nature of Alexander's contributions. After receiving a briefing on cloud technology in December 2007, he immediately grasped its potential to enhance the work of NSA and to become the next-generation architecture for the Intelligence Community and the Department of Defense. He therefore initiated an effort in early 2008 to transform the manner in which NSA collects, stores, and analyzes data to better meet the Agency's needs to extract information from

very large data sets and to do analytic discovery. As part of this effort, NSA has established that it is possible to use cloud technology in a secure fashion. The source code underlying this innovation has been released back to the open-source community, fostering mutually beneficial relationships across the public and private sectors.

"IF YOU CAN THINK IT, YOU CAN DO IT," SAID ALEXANDER.

The establishment of United States Cyber Command in 2010 reflects, to a large extent, key elements of Alexander's long-standing approach to his responsibilities: never follow the path of least resistance or accept the status quo but instead ask how things could be better. With regard to cyber, that meant conceiving of cyberspace as a new domain – not an extension

Lieutenant Colonel Alexander being greeted by his daughters upon his return from Operation Desert Storm.

of others – requiring the United States military to establish new organizations, doctrine, training, and capabilities to meet its responsibility to defend the country. His approach to cyber is one that continues to emphasize collaboration, in this case between United States Cyber Command and NSA, across the United States government, and with various partners: the private sector, academia, and United States allies. Through his leadership on these issues, Alexander has come to be recognized by technologists, industry leaders, researchers, and national elected officials on both sides of the aisle as a thought leader on one of the most vital national security issues of the current era.

Although General Alexander's accomplishments are extraordinary, what stands out just as much in the minds of those who know him well are his leadership abilities and strength of character. His great intel-

lect and enormous talent are accompanied by natural humility, a mischievous wit, and impeccable integrity. While he often sets what initially seem to be unachievable goals, he also empowers and inspires those who work for him to achieve more than they thought possible and then gives credit generously. People are inspired to take the risks associated with striking out in new directions by their confidence in Alexander's vision and integrity and by the knowledge that their efforts will be valued. And the long hours and hard work associated with effecting positive change are made easier through humor, as well as trust.

While his professional life has been demanding, Keith Alexander is also extremely devoted to his family. He and his wife, Debbie, have four married daughters; Jennifer and Mike, Julie and Brian, Diana and Dan, and Heather and Bill have 14

children among them with a 15th on the way. One can only imagine that his example will one day inspire his grandchildren with the same sense of possibility that his 86-year-old grandfather once gave to him: "If you can think it, you can do it." With these words, Alexander's grandfather described with prescience the course of his grandson's future career.

Secretary of Defense Robert Gates administering the Oath of Office to General Alexander after his promotion to General, with Mrs. Debbie Alexander standing at his side.

Alexander family 4th of July gathering in 2012.

When he arrived in Panama in March of 1907, the men digging the Panama Canal met Lieutenant Colonel George Goethals with cautious indifference. President Roosevelt had hired Goethals, who was already a seasoned Army engineer at 48 years old, to complete the construction that had been burdened by decades of delays, both man-made and natural. The canal laborers resented Goethals for the very reason that he had been sent – his military experience and engineering expertise. They feared that he would treat them like soldiers marching into battle, drilling them to dig to the march of a drum. But the West Point engineer proved to be a more capable, just, and reasonable leader than any could have imagined. To be sure, Goethals represented the very best that Military Academy graduates had to offer at the turn of the nineteenth century. Roosevelt expected certain success with Goethals spearheading the digging and building of the locks. For the next seven years, Colonel Goethals wielded supreme authority over the Canal Zone and all who labored to complete the 50-mile path between the oceans. By 1914, Congress and the country celebrated Goethals as the master engineer and administrator who had accomplished the impossible – overcoming disease, nature, and geography to connect the Atlantic and the Pacific.

George Washington Goethals was the epitome of a West Point–trained engineer. He was competent, disciplined, and loyal, while at the same time he was friendly and approachable. A favorite of his peers, he graduated second in the Class of 1880 and consistently demonstrated leadership potential at every post. After completing his engineer training at Willet's Point, New York, he escorted General William T. Sherman on an inspection of the Columbia River District in the Northwest. Sherman "predicted…a brilliant future" for the young Goethals. Between 1884 and 1903, Goethals served in the Ohio River valley, taught civil and military engineering at West Point, built record setting locks on the Muscle Shoals Canal in Tennessee, and improved the harbor works across Rhode Island and southern Massachusetts. During the Spanish-American War, he served briefly under General John R. Brooke's occupation of Puerto Rico. By the time Goethals was selected to serve on the General Staff in 1903, his reputation and accomplishments established him as the most-qualified officer to send to Panama for the canal construction.

Secretary of War William H. Taft noticed Goethals in 1905, and later recommended him to President Roosevelt as the best candidate to replace John Stevens, the railroad engineer leading the American canal effort. Stevens had resigned under the pressures of heading the Isthmus Canal Commission. Under Stevens, the canal construction languished in landslides, malaria, and hundreds of worker fatalities. Whatever Stevens lacked in leadership qualities and engineering experience, Goethals possessed and then some. As Chief Engineer and Chairman of the Isthmus Canal Commission, Goethals devoted all of his energy into the project. He hosted Sunday -afternoon town halls to address worker grievances. Subordinates recalled seeing Goethals in his office until 10 o'clock every night studying and planning the canal's design. During Goethals's daily inspections of the construction, he could quote every detail and specification from memory. Indeed, Goethals's ability to be "omnipotent, omniscient, omnipresent" made him indispensable to the whole enterprise.

Goethals was also an astute politician, keen to the significance of shaping public opinion in his favor. Several months after taking the canal post, he began publishing the *Canal Record* as an account of the progress being made in Panama. Initially, the weekly paper was sent to every member of Congress to ensure funding continued and to counter mounting criticism of the canal. By 1909, the American public was behind Goethals

Major General George W. Goethals, USMA 1880

- ARCHITECT AND BUILDER OF THE PANAMA CANAL
- PROFESSOR OF CIVIL AND MECHANICAL ENGINEERING, WEST POINT
- SERVED IN SPANISH-AMERICAN WAR
- APPOINTED CIVIL GOVERNOR OF THE PANAMA CANAL ZONE
- GOETHALS BRIDGE BETWEEN NEW YORK AND NEW JERSEY NAMED IN HIS HONOR
- BURIED AT THE WEST POINT CEMETERY

War Industries Board, Major General Goethals is second from right.

and the criticism waned. Upon completion of the canal, praise for Goethals was endless. Congress gave him a standing ovation, while Yale, Columbia, and Harvard all awarded honorary degrees to the engineer hero.

What is often overlooked in Goethals's canal

BY 1914, CONGRESS AND THE COUNTRY CELEBRATED GOETHALS AS THE MASTER ENGINEER AND ADMINISTRATOR WHO HAD ACCOMPLISHED THE IMPOSSIBLE – OVERCOMING DISEASE, NATURE, AND GEOGRAPHY TO CONNECT THE ATLANTIC AND THE PACIFIC.

appointment is that he reported directly to the President, and the commission was independent of the Corps of Engineers. Granted the core of Goethals's staff were Army engineers, they all worked for a civilian organization, wearing civilian clothes in lieu of their officer uniforms. As they were beyond the supervision of the Army, Goethals and his men learned the art of power and persuasion to achieve their goals. At the height of the digging and blasting in 1912, Goethals was even mentioned as a potential candidate for the Presidency. When the canal opened in 1914, Congress named Goethals as the first Governor of the Canal Zone, and later passed a special law promoting him to Major General. Goethals retired from the Army in 1916 and remained in charge of the canal until 1917.

When the United States entered World War I, Goethals was in New York running his private engineering firm. Secretary of War Newton Baker called General Goethals to active duty again in late 1917, first as Acting Quartermaster General of the Army and then as Director of Storage and Traffic. In these positions, Goethals attempted to overhaul an antiquated military supply system and link it with the efforts of Bernard Baruch's War Industries Board. Here, Goethals was less successful in creating an efficient organization to supply the American Expeditionary Force. Unlike his tenure at the Panama Canal, Goethals lacked the power and influence to overcome the resistance he experienced from the General Staff managing the war.

After the war, Goethals returned to New York as the Chief Consulting Engineer of the Port Authority of New York. There, he helped design the bridge connecting New Jersey and New York that eventually was named in his honor. When he died in 1928, he was buried at the West Point cemetery beneath a rock tombstone that resembled the type of rock he had cut through to make the Panama Canal.

The Panama Canal remains invariably George Goethals greatest achievement and legacy. In building the canal, Goethals was a West Point leader who was ahead of his time. His mastery of engineering and organization management, combined with his natural ability to gain and maintain the trust of those under him, became the model for twentieth-century Academy graduates. When considering the careers of the generation that followed Goethals, it is difficult to imagine a better example for graduates like Douglas MacArthur, Dwight D. Eisenhower, and Omar Bradley to have followed. It is a legacy that should continue to inspire West Point's graduates for generations to come.

Written by: Lieutenant Colonel Jon Scott Logel, PhD (USA, Retired).

Major General George Goethals's gravesite at West Point Cemetery.

USS Iowa *sailing through Panama Canal.*

Plaque in Cullum Hall at West Point.

>>> Spotlight

The Panama Canal Commission was established by the Panama Canal Act of 1979 and began operations on October 1, 1979. The Commission functioned as an independent agency with the primary purposed of operating and maintaining the Panama Canal and associated facilities in cooperation with the Republic of Panama. On December 31, 1999, the Commission's duties and sovereignty over the canal were transferred to the Republic of Panama, upon the termination of the Panama Canal Treaty of 1977. *www.federalregister.gov*

Major General Goethals at right on the site of the Pacoima Dam in Los Angeles, October 6, 1924.

Lieutenant General Groves and Oppenheimer inspect nuclear blast damage, September 9, 1945.

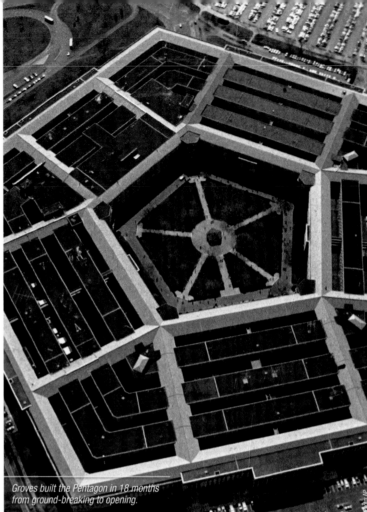

Groves built the Pentagon in 18 months from ground-breaking to opening.

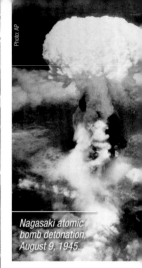

Nagasaki atomic bomb detonation, August 9, 1945.

Lieutenant General Leslie Groves, USMA 1918

- LED THE MANHATTAN PROJECT CREATING THE FIRST ATOMIC BOMBS
- BUILT THE PENTAGON IN 18 MONTHS
- CHIEF OF THE ARMED FORCES SPECIAL WEAPONS PROJECT
- PRESIDENT WEST POINT ASSOCIATION OF GRADUATES
- PRESENTED THE THAYER AWARD TO GENERAL DOUGLAS MACARTHUR IN 1961
- VICE PRESIDENT SPERRY-RAND (UNISYS)

Few Generals ever make a name for themselves sitting behind the proverbial desk. Leslie Richard Groves, however, helped end the Second World War by sheer force of will and administrative dexterity. While he was hardly the typical General, Groves's abilities were vital to the success of the Manhattan Project.

Groves's father was an Army Chaplain who served in the Spanish-American War, the Philippine War, and the Boxer Rebellion.

From an early age, "Dick" Groves knew he wanted to be an officer and made it his goal to attend the United States Military Academy. After failing his initial attempt to gain admission, he attended the Massachusetts Institute of Technology for several years before successfully passing the West Point entrance examinations in 1916.[1]

Groves excelled at the Academy, graduating fourth in his class in November 1918. (His class graduated 18 months early because of

the need for officers in World War I).[2] Groves joined the prestigious Engineer Branch, but the war had already ended before he saw service. By 1940, he was still a Captain.[3] As a new war loomed and the Army grew, however, he was assigned a role supervising the construction of military facilities throughout the nation. The largest of these projects was the massive new War Department building – the Pentagon – in Arlington, Virginia.[4]

His capable performance in these chal-

lenging assignments led to rapid promotion and opened the way for his career-defining (and history-making) role as director of the Manhattan Engineering District, better known as the Manhattan Project. The project, directed to create atomic weapons before our enemies did, had been struggling for several years because of bureaucratic infighting and a lack of adequate resources. Groves's arrival in September 1942 changed all that. As he said later, Groves took very

>>> Spotlight

On May 12, 1962, Lieutenant General Groves as President of the West Point Association of Graduates presented General Douglas MacArthur with the Sylvanus Thayer Award. General MacArthur's acceptance speech referred to as the "Duty, Honor, Country" speech is considered one of the greatest speeches in American history.

The crew of the "Enola Gay" that dropped the first atomic bomb on Hiroshima, August 6, 1945.

Photo: AP

and colleagues complained about his lack of tact, his smugness, and his overbearing nature.[7] His engineering mind-set and drive did not always impress the physicists and other academics with whom he worked.[8] The intense focus on secrecy and security upset those used to academic collaboration. Groves's rule was that "each man should know everything he needed to know to do his job and nothing else." The draconian compartmentalization of the vast undertaking meant that very few involved had a clear picture of what was going on, and only Groves had a complete picture of the program. A biographer argues that Groves embraced compartmentalization of the nuclear effort in part because it was the way his own mind worked; he managed his time very efficiently, giving each problem full attention until it was solved, then moving onto the next challenge.[9]

One of Groves's most important decisions was the selection of noted physicist J. Robert Oppenheimer to take the lead on designing the actual bombs. Despite Groves's brusque manner and conservative outlook, he worked very capably with the brilliant, cosmopolitan, gregarious Oppenheimer. So close were they, in fact, that Groves seems to have helped Oppenheimer avoid security scrutiny. Given Oppenheimer's left-leaning (and possibly communist) political past, this would prove problematic during the Cold War.[10]

The years of intense effort paid off. "For the first time in history, there was a nuclear explosion," he wrote Stimson after the successful test in New Mexico. "And what an explosion!" Contrary to his friend Oppenheimer's woeful reaction to the awesome spectacle, Groves gleefully recounted how the test succeeded "beyond the most optimistic expectations of anyone", describing the fireball, mushroom cloud, and damage to nearby structures, admitting that he "no longer consider[ed] the Pentagon a safe shelter from such a bomb."[11]

Beyond his efforts to build the bomb, Groves was responsible for the training of the special bombing unit and the selection of targets.[12] He argued against attempting multiple atomic strikes at the same time on the first bombing raid, because it would be more difficult to study the results and "would not be sufficiently distinct from a regular Air Force bombing program…"[13] Groves wanted the first bombing to be a memorable episode, and it was.

Groves viewed those who questioned the

use of the bombs with scarcely concealed scorn. "I have no qualms of conscience about the making or using of it," he said later. "It has been responsible for saving perhaps thousands of lives."[14] While his single-mindedness and self-promotion had served his nation well during the Manhattan project, they caused him trouble later in his career. He fought unsuccessfully and angrily against efforts to shift control of the nation's atomic energy to civilian officials, and may have agitated for promotion to Lieutenant General in an unbecoming way.[15] After retiring, though, he continued to serve the Army as President of the West Point Association of Graduates.[16]

ONE OF GROVES'S MOST IMPORTANT DECISIONS WAS THE SELECTION OF NOTED PHYSICIST J. ROBERT OPPENHEIMER TO TAKE THE LEAD ON DESIGNING THE ACTUAL BOMBS.

"He's the biggest sonavabitch I've ever met in my life," wrote a military colleague, "but also one of the most capable individuals."[17] Brusque, overbearing, and portly (if not plain fat), Groves was hardly a model officer in the normal sense. His drive and will to win, however, played a critical role in the most important wartime scientific-engineering project in our nation's history, and helped to end the greatest war the world has ever seen.

Written by: Major Joseph C. Scott.

seriously his mission to produce a weapon quickly "so as to bring the war to a conclusion." Secretary of War Henry Stimson had directed "that any time that a single day could be saved [Groves] should save that day," so Groves barreled through bureaucratic obstacles with exceptional single-mindedness. In his first few days on the job, he coordinated the purchase of more than 1,000 tons of uranium and obtained first priority for government resources. He coordinated the purchase of huge tracts of land

in Tennessee, Washington state, and New Mexico on which to build massive plants for the production of nuclear materials. By early 1943, Groves had complete control over the nation's atomic efforts.[5] The massive effort to build this incredible weapon had become simply "Groves's project."[6]

To say that Groves was a difficult man to work with would be a vast understatement. He was a big, portly man who barely fit into his uniform. His civilian subordinates

THE AVIATORS

The Wright brothers trained the first two military aviators in 1911. One of those initial aviators was Captain Henry "Hap" Arnold (USMA 1907), who would become a Five-Star General and build the Army Air Corps into a force of more than 78,000 aircrafts by the end of World War II. The earliest military aviators came from the ranks of the Army, and later from the Navy as well with the advent of aircraft carriers. The United States Air Force eventually emerged from the Army Air Corps and became an independent service in 1947; therefore, many of the most famous World War II aviators unsurprisingly were West Point graduates. The United States Air Force Academy (USAFA) then followed with its founding in 1954 and first graduating class in 1959. Even after the formation of the Air Force and emergence of USAFA, up to 25 percent of each West Point class could choose another branch of service, and many selected the Air Force until it was able to produce enough of its own officers. The first superintendents, commandants, and deans of USAFA were West Point graduates, as would be many Air Force senior leaders in its first couple of decades, until USAFA graduates came of age and filled the ranks of the Air Force's senior leadership. This chapter highlights some of West Point's most influential aviators.

"A modern, autonomous, and thoroughly trained Air Force in being at all times will not alone be sufficient, but without it there can be no national security."
—General of the Air Force Hap Arnold, USMA 1907

"Airpower has become predominant, both as a deterrent to war, and – in the eventuality of war – as the devastating force to destroy an enemy's potential and fatally undermine his will to wage war."
—General of the Army Omar Bradley, USMA 1915

"The first and absolute requirement of strategic air power in this war was control of the air in order to carry out sustained operations without prohibitive losses."
—General Carl Andrew Spaatz, USMA 1914, First Chief of Staff of the U.S. Air Force

"If we mean that we are to hold Europe against communism, we must not budge. We can take humiliation and pressure short of war in Berlin without losing face. I believe the future of democracy requires us to stay here until forced out."
—General Lucius Clay, USMA 1918, "Father of the Berlin Airlift"

"My own opinion was that blacks could best overcome racist attitudes through achievements, even though those achievements had to take place within the hateful environment of segregation."
—General Benjamin O. Davis, USMA 1936, Commander of the Tuskegee Airmen

B-17 Flying Fortresses dropping their payload over Germany.

General of the Army & Air Force Henry "Hap" Arnold, USMA 1907

- **SECOND U.S. MILITARY AVIATOR TO EARN HIS WINGS**
- **GENERAL OF THE ARMY**
- **GENERAL OF THE AIR FORCE**
- **CONSIDERED "FATHER OF THE U.S. AIR FORCE"**

President Truman awarding General Arnold the Distinguished Service Medal.

>>> Spotlight

There have only been five officers in history to be promoted to Five-Star "General of the Army": Marshall, MacArthur, Eisenhower, Arnold, and Bradley (in rank order). Arnold retired in 1946 when the air component of the military was still a component of the United States Army Air Corps. The United States Air Force (USAF) was formed in 1947, and after being formed, General Arnold's rank was retroactively made from General of the Army to General of the Air Force, so he never formally wore the rank while on active duty. General Arnold is the only "General of the United States Air Force" in history.

General Arnold Statue at the U.S. Air Force Academy.

Henry Harley "Hap" Arnold, one of only five Five-Star Generals of the Army and the only General of the Air Force in American history, was born on June 25, 1886, in Gladwyne, Pennsylvania. Arnold was raised in a very strict home environment and was excited about the opportunity to attend West Point in 1903, when his older brother, against his father's wishes, declined to attend. Acceptance into the Academy was not automatic, however, as Arnold was not initially selected. It was only in July, upon the disqualification of the primary candidate, that Arnold was appointed as a replacement.[1]

While at West Point, Arnold earned a reputation as a prankster and given a pair of nicknames to reflect this tendency: "Pewt," after a character in a popular newspaper serial; and "Benny," for his fondness of the local pub, Benny Havens.[2] Although intelligent, his numerous escapades hurt his overall class standing, and he graduated only 66th out of his class of 111 in 1907, but near the top of his class in number of demerits earned, with 252.[3] At the Academy, Arnold was a member of the football and track teams, although never an athletic standout. He also was an avid polo player, which enabled him to advance his personal love of horsemanship. Upon graduation, he was devastated to be assigned to the Infantry rather than the Cavalry, and he seriously contemplated refusing his commission. After reconsideration, though, he accepted and was assigned to the Philippines, where he began to pursue ways in which he could transfer to another branch of service.

While in the Philippines, one of his assignments involved working for Captain Arthur Cowan, a Signal Corps Officer in charge of mapping the island of Luzon.[4] Cowan learned of Arnold's dissatisfaction with the Infantry, and upon reassignment to Washington, recruited the young Infantryman to join the Signal Corps and to attend the fledgling Army Flying School. Arnold gladly accepted, although he had shown little early affinity for aviation. Upon his completion of training in 1911, he became one of the first two active pilots in the United States Army.[5]

As one of the aviation pioneers in the Army, Arnold learned the intricacies of flight early on, and was part of the growth of the Air Services almost from its inception. Although grounded in 1912 for a number of years after a near-fatal crash, Arnold spent World War I as one of the Air Service leaders in organizing, planning, and developing aviation assets, earning a reputation in Washington as a highly capable, intelligent, and forward-thinking young officer, as well as gaining valuable experience he would apply 25 years later.[6] His greatest disappointment during the war was that he never saw combat, a fact that irritated him throughout his life.[7]

The interwar years saw Arnold serve in numerous staff and leadership positions in the Air Corps, where he championed and implemented many of his ideas on airpower. His selection to the Army Industrial College in 1924 gave him insight and familiarization to the procurement and logistics systems of the military, in addition to introducing him to many key civilian aviation leaders, which would prove invaluable in the coming decades.[8] Briefly in professional exile from 1925 to 1928 for his vocal and enduring support of Billy Mitchell, Arnold nonetheless remained a fixture in the development of air power, and he participated in many notable initiatives following his rehabilitation. Most importantly, in 1934, he led an historic round-trip flight of B-10 bombers between Washington, D.C., and Alaska that demonstrated the capabilities of long-range bombers.[9]

IN 1911, ARNOLD BECAME ONE OF THE FIRST TWO ACTIVE PILOTS IN THE U.S. ARMY.

In September 1938, Arnold became the Chief of the Army Air Corps and was promoted to Major General. As the Senior Air Corps Officer in the Army, he would continue developing American military aviation according to his vision. Over the next three years, Arnold demonstrated remarkable energy in strengthening those areas in which he felt American airpower would be most necessary in the coming war. He recognized the need not only to create a large aviation service, but also to train the necessary leaders and pilots, as well as the difficulties each task would entail.[10] Arnold was a fervent believer in the possibilities of strategic bombing against specific targets and became a staunch proponent of bomber development. He emphasized research and development, specifically the production and fielding of the B-17 bomber and the progression of jet engine technology.

Arnold was an administrative master and was central to the creation of the Army Air Force in 1941, when he was named Chief of Army Air Forces, six months prior to America's entry into World War II.[11] During the initial years of the war, he viewed his tactical planning decisions directing fast, maneuverable escort fighters for the bomber force to be of critical importance, along with his insistence on the development of incendiary bombs.[12] Arnold spent 1943 driving his subordinate commanders to achieve success in Europe and to develop the B-29 Superfortress, destined for service primarily in the Pacific theater.[13] The advent of long-range P-51 and P-47 fighter escorts in Europe by the beginning of 1944 and the steady depletion of German defenses allowed Arnold to gradually focus more effort on the development of the B-29, which became his focus in the closing year of the war.[14]

In the final two years of World War II, numerous health issues prohibited Arnold from being as active as he had been in the previous decades. In May 1943, he suffered his first of four heart attacks that would strike in the final two years of the war, each of which limited his activity for periods of time.[15] Additionally, in early 1945, his beloved wife, Bee, suffered a nervous breakdown, further distracting him from the war effort.[16] As the end of hostilities approached, Arnold decided to retire, and left service in February 1946. Post-war life in California saw a continuation of health issues, and he died of a heart attack in January 1950, shortly after the publication of his autobiography.

An outgoing and expressive man, perhaps his greatest contribution to the war effort was his perseverance in the face of adversity and his determination to achieve his goals. His close personal and professional relationships with industry and civilian leaders (notwithstanding a significant but temporary disagreement with President Roosevelt on the level of support given to Britain under Lend-Lease) proved crucial to the development of American production initiatives.[17] He was determined to pursue the latest technological advancements, particularly the heavy bomber as a pivotal weapon in the future to directly attack an enemy's economy and industrial base, as well as to defeat enemy air forces.[18] Arnold dedicated his professional life to the development of airpower on a holistic scale and was the principal individual responsible for building an American strategic Air Force almost from scratch.[19]

Written by: Lieutenant Colonel Michael A. Boden, PhD (USA, Retired), USMA 1988.

General Carl Andrew Spaatz, the first Chief of Staff of the United States Air Force, graduated from West Point in 1914. In a career that encompassed 34 years, Spaatz witnessed nearly every key event that brought the United States Air Force to its independence. The fact that he was the first leader of the Air Force as an independent service is appropriate considering his importance in bringing about that development.

Spaatz was not a typical Academy aspirant. Born Carl A. Spatz (he changed his name to Spaatz in the late 1930s, to please his wife and to maintain consistency of pronunciation) in 1891, he entered West Point in March 1910, and initially was so unimpressed with Academy life that he submitted a letter of resignation after only three weeks. His father talked him out of resigning, but Spaatz never achieved great success as a Cadet, earning numerous punishment hours and gaining a reputation as a smoker, drinker, and poker player.[1] He graduated in the bottom half of his class and was still walking punishment tours on graduation day.[2] At West Point, though, he did gain his well-known nickname of "Tooey," awarded for his close resemblance to an upperclassman, F.J. Toohey.

Unable to branch directly to the Air Services, he was commissioned an Infantryman and assigned to the 25th Infantry Division in Hawaii prior to his acceptance to the flying school. By May 1916, Spaatz had earned his junior military aviator wings and was assigned to the 1st Aero Squadron in New Mexico. With America's involvement in the First World War, Spaatz soon found himself in combat in Europe. Spending a year with both Pursuit Groups and Bomber units, Spaatz earned rapid promotion to Major and a reputation as a highly skilled, intelligent pilot; he shot down three German aircraft, crash-landed in French territory, and served as the Officer in Charge of the Issoudun Instruction Center for pilots arriving in theater.[3]

During the interwar years, Spaatz was fortunate enough to serve in numerous tactical, operational, and strategic assignments with Pursuit and Bomber units, the Air Force staff in Washington, and service schools. In 1928 to 1929, Spaatz commanded the Question Mark Operation, which demonstrated the challenges and possibilities of in-flight refueling, and was awarded the Distinguished Flying Cross for his actions. Question Mark had a profound influence on Spaatz and significantly influenced him in later years as he developed American ideas of strategic bombing. In the 1930s, he became one of the first theorists in America to examine the possibilities of bombers penetrating beyond enemy coastlines, without escort protection, to attack strategic targets.[4] Assignments to the Operations and Training Division of the Office of the Chief of the Air Corps in 1933 and as the Executive Office for the 2nd Wing

General Carl Andrew Spaatz, USAF, USMA 1914

- **FIRST CHIEF OF STAFF U.S. AIR FORCE**
- **SHOT DOWN THREE GERMAN AIRCRAFT IN WORLD WAR I**
- **CRASH LANDED IN FRANCE IN WORLD WAR I**
- **COMMANDER, U.S. STRATEGIC AIR FORCES IN EUROPE**
- **FOUNDER AND COMMANDER, 8TH AIR FORCE**
- **ONLY SENIOR AMERICAN COMMANDER TO PARTICIPATE IN BOTH GERMAN AND JAPANESE SURRENDERS**

>>> Spotlight

On July 26, 1947, while aboard the Presidential C-54 aircraft *Sacred Cow*, President Harry S. Truman signed the National Security Act of 1947, officially establishing the United States Air Force as a separate service under the National Military Establishment (renamed in 1949 the Department of Defense). The Act set out requirements for the Air Force that "it shall be organized, trained, and equipped primarily for prompt and sustained offensive and defensive air operations. The Air Force shall be responsible for the air forces necessary for the effective prosecution of war except otherwise assigned and, in accordance with integrated joint mobilization plans, for the expansion of the peacetime components of the Air Force to meet the needs of war." *National Museum of the United States Air Force*

of the GHQ Air Force in 1936 placed him in critical positions to observe and influence American airpower development in the years immediately preceding war.[5] In these roles, he was able to implement many of his organizational visions to structure the growing American bomber force, and to be present when the B-17 Flying Fortress first arrived in service.[6]

Upon the outbreak of World War II, Spaatz was given command of the Air Forces Combat Command, which soon became the 8th Air Force. He initially focused on developing a strategic bombing campaign that would weaken Germany to the point that Hitler's forces would be unable to effectively respond to any invasion of the continent.[7]

Almost immediately, however, Spaatz was diverted to North Africa, where he served as General D.D. Eisenhower's Principal Air Advisor and subsequently as Commander of United States Strategic Air Forces in Europe.

During his year in the Mediterranean, Spaatz gained tremendous insight into combat operations and refined his ideas on the strategic application of airpower and the challenges of creating a strategic force from the ground up in terms of organization, logistics, personnel management, and materiel. Additionally, he was introduced to the full spectrum of air operations: air-to-air fighter combat, strategic and tactical bombing, amphibious landings, airborne drops, joint operations with the Army and Navy,

operations with allied forces, and logistical missions. Perhaps most importantly to the successful progress of the war, though, was his development of a trusting and friendly relationship with Eisenhower.[8]

Returning to Europe in preparation for Operation Overlord in January 1944, Spaatz directed the development of Operation Pointblank, the American component of the Combined Bomber Offensive. As part of Pointblank, Spaatz emphasized three targets for the strategic air campaign: single-engine fighter plane production, twin-engine fighter plane production, and "antifriction bearing manufacturing."[9] Three months later, he "reclarified" Pointblank, to include production facilities for oil, rubber, and bomber aircraft.[10] Adhering to these tenets of Pointblank, however, was difficult, owing to British insistence, championed by Air Chief Marshal Trafford Leigh-Mallory, that the strategic bombing effort must focus on the German transportation network in preparation for the coming invasion. Spaatz believed, and was vindicated by ensuing operations, that the greatest impact on German resistance to invasion would be through devastating the industries specified by Pointblank. Spaatz remained steadfast in his adherence to targeting German oil-producing capabilities, at one point even threatening resignation if Eisenhower redirected United States assets.[11]

Soon after the Normandy landings, most of the initial strategic targets of Pointblank had been rendered ineffective, and Spaatz dedicated more U.S assets to other strategic targets, including transportation and rail centers, although he never deviated from his oil-first targeting philosophy.[12] While he never believed that terror-bombing was as successful as targeted attacks on key industries, Spaatz's operations did result in significant collateral damage. To his credit, Spaatz always insisted on specifying specific targets of worth, rather than

attacking broader "industrial areas," as the British did.[13]

In recognition of his contribution to Allied victory, Spaatz was selected as a representative to the May 1945, German surrender in Berlin. He was then assigned to the Pacific, where he arrived too late to accomplish anything of significance militarily other than give the order to the *Enola Gay* to drop the atomic bomb on Hiroshima.[14] He was, however, present for the Japanese surrender at Manila Bay in September, becoming the only senior American Commander to participate in both German and Japanese capitulations.

After the war, with Hap Arnold in failing health, Spaatz was the logical choice to lead the Army Air Forces in the coming fight for service independence. His experience before and during the war largely ensured that in 1947, when the Air Force achieved independence, it was created in accordance to his vision. With an independent Air Force a reality, Spaatz retired in June, 1948. After retirement, he worked as the *Newsweek* military editor for a dozen years and frequently supported President Eisenhower's NATO and Europe-first policies.[15] He also was involved with the development of the United States Air Force Academy, where he was buried following his death on July 14, 1974.

While never a traditional military intellectual, Spaatz without question possessed a keen mind. Throughout his career, he demonstrated tremendous common-sense and courage, and surrounded himself with subordinates whom he trusted and were (for the most part) talented. Spaatz's orders were intentionally broad, allowing his subordinates the greatest possible leeway to accomplish the mission without any micromanagement. In World War II, he possessed all the key attributes necessary to succeed in a long-term, coalition war against a resilient enemy, and his insistence and determination to attack German oil industries was without question critical in the ultimate defeat of Germany.

Written by: Lieutenant Colonel Michael A. Boden, PhD (USA, Retired), USMA 1988.

> **AFTER THE WAR, WITH HAP ARNOLD IN FAILING HEALTH, SPAATZ WAS THE LOGICAL CHOICE TO LEAD THE ARMY AIR FORCES IN THE COMING FIGHT FOR SERVICE INDEPENDENCE.**

Photo: AP

B-17 Flying Fortress.

Discussing aerial tactics with an instructor at Tuskegee.

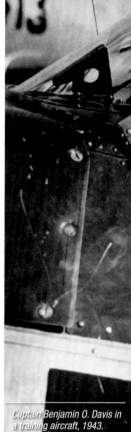

Captain Benjamin O. Davis in a training aircraft, 1943.

General Benjamin O. Davis, USAF, USMA 1936

- COMMISSIONED AS AN INFANTRY OFFICER BECAUSE THE AIR CORPS DID NOT ACCEPT AFRICAN-AMERICANS
- FIRST ASSIGNMENT WAS 24TH INFANTRY REGIMENT (BUFFALO SOLDIERS)
- FIRST AFRICAN-AMERICAN GENERAL OFFICER AND FIRST AFRICAN-AMERICAN FOUR-STAR U.S. AIR FORCE GENERAL
- FIRST AFRICAN-AMERICAN MILITARY PILOT
- FOUNDER AND COMMANDER, THE 332ND FIGHTER GROUP (TUSKEGEE AIRMEN)
- COMMANDER, 51ST FIGHTER WING KOREAN WAR
- COMMANDER, 13TH U.S. AIR FORCE

General Benjamin O. Davis is an icon in American history. He attended West Point and graduated at a time when black Americans still endured segregation and discrimination. Despite overwhelming odds against him, he rose to the greatest heights in his fighter plane, his career, and his personal life. He was a trailblazer and a great American hero, who not only helped win our nation's wars, but helped eliminate discrimination and segregation in America. He was the first General Officer in the United States Air Force.

He was the second child born on December 18, 1912, to career Army Officer Benjamin O. Davis, Sr., and his wife, Elnora. Sadly, Elnora died in 1916 giving birth to their third child. His father served as a black Cavalry Officer from 1889 to 1948. His father was the first black General Officer in the United States Army when he was promoted to Brigadier General in October 1940, just prior to World War II.

Davis, Jr., flew as a passenger in a barnstormer in 1926 and fell in love with flight. He was convinced he needed to learn to fly, so he attended West Point in 1932. As a black cadet, he was shunned, roomed alone, and had very little interaction with his classmates. He applied to flight school but was rejected – simply because he was black. There were no black pilots in 1936 and no black-only units. Instead, he was commissioned in the Infantry and assigned to an all-black unit in Fort Benning, Georgia. He later was assigned to be a Military Tactics Instructor at Tuskegee, Alabama.

Blacks suffered even in the Army under segregation and could not serve in the majority of positions. The administration of President Franklin Delano Roosevelt was under pressure to include blacks in the mobilization of forces in preparation for World War II. A decision was made to create an all-black flying unit, and Captain Davis was assigned

to the first class of student pilots. In March 1942, he became the first black military pilot to receive his wings. He was promoted to Lieutenant Colonel and given command of the first black pursuit squadron – the 99th Pursuit Squadron.

The 99th Pursuit Squadron first saw action in Operation Torch in the invasion of North Africa in November 1942. They participated in the invasion of Sicily in 1943. Davis was given command of the 332nd Fighter Group being formed in the United States He returned to the United States to take command and found that opponents, who had political agendas to eliminate all-black units, were lobbying to have his 99th Pursuit Squadron deactivated. Lieutenant Davis fought this decision vigorously and appeared before an inquiry formed by General George C. Marshall, the Chief of Staff of the Army. Meanwhile, the 99th continued to serve in combat and shot down 12 enemy planes

over the first two days of the invasion of Anzio.

Lieutenant Davis returned to combat leading the 332nd Fighter Group out of a base in Italy. They escorted bombers on long-range missions into the heart of Germany flying P-47s. Davis was promoted to Colonel in September 1944. While he was serving in Italy as a Colonel, his father was also serving in European theater as a Brigadier General – making their father-son team the two top-ranking black officers in the European Theater.

Davis himself flew many missions in both P-47s and P-51s. He was awarded the Silver Star and the Distinguished Flying Cross for missions over Austria and German. The United States Air Force was formed in 1947 and Colonel Davis's commission was transferred from the Army Air Corps to the United States Air Force. In July 1948, President Truman signed an executive order

>> Spotlight

Davis was shunned at West Point by his classmates who would only speak with him for official duties because he was black. He lived alone with no roommates yet graduated near the top of his West Point class. When he graduated he was the only living African-American West Point graduate and therefore was chosen to lead the segregated new all-black aviation unit training at Tuskegee, Alabama. He and four other black pilots received their pilot wings on March 7, 1942, followed by nearly 1,000 other black pilots in World War II. His courageous leadership would help end segregation in the Armed Forces, which would help America integrate other institutions, eventually ending segregation two decades later.

to integrate blacks into the Armed Forces. This was far ahead of the American public, which maintained segregation for the next 16 years.

In 1953, Colonel Davis was given command of the 51st Fighter Squadron in Korea, where he saw combat again leading a squadron of F-86's in the modern jet fighter age. He returned from Korea and became the first General Officer in the United States Air Force when he was promoted to Brigadier General, the same rank his father had held before him as the first black Army General Officer. For the next 16 years, he served in a variety of positions in the United States and overseas. He was promoted to Major General in 1959 (another first). In 1964, President Lyndon Johnson signed the Civil Rights Act of 1964. Davis was promoted to Lieutenant General in 1965 (another first). Much of this success was the result of trailblazers like Henry O. Flipper and his father. Davis and others, like Roscoe Robinson, helped take

IN MARCH 1942, DAVIS BECAME THE FIRST BLACK MILITARY PILOT TO RECEIVE HIS WINGS. HE WAS PROMOTED TO LIEUTENANT COLONEL AND GIVEN COMMAND OF THE FIRST BLACK PURSUIT SQUADRON, THE 99TH PURSUIT SQUADRON.

the baton from former trailblazers and took it to the next level.

He retired in 1970, after the military had been fully integrated in the 1940s and the 1960s had brought about integration into the American public. On December 9, 1998, President Clinton promoted Lieutenant Davis to Four-Star General and pinned on his fourth star. He headed the

Federal Air Marshal program and then the Battle Monuments Commission. He served as an Assistant Secretary of Transportation and helped implement the 55-miles-per-hour speed limit, well below that of his P-51 that he had flown decades before.

He served a total of 34 years in uniform but will be forever remembered for his wartime exploits in World War II as the Commander of the Tuskegee Airmen – the all-black fight squadron with the red tails. He was the first African-American to solo in a military aircraft and to become General Officer in the United States Air Force. He personally helped to bring about the policies that brought down discrimination.

Over the years, the Tuskegee Airmen have come to symbolize all the tragedy, obstacles, and success of African-Americans overcoming the greatest odds to fight for a country that didn't give them full rights. All the Tuskegee Airmen are heroes and Davis

was their heroic leader. Hollywood made a film called *The Tuskegee Airmen*, in which Davis was portrayed by Andre Braugher in the 1995.

General Davis died on the July 4, 2002, the year of the West Point Bicentennial. President Bill Clinton, who had pinned on his fourth star only four years earlier, attended the funeral and stated that "General Davis is here today as living proof that a person can overcome adversity and discrimination, achieve great things, turn skeptics into believers, and through example and perseverance, one person can bring truly extraordinary change." A single red-tailed P-51 flew over Arlington National Cemetery to honor the fallen soldier and the first African-American Air Force General.

The McInerney Family is a family of West Point graduates who exemplify the spirit of "Duty, Honor, Country." The McInerney's served in the air and on the ground during nearly every major conflict in the twentieth century, and one member family made the ultimate sacrifice for our country. Members of the family served with distinction in World War I, World War II, the Cold War, the Korean War, The Berlin Airlift, The Cuban Missile Crisis, the Vietnam War, the 1986 bombing of Libya and the Afghanistan War. The five family members are the patriarch James, Sr. (USMA 1923), and the four sons: James, Jr. (USMA 1952), John and Tom (both USMA 1959) and Richard, KIA Vietnam (USMA 1960)

James E. B. McInerney. The original patriarch was James E. B. McInerney (USMA 1923). He enlisted in the Army in May 1917 and served in France from July 1917 to May 1919, serving in five major battles at the Somme, Lys, St. Mihiel, and the Meuse-Argonne. He entered West Point in 1919 and graduated in 1923. He married Rose between the wars and they had five children – four boys and a girl. All four boys attended and graduated from West Point (1952, 1959, 1959, and 1960).

In 1944, Jim returned to combat in Europe as a Colonel, where he helped introduce the M-24 light tank to units in the field. He served in England, France, and Germany as part of the 9th Army and then returned home after the war. Jim returned to Europe in February 1949 as the commander of all of the ordnance rebuild shops in Western Europe in what preceded the Marshall Plan. He remained on active duty for 37 years and retired as a Colonel in 1954.

James E. McInerney, Jr. Jim and Rose's first son, James E. McInerney, Jr., enlisted in the Army in 1947 and attended Airborne School and the 82nd Airborne Division. He

Lieutenant General Thomas McInerney, USAF, USMA 1959

- AIR FORCE FIGHTER PILOT
- ONE OF FIVE MCINERNEY MEN WHO GRADUATED FROM WEST POINT
- COMMANDED 1986 BOMBING OF LIBYA
- FLEW 407 COMBAT MISSIONS IN VIETNAM
- PARTICIPATED IN BERLIN AIRLIFT AND CUBAN MISSILE CRISIS
- BROTHER RICHARD WAS KILLED IN ACTION IN VIETNAM IN THE INFANTRY

Captain Richard McInerney, USMA 1960, Killed In Action, Vietnam.

Colonel James McInerney (father) and two sons, John and Richard, are all buried in the West Point Cemetery.

>>> Spotlight

The McInerney family had five members of the family graduate from West Point. The patriarch, Colonel Jams McInerney, served in World War I and World War II. His four sons all attended West Point. John passed away just after graduation in 1959. Another, Richard, was Killed In Action in Vietnam as an Infantry Company Commander. Two became General Officers in the United States Air Force. Lieutenant General Tom McInerney (profiled here) and Major General James McInerney hold the record for most SAM sites destroyed in Vietnam.

entered West Point in 1948 with the Class of 19152 and was the Eastern Intercollegiate Boxing Champion in 1951 and 1952. He was commissioned as a fighter pilot flying F-86s and was the last Air Force pilot to shoot down a North Korean MiG-15 when he was attacked May 10, 1955, well after the armistice had been signed. He was a command pilot with thousands of hours in F-86s, F-100s, F-105s, and F-4s. In 1967, as a Lieutenant Colonel, Jim was assigned to be an F-105 Wild Weasel Squadron Commander at Korat Royal Thai Air Force Base, Thailand. Sadly, Jim arrived at Korat on March 11, 1967, ferrying an F-105 from the United States on the same day as his younger brother Dick was Killed In Action on the Bong Son Plains in South Vietnam while serving as a Company Commander with the 1st Cavalry Division (Airmobile). After a quick trip home for the funeral at West Point, Jim returned to Korat to fly during the spring and summer of 1967, which turned out to be some of the heaviest fighting in North Vietnam by our tactical fighters.

Jim led the Air Force's toughest mission and largest fighter squadron in the USAF, comprised of 18 Wild Weasel F-105F aircraft (a two-seat configuration with a Weapons System Officer in the back) and a full complement of 18 single seat F-105D aircraft for strike operations. In his tour as the Wild Weasel Commander, Jim did not lose any squadron pilots in combat, an enviable record of leadership. He flew 101 combat missions, personally destroyed 17 SAM sites (a world record), and was awarded the Air Force Cross, three Silver Stars, and seven Distinguished Flying Crosses. He served in consecutive positions of command and retired as a Major General. Jim became a Vice President for Membership Development at NDIA and played a crucial role in the funding of the American Air Museum in the U.K. For this effort he was designated a Commander of the British Empire (CBE) by the Queen in 1999.

Jim and his wife, Mary Catherine, were married in July 1963 at West Point and had two children, Anne and Jake. On July 8, 2011, Mary Catherine passed away from a fatal stroke.

John A. McInerney John entered West Point in July 1955 as a member of the Class of 1959, along with his twin brother, Tom. Shortly into his third class year at Camp Buckner, a routine physical discovered that he had incurred Hodgkin's disease in his left lung. John endured a very successful operation that put the Hodgkin's disease into remission. John returned to West Point, where he resumed academics and played B squad football and lacrosse as if nothing had happened. During John's commissioning physical in the fall of 1958 that the doctors determined the Hodgkin's disease had returned, so again he returned to Walter Reed for treatment during part of his first class year. Despite the difficulty John still managed to complete all his academics and graduate with his class on June 3, 1959. John was not granted a commission because of the Hodgkin's disease and he returned to Walter Reed during graduation summer for further treatment in the hopes that he again would go into remission. John passed away on December 27, 1959, with his dad and brothers, Jim and Tom, there for his last Christmas.

Thomas G. McInerney Tom graduated with his brother, John, with the Class of 1959 and was commissioned in the Infantry. He attended the basic Infantry Officers' course, as well as Airborne School before receiving the first interservice transfer to the Air Force. His first fighter squadron was in F-104s at George Air Force Base in California, where he participated in a number of Cold War hot spots. The first was the Berlin crisis in 1962 where Tom flew with his squadron out of Hahn Air Base in West Germany on contingency escort missions for the Berlin Airlift flights in case the Russians tried to close the vital air links to Berlin.

Upon his return to George Air Force Base in the early fall of 1962, his second hot spot suddenly appeared. Tom and his squadron were deployed to Key West Naval Air Station in Florida two days ahead of President Kennedy's October 22nd announcement of the Cuban Missile Crisis to the world. Tom was actually flying escort missions three miles off the coast of Cuba just before the President made this historic announcement.

By the time Cuban Missile Crisis was over Tom received orders to go to Vietnam in April 1963 as part of the first Air Force Forward Air Controllers (FAC) permanently assigned to Army of the Republic of Vietnam (ARVN) divisions. Following this incredible experience as a FAC Tom debriefed the AF Chief of Staff General Curtis Lemay and proceeded to the newly formed Tactical Air Warfare Center (TAWC) at Eglin Air Force Base in Florida where the Air Force was training pilots and ground controllers for joint combat operations. In April 1964, Tom was assigned to fly the brand new Air Force F-4Cs that were doing weapons testing at the time. It was here that Tom met the love of his life, Mona Hunt, and they were married in January 1966, just prior to being assigned to Nellis Air Force Base to Fighter Weapons School where he later served as an F-4 instructor pilot.

This experience led to his being assigned to the operational test and evaluation section of the Fighter Weapons School where Tom ran the category three testing on the F-4D and the F-4E models, as well as led the combat evaluations for both aircraft in Southeast Asia (SEA). Combat evaluations involved four month long deployments into SEA flying these newly arrived fighters in all kinds of combat conditions and reporting back to tactical air command and the air staff on their operational evaluation.

In January 1969, Tom volunteered to return to Korat RTAir Force Base to fly with the

Lieutenant General McInerney with President George H.W. Bush.

Lieutenant Colonel JE McInerney (left) and Captain Fred Shannon, his EWO on the two-man Wild Weasel team in front of their F-105G at Korat, Thailand, Air Force Base, July 1967.

first F-4E combat squadron that he had introduced into theater. By then, Tom's older brother, Jim, had left Korat and his younger brother, Dick, had been Killed In Action more than a year earlier. This final SEA tour and 407 combat missions was invaluable and served Tom well in future command assignments both in Asia and Europe.

Tom was assigned to the air staff in the Pentagon to work on the newly designed but not yet flying F-15 air superiority fighter. Thus began a long relationship with the world's best air superiority fighter. In July 1973, after graduating from the National War College and George Washington University, Tom was assigned to be Director of Operations at the 56th Tactical Fighter Wing at Luke Air Force Base in Arizona, which was the largest Air Force base in the world. Tom was then assigned to London as the Air Attaché to the Court of Saint James under three different American Ambassadors:

Walter Annenberg, Elliott Richardson, and Anne Armstrong. Following London Tom was assigned to be Vice Commander of the 20th Tactical Fighter Wing at RAF Upper Heyford in the United Kingdom. The 20th TFW flew F-111s with a tactical nuclear strike mission that was extremely important for NATO's deterrent mission in the Cold War. He returned to the Pentagon to the Office of the Secretary of Defense (OSD) as the senior military assistant to Ambassador Bob Komer, Secretary of Defense Harold Brown's advisor on NATO Affairs. Ambassador Komer was responsible for NATO's long-term defense plan and the NATO summit of 1978 in Washington, D.C.

Tom took command of the 3rd Tactical Fighter Wing at Clark Air Base in the Philippines in March 1979. Clark was one of the largest air bases in the world, with numerous military tenants, two F-4E squadrons, an aggressor squadron comprised

of T-38s, and 35,000 people on the base, including the Philippine civilians. Tom was promoted to Brigadier General in December 1980, along with his assignment to be the

MEMBERS OF THE FAMILY SERVED WITH DISTINCTION IN WORLD WAR I, WORLD WAR II, THE COLD WAR, THE KOREAN WAR, THE BERLIN AIRLIFT, THE CUBAN MISSILE CRISIS, THE VIETNAM WAR, THE 1986 BOMBING OF LIBYA, AND THE AFGHANISTAN WAR.

313th Air Division Commander at Kadena AB in Okinawa, which was comprised of three F-15 Squadrons and one RF-4 squadron, plus all joint housing on the island.

As a Major General, Tom took command of the 3rd Air Force at RAF Mildenhall in the United Kingdom. On April 15, 1986, President Reagan directed air strikes on

Tripoli and Colonel Ghaddafi by planes from the 3rd Air Force and carriers of the United States 6th Fleet. The predominant strike forces were F-111Fs from RAF Lakenheath, with EF-111s from RAF Upper Heyford and Navy A-7s providing SAM suppression for the more than 70 missiles fired at the Tripoli strike force. In addition two other RAF bases were used to launch the largest KC-10 tanker refueling force assembled to date.

In July 1986, Tom was promoted to Lieutenant General and assigned as Vice Commander in Chief at Headquarters, United States Air Forces Europe, at Ramstein AB in West Germany. On June 20, 1994, Tom retired after 35 years in the Air Force and

John and Tom McInerney, USMA 1959.

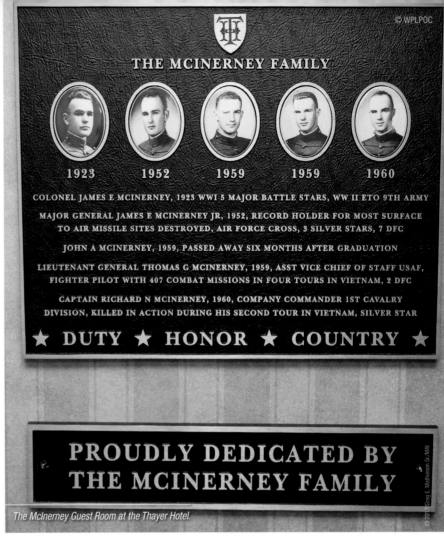

THE MCINERNEY FAMILY

1923 — 1952 — 1959 — 1959 — 1960

COLONEL JAMES E MCINERNEY, 1923 WWI 5 MAJOR BATTLE STARS, WW II ETO 9TH ARMY

MAJOR GENERAL JAMES E MCINERNEY JR, 1952, RECORD HOLDER FOR MOST SURFACE TO AIR MISSILE SITES DESTROYED, AIR FORCE CROSS, 3 SILVER STARS, 7 DFC

JOHN A MCINERNEY, 1959, PASSED AWAY SIX MONTHS AFTER GRADUATION

LIEUTENANT GENERAL THOMAS G MCINERNEY, 1959, ASST VICE CHIEF OF STAFF USAF, FIGHTER PILOT WITH 407 COMBAT MISSIONS IN FOUR TOURS IN VIETNAM, 2 DFC

CAPTAIN RICHARD N MCINERNEY, 1960, COMPANY COMMANDER 1ST CAVALRY DIVISION, KILLED IN ACTION DURING HIS SECOND TOUR IN VIETNAM, SILVER STAR

★ DUTY ★ HONOR ★ COUNTRY ★

PROUDLY DEDICATED BY THE MCINERNEY FAMILY

The McInerney Guest Room at the Thayer Hotel.

moved in to the civilian world. He was a vice President successively for Unisys and Loral and President of the Business Executives for National Security (BENS). Tom also was successful in assisting the Clinton Administration in securing passage by the Senate of the Chemical Warfare Treaty in 1997. In addition Tom played an instrumental role in moving BENS toward generating a terrorism strategy before the global war on terror struck us on 9/11. He has been a Fox News Military Analyst for more than 10 years.

Richard N. McInerney. Dick entered West Point following in his father and three older brothers' footprints. Dick excelled in all endeavors, from being on the 150-pound football team and lettering for four years to becoming an airborne Ranger Infantry Officer upon graduation in 1960. His first assignment with the 82nd Airborne Division as a Platoon Leader was symbolic of his desire to follow the sound of the cannons.

In January 1963, Dick volunteered to go to South Vietnam at a time when most of America did not even know where Vietnam was. As an advisor to a battalion of the Army of the Republic of Vietnam (ARVN) battalion stationed at Dak To in the northern highlands Dick spent a year in combat gaining a clear understanding of the challenges America would face in its endeavor under Presidents Kennedy, Johnson, Nixon, and Ford. Dick returned to be the S-4 and then a Company Commander for the 3rd Infantry Division, the Old Guard, at Fort Myer. The Old Guard is world famous for what they do and only the best command their companies.

In 1966, Dick proceeded to the 1st Cavalry Division (Airmobile) at An Khe. Initially he was assigned as headquarters Company Commander for the 2nd Battalion, but Dick persisted in requesting a rifle company. This happened after six months and Dick was given command of D Company, 2nd Battalion, 5th Calvary Regiment. D Company was his pride and life for the next two and a half months. His battalion was conducting numerous operations against regular units of the North Vietnamese Army (NVA) as the NVA escalated their efforts to destabilize South Vietnam.

On March 11, 1967, as older brother Jim was flying in to Korat RTAir Force Base, Dick's company was airlifted into an area adjacent to another company that was pinned down by an enemy force of unknown size. Dick led his men into immediate contact with the enemy force. When one of his platoons was pinned down in an open area by hostile fire, Dick – realizing that a quick fix on the enemy positions was necessary due to the steadily increasing casualties – seized a machine gun and ran forward 25 meters where he was wounded by a rifle bullet. He asked casualties of his unit in a ditch nearby to indicate the location of the enemy position. His men said the enemy was 20 meters to the front. Ignoring the hostile fire, Dick rose up to throw a grenade and was mortally wounded by enemy fire. For his gallantry in action, Dick was posthumously awarded the Silver Star.

Dick and Mary Grace had three children – John, Mike and Julie. Dick was a true warrior, and his son Mike is of the same mold, Mike having been awarded the Silver Star himself for combat action in Afghanistan.

The McInerney Room at the Thayer Hotel is proudly dedicated by the McInerney family.

Colonel Robin Olds, with distinctive handlebar mustache, discussing fighter-pilot strategy and tactics over Vietnam.

Robin Olds, his wife, actress Ella Raines, and two daughters, Christina and Susan.

Brigadier General Robin Olds, USAF, USMA 1943

- FIGHTER PILOT IN WORLD WAR II AND VIETNAM
- TRIPLE ACE WITH 16 KILLS
- COMMANDANT OF CADETS AT THE U.S. AIR FORCE ACADEMY
- AIR FORCE CROSS AND FOUR SILVER STARS

The flying ace is widely viewed as the pinnacle of the excellence in aerial combat. These elite war fighters are the core of the estimated five percent of pilots who account for the majority of air-to-air "kills."[1] Although achieving "ace" status is rare, a few warriors have managed to accomplish the feat multiple times. Notable among the rolls of fighter aces is Brigadier General Robin Olds, the only American to score air-to-air victories in both World War II and Vietnam.

Robin Olds was born to be a fighter pilot. His father, Major General Robert Olds, had flown for the Army Air Corps in France during the First World War and later served as the aide to General Billy Mitchell. The younger Olds spent most of his early years at Langley Field in Virginia, where his neighbors included many officers who would

become central figures in the development of American airpower.

Growing up in Virginia, Olds first came into his own on the football field, leading the Hampton High School team to the State Championship. Olds played tackle on the Army team for the first two years of Colonel "Red" Blaik's tenure and earned All-American honors for his superior performance on the field. In 1942, he was recognized as "Lineman of the Year" by *Collier's Weekly* and famed sportswriter Gartland Rice labeled him "Player of the Year." In 1985, Olds was elected to the College Football Hall of Fame.

Olds had entered West Point with the Class of 1944, but the war accelerated graduation for his class and he graduated in June of 1943. Olds applied for the Air Corps and

completed his pilot training as a Cadet. The day before graduation, Olds's pilot's wings were pinned on his uniform by General Henry H. "Hap" Arnold.

Olds flew his first combat mission in a P-38J in May of 1944, just prior to the D-Day invasion. Within three months, he had earned his first air-to-air "kills," shooting down two German Focke-Wulf FW-190s on the same mission.[3] Olds became an "Ace" in the P-38 with at least five confirmed victories and was the top-scoring P-38 pilot in the European Theater when he transitioned to flying the P-51 Mustang.[4] By the end of the war, Olds had achieved 12 aerial victories and been promoted to the rank of Major.

During the Korean War, Olds made repeated requests to join the fight, but spent the majority of the war serving with a unit of

the Air Defense Command in Pittsburgh. Olds later wrote that he had learned, after his retirement, he had been denied an assignment to Korea because his wife, actress Ella Raines, and her producers had persuaded the prominent philanthropist Laurance Rockefeller to use his influence inside the Pentagon to keep Olds's from combat. Ella had starred in almost 20 films by this time and was now beginning to work in television, as well; keeping Olds from Korea would keep the actress from being distracted in her work.[5] By the end of the Korean War, less than 10 years after graduating from West Point, Olds had already been promoted to Colonel. In September of 1966, Colonel Olds was again given the opportunity to prove himself as a fighter pilot and as a Combat Commander when he was placed in command of the 8th Tactical Fighter Wing

>>> Spotlight

Fighter Pilot: The Memoirs of Legendary Ace Robin Olds was written by Robin Olds and his daughter, Christina. It tells the stories of World War II, Vietnam, marrying a Hollywood star and time at the United States Air Force Academy.

Courtesy: Fighter Pilot

Lockheed P-38 Lightning over Los Angeles, 1940.

Brigadier General Robin Olds as the Commandant of the U.S. Air Force Academy.

Photo: AP

(TFW) at Ubon Royal Thai Air Force Base.

Olds scored another four aerial victories while piloting an F-4C as Commander of the 8th TFW, but his greatest impact came as a tactical planner. In late 1966, Olds crafted a plan designed to draw out North Vietnamese MiG-21s to engage with the F-4s of the 8th TFW. The plan, named Operation Bolo, used deception to entice the North Vietnamese pilots into a fight. The F-4s would fly the same flight routes and use the same radio call signs as the less-maneuverable F-105s that the MiG pilots preferred to engage. The plan work and by the end of the day, Olds's 8th TFW (which he dubbed the "Wolfpack"), had downed seven MiG-21s — almost half of the 16 MiG-21s which the enemy possessed. Olds himself had scored two aerial victories during Operation Bolo, giving him a total of four victories in a jet-powered fighter. After scoring his fourth victory in Vietnam, Olds was told that the Air Force would remove him from Vietnam as a public-

"FIGHTING SPIRIT ONE MUST HAVE. EVEN IF A MAN LACKS SOME OF THE OTHER QUALIFICATIONS, HE CAN OFTEN MAKE UP FOR IT IN FIGHTING SPIRIT," SAID OLDS.[2]

ity asset if he were to score a fifth aerial victory and become the first "Ace" of the war.[6] Olds never reported scoring a fifth victory in Vietnam. Years later, Olds was asked if he had actually shot down a fifth MiG; he replied, "I choose not to answer that question."[7]

Olds left Southeast Asia in the autumn of 1967 having amassed a total of 16 confirmed kills during his career — becoming a "Triple Ace." He had also earned the Air Force Cross, the Silver Star, and numerous other decorations for his gallantry. Olds was promoted to Brigadier General and reassigned to duty as the 6th Commandant of Cadets at the United States Air Force Academy. Before reporting to the Air Force Academy, Olds met with the Air Force Chief of Staff, General John P. McConnell, who pointed at the well-groomed handlebar mustache that Olds had cultivated as Commander of the Wolfpack, and directed Olds to "Take it off." Olds dutifully complied.

After concluding his tenure at the Air Force Academy, Olds offered to accept a reduction in rank to Colonel so that he could return to the fight in Vietnam. This request was denied and Olds retired from the Air Force as a Brigadier General in 1973.

Olds was a warrior and a leader who earned the admiration and respect of those with whom he served. He was also a visionary whose ideas about the role of fighter aircraft in conventional warfare were often seen as iconoclastic at the time, but ultimately proved prophetic. One of the largest personas in the early years of the United States Air Force, General Olds died in 2007 and was laid to rest in the cemetery at the Air Force Academy.

Written by: Lieutenant Colonel Craig Morrow, PhD, USMA 1991.

THE ASTRONAUTS

President Dwight D. Eisenhower (USMA 1915) led the formation of the National Aeronautics and Space Administration (NASA) during the height of the Cold War, when he signed the act creating NASA on July 29, 1958. The United States and the Soviet Union were in a heated "race to space" after the Soviets launched the first successful satellite to orbit the Earth, *Sputnik*, much to the surprise and shock of the American public. The creation of NASA thus signified America's commitment to ultimately win that race. President John F. Kennedy raised the bar further when he set a goal to land a man on the moon by the end of the 1960s.

Eighteen West Point graduates have been at the forefront of that earlier space race effort and beyond by becoming NASA astronauts. In doing so, they have led some of the most critical missions, including the historic *Apollo 11* mission, which ultimately realized Kennedy's goal, as two of the three astronauts were West Point graduates. This chapter highlights four West Point Astronauts: Borman, Aldrin, Collins, and White.

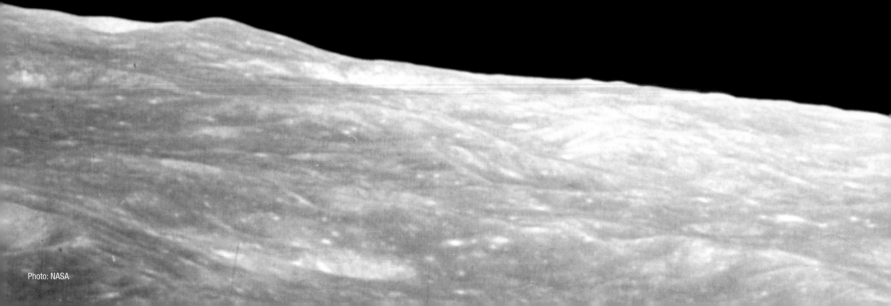

Photo: NASA

President Dwight D. Eisenhower – USMA 1915 – founded NASA by signing the National Aeronautics and Space Act of 1958 on July 29, 1958.

"I believe that this nation should commit itself to achieving the goal, before this decade is out, of landing a man on the moon and returning him safely to Earth."

–President John F. Kennedy, May 1961

"I felt red, white, and blue all over."

–Lieutenant Colonel Ed White, USAF, USMA 1952, Pilot of Gemini 4, *when he was quoted in* Life *magazine after being the first man to walk in space on June 3, 1965 (he was later killed in a launchpad accident January 27, 1967, on Apollo 1, along with Lieutenant Colonel Gus Grissom, USAF, and Lieutenant Commander Roger Chaffee, USN)*

"The view of the Earth from the moon fascinated me – a small disk, 240,000 miles away… Raging nationalistic interests, famines, wars, pestilence don't show from that distance."

–Commander Apollo 8 Frank Borman (USMA 1950), December 1968

"Houston, Tranquility Base here. The Eagle has landed."

–Colonel Buzz Aldrin, USMA 1951, Commander, Apollo 11 and his first words spoken upon man first landing on the moon July 20, 1969

"Here men from the planet Earth first set foot upon the moon, July 1969 A.D. We came in peace for all mankind."

–The inscription on a plaque left behind on the surface of the moon by Colonel Buzz Aldrin (USMA 1951), Lieutenant Colonel Michael Collins (USMA 1952), and Neil Armstrong, Apollo 11

Borman receives Space Medal of Honor from President Lyndon Johnson.

Colonel Frank Borman, USAF, USMA 1950

- COMMANDER, *APOLLO 8*, THE FIRST MISSION TO ORBIT THE MOON
- *APOLLO 8* CREW NAMED *TIME MAGAZINE* "MEN OF THE YEAR," 1968
- CHAIRMAN AND CHIEF EXECUTIVE OFFICER, EASTERN AIRLINES
- WEST POINT ASSISTANT PROFESSOR OF THERMODYNAMICS AND FLUID MECHANICS
- WEST POINT DISTINGUISHED GRADUATE AWARD
- CONGRESSIONAL SPACE MEDAL OF HONOR
- BOARD OF DIRECTORS HOME DEPOT, NATIONAL GEOGRAPHIC, OUTBOARD MARINE CORPORATION, AUTO FINANCE GROUP, THERMO INSTRUMENT SYSTEMS, AND AMERICAN SUPERCONDUCTOR

Although he was born in Gary, Indiana, Frank Borman spent most of his childhood in Arizona. The spirit of adventure, so prevalent in the American West, drove Borman. He was fascinated by airplanes early in life, and before he was old enough to drive a car, he had already earned his pilot's license. He would later comment that "Exploration really is the essence of the human spirit, and to pause, to falter, to turn our back on the quest for knowledge, is to perish." As Commander of the first mission to the moon, Borman's life exemplifies that drive to explore and understand the universe in which we exist.

Borman graduated from West Point ranked eighth in the Class of 1950 – a class that counts among its members President Fidel Ramos of the Philippines, General John Wickham, Jr., the 30th Chief of Staff of the Army, and Lieutenant General Winfield Scott, Jr., the 10th Superintendent of the United States Air Force Academy.

After graduation, Borman entered the United States Air Force, which had become an independent service during Borman's second year at West Point. In 1957, Borman returned to West Point as an Assistant Professor of Thermodynamics and Fluid Mechanics.[1]

Borman was selected by NASA to become an astronaut in 1962. He was one of four astronauts in his cohort to be chosen to command one of the flights in the *Gemini* program. In 1965, he commanded *Gemini 7*. Astronaut James A. Lovell, Jr., accompanied Borman on the *Gemini 7* flight. This flight was a long-endurance flight and as part of the mission, Borman participated in the first space rendezvous when his *Gemini 7* spacecraft came within one foot of the *Gemini 6A* craft while orbiting the Earth.

After the conclusion of the *Gemini* program, Borman remained with NASA as a member of the *Apollo* program. Disaster befell the *Apollo* program in January 1967, when the crew of *Apollo 1* were tragically killed in a fire in their capsule during a launch pad test, including Ed White (USMA

BORMAN AND THE *APOLLO 8* CREW WERE THE FIRST HUMANS TO ORBIT THE MOON AND SEE THE "DARK SIDE" OF THE LUNAR SURFACE AND RETURNED AS HEROES.

1952). Borman was selected to serve as the only astronaut on the board charged with investigating the *Apollo 1* accident and his testimony to the United States Congress helped convince the legislature that *Apollo* program would be made safe to fly again.

Following the *Apollo 1* fire, Borman was assigned to the *Apollo 8* mission. Borman

reunited with James Lovell for this mission and the crew successfully entered lunar orbit on Christmas Eve of 1968. The *Apollo 8* crew were the first humans to orbit the moon and see the "dark side" of the lunar surface. After 10 orbits around the Moon, the *Apollo 8* crew returned safely to Earth as heroes. Borman, Lovell, and Anders were chosen by *Time* magazine as the 1968 "Men of the Year."

After Astronaut Virgil Grissom was killed in the *Apollo 1* fire, Deke Slayton selected Borman to replace Grissom as Commander of the first lunar landing mission; however, Borman elected to retire after the *Apollo 8* mission and Neil Armstrong was ultimately selected to command the *Apollo 11* mission.[2] Had Borman rather than Armstrong flown on *Apollo 11*, he would have joined fellow USMA graduates Buzz Aldrin (USMA 1951)

>>> Spotlight

In 1968, *Time* magazine deviated from its normal protocol; instead of choosing one "Man of the Year," it chose three "Men of the Year." Frank Borman, Will Anders, and James Lovell had just completed their *Apollo 8* mission and been the first humans to orbit the moon. The three were hailed as heroes for achieving this space race accomplishment, which brought the United States even closer to landing men on the moon.

Courtesy: Time, Inc.

Apollo 8 *crew prior to launch, Frank Borman, James Lovell, and Will Anders.*

Borman meeting with cadets at West Point.

and Michael Collins (USMA 1952) on the mission. Had this happened, the entire crew of first moon landing would have been members of the Long Gray Line.

After a distinguished career in the Air Force and with NASA, Borman left government service in 1970 and accepted a position as Senior Vice President at Eastern Airlines. In December of 1975, Borman was appointed the Chief Executive Officer of Eastern; the following year, he was also appointed Chairman of the Board.[3] Under Borman's leadership, a company that had lost $95.6 million the year before he took the reins posted a profit of $39.1 million in his first year as Chief Executive Officer and remained profitable in the years that followed.[4,5] In 1978, Borman introduced the first profit-sharing program in the industry — this helped boost Eastern profits for that year to $67.3 million.[6] Colonel Borman retired from Eastern Airlines in 1986. Since retiring from the Eastern, he

has continued to be active in the corporate world, serving on the Board of Directors of the Home Depot, National Geographic, Outboard Marine Corporation, Auto Finance Group, Thermo Instrument Systems, and American Superconductor.[7]

Among the many accolades earned during Colonel Borman's distinguished career are the Congressional Space Medal of Honor, the Harmon International Aviation Trophy, the Robert J. Collier Trophy, the Tony Jannus Award, West Point Distinguished Graduate Award, and the National Geographic Society's Hubbard Medal.[8]

Borman meeting with Pope Paul VI, February 15, 1969, after Apollo 8 mission.

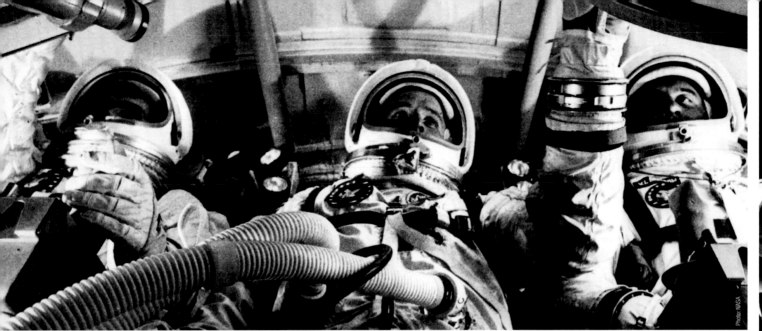

Lieutenant Colonel Edward White, USAF, USMA 1952

- COMMISSIONED IN THE U.S. AIR FORCE
- NASA ASTRONAUT AND PILOT FOR THE *GEMINI 4* MISSION
- PERFORMED AMERICA'S FIRST EXTRAVEHICULAR ACTIVITY (EVA) IN SPACE
- SELECTED AS SENIOR PILOT FOR THE *APOLLO I* MISSION
- ALL-AMERICAN ARMY SOCCER PLAYER
- KILLED ON THE LAUNCHPAD ACCIDENT IN *APOLLO I*, ALONG WITH GUS GRISSOM AND ROGER CHAFEE

>>> Spotlight

The crew of *Apollo 1* was killed on January 27, 1967, when a fire erupted in their spacecraft on the launchpad. Lieutenant Colonel (USAF) Virgil "Gus" Grisson, Lieutenant Colonel Edward White, and LCRN Roger Chaffee were all killed during a training accident.

When Ed White was just large enough to safely wear a parachute, his father, a United States Army Air Corps Officer, gave his 12-year-old son a ride in a two-seat T-6 trainer aircraft. It was a defining moment for the youngster when he was given control of the aircraft. Flying came so natural to him; he knew at that instant he would follow in his father's footsteps. Ed White, Sr., a West Point graduate who would, in 1957, retire from the United States Air Force as a Major General, instilled in his son single-minded determination, a hard work ethic, persistence, and self-control.[1]

Edward Higgins White, II, was born in San Antonio, Texas, on November 14, 1930. As a child, White moved throughout the United States with each of his father's new assignments. As a teenager, he was fortunate not only to spend his last three years of high school in one location, but to live in Arlington, Virginia, a suburb of Washington, D.C. He received a Congressional appointment to attend West Point from Ross Rizley, a United States Representative from Oklahoma. He became a West Point Cadet in 1948.[2]

At West Point, White quickly distinguished himself. Classmates, impressed with his quiet self-confidence, his goal-oriented mind-set, his no-nonsense approach to work and ethics, and his refinement and dignity, instantly recognized him as a born leader. It was in sports, however, that White excelled most. He was cocaptain of the track team and an All-American half-back on the Army soccer team. Teammate Michael Collins admired that he played sports like he lived, with passion, enthusiasm, and self-confidence. He had a unique quality that made his teammates better simply with his presence. White graduated from West Point in 1952, 128th out of 523, with Michael Collins and received his commission from the Air Force.[3]

After initial flight training at Bartow Air Force Base in Florida, jet flight training at James Connally Air Force Base in Texas, and Fighter Gunnery School at Luke Air Force Base in Arizona, White was assigned to the 22nd Day Fighter Squadron in Bitburg, West Germany. While stationed there, White became inspired by an unlikely source – a humorous newspaper article on would-be astronauts. With his typical steadfast determination, he set his sights on the space program. In order to improve his chances of selection, he earned a master's degree in aeronautical engineering in 1959 from the University of Michigan. After graduation, he was accepted into the USAF Flight Test Pilot School at Edwards Air Force Base in California. Following the yearlong training program, he became a test pilot assigned to Wright-Patterson Air Force Base in Ohio. White was accepted into the second group of NASA candidates in September 1962[4], one of nine that also included fellow West Point graduate, Frank Borman, Class of 1950.[5]

In July 1964, NASA announced the crew for *Gemini 4*, the second manned *Gemini* mission: Jim McDivitt, Mission Commander, and Ed White, Mission Pilot. It launched on June 3, 1965, from the Kennedy Space Center. Mission objectives were to test the feasibility of orbital rendezvous and to observe medical complications due to long duration space flights. However, in the wake of Soviet Cosmonaut Alexei Leonov's Extravehicular Activity, or EVA, in April 1965, NASA added a third objective: a space walk. On June 3, 1965, as Jim McDivitt photographed the event, White performed the first American EVA. It was a 21-minute experience that White would later describe as euphoric. The mission was an enormous success, even though the crew experienced unforeseen difficulties in the approach of another orbiting vehicle. During the mission, the spacecraft made 62 orbits around the Earth and traveled 1,609,700 miles.[6] Remarkably, the post-mission medical examination of the astronauts showed no effect of long duration space flight. After their return to Earth, President Johnson promoted both astronauts to Air Force Lieutenant Colonel and the press made White a celebrity.

On March 21, 1966, NASA announced the team for mission AS-204, unofficially known as *Apollo I*. It would consist of Virgil "Gus" Grissom, Commander; Edward White, Senior Pilot; and Roger Chaffee, Pilot. Mission objectives were to evaluate the launch vehicle, the Saturn IB, and the *Apollo* Command Module, as well as ground tracking and launch operations. As the launch date approached, several astronauts, including the mission's crew, voiced concerns to NASA officials over the many problems that plagued the *Apollo* Command Module. However, their concern over the spacecraft was overshadowed by their fear of being replaced if they raised too many alarms. As the February 21, 1967, launch date approached, NASA, which had unrealistic scheduling demands and feared a Soviet lunar mission, preceded with comprehensive testing of the *Apollo* Command Module. On the morning of January 27, 1967, NASA, despite misgivings by the crew, performed the "plugs out" test. As the crew performed various systems checks while locked inside the Command Module, pure oxygen, to a final pressure exceeding one atmosphere, was pumped into the orbiter. At 6:30 p.m., a spark ignited flammable materials and, in the oxygen-rich environment, quickly erupted into a raging fire.[8] Several attempts were made by frantic ground crew members to rescue the astronauts but were turned away by the intense heat. By the time the ground crew finally opened the hatch, White and the other two crewmen had perished.[9] Several days later, following a service at the Cadet Chapel, White was buried at West Point.[10]

As tragic as his death was, an even greater tragedy would be to remember White for that catastrophic event alone. He left a legacy of inspiration to those who not only met him, but to anyone who witnessed his achievements. His West Point classmates and fellow astronauts admired him not only for his intelligence and hard work ethic but for his sense of duty, his upright honor code, and loyalty to the country. Before the *Gemini 4* mission, White, in a small but meaningful demonstration of loyalty, fastened a patch of the American Flag onto his spacesuit. It was started a tradition that remains in place to this day.[11] To White, "Duty, Honor, Country" was more than a motto; it was his credo.

Written by: Robert Beres.

THEIR CONCERN OVER THE SPACECRAFT WAS OVERSHADOWED BY THEIR FEAR OF BEING REPLACED IF THEY RAISED TOO MANY ALARMS.

White's gravesite at the West Point Cemetery.

With the colorful and iconic – and now legal – given name of "Buzz" there are few Americans more closely associated with space exploration and the first landing on the moon than Buzz Aldrin. Still going strong at the time of this writing, retired United States Air Force Colonel Aldrin has lived a life and career dedicated to excellence in every way. Forever remembered as the lunar module pilot for *Apollo 11* and one of the first men to step foot on the moon, Buzz Aldrin

represents the best of the West Point tradition.

Hailing from Montclair, New Jersey, and born Edwin Eugene Aldrin, Jr., (nicknamed "Buzz" by his sister, Fay Ann, since childhood) Aldrin distinguished himself at Montclair High School, Class of 1947, and despite being offered a scholarship to the Massachusetts Institute of Technology, he applied for and received an appointment to the United States Military Academy at West Point for the Class of 1951.[1] At West Point, he was a member

of the varsity track-and-field and swimming teams. Aldrin excelled at West Point and graduated third in a class of 475.[2] As was customary in those days, with such a high class rank graduating from West Point, he chose the United States Air Force as his service and sought to become a fighter pilot. By the time he completed his pilot training from 1951 to 1952, the Korean War was well under way, and his first operational posting was with the 51st Fighter Wing of the 5th Air

Force in Korea from 1952 to 1953.[3] In the course of 66 combat missions while piloting the vaunted F-86 Sabre, the United States's first operational swept wing jet fighter, he shot down two MiG-15s. Perhaps foreshadowing the fame that would later surround him, *Life* magazine published photographs taken from his aircraft showing the enemy pilot ejecting from the aircraft he had shot down.[4]

Following his Korean War service, Aldrin received a number of routine postings for an

Colonel Buzz Aldrin, USAF, USMA 1951

- ONE OF THE FIRST TWO HUMANS TO WALK ON THE MOON ON THE *APOLLO 11* MISSION
- LUNAR MODULE PILOT OF THE FIRST LUNAR LANDING
- F-86 FIGHTER PILOT, KOREAN WAR, 66 COMBAT MISSIONS AND 2 KILLS
- MASSACHUSETTS INSTITUTE OF TECHNOLOGY, DOCTORATE IN ASTRONAUTICS
- ASTRONAUT ON *APOLLO 11* AND *GEMINI 12* MISSIONS
- COMMANDANT U.S. AIR FORCE TEST PILOT SCHOOL, EDWARDS AIR FORCE BASE
- FLIGHT COMMANDER, 22ND FIGHTER SQUADRON
- WEST POINT DISTINGUISHED GRADUATE AWARD
- PRESIDENTIAL MEDAL OF FREEDOM, CONGRESSIONAL GOLD MEDAL, DISTINGUISHED SERVICE MEDAL (TWO), DISTINGUISHED FLYING CROSS (TWO)

>>> Spotlight

Buzz Aldrin poses with 12-inch-tall Buzz Lightyear on October 2, 2009, at the Magic Kingdom in Florida. The toy spent 15 months aboard the International Space Station (ISS) as an initiative to encourage students to study science, technology, engineering, and mathematics. Disney released this photo to the Associated Press (AP).

Apollo 11 *lifts off,*
July 16, 1969.

Air Force Officer, including an aerial gunnery instructor at Nellis Air Force Base, Nevada, and as an aide to the Dean of Faculty at the United States Air Force Academy in Colorado Springs, Colorado. He then received a coveted posting as F-100 Flight Commander at the Bitburg Air Base, Germany, with the 22nd Fighter Squadron from 1956 to 1959.[5] Following his tour in Germany, the Air Force sent him as a full-time graduate student to the Massachusetts Institute of Technology

from where he earned his doctorate in science in the field of astronautics. Not surprisingly given his focus on manned space flight, he sought and was accepted in the third group of astronauts by the National Aeronautics and Space Administration (NASA).[6] He spent a year in the Air Force Space Systems Division in Los Angeles and Houston before he formally joined the astronaut corps in 1964.

For the remainder of the decade, Aldrin was

closely connected with the *Gemini* program that focused on using extra-vehicle craft to rendezvous and dock with spacecraft. In this capacity, he set a number of records for working in open space during the *Gemini 12* mission and became the recognized expert on extra-vehicle activity. However, it was the *Apollo 11* program that propelled Aldrin to be forever remembered in the history books when he became one of the first humans on the surface of the moon on July 20, 1969.

Hundreds of millions people watched the landings from around the world – the largest television event in history. Following this first-in-world-history achievement, Aldrin returned to regular Air Force assignments and became the commandant of the United States Air Force Test Pilot School at Edwards Air Force Base, California, from 1971 to 1972. He retired from active service in 1972, although he remained as an unofficial advisor to NASA to the present day. Unfortunately, depression and struggles with alcohol compounded with personal problems removed him from the public eye. However, he chose the road to recovery and now has 34 years of sobriety, and within recent years, he has become an outspoken advocate for seeking treatment and his life has become the model of stability and service.

THE LARGEST TELEVISION AUDIENCE IN HISTORY, AN ESTIMATED 600 MILLION PEOPLE WATCHED BUZZ ALDRIN AND NEIL ARMSTRONG WALK ON THE MOON ON JULY 20, 1969.

The recipient of dozens of awards and formal recognitions, Buzz Aldrin has led a life dedicated not only to advancing the cause of the United States, but also an untiring crusade for the betterment of mankind. In the 1980s he changed his legal name to "Buzz Aldrin." With an engaging personality, boundless energy, and a great sense of humor, West Point Graduate Buzz Aldrin has indeed lived his life according to the principles of "Duty, Honor, Country."

Written by: Colonel Kevin W. Farrell, PhD (USA, Retired), USMA 1986.

This photo of Colonel Buzz Aldrin is one of the most iconic photos in American history.

Buzz Aldrin Guest Room at the Thayer Hotel.

The Colonel Buzz Aldrin Room at the Thayer Hotel is proudly dedicated by Principal Solar.

When he was 11 years old, Michael Collins took the first step of a journey that would lead to places and sights that have only been shared by a scant few. His journey started in the cockpit of a twin engine Grumman Widgeon the instant the pilot handed to him control of the aircraft. With his innate ability and the pilot's vague instruction of "keep her on the horizon,"[1] the youngster, after initial difficulties, controlled the aircraft that delighted the pilot and amused his father who sat behind him. Collins's father, who was no stranger to flying, often told his son how, in 1911, he had flown with a military pilot who had been trained by the Wright brothers. This helped instill in Collins an interest in flying which, although intriguing, did not seem to be a likely career. It eventually would, of course, take Michael Collins to the moon and back.

Michael Collins was born in Rome, Italy, on October 31, 1930. Following many years of overseas deployments, his father, a United States Army Major General and West Point graduate, moved his family to the Washington, D.C., area at the outbreak of the Second World War. The young Collins attended the prestigious St. Albans School, and later, following in the footsteps of many family members, attended West Point and graduated, 185th out of 527 in 1952, with future astronaut Ed White. The Cadet, known for his casual demeanor and quick wit, was a member of the wrestling team, soccer team, and Policy Committee.[2] Collins received his commission from the Air Force to avoid the potential for nepotism; his uncle was the current Army Chief of Staff.[3]

After initial flight training in Columbus, Mississippi, and Waco, Texas, Michael Collins endured the rigors of advanced day fighter training at Nellis Air Force Base in Las Vegas, where he learned combat techniques flying the Air Force's most modern jet, the F-86 *Sabrejet*. After graduation, he was assigned to the 21st Fighter Bomber Wing in California. For the next few years, he served in Europe and North America. Although initially exciting, the F-86 was no longer a "cutting-edge" fighter, and by 1957, Collins was in need of a change. Inspired by his brother-in-law, a recent graduate of the Navy test pilot school, he was accepted into the USAF Experimental Flight Test Pilot School at Edwards Air Force Base, after which he was assigned to Fighter Ops. In February 1962, Collins found the source of his next inspiration as he witnessed John Glenn's historic three-orbit flight. After an unsuccessful attempt, Collins was accepted into the third group of NASA candidates in 1963[4], one of 14 that also included two other West Point graduates, Edwin Aldrin, Jr., Class of 1951, and David R. Scott, Class of 1954.[5]

After years of training, Mission Pilot Michael Collins and Command Pilot John Young left the confines of Earth atop a two-stage Titan II rocket. *Gemini 10* was launched from Cape Canaveral on July, 18, 1966, and was NASA's most daring mission to date. Not only did the mission establish a new height record – 475 miles – and feature a complicated docking procedure with an Agena Target Vehicle, which had only been accomplished once before, but Collins performed two EVA (Extra-Vehicular Activity, or "space walk"). On his second EVA, Collins became the first astronaut to venture to a non-docked space vehicle. The two astronauts also performed various experiments – 15 in

AS A RESULT OF THE MISSION, HE FELT AN OBLIGATION TO REPAY SOCIETY FOR THE HONOR BESTOWED UPON HIM.

Brigadier General Michael Collins, USAF, USMA 1952

- NASA ASTRONAUT FOR BOTH *GEMINI* AND *APOLLO* PROGRAMS
- FIRST ASTRONAUT TO CONDUCT A "SPACE WALK" TO A NON-DOCKED SPACE VEHICLE
- *APOLLO 11* CREW MEMBER DURING THE FIRST MOON WALK MISSION
- DIRECTOR OF THE NATIONAL AIR AND SPACE MUSEUM
- UNDER-SECRETARY FOR THE SMITHSONIAN INSTITUTION
- RECIPIENT OF THE 1998 WEST POINT DISTINGUISHED GRADUATE AWARD

all – involving various types of photography, micrometeorite study and collection, ion wake measurement, and radiation monitoring.[6] The mission was a resounding success and helped pave the way for the *Apollo* program.

Compared to *Gemini*, the path to *Apollo* was more difficult for Collins. As *Gemini* was winding down, Collins had been assigned to an *Apollo* mission. However, in the aftermath of the *Apollo 1* tragedy, scheduling revisions caused the mission to be cancelled. With fewer experienced astronauts available, Collins was promoted from Lunar Module pilot to Command Service Module pilot that meant that he would orbit the moon and not land. Although disappointed, he had a more important issue to contend with. In July, 1968, Collins underwent surgery to relieve spinal pressure caused by a bone growth between his fifth and sixth cervical vertebrae. Following USAF requirements,

the affected vertebrae were fused together temporarily grounding him from space flight. Two weeks after *Apollo 8* returned from orbiting the moon on December 27, 1968, NASA announced the crew of *Apollo 11*. Collins, now cleared for space flight, replaced the initial Command Service Module Pilot, Fred Haise.[7]

On July 16, 1969, *Apollo 11* lifted off atop a three-stage Saturn V Launch Vehicle from Platform 39A at Cape Canaveral. The goal of the mission was achieved after Neil Armstrong and Buzz Aldrin walked on the surface of the moon and safely returned. While the crew members were on the lunar surface, Michael Collins maintained a lunar orbit alone for nearly 22 hours in the Command Service Module, Columbia. The crew returned to Earth as world-renowned celebrities on July 24th.[8]

The path on which Michael Collins had embarked many years before did not end

with *Apollo 11*. As a result of the mission, he felt an obligation to repay society for the honor bestowed upon him.[9] He left the Space Agency and active military service a few months later to serve in the Nixon Administration as Assistant Secretary of State for Public Affairs. After his term, he was named the Director of the National Air and Space Museum and oversaw its development and operation. In 1978, he became Under Secretary for the Smithsonian Institution. He retired from the Air Force Reserve in 1982 as a Major General. In spite of the fame and the decorations he received for the *Apollo 11* mission, Michael Collins never lost his down-to-earth humility. The West Point Association of Graduates honored Collins with the 1998 "Distinguished Graduate Award" for a career that "…exemplifies the purpose of the Military Academy: to produce graduates who will give a lifetime of service to this country. In more than 30 years of dedica-

tion to the ideals of West Point, Collins has made permanent and invaluable contributions to the national security."[10] He has authored several books and is currently enjoying his retirement in Florida with his wife, Patricia.

Written by: Robert Beres.

>>> Spotlight

On July 24, 1969, *Apollo 11* splashed down in the Pacific Ocean east of Wake Island and was recovered by the *USS Hornet* (CV-12) aircraft carrier. The Captain of the carrier, Captain (later Rear Admiral) Carl J. Sieberlich, stated in 2005 that he was given orders to "never return to port" if the astronauts were infected with "space bugs" and infected the crew of the *USS Hornet*, which was a significant concern at the time. An entire section of the carrier was designated as a morgue in case the sailors of the *USS Hornet* became ill and died from some pathogens brought back from the moon. The astronauts were quarantined for 21 days after splash down. In the interview, Sieberlich states that he was only allowed to open the sealed orders once they were at sea. He told his Executive Officer that if the worst-case situation occurred, they would remain at sea until some "smart guy from NASA" figured it out. Here, President Nixon congratulates the astronauts after they entered the Mobile Quarantine Facility (MQF). The MQF is still on display aboard the *USS Hornet* Aircraft Carrier Museum in Alameda, California.

Apollo 11 *lifts off, July 16, 1969.*

APOLLO 11

The first mission to the moon took off July 16, 1969 with three astronauts: Colonel Buzz Aldrin, Lieutenant Colonel Michael Collins, and Mr. Neil Armstrong. Two of three are West Point graduates: Aldrin (USMA 1951) and Collins (USMA 1952). Armstrong and Aldrin were the first two humans to walk on the moon when they landed on July 20, 1969, one of the greatest moments in recorded history.

POLITICIANS AND GOVERNMENT OFFICIALS

The mission of the United States Military Academy at West Point focuses on producing commissioned leaders of character for service to the nation in the military. Upon graduation, cadets serve at least five years in the military. For graduates who either spend an entire career in uniform or leave the service after their initial commitment, many remain involved in serving the nation through politics, government service, defense companies, philanthropy, or supporting service-members in myriad ways. Many of them also move back and forth between the private sector and federally appointed or elected positions. Nearly every Presidential administration has had West Point graduates involved at the highest levels of government in some capacity whether in or out of uniform. In addition to the graduates who have become heads of states, others have served in Congress as Senators or Representatives, or have become Governors, Mayors, National Security Advisors, Ambassadors, and Presidential Cabinet Members. This chapter highlights some of them.

"Politics is a profession; a serious, complicated and, in its true sense, a noble one."
—*34th President Dwight D. Eisenhower, USMA 1915*

"Practice rather than preach. Make of your life an affirmation, defined by your ideals, not the negation of others. Dare to the level of your capability then go beyond to a higher level."
—*U.S. Secretary of State Al Haig, USMA 1947*

"You must love those you lead before you can be an effective leader. You can certainly command without that sense of commitment, but you cannot lead without it."
—*Secretary of Veteran Affairs Eric Shinseki, USMA 1965*

"An idea can be as flawless as can be, but its execution will always be full of mistakes."
—*Brent Scowcroft, USMA 1947, 9th and 17th U.S. National Security Advisor to President Ford and President George H.W. Bush.*

"We can best honor the memories of those who were killed on September 11th, and those who have been killed fighting the war on terrorism, by dedicating ourselves to building a free and peaceful world safe from the threat of terrorism."
—*U.S. Senator Jack Reed, USMA 1971*

In an era in which partisan politics is the norm, Senator Jack Reed is a unique politician with a proven history of "reaching across the aisle" in a bipartisan effort to take action on behalf of the people of Rhode Island and the United States. Hollywood could not have scripted a more relevant background and ideal persona for a United States Senator to speak authoritatively on issues related to national security, education, and on behalf of America's working class. As a proud member of the Class of 1971 and the Long Gray Line, Reed also has other important connections to West Point, including serving as a former faculty member, service on the prestigious West Point Board of Visitors, and his marriage to Julia Hart Reed on April 16, 2005, at West Point.

John Francis "Jack" Reed was born in Providence, Rhode Island, on November 12, 1949, into a working-class family. His father, Joe, served in World War II and worked as a janitor in the Cranston school district, ultimately working his way up to custodial supervisor. His mother never attended college but ensured her three children studied hard and had the opportunity to pursue a higher education.

Jack attended St. Matthew's Elementary School in Cranston and then attended LaSalle Academy in Providence. He received a nomination to West Point and entered in 1967 as a member of the Class of 1971.

During his years at West Point, the faculty was dominated by Korean War veterans or officers fresh out of combat from Vietnam. A sad but not uncommon lunchtime ritual in the cadet mess hall was to announce to the entire Corps of Cadets each West Point graduate recently Killed In Action in Vietnam. Unfortunately, Reed would hear many of these lunchtime announcements during his cadet years as a large majority of the 273 West Point graduates killed in the war occurred during Reed's years as a cadet. Given the increasing casualty numbers, particularly among Infantry Officers, the Infantry Branch became a very unpopular choice for cadets in the Classes of 1970, 1971, and 1972. Despite its unpopularity, Reed chose the Infantry Branch because he believed it was the best way to lead from the front. By the time his class graduated, however, the war was winding down with the continued American withdrawal.

JACK REED IS A CHAMPION FOR MIDDLE-CLASS FAMILIES AND A STRONG BELIEVER THAT, THROUGH HARD WORK, ALL AMERICANS SHOULD HAVE THE OPPORTUNITY TO BUILD A BETTER LIFE.

Members of the Class of 1971 were not given the option to request an assignment to Vietnam. Because Reed graduated near the top of his class, he was offered an opportunity to further his education at Harvard's John F. Kennedy School of government.

Reed graduated from the Kennedy School with a master's in Public Policy (MPP) in 1973 and returned to the Army and Fort Bragg, North Carolina, to pursue his career in the Infantry. He served as a Platoon Leader, Company Commander, and Battalion Staff Officer in the elite 82nd Airborne Division before returning to teach at West Point. While at the Academy, he taught cadets in economics and international relations — both hallmark courses within the Department of Social Sciences. The Department of Social Sciences has also historically been well known as a stepping-stone toward the Army's senior leadership, with many of its former military faculty members becoming the Army's senior leaders.

In 1979, Captain Reed decided to leave the active-duty Army, attend Harvard Law School as a full-time student, then to pursue a civilian law practice. He graduated Harvard Law School with distinction (cum laude) and started practicing law in Rhode Island while simultaneously serving in the Rhode Island State Senate and remaining in the Army Reserves. Having seen others make unsuccessful bids for Congress, Reed decided upon a methodical approach. He leveraged his law degree and started at the local level in state politics, proved himself to his constituents while building a strong network within the state, then ran for Congress. His strategy

Senator John Francis "Jack" Reed, USMA 1971

- **U.S. SENATOR, STATE OF RHODE ISLAND, 1997–PRESENT**
- **U.S. HOUSE OF REPRESENTATIVES, STATE OF RHODE ISLAND, 1991–96**
- **RHODE ISLAND STATE SENATE, 1984–90**
- **ASSOCIATE PROFESSOR, WEST POINT DEPARTMENT OF SOCIAL SCIENCES**
- **HARVARD UNIVERSITY KENNEDY SCHOOL OF GOVERNMENT, MASTER'S IN PUBLIC POLICY**
- **HARVARD LAW SCHOOL, J.D., CUM LAUDE**
- **AIRBORNE AND RANGER QUALIFIED INFANTRY OFFICER, MAJOR (RETIRED), USAR**
- **WEST POINT BOARD OF VISITORS**

worked, and he was elected in 1991 to the United States House of Representatives from Rhode Island's 2nd District, where he served three terms prior to running for the United States Senate. In 1997, he won the United States Senate seat and became the 43rd Senator from Rhode Island.

Jack Reed also became the eighth West Point graduate elected to the United States Senate and the second from Rhode Island – Senator Ambrose Burnside (USMA 1847) was the first. The other six US. Senators include: Senator Henry DuPont (USMA 1861) from Delaware; Senators Jefferson Davis (USMA 1828) and Adelbert Ames (USMA 1861) from Mississippi; Senator Samuel Maxey (USMA 1846) from Texas; Senator Frank Briggs (USMA 1872) from New Jersey; and Senator Lawrence Tyson (USMA 1883) from Tennessee.

Senator Reed has served 16 years in the Senate and is a member of the Senate's Appropriations Committee, Armed Services Committee, and Banking, Housing, and Urban Affairs Committee, along with membership on several subcommittees. During his tenure,

he has worked with the administrations of President Bill Clinton, President George W. Bush, and President Barack Obama, while also experiencing a five-time shift in the Senate's majority party. He has provided invaluable experience, counsel, and legislation through several economic, political, and military cycles that included the Internet boom and bust, the attacks of 9/11 and the two subsequent wars, and the 2008 global recession. Throughout these cycles, Reed has always been perceived by his constituents and colleagues as a solid professional seeking the best interests of the American people and avoiding partisan politics.

A member of the powerful Armed Services Committee, Reed's military education, academic background, and experience make him one of the top national security experts in the United States Senate. In 2002, he was one of 27 Senators who voted against authorizing President George W. Bush's invasion of Iraq. Reed believed the plan was not well conceived and that it diverted resources away from the primary mission of hunting down Osama Bin Laden and destroying the

Al Qaeda network. Within the Armed Services Committee, he is also the Chairman of the Subcommittee on Seapower. Since the state of Rhode Island is the home of the Naval War College in Newport, Senator Reed frequently leverages the intellectual capital residing within the home base of the Navy's Officer professional education system.

A member of yet another powerful committee, the Senate Appropriations Committee, which controls the purse strings of the federal government, Reed has been described by the *Boston Globe* as "a relentless advocate for his home state."[1] He currently chairs the Subcommittee on Interior and Environment and works tirelessly to direct federal funding to the Ocean State in order to create jobs, strengthen Rhode Island's infrastructure, and support economic and community development projects.

Although Reed has risen to the highest level of the United States government, he remains humble and has always kept true to his Rhode Island roots. Recognizing that he was afforded some of the nation's finest educational opportunities at West Point and

Harvard, Reed is an outspoken authority on the need to provide affordable education to all Americans, which he sees as critical in preparing America for the future and providing its citizens with opportunity and hope. More importantly, Reed never forgot the lessons and values he learned from his father's blue-collar work ethic and the challenges he faced in providing for a family of five – values Reed and his wife hope to instill in their daughter, Emily. As a result, Senator Jack Reed understands and relates to the needs of working class families like few Senators do.

Senator Reed and Julia Hart's wedding at Trophy Point, West Point, on April 16, 2005.

Senator Jack Reed (USMA 1971), with his classmate Lieutenant General Franklin "Buster" Hagenbeck (USMA 1971) at a West Point Board of Visitors Meeting on Capitol Hill.

>>> Spotlight

Rhode Island was one of the original 13 colonies and was the 13th to ratify the Constitution on May 29, 1790. It is currently the smallest state in the United States in size and ranked 43rd in overall population with more than 1,000,000 citizens. Senator Jack Reed has served as a United States Senator, representing Rhode Island since 1997. Prior to being elected as Senator, he was a three-term member of the United States House of Representatives, representing Rhode Island from 1991 to 1997. He is the second West Point graduate to serve as a United States Senator from Rhode Island after Senator Burnside served from 1875 to 1881.

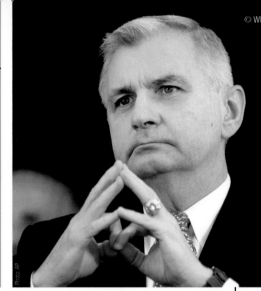

General Jim Jones, USMC, speaking with General John Abizaid and Senator Jack Reed.

Eric Shinseki's military career nearly ended at age 27 after he was seriously wounded in Vietnam by an enemy mine and lost part of his foot. Despite this potentially devastating setback, Shinseki not only had the courage and perseverance to face the injury and amputation of part of his foot, but he thrived and remained in the military serving 38 years while ascending to the United States Army's highest position as its 34th Chief of Staff. Even after retiring, he continued serving his Army and his nation when he was appointed to a Presidential Cabinet position as the 7th Secretary of the Department Veterans Affairs – leading the second largest US agency behind the Department of Defense.

Eric Shinseki was born November 28, 1942, on the island of Kauai, Hawaiian Islands[2] – before Hawaii's statehood – in a Japanese-American internment camp where his parents had been sent along with thousands of other innocent Japanese-Americans following the attack on Pearl Harbor.

Despite being born under such circumstances, Shinseki excelled in grammar school and high school where he was elected as his class president in 1960. He graduated high school on Kauai, entered West Point, and graduated in 1965 with a commission in the Field Artillery. Shortly after his graduation, he married his high school sweetheart, Patricia "Patty" Yoshinobu, on June 26, 1965, and they would raise two children, Lori and Ken.

Graduating West Point during the earliest stages of the Vietnam War, Shinseki and the Class of 1965 experienced the brunt of the war as junior officers leading soldiers at the proverbial "tip of the spear." As a result, 25 members of the Class of 1965 – living up to its motto "Strength and Drive" – would make the ultimate sacrifice for their country while many more, including Shinseki, were seriously wounded in the process.

Upon arriving in Vietnam at the end of 1965, Shinseki was assigned as a forward artillery observer with the 25th Infantry Division when he was wounded for the first time. For his actions in that tour, he received the Bronze Star and Purple Heart. After returning to the US, he transferred branches from the artillery to armor and again returned to Vietnam in 1969 as a troop commander in the 3/5 Cavalry Regiment. By this time, American public support for the war had drastically declined in the wake of the 1968 TET Offensive and US policy-makers struggled to redefine America's strategic objectives in the conflict. Leading Soldiers in such an environment was challenging, but Shinseki was up to the task. His unit faced combat regularly and Shinseki received two Bronze Stars for Valor while also being seriously wounded by the Vietnamese mine that cost him much of his foot. After being evacuated back to the United States, the Army pressed to discharge him. Shinseki successfully fought to stay on active duty and was one of only a few amputees from Vietnam who were allowed to remain

on active duty – General Frederick Franks (USMA 1959) was among that small number. Years later when leading the Department of Veterans Affairs, those lessons he learned from personally battling the defense bureaucracy on his own behalf in order to remain on active duty would undoubtedly prove invaluable – he has leveraged his own personal experience to serve veterans and champion their cause through his unique perspective.

Shinseki recovered from his wounds at Duke University while receiving a Master of Arts degree in English and returned to West Point for three years to teach English as a member of the faculty. Following his tour at the Academy, he then held a series of command and staff positions during the waning years of the Cold War. Fittingly, a part of Shinseki's more than 10 years of service in Europe included the fall of the Berlin Wall in 1989 and the eventual collapse of the Soviet Union, which signaled the ending of the nearly 45-year Cold War struggle and validated the

Secretary Eric Ken Shinseki, USMA 1965

- 7TH SECRETARY OF THE DEPARTMENT OF VETERANS AFFAIRS/PRESIDENTIAL CABINET MEMBER
- 34TH CHIEF OF STAFF, US ARMY
- VICE CHIEF OF STAFF, US ARMY
- COMMANDING GENERAL, US ARMY EUROPE
- COMMANDING GENERAL, 1ST CAVALRY DIVISION
- MASTERS OF ARTS IN ENGLISH LITERATURE, DUKE UNIVERSITY
- WEST POINT PROFESSOR OF ENGLISH
- BRONZE STAR FOR VALOR (2), PURPLE HEART (2)[1]
- WEST POINT DISTINGUISHED GRADUATE AWARD
- BOY SCOUTS OF AMERICA, YOUTH MEMBER

President Obama's Afghanistan War speech at Eisenhower Hall, West Point 2009. Director Petraeus, Admiral Mullen, Secretary Shinseki, Secretary Gataes and Secretary Clinton.

US strategy in that conflict. Shinseki was next promoted to Major General and Commanded the 1st Cavalry Division at Fort Hood Texas. In 1997, he was promoted to four-star general and returned to Germany as Commander, US Army Europe. In that role, Shinseki directed operations in Bosnia-Herzogovian. Shinseki was soon appointed to a brief tour as Vice Chief of Staff of the US Army and then subsequently as the 34th Chief of Staff of the US Army in 1999, where he became the highest-ranking Asian-American in US Army history.

Shinseki held the role of Chief of Staff of the Army for four years, focusing on the unenviable transformation of a Cold War-era Army focused in a singular Soviet threat, to one that was able to counter a variety of threats evolving from the post-Cold War world. Specifically, Shinseki faced the challenge "to make the Army lighter, more modular, and – most importantly – more deployable."[3] Most significantly, his efforts helped prepare the Army for how it would organize in the coming war with Iraq to face both a conventional and potential unconventional threat.

SHINSEKI'S ESTIMATE OF THE NUMBER OF TROOPS NEEDED IN IRAQ POST-INVASION WAS HIGHLY CONTROVERSIAL AT THE TIME, BUT PROVED PRESCIENT

A seminal moment in Shinseki's career came during his Senate Armed Service Committee testimony on February 25, 2003, when he was asked how many US troops would be needed to occupy Iraq if indeed the US were to invade. Although civilian officials argued that a US occupying force would be relatively smaller than the invading force, Shinseki disagreed. In his estimation:

"I would say that what's been mobilized to this point, something on the order of several hundred thousand soldiers, are probably, you know, a figure that would be required. We're talking about post-hostilities control over a piece of geography that's fairly significant with the kinds of ethnic tensions that could lead to other problems [4]."

Shinseki's response was honest, courageous, and characteristic of his ability to provide sound advice – as his role required – even if it was counter to the main stream. The civilian leadership was caught off guard by his response and disputed it publically for days after the hearings. Many military and political pundits would claim that Shinseki's estimates and assessments were incorrect; however, on the contrary, Shinseki's very prescient forecast unfortunately proved to be correct. Like the courage and perseverance that characteristically defined Shinseki's life – his rise from the internment camps, graduation from West Point, triumph over a serious injury, successful bureaucratic challenge to remain in the Army as an amputee, and his rise to the top spot in the US Army – Shinseki responded to Congress the only way he knew how, with courage and honesty. In the wake of those hearings, Shinseki retired shortly afterward on June 11, 2003. After a series of poor political decisions, America remained in Iraq for nearly a decade to counter and pacify the resulting insurgency – even requiring a surge of soldiers in 2007 to meet the post-invasion operational requirements as Shinseki had predicted.[5]

On January 21, 2009, President Barack Obama appointed Shinseki as the 7th Secretary of Veterans Affairs. Shinseki continues to serve the Soldiers and Army he has so positively influenced throughout his life.

>>> Spotlight

The Department of Veterans Affairs (VA) is responsible for all health care, benefits and cemeteries for all 22 million American veterans (except Arlington National Cemetery). The VA operates 152 hospitals, 800 community based outpatient clinics, 126 nursing home care units and 35 domiciliaries. The Secretary of the Veterans Administration is a Presidential Cabinet level position which was created in 1989. Secretary Shinseki is the seventh Secretary of the VA.

Jefferson Davis Statue in Montgomery, Alabama, 1943.

Secretary Jefferson Davis, USMA 1828

- **PRESIDENT OF THE CONFEDERATE STATES OF AMERICA (C.S.A.)**
- **U.S. SECRETARY OF WAR**
- **U.S. SENATOR, STATE OF MISSISSIPPI**
- **WOUNDED AS A COMBAT COMMANDER, MEXICAN-AMERICAN WAR**
- **JEFFERSON DAVIS MONUMENT ERECTED IN HIS HONOR MONUMENT AVENUE, RICHMOND, VIRGINIA**
- **BURIED IN HOLLYWOOD CEMETERY, RICHMOND, VIRGINIA**
- **U.S. CITIZENSHIP RESTORED BY JOINT RESOLUTION OF THE U.S. CONGRESS IN 1978**

Courtesy: CSA

Jefferson Davis was born in 1808, the son of Samuel Davis and Jane (Cook) Davis. Samuel had served in the Continental Army; as a Captain, he commanded a company defending Savannah against an attack by the British. When Samuel's son was born, he was named Jefferson, in honor of one of the founders of the republic that the elder Davis had fought to establish. Jefferson Davis's birth preceded that of Abraham Lincoln by a mere eight months, the distance between the Kentucky birthplaces of Davis and Lincoln were separated by a mere 40-mile distance.[1]

During his youth, Davis was educated at a number of schools in Kentucky and Mississippi. At the age of 16, he entered Transylvania University with the sophomore class.[2] Davis spent only one year at Transylvania University before he was offered an appointment as a Cadet at West Point.[3]

Upon graduation from the Military Academy,

Davis was commissioned into the Infantry and assigned to the 1st Infantry. While serving with the Infantry, Lieutenant Davis saw action in the Black Hawk War, as well as encounters against the Pawnee and Comanche, before resigning his commission in June of 1835. Shortly after his resignation was accepted, he married the daughter of Zachary Taylor, Davis's former Commander in the 1st Infantry, and the future President of the United States.

Davis and his new bride returned to Mississippi. Sallie (Taylor) Davis died of malaria a mere three months after the wedding. Jefferson Davis re-entered the service of the United States when he was elected to the United States Congress in 1845. His first term in the legislature was cut short by the Mexican War, when Davis resigned his seat in Congress June 1846, after being elected Colonel of the 1st Mississippi Volunteers. As Commander of the 1st Mississippi, Colonel Davis returned to service under Zachary

Taylor. Davis trained his soldiers and created a well-disciplined command, which he lead in a gallant charge to capture Fort Teneria in Monterey. Colonel Davis led several successful assaults and was severely wounded during the war. President Polk appointed Davis a Brigadier General, but Davis declined the commission.[4]

Shortly after Davis returned from the war, the death of Senator Speight created a vacant seat in the United States Senate. Davis was appointed by the Governor of Mississippi to fill the vacancy; he was re-elected for a full term. At the commencement of what would have been Davis's first full term in the Senate, President Pierce appointed Davis to be the Secretary of War. Pierce's appointment was likely due to Davis's support of Pierce's platform of compromise rather than secession. After President Pierce left office, Davis was re-elected to represent the people of Mississippi in the Senate.

The tensions between Northern and the Southern states peaked during Davis's final term in the Senate. In December of 1860, shortly after the election of Abraham Lincoln, a motion was made to adjourn for the holiday; Senator Davis opposed the motion. Knowing that Lincoln's recent election would push the nation further down a path of disunion and potentially civil war, Senator Davis stated, "I do not know that we shall achieve much good by meeting, but in the present perilous condition of the country I am not willing to take a holiday. I propose that we shall continue our sessions, for good if God grants it, and for evil if we will have it so."[5]

On January 9, 1861, a Mississippi state convention adopted an ordinance of secession. This compelled Davis to resign his seat in the Senate shortly thereafter. On January 21, he bid farewell to his fellow Senators. In his remarks on the Senate floor, he noted, "I am sure I feel no hostility toward you, Senators of the North. I am sure there is

Stone Mountain Georgia Marble Sculpture of Confederate leaders Jefferson Davis, Robert E. Lee, and Stonewall Jackson.

Jefferson Davis's gravesite in Hollywood Cemetery, Richmond, Virginia.

>>> Spotlight

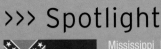

Mississippi became the 20th state in admitted into the Union on December 10, 1817. On January 9, 1861, Mississippi became the second state (after Virginia) to succeed from the Union to join the Confederate States of America and Mississippi became a major battlefield over control of the Mississippi River, where Major General Ulysses S. Grant finally won control at the Battle of Vicksburg in 1864. Jefferson Davis was a Mississippi Member of the United States House of Representatives from Mississippi from 1845 to 1846 and then a Mississippi Senator from 1847 to 1851 and again from 1857 to 1861 prior to serving as the United States Secretary of War from 1853 to 1857. He was elected President of the Confederate States of America and served from 1861 to 1865.

Close-up of grave inscription.

Jefferson Davis Monument on Monument Avenue, Richmond, Virginia.

not one of you, whatever sharp discussion there may have been between us, to whom I cannot say in the presence of my God, I wish you well, and such I am sure is the feeling of the people whom I represent toward those whom you represent. I carry with me no hostile remembrance. Whatever

NOT EVEN HIS MOST RELENTLESS ENEMY EVER ALLEGED THAT IN DEED OR ACT, IN SUNSHINE OR SHADOW, DAVIS VIOLATED A SINGLE ONE OF THE GREAT VIRTUES THAT WEST POINT HAD HELPED TO DEVELOP IN HIS CHARACTER.

offense I have given which has not been redressed or for which satisfaction has not been demanded, I have, Senators, in this hour of our parting, to offer you my apology for any pain which in the heat of discussion I have inflicted. I go hence unencumbered by the remembrance of any injury received, and having discharged the duty of making the only reparation in my power for any injury offered, Mr. President and Senators, having made the announcement which the occasion seemed to me to require, it only remains for me to bid you a final adieu."[6] Moved by Senator Davis's comments, the Senate "burst into deafening applause."[7]

Shortly after resigning for the United States Senate, Davis was appointed a Major General in the Army of the State of Mississippi.[8] But Davis would never serve in the military forces of the confederacy; fate held other plans as Davis was elected provisional President of the Confederate States of America and assumed that office on February 18, 1861. Davis was to be the only President of the Confederate States of America. He presided over the fledgling government from its inception until its abolition. At the end of the Civil War, Davis was charged with treason and imprisoned at Fort Monroe in Virginia. Davis, to his dismay, was never tried. The government released him from confinement after two years and dropped the case against him in 1869. Although Davis was again elected to the Senate in 1874, he was barred from taking office by the Fourteenth Amendment to the U.S. Constitution.

Davis died in December of 1889 and interred in a temporary vault in New Orleans. In May of 1893, his body was removed from the vault and transported to Richmond, Virginia, for re-internment. While in transit to Virginia, Davis's body would lie in state at the capitols of Alabama, Georgia, and North Carolina. Following a 21-gun salute, the former-President's body was laid to rest in the former capitol of the Confederacy.

Morris Schaff, an officer in the United States Army during the Civil War, later wrote about Davis that "not even his most relentless enemy ever alleged that in deed or act, in sunshine or shadow, Jefferson Davis violated a single one of the great virtues which West Point had helped to develop in his character."[9] Davis regretted not being allowed a trial after the war, and it would be more than a century after the war before he would receive partial vindication when, in October of 1978, a joint resolution of the United States Congress posthumously removed the ban on Davis holding elected office and restored his citizenship, effective Christmas day, 1868.

Written by: Lieutenant Colonel Craig Morrow, PhD, USMA 1991.

imon Bolivar Buckner, Sr., was born on April 1, 1823, in Mumfordville, Kentucky. After graduating from West Point in 1844, Buckner was commissioned in the Infantry and served as an assistant professor of geography, history, and ethics and then tactical officer at West Point.[1] He served in the Mexican-American War, where he participated in several major battles. He was wounded at Churubusco[2] and served bravely and was cited for his actions in the Battle of Chapultepec, the Battle of Belen Gate and the storming of Mexico City. When United States forces left Mexico City, Buckner was given the honor of lowering the American flag over Mexico City for the last time.[3]

On March 26, 1855, Buckner resigned from the Army to work with his father-in-law's real estate business in Chicago. Before leaving the Army, however, Buckner had the opportunity to help an old friend (and future adversary) from West Point and the Mexican-American War, Captain Ulysses S. Grant (USMA 1843). Captain Grant was in New York and did not have money available to pay for his hotel. Buckner loaned Grant the money until his funds arrived from Ohio.[4]

On the eve of the Civil War, Simon Buckner, as a former American soldier and current politician, was torn between loyalty to his country and loyalty to his home state like many others. The state of Kentucky was divided in its sentiments at the start of the war – the Governor supported the Confederacy, while the legislature supported the Union. This divided loyalty resulted in Kentucky declaring itself neutral as a "border state" but remaining as part of the Union since it did not secede. Buckner fought to maintain the state's neutrality; however, when that neutrality was compromised by the occupation of a force under Confederate Major General Leonidas Polk

(USMA 1827), Buckner accepted a commission as Brigadier General in the Confederacy. He had previously been offered a commission on two separate occasions by the Union Army, but he respectfully declined.

In 1862, the Confederacy's Western Theater Commander, General Albert Sydney Johnston (USMA 1826), sent Buckner's division as part of a larger force to defend Fort Donelson. Union Brigadier General Ulysses S. Grant had recently turned his attention to this fort near the town of Dover, Tennessee. Buckner and three other Brigadier Generals were tasked to defend the fort and nearby

Governor Simon Bolivar Buckner, Sr., USMA 1844

- 30TH GOVERNOR OF KENTUCKY
- LIEUTENANT GENERAL, CONFEDERATE STATES OF AMERICA (C.S.A.)
- FIRST CONFEDERATE GENERAL TO SURRENDER AN ARMY IN THE CIVIL WAR, 1862
- LAST CONFEDERATE GENERAL TO SURRENDER AN ARMY IN THE CIVIL WAR, 1865
- LAST AMERICAN TO LOWER THE AMERICAN FLAG OVER MEXICO CITY IN MEXICAN-AMERICAN WAR
- FATHER OF GENERAL SIMON BOLIVAR BUCKNER, JR. (USMA 1904)
- ASSOCIATE PROFESSOR AT WEST POINT

Courtesy: CSA

Confederate General Simon Bolivar Buckner, Sr.

Governor Simon Bolivar Buckner, Sr.

town. Brigadier General John Floyd, who was a military novice but well-connected politically, was placed in overall command. The Confederates enjoyed initial success pushing Grant's Army back nearly two miles. Buckner held back his supporting attack, however, because he lacked confidence it its success. As a result, Grant was able to reinforce his troops and recapture lost ground. That evening, Floyd held a commanders meeting and determined that their best chance of survival was to retreat. General Floyd was concerned that, if captured, he would be tried for treason and decided to leave the fort with a major part of the force. Buckner agreed to remain so Floyd relinquished command to him.[5]

The following day, Buckner requested an armistice and suggested a meeting with General Grant to discuss surrender terms. Although the friendship between these two Generals was strong, General Grant's reply was succinct: "No terms except unconditional and immediate surrender can be accepted. I propose to move immediately upon your works."[6] To this, Buckner responded: "SIR:—The distribution of the forces under my command, incident to an unexpected change of commanders, and the overwhelming force under your command, compel me, notwithstanding the brilliant success of the Confederate arms yesterday, to accept the ungenerous and unchivalrous terms which you propose.[7]"

The surrender was a strategic defeat for the Confederates, who lost more than 12,000 men, as well as control of the Cumberland River, which led to the evacuation of Nashville. It was also the first time a Confederate General surrendered an Army to the Union and redefined Grant's "U.S." initials as "Unconditional Surrender."

Following a prisoner exchange, Buckner was returned to the Confederacy. He was promoted and ordered to join General Braxton Bragg (USMA 1837) and his Army of the Mississippi. Days after joining General Bragg, the Army pushed north in order to reclaim Kentucky for the Confederacy. Although the Confederacy enjoyed initial success, Bragg resisted the advice of his commanders and delayed attacking General Don Carlos Buell's Army, which was moving toward Louisville. This hesitation in consolidating forces for an attack resulted in a strategic draw at the Battle of Perryville, forcing Bragg to abandon his campaign to re-capture Kentucky and drawing great criticism from General Buckner.[8]

Buckner was then ordered to join General Edmund Kirby Smith (USMA 1845), where Buckner was promoted to Lieutenant General. After Lee's surrender at Appomattox on April 9, 1865, many remaining armies and soldiers of the Confederacy deserted at an alarming rate. On April 19, 1865, Smith consolidated his armies and placed Buckner in command. On May 9, 1865, Smith named Buckner his Chief of Staff. Many people within the Confederacy believed that neither Smith nor Buckner would surrender, but would retreat with their units into Mexico; instead, Buckner traveled to New Orleans on May 26, 1865, and arranged terms of surrender signifying the last surrender of a major Confederate force in the Civil War.[9]

As a condition of his parole, Buckner was not allowed to return to Kentucky for three years. When he did return he became very active in politics during Reconstruction and reconciliation. In 1885, his old friend Ulysses S. Grant passed away. In a public gesture of reconciliation, Buckner served as a pallbearer at President Grant's funeral, along with fellow Confederate General Joseph Johnston (USMA 1829), side by side with former enemy Union Generals Phil Sheridan (USMA 1853) and William Tecumseh Sherman (USMA 1840).[10] At age 62, Buckner married 26-year-old Delia Claiborne, and she gave birth to Buckner's only son, Simon Bolivar Buckner, Jr., in 1886. In 1887, Buckner was elected Governor of the state of Kentucky. Much of his term as Governor was spent trying to curb violence in the eastern part of the state. Most notable was in 1888, when a posse from Kentucky crossed into West Virginia and killed a leader of the Hatfield Clan as part of the infamous Hatfield-McCoy feud.[11]

Simon Buckner remained active in politics for the remainder of his life. In 1896, he was an unsuccessful Vice Presidential candidate on the Democratic Gold ticket. As a result of his political activity, Buckner visited President Theodore Roosevelt in 1904 and successfully petitioned the President to appoint his only son, Simon Bolivar Buckner, Jr., to West Point.[12] Buckner, Jr., would later serve as commander of ground troops in the Battle of Okinawa during World War II. During this battle, General Buckner, Jr., would be killed, making him the highest-ranking officer to be killed by enemy fire in World War II. The Buckner father and son, both West Point graduates and separated by 80 years, played critical roles in America's two bloodiest wars. The Buckner name lived on, though. At the time of his son's death on Okinawa, his grandson, William Claiborne Bucker, was a cadet at West Point and would graduate in 1948.

On January 8, 1914, as the last surviving member of his class and the oldest living West Point graduate, Simon Bolivar Buckner, Sr., died at age 90 as a result of uremic poisoning and was buried in Frankfort, Kentucky.[13] At the time of his death, he was also the only surviving Confederate Lieutenant General.

Written by: Frank Flowers, USMA 1986.

> **IN 1887, BUCKNER, A FORMER CONFEDERATE GENERAL, WAS ELECTED GOVERNOR OF KENTUCKY, WHICH HAD BEEN A BORDER STATE DURING THE CIVIL WAR.**

Glen Lily, the Kentucky estate of the Buckner's, where Governor Buckner raised the future General Simon Bolivar Buckner, Jr.

James Longstreet was born on January 8, 1821, in Edgefield District, on the South Carolina bank of the Savannah River. His family moved shortly thereafter to Habersham County in the mountains of north Georgia, where he lived the first 12 years of his life. Longstreet, known as "Pete" to differentiate him from his father, also James, was not a good student. Fortunately for him, his uncle's patronage and his education at Augusta's Richmond County Academy were sufficient to gain him an appointment to the United States Military Academy, though he had to secure an Alabama Congressman's nomination for his application. Longstreet, already called "Old Pete" by his West Point classmates, graduated third to last among the 56 graduates

in the Class of 1842, but excelled enough in the military arts to earn his commission as a Second Lieutenant in the Infantry. More lasting than any of Longstreet's academic lessons were the friendships he formed while a cadet. Longstreet was classmates with future Civil War Generals Lafayette McLaws, D. H. Hill, Richard Anderson, and Abner Doubleday. During his years at the Academy, he also formed friendships with William S. Rosecrans, John Pope, and Alexander P. Stewart. His closest friend from West Point, however, was with U.S. "Sam" Grant, with whom he would later serve as a Lieutenant.[1]

Longstreet first experienced combat as a Lieutenant during the Mexican-American War.

Under General Zachary Taylor's command, he fought in the battles of Palo Alto, Resaca de la Palma, and Monterrey — all in 1846. The following year, under General Winfield Scott, he served with distinction at Churubusco, carrying the regimental colors during the assault, and was decorated for his valor. He advanced the regimental colors again at Chapultepec, where he was wounded.[2]

In the years between the Mexican-American War and the United States Civil War, Longstreet served in command and staff positions in the wars against the American Indians of the Southwest. He married Louise Garland, with whom he had 10 children, though several of them would die in adolescence.

Longstreet was serving as a quartermaster when South Carolina seceded from the Union. Before Alabama had even seceded, he petitioned that state's Governor for a commission in the Army of the Confederate States of America. As the senior West Pointer from Alabama currently serving, he was commissioned as a Lieutenant Colonel in the C.S.A., though he continued to serve in his United States Army officer capacity for almost three concurrent months.[3]

On June 17, 1861, C.S.A. President Jefferson Davis promoted Longstreet to the rank of Brigadier General and gave him command of an Infantry brigade under Lieutenant General P.G.T. Beauregard, the senior serving Army

Lieutenant General James Longstreet, C.S.A., USMA 1842

- **DECORATED FOR VALOR AND WOUNDED IN THE MEXICAN-AMERICAN WAR**
- **COMMANDER OF CONFEDERATE FIRST CORPS FROM ITS CREATION TO THE END OF THE CIVIL WAR**
- **KNOWN AS GENERAL LEE'S "OLD WARHORSE"**
- **ONLY SENIOR CONFEDERATE OFFICER TO JOIN THE REPUBLICAN PARTY DURING RECONSTRUCTION**
- **US AMBASSADOR TO THE OTTOMAN EMPIRE**
- **US COMMISSIONER OF RAILROADS UNDER PRESIDENTS WILLIAM MCKINLEY AND THEODORE ROOSEVELT**

Officer to take a commission in the C.S.A. Longstreet demonstrated his tremendous capacity as a war-fighter in the Confederate victory at First Manassas, and in October of 1861, General Joseph E. Johnston promoted him to the rank of Major General.[4]

The following two years were not marked with the same successes for either Longstreet or for the South. In fact, Longstreet's fortunes were very closely aligned with those of the Confederacy. He participated in every major campaign of the war in the East during this time. He commanded the rear guard during the Peninsula Campaign without event, and added to the confusion at the Battle of Seven Pines. He

performed better at Gaines Mill, Frayser's Farm, and Malvern Hill, during which time he fought alongside "Stonewall" Jackson and developed a close relationship with the Army of Northern Virginia's new commander, Robert E. Lee.[5]

Shortly after the Antietam Campaign of September 1862, Lee promoted Longstreet to the rank of Lieutenant General and gave him command of one of his two newly created corps, Jackson commanding the second. With his new command came a new mission. While Lee, Jackson, and the rest of the Army of Northern Virginia defended Richmond from the Union's next invasion under General Hooker, Lee ordered Longstreet to

secure the Confederate logistics and rail hub in southeastern Virginia. His mission in that region he accomplished, though the threat of Union invasion there had probably been vastly overestimated. His siege of Suffolk during this time prevented him from answering Lee's call for reinforcements for the Battle of Chancellorsville in May 1863. Lee won, but with insufficient numbers to pursue and destroy Hooker's fleeing Army of the Potomac.

In contrast with Jackson's reputation as somewhat overly aggressive in the tactical offense, Longstreet was much more calculating and deliberate. This tendency of his was especially apparent at the battles of Second

Manassas and Gettysburg, where his tactical decisions have deeply divided military decisions, who argue alternatively whether he was sluggish or prudent. Criticism is greatest for his actions at Gettysburg, and he spent many of the later years of his life trying to rebuild his lost reputation. Longstreet and his corps had arrived at Gettysburg at the end of the first day of fighting. He sharply disagreed with the plan Lee outlined. Longstreet wanted to assume a defensive position between the rapidly growing Union Army and Washington, D.C. Lee wanted to attack. On day two, Longstreet characteristically took too long to attack, but when he did, his assault narrowly missed its objective of seizing the critical ground of Little Round Top. The third and final day of the battle brought Longstreet Lee's most ignominious orders, those that led to the notorious Pickett's Charge.

Longstreet and his corps spent the last few months of the following year assigned to Braxton Bragg in Tennessee. He fought with distinction at Chickamauga, staving off a decisive defeat of Bragg's Army until Sherman's arrival. Longstreet returned with his corps to Virginia, where he served out the remainder of the year in Lee's defense of Richmond.[6]

After Appomattox, Longstreet and Louise settled in New Orleans. There, he quickly fell from favor among Southern Democrats, who perceived him as a Radical Republican. He further alienated his former troops by resuming his friendship with Sam Grant, receiving a full pardon, endorsing Grant for President in 1868, and being awarded a lucrative appointment in his new administration.[7] What was perhaps the most damaging event of his career occurred in 1874, when he led a New Orleans militia, including some black troops, against rioting Confederate veterans.[8] The following year, he moved back to Gainesville, where he would live out the rest of his days. In 1880, he was appointed as the United States Minister to the Ottoman Empire, where he lived for two years. Fortunately for Longstreet, he outlived the harshest treatment that accompanied his post-war political reputation, dying on January 2, 1903, at the age of 83.

Longstreet is remembered predominantly for his role among the Confederacy's most elite commanders – Lee's "Old Warhorse." Like many of his generation, the leading role he played in the Rebellion is overlooked because of contemporary understandings of honor and loyalty. Rather, Longstreet's legacy is that of one of the great Generals of his era.

Written by: Major Christian G. Teutsch, USMA 1997.

Longstreet Equestrian Statue at Gettysburg.

Widely remembered as the youngest Division Commander of the United States Army during the Second World War, "Jumpin' Jim" Gavin will forever be associated with his heroic and inspired command of the fabled 82nd Airborne Division. Rising from the most humble of origins, Gavin found his life's calling in uniform and epitomized the fundamental leadership principle of leading by example in everything he did. An open and early critic of segregation of the Armed Forces, General Gavin continued his service to the nation following his retirement and served as the Ambassador to France during the Kennedy administration. To this day, his grave at the United States Military Academy Cemetery is a site of pilgrimage for paratroopers from around the globe.

Born in Brooklyn, New York, on March 22, 1907, the parentage of James Gavin remains unclear.[1] Only a few months old when his mother placed him into a Catholic orphanage, Martin Gavin, a coal miner from Mount Carmel, Pennsylvania, and his wife, Mary, adopted him shortly after his second birthday. Although the Gavins were a hardworking family, money was always tight and young James held jobs ranging from newspaper delivery to store clerk to help support his family. Forced to leave school after eighth grade to support his struggling family, he never lost his interest in learning, particularly military history. Not wanting to become a coal miner, he left home on his 17th birthday and took a night train to New York City, where he told a recruiter he was orphaned because parental consent was required for soldiers under 18.[2]

During Jim Gavin's first duty assignment with coastal artillery in Panama, he impressed everyone with his desire to learn, all the while dutifully sending money home. Tutoring from his Company First Sergeant and a Junior Officer enabled Private Gavin to pass the entrance examinations for West Point. Reporting in July 1925, he graduated 185th out of 299 with the Class of 1929.[3] As an Infantry Officer, his assignments were typical of those years. It was the United States Army Infantry School at Fort Benning, Georgia, that profoundly affected his professional development. Under the leadership of two legendary officers, George C. Marshall, Commandant, and Joseph Stilwell, Chief of Tactics, Gavin experienced a new command philosophy. The precursor of today's "mission-type orders" that encourages field commanders to solve battlefield problems in support of higher guidance, Stilwell's approach differed considerably from mainstream thought at the time and if would have a profound effect on Gavin's highly successful combat leadership.

Deeply troubled by the poor state of readi-

Ambassador James Gavin, USMA 1929

- **KNOWN AS THE "JUMPIN' JIM" AND THE "JUMPING GENERAL"**
- **COMMANDING GENERAL OF THE 82ND AIRBORNE DIVISION DURING WORLD WAR II**
- **YOUNGEST DIVISION COMMANDER IN THE U.S. ARMY DURING WORLD WAR II**
- **CHIEF OF THE U.S. ARMY RESEARCH AND DEVELOPMENT OFFICE**
- **U.S. AMBASSADOR TO FRANCE DURING PRESIDENT JOHN F. KENNEDY'S ADMINISTRATION**
- **BURIED AT THE WEST POINT CEMETERY**

Gavin's gravesite at West Point Cemetery.

Major General Ridgway and Major General Gavin in Holland.

>>> Spotlight

The 82nd Airborne Division was first formed in 1917 and deployed to France in World War I. Brigadier General James Gavin "Jumpin Jim" served the entire war in World War II with the 82nd. He jumped into Sicily and Normandy with the 82nd as a Regimental Commander and then became Commanding General of the 82nd Airborne Division on August 27, 1944. Major General Gavin then led the division through the remainder of World War II, including airborne drops on Operations Market Garden and temporarily led both the 82nd Airborne and 101st Airborne Divisions at the Battle of the Bulge until Lieutenant General Ridgeway returned from the United States.

Major General Gavin, Commander 82nd Airborne Division World War II.

Photo: AP

ness of the United States Army, he continued his study of the theory and practice of war, with special interest in the writings of J.F.C. Fuller, an early advocate of mechanized warfare. A series of stateside tours punctuated with an 18-month posting to the Philippines culminated with an assignment teaching tactics at West Point. Gavin had completed 10 full years of commissioned service when he was at last promoted to Captain on June 1, 1939, but promotions then followed in short order: Major on October 10, 1941; Lieutenant Colonel on February 1, 1942; and Colonel on September 25, 1942.[4] Continued schooling furthered his preparation for higher levels of responsibility, but his private life suffered.

Married shortly after graduation in 1929, he and his wife, Irma Baulsir, had a troubled marriage. The fact that Gavin was not present for the birth of their first child because he was away on a hunting trip gives some idea of the strained nature of the relationship. The two later divorced shortly after World War II.

The spectacular successes of German airborne troops inspired Gavin to volunteer for airborne training and he reported to Fort Benning in August 1941. Upon completion of airborne training, he took command of C Company, 503rd Parachute Infantry, an experimental formation. Gavin quickly distinguished himself and became

the Operations Officer of the Provisional Airborne Group. Building upon his practice of continuous learning and borrowing from the airborne doctrines of the Soviet Union and Nazi Germany, he authored the first United States Army airborne field manual, *FM 31-30: Tactics and Technique [sic] of Air-Borne Troops*, dated May 20, 1942.[5]

Gavin's first combat leadership occurred on July 9, 1943, when the regiment he was commanding, the 505th Parachute Infantry Regiment, of the 82nd Airborne Division commanded by Major General Matthew B. Ridgeway, jumped onto the high ground overlooking the beaches at Gela, Sicily. This was the main site of the American invasion of Sicily, code named Operation Husky, and it witnessed the first mass regimental combat jump in American history. Gavin was the first of his soldiers to jump. In the ensuing fighting, he took part in numerous small unit combat actions and repeatedly demonstrated heroic combat leadership that would be his trademark throughout the war. His actions and those of his men saved the precarious American bridgehead and Gavin subsequently received the Distinguished Service Cross for his heroism. For his inspired and successful leadership, Gavin was promoted to Brigadier General and made the deputy to General Ridgeway.

The airborne assault launched by the 82nd Airborne Division early in the morning of June 6, 1944, has forever immortalized the feats of bravery of the soldiers, noncommissioned officers, and officers of the "All-American Division." As Deputy Commander, Gavin played an important role, but when he succeeded Matthew Ridgeway as the Commanding General of the 82nd Airborne Division in August 1944, he attained international celebrity as the youngest Division Commander of the United States Army of the Second World War at the age of 37. He would be promoted to Major General in October 1944, but he had already achieved great fame and the undying loyalty of his troops for his fearlessness in battle and relenting willingness to endure the same sacrifices as his men. During the Battle of Arnhem in Holland in September 1944, the performance of his division was legendary as it fought valiantly in Operation Market Garden, the largest airborne operation of World War II up to that point.

Known for carrying the M-1 Garand Rifle into battle – the same heavy weapon that the vast majority of United States Army Infantrymen carried into battle – Gavin's willingness to endure the same hardships

as his men was well known.[6] He refused special accommodations and insisted upon sleeping in conditions similar to his men. Perhaps the best example of his leadership ethos is demonstrated by an incident during the Battle of the Bulge. When checking on his troops he encountered a soldier who lacked socks and personally ordered his aide to provide him a pair of the General's own socks.[7]

Gavin remained in command of the 82nd Airborne Division through the end of the war and led it during the victory parade in New York City on January 12, 1946. Unlike many of his famous peers who became national heroes and achieved high rank during the war, Gavin did not attain the rank of full General; however, he still achieved great success following the war, most notably as the Chief of the United States Army's Research and Development Office where he commissioned a number of important programs. However, he grew disillusioned with the direction of the United States Army of the 1950s and retired in March 1958 with the rank of Lieutenant General.

Following his retirement from active service, he accomplished a great deal in the corporate world but took a two-year leave of absence when President Kennedy asked Gavin to serve as United States Ambassador to France in 1961 because of the deteriorating relationship between the two countries. Kennedy believed Gavin's wartime success in France and relations with the French people would help improve relations with French President Charles de Gaulle. His private life fared better also in the post-war years and his second marriage to Jean E. Duncan of Knoxville, Tennessee, in July 1948, lasted until his death on February 23, 1990.

The hardscrabble beginnings provided little indication of the international fame and lasting legacy Gavin would achieve in life. In addition to his incredibly successful and charismatic leadership, which was recognized by rapid promotion and multiple awards for heroism – two Distinguished Service Crosses, the Silver Star, and the Purple Heart – Gavin never used his rank or position for personal gain and always retained his appreciation and consideration for the ordinary soldier. General Gavin fulfilled the absolute highest expectations accorded to any West Point graduate and his name has ever since been synonymous with leadership by example.

Written by: Colonel Kevin W. Farrell, PhD (USA, Retired), USMA 1986.

Ambassador Lucius Clay and Ambassador James Gavin during the Berlin Wall Crisis.

The battlefield successes of America's greatest military leaders are well documented in every American conflict. Not surprisingly, this success is generally the primary metric to judge wartime performance and why these leaders have rightfully earned their honored places in the pantheon of American history. Often overlooked, however, is that wartime success can be as much a function of setting the conditions off the battlefield as it is in execution on the battlefield. Additionally, winning the peace can be as important as winning the war and sometimes more difficult. Consequently, successful leaders in these areas are much less documented and frequently absent in any discussion about great military leaders. General Lucius D. Clay was one of these leaders. A gifted executive with keen technical skills and management acumen, Clay was also politically savvy, hard-working, and a coalition-builder. As a result, Clay's 31-year military career followed a unique path as did his life after retirement. In both worlds – comprising nearly 60 years of public service – Clay was extremely influential, often behind the scenes, as a problem solver and trusted advisor who set the conditions for success in times of war and peace.

Born on April 23, 1897, in Marietta, Georgia, Clay was the youngest of three-term United States Senator Alexander Stephens Clay's six children and grew up in the heart of poor, rural Georgia and the post-Reconstruction South.[1] As the son of a United States Senator, Clay spent his youth traveling between Washington, D.C., and Georgia, where he was immersed in both the public and personal sides of politics. As a result, he received a very unique education and perspective while also developing a fiercely independent and self-confident personality.[2] Clay took these traits to West Point as part of the Class of 1918 where he graduated in three years as a member of a wartime class. His academic record was excellent ranking 27th out of 137, and he was the top-ranked cadet in both History and English. His conduct record, however, was not. He ranked 128th and was a major critic of the Academy's rote habits he viewed as unnecessary. Despite this criticism, the intellectually curious Clay greatly appreciated the academic discipline, personal values, and service-oriented focus West Point instilled in him. Upon graduation, Clay was mistakenly commissioned in the Field Artillery before changing to the Corps of Engineers. This switch upset Clay because he believed he had a better chance of seeing combat in World War I as an Artillery Officer than as an enigneer.[3]

Clay's prediction proved correct and he never saw combat, but his unique assignments during the interwar years highlighted his executive, management, and political talents that would be critical during World War II. Assignments that included teaching engineering at West Point and serving on General Douglas MacArthur's staff in the Philippines, to working with "New Dealers" in Washington, D.C., on public works projects and serving as the District Engineer for the Texas Red River Dam not only showcased his abilities, but also earned him a great reputation in both military and political circles. The culmination of his interwar assignments was as the head of the Civil Aeronautics Authority's Defense Airport Program prior to WWII. In this capacity, he oversaw the repair or construction of more than 450 airports that became the foundation of America's commercial air network.[4] Thus, few officers were as qualified to set the conditions for success away from the battlefield as Clay was when the United States entered WWII.

Like many officers at the start of the war, Clay petitioned for a combat command but was unsuccessful. Because of his stellar reputation, Clay was assigned as the War

Ambassador Lucias Clay, USMA 1918

- **MILITARY GOVERNOR OF GERMANY AND COMMANDER OF U.S. FORCES GERMANY**
- **LED THE COMMISSION TO DESIGN AND BUILD THE EISENHOWER FEDERAL HIGHWAY SYSTEM IN THE 1950S**
- **LED THE DESIGN AND CONSTRUCTION OF THE U.S. AIRPORTS SYSTEM IN THE 1930S**
- **INITIATED AND COMMANDED THE BERLIN AIRLIFT**
- **WAR DEPARTMENT DIRECTOR OF MATERIAL DURING WORLD WAR II**

Berlin residents watch aircraft arrive during the Berlin Airlift.

Department's Director of Material instead and headed all wartime procurement for Army Services Forces (ASF) for most of the war. His carrot for this position was becoming the youngest Brigadier General in the United States Army.[5] It was here that Clay helped set in motion the seemingly endless flow of supplies from America's industrial might that fueled both the United States and Allied forces on all fronts. The ASF's mission was a wartime priority that Army Chief of Staff, General George Marshall,

BERLINERS STILL REFER TO HIM AS "THE HERO OF BERLIN," HAVING HONORED HIM BY NAMING ONE OF BERLIN'S LONGEST STREETS CLAY ALEE.

described as "difficult and complex beyond description," but one in which Clay performed brilliantly.[6] When the supply flow became problematic after the Normandy invasion, General Dwight Eisenhower personally requested Clay to resolve the bottleneck in Cherbourg, France. Clay did so quickly and efficiently thinking this would finally earn him a combat command. Instead, his success elevated him to the Deputy Director of War Mobilization and Reconversion in December 1944, making him second only to Director James F. Byrnes in running America's wartime economy. This move also closely associated him with key political figures, such as Treasury Secretary Henry Morgenthau, Presidential Advisor Harry Hopkins, and Representative Sam Rayburn. Although Clay noted that it was a job he "had no desire for...[as] an officer in wartime," it was one for which he was clearly well suited.[7] In fact, his efforts were so noteworthy that Assistant Secretary of

War John J. McCloy concluded after the war that "whenever a difficult problem arose, particularly in the international arena, General Clay was called upon to solve it."[8] By the war's end, Clay's talent for setting the conditions off the battlefield were monumental to America's battlefield success and that reputation sealed his selection to lead the difficult task of occupying a divided Germany.

Clay brought a fresh set of eyes and viewpoints to his new assignment since he was never involved in any previous discussions about post-war Germany. He was also insulated from the wartime devastation in Germany and throughout Europe. Arriving as the Deputy Military Governor in charge of the American occupation in April 1945, Clay, now a Lieutenant General, emerged by March 1947 as the Commander of United States forces in Germany and Military Governor under the Office of Military Government, United States

(OMGUS) until his retirement in May 1949. In that time, Clay also served as an American *proconsul* in Europe, answering only to the State Department and with almost unlimited authority.[9] He had the flexibility in these roles to help restore Germany as a linchpin in the recovery of all Western Europe.

Appalled at the war's devastation, Clay's own childhood experiences arguably made him better able to relate with those being occupied. Along with this compassion, however, he also aggressively pursued policies that ensured United States interests by reviving the United States, British, and French zones of Germany as a bulwark against the spread of Soviet communism after the Grand Alliance fell apart, the Soviet Union parted ways with the United States and Great Britain, and the Cold War began. In Clay's estimation, a stable Germany was a "major constructive step toward peace" in the long run.[10] To accomplish this, Clay's policies centered on being fair and impartial,

General (Retired) Lucius Clay showing President Eisenhower the proposed federal Defense Interstate Highway System.

JFK in West Berlin giving his famous "Ich bin ein Berliner" speech with Ambassador Lucius Clay as his special Ambassador to Berlin.

LUCIUS DuBIGNON CLAY
GENERAL
UNITED STATES ARMY
APRIL 23, 1897 — APRIL 16, 1978
USMA JUNE 1918
COMMANDER-IN-CHIEF EUROPEAN COMMAND
MILITARY GOVERNOR OF GERMANY

MARJORIE McKEOWN
HIS BELOVED WIFE
MAY 2, 1897 — FEBRUARY 8, 1992

General Lucius Clay's gravesite at West Point.

General Clay as Military Governor of Germany.

Ambassador Clay advising President Kennedy on the Berlin Wall Crisis, 1961.

creating a democratic government, and on keeping people fed, which was a priority. He argued that "there is no choice between becoming a communist on 1,500 calories, and a believer in democracy on 1,000 calories."[9]

With the economic strength of the Marshall Plan as a foundation for European recovery, Clay instituted free elections, returned currency control, and regularly provided for the basic needs of the German people. In fact, these efforts were so effective and successful toward creating a revived and unified West Germany, that the Soviets blockaded access to Berlin on June 25, 1948, in an attempt to drive the Western

powers from Germany.[10] Instead, the Soviet blockade only served to solidify the Cold War and led to Clay's finest hour. Rather than capitulate, Clay conceived and directed the Berlin Airlift, or Operation Vittles, where the United States and Great Britain delivered more than 8,000 tons of supplies daily by aircraft for 11 months to the people of West Berlin – an effort that forced the Soviets to relent and finally lift the blockade on May 12, 1949. The United States had won an important first victory in the early Cold War without a shot being fired.[11] Perhaps more importantly, Clay's actions precipitated the immediate unification and formation of the Federal Republic of Germany (West Germany) in May 1949 and proved the

Western resolve to maintain an enduring, free West Berlin. Clay's action in Berlin was so lauded that upon his retirement and return to the United States, he was given a ticker-tape parade in New York City. In the end, West Germany and West Berlin would remain solidly in the United States sphere and provide a foundation of European stability for the remainder of the Cold War.

After retiring, Clay continued putting his talents to use with great success in both the private sector and behind the scenes as a public servant. In the private sector, Clay served as the Chairman of the Board and Chief Executive Officer of the Continental Can Company for 12 years, elevating it

to the top of the packaging industry. As a managing partner for Lehman Brothers, he reorganized and revitalized the failing, but prestigious, investment firm where he worked until age 75.[12] In the public sector, leaders continually sought Clay's counsel and efforts on major policy issues and Clay always willingly obliged. President Harry Truman sought his counsel to organize the home front during the Korean War. He was instrumental in convincing General Eisenhower to run for the Presidency and then assisted the newly elected President Eisenhower in identifying potential Cabinet Members. Also during Eisenhower's administration, one of the President's top priorities was to build a federal highway

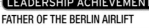

LEADERSHIP ACHIEVEMENT
FATHER OF THE BERLIN AIRLIFT

>>> Spotlight

EISENHOWER INTERSTATE SYSTEM

The Interstate System has been called the Greatest Public Works Project in History. From the day President Dwight D. Eisenhower signed the Federal-Aid Highway Act of 1956, the Interstate System has been a part of our culture — as construction projects, as transportation in our daily lives, and as an integral part of the American way of life. Every citizen has been touched by it, if not directly as motorists, then indirectly because every item we buy has been on the Interstate System at some point. President Eisenhower considered it one of the most important achievements of his two terms in office, and historians agree. *www.fhwa.dot.gov*

Courtesy: D.O.T.

Photo: AP

Map of the Berlin Airlift Operation

Photo: AP

Clay arriving at Templehof Airport.

system. Eisenhower's experience with the German autobahn during WWII convinced him of the value of a national transportation network, and he specifically asked for Clay by name to lead a committee to lay the groundwork. Under Clay's leadership, the President's Advisory Committee on a National Highway Program, or the "Clay Commission," did just that by organizing and planning the largest public works project in United States history. Clay then took the reins in helping the President successfully steer the National Interstate and Defense Highway Act, or the Eisenhower Interstate System named in the President's honor, through Congress.[15] Thus, Clay was instrumental in fundamentally transforming

America's transportation infrastructure through his designing of the United States airport system in the 1930s and federal highway system in the 1950s. He also served as a government advisor to the Federal Home Mortgage Association.

Most notably, however, Clay was a senior governmental advisor on German matters for three Presidential administrations, as well as President John Kennedy's personal envoy to Berlin during the second Berlin Crisis from September 1961 to May 1962 with the official rank of Ambassador. Although this crisis ended with the building of the Berlin Wall and the physical division of Germany, Clay's efforts once again helped win the

peace by diffusing a Cold War flash point, maintaining West Berlin's autonomy, and restoring stability to East-West tensions in Europe.[16] Berliners still refer to him as "the Hero of Berlin," having honored him by naming one of Berlin's longest streets Clay Alee. This street was also the home of Clay Headquarters, the former headquarters of the United States Army's Berlin Brigade.

With his health failing after contracting emphysema, General Clay died on April 16, 1978, and was buried at the United States Military Academy. In honor of his legacy, his gravesite bears a telling tribute from the German people etched on a small plaque that reads "*Wir danken dem bewahrer*

unserer freiheit," or "We thank the preserver of our freedom." Ironically, preserving that freedom was not accomplished on the battlefield or even during a time of war; rather, it was through Clay's monumental efforts after the war in winning and maintaining the peace. Likewise, his efforts in setting the conditions off the battlefield during WWII were critical to victory on the battlefield. In the end, the documentation of General Lucius Clay's career and life merit his inclusion in any conversation about America's great military leaders.

General McCaffrey and his wife, Jill, at the 1996 State of the Union with Hillary and Chelsea Clinton.

General Barry McCaffrey, USMA 1964

- **PRESIDENTIAL CABINET MEMBER**
- **COMMANDER, U.S. SOUTHERN COMMAND (SOUTHCOM)**
- **COMMANDER, 24TH INFANTRY DIVISION (MECHANIZED), DESERT STORM**
- **TWO DISTINGUISHED SERVICE CROSSES, TWO SILVER STARS**
- **BOY SCOUTS OF AMERICA, YOUTH MEMBER**

General Barry McCaffrey speaking with troops as the Commander of SOUTHCOM (Southern Command).

>>> Spotlight

The Distinguished Service Cross is the second-highest award for valor awarded to soldiers in the United States Army for extraordinary heroism and risk of life against an enemy of the United States. During World War I, the Army created the Distinguished Service Medal (DSM) at the request of General John J. "Blackjack" Pershing (USMA 1886) to create a valor award that would rank second to the Medal of Honor. President Woodrow Wilson established the award on January 2, 1918. The Distinguished Service Cross is awarded to a person who, while serving in any capacity with the Army, distinguished himself or herself by extraordinary heroism not justifying the award of a Medal of Honor. The act or acts of heroism must have been so notable and have involved risk of life so extraordinary as to set the individual apart from his or her comrades.

Photo © 2013/Greg E. Mathieson Sr./MAI

Jill McCaffrey greeting Major General McCaffrey on the return to Fort Stewart, GA from Desert Storm as Commander 4th Infantry Division, 1991.

Barry McCaffrey being sworn in by his father, Lieutenant General William J. McCaffrey (USMA 1939), in the Commandant's backyard at West Point, 1964.

First Lieutenant McCaffrey being awarded the first of two Distinguished Service Crosses (DSC) by General Creighton Abrams in Vietnam, 1966.

General Barry McCaffrey is a decorated war hero, a Four-Star General, and an appointed Cabinet Member who has served our country for more than 50 years. When he retired from active duty, he was the youngest and most highly decorated Four-Star General.

Barry McCaffrey was born November 17, 1942, and attended Philips Academy in Andover, Massachusetts. He entered West Point in 1960 and graduated in 1964 – just as the bugle was sounding for the War in Vietnam. He chose the Infantry Branch, graduating from Airborne and Ranger Schools, before joining the prestigious 82nd Airborne. Shortly after arriving at Fort Bragg in North Carolina, he deployed to the American intervention in the Dominican Republic in 1965 as a Platoon Leader. He then deployed to Vietnam in an advisory role, advising the Vietnamese 2nd Parachute Infantry Battalion from 1966 to 1967. He was again deployed to Vietnam in 1969 as an Infantry Company Commander with the 1st Cavalry Division. During his two tours in Vietnam, he was very highly decorated for multiple acts of courage, receiving two Distinguished Service Crosses (DSC), two Silver Stars, three Purple Hearts, and the Combat Infantryman Badge.

His first Distinguished Service Cross (DSC) was awarded for his actions as a First Lieutenant in Vietnam in January 1967, when he was wounded twice in a 12-hour battle. The senior American advisor was killed, so he took command, courageously leading a South Vietnamese unit that was besieged by a larger force.

His second DSC was awarded for actions on March 9, 1969, when, as a Company Commander on a reconnaissance-in-force mission, his unit came under fire from an entrenched bunker complex. With one of his squad's pinned down, he single-handedly led an assault on the bunker destroying the machine gun emplacement. Although wounded in the assault, he continued to lead until the bunker complex had been eliminated and all his wounded had been evacuated.

When awarded his second DSC, the citation read "Captain McCaffrey's extraordinary heroism and devotion to duty were in keeling with the highest traditions of the military service and reflect great credit upon himself, his unit, and the United States Army."

He received two Silver Stars: one for attacking two Viet Cong and killing them with his pistol during a reconnaissance-in-force mission in January 1969; the second for attacking and neutralizing an enemy bunker with a hand grenade in June 1969. He returned to the United States a hero in an unpopular war.

After Vietnam, McCaffrey graduated with a master's degree from D.C.'s American University and then returned to West Point to serve as a professor in the Department of Social Sciences. The late 1970s and 1980s were peaceful times for the United States military, and McCaffrey – a highly decorated combat leader from Vietnam – rose quickly up the ranks, leading Infantry, Battalion, Brigade, and Division. In 1990, Saddam Hussein invaded Kuwait and threatened to invade Saudi Arabia. President Bush mobilized the United States military to defend Saudi Arabia and liberate Kuwait. As the Commanding General of the 24th Infantry Division, McCaffrey led the 370-kilometer "Left Hook" mission, enveloping the Iraqi Army and crushing the Republican Guard in Iraq in less than 100 hours.

His last command was as the Commander of Southern Command (USSOUTHCOM), before retiring after 32 years of service as a Four-Star General. But another threat to United States National Security had developed: the drug war. Upon retirement, General

WITH ONE OF HIS SQUAD'S PINNED DOWN, MCCAFFREY SINGLE-HAND-EDLY LED AN ASSAULT ON THE BUNKER, DESTROY-ING THE MACHINE GUN EMPLACEMENT. ALTHOUGH WOUNDED, HE CONTINUED TO LEAD UNTIL THE BUNKER COM-PLEX HAD BEEN ELIMINATED AND ALL HIS WOUNDED HAD BEEN EVACU-ATED.

McCaffrey was appointed as a member of President Clinton's cabinet as the Director of White House Office of National Drug Policy from 1996 to 2001. From 2001 to 2005, McCaffrey served as the Bradley Distinguished Professor of International Studies. From 2005 to 2010, he served as the adjunct professor of International Studies at West Point. He is the President of his own consulting firm and serves as a national security and terrorism expert for NBC News.

General McCaffrey is one of the most highly decorated and respected Four-Star Generals in American history. His public appearances in thousands of television shows, articles, and publications have helped shape our national security direction.

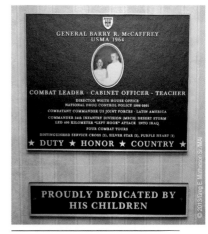

McCaffrey Room at the Thayer Hotel.

The General McCaffrey Room at the Thayer Hotel is dedicated by his family.

Jim Nicholson and his six siblings grew up in a five-room house in Struble, Iowa, with no plumbing and an alcoholic father. They often went to sleep hungry. Undeterred, their mother used to gather the seven children around a kerosene lantern and read the bible every night, saying, "If you work hard, study hard, and pray hard, you'll succeed in this country." She turned out to be very prophetic – all seven children went to college, and five of them earned graduate degrees. Nicholson, "working hard, studying hard, and praying hard," graduated from West Point in 1961 and was knighted by Pope John Paul II in 2003 as the United States Ambassador to the Holy See for his work in Europe on human rights.

Jim Nicholson was the third of seven children. His father suffered from chronic alcoholism, so the family was very poor – so much so that Nicholson and his siblings were nearly split up among relatives in order to provide a better environment for them. His mother, however, a former high school valedictorian, who had studied Latin for four years, was the family's strength and managed to keep the family together.

Nicholson attended a two-room school that had one room for grades one through four, and the other for grades five through eight. His high school in a neighboring town was larger with 96 students in his class. Nicholson was a solid athlete, earning All-State Honors for his undefeated football team and playing baseball. While in school, Nicholson's older brother, Jack, was accepted to West Point and entered in 1952. Nicholson visited him in the fall of 1955 and was in such awe of the Academy that he wanted to attend himself. Unfortunately, he failed to receive a nomination his senior year in high school.

Secretary Robert James Nicholson, USMA 1961

- **U.S. SECRETARY OF DEPARTMENT OF VETERANS AFFAIRS**
- **U.S. AMBASSADOR TO THE HOLY SEE (VATICAN)**
- **CHAIRMAN, REPUBLICAN NATIONAL COMMITTEE**
- **VICE CHAIRMAN, REPUBLICAN NATIONAL COMMITTEE**
- **VIETNAM VETERAN**
- **SENIOR COUNSEL, BROWNSTEIN HYATT FARBER SCHRECK, LLP**

Photo: AP

Captain Jim Nicholson with his Vietnamese Counterpart in Hau Bong, South Vietnam, in November 1965.
Courtesy: Jim Nicholson

President George W. Bush announcing the appointment of Ambassador Jim Nicholson to be the Secretary of Veterans Affairs in December 2004.
Photo: AP

>>> Spotlight

Courtesy: The Vatican

Vatican City State was founded following the signing of the Lateran Pacts between the Holy See and Italy on February 11, 1929. These were ratified on June 7, 1929. Its nature as a sovereign state distinct from the Holy See is universally recognized under international law.[1]

Courtesy: White House

He went on to attend Iowa State, where he started on the freshman baseball team. He continued to pursue his West Point dream, however, and received a nomination the following year from Senator Bourke B. Hickenlooper. With no telephone in his home, Nicholson received his acceptance notification by a Morse code message sent to the railroad depot next to his house. In fact, it was the railroad depot agent, Jack Whalen, a former World War II Marine Corps veteran, who hand-delivered the message. Whalen had become a mentor to young Nicholson and coached the local baseball team. Whalen had tears in his eyes when he delivered the message because he was so proud of Nicholson and knew that he was being afforded the opportunity of a lifetime.

Nicholson entered West Point in July 1957. Since he loved sports and was such a strong athlete, he played baseball, sprint football, and was on the intercollegiate wrestling team during his Plebe year. While he excelled as an athlete, Nicholson nearly failed a class that year – which typically led to separation – and he realized he needed to set different priorities. As much as he loved sports, he dropped baseball and football in order to focus more on academics, only continuing wrestling. This change provided the right balance and he was able to excel in both athletics and academics for his remaining three years.

During his senior year, his Tactical Officer, Major Hal deMoya (USMA 1946), a man whom he respected tremendously, asked him to lead all intramurals for his Cadet Company, Company I-1. Major deMoya wanted to leave his legacy at the Academy by winning the "Bankers Trophy," which was awarded to the Cadet Company with the best intramural sports program. At the same time, the Sprint Football coach, Eric Tipton, asked Nicholson to coach the Plebe Sprint Football Squad. Despite his full schedule, Nicholson accomplished both with great success – Company I-1 ultimately received the Bankers Trophy from the United States Military Academy Superintendent, Major General William C. Westmoreland, and the Plebe Sprint Football Squad went undefeated.

His last two months at West Point pointed to the historical events soon to take place. In May, President Eisenhower accepted the Sylvanus Thayer Award. Then, at graduation, the Class of 1961 heard Vice President Lyndon Johnson deliver the commencement address and received their diplomas from him, while Major General Westmoreland was the ranking officer. Both leaders would be inextricably linked to America's involvement and escalation in Vietnam.

Commissioned as an Infantry Officer after his graduation, Second Lieutenant Nicholson attended the Infantry Officer Basic Course, Ranger School, then Airborne School. His first assignment was with the 4th Infantry Division at Fort Lewis, Washington. Shortly thereafter, he was disappointed with his first duty position – Platoon Leader of the Davy Crockett Platoon housing the newly fielded, handheld, Davy Crockett tactical nuclear weapons system. To lead this high-visibility platoon was an honor for any Platoon Leader, however, and it was also the division's top priority. As a result, Second Lieutenant Nicholson was given his pick of non-commissioned officers, soldiers, and equipment in the entire division. On the other hand, with this unit came incredible responsibility and stress – any failed nuclear inspection would result in the Division Commander's relief, not to mention the sensitivity and danger inherent in tactical-level nuclear weapons. At one point, Nicholson escorted Attorney General Robert Kennedy to Nevada during a live-fire exercise using these weapons. It was during that trip that Nicholson experienced the relationship between senior Army and civilian leadership, and where he concluded that at some point he would rather operate on the civilian side of that relationship.

His reward for outstanding performance as the Davy Crockett Platoon Leader was an early command of Company C, 22nd Infantry, 1st Battle Group. Following this command, he attended military intelligence school and language school in Monterey, California, to study French, special warfare training at Fort Bragg, North Carolina, then deployment to Vietnam in 1965 as a Senior Advisor to an Army of the Republic of Vietnam (ARVN) Infantry Scout Battalion. The battalion was part of South Vietnam's ARVN II Corps, comprised mainly of Montagnards, and operated in the Central Highlands region. It was during this assignment that Nicholson saw the value of his Ranger school training. Patrolling in the mountainous jungle, understanding land navigation, survival training, and remaining calm and alert under stress were essential for his success. This area was the most active in Vietnam at the time, and it was during this early phase of the war when the North Vietnamese began to send full battalions of regular soldiers into South Vietnam and Nicholson's area of operations. As Nicholson rotated back to America at the end of his tour of duty, the United States Army began to escalate its commitment of larger combat units, including the 173rd Airborne Brigade.

After Vietnam, Captain Nicholson returned to West Point, where he worked in the Admissions Office and attended graduate school at Columbia University in New York City. Having just left a combat zone, the last thing he expected then was another life-changing event, soon after arriving he met Suzanne Marie Ferrell of Highland Falls, whom he would marry one year later. Suzanne had recently graduated from Vassar and was headed to graduate school at Cornell when they fell in love. They married

Veterans Affairs Secretary Jim Nicholson with President George W. Bush on Veterans Day in Arlington Cemetery in 2006.

Secretary Jim Nicholson and wife, Suzanne, sharing a laugh at the White House with President George W. Bush in 2007.

and have been together for 45 years.

While studying public policy at Columbia, Nicholson took two constitutional law courses and decided he wanted to become a lawyer. The Army had a program for company-grade officers to attend law school at their own personal expense if they were accepted, and he applied for the program, but he was promoted to Major and no longer eligible for the program. Instead, he submitted his resignation, but the Army rejected active-duty wartime resignations from regular officers, and he remained on active duty two additional years at West Point until 1970.

Nicholson and Suzanne left the Regular Army (he remained in the Army Reserves) and moved to Denver, where Nicholson entered law school at the University of Denver. Suzanne was pregnant when they arrived in Denver and would give birth to their second son, while Nicholson was in law school. Nicholson attended school at night and worked full time as an administrative assistant in the Denver Mayor's office. He would leave home for work at 0630 hours and return from school after 2200 hours, while Suzanne cared for their two children. Following law school graduation, Nicholson was hired by a top-tier Denver firm and made partner after two years of practice.

Nicholson next became General Counsel to the Colorado Association of Housing and Building. When his law school advisor, Dick Hamm, was elected as Colorado Governor in 1975, Nicholson's legal and Housing Council experience then brought him into the political spotlight during Denver's bid to host the XII Winter Olympiad, in which he became the public point person focused on the economic growth and expansion the Olympics could bring. From here, Nicholson became more involved in politics and was soon working with Colorado's Republican Party to elect candidates to the state legislature.

But, despite his thriving legal practice, Nicholson chose to leave law and move into the business world. After a thorough market study, he found an opportunity to develop an old dairy farm between Denver and Boulder. The location was ideal for an upscale residential development on what was otherwise undeveloped farmland. So from the humble workspace of a rented double-wide in 1978, he created Nicholson Enterprises Incorporated, a developer of planned residential communities. Overcoming difficult economic challenges during President Jimmy Carter's administration,

Nicholson Enterprises created the Ranch Country Club development, which was rated the Colorado Project of the Year in 1982. By 1984, he completed that project and pursued an even larger and more successful venture. He purchased a small town in the southeast sector of greater Denver called Parker. His group bought the entire 2,300-acre town from Bankers Trust for $10 million, developed a master plan, installed a new sewer plant, and began to sell parcels to successfully spur the rapid development of that region. Parker, Colorado, has grown to more than 50,000 people from its 1984 count of 55 families. Parallel with these business efforts, Nicholson continued his political involvement becoming Colorado's representative to the Republican National Committee (RNC). He also remained in the active Army Reserve until retiring in 1991 with the rank of Colonel.

"IF YOU WORK HARD, STUDY HARD...AND PRAY HARD...YOU'LL SUCCEED IN THIS COUNTRY," SAID NICHOLSON'S MOTHER.

The Republican Party continued to recognize Nicholson's valuable political acumen and service by placing him as Chairman of the RNC Rules Committee and then electing him Vice Chairman. Following Senator Bob Dole's failed 1996 Presidential bid against President Bill Clinton, the Republican party took a downturn. With low morale, organizational disarray, and a $13-million debt, the RNC was in peril. Nicholson recognized the state of the organization, decided to run for RNC Chairman against four other challengers and won the election on January 17, 1997. In order to put all of his efforts into the position, Nicholson and Suzanne sold the business to the employees and moved to Washington, D.C., where Nicholson took over the Committee that was short on staff and funds. Nicholson likened the RNC atmosphere and morale when he took over to that of "a battalion having been overrun in Vietnam." He immediately changed the RNC strategy by appealing to the Republican Party's "grassroots" base and focused on smaller donors. The strategy worked. In 1997, the Republican Party won 19 elections in a row to include the New Jersey and Virginia gubernatorial races, the Mayoral races in New York City and Los Angeles while losing none. Most importantly, under Nicholson's RNC

Ambassador Jim Nicholson being welcomed to the Vatican as Ambassador on September 13, 2001, by Pope John Paul II.

Superintendent Major General Westmoreland presenting the Bankers Trophy to Cadet Jim Nicholson during June week in 1961.

direction, Republican George W. Bush was elected President in 2000 after weathering a dispute in Florida's election results that went all the way to the Supreme Court before declaring Bush as the victor. In the process, Nicholson managed a small Army of 262 lawyers working the dispute.

Following his successful leadership as RNC Chairman, Nicholson turned down President-elect Bush's suggestion that he serve as Secretary of the Army, and instead told the President that he preferred to go abroad as an Ambassador. Reflecting on his own Catholic upbringing, and recalling the importance of the childhood prayer sessions with his mother and siblings, Nicholson requested to go to the Vatican as the United States Ambassador to the Holy See, for which he was unanimously confirmed. His entire family planned to travel to the Vatican for the presentation of his credentials ceremony scheduled for September 13, 2001. Then came the catastrophic attacks of September 11th, which prevented those plans. Ambassador Nicholson, instead of meeting with the Pope in a celebratory ceremony, prayed together with Pope John Paul II for the victims and their families. Nicholson recalls the Pope saying, "We have to stop those people who kill in the name of God." Such words of support from the Pope provided a

critical lift to the United States in building coalition forces in the days leading up to the attacks against the Taliban in Afghanistan.

While the Pope's comments echoed support for allied efforts in Afghanistan, he was not supportive of the war in Iraq, which he viewed as preemptive war. Although the Pope never openly condemned as being immoral, President Bush's decision to invade Iraq, his actions, such as holding general diplomatic summits against war, clearly signaled his strong disagreement. The lack of Vatican support also created diplomatic challenges among a coalition consisting of allies with large Catholic populations. Nevertheless, Ambassador Nicholson continually dialogued with the Pope and the Vatican to debate "just" war issues, and he even brought several prominent theologians to the Vatican to discuss why the United States was justified in invading Iraq. Along the way, President Bush visited the Vatican three times during his presidency – the most of any President in history – and had a close relationship with Pope John Paul II, in spite of Iraq.

In addition to Ambassador Nicholson's diplomatic efforts regarding the wars, he also saw his time at the Vatican as an opportunity to pursue "the fulfillment of

the U.S. commitment to enhance human dignity worldwide." He did this by focusing his diplomatic efforts on reducing human trafficking, increasing religious freedom, reducing the spread of HIV AIDS, reducing international terrorism, and reducing worldwide starvation. Having grown up poor and often hungry, starvation and hunger were especially sensitive issues for him. In his three and a half years at the Vatican, he held many conferences addressing these critical issues, to include organizing the largest global conference ever held to address human trafficking to which 38 countries sent Representatives.

When Nicholson completed his Ambassadorship at the Vatican, President Bush asked him to return to Washington to join his cabinet as Secretary of the Department of Veterans Affairs. The Senate confirmed him unanimously again, and, on February 1, 2005, Nicholson departed the United States Embassy at the Vatican and was sworn in the next day as VA Secretary. Nicholson assumed responsibility for the second-largest United States government organization – second only to the Department of Defense – consisting of more than 244,000 employees. With the United States involved in two separate wars, there was a high volume of wounded warriors returning from those conflicts that

stressed the VA system. While Secretary, he implemented transformative policies to process claims faster and adapt to the high number of traumatic brain injuries. In particular, he developed Traumatic Brain Injury centers and instituted policies to test every returning soldier for brain injury. After three years as VA Secretary, Nicholson resigned on October 1, 2007, and returned to the private sector to practice law in Washington, D.C. with Brownstein Hyatt Farber Schreck, LLP.

Hailing from a most humble childhood in rural Iowa, Nicholson had the odds stacked against him, yet he rose to achieve success at the highest levels of the military, politics, business, and government. What Nicholson has proved over his lifetime – one that includes more than 50 years of serving and leading in the public and private sectors – is that success is not always a function of being born of advantage; rather, as his mother taught him, success can be every bit a function of working, studying, and praying hard. And, oh yes, along the way, Nicholson was named a Distinguished Graduate of the United States Military Academy.

The Secretary Nicholson Room at the Thayer Hotel is proudly dedicated by PenFed.

Major General Dick Bresnahan and Jim's wife, Suzanne, promoting him to Colonel.

Cadet Jim Nicholson being welcomed to Germany by his brother, Captain Jack Nicholson, in 1960.

Senator Bob Dole and Governor Heineman thank WWII veterans at the WWII Memorial Washington, D.C.

Second Lieutenant Bradley Larson is awarded the Silver Star and Purple Heart by Governor Heineman.

Governor David Heineman, USMA 1970

- **CHAIR OF THE NATIONAL GOVERNOR'S ASSOCIATION**
- **GOVERNOR OF THE STATE OF NEBRASKA, 2005–PRESENT**
- **LIEUTENANT GOVERNOR OF THE STATE OF NEBRASKA**
- **TREASURER OF THE STATE OF NEBRASKA**
- **AIRBORNE-RANGER QUALIFIED ARTILLERY OFFICER**

Governor Heineman is the Governor of Nebraska and was elected by the Governors of the United States as the Chairman of the National Governors Association. When Governor Heineman leaves office in 2015, he will be the longest-serving Governor in the history of Nebraska with a total of 10 consecutive years in office. Under his leadership during a national recession, the State of Nebraska has seen incredible economic growth,

resulting in a record low unemployment rate of 3.8 percent (second lowest in the United States). He uses leadership principles that he learned at West Point to serve his state and the people of Nebraska, and he selflessly displays a "lifetime of service to the nation" as stated in the mission of the United States Military Academy.

Heineman was born May 12, 1948, and raised in Wahoo, Nebraska. His father,

Jean, a World War II Navy veteran, worked at JCPenney first as an assistant manager and then as a store manager of a small store. His dad always spoke to Heineman about leadership and leading by example – whether managing a small store or in any role. His mother, Irene, raised the four children: Heineman, Bill, Don, and Evelyn. Heineman graduated from Wahoo High School in what Heineman describes as an "ideal small community." Growing up

in a small town of 3,500 people allowed him to participate in all types of activities that he believes allowed himself and his classmates to become well-rounded individuals. His parents, both high school graduates, stressed to their children the importance of education and the need for them to pursue the best education they could attain. They had small classrooms and the teachers challenged kids to take challenging classes. In this small

>>> Spotlight

Nebraska was admitted as the 37th state in the Union on March 1, 1857. Dave Heineman served as the Lieutenant Governor from 2001 to 2005 and was appointed Governor in 2005 when Governor Mike Johanns was appointed as United States Secretary of Agriculture. Governor Heineman was elected as Governor in 2007 and 2011. When his four-year term is completed in 2015, he will have served a total of more than 10 years as Governor – the longest serving Governor in the more than 150 years of Nebraska history.

Governor Heineman greets President George W. Bush in Omaha, Nebraska.

West Point, and essentially, he remembers jokingly, the community made the choice for him. When he attended West Point, he felt the entire community took pride in him attending; he was the first from the community to attend West Point in more than 20 years.

The first year at West Point, he remembers as incredibly challenging, but he recalls the camaraderie with his classmates as they endured Plebe year together. While he didn't know whether he would make the Army a career, he found the public service emphasis intriguing; with the mission of the Academy emphasizing cadets should pursue a "lifetime of service to the nation." Classes in those days were six days a week, and while every cadet needed to major in engineering, Heineman chose his electives in economics and management. His interests in public service and specifically interests in economics would remain a theme in his life and career.

Upon graduation, Second Lieutenant Heineman chose the Field Artillery Branch, and his first assignment was in Hawaii at Schofield Barracks with the 25th Infantry Division. Before deploying to Hawaii, he attended Airborne and Ranger Schools, both which helped him formulate his leadership philosophy and style. He realized early on that he never wanted to ask a soldier to do anything he wasn't willing to do himself. Ranger School taught him that mental toughness and discipline under extremely stressful and challenging conditions.

For his first assignment in Hawaii, he was an Executive Officer of a 100-man artillery battery. At age 22, he was responsible for millions of dollars in equipment and leading a unit of 100 men – far more responsibility than he would ever have in the civilian world graduating from any other college. In this role, he learned small-unit tactics and how the small unit fit into bigger picture. He also learned quickly that as a young 22-year-old, he needed to identify and trust the older and more experienced non-commissioned officers to help build and mold the organization. This experience helped him in his next role, when he was selected after a very competitive process to be the aide-de-camp to Brigadier General Andy Gatsis, the Assistant Division Commander of the 25th Infantry Division. While his first assignment as the Executive Officer of the 100-man unit gave him exposure to the small unit at the "tip of the spear,"

the role as Aide-de-Camp gave him exposure to the high level or a large organization. In particular, he learned how leadership of a large organization and communicating effectively to get the message out to hundreds of smaller units was vital to effective leadership of a large organization.

While he loved the Army and enjoyed the camaraderie and the physical challenges, Heineman felt that the need to serve in a broader sense compelled him to leave the Army. However, at the time, he had no idea how to pursue that end goal. He started in business as a stepping-stone to find the role he wanted in the public sector. His first job was with Procter & Gamble (P&G) in sales and marketing, bringing him back to Nebraska. P&G is world renowned as one as the best marketing consumer products companies in the world. The lessons in effective communication and messaging were similar in the business world as he found in leading an Army. These lessons would later serve him well in government.

UNDER HIS LEADERSHIP DURING A NATIONAL RECESSION, THE STATE OF NEBRASKA HAS SEEN INCREDIBLE ECONOMIC GROWTH.

It was shortly after leaving the Army, that Heineman felt compelled to pursue his public service. As a starting point, he went to a Republican event one Saturday in Omaha. After the party meeting, the organizers invited Heineman to have dinner and to meet some "beautiful Republican women." He was introduced to Sally Ganem, an elementary school teacher on Labor Day weekend 1976. They were engaged by Thanksgiving and married the following May. Sally later became a school principal. They had a son, Sam, in 1984.

From 1983 to 1988, he worked for Congressman Hal Daub of Omaha. Heineman was elected to Fremont City Council in 1990, a community of 25,000, which was a part-time role that paid a meager $1,800 a year, but gave him his first exposure to local politics. In this role, he focused on the economics of the city; how and why projects would get funded seemed to him the most important of all

community, people were supportive of each other and there was an overall sense of community. Heineman played football, basketball, and golf and was President of the Student Council. His senior year, their golf team won the state championship. Heineman first heard about the academies when he attended Boys' State and all three academies sent mail-outs to all the attendees of Boys' State. Heineman read about the three academies and liked the history of the Academy and her graduates

and became interested, but didn't think he would be accepted but pursued the opportunity nonetheless.

He remembers his mother coming to his high school one day crying, and he thought someone in the family must have died. His mother had actually received the telegram from West Point accepting him and she was so excited for him that she was in tears. By nightfall, the entire community knew Heineman had been accepted to

council decisions. In 1994, he decided to run for State Treasurer and won, and served in this role for seven years until 2001. In this role, he learned the finances of the state and the levers that the government could use to encourage and set the conditions for businesses to succeed in the state. In 2001, then Governor Mike Johanns asked Heineman to serve as Lieutenant Governor. Together they won an election in 2002. Running a statewide election was a challenge, but Heineman found that hard work, ethics, and performance would be recognized and rewarded by the people of Nebraska. In 2005, then-Governor Mike Johanns was asked by President George W. Bush to join his Cabinet as United States Secretary of Agriculture, and Governor Johanns was confirmed on January 20, 2005. The next day, Heineman was sworn in as the 39th Governor of Nebraska. Because this was more than halfway through the Governor term, he would still have the ability to be

elected to two terms after the two years were completed.

Having spent seven years as State Treasurer and four years as Lieutenant Governor, now-Governor Heineman had a thorough understanding of the finances of the state and the levers available to him to help the economy of the State of Nebraska. He focused his Governorship on creating jobs, improving the economy, and improving education. Just as his parents had focused Heineman on the value of education, he believed the best way to prepare the future generations would be to provide them with the best education possible.

When Governor Heineman was sworn in January 2005, some people in the state assumed his term as Governor would be short lived. He faced a primary race in May 2006 against one of the most-respected and -revered people in the State of Nebraska, Tom Osborne, who most people

simply called "Coach Osborne," despite the fact that he was a serving member of the United States House of Representatives and technically should have been referred to as Congressman Osborne.

Governor Heineman's staff cannot speak more highly of him and his public service. He and his senior staff often "compete" to see who can arrive earlier and work later. Their day typically starts between 5:30 and 6:00 a.m. each day and routinely work until 8 or 9 p.m. every night. He often has high-level staff and cabinet meetings at the Governor's Residence on weekends and evenings for as long as it takes – and he never asks his staff to put in hours that he wouldn't himself.

Governor Heineman started behind Coach Osborne in the polls by 40 percentage points. Undeterred, Governor Heineman believed if he worked hard, the people of Nebraska would reward him. Heineman jokes that even his mother expected

him to lose. In what turned out to be the most-competitive race in Nebraska history, most people who voted for Governor Heineman actually expected Heineman to lose to Osborne. Yet as he had believed, the people of Nebraska rewarded him for his hard work and he was elected Governor. "Governor Dave" had beaten "Coach Osborne" in a legendary election in 2006. He won a second election in 2010 with more than 70 percent of the vote – the highest percentage of all the 38 gubernatorial elections in the United States that year, making him the most popular Governor in the United States. His term will end January 2015. "Governor Dave" won the race, but Nebraska also benefited from "Coach Osborne," then taking the leadership role as the Athletic Director at the University of Nebraska.

When he took office in 2006, the state was ranked 45th in the United States with some of the highest tax rates. He set

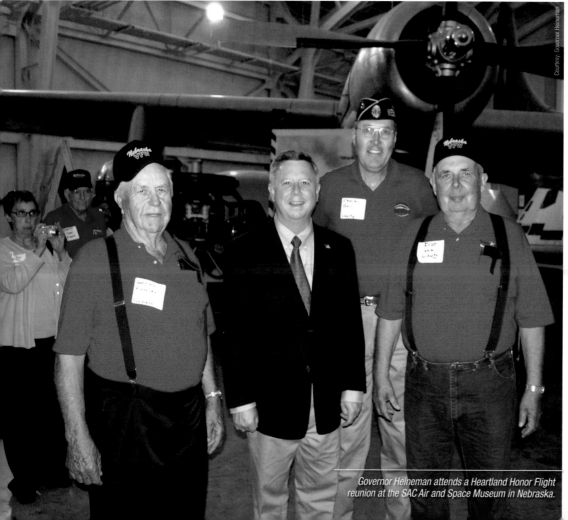

Governor Heineman attends a Heartland Honor Flight reunion at the SAC Air and Space Museum in Nebraska.

Governor and First Lady Heineman.

about making Nebraska more attractive to businesses and by 2011 Nebraska was ranked number one by the Tax Foundation for being the most attractive state for new businesses.

He also took office in the middle of "the Surge" in the Iraq War. Brave Nebraska men and women who volunteered to serve in both the regular Army and the Nebraska National Guard were off fighting for the United States. Many made the ultimate sacrifice. Nebraska men and women were dying in combat at a rate of around one every month, and Governor Heineman as the Commander in Chief of the Nebraska National Guard attended every funeral to honor their sacrifices. As a former Army Captain, he was honored to serve as the Commander in Chief of Nebraska's Guard and enjoys a great relationship with the Adjutant General (TAG) and the soldiers.

Every year, the National Governors Association (NGA) changes leadership with

a Republican and Democrat rotating the Chair and Vice Chair positions. The nation's Governors elected Governor Heineman Vice Chair in 2010, and in 2011, he was elected Chair. In order to be elected to this role, the Governor needed to believe he would have a national focus and be able to lead a bipartisan group of the 55 Governors of states and territories. As Chair of the NGA, he led an initiative to help Governors lead their states economies in the same way that he had led the Nebraska economy. He came to office as Chair with a laudable record in doing so.

During the recession of 2008 to 2011, he grew the Nebraska economy, keeping unemployment below 3.9 percent, second only to North Dakota that was experiencing the oil shale boom. His team created a bipartisan report "Growing States' Economies" with the top 12 ways that each Governor could grow their economies regardless of the decisions or indecisions

at the federal level. When he discusses the politics of federal government, he is concerned at the partisan gridlock. Governors learn to respect healthy opposing views but have to come to bipartisan agreements.

Governor Heineman has led multiple trade missions to Cuba. In 2006, an almost comical "Cold War stare down" occurred between he and Cuban Fidel Castro. In a middle-of-the-night meeting, Governor Heineman and members of the Governor's trade delegation were called to meet with Castro. Governor Heineman and Castro stood toe to toe discussing politics point for point. Neither would show weakness and take a seat, so they stood for four hours staring at each other. He literally stood "toe to toe" with the communist leader.

When asked what the future holds for him after his second term is over, he exposes a typically Midwestern sensibility – that if you do the job you have "here and now"

things will work themselves out. Just as he focused on being the best State Treasurer and was offered the position of Lieutenant Governor, then was made Governor, he focuses now on being the best Governor he can be, and the future will work itself out.

In 2011, as the Chair of the National Governors Association, he led the 50 Governors to a reception at the White House. Traditionally, the President will toast the Governors for the service to the people of their states and to the nation, then the Chair toasts the President. After the President's toast, Governor Heineman toasted, "Only in America can a guy from the small town of Wahoo, Nebraska, find himself in the White House toasting the President." As he reflects upon his amazing journey starting in Wahoo, he credits West Point with giving him the opportunity and the leadership abilities to make the journey possible.

Governor Heineman and Senator Dole in front of the Nebraska section of the World War II monument with Nebraskan veterans.

President George W. Bush in the Oval Office signing legislation initiated by Davis.

Davis with President George W. Bush exiting Air Force One.

Honorable Geoffrey C. Davis, USMA 1981

- MEMBER, U.S. HOUSE OF REPRESENTATIVES, 2004–12
- CHAIRMAN, HUMAN RESOURCES SUBCOMMITTEE, COMMITTEE ON WAYS AND MEANS, U.S. HOUSE OF REPRESENTATIVES
- DEPUTY REPUBLICAN WHIP, U.S. HOUSE OF REPRESENTATIVES
- 82ND AVN BN (CBT) 82ND AIRBORNE DIVISION, TASK FORCE 1-508 PARACHUTE INFANTRY REGIMENT, MULTINATIONAL FORCE AND OBSERVERS (SINAI)
- ARMY AVIATOR, RANGER, SENIOR PARACHUTIST, AIR ASSAULT, RAF PARACHUTE TRAINING SCHOOL

Geoff Davis credits his West Point experience for shaping him as a leader. Indeed, he considered the Army his first real family.

Davis did not know his father growing up. His mother and biological father separated when he was an infant. In hopes of achieving stability, she married a man who turned out to be of poor character. At 6 years old, Davis's first fight was stepping between his mother and a violent drunken stepfather who was physically and verbally abusive to both of them. As a boy, he had to spend much of his time living with relatives due to the problems at home. After the stepfather's sudden death, his mom was able to get her life in order and they moved to Pittsburgh, Pennsylvania.

At 15, he went to work as a janitor at a local hospital to help pay the family bills. It was in this period that his desire to attend West Point began to take root. Because of weak academics, he was not hopeful for admission. One day the first of several turning points came while mopping the floor in the hospital gift shop. An elderly lady who was the volunteer cashier struck up a conversation and asked him what he was going to do after high school. Davis replied that he wanted to attend West Point, but would likely end up enlisting because his grades were not strong.

The elderly woman suggested that he ought to speak with her husband, the legendary General Matthew Ridgway, who had commanded the 82nd Airborne Division in the Normandy Invasion. Two encounters with General Ridgway in November of 1975 were life changing. The visit was inspirational for the young man from the broken family background. General Ridgway decided to personally recommend Davis to the Academy. He saw what Davis did not see in himself: leadership potential.

That same month, Davis visited West Point for the first time and met his Admissions Officer, then Captain Ed Sullivan. Captain Sullivan was candid Davis was not competitive for admission directly to West Point, but he might be able to attend the West Point Prep School, get his grades up, particularly his math grades, then attend West Point.

After returning home, his mother found a nun, Sister Mary Thomas, who was a mathematics professor at nearby LaRoche College, a small local school. Calculus terrified young Davis. Sister Mary Thomas walked him through his first solo solution to a problem set he had repeatedly failed in high school. He got it correct, to his utter dismay. Then the sister shared some life-changing words: "Geoffrey, always remember that big problems are just lots of small problems put together."

Big problems are just lots of small problems put together. Solve the little ones over and over, and the sum will be solutions to the seemingly insurmountable challenges he would later face. It helped him lead in the Army, in business and in the United States government. He later taught that same principle to every person he ever mentored or led, and his teams have always been renowned for their agility and adaptability in gaining success crisis situations.

Davis likes to share that the two biggest things that he gained from his West Point experience were first encountering the reality of Jesus Christ and choosing to follow Him, and second meeting his future wife of 30 years, Pat. Together they have raised six children – three are now successful professionals and they have three younger kids still at home.

As a Firstie, he wrestled over the decision to either become an aviator or be a Ground Combat Arms Officer. After his summer experience with 10th Special Forces Group (Airborne) in Germany, where he saw the actual ground that the Americans had liberated in World War II, combined with his professional research, he decided to branch Armor in the Cavalry Scout track.

© WPLPOC

>>> Spotlight

On June 1, 1792, Kentucky was admitted as the 15th state in the Union. Kentucky did not succeed from the Union during the Civil War but was considered a "border" state with the population divided in sympathies. Kentucky now has more than four million residents. Its two largest metropolitan areas are Louisville and Lexington.

Davis as Chairman Human Resources Subcommittee, U.S. House of Representatives.

President Obama in the Oval Office signing legislation initiated by Davis

Courtesy Congressman Davis

Davis loved the rugged training and service in the Army. Winter Ranger School was a defining experience for him, further developing him as a leader able to function in demanding, unstructured, and fluid environments. All this came to benefit him in later military service and Congressional leadership roles. Following graduation from the Ranger program, Army Aviation and its potential enamored Davis so he applied to flight school and attended the next year.

> **"ALWAYS REMEMBER THAT BIG PROBLEMS ARE JUST LOTS OF SMALL PROBLEMS PUT TOGETHER."**

After graduating from flight school, First Lieutenant Davis was assigned to the 82nd Airborne Division and served as an Assault Helicopter Flight Commander. Later he was selected to run Flight Operations for the United States Army Aviation group as part of the 17 nation coalition the Multinational Force and Observers, Peace Enforcement mission between Israel and Egypt in the Sinai.

After additional assignments, Davis decided to leave active duty to raise his young family. He had committed to God to be the father he never knew himself to his own children. He was successful in the private sector and ran his firm, Capstone, Inc., until answered the call to serve again after the 9/11 attacks.

In 2002, Davis ran for Congress but was narrowly defeated. During his concession speech in November 2002, Davis announced that he was running again. A tough two-year campaign culminated in a 2004 victory over a Hollywood-backed celebrity.

Nearly a quarter century later after graduating from West Point, Davis was elected to the United States House of Representatives representing Kentucky's 4th District. Initially, he served as a Member of the House Armed Services Committee and the House Financial Services Committee. He authored legislation that protected our troops from financial predators and was instrumental in passing Warrior Pay for troops who were serving multiple deployments due to the increasing Operations Tempo of the Wars. These and many other bills he wrote were enacted into law.

He was selected to serve on the prestigious Committee on Ways and Means and became the Chairman of the Human Resources Subcommittee. He had a special passion for this work because of his own challenging upbringing. His subcommittee enacted reforms across a broad spectrum of entitlement programs and focused on fixing broken processes. He led a coalition that passed the first-ever Data Standardization legislation to reduce waste and cost while improving services across all non-Medicare and non-Social Security entitlement programs. In addition, he passed sweeping Regulatory reform ideas like the REINS Acts, to require Congressional Accountability for agencies that seek to impose costly rules on citizens and communities. He was known as a bridge builder across party lines, looking for pragmatic solutions that fit his conservative principles. And all the time, the words of his high school math tutor echoed in his mind, "Big problems are just lots of little problems put together."

By 2012, he had two young sons and a daughter entering their teen years who had known nothing but the intense pace of federal service. Having grown up with a dysfunctional family environment, he sought to provide a better family environment for his children. In 2012, Congressman Davis announced he would not run for office again and would return to Kentucky to spend more time with his family. After rejoining the private sector, Davis went back to work in the technology and data analytics field, as well as providing management consulting services.

Congressman Michael Pompeo, USMA 1986

- MEMBER OF THE U.S. HOUSE OF REPRESENTATIVES, STATE OF KANSAS
- HARVARD UNIVERSITY LAW DEGREE/EDITOR OF HARVARD LAW REVIEW
- CHIEF EXECUTIVE OFFICER, THAYER AEROSPACE
- PRESIDENT, SENTRY INTERNATIONAL
- SERVED IN 2ND ARMORED CAVALRY REGIMENT IN COLD WAR GERMANY

Photo: NARA

>>> Spotlight

KANSAS

Kansas was admitted as the 34th state in the Union on January 29, 1861, as a "slave-free" state. Mike Pompeo was elected as a member of the United States House of Representatives from Kansas in 2010 and again in 2012.

In a list of all the things Mike Pompeo has ever done or will ever do, one fact jumps off the page – the same fact gives Mike Pompeo membership in a club that has existed for more than two centuries, yet consists of only 210 members.

But before we dwell on that accomplishment, let's first take a brief look at the rest of Pompeo's life, starting with the present. Today, Pompeo is a member of the United States House of Representatives. He represents the 4th District of Kansas – 9,531 square miles that are home to more than 177,000 Kansas families. Total population of the district Pompeo serves is just more than 713,000 Kansans.

What motivated Pompeo to want to represent his fellow Kansans in Congress was a profound love for America. Three decades earlier, that love inspired a teenaged Pompeo to set his sights on attending the United States Military Academy at West Point. And it was that same passion for his country that guided Pompeo's actions when he graduated from West Point with an engineering degree and began active duty in the United States Army. Following the lead of a couple of early mentors, Pompeo was assigned to the 2nd Armored Cavalry. Stationed in Germany, his regiment patrolled several hundred kilometers of the border between East Germany and Czechoslovakia and the then-West Germany.

In addition to learning pretty much all a person would ever care to know about armored tank strategy and maintenance, Pompeo had the good fortune of serving with a Platoon Sergeant who, to this day, is still one of the most remarkable people Pompeo has ever known. The insights that Sergeant First Class Pretre shared back then with a young Pompeo are still compelling influences on the decisions and actions of Congressman Pompeo today.

The wisdom of Sergeant First Class Pretre was just part of Pompeo's real-world schooling. Just across the border, Pompeo witnessed firsthand what happens to people when personal freedom and free enterprise are removed from their lives. He saw the drudgery and futility in the eyes of an entire population. And soon after he returned stateside, Pompeo, along with the rest of us, saw the tearing down of the Berlin Wall and with it the collapse of what Ronald Reagan had so rightly called an "evil empire."

Shortly after Pompeo's next assignment at Fort Carson, Colorado, America's armored forces were on the verge of a massive drawdown, and it was time for Pompeo to trade his tank service manuals for a set of law books. He applied for admittance into Harvard Law School and, to this day, is convinced that some kind of affirmative action mandate must have led to his quick acceptance. In Pompeo's words, "Somebody must have told Harvard Law School that they had to admit at least one Army guy every year regardless of how much tank grease he had under his fingernails."

At Harvard, one thing became immediately evident: The only way to succeed there was coincidentally the only way Pompeo was capable of trying to succeed – committing absolutely to the task at hand. Working that hard enabled Pompeo not only to pass his courses and eventually the bar exam, but also to serve as editor of the Harvard Law Review.

Although much was new, some of Pompeo's subjects were more like refresher courses in lessons he'd begun years before. Pompeo was reminded, for instance, that there were lots of people out there who were smarter than he was, but that dedication and commitment to the mission – grinding it out – could fill that gap. Pompeo discovered that the importance of honor is not restricted to the military. Honor matters everywhere. And without it, nothing matters. Finally, Pompeo was reminded that leadership skills come in many forms and that large goals are typically not accomplished by one person applying a specific kind of excellence. What most often leads to success, he discovered, are courageous leaders leading with conviction.

Pompeo spent the first three years after law school at the firm of Williams & Connolly in Washington, D.C. He was surrounded by brilliant people who were very good at what they did and who worked very hard to be that good. It would take an extraordinary opportunity to draw Pompeo away from such a stimulating environment. However, it wasn't long before three of Pompeo's closest friends from his West Point days – Mike Stradinger, Ulrich Brechbuhl, and Brian Bulatao – came to him with just such an opportunity.

It was Pompeo's chance to be an entrepreneur. It meant the exhilaration of free enterprise from a driver's seat he would share with three of the best people he knew. And on top of it all, it meant that he would move to Kansas – the state was where his mother was born and where he as a boy had spent nearly every summer on a farm surrounded by more acres of wheat than any other place on Earth and by almost as many of Pompeo's cousins.

Pompeo and his three West Point buddies named their new company Thayer Aerospace in honor of Colonel Sylvanus Thayer, the father of their alma mater. The young men didn't know a lot about running a business, but they soon discovered that much of what they'd learned at West Point would help them lead their young company to success. Within 10 years, they had created more than 400 good-paying jobs.

Pompeo's next opportunity came in the form of Sentry International, an oil and gas equipment company in need of a President. At Sentry, Pompeo gained additional insight from the small business perspective. Here, his belief in free enterprise was further shaped as he competed in a tough oil and gas industry that was encumbered with an endless muddle of government interference. The more Pompeo saw the more he realized two things: (1.) America's biggest hindrance to success is big government; and (2.) Big government will never shrink itself.

To turn the tide would take a lot of hard work – a lot of grinding – and the commitment of men and women who knew what commitment was. The time and circumstances to reenter service to the country were both right.

Pompeo announced he would run for office and seek election to the United States House of Representatives. The ensuing campaign became the crucible where Pompeo's beliefs were reshaped and forged into a set of objectives and a workable plan for reaching them. At the heart of Pompeo's plan was the kind of hard work and self-reliance that gives every American the opportunity for success, however it's defined. The content and even the style of the campaign were built around the values Pompeo had been taught at West Point: Always answer the question, be to the point about it, give them the whole truth, and when others rest, it's time to work some more.

On January 5, 2010, Pompeo was sworn in to office as the Congressman from the 4th Congressional District of Kansas. He was reelected in November of 2012 and continues to work every day to do precisely what he told the voters he would do.

Beyond all of this, however, it's Pompeo's personal life that provides him with gratification beyond any other. His wife, Susan, is a true partner in every sense. Their son, Nicholas, is the joy of their lives. Pompeo is first to admit that without this strong family, he could not begin to be the person that he is.

West Point graduate, Army veteran, Harvard Law School graduate and former editor of the *Harvard Law Review*, successful businessman and leader of two flourishing companies, second-term member of the United States House of Representatives, dedicated family man – a pretty full life for a guy who is not yet 50. It's a lot of success in a lot of areas, any one of which would make Pompeo noteworthy and maybe even famous in some circles. And yet none of them are what puts Pompeo in the club of 210 extraordinary people throughout history.

That distinction comes from the fact that Pompeo didn't just get accepted into West Point – only one in 10 applicants makes that cut. And it's not because he maintained a 4.0 grade point average. And it's not because he graduated with honors. It's because he graduated first in his class. Not just grades, but demonstrated leadership and self-discipline, along with physical skill, put him at the very top of his class of just more than 1,000 cadets.

Ask Pompeo about that accomplishment today, and he will tell you that the experience was invaluable in one way above all others: It taught him what it takes to be number one. It made him both a dreamer and a realist. That's a rare combination, and one seemingly custom made for leadership in the days that lie ahead for all of us who call America our home.

Charlie Ruppert, Mark Conroe, and John Shimkus at a FCA retreat in upstate New York.

Congressman John Shimkus, USMA 1980

- MEMBER OF THE U.S. HOUSE OF REPRESENTATIVES, 1996-PRESENT
- LIEUTENANT COLONEL, USAR (RETIRED)
- INFANTRY, AIRBORNE RANGER-QUALIFIED
- MBA, SOUTHERN ILLINOIS UNIVERSITY EDWARDSVILLE

At the White House with his wife, Karen, and President and Mrs. Bush.

>>> Spotlight

ILLINOIS

Illinois was admitted as the 21st state in the Union on December 3, 1818, and is the fifth most populous state in the United States. John Shimkus was elected to the United States House of Representatives from Illinois in 1996 and has been a member of Congress since January 3, 1997.

John Shimkus is a 16-year veteran of the United States House of Representatives, currently representing the 19th district of Illinois. He served five years in the active Army, three of which were in the former West Germany. His life revolves around his church, his family, and public service. West Point did as advertised in taking a nice young man and turning him into a leader of character for service to the nation.

He was born February 21, 1958, to Gene and Kathleen Shimkus. His dad was a telephone lineman, and his mother stayed at home raising seven children. Collinsville is a blue-collar bedroom community on the bluffs of the American Bottoms just east of St. Louis, Missouri. At Holy Cross Grade School and Collinsville High School, he got good grades, played sports, and was involved in student government.

When his father brought him a book on the service academies, Shimkus was drawn to the physical beauty and history of West Point. He was enthralled with graduates, such as Grant, Lee, Patton, and MacArthur. He later received a nomination to the Academy from Congressman Mel Price, then-Chairman of the House Armed Services Committee.

Shimkus's first flight was to New York City to attend cadet basic training, commonly known as "Beast Barracks." Although he was physically prepared, nothing could have prepared him mentally for "beast," but he endured. Much attention was given to the Class of 1980, as it was the first class with women. Their story, commitment, and struggle is forever etched in his mind. They were true pioneers.

He struggled academically for the first two years, but improved the last two. Shimkus took advantage of the many activities offered at the Academy, even playing junior varsity baseball as a Yearling, taking jumps with the sport parachute club, running the Jersey Shore Marathon, and bowling with the bowling club. Shimkus enjoyed trying new things, but his most consistent and passionate activity revolved around the Cadet Chapel programs, and he became an officer with the Fellowship of Christian Athletes his Firstie year.

West Point provided more opportunities than a boy from the Midwest could ever dream. In just one summer, Shimkus attended Cadet Troop Leader Training at Fort Benning, Jungle School in Panama, and was an exchange cadet in Bolivia. Upon his return to the Academy, he was able to observe another first when his classmate, Vince Brooks, was named the first African-American First Captain in the Academy's history.

Shimkus felt if he was going to be in the Army, he might as well do "real soldiering," compelling him to choose the Infantry Branch, and it was back to Fort Benning. While at Benning, Shimkus completed Airborne, Infantry Basic, and Ranger Schools. He still considers graduating from Winter Ranger one of his proudest accomplishments. He is thankful to his classmates and Ranger buddies for getting him through.

Single and adventuresome, Shimkus chose to be stationed in southern Germany. He was able to travel throughout Europe and had a memorable trip to the Middle East. As a mechanized Platoon Leader, he was stationed in Bamberg, FRG. The Cold War was raging, and the mission of protecting Western Europe was prevalent. Marktrevwidts was the town his unit was to defend. He knew and still knows the order: first the Czechs, then the East Germans, and if the unit was still standing, the Soviets would arrive.

After his tour, it was back to Benning for the Advance Course. In the United States, the battle lines felt far away. Shimkus looked to other interests and started thinking about a chance to teach. But first he had a commitment to complete, so he was sent to Fort Ord, California, to help the 7th ID transition to a new light division. He loved the Monterey Bay area, and met his soon-to-be wife, Karen, at the local Lutheran Church. He left Fort Ord to get his California Teaching Certificate from Christ College (now Concordia University) in Irvine, California.

Shimkus was asked to return close to his home to teach at Metro East Lutheran High School in Edwardsville, Illinois. Working at this small Christian school was challenging, as he taught six periods and four different classes. Being nimble on your feet is a requirement for teaching high school and was a great preparation for public policy debates. After marriage, Karen joined him the second year, and they set up a home in Collinsville.

The military ethos of "lead by example" and "know your subject" was never far from Shimkus's mind. He self-identified as a Republican because of Reagan's successful peace-through-strength position, the benefits of economic freedom, and the respect for life. While teaching government and history, he would require his students to observe local government in action. The one-party domination of local government was not impressive to Shimkus, who believed that competition was needed, and he decided to join the fray.

An unsuccessful bid for county board was followed by a successful campaign for Collinsville Township Board. From there, Shimkus became Madison County Treasurer, the only Republican countywide official, then the first to be reelected in 50 years. He ran for the United States House of Representatives in 1992 and lost but followed up by winning an open seat in 1996.

Shimkus received a master's of Business Administration from Southern Illinois University-Edwardsville in ceremonies in the summer of 1997.

His family grew, too, with son David arriving in 1993, Joshua in 1995, and Daniel in 1999. When asked, he always responds that the most difficult challenge in serving in Congress is the separation from his family. Many days and nights are spent in Washington, D.C., while others are spent in a continually expanding geographical district in southern Illinois.

He believes service to the nation is service to the nation, whether in the halls of Congress, at the Hohenfells Training area in Germany, or at home.

Shimkus's district is fiscally and socially conservative, and he is proud to be their vote in Congress. He serves on the Energy and Commerce Committee, which has broad jurisdictions that he enjoys. Whether it is the challenges of the nation's health care system, a national energy policy, the new digital world, or the challenges of the use of toxic chemicals and their waste, you can always find Shimkus in the middle of these discussions.

As any officer knows, there are always additional duties, some welcome and some not so much. Shimkus has enjoyed chairing the Baltic Caucus and being a delegate to the NATO Parliamentary Assembly. He is a fourth-generation Lithuanian-American who values freedom. The falling of the Iron Curtain has allowed many former captive nations to experience and profit from freedom. Shimkus stood in Vilnius Square to listen to President George W. Bush welcome Lithuania into NATO.

Shimkus is also loyal to his alma mater. As a reservist, he taught intercession. As a member of Congress, he has returned many times to speak to cadets and always welcomes them in his office in Washington, D.C. In addition, he serves as Vice Chairman of the Board of Visitors.

Jinx (Rick Jenkins), John Shimkus, (John) Agoglia, and Brownie (David Brown) at Saddam's Palace in Baghdad.

First Lady Laura Bush introduces Brett Guthrie shortly before being elected to Congress.

Congressman Brett Guthrie, USMA 1987

- **MEMBER, U.S. HOUSE OF REPRESENTATIVES, 2ND DISTRICT OF KENTUCKY**
- **VICE PRESIDENT, TRACE DIE CAST, INC.**
- **FIELD ARTILLERY OFFICER, 101ST AIRBORNE DIVISION, FORT CAMPBELL, KENTUCKY**
- **YALE UNIVERSITY, MASTER'S IN PRIVATE AND PUBLIC MANAGEMENT**

Brett Guthrie grew up in a typical middle class home in Alabama, attended West Point, served as an Army Officer, then helped grow a family business in Kentucky for 18 years before he was elected as a member of the United States House of Representatives. The incredible path that took him to the halls of Congress wove through the Gothic granite halls of West Point, and he credits West Point as having given him opportunities that he could never have imagined.

Guthrie was born February 18, 1964, in Florence, Alabama, to Lowell and Carolyn Guthrie. He was one of four brothers to Greg, Chris, and Kent. At that time one of the best opportunities in his hometown for a kid graduating high school was to start working in the auto industry and spend a career working in the same role with a pension upon retirement after 30 years, which is exactly the path that his father had chosen. His father worked in the auto industry as a union employee working for Ford Motor Company in Sheffield, Alabama; however,

during Guthrie's senior year in high school, Ford closed the plant and laid off 1,000 employees to outsource those jobs overseas. This unfortunate event and its implications on Guthrie's family and hometown would have a major impact on Guthrie's world vision and on his father's future.

Fortunately, prior to the plant closing, Guthrie's father had worked hard to educate himself, attending college at night while working full time and raising a family. When the factory closed, he and all his friends were unemployed and there were no trade jobs available in the area. The entire town suffered and those who hadn't educated themselves had few opportunities available.

His father moved to Bowling Green, Kentucky, and became an entrepreneur, starting a tool company, called Trace Die Cast, to distribute and sell to the major auto manufacturers. At the same time as the Ford factory was closing in Alabama, Guthrie was accepted to the University of Northern Alabama and started as a fresh-

man in 1982. Ronald Reagan had recently been inaugurated President in 1981, the Soviet Union was embroiled in a war in Afghanistan, and the Reagan revolution had inspired an era of patriotism, optimism, and a significant defense buildup. It was at this time that Guthrie was inspired to attend West Point and received his nomination from Congressman Ronnie Flippo. He was accepted to West Point in 1983 and entered with the Class of 1987. The entire focus of all studies and training during the 1980s was preparation for a European battlefield against the Soviet Union. A number of Guthrie's mentors were Artillery Officers, and they convinced him the most important strategic position on the battlefield was the Artillery Officer, and Guthrie was commissioned as an Artillery Officer.

Upon graduation, Guthrie chose the elite 101st Airborne Division at Fort Campbell, Kentucky, near his father's new home in Bowling Green, Kentucky. After attending Field Artillery Officer Basic Training, Guthrie arrived at Fort Campbell in 1988. While

visiting his grandmother in Bowling Green in 1989, he met Beth Clemmons (they were married in Bowling Green in 1990). The Berlin Wall fell in 1989 and the military started a significant downsizing as Congress sought to achieve a "Peace Dividend" after the 45-year Cold War ended so peacefully and suddenly. Guthrie expected the future for his class remaining in the Army to be peaceful and boring, with the collapse of the only other Superpower. With his father's company, Trace Die Cast, now thriving, he chose to leave the downsizing military to join his father's growing company, which at that time had 70 employees in July 1990.

Guthrie started business with his father at Trace Die Cast and worked for five years before attending business school. He attended Yale School of Management and graduated with a master's in Public and Private Management in 1997. Guthrie and Beth returned to Bowling Green and started their family with three children: Caroline (born in 1993), Robby (1995), and Elizabeth (1998). Guthrie also began

>>> Spotlight

On June 1, 1792, Kentucky was admitted as the 15th state in the Union. Kentucky did not succeed from the Union during the Civil War but was considered a "border" state with the population divided in sympathies. Kentucky now has more than four million residents. Its two largest metropolitan areas are Louisville and Lexington.

Congressman Guthrie meeting with farmers to discuss the drought and the Farm Bill.

getting involved in local politics. After his father's experience with the factory closing in 1982 and now involved in managing a manufacturing company, Guthrie became passionate about adult vocational training and learning. Guthrie was elected to Kentucky State Senate in 1998 and served as the State Senator for the 32nd District in Kentucky. He was also the Chair of the Transportation Committee and served on the Economic Development, Tourism, and Labor Committee, as well as the Education Committee. Trace Die Cast grew and helped create jobs in the district, growing from 70 employees when Guthrie joined the company in 1900 to more than 400 employees by 2008. In 2008, after living in Kentucky for two decades, managing a growing business, and participating in state politics, Guthrie was asked to run for Congress to fill a vacant seat when the incumbent retired.

Despite the Berlin Wall falling in 1989 and the downsizing of the Army that followed, the world had not become a more peaceful place as had been hoped. In fact, his class

had been involved in countless operations in Kuwait (Operation Desert Storm), Bosnia, Afghanistan, and Iraq. Guthrie felt compelled to serve and was anxious to get involved in national and international issues, and ran as a Republican for the 2nd Congressional District. Despite the Democratic Party spending considerably, Guthrie won his first election by a large margin in 2008 followed by reelections in 2010 and 2012. He has served on both the House Committee on Education and the Workforce and the House Energy and Commerce Committee. In 2013, he will serve on both committees simultaneously, a rare and distinguished honor due to his work and success on both committees.

In his role as a member of Congress, he has had the opportunity to work with several classmates and other West Point graduates on national security related issues, particularly in regards to the wars in Iraq and Afghanistan. He has a tremendous respect for classmates and all soldiers who have served for the past 25 years, making great sacrifices for the country.

Given his family experiences and his experience in state economic development, he strongly believes that government can set the conditions for people to have upward mobility by providing vocational and educational opportunities. While it wasn't easy for his father to attend school at night while raising a family and working a full-time job in the factory, that education allowed him to later build a successful business, even after the economy had take a turn for the worse. Guthrie's grandparents, who grew up in a tiny house in Alabama, would be proud of the upward mobility that their family has achieved and would be proud of the lives that their great-grandchildren now live, much more than simply the material wealth that they have built. Guthrie sees his role in Congress as helping to shape United States policy to allow upward mobility and opportunities for hard working Americans to grow and prosper.

He believes that many leaders in America are failing future generations by not addressing issues now, harming the

country's future in order to protect their own reelections. Americans for the first time are pessimistic about the future. Economic policies are putting a burden on future generations that will limit opportunities and upward mobility, and he believes we need to make difficult decisions now. And that is the leadership style that he learned at West Point: "doing the harder right over the easier wrong." One of his favorite stories is of President Lyndon Johnson, when his staff was recommending he not take on the issue of civil rights because it wasn't popular and wasn't going to make him popular. "Then why am I here?" was President Johnson's reply.

Guthrie never envisioned serving in Congress, but attending West Point provided endless opportunities for him that he never envisioned, including the opportunity to serve in Congress. He now proudly serves the people of Kentucky and the United States as a member of Congress.

One of only three career United States Army Officers to serve as United States Secretary of State, Alexander Haig attained the very rare distinction of being a highly decorated Infantry Officer who also reached the highest levels of political power. Although he is best remembered for his high military rank and great prominence during the attempted assassination of President Ronald Reagan, Haig was a genuine combat hero whose battlefield exploits and outstanding leadership alone would have marked him as one of West Point's finest sons. His entire adult life represented selfless service to the nation, but the moment for which he will forever be remembered was when he stepped forward to calm the nation following the attempted assassination of President Ronald Reagan in March 1981.

Born the middle child to a lawyer and homemaker, Alexander M. Haig and Regina A. (Murphy) Haig, near Philadelphia, Pennsylvania, on December 2, 1924, young Alexander's happy childhood was marred by tragedy when his father died of cancer when he was only 10. Raised in a devout Catholic family (his younger brother, Frank R. Haig, became an accomplished Jesuit Priest and university professor), Haig had a solid high school record and briefly attended the University of Notre Dame in 1943, but subsequently sought admission to the United States Military Academy. Graduating 213th in a graduating class of 310 with the West Point Class of 1947, he was commissioned as an Infantry Officer, and his first assignment was with the Army of occupation in postwar Japan.[1] Attracting the favorable notice of General of the Army Douglas MacArthur, Haig performed very well on his staff and remained with MacArthur through the early stages of the Korean War. While MacArthur commanded all United Nations forces in Korea, Haig was responsible for maintaining his operational map. Haig's duties required evening briefings on the war and these responsibilities provided him great exposure to the Senior Officers leading the Korean War. Following service for MacArthur, Haig became the Aide-de-Camp to General Edward Almond, Commanding General X Corps. During his time with Almond, Haig observed and participated in numerous combat actions for which he earned two Silver Stars, the Bronze star for Valor, and two Air Medals.[2]

Following his time in Korea, Haig returned to the United States and held a number of stateside command and staff assignments appropriate for a Junior Officer, including a tour as a Company Tactical Officer at West Point from 1953 to 1955. After additional stateside duties, he attended and graduated from the Naval War College in 1960 and Georgetown University in 1961, for which he received the master's of Science degree. With this additional education, Haig held a number of important positions in the Pentagon that exposed him to senior

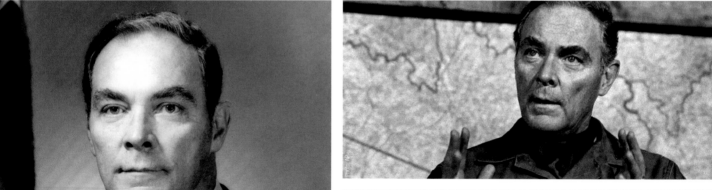

Secretary Alexander Haig, USMA 1947

- **U.S. SECRETARY OF STATE**
- **SUPREME ALLIED COMMANDER EUROPE**
- **WHITE HOUSE CHIEF OF STAFF**
- **DEPUTY NATIONAL SECURITY ADVISOR**
- **DISTINGUISHED SERVICE CROSS, SILVER STAR, PURPLE HEART**
- **HAIG ROOM IN THE JEFFERSON LIBRARY AT WEST POINT DEDICATED IN HIS HONOR**

Haig Grave at Arlington National Cemetery.

>>> Spotlight

The Department of State was formed in 1789 as the first federal United States agency to formulate United States foreign policy and was originally called "Department of Foreign Affairs." The Secretary of State is a Cabinet Member who reports in directly to the United States President. General Al Haig was appointed as the 59th United States Secretary of State in 1981 under President Ronald Reagan and served in this role from January 1981 from July 1982.

Courtesy: Department of State

leaders in the United States Army and Department of Defense, most significantly when he became Military Assistant to the Secretary of the Army in 1964 and Deputy Special Assistant to the Secretary and Deputy Secretary of Defense in 1964 and 1965.[3] The Secretary of Defense throughout these years was Robert S. McNamara.

After the years spent in the Pentagon and possessing a deep appreciation for how the Department of Defense operated at the highest level, Lieutenant Colonel Alexander Haig returned to the field Army and deployed to Vietnam with the 1st Infantry Division from 1966 to 1967. While commanding the famous 1st Battalion, 26th Infantry Regiment in Vietnam, Haig

demonstrated not only outstanding tactical leadership, but also tremendous personal heroism during the Battle of Ap Gu in March 1967. Upon learning that a significantly larger Vietcong force had surrounded two of his Infantry Companies, he flew by helicopter to the center of the fighting and his helicopter was downed by enemy fire. For two days, March 31 and April 1, 1967, Haig and his men battled an enemy force that outnumbered them by more than three to one, often resorting to hand-to-hand combat. Because of his extraordinary heroism during the fighting he earned the Distinguished Service Cross, the United States Army's second-highest award for valor. The official citation of the award, presented to him by the Commanding General

of all United States forces in Vietnam, General William Westmoreland, stated that Haig's actions led directly to 592 Viet Cong casualties.[4] During his year in Vietnam, Haig was promoted to Colonel and given a second combat command, an Infantry Brigade. After this very successful combat tour of duty, he returned once again to West Point, where he was assigned to the Corps of Cadets from 1967 to 1969. His first year he was the Regimental Tactical Officer of the 3rd Regiment of the United States Corps of Cadets and his second he became Deputy Commandant under fellow Big Red One Alumnus, General Bernard Rogers, who was Commandant.[5] General Rogers had been the Assistant Division Commander of the 1st Infantry Division while Haig was a Brigade Commander.

With another assignment to West Point complete, Colonel Haig was posted back to Washington, D.C., where he served in the White House for an extended period. While assigned there, Haig achieved one of the most rapid series of promotions in the history of the United States Army. He also was eyewitness to some of the most controversial periods in American history. Haig's first role was Military Assistant to National Security Advisor Henry Kissinger, but in early 1970, President Richard Nixon appointed him to Deputy Assistant to the President for National Security Affairs. In this capacity, he was intimately involved, along with Henry Kissinger, in the negotiation of the cease-fire talks with North Vietnam to end the Vietnam War. Haig clearly held the confidence of Richard Nixon and consequently rapid military advancement continued, along with his growing influence. Promoted to Brigadier General in September 1969 and Major General in March 1972, Haig skipped the rank of Lieutenant General entirely and instead advanced to the rank of full General. Following Senate confirmation of his appointment to become the 13th United States Army Vice Chief of Staff in October 1972, General Haig held this position from January to May 1973. With the resignation of H.R. Haldeman on April 30, 1974, General Haig, retired from active duty

IN MARCH 1972, HAIG SKIPPED THE RANK OF LIEUTENANT GENERAL ENTIRELY AND INSTEAD ADVANCED TO THE RANK OF FULL GENERAL.

and became the White House Chief of Staff from May 1, 1973, until September 1974.[6] Following a short continuance in office after President Nixon's resignation that August, Donald Rumsfeld replaced him as the White House Chief of Staff. General Haig then returned to active duty and assumed command of arguably the most important combatant command in the Department of Defense of that era, holding a position that actually comprised three roles: Supreme Allied Commander Europe (SACEUR); Commander of the North Atlantic Treaty Organization (NATO); and Commander in Chief United States European Command (CinCUSEUR). He remained in this position until his retirement from active duty in 1979.

Along with his wife, Patricia Fox Haig, whom he had married in 1950, he had three children, and Haig remained active politically and philanthropically to the final days of his life. By all accounts, their marriage was successful and it lasted until Alexander's death on February 19, 2010. Following his retirement from active duty, he served briefly in the corporate world and was named President and Director of United Technologies, but he returned to Washington, D.C., when President Ronald Reagan appointed him Secretary of State in 1981. It was during this assignment he uttered the phrase by which he is most remembered. After the assassination attempt on President Reagan on March 30, 1981, in an effort to reassure the nation he stated unequivocally to assembled reporters, "I am in control here." An effective if combative Secretary of State, Haig resigned on July 5, 1982, and returned to the corporate world. He ran for President in 1988 but failed to receive the Republican Party nomination. The United States Military Academy Association of Graduates awarded him the Distinguished Graduate Award in 1996.[7]

As an Army Officer, Haig demonstrated consistently competent leadership and bravery. As a public servant, he was unwavering supporter and defender of the nation. His ambition served him well and he channeled his extraordinary drive and talent in support of the best interests of the United States of America. Throughout his long and extremely successful career General Haig exemplified the principles of "Duty, Honor, Country."

Written by: Colonel Kevin W. Farrell, PhD (USA, Retired), USMA 1986.

HAIG ROOM
NAMED IN RECOGNITION OF THE LEADERSHIP AND GENEROSITY OF
GENERAL ALEXANDER M. HAIG, JR.
CLASS OF 1947
AND HIS WIFE, PATRICIA HAIG
VICE CHIEF OF STAFF, U.S. ARMY, 1973
WHITE HOUSE CHIEF OF STAFF, 1973-1974
SUPREME ALLIED COMMANDER, EUROPE, 1974-1979
U.S. SECRETARY OF STATE, 1981-1982

Haig Room at the Jefferson Library, West Point.

President Nixon with General Haig.

If not for one other notable graduate in the Class of 1829, General Joseph E. Johnston's military legacy may have been much different. The "Gamecock," as he was known for his appearance and feisty demeanor, was a tactically sound and intelligent commander during his career. Instead, as Robert E. Lee's classmate, Johnston found himself quite often living in the shadow of Lee, even though his own career was marked with bravery and distinction. Born in Farmville, Virginia, on February 3, 1807, Johnston entered West Point in 1825, along with Lee, another one of Virginia's native sons. Linking the two besides their home state and entrance into the Academy, was the fact that Johnston's father served under Lee's father, Henry "Lighthorse Harry" Lee, during the American Revolution. By all accounts, they were good friends at West Point, where Johnston graduated 13th out of 46 in the Class of 1829 behind Lee who graduated number two, and they basically remained friendly throughout their careers.

Both would achieve fame in the Civil War with only one other member of their class becoming a familiar name in that war, but Lee's fame would far surpass that of Johnston's and nearly every other Civil War Commander.[1]

Commissioned in the Field Artillery, Johnston distinguished himself repeatedly before the Civil War both in and out of combat. In combat during the Seminole War and the Mexican War, he earned multiple brevet promotions, along with multiple wounds in Mexico, while also participating in quelling unrest during the 1856 Kansas-Missouri border war. Out of combat, he put his engineer training to use as the Chief Topographic Engineer in the Department of Texas and supervisor of Western River Improvements. Eventually, he was promoted to Brigadier General and appointed Quartermaster General of the United States Army. He served in that position until Virginia seceded from the Union following the April 1861 attack on

JOHNSTON DIED IN WASHINGTON, D.C., FROM PNEUMONIA HE LIKELY CONTRACTED SEVERAL WEEKS EARLIER AT THE FUNERAL OF HIS MAIN WARTIME ADVERSARY, SHERMAN, WITH WHOM HE HAD ESTABLISHED A STRONG POST-WAR FRIENDSHIP.

Fort Sumter, when Johnston, like Lee, broke ties with the Union and set his fate with the Confederacy.[2]

It was Johnston whose performance stood out at the beginning of the war during the July 1861 Confederate victory at First Bull Run, then in opposing the early stages of the Union Peninsula Campaign in May 1862. It was also Johnston who was promoted to full General and the first to command the Army of Northern Virginia. To Johnston, however, the promotion was bittersweet as three other officers, Lee among them, were promoted

ahead of him because of a dispute in dates of rank. His vocal disagreement with the promotion order made Johnston appear petty and obsessive to many of his peers, as well as to Confederate President Jefferson Davis, with whom he would continually feud throughout the war. Unfortunately for Johnston, while defending Richmond during the Battle of Seven Pines, he was wounded on May 31, 1862. Davis placed Lee in charge of the Army of Northern Virginia, and so started Lee's meteoric rise to eternal fame over the course of the war. In the meantime, after six months of recovery, Johnston was assigned as Commander of the Confederacy's Department of the West in 1863 and then the Army of Tennessee. Again unfortunately for Johnston, the Confederacy erroneously considered this operational theater a sideshow and essentially a second-

Courtesy: C.S.A.

General Joseph Johnston, C.S.A., USMA 1829

- QUARTERMASTER GENERAL, U.S. ARMY
- COMMANDER, THE CONFEDERATE DEPARTMENT OF THE WEST
- COMMANDER, THE CONFEDERATE ARMY OF TENNESSEE
- MEMBER, U.S. HOUSE OF REPRESENTATIVES, VIRGINIA, 1879–81
- PRESIDENT GROVER CLEVELAND'S COMMISSIONER OF RAILROADS, 1885–91

General Johnston, C.S.A. statue in Dalton, Georgia

Gen'l R. E.

Photo: NARA

ary priority; rather, it was in the West where the Confederacy arguably sealed its failure as Johnston unsuccessfully tried to keep it afloat with few resources and less support than commanders in the East: Vicksburg fell in July 1863; next Chattanooga fell in November 1863; and finally Atlanta fell in September 1864. In another major dispute, Davis fired Johnston and replaced him with General John Bell Hood after Johnston opted to strategically withdraw his Army in the face of Union General William T. Sherman's advance through Georgia in order to slow the Union Army and preserve his forces to continue fighting. Eventually, Johnston commanded some of the last organized Confederate forces, but finally surrendered on April 26, 1865, at Durham Station, North Carolina, after ignoring directives from Davis to continue the fight. Ironically, it was Johnston and not Lee who received harsh criticism from the now irrelevant Davis for not continuing the fight, even though Lee had surrendered more than two weeks earlier.[3]

Johnston thus entered the post-war era greatly overshadowed by Lee's more visible and successful wartime record.

Where he was unable to surpass Lee's fame in uniform during the Civil War, Johnston outlived his classmate by 21 years and saw great success out of uniform. Although historians have typically been unfavorable to Johnston, and his own attempts to positively shape his wartime legacy in writing largely unsuccessful, Johnston's name and education did help him reach financial success after the war in both the railroad industry and the insurance business. Johnston also continued to serve the reconstructed nation admirably as a Virginia Congressman from 1879 to 1881, then as President Grover Cleveland's Commissioner of Railroads from 1885 until his death in 1891 at the age of 84. Ironically, Johnston died in Washington, D.C., from pneumonia he likely contracted several weeks earlier at the funeral of his main wartime adversary, Sherman, with whom he had

established a strong post-war friendship.[4] In the end, Joseph E. Johnston died a man who was still revered by his soldiers if not always by his former Confederate peers and superiors. He also died a man who had reconciled with his former adversaries, as well as many of his peers. Perhaps most importantly, however, Johnston died a man who finally began emerging from the shadow of his more famous classmate. As fellow Confederate General James Longstreet would later recall in a post-war interview:

"I am inclined to think that General Joe Johnston was the ablest and most accomplished man that the Confederate armies ever produced. He never had the opportunity accorded to others, but he showed wonderful power as a tactician and a commander. I do not think that we had his equal for handling an Army and conducting a campaign."[5]

General Johnston, C.S.A. Statue in Dalton, Georgia.

J. E. JOHNSTON

General Joseph Johnston, C.S.A. Statue in Dalton, Georgia.

>>> Spotlight

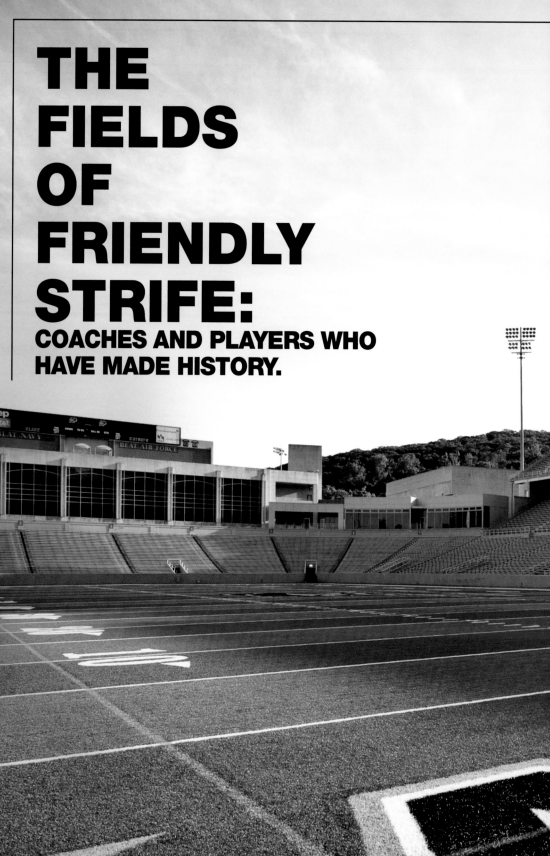

THE FIELDS OF FRIENDLY STRIFE:

COACHES AND PLAYERS WHO HAVE MADE HISTORY.

Since the end of World War I, West Point has had a rigorous physical program to complement every cadet's overall development. As one of the three key pillars of development – the academic and military pillars are the other two – physical and mental fitness are critical to success as a military officer. General Douglas MacArthur (USMA 1903) firmly believed this from his World War I experience, noting his opinion that those who took part in organized sports made the best officers. This belief led to arguably his greatest legacy to West Point, the emphasis on athletics and fitness.[1] MacArthur affirmed this belief in his famous "opinion on athletics" noted on the opposite page. Since every applicant must meet rigorous physical standards and pass a physical aptitude test prior to admittance, West Point as a whole has a very high percentage of top athletes per capita. In addition to a variety of physical education classes, all cadets must play an intercollegiate, club, or intramural sport and pass annual physical fitness tests. West Point intercollegiate teams and athletes have won many national championships and individual accolades, such as three national football championships and three Heisman Trophies. Club sports have been equally successful, including national championships in boxing, judo, orienteering, crew, cycling, triathlon, men's handball, and women's rugby to name a few. The disciplined cadets at West Point make it a favorite place for coaches to practice their craft, and West Point has had world-class coaches, such as Vince Lombardi, Bill Parcells, and Bobby Knight. This chapter highlights some of those athletes and coaches who have represented West Point on the fields of friendly strife.

"I don't look at myself as a basketball coach. I look at myself as a leader who happens to coach basketball."

–Coach Mike Krzyzewski, USMA 1969, Hall of Fame NCAA Basketball Coach and Winningest Coach in NCAA history

"Upon the fields of friendly strife, are sown the seeds, that on other fields, on other days, shall bear the fruits of victory."

–General Douglas MacArthur, written while he was Superintendent, 1919–22

People who work together will win, whether it be against complex football defenses, or the problems of modern society."

–Coach Vince Lombardi, Assistant Army Football Coach, 1949–54, and a Hall of Fame Football Coach

The team that makes the fewest mistakes wins."

–Brigadier General Robert Neyland, USMA 1916, Hall of Fame Coach of the Tennessee Volunteers

"The will to succeed is important, but what's more important is the will to prepare."

–Bobby Knight, Head Coach Army Basketball, 1965–71

"There is no substitute for victory."

–General Douglas MacArthur (his quote inscribed on the MacArthur Trophy, the NCAA Football National Championship Trophy)

There's no substitute for hard work. It is the price of success."

–Colonel Earl "Red" Blaik, USMA 1920, Army Hall of Fame Football Coach

"I have a secret and dangerous mission. Send me an Army football player."

–General George C. Marshall, Army Chief of Staff

Dennis Mahan Michie is synonymous with Army football. A son of West Point, Army football's "Founding Father" was born, raised, and is buried at West Point.

Michie's father, Peter Michie, was an 1863 graduate and Civil War veteran who was present at Appomattox for General Robert E. Lee's surrender. The older Michie then returned to West Point after the war and served as a permanent professor for more than 30 years. In that time, Dennis Michie was born April 10, 1870, raised on West Point, and entered the Academy in 1888. As a cadet, Dennis Michie organized and led the first Army football team. As Team Captain, he then enticed the Naval Academy to challenge West Point in a game for which the Naval Academy accepted. This challenge led to the first Army-Navy football game in 1890, which was held on the Plain at West Point and ended in a 24–0 Navy victory. Unbeknownst to both opponents, this game gave birth to one of the greatest rivalries in all of sports. Following his graduation in 1892, Michie

remained at West Point for a year as the first coach of the Army football team and finished with a record of 3–1–1.

Promoted to Captain, Michie fought in Cuba during the 1898 Spanish-American War. In the battle for Santiago, Michie was leading his men on a patrol along the San Juan River. While organizing his men for an assault, he was struck in the head by a bullet and Killed In Action on July 1, 1898. Sadly, the Navy quarterback and team Captain from the first Army-Navy game, Ensign Worth Bagley (USNA 1895), was also on May 11, 1898 – the only Naval Officer Killed In Action during the conflict. Michie's body was returned to West Point where he is currently buried in the West Point Cemetery. His father passed away three years later in 1901 and is also buried at West Point. A short distance up the hill from the cemetery, Michie's memory is immortalized by the West Point football stadium dedicated and named in his honor in 1924.

In 1999, *Sports Illustrated* ranked its worldwide "Top 20 Sports Venues of the

20th Century," and Michie Stadium cracked the top five at number three. The top five included: Yankee Stadium, Augusta National, Michie Stadium, Cameron Indoor Stadium (Duke University), and Bislett Stadium (Oslo, Norway). *Sports Illustrated* eloquently described the Army football experience:

UNBEKNOWNST TO BOTH OPPONENTS, THIS GAME GAVE BIRTH TO ONE OF THE GREATEST RIVALRIES IN ALL OF SPORTS.

"*Game day at West Point begins three hours before kickoff with the cadet parade on the Plain. It's a scene straight from The Long Gray Line, surpassed only by the view of the Hudson River from the west stands at Michie Stadium. The Corps of Cadets, seated together and dressed in gray and black, evokes memories of when Army was one of the most formidable of college football powers, and cannon blasts shake the*

76-year-old edifice to its foundation every time the Black Knights score. It doesn't matter in the least that national championships are no longer decided here."[1]

Since its initial construction in 1924, Michie Stadium has seen several expansions and now holds 38,000 spectators. Private donations have been instrumental in that process. The Kimsey Auditorium on the south side of the stadium offers skyboxes sponsored by Jim Kimsey, Founder of America Online, while the Hoffman Press Box, sponsored by Sybase founder Mark Hoffman, was added in 1998 and provides spectacular views of the Academy and its surroundings. More than a century after his death, Michie could never have imagined the football legacy he left behind as the "Father of Army Football." One thing is certain, however: Michie was inspirational and selfless as both an athlete and a leader.

Michie Stadium at West Point.

Captain Dennis Michie, USMA 1892

- FOUNDED ARMY FOOTBALL AND THE FIRST ARMY-NAVY GAME
- KILLED IN ACTION, SPANISH-AMERICAN WAR
- MICHIE STADIUM AT WEST POINT NAMED IN HIS HONOR
- BURIED AT THE WEST POINT CEMETERY
- MICHIE STADIUM RANKED AS ONE OF TOP THREE ATHLETIC VENUES IN THE WORLD BY *SPORTS ILLUSTRATED*, 1999

Michie Stadium at West Point.

Captain Dennis Michie's gravesite at West Point Cemetery.

According to a *New York Times* article on January 18, 1908: Had it not been for Captain Pierce it is doubtful if football would have recovered yet from the blows struck at it during the agitation for its abolition, when all educational forces seemed to be arrayed against it. The debt of gratitude that the lovers of the great gridiron sport owe to the former director of athletics at West Point is far greater than any, save a few, recognize.[1]

Such was the praise given to Captain Palmer E. Pierce, an 1891 graduate of West Point and an unlikely savior of college football, as the sport teetered on the brink of extinction. In hindsight, Pierce, who once also served as West Point's athletic director, clearly is one of the unsung heroes of college sports in general. Remarkably, this unlikely sports hero served the nation simultaneously as both a distinguished Army Officer and a fierce advocate of intercollegiate athletics as the National Collegiate Athletic Association's (NCAA) first President for 21 of its first 24 years of existence.

By 1905,college football had proven to be an extremely popular but dangerous sport with few rules, minimal equipment, and no standardization across institutions. In that year alone, 18 football players died on college football fields. Moreover, colleges and universities struggled with fully embracing such an enormously popular sport that provided entertainment, but had little academic purpose and seemed to undermine the true nature of American higher education.[2] In light of this struggle, many institutions largely favored abolishing football, while President Theodore Roosevelt, an ardent fan of the game, also warned academia to reform or abolish football.[3]

While teaching at West Point, Captain Palmer Pierce attended a December 1905 conference of America's 13 football-playing institutions convened to reform the sport. His significant influence at that conference convinced the other members of the need to regulate not only football, but college athletics in general, and encouraged the formation of the Intercollegiate Athletic Association of the United States (IAAUS) – the precursor to the NCAA. Pierce's leadership not only helped save football through greater regulation, standardization, and with a drastic decline in fatalities, but he was also an outspoken advocate of the inherent educational value of sports and

"THE DEBT OF GRATITUDE THAT THE LOVERS OF THE GREAT GRIDIRON SPORT OWE TO THE FORMER DIRECTOR OF ATHLETICS AT WEST POINT IS FAR GREATER THAN ANY, SAVE A FEW, RECOGNIZE.[1]" –*NEW YORK TIMES*.

for integrating college athletics into the academic structure of member institutions.[4] At the 1907 NCAA convention, he prophetically declared, "I firmly believe the [Association] will finally dominate the college athletic world."[5] Indeed, more than a century later, the NCAA is still the governing body regulating the entire college athletic world.

From 1906 through 1930, Pierce's NCAA Presidential span was interrupted twice for his combat service to the nation. In 1916, he was a member of the Punitive Expedition in Mexico against Pancho Villa, then during World War I, where he served in France as Commander of the 54th Infantry Regiment and Assistant Chief of Staff of the American Expeditionary Force. Earlier in his career, Pierce had also seen combat action during the Spanish-American War.

Pierce retired from the military as a Brigadier General in 1930 after 39 years in uniform, but he continued to serve his alma mater as President of the Association of Graduates from 1931 to 1934. He also ended his tenure as NCAA President, but not before institutionalizing and validating the NCAA's role as a legitimate organization within American higher education. Palmer died on January 17, 1940, and is buried in the West Point Cemetery.

One of the largest rooms at the NCAA headquarters in Indianapolis, Indiana, the Palmer E. Pierce Ballroom, honors his legacy and contributions to the world of intercollegiate athletics.

Brigadier General Palmer Pierce, USMA 1891

- ELECTED AS THE FIRST PRESIDENT OF THE NATIONAL COLLEGIATE ATHLETIC ASSOCIATION (NCAA)
- CREDITED WITH SAVING COLLEGE FOOTBALL FROM BEING ABOLISHED IN 1905
- SERVED IN SPANISH-AMERICAN WAR (PHILIPPINES), 1916 PUNITIVE EXPEDITION TO MEXICO, AND WORLD WAR I (FRANCE)
- DIRECTOR OF ATHLETICS, WEST POINT
- PRESIDENT, WEST POINT ASSOCIATION OF GRADUATES
- BURIED IN THE WEST POINT CEMETERY

Pierce's gravesite at West Point Cemetery.

MG Palmer Pierce (left)

Major General Abner Doubleday, USMA 1842

- FIRED THE FIRST SHOT OF THE CIVIL WAR FOR THE UNION ARMY AT THE BATTLE OF FORT SUMTER
- COMMANDED 1ST CORPS AT THE BATTLE OF GETTYSBURG
- CONSIDERED THE "FATHER OF THE GAME OF BASEBALL"
- DOUBLEDAY FIELD AT WEST POINT NAMED IN HIS HONOR

Major General Abner Doubleday (third from right) with his staff during the Civil War.

There are few inventors as synonymous with their creations as Abner Doubleday and baseball. Anyone, from the casual observer to the ardent athlete, knows that all roads lead to our American Mecca, the hallowed grounds of Elihu Phinney's pasture in Cooperstown, New York, where Doubleday, in 1839, invented what would become our national obsession and pastime. His portrait hangs prominently at the National Baseball Hall of Fame, and baseball fields across America are named in his honor, including The United States Military Academy's "Doubleday Field." The connection between Doubleday and baseball was established in 1907 and based on the findings of the Mills Commission. The commission, comprised of team owners, league presidents, Senators, and devout followers, had one task: determine the inventor of baseball. The commission's findings were based

solely on correspondence from Albert Graves, an eyewitness of questionable credibility. The conclusion was strongly influenced by the Commission Chairman, Albert Mills. Mills had been a longtime friend and admirer of Doubleday's. Unfortunately, there is no real evidence that links Doubleday to baseball. It is a myth. Interestingly, West Point records described Doubleday as "…rather averse to outdoor sports."[1] What is not a myth is Doubleday's military career and his service to the preservation of our nation. Doubleday had a part in some of the most important events of the American Civil War, including Fort Sumter and Gettysburg. Quiet and reserved, he prided himself in being morally virtuous, abstaining from drinking, smoking, or using profanity. His meticulous nature earned him the unflattering nickname "Forty-Eight Hours." He was, however, someone who remained calm in the heat of battle and did not

fluster easily.[2]

Doubleday was born in Ballston Spa, New York on June 26, 1819. As a child, he was fascinated by stories told and retold by his grandfather, a Revolutionary War veteran who served under General Anthony Wayne. This may have instilled in him a keen interest of military history and the sense of patriotism that would so dictate course of his life. His father, a New York Congressman, entered Doubleday into a Military Academy in nearby Cooperstown. Afterwards his graduation in 1838, he entered West Point. He graduated in 1842, 24th out of 56 cadets. His graduation class included John Pope, Daniel Harvey Hill, and James Longstreet. After receiving his commission he was stationed at Fort Johnson in North Carolina as a member of the 3rd Artillery Regiment.

He spent his years as a Lieutenant stationed in East Coast batteries and

took part in the military expedition to Mexico, where he first saw combat. By the summer of 1860, Captain Doubleday was stationed at Fort Moultrie near Fort Sumter, second in command under Major Robert Anderson. Charleston was at the center of southern secessionist fervor that grew more vocal after the election of Abraham Lincoln. The garrison moved to the safety of the newly renovated Fort Sumter on the 27th of December, a week after the Charleston Convention passed the Secessionist Ordinance. In the months that followed, Governor Pickens demanded the immediate evacuation of all Federal fortifications in South Carolina, including Fort Sumter. Major Anderson, as well as the Federal government, wanted a diplomatic resolution to diffuse the situation but Doubleday knew this would not be possible. The rebels, he later wrote, "needed blood and the prestige of a victory to rouse the enthusiasm of

Photo: NARA

>>> Spotlight

Courtesy: NPS

The first shot fired in the Civil War was fired by Confederate Lieutenant General post-tramatic growth Beauregard (USMA 1838) against Fort Sumter, South Carolina, on April 12, 1861, commanded by his former West Point instructor Union Commander Major Robert Anderson (USMA 1825). The first Union shot fired back at the rebels from Fort Sumter was fired by Captain Abner Doubleday (USMA 1842). Fort Sumter is now a National Park pictured here in Charleston Harbor.

Doubleday Field at West Point.

Photo: Charleston Sr./MO4

their followers, and cement the rising Confederacy."[3] At dawn on April 12th, rebel forces bombarded the fort. Captain Doubleday fired the first shot in defense of the Union. The next day, Anderson surrendered the fort and, after a brief ceremony, his men boarded a schooner headed to New York where they were treated like conquering heroes.

AT DAWN ON APRIL 12, REBEL FORCES BOMBARDED THE FORT. CAPTAIN DOUBLEDAY FIRED THE FIRST SHOT IN DEFENSE OF THE UNION.

After the surrender of Fort Sumter, Doubleday fought at Second Manassas, Antietam, Fredericksburg, and Chancellorsville. In March 1863, he was promoted to Major General, volunteer service. On the morning of July 1, 1863, Doubleday, five miles south of Gettysburg, was rushing 1st Corps northwest to support General Buford's Cavalry Division. Earlier in the morning, he had been given command of 1st Corps by General Reynolds, Commander of the Union Army's left wing made up of the 1st, 3rd, and 11th Corps. Buford's division was halting Confederate General A.P. Hill's advance, but were being pushed back. In his support of Buford, Doubleday defended against numerous assaults by Hill's corps and even took many prisoners. By late morning, General Shurtz's 11th Corps took position on 1st Corps's right flank as Ewell's corp attacked from the left. By mid-afternoon, General Longstreet's corps arrived and the Union line, hopelessly outnumbered and exhausted, fell back to Cemetery Ridge. 1st Corps regrouped and took position on the Union line's right flank, along Culp's Hill.[4] The Union line had held against a vastly superior force due, in great part, to Doubleday's gallantry and leadership. It should have been his finest moment. Unfortunately, General Meade, who had arrived just before midnight, saw things differently. He had little faith in Doubleday as an effective commander and blamed him for the Union collapse. Meade quickly ordered Major General John Newton to take command of 1st Corps and on July 5th, just two days after the battle, he sent Doubleday to report to the Adjutant-General of the Army In Washington; he was relieved of duty.[5] It was there that Doubleday spent the last two years of the war.

After the Civil War, Doubleday remained in the United States Army. He retired as a full Lieutenant Colonel in 1873. He died in 1893 at the age of 73. During his retirement, he wrote many books on the Civil War. His accounts are filled with critiques, both positive and negative, of many commanders he encountered. His most negative criticisms are understandably directed towards General Meade. His publications on the Battle of Gettysburg describe not only the events, but his justifications and excuses for his corps's retreat. To Doubleday, the events of the first day of the battle must have been as contentious as they were painful. Albert Mills would have been aware of this. Mills may have been motivated to credit Doubleday for inventing baseball, something he never wrote about or even mentioned, to give his old friend something that his military record could not: fame.

Written by: Robert Beres.

Robert Neyland is one of the greatest college football coaches in history. His career was spent transitioning back and forth between military assignments and college football assignments, but he excelled at both. He retired as a Brigadier General from the United States Army and was inducted in to the NCAA College Football Hall of Fame. He won one National Football Championship as an Army football player, then four more as a football coach for the University of Tennessee. Tennessee football fans nicknamed him "The General," a rank that he had actually earned in combat. *Sports Illustrated* named him as the defensive coordinator of its "All-Century College Football Team," and he is considered by many to be the greatest football coach of all time.

Neyland was born February 17, 1892, in Greenville, Texas. Growing up, he was a natural athlete and played multiple sports. He attended Texas A&M for one year, prior to receiving his nomination to West Point from Senator Sam Rayburn. He entered West Point in 1912 and became one of Army's all-time greatest athletes, H-lettering as a football lineman, a baseball pitcher, and a three-time brigade heavyweight boxing champion. He won 20 straight games as an Army pitcher, including all four victories over the Navy. He played football on the Army football team with other legendary cadets, including Dwight D. Eisenhower, Omar Bradley, and James Van Fleet. During his junior year, the 1914 Army football team went 9–0, winning the National Championship. He turned down a lucrative $3,500 contract with the New York Giants, in order to serve in World War I.

He was commissioned in the Corps of Engineers and served in France in World War I. He then attended Massachusetts Institute of Technology (MIT) for his graduate degree and returned to West Point as an Aide-de-Camp to Superintendent Douglas MacArthur, where he also served as assistant football coach. He married Peggy Fitch in 1923, and they had two sons – Robert and Lewis.

Florida and Tennessee evolved to become national powerhouses in football, both tracing the roots of their prominence back to West Point graduate coaches, General James Van Fleet (USMA 1915) and Neyland. Neyland and Van Fleet actually played together on the 1914 undefeated Army National Champion Football Team and went on to be General Officers leading troops in combat, as well as leading both Tennessee and Florida football teams.

Neyland left West Point in 1925 to join the University of Tennessee as an ROTC instructor and assistant football coach to the Tennessee Volunteers. He served as the head coach of Tennessee football three separate times (1926–34, 1936–40, 1946–52), achieving an overall record of 173 wins, 31 losses, and 12 ties with four National Championships (1938, 1940, 1950, 1951) with 112 shutouts and a total of six shutout seasons. During his first seven seasons as head coach, the Volunteers only lost two games with an incredible record of 61–2–5.

He left Tennessee in 1935, recalled to

Brigadier General Robert Neyland, USMA 1916

- "THE GENERAL" NCAA HALL OF FAME FOOTBALL COACH, UNIVERSITY OF TENNESSEE
- LED TENNESSEE TO FOUR FOOTBALL NATIONAL CHAMPIONSHIPS
- SERVED IN BOTH WORLD WAR I AND WORLD WAR II
- DECORATED FOR LEADING LOGISTICS FOR THE CHINA-BURMA-INDIA THEATER OF WAR, WORLD WAR II
- ARMY FOOTBALL PLAYER ON THE UNDEFEATED 1914 TEAM

Unveiling the nine-foot-tall bronze Neyland Statue at Neyland Stadium, University of Tennessee.

active duty by the Army to serve in the Panama Canal Zone, but he returned to Tennessee again to coach the following year. His 1938 National Championship season was won remarkably without giving up a single point all season to the competition – a record that will likely never be matched. It helped secure his position as one of the greatest defensive coaches in history.

He returned to the Army after Pearl Harbor in 1941 and served as the Chief Supply Officer in the incredibly challenging theater of China-Burma-India in World War II, where served under General "Vinegar Joe" Stilwell (USMA 1904). Given the nearly impossible task of supplying Stilwell's Army over the Himalayas, Neyland stepped up and helped win the war. He had been at West Point under General MacArthur when he had uttered the phrase, "Upon the fields of friendly strife, are sown the seeds, that on other fields, on other days, will bear the

fruits of victory," and the football player and coach had taken it to heart, helping to bear the fruits of victory for the United States. Brigadier General Neyland received the Distinguished Service Medal and Legion of Merit and was made an honorary member of the British Empire. He retired as a Brigadier General.

He returned to Tennessee in 1946 in the post-war years and resumed his career as head coach of Tennessee football. The first few years back were challenging, but he managed to cast any doubts of his outstanding leadership abilities when Tennessee won the National Championship in both 1950 and 1951. He retired after the 1952 season, but remained in the role of athletic director from 1952 until his death in 1962. In 1956, he was inducted in to the NCAA Football Hall of Fame.

He died at age 70 in New Orleans. In 1969, which was the centennial of college football, the Coaches Poll selected him

as the second best coach of all time after Notre Dame's Knute Rockne. (Rockne was killed in a plane crash after winning two consecutive National Championships – out of a total of five – in 1929 and 1930.)

The University of Tennessee football stadium bears the name "Neyland Stadium" not only because of Neyland's legacy, but because he personally designed the stadium and its planned expansions that took place after his death. A twice-life-size bronze statue of Neyland was unveiled in 2010 and is displayed in front of the stadium and the legacy. It is the fourth-largest stadium in the nation with a capacity to hold 102,455 people.

Early in his career, Neyland developed seven maxims that he made all his players and coaches memorize. They are still in place today at the University of Tennessee.

Neyland's Seven Maxim's of Football:

1. The team that makes the fewest mistakes will win.

2. Play for and make the breaks, and when one comes your way, score.

3. If at first the game – or the breaks – go against you, don't let up...put on more steam.

4. Protect our kickers, our QB, our lead, and our ball game.

5. Ball, oskie, cover, block, cut and slice, pursue, and gang tackle...for this is the winning edge.

6. Press the kicking game. Here is where the breaks are made.

7. Carry the fight to our opponent and keep it there for 60 minutes.

The Brigadier General Neyland Room at the Thayer Hotel is proudly dedicated by James A. Haslam, II.

Neyland Stadium at University of Tennessee, October 2011.

BRIGADIER GENERAL ROBERT NEYLAND
USMA 1916

COACH · INNOVATOR · WINNER
COMBAT ENGINEER FRANCE - WWI
CHIEF SUPPLY OFFICER, CHINA-BURMA-INDIA (CBI) THEATER-WWII
HEAD COACH UNIVERSITY OF TENNESSEE FOOTBALL
1926-1934, 1936-1940, 1946-1952
COACHED LAST TEAM IN NCAA HISTORY
TO HOLD EVERY OPPONENT SCORELESS
SIX UNDEFEATED SEASONS, FOUR NATIONAL CHAMPIONSHIPS
VOTED DEFENSIVE COORDINATOR OF THE 20TH CENTURY
BY SPORTS ILLUSTRATED

★ DUTY ★ HONOR ★ COUNTRY ★

**PROUDLY DEDICATED BY
JAMES A. HASLAM II**

Brigadier General Neyland Guest Room at the Thayer Hotel.

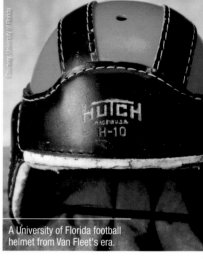

A University of Florida football helmet from Van Fleet's era.

General Clark, President-Elect Eisenhower, and General Van Fleet in Korea, December 1952.

General James A. Van Fleet, Sr., USMA 1915

- **COMMANDER, THE 8TH ARMY, KOREAN WAR**
- **HEAD COACH, FLORIDA GATOR FOOTBALL TEAM**
- **ONLY SON JAMES VAN FLEET, JR., USMA 1946, KILLED IN ACTION, KOREAN WAR**
- **ARMY FOOTBALL PLAYER ON THE UNDEFEATED 1914 ARMY FOOTBALL TEAM**

Football coaches often use wartime analogies to explain their football strategies, but few coaches actually have any professional training or practical experience in war. James Van Fleet was such a man. He led a national college football team to prominence and then commanded the entire Korean War. He is regarded as one of the greatest Generals in American history, which explains in part how he led Florida football to national prominence.

The University of Florida football team is now a national powerhouse. Students on campus might be familiar with Van Fleet Hall, the ROTC building named in honor of General James Van Fleet. But they might not be familiar with how he helped propel Florida football to national prominence in 1922. He led the Gators for two seasons to a 12–3–4 record before the Army reassigned him to the Panama Canal Zone. He set Florida off to what is now thought to be one of the best football programs in the country with four national titles.

Van Fleet fought for America in four wars. Prior to taking the role of head coach of Florida football, he had already led soldiers in two wars – Mexico and World War I. After, he again led soldiers in two additional wars – World War II and the Korean War.

It was no accident that he was a great football coach. He was a standout fullback

>>> Spotlight

In May of 1949, an illustration of Van Fleet's profile adorned the cover of *Time* magazine.

Courtesy: Time, Inc.

Van Fleet with President Kennedy.

He returned a war hero to peacetime and was assigned to teach tactics to University of Florida ROTC students. He coached Florida football for two winning seasons in 1923 and 1924 with a 12–3–4 record. In 1923, the Gators finished the season 6–1–2 overall and third out of 21 in the Southern Conference. The last game was a tremendous 16–6 victory in Alabama on a muddy, rain-soaked field, to upset a previously undefeated Crimson Tide team. The Gators also won their first-ever homecoming with a 19–7 win over the Mercer Bears. The 1924 season was even better, finishing 6–2–2 overall and second in the Southern Conference out of 22 teams. They rose to national prominence with ties against two powerhouses – Texas and Georgia Tech. The team also traveled farther than any other team in the nation.

Little did the players, family, fans, and fund-raisers know, but they were being led by a man who would later be called "America's greatest General" by the 33rd President of the United States.

During World War II, he led a regiment as a Colonel in the first wave on Utah Beach on D-Day during the invasion of France. Generals Eisenhower and Marshall both noted Van Fleet for his outstanding leadership on D-Day and promoted him to Brigadier General. He was given his own division – the 90th Infantry Division. He led the 90th Division under Patton's 3rd Army in relieving the 101st Airborne Division at Bastogne during the Battle of the Bulge. He was promoted to Corps Commander and led the thick of the fighting in the invasion of Germany.

Between World War II and Korea, he was sent to Greece to help fight the communist insurgency developing there, which he helped defeat. General Van Fleet was asked to lead U.N. and U.S. forces in Korean War in April 1951. He did so,

helped take the offensive, and regained lost ground. In April of 1952, his only son, Captain James Van Fleet, Jr., (USMA 1948), a B-26 pilot, went missing in action on only his fourth mission (a bombing mission). General Van Fleet was, suddenly and sadly, commanding a war that took the life of his only son. He remained in combat and did not return home to his wife, but rather rededicated himself to working harder to win the war and get his son and other POW/MIAs back home. General Van Fleet was ordered to not continue the attack in order to secure an armistice in 1953. His son was declared Killed In Action two years later. President Truman said General Van Fleet was "the greatest General we have ever had. I sent him to Greece, and he won the war. I sent him to Korea, and he won the war."

Van Fleet's military decorations make him one of the most decorated Generals in American military history. He fought in Mexico, World War I, World War II, and Korea. He was awarded three Distinguished Services Crosses, three Silver Stars, three Bronze Stars, three Purple Hearts, and the Combat Infantryman Badge. He was awarded the Distinguished Graduate Award from the West Point Association of Graduates.

LITTLE DID THE PLAYERS, FAMILY, FANS, AND FUND-RAISERS KNOW, BUT THEY WERE BEING LED BY A MAN WHO WOULD LATER BE CALLED "AMERICA'S GREATEST GENERAL" BY THE 33RD PRESIDENT OF THE UNITED STATES.

Courtesy: University of Florida

on the undefeated National Championship 9–0 Army football team in 1914 and was professionally trained at West Point in military strategy and tactics. He graduated in the famous Class of 1915, which included future Generals Eisenhower and Bradley and was called "the class the stars fell on."

He served under Major General John J. Pershing in Mexico fighting insurgents in the pursuit of Pancho Villa. He deployed to France in World War I in 1917 under General Pershing as a Battalion Commander of the 17th Machine Gun Battalion. He was wounded after being decorated twice for valor with two Silver Stars.

Blaik in uniform with Blanchard (#35) and Davis (#41).

Colonel Earl "Red" Blaik, USMA 1920

- NCAA HALL OF FAME FOOTBALL COACH
- COACHED TWO NATIONAL CHAMPIONSHIP ARMY FOOTBALL TEAMS, 1944 AND 1945
- COACHED THREE HEISMAN TROPHY WINNERS, BLANCHARD, DAVIS, AND DAWKINS
- PRESIDENTIAL MEDAL OF FREEDOM
- BLAIK FIELD AT MICHIE STADIUM NAMED IN HIS HONOR
- BURIED AT THE WEST POINT CEMETERY

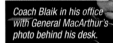

Coach Blaik in his office with General MacArthur's photo behind his desk.

At one point in his young life, Earl Henry "Red" Blaik was of the belief that coaching college football was "scarcely a life's work to aspire to."[1] As it turned out, it was a line of work that made him one of the most notable and highly regarded figures in the history of American sports.

The son of a Scottish immigrant, Blaik was born in Detroit, Michigan, on February 15, 1897.[2] In 1901, the Blaik family moved to Dayton, Ohio, where his father became a construction contractor. While attending Miami University in Oxford, Ohio, Blaik played football for three years – including the team's undefeated 1916 season.

By this time, World War I was well underway but the United States had not yet entered the war, and Blaik, in hopes of becoming an officer, won an appointment to the United States Military Academy at West Point. There he played football for two more seasons and was selected third team All-American, graduating in 1920. By that time, however,

the war had ended and the Army was downsizing. Blaik served two years in the service, then returned to Dayton to work in the home-building business with his father.

Blaik's coaching career began in 1924, when he served as a part-time assistant coach – first at the Miami University (Ohio) for two years, then one year at the University of Wisconsin, then back to West Point. His "temporary" assignment at the Academy eventually led to a full-time assistant coaching position in 1930.[1] Four years later, however, Blaik was passed over for the head-coaching position, due to a long-standing policy requiring that West Point's head coach be an officer on active duty.

In 1934, at the age of 37, Blaik was hired as head football coach at Dartmouth College. By instilling "discipline, sacrifice, and subordination," Blaik molded his players into a consistently winning team.[1] In seven seasons at Dartmouth, he compiled a 45–15–4 record, highlighted by an undefeated season in 1937.[3]

One of Blaik's most notorious victories at Dartmouth was the so-called "fifth-down" game against number-one-ranked Cornell during the 1940 season. Down 3–0 late in the fourth quarter, Cornell scored a touchdown on the final play for an apparent 7–3 victory; however, due to an officiating oversight, Cornell had been given five downs on which to score. Once the mistake was realized, Cornell graciously relinquished the victory and the game went down in the record books as a 3–0 Dartmouth win.[1]

While Blaik was building a football dynasty at Dartmouth, West Point suffered two consecutive losing seasons – 1939 and 1940. Convinced that Blaik was the coach who could things around, West Point's Superintendent arranged to change the school's officer-only coaching policy and offered Blaik the job.

When Blaik requested time to discuss the opportunity with family and the President of Dartmouth, the Superintendent told him, "Take all the time you want, Earl.

Just remember: West Point needs you."[1] As a condition for accepting the position, Blaik requested that West Point amend its restrictive height-to-weight requirements, believing Army's linemen to be significantly handicapped in size.[2] The Academy acquiesced and Blaik said yes to the job.

The assertion that West Point "needed" Blaik was quickly proven true. His Army team won five games in his first year and also achieved a scoreless tie against an undefeated Notre Dame team. West Point players respected Blaik for being a stern and disciplined coach, giving him the nickname "The Colonel." Undeterred by World War II – a time when most other colleges had a depleted supply of football players – Blaik continued to build powerful Army teams. With star running backs and future Heisman Trophy winners, "Doc" Blanchard and Glenn Davis, West Point went undefeated from 1944 through 1946, with 27 wins and one tie. The team won consecutive national titles in 1944 and 1945.

Coach Earl "Red" Blaik's gravesite at West Point Cemetery.

>>> Spotlight

An eight-foot bronze sculpture of Coach Earl "Red" Blaik is displayed at the College Football Hall of Fame in South Bend, Indiana. The statue was created by sculptor Glenna Goodacre, who also designed the Vietnam Women's Memorial in Washington, D.C. The Hall of Fame Executive Director Bernie Kish noted, "We are honored to showcase the Coach Blaik Sculpture here at The Hall. It is truly fitting since he and his mentor, General Douglas MacArthur, were instrumental in creating The National Football Foundation and College Hall of Fame."[1]

Red Blaik Statue at University of Miami (Ohio).

In its 1944 undefeated season, Army's final game was against its perennial nemesis, Navy – a powerhouse team that had just run off six straight wins. With war raging on, Blaik believed at the time there was more interest in that game than "in any ever played."[1] Certainly it was a game that lived up to its hype. After a fourth-quarter Navy score, Army's lead was cut to 9–7. At that point, Army's two star running backs, Blanchard and Davis, took over – with outstanding performances that turned a close contest into a 23–7 Army win.

To underscore the impact of this victory, General Douglas MacArthur sent the following wire upon the game's conclusion:

"The greatest of all Army teams. We have stopped the war to celebrate your success."[1]

When Blaik later reflected on this victory, he said, "I know there must be a moment in every coach's career which surpasses all others … I believe the number one moment for me came in that victory of Army's greatest over Navy's greatest."[1]

After the war, Blaik continued to mold high-caliber teams, with three more undefeated seasons in 1948 through 1950. He was selected as the American Football Coaches Association's (AFCA) Coach of the Year in 1946.[2]

WEST POINT WENT UNDEFEATED FROM 1944 THROUGH 1946, WITH 27 WINS AND ONE TIE. THE TEAM WON CONSECUTIVE NATIONAL TITLES IN 1944 AND 1945.

A significant low spot on Blaik's extraordinary coaching career, it came in the spring of 1951, in what has come to be known as West Point's "Honor Code Scandal." More than 90 cadets, including 51 football players[1], were expelled for cheating on exams. The coach's son and starting quarterback, Cadet Bob Blaik, was among them. Disheartened and deeply disappointed by the mishandling of the cadets involved, Blaik wanted to resign but was persuaded to stay on and rebuild the team.[3]

This scandal caused a setback in the team's success, resulting in two losing seasons. But by 1953, Army was once again a winning team. General Douglas MacArthur, who retired and lived in New York City after 1951 would often attend practices, games and give inspirational speeches to the players. Blaik finished his career with six consecutive winning seasons, and an overall record of 166 wins, 48 losses, and 14 ties.

Earl Blaik retired as Army's head football coach in January 1959. In 1964, he was inducted in to the NCAA College Football Hall of Fame and in 1969, he was inducted in to the Athletic Hall of Fame of his alma mater, Miami University. He received the Presidential Medal of Freedom from President Reagan in 1986.[2] Blaik had been an outstanding mentor, too. Nineteen of his players and assistant coaches went on to become head coaches in college or professional football – the most noteworthy would be Vince Lombardi.

Blaik passed away in 1989 at the age of 92 in Colorado Springs, Colorado. In September of 1999, Michie Stadium's at West Point playing surface was named Blaik Field in his honor. On October 8, 2011, a bronze statue was dedicated of Coach Blaik at Miami University. He is buried at the West Point Cemetery and has a unique football-shaped tombstone.

In describing the unbeaten teams he coached in the 1940s, Earl Blaik himself said it best in these words to his team members: "Seldom in a lifetime's experience is one permitted the complete satisfaction of being part of a perfect performance. From her sons, West Point expects the best. You were the best. In truth, you were a storybook team."[1]

Written by: Steve Chaloult, USMA 1992, and Greg Oliver.

Doc Blanchard with a Heisman pose.

President of the Downtown Athletic Club Wilfred Wottrich poses with Doc Blanchard before the ceremony where he received it, January 5, 1946.

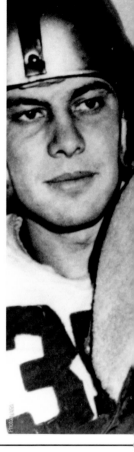

Colonel Felix "Doc" Blanchard, Jr., USAF, USMA 1947

- HEISMAN TROPHY WINNER
- AIR FORCE FIGHTER PILOT IN KOREAN AND VIETNAM WARS
- NICKNAMED "MR. INSIDE"
- DECORATED FOR VALOR AS A FIGHTER PILOT
- COLLEGE HALL OF FAME

After a stunning 59–0 loss to Army during the 1944 season, Notre Dame football coach Ed McKeever sent a telegram back to South Bend declaring, "Have just seen Superman in the flesh. He wears Number 35 and goes by the name of Blanchard."[1] Unfortunately for his opponents, "Superman's" college football heroics were just beginning.

Felix "Doc" Blanchard was born on December 11, 1924, in McColl, South Carolina. He was the son of Mary and Dr. Felix Blanchard. Being the son of a country doctor, Blanchard was nicknamed "Little Doc." He inherited his love of football from his father, who had been a college fullback. Perhaps as a way to help shape his son's destiny, the doctor placed a football in Blanchard's crib when he was an infant.[2]

As Blanchard was growing up, his father continued to encourage his athletic pursuits. "Little Doc" actually wanted to follow in his father's footsteps and become a doctor, but he struggled academically. Instead, Blanchard's sister, Mary Elizabeth, became the family's next physician.[2]

As a teenager, Blanchard attended St. Stanislaus Prep School in Mississippi. Playing fullback his senior year, he scored 165 points and led his team to an undefeated season. His gridiron accomplishments caught the attention of many colleges, including West Point. In recalling the Academy's early interest in recruiting him, Blanchard said, "At that point in time, I really wasn't interested. Academically, I never was too hot, so I never had any idea I would pass the entrance examination."[3]

While Blanchard could have attended just about any college, he chose the University of North Carolina (UNC). He wanted to be close to his father, who was ill at the time. Blanchard spent one year at UNC, helping the freshman team win the state championship in 1942. After his freshman year, Blanchard tried to enlist in Navy, but was rejected for poor eyesight.[1] In the spring of 1943, he enlisted in the Army, where he was trained as a tail gunner.[2] Because of his football skills, he was offered a chance to enter the United States Military Academy at West Point. After preparing for the entrance exams, he was accepted and entered the Academy in the summer of 1944.

Blanchard attended West Point from 1944 to 1946. During the war, course work at the Academy was crammed into three years instead of four to ensure an ample supply of officers. In Blanchard's first season with Army, the team won a national championship. As a two-way starter, he scored nine touchdowns, averaging five-and-a-half yards per rush, and even snared three inceptions. These stats earned Blanchard All-American honors, while finishing third in the voting for the Heisman Trophy.

The primary reason Army dominated its opponents was the pairing of fullback Blanchard and halfback Glenn Davis – aptly dubbed the "Touchdown Twins" – to form one of the greatest backfield duos in college football history. With his speed and strength, Blanchard had an incredible ability to break through defensive lines. He was "Mr. Inside" to Davis's "Mr. Outside." At six feet one inch and 205 pounds, Blanchard was also an excellent blocker. Additionally, he was often used as a pass receiver and occasionally as a kicker.[2]

In assessing Blanchard's skills, Army coach "Red" Blaik said, "I never saw anybody like Blanchard before. He has the weight of a fullback and the speed of a halfback."[1] In 1945, Blanchard had his finest season as a football player. In nine games, he had 19 touchdowns, rushed for 718 yards, and averaged 7.1 yards per rush. He also caught four passes for 166 yards. Blanchard won numerous honors, including

>>> Spotlight

Doc Blanchard and Glenn Davis both appeared multiple times on the covers of *Time* and *Life* magazines. Together, they also starred in *The Spirit of West Point*, filmed during their leave after graduation before deploying to their first assignments.

Courtesy: Time, Inc.

Blanchard (left) and Davis (right).

Photo: NARA

---

the Heisman Trophy, with 860 points, the Sullivan Award (given to the best amateur athlete in the United States) and the Maxwell Award. Blanchard was the first junior to win the Heisman, as well as the first person to win both the Sullivan and Heisman in one year.[2]

"HAVE JUST SEEN SUPERMAN IN THE FLESH. HE WEARS NUMBER 35 AND GOES BY THE NAME OF BLANCHARD."[1] —NOTRE DAME COACH ED MCKEEVER.

In the first game of the 1946 season, Blanchard tore ligaments in his left knee. Despite this setback, he only missed three games and still made key plays throughout the season. One of the most notable plays of his career occurred in a game against Columbia University, in which he scored a touchdown with a 92-yard kick-off return. It was one of 10 touchdowns he scored that year. He also rushed for 613 yards and caught seven passes for 166 yards. Once again, Army had an outstanding season, finishing season with 10 wins, zero losses, and one tie.[2]

Over the course of Blanchard's West Point career, he compiled 38 touchdowns and 1,908 total yards.[3] During Blanchard's tenure, Army averaged 56 points per game, with a record of 27 wins, zero losses, and one tie.[2]

After graduating in 1947, Blanchard joined the Army Air Corps. Both the Pittsburgh Steelers and the San Francisco 49ers were interested in drafting him, but the Army denied his request for an extended furlough to play professionally.[2] However, Blanchard and his former teammate, Davis, did find a way to capitalize on their fame during their first 60-day leave. They played themselves in a low-budget movie entitled *Spirit of West Point*, each earning $20,000 and a percentage of profits.

The film did not exactly earn the praise of critics. Describing the experience in an interview later in his life, Blanchard said, "On a scale of 1 to 10 – 1 being perfect – my acting was a 10. I never went to see the damn movie."[2]

After his three-year tour of duty, Blanchard would have been free to again pursue professional football. Instead, he chose to stay with the military, serving as a pilot for 24 years. During his distinguished military career, Blanchard served in both the Korean and Vietnam Wars, flying 84 missions over North Vietnam. He was cited for bravery in 1959, after a plane he was flying caught fire. Instead of abandoning the plane over a populated area, Blanchard risked his life to safely land it himself.[2]

In 1959, Blanchard was inducted in to the College Football Hall of Fame. He remained involved in amateur football while serving in the military – including coaching under his old coach, "Red" Blaik, as well as scouting recruits. Blanchard retired from the military in 1971 as a Colonel. He then worked for two years as a commandant at the New Mexico Military Institute, before retiring in full. Blanchard died of pneumonia on April 19, 2009, in Bulverde, Texas, where he had been living with his daughter, Mary, and her husband.[3]

At the time of his death, he was the oldest-living Heisman Trophy winner. Of that award, Blanchard said in a *New York Times* interview, "I think it really is more meaningful to me now. At 21, you're kind of all mixed up, I guess … When I first started playing ball, my dream was to be an all-American."[2] Mr. Outside certainly achieved that dream.

Glenn Davis, USMA 1947

- **HEISMAN TROPHY WINNER**
- **NICKNAMED "MR. OUTSIDE"**
- **BURIED AT THE WEST POINT CEMETERY**
- **PLAYED ON THE LOS ANGELES RAMS PROFESSIONAL FOOTBALL TEAM WHO WON THE 1951 NFL CHAMPIONSHIP**
- **ARMY FOOTBALL, BASEBALL, AND TRACK STAR**

Cadet Glenn Davis, Coach Earl "Red" Blaik, and Downtown Athletic Club President Wilfred Wottrich at the Heisman Trophy Award Ceremonies, January 1947.

Davis (#41) and Blanchard (#35).

GLENN W
DAVIS
2ND LT
US ARMY
DEC 24 1924
MAR 9 2005
ASS OF 1947
USMA
MR OUTSIDE

Davis's gravesite at West Point Cemetery

With Olympic-caliber speed and superior agility, Glenn Davis brought a new level of athleticism to college football. His unique combination of skills, along with his remarkable accomplishments on the field, inspired legendary West Point coach, Earl Blaik, to describe Davis as the "best player I have ever seen, anywhere."[1]

Glenn Woodward Davis was born December 26, 1924, in Claremont, California, with a twin brother, Ralph. They were the sons of Ralph Davis, a bank manager, and his wife, Irma. The Davis twins, along with their older sister, Mary, spent most of their youth growing up in LaVerne, California.[2]

By the time he reached high school, Davis was a gifted athlete. While attending Bonita High School, Davis played four sports and won 13 letters. In 1942, after leading Bonita to a Southern California high school scoring record of 236 points, he was named the CIF (California Interscholastic Federation) Football Player of the Year.[2]

After graduating from high school in 1943, Davis's athletic abilities brought him to the attention of many colleges – including the United States Military Academy at West Point. Davis agreed to enter only if his twin brother would be admitted, as well. The Academy was more than happy to oblige.

Davis's primary sport at West Point was football, and he picked up right where he left off in high school. Playing fullback in his first year, he gained 1,028 yards rushing in 144 carries. Army finished the 1943 season with a record of seven wins, two losses, and one tie, and was ranked seventh in the nation in total offense.[2]

Though Davis was well equipped for the demands of college athletics, the academic rigors of West Point were much more challenging. After his first term, he was expelled for failing math. As a consequence, Davis returned to California to attend a four-month math course at a prep school. After successfully completing the course, he was readmitted to West Point for the 1944–45 school year, but was again a first-year student.[1]

At the beginning of the 1944 football season, Davis switched from fullback to halfback because of the arrival of running back, Felix "Doc" Blanchard. The two of them came to be known as "the Touchdown Twins," forming one of the greatest backfield pairings in college football history. Davis was nicknamed "Mr. Outside" for his skill at running around the ends of the defensive line, while Blanchard was "Mr. Inside" for his ability to run through interior linemen.[3] Their skills complemented each other and their combination of speed and strength helped the Academy dominate opposing teams.

Davis played on three of the best teams West Point ever assembled. During the 1944 season, he set NCAA records by averaging 11.5 yards per carry and scoring 20 touchdowns in nine games.[4] For his accomplishments that season, Davis won the Maxwell Award and Walter Camp Trophy as player of the year, and finished second in voting for the Heisman trophy.

The 1945 Army team is often considered one of the best ever. Davis had an equally impressive season, averaging an amazing 11.51 yards per carry and scoring 18 touchdowns. Despite Davis's superb season, teammate Blanchard – who also had a stellar year – won the Heisman, while Davis finished second. Accepting his trophy, Blanchard graciously told the audience, "I'd have voted for Glenn Davis."[1]

In 1946, Davis played two of the best games of his college career. Against Navy, Davis accumulated 265 yards of total offense, leading Army to a 21–18 win. More impressively, he almost single-handedly defeated the University of Michigan. With both Doc Blanchard and quarterback Arnold Tucker injured, Davis rushed for 105 yards, completed seven of eight passes for 160 yards, intercepted two passes, and made a defensive play at the end of the game that ensured Army's 20–13 victory.[2] Due in part to these extraordinary performances, Davis finally won the Heisman Trophy that year.

By the time his college football career had ended, Davis had gained 6,494 yards in 637 carries. He achieved an NCAA record of 59 touchdowns, and passed for 12 more. He averaged one touchdown for every nine plays. These credentials made Davis a three-time All-American.[2]

Football was not Davis's only sport at West Point. He was a guard on the basketball team, as well as a star centerfielder on the baseball team. In fact, the Brooklyn Dodgers offered him a $75,000 contract and significant signing bonus. Davis declined to pursue baseball because he believed he would be too old to be a Major League rookie after fulfilling his military commitment.[2]

Additionally, Davis was a gifted track star, running the 100-yard dash in 9.7 seconds to tie an Army record. He set a West Point record in the 220-yard dash with a time of 20.9 seconds. To this day, Davis holds the highest point total for the Academy's Master of the Sword competition – a series of events testing speed, strength, coordination, and agility. Davis scored a record 962.5 points out of a possible 1,000.[3]

After graduating from West Point in 1947, Davis joined the Army, but still desired a career in professional football. Both Davis and Blanchard were offered generous monetary incentives by professional teams. But the Army had invested too much in training the two to allow them to leave the service to play football.

Davis and Blanchard did find a way to make their first 60-day leave lucrative. They played themselves in a low-budget movie entitled *Spirit of West Point*, each earning $20,000 and five percent of the film's profits. But Davis's role in the film was far more costly; while running for a touchdown for the cameras, he suffered a serious injury to his right knee and had to undergo surgery.[3]

After his discharge from the Army in 1950, Davis finally got the chance to play professionally, spending two seasons with the Rams. Even though his earlier knee injury hindered his ability, he still led the team in rushing during his rookie season. The Rams won the NFL championship that year with Davis selected to the Pro Bowl. His professional career was cut short in 1951 when he re-injured his knee. In his abbreviated professional career, he accumulated 616 yards on 152 rushing carries, and scoring four touchdowns.[2]

After his football career ended, Davis worked in the oil business for several years, and later for the *Los Angeles Times*. Davis was married three times, including a brief marriage to American Actress Terry Moore from 1951 to 1952. Davis died on March 9, 2005, at the age of 80.[4] He is buried at the West Point Cemetery and received special permission to include "Mr. Outside" on his military headstone.

Long after his football career ended, "Mr. Outside" continued to be remembered fondly. In a 1988 interview, he said, "It's amazing, but I still get at least a half dozen fan letters every week. After all these years, that's really something."[2]

Written by: Steve Chaloult, USMA 1992, and Greg Oliver.

BY THE TIME HIS COLLEGE FOOTBALL CAREER HAD ENDED, DAVIS HAD GAINED 6,494 YARDS IN 637 CARRIES. HE ACHIEVED AN NCAA RECORD OF 59 TOUCHDOWNS AND PASSED FOR 12 MORE.

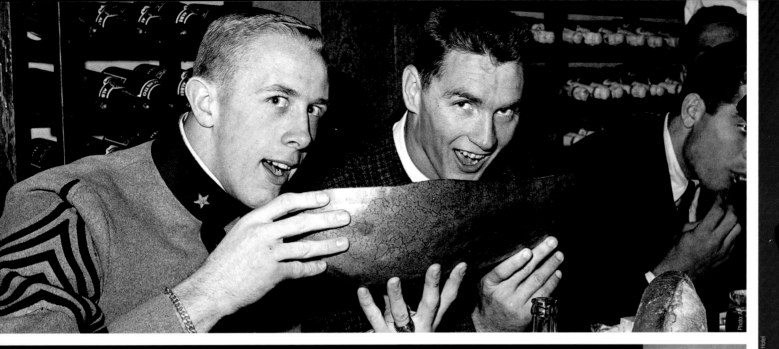

Brigadier General Pete Dawkins, USMA 1959

- HEISMAN TROPHY WINNER, RHODES SCHOLAR, CLASS PRESIDENT, CADET FIRST CAPTAIN
- GENERAL OFFICER
- CHIEF EXECUTIVE OFFICER
- MEMBER OF THE BOARD OF DIRECTORS, THAYER LEADER DEVELOPMENT GROUP
- BUSINESS EXECUTIVES FOR NATIONAL SECURITY (BENS) ANNUAL EISENHOWER AWARD RECIPIENT

>>> Spotlight

On April 8, 1966, Captain Pete Dawkins appeared on the cover of *Life* magazine, entitled "Army's All-American Rhodes Scholar now in Vietnam – Captain Pete Dawkins Keeps on Winning." The story highlighted his award of the Bronze Star for Valor.

Brigadier General Dawkins giving a keynote speech at the Thayer Leader Development Group at the Thayer Hotel.

Cadet Pete Dawkins giving a Heisman pose during the 1958 football season.

Pete Dawkins is one of the most well-known West Point graduates of the twentieth century, having excelled in so many different aspects of American life. He was an outstanding cadet, Army athlete, decorated combat leader, General Officer, and led several large public companies as Chief Executive Officer. It's quite the robust list of accomplishments from a man that, as a child, battled with a bout of polio.

Dawkins was born in Michigan and contracted polio at age 11. He was treated with a very aggressive physical therapy, a breakthrough procedure at the time. That experience inspired him to live a life dedicated to physical fitness, which was an important part of what led him to become an avid athlete. Although he was accepted to attend Yale, he chose West Point instead and never looked back. He did well – very well – at West Point, and credits his cadet years as being the most formative in his life, providing the foundation that launched him onto a career of military leadership and business.

He was, in fact, one of the most successful cadets in West Point history. He is the only cadet to hold all five top titles at once: Class President, First Captain, Captain of the Army football team, Star Man (finishing in the top five percent of the Class of 1959), and Rhodes Scholar. He also was selected as the Heisman Trophy Winner and Maxwell Award Winner, leading the Army football team in 1958 to its last undefeated season, receiving the Lambert Trophy and ranking third in the nation. (The 1958 football team was the last team that was coached by Earl "Red" Blaik.) Dawkins earned consensus All-American, a major honor in college football, and was selected as the "Player of the Year" in 1958 by both *Sports Illustrated* and *Sport Magazine*. He

DAWKINS IS THE ONLY CADET TO HOLD ALL FIVE TOP TITLES AT ONCE: CLASS PRESIDENT, FIRST CAPTAIN, CAPTAIN OF THE ARMY FOOTBALL TEAM, STAR MAN (FINISHING IN THE TOP FIVE PERCENT OF THE CLASS OF 1959), AND RHODES SCHOLAR.

lettered in three sports: football, baseball, and hockey. He was the assistant Captain of the Army hockey team, where he was selected to the All East Hockey Team and was the highest-scoring defenseman. He is one of the three Heisman Trophy Winners from West Point, joining Glenn Davis (Heisman Trophy 1945) and Doc Blanchard (Heisman Trophy 1944).

Dawkins chose the Infantry as his branch selection, and was equally successful after graduation as he had been as a cadet. For his initial assignment, Dawkins attended Oxford University for three years as a Rhodes Scholar, receiving his master's degree. In 1962, he returned to active Army service, attended Infantry Officer Basic, Airborne, and Ranger Schools and was assigned to the 82nd Airborne Division as a Rifle Company Commander. He deployed to Vietnam as Senior Advisor to the 1st Vietnamese Airborne Battalion and was decorated with two Bronze Stars for Valor and three Vietnamese Gallantry Crosses. He returned to the United States, studied for and received his PhD at Princeton, then taught at West Point. He commanded a battalion in the 2nd Infantry Division in Korea, and a brigade at Fort Ord, as well as in the 101st Airborne Division, then became Chief of Staff of the Division. After being promoted to Brigadier General, he completed his career in the Pentagon as the Army's Deputy Director of Strategy, Plans, and Policy.

After retiring from the Army, Dawkins became a partner at Lehman Brothers for four years, heading the Public Finance Banking division. He then took a "furlough" from the world of finance, as the Republican nominee for the United States Senate seat in New Jersey. After a spirited campaign, he lost in a close race to the wealthy incumbent Frank Lautenberg. At that point, he returned to the private sector to head the United States

consulting business of Bain & Company, until he was recruited to head Primerica Financial Services, Inc. as Chief Executive Officer, leading an organization of 125,000 employees from around the world. After being Chief Executive Officer for five years, he moved to become Vice Chairman of Travelers Group, then on to be Vice Chairman of Global Wealth Management at Citigroup. Currently, he serves as Senior Partner of Flintlock Capital Asset Management, a global commodities hedge fund. Through it all, Dawkins has always remained loyal to the Military Academy, working actively on behalf of his alma mater and especially in support of intercollegiate athletics and Army football.

Throughout his career, Dawkins has always believed in public service, and has epitomized the West Point motto of "Duty, Honor, Country." In addition to 24 years of service in the Army and his run for the United States Senate, Dawkins has remained active in the field of national security. He led a panel of Chief Executive Officers in a two-year study for Secretary of Defense Bill Cohen, and was awarded the distinguished Eisenhower Award from the Business Executives for National Security (BENS) for his lifetime of service to the nation.

The BG Dawkins Room at the Thayer Hotel is proudly dedicated by his friends, family, and the Class of 1959.

State at West Point with Hall of Fame Coach Blaik and his three Heisman Trophy Winners: Dawkins, Blanchard, and Davis.

On June 4, 1969, Mike Krzyzewski graduated from West Point. Krzyzewski received his West Point diploma, was commissioned as an officer in the United States Army, and was married to his longtime girlfriend, Mickie, at the Cadet Chapel at West Point; all three ceremonies were held on the same day. It was a symbolic graduation, parting, beginning, and merging of all that was special to Krzyzewski – Mickie and West Point, together, would be the foundation for his incredible life story that followed.

West Point is a university focused entirely on creating leaders of character, and Krzyzewski epitomizes the West Point graduate. Krzyzewski is an NCAA Hall of Fame Basketball Coach with more victories in basketball than any other coach in college basketball history. As the Duke Blue Devils coach, "Coach K" has won four NCAA Championships, has been a 12-time National Coach of the Year, coached the United States Olympic Team to two Olympic Gold Medals, been inducted to the Naismith Memorial Hall of Fame, and received nearly every honor and accolade available to a basketball coach. Yet, with all of this success and the many accolades for his work on the court, he modestly doesn't think of himself a basketball coach: "I don't look at myself as a basketball coach. I look at myself as a leader who happens to coach basketball." He is a leader on and off the court, and a role model for others to follow.

Krzyzewski has traveled throughout the world, but the majority of his life has been focused primarily living in three geographic areas, each of which he holds dear to his heart: Chicago, West Point, and Durham. He spent 18 years growing up in the suburbs of Chicago with his parents, then a total of nine years at West Point (four as a cadet and five later as a coach), then more than 30 years at Duke University in Durham, North Carolina, where he became internationally recognized as a world-class leader, truly in a league of his own.

Coach Mike Krzyzewski, USMA 1969

- **"COACH K"**
- **NCAA HALL OF FAME BASKETBALL COACH**
- **FOUR NCAA BASKETBALL CHAMPIONSHIPS**
- **TWO U.S. OLYMPIC TEAM GOLD MEDALS AS HEAD COACH/ONE AS ASSISTANT COACH**
- **NAISMITH MEMORIAL BASKETBALL HALL OF FAME**
- **2011 *SPORTS ILLUSTRATED* "SPORTSMAN OF THE YEAR"**
- **WEST POINT DISTINGUISHED GRADUATE AWARD**
- **ARMY BASKETBALL TEAM CAPTAIN AND THREE-TIME LETTERMAN**
- **ARMY ATHLETIC HALL OF FAME**

Krzyzewski and Coach Bobby Knight at West Point in 1969.

Krzyzewski was born February 13, 1947, in Chicago, Illinois. He attended Weber High School, where he was a standout point guard and captain of the varsity team. A young 24-year-old Army head coach named Bobby Knight came to Chicago to recruit Krzyzewski in 1964. Knight spoke at length with Krzyzewski's mom and dad, first-generation Americans who encouraged Krzyzewski to attend West Point. Knight would be Krzyzewski's coach, his mentor, and his friend, and a bond was formed that

would last a lifetime.

Krzyzewski entered West Point in July 1965. As a cadet, he attended academic classes, trained to lead soldiers, and played basketball for the Army team. The daily regimen at West Point is all about learning and practicing leadership, discipline, responsibility, and creating a work ethic, and trained on and off the court to lead.

Under Coach Bobby Knight, Cadet Krzyzewski thrived as a leader on the basketball court. Krzyzewski was a three-time letterman and captain his senior year at West Point. He was a second-team NIT (National Invitational Championship) player and played in the North-South game. Before graduation, he chose the Field Artillery as his branch.

Krzyzewski spent one year at West Point as assistant coach before going to Field Artillery Officer Basic Course at Fort Sill, Oklahoma, then on to Fort Carson, Colorado, where he served as a Liaison to the 7/17th Field Artillery. He served in Korea in the 2nd Infantry Division from 1971 to 1972. He returned to United States in 1972 and served as head coach of the West Point Prep School for two years at Fort Belvoir, Virginia. Captain Krzyzewski left the military in 1974, and he and Mickie moved to Bloomington, Indiana, for one

Duke had two NCAA runner-up seasons (1964 and 1978) and four Final Four appearances (1963, 1964, 1966, and 1978). It was an ideal opportunity for 33-year-old Coach K to lead the Duke Basketball team to become the nation's premier basketball program.

Coach K and Mickie moved from West Point to Durham, and he assumed the role of Head Coach on May 4, 1980. There they would raise their three girls: Debbie, Lindy, and Jamie. Over the next three decades, Coach K built up a national franchise that won four NCAA Championships (1991, 1992, 2001, 2010), eight NCAA Finals appearances, 11 Final Four appearances, 13 Atlantic Coast Conference (ACC) championships, and more than 800 wins, bringing his total victories as a coach, including West Point to well over 900. No coach in Division I history has more victories; Knight and Boeheim are the only two with more than 900 victories.

Duke University and its alumni love Coach K. His brand is synonymous with Duke's brand: both are superlative. He has not only led the Duke Blue Devils to four national championships, but also led our United States Olympic Team to two Gold Medals, yet most importantly he has done so with honor, integrity, and has served as a role model for others to follow. At a time when

holds a blue Duke stone. Coach K's youngest daughter, Jamie, married the former Captain of the West Point basketball team, Christopher Spatola (USMA 2002), who is the current Duke Special Assistant to the Director of Athletics/Special Initiatives and is also involved in broadcasting, in addition to his Duke role, covering Patriot League games, including West Point games, for CBS Sports Network. Jamie herself wears a West Point miniature ring as her own engagement ring and tells the story of Coach K's ring: "Many years after graduation and into his career at Duke, my mom had his original stone replaced with a deep, unmistakably Duke-blue one – the same stone that is placed in the class rings of Duke graduates. The symbolism could not be more perfect. Just as the USMA ring supports that Duke-blue stone, West Point has proven to be the foundation for everything that he has done in career, including his nearly 30 years at Duke and, of course, his three years as USA Basketball's National Coach."

Coach K was asked to lead the United States Men's Olympic Team and has led the United States to two Olympic Gold Medals in Beijing 2008 and again in London 2012.

In particular, 2008 was a special year for Coach K and his family as they all traveled to Beijing to represent the United States and then to West Point to be inducted in to the West Point Hall of Fame. Coach K's daughter Jamie articulated the experience:

"For the rest of my life, I will always remember 2008. And when I look back on that won-

Coach K's West Point ring with the Duke Blue Stone

Photo: Duke University Sports Information Department

JUST AS THE USMA RING SUPPORTS THAT DUKE BLUE STONE, WEST POINT HAS PROVEN TO BE THE FOUNDATION FOR EVERYTHING THAT HE HAS DONE IN CAREER, INCLUDING HIS NEARLY 30 YEARS AT DUKE AND, OF COURSE, HIS THREE YEARS AS USA BASKETBALL'S NATIONAL COACH.

year, where he served as graduate assistant at Indiana University for his former coach Bobby Knight.

In 1975, Krzyzewski was offered the Head Coaching role at West Point. He and Mickie returned to West Point, where he coached at Army for five years with a winning 73–59 record, including a birth in the National Invitational Tournament (N.I.T.) in 1978.

In 1980, "Coach K" (as he was now known since his 10-letter name with only two vowels was hard to pronounce) was offered an opportunity to lead the Duke Basketball team as Head Coach. At that time, Duke had a long tradition of basketball but had never won the NCAA National Championship.

many athletic programs have sacrificed principles to achieve victory, Coach K and Duke have won with honor and not sacrificed their principles. His basketball players have outstanding graduation rates and consider Coach K as a father figure. His three daughters call him their "hero."[1] Yet with all these accolades, he is humble in his role: "That's what I do now: I lead and I teach. If we win basketball games from doing that, then that's great, but I lead and teach. Those are the two things I concentrate on."

Though the world associates the Coach K brand with Duke, those close to him know he shares his love of Duke equally with his love of West Point as they are inseparable. In fact, Krzyzewski's West Point ring now

derful year, I will think about our September trip to West Point just as much as our phenomenal August in Beijing. The truth is, in my mind, those two trips are inextricably linked. In Beijing, I saw my dad's dream come true. But, on the trip to the Academy, I saw how that dream became even a possibility. I could see so clearly the connection between my dad's Olympic experience and the values and work ethic instilled in him at West Point. I felt thankful that my grandparents had the foresight to aggressively encourage their 18-year-old son to take advantage of the opportunity he had to attend what my dad now calls 'the best school for leadership in the United States.'"[2]

Coach K with President Obama.

Coach K being inducted in to Army Sports Hall of Fame in 2009.

Coach K and the victorious Duke team give President George H.W. Bush a Duke shirt and basketball

Coach K and Pat Summit honored as the 2011 Sports Illustrated "Sportsman and Sportswoman of the Year."

>>> Spotlight

Home of the Blue Devils, Duke University has about 13,000 undergraduate and graduate students and a world-class faculty helping to expand the frontiers of knowledge. The university has a strong commitment to applying knowledge in service to society, both near its North Carolina campus and around the world.

Courtesy: Duke University Sports Information Department

Coach K and President George H.W. Bush in the Oval Office.

Coach K cutting the net after winning the 1991 NCAA Championship.

MACARTHUR BOWL

NATIONAL FOOTBALL FOUNDATION (NFF)
COLLEGE CHAMPIONSHIP TROPHY

Dedicated in honor of General of the Army Douglas MacArthur, USMA 1903

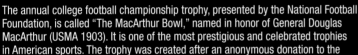

The annual college football championship trophy, presented by the National Football Foundation, is called "The MacArthur Bowl," named in honor of General Douglas MacArthur (USMA 1903). It is one of the most prestigious and celebrated trophies in American sports. The trophy was created after an anonymous donation to the National Football Foundation (NFF) on behalf of General MacArthur in 1959. The trophy is inscribed with the quote "There is no substitute for victory" from General MacArthur's Farewell to Congress delivered on April 24, 1951. General MacArthur was well known for his love of sports, especially football.

The MacArthur Bowl is molded from 400 ounces of silver designed after a college football stadium standing 10 inches tall, 25 inches long, and 18 inches wide. Starting in 1959, the trophy was awarded to the best college football team as determined by a committee comprised of former players, coaches, and sportswriters. Since 1998, the MacArthur Bowl has been awarded to the winner of the Bowl Championship Series (BCS).

The National Football Foundation (NFF) was founded in 1947. The NFF considers General Douglas MacArthur (USMA 1903) and Coach Earl "Red" Blaik (USMA 1920) as two of its key early leaders. The first-annual National Football Foundation awards dinner was not held until 11 years after being founded. In 1958, the NFF held its first-annual awards dinner at the Hotel Astor in New York City with President Dwight D. Eisenhower (USMA 1915) providing the keynote address. The donation to create the trophy was made the next year in 1959, and the National Football Foundation commissioned Tiffany & Company to create the Bowl. The second-annual National Football Foundation awards dinner was held in 1959, but the location was moved to the Waldorf-Astoria in New York City, where it has been held every year since in early December. After returning from Korea in 1951, after 14 years overseas in the Pacific spanning both World War II and the Korean War, General and Mrs. MacArthur took up residence in New York City at the luxurious Waldorf-Astoria, where they lived for the remainder of his life. The winner of the first MacArthur Bowl was Syracuse University with a 10–0–0 record.

Similar to the Stanley Cup Trophy, there is only one MacArthur Bowl and it is presented annually to the championship team. Each year, the name of the new championship team is inscribed on the side of the trophy and displayed at the winning team's campus for the full year following the victory. As of the conclusion of the 2012 season, 54 victorious teams have had their names inscribed on the trophy, several having multiple entries with Alabama (seven), Notre Dame (five), University of Southern California, Miami, and Texas each tied with four.

Pictured above at the 1962 NFF awards ceremony is General MacArthur (center), along with Chester LaRoche (left), President of the National Football Foundation and the winners of the 1962 MacArthur Bowl: the University of Southern California Leonard K. Firestone (USC Chairman of the Board of Trustees), and Jesse Hill (USC Director of Athletics).

LOMBARDI TROPHY

NATIONAL FOOTBALL LEAGUE (NFL) SUPER BOWL TROPHY

Dedicated in honor of Army Football Coach Vince Lombardi

The Lombardi Trophy, awarded each year to the National Football League's (NFL) Super Bowl champion, is named for legendary football coach and "son of West Point," Vince Lombardi. Lombardi, a graduate of Fordham University, served for five years as an assistant football coach at West Point under NCAA Hall of Fame Coach Earl "Red" Blaik (USMA 1920) from 1948 to 1953. He was West Point's offensive line coach and helped lead the Black Knights to a 30–13–2 record during his tenure, to include a 7–1–1 record in his final season. In that same year, Army was also awarded the Lambert Trophy as the best Division I college football team in the Northeast.

Lombardi coached at every level starting with St. Cecilia High School in Englewood, New Jersey, then at the collegiate ranks at both Fordham and Army, reached the NFL as an assistant coach with the New York Giants, and culminated his career as head coach of both the Green Bay Packers and Washington Redskins. As an assistant with the Giants for five years, Lombardi served as the offensive coach while Tom Landry, the future coach of the Dallas Cowboys, was the defensive coach. Lombardi then became head coach of the Green Bay Packers, where he built a football dynasty and sealed his legacy as a football icon. In nine years as Green Bay's head coach from 1959 to 1967, Lombardi compiled a record of 89–29–4 that included five NFL Championships (including the first two Super Bowls) and six conference titles.

Lombardi continued to maintain his connections to West Point and would credit his own coaching experience at Army under Red Blaik with instilling in him the traits of discipline, precision execution, and perseverance – traits he carried with him the rest of his career.[1] General Douglas MacArthur (USMA 1903) frequently attended Army football games when Lombardi was coach and would often give pep talks to the team. That relationship also continued for Lombardi after he went to the NFL but continued to screen Army football games for MacArthur. His connection to and support of former cadets never ceased either. In the fall of 1967, Lombardi went to Arlington National Cemetery to attend the funeral of Army All-American football player Major Don Holleder, who was Killed In Action in Vietnam.

Vince Lombardi passed away from colon cancer on September 3, 1970, and was enshrined in the National Football Hall of Fame in 1971. The NFL renamed the Super Bowl championship trophy the "Vince Lombardi Trophy." The first team to receive the newly named Lombardi Trophy was the Baltimore Colts following its 1971 Super Bowl victory over the Dallas Cowboys and Lombardi's longtime friend Tom Landry in Super Bowl V. The trophy is made of sterling silver, stands 22 inches tall, weighs seven pounds, and is designed after a regulation-sized football in a kicking position. Unlike the MacArthur Bowl Trophy, which is one of a kind and rotates annually to the current college football champion, Tiffany & Company creates a new Lombardi Trophy each year to be presented and retained by the Super Bowl winning team.

Lombardi as Army Football Coach.

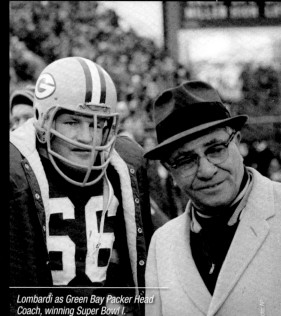

Lombardi as Green Bay Packer Head Coach, winning Super Bowl I.

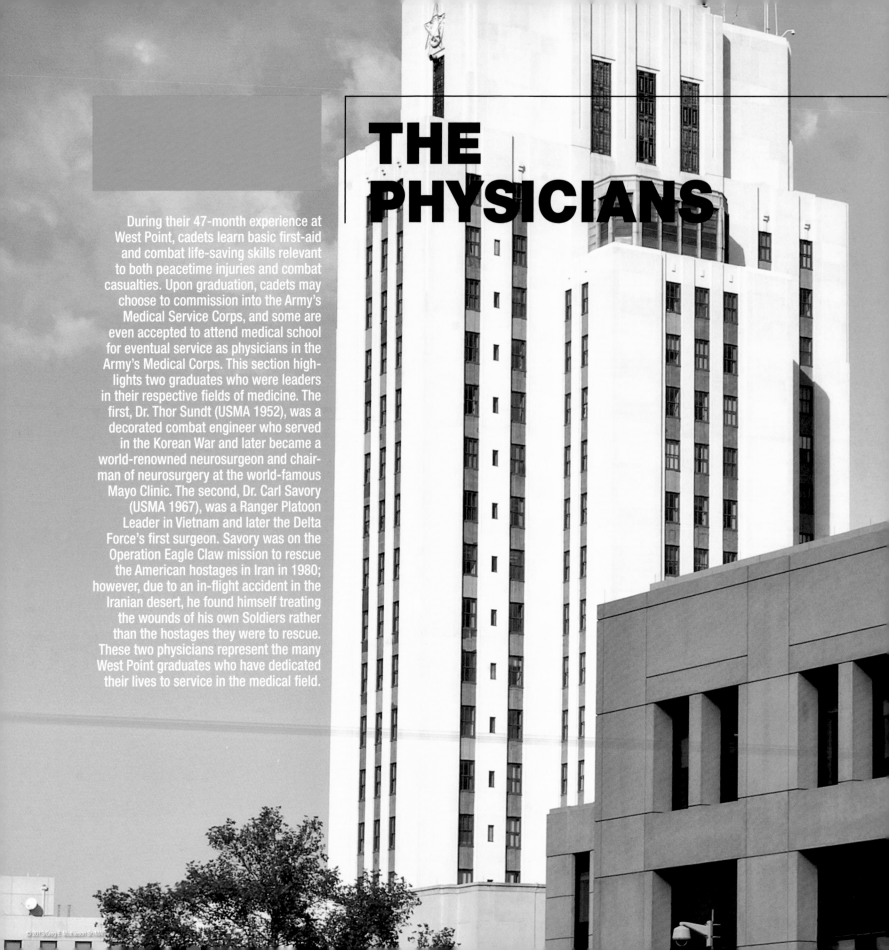

THE PHYSICIANS

During their 47-month experience at West Point, cadets learn basic first-aid and combat life-saving skills relevant to both peacetime injuries and combat casualties. Upon graduation, cadets may choose to commission into the Army's Medical Service Corps, and some are even accepted to attend medical school for eventual service as physicians in the Army's Medical Corps. This section highlights two graduates who were leaders in their respective fields of medicine. The first, Dr. Thor Sundt (USMA 1952), was a decorated combat engineer who served in the Korean War and later became a world-renowned neurosurgeon and chairman of neurosurgery at the world-famous Mayo Clinic. The second, Dr. Carl Savory (USMA 1967), was a Ranger Platoon Leader in Vietnam and later the Delta Force's first surgeon. Savory was on the Operation Eagle Claw mission to rescue the American hostages in Iran in 1980; however, due to an in-flight accident in the Iranian desert, he found himself treating the wounds of his own Soldiers rather than the hostages they were to rescue. These two physicians represent the many West Point graduates who have dedicated their lives to service in the medical field.

"Military medicine has developed into a sophisticated specialty... [and] includes such disciplines as tropical medicine, nuclear warfare, chemical weapons, flight surgery, industrial medicine, hygiene, disaster triage, transport and the care of the wounded during transport, combat nutrition, immunizations, epidemiology, management of venomous bites and stings, and the emotional disorders of military life."

–Colonel Walter J. Pories, M.D., USA (Retired)

"I never want to kill again – I want to save lives."

–Lieutenant Thor Sundt, USMA 1952, after the 1953 Battle of Pork Chop Hill in Korea, where he was decorated for valor, going on to become one of the world's greatest neurosurgeons and chairman of neurosurgery at the Mayo Clinic

"Had our mission been a success, we likely would have considered it a victory and not looked deep at ourselves, the many problems and lack of capabilities that we had at the time. The fact that the mission failed exposed many of the problems that we had, and that caused Congress to create the Hart-Rudman Commission, which then helped create U.S. Special Operations Command, which made the entire military much better and saved American lives in the future."

–Dr. Carl Savory, USMA 1966, 1st Delta Force Surgeon who was a member of the Operation Eagle Claw failed hostage rescue mission to Iran on April 24, 1980

WALTER REED BETHESDA

WALTER REED NATIONAL MILITARY MEDICAL CENTER

One year after graduating from West Point, Thor Sundt walked off the bloody battlefield of Pork Chop Hill, Korea, a decorated combat hero. After the carnage of the battle, Sundt told a classmate that he never wanted to kill again. Instead, he wanted to become a physician and save people, and humanity was the beneficiary. Nearly 40 years later, he would stand on the Plain being recognized as one of the first four Distinguished Graduates in West Point history. Although Sundt only served three years on active duty, he stood being honored with three of the greatest General Officers in American military history: Ridgway, Goodpaster, and Van Fleet. Sundt had fulfilled his dream of spending every day after Pork Chop Hill saving people. He had become arguably the best neurosurgeon in the world. As the leading neurosurgeon and Chairman of Neurosurgery at the world-class Mayo Clinic, he had saved countless lives and led the global development of the tactics, procedures, and policies that fueled the innovation that created this life-saving field.

That day in 1991, when Sundt received his Distinguished Graduate Award, he stood on the Plain, in pain and on crutches, barely able to stand after seven years of battling a cancer that had riddled his body. Yet despite his chronic pain, he continued to work and lead his department, saving patients until the day he died. He passed away only three months after receiving the award. He had lived on determined to stand on the Plain and receive that award, and, primarily, to pass along his life's lessons to the cadets. He credited everything he had achieved in life to learning discipline at West Point as eloquently stated in Schofield's Definition of Discipline. He always treated his soldiers, and later, his patients, as if he served them – not the other way around, following Schofield's words: "He who feels the respect which is due to others cannot fail to inspire in them regard for himself."

Sundt entered West Point in 1948. Sundt, or "Thunder" as his classmates called him, excelled at wrestling. In his Cow year, he met Lois Baker, who would be his soul mate for the next 40 years. He graduated

Dr. Thoralf Sundt, USMA 1952

- **PIONEER IN NEUROLOGICAL MICROSURGERY**
- **CHAIRMAN DEPARTMENT OF NEUROSURGERY, MAYO CLINIC**
- **WEST POINT DISTINGUISHED GRADUATE AWARD**
- **VICE CHAIRMAN OF THE AMERICAN BOARD OF NEUROLOGICAL SOCIETY**
- **COMPANY COMMANDER, 32ND REGIMENTAL COMBAT TEAM, 7TH INFANTRY DIVISION, KOREAN WAR**
- **TWO BRONZE STAR MEDALS FOR VALOR IN KOREAN WAR**

Shaking hands with President Reagan after Reagan's recovery.

>>> Spotlight

Dr. Sundt, though fighting cancer, remained alive long enough to receive the West Point Distinguished Graduate Award, along with Generals Ridgway, Van Fleet ,and Goodpaster as the first group to ever receive the newly established award in 1992. Though cancer was destroying his body, he stood on crutches on the Plain to receive the award as one of the great honors of his lifetime of service. He passed away three months later.

at the top of his class and chose the Corps of Engineers, just as the United States was entering its third year of the Korean War. Before immediately deploying to the ongoing battle raging across the Korean peninsula, however, he and Lois were married in October 1952.

As the Class of 1952 arrived in Korea in the spring of 1953, the United States was in the midst of negotiating an armistice. It was during these negotiations that the second Battle of Pork Chop Hill occurred. Both the United States and Chinese forces battled over Hill 266 for months in a bloody battle that cost more than 1,000 United States casualties. Sundt and many of his 1952 classmates led soldiers on Pork Chop Hill, two of which were Killed In Action: Dick Shea, who would receive the Medal of Honor, and Dick Inman, who would receive the Silver Star – both posthumously for their courageous leadership. Because of the futility with mounting casualties in the midst of negotiating a peace, the United States finally chose to withdraw from Pork Chop Hill. In the withdrawal, Lieutenant Sundt was tasked with destroying the trenches that the United States forces were defending as the Chinese were attacking. Sundt was one of the last soldiers to withdraw from Pork Chop Hill, as he detonated the explosives on the attacking Chinese troops. He was awarded the Bronze Star for Valor for his leadership. Three weeks after the battle of Pork Chop Hill had ended with more than 1,000 United States casualties, the armistice was signed ending hostilities in Korea with 33,686 American soldiers Killed In Action. Humanity benefited from the tragic events on Pork Chop Hill. Sundt left Korea and, in the downsizing of the Army, chose to leave to pursue his dream of saving people, becoming the leading pioneer and the top neurosurgeon in the world.

Sundt returned to Lois in 1955. They moved to Memphis, where he entered medical school at the University of Tennessee in the field of neurosurgery and raised a young family of three. After completing training, he was on staff first at the Semmes-Murphy Clinic in Memphis, then the Mayo Clinic in Rochester, Minnesota, where he would rise to become chairman of neurosurgery at the Mayo Clinic. He was a pioneer in the field and developed innovative approaches, including the first use of the microscope in neurosurgery. Being the best in the field, he always performed surgery on the patients with the most challenging neurological disorders – and he fought for them in the operating room just as he had fought for his country on the battlefield. He once told a patient, who happened to be an Army veteran: "You and I are going to retake this hill from the enemy [brain tumor]. So put your trust in me and together we will win this battle." And they did.

He received top awards in his field, including the Grass Prize and Medal from the Society of Neurological Surgeons. He was the honored guest of the Congress of Neurological Surgeons and was one of the few surgeons to be inducted in to the Institute of Medicine of the National Academy of Science. Sundt received the Medal of Honor of the World Federation of Neurosurgical Societies. He was the neurosurgeon of choice for United States Presidents, kings, farmers, and children, and he loved them all.

In 1985, Sundt was diagnosed with multiple myeloma cancer and given 18 months to live. With the discipline he credited as learning at West Point, he continued to work every day performing surgery on Monday, Wednesday, and Friday for up to seven hours a day, standing while he fought the cancer with everything he had. He loved his patients and said they gave him his strength. His bones became so brittle that he occasionally fractured a rib coughing. He was in chronic pain and was so disciplined in his work that he had a special body cast made to continue to stand on his feet in surgery. In his speech at West Point, when receiving the first Distinguished Graduate award, he spoke eloquently about learning discipline at West Point, and other than self-deprecation, he selflessly spoke nothing about himself, but only of others who had been his heroes and what they had taught him. Of all the accolades he received in his life, he was most proud of being a member of the Long Gray Line, and he had survived against all odds to be honored with three of the greatest Generals of the twentieth century on the "rockbound highland home" that he loved so much.

AFTER THE CARNAGE OF THE BATTLE, THOR TOLD A CLASSMATE THAT HE NEVER WANTED TO KILL AGAIN. INSTEAD HE WANTED TO BECOME A PHYSICIAN AND SAVE PEOPLE, AND HUMANITY WAS THE BENEFICIARY.

In his last year of life, in 1992, Sundt's story was highlighted on *60 Minutes* with Leslie Stahl, when he, Lois, and several patients were interviewed about his leadership under fire, but in regards to the cancer that was destroying his body. The story showcased his strength, humility, brilliance, and courage under extremely challenging conditions. Until the day he died and beyond, Sundt was an inspiration to his profession and to the patients that he believed in, just as he had served and inspired his soldiers in the Korean War. After he passed away, the *60 Minutes* story ran again, as the news show elected him as one of the three most influential people ever interviewed in their esteemed history. He is a hero to all those cadets and graduates who are inspired by him to lead America, both on the field of battle and, later, in life "on other fields, on other days."

The Dr. Sundt Room at the Thayer Hotel is proudly dedicated by his family.

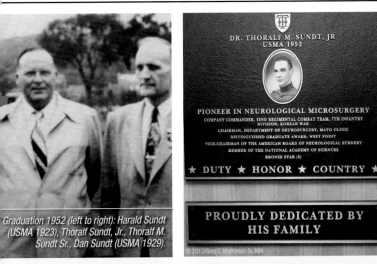

Graduation 1952 (left to right): Harald Sundt (USMA 1923), Thoralf Sundt, Jr., Thoralf M. Sundt Sr., Dan Sundt (USMA 1929).

DR. THORALF M. SUNDT, JR
USMA 1952

PIONEER IN NEUROLOGICAL MICROSURGERY

COMPANY COMMANDER, 32ND REGIMENTAL COMBAT TEAM, 7TH INFANTRY DIVISION, KOREAN WAR

CHAIRMAN, DEPARTMENT OF NEUROSURGERY, MAYO CLINIC

DISTINGUISHED GRADUATE AWARD, WEST POINT

VICE-CHAIRMAN OF THE AMERICAN BOARD OF NEUROLOGICAL SURGERY

MEMBER OF THE NATIONAL ACADEMY OF SCIENCES

BRONZE STAR (I)

★ DUTY ★ HONOR ★ COUNTRY ★

PROUDLY DEDICATED BY HIS FAMILY

© 2013/Greg E. Mathieson Sr./MAI

Dr. Sundt with Nancy and President Reagan preparing for discharge from the hospital wearing a Twins hat.

Colonel Carlton Savory created and led the development of the current Army mobile surgical team after being the founding surgeon of Delta Force and Joint Special Operations Command (JSOC). Savory was an Airborne-Ranger qualified Infantry Officer who led a Ranger platoon in Vietnam and then chose to pursue a medical career. In 1980, he and the newly formed Delta Force embarked on a courageous but ill-fated long-range rescue mission deep into Tehran, Iran to liberate American hostages in Operation Eagle Claw. The mission ended with a collision of two aircraft with eight Americans killed and Savory, instead of treating the liberated prisoners, ended up treating injured members of the air crews.

Carl was born on V-E Day (May 8, 1945) in Binghampton, New York, the only son of Gerald and Emma Savory. When Carl was 3, his father moved the family to Tucson, Arizona, where his father worked in a grocery store, while his mother, Emma, raised him and worked part-time as a hairdresser.

Carl attended Tucson High School, one of the largest high school in the United States at the time with more than 6,000 students. He played basketball and was involved in student politics, including being elected the Youth Governor of Arizona. No one in his immediate family had ever attended college or been in the military. An avid reader, he had read several historical biographies of American military leaders and West Point graduates, and he became very interested in the military.

Savory was accepted to West Point without ever seeing it, and arrived in 1963. He says he "was neither a bad cadet nor a great cadet" and really did not enjoy or appreciate his time at the Academy until years later in hindsight. He participated in intramurals, was trained in SCUBA and joined the SCUBA club, was elected by his classmates to the Honor Committee, and was involved with several other clubs. As his class was graduating, the Vietnam War was escalating rapidly and casualties were mounting, and the Infantry Branch had

become unpopular. In fact, the bottom of the class was forced to go Infantry in what was referred to as having been "branched" involuntarily. Savory was high in the class, and had many options, but he not only chose Infantry, but also volunteered for Vietnam.

After graduation, he attended Airborne and Ranger Schools. Three weeks into Ranger School, he broke his ankle and was hospitalized. He had to beg to be recycled into a later class, and his orders to his unit in Vietnam were canceled because he couldn't meet up with his unit as scheduled. Undeterred, he completed Ranger School and again volunteered for Vietnam. This time he was deployed. He was assigned as a Platoon Leader in A Company 1-503rd Airborne Brigade, and they conducted patrols regularly and had occasional contact with the Viet Cong. While in Vietnam, he volunteered to join a long-range reconnaissance unit and joined E Company, 20th Long Range Patrol, 75th Infantry where his platoon was very active.

Later during his tour, the unit was redesignated as C Co-Ranger 75th Infantry. The lessons learned at West Point and Ranger School had prepared him well for combat and one of the primary lessons was to always lead by example.

After leaving Vietnam, Captain Savory arrived in Germany at a time when the Army was broken, the Vietnam War was ending, and it was the "Hollow Army." He immediately hated the assignment in Germany and tried to be assigned to the Special Forces Qualification Course, intent on being involved in an elite unit, but was told he would have to wait 18 months. While in Germany, he randomly ran into a classmate who told him about an Army program to pay for medical school if any officer was accepted. Savory applied to only one school, the University of Arizona College of Medicine, and was accepted immediately. After four years at the U of A, he graduated with honors and headed to Letterman Army Medical Center in San Francisco, where he completed his surgical

Colonel Carlton Savory, USMA 1967

- 1ST DELTA FORCE SURGEON/1ST JOINT SPECIAL OPERATIONS SURGEON
- OPERATION EAGLE CLAW ASSAULT FORCE MEMBER
- RANGER UNIT PLATOON LEADER VIETNAM WAR
- SURGEON, OPERATION DESERT STORM
- RANGER HALL OF FAME INDUCTEE
- INITIATED THE CONCEPT OF THE CREATION OF THE "FORWARD SURGICAL TEAM," WHICH BECAME ARMY DOCTRINE

C-130 wreckage in the Iranian desert, April 25, 1980.

Savory in Iraq during Operation Desert Storm.

>>> Spotlight

United States Special Operations Command (USSOCOM) was established on April 21, 1987, after the Hart-Rudman Commission of 1986 that investigated the failed rescue attempt in Operation Eagle Claw. USSOCOM is one of seven unified Combatant Commands (COCOMs) that divide the world into area of operations, such as Northern Command (NORTHCOM), European Command (EUCOM), Southern Command (SOUTHCOM), African Command (AFRICOM), Central Command (CENTCOM), and Pacific Command (PACOM), which each have regional authority. Only United States Special Operations Command (USSOCOM) has overall global responsibilities to synchronize operations across all services and commands to prevent any inter-service rivalries that contributed to the failure of Operation Eagle Claw. Each of the seven COCOMs is commanded by a Four-Star Flag Officer from one of the four services.

Courtesy: DOD

DEDICATED TO THE FAC OF TH MILITARY A FOR THEIR HO

NOVEMBER

and orthopedic residency.

In 1978, Major Savory received orders to Fort Ord, California, in Monterey, an ideal assignment. Unfortunately those orders were changed to Fort Bragg, North Carolina, without explanation, to his initial disappointment. It wasn't until he arrived at Fort Bragg that the hospital commander pulled him aside to explain that he had been selected by the legendary Colonel Charlie Beckwith to be the first surgeon of the newly formed 1st Special Forces Operational Detachment–Delta (SFOD-D), which is now commonly referred to as "Delta Force." With Savory's combat Infantry experience, Ranger qualification, and now being a surgeon with a top-secret clearance, he was ideally suited to the new elite unit. The hospital commander explained the new unit's focus on counter-terrorism and asked if Savory would volunteer, which he did on the spot. For the next seven years, Savory's leadership set in motion the systems and procedures that would impact not only Special Operations

but the military medical community as a whole for decades to come.

Starting in April 1979, Savory built up a team of surgical and medical experts to support Delta. They trained hard and unconventionally. For example: The Air Force was typically suited to transport stable patients, not patients that Delta might have in its missions who might need in-flight surgery. So Savory and his team adapted C-130 and stretch C-141s and practiced surgery in-flight on goats and pigs.

Savory and his team were on a validation exercise to showcase Delta's new capabilities in November 1979 when the medical team was awakened and informed that the United States Embassy in Iran had just been taken over by a mob. Initially the Delta thought it was a hypothetical scenario as part of the training exercise, but soon realized the embassy in Tehran had fallen. This event became Deltas focus for the next six months as they trained to rescue the hostages. During this time Doc

Savory attempted to prepare the medical team for every possible contingency by conducting recurrent exercises and training, including the memorization of every hostage's medical records.

In April 1980, Colonel Beckwith briefed President Jimmy Carter, who gave the go-ahead for the mission called Operation Eagle Claw. Beckwith returned to Fort Bragg and the entire team flew to Egypt, from where they would stage the mission deep into Iran, the longest and most dangerous rescue mission ever attempted by any military force. Prior to boarding the aircraft in Egypt, Lieutenant Colonel Bucky Burruss, the charismatic Delta Executive Officer, stood in the hanger and led the group in singing "God Bless America," and they walked out to the flight line to stage the dangerous raid for which they had trained for so long. Savory remembers it being the greatest and proudest moment of his life. Helicopter failures at the refueling site in a location called Desert One caused Colonel Beckwith to abort the mission. In the process of aborting the mission two aircraft collided, killing eight servicemen and destroying a helicopter and C-130. As they flew back, devastated at the failure of the mission with the loss of eight of their fellow servicemen, Savory still recalls it as the worst moment of his life. He now reflects that the greatest moment of his life and the worst both occurred within 24 hours of each other.

Savory believes their mission and sacrifice were not in vain. Under increased interactional pressure after the rescue attempt the Iranians finally released the hostages safely eight months later. The United States military at that time had many organizational design and operational weaknesses. Savory reflects that had the mission been a success there would have been celebrations and there would not have been an investigation and a thorough assessment of those inherent weaknesses, particularly the inter-service failures that were prevalent at the time. Due to the failure of the mission, Congress conducted a thorough investigation and found many problems with the military that needed to

be addressed. Through the Hart-Rudman Commission, Congress created the United States Special Operations Command (USSOCOM) in 1986, which would help the United States military be better prepared for the future conflicts after the end of the Cold War. And although the first mission had ended in failure, Delta Force went on to be known as the most elite group of special operators in the world.

The Iranians released the hostages on the inauguration day of President Ronald Reagan January 20, 1980. President Reagan ordered the hostages to be flown back to the United States and reunited with their families at West Point in the Thayer Hotel – a place Doc Savory knew well. The Delta team never met the hostages; by the time the hostages were released most of the Delta operators were off on other real-world missions.

Colonel Savory retired in 1987, but volunteered to return to duty in 1990 during Operation Desert Storm, where he served in the 274th Forward Airborne Surgical Team attached to the 24th Infantry Division sweeping "left hook" deep into Iraq. In 2009, Doc Savory was inducted in to the Ranger Hall of Fame. He retired from the Army in Columbus, Georgia, and has been a practicing orthopedic surgeon with the internationally renowned Hughston Clinic for more than 25 years.

In 2011, the Thayer Hotel management team invited the remaining living hostages and members of the original Delta Force rescue team to the Thayer Hotel for the 30th anniversary of the hostages return to the Thayer Hotel in 1981. Colonel "Doc" Savory, Colonel Bucky Burruss, Major Wade Ishimoto from Delta and Al Golacinski, Bill Daugherty, and Barry Rosen (former hostages) rang the closing bell at the NASDAQ in Times Square prior to the weekend at the Thayer Hotel and were recognized by the American public for the mission that they had attempted 30 years earlier. The Delta team met some of the former hostages for the first time that evening – two groups united by an international incident and yet separated for three decades. One former hostage introduced himself, and Doc Savory said, "You're O Positive right?" Thirty years later, and he still remembered the medical facts of every American that he and his team had risked their lives to liberate those three decades earlier.

EEPEST GRATITUDE
AFF AND STUDENTS
TED STATES
Y AT WEST POINT
IN WELCOMING US
FREEDOM
AMERICANS HELD
HOSTAGE IN IRAN
–JANUARY 20, 1981

Plaque located in lobby of Thayer Hotel at West Point.

Doc Savory in the desert in Operation Desert Storm.

Savory as a Ranger Platoon Leader in Vietnam.

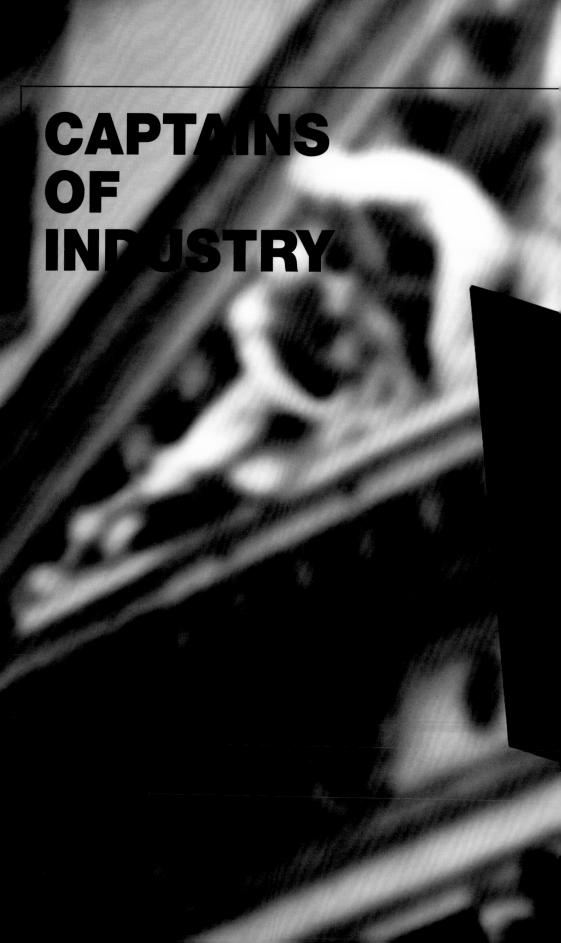

CAPTAINS OF INDUSTRY

Since the founding of West Point, graduates have entered and led the business world after completing their military service beginning with West Point's first graduate, Brigadier General Joseph Swift (USMA 1802), who went on to use the engineer training and leadership he learned at West Point as a canal designer, city planner, and railroad manager. Graduates continued to use their leadership and engineering skills they learned at West Point to influence the continual development and expansion of antebellum America. Just prior to the Civil War, there were more West Point graduates serving as Presidents of railroads than there were serving as General Officers in the Army. West Point graduates have continued this trend for the past 150 years and also have led many of the top corporations as Chief Executive Officers in America and globally, including Procter & Gamble, 7-Eleven Corporation, America Online, Wendy's Restaurants, Foot Locker, Fifth Third Bank, Federated Investors, Kleiner Perkins Caufield & Byers, Nexus Lexus, Marriott International, Northwest Airlines, API Group, Comfort Systems USA, Aptuit, Commerce One, Sybase, Mercedes-Benz USA, EMCOR, Parsons Brinkerhoff, and many others. Many companies now specifically recruit West Point graduates to lead their corporations in middle management and at the C-Suite level because of their proven success across all areas of the private sector. This chapter highlights some of those "captains of industry."

"Nothing of consequence is accomplished without leadership. You are being taught leadership here at the USMA [West Point]. Leadership is the essence of what you will do when you graduate.

–Chief Executive Officer of General Electric Jeff Immelt, Renewing American Leadership address at West Point 2009

Character is the most important trait of a leader."

–Chairman, President and Chief Executive Officer Bob McDonald, USMA 1975

"Values based leadership...it is sorely lacking in the private sector and in my opinion only one institution [West Point] can credibly deliver that message."

–Chief Executive Officer and President of Mercedes-Benz USA (MBUSA) Steve Cannon, USMA 1986

"The penalty for poor ethics in the military is much higher than any place else because people are going to get killed or wounded if a person in combat submits a false report."

–Chairman of the New York Stock Exchange Group, Colonel (USMCR, Retired) Marsh Carter, USMA 1962

"Great leaders achieve results through influence. Their influence is attained through a strong set of values, nobility of character, and by service to others."

–Chief Executive Officer and President of 7-Eleven Corporation Joe DePinto, USMA 1986

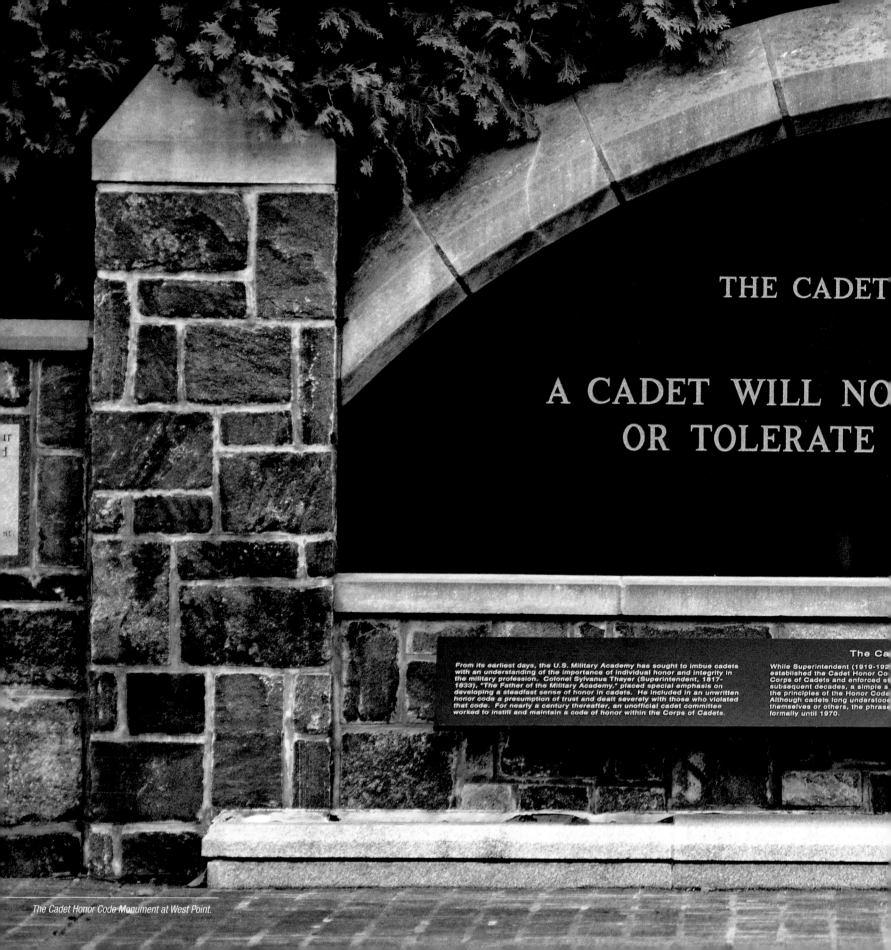

THE CADET

A CADET WILL NO
OR TOLERATE

The Ca

From its earliest days, the U.S. Military Academy has sought to imbue cadets with an understanding of the importance of individual honor and integrity in the military profession. Colonel Sylvanus Thayer (Superintendent, 1817-1833), "The Father of the Military Academy," placed special emphasis on developing a steadfast sense of honor in cadets. He included in an unwritten honor code a presumption of trust and dealt severely with those who violated that code. For nearly a century thereafter, an unofficial cadet committee worked to instill and maintain a code of honor within the Corps of Cadets.

While Superintendent (1919-19
established the Cadet Honor Co
Corps of Cadets and enforced s
subsequent decades, a simple s
the principles of the Honor Code
Although cadets long understoo
themselves or others, the phrase
formally until 1970.

The Cadet Honor Code Monument at West Point.

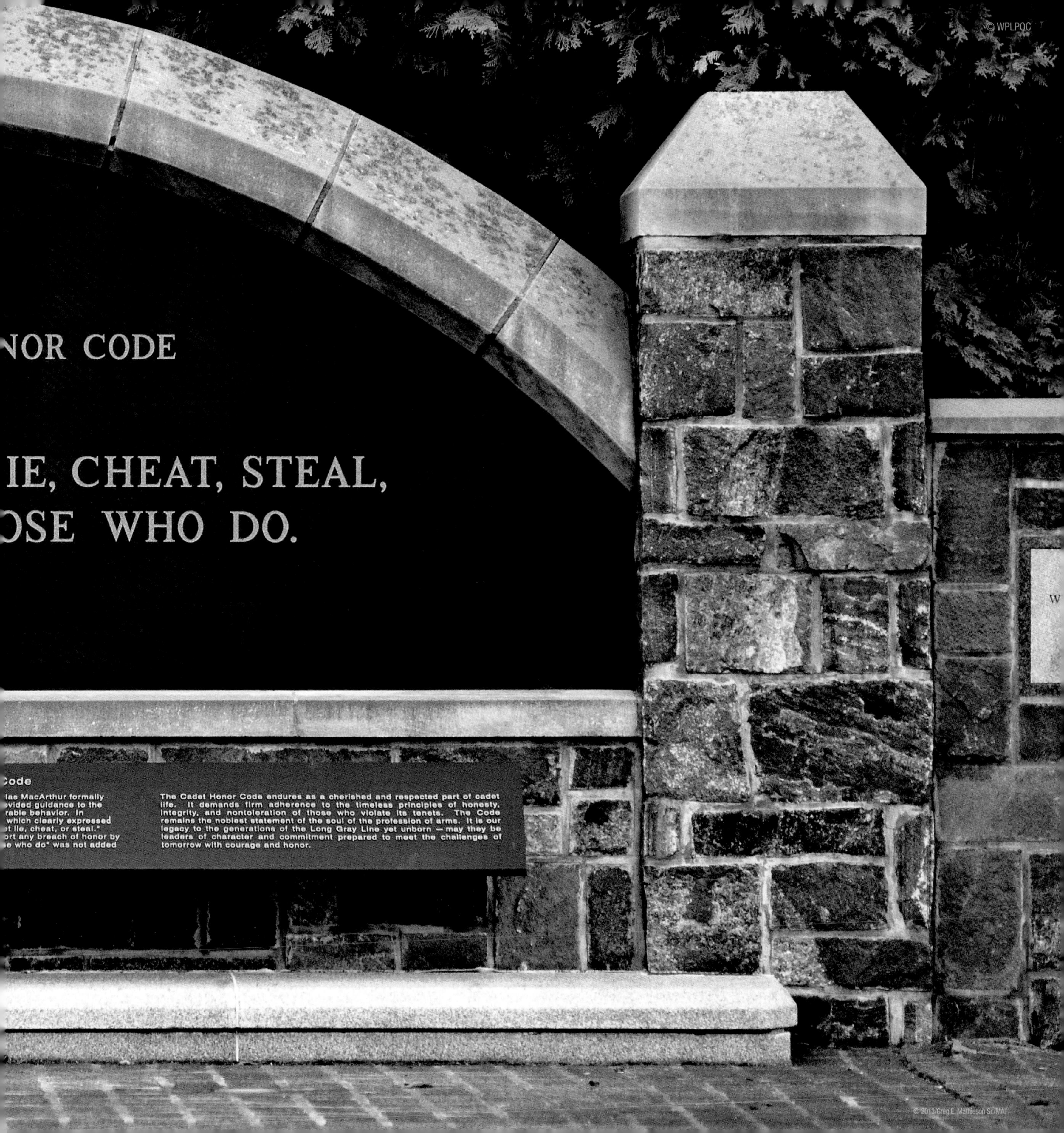
NOR CODE
IE, CHEAT, STEAL,
OSE WHO DO.
Code
las MacArthur formally
vided guidance to the
rable behavior. In
which clearly expressed
t lie, cheat, or steal."
ort any breach of honor by
e who do" was not added
The Cadet Honor Code endures as a cherished and respected part of cadet life. It demands firm adherence to the timeless principles of honesty, integrity, and nontoleration of those who violate its tenets. The Code remains the noblest statement of the soul of the profession of arms. It is our legacy to the generations of the Long Gray Line yet unborn — may they be leaders of character and commitment prepared to meet the challenges of tomorrow with courage and honor.
© WPLPOC
© 2013/Greg E. Mathieson Sr./MAI

Colonel (Retired) Marsh Carter (USMCR), USMA 1962

- **CHAIRMAN OF THE NEW YORK STOCK EXCHANGE GROUP**
- **CHIEF EXECUTIVE OFFICER, STATE STREET BANK & TRUST**
- **NAVY CROSS AND PURPLE HEART RECIPIENT**
- **NAVAL POSTGRADUATE SCHOOL, MASTER'S OF SCIENCE IN OPERATIONS RESEARCH/SYSTEMS ANALYSIS**
- **GEORGE WASHINGTON UNIVERSITY, MASTER'S OF SCIENCE IN TECHNOLOGY AND PUBLIC POLICY**
- **BOY SCOUTS OF AMERICA, EAGLE SCOUT**

Carter celebrating the Marine Corps birthday on the floor of the New York Stock Exchange.

Navy Cross and Purple Heart Medals with Cadet and Marine Sabers on a cadet uniform.

Colonel (Retired) Marsh Carter is a decorated war hero, former White House Fellow, Chief Executive Officer, and role model for ethics and values in corporate America. He is the chairman of the New York Stock Exchange Group (NYSE) and a proud West Point graduate. He was previously the chairman and Chief Executive Officer of State Street Bank & Trust, a major financial firm that grew significantly under his leadership. He has been incredibly successful on Wall Street while maintaining strict ethics and values. He was commissioned as a Marine Corps Officer and served two tours of duty in Vietnam, where he was awarded the Navy Cross, Bronze Star for Valor, Navy Achievement Medal with valor, and the Purple Heart. In 1989, after 14 years of active duty, he retired from the Marine Reserves after a total of 27 years in uniform as a Colonel. After leaving active duty, Carter served for 16 years with Chase Bank, then rose to become the Chief Executive Officer of State Street Bank & Trust, followed by his current role as the chairman of the New York Stock Exchange Group. He was a White House Fellow and has two master's degrees. He has lived his life according to the West Point principles of "Duty, Honor, Country" and is a role model for corporate America.

> **IT IS HARD TO ARGUE ABOUT GREED WITH A PERSON WHO GIVES AWAY HALF HIS EARNINGS. LIKE A GOOD INFANTRY OFFICER, HE LEADS BY EXAMPLE.**

Carter was born in Virginia on April 23, 1940, to a military family. His father, Lieutenant General (Retired) Marshall Carter (USMA 1931), served as an aide to General of the Army George C. Marshall when he was Secretary of State and Secretary of Defense. His father then served as the Deputy Director of the Central Intelligence Agency (CIA) and then was the 5th Director of the National Security Agency. His grandfather Brigadier General Clifton Carter (USMA 1899) graduated early to serve in Cuba during the Spanish-American War, received a graduate degree from MIT, then served in France during World War I. His grandfather was then a professor at West Point from 1917 through 1940. Between the three graduates, the Carters served continuously in uniform from 1895 through Carter's retirement in 1989. His grandfather on the other side of his family and his uncle (on his mother's side) were also Army Officers, having both graduated from Virginia Military Institute (VMI).

Carter entered West Point in 1958, but he decided not to join the Army after graduation. The United States Air Force Academy (USAFA) had only opened in 1959, and, prior to its founding, 25 percent of the West Point class was joining the United States Air Force. Once USAFA opened, the West Point allowance was reduced to 12 percent of the class that could be commissioned in the Air Force or Marine Corps. Carter's class had 601 graduates so 72 were commissioned in the Air Force (64) and Marine Corps (8). Carter chose the Marine Corps because "the Army was our family business, and my Yearling year people, not cadets, would introduce me as so and so's son or grandson," he explained. "I didn't have identity of my own so I wanted to leave family business of the Army." Second Lieutenant Carter chose to be commissioned in the United States Marine Corps to make his own identity – which indeed he would do on a battlefield in a far off land.

Carter's graduation year was an amazing time in West Point history. In May 1962, General Douglas MacArthur gave his legendary "Duty, Honor, Country" speech to the Corps of Cadets at his acceptance speech for the Sylvanus Thayer award, along with the Superintendent Major General William Westmoreland. The next month, President John F. Kennedy spoke at Carter's graduation. His speech ominously warned of "another type of warfare – new in its intensity, ancient in its origin, war by guerillas, subversives…assassins." The Class of 1962 would fight unconventional war in Vietnam, under General Westmoreland, who would be promoted to Four-Star General and command the war in Vietnam for four years.

Carter received his bachelor's of science degree in civil engineering from President Kennedy, was commissioned in the Marine Corps, and deployed to Vietnam in 1966 as a Rifle Company Commander in the 1st Marine Division. During an air assault mission, his company was ambushed in the landing zone. Captain Carter would earn the Navy Cross leading his company through that ambush and successfully extracting a wounded Marine and his entire company. A *New York Times* article that covered the story on January 16, 1967, said, "The Marine withdrawal was planned for 4:30 p.m. It was held up for almost two hours, while one platoon fought its way back to the landing zone picking up Marines dead on the way. The last helicopter carrying Captain Carter left under the illumination of a flare. 'He was real cool' a Marine private said."

A few months later, Captain Carter was wounded when he fell into a punji stake pit in a cemetery that was wired to an M26 grenade. He received shrapnel from the grenade, and for this, he was awarded the Purple Heart Medal.

After returning from his first tour in Vietnam, Carter received a master's degree in operations research and systems analysis from the United States Naval Postgraduate School in Monterey, California, in 1970.

He served a second tour in Vietnam from 1970 to 1971 as an advisor with the Vietnamese Marine Corps. He served in this role as an operations advisor in the Mekong delta and then moved up to Khe Sanh in early 1971 during the Vietnamese invasion of Laos. During his two tours of duty in Vietnam, Carter was awarded the Navy Cross, Bronze Star for Valor, Navy Commendation Medal with valor, Air Medal with valor, and the Purple Heart.

Major Carter's last assignment on active duty was serving as a White House Fellow in Washington, D.C., at the United States Agency for International Development (USAID) from 1975 to 1976. While in Washington, he used his G.I. Bill to receive multiple master's degrees – in science, technology, and public policy from George Washington University in 1976. He left active duty in 1976, but remained in the United States Marine Corps Reserve (USMCR) and retired as Colonel in 1989. After leaving active duty in 1976, Carter was hired by Chase Bank, after an exhaustive search and being turned down by 85 companies. At that time, companies were not supportive of veterans – something that still drives him today. At Chase, he rose in responsibility steadily, eventually becoming Senior Vice President of an international business unit that contributed 15 percent to Chase's bottom line.

Carter joined State Street Bank & Trust in July 1991 as President and Chief Operating Officer, becoming Chief Executive Officer in 1992 and Chairman in 1993. During his nine years as Chief Executive Officer, the company grew more than six times in revenue and to 22,000 employees. While at State Street, he was well known for being a progressive, ethical leader. He was very supportive of minorities – nine of the top 12 Vice President positions reporting to him were women.

His leadership style was typical of an Infantryman: He did a lot of walking around, talking to employees and customers. He led by example and had a very simple leadership philosophy:

There are only three that are really important:

1. Technical competence, know what your business and job are about.

2. Adaptability, because everything changes in six to 18 months now.

3. The ability to communicate.

"I think those are the three leadership traits that every leader needs," said Carter in an interview with *Fortune* magazine.

He retired from State Street Bank & Trust in 2001 after a very successful nine-year growth period with no scandals and a healthy culture. From 2001 to 2004, he served as a visiting senior lecturer at Harvard's Kennedy School of government,

The New York Stock Exchange.

Captain Carter joking around in Vietnam.

Captain Carter in Vietnam.

teaching leadership and management.

In 2003, a scandal at the New York Stock Exchange Group occurred when the outgoing NYSE Chief Executive Officer was given an excessive compensation package. As evidence of the esteem in which Carter is held, he was one of six financial service executives asked to come out of retirement in October 2003 after the Chairman, Chief Executive Officer, and the entire 26-member Board of Directors at the NYSE was asked to resign due to the excessive compensation package given to the Chief Executive Officer. Carter served two years as a board member and was elected Chairman of the Board in 2005.

In an era of excessive executive compensation, Carter is a breath of fresh air, speaking regularly about the abuses of executive compensation and greed. He regularly lectures at Harvard Business School and MIT. When asked about his own compensation, he usually eliminates any attacks by saying he gives away 50 percent of everything he earns. It is hard to argue about greed with a person who gives away half his earnings. Like a good Infantry Officer, he leads by example.

Ethics and leadership are desperately needed in corporate America, and Carter stands at the head of the New York Stock Exchange Group as a role model. When asked where his foundation for ethics comes from, he answers, "For me it was the military, especially at West Point. I went in to West Point the week after graduating high school when I was 18. There are a couple of things about military training. One is you get ethical instructions early. Second, the penalty for poor ethics in the military is much higher than any place else because people are going to get killed or wounded if a person in combat submits a false report."

MARSH CARTER'S MANY LEADERSHIP POSITIONS AND AWARDS:

- Served as Chairman of the Board of Trustees of the Boston Medical Center, 2001–09.
- Cochaired the U.S. Working Group of Thirty that revamped securities laws.
- Served as a member of the board of directors of Honeywell International, 1997–2005.
- Chaired the Massachusetts Governor's Special Advisory Task Force on Massport and Logan Airport following the events of September 11, 2001.
- Inducted into the American Academy of Arts and Sciences 2006.

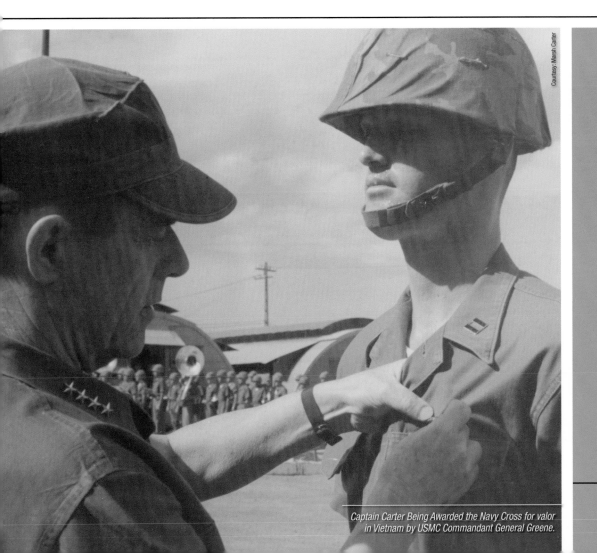

Courtesy: Marsh Carter

Captain Carter Being Awarded the Navy Cross for valor in Vietnam by USMC Commandant General Greene.

>>> Spotlight

NYSE Euronext (NYX) is a leading global operator of financial markets and provider of innovative trading technologies. The company's exchanges in Europe and the United States trade equities, futures, options, fixed-income, and exchange-traded products. With approximately 8,000 listed issues (excluding European Structured Products), NYSE Euronext's equities markets — the New York Stock Exchange, NYSE Euronext, NYSE MKT, NYSE Alternext, and NYSE Arca _ represent one-third of the world's equities trading, the most liquidity of any global exchange group. NYSE Euronext also operates NYSE Liffe, one of the leading European derivatives businesses and the world's second-largest derivatives business by value of trading. The company offers comprehensive commercial technology, connectivity and market data products and services through NYSE Technologies. NYSE Euronext is in the S&P 500 index.

Courtesy: NYSE

Alex Gorsky grew up in a small Midwestern town in a typical middle-class American family, the third of six children whose grandparents had immigrated to the United States and whose father enlisted in the Army during the Korean War. In the sixth grade, Gorsky decided that he wanted to attend the United States Military Academy at West Point; he fulfilled his dream by graduating from West Point in 1982 and serving as

an officer in the United States Army for six years. He now leads Johnson & Johnson, one of the world's the largest and most diversified health care companies with more than 128,000 employees in more than 60 countries and $65 billion in sales. Alex Gorsky's life exemplifies the Horatio Alger story that hard work, perseverance, and honesty can conquer all obstacles.

Gorsky was born in Kansas City, Kansas. His grandparents were immigrants from

Croatia and Russia and his grandfather was in the grocery business. Gorsky's father, Albert Gorsky, voluntarily enlisted in the Army during the Korean War in 1952 and, after proving himself, was selected to attend Officer Candidate School (OCS).

Albert Gorsky served five years of active duty in the Army and then joined the Army reserves while working full-time in sales at Gerber. Albert Gorsky rose to the top of both organizations through hard work,

retiring as Vice President of United States Sales for Gerber and as a Two-Star General in the Army Reserves. Major General Albert E. Gorsky retired from the Army after 38 years and was inducted in to the OCS Hall of Fame.

During Alex Gorsky's childhood, dinner table conversations often included discussions about the military and business. When Gorsky was 12 years old, the family moved to Fremont, Michigan,

Alex Gorsky, USMA 1982

- CHAIRMAN, PRESIDENT, AND CHIEF EXECUTIVE OFFICER OF JOHNSON & JOHNSON
- VICE CHAIRMAN, JOHNSON & JOHNSON
- PRESIDENT, ETHICON, INC. (J&J)
- PRESIDENT, JANSEN PHARMACEUTICALS, INC. (J&J)
- MBA, THE WHARTON SCHOOL, UNIVERSITY OF PENNSYLVANIA
- ALPHA BATTERY COMMANDER, 2/8TH FIELD ARTILLERY, 7TH INFANTRY DIVISION (LIGHT)

Photo: NARA

Courtesy: Alex Gorsky

Courtesy: Alex Gorsky

a small town of only 3,500 people, comprised almost entirely of farmers and Gerber employees. Fremont was very rural, and Gorsky and his friends hunted, fished, hiked, and played sports daily. When a family friend was accepted to West Point, it inspired Alex Gorsky to start reading about the Academy. By sixth grade, his journals show that he was determined to attend West Point. He was the prototypical West Point candidate: captain of the varsity football team, captain of the swimming team, he ran track, and went to Boys' Nation.

Congressman Guy Vander Jagt nominated Gorsky to attend West Point in 1977, and the day he was accepted was one of the greatest days of his life. Gorsky and his family visited the Academy for the first time on "R Day," July 6, 1978, the same day he entered West Point. For Gorsky, coming from a small Midwestern town, the Academy was larger than life. It offered academic and physical challenges and social opportunities that did not exist in Fremont, Michigan. He was very active, joining the pistol, orienteering, marathon, and triathlon teams, and he was always ready to try new experiences. He learned to follow, then to lead. An outstanding athlete and in excellent physical condition, Gorsky tried out for Army Ranger School – the most physically challenging school in the Army – while still a cadet, using up all leave the summer between his Yearling and Cow years. Many cadets competed to gain a slot in Ranger School, and among those accepted there was a high attrition rate. Gorsky was one of the few who earned the coveted Ranger Tab. Due to the high attrition rate in Gorsky's class in 1981, Ranger School was not offered to cadets for several years afterward.

Looking back, Alex Gorsky cites the summer of 1981 as a seminal time in his life. Ranger School gave him the confidence that he could overcome any obstacle, and reinforced his lessons in teamwork, hard work, and commitment. He returned exhausted, having lost 15 pounds, and proceeded to have his worst academic semester of his four years at West Point, which was humbling. At that time, all West Point cadets were required to study engineering (which changed in 1988 to allow some liberal arts majors), and Gorsky majored in engineering and chose as his field of study political science and history. He chose them for two reasons: He had an innate interest in the subject matter, and he had outstanding high-school teachers who had inspired him in those subjects. "I believe that having the combination of an engineering core curriculum, plus a softer science, prepares one for critical thinking combined with understanding organizations, people, and flow of events. In today's world, having a balance between those two domains is more important than ever," says Gorsky.

While some cadets became jaded or cynical while at West Point, Gorsky never did; he always felt privileged to attend the Academy. His belief was reinforced in 1980 through 1981, when the 52 American hostages in Iran were released from captivity after 444 days. After their release, President Ronald Reagan had them flown to West Point, where they were welcomed by their families and cheering cadets. The event was covered by global news media frenzy. "It reinforced my belief in what a special place West Point was – gathering on the Plain and in the Mess Hall, here was an event that the world was watching, and we were right in the midst of it. The event reinforced all my sentiments about the Academy," Gorsky remembered. Having already graduated Ranger School, Gorsky had planned on picking the Infantry Branch, but after spending time with the Field Artillery Officer in Charge his senior year, he was persuaded to choose Artillery. He had been impressed by the Artillery Branch; it included combat arms like the Infantry, but it also placed a major emphasis on strategy and technology.

Artillery Officers needed to understand the strategy and tactics not only of Infantry, but also the Armor and Aviation Branches, and to consider how all of them come together as a combined team. Gorsky's class graduated on May 26, 1982, and he was commissioned in the Army. He attended Airborne School, the Officer Basic Course at Fort Sill, Oklahoma, then language school in Monterey, California, to learn basic Greek. Gorsky served a one-year hardship tour at a base in Northern Greece, which was a great experience for a 23-year-old, and he returned to Fort Ord, California (Monterey), to the 7th Infantry Division. The 7th Infantry Division had recently been designated a "Light Infantry" Division, and the Army was making a tremendous effort to transform it from being a training unit to one of the most effective elite combat units in the Army. It was not unusual for its members to spend more than 200 nights a year in the field training. The Army

> **LEAVING THE ARMY WAS THE TOUGHEST DECISION GORSKY HAS EVER MADE IN HIS LIFE, AND HE STRUGGLED WITH IT AT THE TIME. HE LOVED THE ARMY, THE MISSION, THE SENSE OF PURPOSE, AND THE CULTURE TO ALWAYS "DO THE RIGHT THING" AND FEARED HE MIGHT NOT FIND THAT AGAIN IN CORPORATE AMERICA.**

Captain Gorsky as Artillery Battery Commander at Fort Ord in Monterey, California.

Alex and Patricia Gorsky.

assigned some of its best officers to make this transformation possible, and a huge premium was placed on leadership and small unit tactics. Years later, Gorsky would try to emulate those leadership lessons at Johnson & Johnson. The Army's staff rides and officer professional development sessions had a major impact on him. For instance, while Gorsky was at Fort Ord, they read books such as *We Were Soldiers Once…and Young*, followed by discussions at Officer Professional Development about the leadership challenges faced in the books. In 1985, another seminal event occurred in his life when he met a nurse in Monterey, California, named Patricia. Patricia was an "Army and Air Force brat" who been born in Berchtesgaden, Germany, and had grown up all over the world, living in Morocco, Hawaii, and on multiple bases across the United States. They married in

1987 in Carmel and had their reception at the Defense Language Institute. Gorsky was promoted to Captain and received a command – which is rare at that age and rank – before returning to Officer Advanced Course training. He loved leading soldiers at Fort Ord. Patricia was working as a nurse and head of the family support group there. At his six-year mark, Gorsky had to decide whether to stay in the Army until retirement in 20 years or leave to start his civilian career.

Leaving the Army was the toughest decision Gorsky has made in his life and he struggled with it at the time. He loved the Army, its mission, sense of purpose, and its culture that emphasized always doing the right thing, and he feared he might not find that again in corporate America. In 1988, with Patricia pregnant with their son, Nicholas, Gorsky chose to leave the

Army to pursue a business career. He was offered several positions in the technology sector and in health care and, after much deliberation, he chose a Johnson & Johnson operating company called Janssen Pharmaceutical Inc. The deciding factor in his decision that would remain a tremendous influence in his life was a Credo written in 1943 by General Robert Wood Johnson, a member of the family that founded Johnson & Johnson. The Credo listed the company's top four priorities in order: patients and consumers, employees, community, and lastly, shareholders. When the Credo was written, Johnson & Johnson was still family owned (it would go public in 1944), and General Johnson was the largest single stockholder, yet he listed shareholders last. That resonated with Gorsky, who wanted to find a culture that felt similar to the Army. General Johnson

understood that if you focus on the first three priorities – patients, employees, and the community – then shareholders would benefit, as well. That echoed the Army ethos of always putting the soldier and the mission first. The principles of the Credo were unheard of when it was written in 1943, and terms like "social responsibility" did not come into use until decades later. At Johnson & Johnson, Gorsky believed he had found his new mission. He began his career there as a pharmaceutical sales representative and, over a period of 15 years, he advanced through roles in sales, marketing, and management. In 2001, Gorsky became the President of Janssen Pharmaceutical Inc. During the years he spent at Janssen, the division experienced significant growth in terms of products, people, and overall prominence in the pharmaceutical industry. It had done

>>> Spotlight

"Caring for the world, one person at a time, inspires and unites the people of Johnson & Johnson. We embrace research and science – bringing innovative ideas, products, and services to advance the health and well-being of people. Our approximately 129,000 employees at more than 250 Johnson & Johnson operating companies work with partners in health care to touch the lives of more than a billion people every day, throughout the world." –Alex Gorsky

Courtesy: Johnson & Johnson

Gorsky as a senior at West Point during graduation week.

Gorsky in front of the Johnson & Johnson Credo.

Courtesy: Alex Gorsky

so by launching a variety of life-saving products across a range of important therapeutic areas.

Patricia practiced as a nurse until 2000. "I wouldn't be where I am today without her," says Gorsky, who fondly remembers Patricia teaching him how to in-service various products throughout his career, and keeping their common interest of patient care at the forefront over the years. Johnson & Johnson has always had a very close relationship with the nursing community, and being married to a nurse has given Gorsky a unique and special perspective.

In 2003, Gorsky was named Company Group Chairman of Johnson & Johnson's pharmaceuticals business in Europe, the Middle East, North Africa, and Russia. "It was a tremendous experience working

with so many different regions and people," he says. In 2005, a former mentor who had left Johnson & Johnson asked Gorsky to join him at Novartis, a Swiss pharmaceutical company. Gorsky worked at Novartis for four years, which gave him an excellent perspective from a competitive viewpoint. But deep down, his heart was at Johnson & Johnson, and he returned in 2008 as Company Group Chairman of the Ethicon business in the company's medical devices and diagnostics segment. He was quickly promoted to Worldwide Chairman, Medical Devices and Diagnostics in 2009, then promoted to Vice Chairman of Johnson & Johnson and appointed to its Executive Committee in January of 2011. In April of that year, Gorsky became the seventh Chief Executive Officer of Johnson & Johnson, and in December of 2012, he was elected Chairman of the Board

of Directors. Johnson & Johnson is one of the world's largest diversified health care companies operating in 60 countries, with $65 billion in sales and 128,000 employees. It is also the largest and most-diverse medical devices and diagnostics company in the world, the eighth-largest pharmaceutical company, world's sixth-largest consumer health company, and the world's fifth-largest biologics company. Leading such a complex organization in nearly every country, with so many market-leading products, is certainly both challenging and an incredible opportunity. How does he manage to steer such a large organization? "What's most important is, number one: You establish the right tone for the culture, which starts with our Credo. Number two: Set a common vision and a set of priorities – similar in the military to establishing your 'mission.' Number three:

Provide your team with the resources to allow them to operate with a fair degree of freedom and autonomy to accomplish their objectives. Number four: Give a balance of inspiration and leadership versus just 'management.' And number five: The most important is to pick the right leaders and give them the freedom, since they are closest to what's going on – reward them and hold them accountable."

When asked what he would like to achieve in his role, Gorsky's answer is simple yet monumental, given that he leads a health care company that can reach nearly every person on the planet: "To make a difference so that people can live longer, healthier, and happier lives." Alex Gorsky, West Point Class of 1982, has found his mission.

Brother Pete (left) and sister, Holly Anzani, and her husband, Mark Anzani.

James Patrick "Pat" Mackin, USMA 1988

- **PRESIDENT, MEDTRONIC CRDM DIVISION**
- **VICE PRESIDENT OF WESTERN EUROPE, MEDTRONIC VASCULAR DIVISION**
- **VICE PRESIDENT AND GENERAL MANAGER, MEDTRONIC ENDOVASCULAR BUSINESS**
- **DIRECTOR OF SALES, GENZYME SURGICAL DIVISION**
- **KELLOGG/NORTHWESTERN UNIVERSITY MASTER'S IN BUSINESS ADMINISTRATION**
- **FIELD ARTILLERY OFFICER, 4TH INFANTRY DIVISION**

Testifying on business in Russia before United States Senate.

Pat Mackin is the President of Medtronic's $5-billion Cardiac Rhythm Management business and oversees the 12,000 employees in the division. Medtronic is a Fortune 150 Company and is the world leader in developing sophisticated medical devices with a major focus on cardiovascular disease. He is a 1988 graduate of West Point and served as an Army Officer prior to entering the medical device market in 1991. For the past 20 years, he has been a leader in the medical-device market and has shown that West Point leadership principles can apply in the competitive and complicated American health care market to improve patient care and outcomes.

Pat Mackin was born on October 23, 1966, in Los Angeles, California. Mackin was the youngest of three children, growing up with his sister, Holly, and his brother, Pete. Mackin's father James (Jim) had a big influence on him, as he instilled in his son the importance of determination, perseverance and discipline that became the foundation of his character. His father was raised in a tough neighborhood on

the south side of Chicago and enlisted in the United States Marine Corps at the end of World War II. After the war, his father worked bridge construction in the summers to pay his own way through Northwestern University where he would later graduate with a Journalism degree from the prestigious Merrill School. Jim met his wife, Marge, at Northwestern and they married after graduation in 1952 and then headed to Los Angeles. Jim was an advertising executive and Marge an elementary school teacher. In 1967, Jim was promoted and asked to move to Madison Avenue in New York City. After a couple of years in New York, the family then moved to downtown Chicago and then Augusta, Maine, in 1976, when Jim was recruited to take jobs as the General Manager of large radio stations. Mackin, a standout athlete and at six foot three inches and 200 pounds, played football and hockey, ran track, and was heavily recruited to play football at the collegiate level.

Mackin was appointed to West Point by Senator Bill Cohen (ME) and started on July 2, 1984. Plebe year at West Point

has its share of challenges for any West Point cadet. In addition to the normal Plebe challenges, Mackin went through his own private hell. His mother, Marge, who otherwise was a very healthy, suffered from a stroke and spent the better part of two years learning how to speak again. Unfortunately, at the end of his Cow year, Marge suffered a second massive stroke – one that would keep her hospitalized for the rest of her life. She would never walk or talk again. This sudden loss of his mother's capacities was a shock to Mackin, his two siblings, and his father. After six months in an acute care hospital, she was transferred to the nursing home on a Friday night. The next day, in November of Firstie year, Mackin received a phone call from his brother-in-law, Mark. By the tone of Mark's voice, he feared the worst – that his mother had died. In a total shock, it was not his mother, but his father that had died of a heart attack.

Through this tragedy, Mackin became closer with his brother, sister, and brother-in-law, as well as his new family and friends at West Point, who helped him

through this terrible ordeal. He focused all of his efforts on thriving at West Point. Despite the challenges and knowing how short life can be, he focused on enjoying life as much as possible. The friends he made would be lifelong friends. He proved to be incredibly resilient, which would serve him well later in life.

Mackin graduated from West Point on May 25, 1988, and received his BS in Engineering from then Vice President George W. Bush, Second Lieutenant Mackin chose the Field Artillery Branch, and his first assignment was in the 4th Infantry Division at Fort Carson, Colorado, near Colorado Springs. He was assigned Platoon Leader in the Multiple Launched Rocket System (MLRS) and was promoted to First Lieutenant and Executive Officer in 1990. He loved the Army, leading soldiers, and was recognized by his commanders for his leadership abilities. After the end of the Cold War, the Army experienced significant downsizing as Congress wanted to achieve its "peace dividend." Mackin chose to leave the Army and pursue his business career. As he looked at potential career

>>> Spotlight

Medtronic, Inc. headquartered in Minneapolis, is the global leader in medical technology with a focus on chronic diseases. Medtronic's six major businesses focus their efforts around a condition or therapy type – Cardiac Rhythm Disease Management, Spinal and Biologics, CardioVascular, Neuromodulation, Diabetes, and Surgical Technologies – with a mission focused on alleviating pain, restoring health, and extending life for millions of people around the world.

Courtesy: Medtronic

Courtesy: Medtronic

Courtesy: Paul Mackin

Mackin and his artillery platoon at Fort Carson, Colorado, in 1990.

Courtesy: Paul Mackin

Courtesy: Paul Mackin

options – after having lost his parents to cardiovascular disease and stroke – he was attracted to medical technology businesses that attacked these awful diseases.

Mackin started his business career as a sales representative for a specialty medical device manufacturer that sold surgical instruments, called Snowden-Pencer. He relocated to Boston, and, in this new role, Mackin learned the device industry from the "tip of the spear" – literally and figuratively. He spent day after day in surgery working with surgeons and understanding not only their technical medical needs, but also the business of health care. In Boston, he also met Nicole Sabat, an investment banker for First Boston, whom he married in 1996. Today, they are raising three children, Sloan, Reese, and JP.

Mackin was an outstanding sales representative and was given increased responsibility. He relocated to the company headquarters in Atlanta, where he held sales and marketing management positions. The company was growing

quickly and was acquired by the Kohlberg Group, a private equity firm that combined Snowden-Pencer with a recent Pfizer divestiture, Deknatel. Within a year of the acquisition, the combined company would be sold to Genzyme – one of the top biotechnology companies in the world – for $250 million. The day after the acquisition, at 29 years old, Mackin was made the Director of Sales for a 150-person sales force for Genzyme's Surgical Division.

At this point in his career (1997), Mackin was asked to move into Genzyme's cardiovascular surgery business as the director of marketing and continued to gain increased responsibility and ultimately was made the Senior Vice President and General Manager of the entire cardiovascular surgery business in 2000. From that point on, he has been entirely focused on working on delivering breakthrough medical technology to treat cardiovascular disease and stroke. As he progressed at Genzyme, the senior leadership recognized Mackin's management capabilities and potential, choosing to invest in his professional academic development.

Mackin was accepted to the Kellogg Graduate School of Management to receive his master's in Business Administration (MBA) and was funded by Genzyme. When he graduated in 2000, Kellogg was the number one ranked master's in Business Administration program with a reputation for being the best marketing graduate school in the country.

In 2002, Mackin joined Medtronic, where he would rise through the ranks to senior management. He started in northern California as the Vice President and General Manager of Medtronic's Endovascular Business (stents to protect the thoracic and abdominal aorta from rupturing). He then moved his family to Switzerland in 2004, where he served as the Vice President of Western Europe for the vascular division and, in 2005, successfully launched the company's first drug eluting stent, called Endeavor. The expectations on Wall Street were for the new stent to capture 10 percent of the very competitive stent market in Europe that at the time was led by Johnson & Johnson and Boston Scientific. Mackin led the launch and

delivered 25 percent market share and subsequently caught the attention of Medtronic senior management.

In 2007, Mackin returned from Europe to Medtronic Headquarters in Minneapolis and was promoted to be President of the Medtronic Cardiac Rhythm Disease Management (CRDM). In this role, he has responsibility for the overall strategic direction and profit and loss for a $5-billion division that includes products such as pacemakers and implantable defibrillators. Under his leadership, the Medtronic CRDM commands 50 percent market share and treats more than 750,000 patients a year. He is known as a world-class leader, leading by example. Twenty-five years after his father suffered his fatal heart attack and his mother had a debilitating stroke, Mackin is using West Point leadership principles to manage 12,000 people at the world's leading innovator in cardiovascular devices. His goal: to try and stop these diseases from taking the lives of loved ones from other families.

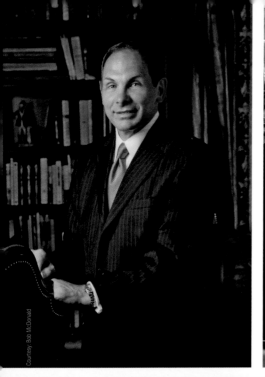

Courtesy Bob McDonald

Briefing President Obama.

Courtesy White House

Robert McDonald, USMA 1975

- **CHAIRMAN, PRESIDENT, AND CHIEF EXECUTIVE OFFICER (CHIEF EXECUTIVE OFFICER), PROCTER & GAMBLE (NYSE: PG)**
- **BOARD OF ADVISORS, THAYER LEADER DEVELOPMENT GROUP**
- **BOY SCOUTS OF AMERICA, YOUTH MEMBER**

Photo: NARA

Meeting Prime Minister Lee Kwan Yew of Singapore.

Bob McDonald is one of the greatest business leaders to ever graduate from West Point. He epitomizes the values taught at West Point and has helped perpetuate those values to hundreds of thousands of people around the world. He is the Chairman of the Board, President and Chief Executive Officer of Procter & Gamble (P&G) — one of the most respected companies in the world. McDonald spent four years at West Point and five years in the Army during the most formative years of his life, learning and practicing values-based leadership before entering the private sector. He then spent more than three decades at P&G, rising from an entry-level management position (in 1980) to become the current Chief Executive Officer. P&G is the largest consumer packaged goods company in the world and has annual sales of more than $83-billion-dollars and operations in more than 180 countries. P&G's brands — Tide, Gillette,

Bounty, Pampers, Crest, Head & Shoulders, Duracell, and others — are known around the world. Billions of consumers use its products daily.

McDonald was born in Gary, Indiana, June 20, 1952. He attended Arlington High School (Arlington Heights, Illinois) and excelled at football and wrestling. It seems he was pre-destined to go to West Point. He first attempt to gain his nomination was from Congressman Donald Rumsfeld when he was just 11 years old. Rumsfeld told young McDonald that, unfortunately, he was just a bit too young, but to keep trying. When he was of age as a high school junior, in 1970, Congressman Philip Crane nominated him to West Point. At West Point, McDonald played on the intercollegiate football, wrestling, rugby, and intramural boxing teams. In his Firstie year, he was the Brigade Adjutant and graduated 22nd out of 863 classmates.

McDonald and his classmates entered West Point in 1971 at the end of the Vietnam War, when entering the military was not popular and the Army was worn down after 10 years of war. Morale was low, recruiting was challenging, and in 1973, the United States had eliminated the draft and made the military an all-volunteer force. Despite these challenges, he and members of his class would lead the Army back to health. Some would stay for 35 years and rise to lead armies, while others, like McDonald, would go on to lead major corporations.

McDonald graduated as a "star man" in the top five percent of his class on June 4, 1975, and was handed his diploma by President Gerald Ford. President Ford's commencement speech presciently stated: "No previous graduating class in the history of West Point will be called upon to fill so many different roles and to perform so many exacting missions as the Class of 1975. Like those who preceded you, you

must know military strategy, tactics, and logistics. You must master the increasingly complex machinery of warfare. You must learn the lessons of leadership."

And this would be the focus of McDonald's life: learning and practicing leadership — and he would excel at it. Graduating at the top of the West Point class had significant rewards. Branches and initial assignments in the Army are based on class rank, and McDonald has had his choice of nearly any job or post in the Army. The Infantry Branch had become very unpopular after it took such heavy casualties in the Vietnam War (1965–73). Yet McDonald chose the Infantry Branch because he wanted to lead soldiers from the front. He chose the elite 82nd Airborne Division at Fort Bragg, North Carolina, as his first post. But before being assigned to Fort Bragg, McDonald volunteered to attend United States Army Ranger School, one of the toughest and most physically and mentally challenging

Touring a P&G plant in the U.S.

Procter&Gamble

courses in the military. Second Lieutenant McDonald endured one of the coldest winters on record during the eight-week course and graduated with his Ranger Tab. He would later go to both Artic and Jungle Warfare Schools.

> **"IF YOU ARE GOING TO GO INTO THE ARMY, GO INTO INFANTRY. IF YOU ARE GOING TO WORK IN MARKETING, WORK FOR P&G," SAYS MCDONALD.**

McDonald spent his five years in the Army at Fort Bragg, first leading a platoon of Infantrymen, and then he served as the Executive Officer in a Rifle Company in the 82nd Airborne with 120 paratroopers. The 82nd Airborne is one of the most elite units in the Army, and McDonald worked hard to maintain the pride and professionalism that made the 82nd so unique. Their mission is to parachute into enemy territory, and McDonald's unit trained for this regularly (McDonald himself logged approximately 60 parachute jumps.) When he discovered that his platoon Sergeant had logged a fictitious jump, he relieved the Sergeant of his leadership role. Honest mistakes could be tolerated, learned from, and even encouraged, but ethical violations were a sign of poor character, something McDonald would never tolerate in the Army or later at P&G.

While at Fort Bragg, when he was commanding a rifle company, McDonald educated himself in business by attending graduate school at night and received his master's in Business Administration from the University of Utah in 1979. He never actually set foot on the campus of the school, taking advantage of a master's in Business Administration program that nearby Pope Air Force Base and the University of Utah ran to bring professors in on the weekends.

McDonald left the Army in 1980 and entered the private sector. He was highly marketable (having graduated at the top of his West Point class), performed exceptionally well as a Company Commander, and already received his MBA. He had his choice of civilian jobs to pursue, but chose P&G. "I figured, and this is the story of my life, really," he says, "If you're gonna be in the Army, go into the Infantry. If you're going to be in marketing, work for P&G. You don't do things halfway." McDonald found the culture at P&G to be a great fit for him: it was similar to the military with a tremendous sense of camaraderie and a common mission and purpose across the company.

It was during his recruitment in 1980 that he met two men that would prove to be significant in his life: John Pepper and A.G. Lafley. Both Navy veterans, they would become the 9th and 11th Chief Executive Officers in P&G history.

Despite being such an old company (founded in 1837), the company has had very few Chief Executive Officers for such a long history. When McDonald joined P&G in 1980, the Chief Executive Officer at the time, Ed Harness, was only the sixth Chief Executive Officer in its history, and all of the Chief Executive Officers had been groomed internally – as would McDonald.

Initially, in 1980, McDonald began working on prominent brands, such as Dawn, Cascade, and Tide. He spent most of the 1990s leading P&G's businesses in the Philippines, Japan and Korea, including responsibility for P&G's Hair Care business in Asia and the P&G Beauty business in Japan.

McDonald led Global Fabric & Home Care, the company's largest and most mature business, which delivered strong sales growth and record-setting profits during his tenure. As vice chair of Global Operations, he led P&G's market development organizations, was a member of the team that created the company's winning Low-Cost Business Model and has championed the integration of P&G's global brand-building capability. He also played a pivotal role in the $57-billion integration of Gillette and led P&G's game-changing "go-to-market" reinvention.

In 2007, McDonald was named Vice Chairman of Global Operations followed by Chief Operating Officer in 2009 and President and Chief Executive Officer in 2010. He was named Chairman in 2010 to replace his friend and mentor, A.G. Lafley. It was an incredibly smooth Chief Executive Officer transition in a corporate environment that, globally, typically sees anything but smooth transitions at the top.

P&G deliberately focuses on leader development and succession planning at every stage of every division. Around the world, leaders are groomed for their character, leadership capabilities, and financial performance. P&G is so well thought of that its top employees are highly sought after by other companies. Like all P&G employees, McDonald was groomed to potentially take over more and more responsibilities, and each time he was given more responsibilities, he excelled, which in turn gained him ever more responsibility.

The mission of the United States Military Academy is to "develop leaders of character" a mission that McDonald internalized as a cadet and then as an Army Officer, perpetuating the same mission at P&G. He has continued to focus on perfecting his own leadership abilities and developing leaders throughout the organization. He routinely speaks around the world to P&G employees about the need to live a life with purpose and the values that those at P&G should aspire to achieve. "Living life driven with purpose is more meaningful and purposeful than meandering through life without direction," says McDonald. When Bob became Chief Executive Officer in July 2009, he reaffirmed the Company's commitment to its purpose – to touch and improve the lives of the world's consumers through branded products of superior quality and value. The company's growth strategy is focused on winning with consumers through innovative, superior performing products that improve the lives of consumers around the world every day. Since P&G touches billions of people around the world with their products, they can literally change the world with the products that they market and sell.

The word "leadership" comes up in nearly every one of McDonald's speeches. As the Chief Executive Officer, he focuses as much time on leader development as he does on any other aspect of the business because in addition to the value of the brands and the patents, the company is really all about its people.

Who would have predicted that by 2010, 35 years after President Ford handed the West Point Class of 1975 their diplomas, McDonald would be leading one of the world's most respected companies? Many of his classmates are not surprised. President Ford's statement, "No previous graduating class in the history of West Point will be called upon to fill so many different roles and to perform so many exacting missions as the Class of 1975," could not have been more prescient than in the example of McDonald. The leadership he studied and practiced at West Point

Meeting President Hu of China.

while preparing to lead soldiers would prove just as applicable in leading one of the largest companies in the world.

With leader development as a primary focus of his career, one of his first acts as Chairman and Chief Executive Officer was to bring his global leadership team to West Point to expose them to the character building lessons he learned there 35 years earlier. He brought his global leadership team to the Thayer Leader Development Group at the Thayer Hotel in 2010, where they spent three days in classrooms and staff rides learning the principles of leadership as taught to cadets. It was all very well received by the leadership team, most of who previously had no exposure to the military.

In 2012, P&G was rated number one as the "Best Company for Leaders" by the Chally Group Worldwide. Their spokesperson said,

"Since 2005, Chief Executive and Chally Group Worldwide have been releasing the "Best Companies for Leaders," a list of corporations who lead the pack when it comes to leadership development. These companies generate significant market share, make leadership development a high priority despite time and financial pressures, and their executives spend more personal time mentoring leaders. This year's top company is Procter & Gamble, led by Chief Executive Officer Bob McDonald."

West Point's primary mission is to train "leaders of character," and all Americans should find pride in the character that is McDonald, who positively represents West Point's values around the world in 180 countries to thousands of employees and billions of consumers.

BOB MCDONALD'S LEADERSHIP POSITIONS AND AWARDS:

- Member of the Board of Directors of Xerox Corporation.
- Vice Chair of the Business Roundtable.
- Chair of the Business Roundtable Fiscal Policy Initiative.
- Chair of the U.S.-China Business Council.
- Serves on the Foreign Investment Advisory Council in Russia and Singapore's International Advisory Council of the Economic Development Board.
- Received the 2007 inaugural Leadership Excellence Award from the U.S. Naval Academy and Harvard Business Review.
- Received 2010 Doctor of Laws, Honorary Degree, from Hampden-Sydney College, and a Doctor of Commercial Science, Honorary Degree, from the University of Cincinnati.
- Boy Scouts of America, Youth Member.

West Point graduation day with President Ford. McDonald graduated 13th in his class.

>>> Spotlight

P&G serves approximately 4.6 billion people around the world with its brands. The company has one of the strongest portfolios of trusted, quality, leadership brands, including Pampers®, Tide®, Ariel®, Always®, Whisper®, Pantene®, Mach3®, Bounty®, Dawn®, Fairy®, Gain®, Charmin®, Downy®, Lenor®, Iams®, Crest®, Oral-B®, Duracell®, Olay®, Head & Shoulders®, Wella®, Gillette®, Braun®, Fusion®, Ace®, Febreze®, Ambi Pur®, SK-II®, and Vicks®. The P&G community includes operations in approximately 75 countries worldwide.

Joe DePinto, Oprah Winfrey, and Igor Finkler on the Oprah Winfrey Show *after* Undercover Boss.

Joseph DePinto, USMA 1986

- **CHIEF EXECUTIVE OFFICER AND PRESIDENT, 7-ELEVEN CORPORATION**
- **MASTER'S IN BUSINESS ADMINISTRATION KELLOGG GRADUATE SCHOOL AT NORTHWESTERN UNIVERSITY**
- **NATIONAL RETAILER OF THE YEAR**
- **BUSINESS EXECUTIVES FOR NATIONAL SECURITY (BENS) BOARD OF DIRECTORS**
- **BOY SCOUTS OF AMERICA, YOUTH MEMBER**

Joe DePinto is a successful business executive who leads 7-Eleven, Inc. one of the largest retail chains in the world with more than 43,000 stores. DePinto had already been a successful global business leader when he came into the public spotlight in 2010 during a reality television show called *Undercover Boss*, in which he went undercover to work as an hourly associate in his own 7-Eleven stores.

The show highlighted DePinto's superb leadership capabilities, his humility, and the strong support his team provided the stores and their employees. *Undercover Boss* went on to become a tremendous success for CBS, featuring dozens of other

Chief Executive Officers going undercover with their own companies. Because of the leadership displayed by DePinto on *Undercover Boss*, he was subsequently asked to appear on the *Oprah Winfrey Show* and share his story. The *Oprah* segment was also seen in a positive light, which again benefited the image of DePinto, West Point, and 7-Eleven.

DePinto was born in Chicago, Illinois, and grew up in the suburbs of Chicago. He attended West Point and graduated in 1986. A superb athlete, DePinto was recruited to play ice hockey and played for the Army team. His chose the Artillery Branch and attended Officer Basic Training at Fort Sill,

Oklahoma, then was assigned to the 2nd Armored Division at Fort Hood, Texas. He served more than four years in the Army and chose to pursue a business career in 1990. He met his wife, Ingrid, in 1987 while stationed in Texas and during the next 20 years, they raised four boys and traveled the world together. (Their oldest son, John, is a member of the West Point Class of 2012.)

When DePinto left the Army in 1990, he had a number of employment options available to him. He chose to start working at KFC, a division of PepsiCo from 1990 to 1995. PepsiCo has an outstanding management-training program and DePinto thrived in this

environment. He was promoted numerous times from District Manager to Director of Operations, and he also helped lead PepsiCo's expansion into multi-branding of restaurants. In these roles, he learned the basics of business at the grassroots level, which would serve him well later as a senior executive. He then became SVP and COO of Thornton Oil Corporation, where he learned about retail and fuel markets. Years later, this understanding of the energy market and its impact on global operations would assist Joe while at 7-Eleven.

In 1997, DePinto attended The Kellogg Graduate School of Management at Northwestern University. With seven

in a few of his own stores. Asking the Chief Executive Officer of a premier corporation to take on this kind of transparency and exposure was a significant risk, and DePinto debated the risks and trade-offs with his senior team. They concluded this would be a great opportunity to publicly showcase (both internally and externally) the company's cultural shift toward Servant Leadership that was initiated by DePinto. Additionally, the team felt that they could highlight the excellent fresh food items that were prepared and delivered daily by 7-Eleven's commissaries and bakeries to their stores. Finally, DePinto believed that this would also be a great opportunity to publicly showcase and recognize some of their unsung company heroes.

DEPINTO WORKED AS AN HOURLY EMPLOYEE AND LEARNED A TREMENDOUS AMOUNT ABOUT HIS CORPORATION AND HIS PEOPLE. MUCH LIKE A GENERAL OFFICER VISITING HIS TROOPS, THIS LEVEL OF UNDERSTANDING OF THE 7-ELEVEN BUSINESS WAS NOT ONLY GOOD FOR TV, BUT FOR HIS 45,000 EMPLOYEES.

He appeared unshaven as a new hourly employee named "Danny," and a film crew followed him around claiming to be a documentary approved by corporate on how to train new associates. He worked in several parts of the business — as an employee working in a store on both the day and night shift, as a bakery assembly line worker, and as a night deliveryman. In one store, he worked with a wonderful woman who suffered from severe kidney disease yet managed the coffee business for the highest volume coffee store in the 7-Eleven system. Another job was working with a hardworking young man in a bakery who was a former Marine and a struggling artist, and a third job was working as a deliveryman with a fun-loving Russian immigrant and former Soviet Union Army Officer on an evening delivery route. DePinto learned a tremendous amount

about his corporation and the great people who work hard every day to make the company operate successfully. He also learned firsthand about the excellent talent dispersed across all parts of the company. Much like a General Officer visiting their troops, this level of understanding of his business and its people was not only good for TV, but was good for the organization. They were able to see their Chief Executive Officer's humility, his humanity and his willingness to roll up his sleeves and work alongside those on the front lines of their stores.

The associates DePinto worked with were all shocked to find out later that they had the Chief Executive Officer of 7-Eleven working under them as an hourly employee. He rewarded each of them for their outstanding work ethic and positive "can-do" attitude, and for being unsung heroes of the company. 7-Eleven donated $150,000 to the National Kidney Foundation and held organ donation card drives on behalf of the associate with the kidney ailment, gave a franchise store to the Russian immigrant who dreamed of owning his own store, and brought the struggling artist inside corporate to work with its internal marketing team.

Oprah was so impressed that she invited DePinto as a guest on her show. 7-Eleven, already well known worldwide received an incredible jump in its image as the episode was shown over and over again in countries across the globe. Both *Undercover Boss* and the *Oprah Winfrey Show* showcased DePinto's West Point leadership training and reflected positively on West Point.

As a global leader in retail business, DePinto has been asked to advise other global companies and institutions. He is a member of the Board of Directors of OfficeMax, Brinker International, SMU's Cox School of Business, Lone Star Big Brother Big Sisters, and the National Italian-American Foundation. He is also a member of the Board of Advisors for the Thayer Leader Development Group at West Point, and Board Member of the Business Executives for National Security (BENS). In 2011, Joe was awarded with the "Retail Leader of the Year Award" by the National Association of Convenience Stores to recognize his industry leadership and success.

The DePinto Room at the Thayer Hotel is proudly dedicated by his 1986 classmates.

years of business experience behind him in multiple roles with considerable responsibility, he was then able to learn from the top business professors in the country. Kellogg is consistently ranked number one as the best marketing school in the country, and DePinto took full advantage of the classroom and the network that he built while there. He graduated with his master's in Business Administration in 1999. Later, he became the President of GameStop Corporation, helping lead GameStop's acquisition of Electronic Boutique to create the world's largest retail video game company.

In 2005, DePinto was named Chief

Executive Officer of 7-Eleven, Inc. Managing such a large global retail organization was a tremendous business and leadership challenge — perfectly suited to test DePinto's leadership capabilities. As the Chief Executive Officer of this global enterprise, the leadership lessons he learned from West Point, the Army, and his business experience proved considerable as 7-Eleven more than doubled their earnings and grew more than 14,000 stores globally in six years.

In 2008, 7-Eleven Marketing executives were approached by a new CBS reality show. CBS asked if DePinto would consider working undercover as an hourly employee

Joe and Ingrid DePinto.

CSP
Serving the Total Convenience & Petroleum

JOE DePINTO
OF 7-ELEVEN
RETAIL
LEADER OF
THE YEAR

>>> Spotlight

What started out as an ice house in Dallas, Texas, back in 1927 has grown and evolved into the world's largest operator, franchisor, and licensor of convenience stores.

The company operates franchises and licenses more than 8,500 stores in the United States and Canada. Of the approximately 7,600 stores the company operates and franchises in the United States, more than 5,700 are franchised.

Outside of the United States and Canada, there are more than 40,900 7-Eleven and other convenience stores in Japan, Taiwan, Thailand, South Korea, China, Malaysia, Mexico, Singapore, Australia, Philippines, Indonesia, Norway, Sweden, and Denmark.

Joe DePinto and his father at graduation from Kellogg/ Northwestern University.

Steve Cannon is the President and Chief Executive Officer of Mercedes-Benz USA (MBUSA), one of the world's most identifiable luxury automobile brands. Cannon graduated with academic honors and ranked number one in physical fitness out of 1,005 cadets in the West Point Class of 1986. It was obvious to everyone in the Class of 1986 that this fierce competitor would accomplish great things in life. Following West Point, Cannon served in the United States Army and was stationed in Germany, where he was front and center when the Soviet Union collapsed, the Berlin Wall fell, and the Cold War ended. Cannon, who speaks fluent German, has spent the past 25 years working in both the United States and Germany, with more than 15 years in marketing, sales, and finance executive positions. Cannon's unique background and proven leadership abilities make him ideally suited to lead one of the world's greatest luxury automobile companies in the USA.

Cannon was born February 10, 1961, and grew up in Wyckoff, New Jersey, where he attended Ramapo High School. He was captain of both the football and wrestling teams and a First-Team All-State Football player and First-Team All-County wrestler.

Congresswoman Marge Roukema nominated Cannon for West Point in the fall of 1981, which marked the first year of Ronald Reagan's presidency and a major growth period for the defense industry. Cannon entered West Point on July 1, 1982, when the Cold War was at its peak, with the Soviet Union embroiled in a costly stalemate in Afghanistan. President Reagan increased the defense budget significantly in a race to bankrupt the economically unsound Soviet empire.

Cannon thrived in the high-intensity West Point environment, which develops leaders of character by focusing on three areas: academic, physical, and military development. Cadets' overall class rank is based on a blended average of these three areas. Every cadet must pass physical standards and every cadet must be an athlete, either intercollegiate or intramural. The vast majority of cadets lettered in a varsity sport in high school and, to be ranked in the top of their class, cadets must be in superb physical condition and be outstanding athletes. Cannon exemplified these traits and quickly

Steve Cannon, USMA 1986

- **PRESIDENT AND CHIEF EXECUTIVE OFFICER, MERCEDES-BENZ USA**
- **TOP CADET IN THE WEST POINT CLASS OF 1986 IN PHYSICAL FITNESS**
- **SERVED AS AN ARMY OFFICER IN WEST GERMANY WHEN THE BERLIN WALL FELL**

Photo: NARA

Courtesy: Steve Cannon

Steve Cannon is the President and Chief Executive Officer of Mercedes-Benz USA, one of the world's most identifiable luxury automobile brands.

Courtesy: Mercedes-Benz

established himself as a leader in his class.

During his first summer at Cadet Basic Training, known as "Beast Barracks," Cannon was the pugil stick champion out of more than 1,400 cadet candidates. He made the Army wrestling team, where he also lettered. Leading into his senior year, he was selected to lead Cadet Basic Training as the "King of Beast," making him the top-ranking cadet for the incoming Plebes at West Point. By this time, he was also ranked number one physically in his class and was an academic standout. Later that same year, he earned the position of Cadet

Regimental Commander for 4th Regiment. This prominent leadership position placed 1,100 cadets under Cannon's leadership and reflected the esteem in which the officers and his classmates held him.

Cannon dominated his class physically, so much so that he "validated" boxing, swimming, wrestling, and gymnastics. This means that when he was pre-screened, he scored so well that he did not have to take the class. He scored a perfect score on every physical test (Army Physical Fitness Test) for four years. He set the one time Academy record for push-ups: 133 in two minutes.

Cannon chose the Field Artillery Branch and reported to Fort Sill, Oklahoma, for Officer Basic, where he competed for a Ranger School slot and naturally won. Attending winter Ranger School is a physical and mental endurance test with an incredibly high attrition rate – little food, sleep, and exposure to cold weather for 61 days causes many to quit. Cannon lost 35 pounds in eight weeks but earned the coveted Ranger Tab.

Following initial officer training in 1987, the Army stationed Cannon in Germany where he was assigned to the 2nd Armored Cavalry Regiment along the West German–Czech border. All training at that time was focused on defending West Germany against the Soviet invasion. Cannon enjoyed living in Germany and learned to speak the language. He ran the last marathon to be held in the isolated city of West Berlin, running a swift 2:57. In 1989, he was on the border and had a front-row seat when suddenly the Cold War ended, not with a battle as the United States Army had prepared, but, thankfully, with a peaceful and quiet end as The Wall came down.

After completing his military service, Cannon returned to the United States in 1991 and began his career in the automotive industry as the assistant to the President and Chief Executive Officer of Mercedes-Benz North America (predecessor to MBUSA), the same Chief Executive Officer role he would personally attain nearly 20 years later. MBUSA is headquartered in Montvale, New Jersey, and is responsible for the distribution, marketing, and customer service for all Mercedes-Benz products, Sprinter Vans, and smart cars in the United States. At the time, Mercedes sold 520,000 cars globally with 58,800 sold in the USA.

From there, Cannon moved to Stuttgart, Germany, and was the first American to join a skunk works team tasked with the design, development, production, and launch of the first Mercedes-Benz series (the M Class) to be manufactured in the United States. Cannon was selected to lead a small team tasked with selecting the site for the future manufacturing location. He led the team through a thorough due diligence process, considering several states, but choosing Tuscaloosa, Alabama, as the site. Hyundai and Toyota followed Mercedes-Benz to the state, and Alabama now is second only to Michigan in automobile manufacturing jobs. The M Class was launched in late 1998 and became the "North American Truck of the Year" that same year. That Mercedes-Benz plant now employs 3,000 American

employees and produces more than 174,000 Mercedes annually that are sold in 135 countries.

After the successful launch of the M Class, Cannon became Director of Marketing for Daimler-owned debis Financial Services. Cannon left Mercedes in 2000 and later served as Principal for The Richards Group, the largest independent full-service advertising agency in the United States.

Cannon returned to MBUSA in 2007 as Chief Marketing Officer with overall responsibility for marketing communications, market research, and product management of the Mercedes-Benz and Maybach brands in the United States. From 2007 to 2011, Cannon and his team successfully moved the brand into some of the most prestigious platforms in sports, including a global partner of The Masters, The U.S. Open Tennis Tournament, and the PGA Championship. The brand's aggressive expansion included a marquis naming-rights deal for The Mercedes-Benz Superdome in New Orleans.

> **CANNON IS LEADING MERCEDES-BENZ TO BE THE NUMBER-ONE LUXURY VEHICLE BRAND IN THE U.S.**

On December 16, 2011, Daimler Board of Management and Dr. Joachim Schmidt, Executive Vice President of Sales & Marketing for Mercedes-Benz Cars in Stuttgart, Germany, announced that Cannon would assume the role of Chief Executive Officer of MBUSA. Cannon is only the second American to lead MBUSA, which has 1,600 direct employees and 358 dealers throughout the U.S. with total indirect employees estimated more than 24,000.[1]

Mercedes-Benz globally sells more than 1.2 million cars per year, and within the United States that number has increased to more than 270,000 per year. Mercedes is in a dog-fight with BMW for the title of the top luxury automobile brand in the United States but has the sales growth and goal to have the number-one position soon under Cannon's leadership. The United States is now one of the fastest growing Mercedes-Benz markets, with 2012 sales growth of 12 percent, and recently overtook Germany as the largest Mercedes-Benz market in the world.

Cannon (right) proudly showing his "Ranger Tab" at Army Ranger School graduation, 1987.

Cannon (right) completing the final West Berlin Marathon prior to the fall of the Iron Curtain.

The Cannon family with all nine children.

>>> Spotlight

Mercedes-Benz USA (MBUSA), headquartered in Montvale, New Jersey, is responsible for the distribution, marketing, and customer service for all Mercedes-Benz products in the United States. MBUSA offers drivers the most diverse lineup in the luxury segment with 14 model lines ranging from the sporty C-Class to the flagship S-Class sedans and the SLS Supercar. MBUSA is also responsible for the distribution, marketing, and customer service of Mercedes-Benz Sprinter Vans and smart in the United States.

Courtesy: Mercedes-Benz

Cannon as a West Point Firstie, 1986.

Cannon (far right) and fellow Firsties just a few days prior to 1986 West Point graduation.

Courtesy: Steve Cannon

Courtesy: Steve Cannon

Cannon (left) conducting East German border patrols, 1988.

Cannon, Cadet Regimental Commander, 4th Regiment USMA, leads 1,100 cadets onto the parade field during "Pass and Review Ceremony," 1986.

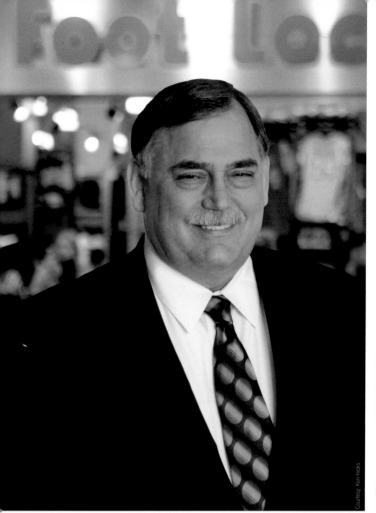

Ken Hicks, USMA 1974

- CHAIRMAN, PRESIDENT, AND CHIEF EXECUTIVE OFFICER, FOOT LOCKER, INC. (NYSE: FL)
- PRESIDENT, JCPENNEY COMPANY, INC.
- PRESIDENT, PAYLESS SHOE SOURCE
- EXECUTIVE VICE PRESIDENT, HOME SHOPPING NETWORK
- MASTER'S IN BUSINESS ADMINISTRATION, HARVARD BUSINESS SCHOOL WITH HIGHEST DISTINCTION
- ARMY FOOTBALL PLAYER
- BOY SCOUTS OF AMERICA, YOUTH MEMBER

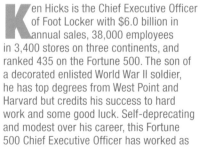

Ken Hicks is the Chief Executive Officer of Foot Locker with $6.0 billion in annual sales, 38,000 employees in 3,400 stores on three continents, and ranked 435 on the Fortune 500. The son of a decorated enlisted World War II soldier, he has top degrees from West Point and Harvard but credits his success to hard work and some good luck. Self-deprecating and modest over his career, this Fortune 500 Chief Executive Officer has worked as

a mechanic, a janitor, a roughneck on an oil rig, a gunner in a field artillery unit, and loves selling shoes. As his friend and West Point classmate General David Petraeus says, "He rolls up his sleeves, gets involved, pitches in, and leads by engaging and walking around."[1]

Hicks's developed a leadership style over four decades that has managed to turn around a global retail giant in the midst of a global recession. Over the past three

years, he and his team have been a shining light in retail, turning Foot Locker around and increasing the stock price from $10 to $35. They have done it by focusing on a clear vision and strategy, reinvigorating the brand, focusing on the customer, and improving productivity of the real estate, sales force, and inventory resulting in a significant increase in shareholder value. He has achieved all of this through leadership he began learning at West Point.

Hicks was born in Tulsa, Oklahoma, in 1953. His dad was in the oil business and moved the family to Calgary when Hicks was 3 months old and then to Texas at age 7. His dad had served in World War II in the Infantry in the 10th Mountain Division Europe. After being hit by a Nazi grenade, he was taken prisoner and sent to the infamous Stalag 17. At the end of World War II Hicks's dad was released after six months as a POW and received the Purple Heart

>>> Spotlight

Foot Locker, Inc. is a specialty athletic retailer that operates approximately 3,370 stores in 23 countries in North America, Europe, Australia, and New Zealand. Through its Foot Locker, Footaction, Lady Foot Locker, Kids Foot Locker, Champs Sports, and CCS retail stores, as well as its direct-to-customer channels, including FootLocker.com, Eastbay, and CCS.com, the company is a leading provider of athletic footwear and apparel.

Ken Hicks and his parents with Congressman George H. W. Bush discussing his nomination to West Point, 1970.

to be a Cadet Company Commander his senior year of Company C-1. His classmate David Petraeus was a company-mate for four years and would later rise to become the commander of the wars in Iraq and then Afghanistan and then the Director of the Central Intelligence Agency. Two other classmates would rise the top of the United States government: General Keith Alexander would lead the National Security Agency, and General Martin Dempsey would become the Chairman of the Joint Chiefs of Staff (Petraeus page 96, Dempsey page 52, Alexander page 264).

All cadets at that time majored in Engineering, and Hicks was allowed to choose his field of concentration in economics. It was the closest field of study he could find to business and he enjoyed numbers and problem solving. He found the professors in the social sciences department to be exemplary and one Bill Murdy (USMA 1964, page 400) evolved over time into a role model for Hicks. Bill would later go on to successfully lead several Fortune 500 companies himself.

Prior to graduating, Hicks chose the field artillery and joined the 3rd Armored Calvary. He liked the strategic importance of the artillery, which had both leadership and analytical challenges. For his first assignment he chose Fort Bliss, Texas, and the 3rd Armored Cavalry Regiment where he served as a forward observer (serving with the calvary, needing to understand tank and calvary tactics, as well as artillery skills to call in fire upon the enemy), then as Fire Direction Officer (with the cannons calculating trajectories and deflections to aim the cannons accurately). First Lieutenant Hicks then deployed to Korea for a year to support the Korean Army with special weapons capability.

While in Korea in 1976, an international crisis occurred. Captain Art Bonifas (USMA 1966) and one of his fellow officers were murdered by North Korean soldiers in the DMZ (Demilitarized Zone). The incident caused the United States and North Korea to nearly go to war (Bonifas biography on page 214). Hicks remembers the next mission after Captain Bonifas was tragically killed, when tensions were high and every artillery piece in South Korea was loaded and aimed at the DMZ in case the North Koreans attacked any of our troops again.

Captain Hicks returned to Fort Bliss and took command of the Howitzer Battery 3rd

Squadron, 3rd Armored Cavalry Regiment. As commander, he had six cannons and 120 men, and he was arguably one of the best gunners in the unit. It was then that he realized it was far more important that he learn to "teach" his soldiers to become better gunners than him – after all, he could only fire one gun at a time himself. This lesson would serve him well later in life as he learned to teach larger and larger groups of employees to "Be all that you can be" as the Army advertisement promised. Prior to leaving the Army, his unit was dubbed "Fastest Guns in the West" on their annual field test by the Department of Army Inspectors.

In 1980, Hicks resigned from the Army to attend the prestigious Harvard Business School (HBS). As he recalls, it seemed everyone in his HBS class had graduated from an Ivy League school, captained minor intercollegiate sports teams, and had already written theses that solved the world's problems. Hicks remembers his thinking sardonically that his only real skill at the time seemed somewhat less useful at business school, being able to shoot cannons very well. But he quickly realized and proved that he had developed more important skill sets than gunnery. Over the previous 10 years, he had learned to be a leader – through experiences that most of his Harvard classmates had not had the opportunity to experience. He reflected "At West Point, leadership is trained in theory in the classroom, but it is also experienced every day which is why I believe it is the premier leadership institute in the world. Cadets lead and follow and get to 'practice' leadership." By the time he was a senior at West Point, he had led 120 cadets every day. He had learned to think and to lead at West Point. When he had entered the Army, he had led soldiers ranging in age from 18 to 50, leaving after commanding a 120-man Field Artillery Battery. Then at Harvard, he learned how to think about business and how to solve problems in the business world.

As stated, some of his Class of 1974 West Point classmates went on to lead wars, armies and United States government agencies. At Harvard, Hicks and many of his Class of 1982 classmates would graduate and go on to lead many large corporations, including Jeff Immelt (General Electric); Jamie Dimon (JP Morgan Chase), Steve Burke (Chief Executive Officer of NBC), Mike Fascitelli (Chief Executive Officer of Vornado), and Naina Lal Kidwai

and the Bronze Star. After the war, Hicks's father returned home to Oklahoma to enter the oil business and marry Pat Carlyle.

Hicks grew up in Houston, Texas, and attended Westbury High School where he was played football and track (shotput), was a leader in the student Senate, key club, national honor society, and worked about 20 hours a week as a mechanic at a gas station and as a janitor. Congressman George Herbert Walker Bush (who would

later be elected as the 41st United States President) nominated Hicks to West Point in 1970.

Cadet Hicks played football as the specialty center (long snapper) for the first two years. He eventually lost the role of long snapper to a USMA 1976 Cadet Bob McClure, who would become the President of the Association of Graduates in 2009. From there, he became involved in intramural lacrosse. Hicks was chosen

(Country Head for HSBC Bank, India) among them. Through both his West Point and his Harvard networks, by proving himself in each of his roles, Hicks was developing both iconic mentors, peers and friends.

At that time in 1981 Hicks was considering a future opportunity in the oil business, so he chose to spend his summer between first and second years at HBS by working as a roughneck in the Mississippi Delta – not the typical summer internship for a Harvard grad. Having been a mechanic in high school, a gunner in the Army, and a roughneck in graduate school, he was not afraid to get his hands dirty. He returned from the Delta for his final year at HBS, and despite having originally felt relatively less skilled than his classmates when he arrived at Harvard, he graduated with the highest distinction as a Baker Scholar in the top five percent of his class – and still the thing he knew how to do best was to shoot cannons.

Upon graduation, he accepted a role as a consultant at the top-tier consulting firm McKinsey & Company to learn more about business. McKinsey gave him the opportunity to practice the business thinking and problem solving that he had learned at Harvard.

He spent five years at McKinsey working on all types of consulting engagements with companies, such as Pepsi, Frito-Lay, and USAA. Hicks still uses many analogies to teach lessons to his team, often using military and sports analogies. He refers to the different levels of that one could experience with a football organization: playing on the field, coaching on the sidelines, and coaching from up in the press box, all important roles for a professional team but all very different experiences. Hicks felt his work at McKinsey was coaching from the skybox and while important and successful, yet Hicks wanted to coach on the sidelines.

So he left consulting to join May Department Stores as the Head of Strategic Planning (moving to the sidelines coaching) with the goal of serving three years and then becoming a line manager (playing on the field). Three years later, he became General Manager of the Home Store. Then he finally got to the line as General Merchandise Manager of Foley's, where he turned around the business to grow sales and profits three years in a row.

As an experienced executive retailer by this time in 1999, Hicks joined Home Shopping Network as the Head Merchant. On the wall in his office at Foot Locker, he has the nine Principles of War displayed, which he believes applies in not only in war, but also in business. In every battle, one of the principles can be identified that was the primary cause of either victory or defeat. The principles are Mass, Offensive, Maneuver, Objective, Simplicity, Unity of Command, Surprise, Maneuver, and Security. Every major military battle in history and every major business success or defeat can be understood through adherence or ignorance of one or more of the principles of war.

In this role at Home Shopping Network, he learned to apply one particular principle of war very effectively: offensive. Every day, 325 items would be sold, 260 of these were brand-new items never before sold. This was speed to market. One particular initial meeting, someone discussed selling a movie video on the Home Shopping Network – it was the movie *Titanic*. They had never sold a video over the network before this time. Without any real props, someone took a photo of Leonardo DiCaprio and stuck it on a video box. The next thing Hicks knew the woman on TV was selling it on the network, and they sold 26,000

units in a few minutes at $20 each. That was speed to market for a retail product a successful example of the "offensive."

Hicks was then recruited to lead Payless Shoes as the President. Payless had previously been a May Company where Hicks had worked earlier in his career but it had been spun off. At the time, Payless sold 320 million pairs of shoes per year at $11 each and was the largest shoe company in the United States.

After Payless, Hicks joined JCPenney as Chief Operating Officer, leading more than 1,200 stores and a supply chain with more than 40 distribution centers across the country. Later, he became Chief Merchant. During Hicks's tenure, he stopped a decade-long decline, turning sales around and returning the chain to profitability – dubbed the "retail

HICKS CREDITS MUCH OF HIS SUCCESS TO THE OPPORTUNITIES AND EXPERIENCES AFFORDED TO HIM BECAUSE OF HIS CHANCE TO ATTEND WEST POINT.

Ken and Lucy met in high school, were married three weeks after graduation from West Point, and have traveled the world together since.

turnaround of the decade" by the *Wall Street Journal*. Hicks was also a part of the JCP leadership team that doubled the stock price during his tenure.

Hicks came to Foot Locker in 2009 when the company was in a slump – sales were down 20 percent since a high in 2006. The global retail company with more than 30,000 employees was struggling and closing stores to try to retain profitability. The global economy was in shambles, and the Foot Locker stock price was at $10. He led his team to develop a strategic plan to better define the business, step up the apparel business, increase their online retail operations, and develop their international opportunities. They developed a five-year plan and achieved it in less than two years. The stock jumped from $10 to $35 in three years after increasing earnings before interest and taxes from 1 percent to 9 percent, and improved net operating income from less than 1 percent to 5 percent after taxes despite the global retail economy lagging throughout the three-year turnaround.

How did he do it? He focuses on teaching and communicating. Everyone knows his vision "To be the leading global retail supplier of athletically inspired shoes and apparel" carrying the most complete assortment from top-tier brands, such as Nike, Adidas, Under Armour, and others. Everyone knows the strategy and the priorities. In fact, he sends every one of the 38,000 employees a pocket pamphlet that clearly states the company's strategies, objectives, and results.

Foot Locker has almost 3,400 stores, 38,000 employees, 30 percent of its business in Europe/Canada/Australia, and has several retail brands under the Foot Locker Corporate umbrella, such as Foot Locker, Lady Foot Locker, Kids Foot Locker, Champs, Footaction, and CCS. It is a global company and it is exposed to the risks of the global economy.

Turning around this giant retailer in the midst of a global recession took all the skills Hicks had developed over four decades: having learned both the formal theory and the real world practice in leadership, engineering, problem solving, and business. The company had previously been a "top-down" retailer. Much as the American military pushes decision-making down to the front line leaders – Captains, Sergeants, and Lieutenants, Hicks pushed down the decision-making, accountability, responsibility, rewards, and promotions to the lowest level – to the guy on the front lines managing in the stores, districts, and buyers and merchandising managers. Just as he learned to teach his gunners instead of trying to be the best gunner himself, he imparts these teachings on his 3,400 store managers. The store managers don't have to be the best salesman, they have to teach all their employees to be the best salesmen. If they succeed, they will be rewarded and promoted. He created a culture to reward and promote those who succeed, and the vast majority of his leadership roles across the company are filled with executives who started as part-time employees at the store level, which helps inspire new workers to join the team at the store level in retail. It is a proven path to management for the successful part-time employee.

Hicks credits much of his success to the opportunities and experiences afforded to him because of his chance to attend West Point. He and his wife give back in time, resources, and funding to the current cadets. The Hicks fund the West Point Model United Nations (Model U.N.) and are proud to say West Point has been the World Champions for five of the last seven years.

As he looks back on his own career, Hicks reflects upon the lessons learned from his mentors both in uniform and in business. His economics professor Captain Bill Murdy went on to lead several large companies in private equity and operating companies (page 400).

Hicks worked for icons in the retail industry, such as Dave Farrell, who had 27 consecutive positive years of growth, for Barry Diller, and Hicks Kolker, and Allen Questrom. He worked directly for each of them at different stages in his career, and he learned a tremendous amount but says "they didn't suffer fools gladly." Although he considers them his role models and coaches, he didn't ask them to be his mentor and he would discourage anyone to look at mentorship as a "favor" to ask of a senior. "Put yourself in a situation where you can "learn," support, and prove yourself instead of putting a mentor in a position of asking for them to "teach." With 38,000 employees, Hicks is teaching them all lessons in leadership.

For over forty years Bill Murdy has led six large corporations at the executive level as either Chief Executive Officer or Chief Operating Officer in several industries. He served three combat tours, received his MBA from Harvard Business School, and has consistently and selflessly supported West Point, veterans and national security organizations for over fifty years. While being very comfortable operating in the boardroom of large public companies, he remains rooted in his modest beginnings of middle class America and his fourteen years in uniform, starting as a Plebe at West Point and rising to Major in the U.S. Army. He credits his success with hard work, luck, timing and always associating himself with great people. When combined, these ingredients make good things happen.

Bill was the oldest of five children in Houston, Texas. His father, who was a commercial photographer, and his Mother raised the children in small Houston home. His father converted the car garage into a photograph studio. As the eldest of three boys and two girls, Bill found himself in an informal leadership position from his early years, first leading his younger siblings and then taking on more and more leadership roles in grade school and public high school. He was a standout student-athlete, attaining nearly every high school title or accolade possible for a young man: Class President, Valedictorian, Eagle Scout and varsity football, tennis and track. After winning scholarships to Dartmouth, Rice, Vanderbilt and being accepted to the three academies, Murdy accepted the appointment

to West Point. He felt an affinity for West Point and the Army since his father had been commissioned in the Army Corps of Engineers in World War II and had served in North Africa, Sicily, Italy, Southern France and Germany. His father had been wounded in the leg on Anzio beach, patched up and never evacuated from the field.

When Bill left for West Point on his first airplane flight, he left behind his high school girlfriend Mary. Over the next fifty-three years they would only be separated for four long periods of time: four years at West Point and then his three tours of combat duty in the Army. Together they would raise two children and live in fourteen different places.

Bill did very well at West Point, rising to the

top of his class and playing both Sprint football for four years as a starter and also one year on the Army tennis team. A few memories of West Point stand out as he reflects on his timing, luck and success. Major General William Westmoreland, who would later command the overall war effort in Vietnam, was an avid tennis player, but Westmoreland didn't want to play and be beaten by a top Army tennis player. Bill was ranked seventh on the Army team. Murdy's classmates would chide him for decades about the time the Superintendent's helicopter flew in to Camp Buckner to pull Cadet Murdy from field training to fly him back to play tennis with the Superintendent...while the class continued roughing it in the field.

William Fordham Murdy, USMA 1964

- CHAIRMAN AND CHIEF EXECUTIVE OFFICER, COMFORT SYSTEMS USA (NYSE: FIX)
- CHAIRMAN AND CHIEF EXECUTIVE OFFICER, LANDCARE (NYSE: GRW)
- CHIEF EXECUTIVE OFFICER, CLUB QUARTERS
- MANAGING GENERAL PARTNER, MORGAN STANLEY VENTURE CAPITAL
- THREE TOURS OF COMBAT IN DOMINICAN REPUBLIC AND SOUTH VIETNAM
- MASTERS IN BUSINESS ADMINISTRATION HARVARD BUSINESS SCHOOL
- ASSOCIATE PROFESSOR, WEST POINT DEPARTMENT OF SOCIAL SCIENCES
- VICE CHAIRMAN, BUSINESS EXECUTIVES FOR NATIONAL SECURITY (BENS)
- CO-FOUNDER AND CHAIRMAN THAYER LEADER DEVELOPMENT GROUP AT WEST POINT
- BOY SCOUTS OF AMERICA: EAGLE SCOUT, DISTINGUISHED EAGLE, SILVER BEAVER AND MEMBER OF THE NATIONAL EXECUTIVE BOARD

COMFORT SYSTEMS USA

FIX LISTED NYSE

JUNE 29 FRIDAY

FIX LISTED NYSE

Tenth anniversary of Comfort Systems listing on the NYSE, June 29, 2007.

Courtesy Bill Murdy

Murdy was chosen as one of only six battalion commanders in the Corps of Cadets his Firstie (senior) year. His battalion was chosen in the spring of 1964 to represent West Point in the funeral procession for General of the Army Douglas MacArthur. In this role, Bill led his battalion down 5th Avenue.

Following in his father's Army footsteps, Bill chose the Corps of Engineers and the 82nd Airborne Division upon graduation. Educated in basic economics by the West Point Social Sciences Department, he vividly recalls the monthly pay for a Second Lieutenant at the time was paid $220/month. Airborne pay was $110/month, so he astutely calculated choosing airborne included a 50% raise. The Class of 1964 was a "guinea pig" class within the Army, and that year the Army chose not to send officers to the traditional Officer Basic Course but instead sent them directly to their military units. En route to the 82nd Airborne, Second Lieutenant Murdy attended Airborne and Ranger Schools at Ft. Benning and arrived at Ft. Bragg in January 1965.

Shortly after arrival, he and his platoon found themselves geared up to parachute into the Dominican Republic in 1965 to eliminate a communist coup in the Caribbean nation. Just after takeoff it was determined the C-130s could land on a newly secure airfield, so instead of jumping in they landed in the Dominican Republic. During these combat operations the Division lost 26 soldiers, including the first member of the Class of 1964, Second Lieutenant Charlie Hutchinson. As a Corps of Engineer platoon leader, Bill's platoon was attached to the 2nd Battalion/504th Infantry. In this role, the city of Santo Domingo had two opposing enemy forces separated by what was affectionately named "All-American Boulevard". Enemy forces were using the sewer system to infiltrate US Army positions and attack friendly forces with snipers. Bill was decorated for personally entering the sewer system and mapping it to help protect friendly forces from attack. For several days he slogged his way around in knee deep in human filth, in enemy territory underground, expecting to encounter an enemy sniper around every corner. Years later, when leading large corporations during crisis, he would fondly remember the smells and the material in the sewers of Santo Domingo to keep his perspective.

Murdy Guest Room at the Thayer Hotel at West Point is proudly dedicated by the senior management and board of directors at Comfort Systems USA.

At Comfort Systems Headquarters in Houston, 2008.

Graduation, June 3, 1964, married one year later.

>>> Spotlight

Comfort Systems is a leading national installation and service provider for heating, ventilation, and air-conditioning systems and related mechanical services in the commercial, industrial, and institutional market. Operating from 75 locations, Comfort has 7,000 employees and revenues of $1.5 billion.

Courtesy: Comfort Systems

Pacific Resources Headquarters Building in Honolulu, 1979.

Courtesy: Bill Murdy

Murdy left the Dominican Republic after six months and returned to the U.S. to attend Pathfinder School with orders to deploy to Vietnam.

He arrived in Vietnam prepared to be a Pathfinder team leader, but was made aide-de-camp to Major General Robert Ploger (USMA 1939), commander of Army Engineer Command Vietnam. MG Ploger was an inspirational leader who had received the Silver Star and Purple Heart for actions on Omaha Beach. In this role Bill saw all of Vietnam and had exposure to the entire war effort in both Army and Marine areas of operation.

After returning to the United States Bill attended Harvard Business School sponsored by the Department of Social Sciences , in order to return to West Point to teach economics. However, upon completion of HBS, while the war was winding down, it was still a major operation in 1971. Instead of leaving

Cambridge and heading to West Point, Bill returned to Vietnam for another yearlong tour.

His first assignment with the 173rd Airborne Brigade in Vietnam was to serve in the Tactical Operations Center managing night operations and moving friendly assets around the area of operations to suppress enemy threats. He frequently went on patrol with his teams to understand their needs. After "doing his time" in the Operations Center Bill finally received combat Company Command of the Engineer Company supporting the 173rd Airborne Brigade. Captain Murdy traveled to his units throughout the Area of Operations (AO) and often went on missions with his subordinate platoons. While he had sought command, he unfortunately took command of an engineering company that was previously not well organized or well led. By this time in 1971, after six years of heavy combat in Vietnam, years of public protests in the United States against the war, with a draftee

army, Army morale had declined, drug use was prevalent, and "fragging" of officers had become commonplace. In hindsight, Bill looks at this command as his first "turnaround"

MURDY HAS VIGOROUSLY AND CONTINUOUSLY SUPPORTED WEST POINT, VETERANS, AND U.S. NATIONAL SECURITY EFFORTS UNSELFISHLY FOR NEARLY FOUR DECADES IN A LIFETIME OF SERVICE TO THE NATION.

opportunity and turn it around he did, by leading from the front, by removing soldiers who lacked discipline and by enforcing standards. Bill returned from the battlefield of Vietnam to the granite walls of West Point to teach economics in the Social Sciences Department in mid-1971.

Bill's considers the team he worked with during his three years at West Point in the Social Sciences Department the best team he's ever been on. At the time, the professors in the Department included Major Barry McCaffrey (later General McCaffrey and Presidential Cabinet Member), Major Jack Jacobs (Medal of Honor recipient and later Colonel), Captain Paul Bucha (Medal of Honor recipient), Captain Dan Christman (later Lieutenant General and Superintendent), Major Howard Graves (later Lieutenant General and Superintendent), Major Wesley Clark (later General and Supreme Allied Commander Europe).

In 1974, after ten years in the Army and a promotion to Major, with the war in Vietnam over and the Army significantly downsizing, Bill chose to leave the army. He was offered

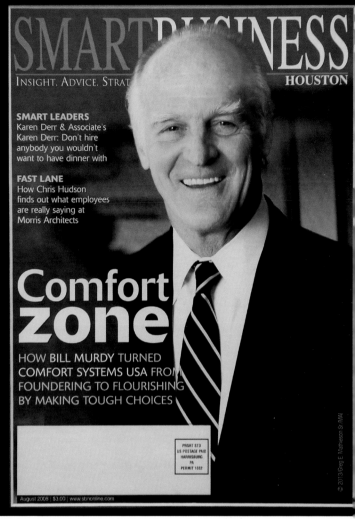

a job in Hawaii with Pacific Resources. Bill and Mary moved the family there in 1974 and would remain in Hawaii until 1981. Soon after arriving he was made Chief Operating Officer of the Pacific Resources (NYSE: PRI). His team took the company public and later negotiated a deal to merge with the Kuwait Oil Company.

While traveling through New York City returning from Kuwait, Bill serendipitously met a recruiter from KornFerry who was in a search for someone to lead a team at Morgan Stanley. Soon after, Bill accepted the position with Morgan Stanley and moved the family back to the mainland. In this new role, Bill created the Morgan Stanley Venture Capital Fund that would later become the private equity group. His leadership helped define an entire industry during its infancy.

To do this, Bill started by convincing the partners (Morgan Stanley was a partner-ship then not a public company) to invest their own capital into an asset pool that he could invest in private companies. He then engaged a major New York financial institu-tion and levered up the assets of the part-ners' six-fold to invest in private companies. His fourteen man team then performed due diligence on private companies to find the most worthwhile risk-adjusted investments. They were very successful in their selections and the returns to the partners were signifi-cant. With the team and concept proven, Bill convinced the partners that it would be even more attractive to offer access to the fund to outside private and institutional investors, with small management and attractive 20% profit sharing agreement for Morgan Stanley. This strategy was incredibly successful for both the firm and for the investors. Twelve of their thirty-six initial investments went public including Cypress Semiconductors, Linear Technology, Nellcor, and 3COM.

Murdy left Morgan Stanley to lead General Investment Development in Boston for eight years until friends and investors in Houston suggested Bill help launch a new company called LandCare, which was a roll up of commercial and residential land care companies (commercial landscaping and tree care). The investors immediately offered Murdy the role of Chairman and CEO. Within a year, he took this start up company public (NYSE: GRW) and sold it to ServiceMaster for $500 million in October 1998.

Bill then led a partnership to help build Club Quarters starting in 1999. In 2000, the same investors who had invited him to lead LandCare asked him to lead a heating and air conditioning (HVAC) company that was underperforming called Comfort Systems USA (NYSE: FIX). At the time FIX was trading at $1.65 a share. Despite a global recession in the midst of his tenure, just over twelve years later the stock had risen to $16/share.

Bill stepped down as CEO & President in 2012 and remains Chairman.

Fred Malek advising President George H.W. Bush.

Frederic Malek, USMA 1959

- CHIEF EXECUTIVE OFFICER, MARRIOTT HOTELS AND NORTHWEST AIRLINES
- FOUNDER AND CHAIRMAN, THAYER LODGING GROUP
- ADVISOR TO FOUR PRESIDENTS OF THE UNITED STATES
- MASTER'S IN BUSINESS ADMINISTRATION, HARVARD BUSINESS SCHOOL
- MALEK TENNIS CENTER AT WEST POINT NAMED IN HIS HONOR
- CO-FOUNDER, THAYER LEADER DEVELOPMENT GROUP
- BOY SCOUTS OF AMERICA, YOUTH MEMBER

Fred Malek advising President Ronald Reagan.

>>> Spotlight

During Malek's eight-year tenure as President of Marriott Hotels, profits quintupled and the stock increased eight fold. He then went on to become President and Chief Executive Officer of Northwest Airlines, where he led the acquisition of the company as a major equity partner.

Fred Malek takes the oath as Chairman of the West Point Board of Visitors, along with Board Member Elizabeth McNally (USMA 2000).

LEADERSHIP ACHIEVEMENT
CHIEF EXECUTIVE OFFICER, MARRIOTT HOTELS & NORTHWEST AIRLINES

Fred Malek is a successful businessman, political figure, and philanthropist. He is one of America's most influential leaders in both American business and politics, leading some of the world's largest corporations (Marriott and Northwest Airlines) and advising four United States Presidents – all of which was after starting his career as an Army Officer in combat. Throughout his life, he has always given incredibly of his time and efforts to support West Point.

Despite his incredible success, Malek remains a humble man. He was raised by his mother and father in a middle-class area of Chicago, graduating from Morton High School in Cicero, Illinois. He attended West Point in 1955 and graduated in 1959. He was commissioned in the Infantry and graduated from Airborne and Ranger Schools. He then went on to serve with a Special Forces Group (Green Beret) in Vietnam in 1961.

IN ADDITION TO HIS BUSINESS CAREER, MALEK CONTINUOUSLY SERVED HIS COUNTRY IN A NUMBER OF CAPACITIES, INCLUDING ACTING AS AN ADVISOR TO FOUR U.S. PRESIDENTS: NIXON, REAGAN, GEORGE H.W. BUSH, AND GEORGE W. BUSH.

After completing his military commitment, Malek attended Harvard Business School and received his master's in Business Administration, which allowed him to land jobs as a consultant at McKinsey & Company (a management consulting firm for national and international businesses, governments, and institutions) and then as chairman of hand-tool manufacturer Triangle Corporation. But it wouldn't be long before he returned to government work in 1969, becoming Deputy Undersecretary of the Department of Health, Education, and Welfare. Then, he became Special Assistant to the President of the United States under President Nixon, then became Deputy Director of the United States Office of Management under President Ford.

In 1974, he left government and became Vice President of Marriott Hotels, eventually rising to the title of President and Chief Executive Officer. During his eight-year tenure as President, profits quintupled and the stock increased eight fold. He then went on to become President and Chief Executive Officer of Northwest Airlines, and Cochairman of CB Richard Ellis (formerly Coldwell Banker).

In addition to being a corporate executive, Malek became a major investment financier, leading the acquisition of the Ritz-Carlton Hotel Company with Marriott International as a major equity partner, the acquisition of Northwest Airlines and the acquisition of CB Richard Ellis. He was also a partner with former President George W. Bush in owning the Texas Rangers Baseball Club. He became the founder and chairman of Thayer Lodging Group, a private equity firm that acquired more than $3 billion of hotel assets and consistently earned top returns for investors. Malek is also the Founder and Chairman of Thayer Capital Partners, a Washington, D.C.–based corporate buyout firm.

In addition to his business career, Malek continuously served his country in a number of capacities, including acting as an advisor to four United States Presidents: Nixon, Reagan, and George H.W. Bush and George W. Bush. He advised President Reagan as a member of the executive committee of the President's Council on Cost Control, the President's Commission on Private Sector Initiatives, and the President's Council on Physical Fitness and Sports. He served President H.W. Bush as director of the 1988 Republican Convention and of the 1990 Economic Summit of Industrialized Nations (with the lifetime rank of Ambassador) and as Campaign Manager for President Bush during 1992. Malek also served as National Finance chairman for the 2008 McCain Presidential Campaign.

Currently, Malek serves on a number of boards, including the Aspen Institute (where he is chairman of the Finance Committee and member of the executive committee), the George H.W. Bush Library Foundation, and the American-Israel Friendship League (where he is also on the executive committee). Malek is also chairman of several organizations, including Virginia Governor Bob McDonnell's Commission on government Reform and Restructuring, the Republican Governors Association Executive Roundtable, The American Action Network and American Action Forum, and the American Friends of the Czech Republic. He also serves on the board of directors at CB Richard Ellis and Dupont Fabros Technologies (where he is also lead director).

For more than half a century, Malek has supported West Point with his time and effort. In 2008, he was appointed to the West Point Board of Visitors by President George W. Bush and currently serves as the Chairman of the Board of Visitors. He has been a major benefactor of West Point, dedicating the Malek Tennis Center.

The Fred Malek Room at the Thayer Hotel was proudly dedicated by Thayer Lodging Group.

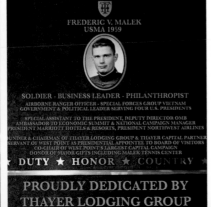

FREDERIC V. MALEK
USMA 1959

SOLDIER - BUSINESS LEADER - PHILANTHROPIST
AIRBORNE RANGER OFFICER - SPECIAL FORCES GROUP VIETNAM
GOVERNMENT & POLITICAL LEADER SERVING FOUR U.S. PRESIDENTS

SPECIAL ASSISTANT TO THE PRESIDENT, DEPUTY DIRECTOR OMB
AMBASSADOR TO ECONOMIC SUMMIT & NATIONAL CAMPAIGN MANAGER
PRESIDENT MARRIOTT HOTELS & RESORTS, PRESIDENT NORTHWEST AIRLINES
FOUNDER & CHAIRMAN OF THAYER LODGING GROUP & THAYER CAPITAL PARTNER
SERVANT OF WEST POINT AS PRESIDENTIAL APPOINTEE TO BOARD OF VISITORS
CO-CHAIR OF WEST POINT'S LARGEST CAPITAL CAMPAIGN
DONOR OF MAJOR GIFTS INCLUDING MALEK TENNIS CENTER

DUTY ★ HONOR ★ COUNTRY

PROUDLY DEDICATED BY
THAYER LODGING GROUP

Lee Anderson, #52, playing on the Army basketball team.

Lee Anderson, USMA 1961

- **CHAIRMAN AND OWNER, API GROUP**
- **TOP DONOR TO WEST POINT IN WEST POINT HISTORY**
- **ANDERSON RUGBY STADIUM NAMED IN HIS HONOR**
- **WEST POINT DISTINGUISHED GRADUATE AWARD**
- **CAPTAIN, ARMY BASKETBALL TEAM**

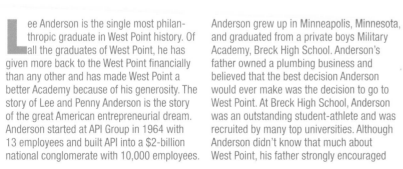

Lee Anderson is the single most philanthropic graduate in West Point history. Of all the graduates of West Point, he has given more back to the West Point financially than any other and has made West Point a better Academy because of his generosity. The story of Lee and Penny Anderson is the story of the great American entrepreneurial dream. Anderson started at API Group in 1964 with 13 employees and built API into a $2-billion national conglomerate with 10,000 employees.

Anderson grew up in Minneapolis, Minnesota, and graduated from a private boys Military Academy, Breck High School. Anderson's father owned a plumbing business and believed that the best decision Anderson would ever make was the decision to go to West Point. At Breck High School, Anderson was an outstanding student-athlete and was recruited by many top universities. Although Anderson didn't know that much about West Point, his father strongly encouraged

Anderson to attend and said "he would never regret going to West Point" and he trusted his father's advice.

At West Point Anderson played football, basketball, and track Plebe year. Yearling year he played football and basketball, but because the seasons overlapped, he chose to focus on the sport he played best Cow and Firstie years: basketball. At six feet seven inches, Anderson was the starting center and earned All East honors his senior year, help-

ing the team to a 17–7 record. Lee Sager, a classmate and fellow basketball player, was later inducted in to the West Point Athletic Hall of Fame. He also played on the team with Robert Foley, who would receive the Medal of Honor for valor in Vietnam and then rise to become the West Point Commandant and a Lieutenant General.

Back then, up to 50 cadets could choose to be commissioned in the United States Air Force and Anderson elected to be commissioned as

>>> Spotlight

The Anderson Rugby Complex is a world-class facility and features home and away locker rooms, a weight training facility, office space, as well as a full-size natural grass competition surface and an artificial turf training pitch. The impact on the program has been profound, while rugby has been successful since it was first played at West Point in 1961, in 2009 the men advanced to the round of four and the women won the National Championship Tournament in 2011.[1]

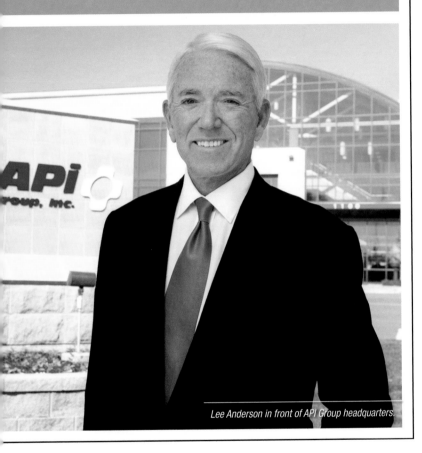

Lee Anderson in front of API Group headquarters.

pany. Shortly after returning to Minneapolis, his father suggested he meet with a company called API Group, that was a small start up company in the fire suppression market to "see what you think about them." Anderson started at API when the company had only 13 employees in 1964. They had little capital and "eked out a profit for the first 10 years" before they were able to acquire another small company that was struggling. This the first of many acquisitions as Anderson built API into a national company through the acquisition and integration of more than 40 small and regional businesses in the construction, manufacturing, and fire suppression businesses. API Group is still privately owned with more than 10,000 employees and $2 billion in annual sales.

Shortly after returning to Minneapolis in 1964, Anderson met Penny Pilney. They married in 1965 and have two children Lee, Jr., and Katharine, who each have three children and all live in the Minneapolis area. In 1993, Anderson and Penny decided to move to Naples, Florida, but have a summer home on northern Lake Superior.

Anderson always was grateful for his father's direction in sending him to West Point and felt that his training at West Point had prepared him to lead in all types of environments. After leaving the military, he and Penny had spent most of their time and effort building API Group. As the company became larger and more profitable, Anderson started to get re-engaged with his alma mater. He started traveling up to West Point for games and events around five times a year and supported the building of the Kimsey Center, started funding "Staff Rides" and other activities, and serves on several committees. Working with the Association of Graduates on several projects, Anderson became aware of the "Pursuit of Excellence" program and the many projects the Superintendent was attempting to pursue with donations.

The Rugby Complex was one of the many "Pursuit of Excellence" programs that the superintendent wanted to have built that went above and beyond the federal funds available to operate the Academy. Anderson had been considering a "legacy gift" and the Rugby Center really appealed to him. Anderson learned that the rugby club had actually started in 1961 when Anderson was a cadet, when a foreign exchange cadet had started the club, though he didn't recall the club at the time. Army Men's Rugby had become the "winningest" program at West Point, typically finishing in the top-five programs annually. Anderson and Penny

generously donated $6 million to fund the Anderson Rugby Complex. This privately funded rugby complex was not only intended for men's rugby, but also for the women's rugby club, which has an equally outstanding women's locker room and facilities. In 2011, the West Point Women's rugby team beat the seven time national championship Penn State women's rugby team to win the National Championship. Without the generous support of Anderson and Penny, it is unlikely that West Point would have a women's national championship winning team.

Anderson's leadership in industry and philanthropy has won him many accolades and awards, including the Ernst & Young Entrepreneur of the Year Award, Thomas Jefferson Award as West Point's most generous donor, being inducted in to the Minnesota Business Hall of Fame, and receiving Minnesota's Outstanding Philanthropist Award. Anderson and Penny have given generously to several other worthy causes, such as University of Saint Thomas; the Boston Children's Muscular Dystrophy Fund, the Boone and Crockett Club, and too many other causes to list.

WITHOUT THE GENEROUS SUPPORT OF LEE AND PENNY, IT IS UNLIKELY THAT WEST POINT WOULD HAVE A WOMEN'S NATIONAL CHAMPIONSHIP WINNING RUGBY TEAM.

As Anderson looks back on his incredible life, he says, "I know that my West Point experience has had a lot to do with my business success. It has really affected my life in total, and I hope to be able to give back to West Point."

a Construction and Procurement Officer in the Air Force. After graduation, he attended USAF Officer basic training at Amarillo Air Force Base and then was permanently assigned to Luke Air Force Base in Phoenix, Arizona. He led a group of 35 people at Luke, many of them civil servants to support the procurement and construction at Luke Air Force Base. He loved the camaraderie and the work. Graduating with a three-year active-duty obligation, Anderson had completed his obligation when his father suffered a

mild heart attack. Anderson had not decided whether or not he would pursue a career in the Air Force, but his father's medical condition helped him make the decision.

He visited his father in Minneapolis, and his father suggested that if Anderson was going to pursue a business career that he do so immediately rather than wait, because his father didn't believe he would be around long enough to advise him later. Anderson left the military and returned to Minneapolis, but never did work for his father's plumbing com-

Lee Anderson Room at the Thayer Hotel was proudly dedicated by the employees of API Group.

Tony Guzzi is the Chief Executive Officer of EMCOR a $6.3 billion company with 27,000 employees. He graduated in the top five percent of his undergraduate university and with distinction from his Harvard Business School (MBA) class. His academic resume is top tier with many awards and accolades and reads like many other Fortune 500 Chief Executive Officers, but Guzzi's leadership style is markedly different than the average Fortune 500 Chief Executive Officer. He earned his undergraduate degree from West Point and served as a Light Infantry Officer in the United States Army. These foundational experiences ingrained in him the belief that the mission comes first and leading people is his mission.

Guzzi was born in Johnstown, Pennsylvania, located in the Western Pennsylvania Mountains. His grandparents were both first-generation Americans from Serbia and Italy. Only one of his four grandparents was able to complete high school – the other three had to go to work in middle of the Great Depression to feed their families. One grandfather entered the coal mines, his grandmother worked as housekeeper, and his other grandfather worked as a fireman – all at age 13. Both sets of grandparents had a combined seven children, and all of their children became college graduates with Guzzi's dad being the first.

His father was an engineer and an entrepreneur, building a company from five people up to 200 that designed and constructed buildings across the Mid-Atlantic. His mother was a nurse with a unique ability to make sure that Guzzi, his older brother, and his younger sister never became too enamored with their own success. Her line: "You have been set up for success, go earn it." Guzzi's father was tragically killed in an auto accident at 63 in December 2000 and his father's untimely death had a profound impact on Guzzi's own outlook on his life. It made him realize that he needed to have balance between his work and family – just as his father had.

Guzzi attended Bishop-McCourt High School in Johnstown, Pennsylvania, and was an excellent student and a good athlete. He was captain of his football team, and lettered three times in football and twice in track. As a result of this success, he was recruited by several Ivy League schools for football.

However, Guzzi had a different goal for his college experience: He wanted to attend West Point. He started to learn about West Point in his junior year in high school through mailings and his own research. His parents and his extended family had always exhibited deep respect for the military and the academies. Guzzi pursued West Point quietly and on his own and his quest was realized when he received a call on Christmas Eve 1981 that he was the principal nominee from the State of Pennsylvania and would gain admission to the United States Military Academy at West Point. Guzzi was attracted to West Point because he wanted to push himself academically, physically, serve his country, and also wanted to further learn how to lead.

Guzzi received his nomination to West Point from Congressman John Murtha, who was a gruff old Marine who told Guzzi, "You have been given a great opportunity, don't screw it up, don't come home without a diploma, you won't be welcome here if you don't finish." Guzzi excelled at West Point in all areas of Academy life-academics, physical fitness, and military training. He graduated as a "star man" in the top five percent of his class.

It was during his second year that he really bought into the ethos of the

Anthony J. "Tony" Guzzi, USMA 1986

- CHIEF EXECUTIVE OFFICER, EMCOR GROUP (NYSE: EME)
- MASTER'S IN BUSINESS ADMINISTRATION, HARVARD BUSINESS SCHOOL
- BOY SCOUTS OF AMERICA, YOUTH MEMBER AND ADULT VOLUNTEER

Cadet Guzzi receives his diploma from West Point in May 1986.

institution of West Point and realized how it was impacting him. That year he realized that a good leader was one who has both competence and character, who does the right thing regardless of personal consequences. West Point is the ultimate laboratory of leadership training, cadets leading cadets and learning to lead soldiers once they join the Army. In this environment, Guzzi developed his leadership style of the "senior serving his subordinates."

Guzzi's performance at West Point resulted in the uncommon distinction of staying in command his entire senior year. He was selected to be a "Beast" (Basic) Training Company Commander, commanded his Cadet Company and then finally served as Cadet Battalion Commander. Graduating at the top of the class, Guzzi had his choice of both branch of service and first assignments. He was torn between Engineers and Infantry, and chose the

Light Infantry because he wanted to lead soldiers in the most challenging physical environment. He chose Schofield Barracks, Hawaii, because at that time the 25th Infantry Division was one of the most deployed units in the Army with a strong Pacific presence.

Guzzi graduated on May 28, 1986, and attended Infantry Officer Basic Course at Fort Benning, Georgia, followed by Ranger School. Ranger School was both a learning experience and also a challenging place to prove leadership skills under pressure. Guzzi entered Ranger School in great shape at 190 pounds. He finished at 156 pounds eight weeks later. Ranger School was a foundational experience for Guzzi, reinforcing that you only succeed if the team succeeds and personal accolades do not mean much of anything. It taught Guzzi that you can push yourself beyond any limits you had thought imaginable, but also you had to still lead and make sure the team succeeded.

Guzzi arrived in Hawaii and loved the Army and leading soldiers. He believed it was his job to help soldiers excel and he trained them hard. He had a strong belief in leading by example and always maintaining the highest physical fitness standards. He had excellent mentors in his Battalion Commanders and each had his own style but all were great leaders.

On Memorial Day 1988, during a beach party, Guzzi walked up and started talking to a stunning young coed named Michelle; Michelle was a University of Oklahoma Physical Therapy student on vacation visiting her sister. Dave Houston, a visiting classmate of Guzzi's, who was with Guzzi offered the following advice: "Forget it; she is out of your league." They were engaged before Labor Day that year and married two years later. They have been married for almost 23 years and have three children: John (19), a sophomore at Boston College; a daughter, Ann Marie (16); and a son,

Louis (11). One of Guzzi's greatest joys has been coaching the kids' teams and spending time with his family remembering the lessons that his father taught him.

After the Gulf War, the Army began cutting back significantly, from 20 divisions to 12 divisions in one year. Guzzi had already applied to graduate school with the hope of either attending through the Army or attending on his own to pursue a civilian career. He was accepted into Harvard Business School and sought his Battalion Commanders' advice. His Battalion Commander was frank, the Army was going through the most significant cutbacks in generations, and it would be hard for Junior Officers like Guzzi to distinguish themselves from the rest of the pack. Guzzi decided to leave the Army and to attend the Harvard master's in Business Administration program. Michelle worked as a physical therapist and put him through business school.

>>> Spotlight

Tony Guzzi (USMA 1986) and Mike Shelton (USMA 1967) at EMCOR.

"The first 90 days were challenging at Harvard, but the rest was pretty easy compared to West Point," says Guzzi humbly, graduating with distinction with his master's in Business Administration from Harvard University. Their son, John, was born two weeks after graduation.

He went to work for McKinsey Consulting in Pittsburgh – back in his home state for the first time in 11 years. He worked with a great team at McKinsey and enjoyed helping companies either work on business strategy or performance improvement. McKinsey taught him two things that would help his future career: (1.) that all decisions should be based in facts and facts are stubborn; and (2.) that great organizations falter or fail if they are not able to change or deal with the harsh realities of business. He loved the McKinsey culture and people but he was not a natural consultant. He struggled between his desire to develop and execute the plan versus helping others

execute the plan. He missed the direct line leadership that he enjoyed in the Army and decided that he wanted to lead a large industrial organization.

United Technologies recruited Guzzi to join their Corporate Strategy Group in 1997. The United Technologies Chief Executive Officer told Guzzi that this would be a short assignment and the goal was to develop Guzzi as a General Manager at the earliest opportunity. In short order, he was sent to Carrier Corporation to take over a business that had four General Managers in five years and had a poor performance record. Guzzi started in this $250 million in the service business and quickly realized that the business had some great products and even better people but had lacked focus, leadership, structure, and, most importantly, a winning spirit. Guzzi and this team accomplished great success in a short period of time and they gained a reputation as turnaround leaders. Senior

leadership at UTC trusted Guzzi to do the right thing and gave him the freedom to operate. The United Technologies President wanted to promote and move Guzzi to another UTC Business Unit after a short 18 months of performance. Guzzi convinced the UT President to leave him in place to prove that the success was not a short-term burst but was sustained and earned success. Guzzi and his team's responsibilities continued to increase and in six short years his scope of responsibilities had increased over tenfold to a $3-billion business leading Carrier, Distribution, and Aftermarket.

As a result of his and his team's success at Carrier, he was offered the opportunity to become the President and Chief Operating Officer of EMCOR a $6.3-billion specialty construction and services company with 27,000 employees. He was attracted to EMCOR as it had great field businesses but they were not performing to their

full potential. He believed a little jolt of discipline and focus was needed. When he started in late 2004, the company was a $4.5-billion company that has grown to a $6.3-billion despite the epic recession in 2008. As a result of the hard work of the EMCOR team, the value of the company more than quadrupled in that period in a flat stock market.

Guzzi loves to spend his time in the field. He learns by touching not by waiting for people to report to him. To work with and for Guzzi, you must have confidence in yourself and trust in him as he will travel throughout the organization and touch it at multiple levels. He does not travel with an entourage but prefers to travel light and go and see the organization in action. He cannot stand "yes men" but rather if he finds one he will encourage them to find another opportunity. He wants frank communication up and down the chain of command and he will often call or visit

LEADERSHIP ACHIEVEMENT
CHIEF EXECUTIVE OFFICER, EMCOR GROUP (NYSE: EME)

Tony coaching youth basketball.

individual project manager to get a "boots on the ground" viewpoint of how not only a job is performing, but also how else can the team be successful and what support they need to be successful. He has a large field presence and spends more than 50 percent of his time in the field.

UNDER GUZZI'S STEWARDSHIP, EMCOR HAS DEVELOPED A ZERO-ACCIDENT PHILOSOPHY. "WE BELIEVE THAT EVERY EMPLOYEE SHOULD RETURN SAFELY TO THEIR FAMILY EACH NIGHT," SAID GUZZI.

He loves leading a large organization and finds it fulfilling. He really believes "it is all about the people." For example, at EMCOR he learned to appreciate their how important improving EMCOR's safety culture and results were. EMCOR's work is inherently dangerous and supports customers in some of the most demanding environments possible. Under Guzzi's stewardship, EMCOR has developed a Zero Accident Philosophy. "We believe that every employee should return every night to his or her family after a day's work. Our front-line supervisors believe in this philosophy and today we work three or four times the total number of man-hours per year than 10 years ago but we have about a tenth of the injuries. Why? We set a policy that makes sense, our front-line leaders bought into this policy, and we hold each other accountable for its implementation and success. Also, we believe it is a competitive advantage as this record makes the best skilled tradespeople want to work here. I believe that this is how we care for our people through concrete results that place people's safety first in and accepts no compromises for our people's safety. Our people deserve to work in this type of environment."

His leadership style can be summed up in four simple words: "Mission first, people always." He believes that an organization must focus on performance and in the long run this performance allows people to be cared for and provides them with long-term careers and personal success. Getting personal stories out of Guzzi is difficult, as he usually prefers to tell the stories of those around him.

His next big mission within EMCOR: He wants to leave a legacy that will have EMCOR recognized as one of the most ethical corporations in America: "We score high marks in the annual Fortune 500 survey as one of the most admired companies in the Engineering and Construction sector however, that is not enough." Guzzi wants EMCOR leaders to be known as leaders of competence and character, the lesson he learned at West Point almost 30 years ago. He hopes to accomplish this with a simple message that seems an awful lot like a commander's intent. "I never want anyone in the public ever thinking that someone at EMCOR is cutting corners. I want our folks to do the right thing by our shareholders, our employees, our customers, our suppliers and our communities we work in. I want them to do what is right and know they have my unqualified support when they do," he says. He plans on supporting this mission and intent with a well-thought training program that has his fingerprints all over it and he will personally go through the training with each of his 200 most senior leaders in small groups. The training is not an ethics program, but a leadership program that focuses on character and trust: "I think this is the next big competitive advantage for EMCOR, being known as the most ethical company with the best leaders in the business."

Briefing President Bush at G8 Leaders Meeting in Heiligendamm, Germany, 2006.

First Lieutenant McCormick 307th Engineer Bn. 82nd Airborne Division.

Dr. David McCormick, PhD, USMA 1987

- CO-PRESIDENT, BRIDGEWATER ASSOCIATES, LP
- UNDERSECRETARY OF THE TREASURY FOR INTERNATIONAL AFFAIRS DURING THE FINANCIAL CRISIS, 2007–09
- DEPUTY NATIONAL SECRETARY ADVISOR FOR INTERNATIONAL ECONOMICS, 2006–07
- PRESIDENT, ARIBA INC.
- CHIEF EXECUTIVE OFFICER, FREEMARKETS INC.
- PHD WOODROW WILSON SCHOOL OF INTERNATIONAL AFFAIRS, PRINCETON UNIVERSITY

Swearing-in ceremony, Undersecretary of Treasury for International Affairs, August 2007.

G8 Summit, Heiligendamm, Germany, 2006.

Prepping President Bush for a meeting with the Japanese Prime Minister.

David McCormick is Co-President and a member of the Management Committee for Bridgewater Associates, a global macro investment firm with more than $140 billion in assets under management, and the world's largest hedge fund.

In his role at Bridgewater, he has helped lead the firm and advise its clients – some of the largest, most sophistical investors in the world – through one of the most challenging periods in modern financial history. This is not the first time McCormick has been tested as a leader in volatile and uncertain times. He has been under fire before as an Army Officer, a business leader in the tech industry, and while serving at the highest levels of government. His most challenging leadership experience was as President Bush's Undersecretary of the Treasury for International Affairs during the 2008–09 global financial crises. In this role, he was a critical player in developing and executing the United States response to the crisis.

McCormick's career has taken a very unconventional path. Reflecting on his life, he is very humble and grateful, saying he had a lot of luck, taking chances that at the time seemed risky and could have turned out much differently. McCormick was born and raised in Bloomsburg, Pennsylvania, where he attended Bloomsburg High School. He was cocaptain of the football and wrestling teams and was recruited to play both sports at West Point. He received his nomination from Senator Arlen Specter and started at West Point on July 1, 1983, during the President Ronald Reagan's first term and at the height of the Cold War.

At West Point, McCormick was a fierce competitor, a four-time letterman on the Army wrestling team and the team's Cocaptain his senior year. He was the two-time East Coast Runner-Up and twice earned a trip to the NCAA Division I championships. He was also a scholar-athlete and awarded the Arvin Award named after Captain Carl Arvin, the USMA 1965 Cadet First Captain who was Killed In Action in Vietnam and awarded two Silver Stars for valor. McCormick's name is inscribed in the Arvin Gymnasium as a West Point Class of 1987 Scholar-Athlete.

McCormick studied Mechanical Engineering and planned to spend a career as an officer in the Army Corps of Engineers. Then in the summer of 1986, prior to his senior year, his career took an unexpected turn when he worked in Washington, D.C., as an intern assigned to the Political Military Bureau of the United States State Department. It was in this role that he became intrigued with international politics and economics, an interest that would later change the course of his career.

McCormick returned to West Point to finish his senior year and was promoted to Cadet Captain and Battalion Commander responsible for approximately 400 cadets. As the Cocaptain of the Army wrestling team, McCormick had hopes of All-American honors, but tore his ACL (knee ligament) partway through his senior year. He delayed the surgery until after the wrestling season (and competed in the Eastern and National Championships despite the injury) and then had his operation just prior to graduation and recovered in time to walk across the podium to receive his diploma from Army Chief of Staff General Wickham on May 27, 1987.

McCormick remained at West Point as the graduate assistant coach of the wrestling team for one semester to give him time to rehabilitate his knee prior to Airborne and Ranger Schools. While there, McCormick took advantage of the setback and enrolled in two classes at Columbia University using the GI Bill. One of the classes was an international politics class taught by Roger Hilsman (USMA 1943), a WWII hero who had served in the Office of Strategic Services (predecessor to the CIA) and in a senior role in the Kennedy administration. This experience, and Roger Hilsman in particular, would further spur McCormick's appetite for a career in public service.

McCormick left West Point in December 1987 to attend the Engineer Officer Basic Training and then to Airborne and Ranger Schools, where he was chosen as the Honor Graduate of Ranger School. Second Lieutenant McCormick arrived at Fort Bragg, North Carolina, to join the 82nd Airborne Division in September 1988. At the 82nd, McCormick found a comfortable home deploying constantly for training and often on alert as the nation's rapid deployment force. The Cold War ended during this assignment and the United States Army struggled to find a post–Cold War mission. That search was short-lived; on August 2, 1990, Saddam Hussein's Iraqi Army forces invaded Kuwait, threatening the world's oil supplies. President George H.W. Bush immediately sent the 82nd Airborne to block the Iraqi Army from continuing on into Saudi Arabia. Days later McCormick and his soldiers found themselves on the ground in the midst of the crisis defending Saudi Arabia and preparing to liberate Kuwait. Several months later, McCormick's unit in the 82nd Airborne was assigned under a French Army Division and was involved in the "left hook" flanking the Iraqi Army in January 1991. First Lieutenant McCormick at age 25 was Executive Officer of combat engineering company of 130 soldiers tasked with clearing minefields and destroying enemy munitions deep in Iraq. He received the Bronze Star Medal for his leadership during Desert Storm.

Upon return to Fort Bragg, McCormick was promoted to Captain and attended the Engineer Officer Advanced Course. While attending the advanced course he started applying to graduate schools, intent on going to Korea on his next Army assignment and then returning to attend graduate studies and hopefully a teaching assignment at West Point. While McCormick loved the Army, in writing his essays for graduate schools he somehow sensed that there was another path for his career and life. After much soul searching, he resigned from the Army in July 1992 and traveled the world – from Greece to Syria, from Borneo to China – for eight months prior to starting graduate study in international affairs on the beautiful Princeton campus.

At Princeton, McCormick initially pursued a master's degree at the Woodrow Wilson School for International Affairs, but during the first year of his master's

THE BUSH ADMINISTRATION REACTED WITH A MASSIVE STIMULUS PACKAGE, AND IT WAS DAVE MCCORMICK'S ROLE THROUGHOUT THIS CRISIS TO COMMUNICATE TO THE WORLD AND TO THE CENTRAL BANKS OF THE MAJOR INDUSTRIALIZED NATIONS.

program, he met Amy, who would become his wife eight years later, and they both opted to pursue their PhDs. Having lived through the end of the Cold War and the dramatic downsizing of the Army, McCormick wrote his doctoral thesis on the future of the Army after the downsizing which later became a book called *The Downsized Warrior*. The Army supported the idea of his doctoral thesis and did something remarkably unique and brought McCormick back on to active duty to perform his research. Captain McCormick returned to the Army for three months temporary duty to perform the research, and with such incredible Army support, McCormick was able to finish his doctoral thesis in record time.

After completing his PhD, McCormick again chose a non-traditional path and joined McKinsey, Inc, a top-tier consulting firm, in Pittsburgh where he worked with Dean Dorman (USMA 1986) and Tony Guzzi (USMA 1986) from 1996 to 1999. In 1999, at the peak of the Internet/tech boom, McCormick was recruited away from McKinsey to join an early stage but high-flying Internet company called FreeMarkets. Soon after joining, the company had an initial public offering, and shortly thereafter McCormick was promoted to President and then Chief Executive Officer. In 2000, he and Amy started their family, having the first of four daughters: Lilah (12), Tess (10), Ava (8), and Elise (6).

FreeMarkets had a meteoric rise, but at that same time, the United States economy collapsed with the bursting of the Internet bubble. While this was a challenging time, with many tech companies failing, McCormick led FreeMarkets through the downturn and continued growth and profitability, and successfully sold the company to Ariba in 2004 for $500 million. He remained at Ariba as the President for the next 18 months before being lured away to join the Bush Administration to serve as Undersecretary for Export Administration in the United States Department of Commerce in 2005. McCormick and Amy and their three daughters, Lilah, Tess, and Ava, moved to Washington, D.C., in summer 2005 and, soon after they arrived, Elise was born.

The role at Commerce was short-lived, however, and six months in to the job, McCormick was asked to join the White House Staff as Deputy National Security Advisor for Economic Affairs. In this

capacity, he negotiated the G-8 and G-20 international summits, closely interacting with President Bush, his cabinet, and the policymakers of the world's leading economies. While in the White House, McCormick also often worked closely with Secretary of the Treasury Henry Paulson. In 2007, Secretary Paulson asked McCormick to join him at the Treasury Department as the Undersecretary of International Affairs serving as the leading United States international economic diplomat. In this role, McCormick interacted with the finance ministers and central bankers of the major economies, placing him in a critical role at an historic time, a job he calls "the greatest job in the U.S. government."

This challenge would bring all of McCormick's experiences and talents together – having been tested and proven at West Point, Ranger School, Desert Storm, and the collapse of the Internet bubble. In October 2008, as the global financial markets began to melt down, the Bush Administration reacted with a massive response. McCormick's role throughout this crisis was to help the economic team craft the required policies and then communicate them to policymakers and market participants around the world. For 18 months, he lived on airplanes, traveling the world, during one of the most volatile and uncertain periods in financial markets history.

McCormick joined Bridgewater in the summer of 2009 where he is Co-President. As the largest hedge fund in the world, his role as Co-President is to advise Bridgewater's clients – some of the most sophisticated institutional investors in the world – not only on their investments, but on the global financial markets overall. Having led soldiers, companies, and our country through some of their largest crises over the past 20 years, McCormick's experiences in the military, business, and government – often during times of crisis – allow him to bring a distinctive and unique perspective to global investors in these challenging times.

As he reflects on the last several decades, McCormick credits his experience at West Point and in the Army as providing the foundation to help him grow and learn through this diverse set of opportunities.

Bridgewater Associates is a global leader in institutional portfolio management, and the largest hedge fund in the world, with approximately $140 billion in assets under management. Founded by Ray Dalio, Bridgewater began investment operations in 1975 and manages portfolios for a wide array of institutional clients globally, including public and corporate pension funds, foreign government and central banks, university endowments and charitable foundations.

Courtesy: Bridgewater

The podium with Treasury Secretary, Henry Paulson, August 2007.

Courtesy: White House

In Rwanda with Dina Powell, Assistant Secretary of State for Educational and Cultural Affairs.

Courtesy: David McCormick

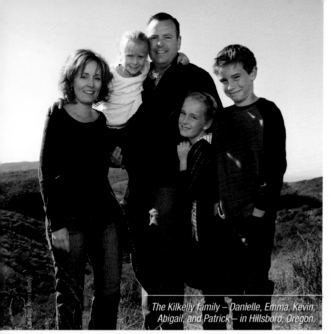

The Kilkelly family – Danielle, Emma, Kevin, Abigail, and Patrick – in Hillsboro, Oregon.

Kevin holding his son, Patrick, inside a Black Hawk helicopter in Geibelstadt, Germany, 1999.

Kevin Kilkelly, USMA 1993

- **PRESIDENT, SOLARWORLD AMERICAS**
- **MASTER'S IN BUSINESS ADMINISTRATION, DUKE UNIVERSITY FUQUA SCHOOL OF BUSINESS**
- **UH-60 BLACK HAWK PILOT**
- **AVIATION COMPANY COMMAND DURING BALKANS CONFLICT**
- **ARMY TRACK AND FIELD AND CROSS-COUNTRY TEAM MEMBER**

Kevin Kilkelly is a 1993 West Point graduate and United States Army veteran of eight years. Kevin served as a UH-60 Black Hawk helicopter pilot and Company Commander during the 1990s, including a deployment to Kosovo to support operations in the Balkans. His military experience, along with a passion for the outdoors, a concern for the environment, and a master's in Business Administration from Duke University, combined to earn him a leadership role atop the solar industry. He is the President of SolarWorld Americas, the commercial arm of the largest solar manufacturer in the United States.

Kilkelly grew up in Kalamazoo, Michigan, and graduated from Portage Northern High School, where he was Captain of the track and cross-country teams, played basketball, and was a student body officer. His grandfather, Joseph McNamara, served in Patton's Army during World War II in the European Theater as a member of the Army Corps of Engineers.

Kilkelly first became aware of West Point when a teammate from high school received an appointment to the Class of 1990. Although

he had been offered multiple scholarship opportunities to run track and cross-country at the collegiate level, Kilkelly was drawn toward West Point and its ideals of selfless service and "Duty, Honor, Country." A few years later, Kilkelly was accepted and entered Beast Barracks in the summer of 1989.

Kilkelly ran cross-country and track at the Academy, and his enjoyment of running has followed ever since. He has since completed the Paris, New York, and Marine Corps Marathons.

While he was in attendance at West Point from 1989 to 1993, the United States entered into two conflicts: Operation Just Cause and Operation Desert Storm. "While the invasion of Panama, during my Plebe year, seemed like a distant headline in a newspaper, Desert Storm felt very real," Kilkelly remembers. "The conflict happened during my final years at West Point, so I had friends who were getting deployed to Kuwait and Iraq. Everyone goes into West Point knowing that we are being trained to serve and lead our nation's military. We study history, so we know conflicts are inevitable, but Desert

Storm made it tangible and immediate."

After the conclusion of Desert Storm, General Norman Schwarzkopf came to West Point. In his address, Schwarzkopf reminded the Corps of Cadets that West Point is about choosing a direction in life that puts service to the nation first and being the standard bearer for not only the military, but also carrying that standard forward into the public and private sector.

Soon after, Kilkelly branched Army Aviation and graduated with a bachelor's degree in Environmental Science. After earning his wings at Fort Rucker, Alabama, he was assigned to the legendary 82nd Airborne Division at Fort Bragg, North Carolina, from 1994 to 1997. During that time, Kilkelly met Danielle – the woman who would become his wife – at a classmate's wedding. They were married in 1997, and, shortly after, he received orders to U.S Army Europe.

The couple moved to Geibelstadt, Germany, where he was assigned to the 12th Aviation Brigade. During his three-year tour in Europe, Captain Kilkelly took over company command while deployed to Albania and Kosovo during

the extended conflicts in the Balkans. In 2001, he chose to leave the Army after eight years, having accomplished many of the goals he set out for himself.

His first corporate job was as a Supply Chain Analyst at General Electric, renowned for its leadership and training programs for executives. GE's bias for action and its emphasis on execution over strategy was a familiar ethos from his 12 years in uniform. Kilkelly earned his Six Sigma Black Belt certification, an achievement that would be invaluable at GE and later in his career.

In 2008, Kilkelly received his master's in Business Administration from Duke University's Fuqua School of Business. He chose Duke because it was a top-tier school that focused on international business and finance.

After nine years at GE and maturing as an executive, Kilkelly chose to perform a search for his next role. He had always had an interest in the energy sector and, with increasing concerns about global climate change, pursuing a career in renewable energy was a logical fit. He carefully set out to earn a

At SolarWorld's U.S. manufacturing plant in Hillsboro, Ohio.

>>> Spotlight

SolarWorld has been the largest solar technology manufacturer in the Americas since 1975. SolarWorld manufactures silicon crystal, wafers, cells, and modules in the United States and offers complete solar-power solutions to all types of customers. At its United States manufacturing plant in Hillsboro, Oregon, and its commercial hub in Camarillo, California, SolarWorld employees more than 900 Americans. SolarWorld is headquartered in Bonn, Germany, and achieved sales of about 1.2 billion Euros for the fiscal year 2011.

On deployment with the 82nd Airborne Division, Fort Bragg, North Carolina, 1995.

leadership role at a solar company and was chosen to lead SolarWorld Americas in 2010.

"WORKING IN SOLAR IS MORE THAN JUST A JOB; IT'S A CALLING TO MAKE THE WORLD A BETTER, CLEANER PLACE FOR THE NEXT GENERATION BY UTILIZING THE WORLD'S MOST ABUNDANT RESOURCE: THE SUN," SAYS KILKELLY.

SolarWorld Americas is the commercial arm of the largest solar manufacturer in the United States. With headquarters in Bonn, Germany, and manufacturing plants in Freiberg, Germany, and Hillsboro, Oregon, SolarWorld achieved more than one billion Euros in annual sales in the fiscal years 2010 and 2011. "SolarWorld has this amazing history of innovation and leadership dating back to the beginning of the solar industry," Kilkelly says. "I would describe the organization and culture as a 35-year-old start-up."

From SolarWorld's commercial hub in Camarillo, California, Kilkelly leads the company's sales, marketing, product development, systems engineering, and logistics operations for the Americas. "Working in solar is more than just a job; it's a calling to make the world a better, cleaner place for the next generation by utilizing the world's most abundant resource – the sun," says Kilkelly. "There is a lot of pride that goes along with working in renewable energy, and solar certainly has a 'cool factor' with my kids."

Today, the solar industry faces daunting challenges. Around the world, solar manufacturers have suffered tremendous business losses as a result of massive over-production by Chinese solar companies, which are propped up by billions of dollars of illegal government subsidies and predatory pricing schemes targeted at export markets. In the United States, about 25 manufacturers were forced to close or downsize in 2011 and 2012, including respected, longtime industry players like Sharp and BP.

Despite these circumstances, SolarWorld Americas has grown and remained competitive under Kilkelly's leadership. During his tenure, the company's annual sales revenue for the Americas grew more than sevenfold. While other companies have shuttered, SolarWorld remains the largest manufacturer in the Western Hemisphere.

In 2011, SolarWorld launched a federal investigation into illegal Chinese trade practices. Under the leadership of SolarWorld's executive team, United States solar manufacturers fought back against the unfair subsidies that China provides to its solar companies and the illegal dumping of Chinese-made solar panels into the American market. The company asked the United States Department of Commerce and International Trade Commission to protect United States workers and their right to fairly compete. As a result of SolarWorld's case, the United States government now imposes duties ranging from 24 to 255 percent on imported Chinese solar cells and panels, helping level the playing field for all United States producers to compete, grow, and thrive.

Kilkelly attributes much of his success to his experience in the military, which gave him the sense of perspective and balance needed to guide a company through turbulent times.

As he reflects on his rise to the top of the solar industry and his path through West Point and the Army, Kilkelly credits West Point with far more than his environmental science degree: "The best friends of my life are those I made at West Point. The relationships I established there have held true over time. Whenever I meet a West Point alumnus, there is an immediate connection, a sense of trust, confidence, and respect that comes from knowing we've be through the same experience. In business, I know that fellow grads share a code of conduct, that we can be relied upon to conduct business professionally and ethically and that we want each other to succeed. I think that bond is unique to the Long Gray Line."

Jim Kimsey remembers the cadet mess hall was so quiet "you could have heard a pin drop" as General MacArthur bid farewell to the Corps of Cadets in 1962 upon receiving the Sylvanus Thayer Award, giving his now famous "Duty, Honor, Country" speech. Many excerpts of that speech are required memorization for Plebes nowadays, but one excerpt was incredibly prescient to foresee the amazing developments of the future, and how Cadet Jim Kimsey would play a major part in that new world.

MacArthur near the end of his famous speech stated, *"You now face a new world – a world of change. The thrust into outer space of the satellite, spheres, and missiles mark the beginning of another epoch in the long story of mankind. In the five or more billions of years the scientists tell us it has taken to form the earth, in the three or more billion years of development of the human race, there has never been a more abrupt or staggering evolution. We deal now not with things of this world alone, but with the illimitable distances and as yet unfathomed mysteries of the universe. We are reaching out for a new and boundless frontier."*

And Jim Kimsey would reach out to that new frontier 30 years after graduation, founding the company that essentially brought the Internet to most American households: America Online, Inc.

James Verlin Kimsey, USMA 1962

- FOUNDING CHIEF EXECUTIVE OFFICER AND CHAIRMAN EMERITUS, AMERICA ONLINE, INC.
- CHAIRMAN EMERITUS, INTERNATIONAL COMMISSION ON MISSING PERSONS (ICMP)
- CHAIRMAN EMERITUS, REFUGEES INTERNATIONAL (R.I.)
- TWO TOURS OF COMBAT IN VIETNAM AND ONE TOUR IN DOMINICAN REPUBLIC

Captain Kimsey at Vietnamese Orphanage.

Jim Kimsey, Chairman Emeritus America Online.

Kimsey with Pope John Paul.

>>> Spotlight

After serving as the President Chief Executive Office of AOL for a decade up until 1995, Kimsey ran the AOL Foundation, a philanthropic organization. The initial focus of the foundation was on interactive learning with grants going to help teach children, particularly the disadvantaged.

The son of a World War I First Sergeant, Jim Kimsey grew up in relatively humble beginnings in Washington, D.C., with four brothers and sisters. He was the atypical West Point applicant; he received a scholarship to Gonzaga High School in Washington, D.C., but was expelled his senior year for being disruptive. With his future at risk, his Irish-Catholic mother convinced the priest at St. John's to allow Jim to graduate from St. John's, which competed locally within D.C. with Gonzaga. Kimsey graduated in 1957 from St. John's High School and then attended Georgetown University on a scholarship for one year. At that time, in 1958, a weekly television show *West Point* was playing (the television was a relatively new luxury for most Americans), and the movie *The Long Grey Line* had just come out, further improving the West Point brand to the American public in the mid-1950s. For the 19-year-old Kimsey, West Point seemed "cool" and he jokes that "the uniform seemed like a good way to get dates."

Kimsey entered West Point July 1958. Unfortunately for Kimsey, although the uniforms were cool, cadets rarely were allowed to leave the all-male campus, so he didn't get many dates the first year. Looking back 50 years later, Kimsey describes his performance as a cadet as "unremarkable, anonymous, and always trying to stay below the radar." He met lifelong friends who would also go on to greatness in their respective fields, including classmates Wayne Downing (later General) and Frank Caufield (Co-Founder of Kleiner, Perkins, Caufield & Byers "KPCB").

Kimsey's Firstie year, General MacArthur received the Sylvanus Thayer Award in May 1962. One month later, President Kennedy drove in a convertible with Superintendent Major General Westmoreland on the Plain to review Graduation Parade (sadly JFK would be shot in the very same Presidential convertible 17 months later in Dallas). The next day after the parade, President Kennedy provided the Commencement Address in which he described the future warfare that the Class of 1962 and their soldiers might expect:

"War by guerrillas, subversives, insurgents, assassins, war by ambush instead of by combat; by infiltration, instead of aggression, seeking victory by eroding and exhausting the enemy instead of engaging him. It is a form of warfare uniquely adapted to what has been strangely called 'wars of liberation,' to undermine the efforts of new and poor countries to maintain the freedom that they have finally achieved. It preys on economic unrest and ethnic conflicts. It requires in those situations where we must counter it, and these are the kinds of challenges that will be before us in the next decade if freedom is to be saved, a whole new kind of strategy, a wholly different kind of force, and therefore a new and wholly different kind of military training."

And then the Class of 1962 headed off to fight those guerilla wars that President Kennedy had predicted, and Kennedy himself would fall to an assassins bullets that he eerily had predicted.

Kimsey chose the Infantry Branch and attended Airborne and Ranger Schools (and was one of the few Ranger School graduates who looks back and actually enjoyed Ranger School). He enjoyed being a field soldier and loved leading under stressful and uncertain environments. His first assignment was as a Platoon Leader in the 82nd Airborne Division at Fort Bragg, North Carolina.

In 1965, Captain Kimsey was an Infantry Company Commander in 1st/508th Airborne and led the first company of soldiers to land in the Dominican Republic after President Johnson ordered Operation Powerpack and ordered the 82nd Airborne Division to invade the Dominican Republic to support the government forces in defending against communist rebels. They had planned to parachute in to liberate the San Isidro airfield east of the capital from guerillas, but en route, friendly government forces secured the airfield and Kimsey's C-130 landed on the airfield. Since it was a hostile environment the air crew treated it as such and ordered Kimsey's men to exit as the aircraft taxied around to take off. Kimsey and his First Sergeant were last off the aircraft as he and his soldiers tumbled out off the rear ramp with ammo strewn all over the runway by the aircrew. This was his first combat experience, and the brigade took two Killed In Action (KIA).

The Vietnam War also escalated significantly in 1965, and many soldiers and officers were sent as individuals. After a few months in the Dominican Republic, Kimsey departed the Dominican Republic individually, to head to Washington, D.C., where his wife and two children were living, to deploy as an individual to Vietnam for one year. He was assigned to a village with a 10-man advisory team to live with the locals as advisors to the South Vietnamese Army in I Corps. The previous American advisory team had been overrun and wiped out by

Jim Kimsey at Mass Grave in Kosovo.

Kimsey Auditorium at Michie Stadium West Point.

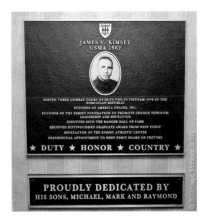

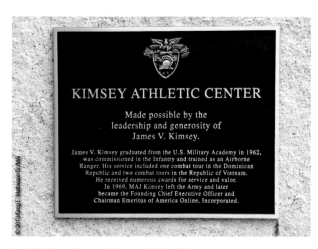

KIMSEY ATHLETIC CENTER

Made possible by the
leadership and generosity of
James V. Kimsey.

James V. Kimsey graduated from the U.S. Military Academy in 1962,
was commissioned in the Infantry and trained as an Airborne
Ranger. His service included one combat tour in the Dominican
Republic and two combat tours in the Republic of Vietnam.
He received numerous awards for service and valor.
In 1969, MAJ Kimsey left the Army and later
became the Founding Chief Executive Officer and
Chairman Emeritus of America Online, Incorporated.

the Viet Cong. He spent a year in the village and built an orphanage that he continued to support after he left, and continues to support to this day.

With his family located in Washington, D.C., he requested the Army send him to Washington, which they did. He rotated out of Vietnam and was sent to Fort Lewis, Washington (unfortunately, the state, not the district). He relocated the family across the country and lived an idyllic life on the general staff of the division. He learned that the more responsibility he would ask for, the more he would get. By the time he left he had been given command of the band, the maintenance outfit and several other randomly assigned units that he offered to fix.

Originally, he had planned to stay in the Army for only his four-year commitment, but he stayed on because he enjoyed the life. He re-deployed to Vietnam as part of the Phoenix Project in 1969, which was one of the most successful programs of the Vietnam War, yet also the most controversial and oft-criticized programs.

In his role with the Phoenix Program, Kimsey worked with Bill Colby (who would later go on to be director of the Central Intelligence Agency from 1973 to 1976) and would go down to the province level to work with LRRP teams (Long Range Reconnaissance Patrols) occasionally patrolling with the team to evaluate the success of the programs. After having lived with the locals for one year on his previous tour, Kimsey was struck by the fact that in 1969 on his second tour, so little was known by most American soldiers about the culture and the people. This experience would shape his opinion on United States operations in future conflicts – as Americans we often operate in areas

where we don't understand the people or the culture – and should avoid doing so.

After eight years in the Army with the war in Vietnam declining, Kimsey could read the tea leaves that his class would remain Majors for many years – and he was right – his classmates who remained in the service would stay at the Major rank for 10 long years. He had also seen that wealthy civilians had far more influence than he would have as a Major, Lieutenant Colonel, or Colonel. He decided to leave the Army and initially wanted to pursue a real estate career, but the real estate industry was struggling.

AT ITS PEAK, AMERICA ONLINE (AOL) [FOUNDED BY KIMSEY] HAD MORE THAN 27 MILLION SUBSCRIBERS AND WAS THE LEADING INDEPENDENT PROVIDER OF INTERACTIVE ONLINE SERVICES TO CONSUMERS.

Kimsey acquired a building at 1831 M Street in Georgetown, D.C., with no money down. It housed a brokerage firm in the upstairs of the building as a tenant and Kimsey opened a bar on the first floor called The Exchange. After a legal dispute with the New York Stock Exchange, he negotiated the rights to have a ticker tape running behind the bar, which was a first. The bar thrived and he opened several other bars, which he sold years later.

Kimsey's good friend and classmate Frank Caufield had served his commitment in the Army, attended Harvard Business School, and started his civilian career in California, founding one of the first private equity firms called KPCB. KPCB had an investment in the DC area that Frank wanted Jim to help with in 1985. It was a small computer company called Control Video. Kimsey started as "adult supervision" over Control Video, but

would turn Control Video into America Online and become the Chief Executive Officer in 1985, take the company public in 1992, and by 1996, he hired Steve Case and Bob Pittman to lead the company, while Kimsey became Chairman until 1998. Between 1985 and 1998, Kimsey led America Online through the Internet revolution, bringing the Internet to corporations and individuals throughout America, which led to a massive investment into Internet companies, software companies, and hardware companies as the Internet reached "out for a new and boundless frontier" as MacArthur had presciently foreseen.

Kimsey founded the AOL Foundation and also formed his own Kimsey Foundation and seeded both with AOL stock near its height. In 1998, Kimsey stepped down while AOL was still riding high with a stock price of $100/share. He focused on running his Kimsey Foundation that is largely dedicated to supporting Washington, D.C.–based educational opportunities. Having come from humble beginnings, with his father a government worker and his mother at home with the five children, Kimsey's own success he credits with educational scholarships to high school and Georgetown, and the government provided education at West Point.

At its height, America Online had more than 28 million users with a market capitalization of $222 billion. The AOL–Time Warner merger and the market challenges for the combined companies that resulted occurred in 2000 long after Jim Kimsey had left the company.

His observation that he could make more impact as a wealthy civilian proved true and his advice and his network have given him influence over many different areas of national security and philanthropy. As a beltway native he remained actively networked in the national security field. In 2000, Senator Bob Dole and Secretary of State Colin Powell convinced Kimsey to take over as Chairman of the International Commission on Missing Persons (ICMP), which was focused on the mass graves in the Balkans with the intent to

sunset the commission after that operation. Despite the initial opposition from those who didn't see its value, the ICMP has identified more missing persons through DNA than all other DNA testing labs in the world combined. In this role as Chairman of ICMP, Kimsey traveled to areas where mass graves and executions were frequent, including the Balkans, Iraq, Afghanistan, and Colombia, often with his friend General Wayne Downing, the former Commander of United States Special Operations. Sadly, General Downing, a great warrior with nearly a dozen valor awards, passed away from a bacterial infection he contracted on a trip to Israel. Kimsey was hospitalized with a bacterial infection a few days later but survived. Kimsey ran the ICMP for 10 years until he convinced Ambassador Tom Miller to succeed him in 2011.

Twenty-five years after being expelled from Gonzaga High School, the headmaster awarded Jim Kimsey with a backdated high-school diploma. Not coincidentally, both St. John's High School and Gonzaga High School now have Kimsey Technology Centers generously funded by the Kimsey Foundation.

In 1999, the Kimsey Athletic Center at West Point was opened, thanks to a generous contribution from West Point graduate Jim Kimsey. It is a massive 120,000-square-foot, four-story, state-of-the-art facility that Kimsey funded in order to boost West Point's intercollegiate competitiveness. The son of a World War II First Sergeant, who heard General MacArthur forecast the new and boundless frontier, had helped America come on line and reach that new frontier.

The Kimsey Room at the Thayer Hotel is proudly dedicated by his sons: Michael, Mark, and Raymond.

Frank Caufield is a pioneer in the global financial markets and helped fund many of America's most successful companies, including America Online, Amazon, Google, eBay, Time Warner, Quest, Caremark, Netscape, Intuit, Electronic Arts, Sybase, Compaq, and Sun Microsystems, to name a few. He has led the development of the venture capital and private equity markets by founding some of the most successful companies in the space, providing investors with superior risk adjusted returns as America's greatest venture capital fund.

Born in Georgia on November 21, 1939, Caufield grew up as an "Army brat," living overseas in Spain, England, and Germany. He followed in his father's footsteps and attended West Point in 1958 as part of the Class of 1962. His father, Frank Caufield, Sr., (USMA 1934) retired as a Brigadier General in 1964 after serving 30 years in the Infantry.

As a cadet, Caufield was somewhat indifferent; however, four decades later, he helped create a world-class crew and sailing center that is one component of the Superintendent's Margin of Excellence Program that has allowed West Point to be ranked as the number-one facilities in the United States according to the Princeton Review annual ranking of 377 universities in the United States.

After graduation, Caufield attended Air Defense Artillery Officer Basic Course and then deployed to Mainz, Germany, with the 6th Artillery Regiment. He resigned from the Army in 1966 to attend Harvard Business School to pursue his master's in Business Administration and was awarded his master's in Business Administration in 1968, founded Oak Grove Ventures in 1971 as Managing General Partner, and co-founded Kleiner, Perkins, Caufield & Byers in 1978. KPCB has backed more than 500 ventures since its founding and helped create many of the most innovative and successful businesses in American history and significant wealth for their investors.

After the fall of the Berlin Wall, Caufield was asked to serve as a Director on the United States government-funded U.S.-Russia Investment fund, the modern-day Marshall Plan for Russia after the collapse of the Soviet Union that helped the transition from a command economy to more open capitalistic markets.

As part of the Superintendent's Margin of Excellence Program, the Superintendent had prioritized building a new crew and sailing facility on the Hudson River. Being attracted to the beautiful setting, Caufield provided the leadership and funding to build the world-class facility that opened with a ribbon-cutting ceremony on May 28, 2002.

> **KPCB HAS BACKED MORE THAN 500 VENTURES SINCE ITS FOUNDING AND HELPED CREATE MANY OF THE MOST INNOVATIVE AND SUCCESSFUL BUSINESSES IN AMERICAN HISTORY.**

Courtesy: Frank Caufield

Frank Joseph Caufield, Jr., USMA 1962

- CO-FOUNDER, KLEINER, PERKINS, CAUFIELD & BYERS
- PRESIDENT, NATIONAL VENTURE CAPITAL ASSOCIATION AND THE WESTERN ASSOCIATION OF VENTURE CAPITALISTS
- DIRECTOR, THE U.S.-RUSSIA FUND
- CHAIRMAN, THE CHILD ABUSE CENTER OF SAN FRANCISCO
- MASTER'S IN BUSINESS ADMINISTRATION, HARVARD UNIVERSITY
- BENEFACTOR OF THE CAUFIELD CREW AND SAILING CENTER AT WEST POINT
- LEAD DIRECTOR, TIME WARNER CORP.

Caufield Crew Center at West Point.

TIMOTHY C. TYSON
USMA 1974

CHAIRMAN AND CEO, APTUIT
PRESIDENT AND CEO, VALEANT PHARMACEUTICALS INTERNATIONAL
PRESIDENT, GLOBAL MANUFACTURING AND SUPPLY, GLAXOSMITHKLINE
BOARD OF DIRECTORS, PHARMACEUTICAL RESEARCH AND MANUFACTURING ASSOCIATION
FOUNDER AND CHAIRMAN, INTERNATIONAL LEADERSHIP FORUM OF INTERNATIONAL
SOCIETY OF PHARMACEUTICAL ENGINEERS
PARTNER, CREERIS VENTURES
CEO ROUNDTABLE ON CANCER
SIX SIGMA HALL OF FAME

★ DUTY ★ HONOR ★ COUNTRY ★

PROUDLY DEDICATED BY
FAMILY AND FRIENDS

The Tim Tyson Guest Room at the Thayer Hotel.

Timothy C. Tyson, USMA 1974

- **CHAIRMAN AND CHIEF EXECUTIVE OFFICER, APTUIT**
- **PRESIDENT AND CHIEF EXECUTIVE OFFICER, VALEANT PHARMACEUTICALS**
- **PRESIDENT, GLAXOSMITHKLINE**
- **CO-FOUNDER, THAYER LEADER DEVELOPMENT GROUP**
- **BOYS SCOUTS OF AMERICA, YOUTH MEMBER**

Tim Tyson is a proud West Point graduate and a global leader in the pharmaceutical industry. In his 35-plus-year career, he has negotiated complex multi-billion-dollar mergers and acquisitions, led major turnarounds that have fueled growth and value, and, most significantly, has been instrumental in bringing more than 50 lifesaving and life-improving medicines to the market.

Tyson was born in 1952 in Hornell, New York, and moved with his family to the Ithaca area

when he was 14. Tyson attended Dryden High School and graduated third in his class. In addition to excelling academically, Tyson lettered in football, basketball, and baseball. During his senior year, Tyson was a leader on the football and baseball teams that won league championships for Dryden High School. He participated in student government, community volunteerism, choir, and theater and played lead guitar for a high-school rock band from Hornell called The Axis Power.

After receiving a Congressional appointment in 1970, Tyson entered West Point with the Class of 1974. As a cadet, Tyson played lacrosse, was a member of the West Point Glee Club and Protestant Chapel Choir, served as a sports editor for the *Howitzer*, and was Regimental Investigating Officer on the Honor Committee. The Class of 1974 graduated after the withdrawal of ground forces from Vietnam and the implementation of the All-Volunteer Army. Tyson was commissioned in the Military Police Corps

and assigned to the 111th Military Police Company at Fort McClellan, Alabama. He served in many positions in the 111th, including Military Police Investigations and Executive Officer. He was well respected by his Commanding Officers, peers, and troops and always pushed himself to overachieve. While on active duty, Tyson attended classes four evenings a week, earning a master's of Public Administration in 1976 and a master's of Business Administration in 1979 from Jacksonville State University. In 2007, he

>>> Spotlight

Tim Tyson was featured on the cover of the November 2005 *Pharmaceutical Executive* magazine. The cover selection is a major accomplishment and recognition within the pharmaceutical industry. A comprehensive article in this edition highlighted the significant turnaround and value created by the team that Tyson had appointed and also highlighted his leadership. Through Tyson's direction, the company was restructured into a long-term profitable growth business, providing life-saving and life-enhancing medicines to patients in need.

Courtesy: Tim Tyson

Courtesy: Tim Tyson

Courtesy: Tim Tyson

Photo: NARA

Photo: NARA

than 4,000 reps and launched 32 new products, eight of which achieved sales greater than $1 billion each. He led the manufacturing merger between GlaxoWellcome and SmithKlineBeecham. As President of GSK's Global Manufacturing and Supply division, Tyson was responsible for 40,000 employees at 130 manufacturing facilities in 41 countries. He made in-person visits to nearly every one of the sites. Tyson's leadership by example inspired the thousands of employees to unprecedented achievements.

From 2002 to 2008, Tyson served as Chief Operating Officer, President & Chief Executive Officer of Valeant Pharmaceuticals International. During this period, sales grew 69 percent and earnings increased 135 percent. He led a major restructuring of the company and established a highly effective research and development capability that developed a best-in-class epilepsy compound and a promising pro-drug for hepatitis C, both in Phase III. Valeant was the first pharmaceutical company to implement the Lean Six Sigma process across all disciplines of the company globally.

> **AS PRESIDENT OF GSK'S GLOBAL MANUFACTURING AND SUPPLY DIVISION, TYSON WAS RESPONSIBLE FOR 40,000 EMPLOYEES AT 130 MANUFACTURING FACILITIES IN 41 COUNTRIES.**

In 2008, Tyson was named Chairman and Chief Executive Officer of Aptuit Inc., a pharmaceutical services company, based in Greenwich, Connecticut. Aptuit was a Scrip Award winner in 2010, for its work partnering on five different development programs with Exelixis. The American Chamber of Commerce in Italy, honored Aptuit with the Transatlantic Award 2010, for its substantial investment in Italy, with the acquisition of GSK's Research Centre of Verona. In 2009, Aptuit was awarded the Chief Executive Officer Cancer Gold Standard accreditation. In addition to implementing Lean Six Sigma practices at GlaxoSmithKline and Valeant, Tyson also introduced the process at Aptuit. In 2011, he was recognized by the International Society of Six Sigma Professionals as Leader of the Year and was honored as the third inductee in to the iSix Sigma Hall of Fame.

Since his graduation from West Point in 1974, Tyson has been an ardent supporter of the Academy and his fellow graduates. He is a Co-Founder of the Thayer Leader Development Group at West Point and an actively involved co-investor in the turnaround and revitalization of the Thayer Hotel at West Point. In 2002, Tyson received a Bicentennial Leadership Award from the United States Military Academy at West Point. He is the West Point Association of Graduates' largest contributor of unrestricted funds and has been inducted in to the Omar N. Bradley Society, which honors leading financial donors to the Long Gray Line.

Tyson and his wife, Amy, were married in 1974 and have a grown son, Matthew; daughter-in-law, Kendra; and two grandchildren, Mira Katherine and Noah Rhys Tyson.

TYSON HAS ALSO SERVED ON/AS A MEMBER OF:

- Pharmaceutical Research and Manufacturing Association (PhRMA) BIOCOM.
- Chief Executive Officer Roundtable, University of California at Irvine.
- Dean's Executive Forum at Cal State Fullerton.
- Chief Executive Officer Roundtable on Cancer.
- Health Sector Advisory Board at Duke University.
- International Leadership Forum of the International Society of Pharmaceutical Engineers.
- Visiting lecturer at Cambridge University.
- Board of Directors, Strike 3 Foundation for Pediatric Cancer.
- Business Executives for National Security.
- Nonprofit boards in Raleigh-Durham, North Carolina, and Orange County, California.

was recipient of JSU's Alumnus of the Year award. Captain Tyson resigned from full-time military service in 1979 and remained in the Army Reserves for the next 14 years, retiring as a Major.

Tyson's first civilian job after leaving the Army was with Procter & Gamble as a manufacturing manager. From 1980 to 1988, he held several executive positions with Bristol-Myers in Syracuse, New York, and Wallingford, Connecticut.

Tyson was hired by Glaxo, Inc. as Director of Engineering in 1988. He successfully led the completion of the construction of a half-billion-dollar research and development facility on the campus in Research Triangle Park, North Carolina. Tyson ran several divisions for Glaxo, GlaxoWellcome, and GlaxoSmithKline and was a member of the Corporate Executive Team reporting to the Chief Executive Officer. Tyson served as Vice President of Sales and Marketing for GlaxoWellcome's United States operations, where he managed a sales force of more

John Garrison, Jr., USMA 1982

- **PRESIDENT AND CHIEF EXECUTIVE OFFICER, BELL HELICOPTER, A TEXTRON COMPANY (NYSE: TXT)**
- **ASSISTANT PROFESSOR OF SOCIAL SCIENCES, UNITED STATES MILITARY ACADEMY**
- **HARVARD BUSINESS SCHOOL, MASTER'S IN BUSINESS ADMINISTRATION WITH DISTINCTION**
- **AIRBORNE AND RANGER QUALIFIED**
- **FOUR-YEAR ARMY FOOTBALL LETTERMAN AND DEAN'S LIST CADET**

On December 30, 2010, John Garrison, President and Chief Executive Officer of Bell Helicopter, presented the Bell Helicopter Armed Forces Bowl trophy to Coach Ellerson and the Army football team after their victory over Southern Methodist University 16–14. The victory was the first bowl game for the Army team in 14 years and first bowl win in 25 years. This moment was particularly special for Garrison as it brought together so many important aspects of his life as scholar, athlete, leader simultaneously: former West Point cadet, Army Officer, West Point professor, and now President and Chief Executive Officer of Bell Helicopter supporting the military – all tied together in this particular moment in time. The employees of Bell Helicopter, 25 percent of whom are veterans and 100 percent of whom support the military, sponsor the Armed Forces Bowl which is billed as "More than a Bowl Game" because it honors all current service members and their families and all veterans of

our Armed Forces. As the presenting sponsor, Garrison needed to be impartial during the game; however, after the victory, he could not contain himself as he awarded the trophy to Coach Ellerson, giving a big "*hooah*" to the Army team.

Garrison was born May 10, 1960, in Massachusetts into an Air Force family – Garrison's parents were both Air Force Officers – his father, John L. Garrison, Sr., a Lieutenant Colonel and pilot, and his mother, Jeanne O'Brien Garrison, an Air Force nurse. He has four brothers and sisters – Jeanne Marie, Donald, Debbie Ann, and Karen Lee. As a military family, they moved every three or four years from Massachusetts, to New Jersey, to Florida, to Germany to Wisconsin. Garrison went to high school in Hales Corners, Wisconsin, and was a standout student-athlete. He played three sports – football, basketball, and baseball – and was captain his senior year of all three teams. He was selected as All-State for both football

and baseball. His high-school coach gave him advice that he remembers vividly today: "Use your athletic ability to get yourself the best education that you can get." Garrison was recruited to play football at all three service academies and also as he says self-deprecatingly, "the bottom half of the Big Ten." He became enamored with West Point, not only for academics, but also for the physical challenges and the leadership training it provided. Even at a young age, Garrison knew that the combination of academic excellence, physical and mental strength, and leadership were cornerstones of personal and professional success. The thought of graduating from West Point and leading a platoon of soldiers intrigued him at a young age. Because his father was on active duty, he was eligible to receive a Vice Presidential nomination, which he received from Vice President Walter Mondale in 1977. He was accepted into West Point and entered in July 1978.

Garrison found West Point academically and

physically challenging. Despite the many challenges, he enjoyed the camaraderie and the scholar-athlete leadership opportunity afforded. His Plebe year, he remembers his first football game – not because of the game itself, but because in those days cadets attended class six days a week, Monday through Saturday. He remembers taking a major test in calculus on Saturday morning at 10 a.m. and having to be dressed and on the field for a 1 p.m. football game up at Michie Stadium. He recalls running up to the stadium thinking to himself that not many Division I football players were taking calculus tests immediately before their games!

Garrison was a four-year Army football letterman, dean's list, and was chosen to be a 3rd Regimental Commander his Firstie year, one of the top cadet leadership positions attainable. As a senior, he struggled with which Army branch to choose. After wise counsel from several Senior Officers, he was convinced that the branch that would give

him the greatest learning experience, with a holistic and strategic view of the battlefield, was the Field Artillery. So he chose Field Artillery and Fort Carson, Colorado, as his first assignment. Before arriving at Fort Carson, he attended Field Artillery Officer Basic Course at Fort Sill, Oklahoma, then Ranger School. He attended Ranger School in the winter of 1983, and even after being a Division I football player for four years, found it to be the most challenging physical and mental experience in his life. Upon graduation, he was selected as one of the Honor Graduates, a coveted award and designation. He looks back at the experience as a great opportunity to learn how to form a team to work collectively under a stressful and challenging environment – a group of individuals who had to all come together to win collectively. It would not be the last time that he would experience the importance of facing adversity as a cohesive team.

After his training, he headed to Fort Carson,

Colorado, south of Colorado Springs. He spent three years at Fort Carson in the typical Lieutenant roles – Fire Support Officer in a Cavalry unit and then Operations Officer in a Multiple Launched Rocket Systems (MLRS) battery. He then attended the Officer Advanced Course (OAC) at Fort Sill, Oklahoma. He deployed to Korea and spent 20 months there culminating as a Battery Commander of an eight-inch artillery battery, leading 138 soldiers where he was awarded the Meritorious Service Medal (MSM).

While in Korea, Garrison was selected by the West Point Social Sciences Department to return to West Point as a professor to teach social sciences to cadets. Prior to teaching, he attended Harvard Business School to receive his master's in Business Administration (MBA). The social sciences department at West Point is renowned for being a stepping-stone to become a General Officer and is a prestigious and extremely competitive assignment to receive.

En route back from Korea in Texas, Garrison married Janet, whom he had met in Fort Worth, Texas, while he attended the Officer Advanced Course at Fort Sill, Oklahoma, just two years earlier. They moved to Boston to attend Harvard, where once again, he graduated with distinction. In doing so, Garrison learned he could compete not only in the military environment, but Harvard gave him the confidence that he could compete in the corporate world. Garrison taught at West Point in the Department of Social Sciences for two years from 1990 to 1992, during which time the world changed radically, more than it had in the past 40 years: The Berlin Wall fell, ending the 45-year Cold War; Saddam Hussein invaded Kuwait; Desert Storm liberated Kuwait; and Congress cut the Army from 20 divisions to 12 divisions in the Peace Dividend. Garrison's Class of 1982 who were remaining in the Army was told that the Army needed to cut his class group by 70 percent within 12 months. This radical cut back was

the "Peace Dividend" that Congress wanted with the end of the Cold War. Having just completed Harvard Business School and with an itch to start in the private sector, Garrison chose to leave the Army after 10 successful years (14, if you include West Point). He was awarded his second Meritorious Service Medal (MSM) and left the Army in June of 1992.

With a West Point BS, Harvard master's in Business Administration, and extensive leadership experience, Garrison had a number of opportunities available to him in a number of lucrative fields. He was offered a role in consulting at a top firm and several investment banking roles, but he did not want to be in consulting or a finance role. Instead, he wanted to be "in the trenches" – involved in creating and building businesses directly rather than advising or financing them from afar. He chose to follow a classmate from HBS to Enron Power Development Corp. In this role he developed power projects and pipelines all over the world, overcoming adversity and challenges, and led the development of a pipeline in Colombia, South America.

After spending two years in this role, Garrison had traveled more than 250 days a year, and while rewarding, it was hard on the family. Another USMA graduate, who was President at Case Corporation (owned by Tenneco), asked Garrison to come to work with him at Case. Garrison started in sales and marketing in their South American operations, promoted to General Manger of their Agricultural System Group, and was eventually promoted to run the Case IH North American Agricultural Division.

In 1999, he was offered an opportunity he could not refuse and returned to Houston to work once again with his HBS classmate who had started a global water company, Azurix, and was in the midst of making several acquisitions. Several months later, Garrison was Chief Operating Officer and President of the company, and shortly thereafter, he was the Chief Executive Officer. Unfortunately, the water company was experiencing challenging times, and its major shareholder, Enron, was also experiencing challenges. Under Garrison's leadership, he restructured the company, selling the public shares, divesting several operating companies, and ultimately repaying the outstanding public debt and closed the company down. It was both difficult and educational for Garrison as he led his team through adversity.

Garrison wanted to return to the manufacturing business, which he was able to do when he was recruited by Textron to be President of E-Z-GO, its global golf car and utility vehicle manufacturer with more than 1,000 employees. Garrison developed the leadership team, and together they, created and executed a strategy that returned E-Z-GO to profitability in the economically challenged golf and utility vehicle markets. Having successfully led one division of Textron, Garrison was then

© Layne Murdock

© Layne Murdock

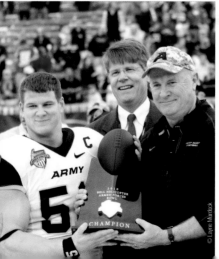

© Layne Murdock

>>> Spotlight

Founded in 1935 as Bell Aircraft Corporation, Bell continues to set the pace for the industry and expand the scope of vertical lift. Now an industry leader with unmatched name recognition, Bell Helicopter was the first to obtain certification for a commercial helicopter. Over its rich history, Bell has delivered more than 35,000 aircraft to customers around the world. With forward thinking in advanced concepts, Bell Helicopter invented tilt rotor aircraft. These unique aircraft lift like a helicopter, then fly like an airplane with twice the speed, three times the payload and five times the range of traditional helicopters. Aerospace and aircraft will never be the same. Headquartered in Fort Worth, Texas, Bell Helicopter has additional plants in Amarillo, Texas, and Mirabel, Canada. As the world's premier provider of vertical lift aircraft, Bell Helicopter continues to provide every customer with products, service, and support second to none.

Courtesy: Bell Helicopter

Courtesy: Bell Helicopter

promoted to run its industrial businesses – representing all of Textron's non-aviation businesses. This was a difficult time for the overall economy during the recession of 2008, and Textron was hit particularly hard with the liquidity crunch, but Garrison looked at this as an opportunity to lead and manage under adversity – yet again. The recession provided the opportunity to implement a structuring plan that enabled the industrial businesses to maintain profitability during the recession and grow

quickly as the global economy recovered. In August 2009, Garrison was asked to become President and Chief Executive Officer of Bell Helicopter based in Fort Worth, where he and his wife, Janet, originally met 23 years earlier.

Bell Helicopter is a 75-year-old company that has approximately 11,500 employees, 8,000 of whom are in Texas. About two-thirds of its business is from the United States government and one-third from

commercial markets with total revenue exceeding $4.5 billion. With his strong military roots, Garrison enjoys interacting with the Marine Corps, Navy, Air Force, and Army customers and supporting, as he says, "their incredible missions." Bell Helicopter also affords him an opportunity to apply

GARRISON'S HIGH-SCHOOL COACH GAVE HIM ADVICE THAT HE REMEMBERS VIVIDLY TODAY: "USE YOUR ATHLETIC ABILITY TO GET YOURSELF THE BEST EDUCATION THAT YOU CAN GET."

his commercial business knowledge and is proud of his company's mission of changing the way the world flies. "The men and women of Bell Helicopter are focused on delivering the mission solutions customer need to be successful. When I think about the incredibly noble missions our customers perform every day – saving lives and preserving freedom – it is humbling," says Garrison.

As experts in vertical lift technology, Bell Helicopter makes the UH-1Y, which is the Marines utility helicopter – the modern platform of the legendary Huey – the AH-1Z Viper, which is the Marines Attack helicopter, and the OH-58D Kiowa Warrior Army Scout Helicopter.

An example of the innovative ways that Bell Helicopter is changing the way the world files is the revolutionary Bell Boeing V-22 Osprey tilt rotor aircraft that is a vertical lift aircraft that

converts to a fixed wing aircraft in flight. This technology has changed the way the Marines operate by giving them increased capabilities, speed, and range. Bell Helicopter's commercial division offers best in class helicopters with the Bell 206-L4, Bell 407, Bell 429, Bell 412, and is developing the newest helicopter the Bell 525 Relentless – all supporting several missions from emergency medical services, airborne law enforcement, search and rescue, oil and gas, and corporate transport.

As he looks back on his life as a soldier, scholar, athlete, and now executive, he sees a theme in his journey. In all aspects of his life, he learns, teaches, coaches, mentors, and leads. That is his role and that is what West Point and the Army taught him as a scholar, an athlete, a leader – first as a follower as a Plebe, then as early as a Yearling, learning to lead as an assistant squad leader. Yet the scholar in him loves to learn and believes in continuous improvement. Having moved every three or four years as an "Air Force brat," then continued moves as an officer and an executive, he enjoys and welcomes change and the challenges and opportunities that it presents. But regardless of whether a leader is an assistant squad leader or the Chief Executive Officer of a multi-billion corporation, Garrison believes leaders need to maintain humility and says, "It's not about you – it's about what your organization can accomplish. People lose their way when they lose sight that the focus needs to be on the organization and its people not on themselves as an individual."

Janet and Garrison have a son and a daughter – both in college.

"He created laughter wherever he went." This epitaph on the tombstone of Herbert Lichtenberg speaks volumes about him. Lichtenberg dedicated his life to making a positive impact on those around him, in general, and to his beloved West Point, in particular. In fact, his positive impact was so great that he was named a Distinguished Graduate of West Point in 2006, an award often reserved for career General Officers.

Lichtenberg and his brother, Alan, grew up in New York City. Alan entered West Point in 1947 and graduated in 1951. Lichtenberg followed his brother to the Academy and started as a Plebe one month after his brother graduated. Lichtenberg graduated in 1955 and was commissioned in the Air Force. He completed his service obligation, joined the family business, and remained in that business for the rest of his life.

Over the next half century, Lichtenberg's leadership, determination, and generosity earned him the honor of being a Distinguished Graduate. A top leader in the home fashion industry, Lichtenberg was particularly recognized for his ethical standards and business acumen as the leader of S. Lichtenberg & Sons. This success eventu-

LICHTENBERG PROVIDED LEADERSHIP THAT HELPED WEST POINT BUILD THE BEST CADET ATHLETIC FACILITIES OF ANY UNIVERSITY IN THE ENTIRE UNITED STATES USING PRIVATE FUNDS.

ally created the economic wealth that allowed him to pursue his passion of supporting West Point.

In 1964, Lichtenberg and Lou Gross led the effort to build a Jewish Chapel on West Point, eventually realizing that vision 20 years later when the United States Military Academy Jewish Chapel opened in 1984. As part of the Superintendent's Margin of Excellence program to build top-tier facilities at West Point, Lichtenberg and his class funded the Lichtenberg Tennis Center. Soon after, the Lichtenberg Tennis Center was opened for Army's 1999 winter/spring season, the United States Tennis Association (USTA) recognized the

center with the "Outstanding Tennis Facility Award." As the first major commitment by a living graduate in support of West Point's Bicentennial Campaign, Lichtenberg's example and leadership in establishing the tennis center inspired other graduates to support the Bicentennial Campaign, resulting in the conception and funding of 10 new athletic facilities. By 2012, this collection of world-class athletic facilities, made possible by the generous donors following Lichtenberg's example, resulted in West Point's number-one ranking by Princeton Review for athletic facilities above 377 other universities. Believing that Army teams practicing in world-class facilities need excellent coaches, Lichtenberg and Lou Gross then led the effort to build eight sets of new housing units to help attract those top coaches who would coach and mentor cadet athletes. Lichtenberg then partnered with Lou Gross to fund a new gymnastics bearing Gross's name. The Lou Gross Sports Center officially opened in February 2002.

While Lichtenberg's generous displays of philanthropy are well known, what is impossible to measure is the enduring positive impact his efforts have had on the cadet

quality of life in the realm of Army athletics and religious activities. Not a single cadet goes through the Academy experience without directly or indirectly benefitting from Lichtenberg's generosity and vision.

While leading S. Lichtenberg & Sons and supporting West Point for more than a half of century, Lichtenberg also raised a family with his wife, Trudy. They have two sons, Michael and Scott, who are both company Vice Presidents, and five grandchildren.

Lichtenberg's leadership and philanthropy were directly responsible for creating the nation's top-ranked, university-level athletic facilities at West Point. He now rests in the West Point Cemetery knowing that he made a monumental impact on the Academy he loved so much. He also continues to bring smiles and laughter to fans of Army athletics as they enjoy intercollegiate sports in the facilities he envisioned.

Herbert Selig Lichtenberg, USMA 1955

- **WEST POINT DISTINGUISHED GRADUATE AWARD**
- **PRESIDENT, S. LICHTENBERG AND SONS**
- **BENEFACTOR, LICHTENBERG TENNIS CENTER AT WEST POINT**
- **LED THE FUND-RAISING EFFORTS TO BUILD THE JEWISH CHAPEL AT WEST POINT**
- **LED THE EFFORT TO BUILD THE COACHES HOUSING AT WEST POINT**
- **AWARDED THE HOME FASHION PRODUCTS ASSOCIATION "MARVIN ROSENBERG HUMANITARIAN AWARD"**
- **DESIGNATED "CURTAIN AND DRAPERY CITIZEN OF INDUSTRY"**
- **NAMED "DEAN OF THE INDUSTRY" AT HOME FASHION PRODUCTS ASSOCIATION**

WEST POINT JEWISH CHAPEL
PRESENTED TO THE
UNITED STATES MILITARY ACADEMY
BY THE
WEST POINT JEWISH CHAPEL FUND

"FOR THE WORK OF RIGHTEOUSNESS SHALL BE PEACE"
והיה מעשה הצדקה שלום
ISAIAH 32:17

Lou Gross grew up in Brooklyn, New York, and attended Brooklyn Technical High School. After graduating from Brooklyn Tech, he attended City College of New York for two years and joined the New York National Guard. He rose to Sergeant First Class before winning a competitive appointment to the United States Military Academy. He entered West Point in 1950 and graduated in 1954, being commissioned in the Corps of Engineers. His first assignment was at Fort Bragg with the 82nd Airborne Division as a combat engineer and he then served in Fort Richardson near Anchorage, Alaska, for two years, assigned to the construction engineers. After the Korean War ended, the Army was downsizing and his options were limited within the Army, so he opted to leave the Army in 1957 and pursue a business career.

Gross started in the plastics industry and joined the Vertrod Corporation in Brooklyn. He built up a niche plastics machinery manufacturing business with 50 employees, which he led until 1999.

In 1965, Gross, Herb Lichtenberg (USMA 1955), and others formed a group of graduates and non-graduates comprised of Jews and non-Jews to raise funds to build a Jewish Chapel at West Point. Together over the next 18 years, they helped lead a capital campaign that raised $7.5 million, while at the same time navigating the administrative and bureaucratic process to build the West Point Jewish Chapel, which opened in 1984. This was the first visible Jewish presence on the Military Academy and helps honor all the Jewish soldiers in the history of the United States military who have served and often made the ultimate sacrifice. In 1995, Gross became the Chairman of the Jewish Chapel Fund and has led this effort to support the Jewish cadet program.

In 1977, Gross, Herb Lichtenberg, and Carl Goldstein started a tradition to host a tailgate at every Army home football game. They invited cadet teams and athlete candidates and their families and today average 500 attendees per game. For the past

IN 1965 GROSS, LICHTENBERG (USMA 1955), AND OTHERS FORMED A GROUP OF GRADUATES AND NON-GRADUATES COMPRISED OF JEWS AND NON-JEWS TO RAISE FUNDS TO BUILD A JEWISH CHAPEL AT WEST POINT.

35 years, they have hosted this tailgate, significantly contributing to Army recruiting and cadet quality of life, while becoming a staple of Army home football games. After the death of Lichtenberg in 2009, Gross led the successful effort to name the plaza at the Holleder Center the Lichtenberg Plaza and make Mr. Goldstein an Honorary Member of the West Point Class of 1955.

In 1998, the Arvin Gymnasium at West Point was being planned as part of a $100 million expansion. Although a considerable amount of funding was coming from private funding, Congress chose to reduce federal funding that eliminated the fifth-floor gym. This change had a negative impact on the gymnastics team that lost its planned space. Herb Lichtenberg and Gross together decided to fund a sports facility to support the gymnastics team and built the Gross Sports Center next to the Lichtenberg Indoor Tennis Center.

Gross has provided support to the cadets and the Academy for more than 50 years that has improved the quality of life for cadets, improved our athletic programs and recruiting, and made West Point a more relevant Military Academy to train our future combat leaders.

Lou Gross, USMA 1954

- BENEFACTOR, GROSS SPORTS FACILITY AT WEST POINT
- CHAIRMAN, WEST POINT JEWISH CHAPEL FUND, 1995–PRESENT
- PRESIDENT, VERTROD CORPORATION, 1967–99
- LICENSED PROFESSIONAL ENGINEER, NEW YORK STATE, 1962
- COLUMBIA UNIVERSITY, MASTER'S DEGREE IN INDUSTRIAL ENGINEERING, 1968
- COLUMBIA UNIVERSITY, PROFESSIONAL DEGREE IN INDUSTRIAL MANAGEMENT, 1969
- SERGEANT FIRST CLASS, U.S. ARMY NATIONAL GUARD, 1948–50

Gross Sports Center at West Point.

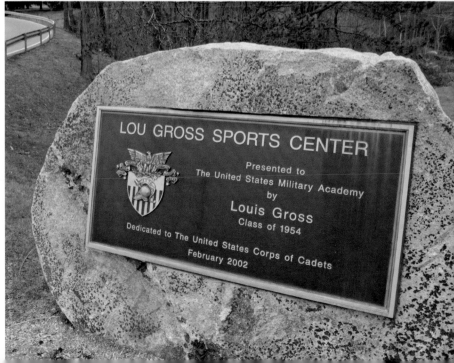

LOU GROSS SPORTS CENTER
Presented to
The United States Military Academy
by
Louis Gross
Class of 1954
Dedicated to The United States Corps of Cadets
February 2002

William P. Foley, II, was born in 1944 just after his father deployed to serve in the United States Army Air Corps as a C-47 Pilot in North Africa and Europe. His father, Captain William P. Foley, Sr., served in North Africa and Sicily and also served as a pilot for the legendary General

FOLEY'S FATHER FLEW FOR GENERAL GEORGE S. PATTON, AND 100 YEARS AFTER PATTON'S GRADUATION, IN 2009, FOLEY DEDICATED THE FOLEY ATHLETIC CENTER IN MEMORY OF HIS FATHER LIEUTENANT COLONEL ROBERT PATRICK FOLEY.

George S. Patton (USMA 1909). One century after Patton graduated from West Point in 2009, William P. Foley, II, dedicated the Foley Athletic Center at West Point in his father's

name. The Foley Athletic Center is a world-class 77,000-square-foot indoor practice facility across the street from the Holleder Center and across from Michie Stadium and the Kimsey Auditorium. The Foley family pledged $15 million to build the facility, the largest single donation in the more than 200-year history of the United States Military Academy. The facility includes a full 100-yard football playing field and is used by the football, lacrosse, soccer, baseball, and softball teams.

This generous donation was part of the Superintendent's "Margin of Excellence" program and has helped West Point become the top-ranked athletic facility of any university in the nation by *Forbes Magazine*.

William P. Foley, II, USMA 1967

- **CHAIRMAN OF THE BOARD, FIDELITY NATIONAL FINANCIAL, INC., (NYSE: FNF), AND EXECUTIVE CHAIRMAN OF THE BOARD FOR FIDELITY NATIONAL INFORMATION SERVICES, INC. (NYSE: FIS)**
- **BENEFACTOR OF THE FOLEY ATHLETIC CENTER AT WEST POINT**
- **CAPTAIN, U.S. AIR FORCE, 1967–71**
- **MASTER'S IN BUSINESS ADMINISTRATION, SEATTLE UNIVERSITY**
- **LAW DEGREE, UNIVERSITY OF WASHINGTON SCHOOL OF LAW**
- **BOARD OF DIRECTORS, WINTER SPORTS, INC. AND REMY INTERNATIONAL, INC.**
- **RANKED IN 2004 BY *GOLF DIGEST* AS ONE OF THE TOP FIVE EXECUTIVE GOLFERS IN THE WORLD**
- **ORANGE COUNTY, CALIFORNIA, "PERSON OF THE YEAR," 1997**

FOLEY ATHLETIC CENTER

GIVEN BY

WILLIAM PATRICK FOLEY II, CLASS OF 1967

IN MEMORY OF HIS FATHER,

LT. COL. ROBERT PATRICK FOLEY, USAF.

A C-47 PILOT IN THE WWII INVASIONS OF

NORTH AFRICA AND SICILY,

HE ALSO SERVED AS A PILOT FOR

GEN GEORGE S. PATTON, CLASS OF 1909,

IN NORTH AFRICA.

>>> Spotlight

The Foley Athletic Center was founded in 2009. It houses a full football field, including end zones. This world-class facility was made possible by a $15 million gift from Mr. William Patrick Foley II (USMA 1967).

The Hoffman name adorns one of the highest relative viewpoints at West Point: on the Hoffman Press Box at Michie Stadium. The press box looks out over the green Astroturf of Blaik Field and across the dark reflective waters of Lusk Reservoir to the colorful fall foliage of the Hudson River Valley, towering over the venue that *Sports Illustrated* rated in 1999 as "one of the top three sports venues of the twentieth century." Michie Stadium is a national treasure and was ranked in the company of the old Yankee Stadium and Augusta National as "one of the top three sports venues of the twentieth century." With the addition of the Hoffman Press Box in 2003, the Army football stadium will continue to be one of the top sports venues of the twenty-first century and beyond.

Hoffman was born and raised in Windom, Minnesota. A standout athlete, he lettered at Windom High School in varsity football, wrestling, and track. He was also selected as a National Merit scholar and attended

Boys State, graduating from high school near the top of his class in 1964. The Windom High School principal, an Air Force veteran, first introduced Hoffman to the idea of West Point and inspired him to apply, which would change the course of Hoffman's life, but not immediately. Hoffman applied but was listed as an alternate candidate to West Point his senior year in high school. Instead, he accepted a wrestling scholarship to Gustavus Adolphus College in St. Peter, Minnesota. His freshman year at Gustavus Adolphus, he was ranked the number-two wrestler in his weight class in the state of Minnesota. Despite his success on the mats, he wanted to be more challenged academically, and showing the resilience and drive that would later define his reputation, he reapplied to West Point while already in college, and was accepted into the Class of 1969.

In June 1965, Hoffman boarded the first plane ride of his life to travel from Minneapolis to New York City, where he first attended the

1965 World Fair. He then traveled up to West Point to start his West Point journey as a Plebe. While at West Point, he wrestled for four years and attended Nationals his senior year. Graduating in June 1969 at the peak of the Vietnam War, Hoffman chose the combat arms and received his first choice in the Field Artillery. In particular, he liked the conceptual role of the Field Artillery Officer: integrating all aspects of combat power on the battlefield and understanding the relationship between the Infantry, Armor, Artillery, and Aviation and how they all came together as a combined arms team.

After graduating from Field Artillery Officer Basic Course at Fort Sill, Second Lieutenant Hoffman deployed to Fort Carson, Colorado, where he then received orders to deploy to Vietnam. Unfortunately, a severe motorcycle accident nearly left him handicapped with a severe leg injury. An enterprising surgeon suggested what at the time was a very progressive surgery and physical therapy for

six months, which Hoffman readily agreed to undertake. The procedure was very successful but the Army felt he would not be at 100 percent, and the Army transferred Hoffman out of combat arms and into the Transportation Corps. Fortunately, this medical diagnosis turned out to be incorrect as Hoffman went on to run marathons, triathlons (Escape from Alcatraz), and many other runs.

After attending the Army Transportation Advanced Course at Fort Eustis, Virginia, Mark returned to Fort Carson with orders again to deploy to Vietnam in 1972. However, with the war winding down, these orders were cancelled, and he was instead deployed to Korea. After an initial battalion staff job in Korea, he commanded A Company, 702nd Transportation Battery with more than 100 soldiers under his command. He loved being a commander and leading soldiers, implementing the leadership lessons he had learned and practiced at West Point. He also valued the new role in the Transportation

Mark Hoffman, USMA 1969

- **BENEFACTOR OF THE HOFFMAN PRESS BOX AT MICHIE STADIUM WEST POINT**
- **CHIEF EXECUTIVE OFFICER, OXYGEN FINANCE**
- **CHAIRMAN, CHIEF EXECUTIVE OFFICER EIGHTFOLD LOGIC**
- **CHAIRMAN, CHIEF EXECUTIVE OFFICER, EVERDREAM**
- **CO-FOUNDER AND CHAIRMAN, CHIEF EXECUTIVE OFFICER, COMMERCEONE**
- **CO-FOUNDER AND CHAIRMAN, CHIEF EXECUTIVE OFFICER, SYBASE**
- **U.S. ARMY 1969–75, COMPANY COMMANDER, A COMPANY, 702ND TRANSPORTATION BATTALION, REPUBLIC OF KOREA**
- **MASTERS IN BUSINESS ADMINISTRATION – UNIVERSITY OF ARIZONA, 1979**
- **ARMY WRESTLING TEAM LETTERMAN**

>>> Spotlight

OXYGEN FINANCE

Oxygen Finance is based on the core principle that spend is an organization's greatest untapped asset.

Oxygen Finance is an enabler for corporate and public sector organizations, unlocking income from their spend and transforming procurement and accounts payable functions into revenue generators. Oxygen Finance's solution is different: it offers a complete, fully resourced service to manage the program on an industrial scale, underpinned by non-intrusive technology.

In addition to delivering a visible income stream, Oxygen Finance provides improved supplier cash flow and increased P2P compliance, together with process efficiencies and enhanced management information.

Corps and learning all aspects of logistics and maintenance, which would serve him well later in the business world. Captain Hoffman returned in 1973 to Fort Eustis, where he remained until 1975, when he resigned from the Army. The post-Vietnam peacetime Army, transitioning to an All-Volunteer Army, was at a modern-day low, morale and recruiting were at a low, drug use and other nefarious activities were at a high. Hoffman chose to leave the Army to pursue a business career but decided first he needed to become educated in business theory before practicing it. His wife was from Arizona so they moved across country to start their civilian career.

While at the University of Arizona, Hoffman and his wife had their first child. With a growing family, he was inspired to study much harder than he had at West Point, and he excelled in academia. Graduating in 1979, he decided he wanted to pursue a career in the technology sector. Pursued by several defense contractors who valued his

West Point degree, command experience, and business graduate degree, he went against the flow and instead chose to pursue a non-defense company called Amdahl. Amdahl was a start-up led by the leading architectural thought leader for mainframe computers, Gene Amdahl, a former IBM executive. The company at that time was on the cutting edge, building the next generation of mainframe computers.

After two years, Hoffman then joined a start-up company called Britton-Lee. The company was on the cutting edge of relational databases. At the time, relational databases were not considered fast enough to run enterprise applications and standard computers were not fast enough to compute for these databases – they needed custom-built hardware that Britton-Lee built. Hoffman learned quickly that while the company was a great idea, it was undercapitalized because the founders wanted to maintain their significant equity positions instead of raising capital that would have diluted them, yet would have allowed them to manage their growth. This was a lesson that would serve him well in later start-ups: having a larger percentage of a company valued at zero was less attractive than giving up some equity to help the company grow to be a billion-dollar company.

At this point in his life (1984), Hoffman believed he understood how companies worked together, how business worked, and the direction that both relational databases and that most importantly general-purpose hardware needed to support them were becoming more and more powerful. As hardware became more capable and processing speeds increased, commercial computers now were capable of processing the databases that previously needed custom made hardware. He saw the future in creating software that could go mass market to all companies. So, he left Britton-Lee with the Vice President of Engineering, Bob Epstein, to co-found a new software company called Sybase.

In 11 years at Sybase as the Co-Founder and Chief Executive Officer, starting with just an idea, he and his team built up the company into a $1-billion company.

In 1995, Hoffman left Sybase to lead CommerceOne, a start-up that was creating electronic market places to connect buyers and sellers in integrated systems. EDI had been the standard communication protocol between buyers and suppliers, but CommerceOne became the leader in the next

protocol, XML technology, taking products to market. CommerceOne grew at a frenzied pace during the tech and Internet booms. The company initially built a marketplace for General Motors, who then wanted to bring in Ford and Chrysler in a consortium deal. After bringing together those traditional arch enemies, CommerceOne did the same thing across multiple industries, building marketplaces and consortiums for traditional competitors. Marketplaces exploded in growth with CommerceOne building consortium marketplaces for the aerospace industry, the mining industry, oil and gas, and many others. CommerceOne was growing revenues at 1,000 percent per quarter over quarter and by 2001, the company had grown exponentially to 5,000 people and a $1-billion run rate.

The tech boom was slipping into a recession in 2001, when the terrorist attacks of September 11th occurred. Together, these two simultaneous seminal events had a disastrous effect on the tech industry and CommerceOne. As quickly as CommerceOne had grown, it shrank just as fast and Hoffman sold the company after seven years as Chief Executive Officer.

John Balen, a venture capitalist friend at Canaan Partners, asked Hoffman to come lead a small start up called Everdream. Together, they built it up and sold to Dell after two-and-a-half years. Hoffman then led a company called Enquisite and then Eightfold Logic (now called Inboundwriter) that still exists as a private company.

By 2011, David Brown, one of the former CommerceOne executives who had worked for Hoffman, had started a company called Oxygen-Finance. David had been trying to get Hoffman involved in the company and asked Hoffman to join his Board of Directors, which he did in January 2012. As the company was located in London, Hoffman also opened up the United States operations in the second quarter of 2012. In November 2012, Hoffman accepted the role of Chief Executive Officer, and he relocated to London to lead the company.

With a proven track record of recognizing and creating game-changing technologies, Hoffman sees Oxygen-Finance as having even more potential than either Sybase or CommerceOne. Oxygen-Finance is in a transformational space for corporations, converting accounts payable from a liability to an asset by negotiating a rebate with all suppliers and providing new income and cash to the buying company. These rebates can

then be recognized as income according to Generally Accepted Accounting Procedures (GAAP). With the credibility of partnerships with world-class companies such as Accenture, KPMG, ATOS, Basware, Deutch Bank, RBS, and others, Hoffman believes Oxygen Finance has the ability to grow faster than CommerceOne, creating a paradigm shift in the global markets, monetizing spend, and turning liabilities into assets for corporations around the globe.

In relation to all the other buildings at West Point, the Hoffman Press Box stands alone. Mark Hoffman's leadership made it happen. Hoffman remembers being courted by the President of the West Point Association of Graduates to provide a major gift to West Point when Hoffman was Chief Executive Officer at Sybase. While the press box had been listed as one of the Superintendent's "Margin of Excellence" programs, the idea did not resonate with Hoffman initially. It was only during an Army football game, back when the press was seated in the old steel container (which was leaking and cold) that he overheard Brent Musburger complain and wonder aloud why the network even bothered to cover Army football games. Hoffman had also formed an excellent relationship with Lieutenant General Dan Christman (USMA 1965), who was passionately promoting an expansion of the athletic facilities using private capital that would transform West Point. Understanding how important media support was for Army football and for overall recruitment to West Point, and considering Musburger's comments, it was then that Hoffman decided to fund the Hoffman Press Box with a $5-million personal gift. The Hoffman Press Box was completed in 2003. It is by far one of the most beautiful press boxes in the country according to the media executives who attend football games across the country. The 8,000-square-foot facility is a two story facility towering over Michie Stadium – the first floor houses up to 100 media members; the second story features radio, television, and coaches booths.

In 2011, *Forbes Magazine* ranked the athletic facilities at West Point as the "#1 University facilities out of 377 Universities in the United States," thanks in large part to generous private donors such as Mark Hoffman. Mark Hoffman has led soldiers in the Army, has created and built game-changing global companies, and in funding the Hoffman Press Box, has immortalized himself on the fields of friendly strife, helping to better prepare cadets to lead "on other fields, on other days."

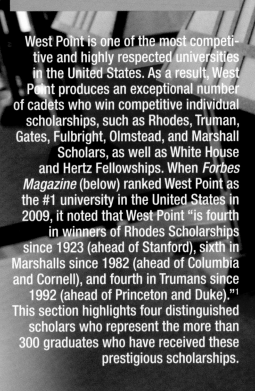

THE SCHOLARS

West Point is one of the most competitive and highly respected universities in the United States. As a result, West Point produces an exceptional number of cadets who win competitive individual scholarships, such as Rhodes, Truman, Gates, Fulbright, Olmstead, and Marshall Scholars, as well as White House and Hertz Fellowships. When *Forbes Magazine* (below) ranked West Point as the #1 university in the United States in 2009, it noted that West Point "is fourth in winners of Rhodes Scholarships since 1923 (ahead of Stanford), sixth in Marshalls since 1982 (ahead of Columbia and Cornell), and fourth in Trumans since 1992 (ahead of Princeton and Duke)."[1] This section highlights four distinguished scholars who represent the more than 300 graduates who have received these prestigious scholarships.

Forbes
THE BEST COLLEGES & B-SCHOOLS
WHY WEST POINT BEATS HARVARD
WHERE YOU GET THE BEST BANG FOR THE BUCK
HOW MIT PUTS ITS M.B.A. CLASS TO WORK

Rhodes Scholars are chosen not only for their outstanding scholarly achievements, but for their character, commitment to others and to the common good, and for their potential for leadership in whatever domains their careers may lead.

—www.rhodescholar.org

As future leaders, with a lasting understanding of British society, Marshall Scholars strengthen the enduring relationship between the British and American peoples, their governments, and their institutions.

—www.marshallscholarship.org

Founded in 1964, the White House Fellows program is one of America's most prestigious programs for leadership and public service.

—www.whitehouse.gov

The mission of the Truman Scholarship Foundation is to find and recognize college juniors with exceptional leadership potential who are committed to careers in government, the non-profit or advocacy sectors, education, or elsewhere in the public service. Then to provide them with financial support for graduate study, leadership training, and fellowship with other students who are committed to making a difference through public service.

—www.truman.gov

Inspecting Iraqi Army weapons with Major Hussein at Camp Habbiniyah, Iraq, 2004.

John Nagl, USMA 1988

- **RHODES SCHOLAR**
- **9TH HEADMASTER, THE HAVERFORD SCHOOL**
- **INAUGURAL MINERVA RESEARCH PROFESSOR, U.S. NAVAL ACADEMY**
- **PRESIDENT, CENTER FOR A NEW AMERICAN SECURITY**
- **ASSISTANT PROFESSOR, WEST POINT DEPARTMENT OF SOCIAL SCIENCES**
- **COMMANDER, 1ST BATTALION 34TH ARMOR**
- **AUTHOR, *LEARNING TO EAT SOUP WITH A KNIFE***
- **TANK PLATOON LEADER, 1ST CAVALRY DIVISION, OPERATION DESERT STORM**

West Point is ranked fifth among United States universities in the number of Rhodes Scholars it has produced. The Class of 1988's John Nagl is a great example of the value Rhodes Scholarship selection committees see in a West Point education and how thought leadership can be as important in war as battlefield prowess.

Nagl became a nationally known thought leader on unconventional warfare during the Iraq and Afghanistan Wars, but the expertise he had developed had started long before, at West Point and at Oxford. Nagl was a Distinguished Graduate from West Point who served 20 years in the Army as an Armor Officer, including combat in both Desert Storm and Operation Iraqi Freedom. He earned his doctorate at Oxford University as a Rhodes Scholar and the George C. Marshall award as the top graduate of his Command and General Staff College class, and returned to West Point to teach. Nagl retired from the Army as a Lieutenant Colonel to become the President of the Center

for a New American Security (CNAS) – one of Washington, D.C.'s most influential think tanks – and is now the Minerva Professor of History, Culture, and War at the United States Naval Academy. Nagl is often described as a classic soldier/scholar in the model of General David Petraeus, who had been one of his teachers at West Point.

Nagl was born at California's Mare Island Naval Station, the son of a Navy submariner, but grew up in Omaha, Nebraska, graduating from Creighton Prep as a nationally ranked member of the speech team and a much less successful distance runner on the track team. Nagl earned appointments to the United States Naval and the Coast Guard academies, but even though he was a "Navy brat," he chose West Point, a foreshadowing of the counterintuitive decision-making that defines him. He entered West Point on July 2, 1984, at the height of the Cold War. Only a decade after Vietnam, the Army had completely forgotten the counterinsurgency lessons from Vietnam;

Cadets trained for a full-scale war against the Soviet Union.

Coming to West Point with the intentions to become an electrical engineer like his father, Nagl instead majored in international relations and continued to excel academically, competing in speech and debate events. The tradition at West Point is that if it rains on your graduation, your class is destined for war. It poured for hours throughout graduation as Nagl sat in the front row of Michie Stadium waiting to shake Vice President George H.W. Bush's hand. The rain omen proved true: Over the next two decades, classmates would serve in combat in Panama, Desert Storm, Somalia, Kosovo, Afghanistan, Iraq, Philippines, and elsewhere.

After attending the Armor Officer Basic Course at Fort Knox, Nagl headed to Oxford University as a Rhodes Scholar to study international relations as the Cold War was coming to an unexpected end. Through the good offices of Doug Fraley – the other Rhodes Scholar from his West Point class – Nagl met Susanne

Varga, a British student of French and German literature, and graduated with a master's degree in International Relations just months before Saddam Hussein invaded Kuwait in the summer of 1990. Nagl led a tank platoon in the 1st Cavalry Division during Desert Storm, returned to Fort Knox, and married Varga with classmate Barry Ives as his best man. Not long after, he began thinking about the nature of international relations in the wake of the Cold War and the triumph of American arms in Desert Storm.

There is a saying that "Generals prepare to fight the last war" but fortunately that doesn't always apply to Captains. Struck by the collapse of the Berlin Wall and of the Iraqi Army, Nagl returned to Oxford to earn his doctorate in preparation for teaching at West Point's famous Department of Social Sciences. It was then that he came to an important realization: America's future wars were likely to look more like Vietnam than like his recent fight in Iraq. Although he had recently led troops in a large-

>>> Spotlight

THE RHODES TRUST

Cecil Rhodes established the postgraduate scholarships to Oxford University, which would bear his name to recognize individuals with exemplary literary and scholastic attainments; the energy to use one's talents to the fullest, as exemplified by fondness for and success in sports; truth, courage, devotion to duty, sympathy for, and protection of the weak, kindliness, unselfishness, and fellowship; and a moral force of character and instincts to lead, and to take an interest in one's fellow beings. West Pointers have performed very well in the competition for Rhodes Scholarships, winning 92 since the program began in 1904 — behind only Harvard, Yale, Princeton, and Stanford.

Courtesy: Rhodes Trust

Nagl with Secretary of Defense Robert Gates after the Landon Lecture, Kansas State University, 2007.

The New York Times Magazine

New York Times Magazine, January 11, 2004.

The Counterinsurgent

Operation Desert Storm, 1990.

---

scale conventional war, Nagl turned his attention to the study of unconventional warfare. He

ALTHOUGH HE FOUGHT ON THE GROUND IN TWO WARS, NAGL'S MOST IMPORTANT CONTRIBUTIONS CAME FROM HIS SCHOLARSHIP – PROOF THAT WEST POINT IS NOT JUST A SCHOOL FOR WARRIORS WHO MAKE HISTORY, BUT FOR SCHOLARS WHOSE STUDY OF IT CAN ALSO CHANGE OUR NATION'S COURSE FOR THE BETTER.

titled his doctoral thesis after an observation by T.E. Lawrence (of Arabia), that making war upon rebellion was messy and slow, like eating soup with a knife. The resulting dissertation, *Learning to Eat Soup with a Knife: Counterinsurgency Lessons from Malaya and Vietnam*, was so far ahead of its time that he struggled to find a publisher until the attacks of September 11th, and the subsequent fall

of the Taliban in Afghanistan brought irregular warfare back into the public consciousness.

Nagl taught international relations and national security studies at West Point and worked to find an outlet for his ideas, ultimately publishing his book on how armies should adapt to the demands of counterinsurgency just before deploying to Iraq in the summer of 2003 as a raging insurgency was developing there. He served as the operations office of a tank battalion in the infamous Sunni Triangle, fighting to develop security and good governance in the area between Ramadi and Fallujah. Nagl came to national attention when *The New York Times Magazine* published a cover story on his fight in Al Anbar, titled "Professor Nagl's War." After a tough year in combat, he returned to the Pentagon to work on Iraq and Afghanistan for Deputy Secretary of Defense Paul Wolfowitz.

The United States was not winning in Iraq, but Nagl was convinced that the history he had studied at Oxford provided lessons that could help the United States do better. He worked with General David Petraeus and Petraeus's West Point classmate Conrad Crane to write a new counterinsurgency field manual that would incorporate historical best practices and change the way the Army fought. The resulting book, *The U.S. Army/Marine Corps Counterinsurgency Field Manual*, was published to international acclaim in 2006, just months before General Petraeus returned to Iraq to implement its lessons. Petraeus led a turnaround in the American way of war, and the results on the ground were dramatic with violence dropping to a level that soon allowed the United States to leave Iraq's future in the hands of their own security forces.

Retiring from the Army, Nagl took over a national security think tank called The Center for a New American Security and continued to advocate for changes in the way America fought its wars, including in Afghanistan. After

three years, he accepted an offer to become the Naval Academy's first Minerva Professor, teaching Midshipmen about the nature of modern conflict and inspiring them to achieve academic excellence. He has since accepted an invitation to become the ninth headmaster of the Haverford School in Philadelphia, where he works to develop young men of character and intellect. Although he fought on the ground in two wars, Nagl's most important contributions came from his scholarship – proof that West Point is not just a school for warriors who make history, but for scholars whose study of it can also change our nation's course for the better.

Guy Filippelli is a Marshall Scholar who has contributed significantly to United States national security through his intellect and leadership in the intelligence space. Soldier, scholar, and now Chief Executive Officer, he has founded and built several innovative companies and established himself as a thought leader for big data analytics. Outwardly relaxed and gregarious but internally disciplined and intellectually curious, Filippelli carefully balances a welcoming personality and a ferocious drive. His success represents a phenomenal story of hard work, mentorship, and serendipity – and embodies the American dream his ancestors sought for their families.

Filippelli was born in Cleveland, Ohio, into a blue-collar, second-generation Italian-American family with a history of service to our nation. His grandfather was born in Italy, came to the United States as a boy, and enlisted in the Army. He rose to the rank of First Sergeant in the 11th Airborne Division at 22 years old, fighting in New Guinea and jumping into combat in the Philippines while leading his soldiers during World War II. Filippelli's father, Philip, served in the 82nd Airborne and later worked for the railroad, while his mother, Kathie, raised their children before returning to work as a secretary.

As a youth, Filippelli focused on math, science, and computers and earned excellent grades and outstanding SAT scores. Recruited by many universities, Filippelli one day noticed a West Point brochure propped up on the kitchen table and his father subtly mentioned an upcoming West Point presentation. After the recruiter's speech, Filippelli's father told him with a massive smile, "This place is for you, buddy." Filippelli applied to

Guy Filippelli, USMA 1997

- **MARSHALL SCHOLAR**
- **AWARDED THE DIRECTOR OF NATIONAL INTELLIGENCE NATIONAL INTELLIGENCE MEDALLION**
- **CO-FOUNDER, BERICO, BTS, REDOWL ANALYTICS**
- **CO-FOUNDER, THE COMMIT FOUNDATION**

Receiving the Intelligence Medallion.

Filippelli with General Petraeus.

Filippelli with the late General Downing.

 >>> Spotlight

Marshall Scholarships finance Americans of high ability to study at a graduate level with any United Kingdom institution in any field of study. Up to 40 scholars are selected each year and West Point cadets have earned 34 Marshall Scholarships since 1982, the Academy's first year competing for the awards.

Courtesy: Marshall Scholarships

West Point and no other university.

Filippelli's first year was difficult, and he soon considered transferring to an Ivy League school. His father's only advice was to stick it out for two years at West Point before making a decision. As a Yearling, life improved dramatically. Filippelli served as a team leader for a foreign exchange cadet, began to excel academically, and joined the Model United Nations club, eventually becoming

Guy Filippelli and Nick Hallem.

club President. Focused on a technical career, he majored in Computer Science until his economics professor, Captain Joe O'Brien, believed Filippelli would best be served studying economics and set up a meeting between Filippelli and Colonel James Golden, the head of the Social Sciences department.

As a Cow and Firstie, his path continued to be shaped by powerful leaders. In Military Art class, he researched his grandfather's World War II paratroop unit, contacting every living soldier who had served in the division, and was deeply inspired by tales of combat leadership about a man he'd only seen in pictures. In economics classes, he studied under Mike Meese, Dennis Smallwood, and Dean Dudley, each of whom left a major mark on his future business career, but it was Lieutenant Colonel Kerry Pierce (USMA 1972) who opened his mind to the history of Western philosophy and thought that inspired his future studies at Oxford. After the course was finished, the class learned that Lieutenant Colonel Pierce was suffering from terminal cancer. Lieutenant Colonel Pierce had wanted to spend his final months imparting wisdom on America's future leaders and passed away shortly after Filippelli's graduation.

After graduation, Filippelli attended Oxford through the Marshall Scholarship (named after General George C. Marshall), one of the most selective postgraduate scholarships available to Americans. While West Point had reinforced him as a leader, Oxford gave him a global perspective. His studies in philosophy, politics, and economics further refined a world view influenced by deep analytic rigor, an appreciation of decision-making, and the importance of information to achieving organizational success. Filippelli also learned Italian, read Frost and T.S. Eliot, quarterbacked the Oxford Cavaliers, and explored his roots by sending out 400 letters to every Filippelli and Barbuto in the Italian phone book and discovering his great-grandfather's long-lost brother.

After graduation, First Lieutenant Filippelli deployed to Korea with the 2nd Infantry Division. When he arrived at his unit, there were no slots for Platoon Leaders; however, thanks to then-Captain John Nagl's (USMA 1988) influence with the local Brigade Commander, Filippelli became a Ground Surveillance Radar Platoon Leader.

Immediately after September 11th, he joined the 66th MI Group in Germany, leading a crack team of software engineers with a special mission to innovate against the overwhelming data problem faced by frustrated intelligence analysts, finally establishing himself as the programmer and software developer he had aspired to become early in his cadet years. He served under then-Major General Keith Alexander (USMA 1974), whose vision and leadership left an indelible mark upon Filippelli. In 2003, he won a coveted assignment in Vicenza, Italy, interfacing with Italian law enforcement and the U.S. Embassy, before being hand-selected to deploy to Afghanistan to again tackle data challenges.

GENERAL PETRAEUS CREDITED FILIPPELLI FOR HAVING MADE A MAJOR DIFFERENCE IN REACHING THE "TIPPING POINT" IN THE IRAQ WAR.

Captain Filippelli arrived in Afghanistan in 2005 with a mission to integrate technology and intelligence as head of the Information Dominance Center, while simultaneously serving as Chief of the Joint Intelligence Support Element. Working with teams of software engineers and analysts, his team focused their efforts on turning overwhelming and underutilized information into relevant intelligence. One morning, he was assigned to escort West Point's McDermott Chair of Social Sciences, who turned out to be General Wayne Downing (USMA 1962). General Downing bonded with Filippelli, bringing him back to West Point several times to support the Combating Terrorism Center and remaining a mentor until his passing in 2007.

Filippelli returned from Afghanistan and served for six months under General Alexander at Fort Meade before leaving the Army. He founded Berico Technologies with Nick Hallam (USMA 1999) and immediately deployed to Baghdad. Working more than 18 hours a day out of a converted shipping container under fellow West Point and Oxford graduate Lieutenant Colonel Jen

Easterly (USMA 1990), he supported the conceptualization, development, and integration of new technical capabilities that fundamentally changed the way signals intelligence could provide real-time support. General Petraeus credited Filippelli for having made a major difference in reaching the "tipping point" in the Iraq War. He was awarded the National Intelligence Medallion, an award typically reserved for a lifetime of service to the nation. Earning the highest accolades a scholar can achieve reflects his dedication to mission accomplishment and the magnitude of his impact on military operations.

As Berico continued to grow and prosper, Filippelli and Hallam began to incubate and invest in new ventures together. In 2009, they teamed with Craig Cummings (USMA 1992) and ex–Air Force Officer Sean Lane to launch BTS, which brought 3G communications devices to the battlefield. In 2012, Filippelli launched RedOwl Analytics, bringing disruptive technology to the financial services sector. He and Hallam continue to invest in young scholars and entrepreneurs through their holding company, Oxpoint Holdings, and launched The COMMIT Foundation, a non-profit focused on creating incredible private-sector opportunities and relationships for veterans and fundamentally closing the information, confidence, and imagination gaps that often hinder successful transition.

Filippelli's story is an evolving tale of a simple kid from Cleveland, hugely affected by great leaders and heroes. He now sees his mission as helping foster similar opportunities for future generations of cadets, scholars, and entrepreneurs.

Filippelli's success as a cadet, Marshall Scholar, soldier, and veteran would certainly make his father and General Marshall proud. He now resides in Baltimore, Maryland, with his wife, Raina, and their daughter, Sienna.

The Harry S. Truman Scholarship is a lasting memorial to a United States President who never attended college but deeply loved his service as an Army National Guard Officer in the First World War. Designed to encourage the most talented college juniors to choose careers in public service, West Point cadets are natural candidates for the honor, and more than two dozen have been selected since the program began in 1972; some, like Elizabeth Young McNally

of the West Point Class of 2000, later win Rhodes Scholarships, as well.

McNally came to West Point from a Catholic all-girls high school in Connecticut. She was drawn by West Point's focus not just on academics, but also on leadership, athletics, and service to country. Despite not possessing any significant exposure to the military when she entered Beast Barracks, McNally knew enough to appreciate that she was embarking on a path not typically taken for

a suburban Connecticut teen. Even so, she could not have begun to imagine where the decade after West Point would take her and her family – two yearlong deployments to Iraq for McNally and for her husband, John, and five shorter deployments to Iraq and Afghanistan for McNally's father, Colonel Rick Young, who followed her into the Army as a doctor in the Connecticut National Guard, and for her younger brother, John, who became a C-130 pilot in the United States Air Force.

At West Point, McNally majored in International Relations and published a prescient article on "Preparing the Army for Operations Other Than War" in the Army's professional journal *Military Review* while still a junior. Ranked in the top 10 in her class, McNally was selected as Brigade Adjutant, sounding off across the famed parade field to call the brigade to attention and making announcements from the poop deck at meals. McNally chose to become a

Elizabeth Young McNally, USMA 2000

- **HARRY S. TRUMAN SCHOLAR**
- **RHODES SCHOLAR**
- **MEMBER OF THE WEST POINT BOARD OF VISITORS**
- **RECIPIENT OF TWO BRONZE STAR MEDALS**
- **ASSOCIATE PRINCIPAL, MCKINSEY & COMPANY**

McNally during her second deployment to Iraq in 2008.

McNally and her husband, John, with classmates George Fees and CJ Kirkpatrick.

>>> Spotlight

TRUMAN
SCHOLARSHIP
FOUNDATION

Courtesy: Truman Foundation

The mission of the Truman Scholarship Foundation is to find and recognize college juniors with exceptional leadership potential and to provide them financial support for graduate study, which will help enable them to make a difference through contributions in the public sector.

McNally during her first deployment to Iraq in 2004.

Military Police Officer and to defer using her Truman Scholarship in order to attend Oxford University as a Rhodes Scholar.

She was studying International Relations there in the prestigious master's of philosophy program when the attacks of September 11, 2001, changed the shape of her future. McNally was the honor graduate of her Military Police Basic Officer course and served as a Platoon Leader in Mannheim, Germany, before deploying to

Baghdad during our second year of combat operations. There, she quickly came to the attention of Lieutenant General David Petraeus, then commanding the Multi-National Security Transition Command; McNally became his Special Assistant, with an initial task of determining the number of border guards, amount of equipment, and type of outposts needed to secure Iraq's borders. Her work on that critical task was so impressive that the Commanding General

then asked her to become part of his personal staff, and despite her rank as a Junior Captain, she assumed strategic responsibilities in the MNSTC-I Headquarters. General Petraeus, famous for recognizing and utilizing talent regardless of rank, described McNally as "truly a once-in-a-career officer; one of top three writers I've ever known."

Returning to the United States, McNally was the honor graduate of her Captain's Course before commanding a military police company at Fort Shafter, Hawaii. General Petraeus asked for her help as he returned to Iraq to command the "Surge" that changed the course of that war; McNally wrote his Congressional testimony and sat behind him during those historic moments when Petraeus single-handedly won from a skeptical Congress and American population the time his troops needed to implement his strategy. He gives credit to McNally for helping shape the language that all Americans heard with hope and fear during those dark days of that war, and for helping him win the support he needed to carry back to his soldiers.

After two tours in Iraq and earning two Bronze Stars for her service, McNally and her classmate husband, John McNally, made the difficult decision to leave the Army and return home to the Northeast to start a family. Following his love of mentoring soldiers, John became a history teacher in New York City, spending two years at a world-renowned charter school before moving to a similarly well-known independent day school. And in September 2010, they welcomed their son, James, into the world. His sister, Olivia, arrived two years later.

McNally is now an Associate Principal at the global management consulting firm McKinsey and Company, demonstrating the same level of performance in the corporate arena that she displayed in combat. At McKinsey, she is an expert on how to drive sustainable change across large and distributed groups of employees, bringing to bear lessons she has learned both in the military and in the corporate world. She is also a passionate builder of the firm, focused on recruiting both scholars and veterans alike to its ranks and on improving the leadership capabilities of all McKinsey consultants. Through all of this, McNally has demonstrated the traits that mark the most talented of West Point graduates: a determination to succeed under any circumstances; a deep appreciation for the fact that leadership is, at its essence, all about people; and an ability to complete many competing demands

near-simultaneously.

McNally has continued to seek out opportunities to serve her country in her post-Army life. She is the youngest member of the West Point Board of Visitors, to which she was appointed by the President of the United States. She has also been recognized for her talent and dedication to public service as member of Senator Kirsten Gillibrand's Service Academy Selection Panel, where she ensures that only the most worthy New York residents earn appointments to the Military Academy. For a number of years, she continued her service to the nation in uniform as an Army Reserve Officer detailed to the personal staff of the Central Command Commander in Tampa and then served as a Special Assistant to the Commander of the International Security Assistance Force in Kabul, Afghanistan. And she keeps abreast of national and international affairs in part through her role as a Term Member of the Council on Foreign Relations.

LIKE TRUMAN, THE PUBLIC SERVICE OF CAPTAIN ELIZABETH MCNALLY YOUNG BEGAN ON A BATTLE-FIELD, BUT WILL CONTINUE IN BOTH BUSINESS AND IN GOVERNMENT SERVICE.

Elizabeth Young McNally is a mother and wife, a combat veteran and West Point graduate, an Army wife and daughter, a graduate of Oxford University as a Rhodes Scholar, and a Truman Scholar who is living a life that would fill President Harry S. Truman with pride and admiration. Like Truman, the public service of Captain Elizabeth Young McNally began on a battlefield, but will continue in both business and in government service.

Written by: Lieutenant Colonel John Nagl, PhD (USA, Retired), USMA 1988.

McNally was part of the staff who accompanied General Petraeus and Ambassador Crocker during their Congressional testimony.

McNally was among the veterans profiled in a Time magazine piece on the 'New Greatest Generation'"

Lieutenant General (Retired) John Moellering is the Chairman of the Board of Directors of one of the largest and most well-respected financial institutions in America: USAA. He lived at West Point as a cadet, as a faculty member, then as the Commandant of Cadets before retiring at the rank of Three-Star General. His two sons, John and Matt, are both graduates of West Point, and his grandson, Matt, is a cadet. West Point has become part of the Moellering family's DNA.

At age 17, Moellering's neighbor was applying to West Point and, in the process, was required to take the Civil Service Exam since the local Congressman used these grades as a benchmark for competing cadet nominations. His neighbor encouraged Moellering to take the exam as a way to get out of a day of high school, which Moellering found quite enticing. Soon after taking the exam, Moellering scored so well he was offered a nomination to West Point from the Congressman (the neighbor did not, ironically). Years later, Moellering looks back and laughs that he started West Point without really knowing anything about the Academy. After the first day, he was ready to quit, until some new cadets were brought in front the formation and called "quitters" by the upperclassmen. As a result, Moellering decided not to back down – mainly out of pride. He not only stayed all four years to graduate West Point, but then went on to a stellar 28-year career, leading soldiers in the Army and eventually retiring as a Three-Star General.

After choosing the Corps of Engineers, he served as a Platoon Leader and Company Commander, was selected to serve as a White House Fellow and eventually Battalion Commander of an Engineer Battalion. He served a year in Vietnam. He loved being a commander and he learned his

Lieutenant General John H. Moellering, USMA 1959

- **CHAIRMAN OF THE BOARD OF DIRECTORS, USAA**
- **PRESIDENT AND CHIEF EXECUTIVE OFFICER, LEAR SIEGLER**
- **VIETNAM VETERAN**
- **WEST POINT COMMANDANT OF CADETS**
- **WHITE HOUSE FELLOW**
- **ADJUNCT FACULTY, KENAN-FLAGLER BUSINESS SCHOOL, UNIVERSITY OF NORTH CAROLINA**
- **BOARD OF ADVISORS, THAYER LEADER DEVELOPMENT GROUP**

Colonel Moellering, Vicksburg District Engineer with Senator John Stennis (D-MS), 1978.

Major Moellering in Vietnam as S-3, 937th Combat Engineer Group, 1968.

>>> Spotlight

USAA provides insurance, banking, investment and retirement products and services to 9.3 million members of the United States military and their families. Known for its legendary commitment to its members, USAA is consistently recognized for outstanding service, employee well-being, and financial strength. USAA membership is open to all who are serving or have honorably served our nation in the United States military – and their eligible family members.

own command style by learning from his own commanders. Looking back on his career, he says of his own leadership development, "I learned as much from my bad commanders as I learned from my good commanders." For example: As a young officer, he saw one of his Battalion Commanders struggle with meeting with the subordinate commanders and the staff at the same time, which took away authority from the commanders and caused confusion in the chain of command.

As a Battalion Commander, he resolved never to have a meeting with *both* the commanders and the Staff Officers all together. As a Battalion Commander, he met with his Company Commanders and had his Executive Officer manage the staff. Commanders needed to keep the command line and staff line straight, something he later brought with him to the business world. However, having served himself as both a commander and a staffer, he says, "If you are in a staff position, it doesn't mean you're not a leader. The key is to constantly seek more and more responsibility."

When Colonel Moellering took command of the Vicksburg Engineering District, he was responsible for a $200-million budget and maintaining multiple projects. It was much like a civilian project manager of a large company – more of a business than a traditional Army command.

He went to the Pentagon as the Executive to the Chief of Staff of the Army. After the end of the Vietnam War, the implementation of an All-Volunteer Army, and a decade of cutbacks, the Army was a hollowed-out Army and times were tough. His boss at the time, the Chief of Staff, was incredibly hard on his staff, but by Moellering proving himself, he gained a loyal mentor. Moellering was promoted to Brigadier General and sent to Fort Lewis as the Assistant Division Commander for the 9th Infantry Division – one of the best jobs in his career, until the Chief of Staff asked him to go to West Point. The Chief of Staff thought the Corps of Cadets was lacking in discipline and needed Moellering to set it straight.

Brigadier General Moellering arrived at West Point in 1982 as the Commandant of Cadets. After having spent four years as a cadet and then three more as an instructor, he thought he had a clear understanding of these cadets were all about. He quickly realized he didn't and began setting up small meetings with them – without the ranking cadets and without other officers – to get the real ground truth. He learned that cadets thought summer training was a joke – a waste of time with no discipline. Moellering recalls attending his first summer training event at Camp Buckner and saw cadets disinterested in a presentation and officers not enforcing discipline. He pulled aside the officers and ripped into the Captains, Majors, and Lieutenant Colonels to set an example that training was serious. They implemented bayonet training, a leadership center for underperformers, and brought in outside public speaking groups to teach every cadet public speaking skills. After the challenging years of the 1970s and the hollowed-out Army, Moellering set out to put discipline back into the Corps of Cadets. But Moellering did not look at the position as a command position. He looked at his role as a mentor and told his Tactical Officers (the Captains and Majors reporting to him) that their role was as mentors and not commanders.

He was promoted to a Two-Star General and commanded the Engineer Center at Fort Leonard Wood. After nine months, he was sent to a Three-Star job. He was then assigned as the Assistant to the Chairman of the Joint Chiefs as the only uniformed member on all the National Security interagency groups in Washington, which included the White House staff, the State Department, the National Security Council, the CIA, and the like. His time spent as a young White House Fellow had helped prepare him to understand how all aspects of government came together in both policy and practice. In this role, he had to learn every aspect of all national security issues in order to advise the Chairman. During his time at the Joint Chiefs, the U.S. would face major national security challenges. These included the Iran-Contra Affair, United States hostages in Lebanon, arms control negotiations with the Soviets, the 1986 air raid on Libya, the Achille Lauro hijacking incident, and many others.

> EVERY DECISION IS MADE WITH THE FINAL QUESTION BEING "HOW DOES THIS EFFECT OUR MEMBERS?" IF THE DECISION DOES NOT HELP MEMBERS, IT JUST ISN'T DONE. SO GROWTH ON ITS OWN ISN'T THE PRIMARY MISSION, TAKING CARE OF EXISTING MEMBERS IS THE FIRST PRIORITY.

Ironically, one of the reasons he left the Army was because of his meteoric rise – he had only spent nine months as a Two-Star before being promoted to Three-Star. Moellering knew he would never command again. He was recruited by ADP as a Senior Vice President to lead a 750-person division. Thus, he retired from the Army at age 49 at the rank of a Lieutenant General.

After retiring from the Army and having had significant responsibility over both personnel and projects, Moellering assumed the transition would be seamless. He thought

Brigadier General Moellering, Assistant Division Commander, 9th Infantry Division, Fort Lewis, Washington, with wife, Karla, 1981.

Brigadier General Moellering, Commandant of Cadets, West Point, 1984.

he understood business, maintenance, engineering, and service life extension, but soon learned that he knew how to manage projects and *spend* money, but he didn't know how to *make* money. He pulled aside his Chief Financial Officer and asked him for help in learning the "business of business" – the art of *making* money. He worked with the CFO to understand all areas of financial analysis. He also thought he knew how to "sell," having needed to influence others in uniform, on Capitol Hill, and elsewhere. But "sales" are as a complex and disciplined art, as well as a science. He enrolled in a Stanford Executive Program to learn the theory of business. Now in his 50s, he methodologically set about to learn every aspect of business – just as he

had learned the art of being a soldier three decades earlier.

Nearly three years after joining ADP, a former business mentor from the company asked him to take a day off and come analyze an aircraft business owned by a private equity fund. Lear Siegler was a defense contractor that sold aircraft maintenance and engineering services to the military and with defense cuts looming in the early 1990s, the future of the company looked bleak, and the private equity fund was considering selling and cutting its losses. Moellering thought the company could take advantage of the budget-cutting environment by encouraging the Department of Defense to outsource much more of its maintenance, engineering,

and major overhaul programs (inherently done more efficiently by the private sector than the government) as the military tried to do more with what it already had. He was asked by the private equity fund to come in and implement his vision as the Chief Executive Officer.

Soon after arriving, he found the corporate culture to be severely lacking. Nepotism, three-martini lunches, and a lack of ethics permeated the senior ranks. After the first month, he fired 22 of the most senior executives and set about hiring a motivated, ethical team (with many military veterans). Within three years, they had turned the company around and the business was thriving, doubling the top line (revenues) and tripling

the bottom line (profits). They then sold the company to United Nuclear Corporation, who later sold the company to General Electric, who then spun off a division to the Carlyle Group, where Moellering remained for another six years.

While at Lear Siegler, he was asked to join the Board of Directors of USAA, a leading financial firm that specialized in servicing members of the military and veterans. He served as a member of the Board of Directors for 12 years, until USAA went through a crisis in leadership and the Chief Executive Officer resigned. The board asked Moellering to take over as Chairman of the Board, which he did in 2007. USAA had been rated as a top financial firm by Moody's Corp. and Standard

Lieutenant General Moellering receiving the Defense Distinguished Service Medal from Secretary of Defense, Caspar Weinberger with Admiral William Crowe, Chairman, Joint Chiefs of Staff and wife, Karla, in 1987.

Courtesy: USAA

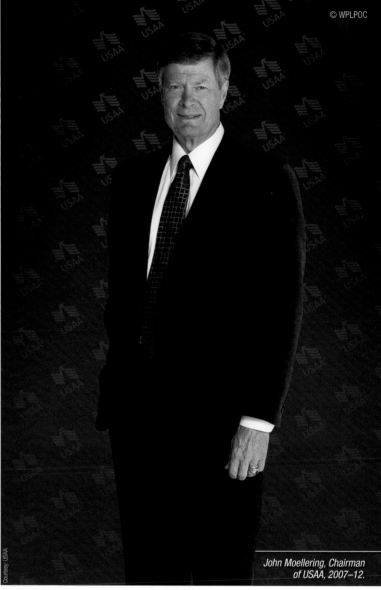

John Moellering, Chairman of USAA, 2007–12.

& Poors. It was also ranked a top Fortune 500 company in America and in customer service by J.D. Power and Associates for many years. They had a devoted, loyal following of more than seven million members. USAA's membership is so incredibly loyal that it has the best retention rate in the industry by far (USAA loses less than two and a half percent of its members annually versus the second best in the industry, which sees a 15 percent annual loss rate). Moellering did exactly as he had when he took command as the Commandant – he set about meeting with small groups of employees without the chain of command present so he could get straight, unfiltered feedback from the troops. His research reinforced his initial beliefs: USAA had incredible people and a unique culture,

but was hurting its own potential growth rate by limiting the type of person who could join (at the time only military veterans could). Being a member-owned company, the culture is not beholden to shareholders on Wall Street. Every decision is made with the final question being "How does this affect our members?" If the decision does not help members, it just isn't done. So growth on its own isn't the primary mission; taking care of existing members is. That alone is a unique culture. When a serviceman gets into financial trouble, the team at USAA does everything they can to stretch the finances to help. These types of actions build an incredibly loyal customer base.

While, at the same time, USSA was signifi-

cantly limiting its potential growth, they also faced increased competition from discount insurance carriers with massive advertising budgets and cartoon birds or reptile spokespeople. Under Moellering, USAA increased its potential market opportunities by including family members of former veterans and increased its potential market pool to 61-million Americans. They also beefed up their marketing and advertising effort in a new outreach program to gain new members. New membership increased tremendously – from 7 million to 9.2 million.

After having had a stellar 28-year career in the Army and leading two very successful businesses, Moellering reminisces on his lessons learned: "The leadership principles

learned in the military are sound. Integrity is the bedrock of leadership in any industry. People have to have trust in your word and character. Whether you are leading troops in the field or leading a bank, as a leader, you need to follow some basic rules. First, do your homework – you need to know everything about your unit or your business. Second, enlightened leadership and persistence are the keys to changing a culture or the direction of a large organization."

The Lieutenant General Moellering Room at the Thayer Hotel is proudly dedicated by his family.

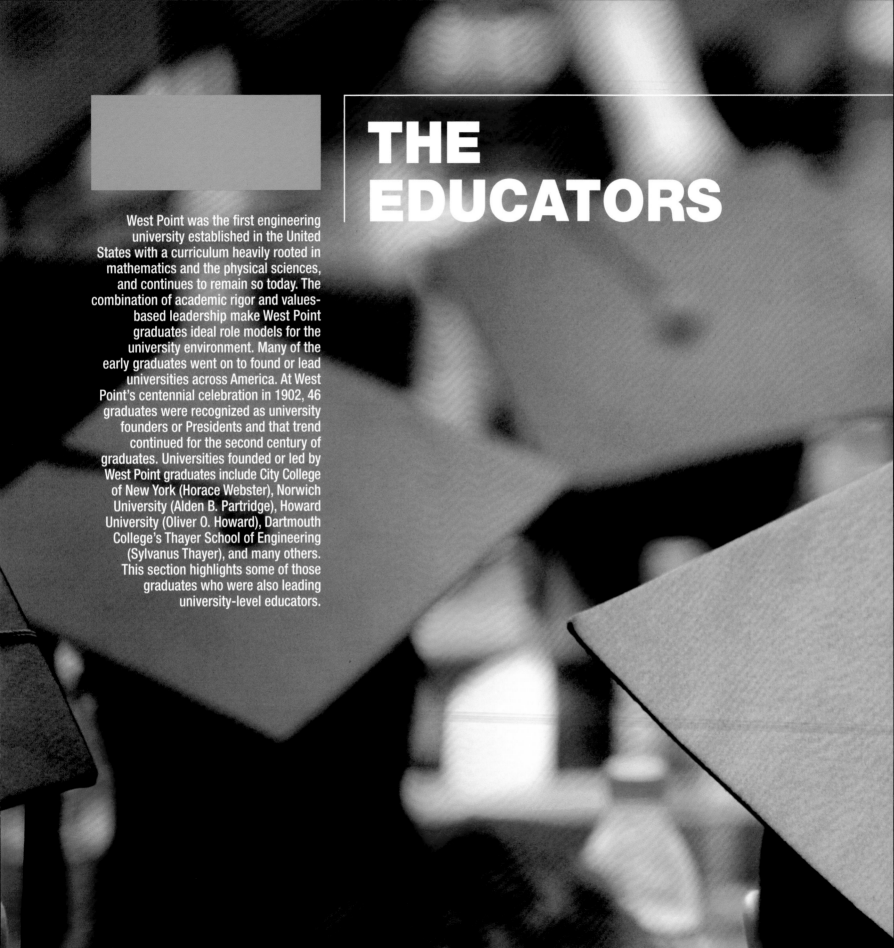

THE EDUCATORS

West Point was the first engineering university established in the United States with a curriculum heavily rooted in mathematics and the physical sciences, and continues to remain so today. The combination of academic rigor and values-based leadership make West Point graduates ideal role models for the university environment. Many of the early graduates went on to found or lead universities across America. At West Point's centennial celebration in 1902, 46 graduates were recognized as university founders or Presidents and that trend continued for the second century of graduates. Universities founded or led by West Point graduates include City College of New York (Horace Webster), Norwich University (Alden B. Partridge), Howard University (Oliver O. Howard), Dartmouth College's Thayer School of Engineering (Sylvanus Thayer), and many others. This section highlights some of those graduates who were also leading university-level educators.

The best means of forming a manly, virtuous, and happy people will be found in the right education of youth. Without this foundation, every other means, in my opinion, must fail.
–President George Washington, who urged Congress to establish a Military Academy at West Point

The education of the officer never ends.
–President Dwight D. Eisenhower, USMA 1915

A better world shall emerge based on faith and understanding.
–General of the Army Douglas MacArthur, USMA 1903

Leadership is intangible, and therefore no weapon ever designed can replace it.
–General of the Army Omar Bradley, USMA 1915

The true purpose of education is to prepare young men and women for effective citizenship in a free form of government.
–President Dwight D. Eisenhower, USMA 1915

Untutored courage is useless in the face of educated bullets.
–General George S. Patton, USMA 1909

Leadership and learning are indispensable to each other.
–President John F. Kennedy

Captain Alden Partridge, USMA 1806

- **SUPERINTENDENT, WEST POINT**
- **FOUNDER, NORWICH UNIVERSITY**
- **WEST POINT PROFESSOR OF MATHEMATICS**

Easily the most controversial figure in the history of the United States Military Academy, Captain Alden Partridge, the Fourth Superintendent, left behind two contradictory legacies: one as a villainous traitor; the other as a hero of military education. A graduate of the Class of 1806, Partridge spent his Army career at West Point, rising from his appointment as mathematics instructor to become the first Superintendent of the Academy who did not also have to serve as the Chief of the Engineers. Ignominiously remembered as a traitor to the Academy who tried to usurp Sylvanus Thayer in 1816 and 1817, Partridge was a more effective leader for the school than the failure and miscreant that George Cullum and others have cast him in history. As head of the Academy from 1815 to 1817, Partridge instilled the military discipline long associated with the Corps of Cadets, and he began the groundwork for the curriculum that Thayer would later

develop. Moreover, Partridge's emphasis on balancing a rigorous course of study with military training established the West Point experience as one of "duty, honor, and morality." After his dismissal from the Army, Partridge established Norwich University in Vermont, starting the first school dedicated to educating "citizen-officers" in 1819.

Given his upbringing in Vermont, his education at Dartmouth College, and transfer to the United States Military Academy, the ideal of the "citizen-soldier" was not foreign to Partridge. His father, Samuel Partridge, Jr., was a Revolutionary War veteran who had fought at Saratoga. Young Alden grew up working his family's farm in the Green Mountains with the expectation that he, too, would eventually serve his nation's Army. After attending Dartmouth for three years, Partridge transferred to the Military Academy in December of 1805 and graduated 10 months later on October 29, 1806. Jonathan Williams, the first

Superintendent, commissioned Partridge as a First Lieutenant due to Partridge's maturity and advance educational experiences. A week later, Partridge was teaching math to the cadets.

For the next 11 years, Partridge was a source of consistent leadership for the nascent Academy, steering the institution through periods of austerity and bureaucratic ambiguity. In effect, he became the "acting superintendent" under Williams and then Joseph Swift as they both found their energy and focus divided between the school and the Corps of Engineers. In this context, Partridge lacked the authority and influence to direct the faculty as a whole. Partridge's demand for control, his inflexible approach to managing the school, and his insistence on the centrality of military training in the cadet program alienated Partridge from the rest of the faculty.

In time, it was the faculty that undid the

young superintendent. Through an effective campaign led by Professor Jared Mansefield, the West Point faculty mounted the effort to remove Partridge and emplace Thayer. Mansefield and others envisioned West Point as a national institution of scientific education, one that emulated France's *Ecole Polytechnique*. In their view, the Presidential guidance from Jefferson gave them the latitude to focus the cadet education less on military training and more on courses of science and math. Partridge saw West Point's purpose more narrowly – a school to produce officers for the Army, nothing more, nothing less.

During his tenure, he sought to make the curriculum more focused on military training and less on academics. Additionally, Partridge officially adopted the gray uniforms as the uniform of the Corps of Cadets. Although Partridge would disagree, there was no standardized academic year or program of study. Partridge practiced

The statue of Captain Alden Partridge at Norwich University in Norwich, Vermont.

>>> Spotlight

NORWICH UNIVERSITY

Norwich University was founded by Alden Partridge in 1819 as "The American Literary, Scientific, and Military Academy." Norwich was the first private institution in the country to teach engineering and the first private military college in the United States. Norwich also had the first collegiate band in the United States. Norwich University now has both undergraduate and graduate programs.

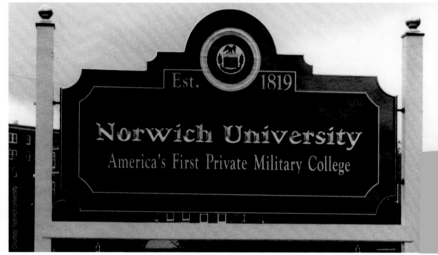

Est. 1819

Norwich University
America's First Private Military College

Courtesy Norwich University

---

favoritism among the Corps of Cadets, which resulted in numerous accusations of scandal and fraud. Eventually, Partridge could not overcome the mounting allegations against him, and President Monroe ordered

NOW KNOWN AS NORWICH UNIVERSITY, PARTRIDGE'S PRIVATE MILITARY COLLEGE WAS THE FORERUNNER TO THE RESERVE OFFICER TRAINING CORPS (ROTC) PROGRAMS, SETTING THE PRECEDENT FOR EDUCATING CIVILIAN MEN TO SERVE SOCIETY, AS WELL AS LEADING SOLDIERS IN THE ARMY.

Thayer to relieve Partridge resulting in the subsequent court-martial proceedings and Partridge's resignation.

Perhaps Partridge's youth and inexperience were as much to blame for his removal

as was his personality. Only 32 when he resigned, he lacked the breadth and depth of knowledge to understand the larger context of running a national Military Academy. Persistent to the end, Partridge sought to create a military Academy that fit his vision and corrected the shortcomings he saw with West Point. In 1819, he established the American Literary, Scientific, and Military Academy at Northfield, Vermont, as a school designed to produce citizen-officers who could lead citizen-soldiers in America's Army. Now known as Norwich University, Partridge's private military college was the forerunner to the Reserve Officer Training Corps (ROTC) programs, setting the precedent for educating civilian men to serve society, as well as leading soldiers in the Army. At Norwich, Partridge was able to

emplace his balanced curriculum of liberal arts, science, and military drill.

For the remainder of his life, Alden Partridge strove to reform the Officer Corps of the United States Army from the "corrupting" influence of the United States Military Academy. He attempted to establish a series of Norwich-like academies across the country, but none of the eight other schools lasted longer than four years.

By 1830, Partridge, under the pen name of "Americanus," had encapsulated his full indictment of West Point in an open letter to Congress and the President. Titled "The Military Academy at West Point Unmasked or Corruption and Military Despotism Exposed," Partridge's letter was a pamphlet detailing 14 "violations" of an "unconstitutional, so aristocratical, so corrupt…and…totally useless" institution. Ultimately, Partridge thought that Thayer and the Academy staff were creating an elitist Officer Corps that

was out of touch with America writ large, and thus, unprepared to lead American men in the event of war. Partridge's views reflected many of the criticisms leveled against West Point in the antebellum era and are still made today.

On balance, Partridge's contributions were vital to the survival of the early Academy, even though they were limited in scope and vision. However, over time, his disparagement of West Point has come to serve as a valuable alternative view to keep the United States Military Academy balanced and true to its national responsibilities over the past two centuries.

Written by: Lieutenant Colonel Jon Scott Logel, PhD (USA, Retired).

Brigadier General Wesley Posvar, USAF, USMA 1946

- 15TH CHANCELLOR, UNIVERSITY OF PITTSBURGH, 1967–91
- GRADUATED FIRST IN THE USMA, CLASS OF 1946
- 1ST U.S. AIR FORCE RHODES SCHOLAR
- FOUNDING HEAD OF DEPARTMENT OF POLITICAL SCIENCE, U.S. AIR FORCE ACADEMY
- CHAIRED SPECIAL COMMISSION ON WEST POINT HONOR CODE

WESLEY WENTZ POSVAR
BRIGADIER GENERAL
UNITED STATES AIR FORCE
CLASS OF 1946 USMA
SEPTEMBER 14, 1925 - JULY 27, 2001

MILDRED MILLER POSVAR
NEÉ MUELLER
HIS BELOVED WIFE

Brigadier General Wesley Posvar's gravesite at West Point Cemetery.

Wesley Posvar Hall at the University of Pittsburgh.

>>> Spotlight

An internationally renowned public research university founded in 1787, the University of Pittsburgh is a leading center of learning and research in the arts, sciences, humanities, professions, and health sciences. It is a member of the prestigious Association of American Universities, a by-invitation-only organization preeminent doctorate-granting research institutions in North America.

Brigadier General Wes Posvar was a West Point graduate, a Rhodes Scholar, a Fighter Pilot, a Brigadier General, and a University President. Or, as a friend once aptly described him, Posvar was "a fighter pilot trapped in the body of a scholar."

Posvar was born September 14, 1925, in Topeka, Kansas, and grew up in Cleveland, Ohio. He excelled at everything he did in life. In fact, he graduated high school as the both the class president and the valedictorian. When he entered West Point on July 1, 1943, the United States was in its second year of involvement in World War II. He thrived at West Point, becoming first in his class academically every year and winning a Rhodes Scholarship upon graduation. After earning his pilot wings, he was commissioned a Second Lieutenant in the Army Air Corps, where his first assignment was as a test pilot at Eglin Air Force Base, Florida, with the 3200th Fighter Test Squadron. But it was his first and last flight assignment as he would dedicate the remainder of his career to academia.

Posvar attended Oxford University during the very challenging post–World War II years of 1948 to 1951, while the United States tried to prevent mass starvation in England with the massive European aid program, called the Marshall Plan. Despite the trying times, he earned a BA and MA in philosophy, politics, and economics at Oxford. In 1950, he married Mildred Miller, and they returned to West Point, where he joined the Department of Social Sciences in 1951 as an assistant professor. With the founding of the United States Air Force Academy (USAFA) in 1957, Posvar was made a professor and eventual promoted to chairman of the Department of Social Sciences at USAFA in Colorado Springs, Colorado. He earned his MPA and PhD from Harvard University and retired from the Air Force as a Brigadier General in 1967 after 21 years of active-duty service.

In 1967, Posvar continued his academic leadership by becoming the chancellor of the University of Pittsburgh, a position he would serve for 24 years until retiring in 1991. He is credited with turning the university, which was on the brink of bankruptcy, into a world-class institution. In May 2000, the university dedicated its largest campus classroom building to Posvar, naming it Wesley Posvar Hall. At the time of the dedication, J.W. Connolly, then Chair of the university's Board of Trustees, said these words about the Brigadier General: "His talent and vision contributed in large measure to the development of the University into one of the world's preeminent centers of academic medicine and research."

Posvar was also actively involved in the community and led many non-profit efforts, including being the Founding Chairman of both the Federal Emergency Management Advisory Board (FEMA) and the National Advisory Council on Environmental Policy and Technology. He was also a Principal Advisor to the Environmental Protection Agency (EPA) and headed a special commission on the West Point Honor Code.

Just more than a year after the dedication of Posvar Hall, Posvar passed away from a

HE IS CREDITED WITH TURNING THE UNIVERSITY, WHICH WAS ON THE BRINK OF BANKRUPTCY, INTO A WORLD-CLASS INSTITUTION. IN MAY 2000, THE UNIVERSITY DEDICATED ITS LARGEST CAMPUS CLASSROOM BUILDING TO POSVAR, NAMING IT WESLEY POSVAR HALL.

heart attack on July 28, 2001. His son, also named Wesley, at the funeral at the West Point Cemetery, summed up his father's achievements with this statement:

"There was a common thread between his first career as an Air Force Officer and second career as a University President – that being public service. There is no question that a strong commitment to public service was his biggest driver...My father was immensely proud of his West Point and military experience. There is a bond between classmates of West Point that, as a civilian, I cannot understand, but I can jealously observe that it is probably the strongest non-family relationship in American society. Today, we add his mortal remains to the earth and foundations of West Point. I gladly and happily leave my father here, so that his presence, both individually and collectively with all the other West Point graduates buried here, will inspire future generations of West Point cadets to greatness, in keeping America free. Even in death, my father lives, as one of The Long Gray Line."

The BG Posvar Room at the Thayer Hotel is proudly dedicated by the University of Pittsburgh.

Hubert Harmon was born two years after his father graduated from West Point and died a few months before his son graduated. Despite his own graduation in the "class the stars fell on" (USMA 1915), Harmon will be remembered as the father of the United States Air Force Academy.

Like many other pioneers of air warfare in the United States Army, Harmon had been a "clean sleeve" at West Point, graduating with no promotions within the Corps of Cadets and garnering a large amount of demerits. And perhaps unique among graduates, Harmon was in fact expelled from the Academy. One week into basic training with the Class of 1914, he was dismissed by the Superintendent on the grounds that his two brothers were upper-class cadets and that no American family deserved three free college educations. One year later, Harmon regained admission under the succeeding Superintendent. A competitive spirit distinguished him on the athletic fields where the 135-pound, five-foot eight-inch Cadet Harmon lettered on West Point's undefeated football team.

The most acclaimed warriors in history are either great combat leaders or visionaries – Harmon was the latter. From his first days in uniform, he anticipated that airpower would change the nature of warfare, and he wanted to be part of the action. Harmon earned his wings in 1917 and was sent to France during WWI as a fighter pilot. Between the wars, he was part of the small cadre of Army Officers who advocated a stronger air arm for the Army and then its own branch of the Armed Forces.

Months before Pearl Harbor was attacked in 1941, Harmon was promoted to Brigadier General and given command of the Gulf Coast Air Corps Training Center at Randolph Field, Texas, which became known as the "West Point of the air" and later one of the USAF's main bases. Early in the war, Harmon was promoted to Major General. In early 1943, he was promoted to Lieutenant General and appointed General Douglas MacArthur's Deputy Commander for the Air Forces in the South Pacific Area. In January 1944, Harmon took command of the 13th Air Force, and later that same year was appointed Commander of

Lieutenant General Hubert Harmon, USAF, USMA 1915

- **FATHER OF THE U.S. AIR FORCE ACADEMY**
- **FIRST SUPERINTENDENT OF THE U.S. AIR FORCE ACADEMY, 1954–56**
- **COMMANDER, THE 13TH AIR FORCE AND OTHER PACIFIC UNITS DURING WWII**
- **WORLD WAR I FIGHTER PILOT**
- **ARMY FOOTBALL PLAYER**

Lieutenant General Harmon Statue at the U.S. Air Force Academy

>>> Spotlight

United States Air Forces were a component of the United States Army from 1911 until 1947, when an independent service was created. The United States Air Force (USAF) was founded in 1947 and the United States Air Force Academy (USAFA) was founded on July 11, 1955, in Colorado Springs, Colorado. Lieutenant General Harmon was the founding Superintendent and is considered the "Father of the Air Force Academy." The first class graduated on June 3, 1959. The founding Superintendent, Dean, and Commandant of Cadets at USAFA were all West Point graduates.

Courtesy: USAFA

the 6th Air Force.

After the war, Harmon served in a number of diplomatic roles, including a stint at the newly formed United Nations. In early 1949, the Joint Chiefs tapped Harmon to head a top-secret study of nuclear strategy that reported to the great displeasure of USAF Chief of Staff General Hoyt Vandenberg that the Air Force alone could not defeat the Soviet Union. Under great pressure to change the report, Harmon stuck to his conclusions. By the end of the year, in admiration of Harmon's integrity, Vandenberg

appointed him to lead the effort to establish a new organization from scratch: the Air Academy. The task required great vision, perseverance, and diplomacy, yet it turned out to be a much greater challenge than either man expected. Harmon dedicated the remaining years of his life to the Air Force Academy.

Without support from President Truman or the other service branches, Harmon expected the project to fade away, even though he had worked diligently on it for nearly four years. However, the elec-

tion of his classmate and friend, Dwight Eisenhower, as President in 1952, changed everything. Ike had served on a board assessing the idea of a new Academy in 1949 and had strongly favored the idea. Although it was still controversial in Congress, when the new President was asked about the Academy he deftly answered that he thought the matter was "all settled." With the project assured of success, Harmon retired – twice – in 1953, only to be called back into the ranks to see it to completion. Eisenhower knew that his old friend and football teammate had a well-deserved reputation as a gifted organizer and administrator that the new institution would need.

Harmon deserves credit for nearly every major aspect of USAFA, including the architecture, the location, and the curriculum. First-time visitors to the Academy, which is nestled at the foot of the Rampart Range in Colorado overlooking the great American plains to the east, are struck by its modernist design. Indeed, the sharp edges and bright aluminum of the buildings, particularly the world-famous Academy chapel, make it easily the most modern campus in the nation and perhaps the world. This radical and architecturally celebrated campus could not have been realized without the easygoing and courageous leadership of General Harmon. The historical record indicates, in fact, that it was his early suggestion that the new Academy take a modern look.

Harmon is known to current cadets as the name that adorns one of the main Halls around the Terrazzo (cadet area), the annual lecture series hosted by the history department, and by the one of the few individual statues. That statue was a gift of the 1959 inaugural class at USAFA, unveiled during their 50th reunion in recognition of Harmon's service as the first Superintendent. Harmon loved the cadets, and they loved him in return. It was that affection which defined the General's leadership style, described by his subordinates as servant-oriented, humble, and self-effacing. Harmon succeeded in crafting the Academy because he never forgot what life was like from the student perspective.

Harmon had spent many years in the educational and training programs of the Army, including the earliest flight schools in the United States and a stint as a West Point Administrator. His experience at the stifling doctrines of the Army, particularly the curriculum of its pre-war Senior Officer training

schools, made him sensitive to the need for military education to be vigilantly open to innovative thinking about the effect of new technologies (such as airpower or advanced communications) on warfare.

In the 1950s, West Point and Annapolis were still heavily focused on math, science, and engineering. Harmon insisted his Academy would balance courses in the social sciences and liberal arts equally. Further, he himself penned the USAFA honor code (West Point's had been unwritten during his cadet years) and had it carved in marble overlooking the campus. To ensure the new Academy did not become dogmatic and insular, Harmon fought for a faculty with ample civilians, unlike the other academies at the time. He lost the battle during his tenure, but won the war. In sum, Harmon's focus on academic excellence propelled the Air Force Academy's reputation far above its peers and literally changed the way all of the service academies were organized, notably the adoption of academic majors and ample elective coursework. One might say that the Superintendent's focus on the philosophical foundations of cadets helped navigate the nation and the world peacefully through the nuclear era.

On July 31, 1956, after five decades in uniform, General Harmon finally retired for good. He had been battling cancer during his entire time as Superintendent and would not survive a full year as a civilian. But he had turned a dream shared by other visionaries and Presidents into a reality. How well was it designed? When the first class marched up the ramp into the cadet area for the first time during the summer of 1958, one of its members (a future General) remarked the whole placed was perfect, but not like new, because it "didn't have any rough edges."

Written by: Dr. Tim Kane, PhD, USAFA 1990.

> **EISENHOWER KNEW THAT HIS OLD FRIEND AND FOOTBALL TEAMMATE HAD A WELL-DESERVED REPUTATION AS A GIFTED ORGANIZER AND ADMINISTRATOR THAT THE NEW INSTITUTION WOULD NEED.**

Courtesy, USAFA Association of Graduates

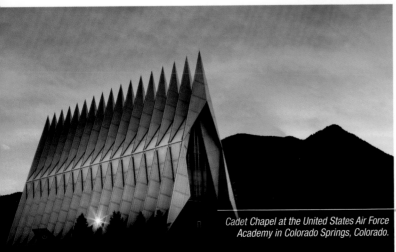

Cadet Chapel at the United States Air Force Academy in Colorado Springs, Colorado.

Every member of USAA is familiar with the name McDermott. The name adorns the USAA headquarters McDermott Building, which overlooks the San Antonio highway I-10 named the McDermott Freeway. Both are named in honor of a West Point graduate and former Air Force Brigadier General Robert McDermott. USAA is now the 62nd largest company in the Fortune 500 in net worth with $22 billion and 9.4 million members[1]. Naming its 3.9-million-square-foot headquarters and a San Antonio highway in his honor is testament to the impact that Brigadier General Robert McDermott had on USAA and the San Antonio area.

Brigadier General Robert McDermott was a pioneer in aviation, education, and finance. He was superlative in all that he did. He served as a World War II Fighter Pilot, as the first Permanent Dean of the United States Air Force Academy, then led USAA as the President, Chairman, and Chief Executive Officer for 25 foundational years.

Robert McDermott was born July 31, 1920, in Boston, Massachusetts, and raised in

Readville, Massachusetts. He graduated from Boston Latin School, then attended Norwich University in Northfield, Vermont, prior to being admitted to West Point in 1939 as a member of the Class of 1943. In the early years of World War II, due to the demand for Army Officers, his class graduated six months early in January 1943 (his original Class of 1943 graduated in January 1943; the original Class of 1944 graduated in June 1943; and the original Class of 1945 graduated a year early on D-Day, June 6, 1944). McDermott was commissioned as a Second Lieutenant in the United States Army Air Corps and attended flight school, earning a coveted role as a fighter pilot in the P-38 Lightning. Lieutenant McDermott deployed to the European Theater of Operations and flew 61 combat missions as a P-38 Lighting pilot. He served as Operations Officer of the 474th Fighter Group in the 9th Air Force from 1944 to 1945[2].

In 1947, when the United States Air Force became an independent service, McDermott and most United States Army Air Corps

Officers became Officers in the United States Air Force.

Prior to leading in academia, he was himself was very well educated. In addition to graduating from West Point, he received a master's in Business Administration (MBA) from Harvard Business School in 1950.

McDermott returned to West Point an Associate Professor in the Department of Social Sciences at West Point from 1950 until 1954. While at West Point, he authored a book to support soldiers with their personal finances called *Principles of Personal Finance for Service Personnel*. The book caught the eye of Charles Cheever, the President of USAA. Based on this book, Cheever and McDermott formed a relationship that later resulted in McDermott joining USAA more than a decade later.[3]

In 1954, McDermott, an Air Force Officer, was assigned as an Economics Professor and Vice Dean of the Faculty at the newly formed United States Air Force Academy in Colorado Springs. There, McDermott and several other

West Point graduates were instrumental in founding the Air Force Academy. All key leadership positions at the new Air Force Academy were filled by West Point graduates: Superintendent, Commandant, and Dean. The first Superintendent of the Air Force Academy was Lieutenant General Hubert Harmon (USMA 1915) who is considered "the Father of the United States Air Force Academy" and the 1st Commandant was Brigadier General Robert Stillman (USMA 1935). In fact, the first nine Commandant of Cadets were West Point graduates, and the first eight Superintendents were West Point graduates. At the same time, Wesley Posvar (USMA 1946) was named the Head of the Department of Social Sciences at the Air Force Academy who also came with McDermott from the faculty at the West Point Department of Social Sciences.

McDermott was selected by President Eisenhower (USMA 1915) to become the first permanent professor at the newly formed Air Force Academy in 1957, then as the first Permanent Dean of the United States Air Force Academy in 1959. This vital position,

Brigadier General Robert Francis McDermott, USAF, USMA 1943

- **CHAIRMAN EMERITUS, USAA**
- **FIRST PERMANENT DEAN, U.S. AIR FORCE ACADEMY**
- **FIRST PERMANENT PROFESSOR, U.S. AIR FORCE ACADEMY**
- **ASSOCIATE PROFESSOR, WEST POINT DEPARTMENT OF SOCIAL SCIENCES**
- **P-38 FIGHTER PILOT, 61 COMBAT MISSIONS**
- **HARVARD BUSINESS SCHOOL, MASTER'S IN BUSINESS ADMINISTRATION**
- **WEST POINT DISTINGUISHED GRADUATE AWARD**

As Dean of the Air Force Academy Brigadier General McDermott teaching a cadet about counterinsurgency warfare in the mid-1960s.

which would be responsible for the selecting the faculty and the curriculum for the new university, came with a promotion to Brigadier General. At the time of his promotion in 1959, McDermott was the youngest Flag-Rank Officer on active duty in any of

AS PRESIDENT AND CHAIRMAN OF USAA, MCDERMOTT ADVOCATED FOR IMPROVED AUTO SAFETY MEASURES TO SAVE LIVES AND REDUCE INSURANCE COSTS, WHICH HELPED MAKE AIR BAGS MANDATORY IN U.S. VEHICLES.

the services at age 39. With the majority of the faculty and leadership at the Air Force Academy being West Point graduates, USAFA was naturally organized in a similar military structure. However, McDermott wanted the Air Force Academy to be more liberal and progressive in its educational program and through his leadership USAFA was the first Academy to introduce academic majors to allow cadets to focus on one particular area

of expertise. He introduced at least 30 majors into the curriculum, decades ahead of West Point, which followed his lead in the 1980s allowing academic majors. Brigadier General McDermott retired from active duty in 1968 after a 25-year military career with the Air Force Academy well established as one of the best academic programs in the United States.

Starting as an Executive Vice President with USAA in 1968, he was promoted to President in 1969. In 1978, he was made Chairman and in 1991 took on the additional responsibility of Chief Executive Officer. He remained in these positions until 1993 when he was made Chairman Emeritus. In total, he led USAA for 25 years.

Under his leadership USAA rose from 16th to the fifth-largest provider of automobile insurance and the fourth-largest provider of homeowner's insurance in 1993. He grew USAA from $200 million in assets to an incredible $30 billion and reduced employee

turnover from 43 percent to an industry low 7 percent. He diversified USAA into mutual funds, banking, and credit cards.[4]

McDermott, summarizing his philosophy, asserted that success had flowed from his application of the Golden Rule to the world of business: "Serve others as you would have them serve you." When he announced his plans to step down, McDermott reminded his colleagues, "We've made customer service our primary goal, and we've encouraged other corporations to do the same." A year later, he was named to the National Business Hall of Fame.[5]

His contributions to West Point, the United States Air Force Academy, USAA, and the City of San Antonio have been recognized with numerous awards from each for his selfless service and extraordinary leadership. In 1993, Brigadier General McDermott was awarded the West Point Distinguished Graduate Award.

His military decorations include two Distinguished Service Medals, Legion of Merit, Bronze Star, and six Air Medals. His

son, David McDermott, is a 1969 graduate of West Point, served in the medical corps as an Army doctor, and retired as a Colonel in 1990. Brigadier General McDermott died August 28, 2006, in San Antonio, Texas.[6]

Brigadier General McDermott Room at the Thayer Hotel is proudly dedicated by USAA.

>>> Spotlight

USAA provides insurance, banking, investment and retirement products and services to 9.3 million members of the United States military and their families. Known for its legendary commitment to its members, USAA is consistently recognized for outstanding service, employee well-being, and financial strength. USAA membership is open to all who are serving or have honorably served our nation in the United States military — and their eligible family members.

Colonel DeBow Freed, PhD, USMA 1946

- **PRESIDENT OF THE UNIVERSITY OF FINDLAY, 2003–10**
- **PRESIDENT OF OHIO NORTHERN UNIVERSITY, 1979–99**
- **PRESIDENT OF MONMOUTH COLLEGE, 1974–79**
- **DEAN OF MOUNT UNION COLLEGE, 1969–74**
- **WEST POINT ASSOCIATE PROFESSOR OF PHYSICS**
- **ACTIVE-DUTY ARMY OFFICER, INCLUDING ASSIGNMENTS IN JAPAN, GERMANY, IRAN, KOREA, AND VIETNAM**

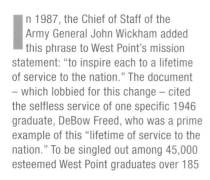

In 1987, the Chief of Staff of the Army General John Wickham added this phrase to West Point's mission statement: "to inspire each to a lifetime of service to the nation." The document – which lobbied for this change – cited the selfless service of one specific 1946 graduate, DeBow Freed, who was a prime example of this "lifetime of service to the nation." To be singled out among 45,000 esteemed West Point graduates over 185 years is a lofty accomplishment.

Freed selflessly served our nation for 65 years – first, in uniform, then, as a University Dean and President at several colleges. He was born August 25, 1925, in Hendersonville, Tennessee, and grew up on his family's farm, graduating from the local Gallatin Tennessee High School. He entered West Point on July 1, 1943, and graduated June 4, 1946, at the age 20, when Secretary of War Honorable Robert P. Patterson presented his diploma to him nine months after World War II ended. Freed was commissioned in the Infantry and served overseas for a total of seven years in Japan, Germany, Iran, Korea, and lived a year in Vietnam during the Vietnam War. He retired as a Colonel after 23 years.

Early in his service, he met Catherine Carol Moore, daughter of an Army physician, whom he married in 1949.

Together, they traveled the globe and raised a son named DeBow, II, while Freed had troop duty in the 1st, 7th, and 25th Army Infantry Divisions. He attended the Infantry School in Fort Benning, Georgia (at which he also taught), the Army Command and Staff College at Fort Leavenworth, Kansas, and the Air War College at Maxwell Air Force Base, Alabama. He was aide to the Assistant Division Commander of the 17th Airborne

they could make a strong contribution. The opportunity for daily association with students and faculty on a college campus was especially appealing to them. At that time, Freed had his PhD and Catherine had her BA, BFA, and MA degrees, a membership in Phi Beta Kappa, and had taught at colleges and universities near their stations throughout Freed's military career.

Freed retired after 23 years of active military duty as an Infantry Colonel and was awarded his second Legion of Merit, on top of his Bronze Star Medal, Air Medal, and many other awards. He went directly into private higher education at Mount Union College in Alliance, Ohio, where he was dean for five years. He was elected President of Monmouth College in Monmouth, Illinois, where he served for another five years, then became President of Ohio Northern University in Ada, Ohio, for 20 years and later served

HE IS AN INSPIRATION TO ALL GRADUATES, WHO SEEK TO CONTINUE SERVICE TO THE NATION AFTER THEY RETIRE THEIR UNIFORM BY EDUCATING AMERICA'S FUTURE GENERATIONS.

as President of the University of Findlay in Findlay, Ohio, for seven years. All of the institutions he served for 32 years as a Dean or President prospered greatly under his leadership, positively influencing the lives of thousands of young people. He presented diplomas to more than 20,000 graduates – thousands of which he and Catherine knew personally – in law, engineering, pharmacy, business, and other degrees. Freed also served as Head of State and on regional academic, scientific, service, and athletic organizations. He was Trustee of a regional hospital, symphony orchestra, center of science and industry, and was a Bank Director.

The document – which added that phrase to the West Point mission statement – cited that during the first 100 years of West Point's history, the Academy had produced 46 university Presidents. The document also stated that "West Point

graduates will advance in the Army as far as their talents and the needs of the service take them. Their dedication to selfless service, even beyond the time in uniform is both a national need and a historical expectation. They are to be leaders for a lifetime." Freed had fulfilled that need and expectation when he served our nation for 65 years – dedicated 23 years in uniform to the nation and 42 years leading the education of tens of thousands of students as a university President. He is an inspiration to all graduates who seek to continue service to the nation after they retire their uniform by educating America's future generations.

The Colonel DeBow Freed Room at the Thayer Hotel.

Division (a training division in the United States) and to the head of the Military Advisory Mission in Tehran, Iran. While chief of the nuclear branch of the Defense Atomic Support Agency at Sandia Base, Albuquerque, New Mexico, and liaison to the Los Alamos Scientific Laboratory for the military services, he concurrently earned a PhD in nuclear engineering at the University of New Mexico.

He was invited to return to West Point

as a faculty member in the physics department. While at West Point, the Freeds lived in one of the large red brick houses on Thayer Road, overlooking the Hudson River. (The home, built in 1907, is about 200 yards from the Thayer Hotel.) DeBow, II, graduated from Highland Falls High School and then received two doctorates from Rice University. The Freeds greatly enjoyed military service and had long considered eventually going into higher education, with the belief

TOURISM TO WEST POINT AND
THE HUDSON VALLEY

LOCAL ATTRACTIONS

Newburgh Airport (15 miles, 24 kilometers) • Newark Airport (54 miles, 87 kilometers) • Laguardia Airport (52 miles, 83.5 kilometers) • JFK Airport (63 miles, 101 kilometers)

© 2013 Craig E. Mathieson SHMR

**The Hudson Valley –
Ranked as one of the top 20
destinations in the world by
National Geographic in 2013.**

West Point, New York

>> Located only 50 miles (80 kilome-
ters) north of New York City

>> 20 minutes from Newburgh
International Airport

>> One-hour drive from JFK, La
Guardia, and Newark Airports

>> One-hour train ride from Grand
Central to Garrison Train Station

Michie Stadium at West Point ranked
by *Sports Illustrated* as one of the top
three venues in the world to watch a
sporting event in the twentieth century after the Old Yankee Stadium
and the Masters at Augusta.

Thayer Hotel and Thayer Leader
Development Group ranked # 1
Leadership, Management & Team
Building Retreats in the U.S., 2013.

Woodbury Commons Premium
Outlets receives 23 million
visitors annually, located only 10
miles (16 kilometers) from
West Point.

THAYER HOTEL
AT WEST POINT

- **TOURISM**
- **WEDDINGS**
- **CORPORATE MEETINGS**
- **LEADERSHIP AND ETHICS TRAINING AT THAYER LEADER DEVELOPMENT GROUP**
- **REUNIONS**
- **GOLF-AND-STAY WEEKENDS – PLAY AT WEST POINT GOLF COURSE, GARRISON GOLF COURSE, AND GARRISON COUNTRY CLUB**
- **SHOP-AND-STAY WEEKENDS AT WOODBURY COMMONS**

THE MOST STORIED OF NEW YORK HOTELS

Experience a true legend among Hudson Valley New York hotels – the Thayer Hotel. As one of the most unique addresses in the world, this landmark West Point New York hotel has been a celebrated part of American history since 1926, when it was established to accommodate United States Military Academy personnel and their guests. It is named in honor of Colonel Sylvanus Thayer, Superintendent of the Academy from 1817 to 1833, and listed on the National Registry of Historic Places. Today, this grand hotel blends its rich sense of tradition with all of the modern luxuries and comforts today's traveler expects. Exquisitely appointed lodging, superb dining, elegant yet contemporary conference and wedding venues – all summarily managed and delivered by an impeccably trained staff to ensure an exceptional stay.

www.thethayerhotel.com

President
Ulysses S. Grant
Room
USMA 1843

THE THAYER
Hotel
AT WEST POINT

ZULUTIME
The Thayer Hotel – West Point, New York

Zulu Time Rooftop Bar at the Thayer Hotel overlooking the majestic Hudson River. The Thayer Hotel is the only full-service Hotel located on the Hudson River between New York City and Albany. Zulu Time was opened in 2010 and is open from April through November.

WEST POINT
MUSEUM

Located only 200 meters outside the Thayer Gate and the Thayer Hotel, the West Point Museum houses one of the best collections of militaria in the world. The museum personnel is also responsible for maintaining and operating Fort Putnam, which is located on West Point and open seasonally.
www.usma.edu/museum

WEST POINT VISITORS CENTER
AND GIFT SHOP

Located just outside the Thayer Gate near the Thayer Hotel, the West Point Visitors Center is a great starting point for visitors arriving at West Point. Tours of West Point can be purchased at the Visitors Center and a gift shop is open to the public inside the Visitors Center.

The Visitors Center is open daily, with the exception of Thanksgiving, Christmas, and New Year's Day. Operating hours are from 9 a.m. to 4:45 p.m.

Call (845) 938-2638 for information. The Gift Shop's number is (845) 446-3085. *www.usma.edu/visitors*

WEST POINT
CADET CHAPEL

Iconic photos of West Point always include the granite Gothic Cadet Chapel overlooking the cadet barracks of West Point and the Plain. The Cadet Chapel is a Protestant denomination church and was built in 1910 designed by Cram, Goodhue, and Ferguson. The majestic granite chapel has the largest pipe organ in the world, containing 23,000 individual pipes. The Protestant services are open to the public and conducted every Sunday at 10:30 a.m. The Cadet Chapel is open daily to the public from 8:15 a.m. to 4:30 p.m. *www.usma.edu*

The beautiful Cadet Chapel is a must-see for any visitor to West Point.

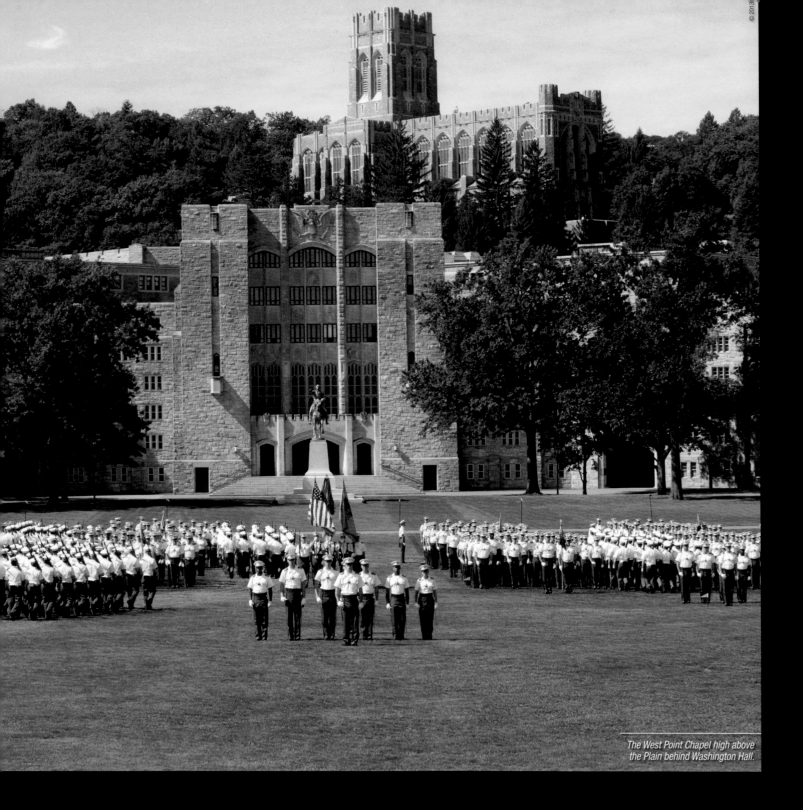

The West Point Chapel high above
the Plain behind Washington Hall.

WEST POINT
JEWISH CHAPEL

The Jewish Chapel was built using $7.5 million in private funds raised by the West Point Jewish Chapel Fund led by Herbert Lichtenberg (USMA 1954) and Lou Gross (USMA 1955). The chapel was first opened in 1984 and deeded to the United States Military Academy in 1986. It is open daily Monday through Friday 9:00 a.m. to 4:30 p.m. Every Friday evening during the academic year, Sabbath services are held at 7:00 p.m. *www.usma.edu/chaplain, 845-938-2710*

WEST POINT JEWISH CHAPEL

PRESENTED TO THE

UNITED STATES MILITARY ACADEMY

BY THE

WEST POINT JEWISH CHAPEL FUND

"FOR THE WORK OF RIGHTEOUSNESS SHALL BE PEACE"
והיה מעשה הצדקה שלום
ISAIAH 32:17

WEST POINT
CATHOLIC CHAPEL

The Catholic Chapel is open to the public and holds services daily at 12:05 p.m. Monday through Friday, Saturday at 5:15 p.m. Sunday mass is held at 9:00 a.m. and 11:00 a.m. during the academic year, and once at 10:00 a.m. during the summer. *www.usma.edu/chaplain/catholic*

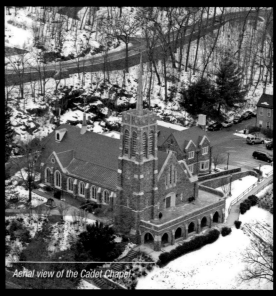

Aerial view of the Cadet Chapel.

© 2013/Greg E. Mathieson Sr./MAI

© 2013/Greg E. Mathieson Sr./MAI

WEST POINT
CEMETERY

The West Point Cemetery is the oldest military post cemetery in the United States. It is a National Historic Landmark and one of the most frequently visited sites on West Point. Soldiers were buried at the site as far back as the Revolutionary War, and the cemetery was officially designated in 1817. The cemetery is available for burial to cadets, graduates, soldiers who pass away while assigned to West Point, and family members of those interred in the West Point Cemetery. Revolutionary War heroine Margaret Corbin is buried here, as are many legendary West Point graduates, such as General H. Norman Schwarzkopf, Ambassador James "Jumpin' Jim" Gavin, Hall of Fame Football Coach Earl "Red" Blaik, Heisman Trophy winner Glenn Davis, Astronaut Lieutenant Colonel Edward White, Lieutenant Colonel George Armstrong Custer, Major General George W. Goethals (builder of the Panama Canal), Major General Daniel Butterfield (composer of "Taps" and Medal of Honor recipient), Colonel Mickey Marcus (first General in the Modern Israeli Army), General Lucius Clay (Father of the Berlin Airlift) and the Colonel Sylvanus Thayer (Father of the United States Military Academy). Graduates from most major conflicts who made the ultimate sacrifice for our country are here, including many men and women who were Killed In Action recently in Iraq and Afghanistan. The cemetery is open to visitors seven days per week all year from sunrise to sunset. The Old Cadet Chapel is located at the entrance to the West Point Cemetery. It was previously located near Barlett Hall and was torn down when the Cadet Chapel was built in 1910. Instead of demolition the cadets chose to relocate the chapel brick by brick to its current location at the West Point Cemetery. It is open to the public and adorned inside with plaques to previous West Point heroes.

George Armstrong Custer's (USMA 1861) gravesite.

General William Westmoreland (USMA 1936), Commander of the War in Vietnam.

Heisman Trophy Winner Glenn Davis (USMA 1947).

Major General John Buford (USMA 1848) hero of the Battle of Gettysburg.

Major General George Washington Goethals
(USMA 1880) Builder of the Panama Canal.

Colonel Sylvanus Thayer (USMA 1808) the
"Father of the United States Military Academy."

General Lucius Clay, the
father of the Berlin Airlift.

Mickey Marcus the First
Modern Israeli General Officer.

Astronaut Colonel Edward White, who was killed in Apollo 1 training accident.

WEST POINT
CEMETERY

Aerial view of the West Point Cemetery with the Old Cadet Chapel in the forefront.

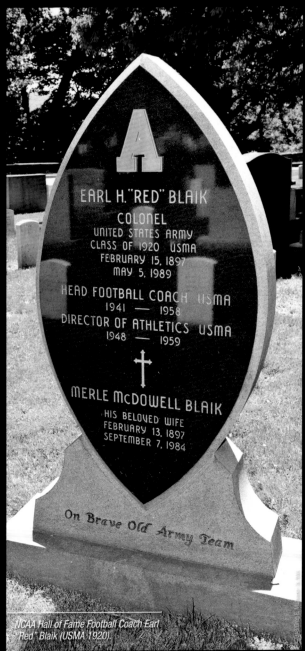

EARL H. "RED" BLAIK
COLONEL
UNITED STATES ARMY
CLASS OF 1920 USMA
FEBRUARY 15, 1897
MAY 5, 1989

HEAD FOOTBALL COACH USMA
1941 — 1958
DIRECTOR OF ATHLETICS USMA
1948 — 1959

MERLE McDOWELL BLAIK
HIS BELOVED WIFE
FEBRUARY 13, 1897
SEPTEMBER 7, 1984

On Brave Old Army Team

NCAA Hall of Fame Football Coach Earl "Red" Blaik (USMA 1920).

Major General Robert Anderson (USMA 1825), Union Commander of Fort Sumter, the first battle of the Civil War.

Margaret Corbin, heroine of the Revolutionary War Battle of Fort Washington, was severely wounded in battle and lived her remaining years at West Point. She is buried at the West Point Cemetery.

Brigadier General Egbert Viele (USMA 1947) Mausoleum, engineer in charge of designing and building New York City Central Park. Brigadier General Viele had been concerned with being buried alive and had a buzzer installed from the Mausoleum to the caretakers house in case he woke up.

Major General Daniel Butterfield, Civil War Medal of Honor Recipient and composer of "Taps."

Lieutenant General James Gavin (USMA 1929), Commander of the 82nd Airborne Division, WWII.

The Old Cadet Chapel at the entrance to the West Point Cemetery.

West Point Old Cadet Chapel.

WEST POINT TROPHY POINT
AND THE PLAIN

The most visible tourist attraction for any visit to West Point is the iconic view of the Plain and Trophy Point, with the gray granite Gothic barracks and the Cadet Chapel high on the hill overlooking the Plain. Parades have been held on the fields of the Plain for more than two centuries, and crowds gather to see the Corps of Cadets parade on most fall and spring weekends.

The Plain holds many statues, such as the Kosciuszko Monument, which was the first monument erected at West Point to honor the Revolutionary War General who trained soldiers on the Plain at West Point. General George Washington is the only equestrian statue on the Plain. Other monuments to West Point graduates, such as Major General Sedgwick, Colonel Sylvanus Thayer, General George S. Patton, General of the Army Douglas MacArthur, and General of the Army (and later President) Dwight D. Eisenhower. Battle Monument was built to honor the regular Army soldiers who were Killed In Action during the Civil War and has every name inscribed, as well as cannon that are named after each of the major battles of the Civil War.

General of the Army Douglas MacArthur (USMA 1903).

Major General Sedgwick Monument.

General of the Armies George Washington, Founder of the Military Base at West Point.

Battle Monument on Trophy Point has the name of every one of the 188 officers and 2,042 soldiers of the Regular Army killed during the Civil War.

General George S. Patton (USMA 1909

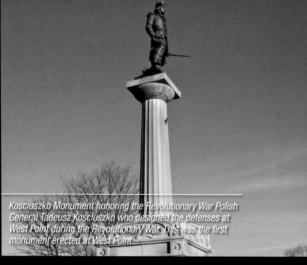

Kosciuszko Monument honoring the Revolutionary War Polish General Tadeusz Kosciuszko who designed the defenses at West Point during the Revolutionary War. This was the first monument erected at West Point.

Colonel Sylvanus Thayer (USMA 1808).

General of the Army Dwight D. Eisenhower (USMA 1915).

Lieutenant General Robert Caslen, Superintendent of West Point on the Plain, August 17, 2013

FORT PUTNAM
WEST POINT

In "Sentiments on a Peace Establishment" in 1783 General George Washington called Fortress West Point "the key of America." He had formally recognized the military value of the Hudson as least as early as May 1775, when he had served on a committee of the Continental Congress that had recommended fortifying both of its sides in the Hudson Highlands.

The initial requirements for fortifying the Hudson River at West Point had been clear from the very first reports by Washington's committee and by Colonel James Clinton and Christopher Tappen, the New York delegates and residents of the Hudson River Valley chosen to pick the location for the fortifications. The Continental Congress and the two New Yorkers had agreed that both sides of the river required posts and garrisons. After surveying other sites, Clinton and Tappen chose the difficult, S-shaped curve at West Point. They believed the narrowness of the channel here and the effects of tide (three to five feet high) and current made this the most appropriate spot. Their report included a description and drawing of a post on Martelaer's Rock with a garrison of 300 men and another at West Point with 200 men. They had also recommended stretching booms across the Hudson between the two posts.[1]

The engineer hired by the New York Committee of Safety, Dutch-born surveyor, cartographer, and botanist Bernard Romans, failed as a military engineer at Martelaer's Rock. He did not locate the fortifications there properly. He also failed to develop them effectively, expeditiously, and economically. On August 29, 1775, Romans began work on a "Grand Bastion," dubbed Constitution Fort. By February 9, 1776, when the Continental and Provincial Congress dismissed him, Romans had completed only an octagonal, wooden blockhouse with eight four-pounder cannons, barracks, a storehouse, and a curtain or wall mounting a battery of 14 cannons. Brigadier General William Alexander, Lord Stirling summarized the issue very succinctly in his report of June 1, 1776: "Mr. Romans has displayed his genius at a very great expence and to very little publik advantage."[2]

From 1776 through October 1777, the focus of fortifying the Hudson River shifted to Forts Clinton and Montgomery on Popolopen Creek. After the British destroyed them before returning to New York City in October, Major General Israel Putnam, the commander of the Hudson Highlands Department, decided that the river and the Highlands would be defended at West Point. Putnam then ordered Colonel Samuel Blachley Webb's Additional Continental Regiment (Connecticut) from Fishkill across the ice at Fort Constitution on January 27, 1778. By January 30th, the huts were far enough along to shelter the men, and they camped on the western side of the river.[3] Fortress West Point, now on both sides of the Hudson, was underway.

French Colonel Louis de la Radière would trace out what would become Fort Clinton/Arnold, Sherburne's Redoubt, and the four water batteries along the Hudson below. It would be left to Polish Colonel Thaddeus Kosciuszko to complete the work after Washington reassigned la Radière. With the help of Captain Thomas Machin, Kosciuszko would oversee the stretching of the Great Chain across the 500 yards from West Point to Constitution Island on April 30, 1778. Weighing some 35 tons and floating on rafts of 50-foot white pine logs, the chain would be the linchpin in West Point's defenses.

Over the next two years, Kosciuszko would add nine additional redoubts and four forts to la Radière's plan to complete the sophisticated defenses. While Fort Clinton/Arnold would be the citadel on the Plain, Fort Putnam would play a crucial role over-watching it from Crown Hill to the west. Built by soldiers of Colonel Rufus Putnam's 5th Massachusetts Regiment, Fort Putnam would depend upon Redoubt 4 on Rocky Hill, some 300 feet higher and 750 meters to the west, to block the likely British avenue of attack. Major General Alexander McDougall made it quite clear that the key to the defense of West Point was Fort Putnam. If it were lost, the fort on the Plain would no longer be tenable. In 1780, it had the following cannons: five iron 18-pounders, two iron 12-pounder, two 6-pounders, one 4-pounder, and four 5.5-inch mortars. It would have been manned by more than 400 soldiers. British General Sir Henry Clinton would deem Fortress West Point so formidable that he would try to buy it from Highland's Commander Major General Benedict Arnold in 1780 rather than attack it. The conspiracy would collapse, Arnold would flee to New York City, and Clinton's Adjutant General Major John André would hang as a spy after his capture as he tried to reach his own lines.

Except during the Yorktown campaign of 1781, General Washington would continue to anchor his Main Army around Fortress West Point for the remainder of the war. In 1784, only two American forts would remain, Fort Pitt and West Point. Today, West Point remains the longest continuously occupied post of the United States Army. In 1802, the United States Military Academy at West Point would rise from the remains of the Revolutionary fortifications. Today, it is one of the premier leader-development institutions in the world. From its Corps of Cadets of more than 4,000 cadets, up to 1,000 new Second Lieutenants graduate each year to serve as officers in the United States Army. West Point continues to play a role as one of the keys to America's security.

Written by: Colonel James Johnson, PhD (USA, Retired), USMA 1979.

Historic Fort Putnam overlooking the Plain at West Point and the Hudson River behind it.

FORT
MONTGOMERY

Fort Montgomery and its sister fortification to the south, Fort Clinton, played a decisive role in the Saratoga campaign of 1777, the turning point of the American Revolution. From 1776 through October 1777, the focus of fortifying the Hudson River shifted from Fort Constitution across from West Point to Popolopen Creek. Captain William Smith laid out Fort Montgomery on the north bank of Popolopen Creek in February 1776, and Lieutenant Thomas Machin supervised the building of Fort Clinton on the hill to the south in August 1776.

Fort Montgomery comprises some 25 archeologically significant features on 14.42 acres of land owned since 1914 by the State of New York. The ramparts of the irregularly shaped fortification follow the contours of the bluffs overlooking the Hudson River and Popolopen Creek and connect three landward redoubts – South, Round Hill, and North – and three river batteries – Grand, Putnam's, and River. Captain Lieutenant Thomas Machin constructed gun batteries on the lower riverbank to protect an iron chain on wooden rafts and a boom of ships' hawsers.

A stone wharf on the north bank of Popolopen Creek provided access to the fort and to the bridge connecting the Twin Forts. Within the fort itself, soldiers built structures to support the outer works and its garrison, including the guard house, the powder magazine, the main barracks, officers' commissary, officers' barracks, storehouse, bake house, soldiers' necessary, provision stores, soldiers' hut, a "spring head," and five additional barracks. All of the outlying works protected the Grand Battery of 32-pounder cannons that in turn guarded the chain and boom.

Fort Clinton, located on the south side of Popolopen Creek, was on high ground from which it could dominate Fort Montgomery. While the rear of the fort facing its sister was incomplete, this roughly circular work was anchored by two star-redoubts, one of four points or bastions and the other of eight. Captain Andrew Moody of the 2nd Artillery referred to the area between the redoubts as an "open field." Fifteen cannons, manned by 40 artillerymen, protected the fort itself, including the eight-pointed redoubt: three 18-pounders, one 12-pounder, ten 6-pounders, and one 4-pounder. The 4-pointed redoubt to the southwest had three 6-pounders fired by nine men. Colonel Lewis Dubois estimated that a garrison of 2,000 men was needed to defend both forts properly; unfortunately, on the day of the battle, fewer than 700 were present.

On October 6, 1777, Forts Montgomery and Clinton earned their places in history. On that day, 1,500 Continental soldiers and New York militiamen confronted Commodore William Hotham's British armada of 47 ships manned by 3,000 British soldiers, sailors, and marines of Lieutenant General Sir Henry Clinton. This was the beginning of the British offensive against the fortifications of the Hudson Highlands. Sir Henry had designed his plan to support Lieutenant General John Burgoyne's expedition into New York from Canada. Clinton began with a feint against Verplanck's Point to keep General Israel Putnam's attention and his force on the east side of the Hudson, while the British General led 2,100 Loyalists, Hessians, and Regulars from Stony Point on the west bank against the landward approaches of Forts Montgomery and Clinton. American Brigadier Generals George and James Clinton had to defend two forts separated by Popolopen Creek with a garrison of only 700 men. On the river there was an iron chain, a boom, and five American warships led by the New York frigates, Congress and Montgomery.

Once his forces were ashore Sir Henry's plan of attack involved a two-prong advance over some 12 miles on Fort Montgomery from the west and Fort Clinton from the south. Clinton constituted under Lieutenant Colonel Mungo Campbell an advance

guard of 500 regulars from the 52nd and 57th regiments and 400 provincials under Colonel Beverly Robinson from the Loyal Americans, New York Volunteers, and Emmerich's Chaussers; he charged Campbell to seize the pass through the Dunderberg, to march behind Bear Mountain, then to attack Fort Montgomery. Clinton designated Major General John Vaughan to lead the main attack through the Dunderberg Pass and Doodletown against Fort Clinton with 1,200 soldiers from the grenadier and light Infantry companies, the 26th and 63rd regiments, one company of the 71st Regiment, a troop of the 17th Light Dragoons, and the Hessian Chausser General Tryon commanded the rear guard of the 7th Royal Fusiliers and the Regime de Trumbach; Clinton charged him to maintain the line of communications with the supporting naval flotilla.

After taking the morning and afternoon to make the difficult approach march and to take a field piece that Governor George Clinton had sent out along Furnace Road, Campbell triggered the main offensive at about 5 p.m. with his final attack on Fort Montgomery. Although he perished as he entered the works leading his 52nd Foot, t momentum of his assault carried Fort Montgomery in about 45 minutes. After Clinto had waited "a favorable moment" following the start of Campbell's fight, he ordered Vaughan to launch his main attack using the bayonet only across an open area of 4 yards filled with abatis and covered by the fire of 10 cannons. The march overland prevented the use of artillery, so this attack was made with courage and discipline b the troops, supported by cannon fire from British row galleys. As undermanned and incomplete as its sister, Fort Clinton fell despite the gallantry of her defenders at abc the same time as Robinson completed his work at Montgomery.

Despite the gallant efforts of the American Clintons, the unfinished twin forts fell to overwhelming British attack by nightfall on October 6th. At the cost of some 70 killed, 40 wounded, and 240 taken prisoners, the Americans nonetheless exacted a substantial price, killing 40 and wounding 150 of the attackers. At 10 p.m., Sir Henr and Hotham also had the pleasure of observing the blazing Montgomery, torched by its crew to prevent it from falling into British hands; the Shark and the Congress would suffer similar fates near Fort Constitution. The Camden would run aground ar become a British prize. With the forts reduced, the ships dispersed, and Putnam and his forces withdrawing northward to protect the pass to Fishkill, over the next few days he would complete his control of the Highlands.[1]

While British forces won the battles of Forts Clinton and Montgomery, Sir Henry Clinton's timetable was disrupted by these fortifications in the Hudson Highlands. Th stubborn defense of the Americans caused the British to delay their northward thrus to join Burgoyne. Thus, Clinton's efforts to save Burgoyne's Army were to be in vain, and General Burgoyne would surrender at Saratoga less than two weeks later. The sacrifices of the American garrisons at Forts Montgomery and Clinton permitted Maj General Horatio Gates to achieve victory at Saratoga; the result might well have bee different had substantial British forces arrived at Saratoga. Most historians credit the defeat of Burgoyne at Saratoga as being the turning point of the war.

WEST POINT
GOLF COURSE

Granite markers sponsored by the Thayer Hotel. All narratives were conceived, written, and copyrighted by Daniel Rice (USMA 1988) and Lieutenant Colonel (Retired) John Vigna (USMA 1988).

U.S. Golf Association Hall of Fame golf course designer Robert Trent Jones, Sr. designed the West Point Golf Course.

The West Point Golf Course

Designed by Robert Trent Jones, Sr., and first opened in 1948, the West Point Golf Course was built by German Prisoners of War at the end of World War II. The West Point Golf Course is dedicated in honor of the soldiers of the United States Army and the West Point graduates who have led those soldiers, our Army, and our nation throughout its storied past that began on and around West Point. The United States Army was established on June 14, 1775. The fortifications system at West Point was established by General Washington in 1778 and is the oldest continuously manned post in the United States. The United States Military Academy at West Point was established on March 16, 1802, in order to provide the United States with a trained, professional Officer Corps who has led America's soldiers in every conflict since the American Revolution. Each of the 18 holes is now named for one of the major military conflicts in which the United States has fought. This idea was conceived and sponsored by the management team at the Thayer Hotel. Each hole has a granite rock marker with information about both that particular hole and about the conflict after which it is named. Each marker also highlights specific contributions of West Point graduates to that conflict in both leadership positions and casualties. Finally, on each hole representing a conflict in which a West Point graduate received the Medal of Honor, there is an additional marker.

#1 REVOLUTIONARY WAR
April 19, 1775–September 3, 1783

America gained its independence from British rule after defeating the British Army and Navy through an alliance with France. With the initial shots fired at Lexington and Concord in Massachusetts, the war lasted eight years as the conflict raged from Canada to South Carolina. Considering West Point the "key to the continent," George Washington and the Continental Congress established a fortification system here – first on Constitution Island in 1775, then expanding across the Hudson River to West Point in 1778 – that included a great chain across the Hudson River supported by artillery fire and multiple smaller forts. Since then, West Point has been continuously garrisoned by the United States Army. After gaining American independence, General Washington urged Congress to establish a Military Academy at West Point, which was eventually founded on March 16, 1802. America lost 4,435 soldiers Killed In Action while gaining our American independence with another 6,618 wounded.

#2 WAR OF 1812
June 18, 1812–February 18, 1815

America's Second War for Independence in 1812 was also its first war fought as an independent nation. America again fought the British Empire in what would later be called the War of 1812 under President James Madison over violations of its economic freedom and territorial integrity. Battles occurred along the Great Lakes, the Atlantic Coast, and in the southern states. West Point graduates saw their first action as they led soldiers and sailors in combat. Lieutenant George Ronan (USMA 1811) was the first West Point graduate Killed In Action falling near Fort Chicago, Illinois, on August 15, 1812. The American Navy, although vastly outnumbered and outgunned, won many major battles and established itself as a respected fighting force. Francis Scott Key, a Maryland lawyer, wrote the "The Star Spangled Banner" while a Prisoner of War aboard a British POW ship in Baltimore Harbor. The United States lost 2,260 Americans, with 4,505 wounded. Six West Point graduates were Killed In Action.

#3 INDIAN WARS
1835–90

Beginning with the first established British colony at Jamestown in 1607, a continuous tension existed between European colonists (eventually Americans) and the Native American Indians for nearly 300 years. This tension frequently erupted into armed conflicts ranging from minor skirmishes, to massacres, to wars as the continued American westward expansion pushed Native American populations westward. Although the earliest of the Indian Wars occurred in 1622 against the Powhatans in Virginia, the first 28 Presidents from George Washington in 1789 to Woodrow Wilson in 1918 all faced varying levels of these conflicts, the brunt of which included the Second Seminole War from 1835 to 1842 (the longest and costliest war waged against Native Americans) and the Black Hills War from 1876 to 1877 (leading to the death of Lieutenant Colonel George A. Custer (USMA 1861) at the Battle of the Little Bighorn in 1876). Numerous West Pointers saw action throughout the Indian Wars, while 21 graduates received the Medal of Honor.

#4 MEXICAN-AMERICAN WAR
April 25, 1846–February 2, 1848

The United States went to war with Mexico in 1846 under President James K. Polk after Mexico refused to recognize America's annexation of Texas and the Rio Grande River as the U.S.–Mexican border. General Zachary Taylor (12th United States President) and General Winfield Scott led the major wings of the American Army during the invasion of Mexico. Taylor won key battles at Monterrey and Buena Vista, while Scott successfully conducted a complex amphibious landing at Veracruz and won a string of impressive battles ending with the capture of Mexico City on September 14, 1847 (while fighting outnumbered, poorly supplied, and deep within enemy territory). Scott was so impressed by the performance of West Point graduates he noted in his "Fixed Opinion" that these officers were invaluable to the rapid and decisive nature of the United States victory. Although a military success leading to the incorporation of present-day California, New Mexico, Arizona, and Utah, the war inflamed tensions over the expansion of slavery in these newly acquired territories that would be a major cause of the American Civil War. Many of the West Point graduates who were Junior Officers in the Mexican-American War later went on to lead both Union and Confederate forces in the Civil War. The United States lost 1,507 killed in combat, while 13,200 died of disease. Another 4,152 were wounded. Forty-eight West Point graduates were Killed In Action.

#5 CIVIL WAR
April 12, 1861–April 9, 1865

America's bloodiest war began after 11 Southern states seceded following the 1860 election of President Abraham Lincoln. Jefferson Davis (USMA 1828) was elected President of the Confederacy. Initially a war to restore the Union, Lincoln's war aims evolved to include, most importantly, the abolition of slavery. Early Confederate victories at First and Second Bull Run, in the Peninsula and Shenandoah Valley Campaigns, Fredericksburg, and Chancellorsville, proved that the war would not end quickly. The Union eventually mobilized its resources and gained key victories at Shiloh, Antietam, Vicksburg, Gettysburg, the Wilderness, and Atlanta. Ultimately, the North overwhelmed and outlasted the Confederacy and restored the Union. West Point graduates led the way for both sides – of the 60 major Civil War battles, 55 had West Point graduates leading both armies with the remainder having a West Point graduate leading on one side. Among these leaders were Union Generals Ulysses S. Grant (USMA 1843 and 18th United States President), William T. Sherman (USMA 1840), and George B. McClellan (USMA 1846), and Confederate Generals Robert E. Lee (USMA 1829) and Thomas J. "Stonewall" Jackson (USMA 1846). The Union lost 364,511 soldiers killed with 281,881 wounded, while the Confederacy lost 258,000 soldiers killed with 137,000 wounded. Sixty West Point graduates died fighting for the Union and 45 graduates died for the Confederacy. Twenty-two West Point graduates and two former cadets received the Medal of Honor.

#6 SPANISH-AMERICAN WAR
April 25, 1898–December 10, 1898

Citing mistreatment of Cubans by the Spanish and following the mysterious bombing of the *USS Maine* in Havana Harbor, Cuba, the United States went to war with Spain in 1898 under President William McKinley. Fighting took place in both the Caribbean and the Philippines in the Pacific. In the Caribbean, the United States won battles at Santiago, San Juan Hill, Kettle Hill, and El Canay. In the Philippines, the United States fleet defeated the Spanish fleet in Manila Bay and later took Manila while aided by Filipino rebels. In defeating the Spanish, the United States became a global empire gaining sovereignty over Cuba and acquiring the Philippines, Puerto Rico, and Guam from Spain. The United States lost 2,446 Americans Killed In Action with 1,662 wounded. Sixteen West Point graduates were Killed In Action. Among them was Dennis M. Michie (USMA 1892), Army football's first head coach and founder of the Army-Navy football game, who was Killed In Action in Santiago, Cuba – West Point's football stadium, Michie Stadium, bears his name. Four West Point graduates received the Medal of Honor.

#7 PHILIPPINE INSURRECTION 1899-1903
February 4, 1899–May 6, 1902

Following America's victory in the Spanish-American War, Spain ceded control of the Philippines to the United States. Filipino leader Emilio Aguinaldo, resistance leader against the Spanish, refused to accept this control and declared Independence under a separate Philippine Republic. After initial engagements with United States

Mayor Rudy Guilliani

forces at Manila and Malolos, Aguinaldo disbanded his Army and led a guerrilla war for the next two years. American forces fought Filipino rebels in brutal campaigns on Luzon, the Visayan Islands, Mindanao, and Sulu until Aguinaldo's capture on March 23, 1901, when he was forced to swear allegiance to the United States and issued a proclamation calling for peace. The guerrilla war lasted another year until most of the Filipino Generals surrendered. Nearly 4,200 United States soldiers were killed and 3,000 wounded – among those Killed In Action were 22 West Point graduates. Nine West Point graduates received the Medal of Honor.

#8 WORLD WAR I
April 6, 1917–November 11, 1918

Europe became embroiled in a global war that consumed the continent from July 28, 1914, to November 11, 1918. For the first three years, America attempted neutrality as the Triple Entente (Britain, France, and Russia) battled the Central Powers (Germany, the Austro-Hungarian Empire, and the Ottoman Empire) to a bitter stalemate – particularly on the Western Front. When Germany resorted to unrestricted submarine warfare in 1917, American felt compelled to declare war on Germany and entered the conflict under President Woodrow Wilson on April 6, 1917. The American Expeditionary Force (AEF), led by General of the Armies John "Blackjack" Pershing (USMA 1886), arrived in France in May 1917 and saw its first action in October 1917. By May 1918, the full weight of fresh United States troops helped turn the tide of the war as the AEF was instrumental in halting the 1918 German Offensives at Chateau-Thierry and Belleau Wood, then going on the offensive at Saint-Mihiel and the Meuse-Argonne. An uncertain post-war settlement at Versailles in 1919 set the stage leading to World War II. America's time in the war was relatively short, but the price was high as the United States lost 116,516 Killed In Action and 204,002 wounded in 13 months of combat. Thirty-two West Point graduates were Killed In Action and one West Point graduate received the Medal of Honor.

#9 WORLD WAR II EUROPEAN THEATER OF OPERATIONS
December 11, 1941–May 8, 1945

The United States under President Franklin D. Roosevelt joined the British and Soviet Allies against the European Axis powers led by Germany and Italy in a war that engulfed much of the globe. From the Battle of the Atlantic, to the Combined Bomber Offensive over Germany, to key land invasions in North Africa (Operation Torch, 1942), Sicily (Operation Husky, 1943), and Italy (Operations Avalanche/Shingle, 1943–44), the allies wore down the Axis until the cross-channel invasion into France. General of the Army Dwight D. Eisenhower (USMA 1915 and 34th United States President) led the Allied invasion of Europe (Operation Overload) on D-Day, June 6, 1944 and opened up the "second front" in France against Germany as the Soviet Union closed in along the eastern front. Following Germany's defeat, post-war Europe became ideologically divided and the Cold War set in. Other West Point graduates who were key leaders in World War II's European Theater included: Generals of the Army Omar N. Bradley (USMA 1915) and Henry H. Arnold (USMA 1907); Generals George S. Patton, Jr. (USMA 1909), Mark W. Clark (USMA 1917), and Matthew B. Ridgeway (USMA 1917); and Lieutenant General James M. Gavin (USMA 1929). There were 405,399 Americas Killed In Action with 670,846 wounded in World War II – among those Killed In Action were 487 West Point graduates. Six West Point graduates and one former cadet received the Medal of Honor in the European Theater of Operations.

#10 WORLD WAR II PACIFIC THEATER OF OPERATIONS
December 7, 1941–September 2, 1945

After Japanese forces attacked Pearl Harbor on December 7, 1941, the United States under President Franklin D. Roosevelt declared war on Japan and fought across the Pacific for the next 45 months. Balancing forces between the Pacific Theater (as the primary combatant against the Japanese), and the European Theater, America followed up these initial defeats with twin offensives that "island-hopped" across the Central Pacific (Midway, 1942; Tarawa and Kwajalein, 1943; Saipan and Peleliu, 1944; and Iwo Jima and Okinawa, 1945) and the South Pacific and Philippines (Coral Sea and Guadalcanal, 1942; New Britain, 1943; and the Philippines, 1944–45). General of the Army Douglas MacArthur (USMA 1903) commanded the drive in the South Pacific and Philippines. The war ended when the Manhattan Project (led by Lieutenant General Leslie Groves, USMA 1918) created the first atomic bombs that were dropped on Hiroshima and Nagasaki in August 1945, forced Japan's surrender, and ushered in the atomic age. Other West Point graduates who were key leaders in World War II's Pacific Theater included: Lieutenant General Jonathon M. Wainwright (USMA 1906); General Simon B. Buckner, Jr. (USMA 1908); and General Joseph W. Stilwell – China-Burma-India Theater (USMA 1904). There were 405,399 Americas Killed In Action with 670,846 wounded in World War II – among those Killed In Action were 487 West Point graduates. Three West Point graduates received the Medal of Honor in the Pacific Theater of Operations.

#11 THE COLD WAR
September 2, 1945–December 25, 1991

The Cold War was an ideological, political, economic, and military conflict that developed after World War II when the Grand Alliance of the United States and Soviet Union, a "marriage of convenience" to defeat Germany, dissolved over irreconcilable differences. Tensions within the alliance developed during the war itself as both the United States and the Soviet Union sought to shape a post-war world that favored their respective systems. As a result, the stage was set that placed the world in two opposing camps: the United States and its allies on one side, and the Soviet Union and its communist allies on the other. Fearful of an uncertain future, both nations competed for nearly half of a century to expand their ideologies through spheres of influence, alliances, economic supremacy, and military strength. A vast arms race that featured nuclear weapons played a central role in nearly every aspect of that competition, and the fear of a United States–Soviet nuclear confrontation always underscored international tensions. Although never directly engaging each other in war, both sides supported numerous regional and proxy wars in Korea, Vietnam, Central America, and elsewhere as the Cold War influenced and shaped political and military leaders spanning nine Presidential administrations. By 1989, the Soviet Union collapsed economically and then completely dissolved by 1991 – liberating the oppressed people of Eastern Europe and the former Soviet Union in its wake.

#12 KOREAN WAR
June 25, 1950–July 27, 1953

The Korean War was the Cold War's first major armed conflict after communist North Korea crossed the 38th parallel and invaded South Korea in an attempt to unify the peninsula. The United States under President Harry S. Truman, with the support of the United Nations, formed a coalition to save South Korea. With United States and South Korean forces driven to a small perimeter around Pusan, General Douglas MacArthur (USMA 1903) led a daring and decisive amphibious invasion at Inchon in September 1950 to aid the forces around Pusan. The United States/United Nations forces eventually drove North Korean forces back across the 38th parallel and continued north to the Yalu River as the war aim changed from liberating South Korea to uniting all of Korea. In the wake of nuclear threats, China entered the war in October 1950 to protect its borders and defend North Korea. Chinese forces pushed U.S./U.N. forces back across the 38th parallel. After re-establishing

the border in June 1951, the remainder of the war saw bitter fighting (Bloody Ridge and Heartbreak Ridge, 1951; the Battle of Triangle Hill, 1952; and the Battle of Pork Chop Hill, 1953) that yielded little exchange of territory. For the next two years, protracted negotiations reached a July 1953 armistice that re-established the border in roughly the same pre-war location and is still in effect today. Officially, the war has not yet ended. The United States lost 36,574 Killed In Action and 103,284 wounded – among those were 157 West Point graduates Killed In Action. Two West Point graduates received the Medal of Honor.

#13 VIETNAM WAR
July 8, 1959–April 30, 1973

America's second major armed conflict of the Cold War was the Vietnam War as the United States replaced the French in support of the Republic of Vietnam (South Vietnam). Initial United States supported included financial aid and military advisors to assist South Vietnam's fight against communist insurgents and prevent "the domino theory" of successive nations falling to communism. This commitment gradually escalated over the next two decades peaking in 1968 with about 540,000 troops under President Lyndon Johnson. Fighting both conventionally and unconventionally against the North Vietnamese Army and Vietcong insurgents, America employed a range of options that included aerial bombing campaigns, "search and destroy" operations, and counterinsurgency operations to achieve "pacification." Conventional operations dominated from 1965 to 1973 and were first led by General William Westmoreland (USMA 1936) and then General Creighton Abrams (USMA 1936). Despite overwhelming tactical success on the battlefield, factors, such as political limitations, changing objectives, and waning support from the American public after the 1968 Tet Offensive, caused America to re-evaluate its commitment. Pursuing a strategy of "Vietnamization" under President Richard Nixon, the United States gradually withdrew its combat forces by 1973. The United States lost 58,200 Americans Killed In Action with 303,644 wounded – among those were 273 West Point graduates Killed In Action. Seven West Point graduates, one former cadet, and one professor received the Medal of Honor.

#14 GRENADA (OPERATION URGENT FURY)
October 25, 1983–December 15, 1983

In its first major Cold War military action since the Vietnam War, the United States, under President Ronald W. Reagan, successfully invaded, then liberated, the small Caribbean Island of Grenada on October 25, 1983 when a Cuban-backed military coup overthrew the democratic government. Initially concerned only with the safety of Americans on the Island and ordering their rescue, the President expanded the objectives to include defeating the coup and restoring the government in order to prevent the spread of Cuban and communist influence throughout the Caribbean. United States Army Rangers, supported by the 82nd Airborne Division – as part of a joint force incorporating all sister services – played a key role in the operation as they parachuted in to seize and secure one of the island's main airfields at Point Salines. The United States lost 19 Americans Killed In Action with 116 wounded.

#15 PANAMA (OPERATION JUST CAUSE)
December 20, 1989–January 12, 1990

At the end of the Cold War, the United States invaded Panama on December 20, 1989, following years of increased tensions between the two nations that culminated with the Panamanian National Assembly giving broad, dictatorial powers to General Manuel A. Noriega and declaring a "state of war" against the United States as long as American forces remained in Panama. Intervening in order to safeguard American lives, defend democracy in Panama, combat drug trafficking, and to protect the integrity of the Panama Canal Zone and treaty, President George H. W. Bush ordered the invasion to depose Noriega. Conducting its first combat jump since

World War II, the 82nd Airborne Division landed at Torrijos International Airport and began combat operations with support from the 7th Infantry Division, United States Southern Command units, and other sister services. Within seven hours, American forces defeated the Panamanian Defense Force to where it unable to provide any organized resistance. General Noriega surrendered January 3, 1990, and operations ceased January 12, 1990. The overwhelming success of Operation Just Cause highlighted America's skillful ability to conduct contingency operations by projecting military force rapidly over long distances in order to protect American interests. The United States lost 23 Americans Killed In Action with 324 wounded.

#16 PERSIAN GULF WAR (OPERATIONS DESERT SHIELD/DESERT STORM)
August 2, 1990–February 28, 1991

After the Cold War, aggressive rogue states became a reality as Iraq invaded Kuwait on August 2, 1990, and threatened much of the world's oil supply. The United States under President George H. W. Bush led a 36-nation international coalition to liberate Kuwait. This coalition, with nearly 530,000 American troops, initially held a defensive posture to protect Saudi Arabia during Operation Desert Shield. Combat operations during Operation Desert Storm began on January 17, 1991, with a six-week aerial bombing campaign until ground forces, under the command of General H. Norman Schwarzkopf, Jr. (USMA 1956), invaded Iraq and Iraqi forces in Kuwait on February 24, 1991. The ground war lasted only 100 hours as coalition forces completely overwhelmed the Iraqi Army and successfully liberated Kuwait. Critical to the ground attack was a surprise flanking maneuver around Iraqi forces by the United States VII Corps commanded by General Frederick Franks (USMA 1959) and the United States XVIII Airborne Corps, which was anchored by General Barry McCaffrey's (USMA 1964) 24th Infantry Division. The magnitude of the coalition victory was so great, that Defense Intelligence Agency estimates included 100,000 Iraqi soldiers Killed In Action, 300,000 wounded in action, 3,700 tanks destroyed, and 42 divisions rendered combat ineffective. The United States lost 145 Americans Killed In Action with 467 wounded in both operations. One West Point graduate, First Lieutenant Donaldson Tiller (USMA 1988), was Killed In Action, along with his crew, on February 27, 1991, when the UH-60 Black Hawk helicopter he piloted was shot down.

(NO HOLE) IN BETWEEN #16 AND #17: SOMALIA (OPERATION RESTORE HOPE/CONTINUE HOPE)
December 4, 1992–March 25, 1994

In December 1992, President George H. W. Bush ordered United States forces to Somalia during Operation Restore Hope in order to provide security for and assist in United Nations humanitarian efforts to ease the suffering that resulted from decades of drought, overpopulation, and religious, ethnic, and clan wars. The United States provided nearly 30,000 troops at its peak to this contingency operation while trying to resist expanding missions from providing humanitarian relief and security for relief efforts to disarming feuding clans and capturing warlords. As fighting in and around Mogadishu increased and more U.N. forces became casualties, the United States began assisting in disarming clans and searching for and capturing responsible warlords. One such operation, led by Major General Scott Miller (USMA 1983 – then CPT Miller), was during the capture attempt of Somali Warlord, General Mohammed Farah Aidid in October 1993. During this operation, two Black Hawk helicopters were shot down and the ensuing Battle of Mogadishu resulted in 19 Americans Killed In Action. Colonel Lee Van Arsdale (USMA 1974), 1st Special Forces Operational Detachment–Delta, led the rescue effort to crash site number one. Shortly after the battle, President William J. Clinton further limited the role of United States forces and ultimately ended operations in Somalia. The United States

lost 42 Americans Killed In Action, while Somalia continued as a failed state with no functioning government.

#17 AFGHANISTAN WAR (OPERATION ENDURING FREEDOM)
October 7, 2001–Present

After the United States was attacked on September 11, 2001, by Taliban-sponsored terrorists, the United States under President George W. Bush initiated Operation Enduring Freedom and invaded Afghanistan on October 7, 2001 to destroy the Taliban and liberate the Afghan people. American forces initially routed the Taliban while liberating Afghanistan. Key to this effort was Operation Anaconda, commanded by Lieutenant General Franklin "Buster" Hagenback (USMA 1971), which saw the first use of a large conventional force in direct combat against the Taliban. The United States also built an Afghan Army and police force while setting out to establish and turn over a legitimate, functioning Afghan national government. West Point graduates who served as commander of coalition forces in Afghanistan include: General David Petraeus (USMA 1974), General Stanley McChrystal (USMA 1976), Lieutenant General Karl Eikenberry (USMA 1973), and Lieutenant General David Barno (USMA 1976). In light of these United States efforts and despite the loss of Al Qaeda leader Osama Bin Laden, who was killed on May 2, 2011, Taliban forces have continued to operate within Afghanistan by infiltrating from bases within Pakistan. As of August 2011, the United States had lost 1,532 Americans Killed In Action with 4,949 soldiers wounded – among those are 21 West Point graduates Killed In Action and 2 deaths in accidents/non-combat actions.

#18 IRAQ WAR (OPERATION IRAQI FREEDOM/NEW DAWN)
March 20, 2003–December 15, 2011

The United States under President George W. Bush led an international coalition in Operation Iraqi Freedom that invaded Iraq on March 20, 2003, and liberated the nation by May 2003. After the invasion, political and military setbacks and poor decisions led to the development of an insurgency that ultimately turned into a civil war between Sunni and Shiite factions. In light of this insurgency, United States–led coalition forces in the Multi-National Security Transition Command under West Point graduates General Martin Dempsey (USMA 1971), Lieutenant General Frank Helmick (USMA 1976), and Lieutenant General Michael Barbero (USMA 1976), built and trained an Iraqi Army and police force that assisted in defeating the insurgency and fostering a legitimate Iraqi government and society. As the United States continued its draw-down and turnover of governance and security to the Iraqi people, the operation entered a new phase on September 1, 2010, known as Operation New Dawn. West Point graduates who served as overall commander of the coalition forces in Iraq include: General David Petraeus (USMA 1974), General Lloyd Austin (USMA 1975), and General Raymond Odierno (USMA 1976). As of August 2011, the United States had lost 4,452 Americans Killed In Action with 31,103 wounded – among those are 47 West Point graduates Killed In Action and 13 deaths in accidents/non-combat actions.

West Point Golf Course has been played by USGA Hall Of Fame Golfer and West Point Graduate President Dwight D. Eisenhower

Revolutionary War re-enactors load a canon in front of the putting green.

Hole #10 World War II Pacific with re-enactor from the time period.

Rudy Guiliani hits a drive in front of the #7 granite marker for the Philippine Insurrection.

Revolutionary War re-enactment on the course.

Hole #2 with War of 1812 re-enactors.

Hole #8 World War I hole with re-enactor.

Hole #13 Vietnam War with a re-enactor from the time period.

THE STAFF RIDES AT FORTRESS WEST POINT
FORTS CLINTON, MONTGOMERY AND STONY POINT

Written by: Colonel James Johnson, PhD (USA, Retired), USMA 1979.

The corporate world has adopted a technique for leader-development and team-building inspired by the United States Army's staff ride. The modern staff ride started in 1906 with a trip to the Civil War battlefield of Chickamauga by student officers from Fort Leavenworth, Kansas. The concept was revived in the 1980s and has been an educational staple for commanders since then. For soldiers, a staff ride allows a commander and his subordinates to study the decisions and actions of historical leaders in a campaign and battle by walking over the same terrain and studying the combat that took place there to develop insights into current tactical doctrine, logistics, communications, and combat systems. It is a systematic analysis of the site of a battle or fortification to learn about the impact of geography, weather, and human interactions on key historical events. The focus in the final analysis is on leadership as participants share a common experience while gaining different frames of reference through the eyes of an actual historical commander.

The German theorist on war, Carl von Clausewitz, wrote in *On War* that "War is the realm of uncertainty; three quarters of the factors on which action in war is based are wrapped in a fog of greater or lesser uncertainty." He therefore reasoned that "A sensitive and discriminating judgment is called for; a skilled intelligence to scent out the truth." That is the purpose of staff rides: to help commanders and staff officers develop their judgment and hone their intelligence so that they can lift the fog of war before they are faced with the pressures of combat or the budget cycle. As participants walk the battlefield, they are forced to confront the realities of terrain, fatigue, and the tactical scenario. The insights that they gain should help them ask more pointed questions about the requirements for the systems they are charged to run. The basic fundamentals of war have not changed from ancient times, and the insights gained from earlier history still have relevance. Corporate leaders have drawn the same value from staff rides.

The Thayer Leader Development Group offers staff rides to corporate and educational groups that explore Fortress West Point and the battles at nearby Forts Clinton and Montgomery and Stony Point from the American Revolution. Corporate Executive Officers (Chief Executive Officers) and Vice Presidents conduct off-site meetings at the Thayer Hotel that use one of these staff rides to re-enforce their meetings' themes or company objectives. By playing roles of commanders from the American Revolution, their subordinate leaders are forced to think out of the box in the language of soldiers. As the experiences unfold, they have discovered that command and leadership involve both art and science. While technology changes, the art of leading soldiers and employees has a continuity through the ages. Assessing the decisions and

Colonel Jim Johnson, dressed in an authentic Revolutionary War uniform, instructs a staff ride starting at the Thayer Hotel.

actions of commanders and soldiers on battlefields from the past allows present leaders to think through their own challenges away from the office and, for soldiers, without the pressure of actual combat. For a few hours, they get to walk in another leader's shoes to gain his experience without paying any real price.

The insights or lessons learned that emerge during the After Action Review have long-term value for organizations. In an age of e-mail and texts, participants get to experience the value to be gained from face-to-face contact, leading while walking around. As General George Washington or New York Governor and Brigadier General George Clinton met with subordinates, they ensured that they knew the mission and the commander's intent; they could also ask questions. They were able to take the measure of their commanders and admonish or encourage them as required. They proved that leaders lead by example. While text and e-mail messages are faster and bridge huge distances, they do not allow

process the relevant information and then to prioritize what is most important so that they can make decisions that move their organizations forward.

One of the great insights that emerges from staff rides is the importance of key terrain. Soldiers and cannons in Fort Clinton/Arnold at West Point protected the water batteries, the Great Chain, and the S-shaped curve in the Hudson River. Fort Putnam dominated the Plain and Fort Clinton/Arnold. Redoubt four over-watched Fort Putnam from Crown Hill 300 feet higher. For soldiers the high ground has a power all its own. The same is true in business. Where a corporation locates a store or factory or places its product on a shelf can determine the ultimate success for the bottom line.

After four hours of walking and riding around the battlefield, participants reach conclusions about what happened in the battle or the strengths and weaknesses of fortifications. As a part of the After Action Review, they then draw insights that

commanders to sense the intangibles made more obvious by human interaction in personal conversations. Great commanders, from Alexander the Great to George Washington to Napoleon to U.S. Grant to Dwight D. Eisenhower, have relied on the power of personal leadership.

The participants in one staff ride to Forts Clinton and Montgomery near Bear Mountain Bridge decided that the rugged terrain would have made even modern satellite, cellular, and radio communications difficult, particularly for the British in the attack. Since communications is vital to corporate and military success, leaders would have had to adapt to new, challenging circumstances. General Henry Clinton did about as well as he could to synchronize and to coordinate the dual attacks on the two forts using the sound of musket fire as the primary signal. Clinton was plagued by the tyranny of time and space as he divided his force for the approach marches, effectively putting them out of supporting distance as they were separated for most of the operation by Bear Mountain and Popolopen Creek. Commanders at Forts Montgomery and Clinton depended on sight, sound, and messages from subordinates to stay abreast of the tactical situation. They depended on what they saw and heard to make judgments. Their orders moved only as fast as couriers could run or ride on horseback. Military and corporate leaders today face an overwhelming volume of correspondence delivered at incredible speeds. Their challenge is to develop systems that allow them to

will make them better leaders in their own organizations – takeaways for life. Teams share these ideas, which can then be carried over into the later discussions of corporate challenges and programs in the off-site meeting or back to their offices around the globe. Winning team members receive staff ride coins as a reward for teamwork and analysis.

Sun Tzu, the ancient Chinese philosopher of war, wrote that "If you know the enemy and know yourself, you need not fear the result of a hundred battles. If you know yourself but not the enemy, for every victory gained you will also suffer a defeat. If you know neither the enemy nor yourself, you will succumb in every battle." Such nuggets gained in a staff ride win battles and make money.

Colonel James M. Johnson, United States Army, Retired, PhD, USMA 1969. Military Historian of the Hudson River Valley, Dr. Frank T. Bumpus Chair of Hudson River Valley History, and Executive Director, Hudson River Valley Institute at Marist College.

To arrange corporate staff rides, contact Dr. Karen Kuhla at kkuhla@ thayerleaderdevelopment.com.

BEAR
MOUNTAIN INN

Bear Mountain State Park is situated in rugged mountains rising from the west bank of the Hudson River. The park features a large play field, shaded picnic groves, lake and river fishing access, a swimming pool, trailside museums and zoo, hiking, biking, and cross-country ski trails. An outdoor rink is open to ice skaters from late October through mid-March. The Perkins Memorial Tower atop Bear Mountain affords spectacular views of the park, the Hudson Highlands, and Harriman State Park. Perkins Memorial Drive and Tower are open from April through late November, weather permitting.

The merry-go-round at Bear Mountain State Park features hand-painted scenes of the park and 42 hand-carved seats of native animals, including black bear, wild turkey, deer, raccoon, skunk, Canada goose, fox, swan, bobcat, rabbit, and more. For general information about the merry-go-round, please contact the Bear Mountain Office at (845) 786-2701 x242. To book a birthday party at the merry-go-round, please contact our concessionaire at 845-786-2731, or visit www.nysparks.com.

STORM KING
ART CENTER

Widely celebrated as one of the world's leading sculpture parks, Storm King Art Center has welcomed visitors from across the globe for 50 years. It is located only one hour north of New York City and only 10 miles from the Thayer Hotel at West Point, in the lower Hudson Valley, where its pristine 500-acre landscape of fields, hills, and woodlands provides the setting for a collection of more than 100 carefully sited sculptures created by some of the most acclaimed artists of our time. *www.stormking.org*, © 2011 Storm King Art Center

View of the South Fields, all works by Mark di Suvero. Photograph by Jerry L. Thompson, ©Storm King Art Center, Mountainville, New York

Mark di Suvero (1933-)
Pyramidian, 1987/1998
Steel, 65' x 46' x 46'
Gift of the Ralph E. Ogden Foundation, Inc.
Photograph by Jerry L. Thompson
©Storm King Art Center, Mountainville, New York

Arnaldo Pomodoro (1926-)
The Pietrarubbia Group: il fondamento, l'uso, il rapporto, 1975-76
Bronze, steel, fiberglass and marble, 9' 2 1/4" x 17' 4 5/8" x 11' 9 1/4"
Given in loving memory of Gabrielle H. Reem, M.D., by her husband, Herbert J. Kayden, M.D. on July 8, 2011,
©Arnaldo Pomodoro
Photograph by Jerry L. Thompson
©Storm King Art Center, Mountainville, New York

BOSCOBEL
HOUSE

Located in the very heart of the Hudson River Valley, the elegant Boscobel House overlooks the mighty Hudson River from its manicured lawns on a bluff in Garrison, New York. Originally built in Montrose, New York, from 1804 to 1808, by British Loyalist States Morris Dyckman and his wife, Elizabeth Corne Dyckman, Boscobel faced demolition in the 1950s and was moved and reconstructed on its current site, thanks to the efforts of a group of pioneers of the preservation movement.

Today, Boscobel is home to one of the nation's leading collections of furniture and decorative arts from the Federal period. It offers a variety of rich cultural, educational, and recreational programs and is one of the area's favorite destinations for international tourists and locals alike. Visitors can take guided house tours, hike the Woodland Trail, and explore the beautiful gardens and grounds that make up the 60-acre property. They can meander along a brick path, through an orchard to the fragrant herb garden and its orangery, continue into the circular rose garden or stroll out to the great lawn and Belvedere, a crescent-shaped scenic overlook, with spectacular views of the Hudson River and its Highlands. Boscobel is open every day from April 1st through December 31st, except Tuesdays, Christmas, and Thanksgiving. For details, please visit www.boscobel.org.

GARRISON
TRAIN
STATION

The Garrison Train Station is located on the east side of the Hudson River just one hour north of New York City and Grand Central Station. Trains depart nearly hourly and shuttles and taxis are available to drive to West Point.

www.mta.info

Garrison View across the River to Thayer Hotel

Garrison View of West Point

THE NATIONAL PURPLE HEART
HALL OF HONOR

The National Purple Heart Hall of Honor is a New York State Historic Site whose mission is to collect, preserve, and share the stories of Purple Heart recipients from all branches of service and across all conflicts for which the award has been available. The Hall of Honor was dedicated on November 10, 2006, and is co-located with the New Windsor Cantonment, the last encampment of the Continental Army at the end of the American Revolution.

The Hall is located here at Temple Hill to commemorate the May 28, 1932, ceremony when 138 veterans of World War I were awarded their Purple Hearts. The ceremony was part of New York's Bicentennial celebration of the birth of George Washington. The commemoration of Purple Heart recipients continues today most visibly through the Roll of Honor, an electronic database. The Hall of Honor is open Monday through Saturday, 10:00 a.m. to 5:00 p.m., and Sunday 1:00 p.m. to 5:00 p.m. 374 Temple Hill Road, New Windsor NY 12553. Call 845-561-1765 for additional information, or visit www.thepurpleheart.com.

"As in any war the hardest part was losing your buddies. This is something that never leaves you. Our country is based on freedom to protect that freedom. Some gave some, they gave all."
Paul Womack, 82nd AAA, (AWBNSP) 2nd Infantry Division

"Life is stripped down to bare essentials for him when he is living from minute to minute, wondering if each is his last..."
— Bill Mauldin, Up Front

VILLAGE OF
COLD SPRINGS

The Village of Cold Spring is located on the east side of the Hudson River 50 miles north of New York City. MTA trains from New York's Grand Central Station service the town nearly hourly. This quaint village is regional tourist destination with bed-and-breakfasts, antique shops, restaurants, and music festivals. *www.coldspringny.gov*

The view from Cold Springs looking up at West Point across the Hudson River.

BANNERMAN
ISLAND

Bannerman Island and Castle is located on the Hudson River just north of West Point. Walking tours, music festivals, and boat tours are available. Check online for details and availability. *www.bannermancastle.org*

CULINARY INSTITUTE
OF AMERICA

The Culinary Institute of America, generally recognized as the world's premier culinary college, is located in historic and picturesque Hyde Park, New York, on the Hudson River's east bank, 40 miles north of West Point. More than 2,800 students from more than 30 countries pursue associate and bachelor's degrees in culinary arts, baking and pastry arts, and culinary science from the internationally acclaimed not-for-profit, four-year institution.

With a wide variety of programs and attractions, the college is a must-see destination for food-lovers.

Known to chefs and food enthusiasts simply as "the CIA," the college operates five award-winning, student-staffed restaurants: The Bocuse Restaurant, American Bounty Restaurant, Ristorante Caterina de' Medici, St. Andrew's Café, and the Apple Pie Bakery Café. Reservations are suggested for all restaurants except the bakery café and can be made by calling 845-471-6608. Menus for all five restaurants can be found and online reservations made at www.ciarestaurants.com.

In addition to the restaurants, visitors can take a tour given by CIA students and shop at the Craig Claiborne Bookstore, a gift shop that features epicurean delights, cookbooks, souvenirs, and high-quality kitchen utensils.

Real food enthusiasts have a chance to experience the ultimate culinary vacation by taking a cooking course under the direction of the college's renowned faculty. Offerings covering many cooking and baking topics, as well as various world cuisines range from single day hands-on and demonstration classes to full five-day "Boot Camp" immersions. Information and course listings are at www.ciachef.edu/enthusiasts/.

BROTHERHOOD
WINERY

100 Brotherhood Plaza Drive, Washingtonville, NY 10992
www.brotherhoodwinery.net | contact@brotherhoodwinery.net | 845-496-3661

Brotherhood, America's oldest winery, was established in the bucolic Hudson Valley in 1839, just an hour visit from metro New York. Jean Jacques was a cobbler by trade and planted vines in Washingtonville, New York, in early 1837. Jacques produced his first commercial vintage in 1839 and sold his wines under the name "Jacques Brothers Winery." The Hudson River was the pulse of commerce in those days and was how wine and grapes were transported from the Hudson Valley to the metro region for sale and distribution.

In 2005, Mr. Baeza and his new partners, The Chadwick and Castro families from Chile, embarked on an extensive renovation and restoration to the Brotherhood property and facilities. Several facets of the facility have been improved upon over the past eight years: Production has tripled, Grand Monarque Hall has been restored in to the Hudson Valley's premier catering facility, the addition of Vinum Cafe to the property, as well as the renovation of a state-of-the-art tasting room and the addition of demonstration vineyards on the property all complement the visitors' experience.

Tours and tastings run seven days a week from 11 a.m. to 5 p.m. Sunday through Friday and 11 a.m. to 6 p.m. on Saturdays from April through December. Open January through March 11 a.m. to 5 p.m. on Friday, Saturday, and Sunday for tours and tastings. Tour and tasting tickets can be purchased for $10, which include Brotherhood's tour, a wine tasting flight (a selection of five wines), and a souvenir wine glass.

Live music is offered in the courtyard during the summer months and a variety of special events throughout the different seasons of the year.

WOODBURY COMMON
PREMIUM OUTLETS

498 Red Apple Court, Central Valley, NY 10917
845-928-4000 | www.premiumoutlets.com

Thirteen million visitors annually visit the 220 outlet stores of Woodbury Commons, only 15 minutes from West Point and the Thayer Hotel. Located 45 miles north of New York City, Woodbury Commons is one of the most frequently visited tourist sites in New York State. Visitors frequently stay at the Thayer Hotel at West Point and tour the Hudson Valley.

Find impressive savings at Ann Taylor, Balenciaga, Banana Republic, Burberry, Calvin Klein, Chloe, Coach, Dior, Dolce & Gabbana, Gucci, Last Call by Neiman Marcus, Michael Kors, Polo Ralph Lauren, Prada, Saks 5th Avenue Off 5th, Tom Ford, Tommy Hilfiger, and more.

Photos courtesy Woodbury Commons

NEW YORK
CITY

New York City is only 50 miles from West Point and is the top tourist destination in the United States according to *Forbes Magazine* (2010 rankings) with approximately 37 million visitors. Times Square, Broadway shows, the Statue of Liberty, the Empire State Building, the *USS Intrepid* Museum, world-class museums, restaurants, and bars make New York City the top attraction in the United States and one of the top destinations in the world. Just north of New York City by 50 miles is West Point and the Hudson River Valley, ranked by *National Geographic* as one of the top 20 places to visit globally according to 2012 rankings. The Historic Thayer Hotel is the ideal location to stay within the Hudson Valley.

EMPIRE STATE
BUILDING

The Empire State Building is a National Historic Landmark and one of the most visited tourist sites in the United States. Built in 1930 it now stands at 1,467 feet and was named "America's Favorite Architecture" in a poll conducted by the American Institute of Architects. Located at 31st Street and 6th Avenue, it is walking distance from Times Square, the most frequently visited tourist site in the United States according to *Forbes Magazine*.

STATUE OF
LIBERTY

The Statue of Liberty is located 50 miles (80 kilometers) south of West Point in New York Harbor. The statue was a gift to the American people from the people of France, originally intended to be opened on the Centennial celebrations of 1876, it opened 10 years later in 1886. The Statue of Liberty is an iconic symbol known around the world. It is often used to represent freedom, democracy, and hope. For millions of immigrants in the 1800s and early 1900s, it was the unmistakable symbol that they had arrived in the country of their dreams after a long and often dangerous trip across the oceans. The Statue of Liberty is managed by the National Park Service (www.statueofliberty.org). The New York Water Taxi offers a number of boat cruises and tours to see the Statue of Liberty (www.newyorkwatertaxi.com).

INTREPID SEA, AIR &
SPACE MUSEUM

1 Intrepid Square, 12th Ave & 46th Street, New York, NY 10036

212-957-7041 | www.intrepidmuseum.org

The Intrepid Sea, Air & Space Museum is the only interactive museum where visitors can explore a legendary aircraft carrier, the first space shuttle, the world's fastest jets, and a secret submarine.

We thrill visitors of all ages and connect them to history through hands-on exploration, stories of heroism, and firsthand accounts by people who were there.

As home to many technological "firsts" and NASA's single largest artifact in the Northeast, the future is bridged by inspiring innovation.

As one of New York City's most original educational institutions, innovation is advanced by developing the next generation of leaders in science, technology, engineering, and math.

Located in New York City on the Hudson River 50 miles south of West Point near 46th Street and West Side Highway.

ROOSEVELT
MANSION

The home of President Franklin Delano Roosevelt is located only 36 miles north of West Point in Hyde Park, New York. FDR is the only United States President to ever be elected four times. He led the United States through World War II and died shortly before the surrender of Nazi Germany.

VANDERBILT
MANSION

Vanderbilt Mansion, in terms of architecture, interiors, mechanical systems, road systems, and landscape, is a remarkably complete example of a Gilded Age country place, illustrating the political, economic, social, cultural, and demographic changes that occurred as America industrialized in the years after the Civil War. Located only 36 miles north of West Point in Hyde Park, New York, it is an ideal tourist destination to visit from the Thayer Hotel.

NEW YORK
WATER TAXI

New York Water Taxi (NYWT) is an affiliate company of The Durst Organization Inc. A partnership venture between Douglas Durst and Tom Fox, NYWT has been a New York fixture since 2002, beginning with a spunky fleet of five distinctive black and yellow checkered vessels. Today, the iconic 12-vessel fleet also includes the vessels of sister organization Circle Line Downtown.

NYWT mission is to provide entertaining, stimulating, and enlightening ways to see New York City's dazzling skyline, celebrated bridges, and lush waterfront parks while maintaining a community-conscious fleet that honors New York's cherished waterways. NYWT provides a wide range of options. New York harbor cruises, September 11th memorial tickets, and Statue of Liberty cruises are just a small selection of the variety of New York City boat tours offered.

NYWT offers custom trips to West Point and has partnered with the Thayer Hotel and Thayer Leader Development Group to offer charter trips from New York City to West Point. NYWT also offers football game trips from New York City to West Point and back to support Army football.

www.newyorkwatertaxi.com

Courtesy: NYWT

INDEPENDENT
HELICOPTERS

www.independenthelicopters.com | 845-549-375

Flight in a helicopter is a unique way to see the Hudson Valley and New York City. A once-in-a-lifetime experience to capture spectacular photos of famous landmarks, including the Statue of Liberty, West Point, Shawangunk Mountains, and more. If you're feeling more adventurous, try an Introductory Helicopter Lessons and experience the thrill of being a pilot. Located by car just 30 minutes North of West Point at Stewart International Airport, a flight to West Point less than 10 minutes.

Courtesy: Independent Helicopters

Courtesy: Independent Helicopters

Courtesy: Walkway Over the Hudson

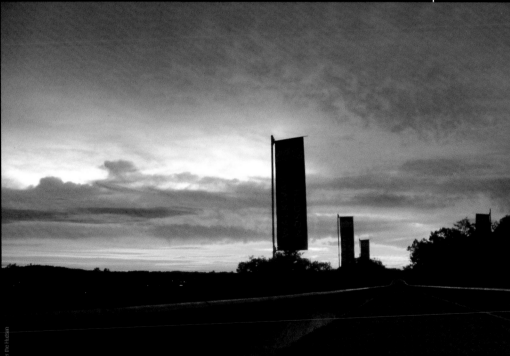

Courtesy: Walkway Over the Hudson

WEST POINT LEADERSHIP PORTRAYED
IN THE MOVIES

West Point graduates have played a major role in American history and therefore have been portrayed in countless Hollywood films. These are a few of the films that have highlighted the leadership shown by West Point graduates in either major movies or in documentaries.

MOVIES

PATTON (1970) General George S. Patton (USMA 1909). George C Scott awarded the Oscar for Best Actor portraying the legendary General.

MACARTHUR (1977) Gregory Peck as MacArthur (USMA 1903).

CAST A GIANT SHADOW (1966). Kirk Douglas as Mickey Marcus (USMA 1924), John Wayne, Frank Sinatra.

THE LONGEST DAY (1962) Two Oscars, General Eisenhower and General Bradley (both USMA 1915) in the invasion of Normandy (D-Day).

WE WERE SOLDIERS (2002) Mel Gibson as Lieutenant Colonel Hal Moore (USMA 1945). Won one Oscar portraying the first major battle of the Vietnam War.

BLACK HAWK DOWN (2001) The story of the battle of Mogadishu. Military Advisor and Mogadishu veteran Colonel Lee Van Arsdale (USMA 1974). Won 2 Oscars.

A BRIDGE TOO FAR (1977) Ryan O'Neil as Brigadier General Gavin, Paul Maxwell as General Maxwell Taylor in Operation Market Garden the invasion of Holland.

THE DESERT FOX (1951) Eisenhower (USMA 1915) and Patton (USMA 1909) as themselves in a movie about German General Rommel.

CUSTER OF THE WEST (1967) Robert Shaw as Lieutenant Colonel Custer, Lawrence Tierney as General Philip Sheridan.

THE GREAT RAID (2005) Benjamin Bratt as Lieutenant Colonel Mucci (USMA 1936) in the raid to free POWs from the Japanese POW camp in the Philippines.

DARBY'S RANGERS (1958) James Garner as Colonel William O. Darby in the 1st Ranger Battalion in Italy in World War II.

THEY DIED WITH THEIR BOOTS ON (1941) Errol Flynn as George Armstrong Custer (USMA 1861).

THE SPIRIT OF WEST POINT (1947) Doc Blanchard and Glenn Davis star as themselves as All-American Army football players.

THE TUSKEGEE AIRMEN (1995) Andre Braugher as Colonel Benjamin O. Davis (USMA 1936), the Founder and Commander of the African-American Tuskegee Airmen.

MERRILL'S MARAUDERS (1962) Jeff Chandler as Colonel Merrill, John Hoyt as General Stilwell in China-Burma-India Theater.

GETTYSBURG (1993) Martin Sheen as General Robert E. Lee, C.S.A. (USMA 1836) and many other graduates in the decisive battle of the Civil War.

NORTH AND SOUTH (1985 TV mini-series) Pickett, McClellan, Stonewall Jackson.

GODS AND GENERALS (2003) Robert Duvall as General Robert E. Lee, C.S.A., Stephen Lang as Stonewall Jackson in Civil War movie.

FAT MAN AND LITTLE BOY (1989) Paul Newman as Lieutenant General Leslie Groves leading the building of the atomic bombs in World War II.

IKE: COUNTDOWN TO D-DAY (2004) Tom Selleck as General Dwight D. Eisenhower, James Remar as General Bradley, Gerald McRaney as General Patton.

CODE BRS (2005) Richard Zeppieri as Assistant Coach Vince Lombardi, Scott Glenn as Coach Red Blaik in a movie about the Cadet Honor Code.

APOLLO 11 (1996) Xander Berkeley as Colonel Buzz Aldrin (USMA 1951) and Jim Metzler at Colonel Michael Collins (USMA 1952).

THE BIG LIFT (1950) General Lucius Clay (USMA 1919) as himself.

WOMEN AT WEST POINT (1979) Linda Perl, Leslie Ackerman star in a film about the first women at West Point.

TO APPOMATTOX (2013) Eight-part TV mini-series about West Point graduates on both sides of the Civil War. Rob Lowe as General Grant, Will Patton as Robert E. Lee.

DOCUMENTARIES

MODERN MARVELS: PANAMA CANAL (2004) History Channel. The building of the Panama Canal led by Major General George Goethals (USMA 1886).

MODERN MARVELS: APOLLO 11 (2004) History Channel. Buzz Aldrin as himself.

MODERN MARVELS: THE MANHATTAN PROJECT (2002). History Channel. Lieutenant General Leslie Groves leads the development of the atomic bombs.

THE BERLIN AIRLIFT: AN AMERICAN EXPERIENCE PBS. The first major battle of the Cold War results in the largest humanitarian effort in history led by General Lucius Clay (USMA 1917).

HAP ARNOLD: THE SKY WARRIOR (1997) Documentary.

BIOGRAPHY: GENERAL OMAR BRADLEY (1994) Documentary.

BIOGRAPHY: PRESIDENT DWIGHT D. EISENHOWER (2004) Documentary.

BIOGRAPHY: GENERAL DOUGLAS MACARTHUR (1962) Documentary.

BEYOND THE GLORY (2005) Coach Mike Krzyzewski "Coach K" Documentary.

A GAME OF HONOR (2011) Documentary on Army-Navy Football.

WEST POINT (2008) PBS documentary.

GENERAL PERSHING: THE IRON GENERAL (2000) The biography of General of the Armies John J. "Blackjack" Pershing (USMA 1886).

U.S. GRANT: WARRIOR (2011) PBS documentary.

CIVIL WAR JOURNAL: WEST POINT CLASSMATES CIVIL WAR ENEMIES (2011).

Movie posters (left to right) courtesy 20th Century Fox, Ted Turner Pictures, Paramount Pictures, United Artists, Miramax Films, Icon Productions, HBO Edge Productions, Warner Brothers Studios, 20th Century Fox, Universal Pictures, Warner Brothers Studios.

Gregory Peck filming MacArthur on the Plain with real cadets.

George C. Scott as Patton.

Hollywood sign, Hollywood, California, 1981.

Gregory Peck as MacArthur on the Plain at West Point.

John Wayne and Kirk Douglas in Cast a Giant Shadow portraying Mickey Marcus.

FRIENDS OF THE AMERICAN REVOLUTION
AT WEST POINT

Written by: Colonel James Johnson, PhD (USA, Retired), USMA 1979.

Friends of the American Revolution (FAR) at West Point, Inc., is a non-profit established to preserve, protect, and publicize known and to be discovered historic sites and remains at West Point from 1775 to 1783.

The goal of the organization, which is a public private partnership, is to restore the fortification system built under the leadership of General George Washington during the American Revolution. Approximately 30 sites from this vast fortification system still exist and remains can be found at West Point, Constitution Island, and in Putnam County directly across the Hudson River. FAR's target is to complete the restoration in time for the 250th anniversary of General Washington being named Commander in Chief of the Continental Army (1775–2025).

In addition, FAR will undertake a comprehensive genealogical survey to identify soldiers stationed at West Point during the Revolution and provide that information to those who wish to trace a direct link to those brave men. In addition, we intend to document civilian personnel who assisted in maintaining the Garrison during this time period.

Cadets at West Point will have a unique opportunity to utilize the fortification system as a staff ride to better understand the complexities of the American Revolution. By studying and visiting the many fortification sites, cadets better understand the key role played by West Point prior to the establishment of the United States Military Academy on this site in 1802.

The Thayer Leader Development Group, located at the historic Hotel Thayer, has utilized the fortification system at West Point for several years as an integral part of its executive leadership training program. Executives from throughout the United States and worldwide have stood on the ground where General Washington stood and learned important leadership skills from Washington's formidable leadership challenge to "protect the West Point."

Lieutenant General Dave Palmer, Distinguished Graduate and former Superintendent at West Point (1986–91), wrote the seminal history of West Point in the Revolution entitled The River and the Rock. FAR is working with the West Point Association of Graduates to reprint this important work in paperback and digital formats so greater numbers of people can learn about West Point's significant history in the American Revolution.

Friends of the American Revolution at West Point, far@farwp.us, www.farwp.us

Redoubt 7 Position on Constitution Island.

Fort Putnam West Point overlooking the Hudson River.

Redoubt 4 Position at West Point.

Cadets taking Class in Kosciuszko's Garden built in 1779.

WEST POINT AND THE AMERICAN CIVIL WAR
150TH ANNIVERSARY – SESQUICENTENNIAL
APRIL 12, 1861–APRIL 9, 1865

The American Civil War was fought from April 12, 1861, to April 9, 1865. Now, 150 years later, the nation is currently in the midst of celebrating the war's sesquicentennial from 2011 from 2015. As America's single costliest conflict, the last conflict to be fought on United States soil, and arguably the most significant event in the nation's history, the Civil War literally and figuratively tore the nation apart when 11 Southern states seceded from the Union over disputes regarding states' rights – specifically the right to maintain the "peculiar institution" of slavery. President Abraham Lincoln initially viewed the war as one to restore the Union, thus testing whether or not a democratic nation, such as America "so conceived and so dedicated, can long endure," as he noted in his famous Gettysburg Address. Over the course of the war, however, the goals radically evolved to include, most importantly, the abolition of slavery. Moreover, the conflict projected to last no more than 90 days, turned out to be a bloody, exhaustive, four-year war that tested the resolve of both sides.

To say the American Civil War was the costliest conflict is an understatement. More than 620,000 Union and Confederate soldiers died in the Civil War – more than in any other American conflict – with at least that many wounded. Recent research further suggests that perhaps as many as 750,000 Americans died.[1] Put into perspective, this figure represented almost two percent of the entire wartime population – a percentage more than double that of the American Revolution and more than six times as great as the Second World War. These percentages only increase in light of the new evidence on casualty figures. So by 1865, it is likely that nearly every American family directly felt the war's reach.

On the eve of the war, the United States proudly displayed 34 stars on its flag with the recent admission to the Union of Kansas in January 1861. Although 11 slave states eventually seceded while four "border states" with legalized slavery maintained their tenuous loyalty to the Union (Delaware, Kentucky, Maryland, and Missouri), the United States continued to fly the 34 star flag during the war symbolizing its refusal to recognize the Confederacy. By the end of the war, the United States flag displayed 36 stars to reflect the establishment of West Virginia when it broke away from Virginia in 1863, and the admission of Nevada in 1864.

The Union had virtually every resource advantage over the Confederacy at the start of the war. It was more industrialized, more commercialized, financially stronger, possessed nearly three times the railroad mileage, and boasted a population of about 23 million. The Confederacy, on the other hand, was predominantly a rural, agrarian society with a population of about nine million, nearly 3.5 million of whom were slaves. In terms of combat power, these differences represented a much greater potential and capacity for the Union to raise, equip, and support a larger Army over a sustained period of time. In spite of these differences, however, both the Union and Confederacy managed to raise armies of unprecedented sizes during the course of the war. From the American Army's modest, pre-war strength of about 16,000 soldiers, the Union produced roughly 2.2 million soldiers and the Confederacy nearly one million soldiers. The vast majority of these soldiers and their leaders on both sides were volunteers – along with conscripts later in the war – who formed around that small professional-Army nucleus. Both sides also soon recognized that armies of this size needed talented leadership in garrison and in combat.[2]

West Point again stepped up to provide the nation with leadership and its graduates played a central role in the war. If the Mexican War was the elementary-level validation of West Point's success in producing junior officers for combat, the Civil War proved to be the graduate-level validation reaffirming West Point's success in producing skilled combat leaders at every level. Approximately 895 West Point graduates collectively fought on both sides. This is a remarkable number given that by 1864, the Academy had only graduated 2,046 cadets since its founding in 1802; essentially 44 percent of the entire alumni filled the ranks of the Civil War armies.[3] On a more personal note, this small, close-knit fraternity of West Point graduates knew each other very well. Like the nation itself, West Point graduates and cadets chose sides. Classmates, close friends, relatives in some instances, and comrades who had fought beside each other in previous conflicts split their loyalties between North and South. In the process, they fought each other and mutually mourned the deaths of graduates killed on both sides.[4]

Academy graduates unsurprisingly found themselves occupying some of the highest positions at every level during the war, leading at the most critical junctures of the war, and constantly crossing paths throughout the war. Jefferson Davis (USMA 1828)

© 2013/Greg E. Mathieson Sr/MAI

served as President of the short-lived Confederate States of America (C.S.A.). Prior to the war, he had also served as a Representative and Senator from Mississippi, as well as the 23rd Secretary of War for the United States. The war's first shots came on April 12, 1861, at the direction of Brigadier General P.G.T. Beauregard, C.S.A. (USMA 1838), who had just recently resigned as the Academy's 12th Superintendent after less than a week in the position following Louisiana's secession, when he ordered the shelling of Fort Sumter, South Carolina. Coincidentally, Major Robert Anderson (USMA 1825), the Union Commanding Officer of Fort Sumter, had been Beauregard's artillery instructor at West Point. In that same engagement, Major General Abner Doubleday (USMA 1842), then a Captain and Anderson's second in command, fired the Union's first shot of the war in defense of the fort. After that initial contact, West Pointers continued to cross paths at every critical point of the war. Major General George B. McClellan (USMA 1846) turned back General Robert E. Lee, C.S.A. (USMA 1829) at the Battle of Antietam in September 1862, which served as the catalyst for Lincoln to issue his "Emancipation Proclamation." Major General George G. Meade (USMA 1835) defeated Lee at the Battle of Gettysburg in July 1863 to stem a second and final Confederate attempt to invade the North. General Ulysses S. Grant (USMA 1843) defeated Lieutenant General John C. Pemberton, C.S.A. (USMA 1837) in the Siege of Vicksburg in July 1863 to split the Confederacy in half. General William T. Sherman (USMA 1840) defeated General Joseph E. Johnston, C.S.A. (USMA 1829),

and Lieutenant General John B. Hood, C.S.A. (USMA 1853) in the Atlanta Campaign in September 1864 and sealed Lincoln's Presidential re-election. In that critical Presidential campaign, Lincoln defeated McClellan, who had campaigned as the Democratic candidate while still serving as a Major General in the Union Army. Ultimately, the war ended when Lee surrendered to Grant at Appomattox Court House on April 9, 1865. In total, West Point graduates directly influenced 60 major Civil War battles as 55 of those battles had graduates commanding both armies, while the remaining five had graduates commanding one side.

With the war over, America faced the daunting task of reconciling past differences and reconstructing the nation. The massive armies demobilized. While the United States Army decreased in size and focused on post-war occupation during Reconstruction, most former soldiers and officers transitioned to civilian life. Grant would eventually go to the White House as a two-term President from 1869 to 1877; Lee, on the other hand, would never be able to return to his Virginia home. Union Quartermaster General Montgomery C. Meigs (USMA 1836) established what would eventually become Arlington National Cemetery in 1864 when he used Lee's former estate to bury Union dead. Although some West Point graduates continued to serve the military at the highest levels, countless other graduates from both sides led the nation through this challenging time after they returned home. Many became become governors, senators, congressmen, ambassadors, diplomats, government officials, university presidents, philanthropists, and captains of industry as they navigated America through Reconstruction and reconciliation.

Just as West Point was one of the last institutions to part ways at the beginning of the war, it was one of the first to reunite after the war.[5] The Academy began readmitting cadets from the former Confederate states in 1868 in an attempt to foster reconciliation. The war that ended slavery was also a catalyst for major social changes at West Point like the rest of the nation when it admitted the first African-American cadet in 1870. By 1877, Henry O. Flipper, a former slave from Georgia, became the first African-American graduate. Upon his commissioning, he also led "Buffalo Soldiers" in the United States Army's famed 10th Cavalry as that unit's first non-white officer. Major General Oliver O. Howard (USMA 1854) also played a lead role in reshaping the social landscape of America during Reconstruction. Howard served as commissioner of the Freedmen's Bureau from 1865 to 1874, the organization charged with integrating former slaves into American society. Firmly believing that education was a critical factor for that integration, Howard founded the university that bears his name, Howard University, in March 1867 as one of the first post–Civil War Historically Black Colleges and Universities.

General George Washington Cullum (USMA 1833), the 16th Superintendent of West Point from 1864 to 1866, also proved to be a key, if not intentional, figure in the post-war reconciliation of West Point graduates. In 1850, Cullum began the monumental task of tracking and chronicling each graduate since the Academy's inception. He established what became known as the "Cullum Number." This number is the chronological number assigned to each graduate in each successive year, starting with the Academy's first graduate, George Swift (USMA 1802), who was assigned Cullum Number One. Following the war, Cullum insisted on excluding all graduates who resigned and fought for the South, but few graduates agreed with him. Instead, Cullum's exclusions inspired City College of New York President, Horace Webster (USMA 1818), to call for the creation of an alumni association. Graduates from both the Union and former Confederacy overwhelmingly responded and formed the Association of Graduates of the United States Military in 1869. Appropriately, the association selected Sylvanus Thayer (USMA 1808), the "Father of the Military Academy," as its first President.[6] West Point then continued Cullum's efforts, but for all graduates. This enduring tradition continues to link members of the Long Gray Line today with Swift and every previous graduate, all of whom are published in 10 volumes of Cullum's *Biographical Register of the Officers and Graduates of the United States Military Academy at West Point, New York*, and in the current descendent of Cullum's work, the *Register of Graduates*. Continuing this chronicle of West Point graduates regardless of their Civil War loyalties became particularly important in the post-war period. In essence, this symbolic gesture of

THE UNION

THE UNION (LEFT TO RIGHT)

General Ulysses S. Grant
USMA 1843
18th President of the United States

Major General George McClellan
USMA 1846
Governor of the State of New Jersey

Major General Ambrose Burnside
USMA 1847
United States Senator of the State of Rhode Island

Major General Joseph Hooker
USMA 1837

Major General George S. Meade
USMA 1835
Fort Meade, Maryland, named in his honor

General John Schofield
USMA 1853
Medal of Honor
Schofield Barracks, Hawaii, named in his honor

General Philip Sheridan
USMA 1853
Sheridan Tank Series named in his honor

Major General William T. Sherman
USMA 1840
Sherman Tanks Series named in his honor

Major General James McPherson
USMA 1853
Killed In Action Battle of Atlanta
McPherson Square, Washington, D.C., named in his honor

Major General George Henry Thomas
USMA 1840
Thomas Circle, Washington, D.C., named in his honor

Major General Oliver Howard
USMA 1840
Medal of Honor
Founder and President of Howard University

Major General John Buford
USMA 1848

Major General John Sedgewick
USMA 1837
Killed In Action at Battle of Spotsylvania

Brigadier General George Stoneman
USMA 1846
Governor of California

Brigadier General George Armstrong Custer
USMA 1861

Brigadier General Joshua Sill
USMA 1853
Killed In Action at Battle of Stones River
Fort Sill, Oklahoma, named in his honor

Major General Abner Doubleday
USMA 1842
Credited with Confederacy Inventing Baseball
Fired the first shots for the Union against the Confederacy at Fort Sumter

Senator Henry DuPont
USMA 1861
Medal of Honor
United States Senator of the State of Delaware

continuity and fraternity resonated with West Pointers by considering them West Point graduates first and foremost, rather than specifically as Union or former Confederate Officers.

In 1875, West Point held a 10-year anniversary on the Plain to commemorate the ending of the Civil War. The event culminated with former Union and Confederate graduates walking across the Plain to shake hands while cadets, such as Henry O. Flipper, likely watched. Other efforts to memorialize West Pointers from the Civil War – although less-inclusive because they focus specifically on Union graduates – include: Cullum Hall, the walls of its main ball room adorned with pictures and plaques in honor of numerous Civil War Generals; Sedgwick's Monument, erected in the honor of Union Major General John Sedgwick (USMA 1837), who was killed in May 1864 at the Battle of Spotsylvania Court House; and the Battle Monument, erected in honor of the Union's regular Army soldiers killed during the war. Most recently in October 2001, the Class of 1961 spearheaded the efforts to establish The Reconciliation Plaza commemorating the Class of 1861, along with West Point graduates in general, throughout the war and its aftermath. The memorial, located between Mahan Hall and Taylor Hall, includes a walking mall of 18 granite markers detailing the story from the beginning of the war through the 50th anniversary of the Battle of Gettysburg. Fittingly, the midpoint of the walking mall includes a bust of Grant facing south, and Lee facing north.[7]

In celebration of the Civil War's sesquicentennial and West Point's central role in the conflict, the History Channel created an interactive feature on its website with one section dedicated to "West Point Warriors." Some of the items noted in this section include[8]:

- 895 graduates served in the Civil War.

- 445 graduates served as General Officers: 294 for the Union and 151 for the Confederacy.

- 45 1861 graduates fought for the Union at the First Battle of Bull Run weeks after graduating

- 20 members of the Class of 1846 became General Officers – the highest of any pre-war class

- George Pickett (USMA 1846) and George A. Custer (USMA 1861) graduated last in their respective classes

Several of the West Point graduates highlighted in this book led the Union and Confederate Armies during the Civil War. They include:

THE CONFEDERATE STATES OF AMERICA (C.S.A.)

THE CONFEDERATE (LEFT TO RIGHT)

President Jefferson Davis, C.S.A.
USMA 1828
President of the Confederate States
of America

General Robert E. Lee, C.S.A.
USMA 1829
General In Chief of Confederate Forces
President of Washington & Lee University

General Joseph Johnston, C.S.A.
USMA 1829
United States Commissioner of Railroads

General P.G.T. Beauregard, C.S.A.
USMA 1838
Fired the first shots of the war and accepted the surrender of Union

General Braxton Bragg, C.S.A.
USMA 1837
Fort Bragg, North Carolina, named in his honor

Lieutenant General Simon B. Buckner, C.S.A.
USMA 1846
Governor of Kentucky

Lieutenant General James Longstreet, C.S.A.
USMA 1842
U.S. Minister to Ottoman Empire

Lieutenant General Leonidas Polk, C.S.A.
USMA 1827
Killed In Action at Battle of Atlanta
Fort Polk, Louisiana, named in his honor

Lieutenant General John Bell Hood, C.S.A.
USMA 1853
Fort Hood, Texas, named in his honor

Lieutenant General Ambrose P. Hill, C.S.A.
USMA 1847
Killed In Action at Third Battle of Petersburg

Major General Stonewall Jackson, C.S.A.
USMA 1846
Killed In Action at Battle of Chancellorsville
USS Stonewall Jackson nuclear submarine named in his honor

Major General George Pickett, C.S.A.
USMA 1846
Led "Pickett's Charge" at Gettysburg

Major General J.E.B. Stuart, C.S.A.,
USMA 1854
Killed In Action at Battle of Yellow Tavern
Stuart Tank Series named in his honor

THE GENEROUS DONORS TO WEST POINT

Written by: Greg Louks, USMA 1988.

Private Donor Leadership that Support the "Margin of Excellence" Making West Point the #1 Athletic Facilities of any University in the United States

West Point's Bicentennial Campaign was the first campaign for a federal service Academy and the first effort to raise a substantial amount of private funds. A comprehensive campaign comprising nearly 100 specific needs for its leadership, academic, and physical programs, its goals were threefold:

1. To raise $150 million in private support for West Point during the course of a five-year campaign.
2. To fully fund each campaign need.
3. To harness the success and momentum of a campaign to create a fund-raising mechanism able to generate at least $25 million each year after the conclusion of the campaign.

The necessity of significant private support for West Point was envisioned as early as 1986 by Lieutenant General Dave Palmer (USMA 1956), who developed the first Academy Needs Book when he was the Superintendent. General Palmer recognized that "Congressional appropriations might provide for a minimum level of sustainment, but would not provide for the pressing need to update its physical plant," particularly in the area of athletic facilities.

In 1997, the West Point Association of Graduates (WPAOG) launched the silent phase of the Bicentennial Campaign and assigned one of its directors, Greg Louks (USMA 1988), as the Campaign Manager. To address concern that a significant influx of private funding might further jeopardize Congressional appropriations, the WPAOG carefully defined the purpose for which private funds would be used:

Congressional appropriations would continue to fund the core needs of the United States Military Academy – those needs requisite to fulfilling its mission of graduating leaders of character with Bachelors of Science degrees and commissions in the United States Army.

Private gifts would be used to fund "Margin of Excellence" needs – those programs and facilities beyond the core needs of West Point for which appropriated funding was not available or not likely.

PRIVATE CONSTRUCTION ON FEDERAL PROPERTY

While comprehensive by definition, the West Point Bicentennial Campaign also included extensive funding for construction of new athletic facilities, including a press box, an athletic center, an indoor football practice facility, a crew and sailing center, an indoor tennis complex, an Olympic sports complex with practice facilities for gymnastics and women's basketball, a golf training center, and a rugby complex with practice and competition pitches, among numerous others; however, capital construction was not limited to athletic facilities. Private funds enabled construction of the Military Heritage Center, with museum-quality exhibit space and distant-learning capability; a skeet and trap lodge; a walkway connecting the new Randall Hall to the existing Holleder Center and in which was built a memorial to West Pointers' contributions during the Cold War; a high-tech classroom; various conference rooms; a state-of-the-art indoor shooting range; and others.

THE PROBLEM

Initially, the WPAOG limited its role to raising and proffering private funds to the United States government. Through a collaborative effort with West Point, the WPAOG would determine the specific amount of funds to be raised for particular facilities. Because the facilities were to be constructed on federal property, the United States Army Corps of Engineers was engaged under private contract by the WPAOG to manage design and construction, utilizing a design-bid-build delivery method.

Unfortunately, this method potentially jeopardized the Bicentennial Campaign. Projects bid through government procurement methods routinely exceeded by at least 40 percent the construction estimates on which fund-raising goals were based, representing numerous and deleterious implications. Concerned that cost overruns on privately funded facilities might give major donor prospects cold feet, the WPAOG Chairman, Jack Hammack (USMA 1949), and the WPAOG President, Seth Hudgins (USMA 1964), directed the Campaign Manager to intervene and find a way to solve the problem.

THE SOLUTION

Upon studying the problem, the WPAOG concluded that rather than proffering gifts of cash for capital construction, it should consider proffering completed construction as gifts in-kind. As a private entity utilizing private funding, the WPAOG – while beholden to West Point building and life-safety codes – was not beholden to standard government procurement policies. With approval from the Board of Directors, the WPAOG Chairman worked with Congress, the Secretary of the Army, the Army Chief of Staff, and the West Point Superintendent, who concurred with the proposal to build privately. While proffers for capital projects still were made to the United States government, they did not include cash. Instead, new proffers included designs, renderings, and certifications of availability of funds.

The WPAOG recognized that selection of the right design and construction team, possessing both competence and character, was integral to its success. Foregoing the construction industry's standard delivery methods, the WPAOG utilized a hybrid of the various models – loosely termed "bridging" – and hired under separate contracts a designer and a builder of its choice, who were engaged throughout design development and construction. Under this new process managed entirely by the WPAOG, the U.S. government formally ceded to the WPAOG the property on which a privately funded project was to be constructed. Upon completion, the facility was turned over to the United States government utilizing DD Form 1354, Transfer and Acceptance of Real Property.

Emboldened by the success of its first project, construction of the Hoffman Press Box, the WPAOG constructed more than a dozen projects valued at approximately $125 million, all of which were built on time and on or under budget with immediate return of construction contingencies. More importantly, the WPAOG was able to fast track construction and identify and hold costs from the onset of design, instilling renewed confidence in donors.

A SUCCESSFUL PUBLIC-PRIVATE PARTNERSHIP

At the conclusion of its campaign in 2002, the WPAOG succeeded in raising nearly a quarter-billion dollars, funded every single campaign need, and created a viable fund-raising mechanism that continued to raise more than $25 million each year. The success of West Point's Bicentennial Campaign cannot be understated, and its implications to other federal service academies cannot be ignored. Rather than jeopardize Congressional appropriations, West Point's success in private fund-raising was appreciated by the Congress, who noted the real commitment of its graduates and friends in preserving and improving that national institution. The Bicentennial Campaign forged a strong partnership between public and private funding that continues to benefit the Military Academy to this day.

In 2012, *Forbes Magazine* ranked West Point as the "#1 University in the United States for Athletic Facilities" out of 377 Universities surveyed. This is testament to the generous donors who made this possible and the USMA leadership that envisioned the need to go above and beyond Congressional funding. Private donors who wish to support the Margin of Excellence program at West Point the Association of Graduates can be contacted at 845-446-1500 or visit www.westpointaog.org.

Written by: Greg Louks, First Captain, USMA 1988, former Director, Association of Graduates. This book is not endorsed or sponsored by the West Point Association of Graduates (WPAOG) but encourages any American to give to this worthy cause.

Johnson Stadium at Doubleday Field.

Jewish Chapel.

Foley Athletic Center.

Caufield Crew & Sailing Center.

Anderson Rugby Complex.

Strength Development Center in the Kimsey Athletic Center.

Counter Terrorism Center.

Tronsrue Marksmanship Center.

Herbert Hall, the home of WPAOG.

Hoffman Press Box at Michie Stadium.

Gross Olympic Center.

Malek Tennis Center.

Lichtenberg Tennis Center.

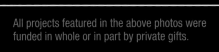

All projects featured in the above photos were funded in whole or in part by private gifts.

WEST POINT BEGINS THE "CLASS RING" TRADITION

American universities, high schools, and sports teams have a long and proud tradition of wearing rings to commemorate affiliations, graduations, and sports championships. While these rings are now a well-established tradition throughout both the academic and athletic worlds, the tradition started in 1835 at West Point. Three decades after West Point's establishment in 1802 as America's first engineering university, cadets in the Class of 1835 collaborated to design and create a ring to symbolize their unique bond as a class, their graduation achievement, and a permanent connection to their West Point roots. Thus, a tradition was born.

Since 1835, each West Point graduating class, with the exception of two, has come together to design and create a one-of-a-kind class ring depicting its unique story. The two exceptions to this tradition are the Class of 1836, which elected not to have a ring, and the Class of 1879, who chose cuff links instead.

West Point classes in those early years produced cadets who would later lead the Union and Confederate armies in America's bloodiest war – the Civil War. General George G. Meade, Class of 1835, for example, was among the first university-level graduates in America ever to wear a class ring (bio page 62). Twenty-eight years later, General Meade commanded the Union's Army of the Potomac at the Battle of Gettysburg in July 1863 and led it to victory over the Confederate Army of Northern Virginia, which was commanded by General Robert E. Lee, Class of 1829 (bio page 122). While the majority of Civil War Generals wore their West Point rings, Lee did not since the tradition had not yet started when he graduated.

Major General Joseph Hooker's Class of 1837 re-instituted the class ring tradition. Hooker would command the Union Army of the Potomac in 1863 (bio page 60) while his classmate, Major General Braxton Bragg, seceded with North Carolina and fought for the Confederacy. Fort Bragg, North Carolina, is named in his honor (bio page 126). General Ulysses S. Grant received his class ring in 1843 and would later lead the Union Army to victory in the Civil War. The ring then traveled with him to the White House where Grant served two terms as President of the United States (bio page 24).

The tradition of the West Point class ring continued into the Twentieth Century with the Class of 1915, also known as "the class the stars fell on" as 59 of its 164 members attained General Officer status. Rising to the very top was Dwight D. Eisenhower, who led the Allies to victory over the Germans in World War II and then also served two terms as President of the United States during the post-war prosperity of the 1950s (bio page 28).

Visitors to the Jefferson Hall Library at West Point have the privilege to see where the tradition of the West Point class ring also becomes legacy. Jefferson Hall houses a collection of class rings representing a major span of West Point's graduating classes since the class ring was institutionalized. Most notable among this collection are the rings from three of America's Five-Star Army Generals: General Douglas MacArthur, General Dwight D. Eisenhower (later President), and General Omar N. Bradley.

The legacy of the West Point class ring was further strengthened with a new tradition that involved the physical transfer of rings from past years to the present. Beginning with the Class of 2002's class rings, the West Point Association of Graduates Ring Memorial Program has provided several donated rings from previous graduates to be forged with the rings of the current year. This "Ring Melt" event mixes the melted gold from the annually donated rings with any remaining gold from each graduating year, and uses that mixture to cast the current class rings. A famous Academy credo states "At West Point, much of the history we teach was made by the people we taught." Through this Ring Melt program, West Point classes of the "Long Gray Line" are now physically connected through the tradition and legacy of the ring just as they are intellectually and emotionally connected through the significant historical actions of previous alumni.

The West Point class ring tradition remains as strong as ever. All four classes at the Academy have Ring and Crest Committees responsible for creating a unique class motto and designing a unique class crest for their respective classes, both of which will eventually don one side of the ring while the Academy crest dons the other side. This work starts at the beginning of the 4th Class, or freshman, year and culminates with First Class Cadets, or seniors, gathering with their family and friends during Ring Weekend. At Ring Weekend, cadets receive their well-earned and highly anticipated rings during a ceremonial process that also includes a banquet, guest speaker, and ball. In the end, the class ring is a constant reminder to each graduate of who they are, from where they graduated, and the institutional values they must uphold.

In January 1967, the National Football League played its first Super Bowl to crown a champion between the National Football League and the American Football League. Legendary head coach Vince Lombardi led the Green Bay Packers to that first Super Bowl championship. Following the victory, Coach Lombardi worked with Jostens to design that first Super Bowl championship ring. Coach Lombardi had been an assistant coach for five years at West Point under Coach Earl "Red" Blaik, and the West Point ring tradition undoubtedly influenced Lombardi's ring design for the 1967 Packers as the resulting championship ring closely resembled West Point class rings.

Coach Lombardi after winning Super Bowl I with the Green Bay Packers.

Coach Lombardi with Jostens's executives with the designs for the Super Bowl I ring.

Lombardi as West Point Football Coach.

In January 1967, Jostens worked with Coach Lombardi to design the first Super Bowl ring, which closely resembled the West Point rings. Vince Lombardi and his two Captains, tackle Bob Skoronski and defensive end Willie Davis, worked with Jostens designer Ken Westerlund to create the ring that tells the story of and commemorates the Super Bowl I championship. Jostens began selling class rings in 1906 and has been providing high-quality rings and yearbooks to high schools, colleges and sports teams for more than a century. Jostens is honored to sponsor *West Point Leadership: Profiles of Courage*.

THE BOY SCOUTS OF AMERICA

West Point exists to train leaders of character for our nation and is the premier leadership institute in the world. Many West Point graduates started their life in uniform by first donning the Cub Scout and Boy Scout uniforms to help them prepare for West Point. The Boy Scouts of America was formed in 1910 with the mission of preparing young people to make ethical and moral choices over their lifetime. There have been more than 110 million members, including many of West Point's most successful graduates. The following West Point graduates are profiled in this book *West Point Leadership: Profiles of Courage* and were proudly involved with the Boy Scouts of America.

MEMBERS OF THE EXECUTIVE BOARD, BOY SCOUTS OF AMERICA

President Dwight David Eisenhower, USMA 1915

William Murdy, USMA 1964, Chairman Comfort Systems USA (NYSE: FIX)

EAGLE SCOUTS

Colonel (USMC, Retired) Marsh Carter, USMA 1962, Chairman, New York Stock Exchange Group (NYSE)

William Murdy, USMA 1964, Chairman Comfort Systems USA (NYSE: FIX)

Dr. Thor Sundt, USMA 1952, Former Chairman, Mayo Clinic Department of Neurosurgery

Rear Admiral Mike Shelton, USMA 1967, Founder of the Modern Seabees, U.S. Navy

Lieutenant Colonel Paul Finken, USMA 1989

General William Westmoreland, Commanding General, Vietnam War

BOY SCOUTS

General Lloyd Austin, USMA 1975, Commander Central Command (CENTCOM)

Brigadier General Pete Dawkins, USMA 1959, Heisman Trophy Winner

Joe DePinto, USMA 1986, Chief Executive Officer, 7-Eleven Corporation (NYSE: SE)

General Keith Alexander, USMA 1974, Commander, CYBERCOMMAND

Paul Bucha, USMA 1965, Medal of Honor Recipient

Alex Gorsky, USMA 1982, Chairman, Chief Executive Officer and President, Johnson & Johnson (NYSE: JNJ)

Tim Tyson, USMA 1974, Chairman, Aptuit

Ken Hicks, USMA 1974, Chief Executive Officer Foot Locker, Inc. (NYSE: FL)

Tony Guzzi, USMA 1986, Chief Executive Officer, EMCOR Group

General John Abizaid, USMA 1973, Commander, Central Command (CENTCOM)

Bob MacDonald, USMA 1975, Chairman, President and Chief Executive Officer, Procter & Gamble (P&G)

Colonel Lee Van Arsdale, USMA 1974, Delta Force Squadron Commander

Lieutenant General Tom McInerney, USMA 1959, USAF Fighter Pilot and Commander

General Fred Franks, USMA 1959, Commander, VII Corps Desert Storm

Lieutenant General Robert Foley, USMA 1962, Medal of Honor Recipient

Senator Jack Reed (D-Rhode Island), USMA 1971

General David Petraeus, USMA 1974, Commander of the Wars in both Iraq and Afghanistan

Colonel James "Nick" Rowe, USMA 1960, Prisoner of War, Escaped after five years, Vietnam

General Eric Shinseki, USMA 1965, Secretary of the Veterans Administration

Fred Malek, Former Chief Executive Officer Marriott International and Northwest Airlines

General Barry McCaffrey, USMA 1964, Presidential Cabinet Member

Captain John Ryan Dennison, USMA 2004

In 2010, Jostens collaborated with the Boy Scouts of America to design and offer personalized Eagle Scout and Wood Rings. Jostens is a proud sponsor of *West Point Leadership: Profiles of Courage* and proud to provide the Boy Scouts of America with rings to remember their lineage, and their association with the former Boy Scouts who are profiled in this book.

As the world's premier leadership institution, West Point's mission is to train commissioned leaders of character for service to the nation. As an organization, the Boy Scouts of America's (BSA) mission is also character-centric as it strives to prepare its members to make moral and ethical choices over their lifetimes by instilling in them the values of the Scout Oath, values also consistent with those instilled at West Point. Thus, the historical relationship between West Point and Scouting is not surprising with many of West Point's graduates first donning Scouting uniforms before entering the Academy. Over 110 million young people have been members of the BSA since its founding in 1910, to include a number of West Point's most successful graduates.[1] This book profiles twenty nine of them who were proudly involved in Scouting before entering West Point.

While numerous former Scouts had always attended West Point, the Academy's Scoutmasters' Council was formally established in 1961 as an official club that enabled cadets to continue their participation in and association with scouting while at the Academy. At that time, nearly 50% of the Corps of Cadets were Eagle Scouts. William J. Dieal, a junior ("Cow") in the Class of 1962, founded the club as a cadet after he had approached the Superintendent, Lieutenant General William J. Westmoreland (USMA 1936), with a group of his friends to seek authorization to conduct the 1st Annual West Point Camporee at Stillwell Lake in late April 1961. Westmoreland, who coincidentally was an Eagle Scout as well as a member of East Coast BSA Organization's Executive Board, readily approved Cadet Dieal's plan. That year, five Boy Scout Troops attended the initial Camporee. The next year as a senior ("Firstie"), Cadet Dieal again organized the 2nd Annual West Point Camporee in late April 1962 at Stillwell Lake. This time, fifteen Boy Scout Troops attended. The year after Cadet Dieal graduated from the Academy, the 3rd Annual West Point Camporee in April 1963 was moved to Lake Frederick where it remains to this day.

Since then, the United States Military Academy has hosted the Annual West Point Invitation Scout Camporee for members of the Boy Scouts of America (BSA), Girl Scouts of America (GSA), and BSA Venturing Crews across the nation. Interestingly, Girl Scouts were invited to the Camporee at about the same time the Academy began admitting women. In the late 1970s, Troop 999 from New Jersey applied for invitation to the West Point Camporee, and was accepted by the Scoutmasters' Council without knowing that the troop was a Girl Scout Troop. Since then, Girls Scouts have been invited, along with Venturing Crews, which were founded in 1998.

West Point's Camporee has become the nation's largest annual Scout Camporee (the BSA National Jamboree is larger but occurs every four years) and now hosts over 4,000 campers annually. With the number of campers exceeding a brigade-sized unit, the annual Camporee at Lake Frederick requires meticulous planning and execution by over 200 cadets in the Scoutmasters' Council.

The Scoutmasters' Council thrives as a result of its rich history and works every year to make the Annual West Point Invitation Scout Camporee better than the previous year. The club organizes itself in the same manner as a military brigade staff and consists of cadets occupying positions of leadership and administrative responsibilities to include Commander, Deputy Commander, Executive Officer, Command Sergeant Major, and primary staff functional areas (personnel administration, operations, supply, etc). During the 52nd Annual Camporee in 2013, a record 5,500 Scouts attended. The annual Camporee has evolved into a weekend-long event in which Scout Troops experience a variety of military and Scouting -based competitions and sites to include: land navigation, first aid, weapons safety and maintenance, zodiac boat race, fire building, military drill, and physical fitness. The Camporee also includes military equipment static displays, mock demonstrations of military operations such as air assault missions with helicopters, a large bonfire, and a military review parade involving the Academy leadership.

Scouting's influence in preparing and shaping young men and women before they enter the Academy remains strong — nearly 20% of the Corps of Cadets are Eagle Scout or Gold Award (Girl Scout equivalent) recipients, and 40% have some former experience in the Scouting program.[2] The Academy further recognizes the importance of that relationship and continues to highly value cadet participation in Scouting with the annual presentation of the Captain Christopher B. Johnson Award to the graduating cadet who contributes the most to Scouting while at West Point. Johnson, who was killed in action in Baghdad, Iraq on 16 October 2004, was a member of the Class of 1998 and the Commander of Scoutmasters' Council as a Firstie. West Point Scouting's "founding father," now-retired Colonel William J. Dieal Jr., continues to be an active member of the Scoutmasters' Council. Dieal, a resident of Cinnaminson, New Jersey and member of the West Point Society of Philadelphia, frequently attends the Camporee every year and also presents another award, the William J. Dieal Memorial Award in honor of his father, to a First Class Cadet making a significant contribution to Scouting while at the Academy.[3] In addition to the annual awards, West Point has also held two special Camporees in honor of former cadet members of the Scoutmasters' Council who have been killed in action in Iraq and Afghanistan. The 43rd Annual Camporee in 2005 memorialized Captain Johnson, while the 51st Annual Camporee memorialized Second Lieutenant David Rylander, Class of 2011, who served as the Scoutmasters' Council Assistant Operations Officer as a Firstie and was killed in action in Afghanistan on 2 May 2012.[4]

ARMY MEDAL OF HONOR

During the American Civil War, Congress created the Army Medal of Honor on February 17, 1862, for those who distinguished themselves in battle. President Abraham Lincoln signed the bill into law on July 12, 1862, and the Army Medal of Honor became official. Since then, the Medal of Honor has become America's highest award for military valor for those who have performed acts of such courageous gallantry so much that they rise "above and beyond the call of duty." In short, there is no higher symbol of American heroism. Eighty-three West Point graduates or former cadets have received the Medal of Honor. There are now three different Medals of Honor: Army, Navy, and Air Force. West Point graduates have earned all three: First Lieutenant Frank Reasoner, USMC, was awarded the Navy Medal of Honor (posthumous); and Colonel William A. Jones, III, USAF, was awarded the Air Force Medal of Honor. The other 81 awards were all Army Medals of Honor. There are only two living West Point graduates who have been awarded the Medal of Honor: Lieutenant General Robert Foley and Captain Paul "Buddy" Bucha. There are only 80 living Medal of Honor recipients from all services as of the writing of this book in May 2013.

The Congressional Medal of Honor Foundation was founded by the Congressional Medal of Honor Society, which consists exclusively of the living Medal of Honor recipients. The Foundation is an IRS 501(c)(3) non-profit with Tax ID #25-1828488.

The foundation, in conjunction with the Congressional Medal of Honor Society, must reach out to the citizens of America, particularly its youth, to promote an awareness of what the Medal of Honor represents and how ordinary Americans through courage, sacrifice, selfless service, and patriotism can challenge fate and change the course of history.

There are no better Ambassadors to take this message to the American people than the Medal of Honor recipients themselves who embody these values through their incredible acts of bravery. The work of the foundation is aimed at promoting awareness of what America's highest military award for valor in combat represents.

Jostens is honored to support both the Medal of Honor Society and the Medal of Honor Foundation by supporting two programs: the Medal of Honor Society Ring and the Medal of Honor Character Development Program.

The Medal of Honor Character Development Program: Lessons of Personal Bravery and Self-Sacrifice is a resource designed by teachers for the Congressional Medal of Honor Foundation (www.cmohfoundation.org) to provide students with opportunities to explore the important concepts of courage, commitment, sacrifice, patriotism, integrity, and citizenship and how these values can be exemplified in daily life. The free program was designed for use in a variety of educational purposes by teachers in any school system in middle and high school. Schools may also video conference with a Medal of Honor recipient.

The Medal of Honor Society Ring, created by Jostens, is a symbol of heroism in honor of the sacrifices of all those who have served and continue to serve around the world. It is only to be worn by Medal of Honor Recipients.

Courtesy Jostens

WEST POINT GRADUATES AND FORMER CADETS WHO HAVE RECEIVED THE MEDAL OF HONOR

Brigadier General John C. Robinson, Former Member of USMA 1839, Laurel Hill, Virginia

Brigadier General John P. Hatch, USMA 1845, U.S. Volunteers, South Mountain, Maryland

Colonel Orlando B. Wilcox, USMA 1847, Bull Run, Virginia

Brigadier General Absalom Baird, USMA 1849, Jonesboro, Georgia

Brigadier General Rufus Saxton, Jr., Class of 1849, Harper's Ferry, Virginia

Colonel Eugene A. Carr, USMA 1850, Pea Ridge, Arkansas

Major General David S. Stanley, USMA 1852, Franklin, Tennessee

Major General John M. Schofield, USMA 1853, Wilson's Creek, Missouri

Brigadier General Oliver O. Howard, USMA 1854, Fair Oaks, Virginia

Major Oliver D. Greene, USMA 1854, Antietam, Maryland

Colonel Zenas R. Bliss, USMA 1854, Fredericksburg, Virginia

Brigadier General Alexander S. Webb, USMA 1855, Gettysburg, Pennsylvania

Captain Abraham K. Arnold, USMA 1859, Davenport Bridge, Virginia

Captain Horace Porter, USMA 1860, Chickamauga, Georgia

First Lieutenant John M. Wilson, USMA 1860, Malvern Hill, Virginia

Captain Henry A. DuPont, USMA 1861, Cedar Creek, Virginia

First Lieutenant Adelbert Ames, USMA 1861, Bull Run, Virginia

First Lieutenant Samuel N. Benjamin, USMA 1861, Bull Run-Spotsylvania, Virginia

Colonel Guy V. Henry, USMA 1861, Cold Harbor, Virginia

Major Eugene B. Beaumont, USMA 1861, Harpeth River, Tennessee

First Lieutenant George L. Gillespie, USMA 1862, Bethesda Church, Virginia

First Lieutenant William H.H. Benyaurd, USMA 1863, Five Forks, Virginia

First Lieutenant William S. Beebe, USMA 1863, Cane River Crossing, Louisiana

Captain Edward S. Godfrey, USMA 1867, Bear Paw, Montana

First Lieutenant William P. Hall, USMA 1868, Near White Rive, Colorado

Private John G. Bourke, USMA 1869, Stones River, Tennessee

Captain William E. Birkhimer, USMA 1870, Luzon, Philippines

Second Lieutenant Edward J. McClernand, USMA 1870, Bear Paw Mountain, Montana

Second Lieutenant Robert G. Carter, USMA 1870, Brazos River, Texas

Captain John B. Kerr, USMA 1870, White River, South Dakota

Captain Charles A. Varnum, USMA 1872, White Clay Creek, South Carolina

First Lieutenant Frank West, USMA 1872, Big Dry Wash, Arizona

First Lieutenant William H. Carter, USMA 1873, Cibicu, Arizona

First Lieutenant Marion P. Maus, USMA 1874, Sierra Madre Mountains, Mexico

Second Lieutenant Oscar F. Long, USMA 1876, Bear Paw, Montana

First Lieutenant Ernest A. Garlington, USMA 1876, Wounded Knee, South Dakota

Lieutenant Colonel James Parker, USMA 1876, Vigon, Luzon, Philippines

First Lieutenant John C. Gresham, USMA 1876, Wounded Knee Creek, South Dakota

First Lieutenant Wilber E. Wilder, USMA 1877, Horshoe Canyon, New Mexico

Second Lieutenant Robert T. Emmet, USMA 1877, Las Animas Canyon, New Mexico

Second Lieutenant Matthias W. Day, USMA 1877, Las Animas Canyon, New Mexico

Colonel Franklin Bell, USMA 1878, Porac, Luzon, Philippines

Second Lieutenant Thomas Cruse, USMA 1879, Big Dry Fork, Arizona

Second Lieutenant Lloyd M. Brett, USMA 1879, O'Fallon's Creek, Montana

Captain Albert Mills, USMA 1879, Near Santiago, Cuba

Captain Hugh J. McGrath, USMA 1880, Luzon, Philippines

Second Lieutenant George M. Morgan, USMA 1880, Big Dry Fork, Arizona

Second Lieutenant George R. Burnett, USMA 1880, Cuchillo Negro Mountains, New Mexico

Captain William H. Sage, USMA 1882, Luzon, Philippines

First Lieutenant John W. Heard, USMA 1883, Cuba

Second Lieutenant Powhatan H. Clarke, USMA 1884, Sonora, Mexico

Major John A. Logan, Former Member USMA 1887, San Jacinco, Philippines (posthumous)

Second Lieutenant Robert L. Howze, USMA 1888, White River, South Carolina

First Lieutenant Louis B. Lawton, USMA 1893, Tientsin, China

Second Lieutenant Charles D. Roberts, USMA 1897, El Caney, Cuba

Second Lieutenant Ira C. Welborn, USMA 1898, Santiago, Cuba

First Lieutenant Louis J. Van Schaick, Batangas, Philippines

Lieutenant Colonel Emory J. Pike, USMA 1901, Vandieres, France (posthumous)

Captain Eli T. Fryer, Former Member USMA 1901, Vera Cruz, Mexico

General of the Army Douglas MacArthur, USMA 1903, Bataan, Philippines

Second Lieutenant Arthur H. Wilson, USMA 1904, Patian Islands, Philippines

Musician Calvin P. Titus, USMA 1905, Peking, China 1900

Lieutenant Jonathan M. Wainwright, USMA 1906, Philippines

Second Lieutenant John T. Kennedy, USMA 1908, Philippines

Colonel William H. Wilbur, USMA 1912, French Morocco

Colonel Demas T. Craw, USMA 1924, French Morocco (posthumous)

Colonel Leon W. Johnson, USMA 1926, Ploesti, Romania

Brigadier General Frederick W. Castle, USMA 1930, Over Germany (posthumous)

Lieutenant Colonel Robert G. Cole, USMA 1839, Carentan, France (posthumous)

Lieutenant Colonel Leon R. Vance, USMA 1939, Wimereaux, France

Second Lieutenant Alexander R. Ninenger, USMA 1941, Bataan, Philippines (posthumous)

Captain Michael J. Daly, Former Member USMA 1945, Nuremberg, Germany

Colonel William A. Jones, III, USMA 1945, Near Dong Hai, Vietnam, Air Force Medal of Honor

First Lieutenant Samuel S. Coursen, USMA 1949, Near Kaesong, Korea (posthumous)

First Lieutenant Richard T. Shea, USMA 1852, Near Sokkogae, Korea (posthumous)

Lieutenant Colonel Andre C. Lucas, USMA 1954, Firebase Ripcord, Vietnam (posthumous)

Captain Humbert R. Versace, USMA 1959, Thoi Binh District, Vietnam (posthumous)

Captain Roger H. Donlon, Former Member USMA 1959, Near Nam Dong, Vietnam

First Lieutenant Frank S. Reasoner, USMC, USMA 1962, Near Da Nang, Vietnam, Navy Medal of Honor (posthumous)

Major Robert R. Foley, USMA 1963, Near Quan Dau Tieng, Vietnam

Captain Paul W. Bucha, USMA 1965, Binh Duong Province, Vietnam

First Lieutenant James A. Gardner, Former Member USMA 1965, My Cahn, Vietnam (posthumous)

Make History

THE THAYER *Hotel* AT WEST POINT

COME AND SEE OUR "MUSEUM" DEDICATED TO THE MOST INSPIRATIONAL GRADUATES OF WEST POINT

We are pleased to announce that the start of our **Room Dedication Program at The Historic Thayer Hotel at West Point** has been a tremendous success! Corporations, individuals, families and West Point classes have come together to dedicate rooms to our honored leaders.

The Historic Thayer Hotel at West Point is a **national historic landmark** that has hosted five US Presidents and countless world leaders and decision makers.

The Hotel recently completed a **multimillion dollar renovation** inclusive of new elaborate high tech meeting and conference rooms and inspirational hallways and displays, **adding 23 Executive Suites**.

These fabulous enhancements have brought this historic property into the modern world of **high-tech conference capabilities,** while restoring the hotel's **old-world grandeur** and inspirational beauty.

West Point has produced US Presidents, foreign heads of state, warrior leaders, astronauts and Captains of Industry. Each beautifully appointed guest room will be dedicated to an inspirational and distinguished graduate of West Point. Customized décor reflects the accomplishments of each named honoree who has made significant contributions to the nation and the world. These dedicated rooms embrace occupants with an abundance of **luxury**, high-tech convenience and **reflective inspiration**.

All **chosen honorees** become part of the storied hotel's history.

These dedicated rooms are enjoyed by world leaders, dignitaries, Academy recruits, cadet parents, returning war heroes, active duty officers and enlisted troops, tourists, and business leaders. **Decision makers in all aspects of world affairs coming to West Point, will see and reflect on both the honorees and the listed sponsors of these rooms.**

Sponsors of the rooms have a **special dedication area in the hallways of the Hotel** outside of the dedicated room. The opportunity for industry sponsors to connect on a deep emotional level with key decision makers from every sector of the economy is extraordinary.

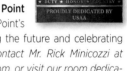

The **Historic Thayer Hotel at West Point** is honored to build awareness of West Point's most accomplished individuals, benefitting the future and celebrating the past. *For more information please contact Mr. Rick Minicozzi at* rick.minicozzi@thayerleaderdevelopment.com. *or visit our room dedication web site at* rdp.thethayerhotel.com.

PARTIAL LIST OF ROOM DEDICATION HONOREES

General Douglas MacArthur, 1903
General Martin Dempsey, 1974
General Anthony McAuliffe, 1919
General Fred Franks, 1959
General Barry McCaffrey, 1964
General Roscoe Robinson Jr., 1951
General Wayne Downing, 1962
General George Alfred Joulwan, 1961
Lieutenant General Harold Moore Jr., 1945
Lieutenant General John H. Moellering, 1959
Major General Frederick A Gorden, 1962
Brigadier General Rebecca Halstead, 1981

Brigadier General Robert McDermott, 1943
Brigadier General Robert Neyland, 1916
Brigadier General Pete Dawkins, 1959
Colonel David "Mickey" Marcus, 1924
Colonel Buzz Aldrin, 1951
Colonel Lee Van Arsdale, 1974
Colonel James "Nick" Rowe, 1960
Dr. Thoralf Sundt, 1952
Mr. Henry O. Flipper, 1877
Mr. Lee Anderson, 1961
Mr. Dana Mead, 1957
Mr. James Kimsey, 1962
Secretary James Nicholson, 1961
Ambassador Michael A. Sheehan, 1977

PARTIAL LIST OF HONOREES AWAITING DEDICATION SPONSORSHIP

President Ulysses S. Grant, 1843
President Dwight D Eisenhower, 1915
Secretary Alexander Haig, 1947
General John J. Pershing, 1886
General Hap Arnold, 1907
General Omar Bradley, 1915
General Norman Schwarzkopf, 1956
General Maxwell Taylor, 1922
General Benjamin O. Davis, 1936
General Creighton Abrams, 1936
General Raymond Odierno, 1976

General Lloyd Austin, 1975
Lieutenant General Leslie Groves, 1918
Lieutenant General Vincent Brooks, 1980
Lieutenant General Brent Scowcroft, 1947
Captain Dennis Michie 1892
Colonel Frank Borman, 1950
Major General George Meade, 1835
Major General George W Goethals, 1880
Major General Luis Esteves, 1915
Major Andrew Rowan, 1890
Colonel Kristin Baker, 1990
Colonel Felix "Doc" Blanchard, 1947
Ms. Andrea Lee Hollen, 1980
Mr. Simon Levy, 1802

A LANDMARK ON THE HUDSON. WHERE HISTORY IS MADE. WEST POINT, NY • WWW.THETHAYERHOTEL.COM • 800-247-5047

THAYER LEADER DEVELOPMENT GROUP AT WEST POINT

As graduates and former leaders of the U.S. Military Academy at West Point, we intimately understand the need to bring more visitors to West Point. Increasing tourism to West Point is in the best interests of the U.S. Military Academy, the U.S. Army and the nation.

Reaching out to the public and gaining exposure to our Alma Mater will help increase applications from the best and the brightest, and help bring potential financial contributors to West Point to help maintain our margin of excellence in academics, physical training and the moral development of tomorrow's leaders of character.

Making a meaningful impact on guests begins with their stay at The Historic Thayer Hotel at West Point. To achieve this, the Hotel has recently undergone a multi-million dollar renovation including the addition of 23 new executive suites and is show casing some of our most inspirational graduates through a room dedication program in which each guest room is named after a graduate. Learn more about the room dedication program at **rdp.thethayerhotel.com**

Yet, most important is the founding of the **Thayer Leader Development Group at West Point** (TLDG). TLDG has hosted corporate conferences and leadership training for hundreds of companies at The Historic Thayer Hotel at West Point. Most executives attending these programs have never had any military experience or

exposure to West Point. These executives are walking away from their experience at TLDG with a new found love and respect for the Armed Forces of the United States and the great work being done here at West Point. Many senior management teams in the Fortune 500 have now visited West Point to either host their own corporate conference at The Hotel or to attend leadership training at TLDG. The average rating from C-Suite executives from these great corporations is 9.5 out of 10 in terms of content, faculty, facilities and overall atmosphere of the program.

We encourage all graduates to bring your friends, family and business teams to West Point for either corporate conferences or tourism…

We are confident that TLDG will add value to your team and will also significantly contribute to enhancing West Point's image throughout this great country. Contact Rick Minicozzi, '86, Managing General Partner, **rick.minicozzi@thayerleaderdevelopment.com** or Bill Murdy, '64, Chairman of the Board, **wfmurdy@thayerleaderdevelopment.com** to discuss how TLDG can tailor a program that suits your organization's needs.

The seven of us encourage all graduates to bring your friends, family and business teams to West Point for either corporate conferences or tourism, to ensure that USMA's reputation continues to be lauded throughout the United States. These are the ideas and the results that we, as former leaders of West Point, envisioned when The Historic Thayer Hotel was privatized.
GO ARMY!

RESPECTFULLY,

LTG (ret) Dan Christman	**LTG (ret) Buster Hagenbeck**	**LTG (ret) Bill Lennox**	**LTG (ret) John Moellering**	**BG (ret) Fletcher Lamkin**	**Mr. Tom Dyer**	**Mr. Jack Hammack**
Former Superintendent of West Point	Former Superintendent of West Point	Former Superintendent of West Point	Former Commandant of Cadets at West Point	Former Dean of Academic Board at West Point	Former Chairman of the Board, Association of Graduates	Former Chairman of the Board, Association of Graduates

| USMA '65 | USMA '71 | USMA '71 | USMA '59 | USMA '64 | USMA '67 | USMA '49 |

SOURCES

THE FOLLOWING PROFILES WERE
BASED ON PERSONAL INTERVIEWS
AND E-MAIL CORRESPONDENCE
BETWEEN THE WPLPOC AND
EACH NOTED INDIVIDUAL:

McInerney, Thomas
Mackin, Pat
Cannon, Steve
DePinto, Joe
Gorsky, Alex
MacDonald, Bob
Meigs, Monty
Murdy, Bill
Carter, Marsh
Anderson, Lee
Malek, Fred
Moellering, John
Kilkelly, Kevin
McCormick, David
Guzzi, Tony
Garrison, John
Viola, Vinnie
Hicks, Ken
Tyson, Tim
Caufield, Frank
Kimsey, Jim
Dawkins, Pete
Krzyzewski, Mike
Figueres, Jose
Bucha, Paul
Barno, Dave
Van Arsdale, Lee
Franks, Fred
Moore, Hal
Kurilla, Erik
Hagenbeck, Buster
Downing, Wayne
Abizaid, John
Sundt, Thor (family interviews)
Savory, Doc
Baker, Kristin
Tien, John
Brooks, Vince
Halstead, Rebecca
Shelton, Mike
Gorden, Fred
McCaffrey, Barry
Pompeo, Mike
Shimkus, John
Young, Elizabeth
Nagl, John
Filippelli, Guy
McChrystal, Stanley
Odierno, Raymond
Austin, Lloyd
Petraeus, David
Eikenberry, Karl
Clark, Wesley
Nicholson, James

COVERS

Front Cover Photos
DePinto: AP
Buzz: NASA
Kristin: NARA
Dempsey: © 2013/Greg E. Mathieson Sr./MAI
Coach K: Duke
Austin: DOD

Back Cover Photos
Carter: NYSE
Benjamin Davis: DOD
Bob McDonald: Courtesy Procter & Gamble
Odierno: DOD
Halstead: DOD
Hicks: Foot Locker

PREFACE - WEST POINT LEADERSHIP: PROFILES OF COURAGE: PAGE #4
[1] United States Military Academy Mission (USMA) Statement as noted on the USMA website: http://www.usma.edu/about/SitePages/Mission.aspx, accessed on March 18, 2013.

CHAPTER INTRODUCTIONS

Page #14: The Founding Fathers of West Point
[1] Francis Casimir Kajencki, *Thaddeus Kosciuszko: Military Engineer of the American Revolution* (El Paso, Texas: Southwest Polonia Press, 1998), 81; Theodore J. Crackel, *West Point: A Bicentennial History* (Lawrence: University of Kansas Press, 2002), 5.

[2] Stephen E. Ambrose, *"Duty, Honor, Country": A History of West Point* (Baltimore: Johns Hopkins Press, 1966), 7; Crackel, 5.

[3] Crackel, 45–48, 59.

Page #38: The Chairman of the Joint Chiefs
[1] Encyclopedia Britannia

Page #340 The Fields of Friendly Strife
[1] Robert Cowley and Thomas Guinzburg eds., *West Point: Two Centuries of Honor and Tradition* (New York: Warner Books, 2002), 172–173.

Page #370: Captains of Industry
DePinto biography written by WPLPOC after phone conversation and e-mail correspondence with Mr. DePinto and the 7-Eleven staff. All photos provided by 7-Eleven with permission to use.

Cannon biography written by WPLPOC after interview at MBUSA in New Jersey with follow-up e-mail and phone conversations. All photos provided by Mr. Cannon and MBUSA with permission to use.

Hicks biography written by WPLPOC after meeting in Foot Locker New York City offices and follow-up e-mail and phone conversations with Foot Locker staff. All photos provided by Mr. Hicks and Foot Locker with permission to use.

Murdy biography written by WPLPOC after in-person meetings and e-mail and phone conversations. All photos provided by Mr. Murdy and Comfort Systems USA with permission to use.

Malek biography written by WPLPOC after phone interview and e-mail correspondence. All photos provide by Mr. Malek and Thayer Capital with permission to use.

Anderson biography written by WPLPOC after phone interview and e-mail correspondence. All photos provided by Mr. Anderson and API with permission to use.

General Meigs biography written by WPLPOC after phone interviews and e-mail correspondence. All photos provided by General Meigs, AP, and BENS with permission to use.

Guzzi biography written by WPLPOC after in-person interview in New York City and follow-up e-mail correspondence. All photos provided by Mr. Guzzi and EMCOR with permission to use.

McCormick biography written by WPLPOC after in-person interview in Stamford, Connecticut and follow-up e-mail correspondence with McCormick and his staff. All photos provided by McCormick and Bridgewater with permission to use.

Kilkelly biography written by WPLPOC after in-person interview in Orlando, Florida, and follow-up e-mail and phone correspondence. All photos provided by Mr. Kilkelly and SolarWorld USA with permission to use.

Caufield biography written by WPLPOC in coordination with Mr. Caufield's staff at KPCB. All photo rights given to use.

Tyson biography written by WPLPOC after interview with Mr. Tyson and follow-up e-mail correspondence. All photos provide by Mr. Tyson and APTUIT with permission to use.

Garrison biography written by WPLPOC after phone interview and follow-up e-mail correspondence. All bios provided by Mr. Garrison and Bell Helicopter with permission to use.

Lichtenberg biography written by WPLPOC with support from Mr. Louis Gross.

Gross biography written by WPLPOC after telephone interview and e-mail correspondence with Mr. Gross.

David Kim biography written by WPLPOC after phone interview and follow-up e-mail correspondence. All photos provided by David Kim, APAX, and Children of the Fallen Patriots Foundation with permission to use.

William Foley bio written by WPLPOC. Attempts were made to get edited by Mr. Foley were unsuccessful.

Dr. Nagl biography written by WPLPOC after phone interview and e-mail correspondence. All photos provided by Dr. Nagl with permission to use.

Guy Filippelli biography written by WPLPOC after in-person interview and e-mail correspondence. All photos provided by Mr. Filippelli with permission to use.

Liz McNally biography written by Dr. John Nagl, her Rhodes Scholar mentor. All photos provided by McNally with permission to use.

Moellering biography written by WPLPOC after phone and in-person meetings with Lieutenant General Moellering. All photos provided by Lieutenant General Moellering and USAA with permission to use.

Alden Patridge photos provided by Norwich University with permission to use.

Lieutenant General Harmon biography written by Dr. Tim Kane, and Air Force Academy graduate.

Dr. Freed biography written by WPLPOC after phone interview and e-mail correspondence with Dr. Freed.

Page #446: The Educators
Hana R. Alberts, "America's Best College: How West Point Beats the Ivy League," in *Forbes Magazine* online, August 24, 2009, at http://www.forbes.com/forbes/2009/0824/colleges-09-education-west-point-america-best-college.html accessed on March 23, 2013.

PROFILES

Page #16: President George Washington
[1] Henry F. Graff, ed. *The Presidents: A Reference History, 2nd Ed.* "George Washinton," by Jacob E. Cook (New York: Simon and Schuster, 1997), 2; John Mack Farragher, ed. *The Encyclopedia of Colonial and Revolutionary America.* "George Washington," by Robert K. Wright, Jr. (New York: De Capo Press, 1996), 443–444; Stephen E. Ambrose. *Duty, Honor, Country: A History of West Point* (Baltimore: The Johns Hopkins Press, 1966), 10–12.

[2] James Thomas Flexner. *Washington: The Indispensable Man* (New York: Little, Brown, and Company, 1974), 3–9; Cook, 2.

[3] Wright, 443; Cooke, 2.

[4] Flexner, 39–41; Cooke, 2; Wright, 444.

[5] Wright, 444; Flexner, 176–178.

[6] Wright, 444; Cooke, 3–19; Flexner, 243–47.

[7] Cooke, 20.

[8] Flexner, 399.

[9] Center for Military History (CMH) website Frequently Asked Questions – see http://www.history.army.mil/html/faq/5star.html (accessed April 21, 2013).

Page #18: President Thomas Jefferson
[1] Merrill D. Peterson, *Introduction to The Portable Thomas Jefferson, xi–xli* (New York: Penguin Books, 1975), xiii–xv.

[2] Peterson, xvi–xvii.

[3] *Ibid.,* xxi–xxii.

[4] Robert Middlekauff, *The Glorious Cause: The American Revolution, 1763–1789* Revised and Expanded Edition (New York: Oxford University Press, 2005), 579–581.

[5] Peterson, xxv–xxx.

[6] Fred Anderson and Andrew Cayton, *The Dominion of War: Empire and Liberty in North America, 1500–2000* (New York: Penguin, 2005), 219.

[7] Stanley Elkins and Eric McKitrick, *The Age of Federalism: The Early American Republic, 1788–1800* (New York: Oxford University Press, 1993), 244–250.

[8] Anderson and Cayton, *The Dominion of War,* 219.

[9] Stephen E. Ambrose, *Duty, Honor, Country: A History of West Point,* Paperback Edition (Baltimore: Johns Hopkins University, 1999), 18–19.

[10] Richard H. Kohn, *Eagle and Sword: The Beginnings of the Military Establishment in America* (New York: The Free Press, 1975), 303.

[11] Peterson, xxxix–xl.

[12] Daniel Walker Howe, *What Hath God Wrought: The Transformation of America, 1815–1848* (New York: Oxford University Press, 2007), 243.

[13] Muir, James N., *Allegorical Sculpture and Monuments in Bronze.* http://www.jamesmuir.com/intro.html (accessed April 18, 2013).

Page #20: Sylvanus Thayer
[1] Theodore J. Crackel, *West Point: A Bicentennial History* (Lawrence, Kansas: The University Press of Kansas, 2002), 102–103; K. Burce Galloway and Robert Bowie Johnson, Jr., *West Point: America's Power Fraternity* (New York: Simon and Schuster, 1973), 147; Stephen E. Ambrose, *Duty, Honor, Country: A History of West Point* (Baltimore: The Johns Hopkins Press, 1966), 67.

[2] James L. Morrison, *The Best School in the World: West Point, the Pre-Civil War Years, 1833–1866* (Kent, Ohio:

Kent State University Press, 1986), 23; also quoted in Crackel, 81.

3 Colonel Charles N. Branham, ed. *Biographical Register of the Officers and Graduates of the United States Military Academy at West Point, New York Since its Establishment in 1802: Supplement, Volume IX, 1940–1950* (West Point, New York: Association of Graduates, 1950), 1–2; Ambrose, 64.

4 Galloway and Johnson, 148; Ambrose, 64.

5 Ambrose, 64–68; Galloway and Johnson, 147–149;

6 Ambrose, 87–90; Crackel, 81–85.

7 Ambrose, 87–98.

8 Crackel, 103.

Page #24: President Ulysses S. Grant
For further reading

Brands, H.W. *The Man Who Saved the Union: Ulysses Grant in War and Peace,* New York: Doubleday, 2012.

Flood, Charles Bracen. *Grant and Sherman: The Friendship that Won the Civil War,* New York: Farrar, Strauss and Giroux, 2005.

Grant, Ulysses S. *Personal Memoirs of U.S. Grant* (Modern Library Edition, Caleb Carr editor), New York: Random House, 1999, reprint of Charles Webster and Company's 1885 edition.

McFeely, William S. *Grant: A Biography,* New York: W. W. Norton, 1981.

Simpson, Brooks D. *Let Us Have Peace: Ulysses S. Grant and the Politics of War and Reconstruction, 1861–1868,* Chapel Hill: University of North Carolina Press, 1991.

Smith, Jean Edward, *Grant.* New York: Simon and Schuster, 2001.

Page #28: President Dwight David Eisenhower
1 Stephen E. Ambrose. *Eisenhower, Soldier and President: The Renowned One-Volume Life* (New York: Simon and Schuster, 1990), 15.

2 Ambrose, 15–16.

3 Ambrose, 22–23.

4 Center for Military History, Publication 71–40. *Dwight David Eisenhower: The Centennial,* March 16, 1990, online version website, http://www.history.army.mil/brochures/Ike/ike.htm accessed 21 April 2013.

5 Colonel (Retired) Charles A. Branham, editor. *Biographical Register of the Officers and Graduates of the US Military Academy at West Point, New York Since its Establishment in 1802: Supplement, Volume IX, 1940–1950* (Association of Graduates, United States Military Academy), 196, 188-207; Smithsonian Institute National Museum of American History: West Point in the Making of America, website, http://americanhistory.si.edu/westpoint/history_6b.html accessed April 21, 2013; Ambrose, 26–28.

6 CMH Pub 71–40 website; Ambrose, 29–35.

7 Eric Larrabee. *Commander in Chief: Franklin Delano Roosevelt, His Lieutenants, and Their War* (New York: Simon and Schuster, 1987), 418; Dwight David Eisenhower (DDE) Presidential Library and Museum – Army Years website http://www.eisenhower.archives.gov/all_about_ike/army_years.html accessed April 21, 2013; CMH Pub 71–40 website.

8 DDE Library website; Larrabee, 412–418.

9 Trevor N. Dupuy, Curt Johnson, and David L. Bongard. *The Harper Encyclopedia of Military Biography* (Edison, New Jersey: Castle Books, 1992), 236; CMH Pub

71–40 website.

10 Michael J. Lyons. World War II: *A Short History, 5th ed.* (New York: Learning Solutions, 2010), 257.

11 DDE Library website; CMH Pub 71–40 website.

12 CMH Pub 71–40 website; DDE Library website.

13 Ambrose, 572–573.

14 DDE Library website, Post-Presidential Speeches.

Page #42: General Nathan Farragut Twining
1 Colonel Charles N. Branham, USA, Retired, ed., *Officers and Graduates of the US Military Academy at West Point, New York Since Its Establishment in 1802: Supplement, Volume IX, 1940–1950* (West Point, New York: Association of Graduates, 1950), 301.

2 Trevor N. Dupuy, Curt Johnson, and David L. Bongard, *The Harper Encyclopedia of Military Biography* (Edison, New Jersey: Castle Books, 1995), 762–763; The Arlington National Cemetery Website, http://www.arlingtoncemetery.net/ntwining.htm accessed April 1, 2013.

3 Dupuy, et. al., 762–763; The Arlington National Cemetery Website, http://www.arlingtoncemetery.net/ntwining.htm accessed April 1, 2013.

4 David M. Jacobs, *The UFO Controversy in America* (Bloomington, Indiana: Indiana University Press, 1975), 156; Hector Quintanilla, Jr., *The Investigation of UFOs: A History and Methodology of "Flying Saucer" Intelligence, Compiled by the Central Intelligence Agency, September 1993* (CIA Historical Review Program, 2012), 97.

5 See US Air Force, Air Material Command, "Unidentified Aerial Objects: Project SIGN, no. F-TR 2274, IA, February 1949, Records of the US Air Force Commands, Activities and Organizations, Record Group 341, National Archives, Washington, DC.

6 See US Air Force, *Projects GRUDGE and BLUEBOOK Reports 1-–12* (Washington, DC; National Investigations Committee on Aerial Phenomena, 1968); and Jacobs, *The UFO Controversy*, 50–54.

7 The Federation of American Scientists cites the current service life of the B-52H as extending to the year 2040.

8 See National Park Service – Vietnam Veterans Memorial at http://www.nps.gov/vive/faqs.htm accessed 1 April 2013.

Page #44: General Lyman Louis Lemnitzer
1 Register of Graduates, West Point, Lemnitzer, Lyman.

2 Binder, L. James. *Lemnitzer: A Soldier of His Time.* New York: Brassey's, 1997.

3 *New York Times*, Obituary, Lemnitzer, Lymon, November 13, 1988.

Page #46: General Maxwell D. Taylor
1 John M. Taylor, *General Maxwell Taylor: The Sword and the Pen* (New York: Doubleday, 1989), 11–13.

2 *Ibid.*, 13–14.

3 Association of Graduates, USMA *1990 Register of Graduates and Former Cadets 1802–1990* (West Point, New York: Association of Graduates Press, 1990), 371.

4 Taylor, 20–21.

5 *Ibid.*, 23.

6 Trevor N. Dupuy, Curt Johnson, and David L. Bongard, *The Harper Encyclopedia of Military Biography* (Edison, New Jersey: Castle Books, 1992), 733.

7 Taylor, 29–30.

8 Dupuy et al., 733.

9 Association of Graduates, 371.

10 Dupuy et al., 733.

11 John Whiteclay Chambers, II, ed., *The Oxford Companion to American Military History* (New York: Oxford University Press, 1999), 713.

Page #48: General Earle Gilmore Wheeler
1 William Gardner Bell, *Commanding Generals and Chiefs of Staff, 1775–2010: Portraits and Biographical Sketches of the United States Army's Senior Officer*, CMH Pub 7014 (Washington, D.C.: Center for Military History, United States Army, 2010), 140.

2 Gilmore Stone Wheeler. *The Forgotten General: Writing a Biography of General Earle G. Wheeler*, http://theforgottengeneral.com/. Biography tab, http://theforgottengeneral.com/wp-content/uploads/2010/12/JCS-Biography.pdf, 88–90, accessed on March 1, 2013.

3 Michael Robert Patterson. Biographical sketch of General Earle Gilmore Weaver, General, United States Army found on the unofficial Arlington National Cemetery Website, http://www.arlingtoncemetery.net/ewheeler.htm, accessed on March 1, 2013; Wheeler, 88–90.

Page #56: Governor George McClellan
McPherson, James M. *Tried by War: Abraham Lincoln as Commander in Chief.* New York: Penguin Press. 2008.

Moten, Matthew. *The Delafield Commission and the American Military Profession,* College Station, TX: Texas A&M University Press, 2000.

Rafuse, Ethan S. *McClellan's War: The Failure of Moderation in the Struggle for Union*, Bloomington: Indiana University Press, 2005.

Rowland, Thomas J. *George B. McClellan and Civil War History: In the Shadow of Grant and Sherman,* Kent, Ohio: Kent State University Press, 1998.

Sears, Stephen W. *George B. McClellan: The Young Napoleon,* Ticknor and Fields, 1988.

Page #58: Senator Ambrose Burnside
Marvel, William. *Burnside,* Chapel Hill, N.C.: University of North Carolina Press, 1991.

Rable, George C. *Fredericksburg! Fredericksburg!* Chapel Hill: University of North Carolina Press, 2002.

Sauers, Richard A. *"A Succession of Honorable Victories": The Burnside Expedition in North Carolina,* Dayton, Ohio: Morningside House, 1996.

Page #60: Major General Joseph Hooker
1 See Stephen W. Sears's essay "In Defense of Fighting Joe Hooker," in Steven E. Woodworth's edited volume, *Civil War Generals in Defeat* (Lawrence, KS: University of Kansas Press, 1999), 119–120, and notes 1–2 on page 223 for several excellent examples. Also see Mark E. Neely, Jr.'s essay "Wilderness and the Cult of Manliness: Hooker, Lincoln, and Defeat," in Gabor S. Boritt's edited volume, *Lincoln's Generals* (New York: Oxford University Press, 1994), 54, as well as several examples in his detailed historiographic overview, 227–237. Walter H. Herbert, *Fighting Joe Hooker* (Indianapolis: Bobs-Merrill, 1944), as his biographer. Herbert even entitles his Chapter 14, "Hooker Loses Confidence in Hooker," pages 192–203, and his Chapter 15, "Army Without a Head," pages 204–221 in his analysis of the Battle of Chancellorsville.

2 Colonel (Retired) Charles A. Branham, editor. *Biographical Register of the Officers and Graduates of the U.S. Military Academy at West Point, New York Since its Establishment in 1802: Supplement, Volume IX, 1940-*

1950 (Association of Graduates, United States Military Academy), 14–15; Herbert, 17–21.

3 Ezra J. Warner, *Generals in Blue: Lives of the Union Commanders* (Baton Rouge: Louisiana State University Press), 233.

4 Herbert, 24–33; Warner, 233; Sears, 131; and Neely, 53.

5 Herbert, 35–46.

6 Warner, 234; Neely, 71.

7 Sears, 134.

8 Neely, 71; Sears, 124–125, 136.

9 Herbert, 171–184; Neely, 69.

10 Sears, 134.

11 Herbert, 269–270.

12 Herbert, 288–293.

Page #62: Major General George G. Meade
Cleaves, Freeman. *Meade of Gettysburg.* Norman, Oklahoma: University of Oklahoma Press, 1960, xii, 5, 14–15, 19–28, 43–44, 57–60, 68–69.

Cullum, George Washington, comp. *Biographical Register of the Officers and Graduates of the U.S. Military Academy, Vol. I.* West Point, NY: Association of Graduates, U.S. Military Academy, 1891, 601–608.

Meade, George. *The Life and Letters of George Gordon Meade, Major General United States Army, Vol. II.* New York: Charles Scribners Sons, 1913, 11, 135–136, 156–159, 246, 281–282.

Register of the Officers and Cadets of the United States Military Academy (West Point: June 1835), 6, 24, United States Military Academy Special Collections.

Page #64: General of the Armies John J. "Blackjack" Pershing
1 Center for Military History (CMH) website Frequently Asked Questions – see http://www.history.army.mil/html/faq/5star.html (accessed 31 July 2013).

2 Frank E. Vandiver, "Pershing, John J. (1860-1948)," in John Whiteclay Chambers II, ed. The Oxford Companion to Military History (New York: Oxford University Press, 1999), 543.

3 Frank E. Vandiver, Black Jack, The Life and Times of John J. Pershing, Volume I (College Station: Texas A&M University Press, 1977), 13-21.

4 Vandiver, Black Jack, Vol I, 40-42.

5 COL (R) Charles A. Branham, editor. Biographical Register of the Officers and Graduates of the US Military Academy at West Point, New York Since its Establishment in 1802: Supplement, Volume IX, 1940-1950 (Association of Graduates, United States Military Academy), 49.

6 Vandiver, Black Jack, Vol I, 94-104; Trevor N . Dupuy, Curt Johnson, and David L. Bongard eds., The Harper Encyclopedia of Military Biography (Edison, NJ: Castle Books, 1995), 587-88.

7 Vandiver, Black Jack, Vol I, 171; Dupuy et. al., 587; and Chambers, 543.

8 Vandiver, Black Jack, Vol I, 194-214; Dupuy et. al., 587; and Chambers, 543.

9 Dupuy et. al., 587; and Chambers, 543.

10 Vandiver, Black Jack, Vol I, 390; Dupuy et. al., 587; and Chambers, 543.

11 Vandiver, Black Jack, Vol I, 593.

12 Vandiver, Black Jack, Vol II, 1094.13 Vandiver, Black

Jack, Vol II, 595-668; Dupuy et. al., 587; and Chambers, 543.

[14] Donald Smythe, Pershing: General of the Armies (Bloomington, IN: Indiana University Press, 1986), 3-4.

[15] Spencer Tucker Introduction in Smythe, xii-xv; Dupuy et. al., 587; and Chambers, 543.

[16] Casualties taken from the Public Broadcasting Service (PBS) website at http://www.pbs.org/greatwar/resources/casdeath_pop.html (accessed 24 September 2013).

[17] Smythe, 307.

Page #68: General of the Army Douglas MacArthur
[1] See Military Times Hall of Valor, website http://projects.militarytimes.com/citations-medals-awards/recipient.php?recipientid=676, accessed April 25, 2013.

[2] Colonel (Retired) Charles A. Branham, editor. Biographical Register of the Officers and Graduates of the US Military Academy at West Point, New York Since its Establishment in 1802: Supplement, Volume IX, 1940–1950 (Association of Graduates, United States Military Academy), 85.

[3] See Military Times Hall of Valor, website http://projects.militarytimes.com/citations-medals-awards/recipient.php?recipientid=676, accessed April 25 2013.

[4] Trevor N. Dupuy, Curt Johnson, and David L. Bongar, The Harper Encyclopdia of Military Biography (Edison, NJ: Castle Books, 1992), 462.

[5] Michael J. Lyons. World War II: A Short History, 5th Ed. (New York: Learning Solutions, 2010), 145-146; Dupuy et. al, 462.

[6] Lyons, 145–146.

[7] Richard B. Frank, MacArthur (New York: Palgrave Macmillan, 2009), 55; The Papers of George Catlett Marshall, vol. 3, "The Right Man for the Job," December 7, 1941-May 31, 1943 (Baltimore and London: The Johns Hopkins University Press, 1991), 147-148.

[8] Douglas MacArthur. Reminiscences (Annapolis, MD: Naval Institute Press, 1964), 146.

[9] Lyons, 146.

[10] Eric Larrabee. Commander in Chief: Franklin Delano Roosevelt, his Lieutenants, and Their War (New York: Simon and Schuster, 1987), 305-353; Dupuy, 462-463; Lyons, 162-165.

[11] John W. Dower. Embracing Defeat: Japan in the Wake of World War II (New York: WW Norton and Company, 1999), 323–325; Dupuy, 463.

[12] Allan R. Millett and Peter Maslowski. For the Common Defense: A Military History of the United States of America (New York: Simon and Schuster, 1994), 508–513.

[13] William Stueck. The Korean War: An International History (Princeton, NJ: Princeton University Press, 1995), 178–184.

[14] General MacArthur's Address to Congress, April 19, 1951. See transcript on the Public Broadcasting Service (PBS), American Experience website http://www.pbs.org/wgbh/amex/macarthur/filmmore/reference/primary/macspeech05.html, accessed April 25, 2013.

[15] Douglas Macarthur, "Duty, Honor, Country" Acceptance Speech for the Thayer Award from West Point, May 12, 1962. See speech text at Famous Speeches website http://www.famous-speeches-and-speech-topics.info/famous-speeches/douglas-macarthur-speech-duty-honor-country.htm, accessed April 27, 2013.

Page #74: General Joseph Stilwell
[1] Barbara W. Tuchman, Stilwell and the American Experience in China, 1911–45, (New York: Grove Press, 2001), 10.

[2] Tuchman, 12.

[3] Official Register of the Officers and Cadets of the United States Military Academy, (West Point, NY: USMA Press and Bindery, 1904), 10.

[4] Tuchman, 25.

[5] Tuchman, 43.

[6] Tuchman, 117.

[7] Tuchman, 519.

Page #76: General Mark Wayne Clark
[1] Register of Graduates, West Point, Mark Clark.

[2] Rick Atkinson, Day of Battle: The War in Sicily and Italy, 1943–1944 (New York: Henry Holt and Co., LLC, 2007), 586.

[3] Atkinson, 183–184.

[4] Atkinson, 183–184.

[5] Trevor N. Dupuy, Curt Johnson, and David L. Bongard, The Harper Encyclopedia of Military Biography (Edison NJ: Castle Books, 1995), 168.

[6] Atkinson, 183.

[7] Dupuy, et. al, 168.

[8] Atkinson, 17–24.

[9] Taken from the text of General Dwight Eisenhower's pre-invasion message to the Allied Expeditionary Force, text found at http://www.army.mil/d-day/message.html, accessed on March 17, 2013.

[10] Atkinson, photo set #2 caption, Chapter 9, "The Murder Space," 398–441.

[11] Atkinson, 581.

[12] Noted in the Council of American Ambassadors website, http://www.americanAmbassadors.org/index.cfm?fuseaction=Publications.article&articleid=44, accessed on March 17, 2013.

[13] Dupuy, et. al, 169.

[14] The official Citadel website, http://www.citadel.edu/citadel-history/Presidents/28-clark.html?q=President-clark, accessed on March 17, 2013.

Page #78: General Matthew B. Ridgway
[1] Russell F. Weigley, The American Way of War (New York: MacMillan Publishing Co., Inc., 1973), xiv.

[2] George C. Mitchell, Matthew B. Ridgway: Soldier, Statesman, Scholar, Citizen (Mechanicsburg, PA: Stackpole Books, 2002), 23.

[3] T.R. Fehrenbach, This Kind of War (Washington, D.C.: Brassey's, 1994), 259.

[4] Jonathan M. Soffer, General Matthew B. Ridgway: From Progressivism to Reaganism, 1895–1993 (London: Praeger, 1998), 118–119.

[5] Matthew B. Ridgway, Soldier: The Memoirs of Matthew B. Ridgway (New York: Harper & Brothers, 1956), 205–211.

[6] Ibid.

Page #84: General H. Norman Schwarzkopf
[1] Schwarzkopf, Norman, "It Doesn't Take a Hero."

[2] http://www.achievement.org/autodoc/page/sch0int-4).

Page #114: General William Tecumseh Sherman

[1] Sherman, William Tecumseh, Memoirs of General William T. Sherman, by Himself. Forward by B.H. Liddell Hart, Bloomington, Indiana University Press, 1957, v.

[2] Sherman, 9.

[3] Ibid., 57–58.

[4] Ibid., 75–79.

[5] B.H. Liddell Hart, Sherman: Soldier, Realist, American, Dodd, Mead & Co., 1920. Reprinted in 1993 by Da Capo Press., 430.

[6] Sherman, 148–149.

[7] Sherman, 152.

[8] Sherman, 153.

[9] Sherman, 166.

[10] Ibid., 178.

[11] Ibid., 182.

[12] Ibid., 181–82.

[13] Sherman, 191.

[14] James Lee McDonough. Shiloh: In Hell Before Night, Knoxville, University of Tennessee Press, 1977, 230.

[15] Sherman, 202.

[16] Letter from Major General William T. Sherman, USA, to the Mayor and City Council of Atlanta, September 12, 1864.

Page #116: Major General George Henry Thomas
[1] Christopher J. Einolf, George Thomas: Virginian for the Union, (Norman: University of Oklahoma Press, 2007), 11–20, 24–30.

[2] Benson Bobrick, Master of War: The Life of General George H. Thomas (New York: Simon & Schuster, 2009), 25–34.

[3] Einolf, 40.

[4] Wayne Wei-Siang Hsieh, "'I Owe Virginia Little, My Country Much': Robert E. Lee, the United States Regular Army, and Unconditional Unionism" in Crucible of the Civil War: Virginia from Secession to Commemoration, edited by Edward L. Ayers, Gary W. Gallagher and Andrew J. Torget, 35–57. (Charlottesville: University of Virginia Press, 2006), 38–40.

[5] Einolf, 133.

[6] Bobrick, 145.

[7] Herman Hattaway and Archer Jones. How the North Won: A Military History of the American Civil War. Paperback Edition. (Champaign: University of Illinois Press, 1991), 267, 453.

[8] Einolf, 115–122.

[9] Bobrick, 149–158. Hattaway and Jones, 450–454.

[10] Hattaway and Jones., 458–462.

[11] Ibid., 546–547, 585.

[12] Einolf, 246–249, 252–255.

[13] Hattaway and Jones, 640, 643, 650–653. Quotation is on p. 651.

Page #120: General Philip Henry Sheridan
[1] Sheridan, Philip Henry, Personal Memoirs of P.H. Sheridan, James and McCowan, NY, 1888, 1.

[2] Sheridan, 5–7.

[3] Morris, Roy, Jr., Sheridan: The Life and Wars of General Phil Sheridan, New York: Crown Publishing, 1992, 15.

[4] Sheridan, 9.

[5] Sheridan, 11–13.

[6] Sheridan, 15–17.

[7] Sheridan 57–63.

[8] Eicher, John H., and David J. Eicher. Civil War High Commands. Stanford, CA: Stanford University Press, 2001, 482–83.

[9] Fredriksen, John C. "Philip Henry Sheridan." In Encyclopedia of the American Civil War: A Political, Social, and Military History, edited by David S. Heidler and Jeanne T. Heidler. New York: W. W. Norton & Company, 2000, 60–62.

[10] Sheridan, 127.

[11] Sheridan, 139–143.

[12] Morris, 67–70, Sheridan 144–166.

[13] Sheridan, 246.

[14] Sheridan, 349.

[15] Sheridan, 375–78,

[16] Sheridan, 456–60.

Page #122: Lieutenant General Robert E. Lee
[1] Emory M. Thomas, Robert E. Lee, (New York: W. W. Norton and Company, 1995), 29.

[2] Thomas, 37.

[3] Thomas, 43.

[4] Richard Harwall, Lee: An Abridgement of the Four-Volume R.E. Lee by Douglas Southall Freeman, (New York: Charles Scribner's Sons, 1961), 22–49.

[5] Harwall, 57–8.

[6] Harwell, 83.

[7] Thomas, 157.

[8] Harwell, 89.

[9] Robert E. Lee, Recollections and Letters of General Robert E. Lee, (New York: Garden City Publishing Company, 1926), 27–8.

[10] Harwell, 119.

[11] Thomas, 197–8.

[12] Pope's Army was not technically called the Army of the Potomac, but, rather, the Army of Virginia.

[13] Shelby Foote, The Civil War: Red River to Appomattox, (New York: Random House Vintage Books, 1974), 951–6. Thomas, 381–5.

[14] Thomas, 380.

Page #124: General John Bell Hood
Cullum, George Washington, comp. Biographical Register of the Officers and Graduates of the U.S. Military Academy, Vol. II. West Point, NY: Association of Graduates, U.S. Military Academy, 1891, 567.

Dyer, John P. The Gallant Hood. New York: Konecky and Konecky, 1950, 15, 20–25, 31, 311–321.

Hood, J.B. Advance and Retreat: Personal Experiences in the United States and Confederate States Armies. New Orleans: G.T. Beauregard, 1880.

Register of the Officers and Cadets of the United States Military Academy (West Point: June 1853), 3, 7–8, United States Military Academy Special Collections.

Warner, Ezra J. Generals in Gray: Lives of the Confederate Commanders. New Orleans: Louisiana State University Press, 1959, 142–143, 378.

Page #127: Major General Frank Dow Merrill
[1] MIT Alumni page.

[2] Marauder's Unit History.

3 Frank McLynn, *The Burma Campaign*.

4 Marauder Unit History.

Page #134: Colonel Henry Andrews Mucci
1 *Register of Graduates*, West Point. Henry Mucci, USMA 1936.

2 David W. Hogan, Jr., *U.S. Army Special Operations in World War II* (Washington, D.C.: Department of the Army CMH Publication 70–42, 1992), 88; Hampton Sides, *Ghost Soldiers: The Epic Account of World War II's Greatest Rescue Mission* (New York: Random House, Anchor Books, 2002).

3 *New York Times*, Obituary, Henry Mucci, April 24, 1997; Sides, 25–26.

4 *Military Times Hall of Valor*.

5 Sides, 25–26; Hogan, 83–85; U.S. Army History, 75th Ranger Regiment, www.history.army.mil.

6 Sides, 17–24; Hogan, 85–89.

7 Hogan, 87–88.

8 Mucci's Rangers: Lieutenant Colonel Henry Mucci: 6th Ranger Battalion Commander. Found at http://www. Rangerfamily.org/Commanders/Henri%20Mucci.htm, accessed March 15, 2013.

9 *Seattle Postintelligencer*, 2009; Sides, 332.

10 Sides, 332.

Page #138: General Wayne Allan Downing
1 Quoted from Brian McEnany's written description of "The Botched Plebe Christmas Escape."

2 https://www.benning.army.mil/Infantry/rtb/rhof/index.html.

3 2006 USMA Association of Graduates Distinguished Graduate Award Citation.

Page #160: Lieutenant General John McAllister Schofield
1 West Point Association of Graduates (AOG): *Gray Matter*, "Schofield's Definition of Discipline," Posted November 4, 2010 – http://www.westpointaog.org/page.aspx?pid=4329, accessed February 4, 2013 – http://www.westpointaog.org/; Dale R. Wilson, *Command Performance Leadership: A Blog Discussing Military and Corporate Leadership Competencies*, Word Press. "Schofield's Definition of Discipline," http://command-performanceleadership.wordpress.com/2012/02/23/schofields-definition-of-discipline/, accessed February 4, 2013.

2 Colonel (Retired) Charles A. Branham, editor, *Biographical Register of the Officers and Graduates of the U.S. Military Academy at West Point, New York Since its Establishment in 1802: Supplement, Volume IX, 1940–1950* (Association of Graduates, United States Military Academy), 24–25.

3 Ezra J. Warner, Generals in Blue: Lives of the Union Commanders (Baton Rouge: Louisiana State University Press, 1964); Trevor N. Dupuy, Curt Johnson, and David L. Bongard, The Harper Encyclopedia of Military Biography (New York: Harper Collins, Inc., 1995), 663–664; James L. McDonough, Schofield: Union General in the Civil War and Reconstruction (Tallahassee, FLA: Florida State University Press, 1972), v–vi; Donald B. Connelly, John M. Schofield and the Politics of Generalship (Chapel Hill, NC: The University of North Carolina Press, Inc., 2006), 1–2.

4 McDonough, 189–191.

5 Connelly, 10–11.

6 Connelly, 9–10.

Page #162: Senator Henry Algernon DuPont
1 DuPont, Colonel H.A. *Henry DuPont: A Brief Recital of His Life and Character by his son, Colonel H.A. DuPont*.

2 Fifty-eighth *Annual Report of the Association of Graduates of the United States Military Academy at West Point, New York*, June 13, 1927, Seemann and Peters, MI, 1927, 124.

3 Letters from Cadet Henry A. DuPont to his father, mother, and aunt, July 7, 1856, to October 16, 1856.

4 Letters to father, October and November 1859.

5 Letter to mother, November 1860.

6 DuPont, *Henry A. DuPont*, 12–13, previous 11.

7 DuPont, *Henry A. DuPont*, 14

8 Letters to mother.

9 General Cullum's *Biographical Register of the Officers and Graduates of the United States Military Academy*, Brookhaven Pres. lacrosse Wisconsin 2002, 768–69.

10 Henry A. DuPont, *The Battle of New Market, Virginia: May 1864*, 1924.

11 There are several fine sources for a full study of the Battle of New Market. Notably *The Battle of New Market and The New Market Campaign May 1864*, Edward Raymond Turner, and B.A. Colonna, "The Battle of New Market" in the *Journal of the Military Service Institution*, as well as a staff ride handbook, Joseph W.A. Whitehorne, "The Battle of New Market," Center of Military History, United States Army Washington, D.C., 1988.

12 Annual Report of the USMA AOG 1927, 125.

13 H.A. DuPont, *The Campaign of 1864 In the Valley of Virginia and The Expedition to Lynchburg*, NY 1925, 157–159.

14 Annual Report, 126.

Page #180: General Jonathan Wainwright
1 Duane Shultz, *Hero of Bataan: The Story of General Jonathan M. Wainwright* (New York: St. Martin's Press, 1981), 56–60, and Jonathan M. Wainwright, *General Wainwright's Story* (Garden City, NY: Doubleday & Company, 1946), 6–18.

2 Shultz, 64.

3 *Ibid.*, 354–356.

4 http://www.history.Army.mil/html/moh/wwll-t-z.html, "Medal of Honor Recipients," U.S. Army Center of Military History, accessed February 20, 2012.

Page #184: Lieutenant General Leonidas Polk
1 Joseph H. Parks, *General Leonidas Polk C.S.A.: The Fighting Bishop* (Baton Rouge: Louisiana State University Press, 1962), 5–9, 11–12.

2 Parks, 21–24, 34–37, 41–45, 52–54, 94.

3 *Ibid.*, 117–131, 149–150.

4 *Ibid.*, 157–168.

5 Herman Hattaway and Archer Jones. *How the North Won: A Military History of the American Civil War*. Paperback Edition. (Champaign: University of Illinois Press, 1991), 164.

6 James McPherson, *Battle Cry of Freedom: The Civil War Era* (New York: Oxford University Press, 1988), 296–297.

7 Ulysses Simpson Grant, *Personal Memoirs of U.S. Grant*. (Mineola, NY: Dover Publications, 1995), 99–104.

8 Hattaway and Jones, 60–68.

9 *Ibid.*, 157–167.

10 *Ibid.*, 259–260.

11 McPherson, 583.

12 *Ibid.*, 672.

13 Hattaway and Jones, 453.

14 McPherson, 676.

15 Grant, 278–269.

16 Hattaway and Jones, 552, 595–596. Parks, 382.

17 Grady McWhiney, quoted in Hattaway and Jones, 257.

18 Hattaway and Jones, 316.

19 *U.S. News & World Report*, Sewanee – University of the South, 2012. http://colleges.usnews.rankingsandreviews.com/best-colleges/sewanee-university-of-the-south-3534 (accessed March 22, 2012).

Page #186: Major General John Sedgwick
1 Salmon, John S. *The Official Virginia Civil War Battlefield Guide*. Mechanicsburg, PA: Stackpole Books, 2001, 253.

2 Eicher, David J. *The Longest Night: A Military History of the Civil War*. New York: Simon & Schuster, 2001, 661.

3 Rhea, Gordon C. *The Battles for Spotsylvania Court House and the Road to Yellow Tavern May 7–12, 1864*. Baton Rouge: Louisiana State University Press, 1997, 95.

4 "Dedication of the Sedgwick Monument at West Point," *New York Times*, retrieved March 8, 2003.

5 Lange, Robie (1984). *Historic Structures Inventory United States Military Academy West Point, NY Vol 2*. Washington, D.C.: National Park Service, 18.

Page #188: Lieutenant General Thomas "Stonewall" Jackson
1 Mary Anna Jackson, *Life and Letter of General Thomas J. Jackson (Stonewall Jackson)*, New York, Harper Brothers, 1891, 14.

2 Jackson, 16

3 Jackson, xii.

4 Douglas S. Freeman, *Lee's Lieutenants A Study in Command*, New York, Scribner 1946, vol. 1, 82.

5 John B. Gordon in *The Life and Letters of Stonewall Jackson*, xiii.

6 Jackson, 32.

7 *Ibid.*, 33.

8 *Ibid.*, 34.

9 Jackson, 34–59 is recalled in Jackson's memoirs; other records show there were 70 students in his class.

10 *Ibid.*, 30.

11 *Ibid.*, 36.

12 Jackson, 37.

13 Report of Captain Magruder to Captain (later Major General) Joseph Hooker, then serving as General Pillow's Assistant Adjutant General.

14 Jackson, 56,

15 Jackson, 151.

16 Jackson, 139–141.

17 *Ibid.*, 141.

18 Jackson, 160.

19 *Ibid.*, 14.

20 *Ibid.*, xiv.

21 *Ibid.*, xv.

Page #192: Lieutenant General Ambrose Powell Hill, Jr.
1 Robertson, James I., *General A.P. Hill: The Story of a*

Confederate Warrior, 4–5.

2 Robertson, James I., *General A.P. Hill: The Story of a Confederate Warrior*, 6–12.

3 Eicher, John H., and David C. Eicher, *Civil War High Commands*, 296.

4 Civil War Trusts. From Civil War Trusts Website: http://www.civilwar.org, accessed February 20, 2013.

5 Robertson, James I., *General A.P. Hill: The Story of a Confederate Warrior*, 62–63.

6 Hassler, William W., *A.P. Hill: Lee's Forgotten General*, 67–71.

7 Robertson, James I., *General A.P. Hill: The Story of a Confederate Warrior*, 133–157.

8 Robertson, James I., *General A.P. Hill: The Story of a Confederate Warrior*, 167–168.

9 Hassler, William W., *A.P. Hill: Lee's Forgotten General*, 73–74, 243–244.

10 Hassler, William W., *A.P. Hill: Lee's Forgotten General*, 112–114, 128–131.

11 Hassler, William W., *A.P. Hill: Lee's Forgotten General*, 136–139.

12 Hassler, William W., *A.P. Hill: Lee's Forgotten General*, 169.

13 Robertson, James I., *General A.P. Hill: The Story of a Confederate Warrior*, 317–324.

14 Civil War Trusts. From Civil War Trusts Website: http://www.civilwar.org, accessed February 20, 2013.

Page #194: Major General James Birdseye McPherson
1 Association of Graduates, USMA *1990 Register of Graduates and Former Cadets 1802–1990* (West Point, New York: Association of Graduates Press, 1990), 277.

2 Trevor N. Dupuy, Curt Johnson, and David L. Bongard, *The Harper Encyclopedia of Military Biography* (Edison, New Jersey: Castle Books, 1992), 475.

3 Association of Graduates, 277.

4 Dupuy *et al.*, 475.

5 *Ibid.*

6 Association of Graduates, 277.

Page #196: Brigadier General Joshua W. Sill
1 West Point *Register of Graduates*.

2 Morris, Roy, Jr., *Sheridan: The Life and Wars of General Phil Sheridan*, New York: Crown Publishing.

3 Sheridan's nickname was "Little Phil" since he stood five-feet, five-inches tall: www.historynet.com/philip-sheridan.

Page #198: Major General James "J.E.B." Stuart
1 Emory M. Thomas, *Bold Dragoon: The Life of J.E.B. Stuart*, 1st ed., New York: Harper and Row, 1986, 1.

2 Thomas, 15.

3 *Ibid.*, 19.

4 *Ibid.*, 43.

5 *Ibid.*, 54.

6 *Ibid.*, 65.

7 *Ibid.*, 69. In truth if there was any tarnish on Jackson's 1862 Valley Campaign a solid case could be made for Ashby being at the center of the stain. Ironically, he became a hero falling during the battle of Port Republic after having been demoted by Jackson for incompetence.

8 *Ibid.*, 71.

[9] Thomas, 3 (Chancellorsville book).

Page #200: Lieutenant Colonel George Armstrong Custer
[1] Thom Hatch, *Clashes of Cavalry: The Civil War Careers of George Armstrong Custer and J.E.B. Stuart* (Mechanicsburg, PA: Stackpole Books, 2001), 18–23.

[2] Hatch, 30–34.

[3] Stan Hoig, *The Battle of the Washita: The Sheridan-Custer Indian Campaign of 1867–69.* (Garden City, NY: Doubleday & Co., 1976), 1–2.

[4] The presence of an "anti-Custer faction" in many of his units is a recurring theme in the literature. See James Donovan, *A Terrible Glory: Custer and the Little Bighorn-the Last Great Battle of the American West* (New York: Back Bay Books, 2008), 55–59, 68, 92–94.

[5] George Armstrong Custer, "In the Air Above Yorktown" in *Battles and Leaders of the Civil War, Vol. 5*, edited by Peter Cozzens, 154–169, (Urbana: University of Illinois Press, 2002).

[6] Stephen W. Sears, *Gettysburg* (New York: Mariner Books, 2004), 34, 460–462.

[7] Ulysses Simpson Grant, *Personal Memoirs of U.S. Grant* (Mineola, NY: Dover Publications, 1995), 310, 336, 355, 370.

[8] Hatch, 213, 217, 224–226.

[9] Grant, 430.

[10] Hoig, 54.

[11] Foreword to John M. Carroll, ed. *General Custer and the Battle of the Washita: The Federal View.* (Bryan, TX: Guidon Press, 1978), xi–xii.

[12] G.A. Custer to P.H. Sheridan, November 28, 1868, in Carroll, ed. *General Custer and the Battle of the Washita: The Federal View*, 37–39.

[13] Hoig, 161–162, 189.

[14] Donovan, 140.

[15] *Ibid.*, 225–226, 261–278.

Page #202: Governor Simon Bolivar Buckner, Sr.
[1] Register of Graduates, West Point, Simon Bolivar Buckner, Sr., USMA 1844.

[2] Register of Graduates, West Point, Simon Bolivar Buckner, Sr., USMA 1844.

[3] Hewitt, 139.

[4] Stickles, 25–29.

[5] Gott, 238–49; Connelly, Army of the Heartland, 123–24.

[6] Stickles, 165–166.

[7] Gott, 257.

[8] Stickles, 204–208.

[9] Stickles, 265–270.

[10] Public Broadcasting System (PBS), *Grant's Funeral March.*

[11] Stickles, 348–355.

[12] Stickles, 420–421.

[13] Stickles, 421.

Page #204: Lieutenant Colonel Joseph Scranton Tate & Captain Frederic Homer Sergeant Tate
[1] *Register of Graduates, West Point Association of Graduates*, Tates, Joseph (1917), Joseph (Jr.) (1941), Daniel (1880), Daniel (1947), and Frederic (1942); 2. Go Army Sports, Tate Rink, www.goarmysports.com

Page #208: Major Donald Holleder
[1] West Point Bugle Notes.

[2] www.coachwyatt.com/holleder.html.

[4] Frank Fitzpatrick, *Philadelphia Inquirer.*

[5] www.coachwyatt.com/holleder.html.

[6] Brian Tumulty, *The Army Times*, April 28, 2012; http://www.Armytimes.com/news/2012/04/ap-soldier-distinguished-service-cross-042812/, accessed March 11, 2013.

[7] www.arlingtoncemetery.net/holleder.html.

[8] Brian Tumulty, *The Army Times*, April 28, 2012; http://www.Armytimes.com/news/2012/04/ap-soldier-distinguished-service-cross-042812/ accessed March 11, 2013.

Page #211: Brigadier General William O. Darby
[1] Darby and Baumer, *Darby's Rangers*, 25–27, 83; Altieri, *The Spearheaders*, 15–22, 66–67; Memo, Colonel I.B. Summers, Adj Gen, U.S. Air Force Base, for Hartle, June 13, 1942, Theodore J. Conway Papers, U.S. Army Military History Institute, (USAMHI), Carlisle, Pa.

[2] Maurice Matloff, ea., *American Military History*, Army Historical Series, 2nd ed. (Washington, D.C.: U.S. Army Center of Military History, government Printing Office, 1973), 444; AFHQ Outline Plan, TORCH, September 20, 1942, U.S. Army Staff, Plans and Operations Division, ABC Decimal File, 1942–48, 381 (7–25–42), Sec. I to 4, RG 319, NARA; Darby and Baumer, *Darby's Rangers*, 10–13; King, *William Orlando Darby*, 44.

[3] Leilyn M. Young, "Rangers in a Night Operation," *Military Review* July 24, 1944): 64–69; Darby and Baumer, Darby's Rangers, 56–60; Darby's Report of Sened, March 5, 1943, WWII Ops Reports, INBN 1-0, RG 407, WNRC.

Page #212: Colonel David "Mickey" Marcus
[1] See the pamphlet, *West Point, The United States Military Academy: Cemetery Walking Tour*, found on the Cemetery Tour link of the United State Military Academy Department of History's website. Colonel Marus's grave is located in Section 6, Row B of the cemetery. The direct link to this pamphlet is http://www.westpoint.edu/history/SiteAssets/SitePages/Navigation%20Bar/Cem%20walk%20tour%2008Jul09.pdf.

[2] Ted Berkman, *Cast a Giant Shadow: The Story of Mickey Marcus, a soldier for All Humanity* (Philadelphia: Jewish Publication Society of America, 1967), 2.

[3] Morris Rosenblum, Heroes of Israel (New York: Fleet Press Corporation, 1972), 77; Berkman, 62–69.

[4] Colonel (Retired) Charles A. Branham, editor. *Biographical Register of the Officers and Graduates of the U.S. Military Academy at West Point, New York Since its Establishment in 1802: Supplement, Volume IX, 1940–1950* (Association of Graduates, United States Military Academy), 445; Berkman, 70; Rosenblum, 77.

[5] Branham, 445; Berkman, 13, 95, 99–100; Rosenblum, 77.

[6] Jeffrey Weiss and Craig Weiss, *I Am My Brother's Keeper: American Volunteers in Israel's War for Independence, 1947–1949* (Atglen, PA: Schiffer Publishing, Ltd., 1998), 76; Rosenblum, 78; Berkman, 25–27, 34, 73, 99–108.

[7] Weiss and Weiss, 20; Berkman, 36.

[8] Weiss and Weiss, 129; Berkman, 46; Rosenblum, 83.

[9] Berkman, 56–61; Rosenblum, 80.

[10] Weiss and Weiss, 132.; Rosenblum, 80–83; Berkman, 115, 149. *BCE* stands for Before the Christian Era, Before the Current Era, or Before the Common Era.

[11] Weiss and Weiss, 139; Rosenblum, 84; Berkman, 179–181.

[12] Berkman, 184; Rosenblum, 84; Weiss and Weiss, 77.

Page #214: Major Arthur Bonifas
[1] Rick Atkinson, *The Long Gray Line: The American Journey of West Point's Class of 1966* (Boston: Houghton Mifflin Company, 1989), 420.

[2] Atkinson, 431, 433–34.

[3] Atkinson, 421–445.

Page #216: Colonel James Nicholas "Nick" Rowe
[1] Register of Graduates, West Point, Rowe, James.

[2] *New York Times*, April 29, 1989, "U.S. Officer is Killed In Manila."

[3] Military Times Hall of Valor, Rowe, James. www.militarytimes.com.

[4] *Washington Post.* "Honoring the Defiant One; Alexandria Family, Friends Await Executed POW's Long-Denied Medal" May 27, 2001.

[5] *New York Times*, April 29, 1989. "U.S. Officer is Killed In Manila."

[6] *Five Years to Freedom*, James Rowe, 1971.

[7] www.army.mil, The Official Home Page of the U.S. Army, March 18, 2013, "Welcome to the Nasty Nick."

Page #234: Lieutenant Colonel Andrew S. Rowan
[1] Headquarters, Department of the Army, *Field Manual 3-0, Operations* (Washington, D.C.: 27 February 2008), 5–10.

[2] FM 3-0, *Operations*, 5–10.

[3] Rowan, Andrew, *How I Carried My Message To Garcia.*

Page #242: Andrea Lee Hollen, USMA 1980
[1] *People*, April 1980

[2] Hollen, Andrea, telephone interviews with WPLPOC November 19, 2012, and January 8, 2013.

Page #238: Major General Frederick A. Gorden
[1] Interview with Major General Fred Gorden and WPLPOC, January 18, 2013.

Page #246: Major (Retired) Priscilla "Pat" Walker Locke
[1] As noted in the LTG Berry's obituary from the Boston Globe at http://www.bostonglobe.com/metro/obituaries/2013/07/16/sidney-berry-general-who-led-westpoint-tumultuous-period-dies/IHgogsFRFeDp2PT2gpexRI/story.html (accessed on 27 August 2013).2 Theodore J. Crackel, West Point: A Bicentennial History (Lawrence, KS: University of Kansas Press), 240; Rick Atkinson, The Long Gray Line: The American Journey of West Point's Class of 1966 (Boston: Houghton-Mifflin), 408.

[2] Theodore J. Crackel, West Point: A Bicentennial History (Lawrence, KS: University of Kansas Press), 240; Rick Atkinson, The Long Gray Line: The American Journey of West Point's Class of 1966 (Boston: Houghton-Mifflin), 408.

Page #268: Major General George W. Goethals
Bishop, Joseph Bucklin, and Farnham. *Goethals: Genius of the Panama Canal. A Biography.* New York: Harper and Bros., 1938.

Center of Military History. *The Panama Canal: An Army's Enterprise.* Washington, D.C.: Government Printing Office, 2009.

McCullough, David. *The Path Between the Seas: The Creation of the Panama Canal, 1870–1914.* New York: Simon and Schuster, 1977.

Zimmerman, Phyllis A. *The Neck of the Bottle: George W. Goethals and the Reorganization of the U.S. Army Supply System, 1917–1918.* College Station, Texas: Texas A&M University Press, 1992.

Page #270: Lieutenant General Leslie Groves
[1] Robert S. Norris, *Racing for the Bomb: General Leslie R. Groves, The Manhattan Project's Indispensable Man* (South Royaltown, Vermont: Steerforth Press, 2002), 28–40, 51–52, 64–69.

[2] Norris, 82–83.

[3] Barton J. Bernstein, "Reconsidering the 'Atomic General': Leslie R. Groves," *The Journal of Military History 67*, no. 3 (2003): 883–920.

[4] Norris, 142–151, 154–159.

[5] Michael Kort, *The Columbia Guide to Hiroshima and the Bomb* (New York: Columbia University Press, 2007), 19–20.

[6] Stimson Memo to Truman and Truman's Response, July 30, 1945, in *The Columbia Guide to Hiroshima and the Bomb*, 228.

[7] Bernstein, 893–896.

[8] McGeorge Bundy, *Danger and Survival: Choices About the Bomb in the First Fifty Years* (New York: Vintage Books, 1988), 56.

[9] Norris, 254–255. On Groves's "compartmentalized" mind, see Norris, 11.

[10] Bernstein, 896–899. For an in-depth account of Oppenheimer's later troubles, see Bundy, 305–318.

[11] Groves Report to Stimson on the Atomic Bomb, July 18, 1945, in *The Columbia Guide to Hiroshima and the Bomb*, 219–221.

[12] Bundy, 60.

[13] Interim Committee Minutes, May 31, 1945, in *The Columbia Guide to Hiroshima and the Bomb*, 181–184. Groves's comments are on p. 184.

[14] Norris, 426.

[15] Bernstein, 914–915.

[16] Norris, 517-518.

[17] General Kenneth D. Nichols, quoted in Bernstein, 901.

Page #274: General of the Air Force Henry "Hap" Arnold
[1] Dik Alan Daso, *Hap Arnold and the Evolution of American Airpower* (Washington, D.C.: Smithsonian Institution Press, 2000), 11–4.

[2] *Ibid.*, 27. There are different theories on the origin of the more famous nickname "Hap," ranging from a sobriquet for his daredevil youthful flying antics in the early 1910s to remembrance of his recently deceased mother in 1931. See *Ibid.*, 126, and DeWitt S. Copp, *A Few Great Captains: The Men and Events that Shaped the Development of U.S. Air Power* (Garden City, NY: Doubleday & Company, Inc., 1980), 6.

[3] Daso, 31, 235.

[4] Thomas M. Coffey, *Hap, Military Aviator: The Story of the U.S. Air Force and the Man Who Built it, General Henry H. "Hap" Arnold* (New York: The Viking Press, 1982), 33.

[5] Herman S. Wolk, *Cataclysm: General Hap Arnold and the Defeat of Japan* (Denton, TX: University of North Texas Press, 2010), 23.

6 Daso, 75.

7 Henry Harley Arnold, *Global Mission* (New York: Harper & Brothers, Publishers, 1949), 48.

8 Daso, 109–10.

9 Wolk, 25.

10 Daso, 160.

11 *Ibid.*, 169.

12 Arnold, 149, 243.

13 Wolk, 75 ff.

14 Daso, 193 and Coffey, 334–8.

15 Wolk, 120.

16 Daso, 198-9.

17 Wolk, 4.

18 Richard Overy, "Foreword," in Daso, x–xi.

19 Wolk, 229.

Works Cited

Arnold, Henry Harley, *Global Mission*. New York: Harper & Brothers, Publishers, 1949.

Coffey, Thomas M. *Hap, Military Aviator: The Story of the U.S. Air Force and the Man Who Built it, General Henry H. "Hap" Arnold*. New York: The Viking Press, 1982.

Copp, DeWitt S. *A Few Great Captains: The Men and Events that Shaped the Development of U.S. Air Power.* Garden City, NY: Doubleday & Company, Inc., 1980.

Daso, Dik Alan. *Hap Arnold and the Evolution of American Airpower.* Washington, D.C.: Smithsonian Institution Press, 2000.

Wolk, Herman S. *Cataclysm: General Hap Arnold and the Defeat of Japan.* Denton, TX: University of North Texas Press, 2010.

Page #276: General Carl Andrew Spaatz
1 David R. Mets, Master of Airpower: General Carl A. Spaatz (Novato, CA: Presidio Press, 1988), 9.

2 Mets,7–8. Spaatz graduated 57th in is class of 107.

3 DeWitt S. Copp, *A Few Great Captains: The Men and Events that Shaped the Development of U.S. Air Power* (Garden City, NY: Doubleday & Company, Inc., 1980), 26–8.

4 Mets, 83–5.

5 Richard G. Davis, *Carl A. Spaatz and the Air War in Europe* (Washington, D.C.: Center for Air Force History, 1993), 66.

6 Mets, 89, 99–100.

7 *Ibid.*, 131–5.

8 *Ibid.*, 172–3.

9 Davis, 284.

10 *Ibid.*, 345.

11 Mets, 255.

12 *Ibid.*, 268.

13 Davis, 592.

14 Mets, 303.

15 *Ibid.*, 334.

Works Cited

Copp, DeWitt S. *A Few Great Captains: The Men and Events that Shaped the Development of U.S. Air Power.* Garden City, NY: Doubleday & Company, Inc., 1980.

Davis, Richard G. *Carl A. Spaatz and the Air War in Europe.* Washington, D.C.: Center for Air Force History, 1993.

Mets, David R. *Master of Airpower: General Carl A. Spaatz.* Novato, CA: Presidio Press, 1988.

Page #284: Brigadier General Robin Olds
1 James F. Dunnigan, *How to Make War: A Comprehensive Guide to Modern Warfare in the Twenty-First Century*, New York: Quill, 149.

2 Robin Olds, as cited in John Roberts (2010). *Cancer: 100 Ways to Fight*, Xlibris Corp., 11.

3 Terry A. Fairfield (2004). *The 479th Fighter Group in World War II: In Action over Europe with the P-38 and P-51*, Altglen, PA: Schiffer Publishing Ltd., 139.

4 Jerry Scutts (1987), *Lion in the Sky: U.S. 8th Air Force Fighter Operations 1942–45*, London: Patrick Stephens Ltd., 73–74.

5 Robin Olds (2010), *Fighter Pilot: The Memoirs of Legendary Ace Robin Olds*, St. Martin's Press, 207. 6 Olds, 318–319.

7 Di Freeze and Deb Smith, (August, 2007), *Robin Olds: Getting to War Wasn't Always Easy*, http://www.airport-journals.com/display.cfm/centennial/0708018.

Page #288: Colonel Frank Borman
1 http://www.jsc.nasa.gov/Bios/htmlbios/borman-f.html.

2 Chaiken, Andrew (1999), *A Man on the Moon*, Time-Life, Inc. 128.

3 NASA (1993), *Astronaut Biography: Frank Borman*, http://www.jsc.nasa.gov/Bios/htmlbios/borman-f.html.

4 Henry Weinstein, *Los Angeles Times*, February 27, 1986, http://articles.latimes.com/1986-02-27/business/fi-12181_1_bad-choices.

5 John McCollister (March 1, 1986), "Frank Borman: Aviation's Most Daring Executive," *Saturday Evening Post*, no. 258.

6 McCollister.

7 NASA.

8 NASA.

Page #290: Lieutenant Colonel Edward White
1 Colin Burgess, Kate Doolan, Bert Vis, *Fallen Astronauts* (Lincoln and London: University of Nebraska Press, 2003) 113.

2 Burgess, 114–115.

3 Burgess, 117–122.

4 Burgess, 122–126.

5 "Picture of the Week," *Life*, September 28, 1962, 8–9.

6 Barton C. Hacker, James M. Grimwood, *On the Shoulders of Titans: A History of Project Gemini*, 1977, 239–245. http://www.hq.nasa.gov/office/pao/History/SP-4203/toc.htm.

7 Burgess, 134.

8 Burgess, 79–88.

9 Burgess, 145–146.

10 "For the Heroes, Salute and Farewell," *Life*, February 10, 1967, 20–23.

11 Burgess, 128.

Bibliography

Burgess, Colin, Doolan, Kate, and Vis, Bert, *Fallen Astronauts*, Lincoln and London: University of Nebraska Press, 2003.

Collins, Michael, *Carrying the Fire*, New York: Farrar, Straus and Giroux, 2009.

Hacker, Barton C. and Grimwood, James M. *On the Shoulders of Titans: A History of Project Gemini*, 1977. http://www.hq.nasa.gov/office/pao/History/SP-4203/toc.htm.

"Picture of the Week." *Life*, September 28, 1962.

"For the Heroes, Salute and Farewell," *Life*, February 10, 1967.

Page #290: Brigadier General Michael Collins
1 Michael Collins, *Carrying the Fire* (New York: Farrar, Straus and Giroux, 2009) 7.

2 United States Military Academy, *The Howitzer for 1952*, (West Point, NY: United States Military Academy), 255

3 Collins, 8–17.

4 Collins, 8.

5 "14 More Astronauts – New and Different," *Life*, November 1, 1963, 40.

6 NSSDC ID: 1966–066A, *Gemini 10*, http://nssdc.gsfc.nasa.gov/nmc/masterCatalog.do?sc=1966-066A.

7 Collins, 270–314.

8 Collins, 364–441.

9 Gene Farmer, "How *Apollo 11* Changed Three Men," *Life*, July 17, 1970, 50.

10 John A. Hammack, "1998 Distinguished Graduate Award," http://www.westpointaog.org/page.aspx?pid=547.

Bibliography

Bilstein, Roger E. *Stages to Saturn*. Washington, D.C.: National Aeronautics and Space Administration, 1996.

Collins, Michael. *Carrying the Fire*. New York: Farrar, Straus and Giroux, 2009.

Compton, William D. *Where No Man Has Gone Before: A History of Apollo Lunar Exploration Missions*. Washington, D.C.: National Aeronautics and Space Administration, 1989.

Farmer, Gene. "How *Apollo 11* Changed Three Men." *Life*, July 17, 1970, 50.

Hammack, John A. "1998 Distinguished Graduate Award." West Point Association of Graduates, http://www.westpointaog.org/page.aspx?pid=547.

Mailer, Norman, "The Psychology of Astronauts," *Life*, November 14, 1969, 50–62.

"14 More Astronauts – New and Different," *Life*, November 1, 1963, 40.

"The Howitzer for 1952," West Point, NY: United States Military Academy, 1952.

Page #292: Colonel Buzz Aldrin
1 James R. Hansen, *First Man: The Life of Neil A. Armstrong* (New York: Simon & Schuster, 2005), 348.

2 Association of Graduates, USMA, *The Register of Graduates and Former Cadets of The United States Military Academy West Point*, New York 2003 (West Point, New York: Association of Graduates Press, 2003).

3 –190.3 *Ibid.*

4 *Life* June 8, 1953.

5 Association of Graduates, 3–190.6

6 *Ibid.*

7 NASA official records.

Page #300: Senator John Francis "Jack" Reed
1 Senator Reed website www.reed.senate.gov.

2 Correspondence with the staff of Senator Reed, April 2013.

Page #304: Secretary Secretary Eric Ken Shinseki
1 Register of Graduates, West Point Association of Graduates, Eric Shinseki, USMA 1965.

2 US News & World Report. December 18, 2008 "Ten Things You Didn't know About Eric Shinseki"

3 US News & World Report. December 18, 2008 "Ten Things You Didn't know About Eric Shinseki"

4 *New York Times*, January 12, 2007 "New Strategy Vindicates Ex-Army Chief" 5 *New York Times*, January 12, 2007 "New Strategy Vindicates Ex-Army Chief"

5 *New York Times*, January 12, 2007 "New Strategy Vindicates Ex-Army Chief"

Page #306: Secretary Jefferson Davis
1 Morris Schaff. (1922), *Jefferson Davis: His Life and Personality*, Boston: John W. Luce & Co., 8.

2 Schaff, 9.

3 William C. Davis. (1996), *Jefferson Davis: The Man and His Hour*, LSU Press, 25.

4 A. C. Bancroft (Ed.). (1889), *The Life and Death of Jefferson Davis*, New York: J. S. Ogilvie, 10.

5 Schaff, 109–110.

6 Wendy Wolff (Ed.). (1994, *The Senate 1789–1989: Classic Speeches 1830–1993*, Washington: U.S. GPO, 415.

7 Allan Tate (1929), *Jefferson Davis: His Rise and Fall, a Biographical Narrative*, 11.

8 Tate, 6.

9 Schaff, 15.

Page #308: General Simon Bolivar Buckner, Jr.
1 The Pacific War Online Encyclopedia, Biography, accessed February 26, 2013.

2 Battle for Okinawa, GlobalSecurity.org, accessed February 25, 2013.

3 (20) Truman, letter to Cate, January 12, 1953, reproduced in Craven and Cate, Army Air Forces. In his memoirs, Truman said that "General Marshall told me that it might cost half a million American lives to force the enemy's surrender on his home grounds." Note: Truman used the alternative spelling, Tokio, in his letter to Cate.

4 Sarantakes, 82–83.

5 *Repertoire Magazine*, Article 743, September 2000.

Page #310: Major General James Longstreet
1 Carol Reardon, *I Have Been a Soldier All My Life*. (Gettysburg, PA: Farnsworth Military Impressions, 1997), 5–6.

2 Reardon, 8.

3 Reardon, 9.

4 Reardon, 11.

5 Reardon, 11–18.

6 Harold M. Knudsen, *General James Longstreet: The Confederacy's Most Modern General*. (Tarentum, PA: Word Association Publishers, 2007), 74–87.

7 Gordon Sawyer, *James Longstreet: Before Manassas and After Appomattox*. (Gainesville, GA: Sawyer House Publishing, 2005), 64–81.

8 Sawyer, 82.

Page #312: Ambassador James Gavin

[1] Mark M. Boatner, *The Biographical Dictionary of World War II* (Novato, CA: Presidio Press, 1996), 177.

[2] Barbara Gavin Fauntleroy, *The General and His Daughter* (New York: Fordham University Press, 2007), xviii.

[3] Association of Graduates, USMA *1990 Register of Graduates and Former Cadets 1802–1990* (West Point, New York: Association of Graduates Press, 1990), 402.

[4] Fauntleroy, xix–xx.

[5] War Department, *Basic Field Manual of Tactics and Technique of Air-Borne Troops* (Washington, D.C.: United States government Printing Office, 1942).

[6] Fauntleroy, xiv.

[7] *Ibid.*

Page #314: Ambassador Lucius Clay
[1] Jean Edward Smith, *Lucius D. Clay: An American Life* (New York: Henry Holt and Company, 1990).

[2] Smith notes that Army records have Clay's birthday as April 23, 1897, but that his actual birth date was April 23, 1898. 2 Smith, 2, 3, and 32.

[3] Colonel (Retired) Charles A. Branham, editor. *Biographical Register of the Officers and Graduates of the U.S. Military Academy at West Point, New York Since its Establishment in 1802: Supplement, Volume IX, 1940–1950* (Association of Graduates, United States Military Academy), 258; Smith, 37–40.

[4] Trevor N. Dupuy, Curt Johnson, and David L. Bongar, *The Harper Encyclopedia of Military Biography* (Edison, NJ: Castle Books, 1992), 171; Smith, 3–4.

[5] Smith, 4–5; Dupuy et. al., 71.

[6] John D. Millett, *United States Army in World War II: The Army Service Forces – The Organization and Role of the Army Service Forces* (Washington, D.C.: Center for Military History, 1954), 2, 365.

[7] DM Giangreco and Robert E. Griffin, *Airbridge to Berlin: The Berlin Crisis of 1948, its Origins and Aftermath* (Topeka, KS: Standard-Hart, 1988), 41–42; Clay quoted from Richard D. McKenzie, "Oral History Interview with Lucius D. Clay" (New York City: July 16, 1974) stored in the Harry S. Truman Library website – http://www.trumanlibrary.org/oralhist/clayl.htm, 3–5; Smith, 4–5; Dupuy, 171.

[8] John H. Backer, *Winds of History: The German Years of Lucius DuBignon Clay* (New York: Van Nostrand Reinhold Company, 1983), vii.

[9] Dupuy, 171; Giangreco and Griffin, 42; Smith 4–7.

[10] Lucius D. Clay, *Decision in Germany* (New York: Doubleday and Company, 1950), ix-x; Smith, 6-7.

[11] Smith, 7.

[12] Smith, 8; Clay, x.

[13] Giangreco and Griffin, 14.

[14] Smith, 10–11, 676; Dupuy, 171.

[15] Smith, 617–621.

[16] Smith, 665; Dupuy, 171.

Page #320: Secretary Robert James Nicholson
[1] www.vaticanstate.va.

Page #336: Secretary Alexander Haig
[1] Association of Graduates, USMA, *The Register of Graduates and Former Cadets of The United States Military Academy West Point, New York 2003* (West Point,

New York: Association of Graduates Press, 2003), 3–159.

[2] *Ibid.*

[3] Trevor N. Dupuy, Curt Johnson, and David L. Bongard, *The Harper Encyclopedia of Military Biography* (Edison, New Jersey: Castle Books, 1992), 305.

[4] Headquarters, U.S. Army, Vietnam, General Orders No. 2318 (May 22, 1967), reproduced in *Military Times Hall of Valor* (website http://militarytimes.com/citations-medals-awards/recipient.php?recipientid=4574) accessed December 10, 2012.

[5] John Whiteclay Chambers, II, ed., *The Oxford Companion to American Military History* (New York: Oxford University Press, 1999), 309.

[6] Association of Graduates, 3–159.

[7] *Ibid.*

Page #338: General Joseph Johnston
[1] Colonel (Retired) Charles A. Branham, editor. *Biographical Register of the Officers and Graduates of the U.S. Military Academy at West Point, New York Since its Establishment in 1802: Supplement, Volume IX, 1940–1950* (Association of Graduates, United States Military Academy), 9; Robert K. Krick, "Snarl and Sneer and Quarrel: Joseph E. Johnston and an Obsession with Rank," in Gary W. Gallagher and Joseph T. Glatthaar eds., Leaders of the Lost Cause: New Perspectives on the Confederate High Command (Mechanicsville, PA, Stackpole Books, 2004), 165–166. Krick notes that only Theophilus H. Holmes achieved notability during the Civil War.; Ezra J. Warner, *Generals in Gray: Lives of the Confederate Commanders* (Baton Rouge: Louisiana State University Press, 1965), 161; Trevor N. Dupuy, Curt Johnson, and David L. Bongard, *The Harper Encyclopedia of Military Biography* (Edison, NJ: Castle Books, 1995), 379.

[2] Warner, 161; Dupuy et. al., 379; Krick, 170–175.

[3] Dupuy et. al., 379; Warner, 161-162; Krick, 182–186 and 189–193.

[4] Dupuy et. al., 379; Warner, 162; Krick, 193–195.

[5] James Longstreet quoted in an August 2, 1879, interview with Henry Grady of the *Philadelphia Weekly Times* when asked who the best Confederate general was. This quote, along with numerous other contemporary Civil War quotes, can be found on James Rosebrock's website: http://jarosebrock.wordpress.com/confederate/Army-of-northern-virginia/joseph-e-johnston/.

Page #342: Captain Dennis Michie
[1] *Sports Illustrated*, June 3, 1999.

Page #343: Brigadier General Palmer Pierce
[1] *New York Times*, January 18, 1908.

[2] Joseph N. Crowley. *The NCAA's First Century: In the Arena* (Digital Edition), 16–19, found on the NCAA website at: http://www.ncaa.org/wps/wcm/connect/public/ncaa/about+the+ncaa/history.

[3] *Ibid.*

[4] *Ibid.*, 27–28.

[5] Steve Rushin, "Inside the Moat: Behind the Forbidding Façade of NCAA Headquarters, The Very People Who Enforce the Organization's Rigid Rules also Question its Godlike Powers and Ultimate Mission," *Sports Illustrated*, Volume 86, Issue No. 9, March 3, 1997, 82.

Page #344: Major General Abner Doubleday
[1] Abner Doubleday, Joseph E. Chance *My Life in the Old Army: Reminiscences of Abner Doubleday* (TCU Press,

1998) 2

[2] Doubleday, Chance 1–3

[3] Abner Doubleday *Reminiscences of Forts Sumter and Moultrie in 1860–61* (New York: Harper & Brothers, 1876) 136–137

[4] Abner Doubleday *Gettysburg Made Plain* (New York: The Century Co., 1888) 26–31

[5] *The War of the Rebellion: A Compilation of the Official Records of the Union and Confederate Armies: Series 1, vol. 27, Part 3 (Gettysburg Campaign)*, eHistory @ The Ohio State University. http://ehistory.osu.edu/osu/sources/recordView.cfm?page=543&dir=045 (accessed November 4, 2012), 543.

Bibliography

Doubleday, Abner, *Reminiscences of forts Sumter and Moultrie in 1960-61* (New York: Harper & Brothers, Publishers, 1876).

Doubleday, Abner, Chance, Joseph E. *My Life in the Old Army: Reminiscences of Abner Doubleday* (TCU Press, 1998).

Doubleday, Abner *Gettysburg Made Plain* (New York: The Century Co., 1888).

Doubleday, Abner *Chancellorsville and Gettysburg* (New York: Charles Scribner's Sons, 1882).

The War of the Rebellion: A Compilation of the Official Records of the Union and Confederate Armies, eHistory @ The Ohio State University. http://ehistory.osu.edu/osu/sources/records/about.cfm.

Page #350: Colonel Earl Henry "Red" Blaik
[1] *New York Times*, William Wallace, May 7, 1989.

[2] *Earl "Red" Blaik*, by Hugh Wyatt; www.coachwyatt.com/blaik1html.

[3] Wikipedia: en.wikipedia.org/wiki/Earl_Blaik.

[4] hickoksports.com/biograph/blaikred.shtml.

Page #352: Colonel Felix "Doc" Blanchard, Jr.
[1] http://www.davidpietrusza.com/Blanchard.html

[2] http://www.answers.com/topic/felix-blanchard

[3] Wikipedia: en.wikipedia.org/wiki/Doc_Blanchard

Page #354: Glenn Davis
[1] http://www.davidpietrusza.com/Davis.html.

[2] www.answers.com/topic/glenn-davis-1.

[3] www.castefootball.us/archives/mr-outside-glenn-davis/.

[4] Wikipedia: en.wikipedia.org/Glenn_Davis (American football).

Page #358: Coach Mike Krzyzewski
[1] Duke University, www.coachk.com.

[2] Jon Jackson, Duke Basketball Media & Public Relations, interview and correspondence, December 2012.

[3] All photos provided by Duke University with permission.

Page #363: The Lombardi Trophy
[1] David Maraniss, *When Pride Still Mattered: A Life of Vince Lombardi* (New York: Simon and Shuster, 1999), 129; Michael MacCambridge, *America's Game: The Epic Story of How Pro Football Captured a Nation* (New York: Anchor Books, 2005), 291.

Page #396: Ken Hicks
[1] *Fortune Magazine*, Hannah Elliott, August 30, 2012.

Page #406: Lee Anderson

[1] West Point Association of Graduates website.

Page #448: Captain Alden Partridge
Crackel, Theodore J. West Point: A Bicentennial History. Lawrence, Kansas: The University of Kansas Press, 2002.

Adams, Cindy, ed., *The West Point Thayer Papers, 1808–1872*, West Point, New York: Association of Graduates, 1965. In the USMA Cadet Library, Special Collections. Available at http://www.library.usma.edu/index.cfm?TablD=6&LinkCategoryID=50#72.

Ambrose, Stephen E. *"Duty, Honor, Country": A History of West Point*. Baltimore: The Johns Hopkins University Press, 1969, 1999.

Webb, Lester A. *Captain Alden Partridge and the United States Military Academy, 1806–1833*. Northport, Alabama: American Southern, 1965.

Page #452: Lieutenant General Hubert R. Harmon
http://www.usafa.edu/df/dfh/docs/Harmon52.pdf.

http://www.usafa.edu/df/dfh/docs/Harmon_bio.pdf.

http://www.af.mil/information/bios/bio.asp?bioID=5713.

Air & Space Power Journal, May–June 2012, 102–105.

Page #454: Brigadier General Robert Francis McDermott
[1] www.usaa.com.

[2] *Register of Graduates*, West Point, McDermott, Robert, 1943.

[3] *Washington Post*, Obituary, Robert McDermott, August 29, 2006.

[4] Harvard Business School Alumni website.

[5] Harvard Business School Alumni website.

[6] West Point Distinguished Graduate Award. Association of Graduates, 1993.

Page #478: Fort Putnam West Point
[1] Report of James Clinton and Christopher Tappen to the New York Provincial Congress, June 13, 1775, Force, 4th ser., 2:1296, map, 736. *New York Journal of the Provincial Congress*, 20, 40-41; Papers of the Continental Congress, 1774-1789 (New York State Papers, 1775-1788), National Archives, Record Group 360, Roll 81, 286, 288-290, microfilm (M247).

[2] Lord Stirling to General Washington, June 1, 1776, Force, 4th ser., 6:672–78.

[3] Washington to Putnam, January 25, 1778, *The Writings of Washington*, 10:348.

Page #512: West Point and the American Civil War
[1] Guy Gugliotta, "New Estimate Raises Civil War Death Toll," The *New York Times*, Science Section, online edition, April 2, 2012, http://www.nytimes.com/2012/04/03/science/civil-war-toll-up-by-20-percent-in-new-estimate.html?_r=0&adxnnl=1&pagewanted=all&adxnnlx=1361296883-wZdqAZepX7dmHMDgCj5t9Q, accessed February 19, 2013; Roy K. Flint, *Notes for Instructors in History of the Military Art: Introduction to the Civil War* (West Point, NY: Department of History, United States Military Academy, 1977), III–3–24.

[2] Thomas E. Griess, ed. The West Point Military History Series: The American Civil War (Garden City Park, NY: Square One Publishers, 2002), 1-7; James M. McPherson, Ordeal by Fire Vol II: The Civil War (New York: Alfred A Knopf, 1982), 163, 181; Roy K. Flint, *Notes for Instructors in History of the Military Art: Introduction to the Civil War* (West Point, NY: Department of History, United States Military Academy, 1977), III–3–9, III–3–13

to III–3–19.

[3] Colonel (Retired) Charles A. Branham, editor. Biographical Register of the Officers and Graduates of the U.S. Military Academy at West Point, New York Since its Establishment in 1802: Supplement, Volume IX, 1940–1950 (Association of Graduates, United States Military Academy), 31, numbers determined by the Cullum Number for every Cadet through the Class of 1864.

[4] Statistics on the number of graduates killed during the war vary. Figures range from 95–105 depending upon cause of death and also include United States actions in the West.

[5] Stephen E. Ambrose, *"Duty, Honor, Country": A History of West Point* (Baltimore: The Johns Hopkins Press, 1966), 188–190.

[6] Ambrose, 188–189.

[7] Description of the memorial can be found on the Civil War News website, Ed Ballam's article, "West Point Class of 1961 give Reconciliation Plaza," in the October 2001 issue announces the dedication, see http://www.civilwarnews.com/archive/articles/class_61_plaza.htm, accessed February 21, 2013.

[8] Selected statistics taken from the History Channel website's interactive feature, "Civil War 150," commemorating the 150th anniversary of the Civil War. See, http://www.history.com/interactives/civil-war-150#/west-point-warriors accessed February 21, 2013.

Page #522: Profiles of Courage West Point Scoutmasters' Council

[1] Alvin Townley. Legacy and Honor: The Values and Influence of America's Eagle Scouts (New York: St. Martin's Press, 2007), 12.

[2] Current statistics taken from the United States Military Academy's Admissions Office.

[3] Interview with COL (Retired) William J. Dieal on 26 March 2012. COL Dieal provided historical background of the Scoutmasters' Council.

[4] Information for CPT Johnson can be found on the West Point.Org website at http://www.west-point.org/users/usma1998/55145/, and for 2LT Rylander at http://www.west-point.org/users/usma2011/67949/; (both accessed on 19 September 2013).

INDEX

" The shadows are lengthening for me. The twilight is here. My days of old have vanished–tone and tint. They have gone glimmering through the dreams of things that were. Their memory is one of wondrous beauty, watered by tears and coaxed and caressed by the smiles of yesterday. I listen vainly, but with thirsty ear, for the witching melody of faint bugles blowing reveille, of far drums beating the long roll.

In my dreams I hear again the crash of guns, the rattle of musketry, the strange, mournful mutter of the battlefield. But in the evening of my memory always I come back to West Point. Always there echoes and re-echoes:

Duty, Honor, Country.

Today marks my final roll call with you. But I want you to know that when I cross the river, my last conscious thoughts will be of the Corps, and the Corps, and the Corps. I bid you farewell."

General of the Army Douglas MacArthur, USMA 1903